D1605086

ADVANCES IN

NEURAL INFORMATION PROCESSING SYSTEMS 3

Other Titles of Interest from
Morgan Kaufmann Publishers

NIPS -2-
Advances in Neural Information Processing Systems
Proceedings of the 1989 Conference
Edited by David S. Touretzky

NIPS -1-
Advances in Neural Information Processing Systems
Proceedings of the 1988 Conference
Edited by David S. Touretzky

Computer Systems That Learn: Classification and Prediction Methods from Statistics, Neural Nets, Machine Learning, and Expert Systems
By Sholom M. Weiss and Casimir A. Kulikowski

Connectionist Models Summer School Proceedings
1990 Edited by David S. Touretzky, Jeffrey L. Elman, Terrence J. Sejnowski, and Geoffrey E. Hinton
1988 Edited by David S. Touretzky, Geoffrey E. Hinton, and Terrence J. Sejnowski

Learning Machines
By Nils J. Nilsson, with an Introduction by Terrence Sejnowski and Halbert White

Readings in Speech Recognition
Edited by Alex Waibel and Kai-Fu Lee

COLT—Proceedings of the Annual Workshops on Computational Learning Theory:
1990 Edited by Mark Fulk and John Case
1989 Edited by Ron Rivest, Manfred Warmuth, and David Haussler
1988 Edited by David Haussler and Leonard Pitt

Genetic Algorithms: Proceedings of the Third International Conference
Edited by David Schaffer

Readings in Cognitive Science: A Perspective from Psychology and Artificial Intelligence
Edited by Allan Collins and Edward Smith

ADVANCES IN

NEURAL INFORMATION PROCESSING SYSTEMS 3

EDITED BY

RICHARD P. LIPPMANN
MIT LINCOLN LABORATORY

JOHN E. MOODY
YALE UNIVERSITY

DAVID S. TOURETZKY
CARNEGIE MELLON UNIVERSITY

MORGAN KAUFMANN PUBLISHERS
2929 CAMPUS DRIVE
SUITE 260
SAN MATEO, CALIFORNIA 94403

Editor *Bruce M. Spatz*
Production Editor *Sharon Montooth*
Cover Design *Jo Jackson*
Compositor *Technically Speaking Publications*

CIP data is available.

ISSN 1049-5258
ISBN 1-55860-184-8
MORGAN KAUFMANN PUBLISHERS, INC.
2929 Campus Drive
San Mateo, CA 94403
(415) 578-9911

Printed in the United States of America

95 94 93 92 91   5 4 3 2 1

Contents

Part VIII Control and Navigation

Part IX Applications

Part X Language and Cognition

Part XI Local Basis Functions

Part XII Learning Systems

Part XIII Learning and Generalization

Part XIV Performance Comparisons

Part XV VLSI

Preface

Since its inception in 1987, the NIPS conference (short for "Neural Information Processing Systems – Natural and Synthetic") has attracted researchers from many disciplines who are applying their expertise to problems in the emerging field of neural networks. The conference and the following two-day workshop have become a forum for presenting to the neural network community the latest research results, and for leading researchers to gather and exchange ideas. This volume contains papers summarizing the talks and posters presented at the most recent NIPS conference, held in Denver, Colorado, from 26-29 November 1990.

The 1990 conference maintained the high level of excitement of its predecessors. Important new theoretical and empirical results were presented concerning the capability and generalization performance of networks. Analyses of biological nervous systems were presented along with mathematical models of some of these networks. Many working analog and digital VLSI chips were described. These chips demonstrated how rapidly VLSI design procedures have advanced in the past few years. New modular learning algorithms were also described, along with significant new industrial applications, new theoretical understanding of network system design issues, and significant advances in speech, robotics, and machine vision systems. Many papers described the application of dynamic temporal networks with recurrent connections. Papers overall demonstrated a better grasp of past neural network research and of past theoretical and practical results in other disciplines.

Multi-disciplinary exchange was promoted this year by grouping papers for presentation according to paper topic instead of by discipline. For example, one session on "Visual Processing" contained papers on theory, algorithms, VLSI implementation, neurobiology, and machine vision applications. Organization by topic instead of by discipline is reflected in this volume. Presentation of papers by researchers outside the United States was promoted this year by the addition of foreign liaisons to the conference organizing committee. Our current liasons represent Australia, Great Britain, continental Europe, Japan, and South America. Presentation of new results by students was promoted this year as in past years. Funds for student travel grants were provided by ATR, the Air Force Office of Scientific Research, Fujitsu, IBM, NASA, Sanyo, Sharp, Siemens, and the University of Colorado, Boulder Optoelectronic Computing Systems Center.

The NIPS conference continues to be an exciting, successful meeting due to the continued efforts of a large group of people. We would first like to thank all the other members of the program and organizing committees who helped make this conference possible. In particular we would like to thank Judy Terrel for her work throughout the year as the conference secretary, Gina Davies and Kathy Hibbard for their work in organizing local arrangements and running the conference desk so smoothly, and Alex Waibel for organizing the post-conference workshops. Finally, we would like to thank everyone who attended and submitted papers and the 85 referees who carefully read and reviewed 20 papers each.

Richard P. Lippmann
John E. Moody
David S. Touretzky
January, 1991

NIPS-91 Organizing Committee

General Chair	Richard P. Lippmann, MIT Lincoln Laboratory
Program Chair	John E. Moody, Yale
Publications	David Touretzky, CMU
Publicity	Stephen Hanson, Siemens Research Center
Treasurer	Kristina Johnson, University of Colorado, Boulder
Local Arrangements	Kathie Hibbard, University of Colorado, Boulder
Workshop Chair	Alex Waibel, CMU
Workshop Local Arrangements	Howard Wachtel, University of Colorado, Boulder
IEEE Liaison	Edward Posner, Caltech
APS Liaison	Larry Jackel, AT&T Bell Laboratories
Neurobiology Liaison	Jim Bower, Caltech
Overseas Liaison (Japan)	Mitsuo Kawato, ATR Research Laboratories
Overseas Liaison (Australia, Singapore, India)	Marwan Jabri, University of Sydney
Overseas Liaison (Europe)	Benny Lautrup, Niels Bohr Institute
Overseas Liaison (United Kingdom)	John Bridle, RSRE
Overseas Liaison (South America)	Andreas Meier, Simon Bolivar University

NIPS-91 Program Committee

CHAIR

John E. Moody, Yale

AREA CO-CHAIRS

Applications:	Lee Giles, NEC Research Institute
Architectures:	Yann LeCun, AT&T Bell Labs
Cognitive Science:	Steve Hanson, Siemens Research Center
Implementations:	Joshua Alspector, Bellcore
Neurobiology:	Terrence Sejnowski, Salk Institute
Theory:	Gerry Tesauro, IBM

REVIEWERS

Asad Abidi, UCLA
David Ackley, Bellcore
Robert Allen, Bellcore
Luis Almeida, INESC, Portugal
P. Anandan, Yale
Dana Anderson, University of Colorado at Boulder
Christopher Atkeson, MIT
Pierre Baldi, Caltech/JPL
Dana Ballard, University of Rochester
Andrew Barto, University of Massachusetts
William Bialek, UC Berkeley
David Bounds, RSRE, England
Herve Bourlard, Philips Research Lab, Belgium
James Bower, Caltech
Thomas Brown, Yale
Joachim Buhmann, USC
David Burr, Bellcore
James Burr, Stanford
Joseph Change, Yale
H.H. Chen, University of Maryland
Jack Cowan, University of Chicago
John Denker, AT&T Bells Labs
Georg Dorffner, Austrian Research Institute
Jeffrey Elman, UCSD
Terrence Fine, Cornell
Walter Freeman, UC Berkeley
Gene Gindi, Yale
Hans Graf, AT&T Bell Labs
Kamil Grajski, Ford Aerospace
Allon Guez, Drexel University
David Haussler, UC Santa Cruz
John Hertz, NORDITA, Denmark
Geoffrey Hinton, University of Toronto
Mark Holler, Intel
Nathan Intrator, Brown University
Larry Jackel, AT&T Bell Labs
Kristina Johnson, University of Colorado at Boulder

Michael Jordan, MIT
Steven Judd, Caltech
Scott Kirkpatrick, IBM
Christoph Koch, Caltech
Thomas Landauer, Bellcore
Benny Lautrup, Neils Bohr Institute, Denmark
Y.C. Lee, Los Alamos
Hong Leung, MIT
Ralph Linsker, IBM
Richard Lippmann, MIT Lincoln Laboratory
Richard Mammone, Rutgers
James Mann, MIT Lincoln Laboratory
Drew McDermott, Yale
Bartlett Mel, Woods Hole
Kenneth Miller, UCSF
Eric Mjolsness, Yale
John Moody, Yale
Ala Murray, University of Edinburgh
Kumpati Narendra, Yale
Stephen Omohundro, ICSI, Berkeley
John Pearson, David Sarnoff Research Center
Sandy Pentland, MIT
Thomas Petsche, Siemens
Fernando Pineda, JPL/Caltech
John Platt, Synaptics
Edward Posner, Caltech
Michael Roth, John Hopkins
Jay Sage, MIT Lincoln Labs
John Schotland, Bellcore
Eric Schwartz, NYU Medical Center
Daniel Schwartz, GTE
Carolo Sequin, UC Berkeley
Gordon Shepard, Yale
Josef Skrzypek, UCLA
Sara Solla, AT&T Bell Laboratories
David Stork, Stanford
Richard Sutton, GTE
Manoel Tenorio, Purdue
Anil Thakoor, JPL
David Touretzky, Carnegie Mellon
David Van Essen, Caltech
Santosh Venkatesh, University of Pennsylvania
Hal White, Stanford

Part I

Neurobiology

Further Studies of a Model for the Development and Regeneration of Eye-Brain Maps

J.D. Cowan & A.E. Friedman
Department of Mathematics, Committee on
Neurobiology, and Brain Research Institute,
The University of Chicago, 5734 S. Univ. Ave.,
Chicago, Illinois 60637

Abstract

We describe a computational model of the development and regeneration of specific eye-brain circuits. The model comprises a self-organizing map-forming network which uses local Hebb rules, constrained by (genetically determined) molecular markers. Various simulations of the development and regeneration of eye-brain maps in fish and frogs are described, in particular successful simulations of experiments by Schmidt-Cicerone-Easter; Meyer; and Yoon.

1 INTRODUCTION

In a previous paper published in last years proceedings (Cowan & Friedman 1990) we outlined a new computational model for the development and regeneration of eye-brain maps. We indicated that such a model can simulate the results of a number of the more complicated surgical manipulations carried out on the visual pathways of goldfish and frogs. In this paper we describe in more detail some of these experiments, and our simulations of them.

1.1 EYE-BRAIN MAPS

We refer to figure 1 from the previous paper which shows the retinal map found in the optic lobe or tectum of a fish or frog. The map is topological, i.e.; neighborhood relationships in the retina are preserved in the optic tectum. As is well-known nearly 50 years ago Sperry (1944) showed that such maps are quite precise and specific, in that maps (following optic nerve sectioning and eye rotation) regenerate in such a way that optic nerve fibers reconnect, more or less, to their previous tectal sites. Some 20 years ago Gaze and Sharma (1970) and Yoon (1972) found evidence for plasticity in the expanded and compressed "maps" which regenerate following eye and brain lesions in goldfish. There are now many experiments which indicate that the regeneration of connections involves both specificity and plasticity.

1. 2. EXPANDED MAPS

Such properties are seen in a series of more complicated experiments involving the expansion of a half-eye map to a whole tectum. These experiments were carried out by Schmidt, Cicerone and Easter (1978) on goldfish, in which following the expansion of retinal fibers from a half-eye over an entire (contralateral) tectum, and subsequent sectioning of the fibers, diverted retinal fibers from the other (intact) eye are found to expand over the tectum, as if they were also from a half-eye. This has been interpreted to imply that the tectum has no intrinsic positional markers to provide cues for incoming fibers, and that all its subsequent markers come from the retina (Chung & Cooke, 1978). However Schmidt et.al. also found that the diverted fibers also map normally. Figure 4 of the previous paper shows the result.

1. 3. COMPRESSED MAPS

Compression is found in maps from entire eyes to ablated half tecta (Gaze & Sharma, 1970; Sharma & Gaze, 1971; Yoon, 1972). There has been considerable controversy concerning the results. Recently Meyer (1982) has shown that although electrophysiological techniques seem to provide evidence for smoothly expanded and compressed maps, autoradiographic techniques do not. Instead of a smooth map there are *patches*, and in many cases no real expansion or compression is seen in irradiated sections, at least not initially. An experiment by Yoon (1976) is relevant here. Yoon noticed that in the early stages of map formation under such conditions, the map is normal. Only after some considerable time does a compressed map form. However if the fibers are sectioned (cut) and allowed to regenerate a second time, compression is immediate. This result has been challenged (Cook, 1979), but it was subsequently confirmed by Schmidt (1983).

1. 4. MISMATCHED MAPS

In mismatch experiments, a half retina is confronted with an inappropriate half tectum. In Yoon's classic "mismatch" experiment (Yoon, 1972) fibers from a half-eye fragment are confronted with the "wrong" half-tectum: the resulting map is normally oriented, even though this involves displacement of retinal fibers from near the tectal positions they normally would occupy.

About 12 years ago Meyer (1979) carried out another important mismatch experiment in which the left half of an eye and its attached retinal fibers were surgically removed, leaving an intact normal half-eye map. At the same time the right half the other eye and its attached fibers were removed, and the fibers from the remaining half eye were allowed to innervate the tectum with the left-half eye map. The result is shown in figure 5 of our previous paper. Fibers from the right half-retina, labelled 1 through 5, would normally make contact with the corresponding tectal neurons. Instead they make contact with neurons 6 through 10, but in a *reversed* orientation. Meyer interprets this result to mean that optic nerve fibers show a tendency to aggregate with their nearest *retinal* neighbors.

2 THE MODEL

We introduced our model in last year's NIPS proceedings (Cowan & Friedman 1990). We here repeat some of the details. Let s_{ij} be the strength or weight of the synapse made by the ith retinal fiber with the jth tectal cell. Then the following system of differential equations expresses the changes in s_{ij}:

$$\dot{s}_{ij} = \lambda_j + c_{ij}\,[\mu_{ij} + (r_i - \alpha)t_j]\,s_{ij} - \tfrac{1}{2}s_{ij}\,(T^{-1}\Sigma_i + R^{-1}\Sigma_j)\{\lambda_j + c_{ij}\,[\mu_{ij} + (r_i - \alpha)t_j]\,s_{ij}\} \qquad (1)$$

where i = 1, 2, ..., N_r, the number of retinal ganglion cells and j = 1, 2, ..., N_t, the number of tectal neurons, c_{ij} is the "stickiness" of the ijth contact, r_i denotes retinal activity and $t_j = \Sigma_i s_{ij} r_i$ is the corresponding tectal activity, and α is a constant measuring the rate of receptor destabilization (see Whitelaw & Cowan (1981) for details). In addition both retinal and tectal elements have fixed lateral inhibitory contacts. The dynamics described by eqn.1 is such that both $\Sigma_i s_{ij}$ and $\Sigma_j s_{ij}$ tend to constant values T and R respectively, where T is the total amount of tectal receptor material available per neuron, and R is the total amount of axonal material available per retinal ganglion cell: thus if sij increases anywhere in the net, other synapses made by the ith fiber will decrease, as will other synapses on the jth tectal neuron. In the current terminology, this process is referred to as "winner-take-all".

In addiiton λ_j represents a general nonspecific growth of retinotectal contacts, presumed to be controlled and modulated by nerve growth factor (Campenot, 1982). Recent observations (Davies *et.al.*, 1987) indicate that the first fibers to reach a given target neuron stimulate it to produce NGF, which in turn causes more fiber growth. We therefore set $\lambda_j = T^{-1}\Sigma_i s_{ij}\lambda$ where λ is a constant. $\Sigma_i s_{ij}$ is the instantaneous value of receptor material used to make contacts, and T is the total amount available, so $\lambda_j \to \lambda$ as the jth neuron becomes innervated. The coefficient μ_{ij} represents a postulated random depolarization which occurs at synapses due to the quantal release of neurotransmitter--the analog of end-plate potentials (Walmsley *et.al.*, 1987). Thus even if $r_i = 0$, map formation can still occur. However the resulting maps are not as sharp as those formed in the presence of retinal activity. Of course if $\mu_{ij} = 0$, as might be the case if α-bungarotoxin is administered, then $\dot{s}_{ij} = \lambda_j(1 - s_{ij})$ and $s_{ij} \rightarrow 1$, i.e.; all synapses of equal strength.

It is the coefficients c_{ij}. which determine the nature of the solution to eqn.1. These coefficients express the contact adhesion strengths of synapses. We suppose that such adhesions are generated by fixed distributions of molecules embedded in neural surface membranes. We postulate that the tips of retinal axons and the surfaces of tectal cells display at least two molecular species, labelled a and b, such that $c_{ij} = \sum \xi_{ab} a_i b_j$ and the sum is over all possible combinations aa, ab etc. A number of possibilities exist in the choice of ξ_{ab} and of the spatial distribution of a and b. One possibility that is consistent with most of the assays which have been carried out (Trisler & Collins (1987), Bonhoffer and Huff (1980), Halfter, Claviez & Schwarz (1981), Boenhoffer & Huff (1985)) is $\xi_{aa} = \xi_{bb} > 0 > \xi_{ab} = \xi_{ba}$ in which each species prefers itself and repels the other, the so-called homophilic case, with a_i and b_i as shown in figure 1.

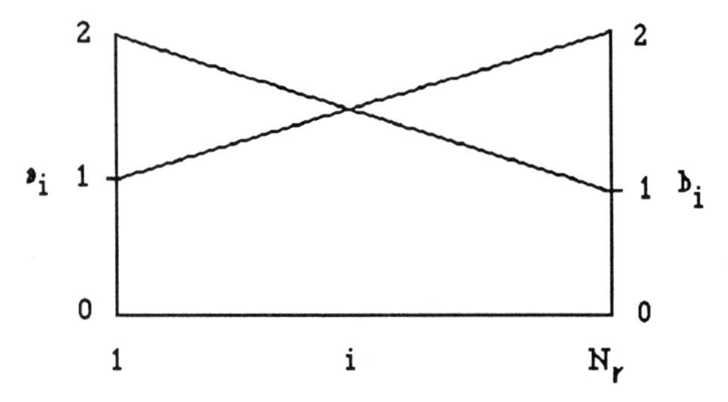

Figure 1: Postulated distribution of sticky molecules in the retina. A similar distribution is supposed to exist in the tectum.

The mismatch and compound eye experiments indicate that map formation depends in part on a tendency for fibers to stick to their retinal neighbors, in addition to their tendency to stick to tectal cell surfaces. We therefore append to c_{ij} the term $\sum'_k \bar{s}_{kj} f_{ik}$ where $\bar{s}_{kj}$ is a local average of s_{kj} and its nearest tectal neighbors, where f_{ik} measures themutual stickiness of the ith and kth retinal fibers, and where $\sum'_k$ means $\sum_{k \neq i}$. Fig. 2 shows the postulated form of f_{ik}. {Again we suppose this stickiness is produced by the interaction of two molecular species etc.; specifically theneural contact adhesion molecules (nCAM) of the sort discovered by Edelman (1983)which seem to mediate the fiber-fiber adhesion observed in tissue cultures by Boenhoffer & Huff (1985), but we do not go into the details}.

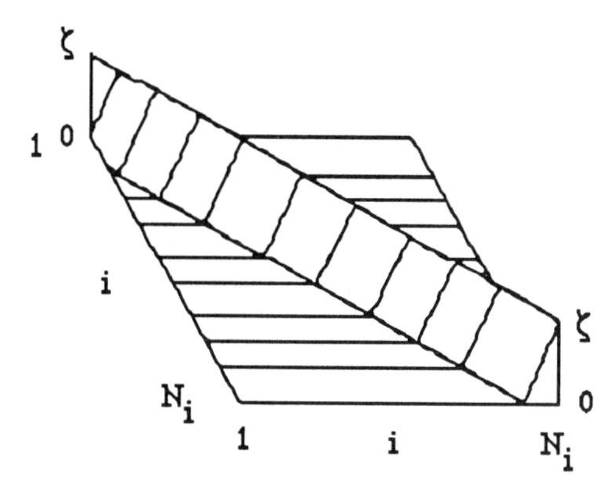

Figure 2: The f_{ik} surface. Retinal fibers are attracted only to themselves or to their immediate retinal neighbors.

Meyer's mismatch experiment also indicate that existing fiber projections tend to exclude other fibers, especially inappropriate ones, from innervating occupied areas. One way to incorporate such geometric effects is to suppose that each fiber which establishes contact with a tectal neuron *occludes* tectal markers there by a factor proportional to its synaptic weight s_{ij}. Thus we subtract from the coefficient c_{ij} a fraction proportional to $T^{-1}\sum'_k s_{kj}$.

With the introduction of occlusion effects and fiber-fiber interactions, it becomes apparent that *debris* in the form of degenerating fiber fragments adhering to tectal cells, following optic nerve sectioning, can also influence map formation. Incoming nerve fibers can stick to debris, and debris can occlude markers. There are in fact four possibilities: debris can occlude tectal markers, markers on other debris, or on incoming fibers; and incoming fibers can occlude markers on debris. All these possibilities can be included in the dependence of c_{ij} on s_{ij}, s_{kj} etc. Note that such debris is supposed to decay, and eventually disappear.

3 SIMULATIONS

The model which results from all these modifications and extensions is much more complex in its mathematical structure than any of the previous models. However computer simulation studies show it to be capable of correctly reproducing the observed details of almost all the experiments cited above. For purposes of illustration we consider the problem of connecting a line of N_r retinal cells to a line of N_t tectal cells. The resulting maps can then be represented by two-dimensional matrices, in which the area of the square at the ijth intersection represents the weight of the synapse between the ith retinal fiber and the jth tectal cell. The normal retino-tectal map is represented by large squares along the matrix diagonal., (see Whitelaw & Cowan (1981) for terminology and further details).

3.1 THE SCHMIDT ET. AL. EXPERIMENT

Figure 3, for example shows a simulation of the retinal "induction" experiments of Schmidt *et.al.* This simulation generated both an expanded map and a nearly normal patch, interacting to form patches. These effects occur because some incoming retinal fibers stick to debris left over from the previous expanded map, and other fibers stick to non-occluded tectal markers. The fiber-fiber markers control the regeneration of the expanded map, whereas the retino-tectal markers control the formation of the nearly normal map.

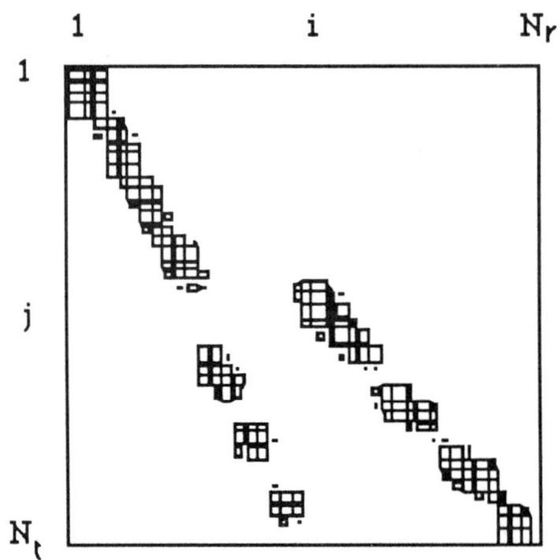

Figure 3: Simulation of the Schmidt et.al. retinal induction experiment. A nearly normal map is intercalated into an expanded map.

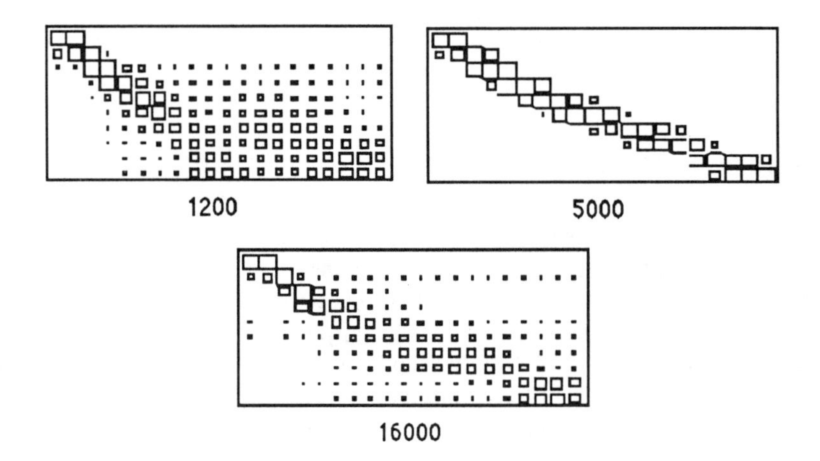

Figure 4: Simulation of the Yoon second compression experiment (see text for details).

3.2 THE YOON SECOND COMPRESSION EXPERIMENT

Yoon's demonstration of immediate second compression can also be simulated. Figure 4 shows details of the simulation. At an early stage just after the first cut, both a normal and a compressed map are forming. The normal map eventually disappears, leaving only a compressed map. After the second cut however, a compressed map forms immediately. Again it is the debris which carries fiber-fiber markers that control map formation.

3.3 THE MEYER MISMATCH EXPERIMENT

It is evident that fiber-fiber interactions are important in controlling map formation. The Meyer mismatch experiment shows this quite clearly. A simulation of this experiment also shows the effect. If f_{ik}, the mutual stickiness of neighboring fibers is not strong enough, retino-tectal markers dominate, and the mismatched map forms with normal polarity. However if f_{ik} is large enough, Meyer's result is found, the mismatched map forms with a reversed polarity. Figure 5 shows the details.

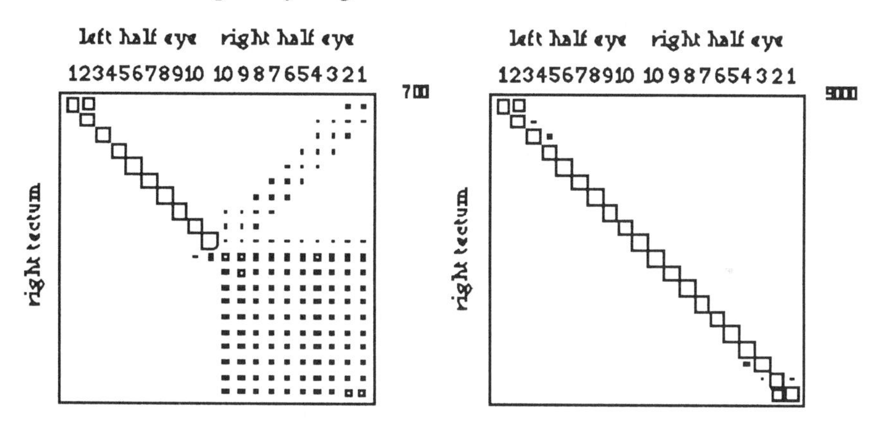

Figure 5: Simulation of the Meyer mismatch experiment (see text for details).

4 CONCLUSIONS

The model we have outlined generates correctly oriented retinotopic maps. It permits the simulation of a large number of experiments, and provides a consistent explanation of almost all of them. In particular it shows how the apparent induction of central markers by peripheral effects, as seen in the Schmidt et. al., can be produced by the effects of debris, as can Yoon's observations of immediate second compression. Affinity markers are seen to play a key role in such effects, as they do in the polarity reversal seen in Meyer's experiment.

In summary much of the complexity of the many regeneration experiments which have been carried out in the last fifty years can be understood in terms of the effects produced by contact adhesion molecules with differing affinities, acting to control an activity-dependent self-organizing mechanism.

Acknowledgements

We thank The University of Chicago Brain Research Foundation for partial support of this work.

References

Boenhoffer, F. & Huf, J. (1980), Nature, **288**, 162-164.; (1985), Nature, **315**, 409-411.
Campenot, R.B. (1982), Develop. Biol., **93**, 1.
Chung, S.-H. & Cooke, J.E. (1978), Proc. Roy. Soc. Lond. **B** *201*, 335-373.
Cowan, J.D. & A.E. Friedman (1990) Advances in NIPS, **2**, Ed. D.S. Touretzky, Morgan-Kaufmann, 92-99.
Cook, J.E. (1979), J. Embryol. exp. Morphol., **52**, 89-103.
Davies, A.M., Bandtlow, C., Heumann, R, Korsching, S., Rohrer, H. & Thoenen, H. (1987), Nature, **326**, 353-358.
Edelman, G.M., (1983), Science, **219**, 450-454.
Gaze, R.M. & Sharma, S.C. (1970), Exp. Brain Res., 10, 171-181.
Halfter, W., Claviez, M. & Schwarz, U. (1981), Nature, **292**, 67- 70.
Meyer, R.L. (1979), Science, **205**, 819-821; (1982), Curr. Top. Develop. Biol., **17**, 101-145.
Schmidt, J.T. (1983), J. Embryol. exp. Morphol., **77**, 39-51.
Schmidt, J.T., Cicerone, C.M. & Easter, S.S. (1978), J. Comp. Neurol., **177**, 257-288.
Sharma, S.C. & Gaze, R.M. (1971), Arch. Ital. Biol., **109**, 357-366.
Sperry, R.W. (1944), J. Neurophysiol., **7**, 57-69.
Trisler, D. & Collins, F. (1987), Science, **237**, 1208-1210.
Walmsley, B., Edwards, F.R. & Tracey, D.J. (1987), J. Neurosci., **7**, *4*, 1037-1046.
Whitelaw, V.A. & Cowan, J.D. (1981), J. Neurosci., **1**, *12*, 1369-1387.
Yoon, M. (1972), Amer. Zool., **12**, 106.; Exp. Neurol., **37**, 451-462; (1976) J. Physiol. Lond., **257**, 621-643.

Development and Spatial Structure of Cortical Feature Maps: A Model Study

K. Obermayer
Beckman-Institute
University of Illinois
Urbana, IL 61801

H. Ritter
Technische Fakultät
Universität Bielefeld
D-4800 Bielefeld

K. Schulten
Beckman-Institute
University of Illinois
Urbana, IL 61801

Abstract

Feature selective cells in the primary visual cortex of several species are organized in hierarchical topographic maps of stimulus features like "position in visual space", "orientation" and "ocular dominance". In order to understand and describe their spatial structure and their development, we investigate a self-organizing neural network model based on the feature map algorithm. The model explains map formation as a dimension-reducing mapping from a high-dimensional feature space onto a two-dimensional lattice, such that "similarity" between features (or feature combinations) is translated into "spatial proximity" between the corresponding feature selective cells. The model is able to reproduce several aspects of the spatial structure of cortical maps in the visual cortex.

1 Introduction

Cortical maps are functionally defined structures of the cortex, which are characterized by an ordered spatial distribution of functionally specialized cells along the cortical surface. In the primary visual area(s) the response properties of these cells must be described by several independent features, and there is a strong tendency to map combinations of these features onto the cortical surface in a way that translates "similarity" into "spatial proximity" of the corresponding feature selective cells (see e.g. [1-6]). A neighborhood preserving mapping between a high-dimensional feature space and the two dimensional cortical surface, however, cannot be achieved, so the spatial structure of these maps is a compromise, preserving some neighborhood relations at the expense of others.

The compromise realized in the primary visual area(s) is a hierarchical representation of features. The variation of the *secondary* features "preferred orientation",

"orientation specifity" and "ocular dominance" is highly repetitive across the *primary* map of retinal location, giving rise to a large number of small maps, each containing a complete representation of the full range of the secondary features. If the neighborhood relations in feature space are to be preserved and maps must be continuous, the spatial distributions of the secondary features "orientation preference", "orientation specifity" and "ocular dominance" can no longer be independent. Interestingly, there is experimental evidence in the macaque that this is the case, namely, that regions with smooth change in one feature (e.g. "ocular dominance") correlate with regions of rapid change in another feature (e.g. "orientation") [7,8]. Preliminary results [9] indicate that these correlations may be a natural consequence of a dimension reducing mapping which preserves neighborhood relations.

In a previous study, we investigated a model for the joint formation of a retinotopic projection and an orientation column system [10], which is based on the self-organizing feature map algorithm [11,12]. This algorithm generates a representation of a given manifold in feature space on a neural network with prespecified topology (in our case a two-dimensional sheet), such that the mapping is continous, smooth and neighborhood relations are preserved to a large extent.[1] The model has the advantage that its rules can be derived from biologically plausible developmental principles [15,16]. Therefore, it can be interpreted not only as a pattern model, which generates a representation of feature combinations subject to a set of constraints, but also as a pattern formation model, which describes an input driven developmental process. In this contribution we will extend our previous work by the addition of another secondary feature, "ocular dominance" and we will concentrate on the hierarchical mapping of feature combinations as a function of the set of input patterns.

2 Description of the Model

In our model the cortical surface is divided into $N \times N$ small patches, *units* $\vec{r}$, which are arranged on a two-dimensional lattice (network layer) with periodic boundary conditions (to avoid edge effects). The functional properties of neurons located in each patch are characterized by a *feature vector* $\vec{w}_{\vec{r}}$, which is associated with each unit $\vec{r}$ and whose components $(\vec{w}_{\vec{r}})_k$ are interpreted as receptive field properties of these neurons. The feature vectors, $\vec{w}_{\vec{r}}$, as a function of unit locations $\vec{r}$, describe the spatial distribution of feature selective cells over the cortical layer, i.e. the cortical map.

To generate a representation of features along the network layer, we use the self-organizing feature map algorithm [1,2]. This algorithm follows an iterative procedure. At each step an *input vector* $\vec{v}$, which is of the same dimensionality as $\vec{w}_{\vec{r}}$, is chosen at random according to a probability distribution $P(\vec{v})$. Then the unit $\vec{s}$, whose feature vector $\vec{w}_{\vec{s}}$ is closest to the input pattern $\vec{v}$, is selected and the components $(\vec{w}_{\vec{r}})_k$ of it's feature vector are changed according to the feature map learning rule:

$$\vec{w}_{\vec{r}}(t+1) \; = \; \vec{w}_{\vec{r}}(t) \; + \; \varepsilon(t)h(\vec{r},\vec{s},t)(\vec{v} - \vec{w}_{\vec{r}}(t)) \tag{1}$$

[1] For other modelling approaches along these lines see [13,14].

where $h(\vec{r},\vec{s},t)$, the *neighborhood function*, is given by:

$$h(\vec{r},\vec{s},t) = \exp\left(-(r_1 - s_1)^2/\sigma_{h1}^2(t) - (r_2 - s_2)^2/\sigma_{h2}^2(t)\right). \quad (2)$$

3 Coding of Receptive Field Properties

In the following we describe the receptive field properties by the feature vector $\vec{w}_{\vec{r}}$ given by $\vec{w}_{\vec{r}} = (x_{\vec{r}},\ y_{\vec{r}},\ q_{\vec{r}}\cos(2\phi_{\vec{r}}),\ q_{\vec{r}}\sin(2\phi_{\vec{r}}),\ z_{\vec{r}})$ where $(x_{\vec{r}},\ y_{\vec{r}})$ denotes the position of the receptive field centers in visual space, $(\phi_{\vec{r}})$ the preferred orientation, and $(q_{\vec{r}})$, $(z_{\vec{r}})$ two quantities, which qualitatively can be interpreted as orientation specificity (see e.g. [17]) and ocular dominance (see e.g. [18]). If $q_{\vec{r}}$ is zero, then the units are unspecific for orientation; the larger $q_{\vec{r}}$ becomes, the sharper the units are tuned. "Binocular" units are characterized by $z_{\vec{r}} = 0$, "monocular" units by a large positive or negative value of $z_{\vec{r}}$. "Similarity" between receptive field properties is then given by the euclidean distance between the corresponding feature vectors.

The components $\vec{w}_{\vec{r}}$ of the input vector $\vec{v} = (x,\ y,\ q\cos(2\phi),\ q\sin(2\phi),\ z)$ describe stimulus features which should be represented by the cells in the cortical map. They denote position in the visual field $(x,\ y)$, orientation ϕ, and two quantities q and z qualitatively describing pattern eccentricity and the distribution of activity between both eyes, respectively. Round stimuli are characterized by $q = 0$ and the more eliptic a pattern is the larger is the value of q. A "binocular" stimulus is characterized by $z = 0$, while a "monocular" stimulus is characterized by a large positive or negative value of z for "right eye" or "left eye" preferred, respectively.

Input vectors were chosen with equal probability from the manifold

$$V = \{\vec{v} \mid x, y \in [0,d];\ \phi \in [0,\pi];\ \ q = q_{pat};\ |z| = z_{pat}\}, \quad (3)$$

i.e. all feature combinations characterized by a fixed value of q and $|z|$ were selected equally often. If the model is interpreted from a developmental point of view, the manifold V describes properties of (subcortical) activity patterns, which drive map formation. The quantities d, q_{pat} and z_{pat} determine the feature combinations to be represented by the map. As we will see below, their values crucially influence the spatial structure of the feature map.

4 Hierarchical Maps

If q_{pat} and z_{pat} are smaller than a certain threshold then "orientation preference", "orientation selectivity" and "ocular dominance" are *not* represented in the map (i.e. $q_{\vec{r}} = z_{\vec{r}} = 0$) but fluctuate around a stationary state of eq. (1), which corresponds to a perfect topographic representation of visual space. In this parameter regime, the requirement of a continous dimension-reducing map leads to the suppression of the additional features "orientation" and "ocular dominance".

Let us consider an ensemble of networks, each characterized by a set $\{\vec{w}_{\vec{r}}\}$ of feature vectors, and denote the time-dependent distribution function of this ensemble by

$S(\vec{w},t)$. Following a method derived in [19], we can describe the time-development of $S(\vec{w},t)$ near the stationary state by the Fokker-Planck equation

$$\frac{1}{\epsilon}\partial_t S(\{\vec{u}_{\vec{r}}\},t) = \sum_{\vec{p}m\vec{q}n} \frac{\partial}{\partial \vec{u}_{\vec{p}m}} B_{\vec{p}m\vec{q}n}\vec{u}_{\vec{q}n} S(\{\vec{u}_{\vec{r}}\},t) + \frac{\epsilon}{2}\sum_{\vec{p}m\vec{q}n} D_{\vec{p}m\vec{q}n}\frac{\partial^2 S(\{\vec{u}_{\vec{r}}\},t)}{\partial \vec{u}_{\vec{p}m}\partial \vec{u}_{\vec{q}n}} \quad (4)$$

where the origin of $S(.,t)$ was shifted to the stationary state $\{\bar{\vec{w}}_{\vec{r}}\}$, using now the new argument variable $\vec{u}_{\vec{r}} = \vec{w}_{\vec{r}} - \bar{\vec{w}}_{\vec{r}}$. The eigenvalues of $\underline{B}$ determine the stability of the stationary state, the topographic representation, while $\underline{B}$ and $\underline{D}$ together govern size and time development of fluctuations $< u_{\vec{p}i}u_{\vec{q}j} >$.

Let us define the Fourier modes $\hat{\vec{u}}_{\vec{k}}$ of the equilibrium deviations $\vec{u}_{\vec{r}}$ by $\hat{\vec{u}}_{\vec{k}} = 1/N \sum_{\vec{r}} e^{i\vec{k}\vec{r}}\vec{u}_{\vec{r}}$. For small values of q_{pat} and z_{pat} the eigenvalues of $\underline{B}$ are all negative, hence the topographic stationary state is stable. If q_{pat} and z_{pat} are larger than[2]

$$q_{thres} = \sqrt{\frac{e}{2}}\,\frac{d}{N}\min(\sigma_{h1},\sigma_{h2}), \qquad z_{thres} = \frac{1}{2}\sqrt{e}\,\frac{d}{N}\min(\sigma_{h1},\sigma_{h2}), \quad (5)$$

however, the eigenvalues corresponding to the set of modes $\hat{\vec{u}}_{\vec{k}}$ which are perpendicular to the (x,y)-plane and whose wave-vectors $\vec{k}$ are given by

$$|\vec{k}| = 2/\sigma_h \;\; if\; \sigma_{h1} = \sigma_{h2}, \qquad \left.\begin{array}{rcl} k_x & = & \pm 2/\sigma_{h1} \\ k_y & = & 0 \end{array}\right\} \; if\; \sigma_{h1} < \sigma_{h2}, \quad (6)$$

become positive. For larger values of q_{pat} and z_{pat} then, the topographic state becomes unstable and a "column system" forms.

For an isotropic neighborhood function ($\sigma_{h1} = \sigma_{h2} = \sigma_h$), the matrices $\hat{B}(\vec{k})$ and $\hat{D}(\vec{k})$ can be diagonalized simultaneously and the mean square amplitude of the fluctuations around the stationary state can be given in explicit form:

$$< u_{\parallel}^2(\vec{k}) > = \pi\frac{\varepsilon}{2}\sigma_h^2\frac{d^2}{N^2}\frac{(\sigma_h^4 k^2/4 + 1/12)\exp(-\sigma_h^2 k^2/4)}{\exp(\sigma_h^2 k^2/4) - 1 + \sigma_h^2 k^2/2} \quad (7)$$

$$< u_{\perp}^2(\vec{k}) > = \pi\frac{\varepsilon}{24}\sigma_h^2\frac{d^2}{N^2}\frac{\exp(-\sigma_h^2 k^2/4)}{\exp(\sigma_h^2 k^2/4) - 1} \quad (8)$$

$$< u_{y1}^2(\vec{k}) > = < u_{y2}^2(\vec{k}) > = \pi\frac{\varepsilon}{4}\sigma_h^2 q_{pat}^2\frac{\exp(-\sigma_h^2 k^2/4)}{\exp(\sigma_h^2 k^2/4) - (N^2 q_{pat}^2 k^2)/(2d^2)} \quad (9)$$

$$< u_z^2(\vec{k}) > = \pi\frac{\varepsilon}{2}\sigma_h^2 z_{pat}^2\frac{\exp(-\sigma_h^2 k^2/4)}{\exp(\sigma_h^2 k^2/4) - (N^2 q_{pat}^2 k^2)/d^2} \quad (10)$$

[2] In the derivation of the following formulas several approximations have to be made. A comparison with numerical simulations, however, demonstrate that these approximations are valid except if the value q_{pat} or z_{pat} is within a few percent of q_{thres} or z_{thres}, respectively. Details of these calculations will be published elsewhere

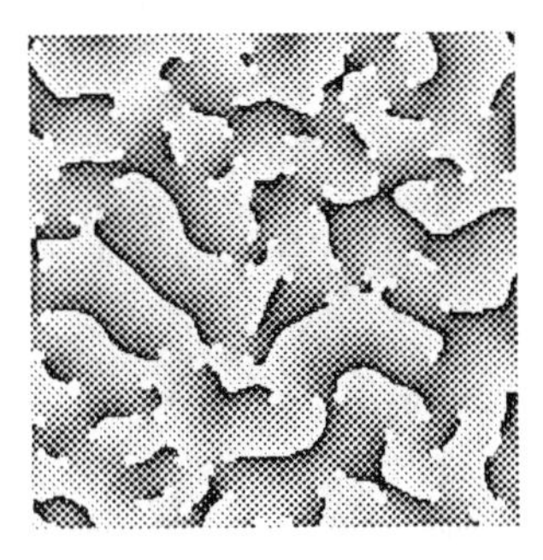
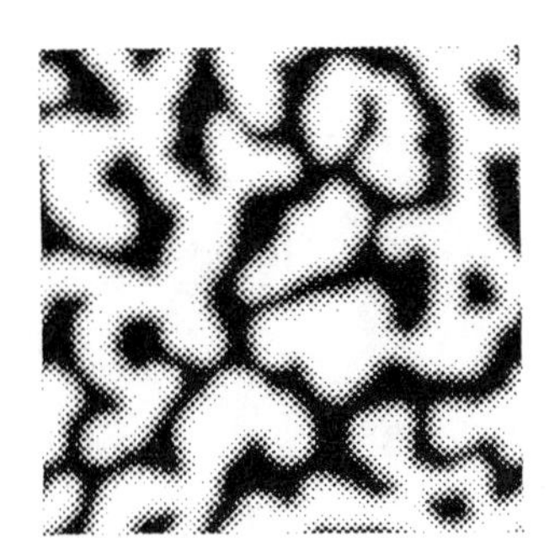
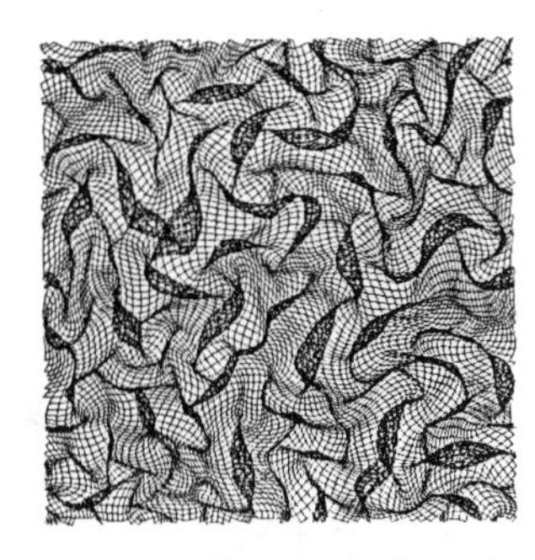

Figure 1: "Orientation preference" (**a**, left), "ocular dominance" (**b**, center) and locations of receptive field centers (**c**, right) as a function of unit loaction. Figure 1a displays an enlarged section of the "orientation map" only. Parameters of the simulation were: $N = 256$, $d = 256$, $q_{pat} = 12$, $z_{pat} = 12$, $\sigma_h = 5$, $\varepsilon = 0.02$

where $u_{\|}$, $u_{\perp}$ denote the amplitude of fluctuations parallel and orthogonal to $\vec{k}$ in the (x, y)-plane, u_{y1}, u_{y2} parallel to the orientation feature dimension and u_z parallel to the ocular dominance feature dimension, respectively.

Thus, for $q_{pat} \rightarrow q_{thres}$ or $z_{pat} \rightarrow z_{thres}$ the mean square amplitudes of fluctuations diverge for the modes which become unstable at the threshold (the denominator of eqs. (9,10) approaches zero) and the relaxation time of these fluctuations goes to infinity (not shown). The fact that either a ring or two groups of modes become unstable is reflected in the spatial structure of the maps above threshold.

For larger values of q_{pat} and z_{pat} orientation and ocular dominance are represented by the network layer, i.e. feature values fluctuate around a stationary state which is characterized by a certain distribution of feature-selective cells. Figure 1 displays orientation preference $\phi_{\vec{r}}$ (Fig. 1a), ocular dominance $z_{\vec{r}}$ (Fig. 1b) and the locations $(x_{\vec{r}}, y_{\vec{r}})$ of receptive field centers in visual space (Fig. 1c) as a function of unit location $\vec{r}$. Each pixel of the images in Figs. 1a,b corresponds to a network unit $\vec{r}$. Feature values are indicated by gray values: black $\rightarrow$ white corresponds to an angle of $0^o \rightarrow 180^o$ (Fig. 1a) and to an ocular dominance value of $0 \rightarrow$ max (Fig. 1b). White dots in Fig. 1a mark regions where units still completely unspecific for orientation are located ("foci"). In Fig. 1c the receptive field center of every unit is marked by a dot. The centers of units which are neighbors in the network layer were connected by lines, which gives rise to the net-like structure.

The overall preservation of the lattice topology, and the absence of any larger discontinuities in Fig. 1c, demonstrate that "position" plays the role of the primary stimulus variable and varies in a topographic fashion across the network layer. On a smaller length scale, however, numerous distortions are visible which are caused by the representation of the other features, "orientation" and "ocular dominance". The variation of these secondary features is highly repetitive and patterns strongly resembling orientation columns (Fig. 1b) and ocular dominance stripes (Fig. 1c) have formed. Note that regions unspecific for orientation as well as "binocular" regions exist in the final map, although these feature combinations were not present in the set of input patterns (3). They are correlated with regions of high magnitude of the "orientation" and "ocular dominance"-gradients, respectively (not shown). These structures are a consequence of the neighborhood preserving and dimension

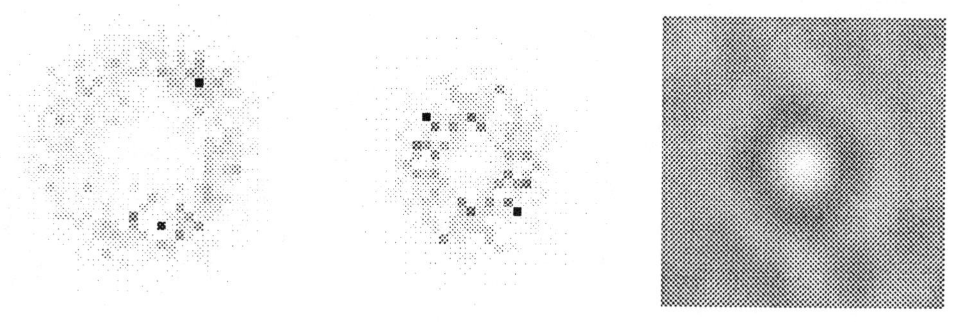

Figure 2: Two-dimensional Fourier spectra of the "orientation" (**a**, left) and "ocular dominance" (**b**, center) coordinates for the map shown in Fig. 1. **c**, right: Autocorrelation function of the feature coordinate $w_{\vec{r}3}$ for the map shown in Fig. 1.

reducing mapping; they do not result from the requirement of representing this particular set of feature combinations.[3]

Figure 2a,b shows the two-dimensional Fourier spectra $\hat{w}_{\vec{k},occ} = \sum_{\vec{r}} e^{i\vec{k}\vec{r}} z_{\vec{r}}$ and $\hat{w}_{\vec{k},ori} = \sum_{\vec{r}} e^{i\vec{k}\vec{r}} q_{\vec{r}}(\cos(2\phi_{\vec{r}}) + i\sin(2\phi_{\vec{r}}))$ for the "ocular dominance" (Fig. 2b) and "orientation" (Fig. 2a) coordinates, respectively. Each pixel corresponds to a single mode $\vec{k}$ and its brightness indicates the mean square amplitude $|\hat{w}_{\vec{k}}|^2$ of the mode $\vec{k}$. For an isotropic neighborhood function the orientation map is characterized by wave vectors from a ring shaped region in the Fourier domain (Fig. 2a), which becomes eccentric with increasing σ_{h1}/σ_{h2} (not shown) until the ring dissolves into two separate groups of modes. The phases (not shown) seem to be random, but we cannot exclude correlations completely. Figure 2c shows the autocorrelation function $S_{33}(\vec{s}) = < w_{(\vec{r}-\vec{s})3}\, w_{(\vec{s})3} >$ as a function of the distance $\vec{s}$ between cells in the network layer. The origin of the $\vec{s}$-plane is located in the center of the image and the brightness indicates a positive (white), zero (medium gray) or negative (black) value of S_{33}. The autocorrelation functions have a Mexican-hat form. The (negative) minimum is located at half the wavelength λ associated with the the wave number $|\vec{k}|$ of the modes with high amplitude in Fig. 2a. At this distance the response properties of the units are anticorrelated to some extent. If cells are separated by a distance larger than λ, the response properties are uncorrelated.

If q_{pat} and z_{pat} are large enough, the feature hierarchy observed in Figs. 1,2 breaks down and "preferred orientation" or "ocular dominance" plays the role of the primary stimulus variable. Figure 3 displays orientation preference $\phi_{\vec{r}}$ (Fig. 3a) and ocular dominance $z_{\vec{r}}$ (Fig. 3b) as a function of unit location $\vec{r}$. There is only one continous region for each interval of "preferred orientation" and for each eye, but each of these regions now contains a representation of a large part of visual space. Consequently the position map shows multiple representations of visual space.

Hierarchical maps are generated by the feature map algorithm whenever there is a hierarchy in the variances of the set of patterns along the various feature dimensions

[3]In the cortex, however, cells unspecific for orientation seem to be important for visual processing. To improve the description of the spatial structure of cortical maps, it is necessary to include these feature combinations into the set V of input patterns (see [9]).

Figure 3: "Orientation preference" (**a**, left) and "ocular dominance" (**b**, center) as a function of unit loaction for a map generated using a large value of q_{pat} and z_{pat}. Parameters were: $N = 128$, $d = 128$, $q_{pat} = 2500$, $z_{pat} = 2500$, $\sigma_h = 5$, $\varepsilon = 0.1$

(In our example a hierarchy in the magnitudes of d, q_{pat} and z_{pat}). The features with the largest variance become the primary feature; the other features become secondary features, which are represented multiple times on the network layer.

Acknowledgements

The authors would like to thank the Boehringer-Ingelheim Fonds for financial support by a scholarship to K. O. This research has been supported by the National Science Foundation (grant number 9017051). Computer time on the Connection Machine CM-2 has been made available by the National Center for Supercomputer Applications at Urbana-Champaign and the Pittsburgh Supercomputing Center both supported by the National Science Foundation.

References

[1] Hubel D.H. and Wiesel T.N. (1974), J. Comp. Neurol. **158**, 267-294
[2] Blasdel G.G. and Salama G. (1986), Nature **321**, 579-585
[3] Grinvald A. et al. (1986), Nature **324**, 361-364
[4] Swindale N.V. et al. (1987), J. Neurosci. **7**, 1414-1427
[5] Löwel S. et al. (1987), **255**, 401-415
[6] Ts'o D.Y. et al., Science **249**, 417-420
[7] Livingstone M.S. and Hubel D.H. (1984), J. Neurosci. **4**, 309-356
[8] Blasdel G.G. (1991), in preparation
[9] Obermayer K. et al. (1991), Proc. of the ICANN-91, Helsinki, submitted
[10] Obermayer K. et al. (1990), Proc. Natl. Acad. Sci. USA **87**, 8345-8349
[11] Kohonen T. (1982a), Biol. Cybern. **43**, 59-69
[12] Kohonen T. (1982b), Biol. Cybern.**44**, 135-140
[13] Nelson M.E. and Bower J.M. (1990), TINS **13**, 401-406
[14] Durbin R. and Mitchison M. (1990), Nature **343**, 644-647
[15] von der Malsburg C. (1973), Kybernetik **14**, 85-100
[16] Kohonen T. (1983), Self-Organization and Associative Memory, Springer-Verlag, New York
[17] Swindale N.V. (1982), Proc. R. Soc. Lond., **B215**, 211-230
[18] Goodhill G.J. and Willshaw D.J. (1990), Network **1**, 41-59
[19] Ritter H. and Schulten K. (1989), Biol. Cybern. **60**, 59-71

INTERACTION AMONG OCULARITY, RETINOTOPY AND ON-CENTER/OFF-CENTER PATHWAYS DURING DEVELOPMENT

Shigeru Tanaka
Fundamental Research Laboratories, NEC Corporation,
34 Miyukigaoka, Tsukuba, Ibaraki 305, Japan

ABSTRACT

The development of projections from the retinas to the cortex is mathematically analyzed according to the previously proposed thermodynamic formulation of the self-organization of neural networks. Three types of submodality included in the visual afferent pathways are assumed in two models: model (A), in which the ocularity and retinotopy are considered separately, and model (B), in which on-center/off-center pathways are considered in addition to ocularity and retinotopy. Model (A) shows striped ocular dominance spatial patterns and, in ocular dominance histograms, reveals a dip in the binocular bin. Model (B) displays spatially modulated irregular patterns and shows single-peak behavior in the histograms. When we compare the simulated results with the observed results, it is evident that the ocular dominance spatial patterns and histograms for models (A) and (B) agree very closely with those seen in monkeys and cats.

1 INTRODUCTION

A recent experimental study has revealed that spatial patterns of ocular dominance columns (ODCs) observed by autoradiography and profiles of the ocular dominance histogram (ODH) obtained by electrophysiological experiments differ greatly between monkeys and cats. ODCs for cats in the tangential section appear as beaded patterns with an irregularly fluctuating bandwidth (Anderson, Olavarria and Van Sluyters 1988); ODCs for monkeys are likely to be straight parallel stripes (Hubel, Wiesel and LeVay, 1977). The typical ODH for cats has a single peak in the middle of the ocular dominance corresponding to balanced response in ocularity (Wiesel and Hubel, 1974). In contrast to this, the ODH for monkeys has a dip in the middle of the ocular dominance (Hubel and Wiesel, 1963). Furthermore, neurons in the input layer of the cat's primary visual cortex exhibit orientation selectivity, while those of the monkey do not.

Through these comparisons, we can observe distinct differences in the anatomical and physiological properties of neural projections from the retinas to the visual cortex in monkeys and cats. To obtain a better understanding of these differences, theoretical analyses of interactions among ocularity, retinotopy and on-center/off-center pathways during visual cortical development were performed with computer simulation based on the previously proposed thermodynamic formulation of the self-organization of neural networks (Tanaka, 1990).

Two models for the development of the visual afferent pathways are assumed: model (A), in which the development of ocular dominance and retinotopic order is taken into account, and model (B), in which the development of on-center/off-center pathway terminals is considered in addition to ocular dominance and retinotopic order.

2 MODEL DESCRIPTION

The synaptic connection density of afferent fibers from the lateral geniculate nucleus (LGN) in a local equilibrium state is represented by the Potts spin variables $\sigma_{j,k,\mu}$'s because of their strong winner-take-all process (Tanaka, 1990). The following function $\pi_{eq}(\{\sigma_{j,k,\mu}\})$ gives the distribution of the Potts spins in equilibrium:

$$\pi_{eq}\left(\{\sigma_{j,k,\mu}\}\right) = \frac{1}{Z} exp\left(-\frac{H(\{\sigma_{j,k,\mu}\})}{T}\right) \tag{1}$$

$$\text{with } Z = \sum_{\{\sigma_{j,k,\mu}=1,0\}} exp\left(-\frac{H(\{\sigma_{j,k,\mu}\})}{T}\right) . \tag{2}$$

The Hamiltonian H in the argument of the exponential function in (1) and (2) determines the behavior of this spin system at the effective temperature T, where H is given by

$$H = -\sum_{j,j'}\sum_{\mu,\mu'}\sum_{\substack{k\in \mathbf{B}_j \\ k'\in \mathbf{B}_{j'}}} V^{\mathrm{VC}}_{j,j'} \Gamma^{\mathrm{LGN}}_{k,\mu,k',\mu'} \sigma_{j,k,\mu}\sigma_{j',k',\mu'} . \tag{3}$$

Function $V^{\mathrm{VC}}_{j,j'}$ represents the interaction between synapses at positions j and j' in layer 4 of the primary visual cortex; function $\Gamma^{\mathrm{LGN}}_{k,\mu,k',\mu'}$ represents the correlation in activity between LGN neurons at positions k and k' of cell types μ and μ'. The set $\mathbf{B}_j$ represents a group of LGN neurons which can project their axons to the position j in the visual cortex; therefore, the magnitude of this set is related to the extent of afferent terminal arborization in the cortex λ^{A}.

Taking the above formulation into consideration, we have only to discuss the thermodynamics in the Potts spin system described by the Hamiltonian H at the temperature T in order to discuss the activity-dependent self-organization of afferent neural connections during development.

Next, let us discuss more specific descriptions on the modeling of the visual afferent pathways. We will assume that the LGN serves only as a relay nucleus and that the signal is transferred from the retina to the cortex as if they were directly connected. Therefore, the correlation function $\Gamma^{\mathrm{LGN}}_{k,\mu,k',\mu'}$ can be treated as that in the retinas $\Gamma^{\mathrm{R}}_{k,\mu;k',\mu'}$. This function is given by using the lateral interaction function in the retina $V^{\mathrm{R}}_{k;k'}$ and the correlation function of stimuli to RGCs $G_{k_1\mu;k_2\mu'}$ in the following:

$$\Gamma^{R}_{k,\mu k',\mu'} = \sum_{k_1,k_2} V^{R}_{k;k_1} G_{k_1,\mu;k_2,\mu'} V^{R}_{k_2;k'} . \tag{4}$$

For simplicity, the stimuli are treated as white noise:

$$G_{k_1,\mu;k_2,\mu'} = \delta_{k_1,k_2} \cdot K_{\mu;\mu'} . \tag{5}$$

Now, we can obtain two models for the formation of afferent synaptic connections between the retinas and the primary visual cortex: model (A), in which ocularity and retinotopy are taken into account:

$$\mu \in \{\text{left, right}\}, \ \mathbf{K} = \begin{bmatrix} 1 & r_1 \\ r_1 & 1 \end{bmatrix} , \tag{6}$$

where r_1 $(0 \le r_1 \le 1)$ is the correlation of activity between the left and right retinas; and model (B), in which on-center and off-center pathways are added to model (A):

$$\mu \in \{(\text{left, on-center}), (\text{left, off-center}), (\text{right, on-center}), (\text{right, off-center})\} ,$$

$$\mathbf{K} = \begin{bmatrix} 1 & r_1+r_2 & r_1 & r_1 \\ r_1+r_2 & 1 & r_1 & r_1 \\ r_1 & r_1 & 1 & r_1+r_2 \\ r_1 & r_1 & r_1+r_2 & 1 \end{bmatrix} , \tag{7}$$

where r_2 $(-1 \le r_2 \le 1)$ is the correlation of activity between the on-center and off-center RGCs in the same retina when there is no correlation between different retinas. A negative value of r_2 means out-of-phase firings between on-center and off-center neurons.

3 COMPUTER SIMULATION

Computer simulations were carried out according to the Metropolis algorithm (Metropolis, 1953; Tanaka, 1991). A square panel consisting of 80×80 grids was assumed to be the input layer of the primary visual cortex, where the length of one grid is denoted by a. The Potts spin is assigned to each grid. Free boundary conditions were adopted on the border of the panel. One square panel of 20×20 grids was assumed to be a retina for each submodality μ. The length of one grid is given as $4a$ so that the edges for the square model cortex and model retinas are of the same length.

The following form was adopted for the interactions $V^{\nu}_{k;k'}$'s (ν = VC or R):

$$V^{\nu}_{k;k'} = \frac{q^{\nu}_{ex}}{2\pi\lambda^{\nu\,2}_{ex}} exp\left(-\frac{d^2_{k,k'}}{2\lambda^{\nu\,2}_{ex}}\right) - \frac{q^{\nu}_{inh}}{2\pi\lambda^{\nu\,2}_{inh}} exp\left(-\frac{d^2_{k,k'}}{2\lambda^{\nu\,2}_{inh}}\right) . \tag{8}$$

All results reported in this paper were obtained with parameters whose values are as follows: $q^{VC}_{ex} = 1.0$, $q^{VC}_{inh} = 5.0$, $\lambda^{VC}_{ex} = 0.15$, $\lambda^{VC}_{inh} = 1.0$, $q^{R}_{ex} = 1$, $\lambda^{R}_{ex} = 0.5$, $\lambda^{R}_{inh} = 1.0$, $\lambda^{A} = 1.6$, $a = 0.1$, $T = 0.001$, $r_1 = 0$, and $r_2 = -0.2$. It is assumed that $q^{R}_{inh} = 0$ for model (A) while $q^{R}_{inh} = 0.5$ for model (B). By considering that the receptive field (RF) of an RGC at position k is represented by $\mu V^{R}_{k;k'}$, RGCs for model (A) and (B) have low-pass and high-pass filtering properties, respectively. Monte Carlo simulation for model (A) was carried out for 200,000 steps; that for model (B) was done for 760,000 steps.

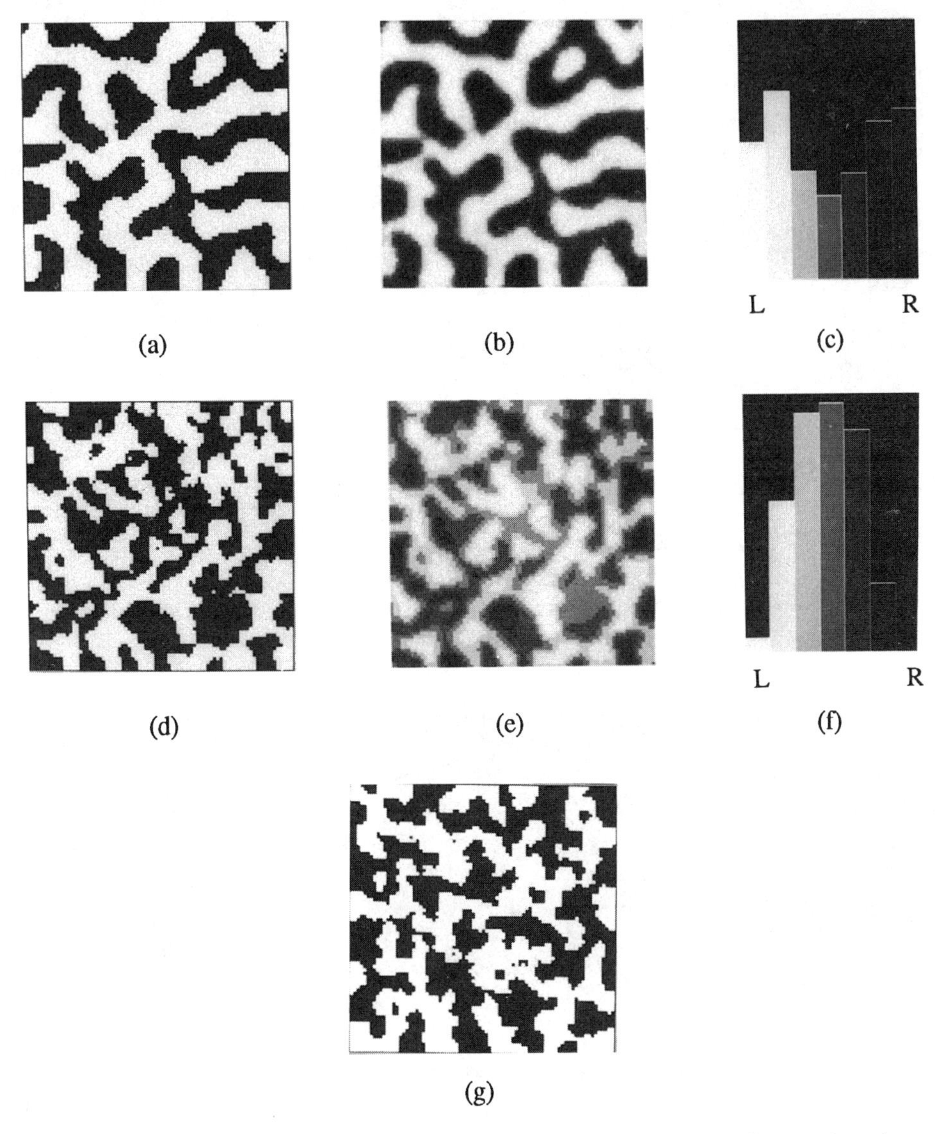

Fig. 1 Simulated results of synaptic terminal and neuronal distributions and ocular dominance histograms for models (A) and (B).

4 RESULTS AND DISCUSSIONS

The distributions of synaptic terminals and neurons, and ocular dominance histograms are shown in Fig. 1, where (a), (b) and (c) were obtained from model (A); (d), (e), (f) and (g) were obtained from model (B). The spatial distribution of synaptic terminals originating from the left or right retina (Figs. 1a and 1d) is a counterpart of an autoradiograph of the ODC by the eye-injection of radiolabeled amino acid. The bandwidth of the simulated ODC (Fig. 1a) is almost constant as well as the observed bandwidth for monkeys (Hubel and Wiesel, 1974). The distribution of ocularity in synaptic terminals shown in Fig. 1d is irregular in that the periodicity seen in Fig. 1a disappears even though a patchy pattern can be seen. This pattern is quite similar to the ODC for cats (Anderson, Olavarria and Van Sluyters 1988).

By calculating the convolution of the synaptic connections $\sigma_{j,k,\mu}$'s with the cortical interaction function $V^{VC}_{j,j'}$, the ocular dominance in response of cortical cells to monocular stimulation and the spatial pattern of the ocular dominance in activity (Figs. 1b and 1e) were obtained. Neurons specifically responding to stimuli presented in the right and left eyes are, respectively, in the black and white domains. This pattern is a counterpart of an electrophysiological pattern of the ODC. The distributions of ocularity in synaptic terminals correspond to those of ocular dominance in neuronal response to monocular stimulation (a to b; d to e in Fig. 1). This suggests that the borders of the autoradiographic ODC pattern coincide with those of the electrophysiological ODC pattern. This correspondence is not trivial since strong lateral inhibition exerts in the cortex.

Reflecting the narrow transition areas between monocular domains in Fig. 1b, a dip appears in the binocular bin in the corresponding ODH (Fig. 1c). In contrast, the profile of the ODH (Fig. 1f) has a single peak in the binocular bin since binocularly responsive neurons are distributed over the cortex (Fig. 1e).

In model (B), on-center and off-center terminals are also segregated in the cortex in superposition to the ODC pattern (Fig. 1g). No correlation can be seen between the spatial distribution of on-center/off-center terminals and the ODC pattern (Fig.1d).

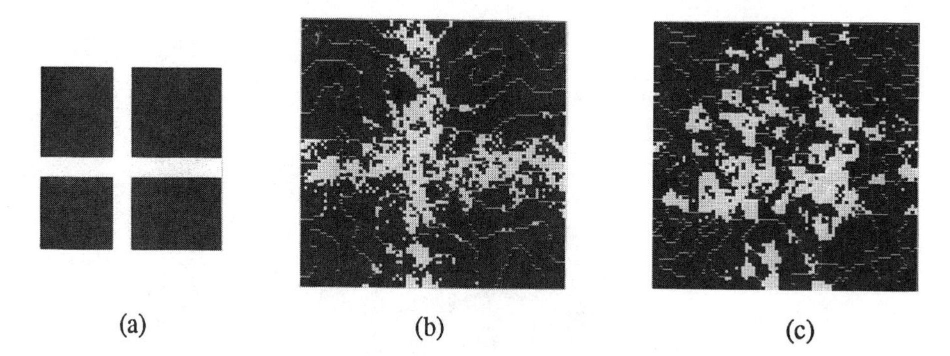

(a) (b) (c)

Fig. 2 A visual stimulation pattern (a) and the distributions of active synaptic terminals in the cortex [(b) for model (A) and (c) for model (B)].

Figures 2b and 2c visualize spatial patterns of active synaptic terminals in the cortex for model (A) and model (B), when the light stimulus shown by Fig.1d is presented to both retinas. A pattern similar to the stimulus appears in the cortex for model (A) (Fig. 1e). This supports the observation that retinotopic order is almost achieved. In other simulations for model (A), the retinotopic order in the final pattern was likely to be achieved when initial patterns were roughly ordered in retinotopy. In model (B), the retinotopic order seems to be broken at least in this system size even though the initial pattern has a well-ordered retinotopy (Fig. 1c). There is a tendency for retinotopy to be harder to preserve in model (B) than in model (A).

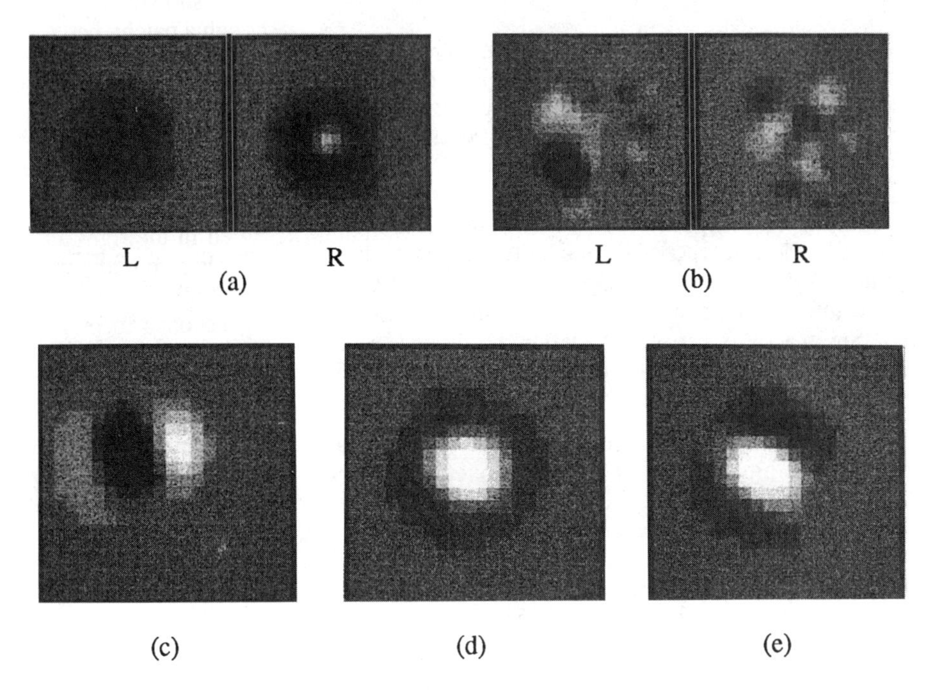

Fig. 3 Representative receptive fields obtained from simulations.

Model (A) reproduced only concentric RFs for both eyes. The dominant RFs of monocular neurons were of the on-center/off-surround type (right in Fig. 3a); the other RFs of the same neurons were of the type of the low-pass filter which has only the off response (left in Fig. 3a). In Model (B), RFs of cortical neurons generally had complex structures (Fig. 3b). It can barely be recognized that the dominant RFs of monocular neurons showed simple-cell-like RFs.

To determine why model (B) produced complex structures in RFs, another simulation of RF formation was carried out based on a model where retinotopy and on-center/off-center pathways are considered. Various types of RFs emerged in the cortex (bottom row in Fig. 3). The difference in structures between Figures. 3c and 3e shows the difference in the orientation and the phase (the deviation of the on region from the RF center) in the simple-cell-like RFs. Fig. 3d shows an on-center concentric RF. Such nonoriented RFs were likely to appear in the vicinity of the singular points around which the orientation rotates by 180 degrees.

Simulations for model (A) with different values of parameters such as q^{VC}_{inh}, λ^{A} and q^{R}_{inh} were also carried out although the results are not visualized here. When q^{VC}_{inh} takes a small value, the ODC bandwidth fluctuates). However large the fluctuation may be, the left-eye or right-eye dominant domains are well connected, and the pattern does not become an irregular beaded pattern as seen in the cat ODC. When afferent axonal arbors were widely spread in the cortex ($\lambda^A >> 1$), segregated ODC stripe patterns had only small fluctuation in the bandwidth. $q^R_{inh} = 0$ corresponds to a monotonically decreasing function $V^R_{k;k'}$ with respect to the radial distance $d_{k,k'}$. When q^R_{inh} was increased from zero, the number of monocular neurons was decreased. Therefore, the profile of the ODH changes from that in Fig. 1c.

In model (B), as the value of r_2 became smaller, on-center and off-center terminals were more sharply segregated, and the average size of the ODC patches became smaller. The segregation of on-center and off-center terminals seems to interfere strongly with the development of the ODC and the retinotopic organization. This may be attributed to the competition between ocularity and on-center/off-center pathways. We have seen that only concentric or simple-cell-like RFs can be obtained (Fig. 3b) unless both the ocularity and the on-center/off-center pathways are taken into account in simulations. However, in model (B) in which the two types of submodality are treated, neurons have complex separated RF structures (Fig. 3b). This also seems to be due to the competition among the ocularity and the on-center/off-center pathways. The simulation of model (B) was performed with no correlation in activity between the left and right eyes r_1. This condition can be realized for binocularly deprived kittens (Tanaka, 1989). By considering this, we may conclude that the formation of normal RFs needs cooperative binocular input.

In this research, we did not consider the effect of color-related cell types on ODC formation. Actually, there are varieties of single-opponent cells in the retina and LGN of monkeys such as four types of red-green opponent cells: a red on-center cell with a green inhibitory surround; a green on-center cell with a red inhibitory surround; a red off-center cell with a green excitatory surround; and a green off-center cell with a red excitatory surround. The correlation of activity between red on-center and green on-center cells or green off-center and red off-center cells may be positive in view of the fact that the spectral response functions between three photoreceptors overlap on the axis of the wavelength. However, the red on-center and green on-center cells antagonize the red off-center and green off-center cells, respectively. Therefore, the former two and latter two can be looked upon as the on-center and off-center cells seen in the retina of cats. This implies that the model for monkeys should be model (B); thereby, the ODC pattern for monkeys should be an irregular beaded pattern despite the fact that the ODC and ODH in model (A) resemble those for monkeys. To avoid such contradiction, the on-center and off-center cells must separately send their axons into different sublayers within layer 4Cβ, as seen in the visual cortex for Tree shrews (Fitzpatrick and Raczkowski, 1990).

5 CONCLUSION

In model (A), the ODC showed the striped pattern and the ODH revealed a dip in the binocular bin. In contrast to this, model (B) reproduced spatially modulated irregular ODC patterns and the single-peak behavior of the ODH. From comparison of these simulated results with experimental observations, it is evident that the ODCs and ODHs for models (A) and (B) agree very closely with those seen in monkeys and cats, respectively. Therefore, this leads to the conclusion that model (A) describes the development of the afferent fiber terminals of the primary visual cortex of monkeys, while model (B) describes that of the cat. In fact, the assumption of the negative correlation ($r_2 < 0$) between the on-center and off-center pathways in model (B) is consistent with the experiments on correlated activity between on-center and off-center RGCs for cats (Mastronarde, 1988).

Finally, we predict the following with regard to afferent projections for cats and monkeys.
[1] In the input layer of the visual cortex for cats, on-center/off-center pathway terminals are segregated into patches, superposing the ocular dominance patterns.
[2] In monkeys, the axons from on-center/off-center cells in the LGN terminate in different sublayers in layer 4Cβ of the primary visual cortex.

Acknowledgment

The author thanks Mr.Miyashita for his help in performing computer simulations of receptive field formation.

References

P.A. Anderson, J. Olavarria & R.C. Van Sluyters. (1988) The overall pattern of ocular dominance bands in the cat visual cortex. J. Neurosci., **8**: 2183-2200.

D.H. Hubel, T.N. Wiesel and S. LeVay. (1977). Plasticity of ocular dominance columns in monkey striate cortex. Philos. Trans. R. Soc. Lond., B**278**: 377-409.

T.N. Wiesel and D.H. Hubel. (1974).Ordered arrangement of orientation columns in monkeys lacking visual experience. J. Comp. Neurol. **158**: 307-318

D.H. Hubel and T.N. Wiesel. (1963). Receptive fields, binocular interaction and functional architecture in the cat's visual cortex. J. Physiol., **160**: 106-154.

S. Tanaka. (1990) Theory of self-organization of cortical maps: Mathematical framework. Neural Networks, **3**: 625-640.

N. Metropolis, A. W. Rosenbluth, M. N. Rosenbluth, A. H. Teller and E. Teller. (1953) Equation of state calculations by fast computing machines. J. Chem. Phys., **21**: 1087-1092.

S. Tanaka. (1991) Theory of ocular dominance column formation: Mathematical basis and computer simulation. Biol. Cybern., in press.

S. Tanaka. (1989) Theory of self-organization of cortical maps. In D. S. Touretzky (ed.), Advances in Neural Information Processing Systems 1, 451-458, San Mateo, CA: Morgan Kaufmann.

D. Fitzpatrick and D. Raczkowski. (1990) Innervation patterns of single physiologically identified geniculocortical axons in the striate cortex of the tree shrew. Proc. Natl. Acad. Sci. USA, **87**: 449-453.

D. N. Mastronarde. (1989) Correlated firing of retinal ganglion cells. Trends in Neurosci. **12**: 75-80.

Simple Spin Models for the Development of Ocular Dominance Columns and Iso-Orientation Patches

J.D. Cowan & A.E. Friedman
Department of Mathematics, Committee on
Neurobiology, and Brain Research Institute,
The University of Chicago, 5734 S. Univ. Ave.,
Chicago, Illinois 60637

Abstract

Simple classical spin models well-known to physicists as the ANNNI and Heisenberg XY Models, in which long-range interactions occur in a pattern given by the Mexican Hat operator, can generate many of the structural properties characteristic of the ocular dominance columns and iso-orientation patches seen in cat and primate visual cortex.

1 INTRODUCTION

In recent years numerous models for the formation of ocular dominance columns (Malsburg, 1979 ; Swindale, 1980; Miller, Keller, & Stryker, 1989) and of iso-orientation patches (Malsburg 1973; Swindale 1982 & Linsker 1986)have been published. Here we show that simple spin models can reproduce many of the observed features. Our work is similar to, but independent of a recent study employing spin models (Tanaka, 1990).

1.1 OCULAR DOMINANCE COLUMNS

We use a one-dimensional classical spin Hamiltonian on a two-dimensional lattice with long-range interactions. Let σ_i be a spin vector restricted to the orientations $\uparrow$ and $\downarrow$ in the lattice space, and let the spin Hamiltonian be:

$$H_{OD} = - \sum_{i} \sum_{j \neq i} w_{ij} \, \sigma_i \cdot \sigma_j \, , \qquad (1)$$

where w_{ij} is the well-known "Mexican Hat" distribution of weights:

$$w_{ij} = a_+ \exp(- |i-j|^2 / \sigma_+^2) - a_- \exp(- |i-j|^2 / \sigma_-^2) \qquad (2)$$

with $\sigma_+ < \sigma_-$ and $a_+ / a_- = \sigma_-^2 / \sigma_+^2$. Evidently $\sigma_i \cdot \sigma_j = \pm |\sigma_i| \, |\sigma_j| = \pm 1$, so that

$$H_{OD} = - \sum_{i} \sum_{j \neq i} w_{ij}^{s} - \sum_{i} \sum_{j \neq i} w_{ij}^{o} \qquad (3)$$

where $w_{ij}^{s} = w_{ij}$ if $\sigma_i = \sigma_j$, and $w_{ij}^{o} = - w_{ij}$ if $\sigma_i \neq \sigma_j$.

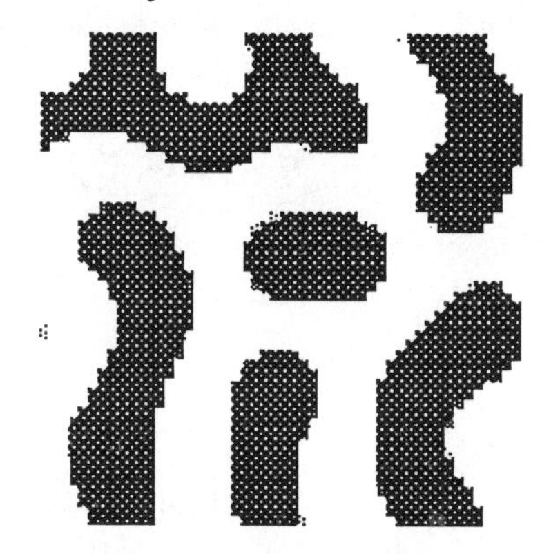

Figure 1. Pattern of Ocular Dominance which results from simulated annealing of the energy function H_{OD}. Light and dark shadings correspond respectively to the two eyes.

Let s denote retinal fibers from the same eye and o fibers from the opposite eye. Then H_{OD} represents the "energy" of interactions between fibers from the two eyes. It is relatively easy to find a configuration of spins which minimizes H_{OD} by simulated annealing (Kirkpatrick, Gelatt & Vecchi 1983). The result is shown in figure 1. It will be seen that the resulting pattern of right and left eye spins σ^R and σ^L is disordered, but at a constant wavelength determined in large part by the space constants σ_+ and σ_-.

Breaking the symmetry of the initial conditions (or letting the lattivce grow systematically) results in ordered patterns.

If H_{OD} is considered to be the energy function of a network of spins exhibiting gradient dynamics (Hirsch & Smale, 1974), then one can write equations for the evolution of spin patterns in the form:

$$\frac{d}{dt}\sigma_i^{\alpha} = -\frac{\partial}{\partial\sigma_i^{\alpha}} H_{OD} = \sum_{j\neq i} w_{ij}^{\alpha\beta}\sigma_j^{\beta}$$

$$= \sum_{j\neq i} w_{ij}^{s}\sigma_i^{\alpha} + \sum_{j\neq i} w_{ij}^{o}\sigma_i^{\beta} = \sum_{j\neq i} w_{ij}\sigma_i^{\alpha} - \sum_{j\neq i} w_{ij}\sigma_i^{\beta}, \qquad (4)$$

where α = R or L, β = L or R respectively. Equation (4) will be recognized as that proposed by Swindale in 1979.

1. 2 ISO-ORIENTATION PATCHES

Now let σ_i represent avector in the plane of the lattice which runs continuously from $\uparrow$ to $\downarrow$ without reference to eye class. It follows that

$$\sigma_i \cdot \sigma_j = |\sigma_i| \, |\sigma_i| \cos(\theta_i - \theta_j) \qquad (5)$$

where θ_i is the orientation of the ith spin vector. The appropriate classical spin Hamiltonian is:

$$H_{IO} = -\sum_i \sum_{j\neq i} w_{ij}\,\sigma_i \cdot \sigma_j = -\sum_i \sum_{j\neq i} w_{ij} \, |\sigma_i| \, |\sigma_i| \cos(\theta_i - \theta_j). \qquad (6)$$

Physicists will recognize H_{OD} as a form of the Ising Lattice Hamiltonian with long-range alternating next nearest neighbor interactions, a type of ANNNI model (Binder, 1986) and H_{IO} as a similar form of the Heisenberg XY Model for antiferromagnetic materials (Binder 1986).

Again one can find a spin configuration that minimizes H_{IO} by simulated annealing. The result is shown in figure 2 in which six differing orientations are depicted, corresponding to 30° increments (note that $\theta + \pi$ is equivalent to θ). It will be seen that there are long stretches of continuously changing spin vector orientations, with intercalated discontinuities and both clockwise and counter-clockwise singular regions around which the orientations rotate. A one-dimensional slice shows some of these features, and is shown in figure 3.

Figure 2. Pattern of orientation patches obtained by simulated annealing of the energy function H_{IO}. Six differing orientations varying from 0° to 180° are represented by the different shadings.

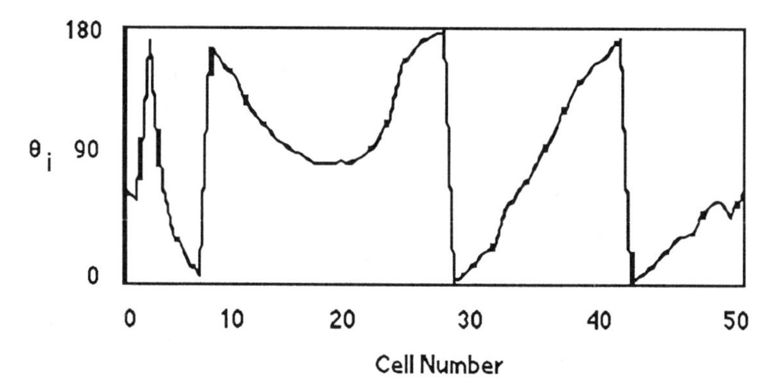

Figure 3. Details of a one-dimensional slice through the orientation map. Long stretches of smoothly changing orientations are evident.

The <u>length</u> of σ_i is also correlated with these details. Figure 4 shows that $|\sigma_i|$ is large in smoothly changing regions and smallest in the neighborhood of a singularity. In fact this model reproduces most of the details of iso-orientation patches found by Blasdel and Salama (1986).

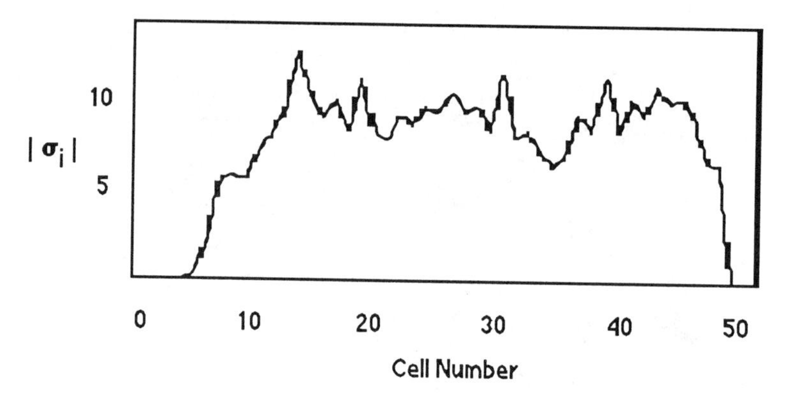

Figure 4. Variation of $|\sigma_i|$ along the same one-dim. slice through the orientation map shown in figure 3. The amplitude drops only near singular regions.

For example, the change in orientation per unit length, $|\mathrm{grad}\theta_i|$ is shown in figure 5. It will be seen that the lattice is "tiled", just as in the data from visual cortex, with max $|\mathrm{grad}\theta_i|$ located at singularities.

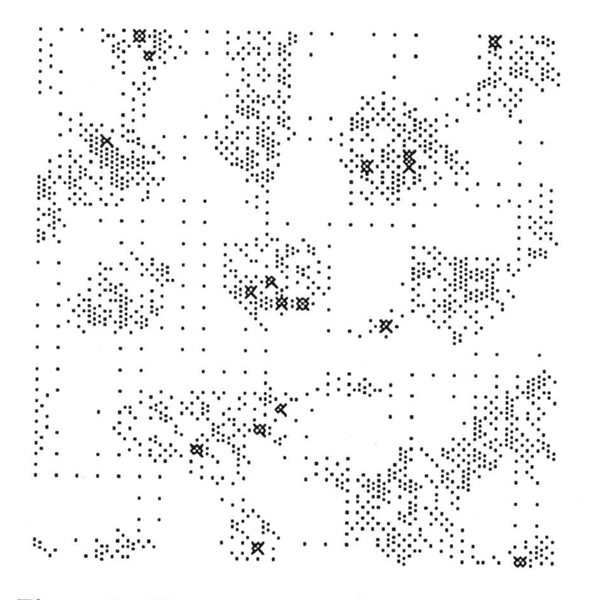

Figure 5. Plot of $|\mathrm{grad}\theta_i|$ corresponding to the orientation map of figure 2. Regions of maximum rate of change of θ_i are shown as shaded. These correspond with the singular regions of figure 2.

Once again, if H_{IO} is taken to be the energy of a gradient dynamical system, there results the equation:

$$\frac{d}{dt}\sigma_i = -\frac{\partial}{\partial\sigma_i}H_{IO} = \sum_{j\neq i} w_{ij}\sigma_j \qquad (7)$$

which is exactly that equation introduced by Swindale in 1981 as a model for the structure of iso-orientation patches. There is an obvious relationship between such equations, and recent similar treatments (Durbin & Mitchison 1990; Schulten, K. 1990 (Preprint); Cherjnavsky & Moody, 1990).

2 CONCLUSIONS

Simple classical spin models well-known to physicists as the ANNNI and Heisenberg XY Models, in which long-range interactions occur in a pattern given by the Mexican Hat operator, can generate many of the structural properties characteristic of the ocular dominance columns and iso-orientation patches seen in cat and primate visual cortex.

Acknowledgements

This work is based on lectures given at the Institute for Theoretical Physics (Santa Barbara) Workshop on Neural Networks and Spin Glasses, in 1986. We thank the Institute and The University of Chicago Brain Research Foundation for partial support of this work.

References

Malsburg, Ch.v.d. (1979), Biol. Cybern., **32**, 49-62.
Swindale, N.V. (1980), Proc. Roy. Soc. Lond. B, **208**, 243-264.
Miller, K.D., Keller, J.B. & Stryker, M. P. (1989), Science, **245**, 605-611.
Malsburg, Ch.v.d. (1973), Biol. Cybern., **14**, 85-100.
Swindale, N.V. (1982), Proc. Roy. Soc. Lond. B, **215**, 211-230.
Linsker, R. (1986), PNAS, **83**, 7508-7512; 8390-8394; 8779-8783.
Tanaka, S. (1990), Neural Networks, **3**, 6, 625-640.
Kirkpatrick, S., Gelatt, C.D. Jr. & Vecchi, M.P. (1983), Science, **229**, 671-679.
Hirsch, M.W. & Smale, S. (1974), Differential Equations, Dynamical Systems, and Linear Algebra. (Academic Press, NY).
Binder, K. (1986), Monte Carlo Methods in Statistical Physics, (Springer, NY.).
Blasdel, G.G. & Salama, G. (1986), Nature, **321**, 579-587.
Durbin, R. & Mitchison, G. (1990), Nature, **343**, 6259, 644-647.
Schulten, K. (1990) (Preprint).
Cherjnavsky, A. & Moody, J. (1990), Neural Computation, **2**, 3, 334-354.

A Recurrent Neural Network Model of Velocity Storage in the Vestibulo-Ocular Reflex

Thomas J. Anastasio
Department of Otolaryngology
University of Southern California
School of Medicine
Los Angeles, CA 90033

Abstract

A three-layered neural network model was used to explore the organization of the vestibulo-ocular reflex (VOR). The dynamic model was trained using recurrent back-propagation to produce compensatory, long duration eye muscle motoneuron outputs in response to short duration vestibular afferent head velocity inputs. The network learned to produce this response prolongation, known as velocity storage, by developing complex, lateral inhibitory interactions among the interneurons. These had the low baseline, long time constant, rectified and skewed responses that are characteristic of real VOR interneurons. The model suggests that all of these features are interrelated and result from lateral inhibition.

1 SIGNAL PROCESSING IN THE VOR

The VOR stabilizes the visual image by producing eye rotations that are nearly equal and opposite to head rotations (Wilson and Melvill Jones 1979). The VOR utilizes head rotational velocity signals, which originate in the semicircular canal receptors of the inner ear, to control contractions of the extraocular muscles. The reflex is coordinated by brainstem interneurons in the vestibular nuclei (VN), that relay signals from canal afferent sensory neurons to eye muscle motoneurons.

The VN interneurons, however, do more than just relay signals. Among other functions, the VN neurons process the canal afferent signals, stretching out their time constants by about four times before transmitting this signal to the motoneurons. This time constant prolongation, which is one of the clearest examples of signal processing in motor neurophysiology, has been termed velocity storage (Raphan et al. 1979). The neural mechanisms underlying velocity storage, however, remain unidentified.

The VOR is bilaterally symmetric (Wilson and Melvill Jones 1979). The semicircular canals operate in push-pull pairs, and the extraocular muscles are arranged in agonist/antagonist pairs. The VN are also arranged bilaterally and interact via inhibitory commissural connections. The commissures are necessary for velocity storage, which is eliminated by cutting the commissures in monkeys (Blair and Gavin 1981).

When the overall VOR fails to compensate for head rotations, the visual image is not stabilized but moves across the retina at a velocity that is equal to the amount of VOR error. This 'retinal slip' signal is transmitted back to the VN, and is known to modify VOR operation (Wilson and Melvill Jones 1979). Thus the VOR can be modeled beautifully as a three-layered neural network, complete with recurrent connections and error signal back-propagation at the VN level. By modeling the VOR as a neural network, insight can be gained into the global organization of this reflex.

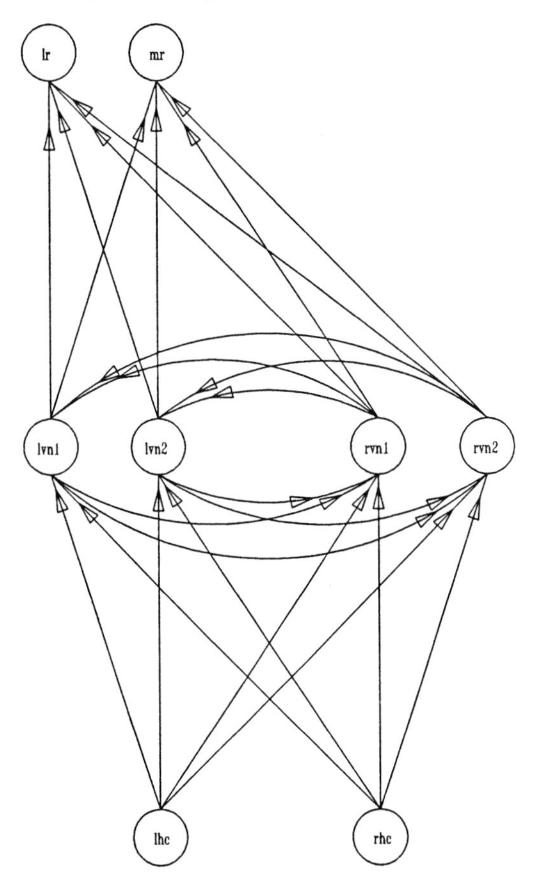

Figure 1: Architecture of the Horizontal VOR Neural Network Model. lhc and rhc, left and right horizontal canal afferents; lvn and rvn, left and right VN neurons; lr and mr, lateral and medial rectus motoneurons of the left eye. This and all subsequent figures are redrawn from Anastasio (1991), with permission.

2 ARCHITECTURE OF THE VOR NEURAL NETWORK MODEL

The recurrent neural network model of the horizontal VOR is diagrammed in Fig. 1. The input units represent afferents from the left and right horizontal semicircular canals (lhc and rhc). These are the canals and afferents that respond to yaw head rotations (as in shaking the head 'no'). The output units represent motoneurons of the lateral and medial rectus muscles of the left eye (lr and mr). These are the motoneurons and muscles that move the eye in the yaw plane. The units in the hidden layer correspond to interneurons in the VN, on both the left and right sides of the brainstem (lvn1, lvn2, rvn1 and rvn2). All units compute the weighted sum of their inputs and then pass this sum through the sigmoidal squashing function.

To represent the VOR relay, input project to hidden units and hidden project to output units. Commissural connections are modeled as lateral interconnections between hidden units on opposite sides of the brainstem. The model is constrained to allow only those connections that have been experimentally well described in mammals. For example, canal afferents do not project directly to motoneurons in mammals, and so direct connections from input to output units are not included in the model.

Evidence to date suggests that plastic modification of synapses may occur at the VN level but not at the motoneurons. The weights of synapses from hidden to output units are therefore fixed. All fixed hidden-to-output weights have the same absolute value, and are arranged in a reciprocal pattern. Hidden units lvn1 and lvn2 inhibit lr and excite mr; the opposite pattern obtains for rvn1 and rvn2. The connections to the hidden units, from input or contralateral hidden units, were initially randomized and then modified by the continually running, recurrent back-propagation algorithm of Williams and Zipser (1989).

3 TRAINING AND ANALYZING THE VOR NETWORK MODEL

The VOR neural network model was trained to produce compensatory motoneuron responses to two impulse head accelerations, one to the left and the other to the right, presented repeatedly in random order. The preset impulse responses of the canal afferents (input units) decay with a time constant of one network cycle or tick (Fig. 2, A and B, solid). The desired motoneuron (output unit) responses are equal and opposite in amplitude to the afferent responses, producing compensatory eye movements, but decay with a time constant four times longer, reflecting velocity storage (Fig. 2, A and B, dashed). Because of the three-layered architecture of the VOR, a delay of one network cycle is introduced between the input and output responses.

After about 5000 training set presentations, the network learned to match actual and desired output responses quite closely (Fig. 2, C and D, solid and dashed, respectively). The input-to-hidden connections arranged themselves in a reciprocal pattern, each input unit exciting the ipsilateral hidden units and inhibiting the contralateral ones. This arrangement is also observed for the actual VOR (Wilson and Melvill Jones 1979). The hidden-to-hidden (commissural) connections formed overlapping, lateral inhibitory feedback loops. These loops mediate velocity storage in the network. Their removal results in a loss of velocity storage (a decrease in output time constants from four to one tick), and also slightly increases output unit sensitivity (Fig. 2, C and D, dotted). These effects on VOR are also observed following commissurotomy in monkeys (Blair and Gavin 1981).

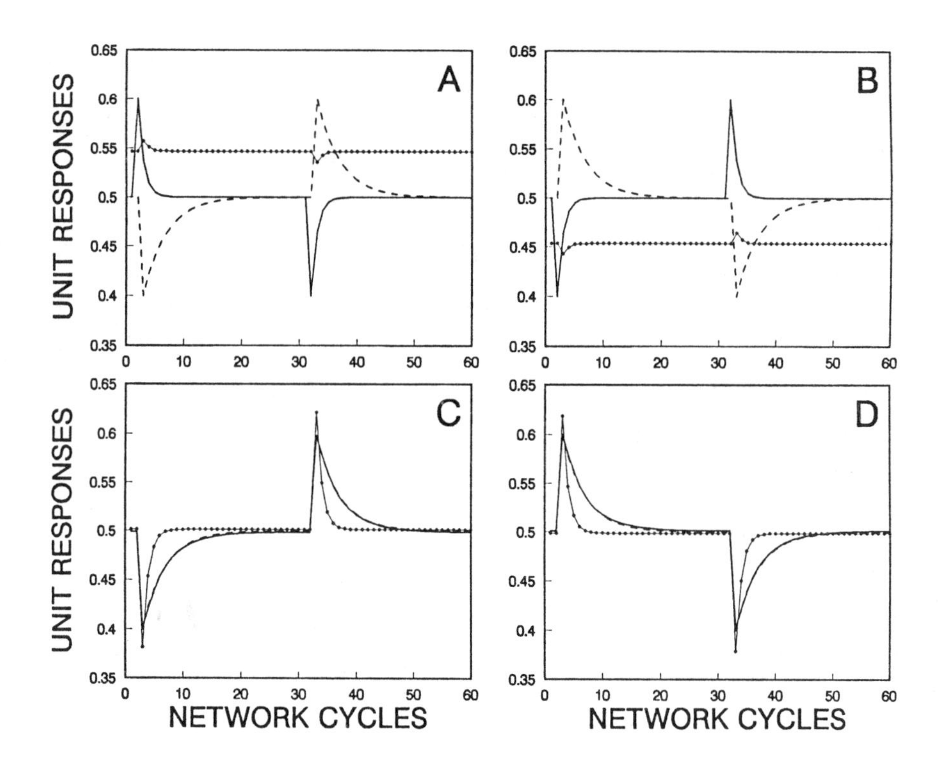

Figure 2: Training the VOR Network Model. A and B, input unit responses (solid), desired output unit responses (dashed), and incorrect output responses of initially randomized network (dotted); lhc and lr in A, rhc and mr in B. C and D, desired output responses (dashed), actual output responses of trained network (solid), and output responses following removal of commissural connections (dotted); lr in C, mr in D.

Although all the hidden units project equally strongly to the output units, the inhibitory connections between them, and their response patterns, are different. Hidden units lvn1 and rvn1 have developed strong mutual inhibition. Thus units lvn1 and rvn1 exert net positive feedback on themselves. Their responses appear as low-pass filtered versions of the input unit responses (Fig. 3, A, solid and dashed). In contrast, hidden units lvn2 and rvn2 have almost zero mutual inhibition, and tend to pass the sharply peaked input responses unaltered (Fig. 3, B, solid and dashed). Thus the hidden units appear to form parallel integrated (lvn1 and rvn1) and direct (lvn2 and rvn2) pathways to the outputs. This parallel arrangement for velocity storage was originally suggested by Raphan and coworkers (1979). However, units lvn2 and rvn2 are coupled to units rvn1 and lvn1, respectively, with moderately strong mutual inhibition. This coupling endows units lvn2 and rvn2 with longer overall decay times than they would have by themselves. This arrangement resembles the mechanism of feedback through a neural low-pass filter, suggested by Robinson (1981) to account for velocity storage. Thus, the network model gracefully combines the two mechanisms that have been identified for velocity storage, in what may be a more optimal configuration than either one alone.

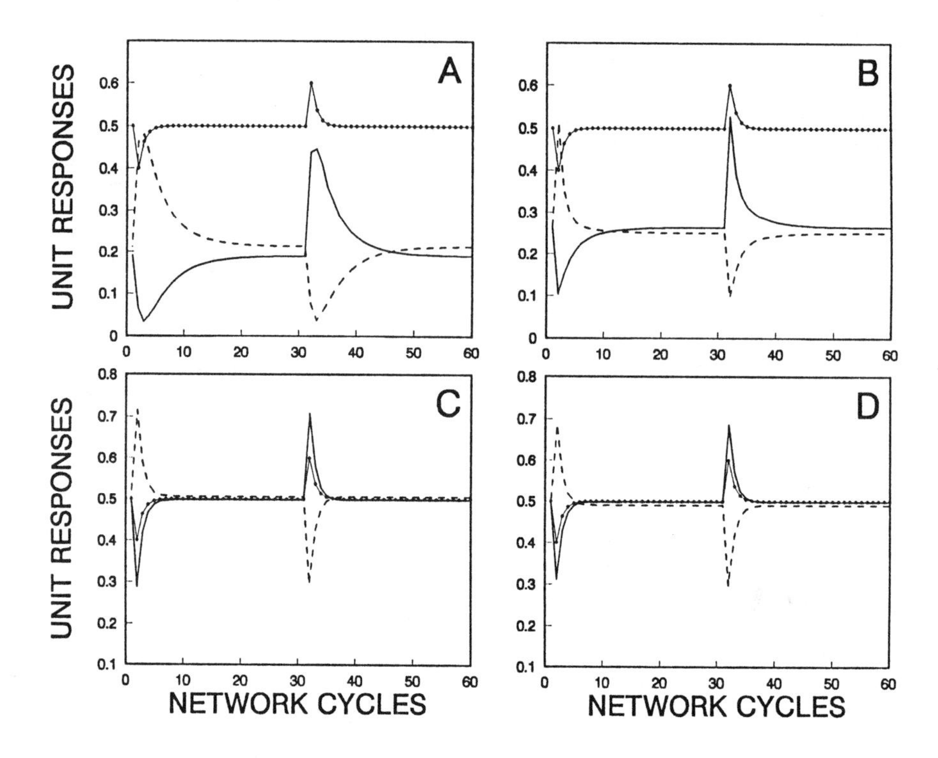

Figure 3: Responses of Model VN Interneurons. Networks trained with (A and B) and without (C and D) velocity storage. A and C, rvn1, solid; lvn1, dashed. B and D, rvn2, solid; lvn2, dashed. rhc, dotted, all plots.

Besides having longer time constants, the hidden units also have lower baseline firing rates and higher sensitivities than the input units (Fig. 3, A and B). The lower baseline forces the hidden units to operate closer to the bottom of the squashing function. This in turn causes the hidden units to have asymmetric responses, larger in the excitatory than in the inhibitory directions. Actual VN interneurons also have higher sensitivities, longer time constants, lower baseline firing rates and asymmetric responses as compared to canal afferents (Fuchs and Kimm 1975; Buettner et al. 1978).

For purposes of comparison, the network was retrained to produce a VOR without velocity storage (inputs and desired outputs had the same time constant of one tick). All of the hidden units in this network developed almost zero lateral inhibition. Although they also had higher sensitivities than the input units, their responses otherwise resembled input responses (Fig. 3, C and D). This demonstrates that the long time constant, low baseline and asymmetric responses of the hidden units are all interrelated by commissural inhibition in the network, which may be the case for actual VN interneurons as well.

4 NONLINEAR BEHAVIOR OF THE VOR NETWORK MODEL

Because hidden units have low baseline firing rates, larger inputs can produce inhibitory hidden unit responses that are forced into the low-sensitivity region of squashing function or even into cut-off. Hidden unit cut-off breaks the feedback loops that subserve velocity storage. This produces nonlinearities in the responses of the hidden and output units.

For example, an impulse input at twice the amplitude of the training input produces larger output unit responses (Fig. 4, A, solid), but these decay at a faster rate than expected (Fig. 4, A, dot-dash). Faster decay results because inhibitory hidden unit responses are cutting-off at the higher amplitude level (Fig. 4, C, solid). This cut-off disrupts velocity storage, decreasing the integrative properties of the hidden units (Fig. 4, C, solid) and increasing output unit decay rate.

Nonlinear responses are even more apparent with sinusoidal input. At low input levels, the output responses are also sinusoidal and their phase lag relative to the input is commensurate with their time constant of four ticks (Fig. 4, B, dashed). As sinusoidal in-

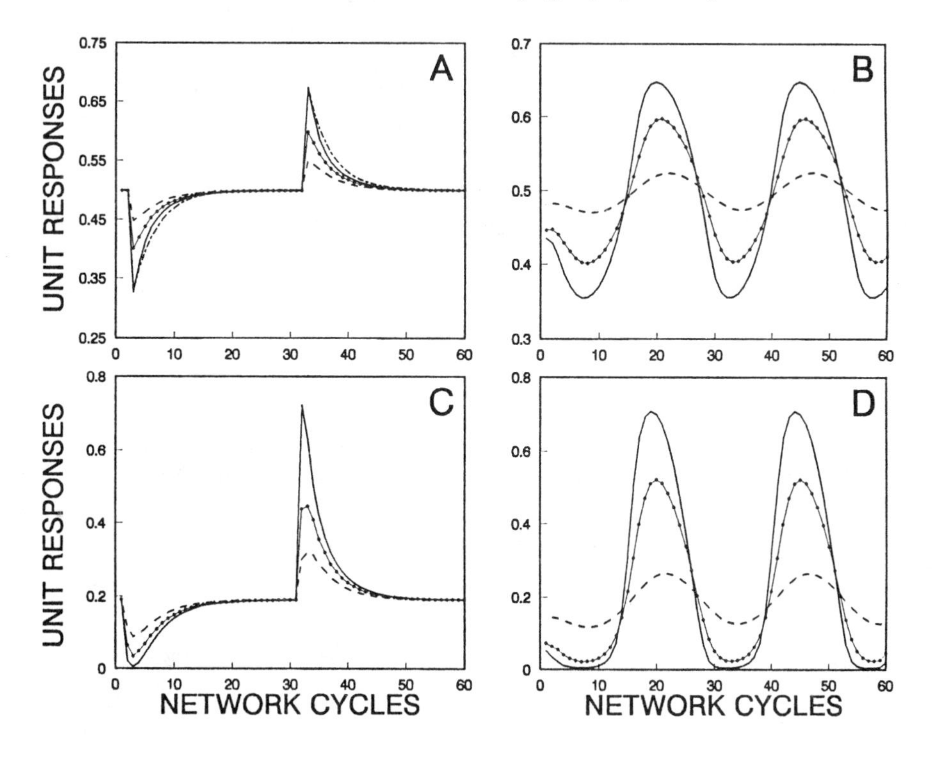

Figure 4: Nonlinear Responses of Model VOR Neurons. A and C, responses of lr (A) and rvn1 (C) to impulse inputs at low (dashed), medium (training, dotted) and high (solid) amplitudes. A, expected lr response at high input amplitude with time constant of four ticks (dot-dash). B and D, response of lr (B) and rvn1 (D) to sinusoidal inputs at low (dashed), medium (dotted) and high (solid) amplitudes.

put amplitude increases, however, output response phase lag decreases, signifying a decrease in time constant (Fig. 4, B, dotted and solid). Also, the output responses skew, such that the excursions from baseline are steeper than the returns. Time constant decrease and skewing with increase in head rotation amplitude are also characteristic of the VOR in monkeys (Paige 1983). Again, these nonlinearities are associated with hidden unit cut-off (Fig. 4, D, dotted and solid), which disrupts velocity storage, decreasing time constant and phase lag. Skewing results as the system time constant is lowered at peak and raised again midrange throughout each cycle of the responses. Actual VN neurons in monkeys exhibit similar cut-off (rectification) and skew (Fuchs and Kimm 1975; Buettner et al. 1978).

5 CONCLUSIONS

The VOR lends itself well to neural network modeling. The results summarized here, presented in detail elsewhere (Anastasio 1991), illustrate how neural network analysis can be used to study the organization of the VOR, and how its organization determines the response properties of the neurons that subserve this reflex.

Acknowledgments

This work was supported by the Faculty Research and Innovation Fund of the University of Southern California.

References

Anastasio, TJ (1991) Neural network models of velocity storage in the horizontal vestibulo-ocular reflex. Biol Cybern 64: 187-196

Blair SM, Gavin M (1981) Brainstem commissures and control of time constant of vestibular nystagmus. Acta Otolaryngol 91: 1-8

Buettner UW, Buttner U, Henn V (1978) Transfer characteristics of neurons in vestibular nuclei of the alert monkey. J Neurophysiol 41: 1614-1628

Fuchs AF, Kimm J (1975) Unit activity in vestibular nucleus of the alert monkey during horizontal angular acceleration and eye movement. J Neurophysiol 38: 1140-1161

Paige GC (1983) Vestibuloocular reflex and its interaction with visual following mechanisms in the squirrel monkey. I. Response characteristics in normal animals. J Neurophysiol 49: 134-151

Raphan Th, Matsuo V, Cohen B (1979) Velocity Storage in the vestibulo-ocular reflex arc (VOR). Exp Brain Res 35: 229-248

Robinson DA (1981) The use of control systems analysis in the neurophysiology of eye movements. Ann Rev Neurosci 4: 463-503

Williams RJ, Zipser D (1989) A learning algorithm for continually running fully recurrent neural networks. Neural Comp 1: 270-280

Wilson VJ, Melvill Jones G (1979) Mammalian Vestibular Physiology. Plenum Press, New York

Self-organization of Hebbian Synapses in Hippocampal Neurons

Thomas H. Brown,[†] Zachary F. Mainen,[†] Anthony M. Zador,[†] and Brenda J. Claiborne[*]

[†] Department of Psychology
Yale University
New Haven, CT 06511

[*] Division of Life Sciences
University of Texas
San Antonio, TX 78285

ABSTRACT

We are exploring the significance of biological complexity for neuronal computation. Here we demonstrate that Hebbian synapses in realistically-modeled hippocampal pyramidal cells may give rise to two novel forms of self-organization in response to structured synaptic input. First, on the basis of the electrotonic relationships between synaptic contacts, a cell may become tuned to a small subset of its input space. Second, the same mechanisms may produce clusters of potentiated synapses across the space of the dendrites. The latter type of self-organization may be functionally significant in the presence of nonlinear dendritic conductances.

1 INTRODUCTION

Long-term potentiation (LTP) is an experimentally observed form of synaptic plasticity that has been interpreted as an instance of a Hebbian modification (Kelso et al, 1986; Brown et al, 1990). The induction of LTP requires synchronous presynaptic activity and postsynaptic depolarization (Kelso et al, 1986). We have previously developed a detailed biophysical model of the LTP observed at synapses onto hippocampal region CA1 pyrami-

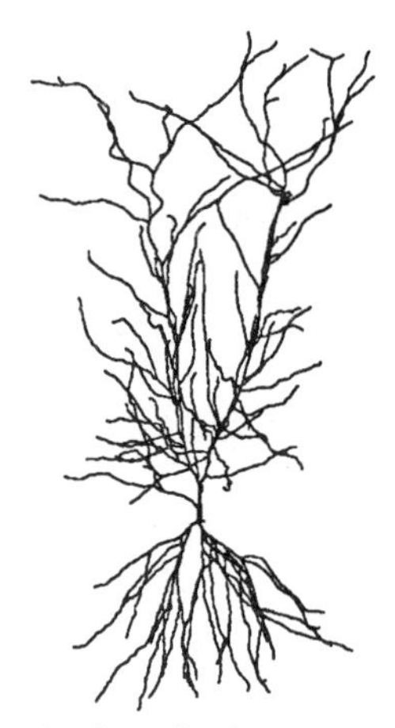

Figure 1: Two-dimensional projection of a reconstructed hippocampal CA1 pyramidal cell.

dal neurons (Zador et al, 1990). The synapses at which this form of LTP occurs are distributed across an extensive dendritic arbor (Fig. 1). During synaptic stimulation, the membrane voltage at each synapse is different. In this way, a biological neuron differs from the processing elements typically used in neural network models, where the postsynaptic activity can be represented by a single state variable. We have developed an electrotonic model based on an anatomically reconstructed neuron. We have used this model to explore how the spatial distribution of inputs and the temporal relationships of their activation affect synaptic potentiation.

2 THE NEURONAL MODEL

Standard compartmental modeling techniques were used to represent the electrical structure of hippocampal CA1 pyramidal cells.

2.1 MORPHOLOGY AND ELECTRICAL PARAMETERS

Morphometric data were obtained from three-dimensional reconstructions (Brown et al., 1991) of hippocampal neurons (Fig. 1). A correction factor was applied to the membrane area based on an estimate for spine density of 2 / μm. The original measurements divided a single neuron into 3000-4000 cylinders with an average length of 5.5 μm. For simulation purposes, this structure was collapsed into 300-400 compartments, preserving the connectivity pattern and changes in process diameter. Electrical constants were $R_m = 70\ k\Omega\text{-}cm^2$, $C_m = 1\ \mu F/cm^2$, $R_i = 200\ \Omega\text{-}cm$ (Spruston & Johnston 1990). The membrane was electrically passive. Synaptic currents were modeled as the sum of fast AMPA and slow NMDA conductances on the head of a two-compartment spine (Zador et al., 1990). The AMPA conductance was represented by an alpha function (Jack et al., 1975) with time constant of 1.5 *msec* (Brown and Johnston, 1983). The NMDA conductance was represented by a more complicated function with two time constants and a voltage dependence due to voltage-sensitive channel blocking by Mg^{2+} ions (see Zador et al., 1990; Brown et al. 1991). The initial peak conductances, g_{AMPA} and g_{NMDA}, were set to 0.5 and 0.1 *nS* respectively.

2.2 SIMULATION AND SYNAPTIC MODIFICATION

Simulations were run on a Sun 4/330 workstation using a customized version of NEURON, a simulator developed by Michael Hines (Hines, 1989). Prior to a simulation, 5 patterns of 40 synapses were selected at random from a pool of synapses distributed uniformly over the apical and basal dendrites. Simulations were divided into *trials* of 100 *msec*. At the beginning of each trial a particular pattern of synapses was activated synchronously (3 stimuli at intervals of 3 *msec*). The sequential presentation of all 5 selected patterns constituted an *epoch*. An entire simulation consisted of 20 presentation epochs. Over the course of each trial, membrane potential was computed at each location in the dendritic tree, and these voltages were used to compute weight changes Δw_{ij} according to the Hebbian algorithm described below. After each trial, the actual peak AMPA conductances (g_{AMPA}, hereafter denoted g_{syn}) were scaled by the sigmoidal function

$$g_{syn} = \frac{g_{max}}{1 + e^{-\sigma (W_{ij} - 0.5 g_{max})}} \tag{1}$$

where σ determines the steepness of the sigmoid, and g_{max} was set to 1.0 *nS*.

The rule for synaptic modification was based on a biophysical interpretation (Kairiss et al., 1991; Brown et al., 1991) of a generalized bilinear form of Hebbian algorithm (Brown et al., 1990):

$$\Delta w_{ij} = \alpha [a_i(t), a_j(t)] - \beta [a_i(t)] - \gamma [a_j(t)] - \delta, \tag{2}$$

where α, β, and γ are functionals, δ is a constant, $a_i(t)$ represents postsynaptic activity and $a_j(t)$ represents presynaptic activity. This equation specifies an interactive form of synaptic enhancement combined with three noninteractive forms of synaptic depression, all of which have possible neurobiological analogs (Brown et al, 1990). The interactive term was derived from a biophysical model of LTP induction in a spine (Zador et al., 1990). A simplified version of this model was used to compute the concentration of Ca^{2+}-bound calmodulin, [CaM-Ca_4]. It has been suggested that CaM-Ca_4 may trigger protein kinases responsible for LTP induction. In general [CaM-Ca_4] was a nonlinear function of subsynaptic voltage (Zador et al., 1990).

The biophysical mechanisms underlying synaptic depression are less well understood. The constant δ represents a passive decay process and was generally set to zero. The functional β represents heterosynaptic depression based on postsynaptic activity. In these simulations, β was proportional the amount of depolarization of the subsynaptic membrane from resting potential (V_{syn} - V_{rest}). The functional γ represents homosynaptic depression based on presynaptic activity. Here, γ was proportional to the AMPA conductance, which can be considered a measure of exclusively presynaptic activity because it is insensitive to postsynaptic voltage. The three activity-dependent terms were integrated over the period of the trial in order to obtain a measure of weight change. Reinterpreting α, β, and γ as constants, the equation is thus:

$$\Delta w_{ij} = \int_{trial} [\alpha [CamCa_4] - \beta (V_{syn} - V_{rest}) - \gamma g_{AMPA} - \delta] \, dt. \tag{3}$$

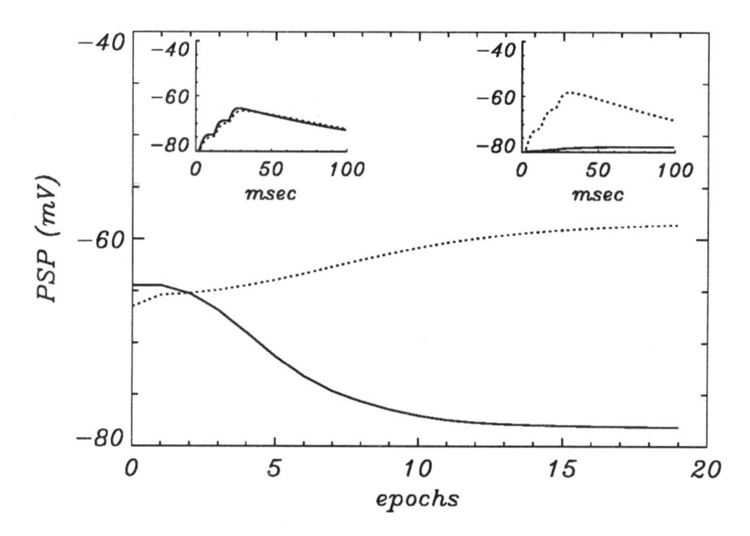

Figure 2: Interactions among Hebbian synapses produce differing global effects ("winning" and "losing" patterns) on the basis of the spatial distribution of synapses. The *PSP* (always measured at the soma) due to two different patterns of 40 synapses are plotted as a function of the presentation epoch. Initially, pattern 1 (*solid line*) evoked a slightly greater *PSP* than pattern 2 (*dotted line*; inset, top right). After 20 epochs these responses were reversed: the *PSP* due to pattern 1 was depressed while the *PSP* due to pattern 2 was potentiated (inset, top left).

3 RESULTS

Analysis of the simulations revealed self-organization in the form of differential modification of synaptic strengths (Mainen et al. 1990). Two aspects of the self-organization phenomena were distinguished. In some simulations, a form of *pattern selection* was observed in which clear "winners" and "losers" emerged. In other simulations, the average synaptic efficacy remained about the same, but spatial heterogeneities—*clustering*—of synaptic strength developed. Different measures were used to assess these phenomena.

3.1 PATTERN SELECTION

The change in the peak postsynaptic potential recorded at the soma (*PSP*) provided one useful measure of pattern selection. In many simulations, pattern selection resulted in a marked potentiation of the *PSP* due to some patterns and a depression of the *PSP* due to others. The *PSP* can be regarded as an indirect measure of the functional consequence of self-organization. In the simulation illustrated in Fig. 2, patterns of 40 synapses produced an average *PSP* of 15 *mV* before learning. After learning, responses ranged from 10% to 150% of this amount. Underlying pattern selection was a change in the average peak synaptic conductance for the pattern $\bar{g}_{syn}()$).[1] The initial value of $\bar{g}_{syn}$ was the same for all patterns, and its final value was bounded by eq. 1. In many simulations, $\bar{g}_{syn}$ approached the upper bound for some patterns and the lower bound for other patterns (Fig. 3). In this way, the neuron became selectively tuned to a subset of its original set of inputs. The specificity

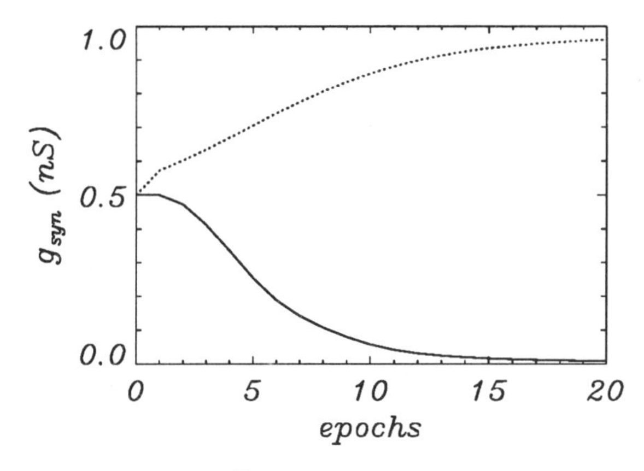

Figure 3. The mean synaptic conductance $\bar{g}_{syn}$ of two patterns is plotted as a function of the presentation epoch. Both patterns began with identical total synaptic strength (40 synapses with g_{syn} = 0.5 *nS*). Synaptic conductances were constrained to the range [0.0, 1.0] *nS*. After twenty epochs, $\bar{g}_{syn}$ of pattern 1 (*solid line*) approached the minimum of 0.0 *nS* while $\bar{g}_{syn}$ of pattern 2 (*dotted line*) approached the maximum of 1.0 *nS*.

of this tuning was dependent on the parameter values of the neuronal model, learning rule, and stimulus set.

3.2 CLUSTER FORMATION

Heterogeneity in the spatial distribution of strengthened and weakened synapses was often observed. After learning, *spatial clusters* of synapses with similar conductances formed. These spatial heterogeneities can be illustrated in several ways. In one convenient method (see Brown et al., 1991), synapses are represented as colored points superimposed on a rendition of the neuronal morphology as illustrated in Fig. 1. By color-coding g_{syn} for each synapse in a pattern, correlations in synaptic strength across dendritic space are immediately apparent. In a second method, better suited to the monochrome graphics available in the present text, the evolution of the variance of g_{syn} is plotted as a function of time (Fig. 4). In the simulation illustrated here, the increase in variance was due to the formation of a single, relatively large cluster of strengthened synapses. Within other parameter regimes, multiple clusters of smaller size were formed.

4 DISCUSSION

The important differences between synaptic modifications in the biophysically-modeled neuron and those in simple processing elements arise from voltage gradients present in the realistic model (Brown et al., 1991; Kairiss et al., 1990). In standard processing elements,

---

[1] Although $\bar{g}_{syn}$ and the somatic *PSP* were generally correlated, the relationship between the two is not linear, as was often evident in simulations (compare initial trials in Figs. 2 and 3).

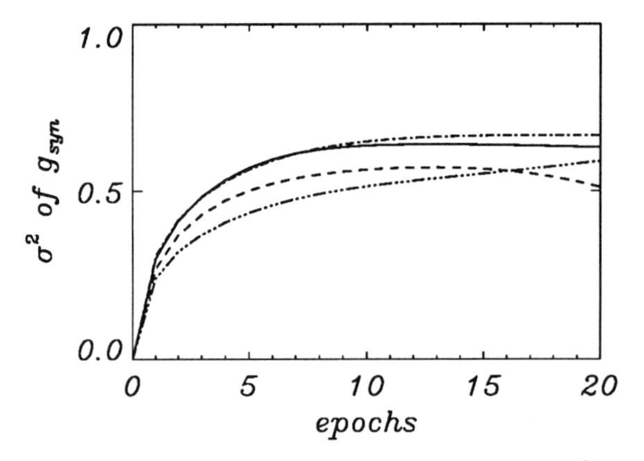

Figure 4: Synaptic heterogeneity is indicated by increases in the variance (σ^2) of the set of synaptic conductances for each pattern. The variances of the peak synaptic conductances (g_{syn}) of 4 patterns are plotted as a function of the epoch. The variance of all 4 patterns approached the theoretical maximum of $\sqrt{0.5}$. In this parameter regime, the variance was due to the potentiation of a single large cluster of synapes combined with the depression of other synapses.

a single state variable represents postsynaptic activity. In contrast, the critical subsynaptic voltages which represent postsynaptic activity in the neuron are correlated but are not strictly equal. The structure and electrical properties of the cell interact with its synaptic input to determine the precise spatiotemporal pattern of membrane voltage. Thus, the voltage at any synapse depends strongly on its electrotonic relationships to other active synapses. The way in which this local depolarization affects the nature of self-organization depends on the specific mechanisms of the synaptic modification rule. We have modeled a pair of opposing voltage-dependent mechanisms. An interactive potentiation mechanism (the functional α) promotes cooperativity between spatially proximal synapses with temporally correlated activity. A heterosynaptic depression mechanism (the functional β), which is independent of presynaptic activity, promotes competition among spatially proximal synapses. Through mechanisms such as these, the specific electrotonic structure of a neuron predetermines a complex set of interactions between any given spatial distribution of synaptic inputs. We have shown that these higher-order interactions can give rise to self-organization with at least two interesting effects.

4.1 SPARSE REPRESENTATION

The phenomenon of pattern selection demonstrates how Hebbian self-organization may naturally tune neurons to respond to a subset of their input space. This tuning mechanism might allow a large field of neurons to develop a sparse coding of the activity in a set of input fibers, since each neuron would respond to a particular small portion of the input space. Sparse coding may be advantageous to associative learning and other types of neural computation (Kanerva, 1988).

4.2 CLUSTERING AND NONLINEAR COMPUTATION

The formation of clusters of strengthened synapses illustrates a property of Hebbian self-organization whose functional significance might only be appreciated in the presence of nonlinear (voltage-dependent) dendritic conductances. We have examined the self-organization process in an electrically passive neuron. Under these conditions, the presence of clustering within patterns has little effect on the observed output. In fact, it is known that hippocampal cells of the type modeled possess a variety of spatially heterogeneous nonlinear dendritic conductances (Jones et al., 1989). The computational role of such nonlinearities is just beginning to be explored. It is possible that interactions between synaptic clustering and nonlinear membrane patches may significantly affect both the performance of dendritic computations and the process of self-organization itself.

Acknowledgments

This research was supported by grants from the Office of Naval Research, the Defense Advanced Research Projects Agency, and the Air Force Office of Scientific Research.

References

Brown, T.H. and Johnston, D. (1983) Voltage-clamp analysis of mossy fiber synaptic input to hippocampal neurons. *J. Neurophysiol.* **50**: 487-507.

Brown, T.H., Kairiss, E.W. and Keenan, C.L. (1990) Hebbian synapses: biophysical mechanisms and algorithms. *Annu. Rev. Neurosci.* **13**: 475-512.

Brown, T.H., Zador, A.M., Mainen, Z.F. and Claiborne, B.J. (1991) Hebbian modifications in hippocampal neurons. In J. Davis and M. Baudry (eds.), *LTP: A Debate of Current Issues* (Cambridge, MA: MIT Press).

Hines, M. (1989) A program for simulation of nerve equations with branching geometries. *Int. J. Bio-Med Comp* **24**: 55-68.

Jack, J., Noble, A. and Tsien, R.W. (1975) *Electrical Current Flow in Excitable Membranes* (London: Oxford Univ. Press).

Jones, O.T., Kunze, D.L and Angelides, K.J. (1989) Localization and mobility of w-conotoxin-sensitive Ca^{2+} channels in hippocampal CA1 neurons. *Science* 244: 1189-1193.

Kairiss, E.W., Mainen, Z.F., Claiborne, B.J. and Brown, T.H. (1991) Dendritic control of hebbian compuations. In F. Eeckman (ed.), *Analysis and Modeling of Neural Systems* (Boston, MA: Kluwer Academic Publishers).

Kanerva, P. (1988) *Sparse distributed memory.* (Cambridge, MA: MIT Press).

Kelso, S.R., Ganong, Brown, T.H. (1986) Hebbian synapses in hippocampus. *Proc. Natl. Acad. Sci. USA* **83**: 5326-5330.

Mainen, Z.M., Zador, A.M., Claiborne, B. and Brown, T.H. (1990) Hebbian synapses induce feature mosaics in hippocampal dendrites. *Soc. Neurosci. Abstr.* **16**: 492.

Spruston, N. and Johnston, D. (1990) Whole-cell patch clamp analysis of the passive membrane properties of hippocampal neurons. *Soc. Neurosci. Abstr.* **16**: 1297.

Zador, A., Koch, C. and Brown, T.H. (1990) Biophysical model of a hebbian synapse. *Proc. Natl. Acad. Sci. USA* **87**: 6718-6722.

Cholinergic Modulation May Enhance Cortical Associative Memory Function

Michael E. Hasselmo* Computation and Neural Systems Caltech 216-76 Pasadena, CA 91125

Brooke P. Anderson† Computation and Neural Systems Caltech 139-74 Pasadena, CA 91125

James M. Bower Computation and Neural Systems Caltech 216-76 Pasadena, CA 91125

Abstract

Combining neuropharmacological experiments with computational modeling, we have shown that cholinergic modulation may enhance associative memory function in piriform (olfactory) cortex. We have shown that the acetylcholine analogue carbachol selectively suppresses synaptic transmission between cells within piriform cortex, while leaving input connections unaffected. When tested in a computational model of piriform cortex, this selective suppression, applied during learning, enhances associative memory performance.

1 INTRODUCTION

A wide range of behavioral studies support a role for the neurotransmitter acetylcholine in memory function (Kopelman, 1986; Hagan and Morris, 1989). However, the role of acetylcholine in memory function has not been linked to the specific neuropharmacological effects of this transmitter within cerebral cortical networks. For several years, we have explored cerebral cortical associative memory function using the piriform cortex as a model system (Wilson and Bower, 1988, Bower, 1990; Hasselmo *et al.*, 1991). The anatomical structure of piriform cortex (represented schematically in figure 1) shows the essential features of more abstract associative

*e-mail: hasselmo@smaug.cns.caltech.edu

†e-mail: brooke@hope.caltech.edu

matrix memory models (Haberly and Bower, 1989) [1]. Afferent fibers in layer 1a provide widely distributed input, while intrinsic fibers in layer 1b provide extensive excitatory connections between cells within the cortex. Computational models of piriform cortex demonstrate a theoretical capacity for associative memory function (Wilson and Bower, 1988; Bower, 1990; Hasselmo *et al.*, 1991). Recently, we have investigated differences in the physiological properties of the afferent and intrinsic fiber systems, using modeling to test how these differences affect memory function. In the experiments described below, we found a selective cholinergic suppression of intrinsic fiber synaptic transmission. When tested in a simplified model of piriform cortex, this modulation enhances associative memory performance.

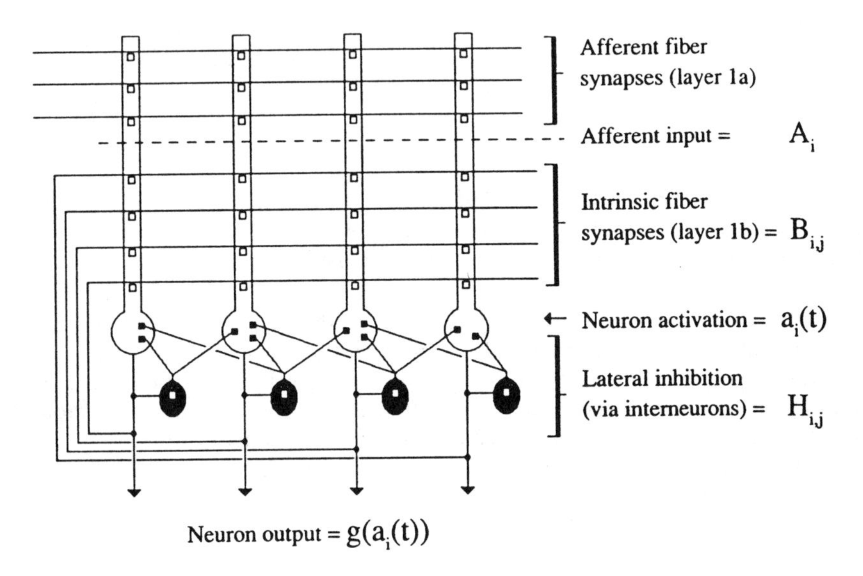

Figure 1: Schematic representation of piriform cortex, showing afferent input A_i (layer 1a) and intrinsic connections B_{ij} (layer 1b)

2 EXPERIMENTS

To study differences in the effect of acetylcholine on afferent and intrinsic fiber systems, we applied the pharmacological agent carbachol (a chemical analogue of acetylcholine) to a brain slice preparation of piriform cortex while monitoring changes in the strength of synaptic transmission associated with each fiber system. In these experiments, both extracellular and intracellular recordings demonstrated clear differences in the effects of carbachol on synaptic transmission (Hasselmo and Bower, 1991). The results in figure 2 show that synaptic potentials evoked by activating intrinsic fibers in layer 1b were strongly suppressed in the presence of

[1] For descriptions of standard associative memory models, see for example (Anderson *et al.*, 1977; Kohonen *et al.*, 1977).

100μM carbachol, while at the same concentration, synaptic potentials evoked by stimulation of afferent fibers in layer 1a showed almost no change.

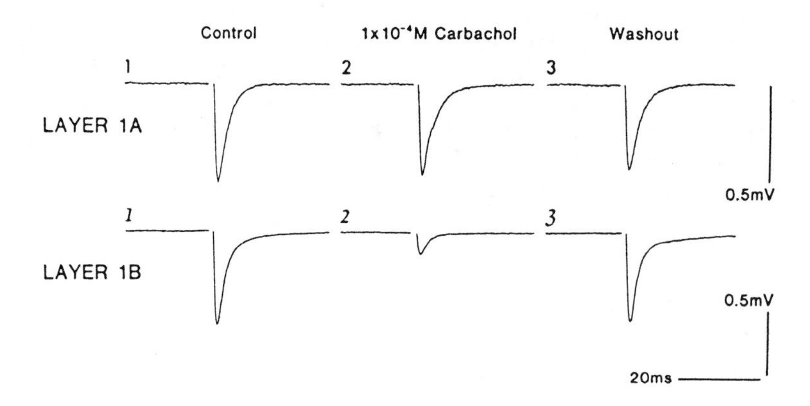

Figure 2: Synaptic potentials recorded in layer 1a and layer 1b before, during, and after perfusion with the acetylcholine analogue carbachol. Carbachol selectively suppresses layer 1b (intrinsic fiber) synaptic transmission.

These experiments demonstrate that there is a substantial difference in the neurochemical modulation of synapses associated with the afferent and intrinsic fiber systems within piriform cortex. Cholinergic agents selectively suppress intrinsic fiber synaptic transmission without affecting afferent fiber synaptic transmission. While interesting in purely pharmacological terms, these differential effects are even more intriguing when considered in the context of our computational models of memory function in this region.

3 MODELING

To investigate the effects of cholinergic suppression of intrinsic fiber synaptic transmission on associative memory function, we developed a simplified model of the piriform cortex. This simplified model is shown schematically in figure 1. At each time step, a neuron was picked at random, and its activation was updated as

$$a_i(t+1) = A_i(t) + \sum_{j=1}^{N}[(1-c)B_{ij} - H_{ij}]g(a_j(t)).$$

where N = the number of neurons; t = time $\in \{0, 1, 2, \ldots\}$; c = a parameter representing the amount of acetylcholine present. $c \in [0, 1]$; a_i = the activation or membrane potential of neuron i; $g(a_i)$ = the output or firing frequency of neuron i given a_i; A_i = the input to neuron i, representing the afferent input from the olfactory bulb; B_{ij} = the weight matrix or the synaptic strength from neuron j to neuron i; and H_{ij} = the inhibition matrix or the amount that neuron j inhibits neuron i. To account for the local nature of inhibition in the piriform cortex, $H_{ij} = 0$

for $|i-j| > r$ and $H_{ij} = h$ for $|i-j| \leq r$, where r is the inhibition radius. The function $g(a_i)$ was set to 0 if $a_i < \theta_a$, where θ_a = a firing threshold; otherwise, it was set to $\gamma_a \tanh(a_i - \theta_a)$, where γ_a = a firing gain.

The weights were updated every N time steps according to the following hebbian learning rule.

$$B_{ij} = f(W_{ij})$$
$$\Delta W_{ij} = W_{ij}(t+N) - W_{ij}(t) = (1-c)\gamma_\ell(a_i - \theta_\ell)g(a_j)$$

The function $f(\cdot)$ is a saturating function, similar to $g(\cdot)$, used so that the weights could not become negative or grow arbitrarily large (representing a restriction on how effective synapses could become). γ_ℓ is a parameter that adjusts learning speed, and θ_ℓ is a learning threshold. The weights were updated every N time steps to account for the different time scales between synapse modification and neuron settling.

3.1 TRAINING OF THE MODEL

During learning, the model was presented with various vectors (taken to represent odors) at the input ($A_i(t)$). The network was then allowed to run and the weights to adapt.

The procedure for creating the set of vectors $\{A^m \mid m \in \{1, \ldots, M\}\}$ was: set $A_i^m = \max\{0, G(\mu, \sigma)\}$, where G = gaussian with average μ and standard deviation σ, and normalize the whole vector so that $\|A^m\|^2 = N(\sigma^2 + \mu^2)$. M = number of memories or odors presented to network during training, and A_i^m = the input to neuron i while odor m is present.

During learning, in the asynchronous update equation, $A_i(t) = A_i^1$ for τ time steps, then $A_i(t) = A_i^2$ for the next τ time steps, and so on; i.e., the various odors were presented cyclically.

3.2 PERFORMANCE MEASURE FOR THE MODEL

The piriform cortex gets inputs from the olfactory bulb and sends outputs to other areas of the brain. Assuming that during recall the network receives noisy versions of the learned input patterns (or odors), we presume the piriform cortex performs a useful service if it reduces the chance of error in deciding which odor is present at the input. One way to quantify this is by using the minimum probability of classification error, P_e (from the field of pattern recognition [2]).

For the case of 2 odors corrupted by gaussian noise, P_e = the area underneath the intersection of the gaussians. For spherically symmetric gaussians with mean vectors μ_1 and μ_2 and identical standard deviations σ,

$$P_e = \frac{2}{\sqrt{\pi}} \int_{\frac{1}{2\sqrt{2}}\frac{d}{\sigma}}^{\infty} e^{-u^2} du$$

where $d = \|\mu_1 - \mu_2\|$. Thus, the important parameter is the amount of overlap as quantified by d/σ — the larger the d/σ, the lower the overlap and P_e.

[2] See, for example, (Duda and Hart, 1973).

For more than 2 odors and for non-gaussian noise or non-spherically-symmetric gaussian noise, the equation for P_e becomes less tractable. But keeping with the above calculations, an analogue of d/σ was developed as follows. σ_i^2 was set $=$ $\langle \|x - \mu_i\|^2 \rangle$, and then β was defined as

$$\beta \equiv \sum_{i<j} \frac{\|\mu_i - \mu_j\|}{\frac{1}{2}(\sigma_i + \sigma_j)}$$

where $i, j \in \{1, \ldots, M\}$. Here, β is the analogue of d/σ in the previous paragraph and is similar to an average over all odor pairs of d/σ.

For the model, if β is larger for the output vectors than for the input vectors, there is less overlap in the outputs, classification of the outputs is easier than classification of the inputs, and the model is serving a useful purpose. Thus, we use $\rho = \beta_{out}/\beta_{in}$ as the performance measure.

3.3 TESTING THE MODEL

The model was designed to show whether the presence of acetylcholine has any influence on learning performance. To that end, the model was allowed to learn for a time with various levels of acetylcholine present, and then acetylcholine was turned off and the model was tested.

For testing, weight adaptation was turned off, acetylcholine influence was turned off ($c = 0$), noisy versions of the various odors presented during learning were presented at the input, and the network was allowed to settle. From these noisy input/output pairs, σ's could be estimated, β_{in} and β_{out} could be calculated, and finally ρ could be calculated. Then, the state of the network could either be reset (for a new learning run) or be set to what it was before the test (so that learning could continue as if uninterrupted).

3.4 RESULTS OF TESTING

A typical example of a test run is shown in figure 3. There, c was varied from 0 (no acetylcholine) to .9 (a large concentration), and the various other parameters were: $N = 10$, $M = 10$, $r = 2$, $h = .3$, $\gamma_a = 1$, $\theta_a = 1$, $\gamma_\ell = 10^{-3}$, $\theta_\ell = 1$, and $\tau = 10$. In the figure, large dark rectangles represent larger values of ρ. Small or non-existant rectangles represent values of $\rho \leq 1$.

Notice that, for a fixed amount of acetylcholine, the model's performance rises and then falls over time. Ideally, the performance should rise and then flatten out, as further learning should not degrade performance. The weight adaptation equation used in the model was not optimized to preclude overlearning (where all of the weights being reinforced have saturated to the largest allowed value). In principle, the function $f(\cdot)$ could be used for this, perhaps in conjunction with a weight decay term. This was not of great concern since the peak performance is what indicates whether or not acetylcholine has a useful effect. Also, the more acetylcholine present, the longer the learning took. This is reasonable as, before saturation, $\Delta W \propto (1-c)$.

Figure 4 shows maximum average performance for various values of acetylcholine. Averages were calculated by doing many tests like the one above. This is useful as the odor inputs and the individual tests are stochastic in nature. Obviously, the larger values of acetylcholine enhance performance.

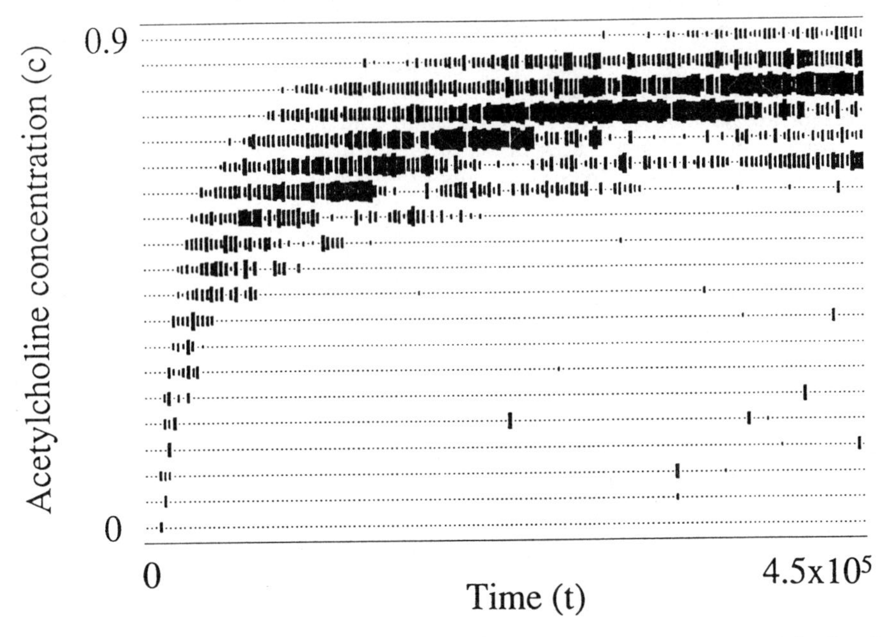

Figure 3: Sample test run, with time on the horizontal axis and acetylcholine level on the vertical axis. Larger black rectangles indicate better performance.

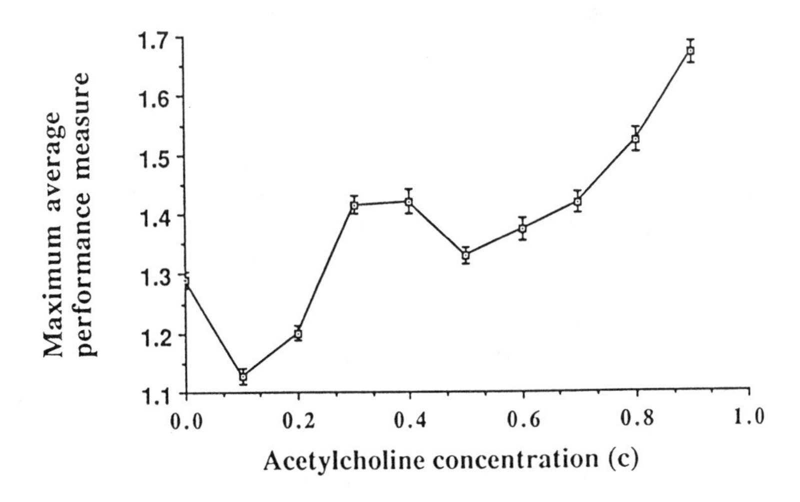

Figure 4: Maximum average performance vs. acetylcholine level. Acetylcholine increases the performance level attained.

4 CONCLUSION

The results from the model show that suppression of connections between cells within the piriform cortex during learning enhances the performance during recall. Thus, acetylcholine released in the cortex during learning may enhance associative memory function. These results may explain some of the behavioral evidence for the role of acetylcholine in memory function and predict that acetylcholine may be released in cortical structures preferentially during learning. Further biological experiments are necessary to confirm this prediction.

Acknowledgements

This work was supported by ONR contracts N00014-88-K-0513 and N00014-87-K-0377 and NIH postdoctoral training grant NS07251.

References

J.A. Anderson, J.W. Silverstein, S.A. Ritz and R.S. Jones (1977) Distinctive features, categorical perception, and probability learning: Some applications of a neural model. *Psychol. Rev.* 84: 413-451.

J.M. Bower (1990) Reverse engineering the nervous system: An anatomical, physiological and computer based approach. In S. Zornetzer, J. Davis and C. Lau (eds.), *An Introduction to Neural and Electronic Networks.* San Diego: Academic Press.

R. Duda and P. Hart (1973), *Pattern Classification and Scene Analysis*, New York: Wiley.

L.B. Haberly and J.M. Bower (1989) Olfactory cortex: Model circuit for study of associative memory? *Trends Neurosci.* 12: 258-264.

J.J. Hagan and R.G.M. Morris (1989) The cholinergic hypothesis of memory: A review of animal experiments. In L.L. Iversen, S.D. Iversen and S.H. Snyder (eds.) *Handbook of Psychopharmacology* Vol. 20 New York: Plenum Press.

M.E. Hasselmo, M.A. Wilson, B.P. Anderson and J.M. Bower (1991) Associative memory function in piriform (olfactory) cortex: Computational modeling and neuropharmacology. In: *Cold Spring Harbor Symposium on Quantitative Biology: The Brain.* Cold Spring Harbor: Cold Spring Harbor Laboratory.

M.E. Hasselmo and J.M. Bower (1991) Cholinergic suppression specific to intrinsic not afferent fiber synapses in piriform (olfactory) cortex. *J. Neurophysiol.* in press.

T. Kohonen, P. Lehtio, J. Rovamo, J. Hyvarinen, K. Bry and L. Vainio (1977) A principle of neural associative memory. *Neurosci.* 2:1065-1076.

M.D. Kopelman (1986) The cholinergic neurotransmitter system in human memory and dementia: A review. *Quart. J. Exp. Psychol.* 38A:535-573.

M.A. Wilson and J.M. Bower (1988) A computer simulation of olfactory cortex with functional implications for storage and retrieval of olfactory information. In D. Anderson (ed.) *Neural Information Processing Systems.* AIP Press: New York.

Part II

Neuro-Dynamics

Order Reduction for Dynamical Systems Describing the Behavior of Complex Neurons

Thomas B. Kepler — Biology Dept.
L. F. Abbott — Physics Dept.
Eve Marder — Biology Dept.

Brandeis University
Waltham, MA 02254

Abstract

We have devised a scheme to reduce the complexity of dynamical systems belonging to a class that includes most biophysically realistic neural models. The reduction is based on transformations of variables and perturbation expansions and it preserves a high level of fidelity to the original system. The techniques are illustrated by reductions of the Hodgkin-Huxley system and an augmented Hodgkin-Huxley system.

INTRODUCTION

For almost forty years, biophysically realistic modeling of neural systems has followed the path laid out by Hodgkin and Huxley (Hodgkin and Huxley, 1952). Their seminal work culminated in the accurately detailed description of the membrane currents expressed by the giant axon of the squid *Loligo*, as a system of four coupled non-linear differential equations. Soon afterward (and ongoing now) simplified, abstract models were introduced that facilitated the conceptualization of the model's behavior, *e.g.* (FitzHugh, 1961). Yet the mathematical relationships between these conceptual models and the realistic models have not been fully investigated. Now that neurophysiology is telling us that most neurons are complicated and subtle dynamical systems, this situation is in need of change. We suggest that a systematic program of simplification in which a realistic model of given complexity spawns a family of simplified meta-models of varying degrees of abstraction could yield considerable advantage. In any such scheme, the number of dynamical variables, or order, must be reduced, and it seems efficient and reasonable to do this first. This paper will be concerned with this step only. A sketch of a more thoroughgoing scheme proceeding ultimately to the binary formal neurons of

Hopfield (Hopfield, 1982) has been presented elsewhere (Abbott and Kepler, 1990). There are at present several reductions of the Hodgkin-Huxley (HH) system (FitzHugh, 1961; Krinskii and Kokoz, 1973; Rose and Hindmarsh, 1989) but all of them suffer to varying degrees from a lack of generality and/or insufficient realism.

We will present a scheme of perturbation analyses which provide a power-series approximation of the original high-order system and whose leading term is a lower-order system (see (Kepler et al., 1991) for a full discussion). The techniques are general and can be applied to many models. Along the way we will refer to the HH system for concreteness and illustrations. Then, to demonstrate the generality of the techniques and to exhibit the theoretical utility of our approach, we will incorporate the transient outward current described in (Connor and Stevens, 1972) and modeled in (Connor et al., 1977) known as I_A. We will reduce the resulting sixth-order system to both third- and second-order systems.

EQUIVALENT POTENTIALS

Many systems modeling excitable neural membrane consist of a differential equation expressing current conservation

$$C\frac{dV}{dt} + I(V,\{x_i\}) = I_{external}(t) \tag{1}$$

where V is the membrane potential difference, C is the membrane capacitance and I(V,x) is the total ionic current expressed as a function of V and the x_i, which are gating variables described by equations of the form

$$\frac{dx_i}{dt} = k_i(V)(\bar{x}_i(V) - x_i). \tag{2}$$

providing the balance of the system's description. The ubiquity of the membrane potential and its role as "command variable" in these model systems suggests that we might profit by introducing potential-like variables in place of the gating variables. We define the equivalent potential (EP) for each of the gating variables by

$$V_i = \bar{x}_i^{-1}(x_i). \tag{3}$$

In realistic neural models, the function $\bar{x}$ is ordinarily sigmoid and hence invertible. The chain rule may be applied to give us new equations of motion. Since no approximations have yet been made, the system expressed in these variables gives exactly the same evolution for V as the original system. The evolution of the whole HH system expressed in EPs is shown in fig.1. There is something striking about this collection of plots. The transformation to EPs now suggests that of the four available degrees of freedom, only two are actually utilized. Specifically, V_m is nearly indistinguishable from V, and V_h and V_n are likewise quite similar. This strongly suggests that we form averages and differences of EPs within the two classes.

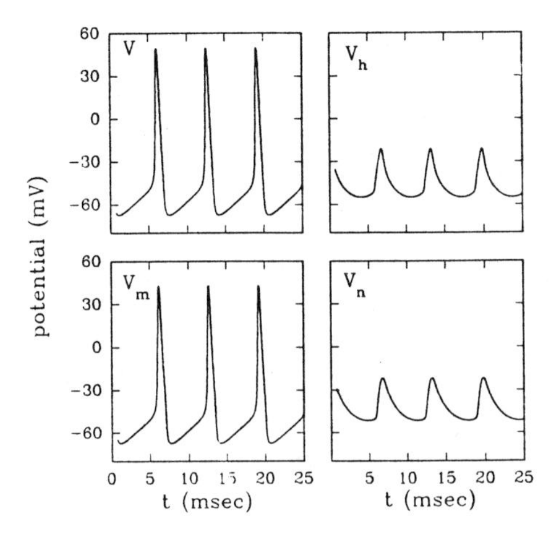

Figure 1: Behavior of equivalent potentials in repetetive firing mode of Hodgkin-Huxley system.

PERTURBATION SERIES

In the general situation, the EPs must be segregated into two or more classes. One class will contain the true membrane potential V. Members of this class will be subscripted with greek letters μ, ν, etc. while the others will be subscripted with latin indices i, j, etc. We make, within each class, a change of variables to 1) a new *representative* EP taken as a weighted average over all members of the class, and 2) differences between each member and their average. The transformations and their inverses are

$$\phi = \sum_{\mu} \alpha_{\mu} V_{\mu} \qquad \psi = \sum_{i} \alpha_i V_i$$
$$\delta_{\mu} = V_{\mu} - \langle V_{\nu} \rangle \qquad \delta_i = V_i - \langle V_j \rangle \tag{4}$$

and

$$V_{\mu} = \phi - \sum_{\nu} \alpha_{\nu} \delta_{\nu} + \delta_{\mu} \qquad V_i = \psi - \sum_{j} \alpha_j \delta_j + \delta_i. \tag{5}$$

We constrain the α_i and the α_{μ} to sum to one. The α's will not be taken as constants, but will be allowed to depend on ϕ and ψ. We expect, however, that their variation will be small so that most of the time dependence of ϕ and ψ will be carried by the V's. We differentiate eqs.(4), use the inverse transformations of eq.(5) and expand to first order in the δ's to get

$$\frac{d\psi}{dt} = \sum_{i} \alpha_i \, k_i(\phi)\left(\bar{x}_i(\phi) - \bar{x}_i(\psi)\right) + O(\delta) \tag{6}$$

and the new current conservation equation,

$$C\frac{d\phi}{dt} + \alpha_0 I(\phi, \{\bar{x}_{\mu}(\phi)\}, \{\bar{x}_i(\psi)\}) = I_{external}(t) + O(\delta). \tag{7}$$

This is still a current conservation equation, only now we have renormalized the capacitance in a state-dependent way through α_0. The coefficient the of δ's in eq.(6) will be small, at least in the neighborhood of the equilibrium point, as long as the basic premise of the expansion holds. No such guarantee is made about the corresponding coefficient in eq.(7). Therefore we will choose the α's to make the correction term *second* order in the δ's by setting the coefficient of each δ_i and δ_μ to zero. For the δ_μ we get,

$$\alpha_0 \alpha_\mu A - \alpha_0 I_{,\mu} + C \alpha_\mu k_\mu + C \dot{\alpha}_\mu = 0 \tag{8}$$

for $\mu \neq 0$, where

$$I_{,j} \equiv \frac{\partial I}{\partial x_j} \bar{x}_j^{-1} \tag{9}$$

and we use the abbreviation $A \equiv \Sigma I_{,\nu}$. And for $\mu = 0$,

$$\alpha_0^2 A - \alpha_0 I_{,0} - C \sum_{\nu \neq 0} \alpha_\nu k_\nu + C \dot{\alpha}_0 = 0 \tag{10}$$

Now the time derivatives of the α's vanish at the equilibrium point, and it is with the neighborhood of this point that we must be primarily concerned. Ignoring these terms yields surprisingly good results even far from equilibrium. This choice having been made, we solve for α_0, as the root of the polynomial

$$\alpha_0 A - I_{,0} - C \sum_{\mu \neq 0} k_\mu I_{,\mu} [\alpha_0 A + C k_\mu]^{-1} = 0 \tag{11}$$

whose order is equal to the number of EPs combining to form ϕ. The time dependence of ψ is given by specifying the α_i. This may be done as for the α_μ to get

$$\alpha_i = I_{,i} \, [\sum_j I_{,j}]^{-1} \tag{12}$$

EXAMPLE: HODGKIN-HUXLEY + I_A

For the specific cases in which the HH system is reduced from fourth order to second, by combining V and V_m to form ϕ and combining V_h and V_n to form ψ, the plan outlined above works without any further meddling, and yields a very faithful reduction. Also straightforward is the reduction of the sixth-order system given by Connor et al. (Connor et al., 1977) in which the HH system is supplemented by I_A (HH+A) to third order. In this reduction, the EP for the I_A activation variable, a, joins V_h and V_n in the formation of ψ. Alternatively, we may reduce to a second order system in which V_a joins with V and V_m to form ϕ and the EPs for n,h and the I_A inactivation variable, b, are combined to form ψ. This is not as straightforward. A direct application of eq.(12) produces a curve of singularities where the denominator vanishes in the expression for $d\psi/dt$; on one side $d\psi/dt$ has the same sign as $\phi - \psi$, (which it should) and on the other side it does not. Some additional decisions must be made here. We may certainly take this to be an indication that the reduction is breaking down, but through good fortune we are able to salvage it. This matter is dealt with in more detail elsewhere (Kepler et al., 1991). The reduced models are related in that the first is recovered when the maximum conductance of I_A is set to zero in either of the other two.

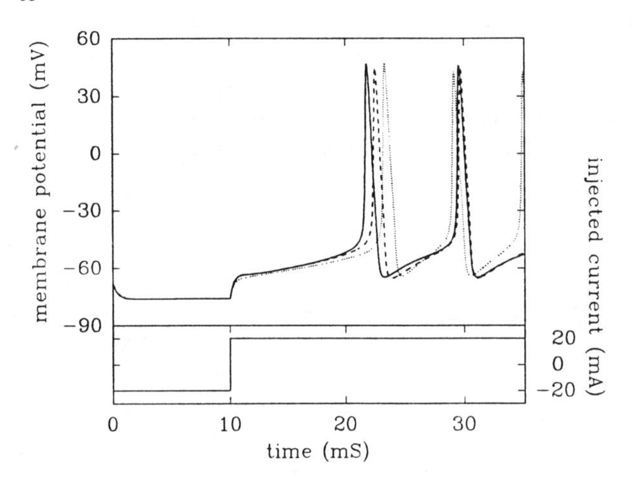

Figure 2: Response of full HH+A (solid line), 3rd order (dashed) and 2nd order systems to current step, showing latency to firing.

Figure 2 shows the voltage trace of a HH+A cell that is first hyperpolarized and then suddenly depolarized to above threshold. Traces from all three systems (full, 3rd order, 2nd order) are shown superimposed. This example focuses on the phenomenon of post inhibitory latency to firing. When a HH cell is depolarized sufficiently to produce firing, the onset of the first action potential is immediate and virtually independent of the degree of hyperpolarization experienced immediately beforehand. In contrast, the same cell with an I_A now shows a latency to firing which depends monotonically on the depth to which it had been hyperpolarized immediately prior to depolarization.

This is most clearly seen in fig.3 showing the phase portrait of the second-order system. The $d\phi/dt = 0$ nullcline has acquired a second branch. In order to get from the initial (hyperpolarized) location, the phase point must crawl over this obstacle, and the lower it starts, the farther it has to climb.

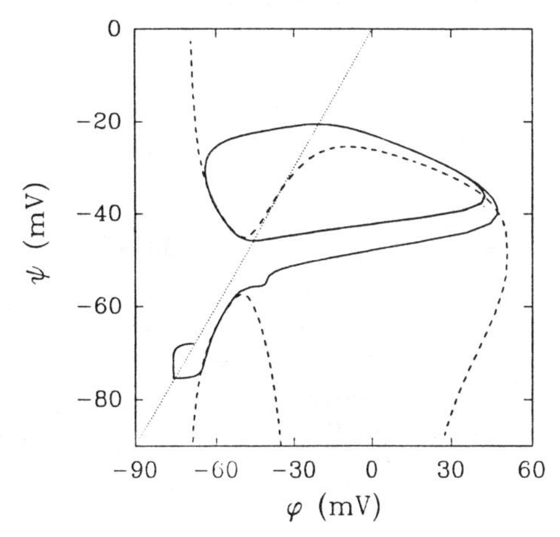

Figure 3: Phase portrait of event shown in fig.3 for 2nd order reduced system.

Figure 4 shows the firing frequency as a function of the injected current, for the full HH and HH+A sytems (solid lines), the HH second order HH+A third order (dashed lines) and HH+A second order (dotted line).* Note that the first reduction matches the full system quite well in both cases. The second reduction, however, does not do as well. It does get the qualitative features right, though. The expansion of the dynamic range for the frequency of firing is still present, though squeezed into a much smaller interval on the current axis. The bifurcation occurs at nearly the right place and seems to have the proper character, *i.e.*, saddle rather than Hopf, though this has not been rigorously investigated.

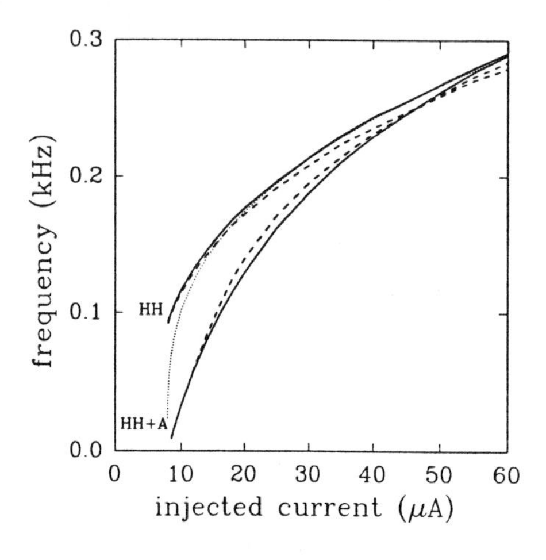

Figure 4: Firing frequency as a function of injected current. Solid: full systems, dashed: 2nd order HH & 3rd order HH+A, dotted: 2nd order HH+A. (From Kepler et al., 1991)

The reduced systems are intended to be dynamically realistic, to respond accurately to the kind of time-dependent external currents that would be encountered in real networks. To put this to the test, we ran simulations in which $I_{external}(t)$ was given by a sum of sinusoids of equal amplitude and randomly chosen frequency and phase. Figure 5 illustrates the remarkable match between the full HH+A system and the third-order reduction, when such an irregular (quasiperiodic) current signal is used to drive them.

CONCLUSION

We have presented a systematic approach to the reduction of order for a class of dynamical systems that includes the Hodgkin-Huxley system, the Connor et al. I_A extension of the HH system, and many other realistic neuron models. As mentioned at the outset, these procedures are merely the first steps in a more comprehensive program of simplification. In this way, the conceptual advantage of abstract models may be joined to the biophysical realism of physiologically derived models in a smooth and tractable manner, and the benefits of simplicity may be enjoyed with a clear conscience.

---

*For purposees of comparison, the HH system used here is as modified by (Connor et al., 1977), but with I_A removed and the leakage reversal potential adjusted to give the same resting potential as the HH+A cell.

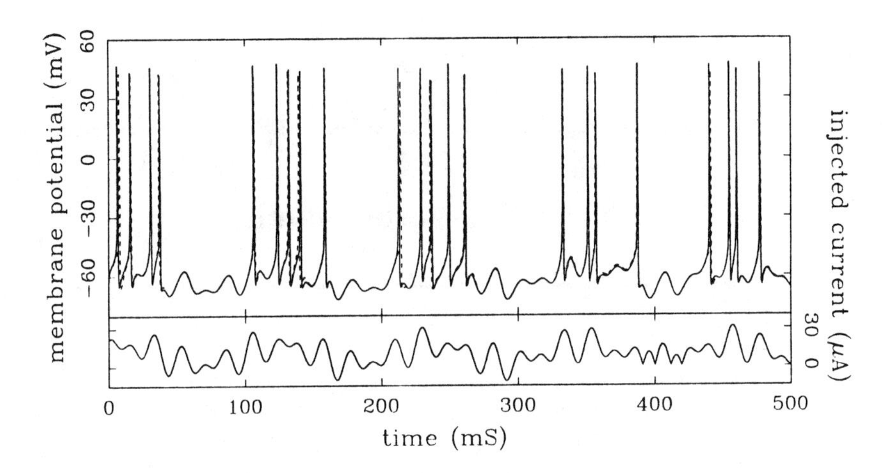

Figure 5: Response of HH+A system to irregular current injection. Solid line: full system, dashed line: 3rd order reduction.

Acknowledgment

This work was supported by National Institutes of Health grant T32NS07292 (TBK), Department of Energy Contract DE-AC0276-ER03230 (LFA) and National Institutes of Mental Health grant MH46742 (EM).

REFERENCES

L.F.Abbott and T.B.Kepler, 1990 in *Proceedings of the XI Sitges Conference on Neural Networks* in press

J.A.Connor and C.F.Stevens, 1971 *J.Physiol.,Lond.* **213** 31

J.A.Connor, D.Walter and R.McKown, 1977 *Biophys.J.* **18** 81

R.FitzHugh, 1961 *Biophys. J.* **1** 445

A.L.Hodgkin and A.F.Huxley, 1952 *J. Physiol.* **117**, 500

J.J.Hopfield, 1982 *Proc.Nat.Acad.Sci.* **79** 2554

T.B.Kepler, L.F. Abbott and E.Marder, 1991 submitted to *Biol.Cyber.*

V.I.Krinskii and Yu.M.Kokoz, 1973 *Biofizika* **18** 506

R.M.Rose and J.L.Hindmarsh, 1989 *Proc.R.Soc.Lond.* **237** 267

Stochastic Neurodynamics

J.D. Cowan
Department of Mathematics, Committee on
Neurobiology, and Brain Research Institute,
The University of Chicago, 5734 S. Univ. Ave.,
Chicago, Illinois 60637

Abstract

The main point of this paper is that stochastic neural networks have a mathematical structure that corresponds quite closely with that of quantum field theory. Neural network Liouvillians and Lagrangians can be derived, just as can spin Hamiltonians and Lagrangians in QFT. It remains to show the efficacy of such a description.

1 INTRODUCTION

A basic problem in the analysis of large-scale neural network activity, is that one can never know the initial state of such activity, nor can one safely assume that synaptic weights are symmetric, or skew-symmetric. How can one proceed, therefore, to analyse such activity? One answer is to use a "Master Equation" (Van Kampen, 1981). In principle this can provide statistical information, moments and correlation functions of network activity by making use of ensemble averaging over all possible initial states. In what follows I give a short account of such an approach.

1.1 THE BASIC NEURAL MODEL

In this approach neurons are represented as simple gating elements which cycle through several internal states whenever the net voltage generated at their activated post-synaptic sites exceeds a threshold. These states are "quiescent", "activated", and "refractory", labelled 'q', 'a', and 'r' respectively. There are then four transitions to consider: q → a, r → a, a → r, and r → q. Two of these, q → a, and r → a, are functions of the neural membrane current. I assume that on the time scale measured in units of τ_m, the membrane time constant, the instantaneous transition rate $\lambda(q \rightarrow a)$ is a smooth function of the input current. $J_i(T)$. The transition rates $\lambda(q \rightarrow a)$ and $\lambda(r \rightarrow a)$ are then given by:

$$\lambda_q = \theta[(J(T)/J_q)-1] = \theta_q[J(T)], \quad (1)$$

and

$$\lambda_r = \theta[(J(T)/J_r)-1] = \theta_r[J(T)], \quad (2)$$

respectively, where J_q and J_r are the threshold currents related to θ_q and θ_r, and where $\theta[x]$ is a suitable smoothly increasing function of x, and $T = t/\tau_m$. . The other two transition rates, $\lambda(a \rightarrow r)$ and $\lambda(r \rightarrow q)$ are defined simply as constants α and β. Figure 1 shows the "kinetic" scheme that results. Implicit in this scheme is the smoothing of input current pulses that takes place in the membrane,and also the smoothing caused by the

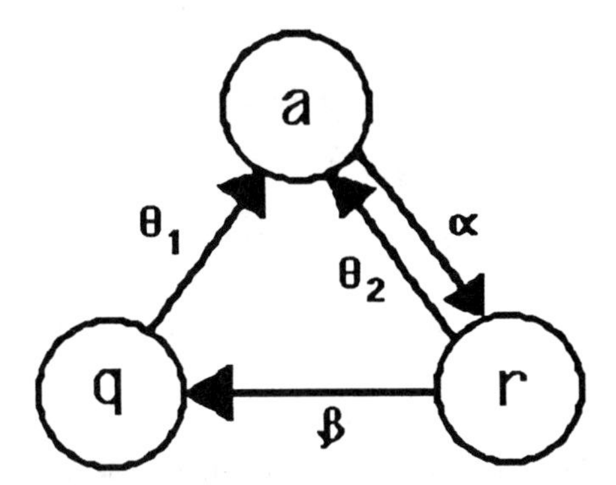

Figure 1. Neural state transition rates

presumed <u>asynchronous</u> activation of synapses. This simplified description of neural state transitions is essential to our investigation of cooperative effects in large nets.

1.2 PROBABILITY DISTRIBUTIONS FOR NEURAL NETWORK ACTIVITY

The configuration space of a neural network is the space of distinguishable patterns of neural activity. Since each neuron can be in the state q, a or r, there are 3^N such patterns in a network of N neurons. Since N is $0(10^{10})$, the configuration space is in principle very large. This observation, together with the existence of random fluctuations of neural activity, and the impracticability of specifying the initial states of all the neurons in a large network, indicates the need for a probabilistic description of the formation and decay of patterns of neural activity.

Let Q(T), A(T), R(T) denote the numbers of quiescent, activated, and refractory neurons in a network of N neurons at time T. Evidently,

$$Q(T)+A(T)+R(T) = N, \qquad (3)$$

Consider therefore N neurons in a d-dimensional lattice. Let a neural state vector be denoted by

$$|\,\Omega> = |v_1 v_2 \ldots\ldots\ldots v_N> \qquad (4)$$

where v_i means the neuron at the site i is in the state v = q, a , or r. Let $P[\Omega(T)]$ be the probability of finding the network in state $|\,\Omega>$ at time T, and let

$$|\,P(T)\rangle = \sum_{\Omega} P[\Omega(T)]|\,\Omega> \qquad (5)$$

be a neural probability state vector. Evidently $\sum_{\Omega} P[\Omega(T)] = 1.$ (6)

1.3 A NEURAL NETWORK MASTER EQUATION

Now consider the most probable state transitions which can occur in an asynchronous noisy network. These are:

(Q, A, R) → (Q, A, R) no change

(Q+1, A-1, R) → (Q, A, R) activation of a quiescent cell

(Q, A-1, R+1) → (Q, A, R) activation of a refractory cell

(Q, A+1, R-1) → (Q, A, R) an activated cell becomes refractory

(Q-1, A, R+1) → (Q, A, R) a refractory cell beomes quiescent.

All other transitions, e.g., those involving two or more transitions in time dT, are assumed to occur with probability O(dT).

These state transitions can be represented by the action on a set of basis vectors, of certain matrices. Let the basis vectors be:

$$|q> = \begin{pmatrix} \cdot \\ \cdot \\ 1 \end{pmatrix}, \quad |a> = \begin{pmatrix} 1 \\ \cdot \\ \cdot \end{pmatrix}, \quad |r> = \begin{pmatrix} \cdot \\ 1 \\ \cdot \end{pmatrix} \tag{7}$$

and consider the Gell-Mann matrices representing the Lie Group SU(3) (Georgi, 1982) :

$$\lambda_1 = \begin{pmatrix} \cdot & 1 & \cdot \\ 1 & \cdot & \cdot \\ \cdot & \cdot & \cdot \end{pmatrix} \quad \lambda_2 = \begin{pmatrix} \cdot & -i & \cdot \\ i & \cdot & \cdot \\ \cdot & \cdot & \cdot \end{pmatrix} \quad \lambda_3 = \begin{pmatrix} 1 & \cdot & \cdot \\ \cdot & -1 & \cdot \\ \cdot & \cdot & \cdot \end{pmatrix} \quad \lambda_4 = \begin{pmatrix} \cdot & \cdot & 1 \\ \cdot & \cdot & \cdot \\ 1 & \cdot & \cdot \end{pmatrix}$$

$$\lambda_5 = \begin{pmatrix} \cdot & \cdot & -i \\ \cdot & \cdot & \cdot \\ i & \cdot & \cdot \end{pmatrix} \quad \lambda_6 = \begin{pmatrix} \cdot & \cdot & \cdot \\ \cdot & \cdot & 1 \\ \cdot & 1 & \cdot \end{pmatrix} \quad \lambda_7 = \begin{pmatrix} \cdot & \cdot & \cdot \\ \cdot & \cdot & -i \\ \cdot & i & \cdot \end{pmatrix} \quad \lambda_8 = \frac{1}{\sqrt{3}} \begin{pmatrix} 1 & \cdot & \cdot \\ \cdot & 1 & \cdot \\ \cdot & \cdot & -2 \end{pmatrix} \tag{8}$$

and the raising and lowering operators:

$$\Lambda_{\pm 1} = \frac{1}{2}(\lambda_4 \pm i\lambda_5), \quad \Lambda_{\pm 2} = \frac{1}{2}(\lambda_1 \pm i\lambda_2), \quad \Lambda_{\pm 3} = \frac{1}{2}(\lambda_6 \pm i\lambda_7). \tag{9}$$

It is easy to see that these operators act on the basis vectors $|\nu>$ as shown in figure 2.

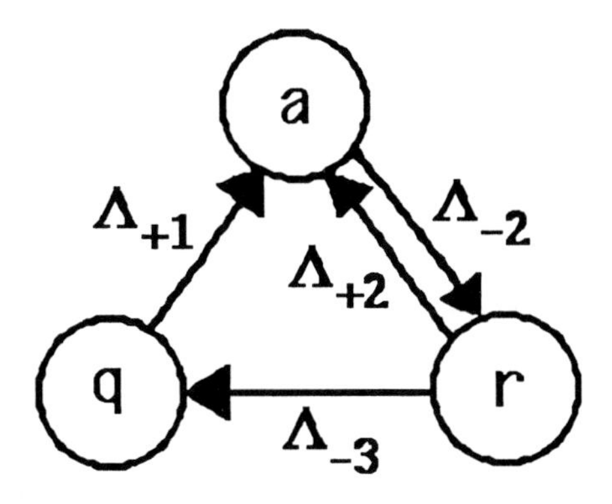

Figure 2. Neural State Transitions generated by the raising and lowering operators of the Lie Group SU(3).

It also follows that:

$$A = \sum_i \Lambda_{+1i} \Lambda_{-1i} = \sum_i \Lambda_{+2i} \Lambda_{-2i} \tag{10}$$

and that:

$$J_i = \sum_j w_{ij} \Lambda_{+1j} \Lambda_{-1j} = \sum_j w_{ij} \Lambda_{+2j} \Lambda_{-2j}. \tag{11}$$

The entire sequence of neural state transition into (Q,A,R) can be represented by the operator "Liouvillian":

$$L = \alpha \sum_i (\Lambda_{+2i} - 1)\Lambda_{-2i} + \beta \sum_i (\Lambda_{+3i} - 1)\Lambda_{-3i}$$

$$+ \frac{1}{N}\sum_i (\Lambda_{-1i} - 1)\Lambda_{+1i}\,\theta_q[J_i] + \frac{1}{N}\sum_i (\Lambda_{-2i} - 1)\Lambda_{+2i}\,\theta_r[J_i]\,. \qquad (12)$$

This operator acts on the state function $| P(T)>$ according to the equation:

$$\frac{\partial}{\partial T} | P(T)> = - L | P(T)>. \qquad (13)$$

This is the neural network analogue of the Schrödinger equation, except that $P[\Omega(T)] = < \Omega | P(T)>$ is a real probability distribution, and L is not Hermitian. In fact this equation is a Markovian representation of neural network activity (Doi, 1976; Grassberger & Scheunert, 1980), and is the required master equation.

1.4 A SPECIAL CASE: TWO-STATE NEURONS

It is helpful to consider the simpler case of two state neurons first, since the group algebra is much simpler. I therefore neglect the refractory state, and use the two dimensional basis vectors:

$$| q > = \begin{pmatrix} \cdot \\ 1 \end{pmatrix}, \qquad | a > = \begin{pmatrix} 1 \\ \cdot \end{pmatrix} \qquad (14)$$

corresponding to the kinetic scheme shown in figure 3a:

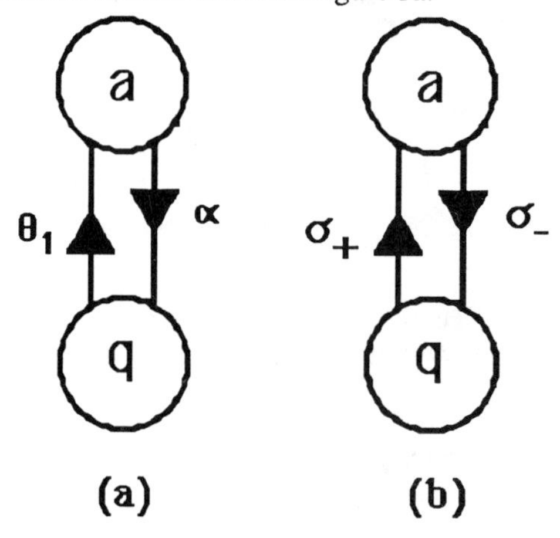

Figure 3. (a) Neural State Transitions in the two-state case, (b) Neural State Transitions generated by the raising and lowering operators of the Lie Group SU(2).

The relevant matrices are the well-known Pauli spin matrices representing the Lie Group SU(2) (Georgi, 1982):

$$\sigma_1 = \begin{pmatrix} . & 1 \\ 1 & . \end{pmatrix} \qquad \sigma_2 = \begin{pmatrix} . & -i \\ i & . \end{pmatrix} \qquad \sigma_3 = \begin{pmatrix} 1 & . \\ . & -1 \end{pmatrix} \tag{15}$$

and the raising and lowering operators:

$$\sigma_{\pm} = \frac{1}{2}(\sigma_1 \pm i\sigma_2) \tag{16}$$

giving the state transiiton diagram shown in figure 3(b). The corresponding neural Liouvillian is:

$$L = \alpha \sum_i (\sigma_{+i} - 1)\sigma_{-i} + \frac{1}{N}\sum_i (\sigma_{-1} - 1)\sigma_{+i}\theta_q[J_i] \tag{17}$$

where

$$J_i = \sum_j w_{ij}\, \sigma_{+j}\sigma_{-j}\,. \tag{18}$$

Physicists will recognize this Liouvillian as a generalization of the Regge spin Hamiltonian of QFT:

$$L = \alpha \sum_i (\sigma_{+i} - 1)\sigma_{-i} + \frac{\kappa}{N}\sum_i\sum_j (\sigma_{-1} - 1)\sigma_{+i}\sigma_{+j}\sigma_{-j}\,. \tag{19}$$

In principle, eqn. (13) with L given by eqn. (12) or (17), together with initial conditions, contains a complete description of neural network activity, since its formal solution takes the form:

$$| P(T)> = \exp\{-\int_0^T L(T')dT'\} | P(0)>\,. \tag{20}$$

1.5 MOMENT GENERATING EQUATIONS AND SPIN-COHERENT STATES

Solving this system of equation in detail however, is a difficult problem. In practice one is satisfied with the first few statistical moments. These can be obtained as follows (I describe here the two-state case. Similar but more complicated calculations obtain for the three-state case).

Consider the following "spin-coherent states" (Perelomov 1986; Hecht 1987):

$$< \alpha | = < 0 | \exp\left(\sum_i \alpha_i \sigma_{-i}\right), \qquad | \alpha > = \exp\left(\sum_i \alpha_i^* \sigma_{+i}\right) | 0 > \tag{21}$$

where α is a complex number, and $< 0 |$ is the "vacuum" state $< q_1 q_2 \ldots\ldots q_N |$.
Evidently

$$< \alpha | P > = < \alpha | \sum_{\Omega} P[\Omega(T)] | \Omega> = \sum_{\Omega} P[\Omega(T)] < \alpha | \Omega> .$$

It can be shown that $< \alpha | \Omega> = \alpha_1^{\nu_1} \alpha_2^{\nu_2} \ldots\ldots\ldots\ldots \alpha_N^{\nu_N}$ and that $< \alpha | P > =$ $G(\alpha_1 \alpha_2 \ldots \alpha_N)$ the moment generating function for the probability distribution P(T).

It can then be shown that:

$$\frac{\partial G}{\partial T} = \left[\alpha \sum_i (D\alpha_i - 1) \frac{\partial}{\partial \alpha_i} + \frac{1}{N} \sum_i \left(\frac{\partial}{\partial \alpha_i} - 1\right) D\alpha_i \theta_q[J_i] \right] G \qquad (22)$$

where

$$D\alpha_i = \alpha_i (1 - \alpha_i \frac{\partial}{\partial \alpha_i}) \quad \text{and} \quad J_i = \sum_j w_{ij} D\alpha_j \frac{\partial}{\partial \alpha_j} . \qquad (23)$$

i.e.; the moment generating equation expressed in the "oscillator-algebra" representation.

1.5 A NEURAL NETWORK PATH INTEGRAL

The content of eqns. (22) and (23) can be summarized in a Wiener-Feynman Path Integral (Schulman 1981). It can be shown that the transition probability of reaching a state $\Omega'(T)$ given the initial state $\Omega(T_0)$, the so-called propagator $\mathfrak{G}(\Omega', T | \Omega, T_0)$, can be expressed as the Path Integral:

$$\int \prod_i \mathfrak{D}\alpha_i(T') \exp \left[\int_T^{T_0} \{ \sum_i \tfrac{1}{2} (D'\alpha_i D\alpha_i^* - D\alpha_i D'\alpha_i^*) - L(D\alpha_i, D\alpha_i^*) \} \right], \qquad (24)$$

where $D'\alpha_i = \frac{\partial}{\partial T} D\alpha_i$ and $\mathfrak{D}\alpha_i(T') = (\frac{2}{\pi})^n \lim_{n \to \infty} \prod_{j=1}^{n} \frac{d^2\alpha_i(j)}{(1+\alpha_i(j)\alpha_i^*(j))^3}$, and

where $d^2\alpha = d(\mathrm{Rl}\,\alpha)\, d(\mathrm{Im}\,\alpha)$. This propagator is sometimes written as an expectation with respect to the Wiener measure $\int \prod_i \mathfrak{D}\alpha_i(T')$ as:

$$\mathfrak{G}(\Omega' | \Omega) = < \exp \left[- \int_T^{T_0} dT' \, \mathfrak{L} \right] > \qquad (25)$$

where the neural network Lagrangian is defined as:

$$\mathcal{L} = L(D\alpha_i, D\alpha_i^*) - \sum_i \frac{1}{2} (D'\alpha_i D\alpha_i^* - D\alpha_i D'\alpha_i^*). \quad (26)$$

The propagator $\mathcal{G}$ contains all the statistics of the network activity. Steepest descent methods, asymptotics, and Liapunov-Schmidt bifurcation methods may be used to evaluate it.

2 CONCLUSIONS

The main point of this paper is that stochastic neural networks have a mathematical structure that corresponds quite closely with that of quantum field theory. Neural network Liouvillians and Lagrangians can be derived, just as can spin Hamiltonians and Lagrangians in QFT. It remains to show the efficacy of such a description.

Acknowledgements

The early stages of this work were carried out in part with Alan Lapedes and David Sharp of the Los Alamos National Laboratory. We thank the Santa Fé Institute for hospitality and facilities during this work, which was supported in part by grant # N00014-89-J-1099 from the US Department of the Navy, Office of Naval Research.

References

Van Kampen, N. (1981), Stochastic Processes in Physics & Chemistry (N. Holland, Amsterdam).
Georgi, H. (1982), Lie Algebras in Particle Physics (Benjamin Books, Menlo Park)
Doi, M. (1976), J.Phys. A. Math. Gen. **9**, 9, 1465-1477; 1479-1495
Grassberger, P. & Scheunert, M. (1980), Fortschritte der Physik **28**, 547-578.
Hecht, K.T. (1987), The Vector Coherent State Method (Springer, New York)
Perelomov, A. (1986), Generalized Coherent States and Their Applications (Springer, New York).
Matsubara, T & Matsuda, H. (1956). A lattice model of Liquid Helium, I. Prog. Theoret. Phys. **16**, 6, 569-582.
Schulman, L. (1981), Techniques and Applications of Path Integration (Wiley, New York).

Dynamics of Learning in Recurrent Feature-Discovery Networks

Todd K. Leen
Department of Computer Science and Engineering
Oregon Graduate Institute of Science & Technology
Beaverton, OR 97006-1999

Abstract

The self-organization of recurrent feature-discovery networks is studied from the perspective of dynamical systems. Bifurcation theory reveals parameter regimes in which multiple equilibria or limit cycles coexist with the equilibrium at which the networks perform principal component analysis.

1 Introduction

Oja (1982) made the remarkable observation that a simple model neuron with an Hebbian adaptation rule develops into a filter for the first principal component of the input distribution. Several researchers have extended Oja's work, developing networks that perform a complete principal component analysis (PCA). Sanger (1989) proposed an algorithm that uses a single layer of weights with a set of cascaded feedback projections to force nodes to filter for the principal components. This architecture singles out a particular node for each principal component. Oja (1989) and Oja and Karhunen (1985) give a related algorithm that projects inputs onto an orthogonal basis spanning the principal subspace, but does not necessarily filter for the principal components themselves.

In another class of models, nodes are forced to learn different statistical features by a set of lateral connections. Rubner and Schulten (1990) use cascaded lateral connections; the ith node receives signals from the input and all nodes j with $j < i$. The lateral connections are modified by an anti-Hebbian learning rule that tends to de-correlate the node responses. Like Sanger's scheme, this architecture singles out a particular node for each principal component. Kung and Diamantaras (1990) propose a different learning rule on the same network topology. Foldiak (1989) simulates a network with full lateral connectivity, but does not discuss convergence.

The goal of this paper is to help form a more complete picture of feature-discovery models that use lateral signal flow. We discuss two models with particular emphasis on their learning dynamics. The models incorporate Hebbian and anti-Hebbian adaptation, and recurrent lateral connections. We give stability analyses and derive bifurcation diagrams for the models. Stability analysis gives a lower bound on the rate of adaptation the lateral connections, below which the equilibrium corresponding to PCA is unstable. Bifurcation theory provides a description of the behavior near loss of stability. The bifurcation analyses reveal stable equilibria in which the weight vectors from the input are combinations of the eigenvectors of the input correlation. Limit cycles are also found.

2 The Single-Neuron Model

In Oja's model the input, $x \in R^N$, is a random vector assumed to be drawn from a stationary probability distribution. The vector of synaptic weights is denoted ω and the post-synaptic response is linear; $y = x \cdot \omega$. The continuous-time, ensemble averaged form of the learning rule is

$$\begin{aligned} \dot{\omega} &= < x\, y > - < y^2 > \omega \\ &= R\omega \; - \; (\omega \cdot R\omega)\, \omega \end{aligned} \tag{1}$$

where $< \ldots >$ denotes the average over the ensemble of inputs, and $R = < x\, x^T >$ is the correlation matrix. The unit-magnitude eigenvectors of R are denoted e_i, $i = 1 \ldots N$ and are assumed to be ordered in decreasing magnitude of the associated eigenvalues $\lambda_1 > \lambda_2 > \ldots > \lambda_N > 0$. Oja shows that the weight vector asymptotically approaches $\pm e_1$. The variance of the node's response is thus maximized and the node acts as a filter for the first principal component of the input distribution.

3 Extending the Single Neuron Model

To extend the model to a system of $M \leq N$ nodes we consider a set of linear neurons with weight vectors (called the forward weights) $\omega_1 \ldots \omega_M$ connecting each to the N-dimensional input. Without interactions between the nodes in the array, all M weight vectors would converge to $\pm e_1$.

We consider two approaches to building interactions that force nodes to filter for different statistical features. In the first approach an internode potential is constructed. This formulation results in a *non-local* model. The model is made local by introducing lateral connections that naturally acquire *anti*-Hebbian adaptation. For reasons that will become clear, the resulting model is referred to as a minimal coupling scheme. In the second approach, we write equations of motion of the forward weights based directly on (1). The evolution of the lateral connection strengths will follow a simple anti-Hebbian rule.

3.1 Minimal Coupling

The response of the ith node in the array is taken to be linear in the input

$$y_i = x \cdot \omega_i . \tag{2}$$

The adaptation of the forward weights is derived from the potential

$$\begin{aligned} U &= -\frac{1}{2}\sum_{j}^{M} < y_j^2 > + \frac{C}{2}\sum_{j,k;j\neq k}^{M} < y_j\, y_k >^2 \\ &= -\frac{1}{2}\sum_{j}^{M} (\omega_j \cdot R\omega_j) + \frac{C}{2}\sum_{j,k;j\neq k}^{M} (\omega_j \cdot R\omega_k)^2, \end{aligned} \tag{3}$$

where C is a coupling constant. The first term of U generates the Hebb law, while the second term penalizes correlated node activity (Yuille *et al.* 1989). The equations of motion are constructed to perform gradient descent on U with a term added to bound the weight vectors,

$$\begin{aligned} \dot{\omega}_i &= -\nabla_{\omega_i} U - < y_i^2 > \omega_i \\ &= < x\, y_i > - C\sum_{j\neq i}^{M} < y_i\, y_j >< x\, y_j > - < y_i^2 > \omega_i \\ &= R\omega_i - C\sum_{j\neq i}^{M} (\omega_i \cdot R\omega_j)\, R\omega_j - (\omega_i \cdot R\omega_i)\, \omega_i. \end{aligned} \tag{4}$$

Note that ω_i refers to the weight vector from the input to the ith node, *not* the ith component of the weight vector.

Equation (4) is *non-local* as it involves correlations, $< y_i\, y_j >$, between nodes. In order to provide a purely local adaptation, we introduce a symmetric matrix of lateral connections

$$\begin{aligned} &\eta_{ij} \qquad i,j = 1,\ldots, M \\ &\eta_{ii} \quad = 0. \end{aligned}$$

These evolve according to

$$\begin{aligned} \dot{\eta}_{ij} &= -d(\eta_{ij} + C < y_i\, y_j >) \\ &= -d(\eta_{ij} + C\, \omega_i \cdot R\omega_j) \end{aligned} \tag{5}$$

where d is a rate constant. In the limit of fast adaptation (large d)

$$\eta_{ij} \rightarrow -C < y_i\, y_j > .$$

With this limiting behavior in mind, we replace (4) with

$$\begin{aligned} \dot{\omega}_i &= < xy_i > + \sum_{j\neq i}^{M} \eta_{ij} < xy_j > - < y_i^2 > \omega_i \\ &= R\omega_i + \sum_{j\neq i}^{M} \eta_{ij}\, R\omega_j - (\omega_i \cdot R\omega_i)\, \omega_i. \end{aligned} \tag{6}$$

Equations (5) and (6) specify the adaptation of the network.

Notice that the response of the ith node is given by (2) and is thus independent of the signals carried on the lateral connections. In this sense the lateral signals affect node plasticity but not node response. This minimal coupling can also be derived as a low-order approximation to the model in §3.2 below.

3.1.1 Stability and Bifurcation

By inspection the weight dynamics given by (5) and (6) have an equilibrium at

$$X_0 \equiv (\omega_i = e_i, \ \eta_{ij} = 0). \tag{7}$$

At this equilibrium the outputs are the first M principal components of input vectors. In suitable coordinates the linear part of the equations of motion break into block diagonal form with any possible instabilities constrained to 3×3 sub-blocks. Details of the stability and bifurcation analysis are given in Leen (1991). The principal component subspace is *always* asymptotically stable. However the equilibrium X_0 is linearly stable if and only if

$$d > d_0 = \frac{(\lambda_i - \lambda_j)^2 (\lambda_i + \lambda_j)}{\lambda_i^2 + \lambda_j^2} \tag{8}$$

$$C > C_0 = \frac{1}{\lambda_i + \lambda_j}, \quad 1 \leq (i,j) \leq M. \tag{9}$$

At C_0 or d_0 there is a qualitative change (a bifurcation) in the learning dynamics. If the condition on d is violated, then there is a Hopf bifurcation to oscillating weights. At the critical value C_0 there is a bifurcation to multiple equilibria. The bifurcation normal form was found by Liapunov-Schmidt reduction (see e.g. Golubitsky and Schaeffer 1984) performed at the bifurcation point (X_0, C_0). To deal effectively with the large dimensional phase space of the network, the calculations were performed on a symbolic algebra program.

At the critical point (X_0, C_0) there is a supercritical pitchfork bifurcation. Two *unstable* equilibria appear near X_0 for $C > C_0$. At these equilibria the forward weights are mixtures of e_M and e_{M-1} and the lateral connection strengths are non-zero. Generically one expects a saddle-node bifurcation. However X_0 is an equilibrium for all values of C, and the system has an inversion symmetry. These conditions preclude the saddle-node and transcritical bifurcations, and we are left with the pitchfork.

The position of *stable* equilibria away from (X_0, C_0) can be found by examining terms of order five and higher in the bifurcation expansion. Alternatively we examine the bifurcation from the homogeneous solution, X_h, in which all weight vectors are proportional to e_1. For a system of two nodes this equilibrium is asymptotically stable provided

$$C < C_h \equiv \min \left\{ \begin{array}{c} (\lambda_1 - \lambda_2)/(2\lambda_1\lambda_2) \\ 1/\lambda_1 \end{array} \right\} \tag{10}$$

If $\lambda_1 < 3\lambda_2$, then there is a supercritical pitchfork bifurcation at C_h. Two *stable* equilibria emerge from X_h for $C > C_h$. At these stable equilibria, the forward weight vectors are mixtures of the first two correlation eigenvectors and the lateral connection strengths are nonzero.

The complete bifurcation diagram for a system of two nodes is shown in Fig. 1. The upper portion of the figure shows the bifurcation at (X_0, C_0). The horizontal line corresponds to the PCA equilibrium X_0. This equilibrium is stable (heavy line) for

$C > C_0$, and unstable (light line) for $C < C_0$. The subsidiary, unstable, equilibria that emerge from (X_0, C_0) lie on the light, parabolic branches of the top diagram. Calculations indicate that the form of this bifurcation is independent of the number of nodes, and of the input dimension. Of course the value of C_0 increases with increasing number of nodes, c.f. (9).

The lower portion of Fig. 1 shows the bifurcation from (X_h, C_h) for a system of two nodes. The horizontal line corresponds to the homogeneous equilibrium X_h. This is stable for $C < C_h$ and unstable for $C > C_h$. The stable equilibria consisting of mixtures of the correlation eigenvectors lie on the heavy parabolic branches of the diagram. For networks with more nodes, there are presumably further bifurcations along the supercritical stable branches emerging from (X_h, C_h); equilibria with qualitatively different eigenvector mixtures are observed in simulations.

Each inset in the figure shows equilibrium forward weight vectors for both nodes in a two-node network. These configurations were generated by numerical integration of the equations of motion (5) and (6). The correlation matrix corresponds to an ensemble of noise vectors with short-range correlations between the components. Simulations of the corresponding *discrete*, pattern-by-pattern learning rule confirm the form of the weight vectors shown here.

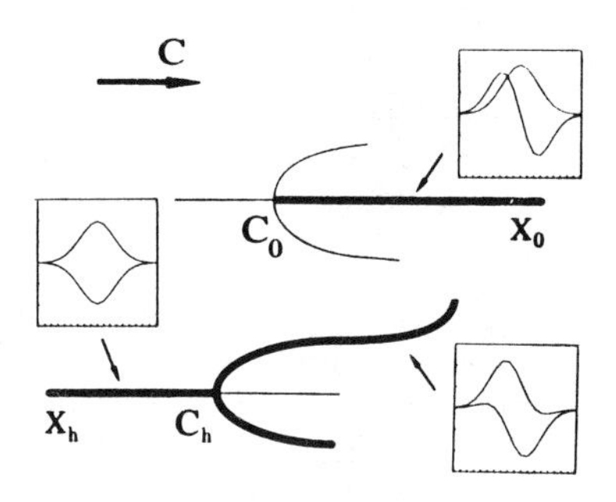

Figure 1: Bifurcation diagram for the minimal model

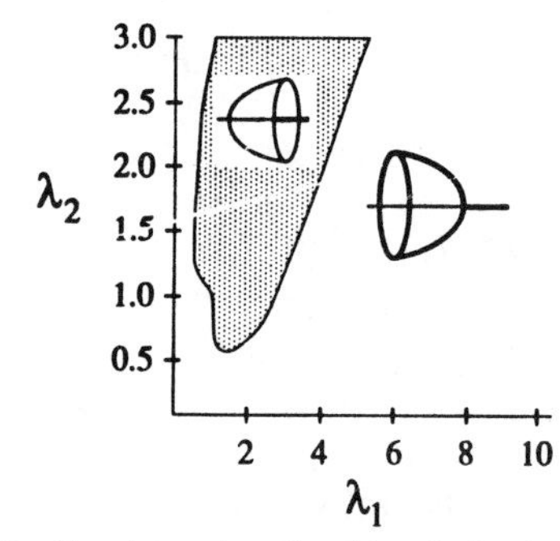

Fig 2: Regions in the (λ_1, λ_2) plane corresponding to supercritical (shaded) and subcritical (unshaded) Hopf bifurcation.

3.2 Full Coupling

In a more conventional coupling scheme, the signals carried on the lateral connections affect the node activities directly. For linear node response, the vector of activities is given by

$$y = (1-\eta)^{-1}\,\omega x \equiv u\,\omega\,x \tag{11}$$

where $y \in R^M$, η is the $M \times M$ matrix of lateral connection strengths and ω is an $M \times N$ matrix whose i^{th} row is the forward weight vector to the ith node. The adaptation rule is

$$\dot{\omega} = < yx^T > - Diag(< yy^T >)\,\omega \tag{12}$$

$$\dot{\eta} = D\,\eta - C < yy^T >, \quad \eta_{ii} = 0, \tag{13}$$

where D and C are constants and $Diag$ sets the off-diagonal elements of its argument equal to zero. This system also has the PCA equilibrium X_0. This is linearly stable if

$$D > 0 \tag{14}$$

$$C > C_0 \equiv \frac{D}{\lambda_i + \lambda_j} + \frac{(\lambda_i - \lambda_j)^2}{\lambda_i^2 + \lambda_j^2}. \tag{15}$$

Equation (14) tells us that the PCA equilibrium is structurally unstable without the $D\eta$ term in (13). Without this term, the model reduces to that given by Foldiak (1989). That the latter generally does not converge to the PCA equilibrium is consistent with the condition in (14).

If, on the other hand, the condition on C is violated then the network undergoes a Hopf bifurcation leading to oscillations. Depending on the eigenvalue spectrum of the input correlation, this bifurcation may be subcritical (with stable limit cycles near X_0 for $C < C_0$), or supercritical (with unstable limit cycles near X_0 for $C > C_0$). Figure 2 shows the corresponding regions in the (λ_1, λ_2) plane for a network of two nodes with $D = 1$. Simulations show that even in the supercritical regime, stable limit cycles are found for $C < C_0$, and for $C > C_0$ sufficiently close to C_0. This suggests that the complete bifurcation diagram in the supercritical regime is shaped like the bottom of a wine bottle, with only the indentation shown in figure 2. Under the approximation $u \approx 1 + \eta$, the super-critical regime is significantly narrowed.

4 Discussion

The primary goal of this study has been to give a theoretical description of learning in feature-discovery models; in particular models that use lateral interactions to ensure that nodes tune to different statistical features. The models presented here have several different limit sets (equilibria and cycles) whose stability and location in the weight space depends on the relative learning rates in the network, and on the eigenvalue spectrum of the input correlation. We have applied tools from bifurcation theory to qualitatively describe the location and determine stability of these different limiting solutions. This theoretical approach provides a unifying framework within which similar algorithms can be studied.

Both models have equilibria at which the network performs PCA. In addition, the minimal model has stable equilibria for which the forward weight vectors are mixtures of the correlation eigenvectors. Both models have regimes in which the weight vectors oscillate. The model given by Rubner *et al.* (1990) also loses stability through Hopf bifurcation for small values of the lateral learning rate.

The minimal values of C in (9) and (15) for the stability of the PCA equilibrium can become quite large for small correlation eigenvalues. These stringent conditions can be ameliorated in both models by the replacement

$$d\,\eta_{ij} \rightarrow (<y_i^2> + <y_j^2>)\,\eta_{ij}.$$

However in the minimal model, this leads to degenerate bifurcations which have not been thoroughly examined.

Finally, it remains to be seen whether the techniques employed here extend to similar systems with non-linear node activation (e.g. Carlson 1991) or to the problem of locating multiple minima in cost functions for *supervised* learning models.

Acknowledgments

This work was supported by the Office of Naval Research under contract N00014-90-1349 and by DARPA grant MDA 972-88-J-1004 to the Department of Computer Science and Engineering. The author thanks Bill Baird for stimulating e-mail discussion.

References

Carlson, A. (1991) Anti-Hebbian learning in a non-linear neural network *Biol. Cybern.*, 64:171–176.

Foldiak, P. (1989) Adaptive network for optimal linear feature extraction. In *Proceedings of the IJCNN*, pages I 401–405.

Golubitsky, Martin and Schaeffer, David (1984) *Singularities and Groups in Bifurcation Theory, Vol. I.* Springer-Verlag, New York.

Kung, S. and Diamantaras K. (1990) A neural network learning algorithm for adaptive principal component extraction (APEX). In *Proceedings of the IEEE International Conference on Acoustics Speech and Signal Processing*, pages 861–864.

Leen, T. K. (1991) Dynamics of learning in linear feature-discovery networks. *Network : Computation in Neural Systems*, to appear.

Oja, E. (1982) A simplified neuron model as a principal component analyzer. *J. Math. Biology*, 15:267–273.

Oja, E. (1989) Neural networks, principal components, and subspaces. *International Journal of Neural Systems*, 1:61–68.

Oja, E. and Karhunen, J. (1985) On stochastic approximation of the eigenvectors and eigenvalues of the expectation of a random matrix. *J. of Math. Anal. and Appl.*, 106:69–84.

Rubner, J. and Schulten K. (1990) Development of feature detectors by self-organization: A network model. *Biol. Cybern.*, 62:193–199.

Sanger, T. (1989) An optimality principle for unsupervised learning. In D.S. Touretzky, editor, *Advances in Neural Information Processing Systems 1.* Morgan Kauffmann.

Yuille, A.L, Kammen, D.M. and Cohen, D.S. (1989) Quadrature and the development of orientation selective cortical cells by Hebb rules. *Biol. Cybern.*, 61:183–194.

A Lagrangian Approach to Fixed Points

Eric Mjolsness
Department of Computer Science
Yale University
P.O. Box 2158 Yale Station
New Haven, CT 16520-2158

Willard L. Miranker
IBM Watson Research Center
Yorktown Heights, NY 10598

Abstract

We present a new way to derive dissipative, optimizing dynamics from the Lagrangian formulation of mechanics. It can be used to obtain both standard and novel neural net dynamics for optimization problems. To demonstrate this we derive standard descent dynamics as well as nonstandard variants that introduce a computational attention mechanism.

1 INTRODUCTION

Neural nets are often designed to optimize some objective function E of the current state of the system via a dissipative dynamical system that has a circuit-like implementation. The fixed points of such a system are locally optimal in E. In physics the preferred formulation for many dynamical derivations and calculations is by means of an objective function which is an integral over time of a "Lagrangian" function, L. From Lagrangians one usually derives time-reversable, non-dissipative dynamics which cannot converge to a fixed point, but we present a new way to circumvent this limitation and derive optimizing neural net dynamics from a Lagrangian. We apply the method to derive a general attention mechanism for optimization-based neural nets, and we describe simulations for a graph-matching network.

2 LAGRANGIAN FORMULATION OF NEURAL DYNAMICS

Often one must design a network with nontrivial temporal behaviors such as running longer in exchange for less circuitry, or focussing attention on one part of a problem at a time. In this section we transform the original objective function (c.f. [Mjolsness and Garrett, 1989]) into a Lagrangian which determines the detailed dynamics by which the objective is optimized. In section 3.1 we will show how to add in an extra level of control dynamics.

2.1 THE LAGRANGIAN

Replacing an objective E with an associated Lagrangian, L, is an algebraic transformation:

$$E[\mathbf{v}] \quad \rightarrow \quad L[\dot{\mathbf{v}}, \mathbf{v}|\mathbf{q}] = K[\dot{\mathbf{v}}, \mathbf{v}|\mathbf{q}] + \frac{dE}{dt}. \tag{1}$$

The "action" $S = \int_{-\infty}^{\infty} L dt$ is to be extremized in a novel way:

$$\delta S/\delta \dot{v}_i(t) = 0 \quad (\text{i.e.} \partial L/\partial \dot{v}_i(t) = 0). \tag{2}$$

In (1), $\mathbf{q}$ is an optional set of control parameters (see section 3.1) and K is a cost-of-movement term independent of the problem and of E. For one standard class of neural networks,

$$E[\mathbf{v}] = -(1/2) \sum_{ij} T_{ij} v_i v_j - \sum_i h_i v_i + \sum_i \phi_i(v_i) \tag{3}$$

so

$$-\partial E/\partial v_i = \sum_j T_{ij} v_j + h_i - g^{-1}(v_i), \tag{4}$$

where $g^{-1}(v) = \phi'(v)$. Also dE/dt is of course $\sum_i (\partial E/\partial v_i)\dot{v}_i$.

2.2 THE GREEDY FUNCTIONAL DERIVATIVE

In physics, Lagrangian dynamics usually have a conserved total energy which prohibits convergence to fixed points. Here the main difference is the unusual functional derivative with respect to $\dot{v}$ rather than v in equation (2). This is a "greedy" functional derivative, in which the trajectory is optimized from beginning to each time t by choosing an extremal value of $\mathbf{v}(t)$ without considering its effect on any subsequent portion of the trajectory:

$$\frac{\delta}{\delta v_i(t)} \int_{-\infty}^{t} dt' L[\dot{\mathbf{v}}, \mathbf{v}] \approx \delta(0) \frac{\partial L[\dot{\mathbf{v}}, \mathbf{v}]}{\partial \dot{v}_i(t)} = \delta(0) \frac{\delta}{\delta \dot{v}_i(t)} \int_{-\infty}^{\infty} dt' L[\dot{\mathbf{v}}, \mathbf{v}] \propto \frac{\delta S}{\delta \dot{v}_i(t)}. \tag{5}$$

Since

$$\frac{\delta S}{\delta \dot{v}_i} = \frac{\partial L}{\partial \dot{v}_i} = \frac{\partial K}{\partial \dot{v}_i} + \frac{\partial E}{\partial v_i}, \tag{6}$$

equations (1) and (2) preserve fixed points (where $\partial E/\partial v_i = 0$) if $\partial K/\partial \dot{v}_i = 0 \Leftrightarrow \dot{\mathbf{v}} = 0$.

2.3 STEEPEST DESCENT DYNAMICS

For example, with $K = \sum_i \phi(\dot{v}_i/r)$ one may recover and generalize steepest-descent dynamics:

$$E[\mathbf{v}] \quad \rightarrow \quad L[\dot{\mathbf{v}}|r] = \sum_i \phi(\dot{v}_i/r) + \sum_i \frac{\partial E}{\partial v_i} \dot{v}_i, \tag{7}$$

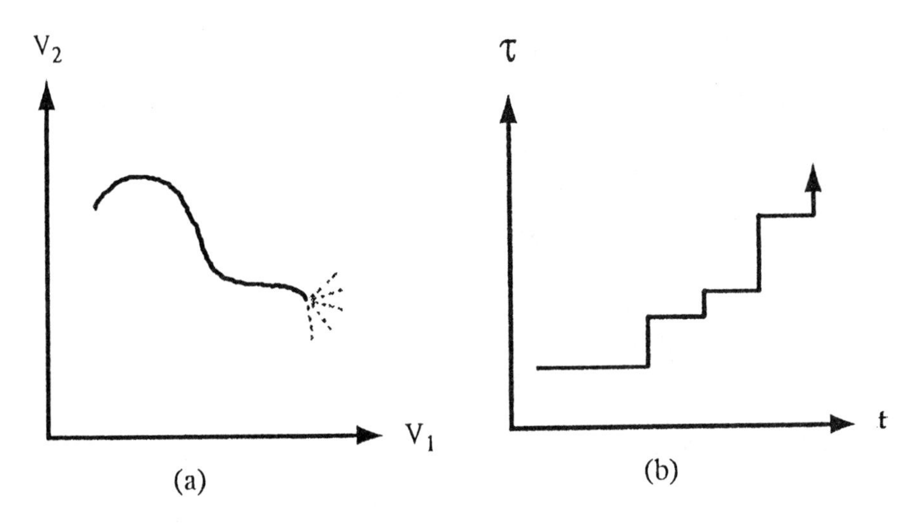

Figure 1: **(a)** Greedy functional derivatives result in greedy optimization: the "next" point in a trajectory is chosen on the basis of previous points but not future ones. **(b)** Two time variables t and τ may increase during nonoverlapping intervals of an underlying physical time variable, T. For example $t = \int dT \phi_1(T)$ and $\tau = \int dT \phi_2(T)$ where ϕ_1 and ϕ_2 are nonoverlapping clock signals.

$$\partial L / \partial \dot{v}_i(t) = 0 \Rightarrow \phi'(\dot{v}_i / r)/r + \partial E / \partial v_i = 0, \text{ i.e.} \tag{8}$$

$$\dot{v}_i = r g\Big(- r\, \partial E / \partial v_i \Big). \tag{9}$$

As usual $g = (\phi')^{-1}$. A transfer function with $-1 \leq g(x) \leq 1$ could enforce a velocity constraint $-r \leq \dot{v}_i \leq r$.

2.4 HOPFIELD/GROSSBERG DYNAMICS

With a suitable K one may recover the analog neuron dynamics of Hopfield (and Grossberg):

$$L = \sum_i \frac{1}{2} \dot{u}_i^2 g'(u_i) + \sum_i \frac{\partial E}{\partial v_i} \dot{v}_i, \quad v_i \equiv g(u_i). \tag{10}$$

$$\partial L / \partial \dot{u}_i(t) = 0 \Rightarrow \dot{u}_i + \partial E / \partial v_i = 0, \text{ i.e.} \tag{11}$$

$$\dot{u}_i = -\partial E / \partial v_i \quad \text{and} \quad v_i = g(u_i). \tag{12}$$

We conjecture that this function $K[\dot{u}_i, u_i]$ is **optimal** in a certain sense: if we linearize the $\mathbf{u}$ dynamics and consider the largest and smallest eigenvalues, extremized separately over the entire domain of $\mathbf{u}$, with $-T$ constrained to have bounded positive eigenvalues, then the ratio of such largest and smallest eigenvalues is minimal for this K. This criterion is of practical importance because the largest eigenvalue should be bounded for circuit implementability, and the smallest eigenvalue should be bounded away from zero for circuit convergence in finite time.

2.5 A CHANGE OF VARIABLES SIMPLIFIES L

We note a change of variable which simplifies the kinetic energy term in the above dynamics, for use in the next section:

$$\begin{aligned} &L[\dot{\mathbf{w}}] = \sum_i \tfrac{1}{2}\dot{w}_i^2 + \sum_i \tfrac{\partial E}{\partial w_i}\dot{w}_i, \\ &\partial L/\partial \dot{w}_i(t) = 0 \Rightarrow \dot{w}_i + \partial E/\partial w_i = 0, \text{ i.e.} \\ &\dot{w}_i = -\partial E/\partial w_i \end{aligned} \tag{13}$$

which is supposed to be identical to $\dot{u}_i = -\partial E/\partial v_i$, $v_i = g(u_i)$ (c.f. (12)). This can be arranged by choosing w:

$$\begin{aligned} &\tfrac{dw_i}{du_i}\dot{u}_i = -\tfrac{\partial E}{\partial v_i}\tfrac{dv_i}{dw_i} \\ &\Rightarrow \tfrac{dw_i}{du_i} = \tfrac{dv_i}{dw_i} = \tfrac{dv_i/du_i}{dw_i/du_i} \\ &\Rightarrow \tfrac{dw_i}{du_i} = \sqrt{g'(u_i)} \end{aligned} \tag{14}$$

i.e.

$$w_i = \int^{u_i} du\sqrt{g'(u)} \text{ and } v_i = \int^{w_i} dw\sqrt{g'(u(w))}. \tag{15}$$

3 APPLICATION TO COMPUTATIONAL ATTENTION

We can introduce a computational "attention mechanism" for neural nets as follows. Suppose we can only afford to simulate A out of $N \gg A$ neurons at a time in a large net. We shall do this by simulating A **real neurons** indexed by $a \in \{1 \ldots A\}$, corresponding to a dynamically chosen subset of the N **virtual neurons** indexed by $i \in \{1 \ldots N\}$.

3.0.1 Constraints

In great generality, the correspondance can be chosen dynamically via a sparse matrix of control parameters

$$\begin{aligned} &q_{ia} = r_{ia} \in [0,1] \quad \text{constrained so that} \\ &\sum_i r_{ia} = 1, \\ &\sum_a r_{ia} \leq 1. \end{aligned} \tag{16}$$

Alternatively, the r variables can be coordinated to describe a "window" or "focus" of attention by taking r_{ia} to be a function of a small number of parameters $\mathbf{q}$ specifying the window, which are adjusted to optimize $\hat{E}[r[q]]$. This procedure, which can result in significant economies, was used for our computer experiments.

3.0.2 Neuron Dynamics

The assumed control relationship is

$$\dot{w}_i = \sum_a r_{ia}\dot{k}_a, \tag{17}$$

i.e. virtual neuron w_i follows the real neuron to which r assigns it. Equation (15) then determines $u_i(t)$ and $v_i(t)$. A plausible kinetic energy term for $\mathbf{k}$ is the same as for $\mathbf{w}$ (c.f. equation (13)), since that choice (equivalent to the Hoplield case) has a good eigenvalue ratio for the $\mathbf{u}$ variables. The Lagrangian for the real neurons becomes

$$L[\dot{\mathbf{k}}] = \frac{1}{2}\sum_a \dot{k}_a^2 + \sum_{ia} \frac{\partial E}{\partial w_i} r_{ia} \dot{k}_a \tag{18}$$

and the equations of motion (greedy variation) may be shown to be

$$\dot{k}_a = \sum_i r_{ia} \sqrt{g'(u(w_i))} \left[\sum_j T_{ij} v_j + h_i - u_i\right]. \tag{19}$$

3.1 CONTROL DYNAMICS FOR ATTENTION

Now we need dynamics for the control parameters $\mathbf{r}$ or more generally $\mathbf{q}$. An objective function transformation (proposed and subjected to preliminary experiments in [Mjolsness, 1987]) can be used to construct a new objective for the control parameters, $\mathbf{q}$, which rewards speedy convergence of the original objective E as a function of the original variables $\mathbf{v}$ by measuring dE/dt:

$$\begin{aligned} E[\mathbf{v}] \rightarrow \hat{E}[\mathbf{q}] &= b(dE/dt) + \hat{E}_{\text{cost}}[\mathbf{q}] \\ &= b[\textstyle\sum_i (\partial E/\partial v_i) \dot{v}_i] + \hat{E}_{\text{cost}}[\mathbf{q}], \end{aligned} \tag{20}$$

where b is a monotonic, odd function that can be used to limit the range of $\hat{E}$. We can calculate dE/dt from equations (17) and (19):

$$\hat{E}_{\text{benefit}}(r) \equiv b(\frac{dE}{dt}) = b\left[\sum_{ia} r_{ia} \frac{\partial E}{\partial w_i} \dot{k}_a\right] = -b\left[\sum_a \left(\sum_i r_{ia} \sqrt{g'(u_i)} \frac{\partial E}{\partial v_i}\right)^2\right], \tag{21}$$

where $\partial E/\partial v_i = \sum_j T_{ij} v_j + h_i - u_i$. If we assume that $\hat{E}_{\text{cost}}$ favors fixed points for which $r_{ia} \approx 0$ or 1 and $\sum_i r_{ia} \approx 0$ or 1, there is a fixed-point-preserving transformation of (21) to

$$\tilde{E}_{\text{benefit}}(r) = -b\left[\sum_{ia} r_{ia} g'(u_i) (\frac{\partial E}{\partial v_i})^2\right]. \tag{22}$$

This is monotonic in a linear function of r. It remains to specify $\hat{E}_{\text{cost}}$ and a kinetic energy term K.

3.2 INDEPENDENT VIRTUAL NEURONS

First consider independent r_{ia}. As in the Tank-Hopfield [Tank and Hopfield, 1986] linear programming net, we could take

$$\hat{E}_{\text{cost}} = \frac{1}{2}\sum_a \left(\sum_i r_{ia} - 1\right)^2 + \sum_i F\left(\sum_a r_{ia} - 1\right) + \sum_{ia} \phi_r(r_{ia}). \tag{23}$$

Thus the $\mathbf{r}$ dynamics just **sorts** the virtual neurons and chooses the A neurons with largest $g'(u_i)\partial E/\partial v_i$. For dynamics, we introduce a new time variable τ that may not even be proportional to t (see figure 1b) and imitate the Lagrangians for Hopfield dynamics:

$$L = \sum_{ia} \frac{1}{2} \left(\frac{d\rho_{ia}}{d\tau} \right)^2 g'(\rho_i) + \frac{d}{d\tau} \left(\tilde{E}_{\text{benefit}} + \hat{E}_{\text{cost}} \right); \quad (24)$$

$$d\rho_{ia}/d\tau = -\partial(\tilde{E}_{\text{benefit}} + \hat{E}_{\text{cost}})/\partial r_{ia} \quad \text{and} \quad r_{ia} = g_r(\rho_{ia}). \quad (25)$$

3.3 JUMPING WINDOW OF ATTENTION

A far more cost-effective net involves partitioning the virtual neurons into real-net-sized blocks indexed by α, so $i \rightarrow (\alpha, a)$ where a indexes neurons within a block. Let $\chi_\alpha \in [0,1]$ indicate which block is the current window or focus of attention, i.e.

$$r_{\alpha a,b} = \delta_{ab} \chi_\alpha. \quad (26)$$

Using (22), this implies

$$\tilde{E}_{\text{benefit}}[\chi] = -b \left[\sum_\alpha \chi_\alpha \sum_a g'(u_{\alpha a}) (\frac{\partial E}{\partial v_{\alpha a}})^2 \right], \quad (27)$$

and

$$\hat{E}_{\text{cost}}[\chi] = \frac{1}{2} (\sum_\alpha \chi_\alpha - 1)^2 + \sum_\alpha \phi_\chi(\chi_\alpha). \quad (28)$$

Since $\hat{E}_{\text{cost}}$ here favors $\sum_\alpha \chi_\alpha = 1$ and $\chi_\alpha \in \{0,1\}$, $\tilde{E}_{\text{benefit}}$ has the same fixed points as, and can be replaced by,

$$\check{E}_{\text{benefit}}[\chi] = -\sum_\alpha \chi_\alpha b \left[\sum_a g'(u_{\alpha a}) (\frac{\partial E}{\partial v_{\alpha a}})^2 \right]. \quad (29)$$

Then the dynamics for χ is just that of a winner-take-all neural net among the blocks which will select the largest value of $b[\sum_a g'(u_{\alpha a})(\partial E/\partial v_{\alpha a})^2]$. The simulations of Section 4 report on an earlier version of this control scheme, which selected instead the block with the largest value of $\sum_a |\partial E/\partial v_{\alpha a}|$.

3.4 ROLLING WINDOW OF ATTENTION

Here the r variables for a neural net embedded in a d-dimensional space are determined by a vector $\mathbf{x}$ representing the geometric position of the window. E_{cost} can be dropped entirely, and $\tilde{E}$ can be calculated from $\mathbf{r}(\mathbf{x})$. Suppose the embedding is via a d-dimensional grid which for notational purposes is partitioned into window-sized squares indexed by integer-valued vectors $\boldsymbol{\alpha}$ and $\mathbf{a}$. Then

$$r_{\alpha a,b} = \delta_{ab} w(L\boldsymbol{\alpha} + \mathbf{a} - \mathbf{x}), \quad (30)$$

where

$$\frac{\partial w(\mathbf{x})}{\partial x_\mu} = \begin{cases} 6[1/4 - (x_\mu + L)^2] & \text{if} \quad -1/2 \leq x_\mu + L \leq 1/2 \\ 6[(x_\mu - L)^2 - 1/4] & \text{if} \quad -1/2 \leq x_\mu - L \leq 1/2 \\ 0 & \text{otherwise} \end{cases} \quad (31)$$

and

$$\tilde{E}[\mathbf{x}] = -b\left[\sum_{\boldsymbol{\alpha}\mathbf{a}} w(L\boldsymbol{\alpha} + \mathbf{a} - \mathbf{x})g'(u_{\boldsymbol{\alpha}\mathbf{a}})(\frac{\partial E}{\partial v_{\boldsymbol{\alpha}\mathbf{a}}})^2\right]. \tag{32}$$

The advantage of (30) over, for example, a jumping or sliding window of attention is that only a small number of real neurons are being reassigned to new virtual neurons at any one time.

3.4.1 Dynamics of a Rolling Window

A candidate Lagrangian is

$$L[\mathbf{x}] = \frac{1}{2}\sum_{\mu}\left(\frac{dx_\mu}{d\tau}\right)^2 + \sum_{\mu}\frac{\partial\tilde{E}}{\partial x_\mu}\frac{dx_\mu}{d\tau}, \tag{33}$$

whence greedy variation $\delta S/\delta\dot{x} = 0$ yields

$$\frac{dx_\mu}{d\tau} = -\left[\sum_{\boldsymbol{\alpha}\mathbf{a}}\frac{\partial w(\mathbf{x} - L\boldsymbol{\alpha} - \mathbf{a})}{\partial x_\mu}g'(u_{\boldsymbol{\alpha}\mathbf{a}})(\frac{\partial E}{\partial v_{\boldsymbol{\alpha}\mathbf{a}}})^2\right] \times b'\left[\sum_{\boldsymbol{\alpha}\mathbf{a}} wg'(u_{\boldsymbol{\alpha}\mathbf{a}})(\frac{\partial E}{\partial v_{\boldsymbol{\alpha}\mathbf{a}}})^2\right]. \tag{34}$$

We may also calculate that the linearized dynamic's eigenvalues can be bounded away from infinity and zero.

4 SIMULATIONS

A jumping window of attention was simulated for a graph-matching network in which the matching neurons were partitioned into groups, only one of which was active ($r_{ia} = 1$) at any given time. The resulting optimization method produced solutions of similar quality as the original neural network, but had a smaller requirement for computational space resources at any given time.

Acknowledgement: Charles Garrett performed the computer simulations.

References

[Mjolsness, 1987] Mjolsness, E. (1987). Control of attention in neural networks. In *Proc. of First International Conference on Neural Networks*, volume vol. II, pages 567–574. IEEE.

[Mjolsness and Garrett, 1989] Mjolsness, E. and Garrett, C. (1989). Algebraic transformations of objective functions. Technical Report YALEU/DCS/RR686, Yale University Computer Science Department. Also, in press for Neural Networks.

[Tank and Hopfield, 1986] Tank, D. W. and Hopfield, J. J. (1986). Simple 'neural' optimization networks: An a/d converter, signal decision circuit, and a linear programming circuit. *IEEE Transactions on Circuits and Systems*, CAS-33.

Associative Memory in a Network of 'biological' Neurons

Wulfram Gerstner *
Department of Physics
University of California
Berkeley, CA 94720

Abstract

The Hopfield network (Hopfield, 1982,1984) provides a simple model of an associative memory in a neuronal structure. This model, however, is based on highly artificial assumptions, especially the use of formal-two state neurons (Hopfield, 1982) or graded-response neurons (Hopfield, 1984). What happens if we replace the formal neurons by 'real' biological neurons? We address this question in two steps. First, we show that a simple model of a neuron can capture all relevant features of neuron spiking, *i.e.*, a wide range of spiking frequencies and a realistic distribution of interspike intervals. Second, we construct an associative memory by linking these neurons together. The analytical solution for a large and fully connected network shows that the Hopfield solution is valid only for neurons with a short refractory period. If the refractory period is longer than a critical duration γ_c, the solutions are qualitatively different. The associative character of the solutions, however, is preserved.

1 INTRODUCTION

Information received at the sensory level is encoded in spike trains which are then transmitted to different parts of the brain where the main processing steps occur. Since all the spikes of any particular neuron look alike, the information of the spike train is obviously not contained in the exact shape of the spikes, but rather in their arrival times and in the correlations between the spikes. A model neuron which tries to keep track of the voltage trace even during the spiking—like the

*present address: Physik-Department der TU Muenchen, Institut fuer Theoretische Physik,D-8046 Garching bei Muenchen

Hodgkin Huxley equations (Hodgkin, 1952) and similar models—carries therefore non-essential details, if we are only interested in the information of the spike train. On the other hand, a simple two-state neuron or threshold model is too simplistic since it cannot reproduce the variety of spiking behaviour found in real neurons. The same is true for continuous or analog model neurons which disregard the stochastic nature of neuron firing completely. In this work we construct a model of the neuron which is intermediate between these extremes. We are not concerned with the shape of the spikes and detailed voltage traces, but we want realistic interval distributions and rate functions. Finally, we link these neurons together to capture collective effects and we construct a network that can function as an associative memory.

2 THE MODEL NEURON

From a neural-network point of view it is often convenient to consider a neuron as a simple computational unit with no internal parameters. In this case, the neuron is described either as a 'digital' theshold unit or as a nonlinear 'analog' element with a sigmoid input-output relation. While such a simple model might be useful for formal considerations in abstract networks, it is hard to see how it could be modified to include realistic features of neurons: How can we account for the statistical properties of the spike train beyond the mean firing frequencies? What about bursting or oscillating neurons? - to mention but a few of the problems with real neurons.

We would like to use a model neuron which is closer to biology in the sense that it produces spike trains comparable of those in real neurons. Our description of the spiking dynamics therefore emphasizes three basic notions of neurobiology: *threshold, refractory period, and noise.* In particular we describe the internal state of the neuron by the membrane voltage h which depends on the synaptic contributions from other neurons as well as on the spiking history of the neuron itself. In a simple threshold crossing process, a spike would be initiated as soon as the voltage $h(t)$ crosses the threshold θ. Due to the statistical fluctuations of the momentary voltage around $h(t)$, however, the spiking will be a statistical event, the spikes coming a bit too early or a bit too late compared to the formal threshold crossing time, depending on the direction of the fluctuations. This fact will be taken into account by introducing a probabilistic spiking rate r, which depends on the difference between the membrane voltage h and the threshold θ in an exponential fashion:

$$r = \frac{1}{\tau_0} \exp[\beta(h - \theta)], \tag{1}$$

where the formal temperature β^{-1} is a measure for the noise and τ_0 is an internal time constant of the neuron. If h changes only slowly during a conveniently chosen time τ_1, we can integrate over τ_1, which yields the probability $P_F(h)$ of firing during a time step of length τ_1. This gives us an analytic procedure to switch from continuous time to the discrete time step representation used later on.

If a spike is initiated in a real neuron, the neuron goes through a cycle of ion influx and efflux which changes the potential on a fast time scale and prevents immediate firing of another spike. To model this we reset the potential after each spike by adding a negative refractory field $h^r(t)$ to the potential:

$$h(t) = h^s(t) + h^r(t), \quad (2)$$

with

$$h^r(t) = \sum_i \epsilon^r(t - t_i), \quad (3)$$

where t_i is the time of the ith spike and $h^s(t)$ is the postsynaptic potential due to incoming spikes from other neurons. The form of the refractory function $\epsilon^r(\tau)$ together with the noise level β determine the firing characteristics of the neuron. With fairly simple refractory fields we can achieve a sigmoid dependence of the firing frequency upon the input current (figure 1) and realistic spiking statistics (figure 3).

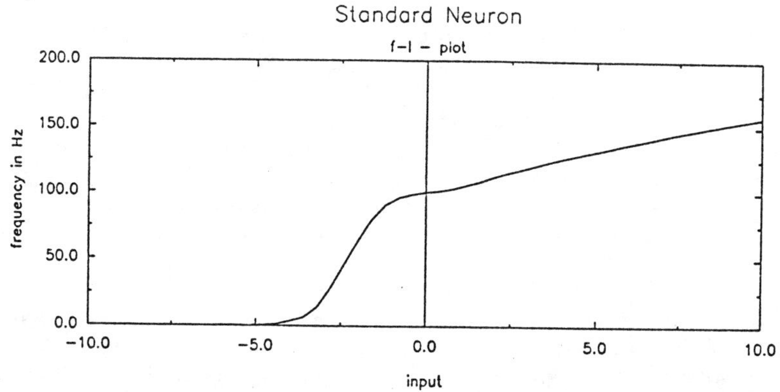

Figure 1: f-I–plot (frequency versus input current) for a standard neuron with absolute and relative refractory period. The absolute refractory period lasts for $a = 5ms$ followed by an exponentially decaying relative refractory function (time constant $2ms$). The refractory function is shown in figure 2.

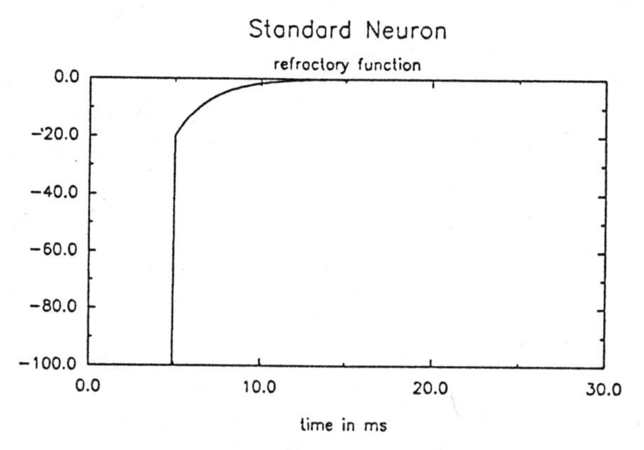

Figure 2: Refractory function of the model used in figure 1.

Indeed, the interval distribution changes from an approximate Poisson distribution for driving currents below threshold to an approximate Gaussian distribution above threshold. Different forms of the refractory function can lead to bursting behavior or to model neurons with adaptive behavior.

In figure 4 we show a bursting neuron defined by a long-tailed refractory function with a slight overshooting at intermediate time delays. At low input level, the bursts are noise induced and appear in irregular intervals. For larger driving currents the spiking changes to regular bursting. Even a model with a simple absolute refractory period

$$\epsilon^r(\tau) = \begin{cases} -\infty & \text{if } 0 \leq \tau \leq \gamma \\ 0 & \text{otherwise} \end{cases} \tag{4}$$

has many interesting features. The explicit solution for a network of these neurons is given in the following sections.

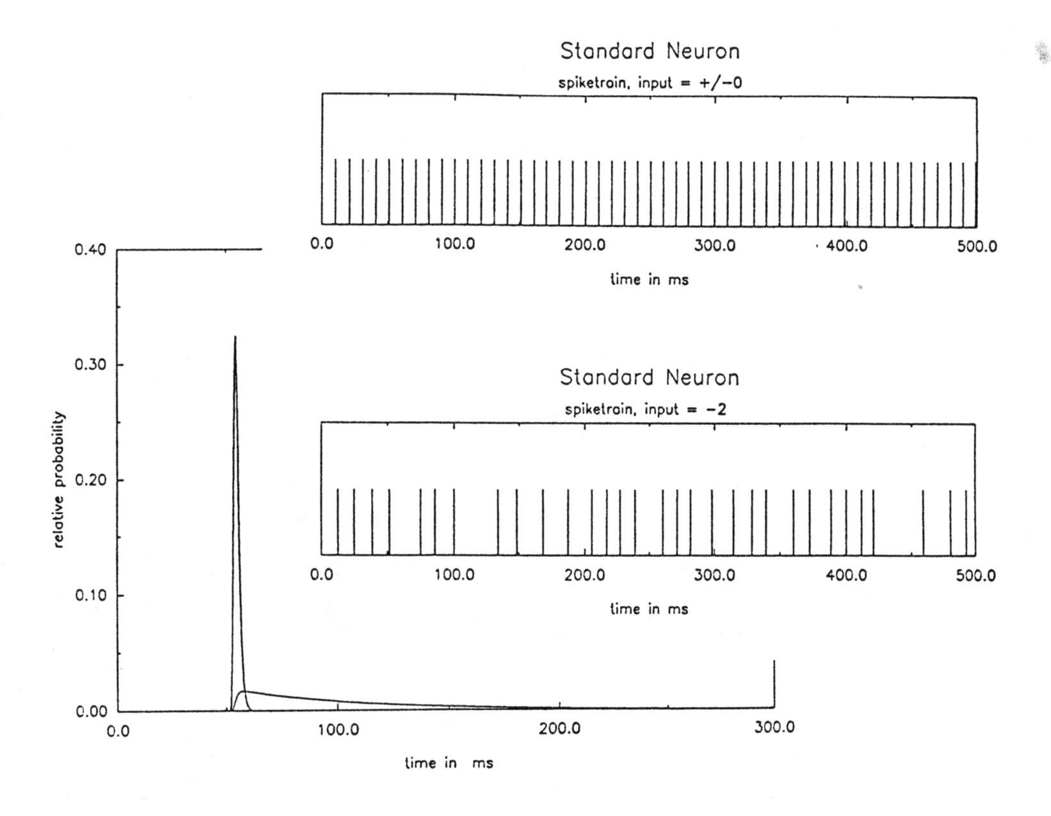

Figure 3: Spike trains and Interval distributions for the model of figure 1 at two different input levels.

3 THE NETWORK

So far we have only described the dynamics which initiates the spikes in the neurons. Now we have to describe the spikes themselves and their synaptic transmission to other neurons. To keep track of the spikes we assign to each neuron a two state variable S_i which usually rests at -1 and flips to $+1$ only when a spike is initiated. In the discrete time step representation that we assume in the following the output of each neuron is then described by a sequence of Ising spins $S_i(t_n)$.

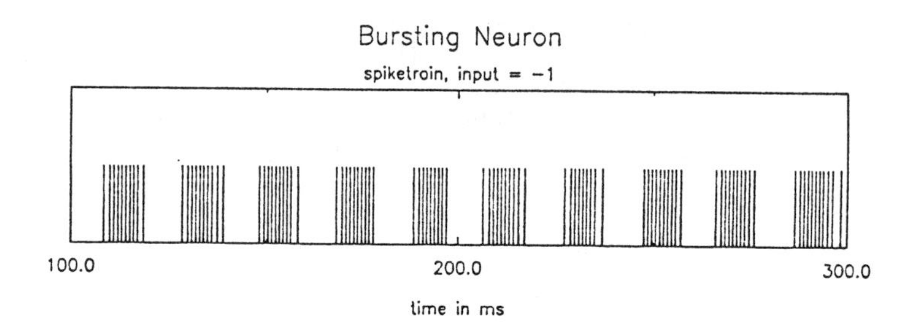

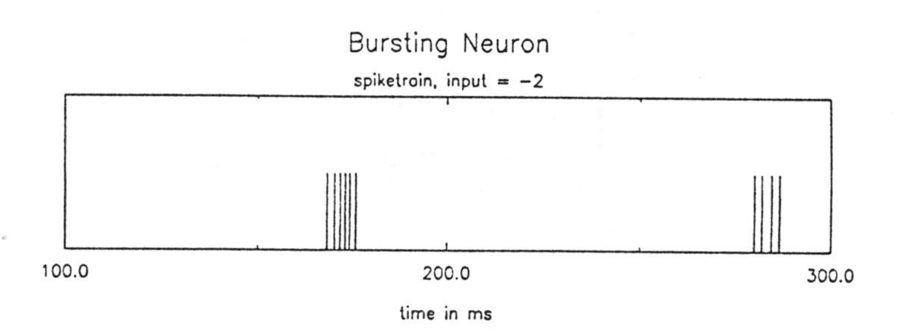

Figure 4: Spike trains for a bursting neuron. At low input level the bursts are noise induced and appear in irregular intervals, at high input level the bursting is regular.

In a network of neurons, neuron i may recieve a spike from neuron j via the synaptic connection, and the spike will evoke a postsynaptic potential at i. The strength of this response will depend on the synaptic efficacy J_{ij}. The time course of this response, however, can be taken to have a generic form independent of the strength of the synapse. We formalize these ideas assuming linearity and write

$$h_i^s(t_n) = \sum_j J_{ij} \sum_{\tau_m} \epsilon(\tau_m) \tilde{S}_j(t_n - \tau_m), \tag{5}$$

where $\epsilon(\tau)$ might be an experimental response function and $\tilde{S}_j$ is a conveniently normalized variable proportional to S_j.

For the synaptic efficacies we assume the Hebbian matrix also taken by Hopfield

$$J_{ij} = \frac{1}{N} \sum_{\mu=1}^{p} \xi_i^\mu \xi_j^\mu, \tag{6}$$

where the varables $\xi_i^\mu = \pm 1, (1 \leq i \leq N, 1 \leq \mu \leq p)$ describe the p random patterns to be stored. We can obtain these synaptic weights by a Hebbian learning procedure. It is now straightforward to incorporate the internal dynamics of the neurons, which we described in the preceding section. The refractory field can be introduced as the diagonal elements of the synaptic connection matrix

$$h_i^r(t_n) = \sum_{\tau_m} J_{ii}(\tau_m)[\tilde{S}_i(t_n - \tau_m) + 1]. \tag{7}$$

If all the neurons are equivalent, the diagonal elements must be independent of i and $J_{ii}(\tau) = \epsilon^r(\tau)$ describes the generic voltage response of our model neuron after firing of a spike.

4 RESULTS

We can solve this model analytically in the limit of a large and fully connected network. The solution depends on an additional parameter ρ which characterizes the maximum spiking frequency of the neurons. To compare our results with the Hopfield model, we replace $P_F(h)$, calculated from (1), by the generic form $\frac{1}{2}(1 + \tanh(\beta h))$ and we take the case of the simple refractory field (4). In this case the parameter ρ is related to the absolute refractory period by $\rho = \frac{1}{\gamma+1}$. For a large maximum spiking frequency or $\gamma \to 0$, we recover the Hopfield solutions. For γ larger than a critical value γ_c the solutions are qualitatively different: there is a regime of inverse temperatures in which both the retrieval solution and the trivial solution are stable. This allows the network to remain undecided, if the initial overlap with one of the patterns is not large enough. This is in contrast to the Hopfield model (Hopfield 1982,1984) where the network is always forced into one of the retrieval states. We compared our analytic solutions with computersimulations which verified that the calculated stationary solutions are indeed stable states of the network with a wide basin of attraction. Thus the basic associative memory characteristics of the standard Hopfield model are robust under the replacement of the two state neurons by more biological neurons.

5 CONCLUSIONS

We constructed a network of neurons with intrinsic spiking behaviour and realistic postsynaptic response. In addition to the standard solutions we have undecided network states which might have a biological significance in the process of decision making. There remain of course a number of unbiological features in the network, *e.g.* the assumption of full connectivity, the symmetry of the connections and the linearity of the learning rule. But most of these assumptions can be overcome at least in principle (see *e.g.* Amit 1989 for references). Our results confirm the general robustness of attractor neural networks to biological modifications, but they suggest that including more biological details also adds interesting features to the variety of states available to the network.

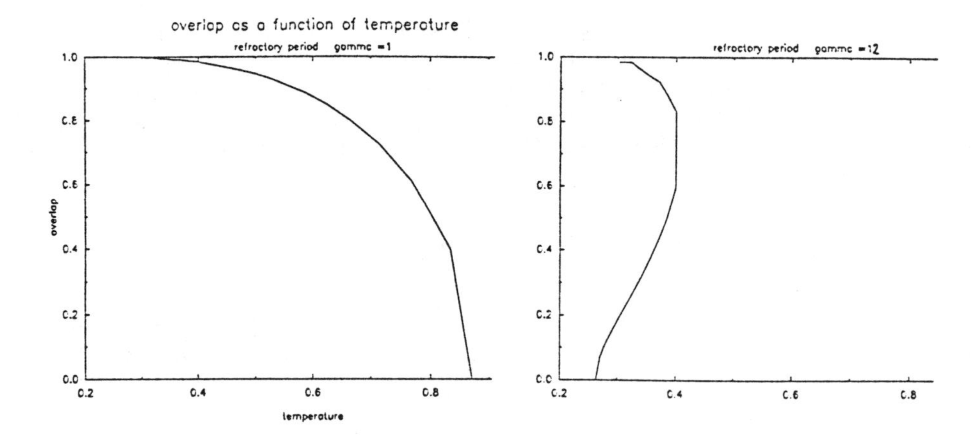

Figure 5: Stationary states of the network. Depending on the length of the refractory period the retrieval behavior varies. Figures *a* and *b* show the overlap with one of the learned patterns for different noise level $T = 1/\beta$. For a neuron a with short refractory period (figure *a*) the overlap curve is similar to those of the Hopfield model. For longer refractory periods (figure *b*) the curve is qualitatively different, showing a regime of bistability at intermediate noise levels. If the network is working at these noise levels it depends on the initial overlap with the learned pattern whether the network will go to the trivial state with overlap 0 or to the retrieval state with large overlap (overlap $m = 1$ corresponds to perfect retrieval.).

Acknowledgements

I would like to thank William Bialek and his students at Berkeley for their generous hospitality and numerous stimulating discussions. Thanks also to J.L.vanHemmen and to Andreas Herz for many helpful comments and advice. I acknowledge the financial support of the German Academic Exchange Service (DAAD) who made my stay at Berkeley possible.

References

Hopfield,J.J. (1982), Neural Networks and Physical Systems with Emergent Collective Computational Abilities, Proc.Natl.Acad.Sci USA **79**, 2554-2558.

Hopfield,J.J. (1984), Neurons with Graded Response have Collective Computational Properties like those of Two-State-Neurons, Proc.Natl.Acad.Sci USA **81**, 3088-3092.

Hodgkin,A.L. and Huxley,A.F. (1952) A Quantitative Description of Membrane Current and its Application to Conduction and Excitation in Nerve, J.Physiology **117**, 500-544.

Amit,D.J., (1989) Modeling Brain Function: The World of Attractor Neural Networks, CH.7. Cambridge University Press.

CAM Storage of Analog Patterns and Continuous Sequences with $3N^2$ Weights

Bill Baird
Dept Mathematics and
Dept Molecular and Cell Biology,
129 LSA, U.C.Berkeley,
Berkeley, Ca. 94720

Frank Eeckman
Lawrence Livermore
National Laboratory,
P.O. Box 808 (L-426),
Livermore, Ca. 94550

Abstract

A simple architecture and algorithm for analytically guaranteed associative memory storage of analog patterns, continuous sequences, and chaotic attractors in the same network is described. A matrix inversion determines network weights, given prototype patterns to be stored. There are N units of capacity in an N node network with $3N^2$ weights. It costs one unit per static attractor, two per Fourier component of each sequence, and four per chaotic attractor. There are no spurious attractors, and there is a Liapunov function in a special coordinate system which governs the approach of transient states to stored trajectories. Unsupervised or supervised incremental learning algorithms for pattern classification, such as competitive learning or bootstrap Widrow-Hoff can easily be implemented. The architecture can be "folded" into a recurrent network with higher order weights that can be used as a model of cortex that stores oscillatory and chaotic attractors by a Hebb rule. Hierarchical sensory-motor control networks may be constructed of interconnected "cortical patches" of these network modules. Network performance is being investigated by application to the problem of real time handwritten digit recognition.

1 Introduction

We introduce here a "projection network" which is a new network for implementation of the "normal form projection algorithm" discussed in [Bai89, Bai90b]. The autoassociative case of this network is formally equivalent to the previous higher order network realization used as a biological model [Bai90a]. It has $3N^2$ weights instead of $N^2 + N^4$, and is more useful for engineering applications. All the mathematical results proved for the projection algorithm in that case carry over to this

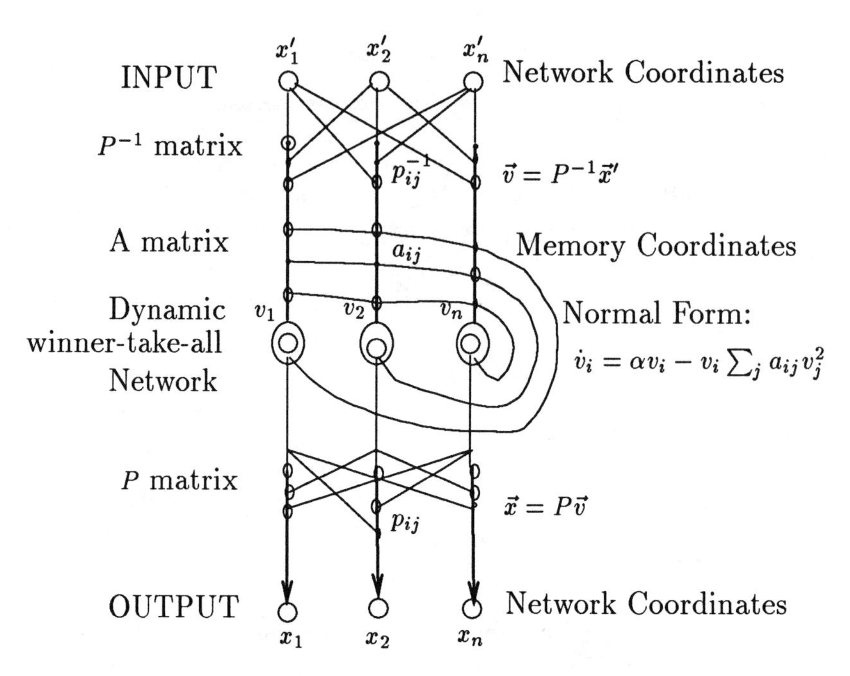

Figure 1: Projection Network - $3N^2$ weights. The A matrix determines a k-winner-take-all net - programs attractors, basins of attraction, and rates of convergence. The columns of P contain the ouptut patterns associated to these attractors. The rows of P^{-1} determine category centroids

new architecture, but more general versions can be trained and applied in novel ways. The discussion here will be informal, since space prohibits technical detail and proofs may be found in the references above.

A key feature of a net constructed by this algorithm is that the underlying dynamics is explicitly isomorphic to any of a class of standard, well understood nonlinear dynamical systems - a "normal form" [GH83]. This system is chosen in advance, independent of both the patterns to be stored and the learning algorithm to be used. This control over the dynamics permits the design of important aspects of the network dynamics independent of the particular patterns to be stored. Stability, basin geometry, and rates of convergence to attractors can be programmed in the standard dynamical system.

Here we use the normal form for the Hopf bifurcation [GH83] as a simple recurrent competitive k-winner-take-all network with a cubic nonlinearity. This network lies in what might considered diagonalized or "overlap" or "memory coordinates" (one memory per k nodes). For temporal patterns, these nodes come in complex conjugate pairs which supply Fourier components for trajectories to be learned. Chaotic dynamics may be created by specific programming of the interaction of two pairs of these nodes.

Learning of desired spatial or spatio-temporal patterns is done by projecting sets of these nodes into network coordinates(the standard basis) using the desired vectors as corresponding columns of a transformation matrix P. In previous work, the differential equations of the recurrent network itself are linearly transformed or "projected", leading to new recurrent network equations with higher order weights corresponding to the cubic terms of the recurrent network.

2 The Projection Network

In the projection net for autoassociation, this algebraic projection operation into and out of memory coordinates is done explicitly by a set of weights in two feed-forward linear networks characterized by weight matrices P^{-1} and P. These map inputs into and out of the nodes of the recurrent dynamical network in memory coordinates sandwiched between them. This kind of network, with explicit input and output projection maps that are inverses, may be considered an "unfolded" version of the purely recurrent networks described in the references above.

This network is shown in figure 1. Input pattern vectors $\vec{x}'$ are applied as pulses which project onto each vector of weights (row of the P^{-1} matrix) on the input to each unit i of the dynamic network to establish an activation level v_i which determines the initial condition for the relaxation dynamics of this network. The recurrent weight matrix A of the dynamic network can be chosen so that the unit or predefined subspace of units which recieves the largest projection of the input will converge to some state of activity, static or dynamic, while all other units are supressed to zero activity.

The evolution of the activity in these memory coordinates appears in the original network coordinates at the output terminals as a spatio-temporal pattern which may be fully distributed accross all nodes. Here the state vector of the dynamic network has been transformed by the P matrix back into the coordinates in which the input was first applied. At the attractor $\vec{v}*$ in memory coordinates, only a linear combination of the columns of the P weight matrix multiplied by the winning nonzero modes of the dynamic net constitute the network representation of the output of the system. Thus the attractor retrieved in memory coordinates reconstructs its learned distributed representation $\vec{x}^*$ through the corresponding columns of the output matrix P, e.g. $P^{-1}\vec{x}' = \vec{v}$, $\vec{v} \rightarrow \vec{v}^*$, $P\vec{v}^* = \vec{x}^*$.

For the special case of content addressable memory or autoassociation, which we have been describing here, the actual patterns to be learned form the columns of the output weight matrix P, and the input matrix is its inverse P^{-1}. These are the networks that can be "folded" into higher order recurrent networks. For orthonormal patterns, the inverse is the transpose of this output matrix of memories, $P^{-1} = P^T$, and no computation of P^{-1} is required to store or change memories - just plug the desired patterns into appropriate rows and columns of P and P^T.

In the autoassociative network, the input space, output space and normal form state space are each of dimension N. The input and output linear maps require N^2 weights each, while the normal form coefficients determine another N^2 weights. Thus the net needs only $3N^2$ weights, instead of the $N^2 + N^4$ weights required by the folded recurrent network. The $2N^2$ input and output weights could be stored off-chip in a conventional memory, and the fixed weights of the dynamic normal form network could be implemented in VLSI for fast analog relaxation.

3 Learning Extensions

More generally, for a heteroassociative net (i. e., a net designed to perform a map from input space to possibly different output space) the linear input and output maps need not be inverses, and may be noninvertible. They may be found by any linear map learning technique such as Widrow-Hoff or by finding pseudoinverses.

Learning of all desired memories may be instantaneous, when they are known in advance, or may evolve by many possible incremental methods, supervised or unsupervised. The standard competitive learning algorithm where the input weight vector attached to the winning memory node is moved toward the input pattern can be employed. We can also decrease the tendency to choose the most frequently selected node, by adjusting paratmeters in the normal form equations, to realize the more effective frequency selective competitive learning algorithm [AKCM90]. Supervised algorithms like bootstrap Widrow Hoff may be implemented as well, where a desired output category is known. The weight vector of the winning normal form node is updated by the competitive rule, if it is the right category for that input, but moved away from the input vector, if it is not the desired category, and the weight vector of the desired node is moved toward the input.

Thus the input map can be optimized for clustering and classification by these algorithms, as the weight vectors (row vectors of the input matrix) approach the centroids of the clusters in the input environment. The output weight matrix may then be constructed with any desired output pattern vectors in appropriate columns to place the attractors corresponding to these categories anywhere in the state space in network coordinates that is required to achieve a desired heteroassociation.

If either the input or the output matrix is learned, and the other chosen to be its inverse, then these competitive nets can be folded into oscillating biological versions, to see what the competive learning algorithms correspond to there. Now either the rows of the input matrix may be optimized for recognition, or the columns of the output matrix may be chosen to place attractors, but not both. We hope to be able to derive a kind of Hebb rule in the biological network, using the unfolded form of the network, which we can prove will accomplish competitive learning. Thus the work on engineering applications feeds back on the understanding of the biological systems.

4 Programming the Normal Form Network

The key to the power of the projection algorithm to program these systems lies in the freedom to chose a well understood normal form for the dynamics, independent of the patterns to be learned. The Hopf normal form used here, (in Cartesian coordinates) $\dot{v}_i = \sum_{j=1}^{N} J_{ij} v_j - v_i \sum_{j=1}^{N} A_{ij} v_j^2$ is especially easy to work with for programming periodic attractors, but handles fixed points as well. J is a matrix with real eigenvalues for determining static attractors, or complex conjugate eignevalue pairs in blocks along the diagonal for periodic attractors. The real parts are positive, and cause initial states to move away from the origin, until the competitive (negative) cubic terms dominate at some distance, and cause the flow to be inward from all points beyond. The off-diagonal cubic terms cause competition between directions of flow within a spherical middle region and thus create multiple attractors and basins. The larger the eigenvalues in J and off-diagonal weights in

A, the faster the convergence to attractors in this region.

It is easy to choose blocks of coupling along the diagonal of the A matrix to produce different kinds of attractors, static, periodic, or chaotic, in different coordinate subspaces of the network. The sizes of the subspaces can be programmed by the sizes of the blocks. The basin of attraction of an attractor determined within a subspace is guaranteed to contain the subspace [Bai90b]. Thus basins can be programmed, and "spurious" attractors can be ruled out when all subspaces have been included in a programmed block.

This can be accomplished simply by choosing the A matrix entries outside the blocks on the diagonal (which determine coupling of variables within a subspace) to be greater (more negative) than those within the blocks. The principle is that this makes the subspaces defined by the blocks compete exhaustively, since intersubspace competition is greater than subspace self-damping. Within the middle region, the flow is forced to converge laterally to enter the subspaces programmed by the blocks.

An simple example is a matrix of the form,

$$A = \begin{bmatrix} d & & & & & \\ & d & & & (g) & \\ & & \begin{bmatrix} d & c \\ c & d \end{bmatrix} & & & \\ & & & \begin{bmatrix} d & d & c & c \\ d & d & c & c \\ c & c & d & d \\ c & c & d & d \end{bmatrix} & & \\ & & & & & \\ & (g) & & & & \ddots \end{bmatrix},$$

where $0 < c < d < g$. There is a static attractor on each axis (in each one dimensional subspace) corresponding to the first two entries on the diagonal, by the agrument above. In the first two dimensional subspace block there is a single fixed point in the interior of the subspace on the main diagonal, because the off-diagonal entries within the block are symmetric and less negative than those on the diagonal. The components do not compete, but rather combine. Nevertheless, the flow from outside is into the subspace, because the entries outside the subspace are more negative than those within it.

The last subspace contains entries appropriate to guarantee the stability of a periodic attractor with two frequencies (Fourier components) chosen in the J matrix. The doubling of the entries is because these components come in complex conjugate pairs (in the J matrix blocks) which get identical A matrix coupling. Again, these pairs are combined by the lesser off-diagonal coupling within the block to form a single limit cycle attractor. A large subspace can store a complicated continuous periodic spatio-temporal sequence with many component frequencies.

The discrete Fourier transform of a set of samples of such a sequence in space and time can be input directly to the P matrix as a set of complex columns corresponding to the frequencies in J and the subspace programmed in A. $N/2$ total DFT samples of N dimensional time varying spatial vectors may be placed in the P matrix, and parsed by the A matrix into $M < N/2$ separate sequences as desired, with separate basins of attraction guaranteed [Bai90b]. For a symmetric A matrix, there is a

Liapunov function, in the amplitude equations of a polar coordinate version of the normal form, which governs the approach of initial states to stored trajectories.

5 Chaotic Attractors

Chaotic attractors may be created in this normal form, with sigmoid nonlinearities added to the right hand side, $v_i \rightarrow tanh(v_i)$. The sigmoids yield a spectrum of higher order terms that break the phase shift symmetry of the system. Two oscillatory pairs of nodes like those programmed in the block above can then be programmed to interact chaotically. In our simulations, for example, if we set the upper block of d entries to -1, and the lower to 1, and replace the upper c entries with 4.0, and the lower with -0.4, we get a chaotic attractor of dimension less than four, but greater than three.

This is "weak" or "phase coherent" chaos that is still nearly periodic. It is created by the broken symmetry, when a homoclinic tangle occurs to break up an invariant 3-torus in the flow [GH83]. This is the Ruelle-Takens route to chaos and has been observed in Taylor-Couette flow when both cylnders are rotated. We believe that sets of Lorentz equations in three dimensional subspace blocks could be used in a projection network as well. Experiments of Freeman, however, have suggested that chaotic attractors of the above dimension occur in the olfactory system [Fre87]. These might most naturally occur by the interaction of oscillatory modes.

In the projection network or its folded biological version, these chaotic attractors have a basin of attraction in the N dimensional state space that constitues a category, just like any other attractor in this system. They are, however, "fuzzy" attractors, and there may be computational advantages to the basins of attraction (categories) produced by chaotic attractors, or to the effects their outputs have as fuzzy inputs to other network modules. The particular N dimensional spatio-temporal patterns learned for the four components of these chaotically paired modes may be considered a coordinate specific "encoding" of the strange attractor, which may constitute a recognizable input to another network, if it falls within some learned basin of attraction. While the details of the trajectory of a strange attractor in any real physical continuous dynamical system are lost in the noise, there is still a particular statistical structure to the attractor which is a recognizable "signature".

6 Applications

Handwritten characters have a natural translation invariant analog representation in terms of a sequence of angles that parametrize the pencil trajectory, and their classification can be taken as a static or temporal pattern recognition problem. We have constructed a trainable on-line system to which anyone may submit input by mouse or digitizing pad, and observe the performance of the system for themselves, in immediate comparison to their own internal recognition response. The performance of networks with static, periodic, and chaotic attractors may be tested simultaneously, and we are presently assessing the results.

These networks can be combined into a hierarchical architecture of interconnected modules. The larger network itself can then be viewed as a projection network, transformed into biological versions, and its behavior analysed with the same tools that were used to design the modules. The modules can model "patches" of cortex interconnected to form sensory-motor control networks. These can be configured to yield autonomous adaptive "organisms" which learn useful sequences of behaviors by reinforcement from their environment.

The A matrix for a network like that above may itself become a sub-block in the A matrix of a larger network. The overall network is then a projection network with zero elements in off-diagonal A matrix entries outside blocks that define multiple attractors for the submodules. The modules neither compete nor combine states, in the absence of A matrix coupling between them, but take states independently based on their inputs to each other through the weights in the matrix J (which here describes full coupling). The modules learn connection weights J_{ij} between themselves which will cause the system to evolve under a clocked "machine cycle" by a sequence of transitions of attractors (static, oscillatory, or chaotic) within the modules, much as a digital computer evolves by transitions of its binary flip-flop states. This entire network may be folded to use more fault tolerant and biologically plausible distributed representations, without disrupting the identity of the subnetworks.

Supervised learning by recurrent back propagation or reinforcement can be used to train the connections between modules. When the inputs from one module to the next are given as impulses that establish initial conditions, the dynamical behavior of a module is described exactly by the projection theorem [Bai89]. Possible applications include problems such as system identification and control, robotic path planning, gramatical inference, and variable-binding by phaselocking in oscillatory semantic networks.

Acknowledgements:

Supported by AFOSR-87-0317, and a grant from LLNL. It is a pleasure to acknowledge the support of Walter Freeman and invaluable assistance of Morris Hirsch.

References

[AKCM90] C. Ahalt, A. Krishnamurthy, P. Chen, and D. Melton. Competitive learning algorithms for vector quantization. *Neural Networks*, 3:277–290, 1990.

[Bai89] B Baird. A bifurcation theory approach to vector field programming for periodic attractors. In *Proc. Int. Joint Conf. on Neural Networks, Wash. D.C.*, pages 1:381–388, June 1989.

[Bai90a] B. Baird. Bifurcation and learning in network models of oscillating cortex. In S. Forest, editor, *Emergent Computation*, pages 365–384. North Holland, 1990. also in Physica D, 42.

[Bai90b] B. Baird. A learning rule for cam storage of continuous periodic sequences. In *Proc. Int. Joint Conf. on Neural Networks, San Diego*, pages 3: 493–498, June 1990.

[Fre87] W.J. Freeman. Simulation of chaotic eeg patterns with a dynamic model of the olfactory system. *Biological Cybernetics*, 56:139, 1987.

[GH83] J. Guckenheimer and D. Holmes. *Nonlinear Oscillations, Dynamical Systems, and Bifurcations of Vector Fields.* Springer, New York, 1983.

Connection Topology and Dynamics in Lateral Inhibition Networks

C. M. Marcus, F. R. Waugh, and R. M. Westervelt
Department of Physics and Division of Applied Sciences, Harvard University
Cambridge, MA 02138

ABSTRACT

We show analytically how the stability of two-dimensional lateral inhibition neural networks depends on the local connection topology. For various network topologies, we calculate the critical time delay for the onset of oscillation in continuous-time networks and present analytic phase diagrams characterizing the dynamics of discrete-time networks.

1 INTRODUCTION

Mutual inhibition in an array of neurons is a common feature of sensory systems including vision, olfaction, and audition in organisms ranging from invertebrates to man. A well-studied instance of this configuration is lateral inhibition between neighboring photosensitive neurons in the retina (Dowling, 1987). Inhibition serves in this case to enhance the perception of edges and to broaden the dynamic range by setting a local reference point for measuring intensity variations. Lateral inhibition thus constitutes the first stage of visual information processing. Many artificial vision systems also take advantage of the computational power of lateral inhibition by directly wiring inhibition into the photodetecting electronic hardware (Mead, 1989).

Lateral inhibition may create extensive feedback paths, leading to network-wide collective oscillations. Sustained oscillations arising from lateral inhibition have been observed in biological visual systems—specifically, in the compound eye of the horseshoe crab *Limulus* (Barlow and Fraioli, 1978; Coleman and Renninger, 1978)—as well as in artificial vision systems, for instance plaguing an early version of the electronic retina chip built by Mead *et al.* (Wyatt and Standley, 1988; Mead, 1989).

In this paper we study the dynamics of simple neural network models of lateral inhibition in a variety of two-dimensional connection schemes. The lattice structures we study are shown in Fig. 1. Two-dimensional lattices are of particular importance to artificial vision systems because they allow an efficient mapping of an image onto a network and because they are well-suited for implementation in VLSI circuitry. We show that the stability of these networks depends sensitively on such design considerations as local connection topology, neuron self-coupling, the steepness or gain of the neuron transfer function, and details of the network dynamics such as connection delays for continuous-time dynamics or update rule for discrete-time dynamics.

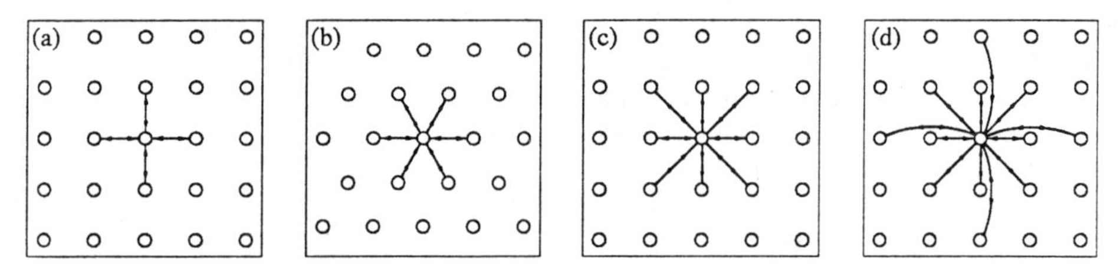

Figure 1: Connection schemes for two-dimensional lateral inhibition networks considered in this paper: (a) nearest-neighbor connections on a square lattice; (b) nearest-neighbor connections on a triangular lattice; (c) 8-neighbor connections on a square lattice; and (d) 12-neighbor connections on a square lattice.

The paper is organized as follows. Section 2 introduces the dynamical equations describing continuous-time and discrete-time lateral inhibition networks. Section 3 discusses the relationship between lattice topology and critical time delay for the onset of oscillation in the continuous-time case. Section 4 presents analytic phase diagrams characterizing the dynamics of discrete-time lateral inhibition networks as neuron gain, neuron self-coupling, and lattice structure are varied. Our conclusions are presented in Section 5.

2 NETWORK DYNAMICS

We begin by considering a general neural network model defined by the set of electronic circuit equations

$$C_i\, du_i(t')/dt' = -u_i(t')/R_i + \sum_j T_{ij} f_j\big(u_j(t'-\tau_{ij}')\big) + I_i \quad , \quad i=1,\ldots,N, \tag{1}$$

where u_i is the voltage, C_i the capacitance, and $R_i^{-1} = \sum_j |T_{ij}|$ the total conductance at the input of neuron i. Input to the network is through the applied currents I_i. The nonlinear transfer function f_i is taken to be sigmoidal with odd symmetry and maximum slope at the origin. A time delay τ_{ij}' in the communication from neuron i to neuron j has been explicitly included. Such a delay could arise from the finite operating speed of the elements—neurons or amplifiers—or from the finite propagation speed of the interconnections. For the case of lateral inhibition networks with self-coupling, the connection matrix is given by

$$T_{ij} = \begin{cases} \gamma & \text{for } i=j \\ -1 & \text{for } i, j \text{ connected neighbors} \\ 0 & \text{otherwise,} \end{cases} \tag{2}$$

which makes $R_i^{-1} = |\gamma| + z$ for all i, where z is the number of connected neighbors. For simplicity, we take all neurons to have the same delay and characteristic relaxation time ($\tau_i' = \tau_{delay}$, $R_i C_i = \tau_{relax}$ for all i) and identical transfer functions. With these assumptions, Eq. (1) can be rescaled and written in terms of the neuron outputs $x_i(t)$ as

$$dx_i(t)/dt = -x_i(t) + F\left(\sum_j T_{ij} x_j(t-\tau) + I_i\right) , \quad i=1,\ldots,N, \tag{3}$$

where the odd, sigmoidal function F now appears outside the sum. The function F is characterized by a maximum slope β (> 0), and its saturation amplitude can be set to ±1 without loss of generality. The commonly used form $F(h) = \tanh(\beta h)$ satisfies these requirements; we will continue to use F to emphasize generality. As a result of rescaling, the delay time τ is now measured in units of network relaxation time (i.e. $\tau = \tau_{delay}/\tau_{relax}$), and the connection matrix is normalized such that $\sum_j |T_{ij}| = 1$ for all i. Stability of Eq. (3) against coherent oscillation will be discussed in Section 3.

The discrete-time iterated map,

$$x_i(t+1) = F\left(\sum_j T_{ij} x_j(t) + I_i\right) \quad , \quad i=1,\ldots,N, \tag{4}$$

with parallel updating of neuron states $x_i(t)$, corresponds to the long-delay limit of Eq. (3) (care must be taken in considering this limit; not all aspects of the delay system carry over to the map (Mallet-Paret and Nussbaum, 1986)). The iterated map network, Eq. (4), is particularly useful for implementing fast, parallel networks using conventional computer clocking techniques. The speed advantage of parallel dynamics, however, comes at a price: the parallel-update network may oscillate even when the corresponding sequential update network is stable. Section 4 gives phase diagrams based on global stability analysis which explicitly define the oscillation-free operating region of Eq. (4) and its generalization to a multistep updating rule.

3 STABILITY OF LATTICES WITH DELAYED INHIBITION

In the absence of delay ($\tau = 0$) the continuous-time lateral inhibition network, Eq. (3), always converges to a fixed point attractor. This follows from the famous stability criterion based on a Liapunov (or "energy") function (Cohen and Grossberg, 1983; Hopfield, 1984), and relies on the symmetry of the lateral inhibitory connections (i.e. $T_{ij} = T_{ji}$ for all connection schemes in Fig. 1). This guarantee of convergence does not hold for nonzero delay, however, and it is known that adding delay can induce sustained, coherent oscillation in a variety of symmetrically connected network configurations (Marcus and Westervelt, 1989a). Previously we have shown that certain delay networks of the form of Eq. (3)—including lateral inhibition networks—will oscillate coherently, that is with all neurons oscillating in phase, for sufficiently large delay. As the delay is reduced, however, the oscillatory mode becomes unstable, leaving only fixed point attractors. A critical value of delay τ_{crit} below which sustained oscillation vanishes for any value of neuron gain β is given by

$$\tau_{crit} = -\ln\left(1 + \lambda_{max}/\lambda_{min}\right) \qquad \left(0 < \lambda_{max} < -\lambda_{min}\right) \tag{5}$$

where λ_{max} and λ_{min} are the extremal eigenvalues of the connection matrix T_{ij}. The analysis leading to (5) is based on a local stability analysis of the coherent oscillatory mode. Though this local analysis lacks the rigor of a global analysis (which can be done for $\tau = 0$ and for the discrete-time case, Eq. (4)) the result agrees well with experiments and numerical simulations (Marcus and Westervelt, 1989a).

It is straightforward to find the spectrum of eigenvalues for the lattices in Fig. 1. Assuming periodic boundary conditions, one can expand the eigenvalue equation $\mathbf{T}x = \lambda x$ in terms of periodic functions $x_j = x_o \, exp(i \, \boldsymbol{q} \cdot \boldsymbol{R}_j)$, where $\boldsymbol{R}_j$ is the 2D vector position of neuron j and $\boldsymbol{q}$ is the reciprocal lattice vector characterizing a particular eigenmode. In the large network limit, this expansion leads to the following results for the square and triangular lattices with nearest neighbor connections and self-connection γ [see next section for a table of eigenvalues]:

$$\tau_{crit} \to ln(1/2 - 2/\gamma) \qquad (-4 < \gamma < 0) \qquad \text{[n.n. square lattice, Fig. 1(a)]}, \qquad (6a)$$

$$\tau_{crit} \to ln[(\gamma - 6)/(2\gamma - 3)] \qquad (-3 < \gamma < 3/2) \qquad \text{[n.n. triangular lattice, Fig. 1(b)]}. \qquad (6b)$$

Curves showing τ_{crit} as a function of self-connection γ are given in Fig. 2. These reveal the surprising result that *the triangular lattice is much more prone to delay-induced oscillation than the square lattice.* For instance, with no self connection ($\gamma = 0$), the square lattice does not show sustained oscillation for any finite delay, while the triangular lattice oscillates for $\tau > \ln 2 \cong 0.693$.

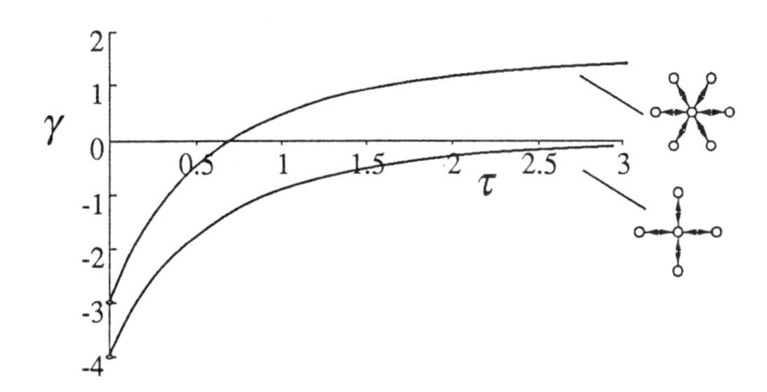

Figure 2: Critical delay τ_{crit} as a function of self-connection γ, from Eq. (6). Note that for $\gamma = 0$ only triangular lattice oscillates at finite delay. The analysis does not apply at exactly $\tau = 0$, where both networks are stable for all values of γ.

The important difference between these two lattices—and the quality which accounts for their dissimilar stability properties—is *not* simply the number of neighbors, but is the presence of *frustration* in the triangular lattice but not in the square lattice. Lateral inhibition, like antiferromagnetism, forms closed loops in the triangular lattice which do not allow all of the connections to be satisfied by any arrangement of neuron states. In contrast, lateral inhibition on the square lattice is not frustrated, and is, in fact, exactly equivalent to lateral excitation via a gauge transformation. We note that a similar situation exists in 2D magnetic models: while models of 2D ferromagnetism on square and triangular lattices behave nearly identically (both are nonfrustrated), the corresponding 2D antiferromagnets are quite different, due to the presence of frustration in the triangular lattice, but not the square lattice (Wannier, 1950).

4 LATTICES WITH ITERATED-MAP DYNAMICS

Next we consider lateral inhibition networks with discrete-time dynamics where all neuron states are updated in parallel. The standard parallel dynamics formulation was given above as Eq. (4), but here we will consider a generalized updating rule which offers some important practical advantages. The generalized system we consider updates the neuron states based on an average over M previous time steps, rather than just using a single previous state to generate the next. This multistep rule is somewhat like including time delay, but as we will see, increasing M actually makes the system more stable compared to standard parallel updating. This update rule also differs from the delay-differential system in permitting a rigorous global stability analysis. The dynamical system we consider is defined by the following set of coupled iterated maps:

$$x_i(t+1) = F\left(\sum_j T_{ij} z_j(t) + I_i\right) \ ; \qquad z_j(t) = M^{-1} \sum_{\tau=0}^{M-1} x_j(t-\tau) \ , \tag{7}$$

where $i, j = 1, \ldots, N$ and $M \in \{1, 2, 3, \ldots\}$. The standard parallel updating rule, Eq.(4), is recovered by setting $M = 1$.

A global analysis of the dynamics of Eq. (7) for any symmetric T_{ij} is given in (Marcus and Westervelt, 1990), and for M=1 in (Marcus and Westervelt, 1989b). It is found that for any M, if all eigenvalues λ satisfy $\beta|\lambda| < 1$ then there is a single attractor which depends only on the inputs I_i. For $I_i = 0$, this attractor is the origin, i.e. all neurons at zero output. Whenever $\beta|\lambda| > 1$ for one or more eigenvalues, multiple fixed points as well as periodic attractors may exist. There is, in addition, a remarkably simple global stability criterion associated with Eq. (7): satisfying the condition $1/\beta > -\lambda_{min}(T_{ij})/M$ insures that no periodic attractors exist, though there may be a multiplicity of fixed point attractors. As in the previous section, λ_{min} is the most negative eigenvalue of T_{ij}. If T_{ij} has no negative eigenvalues, then λ_{min} is the smallest positive eigenvalue, and the stability criterion is satisfied trivially since β is defined to be positive.

These stability results may be used to compute analytic phase diagrams for the various connection schemes shown in Fig. 1 and defined in Eq. (3). The extremal eigenvalues of T_{ij} are calculated using the Fourier expansion described above. In the limit of large lattice size and assuming periodic boundary conditions, we find the following:

	square n. n.	triangle n. n.	square 8 - n.	square 12 - n.
λ_{max}:	$\frac{\gamma+4}{\|\gamma\|+4}$	$\frac{\gamma+3}{\|\gamma\|+6}$	$\frac{\gamma+4}{\|\gamma\|+8}$	$\frac{\gamma+13/3}{\|\gamma\|+12}$
λ_{min}:	$\frac{\gamma-4}{\|\gamma\|+4}$	$\frac{\gamma-6}{\|\gamma\|+6}$	$\frac{\gamma-8}{\|\gamma\|+8}$	$\frac{\gamma-12}{\|\gamma\|+12}$

The resulting phase diagrams characterizing regions with different dynamic properties are shown in Fig. 3. The four regions indicated in the diagrams are characterized as follows: (1) *orig*: low gain regime where a unique fixed point attractor exists (that attractor is the origin for $I_i = 0$); (2) *fp*: for some inputs I_i multiple fixed point attractors may exist, each with an attracting basin, *but no oscillatory attractors exist in this region (i.e. no attractors with period >1)*; (3) *osc*: at most one fixed point attractor, but one or more oscillatory modes also may exist; (4) *fp* + *osc*: multiple fixed points as well as oscillatory attractors may exist.

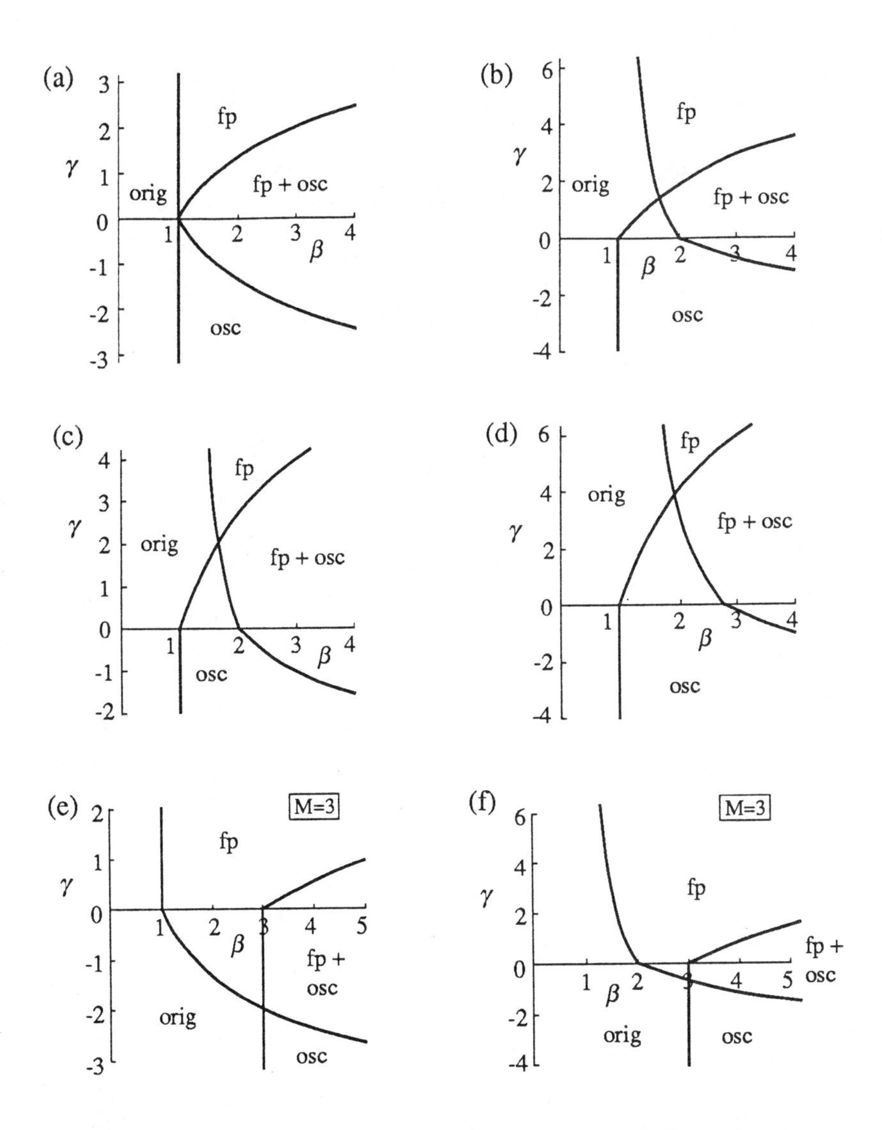

Figure 3: Phase diagrams based on global analysis for lateral inhibition networks with discrete-time parallel dynamics [Eq.(7)] as a function of neuron gain β and self-connection γ. Regions *orig*, *fp*, *osc*, and *fp+osc* are defined in text. (a) Nearest-neighbor connections on a square lattice and single-step updating (M=1); (b) nearest-neighbor connections on a triangular lattice, M=1; (c) 8-neighbor connections on a square lattice, M=1; (d) 12-neighbor connections on a square lattice, M=1; (e) nearest-neighbor connections on a square lattice, M=3; (f) nearest-neighbor connections on a triangular lattice, M=3.

5 CONCLUSIONS

We have shown analytically how the dynamics of two-dimensional neural network models of lateral inhibition depends on both single-neuron properties—such as the slope of the sigmoidal transfer function, delayed response, and the strength of self-connection—and also on the topological properties of the network.

The design rules implied by the analysis are in some instances what would be expected intuitively. For example, the phase diagrams in Fig. 4 show that in order to eliminate oscillations one can either include a positive self-connection term or decrease the gain of the neuron. It is also not surprising that reducing the time delay in a delay-differential system eliminates oscillation. Less intuitive is the observation that for discrete-time dynamics using a multistep update rule greatly expands the region of oscillation-free operation (compare, for example Figs. 4(a) and 4(e)). One result emerging in this paper that seems quite counterintuitive is the dramatic effect of connection topology, which persists even in the limit of large lattice size. This point was illustrated in a comparison of networks with delayed inhibition on square and triangular lattices, where it was found that in the absence of self-connection, only the triangular lattices will show sustained oscillation.

Finally, we note that it is not clear to us how to generalize our results to other network models, for example to models with *asymmetric* connections which allow for direction-selective motion detection. Such questions remain interesting challenges for future work.

Acknowledgments

We thank Bob Meade and Cornelia Kappler for informative discussions. One of us (C.M.M.) acknowledges support as an IBM Postdoctoral Fellow, and one (F.R.W.) from the Army Research Office as a JSEP Graduate Fellow. This work was supported in part by ONR contract N00014-89-J-1592, JSEP contract N00014-89-J-1023, and DARPA contract AFOSR-89-0506.

References

Barlow, R. B. and A. J. Fraioli (1978), J. Gen. Physiol., **71**, 699.

Cohen, M. A., and S. Grossberg (1983), IEEE Trans. SMC-**13**, 815.

Coleman, B. D. and G.H. Renninger (1978), Math. Biosc. **38**, 123.

Dowling, J. E. (1987), *The Retina: An Approachable Part of the Brain* (Harvard University Press, Cambridge, MA).

Hopfield, J. J. (1984), Proc. Nat. Acad. Sci. USA **81**, 3008.

Mallet-Paret, J. and R. D. Nussbaum (1986) in *Chaotic Dynamics and Fractals*, edited by M. F. Barnsley and S. G. Demko, (Academic Press, Orlando) p. 263.

Marcus, C. M. and R. M. Westervelt (1989a), Phys. Rev. A **39**, 347.

Marcus, C. M. and R. M. Westervelt (1989b), Phys. Rev. A **40**, 501.

Marcus, C. M. and R. M. Westervelt (1990), Phys. Rev. A **42**, 2410.

Mead, Carver A. (1989), *Analog VLSI and Neural Systems* (Addison-Wesley, Reading, MA).

Wyatt, Jr., J. L., and D. L. Standley (1988), in *Neural Information Processing Systems, Denver CO, 1987*, edited by D. Z. Anderson, (AIP, New York), p. 860.

Wannier, G. M. (1950), Phys. Rev. **79**, 357.

Shaping the State Space Landscape in Recurrent Networks

Patrice Y. Simard *
Computer Science Dept.
University of Rochester
Rochester, NY 14627

Jean Pierre Raysz
LIUC
Université de Caen
14032 Caen Cedex
France

Bernard Victorri
ELSAP
Université de Caen
14032 Caen Cedex
France

Abstract

Fully recurrent (asymmetrical) networks can be thought of as dynamic systems. The dynamics can be shaped to perform content addressable memories, recognize sequences, or generate trajectories. Unfortunately several problems can arise: First, the convergence in the state space is not guaranteed. Second, the learned fixed points or trajectories are not necessarily stable. Finally, there might exist spurious fixed points and/or spurious "attracting" trajectories that do not correspond to any patterns. In this paper, we introduce a new energy function that presents solutions to all of these problems. We present an efficient gradient descent algorithm which directly acts on the stability of the fixed points and trajectories and on the size and shape of the corresponding basin and valley of attraction. The results are illustrated by the simulation of a small content addressable memory.

1 INTRODUCTION

Recurrent neural networks have the capability of storing information in the state of their units. The temporal evolution of these states constitutes the dynamics of the system and depends on the weights and the input of the network. In the case of symmetric connections, the dynamics have been shown to be convergent [2] and various procedures are known for finding the weights to compute different tasks. In unconstrained neural networks however, little is known about how to train the weights of the network when the convergence of the dynamics is not guaranteed. In his review paper [1], Hirsh defines the conditions which must be satisfied for

*Now with AT&T Bell Laboratories, Crawfords Corner Road, Holmdel, NJ 07733

some given dynamics to converge, but does not provide mechanisms for finding the weights to implement these dynamics.

In this paper, a new energy function is introduced which reflects the convergence and the stability of the dynamics of a network. A gradient descent procedure on the weights provides an algorithm to control interesting properties of the dynamics including contraction over a subspace, stability, and convergence.

2 AN ENERGY FUNCTION TO ENFORCE STABILITY

This section introduces a new energy function which can be used in combination with the backpropagation algorithm for recurrent networks (cf. [6; 5]). The continuous propagation rule is given by the equation:

$$T_i \frac{\partial x_i}{\partial t} = -x_i + g_i \left(\sum_j w_{ij} x_j \right) + I_i \tag{1}$$

where x_i^t is the activation of unit i, g_i is a differentiable function, w_{ij} is the weight from unit j to unit i, and T_i and I_i are respectively the time constant and the input for unit i. A possible discretization of this equation is

$$\tilde{x}_i^{t+1} = \tilde{x}_i^t + \frac{dt}{T_i} \left(-\tilde{x}_i + g \left(\sum_j w_{ij} \tilde{x}_j \right) + I_i \right) \tag{2}$$

$$= G_i(\tilde{x}_1^t, \tilde{x}_2^t, ..., \tilde{x}_n^t) \tag{3}$$

Where $\tilde{x}_i^t$ is the activation of unit i at the discrete time step t. Henceforth, only the discrete version of the propagation equation will be considered and the tilda in $\tilde{x}$ will be omitted to avoid heavy notations.

2.1 MAKING THE MAPPING CONTRACTING OR EXPANDING IN A GIVEN DIRECTION

Using the Taylor expansion, $G(x^t + dx^t)$ can be written as

$$G(x^t + dx^t) = G(x^t) + G'(x^t) \cdot dx^t + o(||x^t||) \tag{4}$$

where $G'(x^t)$ is the linear application derived from $G(x^t)$ and the term $o(||x^t||)$ tends toward 0 faster than $||x^t||$. The mapping G is contracting in the direction of the unitary vector D if

$$\begin{aligned} ||G(x^t + \epsilon D) - G(x^t)|| &\leq ||\epsilon D|| \\ \epsilon ||G'(x^t) \cdot D|| &\leq \epsilon \\ ||G'(x^t) \cdot D|| &\leq 1 \end{aligned} \tag{5}$$

where ϵ is a small positive constant.

Accordingly, the following energy function is considered

$$E_s(X, D) = \frac{1}{2}(||G'(X) \cdot D||^2 - K_X)^2 \tag{6}$$

where K_X is the target contracting rate at X in the direction D. Depending on whether we choose K_X larger or smaller than 1, minimizing $E_s(X, D)$ will make the mapping at X contracting or expanding in the direction D. Note that D can be a complex vector.

The variation of $E_s(X, D)$ in respect to w_{mn} is equal to:

$$\frac{\partial E_s(X,D)}{\partial w_{mn}} = 2(\|G'(X)D\|^2 - K_X)\sum_i \left(\sum_j \frac{\partial G_i(X)}{\partial x_j} D_j\right)\left(\sum_j \frac{\partial^2 G_i(X)}{\partial w_{mn}\partial x_j} D_j\right) \tag{7}$$

Assuming the activation function is of the form 2, the gradient operator yields:

$$\frac{\partial G_i(X)}{\partial x_j} = \delta_{ij}(1 - \frac{dt}{T_i}) + \frac{dt}{T_i} g'(u_i) w_{ij} \tag{8}$$

where $u_i = \sum_k w_{ik} x_k$. To compute $\frac{\partial E(X,D)}{\partial w_{mn}}$ the following expression needs to be evaluated:

$$\frac{\partial^2 G_i(X)}{\partial w_{mn}\partial x_j} = \frac{dt}{T_i}\left(g''(u_i)\sum_k (\delta_{im}\delta_{kn}x_k + w_{ik}\frac{\partial x_k}{\partial w_{mn}})w_{ij} + \delta_{im}\delta_{jn}g'(u_i)\right) \tag{9}$$

which in turn requires the evaluation of $\frac{\partial x_k}{\partial w_{mn}}$. If we assume that for output units, $x_k = X_k$ and $\frac{\partial x_k}{\partial w_{mn}} = 0$, we will improve the stability of the fixed point when the visible units are clamped to the input. What we want however, is to increase stability for the network when the input units are unclamped (or hidden). This means that for every unit (including output units), we have to evaluate $\frac{\partial x_k}{\partial w_{mn}}$. Since we are at the (unstable) fixed point, we have:

$$x_i = g\left(\sum_k w_{ik} x_k\right) + I_i \tag{10}$$

If we derived this equation with respect to w_{mn} we get:

$$\frac{\partial x_i}{\partial w_{mn}} = g'\left(\sum_j w_{ij} x_j\right)(\delta_{mi} x_n + \sum_j w_{ij} \frac{\partial x_j}{\partial w_{mn}}) \tag{11}$$

In matrix form:

$$c = g'(y + wc) \tag{12}$$

Where $c_i = \frac{\partial x_i}{\partial w_{mn}}$, g' is a diagonal (square) matrix such that $g'_{ii} = g'_i\left(\sum_j w_{ij} x_j\right)$ and $g'_{ij} = 0$ for $i \neq j$ (note that $g'w \neq wg'$), y is a vector such that $y_i = \delta_{mi} x_n$ and w is the weight matrix. If we solve this we get:

$$c = (Id - g'w)^{-1} g'y \tag{13}$$

That is:

$$\frac{\partial x_i}{\partial w_{mn}} = (L^{-1})_{im} g'(u_m) x_n \tag{14}$$

where the matrix L is given by:

$$L_{ij} = \delta_{ij} - g'\left(\sum_k w_{ik} x_k\right) w_{ij} \tag{15}$$

x_k is the activation of the unit at the fixed point so it is the clamped value for the visible unit, and x_k^∞ for the hidden unit (the system converges to a stable fixed point when the visible units are clamped).

To obtain the target rate of contraction K_X at X in the direction D, the weights are updated iteratively according to the delta rule:

$$\Delta w_{ij} = -\eta \frac{\partial E_s(X, L)}{\partial w_{ij}} \tag{16}$$

This updating rule has the advantages and disadvantages of gradient descent algorithms.

2.2 COMPLEXITY

The algorithm given above can be implemented in $O(N^2)$ storage and $O(N^3)$ steps, where N is the number of units. This complexity however can be improved by avoiding inverting the matrix L using a local algorithm such as the one presented in [7]. Another implementation of this energy function can be achieved using Lagrange multipliers. This method exactly evaluates $\frac{\partial x_i}{\partial w_{mn}}$ by using a backward pass [9]. Its complexity depends on how many steps the network is unfolded in time.

2.3 GLOBAL STABILITY

Global convergence can be obtained if D is parallel the eigenvector corresponding to the largest eigenvalue of $G'(X)$. Indeed, in that case $G'(X) \cdot D$ is the largest eigenvalue of $G'(X)$. If X is a fixed point, the Ostrowski theorem [4; 3] guarantees X is stable if and only if the maximum eigenvalue of the Jacobian of G is less than 1 in modulus.

Fortunately, the eigenvector corresponding to the largest eigenvalue can easily be computed using an efficient iterative method [8]. By choosing D in that direction, fixed points can be made stable.

3 RESULTS

To simplify the following discussion, V is defined to be the unitary eigenvector corresponding to the largest eigenvalue of the Jacobian of G.

The energy function E_s can be used in at least three ways. First it can be used to accelerate the convergence toward an internal state upon presentation of a specific input p. This is done by increasing the rate of contraction in the direction of V. The chosen value for K_{X_p} is therefore small with respect to 1. The resulting network will settle faster and therefore compute its output sooner. Second, E_s can be used to neutralize spurious fixed points by making them unstable. If the mapping G

is expanding in the direction of V the fixed point will be unstable, and will never be reached by the system. The corresponding target value K_{X_p} should be larger than 1. Third, and most importantly, it can be used to force stability of the fixed points when doing associative memory. Recurrent backpropagation (RBP) [7] can be used to make the patterns fixed points, but there is no guarantee that these will be stable. By making G contract along the direction V, this problem can be solved. Furthermore, one can hope that by making the eigenvalue close to 1, smoothness in the derivatives will make the basins of attraction larger. This can be used to absorb and suppress spurious neighboring stable fixed points.

The following experiment illustrates how the unstable fixed points learned with RBP can be made more stable using the energy function E_s. Consider a network of eight fully connected units with two visible input/output units. The network is subject to the dynamic specified by the equation 2. Three patterns are presented on the two visible units. They correspond to the coordinates of the three points $(0.3, 0.7)$, $(0.8, 0.4)$ and $(0.2, 0.1)$ which were chosen randomly. The learning phase for each pattern consists of 1) clamping the visible units while propagating for five iterations (to let the hidden units settle), 2) evaluating the difference between the activation resulting from the incoming connections of the visible units and the value of the presented pattern (this is the error), 3) backpropagating the corresponding error signals and 4) updating the weight. This procedure can be used to make a pattern a fixed point of the system [6]. Unfortunately, there is no guarantee that these fixed points will be stable. Indeed, after learning with RBP only, the maximum eigenvalue of the Jacobian of G for each fixed point is shown in table 1 (column EV, no E_s). As can be seen, the maximum eigenvalue of two of the three patterns is larger than one.

	unit 0	unit 1	EV, no E_s	EV, using E_s
pattern 0	0.30	0.70	1.063	0.966
pattern 1	0.80	0.40	1.172	0.999
pattern 2	0.20	0.10	0.783	0.710

Table 1: Patterns and corresponding norms of maximum eigenvalues (EV) of the free system, with and without the stability constraint.

For a better understanding of what this means, the network can be viewed as a dynamic system of 8 units. A projection of the dynamics of the system on the visible units can be obtained by clamping these units while propagating for five iterations, and computing the activation resulting from the incoming connection. The difference between the latter value and the pattern value is a displacement (or speed) indicating in which direction in the state space the activations are going. The corresponding vector field is plotted on the top figure 1. It can easily be seen that as predicted by the eigenvalues, patterns 0 and 1 are unstable (pattern 1 is at a saddle point) and pattern 2 is stable. Furthermore there are two additional spurious fixed points around $(0.83, 0.87)$ and $(0.78, 0.21)$.

The energy function E_s can be combined with *RBP* using the following procedure: 1) propagate a few epochs until the error is below a certain threshold (10^{-5}), 2) for each pattern, estimate the largest eigenvalue λ and the corresponding eigenvector V and 3), update the weights using E_s until $|\lambda| < K$ in direction V. Steps 1 to 3

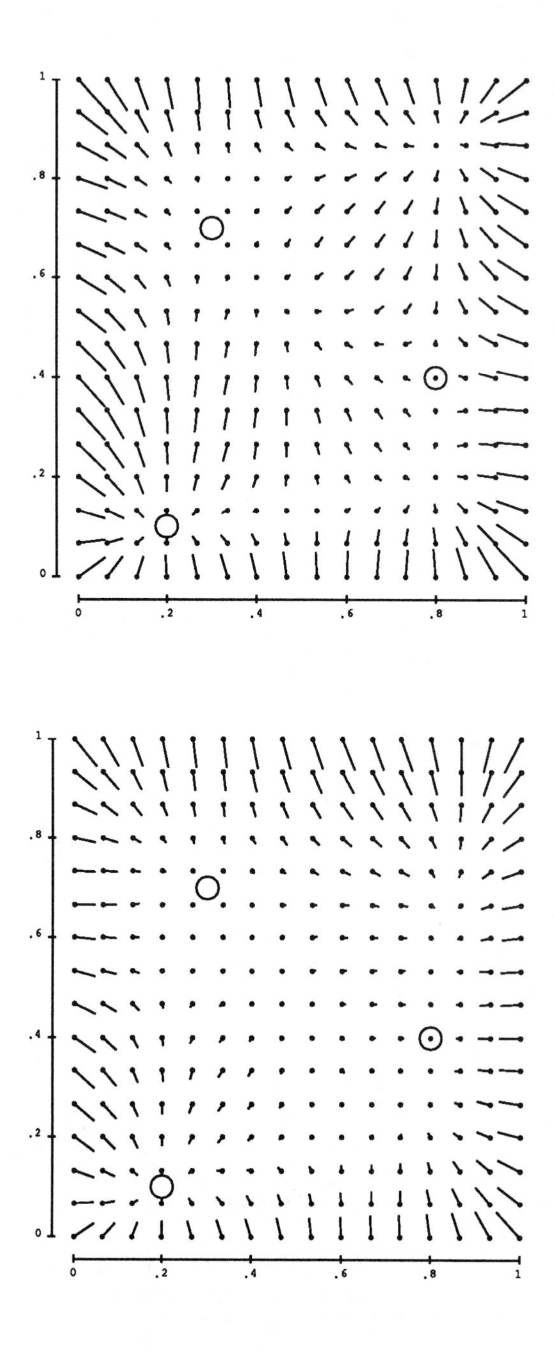

Figure 1: Vector fields representing the dynamics of the state space after learning the patterns (0.3, 0.7), (0.8, 0.4) and (0.2, 0.1). The field on the top represents the dynamics of the network after training with the standard backpropagation algorithm. The field on the bottom represents the dynamics of the network after training with the standard backpropagation algorithm combined with E_s.

are repeated until no more progress is made. The largest eigenvalues after learning are shown in table 1 in the last column. As can be noticed, all the eigenvalues are less than one and therefore the mapping G is contracting in all directions. The dynamics of the network is plotted at the bottom of figure 1. As can clearly be seen, all the patterns are now attractors. Furthermore the two spurious fixed points have disappeared in the large basin of attraction of pattern 1. This is a net improvement over RBP used alone, since the network can now be used as a content addressable memory.

4 DISCUSSION

In this paper we have introduced mechanisms to control global aspects such as stability, attractor size, or contraction speed, of the dynamics of a recurrent network. The power of the algorithm is illustrated by implementing a content addressable memory with an asymmetric neural network. After learning, the stable fixed points of the system coincide with the target patterns. All spurious fixed points have been eliminated by spreading the basins of attraction of the target patterns.

The main limitation of the algorithm resides in using a gradient descent to update the weights. Parameters such as the learning rate have to be carefully chosen, for optimal performance. Furthermore, there is always a possibility that the evolution of the weights might be trapped in a local minimum.

The complexity of the algorithm can be further improved. In equation 10 for instance, it is assumed that we are at a fixed point. This assumption is not true unless the RBP error is really small. This requires that the RBP and the E_s algorithms are run alternatively. A faster and more robust method consists in using backpropagation in time to compute $\frac{\partial x}{\partial w_{mn}}$ and is presently under study.

Finally, the algorithm can be generalized to control the dynamics around target trajectories, such as in [5]. The dynamics is projected onto the hyperplane orthogonal to the state space trajectory and constraints can be applied on the projected dynamics.

Acknowledgements

This material is based upon work supported by the National Science Foundation under Grant number IRI-8903582.

We thank the S.H.S department of C.N.R.S (France), Neuristic Inc. for allowing the use of its neural net simulator SN2, and Corinna Cortes for helpful comments and support.

References

[1] Morris W. Hirsch. Convergent activation dynamics in continuous time networks. *Neural Networks*, 2:331–349, 1989.

[2] J. J. Hopfield. Neural networks and physical systems with emergent collective computational abilities. *Proceedings of the National Academy of Sciences*, 79:2554–2558, April 1982.

[3] J. Ortega and M. Rockoff. Nonlinear difference equations and gauss-seidel type iterative methods. *SIAM J. Numer. Anal.*, 3:497–513, 1966.

[4] A Ostrowski. *Solutions of Equations and Systems of Equations.* Academic Press, New York, 1960.

[5] Barak Pearlmutter. Learning state space trajectories in recurrent neural networks. *Neural Computation*, 1(2):263–269, 1989.

[6] Fernado J. Pineda. Dynamics and architecture in neural computation. *Journal of Complexity*, 4:216–245, 1988.

[7] Fernando J. Pineda. Generalization of backpropagation to recurrent and higher order networks. In *IEEE Conference on Neural Information Processing Systems*, pages 602–601. American Institute of Physics, 1987.

[8] Anthony Ralston and Philip Rabinowitz. *A First Course in Numerical Analysis.* McGraw-Hill, New York, 1978.

[9] Patrice Y. Simard. *Learning State Space Dynamics in Recurrent Networks.* PhD thesis, University of Rochester, 1991.

Adjoint-Functions and Temporal Learning Algorithms in Neural Networks

N. Toomarian and J. Barhen
Jet Propulsion Laboratory
California Institute of Technology
Pasadena, CA 91109

Abstract

The development of learning algorithms is generally based upon the minimization of an energy function. It is a fundamental requirement to compute the gradient of this energy function with respect to the various parameters of the neural architecture, e.g., synaptic weights, neural gain,etc. In principle, this requires solving a system of nonlinear equations for each parameter of the model, which is computationally very expensive. A new methodology for neural learning of time-dependent nonlinear mappings is presented. It exploits the concept of adjoint operators to enable a fast global computation of the network's response to perturbations in all the systems parameters. The importance of the time boundary conditions of the adjoint functions is discussed. An algorithm is presented in which the adjoint sensitivity equations are solved *simultaneously* (i.e., forward in time) along with the nonlinear dynamics of the neural networks. This methodology makes real-time applications and hardware implementation of temporal learning feasible.

1 INTRODUCTION

Early efforts in the area of training artificial neural networks have largely focused on the study of schemes for encoding nonlinear mapping characterized by time-independent inputs and outputs. The most widely used approach in this context has been the error backpropagation algorithm (Werbos, 1974), which involves either static i.e., "feedforward" (Rumelhart, 1986), or dynamic i.e., "recurrent" (Pineda, 1988) networks. In this context (Barhen et al, 1989, 1990a, 1990b), have exploited the concepts of adjoint operators and terminal attractors. These concepts provide a firm mathematical foundation for learning such mappings with dynamical neural networks, while achieving a considerable reduction in the overall computational costs (Barhen et al, 1991).

Recently, there has been a wide interest in developing learning algorithms capable of modeling time-dependent phenomena (Hirsh, 1989). In a more restricted application oriented, domain attention has focused on learning temporal sequences. The problem can be formulated as minimization, over an arbitrary but finite time interval, of an appropriate error functional. Thus, the gradients of the functional with respect to the various parameters of the neural architecture, e.g., synaptic weights, neural gains, etc. must be computed.

A number of methods have been proposed for carrying out this task, a recent survey of which can be found in (Pearlmutter, 1990). Here, we will briefly mention only those which are relevant to our work. Williams and Zipser(1989) discuss a scheme similar to the well known "Forward Sensitivity Equations" of sensitivity theory (Cacuci, 1981 and Toomarian et al, 1987), in which the same set of sensitivity equations has to be solved again and again for each network parameter of interest. Clearly, this is computationally very expensive, and scales poorly to large systems. Pearlmutter (1989), on the other hand, describes a variational approach which yields a set of equations which are similar to the "Adjoint Sensitivity Equations" (Cacuci, 1981 and Toomarian et al, 1987). These equations must be solved backwards in time and involve storage of the state variables from the activation network dynamics, which is impractical. These authors (Toomarian and Barhen, 1990) have suggested a new method which, in contradistinction to previous approaches, solves the adjoint system of equations forward in time, concomitantly with the neural activation dynamics. A potential drawback of this method lies in the fact that these adjoint equations have to be treated in terms of distributions which precludes straight-forward numerical implementation. Finally, Pineda (1990), suggests combining the existence of disparate time scales with a heuristic gradient computation. However, the underlying adiabatic assumptions and highly "approximate" gradient evaluation technique place severe limits on the applicability of his approach.

In this paper we introduce a rigorous derivation of two novel systems of adjoint equations, which can be solved *simultaneously* (i.e., forward in time) with the network dynamics, and thereby enable the implementation of temporal learning algorithms in a computationally efficient manner. Numerical simulations and comparison with previously available results will be presented elsewhere(Toomarian and Barhen, 1991).

2 TEMPORAL LEARNING

We formalize a neural network as an adaptive dynamical system whose temporal evolution is governed by the following set of coupled nonlinear differential equations:

$$\dot{u}_n + \kappa_n u_n = g_n[\gamma_n(\sum_m T_{nm} u_m + I_n)] \qquad t > 0 \tag{1}$$

where u_n represents the output of the nth neuron [$u_n(0)$ being the initial state], and T_{nm} denotes the synaptic coupling from the $m-$th to the $n-$th neuron. The constant κ_n characterizes the decay of neuron activity. The sigmoidal function $g(\cdot)$ modulates the neural response, with gain given by γ; typically, $g(\gamma x) = \tanh(\gamma x)$. The time-dependent "source" term, $I_n(t)$, encodes component-contribution of the target temporal pattern $a(t)$ via the expression

$$I_n(t) = \begin{cases} a_n(t) & \textbf{if } n \in S_X \\ 0 & \textbf{if } n \in S_H \cup S_Y \end{cases} \tag{2}$$

The topographic input, output, and hidden network partitions S_X, S_Y and S_H, respectively, are architectural requirements related to the encoding of mapping-type problems. Details are given in Barhen et al (1989).

To proceed formally with the development of a temporal learning algorithm, we consider an approach based upon the minimization of a "neuromorphic" energy functional E, given by the following expression

$$E(\bar{u}, \bar{p}) = \int_t \frac{1}{2} \sum_n \Gamma_n^2 \, dt = \int_t F dt \tag{3}$$

where

$$\Gamma_n(t) = \begin{cases} a_n(t) - u_n(t) & \textbf{if } n \in S_Y \\ 0 & \textbf{if } n \in S_X \cup S_H \end{cases} \tag{4}$$

In our model the internal dynamical parameters of interest are the synaptic strengths T_{nm} of the interconnection topology, the characteristic decay constants κ_n, and the gain parameters γ_n. Therefore, the vector of system parameters (Barhen et al, 1990b) should be

$$\bar{p} = \{| \; T_{11}, \cdots, T_{NN} \mid \kappa_1, \cdots, \kappa_N \mid \gamma_1, \cdots, \gamma_N \; |\} \tag{5a}$$

In this paper, however, for illustration purposes and simplicity, we will limit ourselves in terms of parameters to the synaptic interconnections only. Hence, the vector of system parameters will have $M = N^2$ elements

$$\bar{p} = \{ T_{11}, \cdots, T_{NN} \} \tag{5b}$$

We will assume that elements of $\bar{p}$ are, in principle, independent. Furthermore, we will also assume that, for a specific choice of parameters and set of initial conditions, a unique solution of Eq. (1) exists. Hence, $\bar{u}$ is an implicit function of $\bar{p}$.

Lyapunov stability requires the energy functional to be monotonically decreasing during learning time, τ. This translates into

$$\frac{dE}{d\tau} = \sum_{\mu=1}^{M} \frac{dE}{dp_\mu} \cdot \frac{dp_\mu}{d\tau} < 0 \tag{6}$$

Thus, one can always choose, with $\eta > 0$

$$\frac{dp_\mu}{d\tau} = -\eta \frac{dE}{dp_\mu} \tag{7}$$

Integrating the above dynamical system over the interval $[\tau, \tau + \Delta\tau]$, one obtains,

$$p_\mu(\tau + \Delta\tau) = p_\mu(\tau) - \eta \int_\tau^{\tau+\Delta\tau} \frac{dE}{dp_\mu} d\tau \tag{8}$$

Equation (8) implies that, in order to update a system parameter p_μ, one must evaluate the gradient of E with respect to p_μ in the interval $[\tau, \tau+\Delta\tau]$. Furthermore, using Eq. (3) and observing that the time integral and derivative with respect to p_μ, permute one can write;

$$\frac{dE}{dp_\mu} = \int_t \frac{dF}{dp_\mu}\, dt = \int_t \frac{\partial F}{\partial p_\mu}\, dt + \int_t \frac{\partial F}{\partial \bar{u}} \cdot \frac{\partial \bar{u}}{\partial p_\mu}\, dt \tag{9}$$

Since F is known analytically [viz. Eq. (3)] computation of $\partial F/\partial u_n$ and $\partial F/\partial p_\mu$ is straightforward.

$$\frac{\partial F}{\partial u_n} = -\,\Gamma_n \tag{10a}$$

$$\frac{\partial F}{\partial p_\mu} = 0 \tag{10b}$$

Thus, the quantity that needs to be determined is the vector $\partial\bar{u}/\partial p_\mu$. Differentiating the activation dynamics, Eq. (1), with respect to p_μ, we observe that the time derivative and partial derivative with respect to p_μ commute. Using the shorthand notation $\partial(\cdots)/\partial p_\mu = (\cdots)_{,\mu}$ we obtain a set of equations to be referred to as "Forward Sensitivity Equations-FSE":

$$\begin{cases} \dot{u}_{n,\mu} + \sum_m A_{nm}\, u_{m,\mu} = S_{n,\mu} & t > 0 \\ u_{n,\mu} = 0 & t = 0 \end{cases} \tag{12}$$

in which

$$A_{nm} = \kappa_n\, \delta_{nm} - \gamma_n\, \hat{g}_n\, T_{nm} \tag{13}$$

$$S_{n,\mu} = \gamma_n\, \hat{g}_n \sum_m T_{nm}\, u_m\, \delta_{p_\mu, T_{nm}} \tag{14}$$

where $\hat{g}_n$ represents the derivative of g_n with respect to u_n, and δ denotes the Kronecker symbol. Since the initial conditions of the activation dynamics, Eq.(1), are excluded from the system parameter vector $\bar{p}$, the initial conditions of the forward sensitivity equations will be taken as zero. Computation of the gradients, via Eq. (9), using the forward sensitivity scheme as proposed by William and Zipser (1989), would require solving Eq. (12), N^2 times, since the source term explicitly depends on p_μ. The system of equations (12) has N equations, each of which requires summation over all N neurons. Hence, the amount of computation (measured in multiply-accumulates, scales like N^4 per time step. We assume that the interval between t_0 to t_f is divided to L time steps. Therefore, the total number of multiply-accumulates scales like N^4L. Clearly, the scaling properties of this approach are very poor and it can not be practically applied to very large networks. On the other hand, this method has also inherent advantages. The FSE are solved forward in time along with the nonlinear dynamics of the neural networks. Therefore, there is no need for or a large amount of memory. Since $u_{n,\mu}$ has N^3 components, that is all needed to be stored.

In order to reduce the computational costs, an alternative approach can be considered. It is based upon the concept of adjoint operators, and eliminates the need for explicit appearance of $\bar{u}_{,\mu}$ in Eq. (9). A vector of adjoint functions, $\bar{v}$ is obtained, which contain all the information required for computing all the "sensitivities", dE/dp_{μ}. The necessary and sufficient conditions for constructing adjoint equations are discussed elsewhere (Toomarian et al, 1987 and references therein).

It can be shown that an Adjoint System of Equations-ASE, pertaining to the forward system of equations (12), can be formally written as

$$-\dot{v}_n + \sum_m A^T_{nm}\, v_m = S^*_n \qquad t > 0 \tag{15}$$

In order to specify Eq. (15) in closed mathematical form , we must define the source term S^*_n and time- boundary conditions for the system. Both should be independent of p_{μ} and its derivatives.

By identifying S^*_n with $\partial F/\partial\, u_n$ and selecting the final time condition $\bar{v}(t = t_f) = 0$, a system of equations is obtained, which is similar to those proposed by Pearlmutter. The method requires that the neural activation dynamics, i.e., Eq. (1), be solved first forward in time, as followed by the ASE, Eq. (15), integrated backwards in time. The computation requirement of this approach scales as N^2L. However, a major drawback to date has resided with the necessity to store quantities such as $\bar{\bar{g}}$, $\bar{S}^*$ and $\bar{S}_{,\mu}$ at each time step. Thus, the memory requirements for this method scale as N^2L.

By selecting $\bar{S}^* = \frac{\partial F}{\partial\, \bar{u}} - \bar{v}\delta(t-t_f)$ and initial conditions $\bar{v}(t = 0) = 0$, these authors (Toomarian and Barhen 1990) have suggested a method which, in contradistinction to previous approaches, enables the ASE to be integrated forward in time, i.e., concomitantly with the neural activation dynamics. This approach saves a large amount of storage, which scales only as N^2. The computation complexity of this method, is similar to that of backward integration and scales as N^2L. A potential drawback lies in the fact that Eq. (15) must then be treated in terms of distributions, which precludes straightforward numerical implementation.

At this stage, we introduce a new paradigm which will enable us to evolve the adjoint dynamics, Eq. (15) forward in time, but without the difficulties associated with solutions in the sense of distributions. We multiply the FSE, Eq. (12), by $\bar{v}$ and the ASE, Eq. (15), by $\bar{u}_{,\mu}$, subtract the two resulting equations and integrate over the time interval (t_o, t_f). This procedure yields the bilinear form:

$$(\bar{v}\ \bar{u}_{,\mu})_{t_f} - (\bar{v}\ \bar{u}_{,\mu})_{t_o} = \int_{t_o}^{t_f} [(\bar{v}\ \bar{S}_{,\mu}) - (\ \bar{u}_{,\mu}\ \bar{S}^*)]dt \tag{16}$$

To proceed, we select

$$\begin{cases} \bar{S}^* = \frac{\partial F}{\partial\, \bar{u}} \\ \bar{v}(t = 0) = 0. \end{cases} \tag{17}$$

Thus, Eq. (16) can be rewritten as:

$$\int_t \frac{\partial F}{\partial\, \bar{u}} \bar{u}_{,\mu} dt \equiv \int_t \bar{S}^*\ \bar{u}_{,\mu} dt = \int_t \bar{v}\ \bar{S}_{,\mu} dt - [\bar{v}\ \bar{u}_{,\mu}]_{t_f} \tag{18}$$

The first term in the RHS of Eq. (18) can be computed by using the values of $\bar{v}$ obtained by solving the ASE, (Eqs. (15) and (17)), forward in time. The main difficulty resides in the evaluation of the second term in the RHS of Eq. (18), i.e., $[\bar{v}\ \bar{u}_{,\mu}]_{t_f}$. To compute it, we now introduce an auxiliary adjoint system:

$$-\dot{z}_n + \sum_m A^T_{nm}\ z_m = \hat{S}_n \qquad t > 0 \tag{19}$$

in which we select

$$\begin{cases} \hat{\bar{S}} = \bar{v}(t)\delta(t - t_f) \\ \bar{z}(t_f) = 0. \end{cases} \tag{20}$$

Note that, eventhough we selected $\bar{z}(t_f) = 0$, we are also interested in solving this auxiliary adjoint system forward in time. Thus, the critical issue is how to select the initial condition (i.e. $\bar{z}(t_o)$), that would result in $\bar{z}(t_f) = 0$. The bilinear form associated with the dynamical systems $\bar{u}_{,\mu}$ and $\bar{z}$ can be derived in a similar fashion to Eq. (16). Its expression is:

$$(\bar{z}\ \bar{u}_{,\mu})_{t_f} - (\bar{z}\ \bar{u}_{,\mu})_{t_o} = \int_{t_o}^{t_f} [(\bar{z}\ \bar{S}_{,\mu}) - (\ \bar{u}_{,\mu}\ \hat{\bar{S}})]dt \tag{21}$$

Incorporating $\hat{\bar{S}}$, $\bar{z}(t_f)$ and the initial condition of Eq. (12) into Eq. (21), we obtain;

$$\int_{t_o}^{t_f} (\bar{u}_{,\mu}\ \hat{\bar{S}})dt \ = \ [\bar{v}\ \ \bar{u}_{,\mu}]_{t_f} \ = \ \int_{t_o}^{t_f} (\bar{z}\ \bar{S}_{,\mu})dt \tag{22}$$

In order to provide a simple illustration on how the problem of selecting the initial conditions for the $\bar{z}$-dynamics can be addressed, we assume, for a moment, that the matrix A in Eq. (19) is time independent. Hence, the formal solution of Eq. (19) can be written as:

$$\bar{z}(t) \ = \ \bar{z}(t_o)e^{A^T(t-t_o)} \tag{23a}$$

$$\bar{z}(t_f) \ = \ \bar{z}(t_o)e^{A^T(t_f-t_o)} \ - \ \bar{v}(t_f) \tag{23b}$$

Therefore, in principle, Eq. (22) can be expressed in terms of $\bar{z}(t_o)$, using Eq. (23a). At time t_f, where $\bar{v}(t_f)$ is known from the solution of Eq. (15), one can calculate the vector $\bar{z}(t_o)$, from Eq. (23b), with $\bar{z}(t_f) \ = 0$.

In the problem under consideration, however, the matrix A in Eq. (19) is time dependent (viz Eq. (13)). Thus the auxiliary adjoint equations will be solved by means of finite differences. Usually, the same numerical scheme that is used for Eqs. (1) and (15) will be adopted. For illustrative purposes, we limit the discussion in the sequel to the first order approximation i.e.;

$$-\ \frac{(\bar{z}^{l+1}\ -\ \bar{z}^l)}{\Delta t}\ +\ A^l\bar{z}^l\ =\ 0 \qquad 0 < l < L \tag{24}$$

From this equation one can easily show that

$$\bar{z}^{l+1} = B^l \cdot B^{l-1} \cdots B^1 \cdot B^0 \bar{z}(t_o) = B^{l!} \bar{z}(t_o) \quad (25)$$

in which

$$B^l = I + \Delta t \, A^l \quad (26)$$

where I is the identity matrix. Thus, the RHS of Eq. (22) can be rewritten as:

$$[\bar{v} \, \bar{u}_{,\mu}]_{t_f} = [\sum_l B^{(l-1)!} \bar{S}_{,\mu}] \bar{z}(t_o) \, \Delta t \quad (27)$$

The initial conditions $\bar{z}(t_o)$ can easily be found at time t_f, i.e., at iteration stop L, by solving the algebraic equation:

$$B^{(L-1)!} \bar{z}(t_o) = \bar{v}(t_f) \quad (28)$$

In summary, the computation of the gradients i.e. Eq. (8) involves two stages, corresponding to the two terms in the RHS of Eq. (18). The first term is calculated using the adjoint functions $\bar{v}$ obtained from Eq. (15). The computational complexity is N^2L. The second term is calculated via Eq. (27), and involves two steps: a) kernel propagation, which requires multiplication of two matrices B^l and $B^{(l-1)}$ at each time step; the computational complexity scales as N^3L; b) numerical integration via Eq. (24) which requires a matrix vector multiplication at each time step; hence, it scales as N^2L. Thus, the overall computational complexity of this approach is of the order N^3L. Notice, however, that here the storage needed is minimal and equal to N^2.

3 CONCLUSIONS

A new methodology for neural learning of time-dependent nonlinear mappings is presented. It exploits the concept of adjoint operators. The resulting algorithm enables computation of the gradient of an energy function with respect to various parameters of the network architecture in a highly efficient manner. Specifically, it combines the advantage of dramatic reductions in computational complexity inherent in adjoint methods with the ability to solve the equations forward in time. Not only is a large amount of computation and storage saved, but the handling of real-time applications becomes also possible. This methodology also makes the hardware implementation of temporal learning attractive.

Acknowledgments

This research was carried out at the Center for Space Microelectronics Technology, Jet Propulsion Laboratory, California Institute of Technology. Support for the work came from Agencies of the U.S. Department of Defense including the Naval Weapons Center (China Lake, CA), and from the Office of Basic Energy Sciences of the Department of Energy, through an agreement with the National Aeronautics and Space Administration. The authors acknowledge helpful discussions with J. Martin and D. Andes from Navel Weapons Center.

References

Barhen, J., Gulati, S., and Zak, M., 1989, "Neural Learning of Constrained Nonlinear Transformations",*IEEE Computer*, 22(6), 67-76.

Barhen, J., Toomarian, N., and Gulati, S., 1990a, " Adjoint Operator Algorithms for Faster Learning in Dynamical Neural Networks", *Adv. Neur. Inf. Proc. Sys.*, 2, 498-508.

Barhen, J., Toomarian, N., and Gulati, S., 1990b, "Application of Adjoint Operators to Neural Learning", *Appl. Math. Lett.*, 3 (3), 13-18.

Barhen, J., Toomarian, N., and Gulati, S., 1991, "Fast Neural Learning Algorithms Using Adjoint Operators", Submitted to *IEEE Trans. of Neural Networks*

Cacuci, D. G., 1981, "Sensitivity Theory for Nonlinear Systems", *J. Math. Phys.*, 22 (12), 2794-2802.

Hirsch, M. W., 1989, "Convergent Activation Dynamics in Continuous Time Networks",*Neural Networks*, 2 (5), 331-349.

Pearlmutter, B. A., 1989,"Learning State Space Trajectories in Recurrent Neural Networks", *Neural Computation*, 1 (2), 263-269.

Pearlmutter, B. A., 1990, "Dynamic Recurrent Neural Networks", Technical Report CMU-CS-90-196, School of Computer Science, Carnegie Mellon University, Pittsburgh, Pa.

Pineda, F., 1988, "Dynamics and Architecture in Neural Computation", *J. of Complexity, 4*, 216-245.

Pineda, F., 1990, "Time Dependent Adaptive Neural Networks", *Adv. Neur. Inf. Proc. Sys.*, 2, 710-718.

Rumelhart, D. E., and McC.and, J. L., 1986, *Parallel and Distributed Processing*, MIT Press.

Toomarian, N., Wacholder, E., and Kaizerman, S., 1987, "Sensitivity Analysis of Two-Phase Flow Problems", *Nucl. Sci. Eng.*, 99 (1), 53-81.

Toomarian, N. and Barhen, J., 1990, "Adjoint Operators and Non- Adiabatic Algorithms in Neural Networks", *Appl. Math. Lett.*, (in press).

Toomarian, N. and Barhen, J., 1991, " Learning a Trajectory Using Adjoint Functions", submitted to *Neural Networks*

Werbos, P., 1974, "Beyond Regression: New Tools for Prediction and Analysis in The Behavioral Sciences", Ph.D. Thesis, Harvard Univ.

Williams, R. J., and Zipser, D., 1989, "A Learning Algorithm for Continually Running Fully Recurrent Neural Networks", *Neural Computation*, 1 (2), 270-280.

Part III

Oscillations

Phase-coupling in Two-Dimensional Networks of Interacting Oscillators

Ernst Niebur, Daniel M. Kammen, Christof Koch, Daniel Ruderman[1] & Heinz G. Schuster[2]
Computation and Neural Systems
Caltech 216-76
Pasadena, CA 91125

ABSTRACT

Coherent oscillatory activity in large networks of biological or artificial neural units may be a useful mechanism for coding information pertaining to a single perceptual object or for detailing regularities within a data set. We consider the dynamics of a large array of simple coupled oscillators under a variety of connection schemes. Of particular interest is the rapid and robust phase-locking that results from a "sparse" scheme where each oscillator is strongly coupled to a tiny, randomly selected, subset of its neighbors.

1 INTRODUCTION

Networks of interacting oscillators provide an excellent model for numerous physical processes ranging from the behavior of magnetic materials to models of atmospheric dynamics to the activity of populations of neurons in a variety of cortical locations. Particularly prominent in the neurophysiological data are the $40-60$ Hz oscillations that have long been reported in the rat and rabbit olfactory bulb and cortex on the basis of single-and multi-unit recordings as well as EEG activity (Freeman, 1978). In addition, periodicities in eye movement reaction times (Pöppel and Logothetis, 1986), as well as oscillations in the auditory evoked potential in response to single click or a series of clicks (Madler and Pöppel, 1987) all support a $30-50$ Hz framework for aspects of cortical activity. Two groups (Eckhorn *et al.*, 1988, Gray

[1] Permanent address: Department of Physics, University of California, Berkeley, CA 94720
[2] Permanent address: Institut für Theoretische Physik, Universität Kiel, 2300 Kiel 1, Germany.

and Singer, 1989; Gray *et al.*, 1989) have recently reported highly synchronized, stimulus specific oscillations in the 35 – 85 Hz range in areas 17, 18 and PMLS of anesthetized as well as awake cats. Neurons with similar orientation tuning up to 7 mm apart show phase-locked oscillations with a phase shift of less than 1 $msec$ that have been proposed to play a role in the coding of visual information (Crick and Koch, 1990, Niebur *et al.* 1991).

The complexity of networks of even relatively simple neuronal units – let alone "real" cortical cells – warrants a systematic investigation of the behavior of two dimensional systems. To address this question we begin with a network of mathematically simple limit-cycle oscillators. While the dynamics of pairs of oscillators are well understood (Sakaguchi, *et al.* 1988, Schuster and Wagner, 1990a,b), this is not the case for large networks with nontrivial connection schemes. Of general interest is the phase-coupling that results in networks of oscillators with different coupling schemes. We will summarize some generic features of simple nearest-neighbor coupled models, models where each oscillator receives input from a large neighborhood, and of "sparse" connection geometries where each cell is connected to only a tiny fraction of the units in its neighborhood, but with large coupling strength. The numerical work was performed on a CM-2 Connection Machine and involved 16,384 oscillators in a 128 by 128 square grid.

2 The Model

The basic unit in our networks is an oscillator whose phase θ_{ij} is 2π periodic and which has the intrinsic frequency ω_{ij}. The dynamics of an isolated oscillator are described by:

$$\frac{d\theta_{ij}}{dt} = \omega_{ij}. \tag{1}$$

The influence of the network can be expressed as an additional interaction term,

$$\frac{d\theta_{ij}}{dt} = \omega_{ij} + f_{ij}(\theta_0, \theta_1, ...\theta_n). \tag{2}$$

The coupling function, f_{ij} we used is expressed as the sum of terms, each one consisting of the product of a coupling strength and the sine of a phase difference (see below, eq. 3). The sinusoidal form of the interaction is, of course, linear for small differences.

This system, and numerous variants, has received a considerable amount of attention from solid state physicists (see, e.g. Kosterlitz and Thouless 1973, and Sakaguchi *et al.* 1988), although primarily in the limit of $t \to \infty$. With an interest in the possible role of networks of oscillators in the parsing or segregating of incident signals in nervous systems, we will concentrate on short time, non-equilibrium, properties.

We shall confine ourselves to two generic network configurations described by

$$\frac{d\theta_{ij}}{dt} = \omega_{ij} + \alpha \sum_{kl} J_{ij,kl} sin(\theta_{ij} - \theta_{kl}), \tag{3}$$

where α designates the global strength of the interaction, and the geometry of the interactions is incorporated in $J_{ij,kl}$.

The networks are all defined on a square grid and they are characterized as follows:

1: Gaussian Connections. The cells are connected to every oscillator within a specified neighborhood with Gaussian weighted connections. Hence,

$$J_{ij,kl} = \frac{1}{2\pi\sigma} exp \left(\frac{(i-k)^2 + (j-l)^2}{2\sigma^2} \right). \quad (4)$$

We truncate this function at 2σ, i.e. $J_{ij,kl} = 0$ if $(i-k)^2 + (j-l)^2 \geq (2\sigma)^2$. While the connectivity in the nearest neighbor case is 4, the connectivity is significantly higher for the Gaussian connection schemes: Already $\sigma = 2$ yields 28 connections per cell, and the largest network we studied, with $\sigma = 6$, results in 372 connections per cell.

2: Sparse Gaussian Connections. In this scheme we no longer require symmetric connections, or that the connection pattern is identical from unit to unit. A given cell is connected to a fixed *number*, n, of neighboring cells, with the probability of a given connection determined by

$$\mathcal{P}_{ij,kl} = \frac{1}{2\pi\sigma} exp \left(\frac{(i-k)^2 + (j-l)^2}{2\sigma^2} \right). \quad (5)$$

$J_{ij,kl}$ is unity with probability $\mathcal{P}_{ij,kl}$ and zero otherwise. This connection scheme is constructed by drawing for each lattice site n coordinate pairs from a Gaussian distribution, and use these as the indices of the cells that are connected with the oscillator at location (i,j). Therefore, the probability of making a connection decreases with distance. If a connection is made, however, the weight is the same as for all other connections. We typically used $n = 5$, and in all cases $2 \leq n \leq 10$.

For all networks, the sum of the weights of all connections with a given oscillator i,j was conserved and chosen as $\alpha \sum_{kl} J_{ij,kl} = 10 * \overline{\omega}$, where $\overline{\omega}$ is the average frequency of all N oscillators in the system, $\overline{\omega} = \frac{1}{N} \sum_{ij} \omega_{ij}$. By this procedure, the total impact of the interaction term is identical in all cases.

3 RESULTS

Perhaps the most basic, and most revealing, comparison of the behavior of the models introduced above is the two-point correlation function of phase-coupling, which is defined as

$$C(R,t) = < cos\, [\theta_{ij}(t) - \theta_{kl}(t)] >, \quad (6)$$

where R is defined as the separation between a pair of cells, $R = |r_{ij} - r_{kl}|$. We compute and then average $C(R,t)$ over 10,000 pairs of oscillators separated by R in the array. In all cases, the frequencies ω_{ij} are chosen randomly, with a Gaussian distribution with mean 0.5 and variance 1. In Figure 1 we plot $C(R,t)$ for separations of $R = 20$, 30, 40, 50, 6, and 70 oscillators. Time is measured in oscillation periods of the mean oscillator frequency, $\overline{\omega}$. At $t = 0$, phases are distributed randomly between 0 and 2π with a uniform distribution. The case of Gaussian connectivity with $\sigma = 6$ and hence 372 connection per cell is seen in Figure 1(a), and the sparse connectivity scheme with $\sigma = 6$ and $n = 5$ is presented in Figure 1(b). The most striking difference is that correlation levels of over 0.9 are rapidly achieved in the sparse scheme for all cases, even for separations of 70 oscillators (plotted as asterisks, *), while there are clear separation-dependent differences in the phase-locking behavior of the Gaussian model. In fact, even after $t = 10$ there is no significant locking over the longer distances of $R = 50, 60$, or 70 units. For local connectivity schemes, like Gaussian connectivity with $\sigma = 2$ or nearest neighbors connections, no long-range order evolves even at larger times (data not shown).

Data in Fig. 1 were computed with a uniform phase distribution for $t = 0$. An interesting and robust feature of the dynamics emerges when the influence of different types of initial phase distributions are examined. In Figure 2 we plot the probability distribution of phases at different early times. In Figure 2(a) the distribution of phases is plotted at $t = 0$ (diamonds), $t = 0.2$ ("plus signs, +) and at $t = 0.4$ (squares) for the sparse scheme with a uniform initial distribution. In Figure 2(b), the evolution of a Gaussian initial distribution centered at $\theta = \pi$ of the phases is plotted. Note the slight curve in the distribution at $t = 0$, indicating that the Gaussian initial seeding is rather slight (variance $\sigma = 2\pi$). Remarkably, however, this has a dramatic impact on the phase-locking as after two-tenth of an average cycle time ("plus" signs) there is already a pronounced peak in the distribution. At $t = 0.4$ (squares) the system that started with the uniform distribution begins to only exhibit a slight increase in the phase-correlation while the system with Gaussian distributed initial phases is strongly peaked with virtually no probability of encountering phase values that differ significantly from the mean.

4 DISCUSSION

The power of the sparse connection scheme to rapidly generate phase-locking throughout the network that is equivalent, or superior, to that of the massively interconnected Gaussian scheme highlights a trade-off in network dynamics: massive averaging versus strong, long-range, connections. With $n = 5$, the sparse scheme effectively "tiles" a two-dimensional lattice and tightly phase-locks oscillators even at opposite corners of the array. Similar results are obtained even with $n = 2$ (data not shown).

In many ways the Gaussian and sparse geometries reperent opposing avenues to achieve global coherence: exhaustive local coupling or distributed, but powerful long-range coupling. The amount of wiring necessary to implement these schemes is, however, radically different.

Acknowledgement

EN is supported by the Swiss National Science Foundation through Grant No. 8220-25941. DMK is a recipient of a Weizman Postdoctoral Fellowship. CK acknowledges support from the Air Force Office of Scientific Research, a NSF Presidential Young Investigator Award and from the James S. McDonnell Foundation. HGS is supported by the Volkswagen Foundation.

References

Crick, F. and Koch, C. 1990. Towards a neurobiological theory of consciousness. *Seminars Neurosci.*, **2**, 263 - 275.

Eckhorn, R., Bauer, R., Jordan, W., Brosch, M., Kruse, W., Munk, M. and Reitboeck, H. J. 1988. Coherent oscillations: A mechanism of feature linking in the visual cortex? *Biol. Cybern.*, **60**, 121 - 130.

Freeman, W. J. 1978. Spatial properties of an EEG event in the olfactory bulb and cortex. *Elect. Clin. Neurophys.*, **44**, 586 - 605.

Gray, C. M., König, P., Engel, A. K. and Singer, W. 1989. Oscillatory responses in cat visual cortex exhibit inter-columnar synchronization which reflects global stimulus properties. *Nature*, **338**, 334 -337.

Kosterlitz, J. M. and Thouless, D. J. 1973. Ordering, metastability and phase transitions in two-dimensional systems. *J. Physics C.*, **6**, 1181 - 1203.

Madler, C. and Pöppel, E. 1987. Auditory evoked potentials indicate the loss of neuronal oscillations during general anaesthesia. *Naturwissenschaften*, **74**, 42 - 43.

Niebur, E., Kammen, D. M., and Koch, C. 1991. Phase-locking in 1-D and 2-D networks of oscillating neurons. In *Nonlinear dynamics and neuronal networks*, Singer, W., and Schuster, H. G. (eds.). VCH Verlag: Weinheim, FRG.

Pöppel, E. and Logothetis, N. 1986. Neuronal oscillations in the human brain. *Naturwissenschaften*, **73**, 267 - 268.

Sakaguchi, H., Shinomoto, S. and Kuramoto, Y. 1988. Mutual entrainment in oscillator lattices with nonvariational type interaction. *Prog. Theor. Phys.*, **79**, 1069 - 1079.

Schuster, H. G. and Wagner, P. 1990a. A model for neuronal oscillations in the visual cortex 1: Mean-field theory and derivation of phase equations. *Biological Cybernetics*, **64**, 77 - 82.

Schuster, H. G. and Wagner, P. 1990b. A model for neuronal oscillations in the visual cortex 2: Phase description of feature dependant synchronization. *Biological Cybernetics*, **64**, 83.

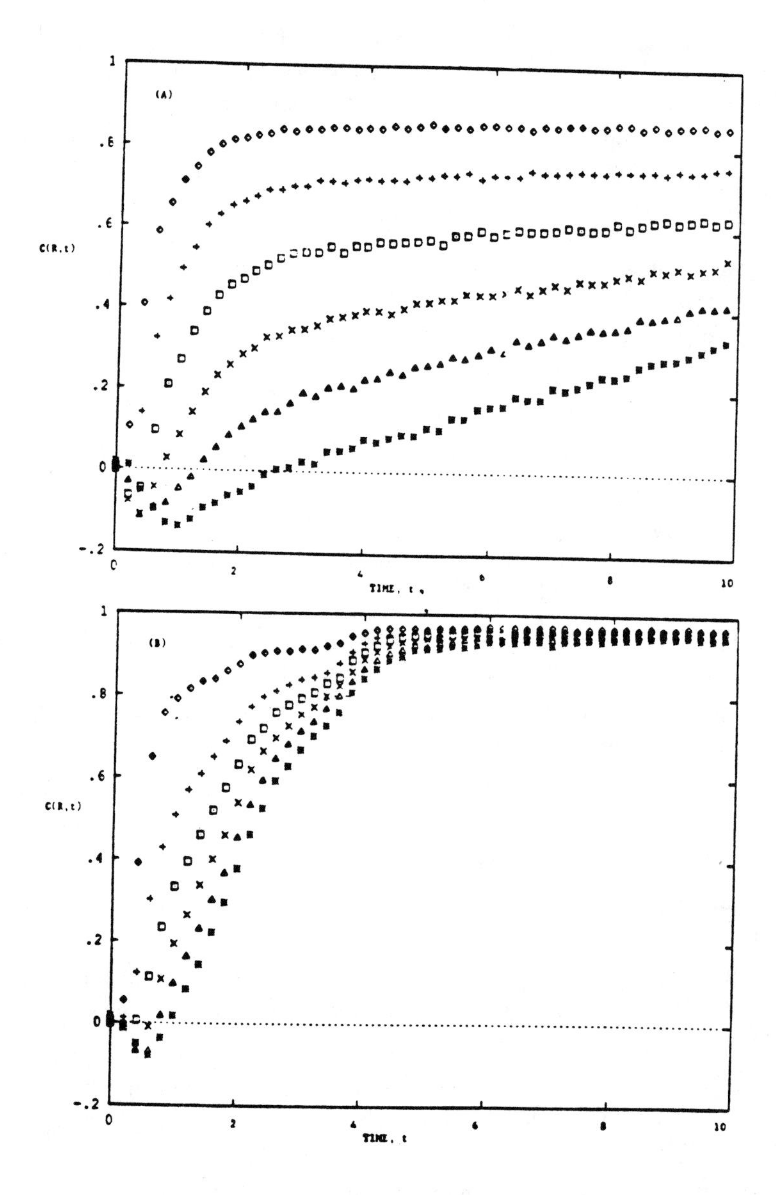

Figure 1: Two-point correlation functions, $C(R,t)$, for various separations, R, in (a) the $\sigma = 6$ Gaussian scheme with 372 connections per cell and (b) the sparse connection scheme with $\sigma = 6$ and $n = 5$ connections per cell. Separations of $R = 20$ (diamonds), $R = 30$ ("plus" signs, $+$), $R = 40$ (squares), $R = 50$ (crosses, $\times$), $R = 60$ (triangles), and $R = 70$ (asterisks, *) are shown. Note the rapid locking for all lengths in the sparse scheme (b) while the Gaussian scheme (a) appears far more "diffusive," with progressively poorer and slower locking as R increases.

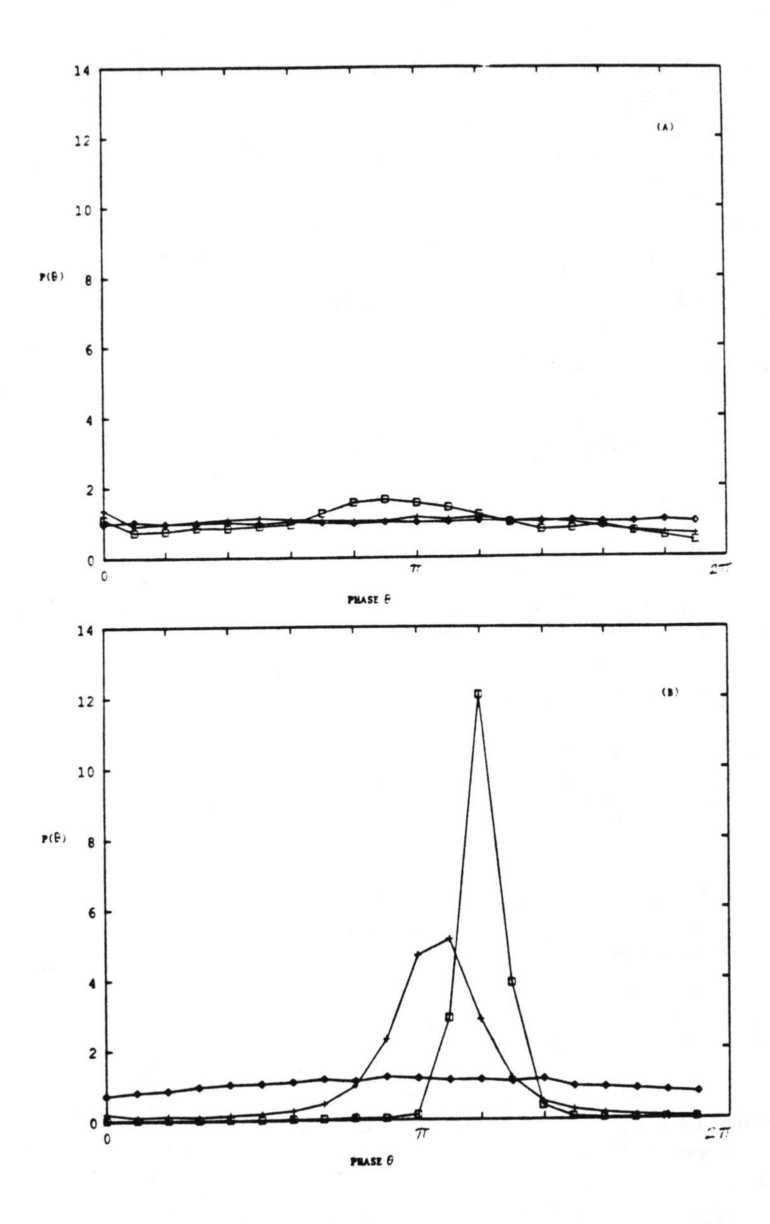

Figure 2: Snapshots of the distribution of phases in the sparse scheme ($n = 5, \sigma = 6$) when the system begins from (a) uniform and (b) a Gaussian "biased" initial distribution. The figures show the probability $P(\theta)$ to find a phase between θ and $\theta + d\theta$ (bin size $\pi/10$). At $t = 0$, the distribution is flat (a) or very slightly curved (b); see text. The difference in the time evolution can clearly be seen in the state of the system after $t = 0.2$ ("plus" signs, +) and $t = 0.4$ (squares).

Oscillation Onset
in
Neural Delayed Feedback

André Longtin
Complex Systems Group and Center for Nonlinear Studies
Theoretical Division B213, Los Alamos National Laboratory
Los Alamos, NM 87545

Abstract

This paper studies dynamical aspects of neural systems with delayed negative feedback modelled by nonlinear delay-differential equations. These systems undergo a Hopf bifurcation from a stable fixed point to a stable limit cycle oscillation as certain parameters are varied. It is shown that their frequency of oscillation is robust to parameter variations and noisy fluctuations, a property that makes these systems good candidates for pacemakers. The onset of oscillation is postponed by both additive and parametric noise in the sense that the state variable spends more time near the fixed point than it would in the absence of noise. This is also the case when noise affects the delayed variable, i.e. when the system has a faulty memory. Finally, it is shown that a distribution of delays (rather than a fixed delay) also stabilizes the fixed point solution.

1 INTRODUCTION

In this paper, we study the dynamics of a class of neural delayed feedback models which have been used to understand equilibrium and oscillatory behavior in recurrent inhibitory circuits (Mackey and an der Heiden, 1984; Plant, 1981; Milton et al., 1990) and brainstem reflexes such as the pupil light reflex (Longtin and Milton, 1989a,b; Milton et al., 1989; Longtin et al., 1990; Longtin, 1991) and respiratory control (Glass and Mackey, 1979). These models are framed in terms of first-order nonlinear delay-differential equations (DDE's) in which the state variable may represent, e.g., a membrane potential, a mean firing rate of a population of neurons or a muscle activity. For example, the negative feedback dynamics of the human pupil light reflex have been shown to be appropriately modelled by the following equation for pupil area (related to the activity of the iris muscles through the nonlinear monotonically decreasing function $g(A)$) (see Longtin and Milton, 1989a,b):

$$\frac{dg(A)}{dA}\frac{dA(t)}{dt} + \alpha g(A) = \gamma \ln\left[\frac{I(t-\tau)A(t-\tau)}{\overline{\phi}}\right] \tag{1}$$

$I(t)$ is the external light intensity and $\overline{\phi}$ is the retinal light flux below which no pupillary response occurs. The left hand side of Eq.(1) governs the response of the system to the state-dependent forcing (i.e. stimulation) embodied in the term on the right-hand side. The delay τ is essential to the understanding of the dynamics of this reflex. It accounts for the fact that the iris muscles move in response to the retinal light flux variations occurring $\sim$ 300 msec earlier.

2 FOCUS AND MOTIVATION

For the sake of discussion, we shall focus on the following prototypical model of delayed negative feedback

$$\frac{dx(t)}{dt} + \alpha x(t) = f(\vec{\mu}; x(t-\tau)) \tag{2}$$

where $\vec{\mu}$ is a vector of parameters and f is a monotonically decreasing function. This equation typically exhibits a Hopf bifurcation (i.e. a qualitative change in dynamics from a stable equilibrium solution to a stable limit cycle oscillation) as the slope of the feedback function or the delay are increased passed critical values.

Autonomous (as opposed to externally forced) oscillations are frequently observed in real neural delayed feedback systems which suggests that these systems may exhibit a Hopf bifurcation. Further, it is clear that these systems operate despite noisy environmental fluctuations. A clear understanding of the properties of these systems can reveal useful information about their structure and the origin of the "noisy" sources, as well as enable us to extract general functioning principles for systems organized according to this scheme.

We now focus our attention on three different dynamical aspects of these systems: 1) the stability of the oscillation frequency and amplitude to parameter variations and to noise; 2) the postponement of oscillation onset due to noise; and 3) the stabilization of the equilibrium behavior in the more realistic case involving a distribution of delays rather than a single fixed delay.

3 FREQUENCY AND AMPLITUDE

Under certain conditions, the neural delayed feedback system will settle onto equilibrium behavior after an initial transient. Mathematically, this corresponds to the fixed point solution x^* of Eq.(2) obtained by setting $\dot{x} = 0$. A supercritical Hopf bifurcation occurs in Eq.(2) when the slope of the feedback function at this fixed point $\left.\frac{df}{dx}\right|_{x^*}$ exceeds some value k_o called the bifurcation value. It can also occur when the delay exceeds a critical value. The case where the parameter α increases is particularly interesting because the system can undergo a Hopf bifurcation at $\alpha = \alpha_1$ followed by a restabilization of the fixed point through a reverse Hopf bifurcation at $\alpha = \alpha_2 > \alpha_1$ (see also Mackey, 1979).

Numerical simulations of Eq.(2) around the Hopf bifurcation point k_o reveal that the frequency is relatively constant while the amplitude *Ampl* grows as $\sqrt{k - k_o}$. However, in oscillatory time series from real neural delayed feedback systems, the frequency and amplitude fluctuate near the bifurcation point, with relative amplitude fluctuations being generally larger than relative frequency fluctuations. This point has been illustrated using data from the human pupil light reflex whose feedback gain is under experimental control (see Longtin, 1991; Longtin et al., 1990). In the case of the pupil light reflex, the variations in the mean and standard deviation of amplitude and period accompanying increases in the bifurcation parameter (the external gain) have been explained in the hypothesis that "neural noise" is affecting the deterministic dynamics of the system. This noise is strongly amplified near the bifurcation point where the solutions are only weakly stable (Longtin et al., 1990). Thus the coupling of the noise to the system is most likely responsible for the aperiodicity of the observed data.

The fact that the frequency is not significantly affected by the noise nor by variation of the bifurcation parameter (especially in comparison to the amplitude fluctuations) suggests that neural delayed feedback circuits may be ideally suited to serve as pacemakers. The frequency stability in regulatory biological systems has previously been emphasized by Rapp (1981) in the context of biochemical regulation.

4 STABILIZATION BY NOISE

In the presence of noise, oscillations can be seen in the solution of Eq.(2) even when the bifurcation value is below that at which the deterministic bifurcation occurs. This does not mean however that the bifurcation has occurred, since these oscillations simply become more and more prominent as the bifurcation parameter is increased, and no qualitative change in the solution can be seen. Such a qualitative change does occur when the solution is viewed from a different standpoint. One can in fact construct a histogram of the values taken on by the solution of the model differential equation (or by the data: see Longtin, 1991). The value of this (normalized) histogram at a given point in the state space (e.g. of pupil area values) provides a measure of the fraction of the time spent by the system in the vicinity of this point. The onset of oscillation can then be detected by a qualitative change in this histogram, specifically when it goes from unimodal to bimodal (Longtin et al., 1990). The distance between the two humps in the bimodal case is a measure of the limit cycle amplitude. For short time series however (as is often the case in neurophysiology), it is practically impossible to resolve this distance and thus to ascertain whether a Hopf bifurcation has occurred.

Intensive simulations of Eq.(2) with either additive noise (i.e. added to Eq.(2)) or parametric noise (e.g. on the magnitude of the feedback function) reveal that the statistical limit cycle amplitude (the distance between the two humps or "order parameter") is smaller than the amplitude in the absence of noise (Longtin et al., 1990). The bifurcation diagram is similar to that in Figure 1. This implies that the solution spends more time near the fixed point, i.e. that the fixed point is stabilized by the noise (i.e. in the absence of noise, the limit cycle is larger and the system spends less time near the unstable fixed point). In other words, the onset of the Hopf bifurcation is postponed in the presence of these types of noise. Hence the noise level in a neural system, whatever its source, may in fact control the onset of an oscillation.

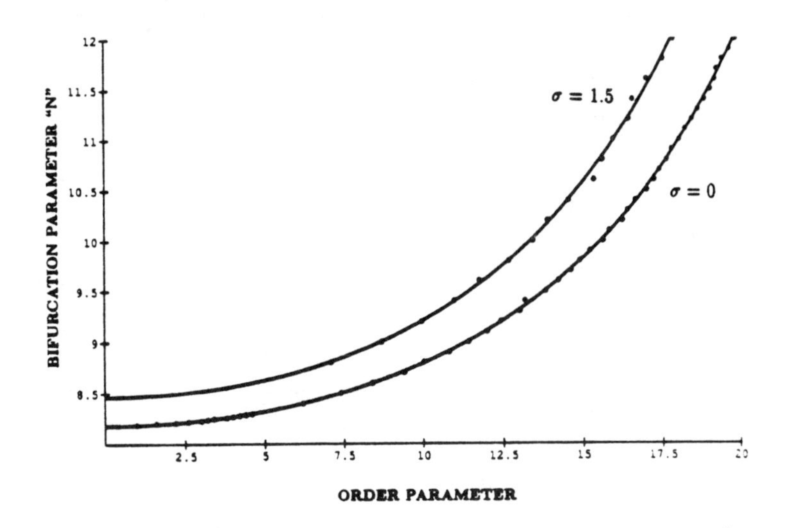

Figure 1. Magnitude of the Order Parameter as a Function of the Bifurcation Parameter n for Noise on the Delayed State of the System.

In Figure 1 it is shown that the Hopf bifurcation is also postponed (the bifurcation curve is shifted to higher parameter values with respect to the deterministic curve) when the noise is applied to the delayed state variable $x(t-\tau)$ and f in Eq.(2) is of the form (negative feedback):

$$f = \frac{\lambda \theta^n}{\theta^n + x^n(t-\tau)}. \tag{3}$$

For parameter values $\alpha = 3.21, \lambda = 200, \theta = 50, \tau = 0.3$, the deterministic Hopf bifurcation occurs at $n = 8.18$. Colored (Ornstein-Uhlenbeck type) Gaussian noise of standard deviation $\sigma = 1.5$ and correlation time $1sec$ was added to the variable $x(t-\tau)$. This numerical calculation can be interpreted as a simulation of the behavior of a neural delayed feedback system with bad memory (i.e. in which there is a small error on the value recalled from the past). Thus, faulty memory also stabilizes the fixed point.

5 DISTRIBUTED DELAYS

The use of a single fixed delay in models of delayed feedback is often a good approximation and strongly warranted in a simple circuit comprising only a small number of cells. However, neural systems often have a spatial extent due to the presence of many parallel pathways in which the axon sizes are distributed according to a certain probability density. This leads to a distribution of conduction velocities down these pathways and therefore to a distribution of propagation delays. In this case, the dynamics are more appropriately modelled by an integro-differential equation of the form

$$\frac{dx}{dt} + \alpha x(t) = f(\vec{\mu}; z(t), x(t)), \quad z(t) = \int_{-\infty}^{t} K(t-u)x(u)\,du. \tag{4}$$

The extent to which values of the state variable in the past affect its present evolution is determined by the kernel $K(t)$. The fixed delay case corresponds to choosing the kernel to be a Dirac delta distribution.

We have looked at the effect of a distributed delay on the Hopf bifurcation in our prototypical delayed feedback system Eq.(2). Specifically, we have considered the case where the kernel in Eq.(4) has the form of a gamma distribution

$$K(t) \equiv G_a^m(t) = \frac{a^{m+1}}{m!} t^m e^{-aq}, \quad a, m \geq 0. \tag{5}$$

The average delay of this kernel is $\overline{\tau} = \frac{m+1}{a}$ and the kernel has the property that it converges to the delta function in the limit where m and a go to infinity all the while keeping the ratio $\overline{\tau}$ constant. For a kernel of a given order it is possible to convert the DDE Eq.(2) into a set of $(m+2)$ coupled ordinary differential equations (ODE's) which approximate the DDE (an infinite set of ODE's is in this case equivalent to the original DDE) (see Fargue, 1973; MacDonald, 1978; Cooke and Grossman, 1982). We have investigated the occurrence of a Hopf bifurcation in the $(m+2)$ ODE's as a function of the order m of the memory kernel (keeping $\overline{\tau}$ equal to the fixed delay of the DDE being approximated). This involves doing a stability analysis around the fixed point of the $(m+2)$ order system of ODE's and numerically determining the value of the bifurcation parameter n at which the Hopf bifurcation occurs.

The result is shown in Figure 2, where we have plotted n versus the order m of approximation. Note that at least a 3 dimensional system of ODE's is required for a Hopf bifurcation to occur in such a system. Note also the fast convergence of n to the bifurcation value for the DDE (5.04). These calculations were done for the Mackey-Glass equation

$$\frac{dx}{dt} + \alpha x(t) = \frac{\lambda \theta^n x(t-\tau)}{\theta^n + x^n(t-\tau)} \tag{6}$$

with parameters $\theta = 1, \alpha = 2, \lambda = 2, \tau = 2$ and $n \in (1, 20)$. This equation is a model for mixed feedback dynamics (i.e. a combination of positive and negative feedback involving a single-humped feedback function). It displays the same qualitative features as Eq.(2) with the feedback given by Eq.(3) at the Hopf bifurcation and was chosen for ease of computation since parameters can be chosen such that the fixed point does not depend on the bifurcation parameter.

We can see that, for a memory kernel of a given order, the Hopf bifurcation occurs at a higher value of the bifurcation parameter (which is proportional to the slope of the feedback function at the fixed point) than for the DDE. This implies that a stronger nonlinearity is required to set the ODE system into oscillation compared to the DDE. In other words, the distributed delay system with the same feedback function as the DDE is less prone to oscillate (see also MacDonald, 1978; Cooke and Grossman, 1982).

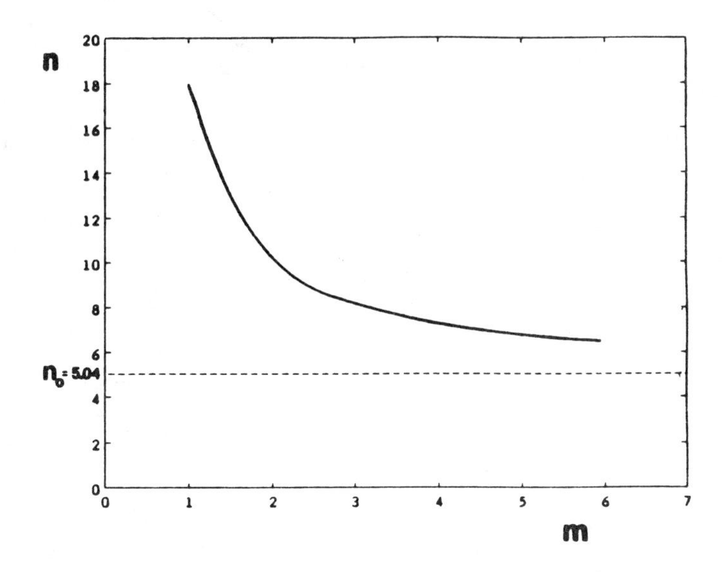

Figure 2. Value of n at Which a Hopf Bifurcation Occurs Versus the Order m of the Memory Kernel.

6 SUMMARY

In summary we have shown that neural delayed negative feedback systems can exhibit either equilibrium or limit cycle behavior depending on their parameters and on the noise levels. The constancy of their oscillation frequency, even in the presence of noise, suggests their possible role as pacemakers in the nervous system. Further, the equilibrium solution of these systems is stabilized by noise and by distributed delays. We conjecture that these two effects may be related as they somewhat share a common feature, in the sense that noise and distributed delays tend to make the retarded action more diffuse. This is supported by the fact that a system with bad memory (i.e. with noise on the delayed variable) also sees its fixed point stabilized.

Acknowledgements

The author would like to thank Mackey for useful conversations as well as Christian Cortis for his help with the numerical analysis in Section 5. This research was supported by the Natural Sciences and Engineering Research Council of Canada (NSERC) as well as the Complex Systems Group and the Center for Nonlinear Studies at Los Alamos National Laboratory in the form of postdoctoral fellowships.

References

K.L. Cooke and Z. Grossman. (1982) Discrete delay, distributed delay and stability switches. *J. Math. Anal. Appl.* **86**:592-627.

D. Fargue. (1973) Réductibilité des systèmes héréditaires a des systèmes dynamiques (régis par des équations différentielles aux dérivées partielles). *C.R. Acad. Sci. Paris* **T.277, No.17** (Serie B, 2e semestre):471-473.

L. Glass and M.C. Mackey. (1979) Pathological conditions resulting from instabilities in physiological control systems. *Ann. N.Y. Acad. Sci.* **316**:214.

A. Longtin. (in press, 1991) Nonlinear dynamics of neural delayed feedback. In D. Stein (ed.),*Proceedings of the 3rd Summer School on Complex Systems, Santa Fe Institute Studies in the Sciences of Complexity, Lect. Vol. III.* Redwood City, CA: Addison-Wesley.

A. Longtin and J.G. Milton. (1989a) Modelling autonomous oscillations in the human pupil light reflex using nonlinear delay-differential equations. *Bull. Math. Biol.* **51**:605-624.

A. Longtin and J.G. Milton. (1989b) Insight into the transfer function, gain and oscillation onset for the pupil light reflex using nonlinear delay-differential equations. *Biol. Cybern.* **61**:51-59.

A. Longtin, J.G. Milton, J. Bos and M.C. Mackey. (1990) Noise and critical behavior of the pupil light reflex at oscillation onset. *Phys. Rev.* **A 41**:6992-7005.

N. MacDonald. (1978) Time lags in biological models. *Lecture Notes in Biomathematics* **27**. Berlin: Springer Verlag.

M.C. Mackey. (1979) Periodic auto-immune hemolytic anemia: an induced dynamical disease. *Bull. Math. Biol.* **41**:829-834.

M.C. Mackey and U. an der Heiden. (1984) The dynamics of recurrent inhibition. *J. Math. Biol.* **19**: 211-225.

J.G. Milton, U. an der Heiden, A. Longtin and M.C. Mackey. (in press, 1990) Complex dynamics and noise in simple neural networks with delayed mixed feedback. *Biomed. Biochem. Acta* **8/9**.

J.G. Milton, A. Longtin, A. Beuter, M.C. Mackey and L. Glass. (1989) Complex dynamics and bifurcations in neurology. *J. Theor. Biol.* **138**:129-147.

R.E. Plant. (1981) A Fitzhugh differential-difference equation modelling recurrent neural feedback. *SIAM J. Appl. Math.* **40**:150-162.

P.E. Rapp. (1981) Frequency encoded biochemical regulation is more accurate then amplitude dependent control. *J. Theor. Biol.* **90**:531-544.

Analog Computation at a Critical Point: A Novel Function for Neuronal Oscillations?

Leonid Kruglyak and William Bialek
Department of Physics
University of California at Berkeley
Berkeley, California 94720
and NEC Research Institute*
4 Independence Way
Princeton, New Jersey 08540

Abstract

We show that a simple spin system biased at its critical point can encode spatial characteristics of external signals, such as the dimensions of "objects" in the visual field, in the temporal correlation functions of individual spins. Qualitative arguments suggest that regularly firing neurons should be described by a planar spin of unit length, and such XY models exhibit critical dynamics over a broad range of parameters. We show how to extract these spins from spike trains and then measure the interaction Hamiltonian using simulations of small clusters of cells. Static correlations among spike trains obtained from simulations of large arrays of cells are in agreement with the predictions from these Hamiltonians, and dynamic correlations display the predicted encoding of spatial information. We suggest that this novel representation of object dimensions in temporal correlations may be relevant to recent experiments on oscillatory neural firing in the visual cortex.

1 INTRODUCTION

Physical systems at a critical point exhibit long-range correlations even though the interactions among the constituent particles are of short range. Through the fluctuation-dissipation theorem this implies that the dynamics at one point in the

*Current address.

system are sensitive to external perturbations which are applied very far away. If we build an analog computer poised precisely at such a critical point it should be possible to evaluate highly non-local functionals of the input signals using a locally interconnected architecture. Such a scheme would be very useful for visual computations, especially those which require comparisons of widely separated regions of the image. From a biological point of view long-range correlations at a critical point might provide a robust scenario for "responses from beyond the classical receptive field" [1].

In this paper we present an explicit model for analog computation at a critical point and show that this model has a remarkable consequence: Because of dynamic scaling, spatial properties of input signals are mapped into temporal correlations of the local dynamics. One can, for example, measure the size and topology of "objects" in a scene using only the temporal correlations in the output of a single computational unit (neuron) located within the object. We then show that our abstract model can be realized in networks of semi-realistic spiking neurons. The key to this construction is that neurons biased in a regime of regular or oscillatory firing can be mapped to XY or planar spins [2,3], and two-dimensional arrays of these spins exhibit a broad range of parameters in which the system is generically at a critical point. Non-oscillatory neurons cannot, in general, be forced to operate at a critical point without delicate fine tuning of the dynamics, fine tuning which is implausible both for biology and for man-made analog circuits. We suggest that these arguments may be relevant to the recent observations of oscillatory firing in the visual cortex [4,5,6].

2 A STATISTICAL MECHANICS MODEL

We consider a simple two-dimensional array of spins whose states are defined by unit two-vectors $\mathbf{S}_n$. These spins interact with their neighbors so that the total energy of the system is $\mathbf{H} = -J \sum \mathbf{S}_n \cdot \mathbf{S}_m$, with the sum restricted to nearest neighbor pairs. This is the XY model, which is interesting in part because it possesses not a critical point but rather a critical *line* [7]. At a given temperature, for all $J > J_c$ one finds that correlations among spins decay algebraically, $\langle \mathbf{S}_n \cdot \mathbf{S}_m \rangle \propto 1/|\mathbf{r}_n - \mathbf{r}_m|^\eta$, so that there is no characteristic scale or correlation length; more precisely the correlation length is infinite. In contrast, for $J < J_c$ we have $\langle \mathbf{S}_n \cdot \mathbf{S}_m \rangle \propto \exp[-|\mathbf{r}_n - \mathbf{r}_m|/\xi]$, which defines a finite correlation length ξ.

In the algebraic phase the dynamics of the spins on long length scales are rigorously described by the spin wave approximation, in which one assumes that fluctuations in the angle between neighboring spins are small. In this regime it makes sense to use a continuum approximation rather than a lattice, and the energy of the system becomes $\mathbf{H} = J \int d^2x |\nabla \phi(\mathbf{x})|^2$, where $\phi(\mathbf{x})$ is the orientation of the spin at position $\mathbf{x}$. The dynamics of the system are determined by the Langevin equation

$$\frac{\partial \phi(\mathbf{x}, t)}{\partial t} = J \nabla^2 \phi(\mathbf{x}, t) + \eta(\mathbf{x}, t), \tag{1}$$

where η is a Gaussian thermal noise source with

$$\langle \eta(\mathbf{x}, t) \eta(\mathbf{x}', t') \rangle = 2 k_B T \delta(\mathbf{x} - \mathbf{x}') \delta(t - t'). \tag{2}$$

We can then show that the time correlation function of the spin at a single site $\mathbf{x}$ is given by

$$\langle \mathbf{S}(\mathbf{x},t)\cdot\mathbf{S}(\mathbf{x},0)\rangle = \exp\left[-2k_BT\int\frac{d\omega}{2\pi}\int\frac{d^2k}{(2\pi)^2}\,\frac{1-e^{-i\omega t}}{\omega^2+J^2k^4}\right]. \tag{3}$$

In fact Eq. 3 is valid only for an infinite array of spins. Imagine that external signals to this array of spins can "activate" and "deactivate" the spins so that one must really solve Eq. 1 on finite regions or clusters of active spins. Then we can write the analog of Eq. 3 as

$$\langle \mathbf{S}(\mathbf{x},t)\cdot\mathbf{S}(\mathbf{x},0)\rangle = \exp\left[-\frac{k_BT}{J}\sum_n|\psi_n(\mathbf{x})|^2\frac{1}{\lambda_n}(1-e^{-J\lambda_n|t|})\right], \tag{4}$$

where ψ_n and λ_n are the eigenfunctions and associated eigenvalues of $(-\nabla^2)$ on the region of active spins. The key point here is that the spin auto-correlation function in time determines the spectrum of the Laplacian on the region of activity. But from the classic work of Kac [8] we know that this spectrum gives a great deal of information about the size and shape of the active region — we can in general determine the area, the length of the perimeter, and the topology (number of holes) from the set of eigenvalues $\{\lambda_n\}$, and this is true regardless of the absolute dimensions of the region. Thus by operating at a critical point we can achieve a scale-independent encoding of object dimension and topology in the temporal correlations of a locally connected system.

3 MAPPING REAL NEURONS ONTO THE STATISTICAL MODEL

All current models of neural networks are based on the hope that most microscopic ("biological") details are unimportant for the macroscopic, collective computational behavior of the system as a whole. Here we provide a rigorous connection between a more realistic neural model and a simplified model with spin variables and effective interactions, essentially the XY model discussed above. A more detailed account is given in [2,3].

We use the Fitzhugh-Nagumo (FN) model [9,10] to describe the electrical dynamics of an individual neuron. This model demonstrates a threshold for firing action potentials, a refractory period, and single-shot as well as repetitive firing — in short, all the qualitative properties of neural firing. It is also known to provide a reasonable quantitative description of several cell types. To be realistic it is essential to add a noise current $\delta I_n(t)$ which we take to be Gaussian, spectrally white, and independent in each cell n.

We connect each neuron to its neighbors in regular one- and two-dimensional arrays. More general local connections are easily added and do not significantly change the results presented below. We model a synapse between two neurons by exponentiating the voltage from one and injecting it as current into the other. Our choice is motivated by the fact that the number of transmitter vesicles released at a synapse is exponential in the presynaptic voltage [11]; other synaptic transfer characteristics, including small delays, give results qualitatively similar to those described here. The resulting equations of motion are

$$\frac{dV_n}{dt} = (1/\tau_1)\left[I_0 + \delta I_n(t) - V_n(V_n^2 - 1) - W_n + \sum_m J_{nm}\exp\{V_m(t)/V_0\}\right],$$
$$\frac{dW_n}{dt} = (1/\tau_2)[V_n - \alpha W_n], \qquad (5)$$

where V_n is the transmembrane voltage in cell n, I_0 is the DC bias current, and the W_n are auxiliary variables; V_0 sets the scale of voltage sensitivity in the synapse. Voltages and currents are dimensionless, and the parameters of the system are expressed in terms of the time constants τ_1 and τ_2 and a dimensionless ratio α. From the voltage traces we extract the spike arrival times in the nth neuron, $\{t_i^n\}$.

With the appropriate choice of parameters the FN model can be made to fire regularly—the interspike intervals are tightly clustered around a mean value. The power spectrum of the spike train $s(t)\sum_i \delta(t - t_i)$ has well resolved peaks at $\pm\omega_0$, $\pm 2\omega_0$, ... We then low-pass filter $s(t)$ to keep only the $\pm\omega_0$ peaks, obtaining a phase-modulated cosine,

$$[Fs](t) \approx \omega_0 \cos[\omega_0 t + \phi(t)], \qquad (6)$$

where $[Fs](t)$ denotes the filtered spike train. By looking at $[Fs](t)$ and its time derivative, we can extract the phase $\phi(t)$ which describes the oscillation that underlies regular firing. Since the orientation of a planar spin is also described by a single phase variable, we can reduce the spike train to a time-dependent planar spin $\mathbf{S}(t)$. We now want to see how these spins interact when we connect two cells via synapses.

We characterize the two-neuron interaction by accumulating a histogram of the phase differences between two connected neurons. This probability distribution defines an effective Hamiltonian, $P(\phi_1, \phi_2) \propto \exp[-\mathbf{H}(\phi_1 - \phi_2)]$. With excitatory synapses ($J > 0$) the interaction is ferromagnetic, as expected (see Fig. 1). The Hamiltonian takes other interesting forms for inhibitory, delayed, and nonreciprocal synapses. By simulating small clusters of cells we find that interactions other than nearest neighbor are negligible. This leads us to predict that the entire network is described by the effective Hamiltonian $\mathbf{H} = \sum_{ij} \mathbf{H}_{ij}(\phi_i - \phi_j)$, where $\mathbf{H}_{ij}(\phi_i - \phi_j)$ is the effective Hamiltonian measured for the pair of connected cells i, j.

One crucial consequence of Eq. 6 is that correlations of the filtered spike trains are exactly proportional to the spin-spin correlations which are natural objects in statistical mechanics. Specifically, if we have two cells n and m,

$$\langle \mathbf{S}_n \cdot \mathbf{S}_m \rangle = \langle \cos(\phi_n - \phi_m) \rangle = \omega_0^{-2} \langle [Fs_n](t)[Fs_m](t) \rangle. \qquad (7)$$

This relation shows us how the statistical description of the network can be tested in experiments which monitor actual neural spike trains.

4 DOES THE MAPPING WORK?

When planar spins are connected in a one-dimensional chain with nearest-neighbor interactions, correlations between spins drop off exponentially with distance. To test this prediction we have run simulations on chains of 32 Fitzhugh-Nagumo neurons connected to their nearest neighbors. Correlations computed directly from the filtered spike trains as indicated above indeed decay exponentially, as seen in the insert to Fig. 1. Fig. 1 shows that the predictions for the correlation length from the simple model are in excellent agreement with the correlation lengths observed in the simulations of spiking neurons; there are no free parameters.

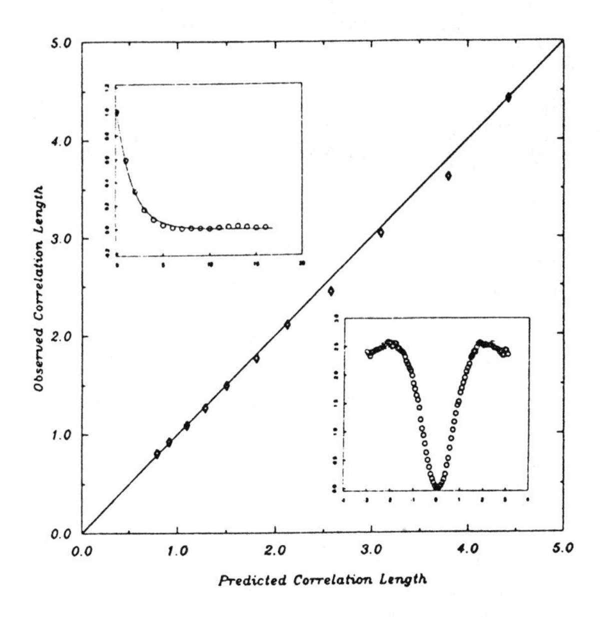

Figure 1: Correlation length obtained from fits to the simulation data vs. correlation length predicted from the Hamiltonians. Inset, upper left: Correlation function vs. distance from simulations, with exponential fit. Inset, lower right: Corresponding Hamiltonian as a function of phase difference.

In the two-dimensional case we connect each neuron to its four nearest neighbors on a square lattice. The corresponding spin model is essentially the XY mode. Hence we expect a low-temperature (high synaptic strength) phase with correlations that decay slowly (as a small power of distance) and a high-temperature (low synaptic strength) disordered phase with exponential decay. These predictions were confirmed by large-scale simulations of two-dimensional arrays [2].

5 OBJECT DIMENSIONS FROM TEMPORAL CORRELATIONS

We believe that we have presented convincing evidence for the description of regularly firing neurons in terms of XY spins, at least as regards their static or equilibrium correlations. In our theoretical discussion we showed that the temporal correlation functions of XY spins in the algebraic phase contained information about the

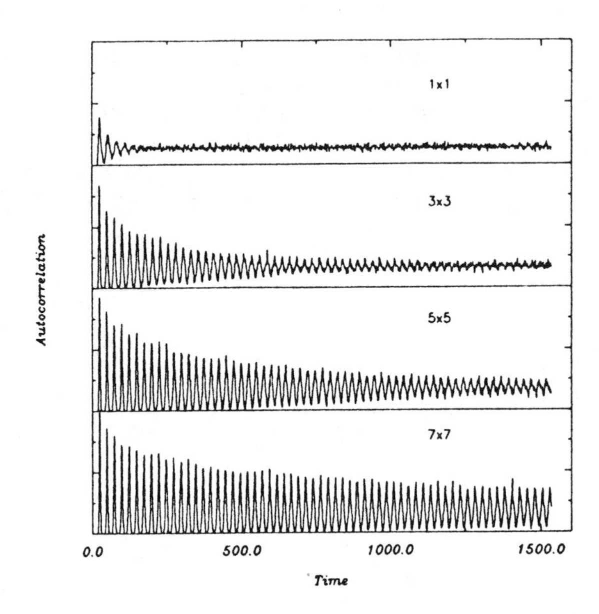

Figure 2: Auto-correlation functions for the spike trains of single cells at the center of square arrays of different sizes.

dimensions of "objects." Here we test this idea in a very simple numerical experiment. Imagine that we have an array of $N \times N$ connected cells which are excited by incoming signals so that they are in the oscillatory regime. Obviously we can measure the size of this "object" by looking at the entire network, but our theoretical results suggest that one can sense these dimensions (N) using the temporal correlations in just one cell, most simply the cell in the center of the array.

In Fig. 2 we show the auto-correlation functions for the spike trains of the center cell in arrays of different dimensions. It is clear that changing the dimensions of the array of active cells has profound effects on these spatially local temporal correlations. Because of the fact that the model is on a critical line these correlations continue to change as the dimensions of the array increase, rather than saturating after some finite correlation length is reached. Qualitatively similar results are expected throughout the algebraic phase of the associated spin model.

Recently it has been shown that when cells in the cat visual cortex are excited by appropriate stimuli they enter a regime of regular firing. These firing statistics are somewhat more complex than simulated here because there are a variable number of spikes per cycle, but we have reproduced all of our major results in models which capture this feature of the real data. We have seen that networks of regularly firing cells are capable of qualitatively different types of computation because these networks can be placed at a critical point without fine tuning of parameters. Most dramatically dynamic scaling allows us to trade spatial and temporal features and thereby encode object dimension in temporal correlations of single cells, as in Fig. 2. To see if such novel computations are indeed mediated by cortical oscillations we suggest the direct analog of our numerical experiment, in which the correlation functions of single cells would be monitored in response to structured stimuli (e.g., textures) with different total spatial extent in the two dimensions of the visual field. We predict that these correlation functions will show a clear dependence on the area of the visual field being excited, with some sensitivity to the shape and topology as well. Most importantly this dependence on "object" dimension will extend to very large objects because the network is at a critical point. In this sense the temporal correlations of single cells will encode any object dimension, rather than being detectors for objects of some critical size.

Acknowledgements

We thank O. Alvarez, D. Arovas, A. B. Bonds, K. Brueckner. M. Crair, E. Knobloch, H. Lecar, and D. Rohksar for helpful discussions. Work at Berkeley was supported in part by the National Science Foundation through a Presidential Young Investigator Award (to W.B.), supplemented by funds from Cray Research, Sun Microsystems, and the NEC Research Institute, by the Fannie and John Hertz Foundation through a Graduate Fellowship (to L.K.), and by the USPHS through a Biomedical Research Support Grant.

References

[1] J. Allman, F. Meizin, and E. McGuiness. *Ann. Rev. Neurosci.*, 8:407, 1985.

[2] L. Kruglyak. *From biological reality to simple physical models: Networks of oscillating neurons and the XY model.* PhD thesis, University of California at Berkeley, Berkeley, California, 1990.

[3] W. Bialek. In E. Jen, editor, *1989 Lectures in Complex Systems, SFI Studies in the Sciences of Complexity*, volume 2, pages 513–595. Addison-Wesley, Reading, Mass., 1990.

[4] R. Eckhorn, R. Bauer, W. Jordan, M. Brosch, W. Kruse, M. Munk, and H. J. Reitboeck. *Biol. Cybern.*, 60:121, 1988.

[5] C. M. Gray and W. Singer. *Proc. Nat. Acad. Sci. USA*, 86:1698, 1989.

[6] C. M. Gray, P. König, A. K. Engel, and W. Singer. *Nature*, 338:334, 1989.

[7] D. R. Nelson. In C. Domb and J. L. Lebowitz, editors, *Phase Transitions and Critical Phenomena*, volume 7, chapter 1. Academic Press, London, 1983.

[8] M. Kac. *The American Mathematical Monthly*, 73:1–23, 1966.

[9] Richard Fitzhugh. *Biophysical Journal*, 1:445–466, 1961.

[10] J. S. Nagumo, S. Arimoto, and S. Yoshizawa. *Proc. I. R. E.*, 50:2061, 1962.

[11] D. J. Aidley. *The Physiology of Excitable Cells.* Cambridge University Press, Cambridge, 1971.

Part IV

Temporal Reasoning

Modeling Time Varying Systems Using Hidden Control Neural Architecture

Esther Levin

AT&T Bell Laboratories
Speech Research Department
Murray Hill, NJ 07974 USA

ABSTRACT

Multi-layered neural networks have recently been proposed for non-linear prediction and system modeling. Although proven successful for modeling time invariant nonlinear systems, the inability of neural networks to characterize temporal variability has so far been an obstacle in applying them to complicated nonstationary signals, such as speech. In this paper we present a network architecture, called "Hidden Control Neural Network" (HCNN), for modeling signals generated by nonlinear dynamical systems with restricted time variability. The approach taken here is to allow the mapping that is implemented by a multi layered neural network to change with time as a function of an additional control input signal. This network is trained using an algorithm that is based on "back-propagation" and segmentation algorithms for estimating the unknown control together with the network's parameters. The HCNN approach was applied to several tasks including modeling of time-varying nonlinear systems and speaker-independent recognition of connected digits, yielding a word accuracy of 99.1%.

I. INTRODUCTION

Layered networks have attracted considerable interest in recent years due to their ability to model adaptively nonlinear multivariate functions. It has been recently proved in [1], that a network with one intermediate layer of sigmoidal units can approximate arbitrarily well any continuous mapping. However, being a static model, a layered network is not capable of modeling signals with an inherent time variability, such as speech.

In this paper we present a hidden control neural network that can implements non-linear and time-varying mapping. The hidden control input signal which allows the network's mapping to change over time, provides the ability to capture the non-stationary properties, and learn the underlying temporal structure of the modeled signal.

II. THE MODEL

II.1 MULTI LAYERED NETWORK

Multi layered neural network is a connectionist models that implements a nonlinear mapping from and input $x \in X \subset R^{N_I}$ to an output $y \in Y \subset R^{N_O}$:

$$y = F_{\omega}(x), \tag{1}$$

where $\omega \in \Omega \subset R^D$, the parameter set of the network, consists of the connection wegihts and the biases, and x and y are the activation vectors of the input and output layers, of dimensionality N_I and N_O, respectively.

Recently layered networks have proven useful for non-linear prediction of signals and system modeling [2]. In these applications one uses the values of a real signal $x(t)$, at a set of discrete times in the past, to predict $x(t)$ at a point in the future. For example, for order-one-predictor, the output of the network y is used as a predictor of the next signal sample, when the network is given past sample as input, e.g. $y=\hat{x}_t=F_{\omega}(x_{t-1})$, where $\hat{x}_t$ denotes the predicted value of the signal at time t, which, in general, differs from the true value, x_t. The parameter set of the network ω is estimated from a training set of discrete time samples from a segment of known signal $\{ x_t, t=0, ..., T \}$, by minimizing a prediction error which measures the distortion between the signal and the prediction made by the network,

$$E(\omega)=\sum_{t=1}^{T} || x_t - F_{\omega}(x_{t-1}) ||^2 , \tag{2}$$

and the estimated parameter set $\hat{\omega}$ is given by $\underset{\Omega}{\operatorname{argmin}} E(\omega)$.

In [2] such a neural network predictor is used for modeling chaotic series. One of the examples considered in [2] is prediction of time series generated by the classic logistic, or Feigenbaum, map,

$$x_{t+1} = 4 \cdot b \cdot x_t (1 - x_t) \tag{3}$$

This iterated map produces an ergodic chaotic time series when b is chosen to equal 1. Although this time series passes virtually every test for randomness, it is generated by the deterministic Eq.(3), and can be predicted perfectly, once the generating system (3) is learned. Using the back-propagation algorithm [3] to minimize the prediction error (2) defined on a set of samples of this time series, the network parameters ω were adjusted, enabling accurate prediction of the next point x_{t+1} in this "random" series given the present point x_t as an input. The mapping F_{ω} implemented by the trained network approximated very closely the logistic map (3) that generated the modeled series.

II.2 HIDDEN CONTROL NETWORK

For a given fixed value of the parameters ω, a layered network implements a fixed input-output mapping, and therefore can be used for time-invariant system modeling or prediction of signals generated by a fixed, time-invariant system. Hidden control network that is based on such layered network, has an additional mechanism that allows the mapping (1) to change with time, keeping the parameters ω fixed. We consider the case where the units in the input layer are divided into two distinct groups. The first input unit group represents the observable input to the network, $x \in X \subset R^p$, and the second represents a control signal $c \in C \subset R^q$, $p+q=N_I$, that controls the mapping between the observable input x, and the network output y.

The output of the network y is given, according to (1), by $F_{\omega}(x, c)$, where (x, c) denotes the concatenation of the two inputs. We focus on the mapping between the observable input x and the output. This mapping is modulated by the control input c :

for a fixed value of x and for different values of c, the network produces different outputs. For a fixed control input, the network implements a fixed observable input-output mapping, but when the control input changes, the network's mapping changes as well, modifying the characteristics of the observed signal:

$$y=F_{\omega}(x,c) \triangleq F_{\omega,c}(x). \tag{4}$$

If the control signal is known for all time t, there is no point in distinguishing between the observable input, x, and the control input c. The more interesting situation is when the control signal is unknown or hidden, i.e., the *hidden control* case, which we will treat in this paper.

This model can be used for prediction and modeling of nonstationary signals generated by time-varying sources. In the case of first order prediction the present value of the signal x_t is predicted based on x_{t-1}, with respect to the control input c_t. If we restrict the control signal to take its values from a finite set, $c \in \{C_1, \cdots, C_N\} \equiv C$, then the network is a finite state network, where in each state it implements a fixed input-output mapping F_{ω,C_i}. Such a network with two or more intermidiate layers can approximate arbitrarily closely any set $\{F_1, \cdots, F_N\}$ of continuous functions of the observable input x [4].

In the applications we considered for this model, two types of time-structures were used, namely

Fully connected model: In this type of HCNN, every state, corresponding to a specific value of the control input, can be reached from any other state in a single time step. It means that there are no temporal restrictions on the control signal, and in each time step, it can take any of its N possible values $\{C_1, ..., C_N\}$. For example, a 2 state fully connected model is shown in Fig. 1a. In a generative mode of operation, when the observable input of the network is wired to be the the previous network's output , the observable signal $x(t)$ is generated in each one of the states by a different dynamics: $x_{t+1}=F_{c_t}(x_t)$, $c_t \in \{0, 1\}$, and therefore this network emulates two different dynamical systems, with the control signal acting as a switch between them.

Left-to-right model: For spoken word modeling, we will consider a finite-state, left-to-right HCNN (see Fig.1b), where the control signal is further restricted to take value C_i only if in the previous time step it had a value of C_i or C_{i-1}. Each state of this network represents an unspecified acoustic unit, and due to the "left-to-right" structure, the whole word is modeled as concatenation of such acoustic units. The time spent in each of the states is not fixed, since it varies according to the value of the control signal, and therefore the model can take into account the duration variability between different utterances of the same word.

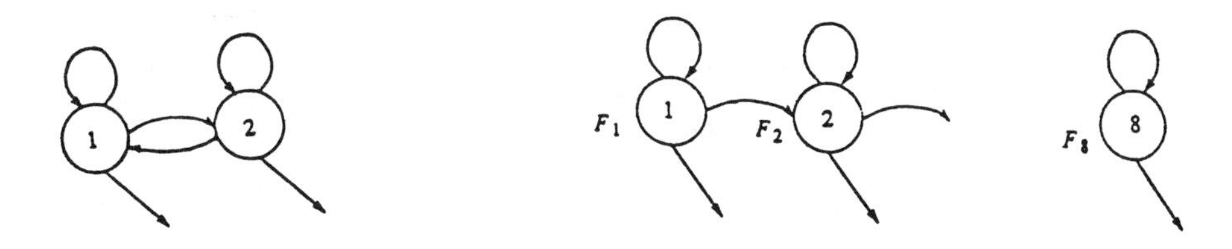

Figure 1: a-Fully connected 2 state HCNN ;
b-Left to right 8 state HCNN for word modeling.

III. USING HCNN

Given the predictive form of HCNN described in the previous section, there are three basic problems of interest that must be solved for the model to be useful in real-world applications. This problems are the following:

Segmentation problem : Here we attempt to uncover the hidden part of the model, i.e., given a network ω and a sequence of observations $\{ x_t, t=0, ..., T \}$, to find the correct control sequence, which best explains the observations. This problem is solved using an optimality criterion, namely the prediction error, similar to Eq.(2),

$$E(\omega, \mathbf{c}_1^T) = \sum_{t=1}^{T} || x_t - F_{\omega, c_t}(x_{t-1}) ||^2 , \tag{5}$$

where $\mathbf{c}_1^T$ denotes the control sequence $c_1, \cdots, c_T$, $c_i \in \mathbf{C}$. For a given network, ω, the prediction error (5) is a function of the hidden control input sequence, and thus segmentation is associated with the minimization:

$$\hat{\mathbf{c}}_1^T = \underset{\mathbf{C}^T}{argmin}\, E(\omega, \mathbf{c}_1^T) , \tag{6}$$

In the case of a finite-state, fully connected model, this minimization can be performed exhaustively, by minimizing for each observation separately, and for a fully connected HCNN with a real-valued control signal (i.e. not the finite state case), local minimization of (5) can be performed using the back-propagation algorithm. For a "left-to-right" model , global minimum of (5) is attained efficiently using the Viterbi algorithm [5].

Evaluation problem, namely how well a given network ω matches a given sequence of observations $\{ x_t, t=0, ..., T \}$. The evaluation is a key point for many applications. For example, if we consider the case in which we are trying to choose among several competing networks, that represent different hypothesis in the hypotheses space, the solution to Problem 2 allows us to choose the network that best matches the observation. This problem is also solved using the prediction error defined in (5). The match, or actually, the distortion, is measured by the prediction error of the network on a sequence of observations, for the best possible sequence of hidden control inputs, i.e.,

$$E(\omega) = \min_{\mathbf{C}^T} E(\omega, \mathbf{c}_1^T) . \tag{7}$$

Therefore, to evaluate a network, first the segmentation problem must be solved.

Training problem, i.e., how to adjust the model parameters ω to best match the observation sequence, or training set, $\{ x_t, t=0, ..., T \}$.

The training in layered networks is accomplished by minimizing the prediction error of Eq.(2) using versions of the back-propagation algorithm. In the HCNN case, the prediction error (5) is a function of the hidden parameters and the hidden control input sequence, and thus training is associated with the joint minimization:

$$\hat{\omega} = \underset{\Omega}{argmin} \{ \min_{\mathbf{C}^T} E(\omega, \mathbf{c}_1^T) \} . \tag{8}$$

This minimization is performed by an iterative training algorithm.

The k-th iteration of the algorithm consists of two stages:

1. Reestimation: For the present value of the control input sequence, the prediction error is minimized with respect to the network parameters.

$$(\hat{\omega})_k = \underset{\Omega}{argmin}\, E(\omega, (\mathbf{c}_1^T)_{k-1}) \tag{9}$$

This minimization is implemented by the back-propagation algorithm.

2. Segmentation: Using the values of parameters, obtained from the previous stage, the control sequence is estimated (as in (6)).

$$(\mathbf{c}_1^T)_k = \underset{C^T}{argmin}\, E((\hat{\omega})_k, \mathbf{c}_1^T) \tag{10}$$

IV. HCNN AS A STATISTICAL MODEL

For further understanding of the properties of the proposed model and the training procedure, it is useful to describe the HCNN by an equivalent statistical vector source of the following form:

$$x_t = F_{\omega,c_t}(x_{t-1}) + n_t, \quad n_t \sim N(0, I), \tag{11}$$

where n_t is a white Gaussian noise. Assuming for simplicity that all the values of the control allowed by the model are equiprobable (this is a special case of Markov process, and can be easily extended for the general case) , we can write the joint likelihood of the data and the control

$$P(x_1^T, c_1^T \mid \omega) = (2\pi)^{-\frac{pT}{2}} \exp[-\frac{1}{2}\sum_{t=1}^{T} \| x_t - F_{\omega,c_t}(x_{t-1}) \|^2], \tag{12}$$

where x_1^T denotes the sequence of observation $\{x_1, x_2, \cdots, x_T\}$.

Eq.(12) provides a probabilistic interpretation of the procedures described in the previous section:

The proposed segmentation procedure is equivalent to choosing the most probable control sequence, given the network and the observations.

The evaluation of the network is related to the probability of the observations given the model, for the best sequence of control inputs,

$$\min_{C^T} E(\omega, c_1^T) <=> \max_{C^T} P(x_1^T, c_1^T \mid \omega), \tag{13}$$

The proposed training procedure (Eq. 8) is equivalent to maximization of the joint likelihood (12):

$$\hat{\omega} = \underset{\Omega}{argmin}\{ \min_{C^T} E(\omega, s_1^T)\} = \underset{\Omega}{argmax}\{ \max_{C^T} P(x_1^T, c_1^T \mid \omega)\}. \tag{14}$$

Thus (8) is equivalent to an approximate maximum likelihood training, where instead of maximizing the marginal likelihood $P(x_1^T \mid \omega) = \sum_{C^T} P(x_1^T, c_1^T \mid \omega)$, only the maximal term in the sum, the joint likelihood (14) is considered. The approximate maximum likelihood training avoids the computational complexity of the exact maximum likelihood approach, and recently [6] was shown to yield results similar to those obtained by the exact maximum likelihood training.

IV.1 HCNN and the Hidden Markov Model (HMM)

During the past decade hidden Markov modeling has been used extensively to represent the probability distribution of spoken words [7]. A hidden Markov model assumes that the modeled speech signal can be characterized as being produced at each time instant by one of the states of a finite state source, and that each observation vector is an independent sample according to the probability distribution of the current state. The transitions between the states of the model are governed by a Markov process

HCNN can be viewed as an extension of this model to the case of Markov output processes. The observable signal in each state is modeled as though it was produced by a dynamical system driven by noise. Here we are modeling the dynamics that generated the signal, F_ω, and the dependence of the present observation vector on the previous one. The assumption that the driving noise (12) is normal is not necessary: instead, we can assume a parametric form of the noise density, and estimate its parameters.

V. EXPERIMENTAL EVALUATION

For experimental evaluation of the proposed model, we tested on two different tasks:

V.1 Time-varying system modeling and segmentation

Here an HCNN was used for a single-step prediction of a signal generated by a time-varying system, described by

$$x_{t+1} = \begin{cases} F_L(x_t) & \text{if } switch=0 \\ 1-F_L(x_t) & \text{if } switch=1 \end{cases}, \tag{15}$$

where F_L is the logistic map from Eq. (3), and *switch* is a random variable, assuming binary values. Both of the systems, F_L, and $1-F_L$, are chaotic and produce signals in the range [0,1]. A fully connected, 2-state HCNN (each state corresponding to one switch position), as in Fig. 1a, was trained on a segment of 400 samples of such a signal, according to the training algorithm described in section V. The performance of the resulting network was tested on an independent set of 1000 samples of this signal. The estimated control sequence differed from the real switch position in only 8 out of 1000 test samples. The evaluation score, i.e., the average prediction error for this estimated control sequence was 7.5×10^{-5} per sample. Fig. 2 compares the mapping implemented by the network in one state, corresponding to control value set to 0, and the logistic map for *switch*=0. Similar results are obtained for c=1 and *switch*=1. These results indicate that the HCNN was indeed able to capture the two underlying dynamics that generated the modeled signal, and to learn the switching pattern simultaneously.

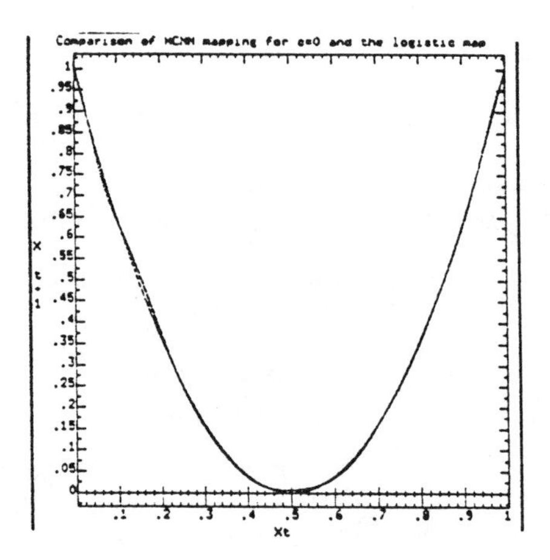

Fig.2 Comparison of the logistic map and the mapping implemented by HCNN with c=0.

V.2 Continuous recognition of digit sequences

Here we tested the proposed HCNN modeling technique on recognition of connected spoken versions of the digits, consisting of "zero" to "nine", and including the word "oh", recorded from male speakers through a telephone handset and sampled at 6.67

kHz. LPC analysis of order 8 was performed on frames of 45 msec duration, with overlap of 15 msec, and 12 cepstral and 12 delta cepstral [8] coefficients were derived for the t-th frame to form the observable signal x_t. Each digit was modeled by an 8 state, left-to-right HCNN, as in Fig.1b. The network was trained to predict the cepstral and delta cepstral coefficients for the next frame. Each network consisted of 32 input units (24 to encode x_t and 8 for a distributed representation of the 8 control values), 24 output units and 30 hidden units, all fully connected. Each network was trained using a training set of 900 utterances from 44 male speakers extracted from continuous strings of digits using an HMM based recognizer [9]. 1666 strings (5600 words), uttered by an independent set of 22 male speakers were used for estimating the recognition accuracy. The mean and the covariance of the driving noise (12) were modeled. The word accuracy obtained was 99.1%.

Fig. 3a illustrates the process of recognition (the forward pass of Viterbi algorithm) of the word "one" by the speaker-independent system. The horizontal axis is time (in frames). 11 models from "zero" to "nine" , and "oh" appear on the vertical axis. The numbers that appear in the graph (from 1 to 8) describe the number of a state. For example, number 2 inside the second row of the graph denotes state number 2 of the model of the word "one". In each frame, the prediction error was calculated for each one of the states in each model, resulting in 88 different prediction errors. The graph in each frame shows the states of the models that are in the vicinity of the minimal error among those 88. This is a partial description of a forward pass of the Viterbi algorithm in recognition, before the left-to-right constraints of the models are taken into account. Figure 3a shows that the main candidate considered in recognition of the word "one" is the actual model of "one", but in the end of the word two spurious candidates arise. The spurious candidates are certain states of the models of "seven" and "nine". Those states are detectors of the nasal 'n' that appears in all these words.

Figure 3b shows the recognition of a four digit string "three - five - oh - four". The spurious candidates indicate detectors of certain sounds, common to different words, like in "four" and in "oh", in "five" and in "nine", in "three", "six" and "eight".

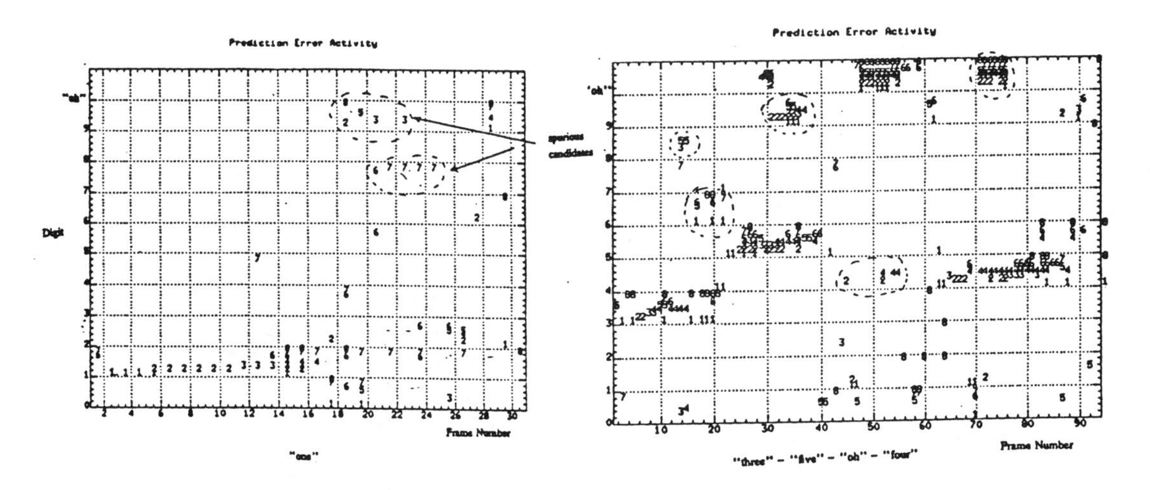

Fig. 3 Illustration of the recognition process.

VI. SUMMARY AND DISCUSSION

This paper introduces a generalization of the layered neural network that can implement a time-varying non-linear mapping between its observable input and output. The variation of the network's mapping is due to an additional, hidden control input, while the network parameters remain unchanged. We proposed an algorithm for finding the network parameters and the hidden control sequence from a training set of examples of observable input and output. This algorithm implements an approximate maximum likelihood estimation of parameters of an equivalent statistical model, when only the dominant control sequence is taken into account. The conceptual difference between the proposed model and the HMM is that in the HMM approach, the observable data in each of the states is modeled as though it was produced by a memoryless source, and a parametric description of this source is obtained during training, while in the proposed model the observations in each state are produced by a non-linear dynamical system driven by noise, and both the parametric form of the dynamics and the noise are estimated. The performance of the model was illustrated for the tasks of nonlinear time-varying system modeling and continuously spoken digit recognition. The reported results show the potential of this model for providing high performance speech recognition capability.

Acknowledgment

Special thanks are due to N. Merhav for numerous comments and helpful discussions. Useful discussions with N.Z. Tishby, S.A. Solla, L.R. Rabiner and J.G. Wilpon are greatly appreciated.

References

1. G. Cybenko, " Approximation by superposition of sigmoidal function," *Math. Control Systems Signals,* in press, 1989.
2. A. Lapedes and R. Farber, " Nonlinear signal processing using neural networks: prediction and system modeling, " *Proc of IEEE,* in press, 1989.
3. D.E. Rumelhart, G.E. Hinton and R.J. Williams, "Learning internal representation by error propagation," *Parallel Distributed Processing: Exploration in the Microstructure of Cognition,* MIT Press, 1986.
4. E. Levin, "Word recognition using hidden control neural architecture," *Proc. of ICASSP,* Albuquerque, April 1990.
5. G.D. Forney, "The Viterbi algorithm," *Proc. IEEE,* vol. 61, pp. 268-278, Mar. 1973.
6. N. Merhav and Y. Ephraim, "Maximum likelihood hidden Markov modeling using a dominant sequence of states," accepted for publication in *IEEE Transaction on ASSP.*
7. L. R. Rabiner, "A tutorial on hidden Markov models and selected applications in speech recognition," *Proc. of IEEE,* vol. 77, No. 2, pp. 257-286, February 1989
8. B.S. Atal, "Effectiveness of linear prediction characteristics of the speech wave for automatic speaker identification and verification," *J. Acoust. Soc. Am.,* vol. 55, No. 6, pp. 1304-1312, June 1974.
9. L.R. Rabiner, J.G. Wilpon, and F.K. Soong, "High performance connected digit recognition using hidden Markov models," *IEEE Transaction on ASSP,* vol. 37, 1989.

The Tempo 2 Algorithm: Adjusting Time-Delays By Supervised Learning

Ulrich Bodenhausen and Alex Waibel
School of Computer Science
Carnegie Mellon University
Pittsburgh, PA 15213

Abstract

In this work we describe a new method that adjusts time-delays and the widths of time-windows in artificial neural networks automatically. The input of the units are weighted by a gaussian input-window over time which allows the learning rules for the delays and widths to be derived in the same way as it is used for the weights. Our results on a phoneme classification task compare well with results obtained with the TDNN by Waibel et al., which was manually optimized for the same task.

1 INTRODUCTION

The processing of pattern-sequences has been investigated with several neural network architectures. One approach to processing of temporal context with neural networks is to implement time-delays. This approach is neurophysiologically plausible, because real axons have a limited conduction speed (which is dependent on the diameter of the axon and whether it is myelinated or not). Additionally, the length of most axons is much greater than the euclidean distance between the connected neurons. This leads to a great variety of different time-delays in the brain. Artificial networks that make use of time-delays have been suggested [10, 11, 12, 8, 2, 3].

In the TDNN [11, 12] and most other artificial neural networks with time-delays the delays are implemented as hat-shaped input-windows over time. A unit j that is connected with unit i by a connection with delay n is only receiving information about the activity of unit i n time-steps ago. A set of connections with consecutive time-delays is used to let each unit gather a certain amount of temporal context. In these networks, weights are automatically trained but the architecture of the network (time-delays, number of connections and number of units) have to be predetermined by laborious experiments [8, 6].

In this work we describe a new algorithm that adjusts time-delays and the width of the input-window automatically. The learning rules require input-windows over time that can be described by a smooth function. With these input-windows it is possible to derive learning rules for adjusting the center and the width of the window. During training, new connections are added if they are needed by splitting already existing connections and training them independently.

Adaptive time-delays in neural networks could have significant advantages for the processing of pattern-sequences, especially if the relevant information is distributed across non-consecutive patterns. A typical example for this kind of pattern sequences are rhythms (relevant in music and speech). In a rhythm, there are many events but also many gaps between these events. Another example is speech, where some parts of an utterance are more important for understanding than others (example: 'hat', 'fat', 'cat'..). Therefore a network that allocates existing and new resources to the parts of the input sequence that are most helpful for the task could be more compact and efficient for various tasks.

2 THE TEMPO 2 NETWORK

The Tempo 2 network is an artificial neural network with *adaptive* weights, *adaptive* time-delays and *adaptive* widths of gaussian input windows over time. It is a generalization of the Back-Propagation network proposed by Rumelhart, Hinton and Williams [9]. The network is based on some ideas that were tested with the Tempo 1 network [2, 3].

The Tempo 2 network is designed to learn about the relevant temporal context during training. A unit in the network is activated by input from a gaussian shaped input-window centered around (t-d) and standard deviation σ, where d (the time-delay) and σ (the width of the input-window) are to be learned [1] (see Fig. 1 and 2). This means that the center and the width of each input-window can be adjusted by learning rules. The adaptive time-delays allow the processing of temporal context that is distributed across several non-consecutive patterns of the sequence. The adaptive width of the window enables the receiving unit to monitor a variable sequence of consecutive activations over time of each sending unit. New connections can be added if they are needed (see section 2.1). The input of unit j at time t, $x(t)_j$, is

$$x(t)_j = \sum_{\tau=0}^{t} \sum_{k} y_k(\tau)\theta(\tau, t, d_{jk}, \sigma_{jk}) w_{jk}$$

with $\theta(\tau, t, d_{jk}, \sigma_{jk})$ representing the gaussian input window given by

$$\theta(\tau, t, d_{jk}, \sigma_{jk}) = \frac{1}{\sqrt{2\pi}\sigma_{jk}} e^{(\tau - t + d_{jk})^2 / 2\sigma_{jk}^2}$$

where y_k is the output of the previous sending unit and w_{jk}, d_{jk} and σ_{jk} are the weights, delays and widths on its connections, respectively.

This approach is partly motivated by neurophysiology and mathematics. In the brain, a spike that is sent by a neuron via an axon is not received as a spike by the receiving cell.

[1] Other windows are possible. The function describing the shape of the window has to be smooth.

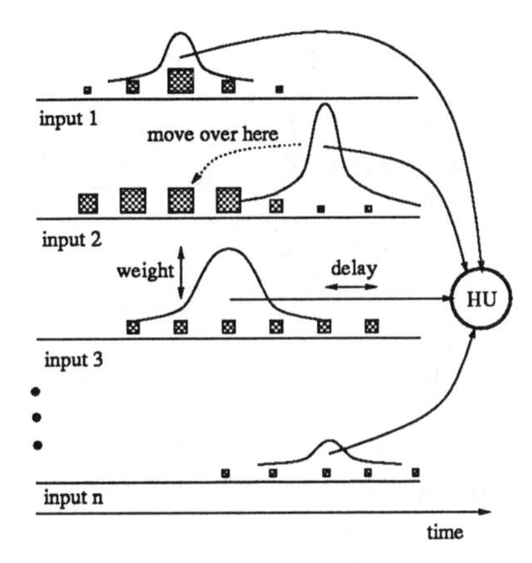

Figure 1: The input to one unit in the Tempo 2 network. The boxes represent the activations of the sending units; a tall box represents a high activity.

Rather, the postsynaptic potential has a short rise and a long tail. Let us assume a situation with two neurons. Neuron A fires at time t-d, where d is the time that the signal needs to travel along the connection and to activate neuron B. Neuron B is activated mostly at time t, but the postsynaptic potential will decrease slowly and neuron B will get some input at time t+1, some smaller input at time t+2 and so on. Functionally, a spike is smeared over time and this provides some "local memory".

For our simulations we simulate this behavior by allowing the receiving unit to be activated by the weighted sum of activations around an input centered at time t-d. If the sending unit ("neuron A") was activated at time t-d, then the receiving unit ("neuron B") will be activated mostly at time t, will be less activated at time t+1, and so on. In our case, the input-window function also allows the receiving unit to be (less) activated at times t-1, t-2 etc.. This enables us to formulate a learning rule that can increase and decrease time-delays.

The gaussian input-window has the advantage that it provides some robustness against temporally misaligned input tokens. By looking at Fig. 2 it is obvious that small misalignments of the input signal do not change the input of the receiving unit significantly. The robustness is dependent on the width of the window. Therefore a wide window would make the input of the receiving unit more robust against signals shifted in time, but would also reduce the time-resolution of the unit. This suggests the implementation of a learning rule that adjusts the width of the input-windows of each connection.

With this gaussian input-window, it is possible to compute how the input of unit j would change if the delay of a connection or the width of the input window were changed. The formalism is the same as for the derivation of the learning rules for the weights in a standard Back-Propagation network. The change of a delay is proportional to the derivative of the output error with respect to the delay. The change of a width is proportional to the derivative of the error with respect to the width. The error at the output is propagated back to the hidden layer. The learning rules for weights w_{ji}, delays d_{ji} and widths σ_{ji} were derived from

$$\Delta w_{ji} = -\epsilon_1 \frac{\partial E}{\partial w_{ji}}$$

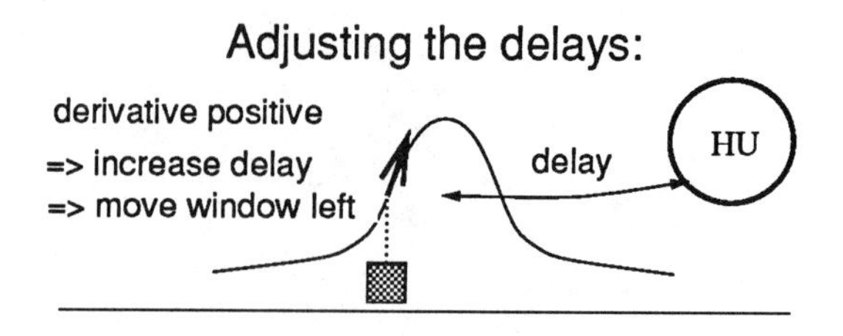

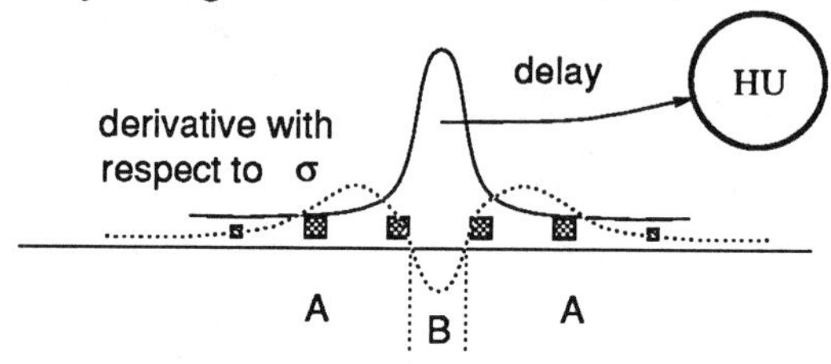

Figure 2: A graphical explanation of the learning rules for delays and widths: The derivative of the gaussian input-window with respect to time is used for adjusting the time-delays. The derivative with respect to σ (dotted line) is used for adjusting the width of the window. A majority of activation in area A will cause the window to grow. A majority of activity in area B will cause the window to shrink.

$$\Delta d_{ji} = -\epsilon_2 \frac{\partial E}{\partial d_{ji}}$$

$$\Delta \sigma_{ji} = -\epsilon_3 \frac{\partial E}{\partial \sigma_{ji}}$$

where ϵ_1, ϵ_2 and ϵ_3 are the learning rates and E is the error. As in the derivation of the standard Back-Propagation learning rules, the chain rule is applied (z = w, d, σ):

$$\frac{\partial E}{\partial z_{ji}} = \frac{\partial E}{\partial x(t)_j} \frac{\partial x(t)_j}{\partial z_{ji}}$$

where $\frac{\partial E}{\partial x(t)_j}$ is the same in the learning rules for weights, delays and widths. The partial derivatives of the input with respect to the parameters of the connections are computed as follows:

$$\frac{\partial x(t)_j}{\partial w_{ji}} = \sum_{\tau=0}^{t} y_i(\tau)\theta(\tau, t, d_{ji}, \sigma_{ji})$$

$$\frac{\partial x(t)_j}{\partial d_{ji}} = \sum_{\tau=0}^{t} y_i(\tau) w_{ji} \frac{\partial}{\partial d_{ji}} \theta(\tau, t, d_{ji}, \sigma_{ji})$$

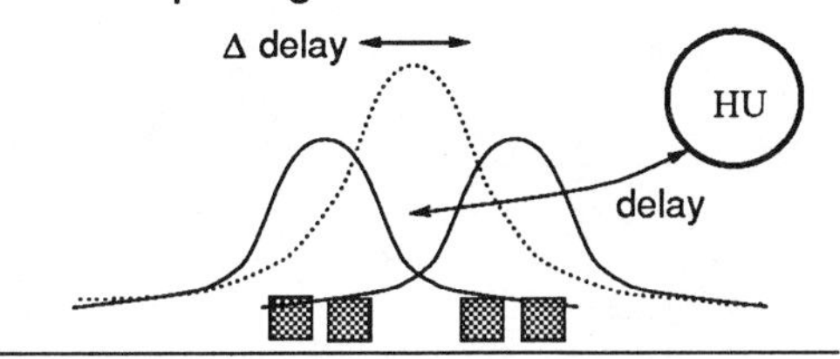

Figure 3: Splitting of a connection. The dotted line represents the "old" window and the solid lines represent the two windows after splitting, respectively.

$$\frac{\partial x(t)_j}{\partial \sigma_{ji}} = \sum_{\tau=0}^{t} y_i(\tau) w_{ji} \frac{\partial}{\partial \sigma_{ji}} \theta(\tau, t, d_{ji}, \sigma_{ji})$$

2.1 ADDING NEW CONNECTIONS

Learning algorithms for neural networks that add hidden units have recently been proposed [4, 5]. In our network connections are added to the already existing ones in a similar way as it is used by Hanson for adding units [5]. During learning, the network starts with one connection between two units. Depending on the task this may be insufficient and it would be desirable to add new connections where more connections are *needed*. New connections are added by splitting already existing connections and afterwards training them independently (see Fig. 3). The rule for splitting a connection is motivated by observations during training runs. It was observed that input-windows started moving backwards and forwards (that means the time-delays changed) after a certain level of performance was reached. This can be interpreted as inconsistent time-delays which might be caused by temporal variability of certain features in the samples of speech. During training we compute the standard deviations of all delay changes and compare them with a threshold:

$$if \sum_{alltokens} (\Delta d_{ji}(token) - \frac{\sum_{alltokens} |\Delta d_{ji}|}{\#tokens})^2 > threshold$$

then split connection ji.

3 SIMULATIONS

The Tempo 2 network was initially tested with rhythm classification. The results were encouraging and evaluation was carried out on a phoneme classification task. In this application, adaptive delays can help to find important cues in a sample of speech. Units should not accumulate information from irrelevant parts of the phonemes. Rather, they should look at parts within the phonemes that provide the most important information for the kind of feature extraction that is needed for the classification task. The network was trained on the phonemes /b/, /d/ and /g/ from a single speaker. 783 tokens were used for training and 759 tokens were used for testing.

adaptive parameters	constant parameters	Training Set	Testing Set
weights	delays, widths	93.2%	89.3%
delays	weights, widths	64.0%	63.0%
widths	weights, delays	63.5%	61.8%
delays, widths	weights	70.0%	68.6%
weights, delays	widths	98.3%	97.8%
weights, delays, widths	-	98.8%	98.0%

Table 1: /b/, /d/ and /g/ classification performance with 8 hidden units in one hidden layer. The network is initialized with random weights and constant widths.

In order to evaluate the usefulness of each adaptive parameter, the network was trained and tested with a variety of combinations of constant and adaptive parameters (see Table 1). In all cases the network was initialized with random weights and delays and constant widths σ of the input windows. All results were obtained with 8 hidden units in one hidden layer.

4 DISCUSSION

The TDNN has been shown to be a very powerful approach to phoneme recognition. The fixed time-delays and the kind of time-window were chosen partly because they were motivated by results from earlier studies [1, 7] and because they were successful from an engineering point of view. The architecture was optimized for the recognition of phonemes /b/, /d/ and /g/ and could be applied to other phonemes without significant changes. In this study we explored the performance of an artificial neural network that can automatically *learn* its own architecture by learning time-delays and widths of the gaussian input windows. The learning rules for the time-delays and the width of the windows were derived in the same way that has been shown successful for the derivation of learning rules for weights.

Our results show that time-delays in artificial neural networks can be learned automatically. The learning rule proposed in this study is able to improve performance significantly compared to fixed delays if the network is initialized with random delays.

The width of an input window determines how much local temporal context is captured by a single connection. Additionally, a large window means increased robustness against temporal misalignments of the input tokens. A large window also means that the connection transmits with a low temporal resolution. The learning rule for the widths of the windows has to compromise between increased robustness against misaligned tokens and decreased time-resolution. This is done by a gradient descent method.

If the network is initialized with the same widths that are used for the training runs with constant widths, 70 - 80% of the windows in the network get smaller during training. Our simulations show that it is possible to let a learning rule adjust parameters that determine the temporal resolution of the network.

The comparison of the performances with one adaptive parameter set (either weights, delays or widths) shows that the main parameters in the network are the weights. Delays and widths seem to be of a lesser importance, but in combination with the weights the delays can improve the performance, especially generalization. A Tempo 2 network with trained delays and widths and *random* weights can classify 70% of the phonemes correctly.

This suggests that learning temporal parameters is effective.

The network achieves results comparable to a similar network with a handtuned architecture. This suggests that the kind of learning rule could be helpful in applying time-delay neural networks to problems where no knowledge about optimal time windows is available. At higher levels of processing such adaptive networks could be used to learn rhythmic (prosodic) relationships in fluent speech and other tasks.

Acknowledgements

The authors gratefully acknowledge the support by the McDonnel-Pew Foundation (Cognitive Neuroscience Program) and ATR Interpreting Telephony Research Laboratories.

References

[1] S.E. Blumstein and K.N. Stevens. Perceptual Invariance And Onset Spectra For Stop Consonants In Different Vowel Environments. *Journal of the Acoustical Society of America*, 67:648–662, 1980.

[2] U. Bodenhausen. The Tempo Algorithm: Learning In A Neural Network With Adaptive Time-Delays. In *Proceedings of the IJCNN 90, Washington D.C.*, January 1990.

[3] U. Bodenhausen. Learning Internal Representations Of pattern Sequences In A Neural Network With Adaptive Time-Delays. In *Proceedings of the IJCNN 90, San Diego*, June 1990.

[4] S. Fahlman and C. Lebiere. The Cascade-Correlation Learning Architecture. In *Advances in Neural Information Processing Systems*. Morgan Kaufmann, 1990.

[5] S. J. Hanson. Meiosis Networks. In *Advances in Neural Information Processing Systems*. Morgan Kaufmann, 1990.

[6] Kamm, C. E.. Effects Of Neural Network Input Span On Phoneme Classification. In *Proceedings of the International Joint Conference on Neural Networks*, June 1990.

[7] D. Kewley-Port. Time Varying Features As Correlates Of Place Of Articulation In Stop Consonants. *Journal of the Acoustical Society of America*, 73:322–335, 1983.

[8] K. J. Lang, G. E. Hinton, and A.H. Waibel. A Time-Delay Neural Network Architecture For Speech Recognition. *Neural Networks Journal*, 1990.

[9] D. E. Rumelhart, G. E. Hinton, and R.J. Williams. Learning Internal Representations By Error Propagation. In J.L. McClelland and D.E. Rumelhart, editors, *Parallel Distributed Processing; Explorations in the Microstructure of Cognition*, chapter 8, pages 318–362. MIT Press, Cambridge, MA, 1986.

[10] D.W. Tank and J.J. Hopfield. Neural Computation By Concentrating Information In Time. In *Proceedings National Academy of Sciences*, pages 1896–1900, April 1987.

[11] A. Waibel, T. Hanazawa, G. Hinton, K. Shikano, and K. Lang. Phoneme Recognition Using Time-Delay Neural Networks. *IEEE, Transactions on Acoustics, Speech and Signal Processing*, March 1989.

[12] A. Waibel. Modular Construction Of Time-Delay Neural Networks For Speech Recognition. *Neural Computation, MIT-Press*, March 1989.

A Theory for Neural Networks with Time Delays

Bert de Vries
Department of Electrical Engineering
University of Florida, CSE 447
Gainesville, FL 32611

Jose C. Principe
Department of Electrical Engineering
University of Florida, CSE 444
Gainesville, FL 32611

Abstract

We present a new neural network model for processing of temporal patterns. This model, the *gamma neural model*, is as general as a convolution delay model with arbitrary weight kernels w(t). We show that the gamma model can be formulated as a (partially prewired) additive model. A temporal hebbian learning rule is derived and we establish links to related existing models for temporal processing.

1 INTRODUCTION

In this paper, we are concerned with developing neural nets with short term memory for processing of temporal patterns. In the literature, basically two ways have been reported to incorporate short-term memory in the neural system equations. The first approach utilizes reverberating (self-recurrent) units of type $\frac{dx}{dt} = -a\sigma(x) + e$, that hold a trace of the past neural net states x(t) or the input e(t). Elman (1988) and Jordan (1986) have successfully used this approach. The disadvantage of this method is the lack of weighting flexibility in the temporal domain, since the system equations are described by first order dynamics, implementing a recency gradient (exponential for linear units).

The second approach involves explicit inclusion of delays in the neural system equations. A general formulation for this type requires a time-dependent weight matrix W(t). In such a system, multiplicative interactions are substituted by temporal convolution operations, leading to the following system equations for an additive *convolution model* -

$$\frac{dx}{dt} = \int_0^t W(t-s)\,\sigma(x(s))\,ds + e. \qquad (1)$$

Due to the complexity of general convolution models, only strong simplifications of the weight kernel have been proposed. Lang et. al. (1990) use a delta function kernel, $W(t) = \sum_{k=0}^{K} W_k \delta(t - t_k)$, which is the core for the Time-Delay-Neural-Network (TDNN). Tank and Hopfield (1987) prewire W(t) as a weighted sum of dispersive delay kernels, $W(t) = \sum_{k=0}^{K} W_k (\frac{t}{\tau_k})^k e^{k(1-\frac{t}{\tau_k})} = \sum_{k=0}^{K} W_k h_k(t, \tau_k)$. The kernels $h_k(t, \tau_k)$ are the integrands of the gamma function. Tank and Hopfield described a one-layer system for classification of isolated words. We will refer to their model as a Concentration-In-Time-Network (CITN). The system parameters were non-adaptive, although a Hebbian rule equivalent in functional differential equation form was suggested.

In this paper, we will develop a theory for neural convolution models that are expressed through a sum of gamma kernels. We will show that such a gamma neural network can be reformulated as a (Grossberg) additive model. As a consequence, the substantial learning and stability theory for additive models is directly applicable to gamma models.

2 THE GAMMA NEURAL MODEL - FORMAL DERIVATION

Consider the N-dimensional convolution model -

$$\frac{dx}{dt} = -ax + W_0 y + \int_0^t ds W(t-s) y(s) + e, \tag{2}$$

where x(t), y(t)=σ(x) and e(t) are N-dimensional signals; W_0 is NxN and W(t) is NxNx $[0, \infty]$. The weight matrix W_0 communicates the direct neural interactions, whereas W(t) holds the weights for the delayed neural interactions. We will now assume that W(t) can be written as a linear combination of normalized gamma kernels, that is, -

$$W(t) = \sum_{k=1}^{K} W_k g_k(t), \tag{3}$$

where -

$$g_k(t) = \frac{\mu^k}{(k-1)!} t^{k-1} e^{-\mu t}, \tag{4}$$

where μ is a decay parameter and k a (lag) order parameter. If W(t) decays exponentially to zero for $t \to \infty$, then it follows from the completeness of Laguerre polynomials that this approximation can be made arbitrarily close (Cohen et. al.,

1979). In other words, for all physical plausible weight kernels there is a K such that W(t) can be expressed as (3), (4). The following properties hold for the gamma kernels $g_k(t)$ -

- *[1] The gamma kernels are related by a set of linear homogeneous ODEs -*

$$\frac{dg_1}{dt} = -\mu g_1$$
$$\frac{dg_k}{dt} = -\mu g_k + \mu g_{k-1}, \quad \text{k=2,..,K} \tag{5}$$

- *[2] The peak value ($\frac{dg_k}{dt} = 0$) occurs at $t_p = \frac{k-1}{\mu}$.*

- *[3] The area of the gamma kernels is a normalized, that is,* $\int_0^\infty ds g_k(s) = 1$.

Substitution of (3) into (2) yields -

$$\frac{dx}{dt} = -ax + \sum_{k=0}^{K} W_k y_k + e, \tag{6}$$

where we defined $y_0(t) = y(t)$ and the *gamma state variables* -

$$y_k(t) = \int_0^t ds g_k(t-s) y_0(s), \quad \text{k=1,..,K}. \tag{7}$$

The gamma state variables hold memory traces of the neural states $y_0(t)$. The important question is how to compute $y_k(t)$. Differentiating (7) using Leibniz' rule yields -

$$\frac{dy_k}{dt} = \int_0^t \frac{\partial}{\partial t} g_k(t-s) y(s) ds + g_k(0) y(t). \tag{8}$$

We now utilize gamma kernel property [1] (eq. (5)) to obtain -

$$\frac{dy_k}{dt} = \int_0^t [-\mu g_k(t-s) + \mu g_{k-1}(t-s)] y(s) ds + g_k(0) y(t) \tag{9}$$

Note that since $g_k(0) = 0$ for $k \geq 2$ and $g_1(0) = \mu$, (9) evaluates to -

$$\frac{dy_k}{dt} = -\mu y_k + \mu y_{k-1}, \quad \text{k=1,..,K}. \tag{10}$$

The gamma model is described by (6) and (10). This extended set of ordinary differential equations (ODEs) is equivalent to the convolution model, described by the set of functional differential equations (2), (3) and (4).

It is a valid question to ask whether the system of ODEs that describes the gamma model can still be expressed as a neural network model. The answer is affirmative, since the gamma model can be formulated as a regular (Grossberg) additive model.

To see this, define the N(K+1)-dimensional augmented state vector $X = \begin{bmatrix} x \\ y_1 \\ | \\ y_K \end{bmatrix}$, the neural output signal $Y = \begin{bmatrix} \sigma(x) \\ y_1 \\ | \\ y_K \end{bmatrix}$, an external input $E = \begin{bmatrix} e \\ 0 \\ | \\ 0 \end{bmatrix}$, a diagonal matrix of decay parameters $M = \begin{bmatrix} a & & 0 \\ & \mu & \\ 0 & & \mu \end{bmatrix}$ and the weight (super)matrix $\Omega = \begin{bmatrix} W_0 & W_1 & \dots & W_K \\ \mu & & & 0 \\ & \ddots & & \\ 0 & & \mu & 0 \end{bmatrix}$. Then the gamma model can be rewritten in the following form -

$$\frac{dX}{dt} = -MX + \Omega Y + E, \tag{11}$$

the familiar Grossberg additive model.

3 HEBBIAN LEARNING IN THE GAMMA MODEL

The additive model formulation of the gamma model allows a direct generalization of learning techniques to the gamma model. Note however that the augmented state vector X contains the gamma state variables $y_1,...,y_K$, basically (dispersively) delayed neural states. As a result, although associative learning rules for conventional additive models only encode the simultaneous correlation of neural states, the gamma learning rules are able to encode temporal associations as well. Here we present Hebbian learning for the gamma model.

The Hebbian postulate is often mathematically translated to a learning rule of the form $\frac{dW}{dt} = \eta x(t) y^T(t)$, where η is a learning rate constant, x the neural activation vector and y^T the neuron output signal vector. This procedure is not likely to encode temporal order, since information about past states is not incorporated in the learning equations.

Tank and Hopfield (1987) proposed a generalized Hebbian learning rule with delays that can be written as -

$$\frac{dW}{dt} = \eta x(t) \left[\int_0^t ds g(s) y(t-s) \right]^T, \qquad (12)$$

where $g(s)$ is a normalized delay kernel. Notice that (12) is a functional differential equation, for which explicit solutions and convergence criteria are not known (for most implementations of $g(s)$). In the gamma model, the signals $\int_0^t ds g_k(s) y(t-s)$ are computed by the system and locally available as $y_k(t)$ at the synaptic junctions W_k. Thus, in the gamma model, (12) reduces to -

$$\frac{dW_k}{dt} = \eta x(t) y_k^T(t) . \qquad (13)$$

This learning rule encodes simultaneous correlations (for k=0) as well as temporal associations (for $k \geq 1$). Since the gamma Hebb rule is structurally similar to the conventional Hebb rule, it is also local both in time and space.

4 RELATION TO OTHER MODELS

The gamma model is related to Tank and Hopfield 's CITN model in that both models decompose W(t) into a linear combination of gamma kernels. The weights in the CITN system are preset and fixed. The gamma model, expressed as a regular additive system, allows conventional adaptation procedures to train the system parameters; μ and K adapt the depth and shape of the memory, while $W_0,..,W_K$ encode spatiotemporal correlations between neural states.

Time-Delay-Neural-Nets (TDNN) are characterized by a tapped delay line memory structure. The relation is best illustrated by an example. Consider a linear one-layer feedforward convolution model, described by -

$$
\begin{aligned}
x(t) &= e(t) \\
y(t) &= \int_0^t W(t-s)\,x(s)\,ds
\end{aligned}
\tag{14}
$$

where x(t), e(t) and y(t) are N-dimensional signals and W(t) a NxNx $[0,\infty]$ dimensional weight matrix. This system can be approximated in discrete time by -

$$
\begin{aligned}
x(n) &= e(n) \\
y(n) &= \sum_{m=0}^{n} W(n-m)\,x(m)
\end{aligned}
\tag{15}
$$

which is the TDNN formulation. An alternative approximation of the convolution model by means of a (discrete-time) gamma model, is described by (figure 1) -

$$
\begin{aligned}
x_0(n) &= e(n) \\
x_k(n) &= (1-\mu)\,x_k(n-1) + \mu x_{k-1}(n-1) \quad \text{k=1,..,K} \\
y(n) &= \sum_{k=0}^{K} W_k x_k(n)
\end{aligned}
\tag{16}
$$

The recursive memory structure in the gamma model is stable for $0 \le \mu \le 2$, but an interesting memory structure is obtained only for $0 < \mu \le 1$. For $\mu = 0$, this system collapses to a static additive net. In this case, no information from past signal values are stored in the net. For $0 < \mu < 1$, the system works as a discrete-time CITN. The gamma memory structure consists of a cascade of first-order leaky integrators. Since the total memory structure is of order K, the shape of the memory is not restricted to a recency gradient. The effective memory depth approximates $\frac{K}{\mu}$ for small μ. For $\mu = 1$, the gamma model becomes a TDNN. In this case, memory is implemented by a tapped delay line. The strength of the gamma model is that the parameters μ and K can be adapted by conventional additive learning procedures. Thus, the optimal temporal structure of the neural system, whether of CITN or TDNN type, is part of the training phase in a gamma neural net. Finally, the application of the gamma memory structure is of course not limited to one-layer feedforward systems. The topologies suggested by Jordan (1986) and Elman (1988) can easily be extended to include gamma memory.

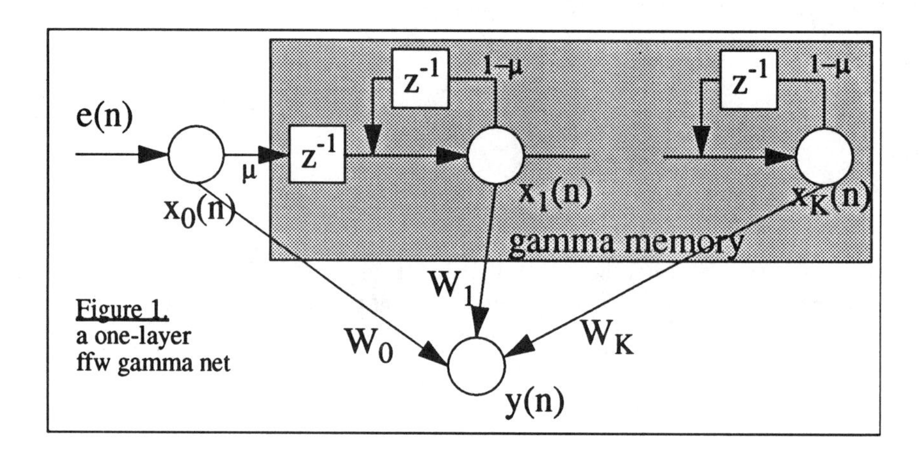

Figure 1.
a one-layer
ffw gamma net

5 CONCLUSIONS

We have introduced the gamma neural model, a neural net model for temporal processing, that generalizes most existing approaches, such as the CITN and TDNN models. The model can be described as a conventional dynamic additive model, enabling direct application of existing learning procedures for additive models. In the gamma model, dynamic objects are encoded by the same learning equations as static objects.

Acknowledgments

This work has been partially supported by NSF grants ECS-8915218 and DDM-8914084.

References

Cohen et. al., 1979. Stable oscillations in single species growth models with hereditary effects. *Mathematical Biosciences* 44:255-268, 1979.

DeVries and Principe, 1990. The gamma neural net - A new model for temporal processing. submitted to *Neural Networks,* Nov.1990.

Elman, 1988. Finding structure in time. *CRL technical report 8801*, 1988.

Jordan, 1986. Attractor dynamics and parallelism in a connectionist sequential machine. *Proc. Cognitive Science* 1986.

Lang et. al. 1990. A time-delay neural network architecture for isolated word recognition. *Neural Networks, vol.3 (1)*, 1990.

Tank and Hopfield, 1987. Concentrating information in time: analog neural networks with applications to speech recognition problems. *1st int. conf. on neural networks,* IEEE, 1987.

ART2/BP architecture for adaptive estimation of dynamic processes

Einar Sørheim*
Department of Computer Science
UNIK, Kjeller
University of Oslo
N-2007 Norway

Abstract

The goal has been to construct a supervised artificial neural network that learns incrementally an unknown mapping. As a result a network consisting of a combination of ART2 and backpropagation is proposed and is called an "ART2/BP" network. The ART2 network is used to build and focus a supervised backpropagation network. The ART2/BP network has the advantage of being able to dynamically expand itself in response to input patterns containing new information. Simulation results show that the ART2/BP network outperforms a classical maximum likelihood method for the estimation of a discrete dynamic and nonlinear transfer function.

1 INTRODUCTION

Most current neural network architectures such as backpropagation require a cyclic presentation of the entire training set to converge. They are thus not very well suited for adaptive estimation tasks where the training vectors arrive one by one, and where the network may never see the same training vector twice. The ART2/BP network system is an attempt to construct a network that works well on these problems.

Main features of our ART2/BP are :

- implements incremental supervised learning
- dynamically self-expanding

*e-mail address: einar@tellus.unik.no or einars@ifi.uio.no

- learning of a novel training pattern does not wash away memory of previous training patterns
- short convergence time for learning a new pattern

2 BACKGROUND

Adaptive estimation of nonlinear functions requires some basic features of the estimation algorithm.

1. *Incremental learning*
   The input/output pairs arrive to the estimation machine one by one. By accumulating the input/output pairs into a training set and rerun the training procedure at every arrival of a new input/output pair, one could use a conventional method. Obvious disadvantages would however be
   - huge learning time required as the size of the training set increases.
   - an upper limit, N, on the number of elements in the training set will have to be set. The training set will then be a gliding horizon of the N last input/output pairs, and information prior to the N last input/output pairs will be lost.
2. *Plasticity*
   Learning of a new input/output pair should not wash away the memory of previously learned nonconflicting input/output pairs. With most existing feed-forward supervised nets this is hard to accomplish, though some efforts have been made (Otwell 90). Some networks, like the ART-family and RCN (Ryan 1988) are plastic but they are self-organizing, not supervised.

To summarize:
Need a supervised network that learns incrementally the mapping of an unknown system and that can be used to predict future outputs. The system in question maps analog vectors to analog vectors.

3 COMBINED ARCHITECTURE

In the proposed network architecture an ART2 network controls a BP network, see Figure 1.

The BP-network consists of many relatively small subnetworks where the subnets are specialized on one particular domain of the input space. ART2 controls how the input space is divided among the subnets and the total amount of subnets needed.

The ART2 network analyzes the input part of the input/output pairs as they arrive to the system. For a given input pattern $\vec{i}_x$, ART2 finds the category C_x which has the closest resemblance to $\vec{i}_x$. If this resemblance is good enough, $\vec{i}_x$ is of category C_x and the LTM-weights of C_x are updated. The BP-subnetwork BP_x, connected to C_x, is as a consequence activated and relearning of BP_x is done. The learning set consists of a "representative" set of the neighbouring subnets patterns and a small number of the previous patterns belonging to category C_x. To summarize the algorithm goes as follows:

1. Send input vector to ART2 network
2. ART2 classification.
3. If in learning mode adjust ART2 LTM weights of the winning node.
4. Send input to the back propagation network connected to the winning ART2 node.
5. If in learning mode :
   - find a representative training set.
   - do epoch learning on training set.

   Otherwise
   - compute output of the selected back propagation network.
6. Go to 1. for new input vector.

The ART2/BP neural network can be used for adaptive estimation of nonlinear dynamic processes. The mapping to be estimated then is

$$\begin{aligned} \vec{y}(t+\delta t) &= \vec{f}(\vec{u}(t), \vec{y}(t)) \\ \vec{u}(t) &\in \Re^m \\ \vec{y}(t) &\in \Re^n \end{aligned} \tag{1}$$

The input/output pairs will be $\vec{io} = [\vec{u}(t), \vec{y}(t), \vec{y}(t+\delta t)]$, denote the input part of $\vec{io}$: $\vec{i} = [\vec{u}(t), \vec{y}(t)]$ and the output part of $\vec{io}$: $\vec{o} = \vec{y}(t+\delta t)$.

4 ART2 MODIFIED

ART2 was developed by Carpenter& Grossberg see (Carpenter 1987) and (Carpenter 1988). ART2 categorizes arbitrary sequences of analog input patterns, and the categories can be of arbitrary coarseness. For a detailed description of ART2, see (Carpenter 1987).

4.1 MODIFICATION

In the standard ART2-algorithm input vectors (patterns) are normalized. For this application it is not desired to classify parallel vectors of different magnitude as belonging to the same category. By adding an extra element to the input vector where this element is simply

$$i_{n+1} = ||\vec{i}||^2 \tag{2}$$

the new input vector becomes

$$\tilde{\vec{i}} = [\vec{i}, ||\vec{i}||^2] \tag{3}$$

From a scaled vector of $\tilde{\vec{i}}$: $\tilde{\vec{x}} = a \cdot \tilde{\vec{i}}$ the original vector $\vec{i}$ could easily be found as :

$$\begin{aligned} i_i &= x_i \cdot \frac{x_{n+1}}{||\tilde{\vec{x}}||^2} \\ \tilde{\vec{x}} &= [x_1, x_2, ..., x_n] \end{aligned} \tag{4}$$

and by using the augmented $\vec{\tilde{i}}$ as the input to ART2 instead of $\vec{i}$ one can at any point in F1(representation layer) and F2(categorization layer) generate the corresponding non-normalized vector. The F2 node competition is modified so that the node having bottom-up LTM weights with the smallest distance (distance being the euclidean norm) to the F1 layer pattern code wins the competition. The distance d_J of F2 node J is given by:

$$
\begin{aligned}
d_J &= \|\vec{p} - \vec{z_J}\| \qquad (5)\\
\|\ \| &: \quad being\ the\ l_2 - norm\\
\vec{p} &: \quad F1\ pattern\ code.\\
\vec{z_J} &: \quad bottom - up\ LTM\ weights\ of\ F2\ node\ J
\end{aligned}
$$

Reset is done by calculating the distance d between the F1 layer pattern code $\vec{p}$ and $\vec{i}$:

$$d = \|\vec{p} - \vec{i}\| \qquad (6)$$

and comparing it to a largest acceptable bound ρ . If $d > \rho$ the winning node is inhibited and a new node will be created. If $d \leq \rho$ LTM-patterns of the winning node J are modified (learning).

5 BACK PROPAGATION NETWORK

The backpropagation network used in this work is of the standard feedforward type, see (Rumelhart 1986) . The number of hidden layers and nodes should be kept low in the subnetworks, for the problems in our simulations we used 1 hidden layer with 2 nodes. As for training algorithms several different kinds have been tried:

- Standard back propagation (SBP)
- A modified back propagation (MBP) method similar to the one used in the BPS simulator from George Mason University.
- Quickprop (Q).
- A quasi-Newton method (BFGS).

All of these except SBP show similar performance in my test cases.

The BP-networks performs as an interpolator in this algorithm and any good interpolation algorithm can be used instead of BP. Approximation theory gives several interesting techniques for approximation/interpolation of multidimensional functions such as Radial Basis Functions and Hyper Basis Functions, for further detail see (Poggio 90). These methods requires a representative training set where the input part determines the location of centers in the input space. The ART2 algorithm can be used for determining these centers in an adaptive way and thus making possible an incremental version of the approximation theory techniques. This idea has not been tested yet, but is an interesting concept for further research.

6 LEARNING

Learning in ART2/BP is a two stage process. First the input patterns is sent to the ART2 network for categorizing and learning . ART2 will then activate the BP subnetwork that is a local expert on patterns of the same category as the input pattern, and learning of this subnetwork will occur. A training set that is representative for the domain of the input space has to be found. Let a small number of the last categorized input/output pairs be allocated to its corresponding subnet to provide a part of the training set. Denote such a set as L_IO_C, (C being the category). Define the location of F2 node J to be its bottom-up weights $\vec{z}_J$. Let the current input $\vec{i}_x$ define an origin, then find the F2 nodes closest to origin in each n-ant of the input space. Call this set of nodes N_x and the set of last input/output pairs stored in these nodes N_IO_x. The training set is then chosen to be:
$T_x = N\_IO_x \cup L\_IO_x$
Before training, the elements in T_x are scaled to increase accuracy and to accelerate learning. BP-learning is then performed, the stopping criteria being a fixed error term or a maximum number of iterations.

7 ESTIMATION

In estimation mode learning in the network is turned off. Given an input thenetwork will produce an output that hopefully will be close to the output of the real system.

The ART2-network selects a winning node in the same way as described before but now the reset assembly is not activated. Then the input is fed to the corresponding BP subnetwork and its output is used as an estimate of the original functions output.

Because each subnetwork is scaled to cover the domain of the input space made up by the complex hull $Co(T_x)$ of its training set T_x, the entire ART2/BP network will cover the complex hull $Co(T) \subset \Re^{n+m}$ where:
$T =$
$\{set\ of\ all\ previous\ \vec{i}'s\ used\ to\ train\ the\ network\}$
Good estimation/prediction can thus be expected if $\vec{i} \in Co(T)$. This means that if the input vector $\vec{i}$ lies in a domain of the input space that has not been previously explored by the elements in the training set, the network will generalize poorly.

8 EXAMPLE

The ART2/BP network has been used to estimate a dynamic model of a tank filled with liquid. The liquid level is sampled every δt time interval and the ART2/BP network is used to estimate the discrete dynamic nonlinear transfer function of the liquid level as a function of inlet liquid flow and previous liquid level. That is, we want to find a good estimate $\hat{f}(\cdot,\cdot)$ of:

$$\begin{aligned} y(t+\delta t) &= f(u(t), y(t)) \qquad (7) \\ u(t) &= inlet\ liquid\ flow\ at\ time\ t \\ y(t) &= liquid\ level\ at\ time\ t \end{aligned}$$

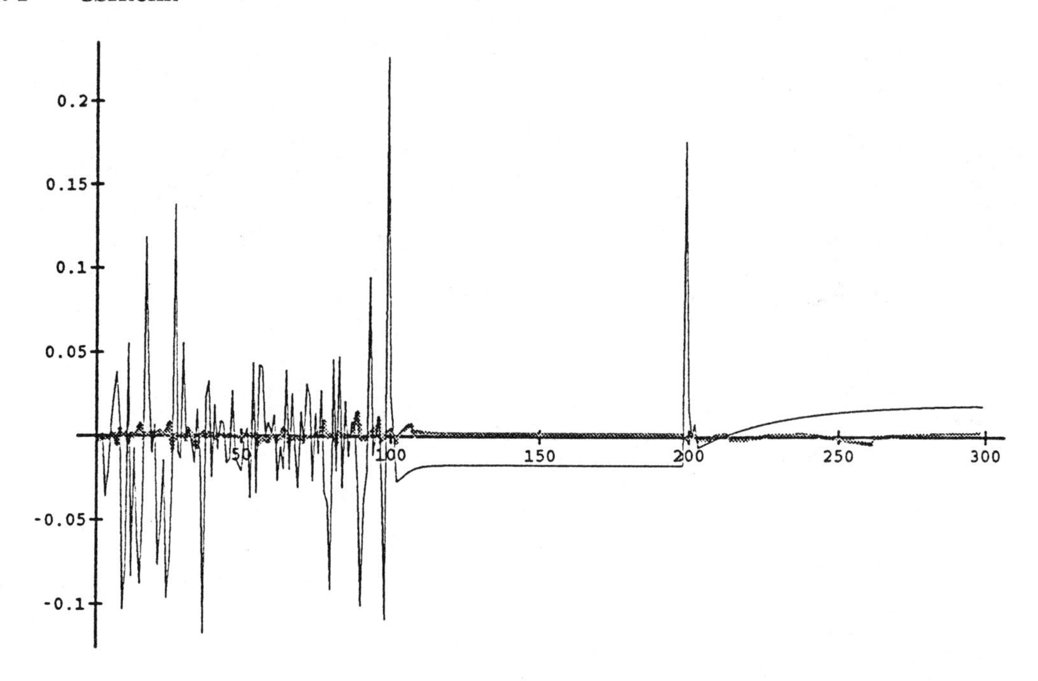

black line : ARMA model estimation error $(y(t+\delta t) - \hat{y}_{ARMA}(t+\delta t))$
grey line : ART2/BP estimation error $(y(t+\delta t) - \hat{y}_{ART2/BP}(t+\delta t))$

Figure 1: Comparison of the estimation error of the ARMA model and the ART2/BP network

To increase the nonlinearities of the transfer function, the area of the tank varies with a step function of the liquid level. The BP subnetworks have 2 input nodes, 1 hidden layer with 2 neurons and a single neuron output layer. In the simulations $\rho = 0.04$ and the last three categorized input/output pairs are stored at every subnetwork. As the input space is 2-dimensional giving 4 neighbouring nodes the maximum size of the training set 7 input/output pairs. After a learning period of 1000 samples with random inlet flow , three test cases are run with the network in estimation mode. The network had then formed about 140 categories. The same set of simulation data is also run through an offline maximum likelihood method to estimate a linear ARMA model of the plant, see (Ljung 1983). /

Figure 1 shows the simulation results of the three test cases where :

samples 1-100 : random input flow.

samples 101-200 : constant input flow at a low level.

samples 201-300 : constant input flow at a high level.

In Figure 1, the estimation errors of the two methods are compared. For the first 100 samples with stochastic input flow, the estimation error variance of the

ART2/BP network is roughly a factor 10 less than that of the ARMA-model. The performance of ART2/BP is also significantly better for the constant input flow cases, here the ARMA model has an error of ~ 0.02 while the ART2/BP-error is ~ 0.002. The overall improvement in estimation error is a reduction of roughly 0.1 . Also keep in mind that ART2/BP is compared to an offline maximum likelihood method while ART2/BP clearly is an online method. The online version of the maximum likelihood would most probably have given a worse performance than the offline version.

9 CONCLUSION/COMMENTS

The proposed ART2/BP neural network architecture offers some unique features compared to backpropagation. It provides incremental learning and can be applied to truly adaptive estimation tasks. In our example it also outperforms a classical maximum likelihood method for the estimation of a discrete dynamic nonlinear transfer function. Future work will be the investigation of ART2/BP's properties for multistep-ahead prediction of dynamic nonlinear transfer functions, and embedding ART2/BP in a neural adaptive controller.

Acknowledgments

Special thanks to Steve Lehar at Boston University for providing me with his ART2 simulation program. It proved to be crucial for getting a quick start on ART2 and understanding the concept.

References

Carpenter, G.A. & Grossberg, S. (1987). ART2: Self-organization of stable category recognition codes for analog input patterns. *Applied Optics* pp 4919-4930.

Carpenter, G.A. & Grossberg, S. (1988). The ART of adaptive pattern recognition by a self-organizing neural network.*Computer* **21** pp 77-88.

Fahlman, S.E. (1988). Faster-Learning Variations on Back-Propagation: An Empirical Study. *Proceedings of the 1988 Connectionist Models Summer School.* Morgan Kaufmann.

Ljung, L. & Søderstrøm (1983). Theory and practice of recursive identification. *The MIT press*, Cambridge, MA.

Otwell, K. (1990). Incremental backpropagation learning from novelty-based orthogonalization. *Proceedings IJNN90* .

Poggio, T., Girosi, F. (1990). Networks for Approximation and Learning. *Proceedings of the IEEE*,Vol. 78, No. 9.

Rumelhart, D.E., Hinton, G.E., & Williams, R.J. (1986). Parallel Distributed Processing: Explorations in the microstructure of Cognition, Vol. 1. *The MIT Press*,Cambridge, MA.

Ryan, T. W. (1988). The resonance correlation network. *Proceedings IJNN88.*

Statistical Mechanics of Temporal Association in Neural Networks with Delayed Interactions

Andreas V.M. Herz
Division of Chemistry
Caltech 139-74
Pasadena, CA 91125

Zhaoping Li
School of Natural Sciences
Institute for Advanced Study
Princeton, NJ 08540

J. Leo van Hemmen
Physik-Department
der TU München
D-8046 Garching, FRG

Abstract

We study the representation of static patterns and temporal associations in neural networks with a broad distribution of signal delays. For a certain class of such systems, a simple intuitive understanding of the spatio-temporal computation becomes possible with the help of a novel Lyapunov functional. It allows a quantitative study of the asymptotic network behavior through a statistical mechanical analysis. We present analytic calculations of both retrieval quality and storage capacity and compare them with simulation results.

1 INTRODUCTION

Basic computational functions of associative neural structures may be analytically studied within the framework of attractor neural networks where *static patterns* are stored as stable *fixed-points* for the system's dynamics. If the interactions between single neurons are instantaneous and mediated by symmetric couplings, there is a Lyapunov function for the retrieval dynamics (Hopfield 1982). The global computation corresponds in that case to a downhill motion in an energy landscape created by the stored information. Methods of equilibrium statistical mechanics may be applied and permit a quantitative analysis of the asymptotic network behavior (Amit et al. 1985, 1987). The existence of a Lyapunov function is thus of great conceptual as well as technical importance. Nevertheless, one should be aware that environmental inputs to a neural net always provide information in *both space and time*. It is therefore desirable to extend the original Hopfield scheme and to explore possibilities for a joint representation of static patterns and temporal associations.

Signal delays are omnipresent in the brain and play an important role in biological information processing. Their incorporation into theoretical models seems to be rather convincing, especially if one includes the distribution of the delay times involved. Kleinfeld (1986) and Sompolinsky and Kanter (1986) proposed models for temporal associations, but they only used a *single* delay line between two neurons. Tank and Hopfield (1987) presented a feedforward architecture for sequence recognition based on multiple delays, but they just considered information relative to the *very end* of a given sequence. Besides these deficiences, both approaches lack the quality to acquire knowledge through a true learning mechanism: Synaptic efficacies have to be calculated by hand which is certainly not satisfactory both from a neurobiological point of view and also for applications in artificial intelligence.

This drawback has been overcome by a careful interpretation of the Hebb principle (1949) for neural networks with a *broad* distribution of transmission delays (Herz et al. 1988, 1989). After the system has been taught stationary patterns and temporal sequences — by the *same* principle ! — it reproduces them with high precission when triggered suitably. In the present contribution, we focus on a special class of such delay networks and introduce a Lyapunov (energy) functional for the deterministic retrieval dynamics (Li and Herz 1990). We thus generalize Hopfield's approach to the domain of temporal associations. Through an extension of the usual formalism of equilibrium statistical mechanics to time-dependent phenomena, we analyze the network performance under a stochastic (noisy) dynamics. We derive quantitative results on both the retrieval quality and storage capacity, and close with some remarks on possible generalizations of this approach.

2 DYNAMICS OF THE NEURONS

Throughout what follows, we describe a neural network as a collection of N two-state neurons with activities $S_i = 1$ for a firing cell and $S_i = -1$ for a quiescent one. The cells are connected by synapses with modifiable efficacies $J_{ij}(\tau)$. Here τ denotes the delay for the information transport from j to i. We focus on a soliton-like propagation of neural signals, characteristic for the (axonal) transmission of action potentials, and consider a model where each pair of neurons is linked by *several* axons with delays $0 \le \tau \le \tau_{\max}$. Other architectures with only a single link have been considered elsewhere (Coolen and Gielen 1988; Herz et al. 1988, 1989; Kerszberg and Zippelius 1990). External stimuli are fed into the system via receptors $\sigma_i = \pm 1$ with input sensitivity γ. The postsynaptic potentials are given by

$$h_i(t) = (1-\gamma) \sum_{j=1}^{N} \sum_{\tau=0}^{\tau_{\max}} J_{ij}(\tau) S_j(t-\tau) + \gamma \sigma_i(t) \ . \tag{1}$$

We concentrate on synchronous dynamics (Little 1974) with basic time step $\Delta t = 1$. Consequently, signal delays take nonnegative integer values. Synaptic noise is described by a stochastic Glauber dynamics with noise level $\beta = T^{-1}$ (Peretto 1984),

$$\text{Prob}\left[S_i(t+1) = \pm 1\right] = \frac{1}{2}\{1 \pm \tanh[\beta h_i(t)]\} \ , \tag{2}$$

where Prob denotes probability. For $\beta \to \infty$, we arrive at a deterministic dynamics,

$$S_i(t+1) = \text{sgn}[h_i(t)] \equiv \begin{cases} 1, & \text{if } h_i(t) > 0 \\ -1, & \text{if } h_i(t) < 0 \end{cases} . \tag{3}$$

3 HEBBIAN LEARNING

During a learning session the synaptic strengths may change according to the Hebb principle (1949). We focus on a connection with delay τ between neurons i and j. According to Hebb, the corresponding efficacy $J_{ij}(\tau)$ will be increased if cell j takes part in *firing* cell i. In its physiological context, this rule was originaly formulated for excitatory synapses only, but for simplicity, we apply it to all synapses.

Due to the delay τ in (1) and the parallel dynamics (2), it takes $\tau+1$ time steps until neuron j actually influences the *state* of neuron i. $J_{ij}(\tau)$ thus changes by an amount proportional to the product of $S_j(t-\tau)$ and $S_i(t+1)$. Starting with $J_{ij}(\tau)=0$, we obtain after P learning sessions, labeled by μ and each of duration D_μ,

$$J_{ij}(\tau) = \varepsilon(\tau)N^{-1}\sum_{\mu=1}^{P}\sum_{t_\mu=1}^{D_\mu} S_i(t_\mu+1)S_j(t_\mu-\tau) \equiv \varepsilon(\tau)\tilde{J}_{ij}(\tau) \ . \tag{4}$$

The parameters $\varepsilon(\tau)$, normalized by $\sum_{\tau=0}^{\tau_{max}} \varepsilon(\tau) = 1$, take morphological characteristics of the delay lines into account; N^{-1} is a scaling factor useful for the theoretical analysis. By (4), synapses act as microscopic feature detectors during the learning sessions and store correlations of the taught sequences in both space (i,j) and time (τ). In general, they will be asymmetric in the sense that $J_{ij}(\tau) \neq J_{ji}(\tau)$.

During learning, we set $T=0$ and $\gamma=1$ to achieve a "clamped learning scenario" where the system evolves strictly according to the external stimuli, $S_i(t_\mu)=\sigma_i(t_\mu-1)$. We study the case where all input sequences $\sigma_i(t_\mu)$ are cyclic with equal periods $D_\mu = D$, i.e., $\sigma_i(t_\mu) = \sigma_i(t_\mu \pm D)$ for all μ. In passing we note that one should offer the sequences already τ_{max} time steps before allowing synaptic plasticity *à la* (4) so that both S_i and S_j are in well defined states during the actual learning sessions. We define patterns $\xi_{ia}^{\mu 0}$ by $\xi_{ia}^{\mu 0} \equiv \sigma_i(t_\mu = a)$ for $0 \leq a < D$ and get

$$J_{ij}(\tau) = \varepsilon(\tau)N^{-1}\sum_{\mu=1}^{P}\sum_{a=0}^{D-1} \xi_{i,a+1}^{\mu 0}\xi_{j,a-\tau}^{\mu 0} \ . \tag{5}$$

Our learning scheme is thus a generalization of outer-product rules to spatio-temporal patterns. As in the following, temporal arguments of the sequence pattern states ξ and the synaptic couplings should always be understood *modulo D*.

4 LYAPUNOV FUNCTIONAL

Using formulae (1)-(5), one may derive equations of motion for macroscopic order parameters (Herz et al. 1988, 1989) but this kind of analysis only applies to the case $P \ll \log N$. However, note that from (4) and (5), we get $\tilde{J}_{ij}(\tau) = \tilde{J}_{ji}(D-(2+\tau))$. For all networks whose *a priori* weights $\varepsilon(\tau)$ obey $\varepsilon(\tau) = \varepsilon(D-(2+\tau))$ we have thus found an "extended synaptic symmetry" (Li and Herz 1990),

$$J_{ij}(\tau) = J_{ji}(D-(2+\tau)) \ , \tag{6}$$

generalizing Hopfield's symmetry assumption $J_{ij} = J_{ji}$ in a natural way to the temporal domain. To establish a Lyapunov functional for the noiseless retrieval dynamics (3), we take $\gamma=0$ in (1) and define

$$H(t) \equiv -\frac{1}{2} \sum_{i,j=1}^{N} \sum_{a,\tau=0}^{D-1} J_{ij}(\tau) S_i(t-a) S_j(t-(a+\tau+1)\%D) , \tag{7}$$

where $a\%b \equiv a \bmod b$. The functional H depends on *all* states between $t+1-D$ and t so that solutions with *constant* H, like D-periodic cycles, need not be static fixed points of the dynamics. By (1), (5) and (6), the difference $\Delta H(t) \equiv H(t)-H(t-1)$ is

$$\Delta H(t) = -\sum_{i=1}^{N} [S_i(t)-S_i(t-D)]\, h_i(t-1) - \frac{\varepsilon(D-1)}{2N} \sum_{\mu=1}^{P} \sum_{a=0}^{D-1} \{\sum_{i=1}^{N} \xi_{ia}^{\mu 0} [S_i(t)-S_i(t-D)]\}^2 . \tag{8}$$

The dynamics (3) implies that the first term is nonpositive. Since $\varepsilon(\tau) \geq 0$, the same holds true for the second one. For finite N, H is bounded and ΔH has to vanish as $t \to \infty$. The system therefore settles into a state with $S_i(t)=S_i(t-D)$ for all i.

We have thus exposed two important facts: (a) the retrieval dynamics is governed by a Lyapunov functional, and (b) the system relaxes to a static state or a limit cycle with $S_i(t)=S_i(t-D)$ — oscillatory solutions with the *same* period as that of the taught cycles or a period which is equal to an integer fraction of D.

Stepping back for an overview, we notice that H is a Lyapunov functional for all networks which exhibit an "extended synaptic symmetry" (6) and for which the matrix $\mathbf{J}(D-1)$ is positive semi-definite. The Hebbian synapses (4) constitute an important special case and will be the main subject of our further discussion.

5 STATISTICAL MECHANICS

We now prove that a limit cycle of the retrieval dynamics indeed resembles a stored sequence. We proceed in two steps. First, we demonstrate that our task concerning cyclic temporal associations can be mapped onto a symmetric network without delays. Second, we apply equilibrium statistical mechanics to study such *"equivalent systems"* and derive analytic results for the retrieval quality and storage capacity.

D-periodic oscillatory solutions of the retrieval dynamics can be interpreted as static states in a "D-plicated" system with D columns and N rows of cells with activities S_{ia}. A network state will be written $A=(A_0, A_1, \ldots, A_{D-1})$ with $A_a \equiv \{S_{ia}; 1 \leq i \leq N\}$. To reproduce the parallel dynamics of the original system, neurons S_{ia} with $a = t\%D$ are updated at time t. The time evolution of the new network therefore has a pseudo-sequential characteristic: synchronous within single columns and sequentially ordered with respect to these columns. Accordingly, the neural activities at time t are given by $S_{ia}(t) \equiv S_i(a+n_t)$ for $a \leq t\%D$ and $S_{ia}(t) \equiv S_i(a+n_t-D)$ for $a > t\%D$, where n_t is defined through $t \equiv n_t + t\%D$. Due to (6), *symmetric* efficacies $J_{ij}^{ab} = J_{ji}^{ba}$ may be contructed for the new system by

$$J_{ij}^{ab} = J_{ij}((b-a-1)\%D) , \tag{9}$$

allowing a well-defined Hamiltonian, equal to that of a Hopfield net of size ND,

$$H = -\frac{1}{2} \sum_{i,j=1}^{N} \sum_{a,b=0}^{D-1} J_{ij}^{ab} S_{ia} S_{jb} . \tag{10}$$

An evaluation of (10) in terms of the former state variables reveals that it is identical to the Lyapunov functional (7). The interpretation, however, is changed: a *limit cycle* of period D in the original network corresponds to a *fixed-point* of the new system of size ND. We have thus shown that the time evolution of a delay network with extended symmetry can be understood in terms of a downhill motion in the energy landscape of its "equivalent system".

For Hebbian couplings (5), the new efficacies J_{ij}^{ab} take a particularly simple form if we define patterns $\{\xi_{ia}^{\mu\alpha}; 1 \leq i \leq N, 0 \leq \alpha \leq D-1\}$ by $\xi_{ia}^{\mu\alpha} \equiv \xi_{i,(a-\alpha)\%D}^{\mu 0}$, i.e., if we create column-shifted copies of the prototype $\xi_{ia}^{\mu 0}$. Setting $\mathcal{E}_{ab} \equiv \varepsilon\big((b-a-1)\%D\big) = \mathcal{E}_{ba}$ leads to

$$J_{ij}^{ab} = \mathcal{E}_{ab} N^{-1} \sum_{\mu=1}^{P} \sum_{\alpha=0}^{D-1} \xi_{ia}^{\mu\alpha} \xi_{jb}^{\mu\alpha} \,. \tag{11}$$

Storing one cycle $\sigma_i(t_\mu) = \xi_{ia}^{\mu 0}$ in the delay network thus corresponds to memorizing D shifted duplicates $\xi_{ia}^{\mu\alpha}$, $0 \leq \alpha < D$, in the equivalent system, reflecting that a D-cycle can be retrieved in D different time-shifted versions in the original network.

If, in the second step, we now switch to the stochastic dynamics (2), the important question arises whether H also determines the equilibrium distribution ρ of the system. This need not be true since the column-wise dynamics of the equivalent network differs from both the Little and Hopfield model. An elaborate proof (Li and Herz, 1990), however, shows that there is indeed an equilibrium distribution *à la* Gibbs,

$$\rho(A) = Z^{-1} \exp[-\beta H(A)] \,, \tag{12}$$

where $Z \equiv \mathrm{Tr}_{\mathrm{A}} \exp[-\beta H(A)]$. In passing we note that for $D = 2$ there are only links with zero delay. By (6) we have $J_{ij}(0) = J_{ji}(0)$, i.e., we are dealing with a symmetric Little model. We may introduce a reduced probability distribution $\tilde{\rho}$ for this special case, $\tilde{\rho}(A_1) \equiv \mathrm{Tr}_{\mathrm{A}_0}\, \rho(A_0 A_1)$, and obtain $\tilde{\rho}(A_1) = Z^{-1} \exp[-\beta \tilde{H}(A_1)]$ with

$$\tilde{H} \equiv -\beta^{-1} \sum_{i=1}^{N} \ln[2 \cosh(\beta \sum_{j=1}^{N} J_{ij} S_j)] \,. \tag{13}$$

We thus have recovered both the effective Hamiltonian of the Little model as derived by Peretto (1984) and the duplicated-system technique of van Hemmen (1986).

We finish our argument by turning to quantative results. We focus on the case where each of the P learning sessions corresponds to teaching a (different) cycle of D patterns $\xi_{ia}^{\mu 0}$, each lasting for one time step. We work with unbiased random patterns where $\xi_{ia}^{\mu 0} = \pm 1$ with equal probability, and study our network at a finite storage level $\alpha = \lim_{N \to \infty}(P/N) > 0$. A detailed analysis of the case where the number of cycles remains bounded as $N \to \infty$ can be found in (Li and Herz 1990).

As in the replica-symmetric theory of Amit et al. (1987), we assume that the network is in a state highly correlated with a *finite* number of stored cycles. The remaining, extensively many cycles are described as a noise term. We define "partial" overlaps by $m_a^{\mu\alpha} \equiv N^{-1} \sum_i \xi_{ia}^{\mu\alpha} S_{ia}$. These macroscopic order parameters measure how close the system is to a stored pattern $\xi^{\mu\alpha}$ at a specific column a. We consider *retrieval solutions*, i.e., $m_a^{\mu\alpha} = m^\mu \delta_{\alpha,0}$, and arrive at the fixed-point equations (Li and Herz 1990)

$$m^\mu = \langle\langle \xi^{\mu 0} \tanh[\beta\{\sum_\nu m^\nu \xi^{\nu 0} + \sqrt{\alpha r} z\}]\rangle\rangle \ , \tag{14}$$

where

$$r = q \sum_{k=1}^{D} \frac{[\lambda_k(\mathcal{E})]^2}{[1 - \beta(1-q)\lambda_k(\mathcal{E})]^2} \quad \text{and} \quad q = \langle\langle \tanh^2[\beta\{\sum_\nu m^\nu \xi^{\nu 0} + \sqrt{\alpha r} z\}]\rangle\rangle. \tag{15}$$

Double angular brackets represent an average with respect to both the "condensed" cycles and the normalized Gaussian random variable z. The $\lambda_k(\mathcal{E})$ are eigenvalues of the matrix $\mathcal{E}$. Retrieval is possible when solutions with $m^\mu > 0$ for a single cycle μ exist, and the storage capacity α_c is reached when such solutions cease to exist. It should be noted that each cycle consists of D patterns so that the storage capacity for *single* patterns is $\tilde{\alpha}_c = D\alpha_c$. During the recognition process, however, each of them will trigger the cycle it belongs to and cannot be retrieved as a static pattern. For systems with a "maximally uniform" distribution, $\mathcal{E}_{ab} = (D-1)^{-1}(1-\delta_{ab})$, we get

D	2	3	4	5	∞
α_c	0.100	0.110	0.116	0.120	0.138

where the last result is identical to that for the corresponding Hopfield model since the diagonal terms of $\mathcal{E}$ can be neglected in that case. The above findings agree well with estimates from a finite-size analysis ($N \leq 3000$) of data from numerical simulations as shown by two examples. For $D=3$, we have found $\alpha_c = 0.120 \pm 0.015$, for $D=4$, $\alpha_c = 0.125 \pm 0.015$. Our results demonstrate that the storage capacity for temporal associations is comparable to that for static memories. As an example, take $D = 2$, i.e., the Little model. In the limit of large N, we see that $0.100 \cdot N$ two-cycles of the form $\xi_{i0}^{\mu 0} \rightleftharpoons \xi_{i1}^{\mu 0}$ may be recalled as compared to $0.138 \cdot N$ static patterns (Fontanari and Köberle 1987); this leads to an 1.45-fold increase of the information content per synapse.

The influence of the weight distribution on the network behavior may be demonstrated by some choices of $\varepsilon(\tau)$ for $D = 4$:

τ	=	0	1	2	3	α_c	m_c
$\varepsilon(\tau)$	=	1/3	1/3	1/3	0	0.116	0.96
$\varepsilon(\tau)$	=	1/2	0	1/2	0	0.100	0.93
$\varepsilon(\tau)$	=	0	1	0	0	0.050	0.93

The storage capacity decreases with decreasing number of delay lines, but measured *per synapse*, it does increase. However, networks with only a few number of delays are less fault-tolerant as known from numerical simulations (Herz et al. 1989). For all studied architectures, retrieved sequences contain less than 3.5% errors.

Our results prove that an extensive number of temporal associations can be stored as spatio-temporal attractors for the retrieval dynamics. They also indicate that dynamical systems with delayed interactions can be programmed in a very efficient manner to perform associative computations in the space-time domain.

6 CONCLUSION

Learning schemes can be successful only if the structure of the learning task is compatible with both the network architecture and the learning algorithm. In the present context, the task is to store simple temporal associations. It can be accomplished in neural networks with a broad distribution of signal delays and Hebbian synapses which, during learning periods, operate as microscopic feature detectors for spatio-temporal correlations within the external stimuli. The retrieval dynamics utilizes the very same delays and synapses, and is therefore rather robust as shown by numerical simulations and a statistical mechanical analysis.

Our approach may be generalized in various directions. For example, one can investigate more sophisticated learning rules or switch to continuous neurons in "iterated-map networks" (Marcus and Westervelt 1990). A generalization of the Lyapunov functional (7) covers that case as well (Herz, to be published) and allows a direct comparison of theoretical predictions with results from hardware implementations. Finally, one could try to develop a Lyapunov functional for a continuous-time dynamics with delays which seems to be rather significant for applications as well as for the general theory of functional differential equations and dynamical systems.

Acknowledgements

It is a pleasure to thank Bernhard Sulzer, John Hopfield, Reimer Kühn and Wulfram Gerstner for many helpful discussions. AVMH acknowledges support from the Studienstiftung des Deutschen Volkes. ZL is partly supported by a grant from the Seaver Institute.

References

Amit D J, Gutfreund H and Sompolinsky H 1985 *Phys. Rev.* **A 32** 1007

— 1987 *Ann. Phys. (N.Y.)* **173** 30

Coolen A C C and Gielen C C A M 1988 *Europhys. Lett.* **7** 281

Fontanari J F and Köberle R 1987 *Phys. Rev.* **A 36** 2475

Hebb D O 1949 *The Organization of Behavior* Wiley, New York

van Hemmen J L 1986 *Phys. Rev.* **A 34** 3435

Herz A V M, Sulzer B, Kühn R and van Hemmen J L 1988 *Europhys. Lett.* **7** 663

— 1989 *Biol. Cybern.* **60** 457

Hopfield J J 1982 *Proc. Natl. Acad. Sci. USA* **79** 2554

Kerszberg M and Zippelius A 1990 *Phys. Scr.* **T33** 54

Kleinfeld D 1986 *Proc. Natl. Acad. Sci. USA* **83** 9469

Li Z and Herz A V M 1990 in *Lecture Notes in Physics* **368** pp287 Springer, Heidelberg

Little W A 1974 *Math. Biosci.* **19** 101

Marcus C M and Westervelt R M 1990 *Phys. Rev.* **A 42** 2410

Peretto P 1984 *Biol. Cybern.* **50** 51

Sompolinsky H and Kanter I 1986 *Phys. Rev. Lett.* **57** 2861

Tank D W and Hopfield J J 1987 *Proc. Natl. Acad. Sci. USA* **84** 1896

Learning Time-varying Concepts

Anthony Kuh
Dept. of Electrical Eng.
U. of Hawaii at Manoa
Honolulu, HI 96822
kuh@wiliki.eng.hawaii.edu

Thomas Petsche
Siemens Corp. Research
755 College Road East
Princeton, NJ 08540
petsche@learning.siemens.com

Ronald L. Rivest
Lab. for Computer Sci.
MIT
Cambridge, MA 02139
rivest@theory.lcs.mit.edu

Abstract

This work extends computational learning theory to situations in which concepts vary over time, e.g., system identification of a time-varying plant. We have extended formal definitions of concepts and learning to provide a framework in which an algorithm can track a concept as it evolves over time. Given this framework and focusing on memory-based algorithms, we have derived some PAC-style sample complexity results that determine, for example, when tracking is feasible. We have also used a similar framework and focused on incremental tracking algorithms for which we have derived some bounds on the mistake or error rates for some specific concept classes.

1 INTRODUCTION

The goal of our ongoing research is to extend computational learning theory to include concepts that can change or evolve over time. For example, face recognition is complicated by the fact that a persons face changes slowly with age and more quickly with changes in make up, hairstyle, or facial hair. Speech recognition is complicated by the fact that a speakers voice may change over time due to fatigue, illness, stress, or background noise (Galletti and Abbott, 1989).

Time varying systems often appear in adaptive control or signal processing applications. For example, adaptive equalizers adjust the receiver and transmitter to compensate for changes in the noise on a transmission channel (Lucky et al., 1968). The kinematics of a robot arm can change when it picks up a heavy load or when the motors and drive train responses change due to wear. The output of a sensor may drift over time as the components age or as the temperature changes.

Computational learning theory as introduced by Valiant (1984) can make some useful statements about whether a given class of concepts can be learned and provide probabilistic bounds on the number of examples needed to learn a concept. Haussler, et al. (1987), and Littlestone (1989) have also shown that it is possible to bound the number of mistakes that a learner will make. However, while these analyses allow the concept to be chosen arbitrarily, that concept must remain fixed for all time. Littlestone and Warmuth (1989) considered concepts that may drift, but in the context of a different accuracy measure than we use. Our research seeks explore further modifications to existing theory to allow the analysis of performance when learning time-varying concept.

In the following, we describe two approaches we are exploring. Section 3 describes an extension of the PAC-model to include time-varying concepts and shows how this new model applies to algorithms that base their hypotheses on a set of stored examples. Section 4 described how we can bound the mistake rate of an algorithm that updates its estimate based on the most recent example. In Section 2 we define some notation and terminology that is used in the remainder of the based.

2 NOTATION & TERMINOLOGY

For a dichotomy that labels each instance as a positive or negative example of a concept, we can formally describe the model as follows. Each instance x_i is drawn randomly, according to an arbitrary fixed probability distribution, from an instance space X. The concept c to be learned is drawn randomly, according to an arbitrary fixed probability distribution, from a concept class C. Associated with each instance is a label $a_i = c(x_i)$ such that $a_i = 1$ if x_i is a positive example and $a_i = 0$ otherwise. The learner is presented with a sequence of examples (each example is a pair $\langle x_i, a_i \rangle$) chosen randomly from X. The learner must form an estimate, $\hat{c}$, of c based on these examples.

In the time-varying case, we assume that there is an adversary who can change c over time, so we change notation slightly. The instance x_t is presented at time t. The concept c_t is *active* at time t if the adversary is using c_t to label instances at that time. The sequence of t active concepts, $\mathbf{c}_t = \{c_1, \ldots, c_t\}$ is called a *concept sequence of length t*. The algorithm's task is to form an estimate $\hat{\mathbf{c}}_t$ of the actual concept sequence $\mathbf{c}_t$, i.e., at each time t, the tracker must use the sequence of randomly chosen examples to form an estimate $\hat{c}_t$ of c_t. A set of length t concept sequences is denoted by $\mathcal{C}(t)$ and we call a set of infinite length concept sequences a *concept sequence space* and denote it by $\mathcal{C}$.

Since the adversary, if allowed to make arbitrary changes, can easily make the tracker's task impossible, it is usually restricted such that only small or infrequent changes are allowed. In other words, each $\mathcal{C}(t)$ is a small subset of C^t.

We consider two different types of different types of "tracking" (learning) algorithms, memory-based (or batch) and incremental (or on-line). We analyze the sample complexity of batch algorithms and the mistake (or error) rate of incremental algorithms.

In the usual case where concepts are time-invariant, batch learning algorithms operate in two distinct phases. During the first phase, the algorithm collects a set of training examples. Given this set, it then computes a hypothesis. In the second phase, this hypothesis is used to classify all future instances. The hypothesis is never again updated. In Section 3 we consider memory-based algoritms derived from batch algorithms.

When concepts are time-invariant, an on-line learning algorithm is one which constantly modifies its hypothesis. On each iteration, the learner (1) receives an instance; (2) predicts a label based on the current hypothesis; (3) receives the correct label; and (4) uses the correct label to update the hypothesis. In Section 4, we consider incremental algorithms based on on-line algorithms.

When studying learnability, it is helpful to define the Vapnik-Chervonenkis (VC) dimension (Vapnik and Chervonenkis, 1971) of a concept class: $\mathrm{VCdim}(C)$ is the cardinality of the largest set such that every possible labeling scheme is achieved by some concept in C. Blumer et al. (1989) showed that a concept class is learnable if and only if the VC-dimension is finite and derived an upper bound (that depends on the VC dimension) for the number of examples need to PAC-learn a learnable concept class.

3 MEMORY-BASED TRACKING

In this section, we will consider memory-based trackers which base their current hypothesis on a stored set of examples. We build on the definition of PAC-learning to define what it means to PAC-track a concept sequence. Our main result here is a lower bound on the maximum rate of change that can be PAC-tracked by a memory-based learner.

A *memory-based tracker* consists of (a) a function $w(\epsilon, \delta)$; and (b) an algorithm $\mathcal{L}$ that produces the current hypothesis, $\hat{c}_t$ using the most recent $w(\epsilon, \delta)$ examples. The memory-based tracker thus maintains a sliding window on the examples that includes the most recent $w(\epsilon, \delta)$ examples. We do not require that $\mathcal{L}$ run in polynomial time.

Following the work of Valiant (1984) we say that an algorithm $\mathcal{A}$ *PAC-tracks a concept sequence space* $C' \subseteq C$ if, for any $\mathbf{c} \in C'$, any distribution D on X, any $\epsilon, \delta > 0$, and access to examples randomly selected from X according to D and labeled at time t by concept c_t; for all t sufficiently large, with t' chosen uniformly at random between 1 and t, it is true that

$$\Pr(d(c_{t'}, \hat{c}_{t'}) \leq \epsilon) \geq 1 - \delta.$$

The probability includes any randomization algorithm $\mathcal{A}$ may use as well as the random selection of t' and the random selection of examples according to the distribution D, and where $d(c, c') = D(x : c(x) \neq c'(x))$ is the probability that c and c' disagree on a randomly chosen example.

Learnability results often focus on learners that see only positive examples. For many concept classes this is sufficient, but for others negative examples are also necessary. Natarajan (1987) showed that a concept class that is PAC-learnable can be learned using only positive examples if the class is closed under intersection.

With this in mind, let's focus on a memory-based tracker that modifies its estimate using only positive examples. Since PAC-tracking requires that $\mathcal{A}$ be able to PAC-learn individual concepts, it must be true that $\mathcal{A}$ can PAC-track a sequence of concepts only if the concept class is closed under intersection. However, this is not sufficient.

Observation 1. *Assume C is closed under intersection. If positive examples are drawn from $c_1 \in C$ prior to time t_0, and from $c_2 \in C$, $c_1 \subseteq c_2$, after time t_0, then there exists an estimate of c_2 that is consistent with all examples drawn from c_1.*

The proof of this is straightforward once we realize that if $c_1 \subseteq c_2$, then all positive examples drawn prior to time t_0 from c_1 are consistent with c_2. The problem is therefore equivalent to first choosing a set of examples from a subset of c_2 and then choosing more examples from all of c_2 — it skews that probability distribution, but any estimate of c_2 will include all examples drawn from c_1.

Consider the set of closed intervals on $[0,1]$, $C = \{[a,b] \mid 0 \leq a,b \leq 1\}$. Assume that, for some $d \geq b$, $c_t = c_1 = [a,b]$ for all $t \leq t_0$ and $c_t = c_2 = [a,d]$ for all $t > t_0$. All the examples drawn prior to t_0, $\{x_t : t < t_0\}$, are consistent with c_2 and it would be nice to use these examples to help estimate c_2. How much can these examples help?

Theorem 1. *Assume C is closed under intersection and* VCdim(C) *is finite; $C_2 \subseteq C$; and $\mathcal{A}$ has PAC learned $c_1 \in C$ at time t_0. Then, for some d such that* VCdim$(C_2) \leq d \leq$ VCdim(C), *the maximum number of examples drawn after time t_0 required so that $\mathcal{A}$ can PAC learn $c_2 \in C$ is upper bounded by* $m(\epsilon,\delta) = \max\left(\frac{4}{\epsilon}\log\frac{2}{\delta}, \frac{8d}{\epsilon}\log\frac{13}{\epsilon}\right)$

In other words, if there is no prior information about c_2, then the number of examples required depends on VCdim(C). However, the examples drawn from c_1 can be used to shrink the concept space towards C_2. For example, when $c_1 = [a,b]$ and $c_2 = [a,c]$, in the limit where $c_1' = c_1$, the problem of learning c_2 reduces to learning a one-sided interval which has VC-dimension 1 versus 2 for the two-sided interval. Since it is unlikely that $c_1' = c_1$, it will usually be the case that $d >$ VCdim(C_2).

In order to PAC-track $\mathbf{c}$, most of the time $\mathcal{A}$ must have $m(\epsilon,\delta)$ examples consistent with the current concept. This implies that $w(\epsilon,\delta)$ must be at least $m(\epsilon,\delta)$. Further, since the concepts are changing, the consistent examples will be the most recent. Using a sliding window of size $m(\epsilon,\delta)$, the tracker will have an estimate that is based on examples that are consistent with the active concept after collecting no more than $m(\epsilon,\delta)$ examples after a change.

In much of our analysis of memory-based trackers, we have focused on a concept sequence space $\mathcal{C}_\lambda$ which is the set of all concept sequences such that, on average, each concept is active for at least $1/\lambda$ time steps before a change occurs. That is, if $N(\mathbf{c},t)$ is the number of changes in the first t time steps of $\mathbf{c}$, $\mathcal{C}_\lambda = \{\mathbf{c} : \limsup_{t\to\infty} N(\mathbf{c},t)/t \leq \lambda\}$. The question then is, for what values of λ does there exist a PAC-tracker?

Theorem 2. *Let $\mathcal{L}$ be a memory-based tracker with $w(\epsilon,\delta) = m(\epsilon,\delta/2)$ which draws instances labeled according to some concept sequence $\mathbf{c} \in \mathcal{C}_\lambda$ with each $c_t \in C$ and* VCdim$(C) < \infty$. *For any $\epsilon > 0$ and $\delta > 0$, $\mathcal{A}$ can UPAC track C if $\lambda < \frac{\delta}{2}m(\epsilon,\delta/2)$.*

This theorem provides a lower bound on the maximum rate of change that can be tracked by a batch tracker. Theorem 1 implies that a memory-based tracker can use examples from a previous concept to help estimate the active concept. The proof of theorem 2 assumes that some of the most recent $m(\epsilon,\delta)$ examples are not consistent with c_t until $m(\epsilon,\delta)$ examples from the active concept have been gathered. An algorithm that removes inconsistent examples more intelligently, e.g., by using conflicts between examples or information about allowable changes, will be able to track concept sequence spaces that change more rapidly.

4 INCREMENTAL TRACKING

Incremental tracking is similar to the on-line learning case, but now we assume that there is an adversary who can change the concept such that $c_{t+1} \neq c_t$. At each iteration:

1. the adversary chooses the active concept c_t;
2. the tracker is given an unlabeled instance, x_t;
3. the tracker predicts a label using the current hypothesis: $\hat{a}_t = \hat{c}_{t-1}(x_t)$;
4. the tracker is given the correct label a_t;
5. the tracker forms a new hypothesis: $\hat{c}_t = \mathcal{L}(\hat{c}_{t-1}, \langle x_t, a_t \rangle)$.

We have defined a number of different types of trackers and adversaries: A *prudent* tracker predicts that $a_t = 1$ if and only if $\hat{c}_t(x_t) = 1$. A *conservative tracker* changes its hypothesis only if $a_t \neq \hat{a}_t$. A *benign adversary* changes the concept in a way that is independent of the tracker's hypothesis while a *malicious adversary* uses information about the tracker and its hypothesis to choose a c_{t+1} to cause an increase in the error rate. The *most malicious adversary* chooses c_{t+1} to cause the largest possible increase in error rate on average.

We distinguish between the error of the hypothesis formed in step 5 above and a mistake made in step 3 above. The *instantaneous error rate* of an hypothesis is $e_t = d(c_t, \hat{c}_t)$. It is the probability that another randomly chosen instance labeled according to c_t will be misclassified by the updated hypothesis. A *mistake* is a mislabeled instance, and we define a mistake indicator function $M_t = 1$ if $c_t(x_t) \neq \hat{c}_{t-1}(x_t)$.

We define the *average error rate* $\varepsilon_t = \frac{1}{t}\sum_{i=1}^{t} e_t$ and the *asymptotic error rate* is $\varepsilon = \liminf_{t\to\infty} \varepsilon_t$. The *average mistake rate* is the average value of the mistake indicator function, $\mu_t = \frac{1}{t}\sum_{i=1}^{t} M_t$, and the *asymptotic mistake rate* is $\mu = \liminf_{t\to\infty} \mu_t$.

We are modeling the incremental tracking problems as a Markov process. Each state of the Markov process is labeled by a triple $\langle c, \hat{c}, \alpha \rangle$, and corresponds to an iteration in which c is the active concept, $\hat{c}$ is the active hypothesis, and α is the set of changes the adversary is allowed to make given c. We are still in the process of analyzing a general model, so the following presents one of the special cases we have examined.

Let X be the set of all points on the unit circle. We use polar coordinates so that since the radius is fixed we can label each point by an angle θ, thus $X = [0, 2\pi)$. Note that X is periodic. The concept class C is the set of all arcs of fixed length π radians, i.e., all semicircles that lie on the unit circle. Each $c \in C$ can be written as $c = [\pi(2\theta - 1) \bmod 2\pi, 2\pi\theta)$, where $\theta \in [0, 1)$. We assume that the instances are chosen uniformly from the circle.

The adversary may change the concept by rotating it around the circle, however, the maximum rotation is bounded such that, given c_t, c_{t+1} must satisfy $d(c_{t+1}, c_t) \leq \gamma$. For the uniform case, this is equivalent to restricting $\theta_{t+1} = \theta_t \pm \beta \bmod 1$, where $0 \leq \beta \leq \gamma/2$.

The tracker is required to be conservative, but since we are satisfied to lower bound the error rate, we assume that every time the tracker makes a mistake, it is told the correct concept. Thus, $\hat{c}_t = \hat{c}_{t-1}$ if no mistake is made, but $\hat{c}_t = c_t$ wherever a mistake is made.

The worst case or most malicious adversary for a conservative tracker always tries to maximize the tracker's error rate. Therefore, whenever the tracker deduces c_t (i.e. whenever the tracker makes a mistake), the adversary picks a direction by flipping a fair coin. The adversary then rotates the concept in that direction as far as possible on each iteration. Then we can define a random direction function S_t and write

$$S_t = \begin{cases} +1, & w.p.\ 1/2\ if\ \hat{c}_{t-1} = c_{t-1}; \\ -1, & w.p.\ 1/2\ if\ \hat{c}_{t-1} = c_{t-1}; \\ S_{t-1}, & if\ \hat{c}_{t-1} \neq c_{t-1}. \end{cases}$$

Then the adversary chooses the new concept to be $\theta_t = \theta_{t-1} + S_t\gamma/2$.

Since the adversary always rotates the concept by $\gamma/2$, there are $2/\gamma$ distinct concepts that can occur. However, when $\theta(t+1/\gamma) = \theta(t)+1/2 \bmod 1$, the semicircles do not overlap and therefore, after at most $1/\gamma$ changes, a mistake will be made with probability one. Because at most $1/\gamma$ consecutive changes can be made before the mistake rate returns to zero, because the probability of a mistake depends only on $\theta_t - \hat{\theta}_t$, and because of inherent symmetries, this system can be modeled by a Markov chain with $k = 1/\gamma$ states. Each state s_i corresponds to the case $|\theta_t - \hat{\theta}_t| = i\gamma \bmod 1$. The probability of a transition from state s_i to state s_{i+1} is $P(s_{i+1}|s_i) = 1 - (i+1)\gamma$. The probability of a transition from state s_i to state s_0 is $P(s_0|s_i) = (i+1)\gamma$. All other transition probabilities are zero. This Markov chain is homogeneous, irreducible, aperiodic, and finite so it has an invariant distribution. By solving the balance equations, for γ sufficiently small, we find that

$$\mathrm{P}(s_l) = \frac{\prod_{i=0}^{l}(1-i\gamma)}{\sum_{j=0}^{\frac{1}{\gamma}-1}\prod_{i=0}^{j}(1-i\gamma)} \approx \sqrt{2\gamma/\pi}\int_{l}^{l+1} e^{-\frac{\gamma}{2}x^2}\,dx \qquad (1)$$

Since we assume that γ is small, the probability that no mistake will occur for each of $k-1$ consecutive time steps after a mistake, $\mathrm{P}(s_{k-1})$, is very small and we can say that the probability of a mistake is approximately $\mathrm{P}(s_0)$. Therefore, from equation 1, for small γ, it follows that $\mu_{\text{malicious}} \approx \sqrt{2\gamma/\pi}$.

If we drop the assumption that the adversary is malicious, and instead assume the the adversary chooses the direction randomly at each iteration, then a similar sort of analysis yields that $\mu_{\text{benign}} = O(\gamma^{2/3})$.

Since the foregoing analysis assumes a conservative tracker that chooses the best hypothesis every time it makes a mistake, it implies that for this concept sequence space and *any* conservative tracker, the mistake rate is $O(\gamma^{1/2})$ against a malicious adversary and $O(\gamma^{2/3b})$ against a benign adversary. For either adversary, it can be shown that $\varepsilon = \mu - \gamma$.

5 CONCLUSIONS AND FURTHER RESEARCH

We can draw a number of interesting conclusions form the work we have done so far. First, tracking sequences of concepts is possible when the individual concepts are learnable and change occurs "slowly" enough. Theorem 2 gives a weak upper bound on the rate of concept changes that is sufficient to insure that tracking is possible.

Theorem 1 implies that there can be some trade-off between the size (VC-dimension) of the changes and the rate of change. Thus, if the size of the changes is restricted, Theorems 1 and 2 together imply that the maximum rate of change can be faster than for the general case. It is significant that a simple tracker that maintains a sliding window on the most recent set of examples can PAC-track the new concept after a change as quickly as a static learner can if it starts from scratch. This suggests it may be possible to subsume detection so that it is implicit in the operation of the tracker. One obviously open problem is to determine d in Theorem 1, i.e., what is the appropriate dimension to apply to the concept changes?

The analysis of the mistake and error rates presented in Section 4 is for a special case with VC-dimension 1, but even so, it is interesting that the mistake and error rates are significantly worse than the rate of change. Preliminary analysis of other concept classes suggests that this continues to be true for higher VC-dimensions. We are continuing work to extend this analysis to other concept classes, including classes with higher VC-dimension; non-conservative learners; and other restrictions on concept changes.

Acknowledgments

Anthony Kuh gratefully acknowledges the support of the National Science Foundation through grant EET-8857711 and Siemens Corporate Research. Ronald L. Rivest gratefully acknowledges support from NSF grant CCR-8914428, ARO grant N00014-89-J-1988, and a grant from the Siemens Corporation.

References

Blumer, A., Ehrenfeucht, A., Haussler, D., and Warmuth, M. (1989). Learnability and the Vapnik-Chervonenkis dimension. *Journal of the Association for Computing Machinery*, 36(4):929–965.

Galletti, I. and Abbott, M. (1989). Development of an advanced airborne speech recognizer for direct voice input. *Speech Technology*, pages 60–63.

Haussler, D., Littlestone, N., and Warmuth, M. K. (1987). Expected mistake bounds for on-line learning algorithms. (Unpublished).

Littlestone, N. (1989). Mistake bounds and logarithmic linear-threshold learning algorithms. Technical Report UCSC-CRL-89-11, Univ. of California at Santa Cruz.

Littlestone, N. and Warmuth, M. K. (1989). The weighted majority algorithm. In *Proceedings of IEEE FOCS Conference*, pages 256–261. IEEE. (Extended abstract only.).

Lucky, R. W., Salz, J., and Weldon, E. J. (1968). *Principles of Data Communications.* McGraw-Hill, New York.

Natarajan, B. K. (1987). On learning boolean functions. In *Proceedings of the Nineteenth Annual ACM Symposium on Theory of Computing*, pages 296–304.

Valiant, L. (1984). A theory of the learnable. *Communications of the ACM*, 27:1134–1142.

Vapnik, V. N. and Chervonenkis, A. Y. (1971). On the uniform convergence of relative frequencies of events to their probabilities. *Theory of Probability and its Applications*, 16:264–280.

The Recurrent Cascade-Correlation Architecture

Scott E. Fahlman
School of Computer Science
Carnegie Mellon University
Pittsburgh, PA 15213

Abstract

Recurrent Cascade-Correlation (RCC) is a recurrent version of the Cascade-Correlation learning architecture of Fahlman and Lebiere [Fahlman, 1990]. RCC can learn from examples to map a sequence of inputs into a desired sequence of outputs. New hidden units with recurrent connections are added to the network as needed during training. In effect, the network builds up a finite-state machine tailored specifically for the current problem. RCC retains the advantages of Cascade-Correlation: fast learning, good generalization, automatic construction of a near-minimal multi-layered network, and incremental training.

1 THE ARCHITECTURE

Cascade-Correlation [Fahlman, 1990] is a supervised learning architecture that builds a near-minimal multi-layer network topology in the course of training. Initially the network contains only inputs, output units, and the connections between them. This single layer of connections is trained (using the Quickprop algorithm [Fahlman, 1988]) to minimize the error. When no further improvement is seen in the level of error, the network's performance is evaluated. If the error is small enough, we stop. Otherwise we add a new hidden unit to the network in an attempt to reduce the residual error.

To create a new hidden unit, we begin with a pool of *candidate units*, each of which receives weighted connections from the network's inputs and from any hidden units already present in the net. The outputs of these candidate units are not yet connected into the active network. Multiple passes through the training set are run, and each candidate unit adjusts its incoming weights to maximize the correlation between its output and the residual error in the active net. When the correlation scores stop improving, we choose the best candidate, freeze its incoming weights, and add it to the network. This process is called "tenure." After tenure, a unit becomes a permanent new feature detector in the net. We then re-train all the weights going to the output units, including those from the new hidden unit. This process of adding a new hidden unit and re-training the output layer is repeated until the error is negligible or we give up. Since the new hidden unit receives connections from the old ones, each hidden unit effectively adds a new layer to the net.

Cascade-correlation eliminates the need for the user to guess in advance the network's size, depth, and topology. A reasonably small (though not minimal) network is built automatically. Because a hidden-unit feature detector, once built, is never altered or cannibalized, the network can be trained incrementally. A large data set can be broken up into smaller "lessons," and feature-building will be cumulative. Cascade-Correlation learns much faster than backprop for several reasons: First only a single layer of weights is being trained at any given time. There is never any need to propagate error information backwards through the connections, and we avoid the dramatic slowdown that is typical when training backprop nets with many layers. Second, this is a "greedy" algorithm: each new unit grabs as much of the remaining error as it can. In a standard backprop net, the all the hidden units are changing at once, competing for the various jobs that must be done—a slow and sometimes unreliable process.

Cascade-correlation, like back-propagation and other feed-forward architectures, has no short-term memory in the network. The outputs at any given time are a function only of the current inputs and the network's weights. Of course, many real-world tasks require the recognition of a sequence of inputs and, in some cases, the corresponding production of a sequence of outputs. A number of recurrent architectures have been proposed in response to this need. Perhaps the most widely used, at present, is the Elman model [Elman, 1988], which assumes that the network operates in discrete time-steps. The outputs of the network's hidden units at time t are fed back for use as additional network inputs at time-step $t+1$. These additional inputs can be thought of as state-variables whose contents and interpretation are determined by the evolving weights of the network. In effect, the network is free to choose its own representation of past history in the course of learning.

Recurrent Cascade-Correlation (RCC) is an architecture that adds Elman-style recurrent operation to the Cascade-Correlation architecture. However, some changes were needed in order to make the two models fit together. In the original Elman architecture there is total connectivity between the state variables (previous outputs of hidden units) and the hidden unit layer. In Cascade-Correlation, new hidden units are added one by one, and are frozen once they are added to the network. It would violate this concept to insert the outputs from new hidden units back into existing hidden units as new inputs. On the other hand, the network must be able to form recurrent loops if it is to retain state for an indefinite time.

The solution we have adopted in RCC is to augment each candidate unit with a single weighted self-recurrent input that feeds back that unit's own output on the previous time-step. That self-recurrent link is trained along with the unit's other input weights to maximize the correlation of the candidate with the residual error. If the recurrent link adopts a strongly positive value, the unit will function as a flip-flop, retaining its previous state unless the other inputs force it to change; if the recurrent link adopts a negative value, the unit will tend to oscillate between positive and negative outputs on each time-step unless the other inputs hold it in place; if the recurrent weight is near zero, then the unit will act as a gate of some kind. When a candidate unit is added to the active network as a new hidden unit, the self-recurrent weight is frozen, along with all the other weights. Each new hidden unit is in effect a single state variable in a finite-state machine that is built specifically for the task at hand. In this use of self-recurrent connections only, the RCC model resembles the "Focused Back-Propagation" algorithm of Mozer[Mozer, 1988].

The output, $V(t)$, of each self-recurrent unit is computed as follows:

$$V(t) = \sigma\left(\sum_i I_i(t)\, w_i \;+\; V(t-1)\, w_s\right)$$

where σ is some non-linear squashing function applied to the weighted sum of inputs I plus the self-weight, w_s, times the previous output. In the studies described here, σ is always the hyperbolic tangent or "symmetric sigmoid" function, with a range from -1 to +1. During the candidate training phase, we adjust the weights w_i and w_s for each unit so as to maximize its correlation score. This requires computing the derivative of $V(t)$ with respect to these weights:

$$\partial V(t)/\partial w_i = \sigma'(t)\ \left(I_i(t) + w_s\ \partial V(t-1)/\partial w_i\right)$$

$$\partial V(t)/\partial w_s = \sigma'(t)\ \left(V(t-1) + w_s\ \partial V(t-1)/\partial w_s\right)$$

The rightmost term reflects the influence of the weight in question on the unit's previous state. Since we computed $\partial V(t-1)/\partial w$ on the previous time-step, we can just save this value and use it in the current step. So the recurrent version of the learning algorithm requires us to store a single additional number for each candidate weight, plus $V(t-1)$ for each unit. At $t = 0$ we assume that the unit's previous value and previous derivatives are all zero.

As an aside, the usual formulation for Elman networks treats the hidden units' previous values as *independent* inputs, ignoring the dependence of these previous values on the weights being adjusted. In effect, the rightmost terms in the above equations are being dropped, though they are not negligible in general. This rough approximation apparently causes little trouble in practice, but it might explain the instability that some researchers have reported when Elman nets are run with aggressive second-order learning procedures such as quickprop. The Mozer algorithm does take these extra terms into account.

2 EMPIRICAL RESULTS: FINITE-STATE GRAMMAR

Figure 1a shows the state-transition diagram for a simple finite-state grammar, called the Reber grammar, that has been used by other researchers to investigate learning and generalization in recurrent neural networks. To generate a "legal" string of tokens from this grammar, we begin at the left side of the graph and move from state to state, following the directed edges. When an edge is traversed, the associated letter is added to the string. Where two paths leave a single node, we choose one at random with equal probability. The resulting string always begins with a "B" and ends with an "E". Because there are loops in the graph, there is no bound on the length of the strings; the average length about eight letters. An example of a legal string would be "BTSSXXVPSE".

Cleeremans, Servan-Schreiber, and McClelland [Cleeremans, 1989] showed that an Elman network can learn this grammar if it is shown many different strings produced by the

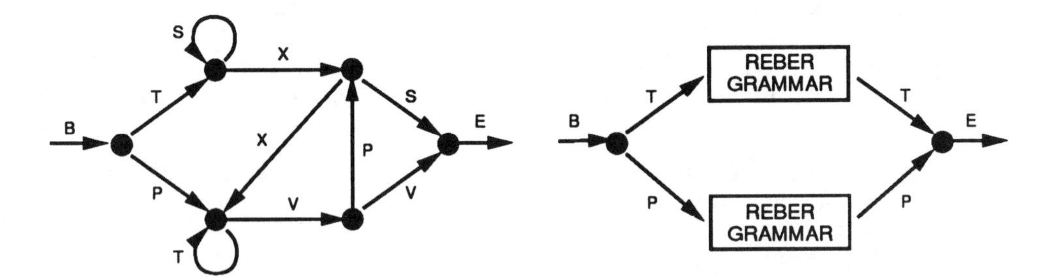

Figure 1: State transition diagram for the Reber grammar (left) and for the embedded Reber grammar (right).

grammar. The internal state of the network is zeroed at the start of each string. The letters in the string are then presented sequentially at the inputs of the network, with a separate input connection for each of the seven letters. The network is trained to predict the next character in the string by turning on one of the seven outputs. The output is compared to the true successor and network attempts to minimize the resulting errors.

When there are two legal successors from a given state, the network will never be able to do a perfect job of prediction. During training, the net will see contradictory examples, sometimes with one successor and sometimes the other. In such cases, the net will eventually learn to partially activate both legal outputs. During testing, a prediction is considered correct if the two desired outputs are the two with the largest values.

This task requires generalization in the presence of considerable noise. The rules defining the grammar are never presented—only examples of the grammar's output. Note that if the network can perform the prediction task perfectly, it can also be used to determine whether a string is a legal output of the grammar. Note also that the successor letter(s) cannot be determined from the current input alone; some memory of of the network's state or past inputs is essential.

Cleeremans *et al.* report that a fixed-topology Elman net with three hidden units can learn this task after 60,000 distinct training strings have been presented, each used only once. A larger network with 15 hidden units required only 20,000 training strings. These were the best results obtained, not averages over a number of runs.

RCC was given the same problem, but using a fixed set of 128 training strings, presented repeatedly. (Smaller string-sets had too many statistical irregularities for reliable training.) Ten trials were run using different training sets. In nine cases, RCC achieved perfect performance after building two hidden units; in the tenth, three hidden units were built. Average training time was 195.5 epochs, or about 25,000 string presentations. (An *epoch* is defined as a single pass through a fixed training set.) In every case, the trained network achieved a perfect score on a set of 128 new strings not used in training. This study used a pool of 8 candidate units.

Cleeremans *et al.* also explored the "embedded Reber grammar" shown in figure 1b. Each of the boxes in the figure is a transition graph identical to the original Reber grammar. In this much harder task, the network must learn to predict the final T or P correctly. To accomplish this, the network must note the initial T or P and must retain this information while processing an "embedded clause" of arbitrary length. It is difficult to discover this rule from example strings, since the embedded clauses may also contain many T's and P's, but only the initial T or P correlates reliably with the final prediction. The "signal to noise ratio" in this problem is very poor.

The standard Elman net was unable to learn this task, even with 15 hidden units and 250,000 training strings. However, the task could be learned partially (correct prediction in about 70% of test strings) if the two copies of the embedded grammar were differentiated by giving them slightly different transition probabilities.

RCC was run six times on the more difficult symmetrical form of this problem. A candidate pool of 8 units was used. Each trial used a different set of 256 training strings and the resulting network was tested on a separate set of 256 strings. As shown in the table below, perfect performance was achieved in about half the trial runs, requiring 7-9 hidden units and and average of 713 epochs (182K string-presentations). Two of the remaining networks perform at the 99+% level, and one got stuck. (Trial 6 is a successful second run on the same test set used in trial 5.)

Trial	Hidden Units	Epochs Needed	Train Set Errors	Test Set Errors
1	9	831	0	0
2	7	602	0	0
3	15	1256	0	2
4	11	910	0	1
5	13	1063	11	16
6	9	707	0	0

Smith and Zipser[Smith, 1989] have studied the same grammar-learning tasks using the time-continuous "Real-Time Recurrent Learning" (or "RTRL") architecture developed by Williams and Zipser[Williams, 1989]. They report that a network with seven visible (combined input-output) units, two hidden units, and full inter-unit connectivity is able to learn the simple Reber grammar task after presentation of 19,000 to 63,000 distinct training strings. On the more difficult embedded grammar task, Smith and Zipser report that RTRL learned the task perfectly in some (unspecified) fraction of attempts. Successful runs ranged from 3 hidden units (173K distinct training strings) to 12 hidden units (25K strings). RTRL is able to deal with discrete or time-continuous problems, while RCC deals only in discrete events. On the other hand, RTRL requires more computation than RCC in processing each training example, and RTRL scales up poorly as network size increases.

3 EMPIRICAL RESULTS: LEARNING MORSE CODE

Another series of experiments tested the ability of an RCC network to learn the Morse code patterns for the 26 English letters. While this task requires no generalization, it does demonstrate the ability of this architecture to recognize a long, rather complex set of patterns. It also provides an opportunity to demonstrate RCC's ability to learn a new task in small increments. This study assumes that the dots and dashes arrive at precise times; it does not address the problem of variable timing.

The network has one input and 27 outputs: one for each letter and a "strobe" output signalling that a complete letter has been recognized. A dot is represented as a logical one (positive input) followed by a logical zero (negative); a dash is two ones followed by a zero. A second consecutive zero marks the end of the letter. When the second zero is seen the network must raise the strobe output and one of the other 26; at all other times, the outputs are zero. For example, the "...-" pattern for the letter V would be encoded as the input sequence "1010101100". The letter patterns vary considerably in length, from 3 to 12 time-steps, with an average of 8. During training, the network's state is zeroed at the start of each new letter; once the network is trained, the strobe output could be used to reset the network.

In one series of trials, the training set included the codes for all 26 letters at once (226 time-steps in all). In ten trials, the network learned the task perfectly in every case, building an average of 10.5 hidden units and requiring an average of 1321 passes through the entire training set. Note that the system does not require a distinct hidden unit for each letter or for each time-slice in the longest sequence.

In a second experiment, we divided the training into a series of short "lessons" of increasing difficulty. The network was first trained to produce the strobe output and to recognize the two shortest letters, E and T. This task was learned perfectly, usually with the creation of 2 hidden units. We then set aside the "ET" set and trained successively on the following sets: "AIN", "DGHKRUW", "BFLOV", and "CJPQXYZ". As a rule, each of these lessons adds one or two new hidden units, building upon those already present. Finally we train on all 26 characters at once, which generally adds 2-3 more units to the existing set.

In ten trials, the incremental version learned the task perfectly every time, requiring an average total of 1427 epochs and 9.6 hidden units—slightly fewer than the number of units added in block training. While the epoch count is slightly greater than in the block-training experiment, most of these epochs are run on very small training sets. The incremental training required only about half as much total runtime as the block training. For learning of even more complex temporal sequences, incremental training of this kind may prove essential.

Our approach to incremental training was inspired to some degree by the work reported in [Waibel, 1989] in which small network modules were trained separately, frozen, and then combined into a composite network with the addition of some "glue" units. However, in RCC only the partitioning of the training set is chosen by the user; the network itself builds the appropriate internal structure, and new units are able to build upon hidden units created during some earlier lesson.

4 CONCLUSIONS

RCC sequential processing to Cascade-Correlation, while retaining the advantages of the original version: fast learning, good generalization, automatic choice of network topology, ability to create complex high-order feature detectors, and incremental learning. The grammar-learning experiments suggest that RCC is more powerful than standard Elman networks in learning to recognize subtle patterns in sequential data. The RTRL scheme of Williams and Zipser may be equally powerful, but RTRL is more complex and does not scale up well when larger networks are needed.

On the negative side, RCC deals in discrete time-steps and not in continuous time. An interesting direction for future research is to explore the use of an RCC-like structure with units whose memory of past state is time-continuous rather than discrete.

Acknowledgments

I would like to thank Paul Gleichauf, Dave Touretzky, and Alex Waibel for their help and useful suggestions. This research was sponsored in part by the National Science Foundation (Contract EET-8716324) and the Defense Advanced Research Projects Agency (Contract F33615-90-C-1465).

References

[Cleeremans, 1989] Cleeremans, A., D. Servan-Schreiber, and J. L. McClelland (1989) "Finite-State Automata and Simple Recurrent Networks" in *Neural Computation 1*, 372-381.

[Elman, 1988] Elman, J. L. (1988) "Finding Structure in Time," CRL Tech Report 8801, Univ. of California at San Diego, Center for Research in Language.

[Fahlman, 1988] Fahlman, S. E. (1988) "Faster-Learning Variations on Back-Propagation: An Empirical Study" in *Proceedings of the 1988 Connectionist Models Summer School*, Morgan Kaufmann.

[Fahlman, 1990] Fahlman, S. E. and C. Lebiere (1988) "The Cascade-Correlation Learning Architecture" in D. S. Touretzky (ed.), *Advances in Neural Information Processing Systems 2*, Morgan Kaufmann.

[Mozer, 1988] Mozer, M. C. (1988) "A Focused Back-Propagation Algorithm for Temporal Pattern Recognition," Tech Report CRG-TR-88-3, Univ. of Toronto, Dept. of Psychology and Computer Science.

[Smith, 1989] Smith, A. W. and D. Zipser (1989) "Learning Sequential Structure with the Real-Time Recurrent Learning Algorithm" in *International Journal of Neural Systems*, Vol. 1, No. 2, 125-131.

[Waibel, 1989] Waibel, A. (1989) "Consonant Recognition by Modular Construction of Large Phonemic Time-Delay Neural Networks" in D. S. Touretzky (ed.), *Advances in Neural Information Processing Systems 1*, Morgan Kaufmann.

[Williams, 1989] Williams, R. J. and D. Zipser (1989) "A learning algorithm for continually running fully recurrent neural networks," Neural Computation 1, 270-280.

Part V

Speech

Continuous Speech Recognition by Linked Predictive Neural Networks

Joe Tebelskis, Alex Waibel, Bojan Petek, and Otto Schmidbauer
School of Computer Science
Carnegie Mellon University
Pittsburgh, PA 15213

Abstract

We present a large vocabulary, continuous speech recognition system based on Linked Predictive Neural Networks (LPNN's). The system uses neural networks as predictors of speech frames, yielding distortion measures which are used by the One Stage DTW algorithm to perform continuous speech recognition. The system, already deployed in a Speech to Speech Translation system, currently achieves 95%, 58%, and 39% word accuracy on tasks with perplexity 5, 111, and 402 respectively, outperforming several simple HMMs that we tested. We also found that the accuracy and speed of the LPNN can be slightly improved by the judicious use of hidden control inputs. We conclude by discussing the strengths and weaknesses of the predictive approach.

1 INTRODUCTION

Neural networks are proving to be useful for difficult tasks such as speech recognition, because they can easily be trained to compute smooth, nonlinear, nonparametric functions from any input space to output space. In speech recognition, the function most often computed by networks is *classification*, in which spectral frames are mapped into a finite set of classes, such as phonemes. In theory, classification networks approximate the optimal Bayesian discriminant function [1], and in practice they have yielded very high accuracy [2, 3, 4]. However, integrating a phoneme classifier into a speech recognition system is nontrivial, since classification decisions tend to be binary, and binary phoneme-level errors tend to confound word-level hypotheses. To circumvent this problem, neural network training must be carefully integrated into word level training [1, 5]. An alternative function which can be computed by networks is *prediction*, where spectral frames are mapped into predicted spectral frames. This provides a simple way to get non-binary distortion measures, with straightforward integration into a speech recognition system. Predictive networks have been used successfully for small vocabulary [6, 7] and large vocabulary [8, 9] speech recognition systems. In this paper we describe our prediction-based LPNN system [9], which performs large vocabulary continuous speech recognition, and which has already been deployed within a Speech to Speech Translation system [10]. We present our experimental results, and discuss the strengths and weaknesses of the predictive approach.

2 LINKED PREDICTIVE NEURAL NETWORKS

The LPNN system is based on canonical phoneme models, which can be logically concatenated in any order (using a "linkage pattern") to create templates for different words; this makes the LPNN suitable for large vocabulary recognition.

Each canonical phoneme is modeled by a short sequence of neural networks. The number of nets in the sequence, $N >= 1$, corresponds to the granularity of the phoneme model. These phone modeling networks are nonlinear, multilayered, feedforward, and "predictive" in the sense that, given a short section of speech, the networks are required to extrapolate the raw speech signal, rather than to classify it. Thus, each predictive network produces a time-varying model of the speech signal which will be accurate in regions corresponding to the phoneme for which that network has been trained, but inaccurate in other regions (which are better modeled by other networks). Phonemes are thus "recognized" indirectly, by virtue of the relative accuracies of the different predictive networks in various sections of speech. Note, however, that phonemes are not classified at the frame level. Instead, continuous scores (prediction errors) are accumulated for various word candidates, and a decision is made only at the word level, where it is finally appropriate.

2.1 TRAINING AND TESTING ALGORITHMS

The purpose of the training procedure is both (a) to train the networks to become better predictors, and (b) to cause the networks to specialize on different phonemes. Given a known training utterance, the training procedure consists of three steps:

1. Forward Pass: All the networks make their predictions across the speech sample, and we compute the Euclidean distance matrix of prediction errors between predicted and actual speech frames. (See Figure 1.)
2. Alignment Step: We compute the optimal time-alignment path between the input speech and corresponding predictor nets, using Dynamic Time Warping.
3. Backward Pass: Prediction error is backpropagated into the networks according to the segmentation given by the alignment path. (See Figure 2.)

Hence backpropagation causes the nets to become better predictors, and the alignment path induces specialization of the networks for different phonemes.

Testing is performed using the One Stage algorithm [11], which is a classical extension of the Dynamic Time Warping algorithm for continuous speech.

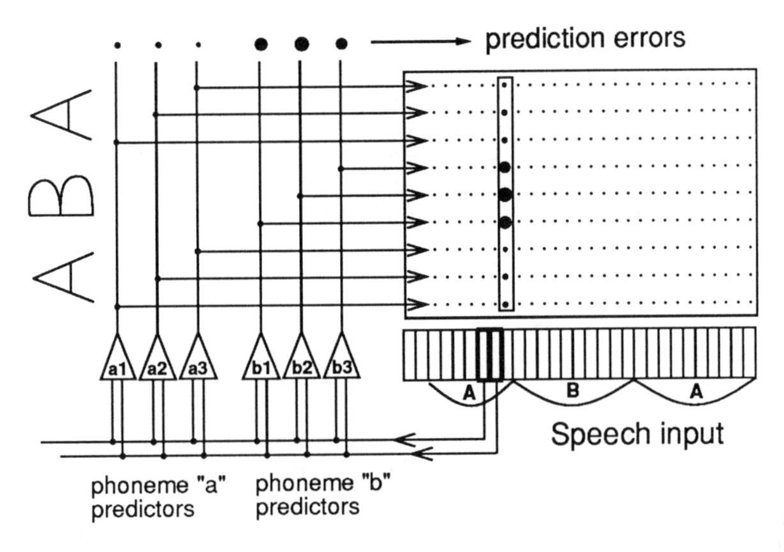

Figure 1: The forward pass during training. Canonical phonemes are modeled by sequences of N predictive networks, shown as triangles (here N=3). Words are represented by "linkage patterns" over these canonical phoneme models (shown in the area above the triangles), according to the phonetic spelling of the words. Here we are training on the word "ABA". In the forward pass, prediction errors (shown as black circles) are computed for all predictors, for each frame of the input speech. As these prediction errors are routed through the linkage pattern, they fill a distance matrix (upper right).

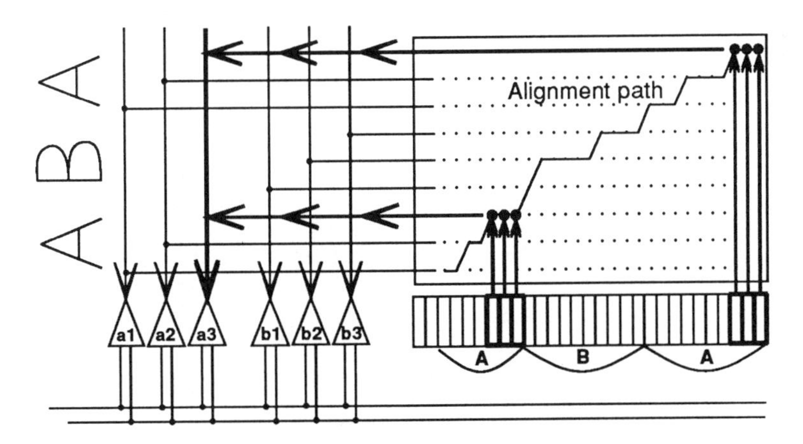

Figure 2: The backward pass during training. After the DTW alignment path has been computed, error is backpropagated into the various predictors responsible for each point along the alignment path. The backpropagated error signal at each such point is the vector difference between the predicted and actual frame. This teaches the networks to become better predictors, and also causes the networks to specialize on different phonemes.

3 RECOGNITION EXPERIMENTS

We have evaluated the LPNN system on a database of continuous speech recorded at CMU. The database consists of 204 English sentences using a vocabulary of 402 words, comprising 12 dialogs in the domain of conference registration. Training and testing versions of this database were recorded in a quiet office by multiple speakers for speaker-dependent experiments. Recordings were digitized at a sampling rate of 16 KHz. A Hamming window and an FFT were computed, to produce 16 melscale spectral coefficients every 10 msec. In our experiments we used 40 context-independent phoneme models (including one for silence), each of which had a 6-state phoneme topology similar to the one used in the SPICOS system [12].

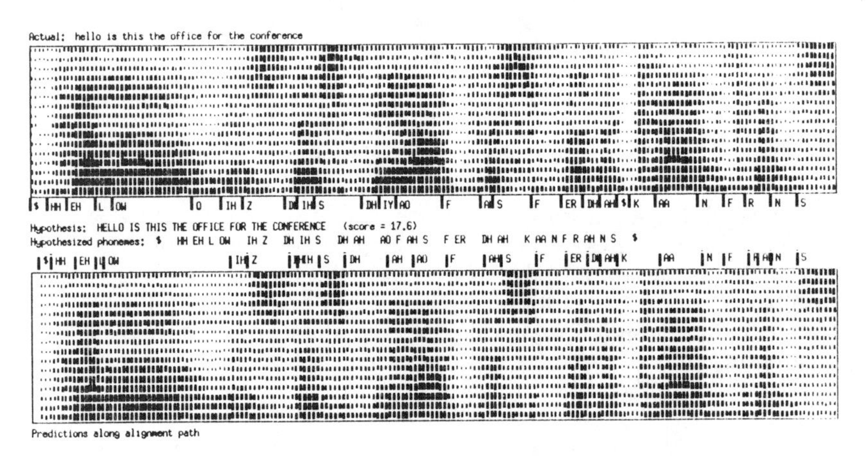

Figure 3: Actual and predicted spectrograms.

Figure 3 shows the result of testing the LPNN system on a typical sentence. The top portion is the actual spectrogram for this utterance; the bottom portion shows the frame-by-frame predictions made by the networks specified by each point along the optimal alignment path. The similarity of these two spectrograms indicates that the hypothesis forms a good acoustic model of the unknown utterance (in fact the hypothesis was correct in this case). In our speaker-dependent experiments using two males speakers, our system averaged 95%, 58%, and 39% word accuracy on tasks with perplexity 5, 111, and 402 respectively.

In order to confirm that the predictive networks were making a positive contribution to the overall system, we performed a set of comparisons between the LPNN and several pure HMM systems. When we replaced each predictive network by a univariate Gaussian whose mean and variance were determined analytically from the labeled training data, the resulting HMM achieved 44% word accuracy, compared to 60% achieved by the LPNN under the same conditions (single speaker, perplexity 111). When we also provided the HMM with delta coefficients (which were not directly available to the LPNN), it achieved 55%. Thus the LPNN was outperforming each of these simple HMMs.

4 HIDDEN CONTROL EXPERIMENTS

In another series of experiments, we varied the LPNN architecture by introducing hidden control inputs, as proposed by Levin [7]. The idea, illustrated in Figure 4, is that a sequence of independent networks is replaced by a single network which is modulated by an equivalent number of "hidden control" input bits that distinguish the state.

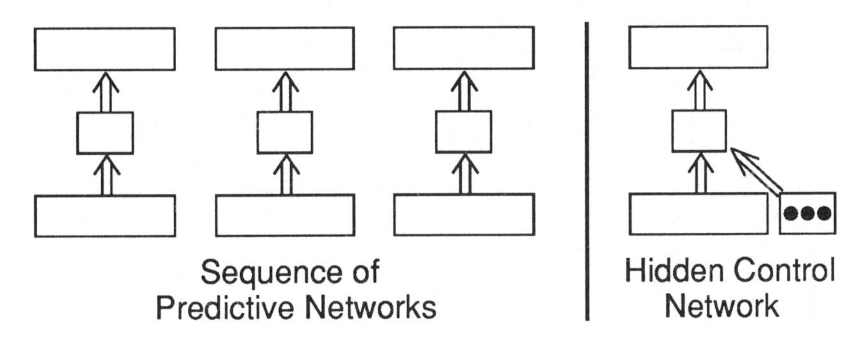

Figure 4: A sequence of networks corresponds to a single Hidden Control network.

A theoretical advantage of hidden control architectures is that they reduce the number of free parameters in the system. As the number of networks is reduced, each one is exposed to more training data, and – up to a certain point – generalization may improve. The system can also run faster, since partial results of redundant forward pass computations can be saved. (Notice, however, that the total number of forward passes is unchanged.) Finally, the savings in memory can be significant.

In our experiments, we found that by replacing 2-state phoneme models by equivalent Hidden Control networks, recognition accuracy improved slightly and the system ran much faster. On the other hand, when we replaced *all* of the phonemic networks in the entire system by a single Hidden Control network (whose hidden control inputs represented the phoneme as well as its state), recognition accuracy degraded significantly. Hence, hidden control may be useful, but only if it is used judiciously.

5 CURRENT LIMITATIONS OF PREDICTIVE NETS

While the LPNN system is good at modeling the acoustics of speech, it presently tends to suffer from poor discrimination. In other words, for a given segment of speech, all of the phoneme models tend to make similarly good predictions, rendering all phoneme models fairly confusable. For example, Figure 5 shows an actual spectrogram and the frame-by-frame predictions made by the /eh/ model and the /z/ model. Disappointingly, both models are fairly accurate predictors for the entire utterance.

This problem arises because each predictor receives training in only a small region of input acoustic space (i.e., those frames corresponding to that phoneme). Consequently, when a predictor is shown any other input frames, it will compute an

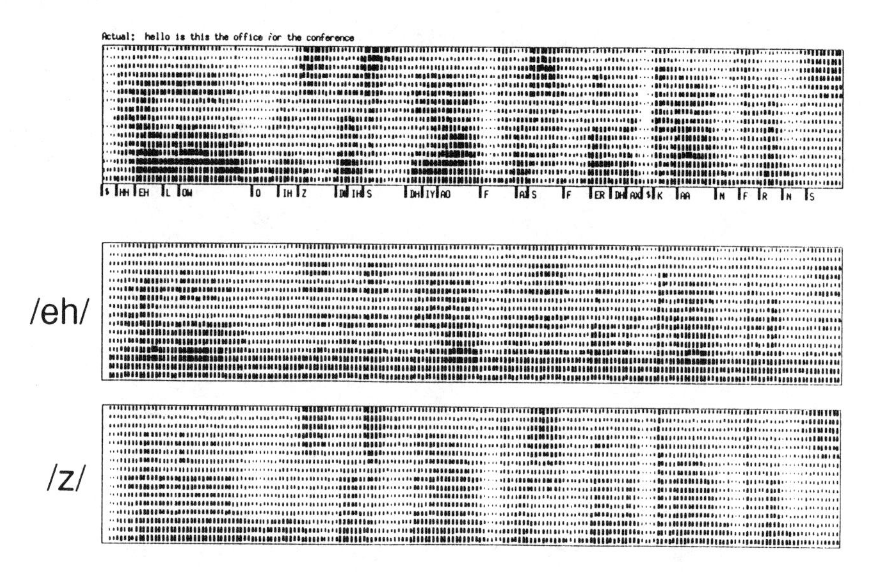

Figure 5: Actual spectrogram, and corresponding predictions by the /eh/ and /z/ phoneme models.

undefined output, which may overlap with the outputs of other predictors. In other words, the predictors are currently only trained on positive instances, because it is not obvious what predictive output target is meaningful for negative instances; and this leads to problematic "undefined regions" for the predictors. Clearly some type of discriminatory training technique should be introduced, to yield better performance in prediction based recognizers.

6 CONCLUSION

We have studied the performance of Linked Predictive Neural Networks for large vocabulary, continuous speech recognition. Using a 6-state phoneme topology, without duration modeling or other optimizations, the LPNN achieved an average of 95%, 58%, and 39% accuracy on tasks with perplexity 5, 111, and 402, respectively. This was better than the performance of several simple HMMs that we tested. Further experiments revealed that the accuracy and speed of the LPNN can be slightly improved by the judicious use of hidden control inputs.

The main advantages of predictive networks are that they produce non-binary distortion measures in a simple and elegant way, and that by virtue of their nonlinearity they can model the dynamic properties of speech (e.g., curvature) better than linear predictive models [13]. Their main current weakness is that they have poor discrimination, since their strictly positive training causes them all to make confusably accurate predictions in any context. Future research should concentrate on improving the discriminatory power of the LPNN, by such techniques as corrective training, explicit context dependent phoneme modeling, and function word modeling.

Acknowledgements

The authors gratefully acknowledge the support of DARPA, the National Science Foundation, ATR Interpreting Telephony Research Laboratories, and NEC Corporation. B. Petek also acknowledges support from the University of Ljubljana and the Research Council of Slovenia. O. Schmidbauer acknowledges support from his employer, Siemens AG, Germany.

References

[1] H. Bourlard and C. J. Wellekens. Links Between Markov Models and Multilayer Perceptrons. *Pattern Analysis and Machine Intelligence*, 12:12, December 1990.

[2] A. Waibel, T. Hanazawa, G. Hinton, K. Shikano, and K. Lang. Phoneme Recognition Using Time-Delay Neural Networks. *IEEE Transactions on Acoustics, Speech, and Signal Processing*, March 1989.

[3] M. Miyatake, H. Sawai, and K. Shikano. Integrated Training for Spotting Japanese Phonemes Using Large Phonemic Time-Delay Neural Networks. In *Proc. IEEE International Conference on Acoustics, Speech, and Signal Processing*, April 1990.

[4] E. McDermott and S. Katagiri. Shift-Invariant, Multi-Category Phoneme Recognition using Kohonen's LVQ2. In *Proc. IEEE International Conference on Acoustics, Speech, and Signal Processing*, May 1989.

[5] P. Haffner, M. Franzini, and A. Waibel. Integrating Time Alignment and Connectionist Networks for High Performance Continuous Speech Recognition. In *Proc. IEEE International Conference on Acoustics, Speech, and Signal Processing*, May 1991.

[6] K. Iso and T. Watanabe. Speaker-Independent Word Recognition Using a Neural Prediction Model. In *Proc. IEEE International Conference on Acoustics, Speech, and Signal Processing*, April 1990.

[7] E. Levin. Speech Recognition Using Hidden Control Neural Network Architecture. In *Proc. IEEE International Conference on Acoustics, Speech and Signal Processing*, April 1990.

[8] J. Tebelskis and A. Waibel. Large Vocabulary Recognition Using Linked Predictive Neural Networks. In *Proc. IEEE International Conference on Acoustics, Speech, and Signal Processing*, April 1990.

[9] J. Tebelskis, A. Waibel, B. Petek, and O. Schmidbauer. Continuous Speech Recognition Using Linked Predictive Neural Networks. In *Proc. IEEE International Conference on Acoustics, Speech, and Signal Processing*, May 1991.

[10] A. Waibel, A. Jain, A. McNair, H. Saito, A. Hauptmann, and J. Tebelskis. A Speech-to-Speech Translation System Using Connectionist and Symbolic Processing Strategies. In *Proc. IEEE International Conference on Acoustics, Speech, and Signal Processing*, May 1991.

[11] H. Ney. The Use of a One-Stage Dynamic Programming Algorithm for Connected Word Recognition. *IEEE Transactions on Acoustics, Speech, and Signal Processing*, 32:2, April 1984.

[12] H. Ney, A. Noll. Phoneme Modeling Using Continuous Mixture Densities. In *Proc. IEEE International Conference on Acoustics, Speech, and Signal Processing*, April 1988.

[13] N. Tishby. A Dynamic Systems Approach to Speech Processing. In *Proc. IEEE International Conference on Acoustics, Speech, and Signal Processing*, April 1990.

A Recurrent Neural Network for Word Identification from Continuous Phoneme Strings

Robert B. Allen
Bellcore
Morristown, NJ 07962-1910

Candace A. Kamm
Bellcore
Morristown, NJ 07962-1910

Abstract

A neural network architecture was designed for locating word boundaries and identifying words from phoneme sequences. This architecture was tested in three sets of studies. First, a highly redundant corpus with a restricted vocabulary was generated and the network was trained with a limited number of phonemic variations for the words in the corpus. Tests of network performance on a transfer set yielded a very low error rate. In a second study, a network was trained to identify words from expert transcriptions of speech. On a transfer test, error rate for correct simultaneous identification of words and word boundaries was 18%. The third study used the output of a phoneme classifier as the input to the word and word boundary identification network. The error rate on a transfer test set was 49% for this task. Overall, these studies provide a first step at identifying words in connected discourse with a neural network.

1 INTRODUCTION

During the past several years, researchers have explored the use of neural networks for classifying spectro-temporal speech patterns into phonemes or other sub-word units (e.g., Harrison & Fallside, 1989; Kamm & Singhal, 1990; Waibel *et al.*, 1989). Less effort has focussed on the use of neural nets for identifying words from the phoneme sequences that these spectrum-to-phoneme classifiers might produce. Several recent papers, however, have combined the output of neural network phoneme recognizers with other techniques, including dynamic time warping (DTW) and hidden Markov models (HMM) (e.g., Miyatake, *et al.*, 1990; Morgan & Bourlard, 1990).

Simple recurrent neural networks (Allen, 1990; Elman, 1990; Jordan, 1986) have been shown to be able to recognize simple sequences of features and have been applied to linguistic tasks such as resolution of pronoun reference (Allen, 1990). We consider whether they can be applied to the recognition of words from phoneme sequences. This paper presents the results of three sets of experiments using recurrent neural networks to locate word boundaries and to identify words from phoneme sequences. The three experiments differ primarily in the degree of similarity between the input phoneme sequences and the input information that would typically be generated by a spectrum-to-phoneme classifier.

2 NETWORK ARCHITECTURE

The network architecture is shown in Figure 1. Sentence-length phoneme sequences are stepped past the network one phoneme at a time. The input to the network on a given time step within a sequence consists of three 46-element vectors (corresponding to 46 phoneme classes) that identify the phoneme and the two subsequent phonemes. The activation of state unit S_i on the step at time t is a weighted sum of the activation of its corresponding hidden unit (H) and the state unit's activation on the previous time step, where β is the weighting factor for the hidden unit activation and μ is the state memory weighting factor: $S_{i,t}=\beta H_{i,t-1}+\mu S_{i,t-1}$. In this research β=1.0 and μ=0.5. The output of the network consists of one unit for each word in the lexicon and an additional unit whose activation indicates the presence of a word boundary.

Weights from the hidden units to the word units were updated based on error observed only at phoneme positions that corresponded to the end of a word (Allen, 1988). The end of the phoneme sequence was padded with codes representing silence. State unit activations were reset to zero at the end of each sentence. The network was trained using a momentum factor of α=0.9 and an average learning rate of η=0.05. The learning rate was adjusted for each output unit proportionally to the relative frequency of occurrence of the word corresponding to that unit.

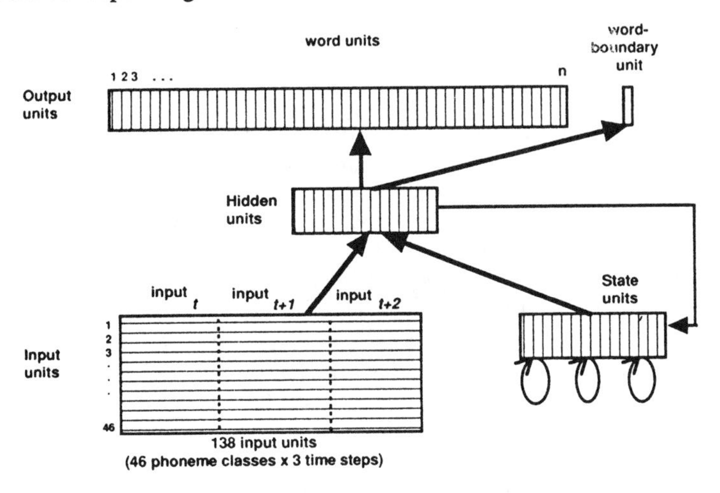

Figure 1: Recurrent Network for Word Identification

3 EXPERIMENT 1: DICTIONARY TRANSCRIPTIONS

3.1 PROCEDURE

A corpus was constructed from a vocabulary of 72 words. The words appeared in a variety of training contexts across sentences and the sentences were constrained to a very small set of syntactic constructions. The vocabulary set included a subset of rhyming words. Transcriptions of each word were obtained from Webster's Seventh Collegiate Dictionary and from an American-English orthographic-phonetic dictionary (Shoup, 1973). These transcriptions describe words in isolation only and do not reflect coarticulations that occur when the sentences are spoken. For this vocabulary, 26 of the words had one pronunciation, 19 had two variations, and the remaining 27 had from 3 to 17 variations. The corpus consisted of 18504 sentences of about 7 words each. 6000 of these sentences were randomly selected and reserved as transfer sentences.

The input to the network was a sequence of 46-element vectors designed to emulate the activations that might be obtained from a neural network phoneme classifier with 46 output classes (Kamm and Singhal, 1990). Since a phoneme classifier is likely to generate a set of phoneme candidates for each position in a sequence, we modified the activations in each input vector to mimic this expected situation. Confusion data were obtained from a neural network classifier trained to map spectro-temporal input to an output activation vector for the 46 phoneme classes. In this study, input activations for phonemes that accounted for fewer than 5% of the confusions with the correct phoneme remained set to 0.0, while input activations for phonemes accounting for higher proportions of the total confusions with the correct phoneme were set to twice those proportions, with an upper limit of 1.0. This resulted in relatively high activation levels for one to three elements and activation of 0.0 for the others. Overall, the network had 138 (46×3) input units, 80 hidden units, 80 state units, and 73 output units (one for each word and one boundary detection unit). The network was trained for 50000 sentence sequences chosen randomly (with replacement) from the training corpus. Each sequence was prepared with randomly selected transcriptions from the available dialectal variations.

3.2 RESULTS

In all the experiments discussed in this paper, performance of the network was analyzed using a sequential decision strategy. First, word boundaries were hypothesized at all locations where the activation of the boundary unit exceeded a predefined threshold (0.5). Then, the activations of the word units were scanned and the unit with the highest activation was selected as the identified word. By comparing the locations of true word boundaries with hypothesized boundaries, a false alarm rate (i.e., the number of spurious boundaries divided by the number of non-boundaries) was computed. Word error rate was then computed by dividing the number of incorrect words at correctly-detected word boundaries by the total number of words in the transfer set. This word error rate includes both deletions (i.e., missed boundaries) and word substitutions (i.e., incorrectly-identified words at correct boundaries). Total error rate is obtained by summing the word error rate and the false alarm rate.

On the 6000 sentence test set, the network correctly located 99.3% of the boundaries, with a word error rate of 1.7% and a false alarm rate of 0.3% Overall, this yielded a total error rate of 2.0%. To further test the robustness of this procedure to noisy input, three networks were trained with the same procedures as above except that the input phoneme sequences were distorted. In the first network, there was a 30% chance that input phonemes would be duplicated. In a second network, there was a 30% chance that input phonemes would be deleted. In the third network, there was a 70% chance that an input phoneme would be substituted with another closely-related phoneme. Total error rates were 11.7% for the insertion network, 20.9% for the deletion network, and 10.0% for the substitution network.

Even with these fairly severe distortions, the network is moderately successful at the boundary detection/word identification task. Experiment 2 was designed to study network performance on a more diverse and realistic training set.

4 EXPERIMENT 2: EXPERT TRANSCRIPTIONS OF SPEECH

4.1 PROCEDURE

To provide a richer and more natural sample of transcriptions of continuous speech, training sequences were derived from phonetic transcriptions of 207 sentences from the DARPA Acoustic-Phonetic (AP) speech corpus (TIMIT) (Lamel, *et al.*, 1986). The training set consisted of 4-5 utterances of each of 50 sentences, spoken by different talkers. One other utterance of each sentence (spoken by different talkers) was used for transfer tests. This corpus contained 277 unique words. For training, the transcripts were also segmented into words. When a word boundary was spanned by a single phoneme because of coarticulation (for example, the transcription /haeǰr/ for the phrase "had your"), the coarticulated phoneme (in this example, /ǰ/) was arbitrarily assigned to only the first word of the phrase. These transcriptions differ from those used in Experiment 1 primarily in the amount of phonemic variation observed at word boundaries, and so provide a more difficult boundary detection task for the network. As in Experiment 1, the input to the network on any time step was a set of three 46-element vectors. The original input vectors (obtained from the phonetic transcriptions) were modified based on the phoneme confusion data described in Section 3.1. The network had 138 (3×46) input units, 80 hidden units, 80 state units, and 278 output units.

4.2 RESULTS

After training on 80000 sentence sequences randomly selected from the 207 sentence training set (approximately 320,000 weight updates), the network was tested on the 50 sentence transfer set. With a threshold for the boundary detection unit of 0.5, the network was 87.5% correct at identifying word boundaries and had a false alarm rate of 2.3%. The word error rate was 15.5%. Thus, using the sequential decision strategy, the total error rate was 17.8%.

Considering all word boundaries (i.e., not just the correctly-detected boundaries), word identification was 90.3% correct when the top candidate only (i.e., the output unit with the highest activation) was evaluated and 96.3% for the top three word choices. Because there were instances where boundaries were not detected, but the word unit activations indicated the correct word, a decision strategy that simultaneously considered both the activation of the word boundary unit and the activation of the word units was also explored. However, the distributions of the word unit activations at non-boundary locations (i.e., within words) and at word boundaries overlapped significantly, so this strategy was unsuccessful at improving performance. In retrospect, this result is not very surprising, since the network was not trained for word identification at non-boundaries.

Many of the transfer cases were similar to the training sentences, but some interesting generalizations were observed. For example, the word "beautiful" always appeared in the training set as /bjuɾəfl/, but its appearance in the test set as /bjuɾəfUl/ was correctly identified. That is, the variation in the final syllable did not prevent correct identification of the word boundary or the word, despite the fact that the network had seen other instances of the phoneme sequence /Ul/ in the words "woolen" and "football" (second syllable). Of the 135 word transcriptions in the transfer set that were unique (i.e., they did not appear in the training set), the net correctly identified 72% based on the top candidate and 85% within the top 3 candidates. Not surprisingly, performance for the 275 words in the transfer set with non-unique transcriptions was higher, with 96% correct for the top candidate and 98% for the top 3 choices.

There was evidence that the network occasionally made use of phoneme context beyond word boundaries to distinguish among confusable transcriptions. For example, the words "an", "and", and "in" all appeared in the transfer set on at least one occasion as /ən/, but each was correctly identified. However, many word identification errors were confusions between words with similar final phonemes (e.g., confusing "she" with "be", "pewter" with "order"). This result suggests that, in some instances, the model is not making sufficient use of prior context.

5 EXPERIMENT 3: MACHINE-GENERATED TRANSCRIPTIONS

5.1 CORPUS AND PROCEDURE

In this experiment, the input to the network was obtained by postprocessing the output of a spectrum-to-phoneme neural network classifier to produce sequences of phoneme candidates. The spectrum-to-phoneme classifier, (Kamm and Singhal, 1990), generates a series of 46-element vectors of output activations corresponding to 46 phoneme classes. The spectro-temporal input speech patterns are stepped past the classifier in 5-ms increments, and the classifier generates output vectors on each step. Since phonemes typically have average durations longer than 5 ms, a postprocessing stage was required to compress the output of the classifier into a sequence of phoneme candidates appropriate for use as input to the boundary detection/word identification neural network.

The training set was a subset of the DARPA A-P corpus consisting of 2 sentences spoken by each of 106 talkers. The postprocessor provided output sequences for the training sentences that were quite noisy, inserting 2233 spurious phonemes and deleting 581 of the 7848 phonemes identified by expert transcription. Furthermore, in 2914 instances, the phoneme candidate with highest average activation was not the correct phoneme. However, this result was not unexpected, since the postprocessing heuristics are still under development. The primary purpose for using the postprocessor output was to provide a difficult input set for the boundary detection/word identification network.

After postprocessing, the highest-activation phoneme candidate sequences were mapped to the input vectors for the boundary detection/word identification network as follows: the vector elements corresponding to the three highest-activation phoneme candidate classes were set to their corresponding average activation values, and the other 43 phoneme classes were set to 0.0 activation. The network had 138 (i.e., 46×3) input units, 40 hidden units, 40 state units and 22 output units (21 words and 1 boundary unit). The network was trained for 40000 sentence sequences and then tested on a transfer set consisting of each sentence spoken by a new set of 105 talkers. The sequences in the transfer set were also quite noisy, with 2162 inserted phoneme positions and 775 of 7921 phonemes deleted. Further, the top candidate was not the correct phoneme in 3175 positions.

5.2 RESULTS

The boundary detection performance of this network was 56%, much poorer than for the networks with less noisy input. Since the network sometimes identified the word boundary at a slightly different phoneme position than had been initially identified, we implemented a more lenient scoring criterion that scored a "correct" boundary detection whenever the activation of the boundary unit exceeded the threshold criterion at the true boundary position *or* at the position immediately preceding the true boundary. Even with this looser scoring criterion, only 65% of the boundaries in the transfer set were correctly detected using a boundary detection threshold of 0.5. The false alarm rate was 9% and the word error rates were 40%, yielding a total error rate of 49%. This is much larger than the error rate for the network in Experiment 2. This difference may be explained in part by the presence of insertions in the input stream in this experiment as compared to Experiment 2, which had no insertions. The results of Experiment 2 indicated that this recurrent architecture has a limited capacity for considering past information (i.e., as evidenced by substitution errors such as "she" for "be" and "pewter" for "order"). As a result, poorer performance might be expected when the information required for word boundary detection or word identification spans longer input sequences, as occurs when the input contains extra vectors representing inserted phonemes.

5.3 NON-RECURRENT NETWORK

To evaluate the utility of the recurrent network architecture for this task, a simple non-recurrent network was trained using the same training set. In addition to the t, $t+1$ and $t+2$ input slots (Fig. 1), the non-recurrent network also included $t-1$ and $t-2$ slots, in an attempt to match some of the information about past context that may be available to the recurrent network through the state unit activations. Thus, the input required 230 (i.e., 5×46) input units. The network had no state units, 40 hidden units and 22 output units, and was trained through 40000 sentence sequences. On the transfer set, using a boundary detection threshold of 0.5, 75% of the word boundaries were correctly detected, and a false alarm rate of 31%. The word error rate was 60%. Thus, the recurrent net performed consistently better than this non-recurrent network both in terms of fewer false alarms and fewer word errors, despite the fact that the non-recurrent network had more weights. These results suggest that recurrence is important for the boundary and word identification task with this noisy input set.

6 DISCUSSION AND FUTURE DIRECTIONS

The current results suggest that this neural network model may provide a way of integrating lower-level spectrum-to-phoneme classification networks and phoneme-to-word classification networks for automatic speech recognition. The results of these initial experiments are moderately encouraging, demonstrating that this architecture can be used successfully for boundary detection with moderately large (200-word) and noisy corpora, although performance drops significantly when the input stream has many inserted and deleted phonemes. Furthermore, these experiments demonstrate the importance of recurrence.

Many unresolved questions about the application of this model for the word boundary/word identification task remain. The performance of this model needs to be compared with that of other techniques for locating and identifying words from phoneme sequences (for example, the two-level dynamic programming algorithm described by Levinson *et al.*, 1990).

Word-identification performance of the model (based on the output class with highest activation) is far from perfect, suggesting that additional strategies are needed to improve performance. First, word identification errors substituting "she" for "be" and "pewter" for "order" suggest that the network sometimes uses information only from one or two previous time steps to make word choices. Efforts to extend the persistence of information in the state units beyond this limit may improve performance, and may be especially helpful when the input is corrupted by phoneme insertions. Another possible strategy for improving performance would be to use the locations and identities of words whose boundaries and identities can be hypothesized with high certainty as "islands of reliability". These anchor points could then help determine whether the word choice at a less certain boundary location is a reasonable one, based on features like word length (in phonemes) or semantic or syntactic constraints. In addition, an algorithm that considers more than just the top candidate at each hypothesized word position and that uses semantic and syntactic constraints for reducing ambiguity might be prove more robust than the single-best-choice word identification strategy used in the current experiments. Schemes that attempt to identify word sequences without specifically locating word boundaries should be explored. The question of whether this network architecture will scale to successfully handle still larger corpora and realistic applications also requires further study. These unresolved issues notwithstanding, the current work demonstrates the feasibility of an integrated neural-based system for performing several levels of processing of speech, from spectro-temporal pattern classification to word identification.

References

Allen, R.B. Sequential connectionist networks for answering simple questions about a microworld. *Proceedings of the Cognitive Science Society,* 489-495, 1988.

Allen, R.B. Connectionist language users. *Connection Science,* **2,** 279-311, 1990.

Elman, J. L. Finding structure in time. *Cognitive Science*, **14**, 179-211, 1990.

Harrison, T. and Fallside, F. A connectionist model for phoneme recognition in continuous speech. *Proc. ICASSP 89*, 417-420, 1989.

Jordan, M. I. Serial order: A parallel distributed processing approach. *(Tech. Rep. No. 8604)*. San Diego: University of California, Institute for Cognitive Science, 1986.

Kamm, C. and Singhal, S. Effect of neural network input span on phoneme classification, *Proc. IJCNN June 1990*, **1**, 195-200, 1990.

Lamel, L., Kassel, R. and Seneff, S. Speech database development: Design and analysis of the acoustic-phonetic corpus. *Proc. DARPA Speech Recognition Workshop*, 100-109, 1986.

Levinson, S. E., Ljolje, A. and Miller, L. G. Continuous speech recognition from a phonetic transcription. *Proc. ICASSP-90*, 93-96, 1990.

Miyatake, M., Sawai, H., Minami, Y. and Shikano, H. Integrated training for spotting Japanese phonemes using large phonemic time-delay neural networks. *Proc. ICASSP 90*, 449-452, 1990.

Morgan, N. and Bourlard, H. Continuous speech recognition using multilayer perceptrons with hidden Markov models. *Proc. ICASSP 90*, 413-416, 1990.

Shoup, J. E. American English Orthographic-Phonemic Dictionary. NTIS Report AD763784, 1973.

Waibel, A., Hanazawa, T., Hinton, G., Shikano, K. and Lang, K. Phoneme recognition using time-delay neural networks. *IEEE Trans. ASSP*, **37**, 328-339, 1989.

Webster's Seventh Collegiate Dictionary. Springfield, MA: Merriam Company, 1972.

Connectionist Approaches to the Use of Markov Models for Speech Recognition

Hervé Bourlard [†,‡]
[†] L & H Speechproducts
Koning Albert 1 laan, 64
1780 Wemmel, BELGIUM

Nelson Morgan [‡] **& Chuck Wooters** [‡]
[‡] Intl. Comp. Sc. Institute
1947, Center St., Suite 600
Berkeley, CA 94704, USA

ABSTRACT

Previous work has shown the ability of Multilayer Perceptrons (MLPs) to estimate emission probabilities for Hidden Markov Models (HMMs). The advantages of a speech recognition system incorporating both MLPs and HMMs are the best discrimination and the ability to incorporate multiple sources of evidence (features, temporal context) without restrictive assumptions of distributions or statistical independence. This paper presents results on the speaker-dependent portion of DARPA's English language Resource Management database. Results support the previously reported utility of MLP probability estimation for continuous speech recognition. An additional approach we are pursuing is to use MLPs as nonlinear predictors for autoregressive HMMs. While this is shown to be more compatible with the HMM formalism, it still suffers from several limitations. This approach is generalized to take account of time correlation between successive observations, without any restrictive assumptions about the driving noise.

1 INTRODUCTION

We have been working on continuous speech recognition using moderately large vocabularies (1000 words) [1,2]. While some of our research has been in speaker-independent recognition [3], we have primarily used a German speaker-dependent database called SPICOS [1,2]. In our previously reported work, we developed a hybrid MLP/HMM algorithm in which an MLP is trained to generate the output probabilities of an HMM [1,2]. Given speaker-dependent training, we have been able to recognize 50-60 % of the words in the SPICOS test sentences. While this is not a state-of-the-art level of performance, it was accomplished with single-state phoneme models, no triphone or allophone representations, no function word modeling, etc., and so may be regarded as a "baseline" system. The main point to using such a simple system is simplicity for comparison of the effectiveness of alternate probability estimation techniques. While we are working on extending our technique to more complex systems, the current paper describes the application of the baseline system (with a few changes, such as different VQ features) to the speaker-dependent portion of the English language Resource Management (RM) database (continuous utterances built up from a lexicon of roughly 1000 words) [4]. While this exercise was primarily intended to confirm that the previous result, which showed the utility of MLPs for the estimation of HMM output probabilities, was not restricted to the limited data set of our first experiments, it also shows how to improve further the initial scheme.

However, potential problems remain. In order to improve local discrimination, the MLP is usually provided with contextual inputs [1,2,3] or recurrent links. Unfortunately, in these cases, the dynamic programming recurrences of the Viterbi algorithm are no longer stricly valid when the local probabilities are generated by these contextual MLPs. To solve this problem, we have started considering, as initially proposed in [9] and [10], another approach in which MLP is used as a nonlinear predictor. Along this line, a new approach is suggested and preliminary results are reported.

2 METHODS AND RESULTS

As shown by both theoretical [5] and experimental [1] results, MLP output values may be considered to be estimates of a posteriori probabilities. Either these or some other related quantity (such as the output normalized by the prior probability of the corresponding class) may be used in a Viterbi search to determine the best time-warped succession of states to explain the observed speech measurements. This hybrid approach has the potential of exploiting the interpolating capabilities of MLPs while using Dynamic Time Warping (DTW) to capture the dynamics of speech. As described in [2], the practical application of the technique requires cross-validation during training to determine the stopping point, division by the priors at the output to generate likelihoods, optimized word transition penalties, and training sentence alignment via iterations of the Viterbi algorithm.

For the RM data, initial development was done on a single speaker to confirm that the techniques we developed previously [2] were still applicable. Although we experimented slightly with this data, the system we ended up with was substantially unchanged, with the exception of the program modifications required to use different vector quantized (VQ) features. Input features used were based on the front end for SRI's DECIPHER system [6], including vector quantized mel-cepstrum (12 coefficients), vector-quantized difference of mel-cepstrum, quantized energy, and quantized difference of energy. Both vector quantization codebooks contained 256 prototypes, while energy and delta energy were quantized into 25 levels. A feature vector was calculated for each 10 ms of input speech. Since each feature was represented by a simple binary input vector with only one bit 'on', each 10 ms frame of speech signal was represented by a 562-dimensional binary vector with only 4 bits 'on'. Some experiments were run with no context (i.e., only one frame was input to the network for each classification). To show the advantage of contextual information, other experiments were run with nine frames of input to the network, allowing four frames of contextual information on each side of the current frame being classified. In this case, the input field contained $9 \times 562 = 5058$ units. The size of the output layer was kept fixed at 61 units, corresponding to the 61 phonemes to be recognized. As we found in our SPICOS experiments, a hidden layer was not useful for this problem, probably because of the high dimension of the binary input space and, as a consequence, of the large number of parameters. Of course, it could be argued that a hidden layer should reduce this huge number of parameters, and thus improve generalization. However, networks with no hidden units always outperformed experimental systems with hidden layers, on both the frame and word levels. The ability of the simpler nets to generalize well, despite the sheer number of parameters, was probably due to the cross-validation technique used during the MLP training [7]. However, as shown in [3], hidden layers are useful for the case of continuous input features. In this case, the dimension of the input layer of the MLP is much lower (even with contextual information), so that large hidden layers (e.g., 1000 units) may be useful.

For each speaker, we used 400 sentences for training, 100 for cross-validation, and a final 100 for recognition tests. Starting from an initial segmentation (derived from the average length of the phonemes), a Viterbi algorithm was then iterated with standard emission probabilities (i.e., by counting, no contextual information and assuming independence of the features) to generate a final segmentation which provided us with initial targets for the MLP training. Training of the MLP was done by an error-back propagation algorithm, using an entropy criterion. In each iteration, the complete training set was presented, and the parameters were updated after each training pattern (stochastic gradient). To avoid overtraining of the MLP, improvement on the cross-validation set was checked after each iteration. If the classification rate on the cross-validation set had not improved more than a small threshold, the learning rate of the gradient procedure was reduced by a factor of two. Compared with the results reported in [11], it has been observed recently that it was still possible to improve significantly the recognition performance [11] by starting from a lower initial learning constant and by adapting the segmentation of the training sentences to the MLP. This has been done by using the final segmentation of the standard Viterbi as a new starting point of a Viterbi training embedding now the MLP for estimating the emission probabilities. In this case, each iteration of the Viterbi is followed by a new optimization of the MLP (according to the new

Table 1: Word Recognition Performance on RM database

	Perplexity = 1000		
speaker	**ML**	**MLP(9)**	**+ FWM**
jws04	48.2	62.3	
bef03	39.3	56.7	
cmr02	59.5	70.9	
dtb03	49.8	61.2	
das12	63.8	76.5	81.8
ers07	45.4	58.3	
dms04	58.0	69.1	
tab07	60.8	70.5	
hxs06	60.9	76.3	
rkm05	37.9	53.8	60.2
pgh01	50.4	63.6	
mean	52.2	65.4	

segmentation generated by the Viterbi alignment). Recognition performance resulting of this process are reported in the column "MLP(9)" of Table 1. Comparison with results presented in [11] clearly shows the additional improvement (which was also observed at the frame level) that can be gained from such modifications.

3 RECOGNITION AND DISCUSSION

For recognition, the output layer of the MLP was evaluated for each frame, and (after division by the prior probability of each phoneme) was used as emission probabilities in a discrete HMM system. In this case, each phoneme k was thus associated with a single conditional density evaluated on the k-th output unit of the MLP. In our system, in order to model state duration, each phoneme was modeled by an HMM with a single state q_k repeated $D/2$ times, where D is the prior estimate of the duration of the phoneme as observed on the training set. Only selfloops and sequential transitions were permitted. A Viterbi decoding was then used for recognition of the first thirty sentences of the cross-validation set to optimize word transition probabilities. Note that this same simplified HMM was used for both the Maximum Likelihood (ML) reference system (estimating probabilities directly from relative frequencies) and the MLP system, and that the same input features were used for both.

The first two columns of Table 1 shows the recognition rates (100 % - error rate, where errors include insertions, deletions, and substitutions) for the 100 test sentences of the 11 speakers which were left out in the development, respectively for standard Maximum Likelihood (ML) and MLP with 9 frames of contextual input (MLP(9)). These results (all obtained with no language model, i.e., with a perplexity of 1000 for a 1000 word vocabulary) show the significant improvements that can be achieved using MLPs for continuous speech recognition (over simpler probability estimators) and that the incorporation of context has a major effect. However, it was also particularly interesting to note that the improvement was already significant with no contextual information at the input [11]. This can be explained by the fact that in standard HMM (denoted ML in Table 1) we must assume the independence of the four features so that we can estimate the joint density by their product, which is not the case with the MLP. This observation was also valid at the frame level [1,11].

However, these results are not the best ones we can expect from such an approach. A way to improve further the performance is to add function word models for small words as it is often done in standard HMMs. This idea was tested by using 28 additional output units (representing 12 word models) to the initial scheme. Results for the best and the worse speaker are reported under the column denoted "+ FWM" in Table 1. In view of the improvements, it can be concluded that many of the tricks valid for standard HMMs are also useful in our approach and can improve significantly the initial results.

4 MLP AS AUTOREGRESSIVE MODEL

As shown in the previous Section, it is clear that the proposed HMM/MLP hybrid approach can achieve significant improvements over standard HMMs. However, it has to be observed that these improvements are obtained despite some theoretical weaknesses. Indeed, it can be shown that the Dynamic Programming (DP) recurrences of the Viterbi algorithm (used for training and recognition) are no longer strictly valid when the local probabilities are generated by MLPs with contextual inputs. For a sequence of acoustic vectors $X = \{x_1, \ldots, x_N\}$ and a Markov model M, $P(X|M)$ cannot simply be obtained by DP recurrences (which are only valid for first order Markov models) using the contextual MLP outputs (divided by the priors). Thus, neither feedback or contextual input to the MLP (followed by the Bayes' rule to estimate $P(X|M)$) are stricly correct to use for the Viterbi algorithm, since both violate the restriction to instantaneous features on the left side of the conditional in local probabilities (in our case, the system is even not causal any more). This problem does not appear in standard HMMs were contextual information is usually provided via dynamic features such as the first and second derivatives (which are, in theory, estimates of instantaneous features) of the time-varying acoustic vectors.

In [9] and [10], another approach, related to autoregressive (AR) HMMs [8], is proposed in which the MLP is used as a nonlinear predictor. The basic idea is to assume that the observed vectors associated with each HMM state are drawn from a particular AR process described by an AR function that can be linear [8] or nonlinear and associated with the transfer function of an MLP. If x_n is the acoustic vector at time n and if $X_{n-p}^{n-1} = \{x_{n-p}, \ldots, x_{n-1}\}$ denotes the input of the MLP (which attempts to predict x_n, the desired output of the MLP associated with X_{n-p}^{n-1}), it can be shown [8,9,12] that, if the prediction error is assumed to be Gaussian with zero mean and unity variance, minimization of the prediction error is equivalent to estimation of $p(x_n|q_k^n, X_{n-p}^{n-1})$ (where q_k^n is the HMM state associated with x_n), which can be expressed as a Gaussian (with unity variance) where the exponent is the prediction error. Consequently, the prediction errors can be used as local distances in DP and are fully compatible with the recurrences of the Viterbi algorithm. However, although the MLP/HMM interface problem seems to be solved, we are now limited to Gaussian AR processes. Furthermore, each state must be associated with its own MLP [10]. An alternative approach, as proposed in [9], is to have a single MLP with additional "control" inputs coding the state being considered. However, in both cases, the discriminant character of the MLP is lost since it is only used as a nonlinear predictor. On preliminary experiments on SPICOS we were unable to get significant results from these approaches compared with the method presented in the previous Section [1,2].

However, it is possible to generalize the former approach and to avoid the Gaussian hypothesis. It is indeed easy to prove (by using Bayes' rule with an additional conditional X_{n-p}^{n-1} everywhere) that:

$$p(x_n|q_k^n, X_{n-p}^{n-1}) = \frac{p(q_k^n|X_{n-p}^{n})\, p(x_n|X_{n-p}^{n-1})}{p(q_k^n|X_{n-p}^{n-1})} . \tag{1}$$

As $p(x_n|X_{n-p}^{n-1})$ in (1) is independent of the classes q_k it can overlooked in the DP recurrences. In this case, without any assumption about mean and covariance of the driving noise, $p(x_n|q_k^n, X_{n-p}^{n-1})$ can be expressed as the ratio of the output values of two "standard" MLPs (as used in the previous Section and in [1,2]), respectively with X_{n-p}^{n-1} and X_{n-p}^{n} as input. In preliminary experiments, this approach lead to better results then the former AR models without however bearing comparison with the method used in the previous Section and in [1,2]. For example, on SPICOS and after tuning, we got 46 % recognition rate instead of 65 % with our best method [2].

5 CONCLUSION

Despite some theoretical nonidealities, the HMM/MLP hybrid approach can achieve significant improvement over comparable standard HMMs. This was observed using a simplified HMM system with single-state monophone models, and no langauge model. However, the reported results also show that many of the tricks used to improve standard HMMs are also valid for our hybrid approach, which leaves the way open to all sort of further developments. Now that we have confirmed the principle, we are beginning to develop a complete system, which will incorporate context-dependent sound units. In this framework, we are studying the possibility of modeling multi-states HMMs and triphones. On the other hand, in spite of preliminary disappointing performance (which seems to corroborate previous experiments done by others [13,14] with AR processes for speech recognition), MLPs as AR models are still worth considering further given their attractive theoretical basis and better interface with the HMM formalism.

References

[1] Bourlard, H., Morgan, N., & Wellekens, C.J., "Statistical Inference in Multilayer Perceptrons and Hidden Markov Models with Applications in Continuous Speech Recognition", *Neurocomputing*, Ed. F. Fogelman & J. Hérault, NATO ASI Series, vol. F68, pp. 217-226, 1990.

[2] Morgan, N., & Bourlard, H., "Continuous Speech Recognition using Multilayer Perceptrons with Hidden Markov Models", *IEEE Proc. of the 1990 Intl. Conf. on ASSP*, pp. 413-416, Albuquerque, NM, April 1990.

[3] Morgan, N., Hermansky, H., Bourlard, H., Kohn, P., Wooters, C., & Kohn, P., "Continuous Speech Recognition Using PLP Analysis with Multilayer Perceptrons" accepted for *IEEE Proc. of the 1991 Intl. Conf. on ASSP*, Toronto, 1991.

[4] Price, P., Fisher, W., Bernstein, J., & Pallet, D., "The DARPA 1000-Word Resource Management Database for Continuous Speech Recognition", *Proc. IEEE Intl. Conf. on ASSP*, pp. 651-654, New-York, 1988.

[5] Bourlard, H., & Wellekens, C.J., "Links between Markov Models and Multilayer Perceptrons", *IEEE Trans. on Pattern Analysis and Machine Intelligence*, Vol. 12, No. 12, pp. 1167-1178, December 1990.

[6] Murveit, H., & Weintraub, M., "1000-Word Speaker-Independent Continuous Speech Recognition Using Hidden Markov Models", *Proc. IEEE Intl. Conf. on ASSP*, pp. 115-118, New-York, 1988.

[7] Morgan, N., & Bourlard, H., "Generalization and Parameter Estimation in Feedforward Nets: Some Experiments", *Advances in Neural Information Processing Systems 2*, Ed. D.S Touretzky, San Mateo, CA: Morgan-Kaufmann, pp. 630-637, 1990.

[8] Juang, B.H. & Rabiner, L.R., "Mixture Autoregressive Hidden Markov Models for Speech Signals", *IEEE Trans. on ASSP*, vol. 33, no. 6, pp. 1404-1412, 1985.

[9] Levin, E., "Speech Recognition Using Hidden Control Neural Network Architecture", *Proc. of IEEE Intl. Conf. on ASSP*, Albuquerque, New Mexico, 1990.

[10] Tebelskis, J., & Waibel A., "Large Vocabulary Recognition Using Linked Predictive Neural Networks", *Proc. of IEEE Intl. Conf. on ASSP*, Albuquerque, New Mexico, 1990.

[11] Morgan, N., Wooters, C., Bourlard, H., & Cohen, M., "Continuous Speech Recognition on the Resource Management Database Using Connectionist Probability Estimation", *Proc. of Intl. Conf. on Spoken Language Processing*, Kobe, Japan, 1990.

[12] Bourlard, H., "How Connectionist Models Could Improve Markov Models for Speech Recognition", *Advanced Neural Computers*, Ed. R. Eckmiller, North-Holland, pp. 247-254, 1990.

[13] de La Noue, P., Levinson, S., & Sondhi M., "Incorporating the Time Correlation Between Successive Observations in an Acoustic-Phonetic Hidden Markov Model for Continuous Speech Recognition", AT&T Technical Memorandum No. 11226, 1989.

[14] Wellekens, C.J., "Explicit Time Correlation in Hidden Markov Models", *Proc. of the IEEE Intl. Conf. on ASSP*, Dallas, Texas, 1987.

Spoken Letter Recognition

Mark Fanty & Ronald Cole
Dept. of Computer Science and Engineering
Oregon Graduate Institute
Beaverton, OR 97006

Abstract

Through the use of neural network classifiers and careful feature selection, we have achieved high-accuracy speaker-independent spoken letter recognition. For isolated letters, a broad-category segmentation is performed Location of segment boundaries allows us to measure features at specific locations in the signal such as vowel onset, where important information resides. Letter classification is performed with a feed-forward neural network. Recognition accuracy on a test set of 30 speakers was 96%. Neural network classifiers are also used for pitch tracking and broad-category segmentation of letter strings. Our research has been extended to recognition of names spelled with pauses between the letters. When searching a database of 50,000 names, we achieved 95% first choice name retrieval. Work has begun on a continuous letter classifier which does frame-by-frame phonetic classification of spoken letters.

1 INTRODUCTION

Although spoken letter recognition may seem like a modest goal because of the small vocabulary size, it is a most difficult task. Many letter pairs, such as M–N and B–D, differ by a single articulatory feature. Recent advances in classification technology have enabled us to achieve new levels of accuracy on this task [Cole *et al.*, 1990, Cole and Fanty, 1990, Fanty and Cole, 1990]. The EAR (English Alphabet Recognition) system developed in our laboratory recognizes letters of the English alphabet, spoken in isolation by any speaker, at 96% accuracy. We achieve this level of accuracy by training neural network classifiers with empirically derived features—features selected on the basis of speech knowledge, and refined through experimentation. This process results in significantly better performance than just using "raw" data such as spectral coefficients.

We have extended our research to retrieval of names from spellings with brief pauses between the letters, and to continuous spellings. This paper provides an overview of these systems with an emphasis on our use of neural network classifiers for several separate components. In all cases, we use feedforward networks, with full connectivity between adjacent layers. The networks are trained using back propagation with conjugate gradient descent.

2 ISOLATED LETTER RECOGNITION

2.1 SYSTEM OVERVIEW

Data capture is performed using a Sennheiser HMD 224 noise-canceling microphone, lowpass filtered at 7.6 kHz and sampled at 16 kHz per second.

Signal processing routines produce the following representations every 3 msecs: (a) zero crossing rate: the number of zero crossings of the waveform in a 10 msec window; (b) amplitude: the peak-to-peak amplitude (largest positive value minus largest negative value) in a 10 msec window in the waveform; (c) filtered amplitude: the peak-to-peak amplitude in a 10 msec window in the waveform lowpass filtered at 700 Hz; (d) DFT: a 256 point FFT (128 real numbers) computed on a 10 msec Hanning window; and (e) spectral difference: the squared difference of the averaged spectra in adjacent 24 msec intervals.

Pitch tracking is performed with a neural network which locates peaks in the filtered (0-700 Hz) waveform that begin pitch periods. described in section 2.2.

Broad-category segmention divides the utterance into contiguous intervals and assigns one of four broad category labels to each interval: CLOS (closure or background noise), SON (sonorant interval), FRIC (fricative) and STOP. The segmenter, modified from [April 1988], uses cooperating knowledge sources which apply rules to the signal representations, most notably ptp0-700, pitch and zc0-8000.

Feature measurement is performed on selected locations in the utterance, based upon the broad-category boundaries. A total of 617 inputs are used by the classifier.

Letter classification is performed by a network with 52 hidden units and 26 output units, one per letter.

2.2 NEURAL NETWORK PITCH TRACKER

Pitch tracking is achieved through a network which classifies each peak in the waveform as to whether it begins a pitch period [Barnard *et al.*, 1991]. The waveform is lowpass filtered at 700 Hz and each positive peak is classified using information about it and the preceding and following four peaks. For each of the nine peaks, the following information is provided. (1) the amplitude, (2) the time difference between the peak and the candidate peak, (3) a measure of the similarity of the peak and the candidate peak (point-by-point correlation), (4) the width of the peak, and (5) the negative amplitude or most negative value preceding the peak. The network was trained on the TIMIT database, and agrees with expert labelers about 98% of the time. It performs well on our data without retraining.

2.3 NEURAL NETWORK LETTER CLASSIFIER

Each letter (except W) has a single SON segment (e.g. the /iy/ in T, the whole letter M). This segment always exists, and provides the temporal anchor for most of the feature measurements. The previous consonant is the STOP or FRIC (e.g. B or C) before the SON. If there is no STOP or FRIC (e.g. E), the 200 msec interval before the SON is treated as a single segment for feature extraction. After dozens of experiments, we arrived at the following feature set:

- DFT coefficients from the consonant preceding the SON. The consonant is divided into thirds temporally; from each third, 32 averaged values are extracted linearly from 0 to 8kHz. All DFT inputs are normalized locally so that the largest value from a given time slice becomes 1.0 and the smallest becomes 0.0. (96 values)
- DFT coefficients from the SON. From each seventh of the SON, 32 averaged values are extracted linearly from 0 to 4kHz. (224 values)
- DFT coefficients following the SON. At the point of maximum zero-crossing rate in the 200 msec after the SON, 32 values are extracted linearly from 0 to 8kHz. (32 values)
- DFT coefficients from the second and fifth frame of the SON—32 values from each frame extracted linearly from 0 to 4kHz. These are not averaged over time, and will reflect formant movement at the SON onset. (64 values)
- DFT coefficients from the location in the center of the SON with the largest spectral difference—linear from 0 to 4kHz. This samples the formant locations at the vowel-nasal boundary in case the letter is M or N. (32 values)
- Zero-crossing rate in 11 18-msec segments (198 msec) before the SON, in 11 equal-length segments during the SON and in 11 18-msec segments after the SON. This provides an absolute time scale before and after the SON which could help overcome segmentation errors. (33 values)
- Amplitude from before, during and after the SON represented the same way as zero-crossing. (33 values)
- Filtered amplitude represented the same way as amplitude. (33 values)
- Spectral difference represented like zero-crossing and amplitude except the maximum value for each segment is used instead of the average, to avoid smoothing the peaks which occur at boundaries. (33 values)
- Inside the SON, the spectral center of mass from 0 to 1000 Hz, measured in 10 equal segments. (10 values)
- Inside the SON, the spectral center of mass from 1500 to 3500 Hz, measured in 10 equal segments. (10 values)
- Median pitch, the median distance between pitch peaks in the center of the SON. (1 value)
- Duration of the SON. (1 value)

- Duration of the consonant before the SON. (1 value)
- High-resolution representation of the amplitude at the SON onset: five values from 12 msec before the onset to 30 msec after the onset. (5 values)
- Abruptness of onset of the consonant before the SON, measured as the largest two-frame jump in amplitude in the 30 msec around the beginning of the consonant. (1 value)
- The label of the segment before the SON: CLOS, FRIC or STOP. (3 values)
- The largest spectral difference value from 100 msec before the SON onset to 21 msec after, normalized to accentuate the difference between B and V. (1 value)
- The number of consistent pitch peaks in the previous consonant. (1 value)
- The number of consistent pitch peaks before the previous consonant. (1 value)
- The presence of the segment sequence CLOS FRIC after the SON (an indicator of X or H). (1 binary value)

All inputs to our network were normalized: mapped to the interval [0.0, 1.0]. We attempted to normalize so that the entire range was well utilized. In some instances, the normalization was keyed to particular distinctions. For example, the center of mass in the spectrum from 0 to 1000 Hz was normalized so that E was low and A was high. Other vowels, such as O would have values "off the scale" and would map to 1.0, but the feature was added specifically for E/A distinctions.

2.4 PERFORMANCE

During feature development, two utterances of each letter from 60 speakers were used for training and 60 additional speakers served as the test set. For the final performance evaluation, these 120 speakers were combined to form a large training set. The final test set consists of 30 new speakers. The network correctly classified 95.9% of the letters.

The E-set {B,C,D,E,G,P,T,V,Z} and MN are the most difficult letters to classify. We trained separate network for just the M vs. N distinction and another for just the letters in the E-set [Fanty and Cole, 1990]. Using these networks as a second pass when the first network has a response in the E-set or in {M,N}, the performance rose slightly to 96%.

As mentioned above, all feature development was performed by training on half the training speakers and testing on the other half. The development set performance was 93.5% when using all the features. With only the 448 DFT values (not spectral difference or center of mass) the performance was 87%. Using all the features except DFT values (but including spectral difference and center of mass), the performance was 83%.

3 NAME RETRIEVAL FROM SPELLINGS

3.1 SYSTEM OVERVIEW

Our isolated letter recognizer was expanded to recognize letters spoken with pauses by (1) Training a neural network to do broad-category segmentation of spelled strings (described in section 3.2); (2) Retraining the letter recognizer using letters extracted from spelled strings; (3) Devising an algorithm to divide an utterance into individual letters based on the broad category segmentation; and (4) Efficiently searching a large list of names to find the best match.

The letter classification network uses the same features as the isolated letter network. Feature measurements were based on segment boundaries provided by the neural network segmenter. The letter classification network was trained on isolated letters from 120 speakers plus letters from spelled strings from 60 additional speakers. The letter recognition performance on our cross-validation set of 8 speakers was 97%; on a preliminary test set of 10 additional speakers it was 95.5%. The letter recognition performance on our final test set was lower, as reported below.

The rules for letter segmentation are simplified by the structure of the English alphabet. All letters (except W—see below) have a single syllable, which corresponds to a single SON segment in the broad-category segmentation. In the usual case, letter boundaries are placed at the last CLOS or GLOT between SONs. A full description of the rules used can be found in [Cole *et al.*, 1991].

The output of the classifier is a score between 0.0 and 1.0 for each letter. These scores are treated as probabilities and the most likely name is retrieved from the database. The names are stored in a tree structure. The number of nodes near the root of the tree is small, so the search is fast. As the search approaches the leaves, the number of nodes grows rapidly, but it is possible to prune low-scoring paths.

3.2 NEURAL NETWORK BROAD-CATEGORY SEGMENTATION

The rule-based segmenter developed for isolated letters was too finely tuned to work well on letter strings. Rather than re-tune the rules, we decided to train a network to do broad category segmentation. At the same time, we added the category GLOT for glottalization, a slowing down of the vocal cords which often occurs at vowel-vowel boundaries.

The rule-based segmenter searched for boundaries. The neural network segmenter works in a different way [Gopalakrishnan, August 1990]. It classifies each 3 msec frame as being in a SON, CLOS, STOP, FRIC or GLOT. A five-point median smoothing is applied to the outputs, and the classification of the frame is taken to be the largest output. Some simple rules are applied to delete impossible segments such as 12 msec SONs.

The features found to produce the best performance are:

- 64 DFT coefficients linear from 0 to 8kHz at the frame to be classified.
- Spectral difference of adjacent 24 msec segments. These values are given for every frame in the 30 msec surrounding the frame to be classified, and for every 5 frames beyond that to 150 msecs before and after the frame to be classified. All subsequent features are sampled in the same manner.
- Spectral difference from 0 to 700 Hz in adjacent 24 msec segments.
- Amplitude of the waveform.
- Amplitude of the waveform lowpass filtered at 700 Hz. The window used to

measure the amplitude is just larger than the median pitch. In normal voicing, there is always at least one pitch peak inside the window and the output is smooth. During glottalization, the pitch peaks are more widely spaced. For some frames, the window used to measure amplitude contains no pitch peaks and the amplitude is sharply lower. Uneveness in this measure is thus an indication of glottalization.

- Zero crossing rate.
- A binary indicator of consistent pitch.
- The center of mass in the DFT coefficients between 0 and 1000 Hz.

A train-on-errors procedure was found to be very helpful. The segmenter resulting from training on the initial data set was used to classify new data. Frames for which it disagreed with hand-labeling were added to the initial data set and the network was retrained. This process was repeated several times.

3.3 SYSTEM PERFORMANCE

The system was evaluated on 1020 names provided by 34 speakers who were not used to train the system. Each subject spelled 30 names drawn randomly from the database of 50,000 surnames. The speaker was instructed to pause briefly between letters, but was not given any feedback during the session.

The list of 50,000 names provides a grammar of possible strings with perplexity 4. Using this grammar, the correct name was found 95.3% of the time. Of the 48 names not correctly retrieved, all but 6 of these were in the top 3 choices, and all but 2 were in the top 10. The letter recognition accuracy was 98.8% (total words minus substitutions plus deletions plus insertions, using a dynamic programming match). Examination of these name-retrieval errors revealed that about 50% were caused by misclassification of a letter, and about 50% were caused by bad letter segmentation. (Sixty percent of the segmentation errors were caused by GLOT insertions; forty percent were due to the speaker failing to pause.)

Without a grammar, the correct name is found only 53.9% of the time; almost half the inputs had at least one segmentation or classification error. The letter recognition accuracy was 89.1% using a dynamic programming match. Ignoring segmentation errors, 93% of the letters were correctly classified.

4 PHONEME RECOGNITION IN CONNECTED LETTERS

We have begun work on a continuous letter recognizer, which does not require pauses between the letters. The current system has two parts: a phonetic classifier which categorizes each frame as one of 30 phonemes (those phonemes found in letters plus glottalization)[Janssen *et al.*, 1989], and a Viterbi search to find the sequence of letters which best matches the frame-by-frame phoneme scores.

The phonetic classifier is given 160 DFT coefficients; 40 for the frame to be classified, for the immediate context (+/- 12 msec), for the near context (+/- 45 msec) and for the far context (+/- 78 msec) In addition, 87 features are added for the waveform amplitude, zero-crossing rate and spectral difference measure in a 183 msec window centered on the frame to be classified. It was trained on 9833 frames from 130 speakers spelling naturally. It was tested on 72 new speakers and achieved 76% frame accuracy with the instances of each phoneme categories equally balanced. When we feed the outputs of this network into a second network in addition to the DFT and other features, performance rose to 81%.

Simple letter models are used in a Viterbi search and enforce order and duration constraints for the phonemes. More work is required on coarticulation modeling, among other things. We are especially anxious to use carefully chosen features as with our isolated letter recognizer.

Acknowledgements

This research was supported by Apple Computer, NSF, and a grant from DARPA to the Computer Science & Engineering Department of the Oregon Graduate Institute. We thank Vince Weatherill for his help in collecting and labeling data.

References

[Barnard *et al.*, 1991] E. Barnard, R. A. Cole, M. Vea, and F. Alleva. Pitch detection with a neural net classifier. *IEEE Transactions on Acoustics, Speech and Signal Processing)*, 1991. To appear.

[Cole and Fanty, 1990] R. A. Cole and M. Fanty. Spoken letter recognition. In *Proceedings of the DARPA Workshop on Speech and Natural Language Processing*, June 1990. Hidden Valley, PA.

[Cole and Hou, April 1988] R. A. Cole and L. Hou. Segmentation and broad classification of continuous speech. In *Proceedings IEEE International Conference on Acoustics, Speech, and Signal Processing*, April, 1988.

[Cole *et al.*, 1990] R. A. Cole, M. Fanty, Y. Muthusamy, and M. Gopalakrishnan. Speaker-independent recognition of spoken english letters. In *Proceedings of the International Joint Conference on Neural Networks*, June 1990. San Diego, CA.

[Cole *et al.*, 1991] R. A. Cole, M. Fanty, M. Gopalakrishnan, and R. Janssen. Speaker-independent name retrieval from spellings using a database of 50,000 names. In *Proceedings IEEE International Conference on Acoustics, Speech, and Signal Processing*, 1991. Toronto, Canada.

[Fanty and Cole, 1990] M. Fanty and R. A. Cole. Speaker-independent english alphabet recognition: Experiments with the e-set. In *Proceedings of the International Conference on Spoken Language Processing*, November 1990. Kobe, Japan.

[Gopalakrishnan, August 1990] M. Gopalakrishnan. Segmenting speech into broad phonetic categories using neural networks. Master's thesis, Oregon Graduate Institute / Dept. of Computer Science, August, 1990.

[Janssen *et al.*,] R. D. T. Janssen, M. Fanty, and R. A. Cole. Speaker-independent phonetic classification of the english alphabet. submitted to *Proceedings of the International Joint Conference on Neural Networks*, 1991.

Speech Recognition Using Demi-Syllable Neural Prediction Model

Ken-ichi Iso and Takao Watanabe
C & C Information Technology Research Laboratories
NEC Corporation
4-1-1 Miyazaki, Miyamae-ku, Kawasaki 213, JAPAN

Abstract

The Neural Prediction Model is the speech recognition model based on pattern prediction by multilayer perceptrons. Its effectiveness was confirmed by the speaker-independent digit recognition experiments. This paper presents an improvement in the model and its application to large vocabulary speech recognition, based on subword units. The improvement involves an introduction of "backward prediction," which further improves the prediction accuracy of the original model with only "forward prediction". In application of the model to speaker-dependent large vocabulary speech recognition, the demi-syllable unit is used as a subword recognition unit. Experimental results indicated a 95.2% recognition accuracy for a 5000 word test set and the effectiveness was confirmed for the proposed model improvement and the demi-syllable subword units.

1 INTRODUCTION

The Neural Prediction Model (NPM) is the speech recognition model based on pattern prediction by multilayer perceptrons (MLPs). Its effectiveness was confirmed by the speaker-independent digit recognition experiments (Iso, 1989; Iso, 1990; Levin, 1990).

Advantages in the NPM approach are as follows. The underlying process of the speech production can be regarded as the nonlinear dynamical system. Therefore, it is expected that there is causal relation among the adjacent speech feature vectors. In the NPM, the causality is represented by the nonlinear prediction mapping $\mathbf{F}$,

$$\mathbf{a}_t = \mathbf{F}_w(\mathbf{a}_{t-1}), \tag{1}$$

where $\mathbf{a}_t$ is the speech feature vector at frame t, and subscript w represents mapping parameters. This causality is not explicitly considered in the conventional speech recognition model, where the adjacent speech feature vectors are treated as independent variables.

Another important model characteristic is its applicability to continuous speech recognition. Concatenating the recognition unit models, continuous speech recognition and model training from continuous speech can be implemented without the need for segmentation.

This paper presents an improvement in the NPM and its application to large vocabulary speech recognition, based on subword units. It is an introduction of "backward prediction," which further improves the prediction accuracy for the original model with only "forward prediction". In Section 2, the improved predictor configuration, NPM recognition and training algorithms are described in detail. Section 3 presents the definition of demi-syllables used as subword recognition units. Experimental results obtained from speaker-dependent large vocabulary speech recognition are described in Section 4.

2 NEURAL PREDICTION MODEL

2.1 MODEL CONFIGURATION

Figure 1 shows the MLP predictor architecture. It is given two groups of feature vectors as input. One is feature vectors for "forward prediction". Another is feature vectors for "backward prediction". The former includes the input speech feature vectors, $\mathbf{a}_{t-\tau_F}, \ldots, \mathbf{a}_{t-1}$, which have been implemented in the original formulation. The latter, $\mathbf{a}_{t+1}, \ldots, \mathbf{a}_{t+\tau_B}$, are introduced in this paper to further improve the prediction accuracy over the original method, with only "forward prediction". This, for example, is expected to improve the prediction accuracy for voiceless stop consonants, which are characterized by a period of closure interval, followed by a sudden release. The MLP output, $\hat{\mathbf{a}}_t$, is used as a predicted feature vector for input speech

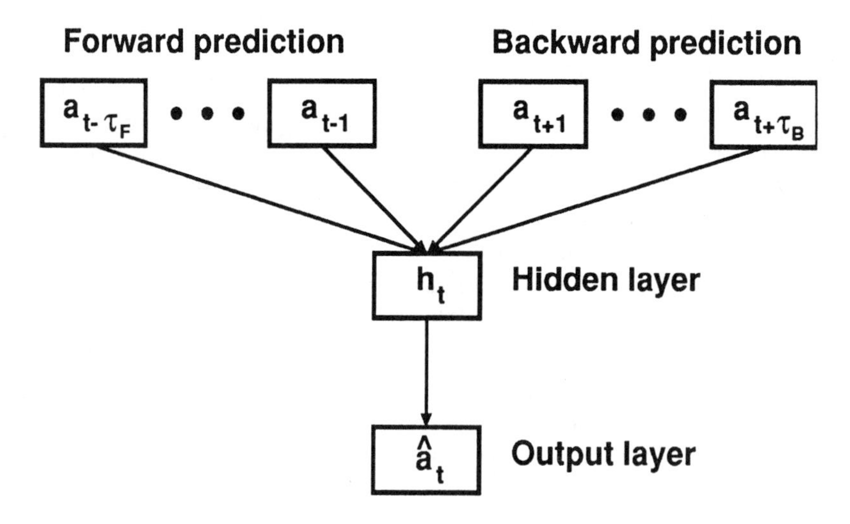

Figure 1: Multilayer perceptron predictor

feature vector $\mathbf{a}_t$. The difference between the input speech feature vector $\mathbf{a}_t$ and its prediction $\hat{\mathbf{a}}_t$ is the prediction error. Also, it can be regarded as an error function for the MLP training, based on the back-propagation technique.

The NPM for a recognition class, such as a subword unit, is constructed as a state transition network, where each state has an MLP predictor described above (Figure 2). This configuration is similar in form to the Hidden Markov Model (HMM), in which each state has a vector emission probability distribution (Rabiner, 1989). The concatenation of these subword NPMs enables continuous speech recognition.

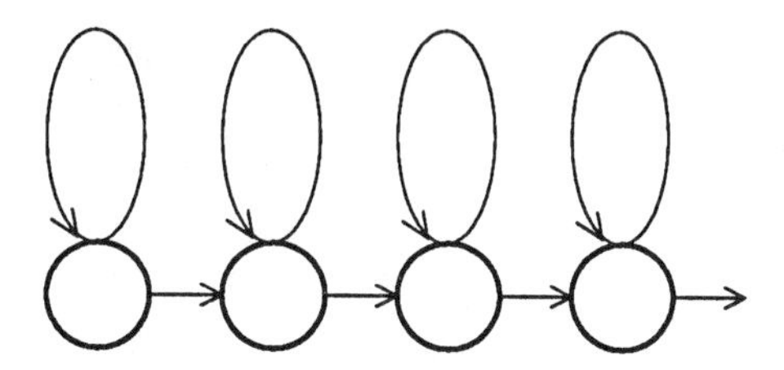

Figure 2: Neural Prediction Model

2.2 RECOGNITION ALGORITHM

This section presents the continuous speech recognition algorithm based on the NPM. The concatenation of subword NPMs, which is also the state transition network, is used as a reference model for the input speech. Figure 3 shows a diagram of the recognition algorithm. In the recognition, the input speech is divided into segments, whose number is equal to the total states in the concatenated NPMs ($= N$). Each state makes a prediction for the corresponding segment. The local prediction error, between the input speech at frame t and the n-th state, is given by

$$d_t(n) = \|\mathbf{a}_t - \hat{\mathbf{a}}_t(n)\|^2, \tag{2}$$

where n means the consecutive number of the state in the concatenated NPM. The accumulation of local prediction errors defines the global distance between the input speech and the concatenated NPMs

$$D = \min_{\{n_t\}} \sum_{t=1}^{T} d_t(n_t), \tag{3}$$

where n_t denotes the state number used for prediction at frame t, and a sequence $\{n_1, n_2, \ldots, n_t, \ldots, n_T\}$ determines the segmentation of the input speech. The minimization means that the optimal segmentation, which gives a minimum accumulated prediction error, should be selected. This optimization problem can be solved by the use of dynamic-programming. As a result, the DP recursion formula is obtained

$$g_t(n) = d_t(n) + \min \left\{ \begin{array}{l} g_{t-1}(n) \\ g_{t-1}(n-1) \end{array} \right\}. \tag{4}$$

At the end of Equation (4) recursive application, it is possible to obtain $D = g_T(N)$. Backtracking the result provides the input speech segmentation.

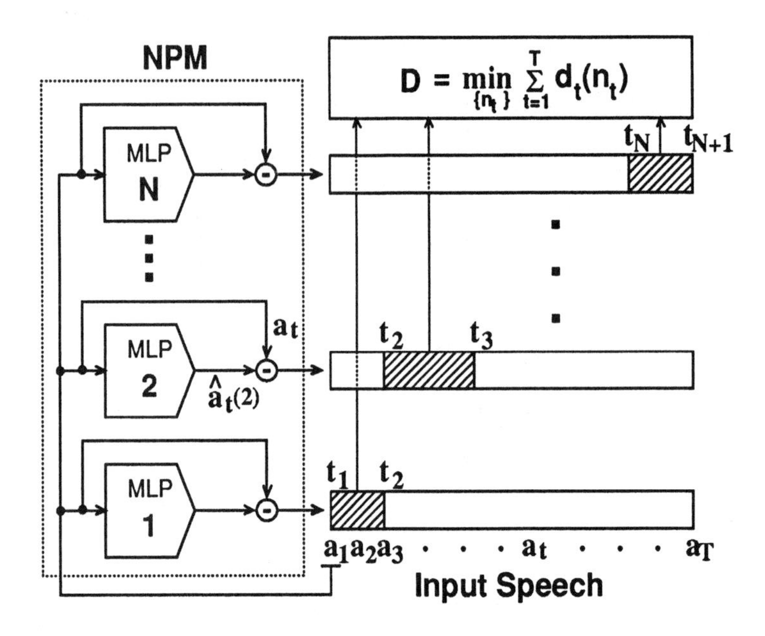

Figure 3: Recognition algorithm based on DP

In this algorithm, temporal distortion of the input speech is efficiently absorbed by DP based time-alignment between the input speech and an MLPs sequence. For simplicity, the reference model topology shown above is limited to a sequence of MLPs with no branches. It is obvious that the algorithm is applicable to more general topologies with branches.

2.3 TRAINING ALGORITHM

This section presents a training algorithm for estimating NPM parameters from continuous utterances. The training goal is to find a set of MLP predictor parameters, which minimizes the accumulated prediction errors for training utterances. The objective function for the minimization is defined as the average value for accumulated prediction errors for all training utterances

$$\bar{D} = \frac{1}{M} \sum_{m=1}^{M} D(m), \tag{5}$$

where M is the number of training utterances and $D(m)$ is the accumulated prediction error between the m-th training utterance and its concatenated NPM, whose expression is given by Equation (3). The optimization can be carried out by an iterative procedure, combining dynamic-programming (DP) and back-propagation (BP) techniques. The algorithm is given as follows :

1. Initialize all MLP predictor parameters.
2. Set $m = 1$.

3. Compute the accumulated prediction error $D(m)$ by DP (Equation (4)) and determine the optimal segmentation $\{n_t^*\}$, using its backtracking.
4. Correct parameters for each MLP predictor by BP, using the optimal segmentation $\{n_t^*\}$, which determines the desired output $\mathbf{a}_t$ for the actual output $\hat{\mathbf{a}}_t(n_t^*)$ of the n_t^*-th MLP predictor.
5. Increase m by 1.
6. Repeat 3 - 5, while $m \leq M$.
7. Repeat 2 - 6, until convergence occurs.

Convergence proof for this iterative procedure was given in (Iso, 1989; Iso, 1990). This can be intuitively understood by the fact that both DP and BP decrease the accumulated prediction error and that they are applied successively.

3 Demi-Syllable Recognition Units

In applying the model to large vocabulary speech recognition, the demi-syllable unit is used as a subword recognition unit (Yoshida, 1989). The demi-syllable is a half syllable unit, divided at the center of the syllable nucleus. It can treat contextual variations, caused by the co-articulation effect, with a moderate unit number. The units consist of consonant-vowel (CV) and vowel-consonant (VC) segments. Word models are made by concatenation of demi-syllable NPMs, as described in the transcription dictionary. Their segmentation boundaries are basically defined as a consonant start point and a vowel center point (Figure 4). Actually, they are automatically determined in the training algorithm, based on the minimum accumulated prediction error criterion (Section 2.3).

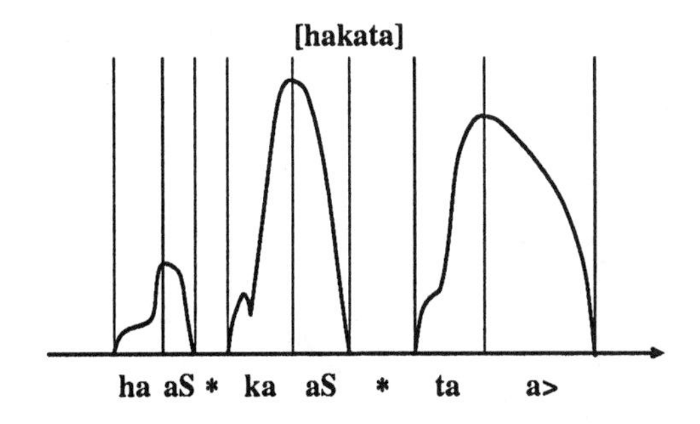

Figure 4: Demi-syllable unit boundary definition

4 EXPERIMENTS

4.1 SPEECH DATA AND MODEL CONFIGURATION

In order to examine the validity of the proposed model, speaker-dependent Japanese isolated word recognition experiments were carried out. Phonetically balanced 250, 500 and 750 word sets were selected from a Japanese word lexicon as training vocabularies. For word recognition experiments, a 250 word test set was prepared. All the words in the test set were different from those in the training sets. A Japanese male speaker uttered these word sets in a quiet environment. The speech data was sampled at a 16 kHz sampling rate, and analyzed by a 10 msec frame period. As a feature vector for each time frame, 10 mel-scaled cepstral parameters, 10 mel-scaled delta cepstral parameters and a changing ratio parameter for amplitude were calculated from the FFT based spectrum.

The NPMs for demi-syllable units were prepared. Their total number was 241, where each demi-syllable NPM consists of a sequence of four MLP predictors, except for silence and long vowel NPMs, which have one MLP predictor. Every MLP predictor has 20 hidden units and 21 output units, corresponding to the feature vector dimensions. The numbers of input speech feature vectors, denoted by τ_F, for the forward prediction, and by τ_B, for the backward prediction, in Figure 1, were chosen for the two configurations, $(\tau_F, \tau_B) = (2,1)$ and $(3,0)$. The former, Type A, uses the forward and backward predictions, while the latter, Type B, uses the forward prediction only.

4.2 WORD RECOGNITION EXPERIMENTS

All possible combinations between training data amounts ($= 250, 500, 750$ words) and MLP input layer configurations (Type A and Type B) were evaluated by 5000 word recognition experiments.

To reduce the computational amount in 5000 word recognition experiments, the similar word recognition method described below was employed. For every word in the 250 word recognition vocabulary, a 100 similar word set is chosen from the 5000 word recognition vocabulary, using the distance based on the manually defined phoneme confusion matrix. In the experiments, every word in the 250 word utterances is compared with its 100 similar word set. It has been confirmed that a result approximately equivalent to actual 5000 word recognition can be obtained by this similar word recognition method (Koga, 1989).

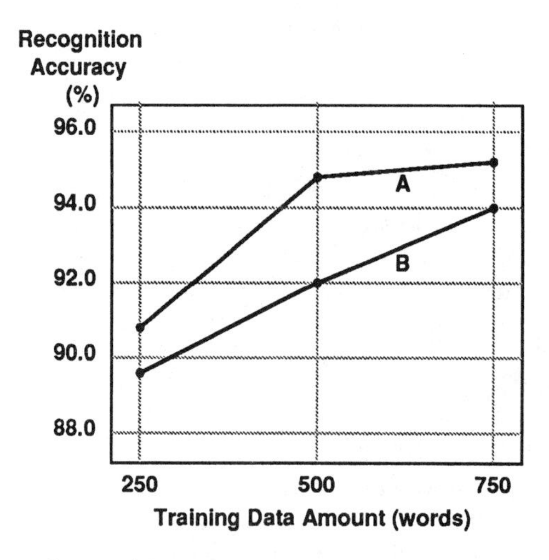

Figure 5: Recognition accuracy vs. training data amounts

The results for 5000 word recognition experiments are shown in Figure 5. As a result, consistently higher recognition accuracies were obtained for the input layer configuration with backward prediction (Type A), compared with the configuration without backward prediction (Type B), and absolute values for recognition accuracies become higher with the increase in training data amount.

5 DISCUSSION AND CONCLUSION

This paper presents an improvement in the Neural Prediction Model (NPM), which is the introduction of backward prediction, and its application to large vocabulary speech recognition based on the demi-syllable units. As a result of experiments, the NPM applicability to large vocabulary (5000 words) speech recognition was verified. This suggests the usefulness of the recognition and training algorithms for concatenated subword unit NPMs, without the need for segmentation. It was also reported in (Tebelskis, 1990) (90 % for 924 words), where the subword units (phonemes) were limited to a subset of complete Japanese phoneme set and the duration constraints were heuristically introduced. In this paper, the authors used the demi-syllable units, which can cover any Japanese utterances, and no duration constraints. High recognition accuracies (95.2 %), obtained for 5000 words, indicates the advantages of the use of demi-syllable units and the introduction of the backward prediction in the NPM.

Acknowledgements

The authors wish to thank members of the Media Technology Research Laboratory for their continuous support.

References

K. Iso. (1989), "Speech Recognition Using Neural Prediction Model," *IEICE Technical Report,* SP89-23, pp.81-87 (in *Japanese*).

K. Iso and T. Watanabe. (1990), "Speaker-Independent Word Recognition Using A Neural Prediction Model," *Proc.ICASSP-90,* S8.8, pp.441-444.

E. Levin. (1990), "Word Recognition Using Hidden Control Neural Architecture," *Proc.ICASSP-90,* S8.6, pp.433-436.

J. Tebelskis and A. Waibel. (1990), "Large Vocabulary Recognition Using Linked Predictive Neural Networks," *Proc. ICASSP-90,* S.8.7, pp.437-440.

L.R.Rabiner. (1989), "A Tutorial on Hidden Markov Models and Selected Applications in Speech Recognition", *Proc. of IEEE,* Vol.**77**, No.2, pp.257-286., February 1989.

K. Yoshida, T. Watanabe and S. Koga. (1989), "Large Vocabulary Word Recognition Based on Demi-Syllable Hidden Markov Model Using Small Amount of Training Data," *Proc.ICASSP-89,* S1.1, pp.1-4.

S. Koga, K. Yoshida, and T. Watanabe. (1989), "Evaluation of Large Vocabulary Speech Recognition Based on Demi-Syllable HMM," *Proc. of ASJ Autumn Meeting* (in Japanese).

RecNorm: Simultaneous Normalisation and Classification applied to Speech Recognition

John S. Bridle
Royal Signals and Radar Est.
Great Malvern
UK WR14 3PS

Stephen J. Cox
British Telecom Research Labs.
Ipswich
UK IP5 7RE

Abstract

A particular form of neural network is described, which has terminals for acoustic patterns, class labels and speaker parameters. A method of training this network to "tune in" the speaker parameters to a particular speaker is outlined, based on a trick for converting a supervised network to an unsupervised mode. We describe experiments using this approach in isolated word recognition based on whole-word hidden Markov models. The results indicate an improvement over speaker-independent performance and, for unlabelled data, a performance close to that achieved on labelled data.

1 INTRODUCTION

We are concerned to emulate some aspects of perception. In particular, the way that a stimulus which is ambiguous, perhaps because of unknown lighting conditions, can become unambiguous in the context of other such stimuli: the fact that they are subject to the same unknown conditions gives our perceptual apparatus enough constraints to solve the problem. Individual words are often ambiguous even to human listeners. For instance a Cockney might say the word "ace" to sound the same as a Standard English speaker's "ice". Similarly with "room" and "rum", or "work" and "walk" in other pairs of British English accents. If we heard one of these ambiguous pronunciations, knowing nothing else about the speaker we could not tell which word had been said. For current automatic speech recognition (ASR) systems such effects are much more frequent, because we do not know how to concentrate on the important aspects of the signal locally, nor how to exploit the fact that some unknown properties apply to whole words, nor how to bring to bear on the task of acoustic disambiguation all the information that is normally latent in the context of the utterance.

Most attempts to construct ASR systems which can be used by many persons have used so-called speaker-independent models. When decoding a short sequence of words there is no way of imposing our knowledge that all the speech is uttered by one person.

To enable adaptation using small amounts of speech from a new speaker we propose to factor the speech knowledge into speaker-independent models, continous speaker-specific parameters and a transformation which modifies the models according to the speaker parameters. (In this paper we shall only use transformations which can just as easily be applied to the input patterns.) We are specially interested in the possibility of estimating such parameters from quite small amounts of *unlabelled* speech, such as a few short words or one longer word. Although the types of models and transformations we have used are very simple, we hope the general approach will be applicable to quite sophisticated models and transformations which will be necessary for future high-performance speech recognition systems.

2 AN ADAPTIVE NETWORK APPROACH

2.1 GENERAL IDEA

Suppose we had a feed-forward network with three (vector-valued) terminals, which encapsulates our knowledge of the relationship between acoustic patterns, $\boldsymbol{X}$, class labels (e.g. word identities) $\boldsymbol{C}$, and speaker parameters, $\boldsymbol{Q}$.

Training such a network seems difficult, because although we can supply ($\boldsymbol{X}$,$\boldsymbol{C}$) pairs, we do not know the appropriate values of $\boldsymbol{Q}$. (We only know the *names* of the speakers, or perhaps some phonetician's descriptive labels.)

In training the network we start with default values of $\boldsymbol{Q}$, feed forward from $\boldsymbol{X}$ and $\boldsymbol{Q}$ to $\boldsymbol{C}$, back-propagate derivatives to internal parameters of the network (weights, transition probabilities, etc.) and also to the $\boldsymbol{Q}$s, enforcing the constraint that the $\boldsymbol{Q}$s for any one speaker stay equal. We can imagine one copy of the network for each utterance, with the $\boldsymbol{Q}$ terminals of networks dealing with the same speaker strapped together. One convenient implementation (for a small number of training speakers) is to adapt one $\boldsymbol{Q}$ vector per speaker in a set of weights from one-from-N coded speaker identity inputs to linear units, as we shall see later.

Once the network is trained we have two modes of use. If we have available one or more known utterances by a new speaker, then we can "tune-in" to the speaker (as during training) except that only the $\boldsymbol{Q}$ inputs are adjusted. The case of most interest in this paper, however, is when we have a few *unknown* words from an unknown speaker. We set up a $\boldsymbol{Q}$-strapped set of networks, one for each word, initialise the $\boldsymbol{Q}$ values to their defaults, propagate forwards to produce a set of distributions across word labels, and then we use a technique which tends to sharpen these distributions. In the simplest case, the sharpening process could be a matter of: for each utterance pick the word label with the largest output, and assuming it to be correct back-propagate derivatives to the common $\boldsymbol{Q}$. In practice, we can use a gentler method in which large outputs get most 'encouragement'. For some networks it is possible to show that such a "phantom target" procedure can lead to hillclimbing on the likelihood of the data given an assumption about the form of the generator of the data (see Appendix).

2.2 SIMPLE NETWORK ILLUSTRATION

We have explored these ideas using a very simple network based on that in figure 1. It can be viewed either as a feedforward network with radial (minus Euclidean distance squared) units and a generalised-logistic (Softmax) output non-linearity, or as a Gaussian classifier in which the covariance matrices are unit diagonal (see [Bri90b]). Training is done by gradient-based optimisation, using back-propagation of partial derivatives. During training the criterion is based on relative entropy (likelihood of the targets given the network outputs) [Bri90c]. (Such *discriminative* training can lead to different results from the usual model-based methods [Bri90b], which in this case would set the reference points at the data means for each class.)

This simple classifier network is preceded by a full linear transformation (6 parameters), so the equivalent model-based classifier has Gaussian distributions with the same arbitrary covariance matrix for each class. We use the biasses of the linear units as speaker parameters, so the weights from speaker identity inputs go straight into the hidden units, is as figure 2.

During adaptation to a new speaker from *unlabelled* tokens, the speaker parameters of the transformation are allowed to adapt, but the ("phantom") targets are derived from the outputs themselves (the targets are just double the outputs) so that the largest outputs are encouraged.

In figure 3 we see the adaptation of the positions of the reference points of the radial units in figure 2 when the input points are essentially the 6 reference points displaced to one side (to represent one example of each word spoken by a new speaker). Adaptation based on tentative classifications pulls the reference points towards a position where the inputs can be given confident, consistent labels.

3 SPEECH RECOGNITION EXPERIMENTS

We have applied these ideas to the problem of recognising a few short, confusable words from a known set, all spoken by the same unknown speaker. If our method works we should be able to recognise each word better (on average) if we also look at a few other unknown words from the same speaker.

The dataset [Sal89], which had been recorded previously for other purposes, comprised the British English isolated pronounciations of the names of the letters of the alphabet, each spoken 3 times by each speaker. The 104 speakers were divided into two groups of 52 (Train and Test), balanced for age and sex. Initial acoustic analysis produced 28-component spectrum vectors, 100 per second. In place of the 2-D input patterns discussed above, each speech pattern was a variable-duration sequence (typically 50) of 28-vectors.

In place of each simple Gaussian density class-models we used a set of Gaussian densities and a matrix of probabilities of transitions between them. Each class-model is thus a hidden Markov model (HMM) of a word. We used 26 HMMs, each

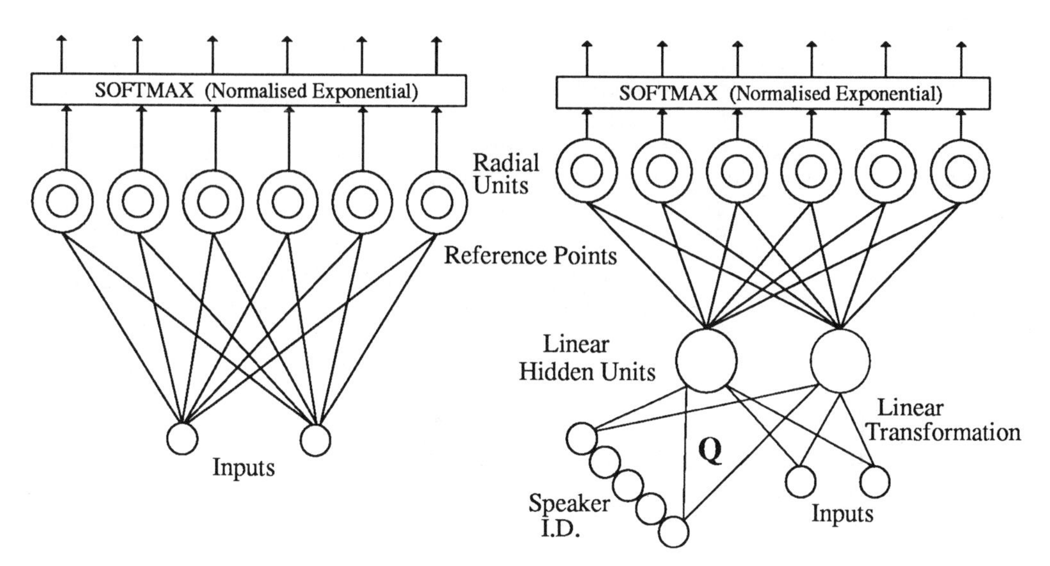

Fig.1 Feedforward Network Implementing Simple Gaussian Classifier

Fig.2 Gaussian classifier network with input transformation and speaker inputs

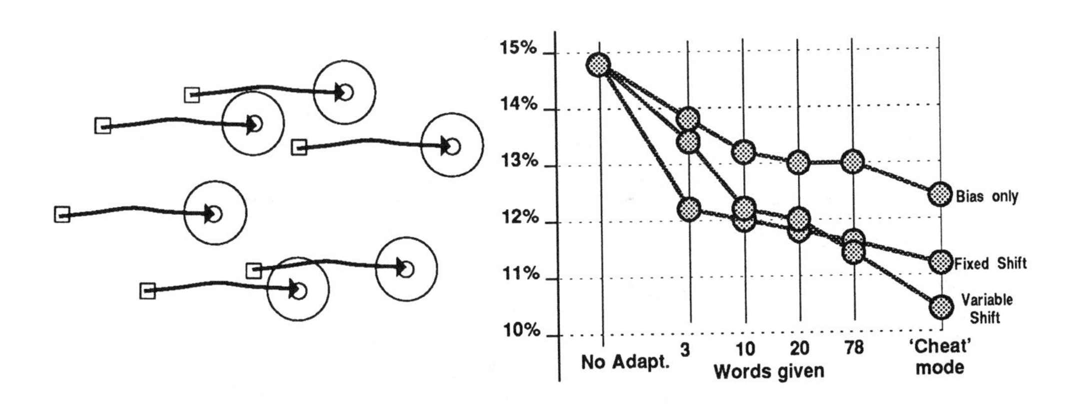

Fig.3 Adaptation to 6 displaced points

Fig.4 Average error rates for alphabet word recognition

with 15 states, each with a 3-component Gaussian mixture output distribution. For further details see [CB90].

The equivalent to the evaluation of a Gaussian density in the simple network is the Forward (or Alpha) computation of the likelihood of the data given a (hidden Markov) model. This calculation can be thought of as being performed by a recurrent network of a special form. When we include the Bayes inversion to produce probabilities of the classes (this is a normalisation if we assume equal prior probabilities) we obtain the equivalent of the simple network of figure 1, which we call an Alphanet[Bri90a].

In place of the 2-component linear transformation in figure 2 we use a constrained linear transformation based on [Hun81] $y_i = a_i x_{i-1} + b_i x_i + c_i x_{i+1} + d_i$, where $x_i, i = 1, \ldots 28$, is the log spectrum amplitude in frequency channel i.

We tried three conditions:

- Bias Only: $a = 0$, $b = 1$, $c = 0$ (28 parameters)
- Fixed Shift: $a_i = a$, $b_i = b$, $c_i = c$ (31 parameters)
- Variable Shift: the general case (107 parameters)

Figure 4 shows average word error rates for the three types of transformation, for different numbers of utterances taken together ($N = 3, 10, 20, 78$). $N = 1$ is the non-adaptive case. 'Cheat' Mode is a check on the power of the transformations: for each test speaker, all 78 utterances were used to set the parameters of the transformation, then recognition performance was measured using those parameters of the same utterances.

We see:

- Use of unsupervised adaptation reduced the error rates.
- The reductions are not spectacular (15% errors to 12% errors, a reduction in error rate by 20%.) but they are statistically significant and may be practically significant too.
- The performance in 'Cheat' Mode is only a little better than in unsupervised mode, so performance is being limited by the power of the transformation.
- The Fixed Shift transformation gives quite good results even on only 3 words at a time.

When tested on a 120 talker telephone-line database of isolated digits collected at British Telecom, the best unsupervised speaker adaptation technique gave a 37% decrease in error-rate (for both supervised and unsupervised adaptation on 5 utterances) using a simple front-end consisting of 8 MFCCs (mel frequency-scale cepstrum coefficients). A more sophisticated front-end (using differential information and energy) improved the unadapted performance by 63% over the 8 MFCC front-end. Using this front-end, the best unsupervised adaptation technique (on 5 utterances) decreased the error-rate by a further 25%

4 CONCLUSIONS

The results reported here show that simultaneous word recognition and speaker normalisation can be made to work, that it improves performance over the corresponding speaker-independent version, and that given 3 to 10 unknown words performance can be almost as good as when the adaptation is done using knowledge of the word identities. The main extensions we are interested in are to use non-linear transformations, and to learn low-dimensional but effective speaker parameterisations.

A Unsupervised Adaptation using Phantom Targets

We aim to motivate the 'phantom target' trick of feeding back twice each output of the network as a target.

Suppose we have a classifier network, with a 1-from-N output coding, and a Softmax output nonlinearity. We write Q_j for an output value, V_j for an input to the Softmax output stage, $\boldsymbol{x}$ for the input to the network, c for a class and $\boldsymbol{\theta}$ for parameters which we may want to adjust. A typical output value is

$$Q_j(\boldsymbol{x}, \boldsymbol{\theta}) = \mathrm{e}^{V_j(\boldsymbol{x}, \boldsymbol{\theta})} \Big/ \sum_k \mathrm{e}^{V_k(\boldsymbol{x}, \boldsymbol{\theta})}.$$

The output values are interpretable as estimates of posterior probabilities: $Q_j \approx \Pr(\mathrm{c} = \mathrm{j} \mid \boldsymbol{x}, \boldsymbol{\theta})$. For the next step we assume there are some implicit probability density functions $P_j(\boldsymbol{x}, \boldsymbol{\theta}) \approx \Pr(\boldsymbol{x} \mid \mathrm{c} = \mathrm{j}, \boldsymbol{\theta})$ Assuming equal prior probabilities of the classes for simplicity, Bayes rule gives

$$Q_j(\boldsymbol{x}, \boldsymbol{\theta}) = P_j(\boldsymbol{x}, \boldsymbol{\theta}) \Big/ \sum_{k=1}^{N} P_k(\boldsymbol{x}, \boldsymbol{\theta}),$$

so we suppose that

$$P_j(\boldsymbol{x}, \boldsymbol{\theta}) = \frac{1}{z_j(\boldsymbol{\theta})} \mathrm{e}^{V_j(\boldsymbol{x}, \boldsymbol{\theta})},$$

where the normalisation is

$$z_j(\boldsymbol{\theta}) = \int \mathrm{e}^{V_j(\boldsymbol{x}, \boldsymbol{\theta})} d\boldsymbol{x}.$$

In the networks we use, the same normalisation applies to all the classes, so we write $z_j(\boldsymbol{\theta}) = z(\boldsymbol{\theta})$.

A maximum-likelihood approach to unsupervised adaptation maximises the likelihood of the data given the set of (equally probable) distributions, which is

$$P(\boldsymbol{x}, \boldsymbol{\theta}) = \sum_{k=1}^{N} P_k(\boldsymbol{x}, \boldsymbol{\theta}) \frac{1}{N},$$

It is simpler to maximise the *log* likelihood:

$$L(\boldsymbol{x}, \boldsymbol{\theta}) \triangleq \log P(\boldsymbol{x}, \boldsymbol{\theta}) = \log \sum_k P_k(\boldsymbol{x}, \boldsymbol{\theta}) - \log N = \log \sum_k \mathrm{e}^{V_k(\boldsymbol{x}, \boldsymbol{\theta})} - \log z(\boldsymbol{\theta}) - \log N.$$

We shall need

$$\frac{\partial L}{\partial V_j} = \frac{1}{\sum_k e^{V_k(\boldsymbol{x}, \boldsymbol{\theta})}} e^{V_j(\boldsymbol{x}, \boldsymbol{\theta})} - \frac{1}{z(\boldsymbol{\theta})} \frac{\partial z(\boldsymbol{\theta})}{\partial V_j(\boldsymbol{x}, \boldsymbol{\theta})}.$$

(The likelihood of the whole training set is the product of the likelihoods of the individual patterns, and the log turns the product into a sum, so we can sum the derivatives of L over the training set.)

We can often assume that the normalisation is independent of $\boldsymbol{\theta}$, giving

$$\frac{\partial L}{\partial V_j} = \frac{e^{V_j(\boldsymbol{x}, \boldsymbol{\theta})}}{\sum_k e^{V_k(\boldsymbol{x}, \boldsymbol{\theta})}} = Q_j(\boldsymbol{x}, \boldsymbol{\theta}).$$

If we have a supervised backprop network using the relative entropy based criterion (rather than squared error) [?], we are minimising $J = -\sum_j T_j \log Q_j$, where T_j is the target for the jth output. We know [Bri90b] that $\frac{\partial J}{\partial V_j} = Q_j - T_j$, so if we set $T_j = 2Q_j$ we have $\frac{\partial J}{\partial V_j} = -\frac{\partial L}{\partial V_j}$, and minimising J is equivalent to maximising L.

For the simple Gaussian network of figure 1, this unsupervised adaptation, applied to the reference points, can be understood as an on-line, gradient descent, relative of the k-means cluster analysis procedure, or of the LBG vector quantiser design method, or indeed of Kohonen's feature map (without the neighbourhood constraints).

References

[Bri90a] J S Bridle. Alphanets: a recurrent 'neural' network architecture with a hidden Markov model interpretation. *Speech Communication*, Special "Neurospeech" issue, February 1990.

[Bri90b] J S Bridle. Probabilistic interpretation of feedforward classification network outputs, with relationships to statistical pattern recognition. In F Fougelman-Soulie and J Hérault, editors, *Neuro-computing: algorithms, architectures and applications*, NATO ASI Series on Systems and computer science. Springer-Verlag, 1990.

[Bri90c] J S Bridle. Training stochastic model recognition algorithms as networks can lead to maximum mutual information estimation of parameters. In *Advances in Neural Information Processing Systems 2*. Morgan Kaufmann, 1990.

[CB90] S J Cox and J S Bridle. Simultaneous speaker normalisation and utterance labelling using Bayesian/neural net techniques. In *Proc. IEEE Int. Conf. Acoustics Speech and Signal Processing*, 1990.

[Hun81] M J Hunt. Speaker adaptation for word-based speech recognition. *J. Acoust. Soc. Amer*, 69:S41–S42, 1981. (abstract only).

[Sal89] J A S Salter. The RT5233 Alphabetic database for the Connex project. Technical Report RT52/G231/89, BT Technology Executive, 1989.

Exploratory Feature Extraction in Speech Signals

Nathan Intrator
Center for Neural Science
Brown University
Providence, RI 02912

Abstract

A novel unsupervised neural network for dimensionality reduction which seeks directions emphasizing multimodality is presented, and its connection to exploratory projection pursuit methods is discussed. This leads to a new statistical insight to the synaptic modification equations governing learning in Bienenstock, Cooper, and Munro (BCM) neurons (1982).

The importance of a dimensionality reduction principle based solely on distinguishing features, is demonstrated using a linguistically motivated phoneme recognition experiment, and compared with feature extraction using back-propagation network.

1 Introduction

Due to the *curse of dimensionality* (Bellman, 1961) it is desirable to extract features from a high dimensional data space before attempting a classification. How to perform this feature extraction/dimensionality reduction is not that clear. A first simplification is to consider only features defined by linear (or semi-linear) projections of high dimensional data. This class of features is used in projection pursuit methods (see review in Huber, 1985).

Even after this simplification, it is still difficult to characterize what interesting projections are, although it is easy to point at projections that are uninteresting. A statement that has recently been made precise by Diaconis and Freedman (1984) says that for most high-dimensional clouds, most low-dimensional projections are approximately normal. This finding suggests that the important information in the data is conveyed in those directions whose single dimensional projected distribution is far from Gaussian, especially at the center of the distribution. Friedman (1987) argues that the most computationally attractive measures for deviation from normality (projection indices) are based on polynomial moments. However they very heavily emphasize departure from normality in the tails of the distribution (Huber, 1985). Second order polynomials (measuring the variance - principal components) are not sufficient in characterizing the important features of a distribution (see example in Duda & Hart (1973) p. 212), therefore higher order polynomials are needed. We shall be using the observation that high dimensional clusters translate to multimodal low dimensional projections, and if we are after such structures measuring multimodality defines an interesting projection. In some special cases, where the data is known in advance to be bi-modal, it is relatively straightforward to define a good projection index (Hinton & Nowlan, 1990). When the structure is not known in advance, defining a general multimodal measure of the projected data is not straight forward, and will be discussed in this paper.

There are cases in which it is desirable to make the projection index invariant under certain transformations, and maybe even remove second order structure (see Huber, 1985) for desirable invariant properties of projection indices). In such cases it is possible to make such transformations before hand (Friedman, 1987), and then assume that the data possesses these invariant properties already.

2 Feature Extraction using ANN

In this section, the intuitive idea presented above is used to form a statistically plausible objective function whose minimization will be those projections having a single dimensional projected distribution that is far from Gaussian. This is done using a loss function whose expected value leads to the desired projection index. Mathematical details are given in Intrator (1990).

Before presenting this loss function, let us review some necessary notations and assumptions. Consider a neuron with input vector $x = (x_1, \ldots, x_N)$, synaptic weights vector $m = (m_1, \ldots, m_N)$, both in R^N, and activity (in the linear region) $c = x \cdot m$. Define the threshold $\Theta_m = E[(x \cdot m)^2]$, and the functions $\hat{\phi}(c, \Theta_m) = c^2 - \frac{2}{3}c\Theta_m$, $\phi(c, \Theta_m) = c^2 - \frac{4}{3}c\Theta_m$. The ϕ function has been suggested as a biologically plausible synaptic modification function that explains visual cortical plasticity (Bienenstock, Cooper and Munro, 1982). Note that at this point c represents the linear projection of x onto m, and we seek an optimal projection in some sense.

We want to base our projection index on polynomial moments of low order, and to use the fact that bimodal distribution is already interesting, and any additional mode should make the distribution even more interesting. With this in mind, consider the following family of loss functions which depend on the synaptic weight vector and on the input x;

$$L_m(x) = -\mu \int_{\Theta_m}^{(x \cdot m)} \hat{\phi}(s, \Theta_m) ds = -\frac{\mu}{3}\{(x \cdot m)^3 - E[(x \cdot m)^2](x \cdot m)^2\}.$$

The motivation for this loss function can be seen in the following graph, which represents the ϕ function and the associated loss function $L_m(x)$. For simplicity the loss for a fixed threshold Θ_m and synaptic vector m can be written as $L_m(c) = -\frac{\mu}{3}c^2(c - \Theta_m)$, where $c = (x \cdot m)$.

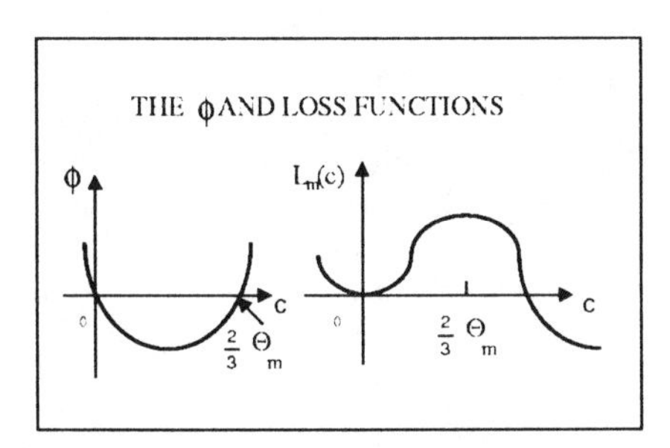

Figure 1: The function ϕ and the loss functions for a fixed m and Θ_m.

The graph of the loss function shows that for any fixed m and Θ_m, the loss is small for a given input x, when either $(x \cdot m)$ is close to zero, or when $(x \cdot m)$ is larger than $\frac{4}{3}\Theta_m$. Moreover, the loss function remains negative for $(x \cdot m) > \frac{4}{3}\Theta_m$, therefore, any kind of distribution at the right hand side of $\frac{4}{3}\Theta_m$ is possible, and the preferred ones are those which are concentrated further away from $\frac{4}{3}\Theta_m$.

We must still show why it is not possible that a minimizer of the average loss will be such that all the mass of the distribution will be concentrated in one of the regions. Roughly speaking, this can not happen because the threshold Θ_m is dynamic and depends on the projections in a nonlinear way, namely, $\Theta_m = E(x \cdot m)^2$. This implies that Θ_m will always move itself to a stable point such that the distribution will not be concentrated at only one of its sides. This yields that the part of the distribution for $c < \frac{4}{3}\Theta_m$ has a high loss, making those distributions in which the distribution for $c < \frac{4}{3}\Theta_m$ has its mode at zero more plausible.

The risk (expected value of the loss) is given by:

$$R_m = -\frac{\mu}{3}\,\{E[(x \cdot m)^3] - E^2[(x \cdot m)^2]\}.$$

Since the risk is continuously differentiable, its minimization can be achieved via a gradient descent method with respect to m, namely:

$$\frac{dm_i}{dt} = -\frac{\partial}{\partial m_i}R_m = \mu\; E[\phi(x \cdot m, \Theta_m)x_i].$$

The resulting differential equations suggest a modified version of the law governing synaptic weight modification in the BCM theory for learning and memory (Bienenstock, Cooper and Munro, 1982). This theory was presented to account for various experimental results in visual cortical plasticity. The biological relevance of the theory has been extensively studied (Soul et al., 1986; Bear et al., 1987; Cooper et al., 1987; Bear et al., 1988), and it was shown that the theory is in agreement with the classical deprivation experiments (Clothioux et al., 1990).

The fact that the distribution has part of its mass on both sides of $\frac{4}{3}\Theta_m$ makes this loss a plausible projection index that seeks multimodalities. However, we still need to reduce the sensitivity of the projection index to outliers, and for full generality, allow any projected distribution to be shifted so that the part of the distribution that satisfies $c < \frac{4}{3}\Theta_m$ will have its mode at zero. The over-sensitivity to outliers is addressed by considering a nonlinear neuron in which the neuron's activity is defined to be $c = \sigma(x \cdot m)$, where σ usually represents a smooth sigmoidal function. A more general definition that would allow symmetry breaking of the projected distributions, will provide solution to the second problem raised above, and is still consistent with the statistical formulation, is $c = \sigma(x \cdot m - \alpha)$, for an arbitrary threshold α which can be found by using gradient descent as well. For the nonlinear neuron, Θ_m is defined to be $\Theta_m = E[\sigma^2(x \cdot m)]$.

Based on this formulation, a network of Q identical nodes may be constructed. All the neurons in this network receive the same input and inhibit each other, so as to extract several features in parallel. A similar network has been studied in the context of mean field theory by Scofield and Cooper (1985). The activity of neuron k in the network is defined as $c_k = \sigma(x \cdot m_k - \alpha_k)$, where m_k is the synaptic weight vector of neuron k, and α_k is its threshold. The *inhibited* activity and threshold of the k'th neuron are given by $\tilde{c}_k = c_k - \eta \sum_{j \neq k} c_j$, $\tilde{\Theta}_m^k = E[\tilde{c}_k^2]$.

We omit the derivation of the synaptic modification equations which is similar to the one for a single neuron, and present only the resulting modification equations for a synaptic vector m_k in a lateral inhibition network of nonlinear neurons:

$$\dot{m}_k = -\mu \; E\{\phi(\tilde{c}_k, \tilde{\Theta}_m^k)\Big(\sigma'(c_k) - \eta \sum_{j \neq k} \sigma'(c_j)\Big)x\}.$$

The lateral inhibition network performs a direct search of Q-dimensional projections together, and therefore may find a richer structure that a stepwise approach may miss, e.g. see example 14.1 Huber (1985).

3 Comparison with other feature extraction methods

When dealing with a classification problem, the interesting features are those that distinguish between classes. The network presented above has been shown to seek multimodality in the projected distributions, which translates to clusters in the original space, and therefore to find those directions that make a distinction between different sets in the training data.

In this section we compare classification performance of a network that performs dimensionality reduction (before the classification) based upon multimodality, and a network that performs dimensionality reduction based upon minimization of misclassification error (using back-propagation with MSE criterion). This is done using a phoneme classification experiment whose linguistic motivation is described below. In the latter we regard the hidden units representation as a new reduced feature representation of the input space. Classification on the new feature space was done using back-propagation[1]

[1] See Intrator (1990) for comparison with principal components feature extraction and with k-NN as a classifier

Consider the six stop consonants [p,k,t,b,g,d], which have been a subject of recent research in evaluating neural networks for phoneme recognition (see review in Lippmann, 1989). According to phonetic feature theory, these stops posses several common features, but only two distinguishing phonetic features, place of articulation and voicing (see Blumstein & Lieberman 1984, for a review and related references on phonetic feature theory). This theory suggests an experiment in which features extracted from unvoiced stops can be used to distinguish place of articulation in voiced stops as well. It is of interest if these features can be found from a single speaker, how sensitive they are to voicing and whether they are speaker invariant.

The speech data consists of 20 consecutive time windows of 32msec with 30msec overlap, aligned to the beginning of the burst. In each time window, a set of 22 energy levels is computed. These energy levels correspond to Zwicker critical band filters (Zwicker, 1961). The consonant-vowel (CV) pairs were pronounced in isolation by native American speakers (two male BSS and LTN, and one female JES.) Additional details on biological motivation for the preprocessing, and linguistic motivation related to child language acquisition can be found in Seebach (1990), and Seebach and Intrator (1991). An average (over 25 tokens) of the six stop consonants followed by the vowel [a] is presented in Figure 2. All the images are smoothened using a moving average. One can see some similarities between the voiced and unvoiced stops especially in the upper left corner of the image (high frequencies beginning of the burst) and the radical difference between them in the low frequencies.

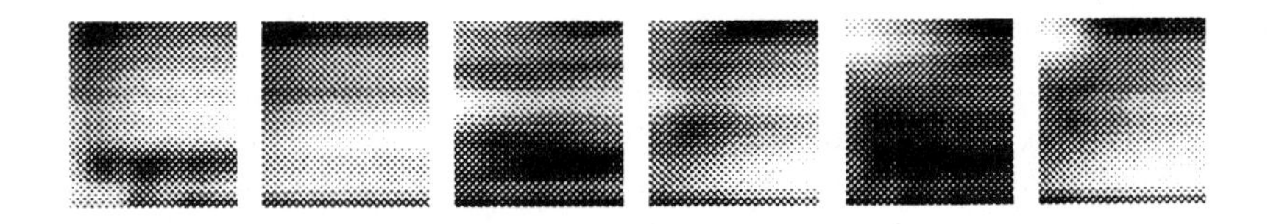

Figure 2: An average of the six stop consonants followed by the vowel [a]. Their order from left to right [pa] [ba] [ka] [ga] [ta] [da]. Time increases from the burst release on the X axis, and frequency increases on the Y axis.

In the experiments reported here, 5 features were extracted from the 440 dimension original space. Although the dimensionality reduction methods were trained only with the unvoiced tokens of a single speaker, the classifier was trained on (5 dimensional) voiced and unvoiced data from the other speakers as well.

The classification results, which are summarized in table 1, show that the back-propagation network does well in finding structure useful for classification of the trained data, but this structure is more sensitive to voicing. Classification results using a BCM network suggest that, for this specific task, structure that is less sensitive to voicing can be extracted, even though voicing has significant effects on the speech signal itself. The results also suggest that these features are more speaker invariant.

Place of Articulation Classification (B-P)		
	B-P	BCM
BSS /p,k,t/	100	100
BSS /b,g,d/	83.4	94.7
LTN /p,k,t/	95.6	97.7
LTN /b,g,d/	78.3	93.2
JES (Both)	88.0	99.4

Table 1: Percentage of correct classification of place of articulation in voiced and unvoiced stops.

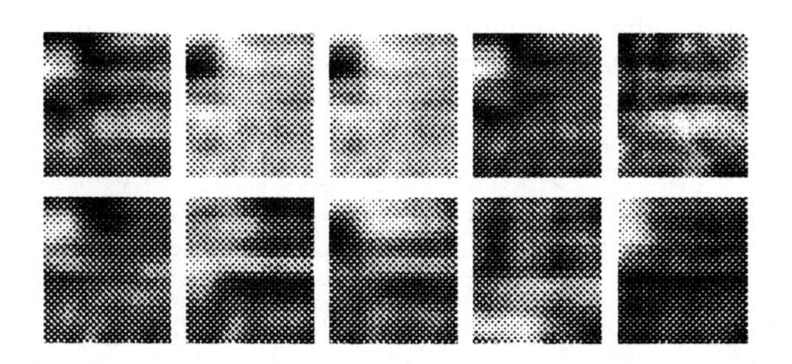

Figure 3 : Synaptic weight images of the 5 hidden units of back-propagation (top), and by the 5 BCM neurons (bottom).

The difference in performance between the two feature extractors may be partially explained by looking at the synaptic weight vectors (images) extracted by both method: For the back-propagation feature extraction it can be seen that although 5 units were used, fewer number of features were extracted. One of the main distinction between the unvoiced stops in the training set is the high frequency burst at the beginning of the consonant (the upper left corner). The back-propagation method concentrated mainly on this feature, probably because it is sufficient to base the recognition of the training set on this feature, and the fact that training stops when misclassification error falls to zero. On the other hand, the BCM method does not try to reduce the misclassificaion error and is able to find a richer, linguistically meaningful structure, containing burst locations and format tracking of the three different stops that allowed a better generalization to other speakers and to voiced stops.

The network and its training paradigm present a different approach to speaker independent speech recognition. In this approach the speaker variability problem is addressed by training a network that concentrates mainly on the distinguishing features of a single speaker, as opposed to training a network that concentrates on both the distinguishing and common features, on multi-speaker data.

Acknowledgements

I wish to thank Leon N Cooper for suggesting the problem and for providing many helpful hints and insights. Geoff Hinton made invaluable comments. The application of BCM to speech is discussed in more detail in Seebach (1990) and in a forthcoming article (Seebach and Intrator, 1991). Research was supported by the National Science Foundation, the Army Research Office, and the Office of Naval Research.

References

Bellman, R. E. (1961) Adaptive Control Processes, Princeton, NJ, Princeton University Press.

Bienenstock, E. L., L. N Cooper, and P.W. Munro (1982) Theory for the development of neuron selectivity: orientation specificity and binocular interaction in visual cortex. *J.Neurosci.* 2:32-48

Bear, M. F., L. N Cooper, and F. F. Ebner (1987) A Physiological Basis for a Theory of Synapse Modification. *Science* 237:42-48

Diaconis, P, and D. Freedman (1984) Asymptotics of Graphical Projection Pursuit. *The Annals of Statistics*, 12 793-815.

Friedman, J. H. (1987) Exploratory Projection Pursuit. *Journal of the American Statistical Association* 82-397:249-266

Hinton, G. E. and S. J. Nowlan (1990) The bootstrap Widrow-Hoff rule as a cluster-formation algorithm. *Neural Computation.*

Huber P. J. (1985) Projection Pursuit. *The Annal. of Stat.* 13:435-475

Intrator N. (1990) A Neural Network For Feature Extraction. In D. S. Touretzky (ed.), *Advances in Neural Information Processing Systems 2.* San Mateo, CA: Morgan Kaufmann.

Lippmann, R. P. (1989) Review of Neural Networks for Speech Recognition. *Neural Computation* 1, 1-38.

Reilly, D. L., C.L. Scofield, L. N Cooper and C. Elbaum (1988) GENSEP: a multiple neural network with modifiable network topology. *INNS Conference on Neural Networks.*

Saul, A. and E. E. Clothiaux, 1986) Modeling and Simulation II: Simulation of a Model for Development of Visual Cortical specificity. *J. of Electrophysiological Techniques,* 13:279-306

Scofield, C. L. and L. N Cooper (1985) Development and properties of neural networks. *Contemp. Phys.* 26:125-145

Seebach, B. S. (1990) Evidence for the Development of Phonetic Property Detectors in a Neural Net without Innate Knowledge of Linguistic Structure. Ph.D. Dissertation Brown University.

Duda R. O. and P. E. Hart (1973) *Pattern classification and scene analysis* John Wiley, New York

Zwicker E. (1961) Subdivision of the audible frequency range into critical bands (Frequenzgruppen) *Journal of the Acoustical Society of America* 33:248

Phonetic Classification and Recognition Using the Multi-Layer Perceptron

Hong C. Leung, James R. Glass,
Michael S. Phillips, and Victor W. Zue
Spoken Language Systems Group
Laboratory for Computer Science
Massachusetts Institute of Technology
Cambridge, Massachusetts 02139, U.S.A.

Abstract

In this paper, we will describe several extensions to our earlier work, utilizing a segment-based approach. We will formulate our segmental framework and report our study on the use of multi-layer perceptrons for detection and classification of phonemes. We will also examine the outputs of the network, and compare the network performance with other classifiers. Our investigation is performed within a set of experiments that attempts to recognize 38 vowels and consonants in American English independent of speaker. When evaluated on the TIMIT database, our system achieves an accuracy of 56%.

1 Introduction

Thus far, the neural networks research community has placed heavy emphasis on the problem of pattern classification. In many applications, including speech recognition, one must also address the issue of *detection*. Thus, for example, one must detect the presence of phonetic segments as well as classify them. Recently, the community has moved more towards recognition of continuous speech. A network is typically used to label every frame of speech in a frame-based recognition system [Franzini 90, Morgan 90, Tebelskis 90].

Our goal is to study and exploit the capability of ANN for speech recognition, based on the premise that ANN may offer a flexible framework for us to utilize our improved, albeit incomplete, speech knowledge. As an intermediate milestone, this paper extends our earlier work on phonetic classification to context-independent phonetic recognition. Thus we need to locate as well as identify the phonetic units. Our system differs from the majority of approaches in that a segmental framework is adopted. The network is used in conjunction with acoustic segmentation procedures to provide a phonetic string for the entire utterance.

2 Segmental Formulation

In our segmental framework, a phonetic unit is mapped to a segment explicitly delineated by a begin and end time in the speech signal. This is motivated by the belief that a segmental framework offers us more flexibility in applying our speech knowledge than is afforded by a frame-based approach. As a result, a segment-based approach could ultimately lead to superior modelling of the temporal variations in the realization of underlying phonological units.

Let $\hat{\alpha}$ denote the best sequence of phonetic units in an utterance. To simplify the problem, we assume that $p(s_i) = p(s_i|\alpha_j)$, where s_i stand for the ith time segment that has *one and only one* phoneme in it, and α_j stands for the best phoneme label in s_i. Thus the probability of the best sequence, $p(\hat{\alpha})$, is:

$$p(\hat{\alpha}) = \prod_{s_i \epsilon \vec{s}} p(\alpha_j)p(s_i); \qquad 1 \leq j \leq N \tag{1}$$

where $\vec{s}$ is any possible sequence of time segments consisting of $\{s_1, s_2, ...\}$, $p(s_i)$ is the probability of a valid time segment, and N is the number of possible phonetic units. In order to perform recognition, the two probabilities in Equation 1 must be estimated. The first term, $p(\alpha_j)$, is a set of phoneme probabilities and thus can be viewed as a classification problem. The second term, $p(s_i)$, is a set of probabilities of valid time regions and thus can be estimated as a segmentation problem.

2.1 Segmentation

In order to estimate the segment probabilities, $p(s_i)$, in Equation 1, we have formulated segmentation into a boundary classification problem. Let b_l and b_r be the left and right boundary of a time segment, s_i, respectively, as shown in Figure 1a. Let $\{b_1, b_2, .., b_K\}$ be the set of boundaries that might exist within s_i. These boundaries can be proposed by a boundary detector, or they can simply occur at every frame of speech. We define $p(s_i)$ to be the joint probability that the left and right boundaries *exist* and all other boundaries within s_i *do not* exist. To reduce the complexity of the problem, assume b_j is statistically independent of b_k for $\forall j \neq k$. Thus,

$$\begin{aligned} p(s_i) &= p(b_l, \bar{b}_1, \bar{b}_2, .., \bar{b}_K, b_r) \\ &= p(b_l)p(\bar{b}_1)p(\bar{b}_2)...p(\bar{b}_K)p(b_r), \end{aligned} \tag{2}$$

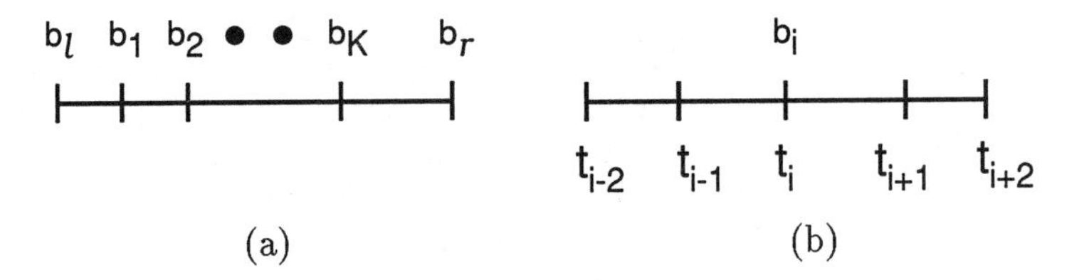

Figure 1: Schematic diagrams for estimation of (a) segment probability, $p(s_{\mathbf{i}})$, and (b) boundary probability, $p(b_{\mathbf{k}})$. The boundaries can be proposed by a boundary detector, or they can simply occur at every frame. See text.

where $p(b_{\mathbf{l}})$ and $p(b_{\mathbf{r}})$ stand for the probability that the left and right boundary exist, respectively, $p(\bar{b}_{\mathbf{k}})$ stands for the probability that the $k^{\mathbf{th}}$ boundary does not exist. As a result, the probability of a segment, $p(s_{\mathbf{i}})$ can be obtained by computing the probabilities of the boundaries, $p(b_{\mathbf{k}})$, subsumed by the segment. As we will discuss in a later section, by using the time-aligned transcription, we can train the boundary probabilities in a supervised manner.

2.2 Phonetic Classification

Once the probability of a segment, $p(s_{\mathbf{i}})$, is obtained, we still need to classify it, i.e. compute the probabilities of the phonetic units in the segment, $p(\alpha_{\mathbf{j}})$. Again, the time-aligned transcription can be used to train the probabilities in a supervised manner. We have discussed this in earlier papers [Leung 89, Leung 90]. In a later section, we will discuss some of our recent experimental results.

3 Experiments

3.1 Tasks and Corpora

The experiments described in this paper deal with classification and recognition of 38 phonetic labels representing 14 vowels, 3 semivowels, 3 nasals, 8 fricatives, 2 affricates, 6 stops, 1 flap and 1 silence. Within the context of classification, the networks are given a segment of the speech signal, and are asked to determine its phonetic identity. Within the context of recognition, the networks are given an utterance, and are asked to determine the identity and locations of the phonetic units in the utterance. All experiments were based on the sentences in the TIMIT database [Lamel 86]. As summarized in Table 1, Corpus I contains 1,750 sx sentences spoken by 350 male and female speakers, resulting in a total of 64,000 phonetic tokens. Corpus II contains 4,400 sx and si sentences spoken by 550 male and female speakers, resulting in a total of 165,000 phonetic tokens.

3.2 Phonetic Classification

As previously discussed, estimation of the probability, $p(\alpha_{\mathbf{j}})$ in Equation 1 can be viewed as a classification problem. Many statistical classifiers can be used. We have

Corpus	Set	Speakers	Sentences	Tokens	Type
I	training	300	1500	55,000	sx
	testing	50	250	9,000	sx
II	training	500	4000	150,000	sx/si
	testing	50	400	15,000	sx/si

Table 1: Corpora I and II extracted from the TIMIT database. Corpus I contains only sx sentences, whereas Corpus II contains both sx and si sentences. The speakers in the testing sets for both Corpus I and Corpus II are the same.

chosen to use the MLP, due to its discriminatory capability, as well as its flexibility in that it does not make assumptions about specific statistical distributions or distance metrics. In addition, earlier work shows that the outputs of MLP can approximate posteriori probabilities [Bourlard 88]. To train the network, we adopt procedures such as center initialization, input normalization, adaptive gain, and modular training [Leung 90]. The input representation was identical to that in the SUMMIT system, and consisted of 82 acoustic attributes [Zue 89]. These segmental attributes were generated automatically by a search procedure that uses the training data to determine the settings of the free parameters of a set of generic property detectors using an optimization procedure [Phillips 88].

3.3 Boundary Classification

In our segmental framework formulated in Equation 1, the main difference between classification and recognition is the incorporation of a probability for each segment, $p(s_i)$. As described previously in Equation 2, we have simplified the problem of estimating $p(s_i)$ to one of determining the probability that a boundary exists, $p(b_k)$.

To estimate $p(b_k)$, a MLP with two output units is used, one for the valid boundaries and the other for the extraneous boundaries. By referencing the time-aligned phonetic transcription, the desired outputs of the network can be determined. In our current implementation $p(b_k)$ is determined using four abutting segments, as shown in Figure 1b. These segments are proposed by the boundary detector in the SUMMIT system. Let t_i stand for the time at which b_i is located, and s_i stand for the segment between t_i and t_{i+1}, where $t_{i+1} > t_i$. The boundary probability, $p(b_i)$, is then determined by using the average mean-rate response [Seneff 88] in s_{i-2}, s_{i-1}, s_i, and s_{i+1} as inputs to the MLP. Thus the network has altogether 160 input units.

3.4 Results

3.4.1 Phonetic Classification

In the phonetic classification experiments, the system classified a token extracted from a phonetic transcription that had been aligned with the speech waveform. Since there was no detection involved in these experiments only substitution errors were possible.

	Classifier	Correct	Parameters
I	SUMMIT	70%	2,200
I	Gaussian	70%	128,000
I	MLP	74%	15,000
II	MLP	76%	30,000

Table 2: Phonetic classification results using the SUMMIT classifier, Gaussian classifier, and MLP. Also shown are the number of parameters in the classifiers.

In the first set of experiments, we compared results based on Corpus I, using different classifiers. As Table 2 shows, the baseline speaker-independent classification performance of SUMMIT on the testing data was 70%. When Gaussian classifiers with full covariance matrices were used, we found that the performance is also about 70%. Finally, when the MLP is used, a performance of 74% is achieved.

Although the sx sentences were designed to be phonetically balanced, the 1,750 sentences in Corpus I are not distinct. In the second set of experiments, we evaluated the MLP classifier on Corpus II, which include both the sx and si sentences.[1] As shown in Table 2, the classifier achieves 76%.

Parameters: The networks used as described in Table 2 have only 1 hidden layer. The number of hidden units in the network can be 128 or 256, resulting in 15,000 or 30,000 connections. For comparison, Table 2 also shows the number of parameters for the SUMMIT and Gaussian classifiers. While the SUMMIT classifier requires only about 2,200 parameters, the Gaussian classifiers require as much as 128,000 parameters, an order of magnitude more than the MLP. These numbers also give us some idea about the computational requirements for different classifiers, since the required number of multiplications is about the same as the number of parameters.

Network Outputs: We have chosen the network to estimate the phoneme probabilities. When the network is trained, the target values are either 1 or 0. However, if the network is over-trained, its output values may approach either 1 or 0, resulting in poor estimates of the posterior probabilities. Figure 2 shows two distributions for the output values of the network for 3600 tokens from the test set. Figure 2a corresponds to the ratio of the highest output value to the sum of the network output values, whereas Figure 2b corresponds to the second highest output value. We can see that both distributions are quite broad, suggesting that the network often makes "soft" decisions about the phoneme labels. We feel that this is important since in speech recognition, we often need to combine scores or probabilities from different parts of the system.

3.4.2 Boundary Classification

We have evaluated the boundary classifier using the training and testing data in Corpus I. By using 32 hidden units, the network can classify 87% of the boundaries in the test set correctly.

[1] All the si sentences in TIMIT are distinct.

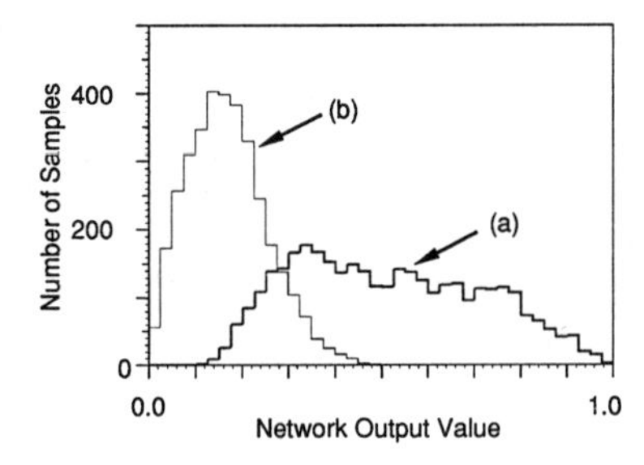

Figure 2: Histograms for the output values of the network extracted from 3600 samples: (a) the highest output values, and (b) the second highest output values.

Corpus	Classifer	Segment	Accuracy
I	Baseline	Binary Hierarchy	47%
I	MLP	Binary Hierarchy	50%
I	MLP	Stochastic Pruning	54%
II	MLP	Stochastic Pruning	56%

Table 3: Phonetic recognition results using binary hierarchy (dendrogram), and boundary pruning. No duration, bigram, or trigram statistics have been used. Errors include substitutions, deletions, and insertions.

3.4.3 Phonetic Recognition

One of the disadvantages of our segmental framework is that the amount of computation involved can be very significant, since a segment can begin and end at any frame of an utterance. We have explored various pruning strategies. In this paper, we will report our results using stochastic pruning and binary hierarchy [Leung 90a]. We have found that such pruning strategies can reduce the amount of computation by about 3 orders of magnitude.

The results of the phonetic recognition experiments are shown in Table 3. No duration, bigram, or trigram statistics have been used. The baseline performance of the current SUMMIT system on Corpus I is 47%, including substitution, deletion, and insertion errors. When the MLP was used in place of the classifier in the current SUMMIT system using also the binary hierarchical representation, the performance improved to 50%. When the MLP was used with stochastic pruning technique, the performance improved to 54%. Finally, by using the network trained and tested on Corpus II, the performance improved to 56%.

4 Discussion

In summary, we have discussed a segmental approach for phonetic recognition. We have also examined the outputs of the network, and compared performance results and computational requirements with different classifiers. We have shown that decisions made by the network are quite "soft", and that the network yields results favorable to other more traditional classifiers. Future work includes the use of context-dependent models for phonetic and boundary classification, utilization of other phonological units, and extension to recognition of continuous speech.

References

[Bourlard 88] Bourlard, H., and C.J. Wellekens, "Links between Markov Models and Multilayer Perceptrons," *Advances in Neural Information Processing Systems 1,* Morgan Kaufmann, 1988.

[Franzini 90] Franzini, M.A., K.F. Lee, and A. Waibel, "Connectionist Viterbi Training: A New Hybrid Method for Continuous Speech Recognition," *Proc. ICASSP-90,* Albuquerque, NM, USA, 1990.

[Lamel 86] Lamel, L.F., R.H. Kassel, and S. Seneff, "Speech Database Development: Design and Analysis of the Acoustic Phonetic Corpus," *Proc. DARPA Speech Recognition Workshop,* 1986.

[Leung 89] Leung, H.C., *The Use of Artificial Neural Networks of Phonetic Recognition,* Ph.D. Thesis, Mass. Inst. of Tech., 1989.

[Leung 90] Leung, H.C., and V.W. Zue, "Phonetic Classification Using Multi-Layer Perceptrons," *Proc. ICASSP-90,* Albuquerque, 1990.

[Leung 90a] Leung, H., Glass, J., Phillips, M., and Zue, V., "Detection and Classification of Phonemes Using Context-independent Error Back-Propagation," *Proc. International Conference on Spoken Language Processing,* Kobe, Japan, 1990.

[Morgan 90] Morgan, N., and H. Bourlard, "Continuous Speech Recognition Using Multilayer Perceptrons with Hidden Markov Models," *Proc. ICASSP-90,* Albuquerque, NM, USA, 1990.

[Phillips 88] Phillips, M.S., "Automatic Discovery of Acoustic Measurements for Acoustic Classification," *J. Acoust. Soc. Amer.,* Vol. 84, 1988.

[Seneff 88] Seneff, S. "A Joint Synchrony/Mean-Rate Model of Auditory Speech Processing," *Proc. J. of Phonetics,* 1988.

[Tebelskis] Tebelskis, J., and A. Waibel, "Large Vocabulary Recognition Using Linked Predictive Neural Networks," Proc. ICASSP-90, Albuquerque, NM, USA, 1990.

[Zue 89] Zue, V., J. Glass, M. Phillips, and S. Seneff, "The MIT SUMMIT Speech Recognition System: A Progress Report," *Proceedings of DARPA Speech and Natural Language Workshop,* February, 1989.

From Speech Recognition to Spoken Language Understanding: The Development of the MIT SUMMIT and VOYAGER Systems

Victor Zue, James Glass, David Goodine, Lynette Hirschman, Hong Leung, Michael Phillips, Joseph Polifroni, and Stephanie Seneff
Room NE43-601
Spoken Language Systems Group
Laboratory for Computer Science
Massachusetts Institute of Technology
Cambridge, MA 02139 U.S.A.

Abstract

Spoken language is one of the most natural, efficient, flexible, and economical means of communication among humans. As computers play an ever increasing role in our lives, it is important that we address the issue of providing a graceful human-machine interface through spoken language. In this paper, we will describe our recent efforts in moving beyond the scope of speech recognition into the realm of spoken-language understanding. Specifically, we report on the development of an urban navigation and exploration system called VOYAGER, an application which we have used as a basis for performing research in spoken-language understanding.

1 Introduction

Over the past decade, research in speech coding and synthesis has matured to the extent that speech can now be transmitted efficiently and generated with high intelligibility. Spoken input to computers, however, has yet to pass the threshold of practicality. Despite some recent successful demonstrations, current speech recognition systems typically fall far short of human capabilities of continuous speech recognition with essentially unrestricted vocabulary and speakers, under adverse acoustic environments. This is largely due to our incomplete knowledge of the encoding of linguistic information in the speech signal, and the inherent variabilities of this process. Our approach to system development is to seek a good understanding of human communication through spoken language, to capture the essential features of the process in appropriate models, and to develop the necessary computational framework to make use of these models for machine understanding.

Our research in spoken language system development is based on the premise that many of the applications suitable for human/machine interaction using speech typically involve interactive problem solving. That is, in addition to converting the speech signal to text, the computer must also understand the user's request, in order to generate an appropriate response. As a result, we have focused our attention on three main issues. First, the system must operate in a realistic application domain, where domain-specific information can be utilized to translate spoken input into appropriate actions. The use of a realistic application is also critical to collecting data on how people would like to use machines to access information and solve problems. Use of a constrained task also makes possible rigorous evaluations of system performance. Second and perhaps most importantly the system must integrate speech recognition and natural language technologies to achieve speech *understanding*. Finally, the system must begin to deal with interactive speech, where the computer is an active conversational participant, and where people produce spontaneous speech, including false starts, hestitations, etc.

In this paper, we will describe our recent efforts in developing a spoken language interface for an urban navigation system (VOYAGER). We begin by describing our overall system architecture, paying particular attention to the interface between speech and natural language. We then describe the application domain and some of the issues that arise in realistic interactive problem solving applications, particulary in terms of conversational interaction. Finally, we report results of some performance evaluations we have made, using a spontaneous speech corpus we collected for this task.

2 System Architecture

Our spoken language language system contains three important components. The SUMMIT speech recognition system converts the speech signal into a set of word hypotheses. The TINA natural language system interacts with the speech recognizer in order to obtain a word string, as well as a linguistic interpretation of the utterance. A control strategy mediates between the recognizer and the language understanding component, using the language understanding constraints to help control the search of the speech recognition system.

2.1 Continuous Speech Recognition: The SUMMIT System

The SUMMIT system (Zue et al., 1989) starts the recognition process by first transforming the speech signal into a representation that models some of the known properties of the human auditory system (Seneff, 1988). Using the output of the auditory model, acoustic landmarks of varying robustness are located and embedded in a hierarchical structure called a dendrogram (Glass, 1988). The acoustic segments in the dendrogram are then mapped to phoneme hypotheses, using a set of automatically determined acoustic attributes in conjunction with conventional pattern recognition algorithms. The result is a phoneme network, in which each arc is characterized by a vector of probabilities for all the possible candidates. Recently, we have begun to experiment with the use of artificial neural nets for phonetic classifiction. To date, we have been able to improve the system's classification performance by over 5% (Leung and Zue, 1990).

Words in the lexicon are represented as pronunciation networks, which are generated automatically by a set of phonological rules (Zue et al., 1990). Weights derived from training data are assigned to each arc, using a corrective training procedure, to reflect the likelihood of a particular pronunciation. Presently, lexical decoding is accomplished by using the Viterbi algorithm to find the best path that matches the acoustic-phonetic network with the lexical network.

2.2 Natural Language Processing: The TINA System

In a spoken language system, the natural language component should perform two critical functions: 1) provide constraint for the recognizer component, and 2) provide an interpretation of the meaning of the sentence to the back-end. Our natural language system, TINA, was specifically designed to meet these two needs. TINA is a probabilistic parser which operates top-down, using an agenda-based control strategy which favors the most likely analyses. The basic design of TINA has been described elsewhere (Seneff, 1989), but will be briefly reviewed. The grammar is entered as a set of simple context-free rules which are automatically converted to a shared network structure. The *nodes* in the network are augmented with constraint filters (both syntactic and semantic) that operate only on locally available parameters. All arcs in the network are associated with probabilities, acquired automatically from a set of training sentences. Note that the probabilities are established *not* on the rule productions but rather on arcs connecting sibling pairs in a shared structure for a number of linked rules. The effect of such pooling is essentially a hierarchical bigram model. We believe this mechanism offers the capability of generating probabilities in a reasonable way by sharing counts on syntactically/semantically identical units in differing structural environments.

2.3 Control Strategy

The current interface between the SUMMIT speech recognition system and the TINA natural language system, uses an N-best algorithm (Chow and Schwartz, 1989; Soong and Huang, 1990; Zue et al., 1990), in which the recognizer can propose its best N complete sentence hypotheses one by one, stopping with the first sentence that is successfully analyzed by the natural language component TINA. In this case, TINA acts as a filter on *whole sentence* hypotheses.

In order to produce N-best hypotheses, we use a search strategy that involves an initial Viterbi search all the way to the end of the sentence, to provide a "best" hypothesis, followed by an A^* search to produce next-best hypotheses in turn, provided that the first hypothesis failed to parse. If all hypotheses fail to parse the system produces the rejection message, "I'm sorry but I didn't understand you."

Even with the parser acting as a filter of whole-sentence hypotheses, it is appropriate to also provide the recognizer with an inexpensive language model that can partially constrain the theories. This is currently done with a word-pair language model, in which each word in the vocabulary is associated with a list of words that could possibly follow that word *anywhere* in the sentence.

3 The VOYAGER Application Domain

VOYAGER is an urban navigation and exploration system that enables the user to ask about places of interest and obtain directions. It has been under development since early 1989 (Zue et al., 1989; Zue et al., 1990). In this section, we describe the application domain, the interface between our language understanding system TINA and the application back-end, and the discourse capabilities of the current system.

3.1 Domain Description

For our first attempt at exploring issues related to a fully-interactive spoken-language system, we selected a task in which the system knows about the physical environment of a specific geographical area and can provide assistance on how to get from one location to another within this area. The system, which we call VOYAGER, can also provide information concerning certain objects located inside this area. The current version of VOYAGER focuses on the geographic area of the city of Cambridge, MA between MIT and Harvard University.

The application database is an enhanced version of the Direction Assistance program developed at the Media Laboratory at MIT (Davis and Trobaugh, 1987). It consists of a map database, including the locations of various classes of objects (streets, buildings, rivers) and properties of these objects (address, phone number, etc.) The application supports a set of retrieval functions to access these data. The application must convert the semantic representation of TINA into the appropriate function call to the VOYAGER back-end. The answer is given to the user in three forms. It is graphically displayed on a map, with the object(s) of interest highlighted. In addition, a textual answer is printed on the screen, and is also spoken verbally using synthesized speech. The current implementation handles various types of queries, such as the location of objects, simple properties of objects, how to get from one place to another, and the distance and time for travel between objects.

3.2 Application Interface to VOYAGER

Once an utterance has been processed by the language understanding system, it is passed to an interface component which constructs a command function from the natural language representation. This function is subsequently passed to the back-end where a response is generated. There are three function types used in the current command framework of VOYAGER, which we will illustrate with the following example:

Query: Where is the nearest bank to MIT?
Function: `(LOCATE (NEAREST (BANK nil) (SCHOOL "MIT")))`

`LOCATE` is an example of a major function that determines the primary action to be performed by the command. It shows the physical location of an object or set of objects on the map. Functions such as **BANK** and **SCHOOL** in the above example access the database to return an object or a set of objects. When null arguments are provided, all possible candidates are returned from the database. Thus, for example, `(SCHOOL "MIT")` and `(BANK nil)` will return the objects MIT and all known banks, respectively. Finally, there are a number of functions in VOYAGER that act as filters, whereby the subset that fulfills some requirements are returned. The function `(NEAREST X y)`, for example, returns the object in the set X that is closest to the object y. These filter functions can be nested, so that they can quite easily construct a complicated object. For example, "the Chinese restaurant on Main Street nearest to the hotel in Harvard Square that is closest to City Hall" would be represented by,

```
(NEAREST
  (ON-STREET
    (SERVE (RESTAURANT nil) "Chinese")
    (STREET "Main" "Street"))
  (NEAREST
    (IN-REGION (HOTEL nil) (SQUARE "Harvard"))
    (PUBLIC-BUILDING "City Hall")))
```

3.3 Discourse Capabilities

Carrying on a conversation requires the use of context and discourse history. Without context, some user input may appear underspecified, vague or even ill-formed. However, in context, these queries are generally easily understood. The discourse capabilities of the current VOYAGER system are simplistic but nonetheless effective in handling the majority of the interactions within the designated task. We describe briefly how a discourse history is maintained, and how the system keeps track of incomplete requests, querying the user for more information as needed to fill in ambiguous material.

Two slots are reserved for discourse history. The first slot refers to the location of the user, which can be set during the course of the conversation and then later referred to. The second slot refers to the most recently referenced set of objects. This slot can be a single object, a set of objects, or two separate objects in the case where the previous command involved a calculation involving both a source and a destination. With these slots, the system can process queries that include pronominal reference as in "What is their address?" or "How far is it from here?"

VOYAGER can also handle underspecified or vague queries, in which a function argument has either no value or multiple values. Examples of such queries would be "How far is a bank?" or "How far is MIT?" when no [FROM-LOCATION] has been specified. VOYAGER points out such underspecification to the user, by asking for specific clarification. The underspecified command is also pushed onto a stack of incompletely specified commands. When the user provides additional information that is evaluated successfully, the top command in the stack is popped for reevaluation. If the additional information is not sufficient to resolve the original command, the command is again pushed onto the stack, with the new information incorporated. A protection mechanism automatically clears the history stack whenever the user abandons a line of discussion before all underspecified queries are clarified.

4 Performance Evaluation

In this section, we describe our experience with performance evaluation of spoken language systems. The version of VOYAGER that we evaluated has a vocabulary of 350 words. The word-pair language model for the speech recognition sub-system has a perplexity of 72. For the N-best algorithm, the number of sentence hypotheses was arbitrarily set at 100. The system was implemented on a SUN-4, using four commercially available signal processing boards. This configuration has a processes an utterance in 3 to 5 times real-time.

The system was trained and tested using a corpus of spontaneous speech recorded from 50 male and 50 female subjects (Zue et al., 1989). We arbitrarily designated the data from 70 speakers, equally divided between male and female, to be the training set. Data from 20 of the remaining speakers were designated as the development set. The test set consisted of 485 utterances generated by the remaining 5 male and 5 female subjects. The average number of words per sentence was 7.7.

VOYAGER generated an action for 51.7% of the sentences in the test set. The system failed to generate a parse on the remaining 48.3% of the sentences, either due to recognizer errors, unknown words, unseen linguistic structures, or back-end inadequacy. Specifically, 20.3% failed to generate an action due to recognition errors or the system's inability to deal with spontaneous speech phenomena, 17.2% were found to contain unknown words, and an additional 10.5% would not have parsed even if recognized correctly. VOYAGER almost never failed to provide a response once a parse had been generated. This is a direct result of our conscious decision to constrain TINA according to the capabilities of the back-end. Although 48.3% of the sentences were judged to be incorrect, only 13% generated the wrong response. For the remainder of the errors, the system responded with the message, "I'm sorry but I didn't understand you."

Finally, we solicited judgments from three naive subjects who had had no previous experience with VOYAGER to assess the capabilities of the back-end. About 80% of the responses were judged to be appropriate, with an additional 5% being verbose but otherwise correct. Only about 4% of the sentences produced diagnostic error messages, for which the system was judged to give an appropriate response about two thirds of the time. The response was judged incorrect about 10% of the time. The subjects judged about 87% of the user queries to be reasonable.

5 Summary

This paper summarizes the status of our recent efforts in spoken language system development. It is clear that spoken language systems will incorporate research from, and provide a useful testbed for a variety of disciplines including speech, natural language processing, knowledge aquisition, databases, expert systems, and human factors. In the near term our plans include improving the phonetic recognition accuracy of SUMMIT by incorporating context-dependent models, and investigating control strategies which more fully integrate our speech recognition and natural language components.

Acknowledgements

This research was supported by DARPA under Contract N00014-89-J-1332, monitored through the Office of Naval Research.

References

Chow, Y, and R. Schwartz, (1989) "The N-Best Algorithm: An Efficient Procedure for Finding Top N Sentence Hypotheses", *Proc. DARPA Speech and Natural Language Workshop*, pp. 199-202, October.

Davis, J.R. and T. F. Trobaugh, (1987) "Back Seat Driver," Technical Report 1, MIT Media Laboratory Speech Group, December.

Glass, J. R., (1988) "Finding Acoustic Regularities in Speech: Applications to Phonetic Recognition," Ph.D. thesis, Massachusetts Institute of Technology, May.

Leung, H., and V. Zue, (1990) "Phonetic Classification Using Multi-Layer Perceptrons," *Proc. ICASSP-90*, pp. 525–528, Albuquerque, NM.

Seneff, S., (1988) "A Joint Synchrony/Mean-Rate Model of Auditory Speech Processing," *J. of Phonetics,* vol. 16, pp. 55–76, January.

Seneff, S. (1989) "TINA: A Probabilistic Syntactic Parser for Speech Understanding Systems," *Proc. DARPA Speech and Natural Language Workshop*, pp. 168–178, February.

Soong, F., and E. Huang, (1990) "A Tree-Trellis Based Fast Search for Finding the N-best Sentence Hypotheses in Continuous Speech Recognition", *Proc. DARPA Speech and Natural Language Workshop*, pp. 199-202, June.

Zue, V., J. Glass, M. Phillips, and S. Seneff, (1989) "Acoustic Segmentation and Phonetic Classification in the SUMMIT System," *Proc. ICASSP-89*, pp. 389–392, Glasgow, Scotland.

Zue, V., J. Glass, D. Goodine, H. Leung, M. Phillips, J. Polifroni, and S. Seneff, (1989) "The VOYAGER Speech Understanding System: A Progress Report," *Proc. DARPA Speech and Natural Language Workshop*, pp. 51–59, October.

Zue, V., N. Daly, J. Glass, D. Goodine, H. Leung, M. Phillips, J. Polifroni, S. Seneff, and M. Soclof, (1989) "The Collection and Preliminary Analysis of a Spontaneous Speech Database," *Proc. DARPA Speech and Natural Language Workshop*, pp. 126–134, October.

Zue, V., J. Glass, D. Goodine, M. Phillips, and S. Seneff, (1990) "The SUMMIT Speech Recognition System: Phonological Modelling and Lexical Access," *Proc. ICASSP-90*, pp. 49–52, Albuquerque, NM.

Zue, V., J. Glass, D. Goodine, H. Leung, M. Phillips, J. Polifroni, and S. Seneff, (1990) "The VOYAGER Speech Understanding System: Preliminary Development and Evaluation," *Proc. ICASSP-90*, pp. 73–76, Albuquerque, NM.

Zue, V., J. Glass, D. Goodine, H. Leung, M. Phillips, J. Polifroni, and S. Seneff, (1990) "Recent Progress on the VOYAGER System," *Proc. DARPA Speech and Natural Language Workshop*, pp. 206–211, June.

Speech Recognition using Connectionist Approaches

Khalid Choukri
SPRINT Coordinator
CAP GEMINI INNOVATION
118 rue de Tocqueville, 75017 Paris. France
e-mail: choukri@capsogeti.fr

Abstract

This paper is a summary of SPRINT project aims and results. The project focus on the use of neuro-computing techniques to tackle various problems that remain unsolved in speech recognition. First results concern the use of feed-forward nets for phonetic units classification, isolated word recognition, and speaker adaptation.

1 INTRODUCTION

Speech is a complex phenomenon but it is useful to divide it into levels of representation. Connectionism paradigms and particularities are exploited to tackle the major problems in relationship with intra and inter speaker variabilities in order to improve the recognizer performance. For that purpose the project has been split into individual tasks which are depicted below:

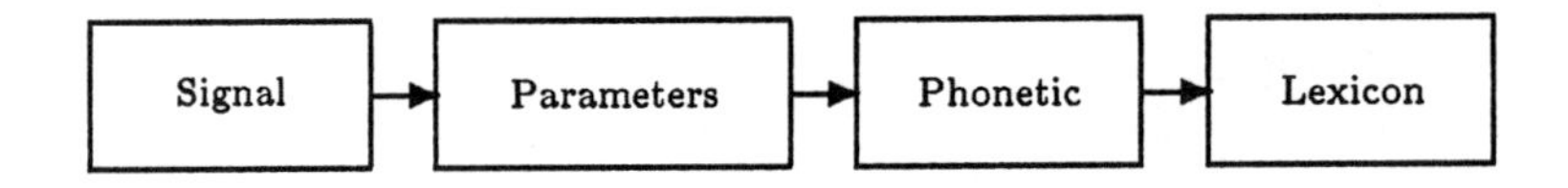

The work described herein concerns :

- Parameters-to-Phonetic: Classification of speech parameters using a set of "phonetic" symbols and extraction of speech features from signal.
- Parameters-to-Lexical: Classification of a sequence of feature vectors by lexical access (isolated word recognition) in various environments.
- Parameters-to-Parameters: Adaptation to new speakers and environments.

The following sections summarize the work carried out within this project. Details, including different nets description, are reported in the project deliverables (Choukri, 1990), (Bimbot, 1990), (Varga, 1990).

2 PARAMETERS-TO-PHONETIC

The objectives of this task were to assess various neural network topologies, and to examine the use of prior knowledge in improving results, in the process of acoustic-phonetic decoding of natural speech. These results were compared to classical pattern classification approaches such as k-nearest neighbour classifiers (K-nn), dynamic programming, and k-means.

2.1 DATABASES

The speech was uttered by one male speaker in French. Two databases were used: DB_1 made of isolated non-sense words (logatomes) which contains 6672 phonemes and DB_2 provided by the recording of 200 sentences which contains 5270 phonemes. DB_2 was split equally into training and test sets (2635 data each). 34 different labels were used : 1 per phoneme (not per allophone) and one for the silence. For each phoneme occurrence, 16 frames of signal (8 on each side of the label) were processed to provide a 16 Mel-scaled filter-bank vector.

2.2 CLASSICAL CLASSIFIERS

Experiments using k-NN and k-means classifiers were conducted to check the sufficient consistency of the data and to have some reference scores. A first protocol considered each pattern as a 256-dimension vector, and achieved k-nearest neighbours with the euclidean distance between references and tests. A second protocol attempted to decrease the time misalignments influences by carrying out some Dynamic Time Warping between references and tests and taking the sum of distances along the best path, as a distance measure between patterns. The same data was used in the framework of a k-means classifier, for various values of k (number of representatives per class). The best results are :

Method	K-means ($K \geq 16$)	K-nn (K=5)	K-nn + DTW (K=5)
Score	61.3 %	72.2 %	77.5 %

2.3 NEURAL CLASSIFIERS

2.3.1 LVQ Classifiers

Experiments were conducted using Learning Vector Quantization technique (LVQ) (Bennani, 1990). A study of the importance of the weights initialization procedure proved to be an important parameter for the classification performance. We have compared three initialization algorithms: k-means, LBG, Multiedit. With k-means and LBG, tests were conducted with different numbers of reference vectors, while for Multiedit, the algorithm discovers automatically representative vectors in the training set, the number of which is therefore not specified in advance.

Initialization by LBG gave better performance for self-consistency (evaluation on the training database: DB_1) , whereas test performance on DB_2 (sentences) were similar for all procedures and very low. Further experiments were carried out on DB_2 both for training and testing. LBG initialization with 16 and 32 classes were tried (since they gave the best performances in the previous experiment). Even though the self-consistency for sentences is slightly lower than the one for logatomes, the improvement of recognition scores are far better as illustrated here:

nb ref per class	16	32
K-means	60.3 %	61.3 %
LBG → LVQ	62.4 % → 66.1 %	63.2 % → 67.2 %

This experiment and some others (not presented here) (Bimbot, 1990) confirm that the failure of previous experiments is more due to a mismatch between the corpora for this recognition method, than an inadequacy of the classification technique itself.

2.3.2 The Time-Delay Neural Network (TDNN) Classifiers

A TDNN, as introduced by A. Waibel (Waibel, 1987), can be described by its set of typological parameters, i.e. :

$$M_0 \times N_0 \ / \ P_0, S_0 \ - \ M_1 \times N_1 \ / \ P_1, S_1 \ - \ M_2 \times N_2 \ - \ K \times 1 \ .$$

In the following a "TDNN-derived" network has a similar architecture, except that M_2 is not constrained to be equal to K, and the connectivity between the last 2 layers is full. Various TDNN-derived architectures were tested on recognizing phonemes from sentences (DB_2) after learning on the logatomes (DB_1). Best results are given below:

TDNN-derived structure	self-consist.	reco score
16x16 / 2,1 - 8x15 / 7,2 - 5x5 - 34x1	63.9 %	48.1 %
16x16 / 2,1 - 16x15 / 7,4 - 11x3 - 34x1	75.1 %	54.8 %
16x16 / 4,1 - 16x13 / 5,2 - 16x5 - 34x1	81.0 %	60.5 %
16x16 / 2,1 - 16x15 / 7,4 - 16x3 - 34x1	79.8 %	60.8 %

The first net is clearly not powerful enough for the task, so the number of free parameters has be increased. This upgraded the results immediately as can be seen for the other nets. The third and fourth nets have equivalent performance, they differ in the local windows width and delays. Other tested architectures did not increase this performance. The main difference between training and test sets is certainly the different speaking rate, and therefore the existence of important time distorsions. Though TDNN-derived architectures seem more able to handle this kind of distorsions than LVQ, as the generalization performance is significantly higher for similar learning self-consistency, but both fail to remove all temporel misalignment effects.

In order to upgrade classification performance we changed the cost function which is minimized by the network : the error term corresponding to the desired output is multiplied by a constant H superior to 1, the terms of the error corresponding to other outputs being left unchanged to compensate the deficiency of the simple mean square error procedure. We obtained our best results with the best TDDN-derived net we experimented for H=2 :

Database	Net :	self-consist.	reco score
DB_1	16x16 / 4,1 - 16x13 / 5,2 - 16x5 - 34x1	87.0 %	63.0 %
DB_2	16x16 / 4,1 - 16x13 / 5,2 - 16x5 - 34x1	87.0 %	78.0 %

The too small number of independent weights (too low-dimensioned TDNN-derived architecture) makes the problem too constrained. A well chosen TDNN-derived architecture can perform as well as the best k-nearest neighbours strategy. Performance gets lower for data that mainly differ by a significant speaking rate mismatch which could indicate that TDNN-derived architectures do not manage to handle all kinds of time distortions. So it is encouraging to combine different networks and classical methods to deal with the temporal and sequential aspects of speech.

2.3.3 Combination of TDNN and LVQ

A set of experiments using a combined TDNN-derived network and LVQ architecture were conducted. For these experiments, we have used the best nets found in previous experiments. The main parameter of these experiments is the number of hidden cells in the last layer of the TDNN-derived network which is the input layer of LVQ (Bennani, 1990).

Evaluation on DB_1 with various numbers of references per class gave the following recognition scores:

refs per class	4	8	16
TDNN +k-means	76.2 %	78.1 %	79.8 %
TDNN +LBG	77.7 %	79.9 %	81.3 %
TDNN +LVQ (LBG for initialization)	78.4 %	82.1 %	81.4 %

Best results have been obtained with 8 references per class and the LBG algorithm to initialize the LVQ module. The best performance on the test set (82.1 %) represents a significant increase (4 %) compared to the best TDNN-derived network.

Other experiments were performed on TDNN + LVQ by using a modified LVQ architecture, presented in (Bennani, 1990), which is an extension of LVQ built to automatically weight the variables according to their importance for the classification. We obtain a recognition score of 83.6 % on DB_2 (training and tests on sentences).

We also used low dimensioned TDNNs for discriminating between phonetic features (Bimbot, 1990), assuming that phonetics will provide a description of speech that will appropriately constrain a priori a neural network, the TDNN structure warranting the desirable property of shift invariance.

The feature extraction approach can be considered as an other way to use prior knowledge for solving a complex problem with neural networks. The results obtained in these experiments are an interesting starting point for designing a large modular network where each module is in charge of a simple task, directly related to a well-defined linguistic phenomenon (Bimbot, 1990).

2.4 CONCLUSIONS

Experiments with LVQ alone, a TDNN-derived network alone and combined TDNN-LVQ architectures proved the combined architecture to be the most efficient with respect to our databases as summarized below (training and tests on DB_2):

k-means	LVQ	k-nn	k-nn + DTW	TDNN	TDNN + LVQ
61.3 %	67.2 %	72.2 %	77.5 %	78.0 %	83.6 %

3 PARAMETERS-TO-LEXICAL

The main objective of this task is to use neural nets for the classification of a sequence of speech frames into lexical items (isolated words). Many factors affect the performance of automatic speech recognition systems. They have been categorized into those relating to speaker independent recognition mode, the time evolution of speech (time representation of the neural network input), and the effects of noise . The two first topics are described herein while the third one is described in (Varga, 1990).

3.1 USE OF VARIOUS NETWORK TOPOLOGIES

Experiments were carried out to examine the performance of several network topologies such as those evaluated in section 2. A TDNN can be thought of as a single Hidden Markov Model state spread out in time. The lower levels of the network are forced to be shift-invariant, and instantiate the idea that the absolute time of an event is not important. Scaly networks are similar to TDDNs in that the hidden units of a scaly network are fed by partially overlapping input windows. As reported in previous sections, LVQ proved to be efficient for the phoneme classification task and an "optimal" architecture was found as a combination of a TDNN and LVQ. It was used herein for isolated word recognition.

From experiments reported in detail in (Varga, 1990) there seems little justification for fully-connected networks with their thousands of weights when TDNNs and Scaly networks with hundreds of weights have very similar performance. This performance is about **83%** (the nearest class mean classifier gave a performance of 69%) on the E-set database (a portion of the larger CONNEX alphabet database which British Telecom Research Laboratories have prepared for experiments on neural networks). The first utterance by each speaker of the "E" words: "B, C, D,

E, G, P, T, V" were used. The database is divided into training and test sets, each consisting of approximately 400 words and 50 speakers.

Other experiments were conducted on an isolated digits recognition task, speaker independent mode (25 speakers for training and 15 for test), using networks already introduced. A summary of the best performance obtained is:

K-means		TDNN		LVQ		TDNN+LVQ	
train.	test	train.	test	train.	test	train.	test
97.38	90.57	98,90	94.0	98.26	92.57	99.90	97.50

Performance for training is roughly equivalent for all algorithms. For generalization, performance of the combined architecture is clearly superior to other techniques.

3.2 TIME EVOLUTION OF SPEECH

In contrast to images as patterns of specific size, speech signals display a temporal evolution. Approaches have to be developed on how a network with its fixed number of input units can cover word patterns of variable size and also account for the dynamic time variations within words.

Different projections onto the fixed-size collection of N×M network input elements (number of vectors × number of coefficients per vector) have been tested, such as :

Linear Normalization : the boundaries of a word are determined by a conventional endpoint detection algorithm and the N' feature vectors linearly compressed or expanded to N by averaging or duplicating vectors,

Time Warp : word boundaries are located initially. Some parts of a word of length N' are compressed, while others are stretched and some remain constant with respect to speech characteristics,

Noise Boundaries : the sequence of N' vectors of a word are placed in the middle of or at random within the area of the desired N vectors and the margins padded with the noise in the speech pauses,

Trace Segmentation : the procedure essentially involves the division of the trace that is followed by the temporal course in the M-dimensional feature vector space, into a constant number of new sections of identical length.

These time normalization procedures were used with the scaly neural network (Varga, 1990). It turned out that three methods for time representation - time normalization, trace segmentation with endpoint detection or with noise boundaries - are well suited to solve the transformation problem for a fixed input network layer. The recognition scores are in the 98.5% range (with±1% deviation) for 10 digits and 99.5% for a 57 words in speaker independent mode. There is no clear indication that one of these approaches is superior to the other ones.

3.3 CONCLUSIONS

The neural network techniques investigated have delivered comparable performance to classical techniques. It is now well agreed that Hybrid systems (Integration of

Hidden Markov Modeling and MLPs) yield enhanced performance. Initial steps have been made towards the integration of Hidden Markov Models and MLPs. Mathematical formulations are required to unify hybrid models. The temporal aspect of speech has to be carefully considered and taken into account by the formalism.

4 PARAMETERS-TO-PARAMETERS

The main objective of this task was to provide the speech recognizer with a set of parameters adapted to the current user without any training phase.

Spectral parameters corresponding to the same sound uttered by two speakers are generally different. Speaker-independent recognizers usually take this variability into account, using stochastic models and/or multi-references. An alternative approach consists in learning spectral mappings to transform the original set of parameters into another one more adapted with respect to the characteristics of the current user and the speech acquisition conditions. The way to proceed can be summed up as follows :

- Load of the standard dictionary of the reference speaker,
- Acquisition of an adaptation vocabulary for the new speaker,
- Each new utterance is time-warped against the corresponding reference utterance. Thus temporal variability is softened and corresponding feature vectors are available (input-output pairs),
- The spectral transformations are learned from these associated vectors,
- The adaptation operator is applied to the reference dictionary, leading to an adapted one,
- The recognizer is evaluated using the obtained adapted dictionary.

The mathematical formulation is based on a very important result, regarding input-output mappings, and demonstrated by Funahashi (Funahashi, 1989) and Hornik, Stinchcombe & White (Hornik, 1989). They proved that a network using a single hidden layer (a net with 3 layers) with an arbitrary squashing function can approximate any Borel measurable function to any desired degree of accuracy.

Experiments were conducted (see details in (Choukri, 1990)) on a speech isolated word database consisting of 20 English words recorded 26 times by 16 different speakers (TI data base (Choukri, 1987)). The first repetition of the 20 words are reference templates, tests are conducted on the remaining 25 repetitions. Before adaptation, the cross-speaker scores is of 68%. On the average adaptation with the multi-layer perceptron provides a 15% improvement compared to the non-adapted results.

5 CONCLUSIONS

For phonetic classifications, sophisticated networks, combinations of TDNNs and LVQ, revealed to be more efficient than classical approaches or simple network architectures; their use for isolated word recognition offered comparable performance. Various approaches to cope with temporal distortions were implemented and demonstrate that combination of sophisticated neural networks and their cooperation with HMM is a promising research axis. It has also been established that basic MLPs are efficient tools to learn speaker-to-speaker mappings for speaker adaptation procedures. We are expecting more sophisticated MLPs (recurrent and context sensitive) to perform better.

Acknowledgements:

This project is partially supported by the European ESPRIT Basic research Actions programme (BRA 3228). The partners involved are: CGInn (F), ENST (F), IRIAC (F), RSRE (UK), SEL (FRG), and UPM (SPAIN).

References

K. Choukri. (1990) *Speech processing and recognition using integrated neurocomputing techniques: ESPRIT Project SPRINT (Bra 3228), First deliverable of Task 2,* June 1990.

F. Bimbot. (1990) *Speech processing and recognition using integrated neurocomputing techniques: ESPRIT project SPRINT (Bra 3228), First deliverable of task 3,* June 1990.

A. Varga. (1990) *Speech processing and recognition using integrated neurocomputing techniques: ESPRIT Project SPRINT (Bra 3228), First deliverable of Task 5,* June 1990.

A. Waibel, T. Hanazawa, G. Hinton, K. Shikano, and K. Lang. (1987) *Phoneme recognition using Time-Delay Neural Networks.*, Technical Report, CMU / ATR, Oct 30, 1987.

Y. Bennani, N. Chaourar, P. Gallinari, and A. Mellouk. (1990) *Comparison of Neural Net models on speech recognition tasks,* Technical Report, Universit of Paris Sud, LRI, 1990.

Ken-Ichi Funahashi. (1989) *On the approximate realization of continuous mappings by neural networks,* in Neural Networks, 2(2):183–192, march 1989.

K. Hornik, M. Stinchcombe, and H. White. (1989) *Multilayer feedforward networks are universal approximators.*, in Neural Networks, vol. 2(number 5):359–366, 1989.

K. Choukri. (1987) *Several approaches to Speaker Adaptation in Automatic Speech Recognition Systems,* PhD thesis, ENST (Télécom Paris), Paris, 1987.

AUTHORS AND CONTRIBUTORS

Y. BENNANI F. BIMBOT J. BRIDLE N. CHAOURAR
K. CHOUKRI L. DODD F. FOGELMAN P. GALLINARI
D. HOWELL M. IMMENDORFER A. KRAUSE K. McNAUGHT
A. MELLOUK C. MONTACIE R. MOORE O. SEGARD
H. VALBRET A. VARGA A. WALLYN

Part VI

Signal Processing

Natural Dolphin Echo Recognition Using an Integrator Gateway Network

Herbert L. Roitblat
Department of Psychology, University of Hawaii, Honolulu, HI 96822

Patrick W. B Moore, Paul E. Nachtigall, & Ralph H. Penner
Naval Ocean Systems Center, Hawaii Laboratory, Kailua, Hawaii, 96734

Abstract

We have been studying the performance of a bottlenosed dolphin on a delayed matching-to-sample task to gain insight into the processes and mechanisms that the animal uses during echolocation. The dolphin recognizes targets by emitting natural sonar signals and listening to the echoes that return. This paper describes a novel neural network architecture, called an integrator gateway network, that we have developed to account for this performance. The integrator gateway network combines information from multiple echoes to classify targets with about 90% accuracy. In contrast, a standard backpropagation network performed with only about 63% accuracy.

1. INTRODUCTION

The study of animals can provide a very important source of information for the design of automated artificial systems such as robots and autonomous vehicles. Animals have evolved in a real world, solving real problems, such as gathering and interpreting essential information. We call the process of using animal studies to inform the design of artificial systems biomimetics because the artificial systems are designed as mimics of biological ones.

2. INVESTIGATIONS OF DOLPHIN ECHOLOCATION PERFORMANCE

Dolphin echolocation clicks emerge from the rounded forehead or melon as a highly directional sound beam with 3 dB (half power) beamwidths of approximately 10° in both the vertical and horizontal planes (Au, et al., 1986). Echolocation clicks have peak energy at frequencies from 40 to 130 kHz with source levels of 220 dB re: 1 μPa at 1 m (Au, 1980; Moore & Pawloski, 1990). Bottlenosed dolphins have excellent directionally selective hearing (Au & Moore, 1984), spanning over 7 octaves, and can detect frequencies as high as 150 kHz (Johnson, 1966).

3. BEHAVIORAL METHODS

We have been studying the performance of a bottlenosed dolphin on an echolocation delayed matching-to-sample (DMTS) task (e.g., Nachtigall, 1980; Nachtigall, et al., 1985; Roitblat, et al., 1990a; Moore, et al., 1990). In this task a sample stimulus is presented underwater to a blindfolded dolphin. The dolphin is allowed to echolocate on this object ad lib. The object is then removed from the water, and after a short delay, three alternative objects are presented (the comparison stimuli). One of these objects is identical to (matches) the sample object, and the dolphin is required to indicate the matching stimulus by touching a response wand in front of it. The object that serves as sample and the location of the correct match vary randomly from trial to trial.

Recent work has concentrated on performance with three sample and comparison stimuli: (a) a PVC plastic tube, (b) a water-filled stainless steel sphere, and (c) a solid aluminum cone (see Roitblat, et al., 1990a). On average the dolphin used 37.2 clicks to identify the sample, and an average of 4.2 scans to examine the three comparison stimuli. A scan is a train of clicks to a single stimulus ended either by the initiation of a scan to another stimulus or by a cessation of clicking

The dolphin's scanning patterns were modeled using sequential sampling theory (see also Roitblat, 1984). Simulations based on this model provide a reasonably good approximation of the dolphin's performance (Roitblat, et al., 1990a). The simulation differed from the dolphin's actual performance, however, in that it was less variable than the live dolphin. We return to the problem of accounting for this difference in variability below after considering some models of the details of echo recognition.

4. ARTIFICIAL NEURAL NETWORKS

We have developed a series of neural-network models of dolphin echolocation processing (see also Gorman and Sejnowski, 1988). We (Moore, et al., 1990; Roitblat, et al., 1989) trained a counterpropagation network (Hecht-Nielsen, 1987, 1988) to classify echoes represented by their spectra into categories corresponding to each of the stimuli in our current stimulus set. The network correctly classified more than 95% of these spectra. This classification suggests two things. First, the spectral information

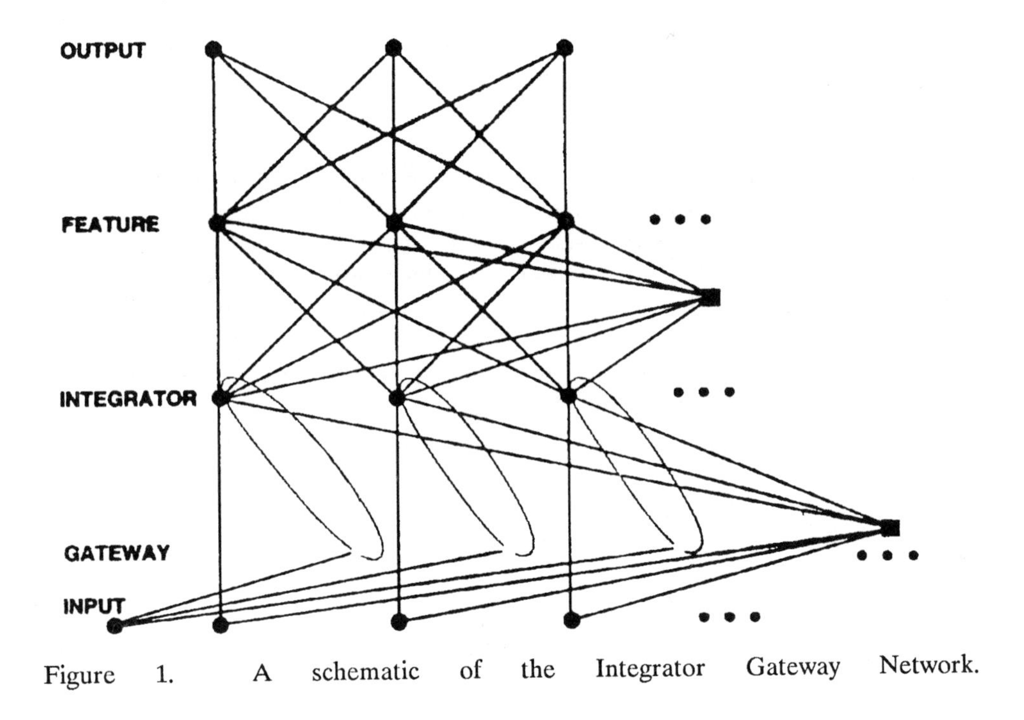

Figure 1. A schematic of the Integrator Gateway Network.

present in the echoes was sufficient to identify the targets on which the dolphin was echolocating. Second, only a single echo was necessary to classify the target. Although the network could identify the target with only a single echo, the dolphin concurrently performing the same task emitted many clicks in identifying the same targets. Further investigation revealed that the clicks emitted by the dolphin were more variable than our initial sample suggested (Roitblat, et al., 1990b). This variability provides one possible explanation for the high performance level, and low variability of our initial model.

4.1 THE INTEGRATOR GATEWAY NETWORK

Our integrator gateway network incorporates features of the sequential sampling model described earlier, including the assumptions that the dolphin averages or sums spectral information from successive echoes and continues to emit clicks and collect returning echoes until it can classify the target producing those echoes with sufficient confidence. It mimics the dolphin's strategy of using multiple echoes to identify each target. Figure 1 shows schematic of the Integrator Gateway Network.

Network inputs were 30-dimensional spectral vectors containing echo amplitudes in 1.95 kHz wide frequency bins. The echoes were captured and digitized during the dolphin's matching-to-sample performance. In addition to the 30 bins of spectral information, each echo was also marked as to whether the echo was (1.00) or was not

(0.00) at the start of an echo train. Recall that the dolphin directs a series of clicks to one target at a time, so it seemed plausible to include information marking the start of a click train. The frequency inputs were then passed to a scalar unit and to the integrator layer. The integrator layer also contained 30 units, connected to the frequency units in the input layer in a corresponding one-to-one pattern. The connections to the scalar unit were fixed at 1/n, where n is the number of frequency inputs. The weights to the integrator layer were fixed at 1.00. The output of the scalar unit, i.e., the sum of all of its inputs, was passed to each unit in the integrator layer via a fixed weight of -1.00. The effect of this scalar unit was to subtract the average activity of the input layer (neglecting the start-of-train marker) from the inputs to the integrator layer. This subtraction preserved all of the relative activity information present in the inputs, but kept the inputs within a manageable range.

The elements in the integrator layer computed a cumulative sum of the inputs they received. The role of this layer was to accumulate and integrate information from successive echo spectra. The outputs of the integrator layer were passed via fixed connections with 1.00 weights to corresponding units in the gateway layer. The integrator layer and the gateway layer each contained the same number of units. Each unit in the gateway layer acted as a reset for the corresponding unit in the integrator layer, and connected back to its corresponding unit with a weight of -1.00. Each unit in the gateway layer employed a multiplicative transfer function that multiplied the input from its corresponding unit in the integrator layer with the value of the start-of-train marker. Because this marker had 1.00 activity at the start of a scan and 0.00 activity otherwise, it functioned as a reset signal, causing the units in the integrator layer to be reset to 0.00 at the start of every scan; their previous activation level was subtracted from their input.

The output of the integrator layer also led via variable-weight connections to each of the elements in the feature layer. The same kind of scalar unit that intervened between the input layer and integrator layer was also used between the integrator layer and feature layer to subtract the average activity of the integrator layer, again to keep activations within a manageable range. The outputs of the feature layer led via variable-weight connections to the classifier layer. The elements in these two layers contained sigmoid transfer functions and were trained using a standard cumulative back-propagation algorithm with the epoch duration set to the number of training samples (60).

The training set consisted of six sets of ten successive echoes each, selected from the ends of haphazardly chosen echo trains. An equal number of cone, tube, and sphere echoes were used. The training set was a relatively small subset (4%) of the total set of available echoes (1,335).

4.2 INTEGRATOR GATEWAY RESULTS AND DISCUSSION

Figure 2 shows the results of generalization testing of the network in the form of a derived confidence measure. The network was given all 30 scans (10 scans of each tar-

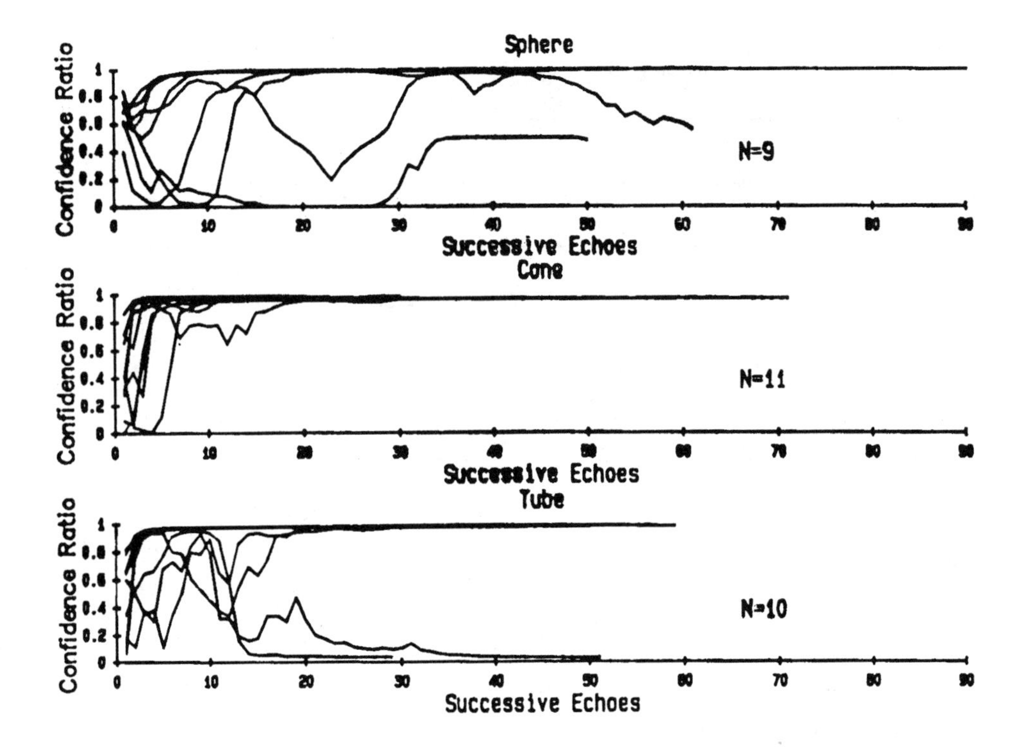

Figure 2. Results of generalization testing of the network in the form of the confidence of the network in assigning the echo train to the proper category. See text.

get for a total of 1,335 sequential echoes), and was required to classify each echo train. "Confidence" was defined as the ratio of the activation level of the correct classification versus the total output of the three classification units. A confidence ratio of 1.00 indicates that only the correct unit is active. Confidence of 0.00 indicates that the correct unit is entirely inactive. Intermediate confidences correspond to intermediate likelihood ratios (Qian & Sejnowski, 1988).

Recall that echo trains varied in length under control of the dolphin. Therefore, it is not entirely clear how to measure the network performance. According to sequential sampling theory (see Roitblat, et al., 1990a) a rational decision maker collects echo evidence only until a sufficiently confident classification is available and then stops. Table 1 shows the number of clicks in each train that were required to reach a confidence ratio of 0.96 and the classification that the network derived. Some of the scans ended before the network could achieve this confidence level. Three erroneous classifications were made (90% correct).

Table 1
Number of Clicks to Network Confidence Criterion

Target Scanned					
Sphere	Cone	Tube	Sphere	Cone	Tube
Integrator Gateway			Backpropagation		
16S	20C	40C	1S	1C	3S
9S	4C	18C	6S	30C	1S
7S	2C	20T	1S	1C	11S[1]
6S	6C	23T	5S	2C	1T
19S	14C	5T	14S	2C	14T
19S	6C	4T	14S	30S[1]	1T
34S	6C	4T	3S	32S[1]	1T
7S	4C	4T	1S	57S	1T
23C	6C	5T	40T	22S	2T
	3C	4T		22S	1T
	11C			27T	

Note: Entries are the number of clicks needed by the network to achieve the 0.96 confidence criterion. C indicates a Cone decision, S indicates a Sphere decision, T indicates a Tube decision. [1]Indicates that the dolphin stopped echolocating before the network reached its confidence criterion. On these scans, the decision is the one with the highest confidence at the end of the scan.

4.3 A SIMPLE BACKPROPAGATION NETWORK

The integrator gateway network reflects the assumption of sequential sampling theory that the dolphin combines information from successive echoes in deriving its identification. In contrast, a standard backpropagation network does not integrate over successive echoes, but instead attempts to identify each echo independently. A backpropagation network can be used as a model of a system that emits multiple clicks because the echoes vary in quality. Rather than integrating the echoes, it simply waits for a single adequate echo that allows it to meet its confidence criterion.

We trained a backpropagation network (using the fast-backpropagation algorithm to adjust the weights (Samad, 1988) on the same data that were submitted to the integrator network in order to determine whether the additional structure of the integrator network contributed to its performance accuracy. The network contained exactly the same number of inputs, hidden units, outputs, and adjustable connections as the integrator network. The networks differed only in absence of the integration apparatus in the backpropagation network.

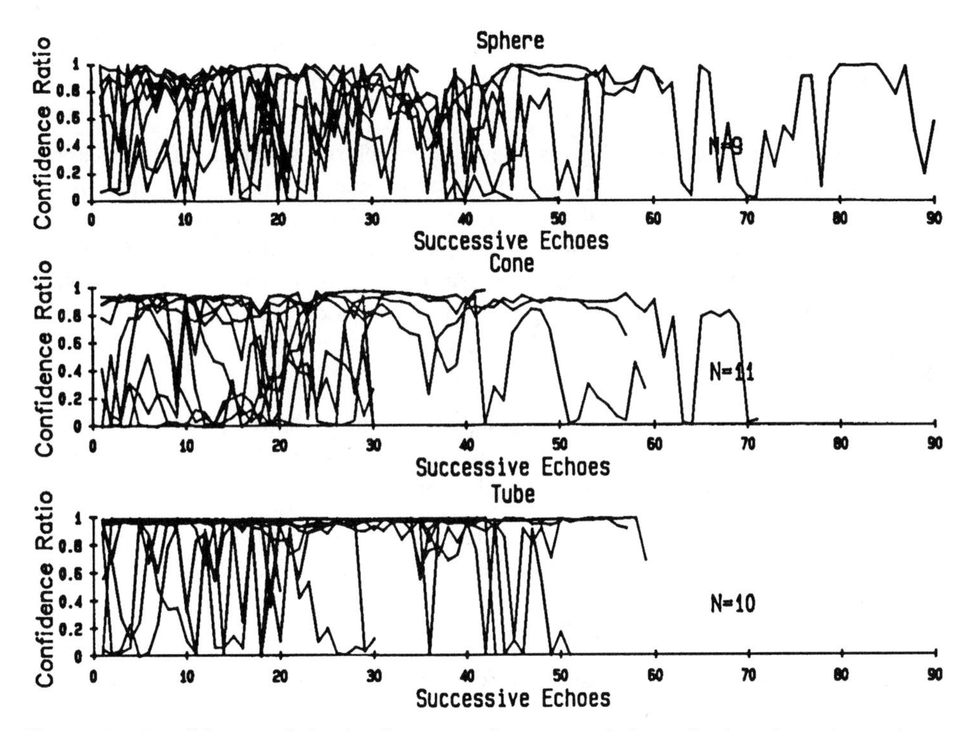

Figure 3. Confidence of the backpropagation network in assigning the echo train to the proper category as a function of the number of echoes received.

4.4 BACKPROPAGATION RESULTS

Figure 3 shows the confidence of the backpropagation network in assigning the echo train to the proper category as a function of the number of echoes received. Compared to the categorization performance of the integrator network, the backpropagation network was much more variable. As Figure 3 shows, the individual echoes were highly variable, and frequently assigned to an erroneous category.

The performance of the backpropagation network when judged by the standards of sequential sampling theory are also shown in Table 1. This table shows the number of clicks necessary to first reach a classification with greater then 0.96 confidence. On average the backpropagation network (11.57 echoes) reached its confidence criterion in the about the same number of clicks (t (df = 58) = 0.03, $p > .05$) as the integrator network (11.67 echoes), but it produced more errors (X^2 (df=1) = 5.96).

These data suggest that the integrator network added significantly to the ability to classify sequentially produced echoes. By implementing a signal "averaging" mechanism in the neural network the system could take advantage of the redundancy inherent in the use of multiple echoes from the same source and in the stochastic properties of the noise in which those echoes are embedded. In contrast, the backpropagation network is required to process not only the characteristics of the echoes themselves, but also the characteristics of the noise. This results in many spurious classifications.

The gateway integrator network adds a level of complexity to the standard backpropagation network architecture that contributes substantially to its performance. Its design is inspired by properties of the dolphin's performance (Nachtigall & Moore, 1988) and it represents one step along a development path that seeks to include more and more of the mechanisms that we can identify from the neurobiology of echolocation and from the performance of dolphins in their aquatic environment.

References

Au, W. W. L. (1980). Echolocation signals of the Atlantic bottlenose dolphin (Tursiops truncatus) in open waters. In R. G. Busnel & J. F. Fish (Eds.) *Animal sonar systems*. (pp. 251-282). New York: Plenum Press.

Au, W. W. L. & Moore, P. W. B. (1984). Receiving beam patterns and directivity indices of the Atlantic bottlenose dolphin *Tursiops truncatus*. *Journal of the Acoustical Society of America*, 75, 255-262.

Au, W. W. L., Moore, P. W. B. & Pawloski, D. (1986). Echolocating transmitting beam of the Atlantic bottlenose dolphin. *Journal of the Acoustical Society of America*, 80, 688-691.

Gorman, R. P. & Sejnowski, T. J. (1988). Analysis of hidden units in a layered network trained to classify sonar targets. *Neural Networks*, 1, 75-89.

Hecht-Nielsen, R. (1987). Counterpropagation networks. *Applied Optics*, 26, 4979-4984.

Hecht-Nielsen, R. (1988). Applications of counterpropagation networks. *Neural Networks*, 1, 131-139.

Johnson, C. S. (1966). *Auditory thresholds of the bottlenosed porpoise, Tursiops truncatus (Montague)* (Naval Ordnance Test Station Technical Publication No 4178). Naval Ordnance Test Station.

Moore, P. W. B. & Pawloski, D. A. (1990). Investigations on the control of echolocation pulses in the dolphin (*Tursiops truncatus*). In J. Thomas & R. Kastelein (Eds.) *Sensory abilities of cetaceans*. New York: Plenum. In press.

Moore, P. W. B., Roitblat, H. L., Penner, R. H., & Nachtigall, P. E., Recognizing Successive Dolphin Echoes with an Integrator Gateway Network. Submitted for publication.

Nachtigall, P. E. (1980). Odontocete echolocation performance on object size, shape, and material, In R. G. Busnel & J. F. Fish (Eds.), *Animal Sonar Systems*, pp. 71-95, New York, Plenum Press.

Nachtigall, P. E., & Moore, P. W. B. (Eds.) (1988). *Animal sonar: Processes and performance*. New York: Plenum.

Nachtigall, P. E., Patterson, S. A., & Bauer, G. B. (1985). Echolocation delayed matching-to-sample in a bottlenose dolphin. Paper presented at the Sixth Biennial Conference on the Biology of Marine Mammals, Vancouver, B.C., Canada. November.

Qian, N. & Sejnowski, T. J. (1988). Predicting the secondary structure of globular proteins using neural network models. *Journal of Molecular Biology*, 202, 865-884.

Roitblat, H. L. (1984). Representations in pigeon working memory, In: H. L. Roitblat, T. G. Bever and H. S. Terrace (Eds.), *Animal cognition*. Hillsdale, NJ: Erlbaum, 79-97.

Roitblat, H. L., Moore, P. W. B., Nachtigall, P. E., Penner, R. H., & Au, W. W. L. (1989). Dolphin echolocation: Identification of returning echoes using a counterpropagation network. *Proceedings of the First International Joint Conference on Neural Networks*. Washington, DC: IEEE Press.

Roitblat, H. L., Penner, R. H. & Nachtigall, P. E. (1990a). Matching-to-sample by an echolocating dolphin. *Journal of Experimental Psychology: Animal Behavior Processes*, 16, 85-95.

Roitblat, H. L., Penner, R. H. & Nachtigall, P. E. (1990b). Attention and decision making in echolocation matching-to-sample by a bottlenose dolphin (*Tursiops truncatus*): the microstructure of decision making. In J. Thomas & R. Kastelein (Eds.) *Sensory abilities of cetaceans*. New York: Plenum. In press.

Samad, T. (1988). Back propagation is significantly faster if the expected value of the source unit is used for update. *International Neural Network Society Conference Abstracts*.

Signal Processing by Multiplexing and Demultiplexing in Neurons

David C. Tam
Division of Neuroscience
Baylor College of Medicine
Houston, TX 77030
dtam@next-cns.neusc.bcm.tmc.edu

Abstract

Signal processing capabilities of biological neurons are investigated. Temporally coded signals in neurons can be multiplexed to increase the transmission capacity. Multiplexing of signal is suggested in bi-threshold neurons with "high-threshold" and "low-threshold" for switching firing modes. To extract the signal embedded in the interspike-intervals of firing, the encoded signal are demultiplexed and multiplexed by a network of neurons with delayed-line circuitry for signal processing. The temporally coded input signal is transformed spatially by mapping the firing intervals topographically to the output of the network, thus decoding the specific firing interspike-intervals. The network also provides a band-pass filtering capability where the variability of the timing of the original signal can be decoded.

1 INTRODUCTION

Signals of biological neurons are encoded in the firing patterns of spike trains or the time series of action potentials generated by neurons. The signal content of the codes encoded by a presynaptic neuron will be decoded by some other neurons postsynpatically. Neurons are often thought to be encoding a single type of codes. But there is evidence suggesting that neurons may encode more than one type of signals. One of the mechanisms for embedding multiple types of signals processed by a neuron is multiplexing. When the signals are multiplexed, they also need to be demultiplexed to extract the useful information transmitted by the neurons. Theoretical and experimental evidence of such multiplexing and demultiplexing scheme for signal processing by neurons will be given below.

2 MULIPLEXING IN NEURONS

Most neurons fire action potentials when the membrane potential is depolarized to a threshold above the resting potential. For some neurons, there are more than a single threshold that can trigger the generation of action potentials. The thresholds occur not only at depolarized membrane potential (above the resting potential) but also at hyperpolarized potential (below the resting potential). This bi-threshold phenomena had been reported in a number of biological neurons including the giant squid axon (Hodgkin & Huxley, 1952), thalamic (Jahnsen & Llinás, 1984), inferior olivary (Yarom & Llinás, 1987), and hippocampal neurons (Stasheff & Wilson, 1990). The phenomena of triggering the firing of action potentials at a membrane potential below the resting potential level following prolonged hyperpolarization have been observed under different conditions in different neurons such as during the anodal break after voltage-clamped at a hyperpolarized potential (Hodgkin & Huxley, 1952), and are called "low-threshold spikes" (Yarom & Llinás, 1987) and "baseline spikes" (Stasheff & Wilson, 1990), which are spikes elicited naturally during the after-hyperpolarization (a.h.p.) period. The generation of low-threshold spikes is a voltage- and time-dependent process occurring during a prolonged hyperpolarization for de-inactivation of ionic conductances.

Given this bi-threshold for firing of action potentials, a neuron can function in two modes of operations: one at depolarization potentials and the other at hyperpolarization potentials. Thus, when the neuron is depolarized from the resting potential, the neuron will process signal based on the "high-threshold", and when the neurons is hyperpolarized for a prolonged duration, the neuron will process signal based on the "low-threshold". Formally, it is described as follows:

$$y(t) = \begin{cases} 1, & if\ V(t) \geq \theta_{hi} \quad or \\ & if\ V(t-i\Delta t) < \theta_{lo}\ and\ V(t) \geq \theta_{lo},\ for\ 1<i<j \\ 0, & otherwise \end{cases} \tag{1}$$

where $y(t)$ denotes the occurrence of the firing of an action potential at time t, $x(t)$ denotes the membrane potential of the neuron at time t, θ_{hi} denotes the "high-threshold" and θ_{lo} denotes the "low-threshold", and $j\Delta t$ represents the duration of hyperpolarization, such that the neuron will fire when depolarized at the hyperpolarization potential. This bi-threshold firing phenomenon was suggested to be involved in the two different rhythms generated by a neuron as a periodic bi-stable oscillator (Rose & Hindmarsh, 1985; Goldbeter & Moran, 1988), which can switch between two different firing frequencies, thus multiplexing the signal depending on the mode of operation or polarization level (Tam, 1990c).

3 DEMULTIPLEXING IN NEURONS

The multiplexed signal encoded in a neuron can be demultiplexed in a number of ways. One of the systematic way of extracting the firing frequency of the encoded signal can be described by a network of neurons. Given the temporally modulated input spike train spike, the firing intervals of the encoded signal can be extracted by a network of neurons such that the firing of these output neurons will decode the interspike-intervals of the input signal. In this network, the temporal codes of the input spike train will be converted into a spatially-distributed topographical code where each output neuron represents a particular firing interval with a specific band-width. Thus, the original signal is demultiplexed by mapping the input firing intervals into the firing of specific neurons based on the spatial location of the neuron in the output layer.

The circuitry of this network of neurons utilizes delay-lines for signal processing (Reiss, 1964; Tam, 1990a, b). Examples of delay-line architecture used for signal processing can be found in the cerebellar cortex (Eccles *et al.*, 1967), inferior colliculus (Yin, *et al.*, 1987, 1986, 1985; Chan *et al.*, 1987) and cochlear nucleus (Carr & Konishi, 1990).

The time-delayed network can be described as follows. Let $x(t)$ be a time-series of spikes (or delta-functions, $\delta(t)$) with a total of $n+1$ spikes:

$$x(t) = \sum_{j=0}^{n} \delta(t - \tau_j) \tag{2}$$

Let the input to the network be a spike train $x(t)$ given by (2). There are k neurons in the first input layer of the network. The input is split into multiple branches, each of which is connected to all k neurons in the first layer. In addition to the direct connection between the input and the first layer neurons, each input branch to the first layer neuron is also split into multiple branches with successive incremental time-delays. Specially, the k-th neuron in the first layer has $k+1$ input lines, each input is successively delayed by a time delay Δt relative to the previous one. That is, the i-th input to this k-th neuron in the first layer at time t is given by $x(t-i\Delta t)$. Thus, the sum of the input to this k-th neuron is given by:

$$X_k(t) = \sum_{i=0}^{k} x(t - i\Delta t) \tag{3}$$

3.1 BAND-PASS FILTERING

Band-pass filtering can be accomplished by the processing at the first layer of neurons. If the threshold for the generation of an output spike for the k-th neuron is set at one, then this neuron will fire only when the interspike-interval, I_j, of the input spike train is within the time-delay window, $k\Delta t$. That is, the output of this k-th neuron is given by:

$$y_k(t) = \begin{cases} 1, & if\ X_k > 1 \\ 0, & otherwise \end{cases} \tag{4}$$

The *interspike-interval*, I_j, is defined as the time interval between any two adjacent spikes:

$$I_j = \tau_j - \tau_{j-1}, \quad for\ 0 < j \le n \tag{5}$$

Therefore, the k-th neuron can be considered as encoding a band-pass filtered input interspike-interval, $0 < I_j \le k\Delta t$. Thus, the k-th neuron in the first layer essentially capture the input interspike-interval firing of less than $k\Delta t$, the band-passed interspike-interval. To ensure that the neuron will fire a spike of Δt in duration, we introduce a refractory period of $(k-1)\Delta t$ after the firing of a spike for the k-th neuron to suppress continual activation of the neuron due to the phase differences of the incoming delayed signal.

3.2 HIGHER-ORDER INTERSPIKE-INTERVAL PROCESSING

Higher-order interspike-intervals can be eliminated by the second layer neurons. The *order* of the interspike-interval is defined by the number of intervening spikes between any two spikes in the spike train. That is, the first-order interspike-interval contains no intervening spike between the two adjacent spikes under consideration. Second-order interspike-interval is the time interval between two consecutive first-order interspike-intervals, i.e., the interval containing one intervening spike.

If the second layer neurons receive excitatory input from the corresponding neuron with a threshold ($\theta > 1$) and inhibitory input from the corresponding neuron with a threshold of ($\theta > 2$), then the higher-order intervals are eliminated, with the output of the second layer (double-primed) neuron given by:

$$y''_k(t) = y_k(t) - y'_k(t) = \begin{cases} 1, & if\ 2 \ge X_k(t) > 1 \\ 0, & otherwise \end{cases} \tag{6}$$

where

$$y'_k(t) = \begin{cases} 1, & if\ X_k > 2 \\ 0, & otherwise \end{cases} \tag{7}$$

This requires that an addition input layer of neurons be added to the network, which we call the *first-parallel layer,* whose input/output relationship is given by (7). In other words, there are k first layer neurons and k first-parallel layer neurons serving as the input layers of the network. The k-th neuron in the first layer and the k-th neuron in the first-parallel layer are similar in their inputs, but the thresholds for producing an output spike are different. The difference between the outputs of the first set of neurons (first layer) in the first layer and the primed set of neurons (first-parallel layer) is computed by the *second* layer by making excitatory connection from the first layer neuron and inhibitory connection from the first-parallel layer neuron for each corresponding k-th neuron respectively as described by (6). This will ensure accurate estimation of only first-order interspike-interval, $0 < I_j \leq k\Delta t$, within the time-delay window $k\Delta t$.

3.3 BAND-WIDTH PROCESSING

The third layer neurons will filter the input signal by distributing the frequency (or interval) of firing of neurons within a specific band-width. Since the k-th neuron in the second layer detects the band-passed first-order interspike-intervals $(0 < I_j \leq k\Delta t)$ and the h-th neuron detects another band-passed interspike-intervals $(0 < I_j \leq h\Delta t)$, then the difference between these two neurons will detect first-order interspike-intervals with a band-width of $(k\text{-}h)\Delta t$. In order words, it will detect the first-order interspike-interval between $k\Delta t$ and $h\Delta t$, i.e., $h\Delta t < I_j \leq k\Delta t$.

This requires that the *third* layer neurons derive their inputs from two sources: one excitatory and the other inhibitory from the second layer. The output of the k-th neuron in the third layer, $y'''_k(t)$, is obtained from the difference between the outputs of k-th and h-th neurons in the second layer:

$$y'''_{kh}(t) = y''_k(t) - y''_h(t) = \begin{cases} 1, & if\ 2 \geq \sum_{i=h}^{k} x(t - i\Delta t) > 1 \\ 0, & otherwise \end{cases} \tag{7}$$

A two-dimensional topographical map of the band-passed interspike-intervals of the input spike train can be represented by arranging the third-layer neurons in a two-dimensional array, with one axis (the horizontal axis) representing the k index (the band-passed interspike-interval) of equation (7) and the other axis (the vertical axis) representing the $(k\text{-}h)$ index (the band-width interspike-interval). Thus the firing of the third layer neurons represents the band-passed filtered version of the original input spike train, extracting the firing interspike-interval of the input signal. The "coordinate" of the neuron in the third layer represents the band-passed interspike-interval $(0 < I_j \leq k\Delta t)$ and the band-width interspike-interval $(h\Delta t < I_j \leq k\Delta t)$ of the original input spike train signal. The band-width can be used to detect the variations (or jittering) in the timing for firing of spikes in the input spike train, since the timing of firing of spikes in biological neurons can be very variable. Thus, the network can be used to detect the variability of timing in firing of spikes by the firing location of the third layer neuron.

3.4 EXTRACTION OF EMBEDDED SIGNAL BY BI-THRESHOLD FIRING

If the neurons in the second and third layers are bi-threshold neurons where one threshold is at the "depolarization" level (i.e., a positive value) and the other threshold is at the "hyperpolarization" level (i.e., a negative value), then addition information may be extracted based on the level of firing threshold. Since the neuron in the second and third layers receive inhibitory inputs from the preceding layer, there are instances where the neuron be "hyperpolarized" or the sum of the inputs to the neuron is negative. Such condition occurs when the order of the interspike-interval is higher than one. In other words, the higher-order interspike-interval signal is embedded in the "hyperpolarization", which is normally suppressed from generating a spike when there is only one threshold for firing at the "depolarized" level (θ_{hi}). But for bi-threshold neurons where there is another threshold at the hyperpolarized level (θ_{lo}), such embedded signal encoded as hyperpolarization can be extracted by sending an external depolarizing signal to this neuron causing the neuron to fire at the low threshold. Thus the hyperpolarization signal can be "read-out" by an external input to the bi-threshold neuron. In summary, a time-delay network can be used to process temporally modulated pulsed-coded spike train signal and extract the firing interspike-intervals by mapping the band-passed intervals topographically on a two-dimensional output array from which the order of the interspike-interval can be extracted using different thresholds of firing.

Acknowledgements

This work is supported by ONR contract N00014-90-J-1353.

References

Carr, C. E. & Konishi, M. (1990) A circuit for detection of interaural time differences in the brain stem of the barn owl. *J. Neurosci.* 10: 3227-3246.

Chan, J. C., Yin, T. C. & Musicant, A. D. (1987) Effects of interaural time delays of noise stimuli on low-frequency cells in the cat's inferior colliculus. II. Responses to band-pass filtered noises. *J. Neurophysiol.* 58: 543-561.

Goldbeter, A. & Moran, F. (1988) Dynamics of a biochemical system with multiple oscillatory domains as a clue for multiple modes of neuronal oscillations. *Eur. Biophys. J.* 15:277-287.

Hodgkin, A. L. & Huxley, A. F. (1952) A quantitative description of membrane current and its application to conduction and excitation in nerve. *J. Physiol. (London)* 117: 500-544.

Eccles, J.C., Ito, M. and Szentágothai, J. (1967) *The Cerebellum as a Neuronal Machine*, Springer-Verlag, New York, Heidelberg.

Jahnsen, H. & Llinás, R. (1984) Electrophysiological properties of guinea-pig thalamic neurones: An *in vitro* study. *J. Physiol. (London)* 349:205-226.

Reiss, R.F. (1964) A theory of resonant networks. In (Ed. R.F. Reiss) *Neural Theory and Modeling: Proceedings of the 1962 Ojai Symposium.* Stanford University Press, Stanford, CA.

Rose, R. M. & Hindmarsh, J. L. (1985) A model of a thalamic neuron. *Proc. R. Soc. Lond.* 225:161-193.

Stasheff, S. F. & Wilson, W. A. (1990) Increased ectopic action potential generation accompanies epileptogenesis in vitro. *Neurosci. Lett.* 111: 144-150.

Tam, D. C. (1990a) Temporal-spatial coding transformation: Conversion of frequency-code to place-code via a time-delayed neural network. *Proceedings of the International Joint Conference on Neural Networks* (H. Caudill, eds.), *Jan., 1990.* Vol. 1, pp. I-130–133.

Tam, D. C. (1990b) Decoding of firing intervals in a temporal-coded spike train using a topographically mapped neural network. *Proc. of International Joint Conference on Neural Networks.* Vol. 3, pp. III-627–632.

Tam, D. C. (1990c) Functional significance of bi-threshold firing of neurons. *Society for Neuroscience Abstract.* Vol. 16, p. 1091.

Yarom, Y. & Llinás, R. (1987) Long-term modifiability of anomalous and delayed rectification in guinea pig inferior olivary neurons. *J. Neurosci.* 7:1166-1177.

Yin, T. C., Chan, J. C. & Carney, L. H. (1987) Effects of interaural time delays of noise stimuli on low-frequency cells in the cat's inferior colliculus. III. Evidence for cross-correlation. *J. Neurophysiol.* 58: 562-583.

Yin, T. C., Chan, J. C. & Irvine, D. R. (1986) Effects of interaural time delays of noise stimuli on low-frequency cells in the cat's inferior colliculus. I. Responses to wideband noise. *J. Neurophysiol.* 55: 280-300.

Yin, T. C., Hirsch, J. A. & Chan, J. C. (1985) Responses of neurons in the cat's superior colliculus to acoustic stimuli. II. A model of interaural intensity sensitivity. *J. Neurophysiol.* 53: 746-758.

Applications of Neural Networks in Video Signal Processing

John C. Pearson, Clay D. Spence and Ronald Sverdlove
David Sarnoff Research Center
CN5300
Princeton, NJ 08543-5300

Abstract

Although color TV is an established technology, there are a number of longstanding problems for which neural networks may be suited. Impulse noise is such a problem, and a modular neural network approach is presented in this paper. The training and analysis was done on conventional computers, while real-time simulations were performed on a massively parallel computer called the Princeton Engine. The network approach was compared to a conventional alternative, a median filter. Real-time simulations and quantitative analysis demonstrated the technical superiority of the neural system. Ongoing work is investigating the complexity and cost of implementing this system in hardware.

1 THE POTENTIAL FOR NEURAL NETWORKS IN CONSUMER ELECTRONICS

Neural networks are most often considered for application in emerging *new* technologies, such as speech recognition, machine vision, and robotics. The fundamental ideas behind these technologies are still being developed, and it will be some time before products containing neural networks are manufactured. As a result, research in these areas will not drive the development of inexpensive neural network hardware which could serve as a catalyst for the field of neural networks in general.

In contrast, neural networks are rarely considered for application in mature technologies, such as consumer electronics. These technologies are based on established principles of information processing and communication, and they are used in millions of products per year. The embedding of neural networks within such mass-market products would certainly fuel the development of low-cost network hardware, as economics dictates rigorous cost-reduction in every component.

2 IMPULSE NOISE IN TV

The color television signaling standard used in the U.S. was adopted in 1953 (McIlwain and Dean, 1956; Pearson, 1975). The video information is first broadcast as an amplitude modulated (AM) radio-frequency (RF) signal, and is then demodulated in the receiver into what is called the composite video signal. The composite signal is comprised of the high-bandwidth (4.2 MHz) luminance (black and white) signal and two low-bandwidth color signals whose amplitudes are modulated in quadrature on a 3.58 MHz subcarrier. This signal is then further decoded into the red, green and blue signals that drive the display. One image "frame" is formed by interlacing two successive "fields" of 262.5 horizontal lines.

Electric sparks create broad-band RF emissions which are transformed into oscillatory waveforms in the composite video signal, called AM impulses. See Figure 1. These impulses appear on a television screen as short, horizontal, multi-colored streaks which clearly stand out from the picture. Such sparks are commonly created by electric motors. There is little spatial (within a frame) or temporal (between frames) correlation between impulses.

General considerations suggest a two step approach for the removal of impulses from the video signal – *detect* which samples have been corrupted, and *replace* them with values derived from their spatio-temporal neighbors. Although impulses are quite visible, they form a small fraction of the data, so only those samples detected as corrupted should be altered. An interpolated average of some sort will generally be a good estimate of impulse-corrupted samples because images are generally smoothly varying in space and time.

There are a number of difficulties associated with this detection/replacement approach to the problem. There are many impulse-like waveforms present in normal video, which can cause "false positives" or "false alarms". See Figure 2. The algorithms that decode the composite signal into RGB spread impulses onto neighboring lines, so it is desirable to remove the impulses in the composite signal. However, the color encoding within the composite signal complicates matters. The subcarrier frequency is near the ringing frequency of the impulses and tends to hide the impulses. Furthermore, the replacement function cannot simply average the nearest

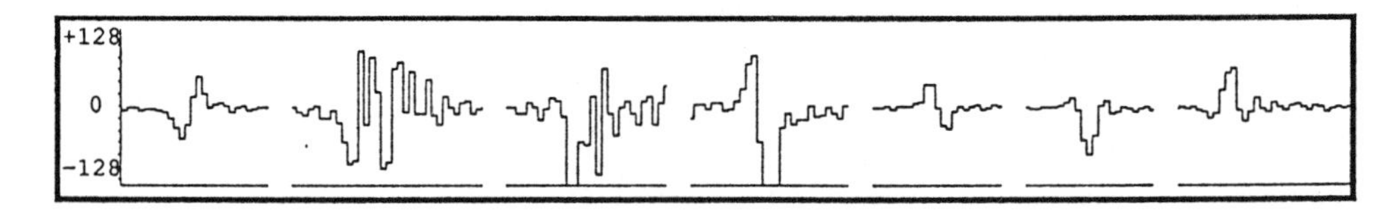

Figure 1: Seven Representative AM Impulse Waveforms. They have been digitized and displayed at the intervals used in digital receivers (8 bits, .07 usec). The largest amplitude impulses are 20-30 samples wide, approximately 3% of the width of one line of active video (752 samples).

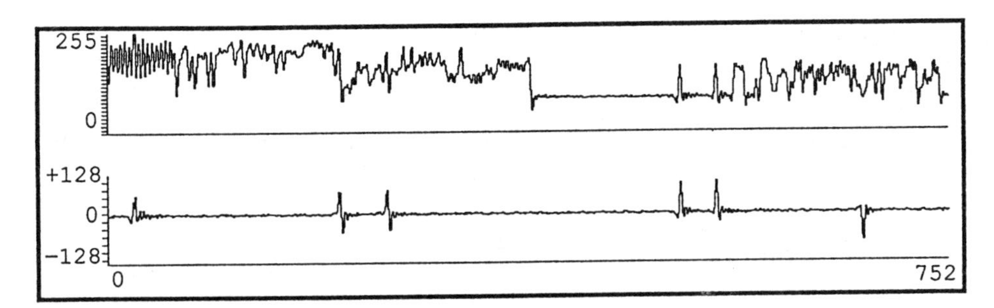

Figure 2: Corrupted Video Scan Line. (Top) Scan line of a composite video signal containing six impulse waveforms. (Bottom) The impulse waveforms, derived by subtracting the uncorrupted signal from the corrupted signal. Note the presence of many impulse-like features in the video signal.

samples, because they represent different color components. The impulses also have a wide variety of waveforms (Figure 1), including some variation caused by clipping in the receiver.

3 MODULAR NEURAL NETWORK SYSTEM

The impulse removal system incorporates three small multi-layer perceptron networks (Rumelhart and McClelland, 1986), and all of the processing is confined to one field of data. See Figure 3. The replacement function is performed by one network, termed the i-net ("i" denotes interpolation). Its input is 5 consecutive samples each from the two lines above and the two lines below the current line. The network consists of 10 units in the first hidden layer, 5 in the second, and one output node trained to estimate the center sample of the current line.

The detection function employs 2 networks in series. (A single network detector has been tried, but it has never performed as well as this two-stage detector.) The inputs to the first network are 9 consecutive samples from the current line centered on the sample of interest. It has 3 nodes in the first layer, and one output node trained to compute a moving average of the absolute difference between the clean and noisy signals of the current inputs. It is thus trained to function as a filter for impulse energy, and is termed the e-net. The output of the e-net is then low-pass filtered and sub-sampled to remove redundant information.

The inputs to the second network are 3 lines of 5 consecutive samples each, drawn from the post-processed output of the e-net, centered on the sample of interest. This network, like the e-net, has 3 nodes in the first layer and one output node. It is trained to output 1 if the sample of interest is contaminated with impulse noise, and 0 otherwise. It is thus an impulse detector, and is called the d-net.

The output of the d-net is then fed to a binary switch, which passes through to the final system output either the output of the i-net or the original signal, depending on whether the input exceeds an adjustable threshold.

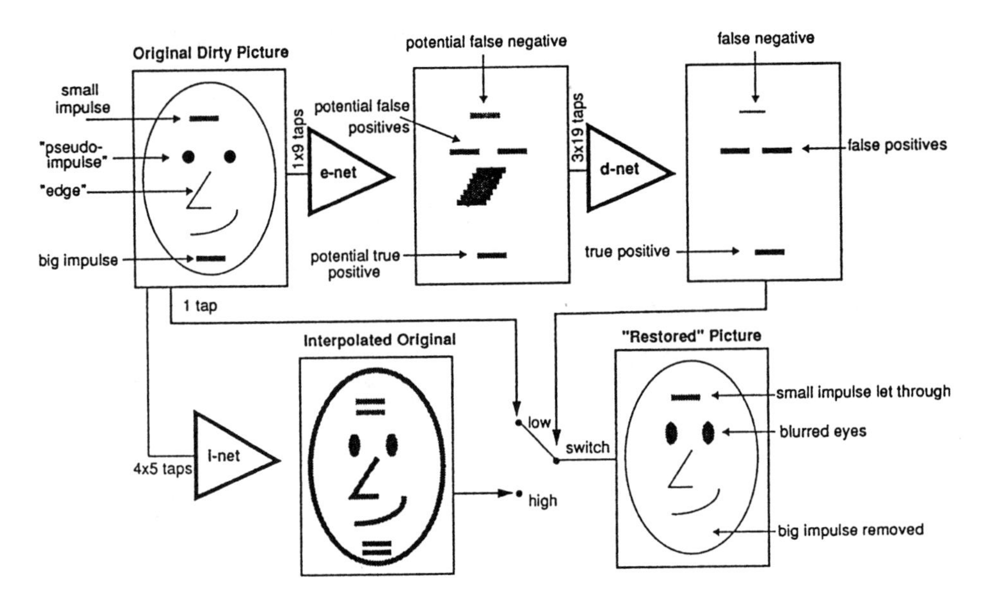

Figure 3: The Neural Network AM Impulse Removal System. The cartoon face is used to illustrate salient image processing characteristics of the system. The e-net correctly signals the presence of the large impulse (chin), misses the small impulse (forehead), and incorrectly identifies edges (nose) and points (eyes) as impulses. The d-net correctly disregards the vertically correlated impulse features (nose) and detects the large impulse (chin), but incorrectly misses the small impulse (forehead) and the non-correlated impulse-like features (eyes). The i-net produces a fuzzy (doubled) version of the original, which is used to replace segments identified as corrupted by the d-net.

Experience showed that the d-net tended to produce narrow spikes in response to impulse-like features of the image. To remove this source of false positives, the output of the d-net is averaged over a 19 sample region centered on the sample of interest. This reduces the peak amplitude of signals due to impulse-like features much more than the broad signals produced by true impulses. An impulse is considered to be present if this smoothed signal exceeds a threshold, the level of which is chosen so as to strike a balance between low false positive rates (high threshold), and high true positive rates (low threshold).

Experience also showed that the fringes of the impulses were not being detected. To compensate for this, sub-threshold d-net output samples are set high if they are within 9 samples of a super-threshold d-net sample. Figure 4 shows the output of the resulting trained system for one scan line.

The detection networks were trained on one frame of video containing impulses of 5 different amplitudes with the largest twenty times the smallest. Visually, these ranged from non-objectionable to brightly colored. Standard incremental back-propagation and conjugate gradient (NAG, 1990) were the training proceedures used. The complexity of the e-net and d-net were reduced in phases. These nets

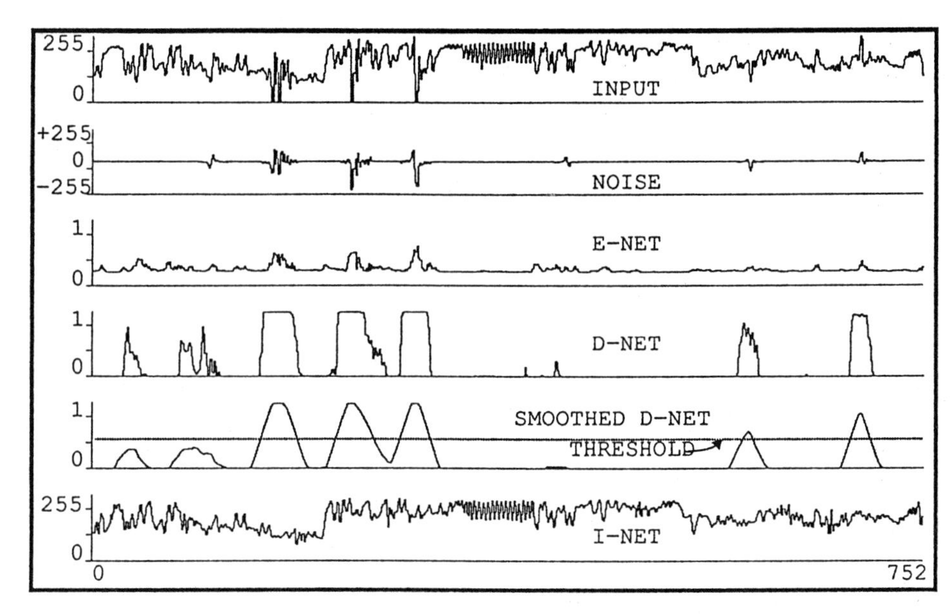

Figure 4: Input and Network Signals.

began as 3 layer nets. After a phase of training, redundant nodes were identified and removed, and training re-started. This process was repeated until there were no redundant nodes.

4 REAL-TIME SIMULATION ON THE PRINCETON ENGINE

The trained system was simulated in real-time on the Princeton Engine (Chin et. al., 1988), and a video demonstration was presented at the conference. The Princeton Engine (PE) is a 29.3 GIPS image processing system consisting of up to 2048 processing elements in a SIMD configuration. Each processor is responsible for the output of one column of pixels, and contains a 16-bit arithmetic unit, multiplier, a 64-word triple-port register stack, and 16,000 words of local processor memory. In addition, an interprocessor communication bus permits exchanges of data between neighboring processors during one instruction cycle.

While the i-net performs better than conventional interpolation methods, the difference is not significant for this problem because of the small amount of signal which is replaced. (If the whole image is replaced, the neural net interpolator gave about 1.5 dB better performance than a conventional method.) Thus it has not been implemented on the PE. The i-net may be of value in other video tasks, such as converting from an interlaced to a non-interlaced display.

16-bit fixed point arithmetic was used in these simulations, with 8 bits of fraction, and 10 bit sigmoid function look-up tables. Comparison with the double-precision arithmetic used on the conventional computers showed no significant reduction in

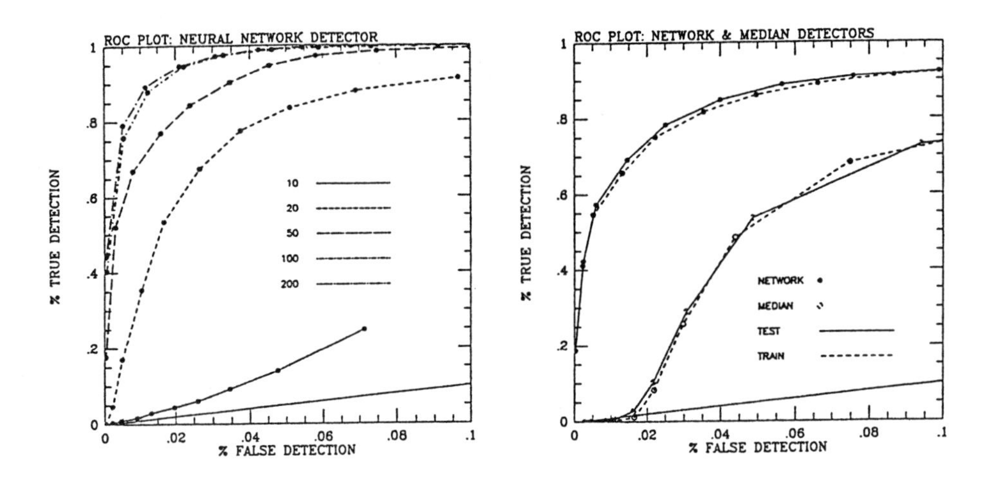

Figure 5: ROC Analysis of Neural Network and Median Detectors.

performance. Current work is exploring the feasibility of implementing training on the PE.

5 PERFORMANCE ANALYSIS

The mean squared error (MSE) is well known to be a poor measure of subjective image quality (Roufs and Bouma, 1980). A better measure of detection performance is given by the receiver operating characteristic, or ROC (Green and Swets, 1966, 1974). The ROC is a parametric plot of the fraction of corrupted samples correctly detected versus the fraction of clean samples that were falsely detected. In this case, the decision threshold for the smoothed output of the d-net was the parameter varied. Figure 5 (left) shows the neural network detector ROC for five different impulse amplitudes (tested on a video frame that it was not trained on). This quantifies the sharp breakdown in performance observed in real-time simulations at low impulse amplitude. This breakdown is not observed in analysis of the MSE.

Median filters are often suggested for impulse removal tasks, and have been applied to the removal of impulses from FM TV transmission systems (Perlman, et al, 1987). In order to assess the relative merits of the neural network detector, a median detector was designed and analyzed. This detector computes the median of the current sample and its 4 nearest neighbors with the same color sub-carrier phase. A detection is registered if the difference between the median and the current sample is above threshold (the same additional measures were taken to insure that impulse fringes were detected as were described above for the neural network detector). Figure 5 (right) shows both the neural network and median detector ROC's for two different video frames, each of which contained a mixture of all 5 impulse amplitudes. One frame was used in training the network (TRAIN), and the other was not (TEST). This verifies that the network was not overtrained, and quantifies the superior performance of the network detector observed in real-time simulations.

6 CONCLUSIONS

We have presented a system using neural network algorithms that outperforms a conventional method, median filtering, in removing AM impulses from television signals. Of course an additional essential criterion is the cost and complexity of hardware implementations. Median filter chips have been successfully fabricated (Christopher et al., 1988). We are currently investigating the feasibility of casting small neural networks into special purpose chips. We are also applying neural nets to other television signal processing problems.

Acknowledgements

This work was supported by Thomson Consumer Electronics, under Erich Geiger and Dietrich Westerkamp. This work was part of a larger team effort, and we acknowledge their help, in particular: Nurit Binenbaum, Jim Gibson, Patrick Hsieh, and John Ju.

References

Chin, D., J. Passe, F. Bernard, H. Taylor and S. Knight, (1988). The Princeton Engine: A Real-Time Video System Simulator. *IEEE Transactions on Consumer Electronics* **34**:2 pp. 285–297.

Christopher, L.A., W.T. Mayweather III, and S. Perlman, (1988). A VLSI Median Filter for Impulse Noise Elimination in Composite or Component TV Signals. *IEEE Transactions on Consumer Electronics* **34**:1 p. 262.

Green, D.M., and J.A. Swets, (1966 and 1974). *Signal Detection Theory and Psychophysics.* New York, Wiley (1966). Reprinted with corrections, Huntington, N.Y., Krieger (1974).

McIlwain, K. and C.E. Dean (eds.); Hazeltine Corporation Staff, (1956). *Principles of Color Television.* New York. John Wiley and Sons.

NAG, (1990). *The NAG Fortran Library Manual, Mark 14.* Downers Grove, IL (The Numerical Algorithms Group Inc.).

Pearson, D.E., (1975). *Transmission and Display of Pictorial Information.* New York. John Wiley and Sons.

Perlman, S.S, S. Eisenhandler, P.W. Lyons, and M.J. Shumila, (1987). Adaptive Median Filtering for Impulse Noise Elimination in Real-Time TV Signals. *IEEE Transactions on Communications* **COM-35**:6 p. 646.

Roufs, J.A. and H. Bouma, (1980). Towards Linking Perception Research and Image Quality. *Proceedings of the SID* **21**:3, pp. 247–270.

Rumelhart, D.E. and J.L. McClelland (eds.), (1986). *Parallel Distributed Processing: Explorations in the Microstructure of Cognition.* Cambridge, Mass., MIT Press.

Part VII

Visual Processing

Discovering Viewpoint-Invariant Relationships That Characterize Objects

Richard S. Zemel and **Geoffrey E. Hinton**
Department of Computer Science
University of Toronto
Toronto, ONT M5S 1A4

Abstract

Using an unsupervised learning procedure, a network is trained on an ensemble of images of the same two-dimensional object at different positions, orientations and sizes. Each half of the network "sees" one fragment of the object, and tries to produce as output a set of 4 parameters that have high mutual information with the 4 parameters output by the other half of the network. Given the ensemble of training patterns, the 4 parameters on which the two halves of the network can agree are the position, orientation, and size of the whole object, or some recoding of them. After training, the network can reject instances of other shapes by using the fact that the predictions made by its two halves disagree. If two competing networks are trained on an unlabelled mixture of images of two objects, they cluster the training cases on the basis of the objects' shapes, independently of the position, orientation, and size.

1 INTRODUCTION

A difficult problem for neural networks is to recognize objects independently of their position, orientation, or size. Models addressing this problem have generally achieved viewpoint-invariance either through a separate normalization procedure or by building translation- or rotation-invariance into the structure of the network. This problem becomes even more difficult if the network must learn to perform viewpoint-invariant recognition without any supervision signal that indicates the correct viewpoint, or which object is which during training.

In this paper, we describe a model that is trained on an ensemble of instances of the same object, in a variety of positions, orientations and sizes, and can then recognize new instances of that object. We also describe an extension to the model that allows it to learn to recognize two different objects through unsupervised training on an unlabelled mixture of images of the objects.

2 THE VIEWPOINT CONSISTENCY CONSTRAINT

An important invariant in object recognition is the fixed spatial relationship between a rigid object and each of its component features. We assume that each feature has an intrinsic reference frame, which can be specified by its *instantiation parameters*, i.e., its position, orientation and size with respect to the image. For a rigid object and a particular feature of that object, there is a *fixed* viewpoint-independent transformation from the feature's reference frame to the object's. Given the instantiation parameters of the feature in an image, we can use the transformation to predict the object's instantiation parameters. The *viewpoint consistency constraint* (Lowe, 1987) states that all of the features belonging to the same rigid object should make consistent predictions of the object's instantiation parameters. This constraint has been played an important role in many shape recognition systems (Roberts, 1965; Ballard, 1981; Hinton, 1981; Lowe, 1985).

2.1 LEARNING THE CONSTRAINT: SUPERVISED

A recognition system that *learns* this constraint is TRAFFIC (Zemel, Mozer and Hinton, 1989). In TRAFFIC, the constraints on the spatial relations between features of an object are directly expressed in a connectionist network. For two-dimensional shapes, an object instantiation contains 4 degrees of freedom: (x,y)-position, orientation, and size. These parameter values, or some recoding of them, can be represented in a set of 4 real-valued *instantiation* units. The network has a modular structure, with units devoted to each object or object fragment to be recognized. In a *recognition module*, one layer of instantiation units represents the instantiation parameters of each of an object's features; these units connect to a set of units that represent the object's instantiation parameters as predicted by this feature; and these predictions are combined into a single object instantiation in another set of instantiation units. The set of weights connecting the instantiation units of the feature and its predicted instantiation for the object are meant to capture the fixed, *linear* reference frame transformation between the feature and the object. These weights are trained by showing various instantiations of the object, and the object's instantiation parameters act as the training signal for each of the features' predictions. Through this supervised procedure, the features of an object learn to predict the instantiation parameters for the object. Thus, when the features of the object are present in the image in the appropriate relationship, the predictions are consistent and this consistency can be used to decide that the object is present. Our simulations showed that TRAFFIC was able to learn to recognize constellations in realistic star-plot images.

2.2 LEARNING THE CONSTRAINT: UNSUPERVISED

The goal of the current work is to use an *unsupervised* procedure to discover and use the consistency constraint.

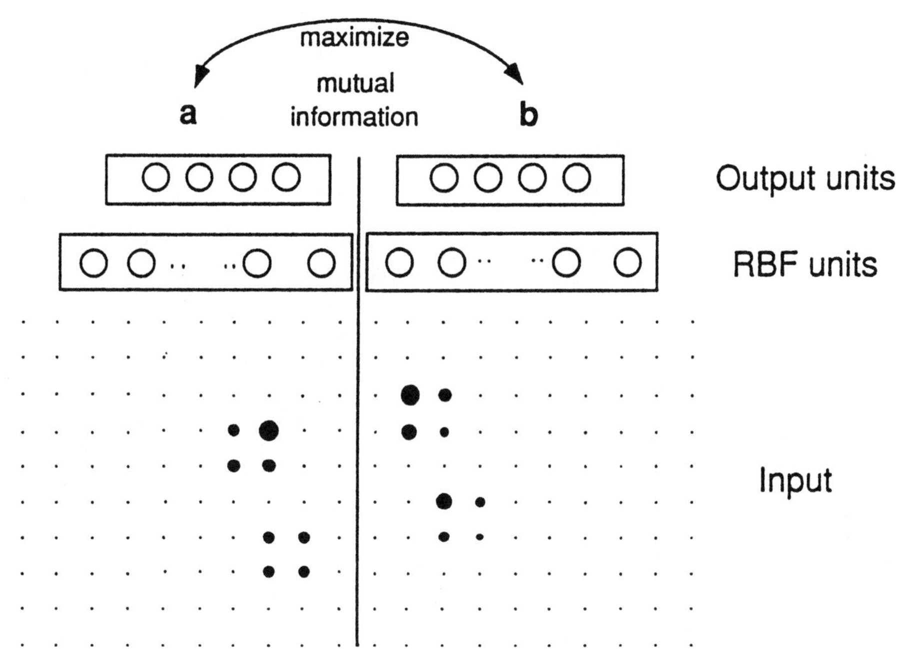

Figure 1: A module with two halves that try to agree on their predictions. The input to each half is 100 intensity values (indicated by the areas of the black circles). Each half has 200 Gaussian radial basis units (constrained to be the same for the two halves) connected to 4 output units.

We explore this idea using a framework similar to that of TRAFFIC, in which different features of an object are represented in different parts of the recognition module, and each part generates a prediction for the object's instantiation parameters. Figure 1 presents an example of the kind of task we would like to solve. The module has two halves. The rigid object in the image is very simple – it has two ends, each of which is composed of two Gaussian blobs of intensity. Each image in the training set contains one instance of the object. For now, we constrain the instantiation parameters of the object so that the left half of the image always contains one end of the object, and the right half the other end. This way, just based on the end of the object in the input image that it sees, each half of the module can always specify the position, orientation and size of the whole object. The goal is that, after training, for any image containing this object, the output vectors of both halves of the module, a and b, should both represent the same instantiation parameters for the object.

In TRAFFIC, we could use the object's instantiation parameters as a training signal for both module halves, and the features would learn their relation to the object. Now, without providing a training signal, we would like the module to learn that what is consistent across the ensemble of images is the relation between the position, orientation, and size of each end of that object. The two halves of a module trained on a particular shape should produce consistent instantiation parameters for any instance of this object. If the features are related in a different way, then these predictions should disagree. If the module learns to do this through an unsupervised procedure, it has found a viewpoint-invariant spatial relationship that characterizes the object, and can be used to recognize it.

3 THE IMAX LEARNING PROCEDURE

We describe a version of the IMAX learning procedure (Hinton and Becker, 1990) that allows a module to discover the 4 parameters that are consistent between the two halves of each image when it is presented with many different images of the same, rigid object in different positions, orientations and sizes. Because the training cases are all positive examples of the object, each half of the module tries to extract a vector of 4 parameters that significantly agrees with the 4 parameters extracted by the other half. Note that the two halves can agree on each instance by outputting zero on each case, but this agreement would not be *significant*. To agree significantly, each output vector must vary from image to image, but the two output vectors must nevertheless be the same for each image. Under suitable Gaussian assumptions, the significance of the agreement between the two output vectors can be computed by comparing the variances across training cases of the parameters produced by the individual halves of the module with the variances of the differences of these parameters.

We assume that the two output vectors, $\mathbf{a}$ and $\mathbf{b}$, are both noisy versions of the same underlying signal, the correct object instantiation parameters. If we assume that the noise is independent, additive, and Gaussian, the mutual information between the presumed underlying signal and the average of the noisy versions of that signal represented by $\mathbf{a}$ and $\mathbf{b}$ is:

$$I(\mathbf{a};\mathbf{b}) = \frac{1}{2}\log\frac{|\sum_{(\mathbf{a}+\mathbf{b})}|}{|\sum_{(\mathbf{a}-\mathbf{b})}|} \tag{1}$$

where $|\sum_{(\mathbf{a}+\mathbf{b})}|$ is the determinant of the covariance matrix of the sum of $\mathbf{a}$ and $\mathbf{b}$ (see (Becker and Hinton, 1989) for details). We train a recognition module by setting its weights so as to maximize this objective function. By maximizing the determinant, we are discouraging the components of the vector $\mathbf{a}+\mathbf{b}$ from being linearly dependent on one another, and thus assure that the network does not discover the same parameter four times.

4 EXPERIMENTAL RESULTS

Using this objective function, we have experimented with different training sets, input representations and network architectures. We discuss two examples here.

In all of the experiments described, we fix the number of output units in each module to be 4, matching the underlying degrees of freedom in the object instantiation parameters. We are in effect telling the recognition module that there are 4 parameters worth extracting from the training ensemble. For some tasks there may be less than 4 parameters. For example, the same learning procedure should be able to capture the lower-dimensional constraints between the parts of objects that contain internal degrees of freedom in their shape (e.g., scissors), but we have not yet tested this.

The first set of experiments uses training images like Figure 1. The task requires an intermediate layer between the intensity values and the instantiation parameters vector. Each half of the module has 200 non-adaptive, radial basis units. The means of the RBFs are formed by randomly sampling the space of possible images of an end of the object; the variances are fixed. The output units are linear. We maximize the objective function I by adjusting the weights from the radial basis units to the output units, after each full sweep through the training set.

The optimization requires 20 sweeps of a conjugate gradient technique through 1000 training cases. Unfortunately, it is difficult to interpret the outputs of the module, since it finds a nonlinear transform of the object instantiation parameters. But the mutual information is quite high – about 7 bits. After training, the predictions made by the two halves are consistent on new images We measure the consistency in the predictions for an image using a kind of generalized Z-score, which relates the difference between the predictions on a particular case ($\mathbf{d_i}$) to the distribution of this difference across the training set:

$$Z(\mathbf{d_i}) = (\mathbf{d_i} - \overline{\mathbf{d}})^t \sum\nolimits_{\mathbf{d}}^{-1} (\mathbf{d_i} - \overline{\mathbf{d}}) \quad (2)$$

A low Z-score indicates a consistent match. After training, the module produces high Z-scores on images where the same two ends are present, but are in a different relationship than the object on which it was trained. In general, the Z-scores increase smoothly with the degree of perturbation in the relationship between the two ends, indicating that the module has learned the constraint.

In the second set of experiments, we remove an unrealistic constraint on our images – that one end of the object must always fall in one half of the image. Instead we assume that there is a feature-extraction process that finds instances of simple features in the image and passes on to the module a set of parameters describing the position, orientation and spatial extent of each feature. This is a reasonable assumption, since low-level vision is generally good at providing accurate descriptions of simple features that are present in an image (such as edges and corners), and can also specify their locations.

In these experiments, the feature-extraction program finds instances of two features of the letter y – the upper u-shaped curve and the long vertical stroke with a curved tail. The recognition module then tries to extract consistent object instantiation parameters from these feature instantiation parameters by maximizing the same mutual information objective as before.

There are several advantages of this second scheme. The first set of training instances were artificially restricted by the requirement that one end must appear in the left half of the image, and the other in the right half. Now since a separate process is analyzing the entire image to find a feature of a given type, we can use the entire space of possible instantiation parameters in the training set. With the simpler architecture, we can efficiently handle more complex images. In addition, no hidden layer is necessary – the mapping from the features' instantiation parameters to the object's instantiation parameters is linear.

Using this scheme, only twelve sweeps through 1000 training cases are necessary to optimize the objective function. The speed-up is likely due to the fact that the input is already parameterized in an appropriate form for the extraction of the instantiation parameters. This method also produces robust recognition modules, which reject instances where the relationships between the two input vectors does not match the relationship in the training set. We test this robustness by adding noise of varying magnitudes separately to each component of the input vectors, and measuring the Z-scores of the output vectors. As expected, the agreement between the two outputs of a module degrades smoothly with added noise.

5 COMPETITIVE IMAX

We are currently working on extending this idea to handle multiple shapes. The obvious way to do this using modules of the type described above is to force the modules to specialize by training each module separately on images of a particular shape, and then to recognize shapes by giving the image to each module and seeing which module achieves the lowest Z-score. However, this requires supervised training in which the images are labelled by the type of object they contain. We are exploring an entirely unsupervised method in which images are *unlabelled*, and every image is processed by many competing modules.

Each competing module has a *responsibility* for each image that depends on the consistency between the two output vectors of the module. The responsibilities are normalized so that, for each image, they sum to one. In computing the covariances for a particular module in Equation 1, we weight each training case by the module's responsibility for that case. We also compute an overall *mixing proportion*, π_m, for each module which is just the average of its responsibilities. We extend the objective function I to multiple modules as follows:

$$I^* = \sum_m \pi_m \, I_m(\mathbf{a}; \mathbf{b}) \tag{3}$$

We could compute the relative responsibilities of modules by comparing their Z-scores, but this would lead to a recurrent relationship between the responsibilities and the weights within a module. To avoid this recurrence, we simply store the responsibility of each module for each training case. We optimize I^* by interleaving updates of the weights within each module, with updates of the stored responsibilities. This learning is a sophisticated form of competitive learning. Rather than clustering together input vectors that are close to one another in the input space, the modules cluster together input vectors that share a common spatial relationship between their two halves.

In our experiments, we are using just two modules and an ensemble of images of two different shapes (either a *g* or a *y* in each image). We have found that the system can cluster the images with a little bootstrapping. We initially split the training set into *g*-images and *y*-images, and train up one module for several iterations on one set of images, and the other module on the other set. When we then use a new training set containing 500 images of each shape, and train both modules competitively on the full set, the system successfully learns to separate the images so that the modules each specialize in a particular shape. After the bootstrapping, one module wins on 297 cases of one shape and 206 cases of the other shape. After further learning on the *unlabelled* mixture of shapes, it wins on 498 cases of one shape and 0 cases of the other.

By making another assumption, that the input images in the training set are *temporally* coherent, we should be able to eliminate the need for the bootstrapping procedure. If we assume that the training images come in runs of one class, and then another, as would be the case if they were a sequence of images of various moving objects, then for each module, we can attempt to maximize the mutual information between the responsibilities it assigns to consecutive training images. We can augment the objective function I^* by adding this temporal coherence term onto the spatial coherence term, and our network should cluster the input set into different shapes while simultaneously learning how to recognize them.

Finally, we plan to extend our model to become a more general recognition system. Since the learning relatively is fast, we should also be able to build a hierarchy of modules that could learn to recognize more complex objects.

Acknowledgements

We thank Sue Becker and Steve Nowlan for helpful discussions. This research was supported by grants from the Ontario Information Technology Research Center, the Natural Sciences and Engineering Research Council, and Apple Computer, Inc. Hinton is the Noranda Fellow of the Canadian Institute for Advanced Research.

References

Ballard, D. H. (1981). Generalizing the Hough transform to detect arbitrary shapes. *Pattern Recognition*, 13(2):111–122.

Becker, S. and Hinton, G. E. (1989). Spatial coherence as an internal teacher for a neural network. Technical Report Technical Report CRG-TR-89-7, University of Toronto.

Hinton, G. E. (1981). A parallel computation that assigns canonical object-based frames of reference. In *Proceedings of the 7th International Joint Conference on Artificial Intelligence*, pages 683–685, Vancouver, BC, Canada.

Hinton, G. E. and Becker, S. (1990). An unsupervised learning procedure that discovers surfaces in random-dot stereograms. In *Proceedings of the International Joint Conference on Neural Networks*, volume 1, pages 218–222, Hillsdale, NJ. Erlbaum.

Lowe, D. G. (1985). *Perceptual Organization and Visual Recognition.* Kluwer Academic Publishers, Boston.

Lowe, D. G. (1987). The viewpoint consistency constraint. *International Journal of Computer Vision*, 1:57–72.

Roberts, L. G. (1965). Machine perception of three-dimensional solids. In Tippett, J. T., editor, *Optical and Electro-Optical Information Processing.* MIT Press.

Zemel, R. S., Mozer, M. C., and Hinton, G. E. (1989). TRAFFIC: Object recognition using hierarchical reference frame transformations. In Touretzky, D. S., editor, *Advances in Neural Information Processing Systems 2*, pages 266–273. Morgan Kaufmann, San Mateo, CA.

A Neural Network Approach for Three-Dimensional Object Recognition

Volker Tresp
Siemens AG, Central Research and Development
Otto-Hahn-Ring 6, D-8000 München 83
Germany

Abstract

The model-based neural vision system presented here determines the position and identity of three-dimensional objects. Two stereo images of a scene are described in terms of shape primitives (line segments derived from edges in the scenes) and their relational structure. A recurrent neural matching network solves the correspondence problem by assigning corresponding line segments in right and left stereo images. A 3-D relational scene description is then generated and matched by a second neural network against models in a model base. The quality of the solutions and the convergence speed were both improved by using mean field approximations.

1 INTRODUCTION

Many machine vision systems and, to a large extent, also the human visual system, are model based. The scenes are described in terms of shape primitives and their relational structure, and the vision system tries to find a match between the scene descriptions and 'familiar' objects in a model base. In many situations, such as robotics applications, the problem is intrinsically 3-D. Different approaches are possible. Poggio and Edelman (1990) describe a neural network that treats the 3-D object recognition problem as a multivariate approximation problem. A certain number of 2-D views of the object are used to train a neural network to produce the standard view of that object. After training, new perspective views can be recognized.

In the approach presented here, the vision system tries to capture the true 3-D structure of the scene. Two stereo views of a scene are used to generate a 3-D

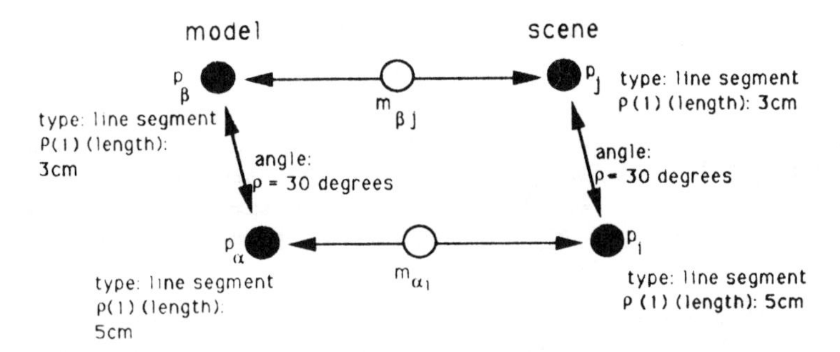

Figure 1: Match of primitive p_α to p_i.

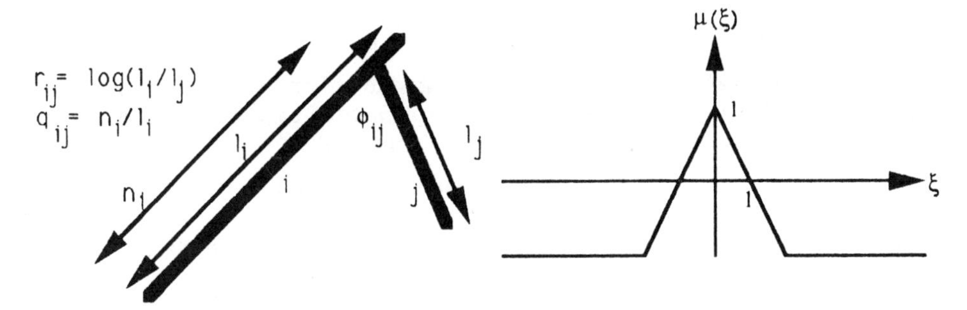

Figure 2: Definitions of r, q, and θ (left). The function $\mu()$ (right).

description of the scene which is then matched against models in a model base. The stereo correspondence problem and the model matching problem are solved by two recurrent neural networks with very similar architectures. A neuron is assigned to every possible match between primitives in the left and right images or, respectively, the scene and the model base. The networks are designed to find the best matches by obeying certain uniqueness constraints.

The networks are robust against the uncertainties in the descriptions of both the stereo images and the 3-D scene (shadow lines, missing lines). Since a partial match is sufficient for a successful model identification, opaque and partially occluded objects can be recognized.

2 THE NETWORK ARCHITECTURE

Here, a general model matching task is considered. The activity of a match neuron $m_{\alpha i}$ (Figure 1) represents the certainty of a match between a primitive p_α in the model base and p_i in the scene description. The interactions between neurons can be derived from the network's energy function where the fixed points of the network correspond to the minima of the energy function. The first term in the energy function evaluates the match between the primitives

$$E_P = -1/2 \sum_{\alpha i} \kappa_{\alpha i} m_{\alpha i}. \quad (1)$$

The function $\kappa_{\alpha i}$ is zero if the type of primitive p_α is not equal to the type of primitive p_i. If both types are identical, $\kappa_{\alpha i}$ evaluates the agreement between parameters $\rho^p_\alpha(k)$ and $\rho^p_i(k)$ which describe properties of the primitives. Here, $\kappa_{\alpha i} = \mu(\sum_k |\rho^p_\alpha(k) - \rho^p_i(k)|/\sigma^p_k)$ is maximum if the parameters of p_α and p_i match (Figures 1 and 2).

The evaluation of the match between the relations of primitives in the scene and data base is performed by the energy term (Mjolsness, Gindi and Anadan, 1989)

$$E_S = -1/2 \sum_{\alpha,\beta,i,j} \chi_{\alpha,\beta,i,j} \, m_{\alpha i} m_{\beta j}. \quad (2)$$

The function $\chi_{\alpha i} = \mu(\sum_k |\rho^r_{\alpha,\beta}(k) - \rho^r_{i,j}(k)|/\sigma^r_k)$ is maximum if the relation between p_α and p_β matches the relation between p_i and p_j.

The constraint that a primitive in the scene should only match to one or no primitive in the model base (column constraint) is implemented by the additional (penalty-) energy term (Utans et al., 1989, Tresp and Gindi, 1990)

$$E_C = \sum_i [((\sum_\alpha m_{\alpha i}) - 1)^2 \sum_\alpha m_{\alpha i}]. \quad (3)$$

E_C is equal to zero only if in all columns, the sum over the activations of all neurons is equal to one or zero and positive otherwise.

2.1 DYNAMIC EQUATIONS AND MEAN FIELD THEORY

2.1.1 MFA_1

The neural network should make binary decisions, match or no match, but binary recurrent networks get easily stuck in local minima. Bad local minima can be avoided by using an annealing strategy but annealing is time-consuming when simulated on a digital computer. Using a mean field approximation, one can obtain deterministic equations by retaining some of the advantages of the annealing process (Peterson and Söderberg, 1989). The network is interpreted as a system of interacting units in thermal contact with a heat reservoir of temperature T. Such a system minimizes the free energy $F = E - T\hat{S}$ where $\hat{S}$ is the entropy of the system. At $T = 0$ the energy E is minimized. The mean value $v_{\alpha i} = < m_{\alpha i} >$ of a neuron becomes $v_{\alpha i} = 1/(1 + e^{-u_{\alpha i}/T})$ with $u_{\alpha i} = -\partial E/\partial v_{\alpha i}$. These equations can be updated synchronously, asynchronously or solved iteratively by moving only a small distance from the old value of $u_{\alpha i}$ in the direction of the new mean field.

At high temperatures T, the system is in the trivial solution $v_{\alpha i} = 1/2 \ \forall \alpha, i$ and the activations of all neurons are in the linear region of the sigmoid function. The system can be described by linearized equations. The magnitudes of all eigenvalues of the corresponding transfer matrix are less than 1. At a critical temperature T_c, the magnitude of at least one of the eigenvalues becomes greater than one and the trivial solution becomes unstable. T_c and favorable weights for the different terms in the energy function can be found by an eigenvalue analysis of the linearized equations (Peterson and Söderberg, 1989).

2.1.2 MFA_2

The column constraint is satisfied by states with exactly one neuron or no neuron 'on' in every column. If only these states are considered in the derivation of the mean field equations, one can obtain another set of mean field equations, $v_{\alpha i} = 1 \times e^{u_{\alpha i}/T}/(1 + \sum_{\beta} e^{u_{\beta i}/T})$ with $u_{\alpha i} = -\partial E/\partial v_{\alpha i}$.

The column constraint term (Equation 3) drops out of the energy function and the energy surface in simplified. The high temperature fixed point corresponds to $v_{\alpha i} = 1/(N+1)\ \forall \alpha, i$ where N is the number of rows.

3 THE CORRESPONDENCE PROBLEM

To solve the correspondence problem, corresponding lines in left and right images have to be identified. A good assumption is that the appearance of an object in the left image is a distortion and shifted version of the appearance of the object in the right image with approximately the same scale and orientation. The machinery just developed can be applied if the left image is interpreted as the scene and the right image as the model.

Figure 3 shows two stereo images of a simple scene and the segmentation of left and right images into line segments which are the only primitives in this application. Lines correspond to the edges, structure and contours of the objects and shadow lines. The length of a line segment $\rho_i^p(1) = l_i$ is the descriptive parameter attached to each line segment p_i. Relations between line segments are only considered if they are in a local neighborhood: $\chi_{\alpha,\beta,i,j}$ is equal to zero if not both a) p_α is attached to line segment p_β and b) line segment p_i is attached to line segment p_j. Otherwise, $\chi_{\alpha,\beta,i,j} = \mu(|\phi_{\alpha\beta} - \phi_{ij}|/\sigma_\phi^r + |r_{\alpha\beta} - r_{ij}|/\sigma_r^r + |q_{\alpha\beta} - q_{ij}|/\sigma_q^r)$ where $\rho_{i,j}^r(1) = \phi_{ij}$ is the angle between line segments, $\rho_{i,j}^r(2) = r_{ij}$ the logarithm of the ratio of their lengths and $\rho_{i,j}^r(3) = q_{ij}$ the attachment point (Shumaker et al., 1989) (Figure 2).

Here, we have two uniqueness constraints: only at most one neuron should be active in each column or each row. The row constraint is enforced by an energy term equivalent to E_C: $E_R = \sum_\alpha [((\sum_i m_{\alpha i}) - 1)^2 \sum_i m_{\alpha i}]$.

4 DESCRIPTION OF THE 3-D OBJECT STRUCTURE

From the last section, we know which endpoints in the left image correspond to endpoints in the right image. If D is the separation of both (in parallel mounted) cameras, f the focal lengths of the cameras, x_l, y_l, x_r, y_r the coordinates of a particular point in left and right images, the 3-D position of the point in camera coordinates x, y, z becomes $z = Df/(x_r - x_l)$, $y = zy_r/f$, $x = zx_r/f + D/2$. This information is used to generate the 3-D description of the visible portion of the objects in the scene.

Knowing the true 3-D position of the endpoints of the line segments, the system concludes that the chair and the wardrobe are two distinct and spatially separated objects and that line segments 12 and 13 in the right image and 12 in the left image are not connected to either the chair or the wardrobe. On the other hand, it is not

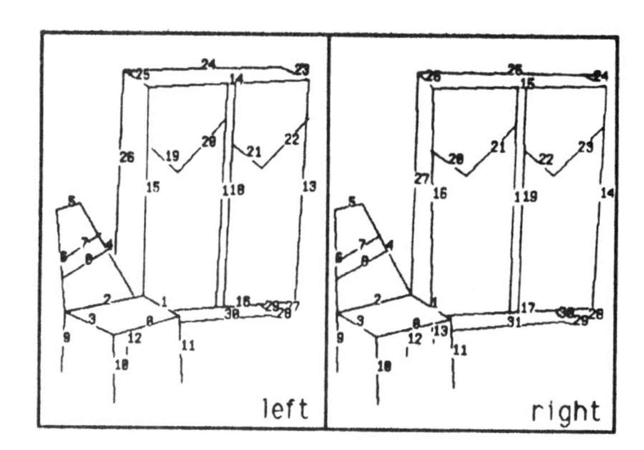

Figure 3: Stereo images of a scene and segmented images. The stereo matching network matched all line segments that are present in both images correctly.

obvious that the shadow lines under the wardrobe are not part of the wardrobe.

5 MATCHING OBJECTS AND MODELS

The scene description now must be matched with stored models describing the complete 3-D structures of the models in the data base. The model description might be constructed by either explicitly measuring the dimensions of the models or by incrementally assembling the 3-D structure from several stereo views of the models. Descriptive parameters are the (true 3-D) length of line segments l, the (true 3-D) angles ϕ between line segments and the (true 3-D) attachment points q. The knowledge about the 3-D structure allows a segmentation of the scene into different objects and the row constraint is only applied to neurons relating to the same object O in the scene $E_{R'} = \sum_O \sum_\alpha [((\sum_{i \in O} m_{\alpha i}) - 1)^2 \sum_{i \in O} v_{\alpha i}]$.

Figure 4 shows the network after convergence. Except for the occluded leg, all line segments belonging to the chair could be matched correctly. All not occluded line segments of the wardrobe could be matched correctly except for its left front leg. The shadow lines in the image did not find a match.

6 3-D POSITION

In many applications, one is also interested in determining the positions of the recognized objects in camera coordinates. In general, the transformation between

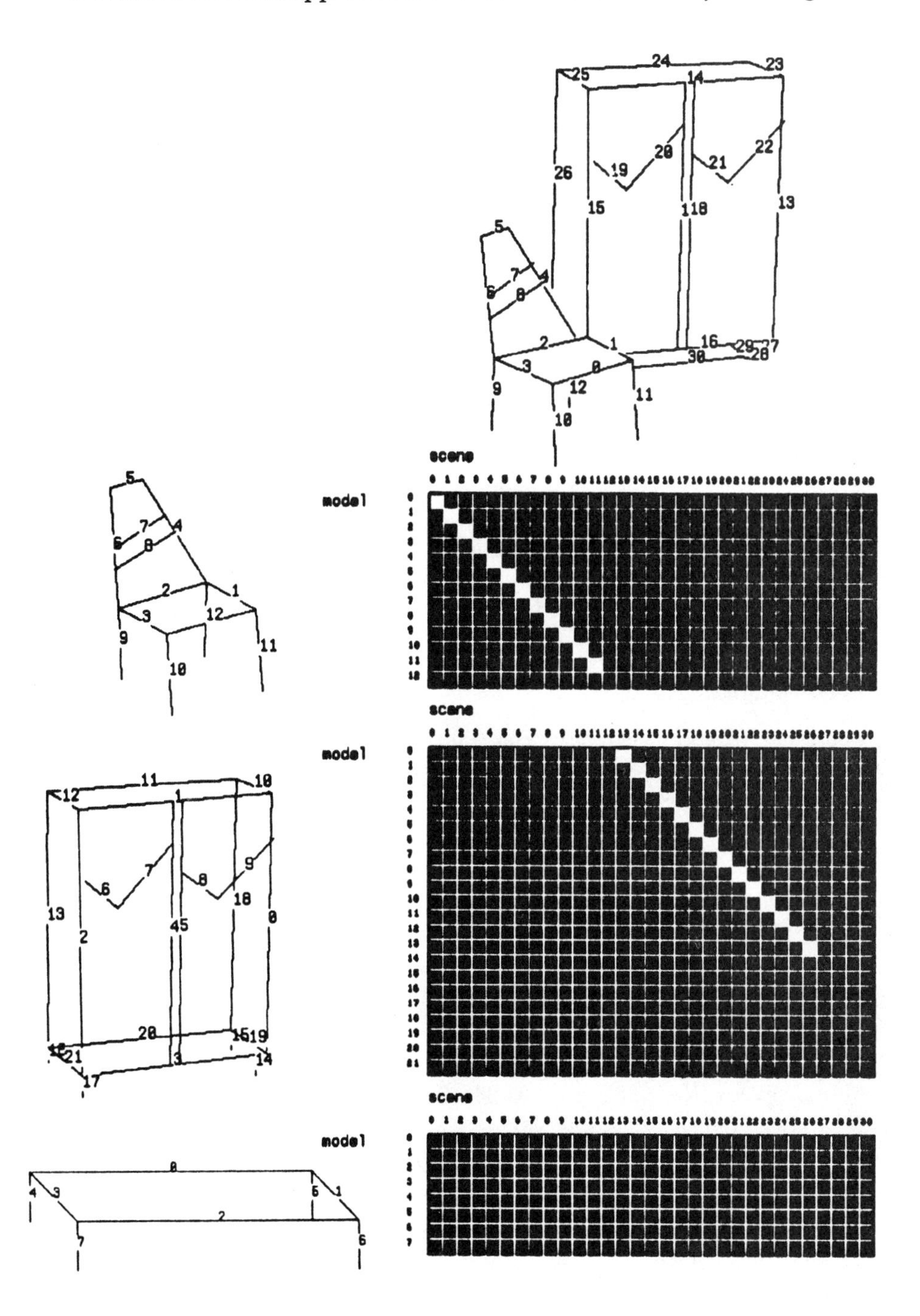

Figure 4: 3-D matching network.

an object in a standard frame of reference $X_0 = (x_0, y_0, z_0)$ and the transformed frame of reference $X_S = (x_s, y_s, z_s)$ can be described by $X_S = RX_0$, where R is a 4×4 matrix describing a rotation followed by a translation. R can be calculated if X_0 and X_S are known for at least 4 points using, for example, the pseudo inverse or an ADALINE. Knowing the coefficients of R, the object position can be calculated. If an ADALINE is used, the error after convergence is a measure of the consistency of the transformation. A large error can be used as an indication that either a wrong model was matched, or certain primitives were misclassified.

7 DISCUSSION

Both MFA_1 and MFA_2 were used in the experiments. The same solutions were found in general, but due to the simpler energy surface, MFA_2 allowed greater time steps and therefore converged 5 to 10 times faster.

For more complex scenes, a hierarchical system could be considered. In the first step, simple objects such as squares, rectangles, and circles would be identified. These would then form the primitives in a second stage which would then recognize complete objects. It might also be possible to combine these two matching nets into one hierarchical net similar to the networks described by Mjolsness, Gindi and Anadan (1989).

Acknowledgements

I would like to acknowledge the contributions of Gene Gindi, Eric Mjolsness and Joachim Utans of Yale University to the design of the matching network. I thank Christian Evers for helping me to acquire the images.

References

Eric Mjolsness, Gene Gindi, P. Anadan. Neural Optimization in Model Matching and Perceptual Organization. *Neural Computation 1*, pp. 218-209, 1989.

Carsten Peterson, Bo Söderberg. A new method for mapping optimization problems onto neural networks. *International Journal of Neural Systems*, Vol. 1, No. 1, pp. 3-22, 1989.

T. Poggio, S. Edelman. A Network That Learns to Recognize Three-Dimensional Objects. *Nature*, No. 6255, pp. 263-266, January 1990.

Grant Shumaker, Gene Gindi, Eric Mjolsness, P. Anadan. Stickville: A Neural Net for Object Recognition via Graph Matching. Tech. Report No. 8908, Yale University, 1989.

Volker Tresp, Gene Gindi. Invariant Object Recognition by Inexact Subgraph Matching with Applications in Industrial Part Recognition. *International Neural Network Conference*, Paris, pp. 95-98, 1990.

Joachim Utans, Gene Gindi, Eric Mjolsness, P. Anadan. Neural Networks for Object Recognition within Compositional Hierarchies, Initial Experiments. Tech. Report No. 8903, Yale University, 1989.

A Second-Order Translation, Rotation and Scale Invariant Neural Network

Shelly D.D. Goggin **Kristina M. Johnson** **Karl E. Gustafson***
Optoelectronic Computing Systems Center and
Department of Electrical and Computer Engineering
University of Colorado at Boulder
Boulder, CO 80309
shellg@boulder.colorado.edu

ABSTRACT

A second-order architecture is presented here for translation, rotation and scale invariant processing of 2-D images mapped to n input units. This new architecture has a complexity of $O(n)$ weights as opposed to the $O(n^3)$ weights usually required for a third-order, rotation invariant architecture. The reduction in complexity is due to the use of discrete frequency information. Simulations show favorable comparisons to other neural network architectures.

1 INTRODUCTION

Multiplicative interactions in neural networks have been proposed (Pitts and McCulloch, 1947; Giles and Maxwell, 1987; McClelland et al, 1988) both to explain biological neural functions and to provide invariances in pattern recognition. Higher-order neural networks are useful for invariant pattern recognition problems, but their complexity prohibits their use in many large image processing applications. The complexity of the third-order rotation invariant neural network of Reid et al, 1990 is $O(n^3)$, which will clearly not scale. For example, when n is on the order of 10^6, as in high definition television (HDTV), $O(10^{18})$ weights would be required in a third-order neural network. Clearly, image processing applications are best approached with neural networks of lower complexity. We present a translation,

*Department of Mathematics

rotation and scale invariant architecture, which has weight complexity of $O(n)$, and requires only multiplicative and additive operations in the activation function.

2 HIGHER-ORDER NEURAL NETWORKS

Higher-order neural networks (HONN) have multiplicative terms in their activation function, such that the output of a unit, o_k, has the form

$$o_k = f[\sum_{(i=0)}^{(n-1)} \sum_{(j=0)}^{(n-1)} \ldots \sum_{l=0}^{(n-1)} w_{ij...lk} x_i x_j ... x_l] \tag{1}$$

where f is a thresholding function, $w_{ij...lk}$ is the weight for each term, and x_i is one of n input values. Some of the x_i could be bias units to give lower order terms. The order of the multiplications is $O(n^m)$ for an m-order network, but the order of the number of weights can be lower. Since the multiplications of data can be done in a preprocessing stage, the major factor in the computational burden is the number of weights. The emphasis on the complexity of the weights is especially relevant for optical implementations of higher-order networks (Psaltis et al, 1988, Zhang et al, 1990), since the multiplications can usually be performed in parallel.

Invariances can be achieved with higher-order neural networks by using the spatial frequencies of the input as a priori information. Wechsler and Zimmerman, 1988, compute the Fourier transform of the data in polar coordinates and use these data as inputs to a neural network to achieve rotation, scale and translation invariance. The disadvantage with this approach is that the Fourier transform and the computation of polar coordinates require more complex operations than addition and multiplication of inputs. It has been shown that second-order networks can be constructed to provide either translation and scale invariance or rotation and scale invariance (Giles et al, 1988). However, their approach does not consider the difficulties in defining scale and rotation for images made up of pixels. Our architecture directly addresses the problem of rotation, translation and scale invariance in pattern recognition for 2-D arrays of binary pixels. Restrictions permit structure to be built into the weights, which reduces their complexity.

3 WEDGE-RING HONN

We present a new architecture for a second-order neural network based on the concept of the wedge-ring detector (Casasent, 1985). When a wedge-ring detector is used in the Fourier plane of an optical processor, a set of features are obtained that are invariant to scale, rotation and translation. As shown in figure 1, the lens performs a spatial Fourier transform on an image, which yields an intensity pattern that is invariant to translations in the image plane. The ring detectors sum the amplitudes of the spatial frequencies with the same radial distance from the zero frequency, to give features that are invariant to rotation and shift changes. The wedge detectors sum the amplitudes of frequencies within a range of angles with respect to the zero frequency to produce features that are invariant to scale and shift changes, assuming the images retain the same zero frequency power as they are scaled.

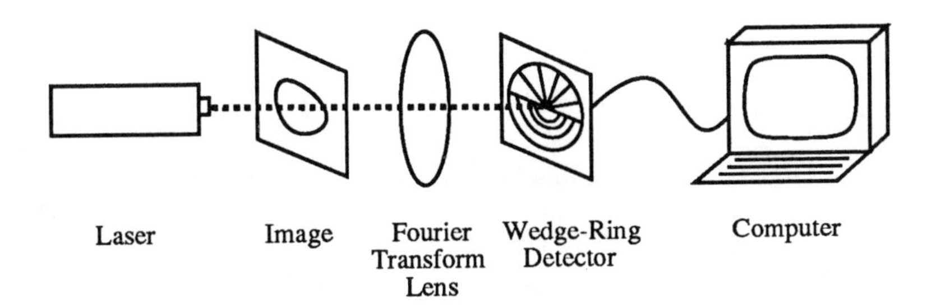

Figure 1: A Wedge-Ring Detector Optical Processor

In a multi-pixel, binary image, a second-order neural network can perform the same function as the wedge-ring detector without the need for a Fourier transform. For an image of dimensions $\sqrt{n} \times \sqrt{n}$, let us define the pixel spatial frequency $f_{i,j}$ as

$$f_{k,l} = \sum_{(i=0)}^{(\sqrt{n}-1-|k|)} \sum_{(j=0)}^{(\sqrt{n}-1-|l|)} x_{i,j}x_{i+|k|,j+|l|}, \quad -(\sqrt{n}-1) \leq k,\ l \leq \sqrt{n}-1 \tag{2}$$

where $x_{i,j}$ is a binary valued pixel at location (i,j). Note that the pixel frequencies have symmetry; $f_{i,j} = f_{-i,-j}$. The frequency terms can be arranged in a grid in a manner analogous to the Fourier transform image in the optical wedge-ring detector. (See figure 2.)

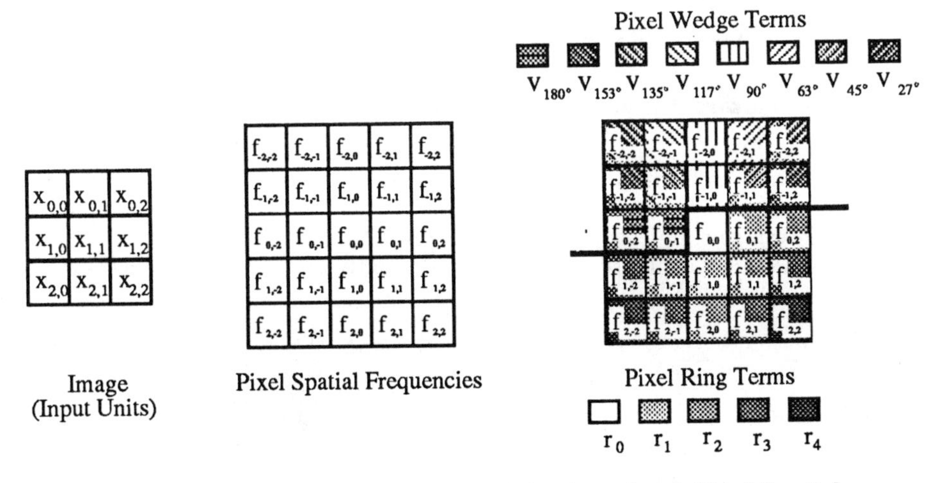

Figure 2: A Simple Input Image and its Associated Pixel Spatial Frequencies, Pixel Ring Terms and Pixel Wedge Terms

For all integers p, $0 \leq p \leq 2(\sqrt{n}-1)$, the ring pixel terms r_p are given by

$$r_p = 2 \sum_{|k|+|l|=p} f_{k,l}, \quad 0 \leq k \leq \sqrt{n}-1, \quad \begin{array}{l} 0 \leq l \leq \sqrt{n}-1, \ if\ k=0. \\ -(\sqrt{n}-1) \leq l \leq \sqrt{n}-1, \ if\ k>0. \end{array} \tag{3}$$

as shown in figure 2. This definition of the ring pixel terms works well for images with a small number of pixels. Larger pixel arrays can use the following definition. For $0 \leq p \leq 2(\sqrt{n}-1)^2$,

$$r_p = 2 \sum_{k^2+l^2=p} f_{k,l}, \quad 0 \leq k \leq \sqrt{n}-1, \quad \begin{array}{l} 0 \leq l \leq \sqrt{n}-1, \ if\ k=0. \\ -(\sqrt{n}-1) \leq l \leq \sqrt{n}-1, \ if\ k>0. \end{array} \tag{4}$$

Note that p will not take on all values less than $2n$. The number of ring pixel terms generated by equation 4 is less than or equal to $\lceil n/2 \rceil + \lfloor \sqrt{n}/2 \rfloor$. The number of ring pixel terms can be reduced by making the rings a fixed width, Δr. Then, for all integers p, $0 \leq p \leq \lceil \sqrt{2}(\sqrt{n}-1)/\Delta r \rceil$.

$$r_p = 2 \sum_{(p-1)\Delta r < \sqrt{k^2+l^2} \leq p\Delta r} f_{k,l}, \quad \begin{array}{l} 0 \leq k \leq \sqrt{n}-1, \\ 0 \leq l \leq \sqrt{n}-1, \ if\ k=0. \\ -(\sqrt{n}-1) \leq l \leq \sqrt{n}-1, \ if\ k>0. \end{array} \tag{5}$$

As the image size increases, the ring pixel terms will approximate continuous rings.

For $0 < \theta \leq 180^o$, the wedge pixel terms v_θ are

$$v_\theta = 2 \sum_{\tan^{-1}(k/l)=\theta} f_{k,l}, \quad -(\sqrt{n}-1) \leq k \leq 0, \quad \begin{array}{l} -(\sqrt{n}-1) \leq l \leq 1, \ if\ k=0, \\ -(\sqrt{n}-1) \leq l \leq \sqrt{n}-1, \ if\ k<0, \end{array} \tag{6}$$

as shown in figure 2. The number of wedge pixel terms is less than or equal to $2n - 2\sqrt{n} + 1$. The number of wedge pixel terms can be reduced by using a fixed wedge width, Δv. Then for all integers q, $1 \leq q \leq \lceil 180^o/\Delta v \rceil$,

$$v_\theta = 2 \sum_{(q-1)\Delta v < \tan^{-1}(k/l) \leq q\Delta v} f_{k,l}, \quad \begin{array}{l} -(\sqrt{n}-1) \leq k \leq 0, \\ -(\sqrt{n}-1) \leq l \leq 1, \ if\ k=0, \\ -(\sqrt{n}-1) \leq l \leq \sqrt{n}-1, \ if\ k<0, \end{array} \tag{7}$$

For small pixel arrays, the pixel frequencies are not evenly distributed between the wedges.

All of the operations from the second-order terms to the pixel frequencies and from the pixel frequencies to the ring and wedge pixel terms are linear. Therefore, the values of the wedge-ring features can be obtained by directly summing the second-order terms, without explicitly determining the individual spatial frequencies.

$$r_p = 2 \sum_{(k^2+l^2=p)} \sum_{(i=0)}^{(\sqrt{n}-1-|k|)} \sum_{(j=0)}^{(\sqrt{n}-1-|l|)} x_{i,j} x_{i+|k|,j+|l|}, \quad \begin{array}{l} 0 \leq k \leq \sqrt{n}-1, \\ 0 \leq l \leq \sqrt{n}-1, \ if\ k=0. \\ -(\sqrt{n}-1) \leq l \leq \sqrt{n}-1, \\ if\ k>0. \end{array} \tag{8}$$

$$v_\theta = 2 \sum_{(\tan^{-1}(k/l)=\theta)} \sum_{(i=0)}^{(\sqrt{n}-1-|k|)} \sum_{(j=0)}^{(\sqrt{n}-1-|l|)} x_{i+|k|,j+|l|} x_{i,j}, \quad \begin{array}{l} -(\sqrt{n}-1) \leq k \leq 0, \\ -(\sqrt{n}-1) \leq l \leq 1, \\ if\ k=0. \\ -(\sqrt{n}-1) \leq l \leq \sqrt{n}-1, \\ if\ k<0. \end{array} \tag{9}$$

A mask can be used to sum the second-order terms directly. For an example of the mask for the 3×3 image, see figure 3.

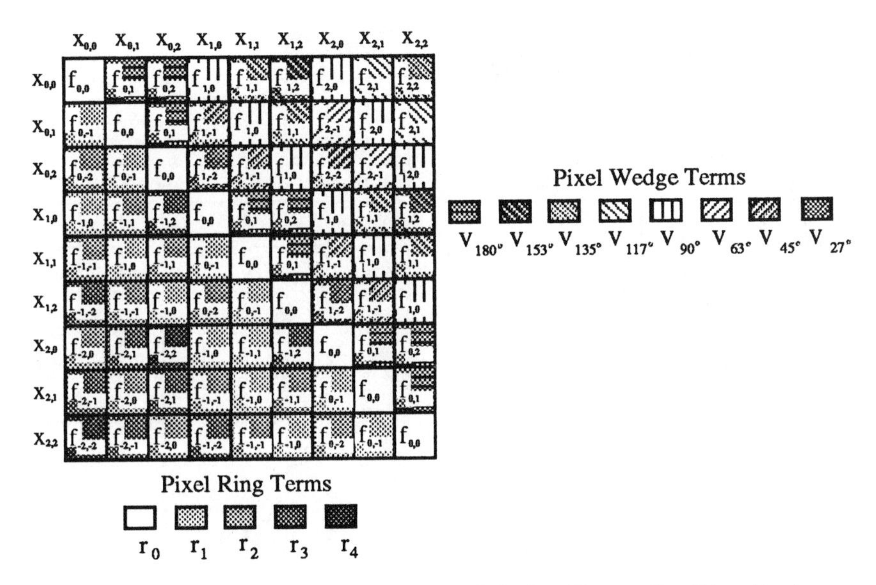

Figure 3: A Mask for Summing Second-Order Terms for Ring Features and Wedge Features for the Image in Figure 2

The ring and wedge pixel terms can be used as inputs for a multilayer neural network that can then perform pattern recognition with general combinations of these features. The output of the first (and possibly only) hidden layer units are for unit j,

$$o_j = f[\sum_p w_{j,p} r_p + \sum_\theta w_{j,\theta} v_\theta], \tag{10}$$

where f here is the threshold function. The total number of ring and wedge terms, which corresponds to the number of weights, is less than or equal to $(5/2)n$.

4 EXAMPLE RESULTS FOR THE TC PROBLEM

Results have been obtained for the 9×9 TC problem (McClelland et al, 1988) (see figure 4). Since wedge and ring pixel terms are used, a solution to the problem is readily seen. Figure 5 shows the final neural network architecture. Equations 4 and 6 are used to calculate the ring and wedge pixel terms, respectively. With two additional layers, the network can distinguish between the T and the C at any of the three scales or four rotations. In the hidden layer, the 180° wedge pixel term is subtracted from the 90° wedge pixel term and vice-versa with a bias unit weighted by 0.5 and a hard-limiting threshold function. This computation results in hidden units with values $(0,1)$ or $(1,0)$ for the C and $(1,1)$ for the T. The next level then performs a binary AND, to get a 1 for T and a 0 for C. The wedge features are also used in a layer to determine whether the image was rotated by $\pm 90^o$ or not. The ring units are used as input to a layer with an output unit for each of the three scales. Due to the reduced complexity of the weights in this second-order neural network, a solution for the architecture and weights is obtained by inspection, whereas the

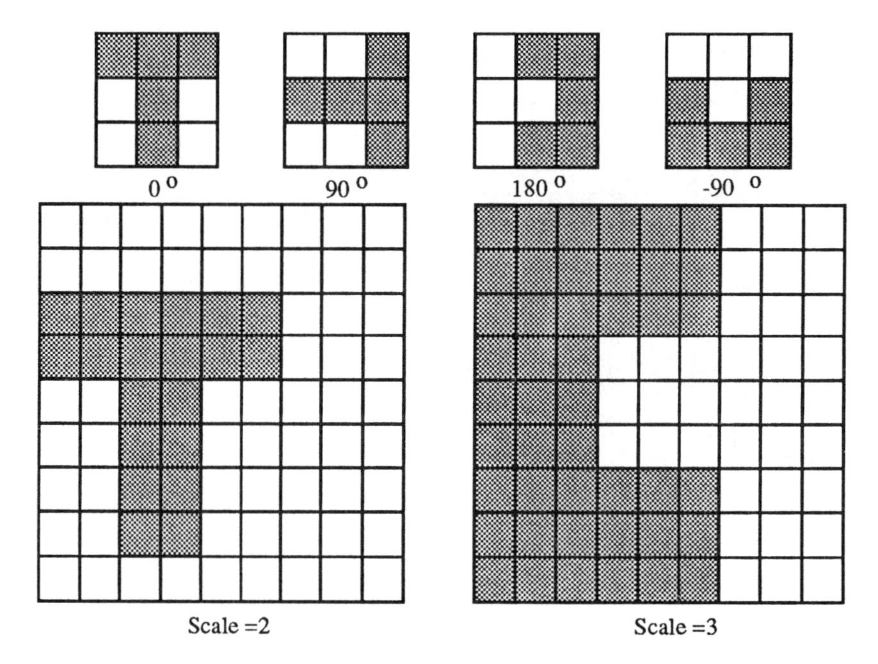

Figure 4: Examples of Rotated and Scaled Input Images for the TC Problem

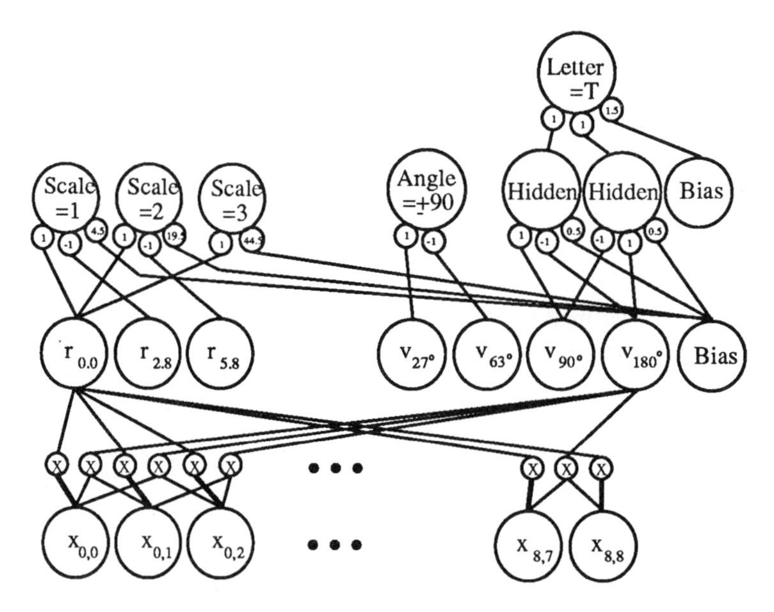

Figure 5: Multilayer Neural Network for the Wedge-Ring Features for the TC Problem

same problem required computer simulation when presented to a third-order neural network (Reid et al, 1990).

5 CONCLUSIONS

In this paper, we show how the weight complexity in a higher-order neural network is reduced from $O(n^3)$ to $O(n)$ by building into the architecture invariances in rotation, translation and scale. These invariances were built into the neural network architecture by analogy to the architecture for feature extraction in the optical wedge-ring detector system. This neural network architecture has been shown to greatly simplify the computations required to solve the classic TC problem.

Acknowledgements

We gratefully acknowledge fellowship support from GTE Research Labs and the NSF Engineering Research Center for Optoelectronic Computing Systems grant CDR8622236.

References

D. Casasent, "Coherent optical pattern recognition: A review," *Optical Engineering,* vol. 24, no. 1, pp. 26-32 (1985).

C.L. Giles, R.D. Griffin, and T. Maxwell, "Encoding geometric invariances in higher-order networks," *In: Neural Information Processing Systems,* D. Z. Anderson (ed.), (New York: American Institute of Physics, 1988) pp. 301-309.

C.L. Giles and T. Maxwell, "Learning, invariance and generalization in high-order neural networks," *Applied Optics,* vol. 26, no. 23, pp. 4972-4978 (1987).

J.L. McClelland, D.E. Rumelhart and the PDP Research Group, *Parallel Distributed Processing, Explorations in the Microstructure of Cognition,* (Cambridge, MA: The MIT Press, 1988).

W. Pitts and W.S. McCulloch, "How we know universals: The perception of auditory and visual forms," *Bulletin of Mathematical Biophysics,* vol. 9, pp. 127-147 (1947).

D. Psaltis, C.H. Park and J. Hong, "Higher order associative memories and their optical implementations," *Neural Networks,* vol. 1, pp. 149-163 (1988).

M.B. Reid, L. Spirkovska and E. Ochoa, "Simultaneous position, scale and rotation invariant pattern classification using third-order neural networks," *To appear in: The International Journal of Neural Networks - Research and Applications.*

H. Wechsler and G.L. Zimmerman, "Invariant object recognition using a distributed associative memory," *In: Neural Information Processing Systems,* D. Z. Anderson (ed.), (New York: American Institute of Physics, 1988) pp. 830-839.

L. Zhang, M.G. Robinson and K.M. Johnson, "Optical implementation of a second order neural network," *International Neural Network Conference,* Paris, July, 1990.

Learning to See Rotation and Dilation with a Hebb Rule

Martin I. Sereno and **Margaret E. Sereno**
Cognitive Science D-015
University of California, San Diego
La Jolla, CA 92093-0115

Abstract

Previous work (M.I. Sereno, 1989; cf. M.E. Sereno, 1987) showed that a feedforward network with area V1-like input-layer units and a Hebb rule can develop area MT-like second layer units that solve the aperture problem for pattern motion. The present study extends this earlier work to more complex motions. Saito et al. (1986) showed that neurons with large receptive fields in macaque visual area MST are sensitive to different senses of rotation and dilation, irrespective of the receptive field location of the movement singularity. A network with an MT-like second layer was trained and tested on combinations of rotating, dilating, and translating patterns. Third-layer units learn to detect specific senses of rotation or dilation in a position-independent fashion, despite having position-dependent direction selectivity within their receptive fields.

1 INTRODUCTION

The visual systems of mammals and especially primates are capable of prodigious feats of movement, object, and scene recognition under noisy conditions--feats we would like to copy with artificial networks. We are just beginning to understand how biological networks are wired up during development and during learning in the adult. Even at this stage, however, it is clear that explicit error signals and the apparatus for propagating them backwards across layers are probably not involved. On the other hand, there is a growing body of evidence for connections whose strength can be modified (via NMDA channels) as functions of the correlation between pre- and post-synaptic activity. The present project was to try to learn to detect pattern rotation and dilation by example, using a simple Hebb rule. By building up complex filters in stages using a simple, realistic learning rule, we reduce the complexity of what must be learned with more explicit supervision at higher levels.

1.1 ORIENTATION SELECTIVITY

Some of the connections responsible for the selectivity of cortical neurons to local stimulus features develop in the absence of patterned visual experience. For example, primary visual cortex (V1 or area 17) contains orientation-selective neurons at birth in several animals. Linsker (1986a,b) has shown that feedforward networks with gaussian topographic interlayer connections, linear summation, and simple hebb rules, develop orientation selective units in higher layers when trained on noise. In his linear system, weight updates for a layer can be written as a function of the two-point correlation characterizing the previous layer. Noise applied to the input layer causes the emergence of connections that generate gaussian correlations at the second layer. This in turn drives the development of more complex correlation functions in the third layer (e.g., difference-of-gaussians). Rotational symmetry is broken in higher layers with the emergence of Gabor-function-like connection patterns reminiscent of simple cells in the cortex.

1.2 PATTERN MOTION SELECTIVITY

The ability to see coherent motion fields develops late in primates. Human babies, for example, fail to see the transition from unstructured to structured motion--e.g., the transition between randomly moving dots and circular 2-D motion--for several months. The transition from horizontally moving dots with random y-axis velocities to dots with sinusoidal y-axis velocities (which gives the percept of a rotating 3-D cylinder) is seen even later (Spitz, Stiles-Davis, & Siegel, 1988). This suggests that the cortex requires many experiences of moving displays in order to learn how to recognize the various types of coherent texture motions.

However, orientation gradients, shape from shading, and pattern translation, dilation, and rotation cannot be detected with the kinds of filters that can be generated solely by noise. The correlations present in visual scenes are required in order for these higher level filters to arise.

1.3 NEUROPHYSIOLOGICAL MOTIVATION

Moving stimuli are processed in successive stages in primate visual cortical areas. The first cortical stage is layer 4Cα of V1, which receives its main ascending input from the magnocellular layers of the lateral geniculate nucleus. Layer 4Cα projects to layer 4B, which contains many tightly-tuned direction-selective neurons. These neurons, however, respond to moving contours as if these contours were moving perpendicular to their local orientation (Movshon et al., 1985).

Layer 4B neurons project directly and indirectly to area MT, where a subset of neurons show a relatively narrow peak in the direction tuning curve for a plaid that is lined up with the peak for a single grating. These neurons therefore solve the aperture problem for pattern translation presented to them by the local motion detectors in layer 4B of V1. MT neurons, however, appear to be largely blind to the sense of pattern rotation or dilation (Saito et al., 1986). Thus, there is a higher order 'aperture problem' that is solved by the neurons in the parts of areas MST and 7a that distinguish senses of pattern rotation and dilation. The present model provides a rationale for how these stages might naturally arise in development.

2 RESULTS

In previous work (M.I. Sereno, 1989; cf. M.E. Sereno, 1987) a simple 2-layer feedforward architecture sufficed for an MT-like solution to the aperture problem for local translational motion. Units in the first layer were granted tuning curves like those in V1, layer 4B. Each first-layer unit responded to a particular range of directions and speeds of the component of movement perpendicular to a local contour. Second layer units developed MT-like receptive fields that solved the aperture problem for local pattern translation when trained on locally jiggled gratings rigidly moving in randomly chosen pattern directions.

2.1 NETWORK ARCHITECTURE

A similar architecture was used for second-to-third layer connections (see Fig. 1--a sample network with 5 directions and 3 speeds). As with Linsker, a new input layer was constructed from a canonical unit, suitably transformed. Thus, second-layer units were granted tuning curves resembling those found in MT (as well as those generated by first-to-second layer learning)--that is, they responded to the local *pattern* translation but were blind to particular senses of local rotation, dilation, and shear. There were 12 different local

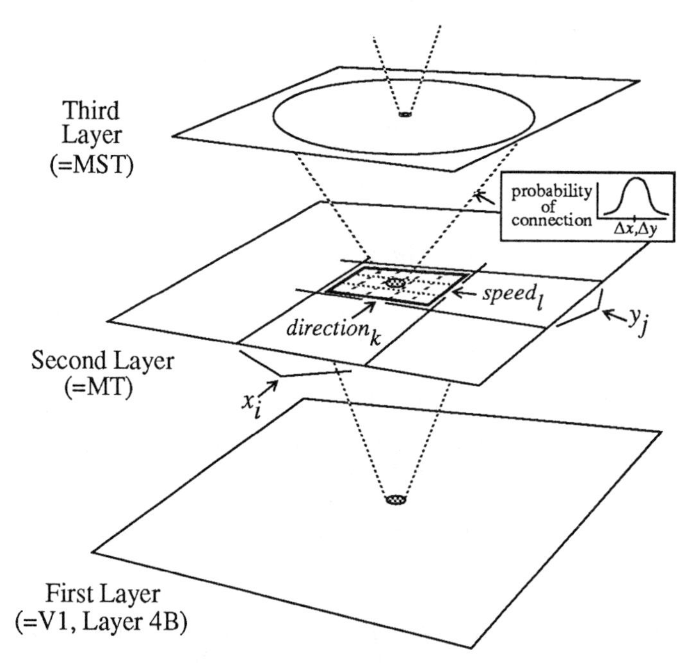

Figure 1: Network Architecture

pattern directions and 4 different local pattern speeds at each x-y location (48 different units at each of 100 x-y points). Second-layer excitatory tuning curves were piecewise linear with half-height overlap for both direction and speed. Direction tuning was set to be 2-3 times as important as speed tuning in determining the activation of input units. Input units generated untuned feedforward inhibition for off-directions and off-speeds. Total inhibition was adjusted to balance total excitation. The probability that a unit in the first layer connected to a unit in the second layer fell off as a gaussian centered on the retinotopically equivalent point in the second layer. Since receptive fields in areas MST and 7a are large, the interlayer divergence was increased relative to the divergence in the first-to-second layer connections. Third layer units received several thousand connections.

The network is similar to that of Linsker except that there is no activity-*in*dependent decay (k_1) for synaptic weights and no offset (k_2) for the correlation term. The activation, out_j, for each unit is a linear weighted sum of its inputs, in_i scaled by α, and clipped to maximum and minimum values:

$$out_j = \begin{cases} \alpha \sum_i in_i weight_{ij} \\ out_{max,\, min} \end{cases}$$

Weights are also clipped to maximum and minimum values. The change in each weight, $\Delta weight_{ij}$, is a simple fraction, δ, of the product of the pre- and post-synaptic values:

$$\Delta weight_{ij} = \delta in_i out_j$$

The learning rate, δ, was set so that about 1,000 patterns could be presented before most weights saturated. The stable second-layer weight patterns seen by Linsker (1986a) are reproduced by this model when it is trained on noise input. However, since it lacks k_2, it cannot generate center-surround weight structures given only gaussian correlations as input.

2.2 TRAINING PATTERNS

Second-to-third layer connections were trained with full or partial field rotations, dilations, and translations. Each stimulus consisted of a set of local pattern motions at each x-y point that were: 1) rotating clockwise or counterclockwise around, 2) dilating or contracting toward, or 3) translating through a randomly chosen location. The singularity was always within the input array. Both full and partial field rotations and dilations were effective training stimuli for generating rotation and dilation selectivity.

2.3 POSITION-INDEPENDENT TUNING CURVES

Post-training rotation and dilation tuning curves for different receptive-field locations were generated for many third-layer units using paradigms similar to those used on real neurons. The location of the motion singularity of the test stimulus was varied across layer two. Third-layer units often responded selectively to a particular sense of rotation or dilation at each visual field test location. A sizeable fraction of units (10-60%) responded in a position-independent way after unsupervised learning on rotating and dilating fields. Similar responses were found using both partial- and full-field test stimuli.

These units thus resemble the neurons in primate visual area MSTd (10-40% of the total there) recorded by Saito et al. (1986), Duffy and Wurtz (1990), and Andersen et al. (1990) that showed position-*independent* responses to rotations and dilations. Other third-layer units had position-*dependent* tuning--that is, they changed their selectivity for stimuli centered at different visual field locations, as, in fact, do a majority of actual MSTd neurons.

2.4 POSITION-DEPENDENT WEIGHT STRUCTURES

Given the position- independence of the selective response to rotations and/or dilations in some of the third-layer units, it was surprising to find that most such units had weight structures indicating that local direction sensitivity varied systematically across a unit's receptive field. Regions of maximum weights in direction-speed subspace tended to vary smoothly across x-y space such that opposite ends of the receptive field were sensitive to opposite directions. This picture obtained with full and medium-sized partial field training examples, breaking down only when the rotating and dilating training patterns were substantially smaller than the receptive fields of third-layer units. In the last case, smooth changes in direction selectivity across space were interrupted at intervals by discontinuities.

An essentially position-independent tuning curve is achieved because any off-center clockwise rotation that has its center within the receptive field of a unit selective for clockwise rotation will activate a much larger number of input units connected with large positive weights than will any off-center counterclockwise rotation (see Fig 2).

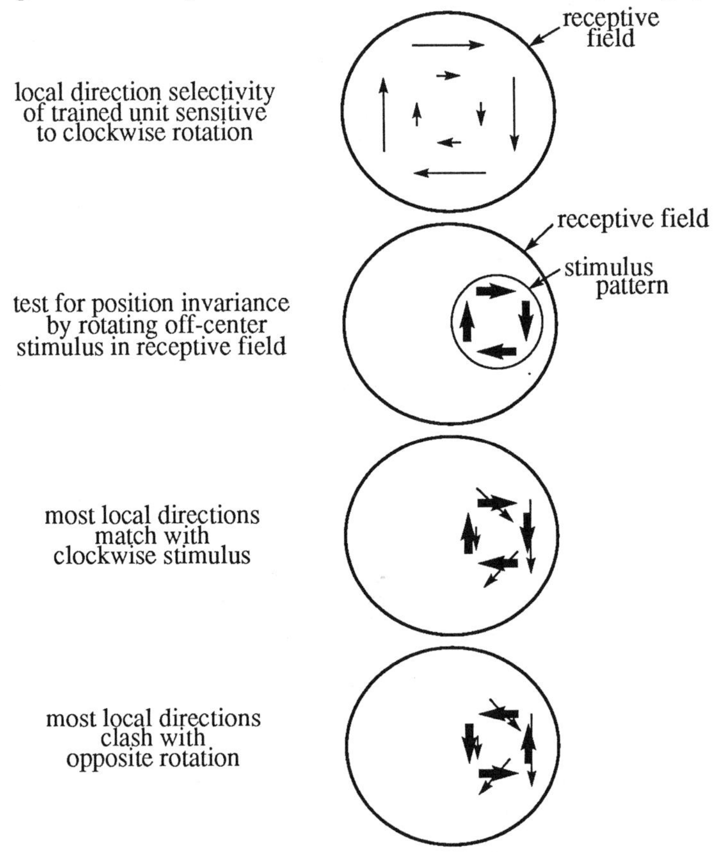

Figure 2: Position-dependent weights and position-independent responses

Saito et al. (1986), Duffy & Wurtz (1990), and Andersen et al. (1990) have all suggested that true translationally-invariant detection of rotation and dilation sense must involve several hierarchical processing stages and a complex connection pattern. The present results show that position-independent responses are exhibited by units with position-*dependent* local direction selectivity, as originally exhibited with small stimuli in area 7a by Motter and Mountcastle (1981).

2.5 WHY WEIGHTS ARE PERIODIC IN DIRECTION-SPEED SUBSPACE

For all training sets, the receptive fields of all units contained regions of all-max weights and all-min weights within the direction-speed subspace at each x-y point. For comparison, if the model is trained on uncorrelated direction noise (a different random local direction at each x-y point), third layer input weight structures still exhibit regions of all-max and all-min weights in the direction-speed subspace at each x-y point in the second layer. In contrast to weight structures generated by rigid motion, however, the location of these regions for a unit are not correlated across x-y space. These regions emerge at each x-y location because the overlap in the input unit tuning curves generates local two-point correlations in direction-speed subspace that are amplified by a hebb rule (Linsker, 1986a). This mechanism prevents more complex weight structures (like those envisaged by the neurophysiologists and those generated by backpropagation) from emerging. The two-point correlations *across x-y* space generated by jiggled gratings, or by the rotation and dilation training sets serve to align the all-max or all-min regions in the case of translation sensitivity, or generate smooth gradients in the case of sensitivity to rotation and dilation.

2.6 WHY MT DOES *NOT* LEARN TO DETECT ROTATION AND DILATION

Saito et al. (1986) demonstrated that MT neurons are not selective for particular senses of pattern rotation and dilation, but only for particular pattern translations (MT neurons will of course respond to a part of a large rotation or dilation that locally approximates the unit's translational directional tuning). MT neurons in the present model do not develop this selectivity even when trained on rotating and dilating stimuli because of the smaller divergence in the first layer (V1) to second layer (MT) connection. The local views of rotations and dilations seen by MT are apparently noise-like enough that any second order selectivity is averaged out. A larger (unrealistic) divergence allows a few units to solve the aperture problem and detect rotation and dilation in one step.

Training sets that contain many pure-translation stimuli along with the rotating and dilating stimuli fail to bring about the emergence of selectivity to senses of rotation and dilation (most units reliably detect only particular translations in this case). Satisfactory performance is achieved only if the translating stimuli are on average smaller than the rotating and dilating stimuli. This may point to a regularity in the poorly characterized stimulus set that the real visual system experiences, and perhaps in this case, has come to depend on for normal development.

DISCUSSION

This exercise found a particularly simple solution to our problem that in retrospect should have been obvious from first principles. The present results suggest that this simple solution is also easily learned with simple Hebb rule. Two points warrant discussion.

First, this model achieves a reasonable degree of translational invariance in the detection of several simple kinds of pattern motion despite having weight structures that approximate a simple centered template. Such a solution to approximately translationally invariant pattern detection may be applicable, and more importantly, practically learnable, for other more complex patterns, as long as the local features of interest vary reasonably smoothly and the pattern is not presented too far off-center. These constraints may characterize many foveated objects.

Second, given that the tuning curves for particular stimulus features often change in a continuous fashion as one moves across the cortex (e.g., orientation tuning, direction tuning), there is likely to be a pervasive tendency in the cortex for receptive fields in higher areas to be constructed from subunits that receive strong connections from nearby cells in the lower area.

Acknowledgements

We thank Udo Wehmeier, Nigel Goddard, and David Zipser for help and discussions. Networks and displays were constructed on the Rochester Connectionist Simulator.

References

Andersen, R., M. Graziano, and R. Snowden (1990) Translational invariance and attentional modulation of MST cells. *Soc. Neurosci., Abstr.* **16**:7.

Duffy, C.J. and R.H. Wurtz (1990) Organization of optic flow sensitive receptive fields in cortical area MST. *Soc. Neurosci., Abstr.* **16**:6.

Linsker, R. (1986a) From basic network principles to neural architecture: emergence of spatial-opponent cells. *Proc. Nat. Acad. Sci.* **83**, 7508-7512.

Linsker, R. (1986b) From basic network principles to neural architecture: emergence of orientation-selective cells. *Proc. Nat. Acad. Sci.* **83**, 8390-8394.

Motter, B.C. and V.B. Mountcastle (1981) The functional properties of the light-sensitive neurons of the posterior parietal cortex studied in waking monkeys: foveal sparing and opponent vector organization. *Jour. Neurosci.* **1**:3-26.

Movshon, J.A., E.H. Adelson, M.S. Gizzi, and W.T. Newsome (1985) Analysis of moving visual patterns. In C. Chagas, R. Gattass, and C. Gross (eds.), *Pattern Recognition Mechanisms*. Springer-Verlag, pp. 117-151.

Saito, H., M. Yukie, K. Tanaka, K. Hikosaka, Y. Fukada and E. Iwai (1986) Integration of direction signals of image motion in the superior temporal sulcus of the macaque monkey. *Jour. Neurosci.* **6**:145-157.

Sereno, M.E. (1987) Modeling stages of motion processing in neural networks. *Proceedings of the 9th Annual Cognitive Science Conference*, pp. 405-416.

Sereno, M.I. (1988) The visual system. In I.W.v. Seelen, U.M. Leinhos, & G. Shaw (eds.), *Organization of Neural Networks*. VCH, pp. 176-184.

Sereno, M.I. (1989) Learning the solution to the aperture problem for pattern motion with a hebb rule. In D.S. Touretzky (ed.), *Advances in Neural Information Processing Systems I*. Morgan Kaufmann Publishers, pp. 468-476.

R.V. Spitz, J. Stiles-Davis & R.M. Siegel. Infant perception of rotation from rigid structure-from-motion displays. *Soc. Neurosci., Abstr.* **14**, 1244 (1988).

Stereopsis by a Neural Network Which Learns the Constraints

Alireza Khotanzad and Ying-Wung Lee
Image Processing and Analysis Laboratory
Electrical Engineering Department
Southern Methodist University
Dallas, Texas 75275

Abstract

This paper presents a neural network (NN) approach to the problem of stereopsis. The correspondence problem (finding the correct matches between the pixels of the epipolar lines of the stereo pair from amongst all the possible matches) is posed as a non-iterative many-to-one mapping. A two-layer feed forward NN architecture is developed to learn and code this nonlinear and complex mapping using the back-propagation learning rule and a training set. The important aspect of this technique is that none of the typical constraints such as uniqueness and continuity are explicitly imposed. All the applicable constraints are learned and internally coded by the NN enabling it to be more flexible and more accurate than the existing methods. The approach is successfully tested on several random-dot stereograms. It is shown that the net can generalize its learned mapping to cases outside its training set. Advantages over the Marr-Poggio Algorithm are discussed and it is shown that the NN performance is superior.

1 INTRODUCTION

Three-dimensional image processing is an indispensable property for any advanced computer vision system. Depth perception is an integral part of 3-d processing. It involves computation of the relative distances of the points seen in the 2-d images to the imaging device. There are several methods to obtain depth information. A common technique is stereo imaging. It uses two cameras displaced by a known distance to generate two images of the same scene taken from these two different viewpoints. Distances to objects can be computed if corresponding points are identified in both frames. Corresponding points are two image points which correspond to the same object point in the 3-d space as seen by the left and the right cameras, respectively. Thus, solving the so called "correspondence problem" is the essential stage of depth perception by stereo imaging.

Many computational approaches to the correspondence problem have been studied in the past. An exhaustive review of such techniques is best left to a survey articles by Dhond and Aggarwal (1989). Common to all such techniques is the employment of some constraints to limit computational requirement and also reduce the ambiguity. They usually consist of strict rules that are fixed *a priori* and are based on a rough model of the surface to-be-solved. Unfortunately, psychophysical evidence of human stereopsis suggest that the appropriate constraints are more complex and more flexible to be characterized by simple fixed rules.

In this paper, we suggest a novel approach to the stereo correspondence problem via neural networks (NN). The problem is cast into a mapping framework and subsequently solved by a NN which is especially suited to such tasks. An important aspect of this approach is that the appropriate constraints are automatically learned and generalized by the net resulting in a flexible and more accurate model.

The iterative algorithm developed by Marr and Poggio (1976) for can be regarded as a crude neural network approach with no embedded learning. In fact, the initial stages of the proposed technique follow the same initial steps taken in that algorithm. However, the later stages of the two algorithms are quite distinct with ours involving a learning process and non-iterative operation.

There have been other recent attempts to solve the correspondence problem by neural networks. Among these are O'Toole (1989), Qian and Sejnowski (1988), Sun et al. (1987), and Zhou and Chellappa (1988). These studies use different approaches and topologies from the one used in this paper.

2 DESCRIPTION OF THE APPROACH

The proposed approach poses the correspondence problem as a mapping problem and uses a special kind of NN to learn this mapping. The only constraint that is explicitly imposed is the "epipolar" constraint. It states that the match of a point in row m of one of the two images can only be located in row m of the other image. This helps to reduce the computation by restricting the search area.

2.1 CORRESPONDENCE PROBLEM AS A MAPPING PROBLEM

The initial phase of the procedure involves casting the correspondence problem as a many to one mapping problem. To explain the method, let us consider a very simple problem involving one row (epipolar line) of a stereo pair. Assume 6 pixel wide rows and take the specific example of [001110] and [111010] as left and right image rows respectively. The task is to find the best possible match between these two strings which in this case is [1110].

The process starts by forming an "initial match matrix". This matrix includes all possible matches between the pixels of the two rows. Fig. 1 illustrates this matrix for the considered example. Each 1 indicates a potential match. However only a few of these matches are correct. Thus, the main task is to distinguish the correct matches which are starred from the false ones.

To distinguish the correct matches from the false ones, Marr and Poggio (1976) imposed two constraints on the correspondences; (1) uniqueness- that there should be a one-to-one correspondence between features in the two eyes, and (2) smoothness - that surfaces should change smoothly in depth. The first constraint means that only one element of the match matrix may have a value of 1 along each horizontal and vertical direction. The second constraint translates into a tendency for the correct matches to spread along the 45° directions. These constraints are implemented through weighted connections between match matrix elements. The uniqueness constraint is modeled by inhibitory (negative) weights along the horizontal/vertical directions. The smoothness constraint gives rise to excitatory (positive) weights along 45° lines. The connections from the rest of elements receive a zero (don't care) weight. Using fixed excitatory and inhibitory constants, they progressively eliminate false correspondences by applying an iterative algorithm.

The described row wise matching does not consider the vertical dependency of pixels in 2-d images. To account for inter-row relationships, the procedure is extended by stacking up the initial match matrices of all the rows to generate a three-dimensional "initial match volume", as shown in Fig. 2. Application of the two mentioned constraints extends the 2-d excitatory region described above to a 45° oriented plane in the volume while the inhibitory region remains on the 2-d plane of the row-wise match. Since depth changes usually happen within a locality, instead of using the complete planes, a subregion of them around each element is selected. Fig. 3 shows an example of such a neighborhood. Note that the considered excitatory region is a circular disc portion of the 45° plane. The choice of the radius size (three in this case) is arbitrary and can be varied. A similar iterative technique is applied to the elements of the initial match volume in order to eliminate incompatible matches and retain the good ones.

There are several serious difficulties with the Marr-Poggio algorithm. First, there is no systematic method for selection of the best values of the excitatory/inhibitory weights. These parameters are usually selected by trial and error. Moreover, a set of weights that works well for one case does not necessarily yield good results for a different pair of images. In addition, utilization of constant weights has no analogy in biological vision systems. Another drawback regards the imposition of the two previously mentioned constraints which are based on assumptions about the form of the underlying scene. However, psychophysical evidence suggests that the stereopsis constraints are more complex and more flexible than can be characterized by simple fixed rules.

The view that we take is that the described process can be posed as a mapping operation from the space of "initial match volume" to the space of "true match volume". Such a transformation can be considered as a one-shot (non-iterative) mapping from the initial matches to the final ones. This is a complex non-linear relationship which is very difficult to model by conventional methods. However, a neural net can learn, and more importantly generalize it.

2.2 NEURAL NETWORK ARCHITECTURE

The described mapping is a function of the elements in the initial match volume. This can be expressed as:

$$t(x_1, x_2, x_3) = f\ (i(a, b, c)\ \mid (a, b, c) \in S)$$

where

$t(x_1, x_2, x_3) =$	state of the node located at coordinate (x_1, x_2, x_3) in the true match volume.
$f =$	the nonlinear mapping function.
$i(a, b, c) =$	state of the node located at coordinate (a, b, c) in the initial match volume.
$S =$	A set of three-dimensional coordinates including (x_1, x_2, x_3) and those of its neighbors in a specified neighborhood.

In such a formulation, if f is known, the task is complete. A NN is capable of learning f through examining a set of examples involving initial matches and their corresponding true matches. The learned function will be coded in a distributive manner as the learned weights of the net.

Note that this approach does not impose any constraints on the solution. No *a priori* excitatory/inhibitory assignments are made. Only a unified concept of a neighboring region, S, which influences the disparity computation is adopted. The influence of the elements in S on the solution is learned by the NN. This means that all the appropriate constraints are automatically learned.

Unlike the Marr-Poggio approach, the NN formulation allows us to consider any shape or size for the neighborhood, S. Although in discussions of next sections we use a Marr-Poggio type neighborhood as shown in Fig. 3, there is no restriction on this. In this work we used this S in order to be able to compare our results with those of Marr-Poggio. In a previous study (Khotanzad & Lee (1990)) we used a standard fully connected multi-layer feed-forward NN to learn f. The main problem with that net is the ad hoc selection of the number of hidden nodes. In this study, we use another layered feed-forward neural net termed "sparsely connected NN with augmented inputs" which does not suffer from this problem. It consists of an input layer, an output layer, and one "hidden layer. The hidden layer nodes and the output node have a Sigmoid non-linearity transfer function. The inputs to this net consist of the state of the considered element in the initial match volume along with states of those in its locality as will be described. The response of the output node is the computed state of the considered element of the initial match volume in the true match volume. The number of hidden nodes are decided based on the shape and size of the selected neighborhood, S , as described in the example to follow. This net is not a fully connected net and each hidden node gets connected to a subset of inputs. Thus the term "sparsely connected" is used.

To illustrate the suggested net, let us use the S of Fig. 3. In this case, each element in the initial match volume gets affected by 24 other elements shown by circles and crosses in the figure. Our suggested network for such an S is shown in Fig. 4. It has 625 inputs, 25 hidden nodes and one output node. Each hidden node is only connected to one set of 25 input nodes. The 625 inputs consist of 25 sets of 25 elements of the initial match volume. Let us denote these sets by $I_1, I_2, \cdots, I_{25}$ respectively. The first set of 25 inputs consists of the state of the element of the initial match volume whose final state is sought along with those of its 24 neighbors. Let us denote this node and its neighbors by t and $S^t = s_1^t, s_2^t, \cdots, s_{24}^t$ respectively. Then $I_1 = \{t, S^t\}$. The second set is composed of the same type of information for neighbor s_1^t. In other words $I_2 = \{s_1^t, S^{s_1^t}\}$. $I_3, \cdots, I_{25}$ are made similarly. So in general

$$I_j=\{s_j^t, S^{s_j^t}\}, \quad j = 2, 3,..., 25.$$

Note that there is a good degree of overlap among these 625 inputs. However, these redundant inputs are processed separately in the hidden layer as explained later. Due to the structure of this input, it is referred to as "augmented input".

The hidden layer consists of 25 nodes, each of which is connected to only one of the 25 sets of inputs through weights to be learned. Thus, each node of the hidden layer processes the result of evolution of one of the 25 input sets. The effects of processing these 25 evolved sets would then be integrated at the single output node through the connection weights between the hidden nodes and the output node. The output node then computes the corresponding final state of the considered initial match element.

Training this net is equivalent to finding proper weights for all of its connections as well as thresholds associated with the nodes. This is carried out by the back-propagation learning algorithm (Rumelhart et. al (1986)). Again note that all the weights used in this scheme are unknown and need to be computed through the learning procedure with the training set. Thus, the concept of *a priori* excitatory and inhibitory labeling is not used.

3 EXPERIMENTAL STUDY

The performance of the proposed neural network approach is tested on several random-dot stereograms. A random dot stereogram consists of a pair of similar structural images filled with randomly generated black and white dots, with some regions of one of the images shifted to either left or right relative to the other image. When viewed through a stereoscope, a human can perceive the shifted structures as either floating upward or downward according to their relative disparities. Stereograms with 50% density (i.e. half black, half white) are used.

Six 32×32 stereograms with varying disparities are used to teach the network. The actual disparity maps (floating surfaces) of these are shown in Fig. 5. Each stereogram contains three different depth levels (disparity regions) represented by different gray levels. Therefore, six three-dimensional initial match volumes and their six corresponding true match volumes comprise the training set for the NN. Each initial match volume and its corresponding true match volume contain 32^3 input-output pairs. Since six stereograms are considered, a total of 6×32^3 input-output pairs are available for training.

The performance of the trained net is tested on several random-dot stereograms. Fig. 5 shows the results for the same data the net is trained with. In addition the performance was tested on other stereograms that are different from the training set. The considered differences include: the shape of the disparity regions, size of the image, disparity levels, and addition of noise to one image of the pair. These cases are not presented here due to space limitation. We can report that all of them yielded very good results.

In Fig. 5, the results obtained using the Marr-Poggio algorithm are also shown for comparison. Even though it was tried to find the best feed backs for Marr-Poggio through trial and error, the NN outperformed it in all cases in terms of number of error pixels in the resulting disparity map.

4 CONCLUSION

In this paper, a neural network approach to the problem of stereopsis was discussed. A multilayer feed-forward net was developed to learn the mapping that retains the correct matches between the pixels of the epipolar lines of the stereo pair from amongst all the possible matches. The only constraint that is explicitly imposed is the "epipolar" constraint. All the other appropriate constraints are learned by example and coded in the nets in a distributed fashion. The net learns by examples of stereo pairs and their corresponding depth maps using the back-propagation learning rule. Performance was tested on several random-dot stereograms and it was shown that the learning is generalized to cases outside the training. The net performance was also found to be superior to Marr-Poggio algorithm.

Acknowledgements

This work was supported in part by DARPA under Grant MDA-903-86-C-0182

References

Dhond, U. R. & Aggarwal, J. K. (1989), "Structure from stereo - A review," *IEEE Trans. SMC*, vol. 19, pp. 1489-1510.

Drumheller, M. & Poggio, T. (1986), "On parallel stereo," *Proc. IEEE Intl. Conf. on Robotics and Automation*, vol. 3, pp. 1439-1448.

Khotanzad, A. & Lee, Y. W. (1990), "Depth Perception by a Neural Network," *IEEE Midcon/90 Conf. Record*, Dallas, Texas, pp. 424-427, Sept. 11-13.

Marr, D. & Poggio, T. (1976), "Cooperative computation of stereo disparity," Science, 194, pp. 238-287.

O'Toole, A. J. (1989), "Structure from stereo by associative learning of the constraints," *Perception*, 18, pp. 767-782.

Poggio, T. (1984), "Vision by man and machine," *Scientific American*, vol. 250, pp. 106-116, April.

Qiang, N. & Sejnowski, T. J. (1988), "Learning to solve random-dot stereograms of dense and transparent surfaces with recurrent backpropagation," in Touretzky & Sejnowski (Eds.), Proceedings of the 1988 Connectionist Models, pp. 435-444, Morgan Kaufmann Publishers.

Rumelhart, D. E., Hinton G. E., and Williams R. J. (1986), "Learning internal representations by error propagation," in D.E. Rumelhart & J.L. McClelland (Eds.), Parallel Distributed Processing: Explorations in the Microstructure of Cognition. vol. 1: Foundations, MIT Press.

Sun, G. Z., Chen, H. H., Lee, Y. C. (1987), "Learning stereopsis with neural networks," *Proc. IEEE First Intl. Conf. on Neural Networks*, San Diego, CA, pp. 345-355, June.

Zhou, Y. T. and Chellappa, R. (1988), "Stereo matching using a neural network," *Proc. IEEE International Conf. Acoustics, Speech, and Signal Processing, ICASSP-88*, New York, pp. 940-943, April 11-14.

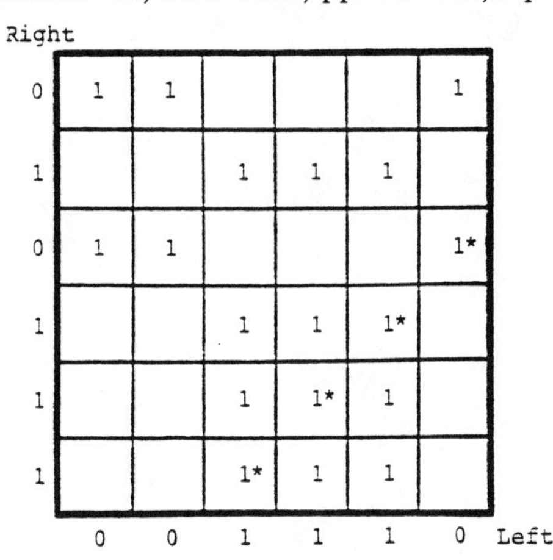

Figure 1: The initial match matrix for the considered example. 1 represents a match. Correct matches are starred.

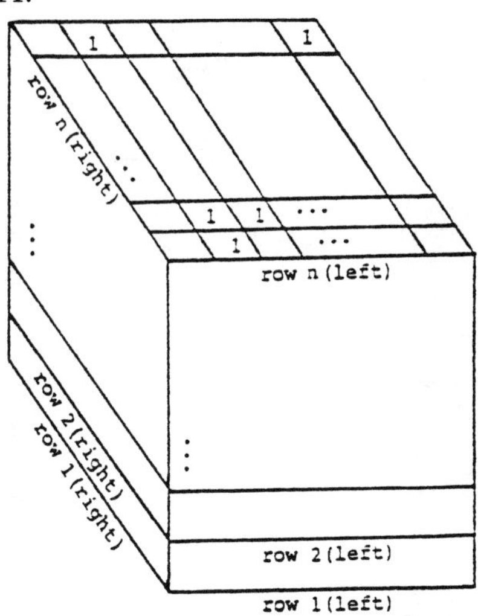

Figure 2: Schematic of the initial match volume constructed by stacking up row match matrices.

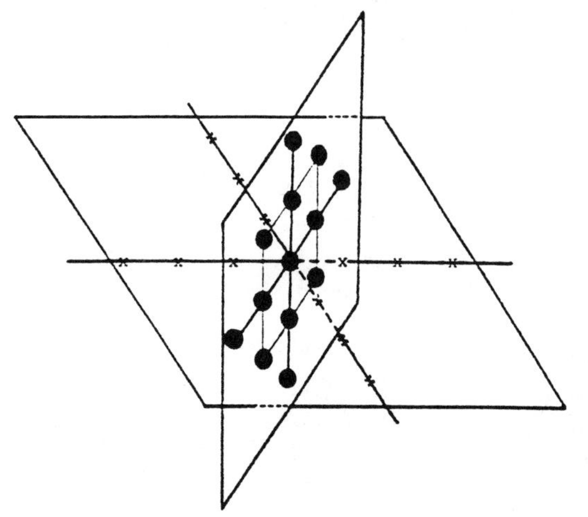

Figure 3: The neighborhood structure considered in the initial match volume. If used with Marr-Poggio, circles and crosses represent excitatory and inhibitory neighbors respectively.

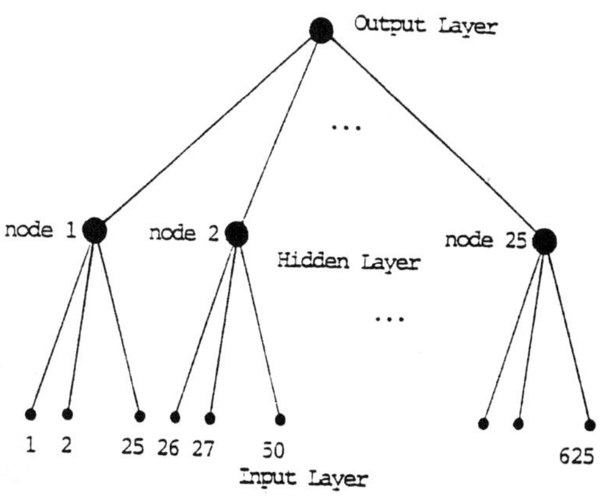

Figure 4: The sparsely connected NN with augmented inputs when the neighborhood of Fig. 3 is used.

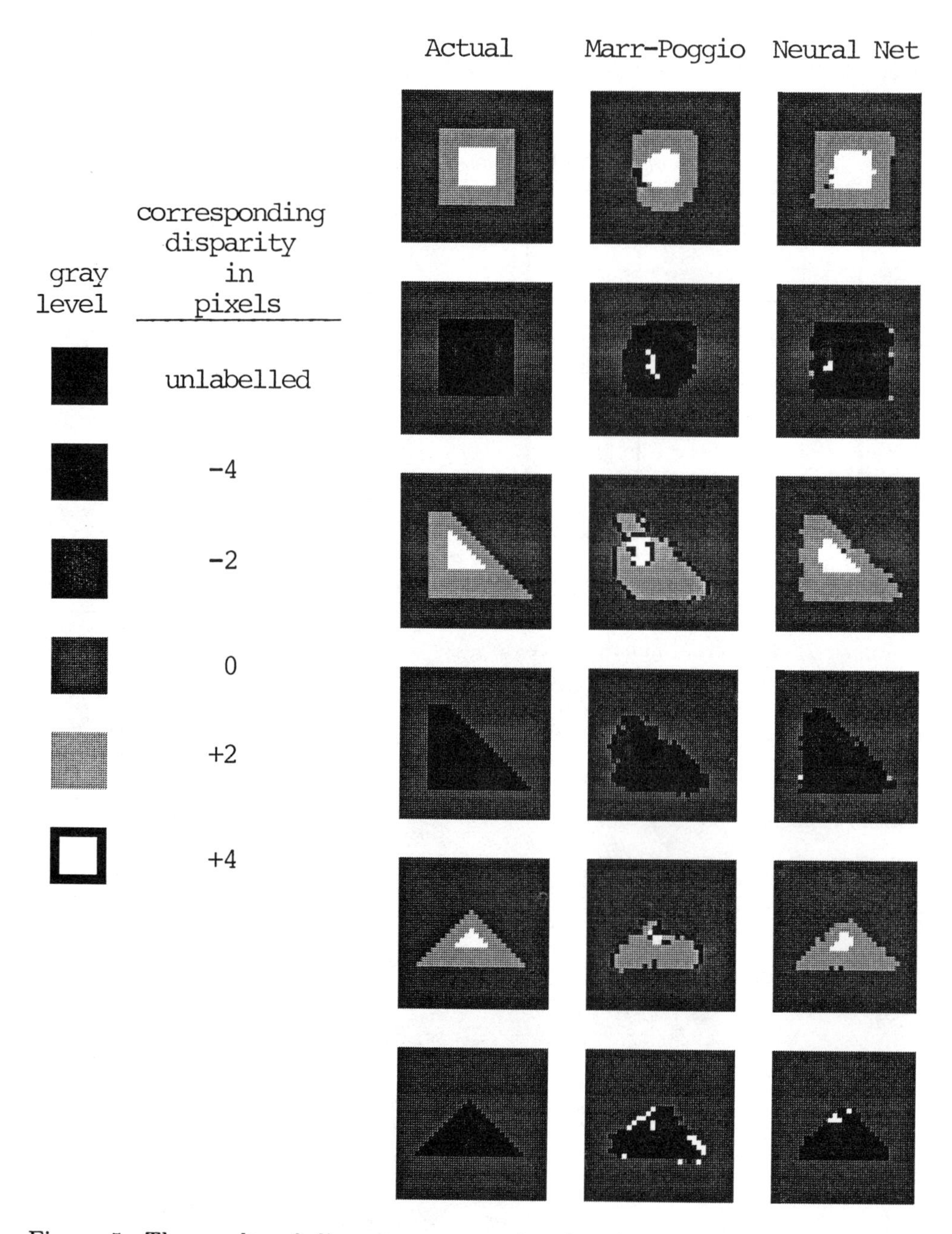

Figure 5: The results of disparity computation for six random-dot stereograms which are used to train the NN. The Marr-Poggio results are also shown.

Grouping Contours by Iterated Pairing Network

Amnon Shashua
M.I.T. Artificial Intelligence Lab., NE43-737
and Department of Brain and Cognitive Science
Cambridge, MA 02139

Shimon Ullman

Abstract

We describe in this paper a network that performs grouping of image contours. The input to the net are fragments of image contours, and the output is the partitioning of the fragments into groups, together with a saliency measure for each group. The grouping is based on a measure of overall length and curvature. The network decomposes the overall optimization problem into independent optimal pairing problems performed at each node. The resulting computation maps into a uniform locally connected network of simple computing elements.

1 The Problem: Contour Grouping

A problem that often arises in visual information processing is the linking of contour fragments into optimal groups. For example, certain subsets of contours spontaneously form perceptual groups, as illustrated in Fig. 1, and are often detected immediately without scanning the image in a systematic manner. Grouping process of this type are likely to play an important role in object recognition by segmenting the image and selecting image structures that are likely to correspond to objects of interest in the scene.

We propose that some form of autonomous grouping is performed at an early stage based on geometrical characteristics, that are independent of the identity of objects to be selected. The grouping process is governed by the notion of saliency in a way that priority is given to forming salient groups at the expense of potentially less salient ones. This general notion can again be illustrated by Fig. 1; it appears that certain groups spontaneously emerge, while grouping decisions concerning the less salient parts of the image may remain unresolved. As we shall see, the computation below exhibits a similar behavior.

We define a grouping of the image contours as the formation of a set of disjoint

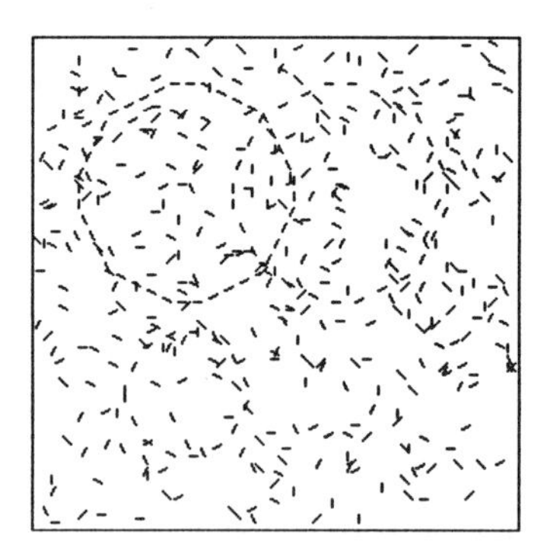

Figure 1: Contours that spontaneously form perceptual groups with various degrees of saliency. On the left is an edge image of a plane surrounded by a car, a house, trees and texture. The image on the right contains three circles, having decreasing degrees of saliency, in a background of randomly placed and oriented segments.

groups, each corresponding to a curve that may have any number of gaps, and whose union covers all the contour fragments in the image. Given a function $F(A)$ that measures some desired property of a group A, we would like to find a disjoint set of groups $\{A_1, ..., A_m\}$ that maximizes $\sum_i F(A_i)$ over all possible groupings. Our definition of the problem is related to, but not identical with, problems studied in the past under headings of "perceptual organization", "segmentation", "cueing" and "figure-ground separation". In our definition of grouping, local grouping decisions based on collinearity of neighboring edge segments may be overridden in favor of more global decisions that are governed by the overall saliency of the groups.

The paper introduces a novel grouping method having the following properties: (i) the grouping optimizes an overall saliency measure, (ii) the optimization problem is mapped onto a uniform locally connected network of simple computing elements, and (iii) the network's architecture and its computation are different in several respects from traditional neural network models.

2 Optimal Grouping

For the purpose of grouping it is convenient to consider the image as a graph of edge elements. The vertices of the graph correspond to image pixels, and the arcs to elementary edge fragments. The input to the grouping problem is a contour image, represented by a subset E^r of the elements in the graph. A path in the graph corresponds to a contour in the image having any number of gaps. This implies that the grouping process implicitly bridges across gaps. This filling-in process is critical to any grouping scheme as demonstrated by the circles in Fig. 1.

The emphasis in this paper is on 1-D chains of elements such as objects' bounding contours. Grouping is therefore a collections of chains of $A_1, ..., A_m$ such that $A_i \cap A_j = \emptyset \;\; i \neq j$ and $\cup_i A_i \supseteq E^r$. To define an optimal grouping we will define a function $F(A)$ that measures the quality of a group A. An optimal grouping is then a grouping that maximizes $\sum_{i=1}^{m} F(A_i)$ over all possible groupings of the elements.

2.1 The Quality Measure of a Group, $F(A)$

The definition of the measure $F(A)$ is motivated by both perceptual and computational considerations. In agreement with perceptual observations, it is defined to favor long smooth contours. Its form is also designed to facilitate distributed multistage optimization, as discussed below.

To define $F(A)$ of a chain of elements $A = \{e_1, ..., e_m\}$, consider first a single element e_i, and the n preceding elements in the chain. We use first a quantity $s_n(i)$ which is the contribution of the n preceding elements to e_i, which is:

$$s_n(i) = \sum_{j=\max\{1,i-n\}}^{i} \sigma_j C_{ij}$$

σ_j is defined as 1 when e_j corresponds to a contour fragment in the image and 0 for gaps. $s_n(i)$ is therefore simply a weighted sum of the contributions of the elements in the chain. The weighting factor C_{ij} is taken to be a decreasing function of the total curvature of the path γ_{ij} between elements e_i and e_j. This will lead to a grouping that prefers curves with small overall curvature over wiggly ones. C_{ij} is given by the formula:

$$C_{ij} = e^{-\int_{\gamma_{ij}} \left(\frac{d\theta}{ds}\right)^2 ds}$$

The exponent is the squared total curvature of the path between elements e_i and e_j, and the resulting C_{ij} lies between 0 (highly curved contour) and 1 (straight line). For a discrete sampling of the curve, C_{ij} can be approximated by the product:

$$C_{ij} = \prod_{p=i}^{j+1} f_{p,p-1} \qquad C_{ii} = 1$$

where $f_{p,q}$ is referred to as the *coupling constant* between adjacent elements e_p and e_q and is given by $f_{p,q} = e^{-\alpha \tan \frac{\alpha}{2}}$ where α is the angle measuring the orientation difference between p and q [3]. In a similar manner, one can define $\bar{s}_n(i)$, the contribution of the n elements following e_i in the chain. $S_n(i) = s_n(i) + \bar{s}_n(i) - \sigma_i$ measures the contribution to element e_i from both direction. This increases monotonically with the length and low total curvature of the curve passing through element e_i. Then then the overall quality of the chain A is finally given by

$$F_n(A) = \sum_{i=1}^{m} S_n(i)$$

$F_n(A)$ increases quadratically with the size of A and is non-linear with respect to the total curvature of A. Maximizing $\sum F(A_j)$ over all possible groupings will, therefore, prefer groups that are long and smooth. As n increases, the measure F_n will depend on larger portions of the curve surrounding each element, resulting in a finer discrimination between groups. In practice, we limit the measure to a finite n, and the optimal grouping is defined as:

$$I_n = arg \max_{m, A_1, \ldots, A_m} \sum_{i=1}^{m} F_n(A_i)$$

where the max is taken over all possible groupings. That is, we are looking for a grouping that will maximize the overall criterion function based on length and smoothness.

3 The Optimization Approach

Optimizing I_n is a nonlinear problem with an energy landscape that can be quite complex making it difficult to find a global optimum, or even good local optima, using straightforward gradient descent methods. We define below a computation that proceeds in two stages, *saliency* and *pairing* stages, of n steps each. In the saliency stage we compute, by iterating a local computation, optimal values of $S_n(i)$ for all elements in the graph. These values are an upper-bound on the saliency values achievable by any grouping. In the pairing stage we further update $S_n(i)$ by repeatedly forming local pairings of elements at each node of the graph. The details of both stages are given below.

3.1 Saliency Stage

For any given grouping $A_1, ..., A_m$, because they are disjoint, we have that

$$\sum_{j=1}^{m} F_n(A_j) = \sum_{i=1}^{N} S_n(i) \leq \sum \max_{\gamma_i} S_n(i)$$

where N is the number of elements in the graph and γ_i is a curve passing through element e_i. We denote $S_n(i)$ to be the *saliency* of element e_i with respect to a curve γ_i. We therefore have that the maximal saliency value $S_n^*(i) = \max_{\gamma_i} S_n(i)$ is an upper-bound on the saliency value element e_i receives on the optimal grouping I_n.

We define a local computation on the grid of elements such that each element e_i computes maximal $S_n(i)$ by iterating the following simple computation, at each step taking the maximal contribution of its neighbors.

$$s_0(i) = \sigma_i$$
$$s_{n+1}(i) = \sigma_i + \max_j s_n(j) f_{ij} \tag{1}$$

where this computation is performed by all elements in parallel. It can be shown that at the n'th iteration $s_n(i)$ is maximal over all possible curves of length n, having any number of gaps, that come into e_i. Since $S_n(i) = s_n(i) + \bar{s}_n(i) - \sigma_i$, we have found the maximal $S_n(i)$ as well. For further details on the properties of this computation, see [3]. Note that since the computation is carried by all elements of the net, including gaps (σ equals 0), the gaps are filled-in as a by-product of the computation. One can show that the filling-in contour between two end-elements has the smallest overall curvature, and therefore has the shape of a cubic spline.

3.2 Pairing Stage

Given the optimal saliency values $S_n^*(i)$ computed at the saliency stage we would like next to find a near-optimal grouping I_n. We first note the one-to-one correspondence between a grouping and a pairing of elements at each node of the graph. We define a pairing to be a partition of the k elements around node P into $\lceil \frac{k}{2} \rceil$ disjoint pairs. A pairing performed over all nodes of the net creates an equivalence relation over the elements of the net and therefore, by transitivity, determines a grouping. We therefore proceed by selecting a pairing at each node of the net that will yield a near optimal grouping I_n.

Given $s_n(i)$, the optimal saliency values computed by (1), and a pairing at node P

we update the saliency values by

$$s_{n+1}(i) = \sigma_i + s_n(j) f_{ij} \tag{2}$$

where e_i and e_j are pairs determined by the pairing. This computation is exactly like (1) with the exception that (2) is applied to a fixed pairing while in (1) each element selects the neighbor with maximal contribution. Further applications of pairing followed by (2) allows the result of pairing decisions to propagate along curves and influence other pairing decisions. This gives rise to the notion of *iterated pairings*, a repetitive pairing procedure applied simultaneously over all nodes of the graph followed by saliency computation (2). We define below a pairing procedure that identifies salient groups in contour images.

For every node P in the graph with elements $e_1, ..., e_k$ coming into P, we have that $s_n(i) \quad i = 1, ..., k$ computed by (1) are measured along optimal, not necessarily disjoint, curves $A_1, ..., A_k$ of length n each. An *optimal pairing* at node P is defined as a disjoint pairing that concatenates $A_1, ..., A_k$ into $\lceil \frac{k}{2} \rceil$ curves such that the sum of their quality measure $F(\cdot)$ is maximal. Because F is defined to prefer smooth curves and because of its non-linearity with respect to total curvature, an optimal pairing agrees with the notion of forming salient groups on the expense of potentially less salient ones. The following proposition shows that an optimal pairing can be determined locally without the need to evaluate the quality measure of the concatenated curves.

Proposition 1 *For a given node P, let $e_1, ..., e_k$ be the elements around P, $A_1, ..., A_k$ be curves coming into P that are associated with the non-zero saliency values $s_1(n), ..., s_k(n)$ with sufficiently large n (at least twice the largest chain A_i), π be a permutation of the indices $(1, ..., k)$ and $J = \{(1,2),(3,4),...,(k-1,k)\}$, then*

$$arg \max_{\pi} \sum_{(i,j)\in J} F_n(A_{\pi_i} A_{\pi_j}) = arg \max_{\pi} \sum_{(i,j)\in J} \omega_{\pi_i,\pi_j}$$

where $A_i A_j$ stands for the concatenation of curves A_i, A_j, and $\omega_{ij} = f_{ij}\,(s_n(i)c_n(j) + s_n(j)c_n(i))$ where c_n is defined as $c_n(i) = \sum_k C_{kj}$ where k is taken over all elements in the chain A_j.

Proof: This is merely a calculation. $F_n(A_i A_j)$, the measure of group-saliency of the chain $A_i A_j$, is equal to $F_n(A_i) + F_n(A_j) + \omega_{ij}$. Finally, without loss of generality, we can assume that k is even, because we can always add another element with zero weights attached to it. □

Proposition 1 shows that an optimal pairing of elements can be determined locally on the basis of the saliency values computed in (1). One way to proceed is therefore the following. The quantities c_n and therefore ω_{ij} can be accumulated and computed during computation (1). Then, the optimal pairing is computed at every node. Finding an optimal pairing is equivalent to finding an optimal *weighted match in a general graph* [2], with weights ω_{ij}. The weighted matching problem on graphs has a polynomial algorithm due to Edmonds [1] and therefore its implementation is not unwieldly.

Below we describe an alternative and more biologically plausible scheme that can be implemented in a simple network using iterative local computations. The computation is in fact almost identical to the saliency computation described in (1).

Since the saliency values s_n computed by (1) are an upper-bound on the final values achievable in any grouping, we would like to find a pairing that will preserve these values as closely as possible. Suppose that at P, e_i receives its maximal contribution from e_j, and at the same time e_i provides the maximal contribution to e_j ('mutual neighbors'). When performing local pairing at P, it is reasonable to select e_i and e_j as a pair. Note that although this is a local decision at P, the values $s_n(i)$ and $s_n(j)$ already take into account the contribution of extended curves. The remaining elements undergo another round of saliency selection and pairing of mutual neighbors, until all elements at P are paired. The following proposition shows that this pairing process is well behaved in the sense that at each selection round there will always be at least one pair that mutually select each other. We therefore have that the number of selection rounds is bounded by $\lceil \frac{k}{2} \rceil$, where k is the number of elements having non-zero saliency value coming into node P.

proposition 2 *Let $x_1, ..., x_k$ be k positive real numbers, $\omega_{ij} = \omega_{ji}$ be positive weights $i, j = 1, ..., k$ and $\delta_i = arg \max_j x_j \omega_{ij}$, then $\exists i, j$ such that $\delta_i = j$ and $\delta_j = i$ (i and j are mutual neighbors).*

Proof: by induction on k. For $k = 3$ assume there exists a cycle in the selection pattern. For any given cycle we can renumber the indecis such that $\delta_1 = 2, \delta_2 = 3$ and $\delta_3 = 1$. Let w_i stand for $w_{i-1,i}$ where $\omega_1 = \omega_{k,1}$. We get (i) $x_2\omega_2 > x_3\omega_1$, (ii) $x_2\omega_3 > x_1\omega_2$ and (iii) $x_1\omega_1 > x_2\omega_3$. From (ii) and (iii) we get an inequality that contradicts (i). For the induction hypothesis, assume the claim holds for arbitrary $k - 1$. We must show that the claim holds for k. Given the induction hypothesis we must show that there is no selection pattern that will give rise to a cycle of size k. Assume in contradiction that such a cycle exists. For any given cycle of size k we can renumber the indecis such that $\delta_i = i + 1$ and $\delta_k = 1$ which implies that $x_i\omega_i > x_j\omega_{ij}$ for all $j \neq i$. In particular we have the following k inequalities: $x_i\omega_i > x_{i-2}\omega_{i-1}$ where $i = 1, ..., k$. From the $k - 1$ inequalities corresponding to $i = 2, ..., k$ we get, by transitivity, that $x_1\omega_1 < x_{k-1}\omega_k$ which contradicts the remaining inequality that corresponds to $i = 1$. □

3.3 Summary of Computation

The optimization is mapped onto a locally connected network with a simple uniform computation. The computation consists of the following steps. (i) Compute the saliency S_n^* of each line element using the computation defined in (1). (ii) At each node perform a pairing of the line elements at the node. The pairing is performed by repeatedly selecting mutual neighbors. (iii) Update at each node the values s_n based on the newly formed pairing (eq. 2). (iv) Go back to step 2.

These iterated pairings allow pairing decisions to propagate along maximally salient curves and influence other pairing decisions. In the implementation, the number of iterations n is equal in both stages and as n increases, the finer the pairing would be, resulting in a finer discrimination between groups. During the computation, the more salient groups emerge first, the less salient groups require additional iterations. Although the process is not guaranteed to converge to an optimal solution, it is a very simple computation that yields in practice good results. Some examples are shown in the next section.

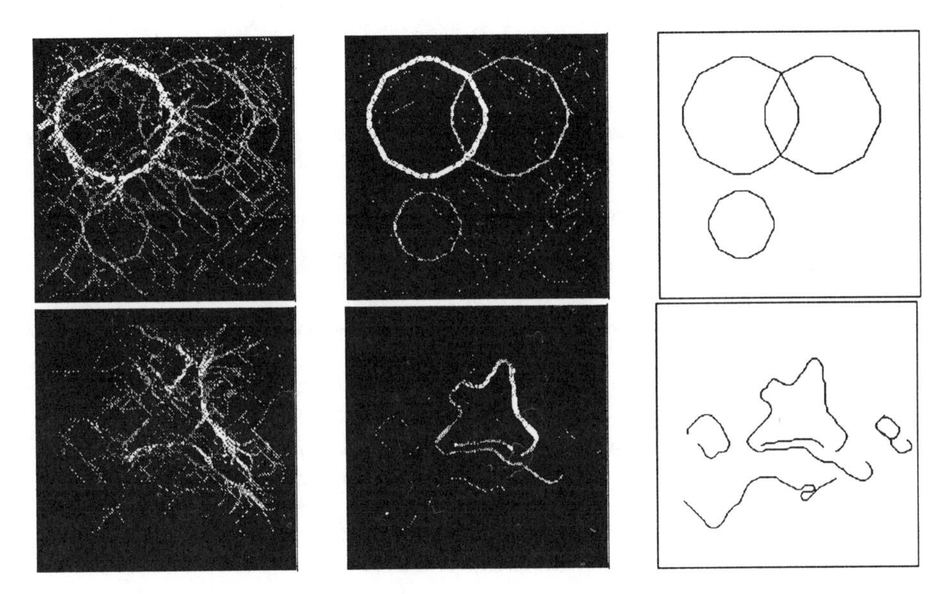

Figure 2: Results after 30 iterations of saliency and pairing on a net of size 128×128 with 16 elements per node. Images from left to right display the saliency map following the saliency and pairing stages and a number of strongest groups. The saliency of elements in the display is represented in terms of brightness and width — increased saliency measure corresponds to increase in brightness and width of element in display.

3.4 Examples

Fig. 2 shows the results of the network applied to the images in Fig. 1. The saliency values following the saliency and pairing stages illustrate that perceptually salient curves are also associated with high saliency values (see also [3]). Finally, in these examples, the highest saliency value of each group has been propagated along all elements of the group such that each group is now associated with a single saliency value. A number of strongest groups has been pulled out showing the close correspondence of these groups to objects of interest in the images.

Acknowledgments

This work was supported by NSF grant IRI-8900267. Part of the work was done while A.S. was visiting the exploratory vision group at IBM research center, Yorktown Heights.

References

[1] J. Edmonds. Path trees and flowers. *Can. J. Math.*, 1:263–271, 1965.

[2] C.H. Papadimitriou and K. Steiglitz. *Combinatorial Optimization: Algorithms and Complexity.* Prentice-Hall, New Jersey, 1982.

[3] A. Shashua and S. Ullman. Structural saliency: The detection of globally salient structures using a locally connected network. In *Proceedings of the 2nd International Conference on Computer Vision*, pages 321–327, 1988.

Neural Dynamics of Motion Segmentation and Grouping

Ennio Mingolla
Center for Adaptive Systems, and
Cognitive and Neural Systems Program
Boston University
111 Cummington Street
Boston, MA 02215

Abstract

A neural network model of motion segmentation by visual cortex is described. The model clarifies how preprocessing of motion signals by a Motion Oriented Contrast Filter (MOC Filter) is joined to long-range cooperative motion mechanisms in a motion Cooperative Competitive Loop (CC Loop) to control phenomena such as as induced motion, motion capture, and motion aftereffects. The total model system is a motion Boundary Contour System (BCS) that is computed in parallel with a static BCS before both systems cooperate to generate a boundary representation for three dimensional visual form perception. The present investigations clarify how the static BCS can be modified for use in motion segmentation problems, notably for analyzing how ambiguous local movements (the aperture problem) on a complex moving shape are suppressed and actively reorganized into a coherent global motion signal.

1 INTRODUCTION: WHY ARE STATIC AND MOTION BOUNDARY CONTOUR SYSTEMS NEEDED?

Some regions, notably MT, of visual cortex are specialized for motion processing. However, even the earliest stages of visual cortex processing, such as simple cells in V1, require stimuli that change through time for their maximal activation and are direction-sensitive. Why has evolution generated regions such as MT, when even V1 is change-sensitive and direction-sensitive? What computational properties are achieved by MT that are not already available in V1?

The monocular Boundary Contour System (BCS) theory of Grossberg and Mingolla (1985a, 1985b, 1987), and its binocular generalization (Grossberg, 1987, Grossberg & Marshall, 1989), has modeled many boundary segmentation properties of V1 and its prestriate projections. The BCS has until now been used to analyze data generated in response to static visual images. Henceforth I will therefore call such a BCS a static BCS model. Nonetheless its model cells can be gated by cells sensitive to image transients to generate receptive fields sensitive to visual motion. How does a motion BCS differ from a static BCS whose cells are sensitive to image transients?

2 STATIC AND MOTION FILTERING: DIRECTION-OF-CONTRAST AND DIRECTION-OF-MOTION

That boundaries of opposite direction-of-contrast are perceptually linked is vividly illustrated by the reverse-contrast Kanizsa square. A fundamental property of the front end of the BCS, which is a Static Oriented Contrast Filter (SOC Filter), is that its output is insensitive to direction-of-contrast, in order to support perception of boundaries in variable illumination. This insensitivity is achieved through the pooling by units identified with complex cells of information of units identified with simple cells, whose receptive fields are elongated and sensitive to opposite contrast polarities. The pooling implies that the complex cell layer of the SOC Filter is insensitive to direction-of-motion, as well as to direction-of-contrast. Evidently, any useful filter that will act as the front-end of a motion segmentation system must be sensitive to direction-of-motion while being insensitive to direction-of-contrast.

3 GLOBAL SEGMENTATION AND GROUPING: FROM LOCALLY AMBIGUOUS MOTION SIGNALS TO COHERENT OBJECT MOTION SIGNALS

In their discussion of "velocity space," Adelson and Movshon (1980, 1982) introduce diagrams similar to Figure 1a to illustrate local motion direction (and speed) ambiguity from information confined to an aperture. In Figure 1a the length of arrows codes possible trajectories of a point which would be consistent with the measured change of contrast over time of the cell in question; for this reason, it is sometimes said that early cells are sensitive to only the normal component of velocity. Figure 1B shows another view of this situation; the length of arrows is roughly proportional to a cell's "prior probability distribution" for interpreting changing stimulation as occurring in one of several directions, of which the direction perpendicular to the cell receptive field's axis of orientation is locally preferred. Note that in this conception, if a cell with an oriented receptive field (e.g. a simple cell) is being stimulated by an edge that is not perfectly aligned with its receptive field's dark-to-light contrast axis, its "preferred direction" will not correspond to that perpendicular to the edge. In this case, however, it is assumed that within a hypercolumn of cells tuned to similar spatial frequency, contrast, and temporal parameters but varying in preferred orientation, some other cell whose preferred orientation was more nearly aligned with the edge would generate a stronger signal than the cell in question. Thus, the distribution of motion signals across cells tuned to all orientations would favor the direction perpendicular to the orientation of the edge.

Figure 1: Motion direction ambiguity along an edge

4 STATIC AND MOTION COOPERATIVE GROUPING

The static BCS contains a process of for long-range completion, regularization, and grouping which is mediated by a cooperative-competitive feedback loop (CC Loop) whose competitive layer is identified with hypercomplex cells of V2 and whose cooperative layer contains units called "bipole cells," which are hypothesized to exist in the projections of V2 cells. The CC Loop seeks to form and sharpen boundaries whenever evidence from bottom-up inputs in two regions indicates that a collinear (possibly curved) continuation of boundary activity is called for. A horizontally tuned bipole cell sends feedback to horizontally tuned cells in the competitive layer.

In considering how the static CC Loop must be modified to deal with motion segmentation, consider that motion is not binary but continuously valued; headings can be, for example, "north by northwest." The analysis of moving contours thus requires one more degree of freedom than the analysis of static contours, for a contour of a given orientation can be moving in an infinity of directions, and conversely contours of any orientation can be moving in the same direction; thus a modification in the structure of the static BCS is required. Consider again the aperture problem. In the barberpole illusion the perception of motion direction along entire contours – whose measurement by cells with localized receptive fields is everywhere subject to the aperture problem – is determined by the perceived motion of their endpoints (Wallach,1976). Endstopping in simple cells of the MOC Filter can provide the enhancement of signals from segment endpoints, enabling the cooperative bipole cells of the motion CC Loop to reorganize the ambiguous local motion signals from the interiors of the diagonal segments into signals that are consistent with those of the endpoints.

5 GENERALIZING THE GROSSBERG-RUDD MOC FILTER FOR SEGMENTATION AND GROUPING

The original Grossberg & Rudd MOC Filter is illustrated in Figure 2. The goal is to generalize certain of its functions to handle 2-D (two-dimensional) motion segmentation issues. The MOC Filter is insensitive to direction-of-contrast but sensitive to direction-of-motion. Level 1 registers the input pattern. Level 2 consists of sustained response cells with oriented receptive fields that are sensitive to direction-of-contrast. Level 3 consists of transient response cells with unoriented receptive fields that are sensitive to direction of change in the total cell input. Level 4 cells combine sustained cell and transient cell signals to become sensitive to direction-of-motion and sensitive to direction-of-contrast. Level 5 cells combine Level 4 cells to become sensitive to direction-of-motion and insensitive to direction-of-contrast.

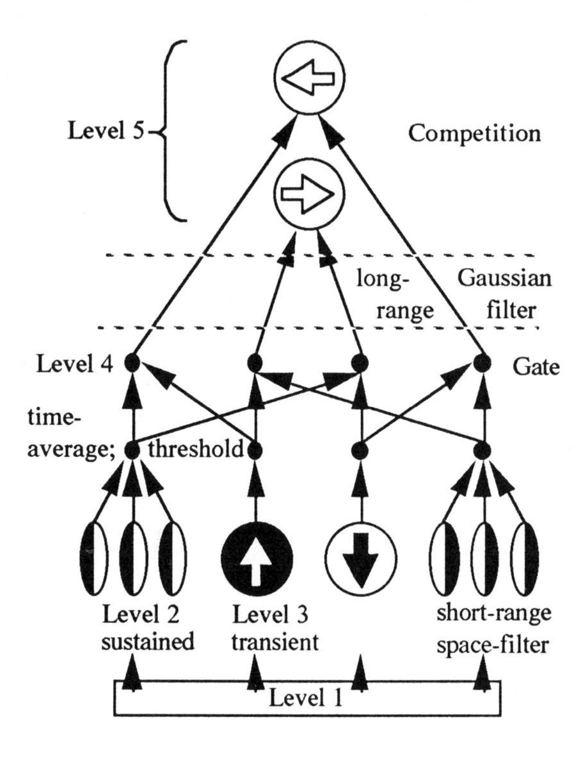

Figure 2: The Motion Oriented Contrast (MOC) Filter

The full domain of motion segmentation and grouping includes such problems as determining structure in depth from motion, motion transparency, and motion grouping amid occlusion. Although the motion BCS is conceived with these and related difficult phenomena in mind, I will instead focus on the elementary grouping operations necessary to perform detections of object motion within the visual field. Even here difficult issues arise. Consider the lower right corner of a homogeneous rectangular form of relatively high luminance that is moving diagonally upward and to the right on a homogeneous background of relatively low luminance. (See Figure 3a.) In region A dark-to-light (luminance increasing over time) transition occurs at a vertical edge, while in region B a light-to-dark (luminance decreasing over time) transition occurs at a horizontal edge. Both the regions of horizontal and vertical contrast near the corner provide signals to the MOC Filter, provided that the sustained cells of Level 2 (Figure 2) are taken to be spatially laid out as indicated in Figure 3b. Over three successive time increments, the contours of the rectangle of Figure 3a occur in the positions indicated, while luminance increases along the vertical edge and decreases along the horizontal edge. If certain of the sustained cell receptive fields sending inputs to Level 4 of the MOC Filter (Figure 2) were arranged as indicated, a diagonal motion signal could be generated from both vertically and horizontally oriented cells, in conjunction with luminance gating signals of opposite signs. (Of course, motion signals of many other directions will also be generated along the lengths of the horizontal and vertical edges; these will be considered subsequently.) In other words, for at least some of the gating nodes of Layer 4 (Figure 2), the layout of receptive field centers of contributing sustained cells of Layer 2 is taken to be in a direction diagonal to the orientational preference of the individual sustained cells. It would make no sense to build a motion filter whose receptive field centers were arrayed collinearly with the contributing sustained cell's orientational preference – although this type of arrangement might be suitable for collinear completion in a static form system. Accordingly, it appears that a variant of a "sine law" exists, whereby the contribution of any sustained cell at Level 2 to Level 4 gating cell is modulated by the (absolute value of the) sine of the angle formed between the sustained cell's orientational preference and the gating cell's directional preference.

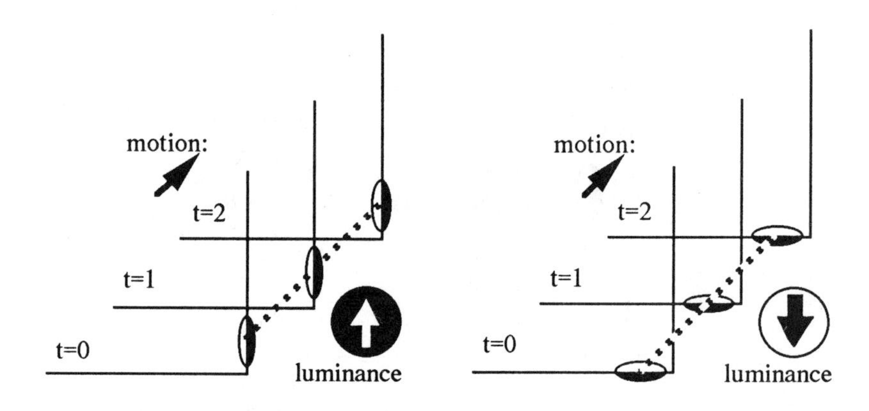

Figure 3: The corner of a light rectangle moving diagonally

The long range filter (Level 5, Figure 2) can simultaneously accept motion signals from both the horizontal and vertical edges of the moving corner, despite the gating of one set of signals by transient "luminance increasing" detectors (Level 3, Figure 2) and gating of another set by "luminance decreasing" detectors. Thus while simultaneous increase and decrease of luminance is logically impossible in an infinitesimal area, and while a too rapid change from increase to decrease may be unresolvable by sustained cells at Level 2, the simultaneous nearby increase and decrease of luminance with a coherent trajectory or direction despite different contour orientations is fodder for the long-range filter. Note that the long-range filter of the MOC Filter is not the same as the long-range grouping stage of the CC Loop.

6 ENDSTOPPING: GENERATION OF A TERMINATOR OR CORNER ADVANTAGE IN MOTION SIGNALS

In discussing the barberpole illusion I referred to an "advantage" for motion signals near terminators or corners of contours. The designation "advantage" connotes that those signals tend to be better indicators of object motion than signals generated from a relatively straight interior of a contour. For this advantage to be manifest in perception, however, that advantage must also be one of signal strength, the more so because the regions or spatial extent of interior motion signals is often larger than the region of terminator or corner signals. The source of the advantage would appear to involve endstopping at the very front end of the MOC Filter. Many simple cells, identified with the orientation and direction-of-contrast sensitive sustained cells of Level 2 of the MOC Filter, exhibit endstopping (Dreher, 1972.) (Note that this endstopping is functionally analogous to the first competitive stage of the SOC Filter.) Strong endstopping, whereby only signals at terminators survive, can reduce the problem of determining motion direction to one of tracking an isolated region of activity. In the case of weak endstopping considered here, however, surviving signals indicating "locally preferred" directions can continue to confound the problem of motion segmentation and grouping.

7 CONSENSUS AT CORNERS: GAUSSIAN SPACE AVERAGING AND DIRECTIONAL COMPETITION

In the weak endstopping case the local motion signals from the lower right corner of the moving rectangle would have roughly the form diagramed in Figure 4a. While there is some preference for diagonal (up-and-to-the-right) signals, local motion signals of other directions also exist. (b) A mechanism is needed to combine different directions signals into a single coherent local direction signal. (c) The signal combination can be accomplished by a motion analog of the second competitive stage among orientations of the SOC Filter, as described in Grossberg & Mingolla, (1987). A excitatory on-center, inhibitory off-surround network organization among cells coding different directions-of-motion at the same position can accomplish the desired pooling and choice through competitive peak summation and sharpening. Note that the domain of spatial averaging of the Gaussian filter (transition from Level 4 to Level 5 of the MOC Filter) is presumed to be large enough to span the signals generated by the ends of the leading vertical and trailing horizontal edges. At Level 5, then, signals of many directions occur for cells coding the same position. Those directions will have the appropriate "central tendency", however, and a simple center-surround competition in the space of directions, analogous to the revised version of the second competitive stage (for orientations) of the static BCS described by Grossberg & Mingolla (1987), suffices to choose the direction which is most consistent with surrounding input data at each location. (See Figure 4b.)

In this article I have described motion analysis mechanisms whereby the visual system frees itself from an excessive reliance on either purely local (short-range filtering) computations or top-down (cognitive or expectancy based) computations. Instead, within a perceptual middle ground, competitive and cooperative interactions withing a parallel and structured network with several scales of interaction help to choose and enhance those aspects of local data which contribute to coherent and consistent measures of object motion.

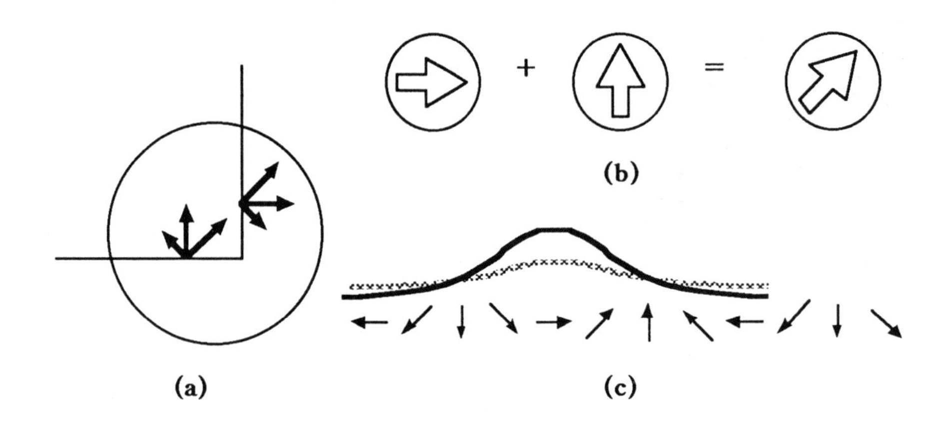

Figure 4: Resolution of ambiguous signals at corners

Acknowledgements

The research described was performed jointly with Stephen Grossberg.

The author was supported in part by AFOSR F49620-87-C-0018.

References

Adelson, E. H. & Movshon, J. A. (1980). *Journal of the Optical Society of America*, **70**, 1605.

Adelson, T. & Movshon, J. A. (1982). *Nature*, **300**, 523-525.

Dreher, B. (1972) investigative Ophthamology, **11**, 355-356.

Grossberg, S. (1987) *Perception and Psychophysics*, **41**, 87-116.

Grossberg, S. & Marshall, J. (1989). *Neural Networks,* **2**, 29-51.

Grossberg, S. & Mingolla, E. (1985a). *Psychological Review*, **92**, 173-211.

Grossberg, S. & Mingolla, E. (1985b). *Perception and Psychophysics*, **38**, 141-171.

Grossberg, S. & Mingolla, E. (1987). *Computer Vision, Graphics, and Image Processing*, **37**, 116-165.

Grossberg, S. & Rudd, M. (1989). *Neural Networks,* **2**, 421-450.

Wallach, H. (1976). *On perception.* New York, Quadrangle.

A Multiscale Adaptive Network Model of Motion Computation in Primates

H. Taichi Wang
Science Center, A18
Rockwell International
1049 Camino Dos Rios
Thousand Oaks, CA 91360

Bimal Mathur
Science Center, A7A
Rockwell International
1049 Camino Dos Rios
Thousand Oaks, CA 91360

Christof Koch
Computation & Neural Systems
Caltech, 216-76
Pasadena, CA 91125

Abstract

We demonstrate a multiscale adaptive network model of motion computation in primate area MT. The model consists of two stages: (1) local velocities are measured across multiple spatio-temporal channels, and (2) the optical flow field is computed by a network of direction-selective neurons at multiple spatial resolutions. This model embeds the computational efficiency of Multigrid algorithms within a parallel network as well as adaptively computes the most reliable estimate of the flow field across different spatial scales. Our model neurons show the same nonclassical receptive field properties as Allman's type I MT neurons. Since local velocities are measured across multiple channels, various channels often provide conflicting measurements to the network. We have incorporated a veto scheme for conflict resolution. This mechanism provides a novel explanation for the spatial frequency dependency of the psychophysical phenomenon called Motion Capture.

1 MOTIVATION

We previously developed a two-stage model of motion computation in the visual system of primates (i.e. magnocellular pathway from retina to V1 and MT; Wang, Mathur & Koch, 1989). This algorithm has these deficiencies: (1) the issue of optimal spatial scale for velocity measurement, and (2) the issue optimal spatial scale for the smoothness of motion field. To address these deficiencies, we have implemented a multi-scale motion network based on multigrid algorithms.

All methods of estimating optical flow make a basic assumption about the *scale* of the velocity relative to the spatial neighborhood and to the temporal discretization step of delay. Thus, if the velocity of the pattern is much larger than the ratio of the spatial to temporal sampling step, an incorrect velocity value will be obtained (Battiti, Amaldi & Koch, 1991). Battiti *et al.* proposed a coarse-to-fine strategy for adaptively determining the optimal discretization grid by evaluating the local estimate of the relative error in the flow field due to discretization. The optimal spatial grid is the one minimizing this error. This strategy both leads to a superior estimate of the optical flow field as well as achieving the speedups associated with multigrid methods. This is important, given the large number of iterations needed for relaxation-based algorithms and the remarkable speed with which humans can reliably estimate velocity (on the order of 10 neuronal time constants).

Our previous model was based on the standard regularization approach, which involves smoothing with weight λ. This parameter controls the smoothness of the computed motion field. The scale over which the velocity field is smooth depends on the size of the object. The larger the object is, the larger the value of λ has to be. Since a real life vision system has to deal with objects of various sizes simultaneously, there does not exist an "optimal" smoothness parameter. Our network architecture allows us to circumvent this problem by having the same smoothing weight λ at different resolution grids.

2 NETWORK ARCHITECTURE

The overall architecture of the two-stage model is shown in Figure 1. In the first stage, local velocities are measured at multiple spatial resolutions. At each spatial resolution p, the local velocities are represented by a set of direction-selective neurons, u(i,j,k,p), whose preferred direction is in direction Θ_k (the Component cells; Movshon, Adelson, Gizzi & Newsome, 1985). In the second stage, the optical flow field is computed by a network of direction-selective neurons (Pattern cells) at multiple spatial resolutions, v(i,j,k,p). In the following, we briefly summarize the network.

We have used a multiresolution population coding:

$$\mathbf{V} = \sum_{k}^{Nor} \sum_{p=0}^{Nres-1} \prod_{p'=p}^{1} \mathbf{I}_{p'}^{p'-1} v_k^p \, \Theta_k \qquad (1)$$

where *Nor* is the number of directions in each grid, *Nres* is the number of resolutions in the network and **I** is a 2-D linear interpolation operator (Brandt, 1982).

In our single resolution model, the input source, $s_0(i,j,k)$, to a pattern cell v(i,j,k) was:

$$\frac{\partial v(i,j,k)}{\partial t} = s_0(i,j,k) = \sum_{k'} \cos(\Theta_k - \Theta_{k'}) \, \{u(i,j,k') - (\mathbf{u} \cdot \mathbf{V}(i,j))\} \, e(i,j,k') \qquad (2)$$

where **u** is the the unit vector in the direction of local velocity and e(i,j,k') is the local edge strength. For our multiscale network, we have used a convergent multi-channel source term, S_0, to a pattern cell v(i,j,k,p) is:

$$s_0^p = \sum_{p' \leq p} \prod_{p''=p'}^{p} \mathbf{R}_{p''-1}^{p''} \, s_0^{p'} \qquad (3)$$

where **R** is a 2-D restriction operator. We use the full weighting operator instead of the injection operator because of the sparse nature of the input data.

The computational efficiency of the multigrid algorithms chas been embedded in our multiresolution network by a set of spatial-filtering synapses, S_1, written as:

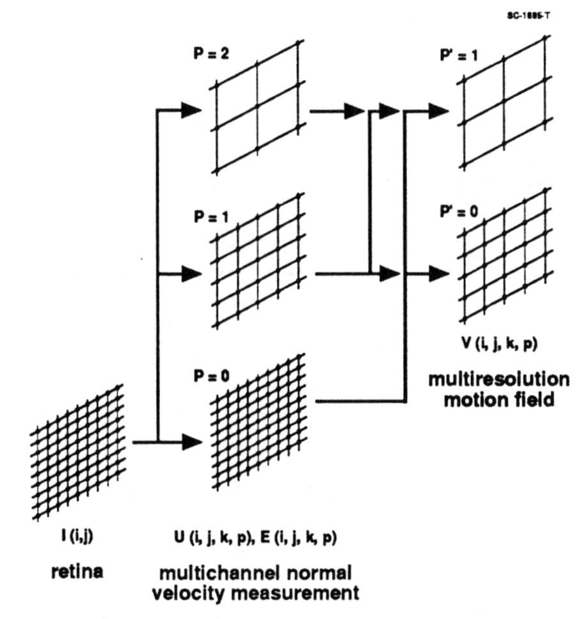

Figure 1. The network architecture.

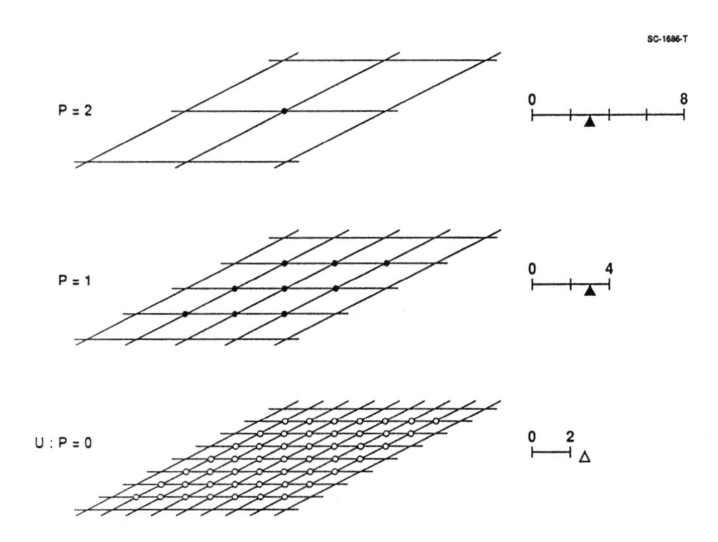

Figure 2. A coarse-to-fine veto scheme.

$$S_1^p = \alpha \mathbf{R}_{p-1}^p v^{p-1} - \beta \mathbf{I}_{p+1}^p \mathbf{R}_p^{p+1} v^p, \quad (4)$$

where α and β are constants.

As discussed in the section 1, the scale over which the velocity field is smooth depends on the size of the object. Consider, for example, an object of certain size is moving with a given velocity across the field of view. The multiresolution representation and the spatial frequency filtering connections will force the velocity field to be represented mostly by a few neurons whose resolution grid matches the size of the object. Therefore, the smoothness constraint should be enforced on the individual resolution grids. If membrane potential is used, the source for the smoothness term, S_2, at resolution grid p, can be written as:

$$S_2^p(i,j,k) = \lambda \sum_{k'} \cos(\theta_k - \theta_{k'}) \{v(i\text{-}1,j,k',p) + v(i+1,j,k',p) + v(i,j\text{-}1,k',p) + v(i,j+1,k',p) - 4v(i,j,k',p)\} \quad (5)$$

where λ is the smoothness parameter. The smoothing weight λ in our formulation is the same for each grid and is independent of object sizes.

The network equation becomes,

$$\frac{\partial v(i,j,k,p)}{\partial t} = S_0^p + S_1^p + S_2^p \quad (6)$$

The multiresolution network architecture has considerably more complicated synaptic connection pattern but only 33% more neurons as compared to the single resolution model, the convergence is improved by about two orders of magnitude (as measured by numbers of iterations needed).

3 CONFLICT RESOLUTION

The velocity estimated by our -- or any other motion algorithm -- depends on the spatial (Δx) and temporal (Δt) discretization step used. Battiti *et al.* derived the following expression for the relative error in velocity due to incorrect derivative estimation:

$$\delta = \left| \frac{\Delta u}{u} \right| \cong \frac{2\pi^2}{3\lambda^2} [(\Delta x)^2 - (u\Delta t)^2] \quad (7)$$

where u is the velocity, λ is the spatial frequency of the moving pattern. As velocity u deviates from Δx=uΔt, the velocity measurement become less accurate. The scaling factor in (7) depends on the spatial filtering in the retina. Therefore, the choice of spatial discretization and spatial filtering bandwidth have to satisfy the requirements of both the *sampling theorem* and the *velocity measurement accuracy*. Even though (7) was derived based on the gradient model, we believe similar constraint applies to correlation models. We model the receptive field profiles of primate retinal ganglion cells by the Laplacian-of-Gaussian (LOG) operators. If we require that the accuracy of velocity measurement be within 10% within u = 0 to u = 2 (Δx/Δt), then the standard deviation, σ, of the Gaussian must be greater or equal to 2Δx.

What happens if velocity measurement at various scales gives inconsistent results? Consider, for example, an object moving at a speed of 3 pixels/sec across the retina. As shown in Figure 2, channels p=1 and p=2 will give the correct measurement, since it is in the reliable ranges of these channels, as depicted by filled circles. The finest channel, p=0, on the other hand will give an erroneous reading. This suggests a coarser-to-fine veto scheme for conflict resolution. We have incorporated this strategy in our network architecture by implementing a shunting term in Eq. (4). In this way, the erroneous input signals from the component cells at grid p=0 are shunted out (the open circles in Figure 2) by the component cells (the filled circles) at coarser grids.

4 MOTION CAPTURE

How does human visual system deal with the potential conflicts among various spatial channels? Is there any evidence for the use of such a coarse-to-fine conflict resolution scheme? We believe that the well-known psychophysical phenomenon of Motion Capture is the manifestation of this strategy.

When human subjects are presented a sequence of randomly moving random dots pattern, we perceive random motion. Ramachandran and Anstis (1983) found, surprisingly, that our perception of it can be greatly influenced by the movement of a superimposed low contrast, low spatial frequency grating. They found that the human subject has a tendency to perceive the random dots as moving with the spatial grating, as if the random dots adhere to the grating. For a given spatial frequency of the grating, the percentage of capture is highest when the phase shift between frames of the grating is about 90°. Even more surprisingly, the lower the spatial frequency of the grating, the higher the percentage of capture.

Other researchers (e.g. Yuille & Grzywacz, 1988) and we have attempted to explain this phenomenon based on the smoothness constraint on the velocity field. However, smoothness alone can not explain the dependencies on spatial frequency and the phase shift of the gratings. The coarser-to-fine shunting scheme provides a natural explanation of these dependencies.

We have simulated the spatial frequency and phase shift dependency. The results are shown in Figure 3. In these simulations, we plotted the relative uniformity of the motion-captured velocity fields. Uniformity of 1 signifies total capture. As can be seen clearly, for a given spatial frequency, the effect of capture increases with phase shift, and for a given phase shift, the effect of capture also increase as the spatial frequency become lower. The lower spatial frequency gratings are more effective, because the coarser the channels are, the more finer component cells can be effectively shunted out, as is clear from the receptive field relationship shown in Figure 2.

5 NONCLASSICAL RECEPTIVE FIELD

Traditionally, physiologists use isolated bars and slits to map out the classical receptive fields (CRF) of a neuron which is the portion of visual field that can be *directly* stimulated. Recently, there is mounting evidence that in many visual neurons stimuli presented outside the CRF strongly and selectively influence neural responses to stimuli presented within the CRF. This is termed nonclassical receptive field.

Allman, Miezin & McGuinness (1985) have found that the true receptive field of more than 90% of neurons in the middle temporal (MT) area extends well beyond their CRF. The surrounds commonly have directional and velocity-selectivity influences that are

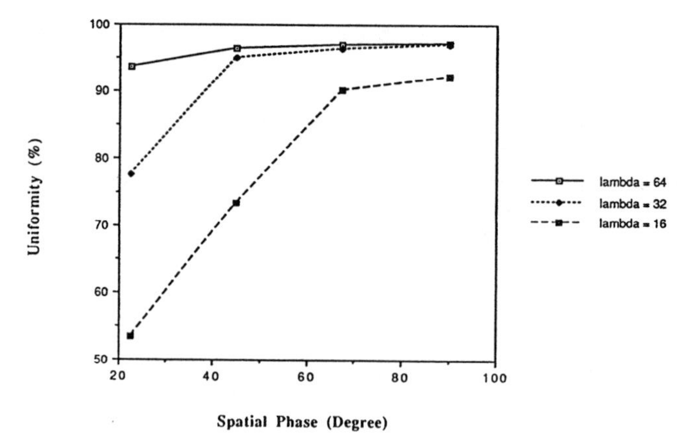

Figure 3. Spatial frequency dependency of Motion Capture.

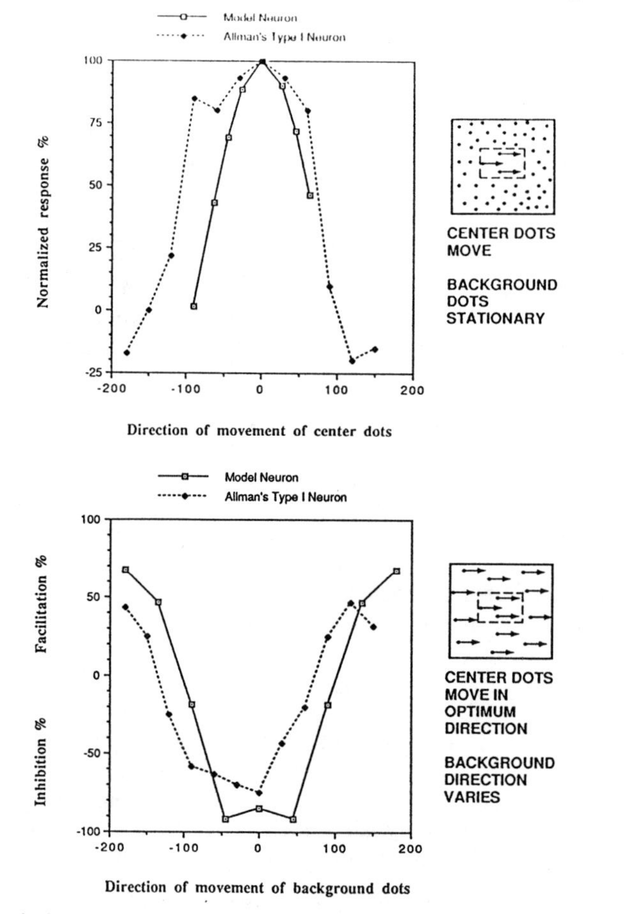

Figure 4. Simulation of Allman's type I non-classical receptive field properties.

antagonistic to the response from the CRF. Based on the surround selectivity, the MT neurons can be classified into three types. Our model neurons show that same type of nonclassical receptive field selectivity as Allman's type I neuron. We have performed a series of simulations similar to Allman's original experiments.

After the CRF of a model is determined, the optimal motion stimulus is presented within the CRF. The surrounds are, however, moved by the same amount but in the various directions. Clearly, the motion in the surround has profound effect of the activity of the cell we are monitoring. The effect of the surround motion on the cell as a function of the the direction of surround motion is plotted in Figure 4 (b). When the surround is moved in a similar direction as the center, the neuron activity of the cell is almost totally suppressed. On the other hand, when the surround is moved opposite to the center, the cell's activity is enhanced. Superimposed on Figure 4 are the similar plots from Allman's paper.

6 CONCLUSION

In conclusion, we have developed a multi-channel, multi-resolution network model of motion computation in primates. The model MT neurons show similar nonclassical surround properties as Allman's type I cells. We also proposed a novel explanation of the Motion Capture phenomenon based on a coarse-to-fine strategy for conflict resolution among the various input channels.

Acknowledgements

CK acknowledges ONR, NSF and the James McDonnell Foundation for supporting this research.

References

Allman, J., Miezin, F., and McGuinness, E. (1985) "Direction- and velocity-specific responses from beyond the classical receptive field in the middle temporal visual area (MT)", *Perception*, **14,** 105 - 126.
Battiti, R., Koch, C. and Amaldi, E. (1991) "Computing optical flow across multiple scales: an adaptive coarse-to-fine approach", to appear in *Intl. J. Computer Vision.*
Brandt, A. (1982) "Guide to multigrid development". In: *Muitlgrid Methods*, Ed. Dold, A. and Eckmann, B., Springer-Verlag.
Movshon, J.A., Adelson, E.H., Gizzi, M.S., and Newsome, W.T. (1985) "The Analysis of Moving Visual Pattern", In *Pattern Recognition Mechanisms*, ed. Chagas, C., Gattas, R., Gross, C.G., Rome: Vatican Press.
Ramachandran, V.S. and Anstis, S.M. (1983) "Displacement thresholds for coherent apparent motion in random dot-patterns", *Vision Res.* **23** (12), 1719 - 1724.
Yuille, A.L. and Grzywacz, N.M. (1988) "A computational theory for the perception of coherent visual motion", Nature, **333**, 71 - 74.
Wang, H. T., Mathur, B. P. and Koch, C. (1989) "Computing optical flow in the primate visual system", *Neural Computation*, **1**(1), 92 - 103.

Qualitative structure from motion

Daphna Weinshall
Center for Biological Information Processing
MIT, E25-201, Cambridge MA 02139

Abstract

Exact structure from motion is an ill-posed computation and therefore very sensitive to noise. In this work I describe how a qualitative shape representation, based on the sign of the Gaussian curvature, can be computed directly from motion disparities, without the computation of an exact depth map or the directions of surface normals. I show that humans can judge the curvature sense of three points undergoing 3D motion from two, three and four views with success rate significantly above chance. A simple RBF net has been trained to perform the same task.

1 INTRODUCTION

When a scene is recorded from two or more different positions in space, e.g. by a moving camera, objects are projected into disparate locations in each image. This disparity can be used to recover the three-dimensional structure of objects that is lost in the projection process. The computation of structure requires knowledge of the 3D motion parameters. Although these parameters can themselves be computed from the disparities, their computation presents a difficult problem that is mathematically ill-posed: small perturbations (or errors) in the data may cause large changes in the solution [9]. This brittleness, or sensitivity to noise, is a major factor limiting the applicability of a number of structure from motion algorithms in practical situations (Ullman, 1983).

The problem of brittleness of the structure from motion algorithms that use the minimal possible information may be attacked through two different approaches. One involves using more data, either in the space domain (more corresponding points in each image frame, Bruss & Horn, 1981), or in the time domain (more frames,

Ullman, 1984). The other approach is to look for, instead of a general quantitative solution, a qualitative one that would still meet the main requirements of the task for which the computation is performed (e.g., object representation or navigation). This approach has been applied to navigation (e.g., Nelson & Aloimonos, 1988) and object recognition (e.g., Koenderink & van Doorn, 1976; Weinshall, 1989).

Under perspective projection, the knowledge of the positions of 7 corresponding points in two successive frames is the theoretical lower limit of information necessary to compute the 3D structure of an object that undergoes a general motion (Tsai & Huang, 1984). As mentioned above, acceptable performance of structure from motion algorithms on real, noisy images requires that a larger number of corresponding points be used. In contrast, the human visual system can extract 3D motion information using as few as 3 points in each of the two frames (Borjesson & von Hofsten, 1973). To what extent can object shape be recovered from such impoverished data? I have investigated this question experimentally (by studying the performance of human subjects) and theoretically (by analyzing the information available in the three-point moving stimuli).

2 THEORETICAL SHORTCUTS

The goal of the structure from motion computation is to obtain the depth map of a moving object: the value of the depth coordinate at each point in the 2D image of the object. The depth map can be used subsequently to build a representation of the object, e.g., for purposes of recognition. One possible object representation is the description of an object as a collection of generic parts, where each part is described by a few parameters. Taking the qualitative approach to vision described in the introduction, the necessity of having a complete depth map for building useful generic representations can be questioned. Indeed, one such representation, a map of the sign of the Gaussian curvature of the object's surface, can be computed directly (and, possibly, more reliably) from motion disparities. The knowledge of the sign of the Gaussian curvature of the surface allows the classification of surface patches as elliptic (convex/concave), hyperbolic (saddle point), cylindrical, or planar. Furthermore, the boundaries between adjacent generic parts are located along lines of zero curvature (parabolic lines).

The basic result that allows the computation of the sign of the Gaussian curvature directly from motion disparities is the following theorem (see Weinshall, 1989 for details):

Theorem 1 *Let FOE denote the Focus Of Expansion – the location in the image towards (or away from) which the motion is directed.*

Pick three collinear points in one image and observe the pattern they form in a subsequent image.

The sign of the curvature of these three points in the second image relative to the FOE is the same as the sign of the normal curvature of the 3D curve defined by these three points.

The sign of the Gaussian curvature at a given point can be found without knowing the direction of the normal to the surface, by computing the curvature sign of point

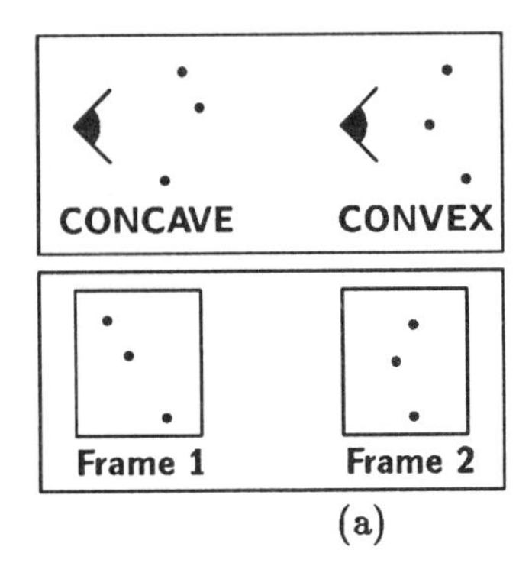

(a)

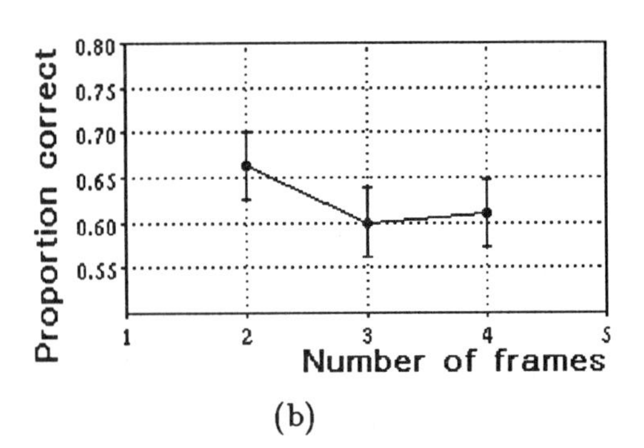

(b)

Figure 1: Experiment 1: perception of curvature from three points in 3D translation. *(a)* Four naive subjects were shown two, three or four snapshots of the motion sequence. The subjects did not perceive the motion as translation. The total extent and the speed of the motion were identical in each condition. The three points were always collinear in the first frame. The back and forth motion sequence was repeated eight times, after which the subjects were required to decide on the sign of the curvature (see text). The mean performance, 62%, differed significantly from chance ($t = 5.55$, $p < 0.0001$). Furthermore, all subjects but one performed significantly above chance. *(b)* The effect of the number of frames was not significant ($\chi^2 = 1.72$, $p = 0.42$). Bars show ± 1 standard error of the mean.

triads in all directions around the point. The sign of the Gaussian curvature is determined by the number of sign reversals of the triad curvatures encountered around the given point. The exact location of the FOE is therefore not important.

The sign operator described above has biological appeal, since the visual system can compute the deviation of three points from a straight line with precision in the hyperacuity range (that is, by an order of magnitude more accurately than allowed by the distance between adjacent photoreceptors in the retina). In addition, this feature must be important to the visual system, since it appears to be detected preattentively (in parallel over the entire visual field; see Fahle, 1990).

It is difficult to determine whether the visual system uses such a qualitative strategy to characterize shape features, since it is possible that complete structure is first recovered, from which the sign of the Gaussian curvature is then computed. In the following experiments I present subjects with impoverished data that is insufficient for exact structure from motion (3 points in 2 frames). If subjects can perform the task, they have to use some strategy different from exact depth recovery.

3 EXPERIMENT 1

In the first experiment four subjects were presented with 120 moving rigid configurations of three points. The number of distinct frames per configuration varied from 2 to 4. The motion was translation only. Subjects had to judge whether the three points were in a convex or a concave configuration, namely, whether the broken 3D line formed by the points was bent towards or away from the subject (figure 1a). The middle point was almost never the closest or the farthest one, so that relative depth was not sufficient for solving the problem. With only two-frame the stimulus was ambiguous in that there was an infinity of rigid convex and concave 3D configurations of three points that could have given rise to the images presented. For these stimuli the correct answer is meaningless, and one important question is whether this inherent ambiguity affects the subjects' performance (as compared to their performance with 3 and 4 frames).

The subjects' performance in this experiment was significantly better than chance (figure 1b). The subjects were able to recover partial information on the shape of the stimulus even with 2 frames, despite the theoretical impossibility of a full structure from motion computation[1]. Moreover, the number of frames presented in each trial had no significant effect on the error rate: the subjects performed just as well in the 2 frame trials as in the 3 and 4 frame trials (figure 1b). Had the subjects relied on the exact computation of structure from motion, one would expect a better performance with more frames (Ullman, 1984; Hildreth et al., 1989).

One possible account (reconstructional) of this result is that subjects realized that the motion of the stimuli consisted of pure 3D translation. Three points in two frames are in principle sufficient to verify that the motion is translational and to compute the translation parameters. The next experiment renders this account implausible by demonstrating that the subjects perform as well when the stimuli undergo general motion that includes rotation as well as translation.

Another possible (geometrical) account is that the human visual system incorporates the geometrical knowledge expressed by theorem 1, and uses this knowledge in ambiguous cases to select the more plausible answer. However, theorem 1 does not address the ambiguity of the stimulus that stems from the dependency of the result on the location of the Focus Of Expansion. If indeed some knowledge of this theorem is used in performing this task, the ambiguity has to be resolved by "guessing" the location of the FOE. The strategy consistent with human performance in the first experiment is assuming that the FOE lies in the general direction towards which the points in the image are moving. The next experiment is designed to check the use of this heuristic.

4 EXPERIMENT 2

This experiment was designed to clarify which of the two proposed explanations to the subjects' good performance in experiment 1 with only 2 frames is more plausible.

First, to eliminate completely the cue to exact depth in a translational motion, the stimuli in experiment 2 underwent rotation as well as translation. The 3D motion was set up in such a manner that the projected 2D optical flow could not be interpreted as resulting from pure translational motion.

Second, if subjects do use an implicit knowledge of theorem 1, the accuracy of their performance should depend on the correctness of the heuristic used to estimate

[1] I should note thal all the subjects were surprised by their good performance. They felt that the stimulus was ambiguous and that they were mostly guessing.

the location of the FOE as discussed in the previous section. This heuristic yields incorrect results for many instances of general 3D motion. In experiment 2, two types of 3-point 2-frame motion were used: one in which the estimation of the FOE using the above heuristic is correct, and one in which this estimation is wrong. If subjects rely on an implicit knowledge of theorem 1, their judgement should be mostly correct for the first type of motion, and mostly incorrect for the second type.

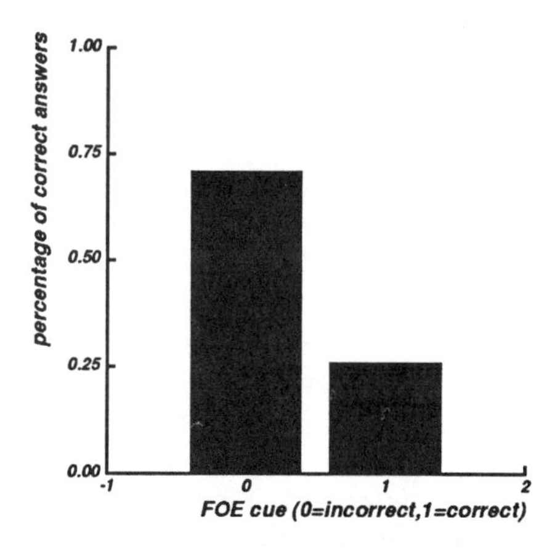

Figure 2: Experiment 2: three points in general motion. The same four subjects as in experiment 1 were shown two-frame sequences of back and forth motion that included 3D translation and rotation. The mean performance when the FOE heuristic (see text) was correct, 71%, was significantly above chance ($t = 5.71$, $p < 0.0001$). In comparison, the mean performance when the FOE heuristic was misleading, 26%, was significantly below chance ($t = -4.90$, $p < 0.0001$). The degree to which the motion could be mistakenly interpreted as pure translation was uncorrelated with performance ($r = 0.04$, $F(1,318) < 1$). The performance in experiment 2 was similar to that in experiment 1 (the difference was not significant $\chi^2 < 1$). In other words, the performance was as good under general motion as under pure translation.

Figure 2a describes the results of experiment 2. As in the first experiment, the subjects performed significantly above chance when the FOE estimation heuristic was correct. When the heuristic was misleading, they were as likely to be wrong as they were likely to be right in the correct heuristic condition. As predicted by the geometrical explanation to the first experiment, seeing general motion instead of pure translation did not seem to affect the performance.

5 LEARNING WITH A NEURAL NETWORK

Computation of qualitative structure from motion, outlined in section 2, can be supported by a biologically plausible architecture based on the application of a three-point hyperacuity operator, in parallel, in different directions around each point and over the entire visual field. Such a computation is particularly suitable to implementation by an artificial neural network. I have trained a Radial Basis Function (RBF) network (Moody & Darken, 1989; Poggio & Girosi, 1990) to identify the sign of Gaussian curvature of three moving points (represented by a coordinate vector of length 6). After a supervised learning phase in which the network was trained to produce the correct sign given examples of motion sequences, it consistently achieved a substantial success rate on novel inputs, for a wide range of parameters. Figure 3 shows the success rate (the percentage of correct answers) plotted against the number of examples used in the training phase.

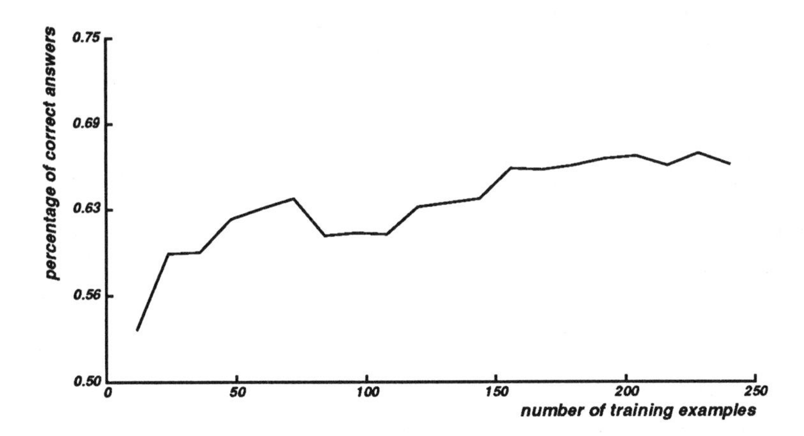

Figure 3: The correct performance rate of the RBF implementation vs. the number of examples in the training set.

6 SUMMARY

I have presented a qualitative approach to the problem of recovering object structure from motion information and discussed some of its computational, psychophysical and implementational aspects. The computation of qualitative shape, as represented by the sign of the Gaussian curvature, can be performed by a field of simple operators, in parallel over the entire image. The performance of a qualitative shape detection module, implemented by an artificial neural network, appears to be similar to the performance of human subjects in an identical task.

Acknowledgements

I thank H. Bülthoff, N. Cornelius, M. Dornay, S. Edelman, M. Fahle, S. Kirkpatrick, M. Ross and A. Shashua for their help. This research was done partly in the MIT AI Laboratory. It was supported by a Fairchild postdoctoral fellowship, and in part by grants from the office of Naval Research (N00014-88-k-0164), from the National Science Foundation (IRI-8719394 and IRI-8657824), and a gift from the James S. McDonnell Foundation to Professor Ellen Hildreth.

References

[1] E. Borjesson and C. von Hofsten. Visual perception of motion in depth: ap-

plication of a vector model to three-dot motion patterns. *Perception and Psychophysics*, 13:169–179, 1973.

[2] A. Bruss and B. K. P. Horn. Passive navigation. *Computer Vision, Graphics, and Image Processing*, 21:3–20, 1983.

[3] M. W. Fahle. Parallel, semi-parallel, and serial processing of visual hyperacuity. In *Proc. SPIE Conf. on Electronic Imaging: science and technology*, Santa Clara, CA, February 1990. to appear.

[4] E. C. Hildreth, N. M. Grzywacz, E. H. Adelson, and V. K. Inada. The perceptual buildup of three-dimensional structure from motion, 1989. Perception & Psychophysics, in press.

[5] J. J. Koenderink and A. J. van Doorn. Local structure of movement parallax of the plane. *Journal of the Optical Society of America*, 66:717–723, 1976.

[6] J. Moody and C. Darken. Fast learning in networks of locally tuned processing units. *Neural Computation*, 1:281–289, 1989.

[7] R. C. Nelson and J. Aloimonos. Using flow field divergence for obstacle avoidance: towards qualitative vision. In *Proceedings of the 2nd International Conference on Computer Vision*, pages 188–196, Tarpon Springs, FL, 1988. IEEE, Washington, DC.

[8] T. Poggio and F. Girosi. Regularization algorithms for learning that are equivalent to multilayer networks. *Science*, 247:978–982, 1990.

[9] T. Poggio and C. Koch. Ill–posed problems in early vision: from computational theory to analog networks. *Proceedings of the Royal Society of London B*, 226:303–323, 1985.

[10] R.Y. Tsai and T.S. Huang. Uniqueness and estimation of three dimensional motion parameters of rigid objects with curved surfaces. *IEEE Transactions on Pattern Analysis and Machine Intelligence*, 6:13–27, 1984.

[11] S. Ullman. Computational studies in the interpretation of structure and motion: summary and extension. In J. Beck, B. Hope, and A. Rosenfeld, editors, *Human and Machine Vision*. Academic Press, New York, 1983.

[12] S. Ullman. Maximizing rigidity: the incremental recovery of 3D structure from rigid and rubbery motion. *Perception*, 13:255–274, 1984.

[13] D. Weinshall. Direct computation of 3D shape and motion invariants. A.I. Memo No. 1131, Artificial Intelligence Laboratory, Massachusetts Institute of Technology, May 1989.

Optimal Sampling of Natural Images: A Design Principle for the Visual System?

William Bialek,[a,b] Daniel L. Ruderman,[a] and A. Zee[c]

[a]Department of Physics, and
Department of Molecular and Cell Biology
University of California at Berkeley
Berkeley, California 94720

[b]NEC Research Institute
4 Independence Way
Princeton, New Jersey 08540

[c]Institute for Theoretical Physics
University of California at Santa Barbara
Santa Barbara, California 93106

Abstract

We formulate the problem of optimizing the sampling of natural images using an array of linear filters. Optimization of information capacity is constrained by the noise levels of the individual channels and by a penalty for the construction of long-range interconnections in the array. At low signal-to-noise ratios the optimal filter characteristics correspond to bound states of a Schrödinger equation in which the signal spectrum plays the role of the potential. The resulting optimal filters are remarkably similar to those observed in the mammalian visual cortex and the retinal ganglion cells of lower vertebrates. The observed scale invariance of natural images plays an essential role in this construction.

1 Introduction

Under certain conditions the visual system is capable of performing extremely efficient signal processing [1]. One of the major theoretical issues in neural computation is to understand how this efficiency is reached given the constraints imposed by the biological hardware. Part of the problem [2] is simply to give an informative representation of the visual world using a limited number of neurons, each of which has a limited information capacity. The information capacity of the visual system is determined in part by the spatial transfer characteristics, or "receptive fields," of the individual cells. From a theoretical point of view we can ask if there exists an optimal choice for these receptive fields, a choice which maximizes the information transfer through the system given the hardware constraints. We show that this optimization problem has a simple formulation which allows us to use the intuition developed through the variational approach to quantum mechanics.

In general our approach leads to receptive fields which are quite unlike those observed for cells in the visual cortex. In particular orientation selectivity is not a generic prediction. The optimal filters, however, depend on the statistical properties of the images we are trying to sample. Natural images have a symmetry — scale invariance [4] — which saves the theory: The optimal receptive fields for sampling of *natural* images are indeed orientation selective and bear a striking resemblance to observed receptive field characteristics in the mammalian visual cortex as well as the retinal ganglion of lower vertebrates.

2 General Theoretical Formulation

We assume that images are defined by a scalar field $\phi(\mathbf{x})$ on a two dimensional surface with coordinates $\mathbf{x}$. This image is sampled by an array of cells whose outputs Y_n are given by

$$Y_n = \int d^2x F(\mathbf{x} - \mathbf{x}_n)\phi(\mathbf{x}) + \eta_n, \tag{1}$$

where the cell is loacted at site $\mathbf{x}_n$, its spatial transfer function or receptive field is defined by F, and η is an independent noise source at each sampling point. We will assume for simplicity that the noise source is Gaussian, with $\langle\eta^2\rangle = \sigma^2$. Our task is to find the receptive field F which maximizes the information provided about ϕ by the set of outputs $\{Y_n\}$.

If the field ϕ is itself chosen from a stationary Gaussian distribution then the information carried by the $\{Y_n\}$ is given by [3]

$$I = \frac{1}{2\ln 2}\mathrm{Tr}\ln\left[\delta_{nm} + \frac{1}{\sigma^2}\int\frac{d^2k}{(2\pi)^2}e^{i\mathbf{k}\cdot(\mathbf{x}_n-\mathbf{x}_m)}|\tilde{F}(\mathbf{k})|^2 S(\mathbf{k})\right], \tag{2}$$

where $S(\mathbf{k})$ is the power spectrum of the signals,

$$S(\mathbf{k}) = \int d^2y e^{-i\mathbf{k}\cdot\mathbf{y}}\langle\phi(\mathbf{x}+\mathbf{y})\phi(\mathbf{x})\rangle, \tag{3}$$

and $\tilde{F}(\mathbf{k}) = \int d^2x e^{-i\mathbf{k}\cdot\mathbf{x}} F(\mathbf{x})$ is the receptive field in momentum (Fourier) space.

At low signal-to-noise ratios (large σ^2) we have

$$I \approx \frac{N}{2\ln 2\sigma^2} \int \frac{d^2k}{(2\pi)^2} |\tilde{F}(\mathbf{k})|^2 S(\mathbf{k}), \tag{4}$$

where N is the total number of cells.

To make our definition of the noise level σ meaningful we must constrain the total "gain" of the filters F. One simple approach is to normalize the functions F in the usual L^2 sense,

$$\int d^2x F^2(\mathbf{x}) = \int \frac{d^2k}{(2\pi)^2} |\tilde{F}(\mathbf{k})|^2 = 1. \tag{5}$$

If we imagine driving the system with spectrally white images, this condition fixes the total signal power passing through the filter.

Even with normalization, optimization of information capacity is still not well-posed. To avoid pathologies we must constrain the scale of variations in $\mathbf{k}$–space. This makes sense biologically since we know that sharp features in $\mathbf{k}$–space can be achieved only by introducing long-range interactions in real space, and cells in the visual system typically have rather local interconnections. We implement this constraint by introducing a penalty proportional to the mean square spatial extent of the receptive field,

$$\int d^2x\, x^2 F^2(x) = \int \frac{d^2k}{(2\pi)^2} |\nabla_k \tilde{F}(\mathbf{k})|^2. \tag{6}$$

With all the constraints we find that, at low signal to noise ratio, our optimization problem becomes that of minimizing the functional

$$C[\tilde{F}] = (1/2)\alpha \int \frac{d^2k}{(2\pi)^2} |\nabla_k \tilde{F}(\mathbf{k})|^2 \;-\; \frac{1}{2\ln 2\sigma^2} \int \frac{d^2k}{(2\pi)^2} |\tilde{F}(\mathbf{k})|^2 S(\mathbf{k}) \;-\; \Lambda \int \frac{d^2k}{(2\pi)^2} |\tilde{F}(\mathbf{k})|^2, \tag{7}$$

where Λ is a Lagrange multiplier and α measures the strength of the locality constraint. The optimal filters are then solutions of the variational equation,

$$-\frac{\alpha}{2}\nabla_k^2 \tilde{F}(\mathbf{k}) - \frac{1}{2\ln 2\sigma^2} S(\mathbf{k})\tilde{F}(\mathbf{k}) = \Lambda \tilde{F}(\mathbf{k}). \tag{8}$$

We recognize this as the Schrödinger equation for a particle moving in $\mathbf{k}$-space, in which the mass $M = \hbar^2/\alpha$, the potential $V(\mathbf{k}) = -S(\mathbf{k})/2\ln 2\sigma^2$, and Λ is the energy eigenvalue. Since we are interested in normalizable F, we are restricted to bound states, and the optimal filter is just the bound state wave function.

There are in general several optimal filters, corresponding to the different bound states. Each of these filters gives the same value for the total cost function $C[\tilde{F}]$ and hence is equally "good" in this context. Thus each sampling point should be served by a set of filters rather than just one. Indeed, in the visual cortex one finds a given region of the visual field being sampled by many cells with different spatial frequency and orientation selectivities.

3 A Near-Fatal Flaw and its Resolution

If the signal spectra $S(\mathbf{k})$ are isotropic, so that features appear at all orientations across the visual field, all of the bound states of the corresponding Schrödinger equation are eigenstates of angular momentum. But real visual neurons have receptive fields with a single optimal orientation, not the multiple optima expected if the filters F correspond to angular momentum eigenstates. One would like to combine different angular momentum eigenfunctions to generate filters which respond to localized regions of orientation. In general, however, the different angular momenta are associated with different energy eigenvalues and hence it is impossible to form linear combinations which are still solutions of the variational problem.

We *can* construct receptive fields which are localized in orientation if there is some extra symmetry or accidental degeneracy which allows the existence of equal-energy states with different angular momenta. If we believe that real receptive fields are the solutions of our variational problem, it must be the case that the signal spectrum $S(\mathbf{k})$ for natural images possesses such a symmetry.

Recently Field [4] has measured the power spectra of several natural scenes. As one might expect from discussions of "fractal" landscapes, these spectra are scale invariant, with $S(\mathbf{k}) = A/|\mathbf{k}|^2$. It is easy to see that the corresponding quantum mechanics problem is a bit sick — the energy is not bounded from below. In the present context, however, this sickness is a saving grace. The equivalent Schrödinger equation is

$$-\frac{\alpha}{2}\nabla_k^2 \tilde{F}(\mathbf{k}) - \frac{A}{2\ln 2\sigma^2|\mathbf{k}|^2}\tilde{F}(\mathbf{k}) = \Lambda\tilde{F}(\mathbf{k}). \tag{9}$$

If we take $\mathbf{q} = (\sqrt{2|\Lambda|/\alpha})\mathbf{k}$, then for bound states ($\Lambda < 0$) we find

$$\nabla_q^2 \tilde{F}(\mathbf{q}) + \frac{B}{|\mathbf{q}|^2}\tilde{F}(\mathbf{q}) = \tilde{F}(\mathbf{q}), \tag{10}$$

with $B = A/\ln 2\sigma^2$. Thus we see that the energy Λ can be scaled away; there is no quantization condition. We are free to choose any value of Λ, but for each such value there are several angular momentum states. Since they correspond to the same energy, superpositions of these states are also solutions of the original variational problem. The scale invariance of natural images is the symmetry we need in order to form localized receptive fields.

4 Predicting Receptive Fields

To solve Eq. (9) we find it easier to transform back to real space. The result is

$$r^2(1+r^2)\frac{\partial^2 F}{\partial r^2} + r(1+5r^2)\frac{\partial F}{\partial r} + [r^2(4+B+\partial^2/\partial\phi^2) + \partial^2/\partial\phi^2]F = 0, \tag{11}$$

where ϕ is the angular variable and $r = (\sqrt{\alpha/2|\Lambda|})|\mathbf{x}|$. Angular momentum states $F_m \sim e^{im\phi}$ have the asymptotic $F_m(r << 1) \sim r^{\pm m}$, $F_m(r >> 1) \sim r^{\lambda_\pm(m)}$, with $\lambda_\pm(m) = -2 \pm \sqrt{m^2 - B}$. We see that for $m^2 < B$ the solutions are oscillatory functions of r, since λ has an imaginary part. For $m^2 > B + 4$ the solution can diverge as r becomes large, and in this case we must be careful to choose solutions which are regular both at the origin and at infinity if we are to maintain the constraint in Eq. (5). Numerically we find that there are no such solutions; the functions which behave as $r^{+|m|}$ near the origin diverge at large r if $m^2 > B + 4$. We conclude that for a given value of B, which measures the signal-to-noise ratio, there exists a finite set of angular momentum states; these states can then be superposed to give receptive fields with localized angular sensitivity.

In fact *all* linear combinations of $m-$states are solutions to the variational problem at low signal to noise ratio, so the precise form of orientation tuning is not determined. If we continue our expansion of the information capacity in powers of the signal-to-noise ratio we find terms which will select different linear combinations of the $m-$states and hence determine the precise orientation selectivity. These higher-order terms, however, involve multi-point correlation functions of the image. At the lowest SNR, corresponding to the first term in our expansion, we are sensitive only to the two-point function (power spectrum) of the signal ensemble, which carries no information about angular correlations. A truly predictive theory of orientation tuning must thus rest on measurements of angular correlations in natural images; as far as we know such measurements have not been reported.

Even without knowing the details of the higher-order correlation functions we can make some progress. To begin, it is clear that at very small B orientation selectivity is impossible since there are only $m = 0$ solutions. This is the limit of very low SNR, or equivalently very strong constraints on the locality of the receptive field (large α above). The circularly symmetric receptive fields that one finds in this limit are center-surround in structure, with the surround becoming more prominent as the signal-to-noise ratio is increased. These predictions are in qualitative accord with what one sees in the mammalian retina, which is indeed extremely local — receptive field centers for foveal ganglion cells may consist of just a single cone photoreceptor. As one proceeds to the the cortex the constraints of locality are weaker and orientation selectivity becomes possible. Similarly in lower vertebrates there is a greater range of lateral connectivity in the retina itself, and hence orientation selectivity is possible at the level of the ganglion cell.

To proceed further we have explored the types of receptive fields which can be produced by superposing $m-$states at a given value of B. We consider for the moment only even-symmetric receptive fields, so we add all terms in phase. One such receptive field is shown in Fig. 1, together with experimental results for a simple cell in the primary visual cortex of monkeys [5]. It is clear that we can obtain reasonable correspondence between theory and experiment. Obviously we have made no detailed "fit" to the data, and indeed we are just beginning a quantitative comparison of theory with experiment. Much of the arbitrariness in the construction of Fig. 1 will be removed once we have control over the higher terms in the SNR expansion, as described above.

It is interesting that, at low SNR, there is no preferred value for the length scale. Thus the optimal system may choose to sample images at many different scales and at different scales in different regions of the image. The experimental variability in spatial frequency tuning from cell to cell may thus not represent biological sloppiness but rather the fact that any peak spatial frequency constitutes an optimal filter in the sense defined here.

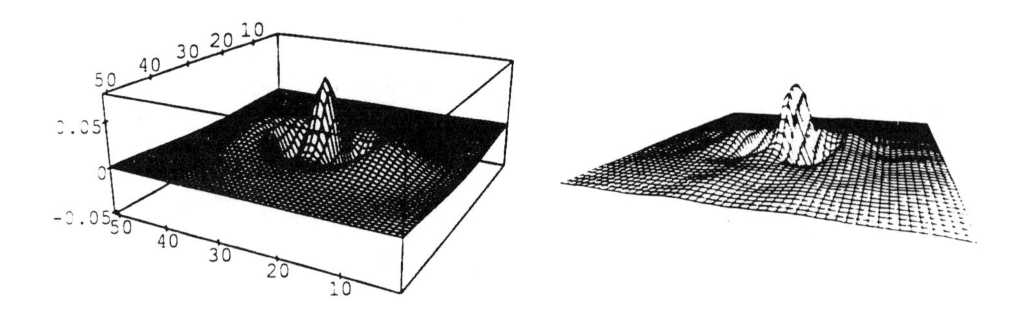

Figure 1: Model (left) and monkey (right) receptive fields. Monkey RF is from reference [5].

5 Discussion

The selectivity of cortical neurons for orientation and spatial frequency are among the best known facts about the visual system. Not surprisingly there have been many attempts to derive these features from some theoretical perspective. One approach is to argue that such selectivity provides a natural preprocessing stage for more complex computations. A very different view is that the observed organization of the cortex is a consequence of developmental rules, but this approach does not address the computational function which may be expressed by cortical organization. Finally several authors have considered the possibility that cortical receptive fields are in some sense optimal, so that they can be predicted from a variational principle [6, 7, 8]. Clearly we have adopted this last hypothesis; the issue is whether one can make a compelling argument for any particular variational principle.

Optimization of information capacity seems like a very natural principle to apply in the early stages of visual processing. As we have emphasized, this principle must be supplemented by a knowledge of hardware constraints and of image statistics. Different authors have made different choices, especially for the constraints. Different formulations, however, may be related — optimization of information transfer at some fixed "gain" of the receptive fields is equivalent, through a Legendre transformation, to minimization of the redundancy at fixed information transfer, a problem discussed by Atick and Redlich [8]. This latter approach has given very successful predictions for the structure of ganglion cell receptive fields in cat and monkey, although there are still some arbitrary parameters to be determined. It is our hope that these ideas of receptive fields as solutions to variational problems can be given more detailed tests in the lower vertebrate retinas, where it is possible to characterize signals and noise at each of three layers of processing cicuitry.

As far as we know our work is unique in that the statistics of natural images, is an essential component of the theory. Indeed the scale invariance of natural images plays a decisive role in our prediction of orientation selectivity; other classes of signals would result in qualitatively different receptive fields. We find this direct linkage between the properties of natural images and the architecture of natural computing systems to be extremely attractive. The semi-quantitative correspondence between predicted and observed receptive fields (Fig. 1) suggests that we have the kernel of a truly predictive theory for visual processing.

Acknowledgements

We thank K. DeValois, R. DeValois, J. D. Jackson, and N. Socci for helpful discussions. Work at Berkeley was supported in part by the National Science Foundation through a Presidential Young Investigator Award (to WB), supplemented by funds from Sun Microsystems and Cray Research, and by the Fannie and John Hertz Foundation through a graduate fellowship (to DLR). Work in Santa Barbara was supported in part by the NSF through Grant No. PHY82-17853, supplemented by funds from NASA.

References

[1] W. Bialek. In E. Jen, editor, *1989 Lectures in Complex Systems, SFI Studies in the Sciences of Complexity, Lect. Vol. II*, pages 513–595. Addison-Wesley, Menlo Park, CA, 1990.

[2] H. B. Barlow. In W. A. Rosenblith, editor, *Sensory Communication*, page 217. MIT Press, Cambridge, MA, 1961.

[3] C. E. Shannon and W. Weaver. *The Mathematical Theory of Communication*. University of Illinois Press, Urbana, IL, 1949.

[4] D. Field. *J. Opt. Soc. Am.*, 4:2379, 1987.

[5] M. A. Webster and R. L. DeValois. *J. Opt. Soc. Am.*, 2:1124–1132, 1985.

[6] B. Sakitt and H. B. Barlow. *Biol. Cybern.*, 43:97–108, 1982.

[7] R. Linsker. In D. Touretzky, editor, *Advances in Neural Information Processing 1*, page 186. Morgan Kaufmann, San Mateo, CA, 1989.

[8] J. J. Atick and A. N. Redlich. *Neural Computation*, 2:308, 1990

A VLSI Neural Network for Color Constancy

Andrew Moore
Computation and Neural Systems Program, 116-81
California Institute of Technology
Pasadena, CA 91125

Geoffrey Fox*
Dept. of Physics
California Institute of Technology
Pasadena, CA 91125

John Allman
Dept. of Biology, 216-76
California Institute of Technology
Pasadena, CA 91125

Rodney Goodman
Dept. of Electrical Engineering, 116-81
California Institute of Technology
Pasadena, CA 91125

Abstract

A system for color correction has been designed, built, and tested successfully; the essential components are three custom chips built using subthreshold analog CMOS VLSI. The system, based on Land's Retinex theory of color constancy, produces colors similar in many respects to those produced by the visual system. Resistive grids implemented in analog VLSI perform the smoothing operation central to the algorithm at video rates. With the electronic system, the strengths and weaknesses of the algorithm are explored.

1 A MODEL FOR COLOR CONSTANCY

Humans have the remarkable ability to perceive object colors as roughly constant even if the color of the illumination is varied widely. Edwin Land, founder of the Polaroid Corporation, models the computation that results in this ability as three identical center-surround operations performed independently in three color planes, such as red, green, and blue (Land, 1986). The basis for this model is as follows.

Consider first an array of grey papers with different reflectances. (Land designated these arrays *Mondrians*, since they resemble the works of the Dutch painter Piet

*Present address: Dept. of Physics, Syracuse University, Syracuse, NY 13244

Mondrian.) Land illuminated a Mondrian with a gradient of illumination, ten times more bright at the top than at the bottom, so that the flux reaching the eye from a dark grey patch at top was identical to the flux from a light grey patch at bottom. Subjects reported that the top paper was dark grey and the bottom paper was light grey. Land accounted for this with a center minus surround model. At each point in an image, the incoming light is compared to a spatial average of light in the neighborhood of the point in question. Near the top of the Mondrian, the abundance of white is sensed and subtracted from the central sensor to normalize the central reading with respect to neighboring values, weighted with distance; near the bottom, the abundance of dark is sensed and used to correct the central reading. Land proposed that the weighting function of the surround is a monotonic decreasing function of distance, such as $1/r^2$.

In earlier work, similar experiments were carried out with color Mondrians (Land, 1977; McCann *et. al.*, 1976). However, instead of varying the intensity of illumination, Land and his colleagues varied the *color* of the illumination. The color of patches in a Mondrian remained nearly constant despite large changes in the illuminant color. This is the phenomenon of color constancy: the ability of observers to judge, under a wide variety of lighting conditions, the approximate reflectance or intrinsic color of objects. Land and his colleagues proposed a variety of different models for this phenomenon, collectively referred to as *Retinex* models. (The term Retinex was coined by Land since he was not sure whether the computation was going on in the retina, the cortex, or both.) In his most recent paper on the subject (Land, 1986), Land simply extended the black-and-white model to the three color dimensions. In each of three independent color planes, the color at a given point is compared to that of the points surrounding it, weighted as $1/r^2$.

2 EFFICIENT CALCULATION OF THE SURROUND

In practical terms, the Retinex algorithm corresponds to subtracting from an image a blurred version of itself. The distance weighting (type of blurring) Land proposes varies as $1/r^2$, so the operation is a center minus surround operation, where the surround is the center convolved with a $1/r^2$ kernel.

$$l'_{out,i}(x,y) = l'_i(x,y) - \log\left[l_i(x,y) \otimes \frac{1}{r^2}\right] \qquad r \neq 0 \tag{1}$$

where l_i is the signal or lightness in color plane i, and l'_i is the log of the signal. The logs are important since the signal is composed of illuminant times reflectance and the log of a product is a sum. By subtracting the blurred version of the image after taking logs, the illuminant is subtracted away in the ideal case (but see below).

This type of Retinex algorithm, then, has a psychophysical basis and sound computational underpinnings (Hurlbert, 1986). But the complexity is too great. Since the required surround is so large, such a convolution across an NxN pixel image entails on the order of N^4 operations. On a chip, this corresponds to explicit connections from each pixel to most if not all other pixels.

A similar operation can be carried out much more efficiently by switching from a convolution to a resistive grid calculation. The operations are similar since the weighting of neighboring points (Green's function) in a resistive grid decreases in the limit as the exponential of the distance from a given location on a resistive grid (Mead, 1989). Again, the kernel is a monotonic decreasing function. With this type of kernel, the operation in each Retinex (color channel) is

$$l'_{out,i}(x, y) = l'_i(x, y) - l'_i(x, y) \otimes e^{-\frac{|r|}{\lambda}} \tag{2}$$

where λ is the length constant or extent of weighting in the grid. Since the calculation is purely local, the complexity is reduced dramatically from $O(N^4)$ to $O(N^2)$. On a chip, a local computation corresponds to connections only between nearest-neighbor pixels.

3 EVALUATION OF THE ALGORITHM WITH COMPUTER SIMULATIONS

3.1 STRENGTHS AND WEAKNESSES OF THE ALGORITHM

Images of a subject holding a color poster were captured under fluorescent and incandescent light with an RGB video camera and a 24 bit frame grabber. First, the camera was adjusted so that the color looked good under fluorescent light. Next, without readjusting the camera, the fluorescents were turned off and the subject was illuminated with incandescent light. The results were unacceptable. The skin color was very red, and, since the incandescent lamp was not very bright, the background was lost in darkness. The two images were processed with the Land algorithm, using resistive grids to form the surround for subtraction. Details of the simulations and color images can be found in (Moore *et. al*, 1991). For the good, fluorescent image, the processing improved the image contrast somewhat. For the poor, incandescent image, the improvement was striking. Skin color was nearly normal, shadows were softened, and the the background was pulled out of darkness.

Computer simulation also pointed out two weaknesses of the algorithm: color Mach bands and the greying out of large monochromatic regions. Color Mach bands arise from this algorithm in the following way. Suppose that a strongly colored region, e.g. red, abuts a grey region. In the grey region, the surround subtracted at a given point has a strong red component. Therefore, after subtraction of the surround, a grey point is rendered as grey minus red, or equivalently, grey plus the complementary color of red, which is blue-green. Since the surround weighting decreases with distance, the points in the image closest to the red area are strongly tinged with blue-green, while points further away are less discolored. Induction of this sort in black-and-white images is known as the Mach band effect. An analogous induction effect in color is intrinsic to this algorithm.

Greying out of large colored areas is also an intrinsic weakness of the algorithm. The surrounds used in the simulations are quite large, with a length constant of nearly one third of the image. Often a large portion of an image is of a single color, e.g. a blue sky commonly fills the upper half of many natural scenes. In the sky region, the surround samples mostly blue, and with subtraction, blue is subtracted from blue, leaving a grey sky. This effect illustrates the essence of the algorithm

- it operates under a *grey world assumption.* The image for which this algorithm is ideal is richly colored, with reds and their green complements, yellows and their blue complements, and whites with their black complements. In such images, the large surround is sampling the color of a grey "mirror", since the sum of a color and its complement is grey. If this condition holds, the color subtracted when the surround is subtracted from a point in the image is the color of the illuminant; the surround acts as a dull grey mirror which reflects the illuminant. [Many color constancy schemes rely on this assumption; for a review see (Lennie and D'Zmura, 1988).]

3.2 AN EXTENSION TO THE LAND ALGORITHM

These two weaknesses arise from too much surround subtraction in solidly colored areas. One way the minimize the effects is to modulate the surround with a measure of image structure, which we call *edginess*, before subtraction. So, while for the original algorithm, the operation is $output = center - surround$, to ameliorate induction effects and lessen reliance on the grey world assumption, the surround weight should be modified pointwise. In particular, if edginess is given a value close to zero in homogeneous regions like the blue sky, and is given a value close to one in detailed areas, a better formulation is $output = center - surround \cdot edginess$. In this relation, the surround is effectively zeroed in smooth areas before it is subtracted, so that induction is diminished - more of the original color is retained. The extended algorithm, then, is a working compromise between color constancy via strict application of the grey world assumption and no color constancy at all. To compute a measure of spatial structure, the average magnitude of the first spatial derivatives is found at each point in each color plane is smoothed on a resistive grid; the output at a given point is multiplied with the surround value from the corresponding point of first resistive grid. In our simulations, the modified algorithm reduces (but does not eliminate) color Mach bands, and returns color to large monochromatic regions such as the the sky in the example image discussed above, at the cost of one additional resistive grid per color channel. This extension is not the whole answer, however. If a large region is highly textured (for example, if there is a flock of birds in the sky), edginess is high, the surround is subtracted at near full strength, and the sky is rendered grey in the textured region. This is a subject of continuing research. We implemented the original algorithm, but not this extension of it, using analog VLSI.

4 VLSI IMPLEMENTATION OF THE RETINEX ALGORITHM

To realize a real-time electronic system of video camera color correction based on Land's algorithm, the three color outputs of a video camera are fed onto three separate resistive grids built from subthreshold analog CMOS VLSI. Each 48 by 47 node resistive grid was built using 2 micron design rules and contains about 60,000 transistors. The circuit details within each pixel are similar to those of the analog retina (Mead, 1989); technical details of the system may be found in (Moore *et.al.*, 1991).

Computer simulations are quite costly in terms of time and disk storage. With a real-time system, it is possible to intensively investigate the strengths and weaknesses of this color correction algorithm quickly and economically.

4.1 REAL-TIME VERIFICATION OF ALGORITHM STRENGTHS

4.1.1 Dynamic range enhancement

A common problem with video imaging is that the range of an image exceeds the dynamic range of the camera sensors. For example, consider an image comprised of an indoor scene and an outdoor scene viewed through a window. The indoor illumination (e.g., direct sunlight) can be one thousand times or more brighter than the indoor illumination (e.g., artificial lights or indirect sunlight). A video camera can only capture one portion of the scene with fidelity. By opening up the camera iris so that a lot of light falls on the camera sensors, the indoor scene looks good, but the outdoor scene is awash in white. Conversely, by closing the camera iris so that less light falls on the camera sensors, the outdoor scene looks good, but the indoor scene is rendered as deep black.

In fact, the image information is often not lost in this troublesome situation. Most sensors are not linear, but instead have a response function that resembles a hyperbolic tangent. Rather than saturating at the extremes of the response range, most sensors compress information near those response extremes. With a center-surround processing stage following a camera, the information "squashed" near the camera range limits can be recovered. In extremely bright portions of an image, white is subtracted from white, "pulling" the signal toward the mid-range, so that details in that portion of the scene become defined. Similarly, in dark portions of the scene, dark is subtracted from dark and the details of the indoor portion of the example image are visible. Thus the Land algorithm as applied to video imaging can enhance the dynamic range of video cameras. [This strength of the algorithm was predicted from the similar capability of the (black-and-white) silicon retina (Mead, 1989) - it has a dynamic range that exceeds by far the range of conventional cameras since it incorporates light sensors and center-surround processing on one chip.]

4.1.2 Color constancy

For a richly colored scene, the Land algorithm can remove strongly colored illumination, with some qualifications. We constructed a color Mondrian with many differently colored patches of paper, and illuminated it with ordinary fluorescent light plus various colored lights. Under a wide range of conditions, the color of the Mondrian as viewed on a video monitor changes with the illumination while it looks fairly stable to an observer. After passing the images through the electronic color compensation system, the image is also fairly stable for a wide variety of illumination conditions. There is a significant difference, however, between what an observer sees and what the corrected camera image reports. The video images passed through the electronic implementation of the Land algorithm take on the illuminant somewhat in portions of the image that are brighter than average, and take on the complementary color of the illuminant in portions that are darker than average. For example, for a blue illumination, the raw video image looks bluer all over. The processed image changes in a different way. White patches are faintly blue (much less as compared to the raw image), and black patches (which remain black in the raw image) are tinged with yellow. There is psychophysical evidence that the same effects are noted by human observers (see Jameson and Hurvich, 1989, for a review), but they are much less pronounced than those produced by the Land algorithm in our experience. Still, the overall effect of constancy in the processed images is convincing as compared to the raw images.

4.2 REAL-TIME VERIFICATION OF ALGORITHM WEAKNESSES

4.2.1 Color Mach bands and greying of large regions

To our surprise, the color Mach band effect, explained above, is less pronounced than we expected; for many scenes the induction effects are not noticeable. It is possible to the see the Mach bands clearly by placing colored cards on a grey background - the complementary color of the card surrounds the card as a halo that diminishes with distance from the card.

Since the Retinex algorithm relies on the grey world assumption, the algorithm fails where this assumption fails to hold. With the real-time system, we have demonstrated this in many ways. For example, if the video camera is pointed at the color Mondrian and the hand of a Caucasian investigator (with a reddish skin tone) is slowly moved in front of the camera lens, the Mondrian in the background slowly grows more green. Green is the complementary color of red. Another example of practical importance is revealed by zooming in on a particular patch of the Mondrian. As more and more of the image is filled with this patch, the patch grows greyer and greyer, because the correction system subtracts the patch color from itself.

4.2.2 Scene dependence of color constancy

As described above, we were impressed with this algorithm after simulating it on a digital computer. The skin tone of a subject, deeply reddened by incandescent light, was dramatically improved by the algorithm. In the computer study, the subject's face was, by accident rather than design, just in the middle of a large white patch and a large black patch. The electronic system yields perfect constancy of skin tone with this configuration also, but not for an arbitrary configuration. In short, the color constancy afforded by this algorithm is scene dependent; to consistently produce perfect color constancy of an object with the real-time system, it is necessary to place the object carefully within a scene. We are still investigating this weakness of the algorithm. Whether it is camera dependent (i.e., the result of camera nonlinearities) remains to be seen.

5 Conclusion

After studying the psychophysics and the computational issues in color constancy, encouraging preliminary results for a particular version of Land's Retinex algorithm were obtained in computer simulation. In order to study the algorithm intensively, an electronic system was developed; the system uses three resistive grids built from subthreshold analog CMOS VLSI to form a blurred version of the image for subtraction from the original. It was found that the system produces images that are more constant, in a sense, than raw video images when the illuminant color varies. However, the constancy is more apparent than real; if absolute constancy of a particular object is desired, that object must be carefully placed in its surroundings. The real-time system allowed us to address this and other such practical issues of the algorithm for the first time.

Acknowledgements

We are grateful to many of our colleagues at Caltech and elsewhere for discussions and support in this endeavor. A.M. was supported by fellowships from the Parsons Foundation and the Pew Charitable Trust and by research assistantships from Office of Naval Research, the Joint Tactical Fusion Program and the Center for Research in Parallel Computation. We are grateful to DARPA for MOSIS fabrication services, and to Hewlett Packard for computing support in the Mead Lab. The California Institute of Technology has filed for a U.S. patent for this and other related work.

References

A. Hurlbert. (1986) Formal connections between lightness algorithms. *J. Opt. Soc. Am.* **A3**: 1684-1693.

D. Jameson & L.M. Hurvich (1989). Essay concerning color constancy. *Ann. Rev. Psychol.* **40**:1-22.

E.H. Land. (1977) The Retinex theory of color vision. *Scientific American* **237**:108-128.

E.H. Land. (1986) An alternative technique for the computation of the designator in the retinex theory of color vision. *Proc. Natl. Acad. Sci. USA* **83**:3078-3080.

P. Lennie & M. D'Zmura. (1988) Mechanisms of color vision. *CRC Crit. Rev. Neurobiol.* **3**(4):333-400.

J.J. McCann, S.P. McKee, & T.H. Taylor. (1976) Quantitative studies in Retinex theory. *Vision Res.* **16**:445-458.

C.A. Mead. (1989) *Analog VLSI and Neural Systems.* Reading, MA: Addison-Wesley.

A. Moore, J. Allman, & R. Goodman. (1991) A Real-time Neural System for Color Constancy. *IEEE Trans. Neural Networks* **2**(2) *In press.*

Optimal Filtering in the Salamander Retina

Fred Rieke[a,c], **W. Geoffrey Owen**[b] **and William Bialek**[a,b,c]

Departments of Physics[a] and Molecular and Cell Biology[b]
University of California
Berkeley, California 94720
and
NEC Research Institute[c]
4 Independence Way
Princeton, New Jersey 08540

Abstract

The dark-adapted visual system can count photons with a reliability limited by thermal noise in the rod photoreceptors — the processing circuitry between the rod cells and the brain is essentially noiseless and in fact may be close to optimal. Here we design an optimal signal processor which estimates the time-varying light intensity at the retina based on the rod signals. We show that the first stage of optimal signal processing involves passing the rod cell output through a linear filter with characteristics determined entirely by the rod signal and noise spectra. This filter is very general; in fact it is the first stage in any visual signal processing task at low photon flux. We identify the output of this first-stage filter with the intracellular voltage response of the bipolar cell, the first anatomical stage in retinal signal processing. From recent data on tiger salamander photoreceptors we extract the relevant spectra and make parameter-free, quantitative predictions of the bipolar cell response to a dim, diffuse flash. Agreement with experiment is essentially perfect. As far as we know this is the first successful predictive theory for neural dynamics.

1 Introduction

A number of biological sensory cells perform at a level which can be called optimal — their performance approaches limits set by the laws of physics [1]. In some cases the behavioral performance of an organism, not just the performance of the sensory cells, also approaches fundamental limits. Such performance indicates that neural computation can reach a level of precision where the reliability of the computed output is limited by noise in the sensory input rather than by inefficiencies in the processing algorithm or noise in the processing hardware [2]. These observations suggest that we study algorithms for optimal signal processing. If we can make the notion of optimal processing precise we will have the elements of a predictive (and hence unequivocally testable) theory for what the nervous system *should* compute. This is in contrast to traditional modeling approaches which involve adjustment of free parameters to fit experimental data.

To further develop these ideas we consider the vertebrate retina. Since the classic experiments of Hecht, Shlaer and Pirenne we have known that the dark-adapted visual system can count small numbers of photons [3]. Recent experiments confirm Barlow's suggestion [4,5] that the reliability of behavioral decision making reaches limits imposed by dark noise in the photoreceptors due to thermal isomerization of the photopigment [6]. If dark-adapted visual performance is limited by thermal noise in the sensory cells then the subsequent layers of signal processing circuitry must be extremely reliable. Rather than trying to determine precise limits to reliability, we follow the approach introduced in [7] and use the notion of "optimal computation" to design the optimal processor of visual stimuli. These theoretical arguments result in parameter-free predictions for the dynamics of signal transfer from the rod photoreceptor to the bipolar cell, the first stage in visual signal processing. We compare these predictions directly with measurements on the intact retina of the tiger salamander *Ambystoma tigrinum* [8,9].

2 Design of the optimal processor

All of an organism's knowledge of the visual world derives from the currents $I_{\mathrm{n}}(t)$ flowing in the photoreceptor cells (labeled n). Visual signal processing consists of estimating various aspects of the visual scene from observation of these currents. Furthermore, to be of use to the organism these estimates must be carried out in real time. The general problem then is to formulate an optimal strategy for estimating some functional $G[R(\mathbf{r},t)]$ of the time and position dependent photon arrival rate $R(\mathbf{r},t)$ from real time observation of the currents $I_{\mathrm{n}}(t)$.

We can make considerable analytic progress towards solving this general problem using probabilistic methods [7,2]. Start by writing an expression for the probability of the functional $G[R(\mathbf{r},t)]$ conditional on the currents $I_{\mathrm{n}}(t)$, $P\{G[R(\mathbf{r},t)]|I_{\mathrm{n}}(t)\}$. Expanding for low signal-to-noise ratio (SNR) we find that the first term in the expansion of $P\{G|I\}$ depends only on a filtered version of the rod currents,

$$P\{G[R(\mathbf{r},t)]|I_{\mathrm{n}}(t)\} = \Im_G[F * I_{\mathrm{n}}] + \text{higher order corrections}, \quad (1)$$

where $*$ denotes convolution; the filter F depends only on the signal and noise characteristics of the photoreceptors, as described below. Thus the estimation task divides naturally into two stages — a universal "pre-processing" stage and a task-dependent stage. The universal stage is independent both of the stimulus $R(\mathbf{r},t)$ and of the particular functional $G[R]$ we wish to estimate. Intuitively this separation makes sense; in conventional signal processing systems detector outputs are first

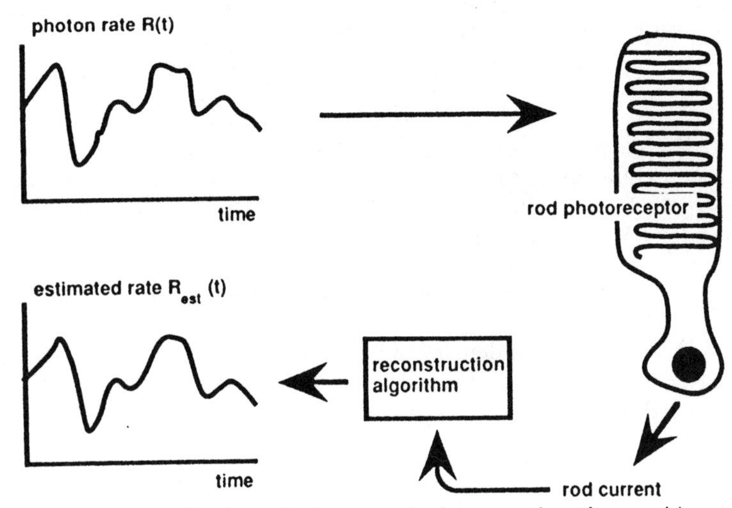

Figure 1: Schematic view of photon arrival rate estimation problem.

processed by a filter whose shape is motivated by general SNR considerations. Thus the view of retinal signal processing which emerges from this calculation is a pre-processing or "cleaning up" stage followed by more specialized processing stages. We emphasize that this separation is a mathematical fact, not a model we have imposed.

To fill in some of the details of the calculation we turn to the simplest example of the estimation tasks discussed above — estimation of the photon arrival rate itself (Fig. 1): Photons from a light source are incident on a small patch of retina at a time-varying rate $R(t)$, resulting in a current $I(t)$ in a particular rod cell. The theoretical problem is to determine the optimal strategy for estimating $R(t)$ based on the currents $I(t)$ in a small collection of rod cells. With an appropriate definition of "optimal" we can pose the estimation problem mathematically and look for analytic or numerical solutions. One approach is the conditional probability calculation discussed above [7]. Alternatively we can solve this problem using functional methods. Here we outline the functional calculation.

Start by writing the estimated rate as a filtered version of the rod currents:

$$\begin{aligned} R_{\text{est}}(t) &= \int d\tau F_1(\tau) I(t-\tau) \\ &+ \int d\tau \int d\tau' F_2(\tau,\tau') I(t-\tau) I(t-\tau') + \cdots . \end{aligned} \tag{2}$$

In the low SNR limit the rods respond linearly (they count photons), and we expect that the linear term dominates the series (2). We then solve analytically for the filter $F_1(\tau)$ which minimizes $\chi^2 = \langle \int dt\, |R(t) - R_{\text{est}}(t)|^2 \rangle$ — *i.e.* the filter which satisfies $\delta\chi^2/\delta F_1(\tau) = 0$. The averages $\langle \cdots \rangle$ are taken over the ensemble of stimuli

$R(t)$. The result of this optimization is*

$$F_1(\tau) = \int \frac{d\omega}{2\pi} e^{-i\omega\tau} \frac{\left\langle \tilde{R}(\omega)\tilde{I}^*(\omega)\right\rangle}{\left\langle |\tilde{I}(\omega)|^2\right\rangle}. \quad (3)$$

In the photon counting regime the rod currents are described as a sum of impulse responses $I_0(t-t_\mu)$ occuring at the photon arrival times t_μ, plus a noise term $\delta I(t)$. Expanding for low SNR we find

$$F_1(\tau) = \int \frac{d\omega}{2\pi} e^{-i\omega\tau} S_R(\omega) \frac{\tilde{I}_0^*(\omega)}{S_I(\omega)} + \cdots, \quad (4)$$

where $S_R(\omega)$ is the spectral density of fluctuations in the photon arrival rate, $\tilde{I}_0(\omega)$ is the Fourier transform of $I_0(t)$, and $S_I(\omega)$ is the spectral density of current noise $\delta I(t)$ in the rod.

The filter (4) naturally separates into two distinct stages: A "first" stage

$$\tilde{F}_{\text{bip}}(\omega) \equiv \tilde{I}_0^*(\omega)/S_1(\omega) \quad (5)$$

which depends only on the signal and noise properties of the rod cell, and a "second" stage $S_R(\omega)$ which contains our *a priori* knowledge of the stimulus. The first stage filter is the matched filter given the rod signal and noise characteristics; each frequency component in the output of this filter is weighted according to its input SNR.

Recall from the probabilistic argument above that optimal estimation of some arbitrary aspect of the scene, such as motion, also results in a separation into two processing stages. Specifically, estimation of *any* functional of light intensity involves only a filtered version of the rod currents. This filter is precisely the universal filter $F_{\text{bip}}(\tau)$ defined in (5). This result makes intuitive sense since the first stage of filtering is simply "cleaning up" the rod signals prior to subsequent computation. Intuitively we expect that this filtering occurs at an early stage of visual processing. The first opportunity to filter the rod signals occurs in the transfer of signals between the rod and bipolar cells; we identify the transfer function between these cells with the first stage of our optimal filter. More precisely we identify the intracellular voltage response of the bipolar cell with the output of the filter $F_{\text{bip}}(\tau)$. In response to a dim flash of light at $t = 0$ the average bipolar cell voltage response should then be

$$V_{\text{bip}}(t) \propto \int d\tau\, F_{\text{bip}}(\tau) I_0(t-\tau). \quad (6)$$

Nowhere in this prediction process do we insert any information about the bipolar response — the shape of our prediction is governed entirely by signal and noise properties of the rod cell and the theoretical principle of optimality.

3 Extracting the filter parameters and predicting the bipolar response

To complete our prediction of the dim flash bipolar response we extract the rod single photon current $I_0(t)$ and rod current noise spectrum $S_I(\omega)$ from experimen-

*We define the Fourier Transform as $\tilde{f}(\omega) = \int dt e^{+i\omega t} f(t)$.

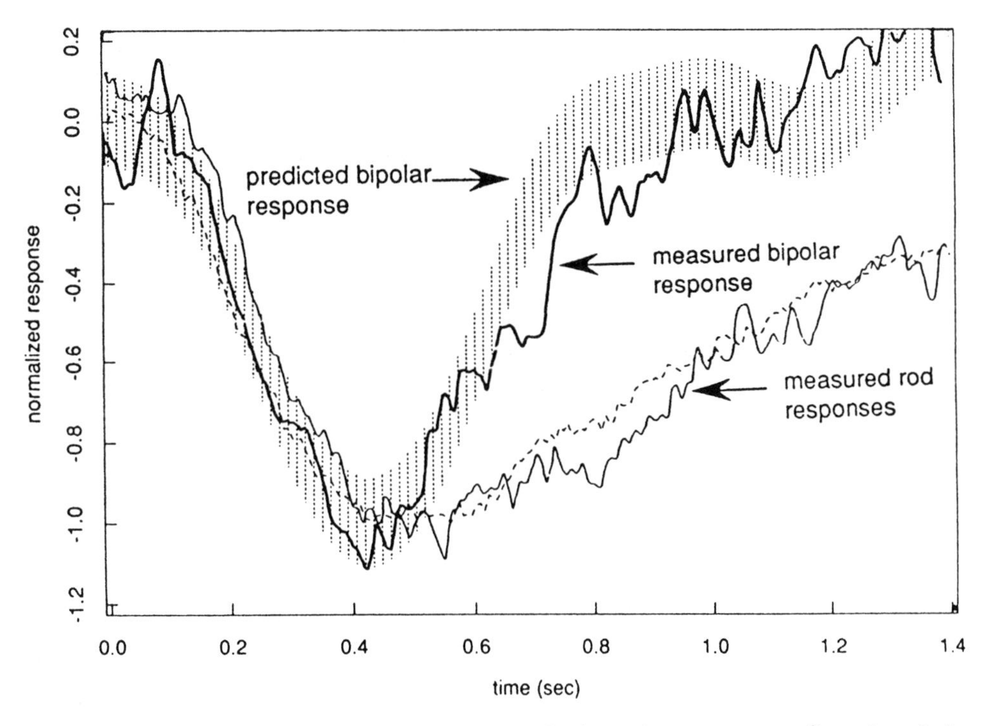

Figure 2: Comparison of predicted dim flash bipolar voltage response (based entirely on rod signal and noise characteristics) and measured bipolar voltage response. For reference we show rod voltage responses from two different cells which show the typical variations from cell to cell and thus indicate the variations we should expect in different bipolar cells. The measured responses are averages of many presentations of a diffuse flash occurring at $t = 0$ and resulting in the absorption of an average of about 5 photons in the rod cell. The errors bars are one standard deviation.

tal data. To compare our prediction directly with experiment we must obtain the rod characteristics under identical recording conditions as the bipolar measurement. This excludes suction pipette measurements which measure the currents directly, but effect the rod response dynamics [10,11]. The bipolar voltage response is measured intracellularly in the eyecup preparation [8]; our approach is to use intracellular voltage recordings to characterize the rod network and thus convert voltages to currents, as in [12]. This approach to the problem may seem overly complicated — why did we formulate the theory in terms of currents and not voltages? It is important we formulate our theory in terms of the *individual* rod signal and noise characteristics. The electrical coupling between rod cells in the retina causes the voltage noise in nearby rods to be correlated; each rod, however, independently injects current noise into the network.

The impedances connecting adjacent rod cells, the impedance of the rod cell itself and the spatial layout and connections between rods determine the relationship between currents and voltages in the network. The rods lie nearly on a square lattice with lattice constant 20 μm. Using this result we extract the impedances from two independent experiments [12]. Once we have the impedances we "decorrelate" the voltage noise to calculate the uncorrelated current noise. We also convert the measured single photon voltage response to the corresponding current $I_0(t)$. It is important to realize that the impedance characteristics of the rod network are experimentally determined, and are not in any sense free parameters!

After completing these calculations the elements of our bipolar prediction are obtained under identical conditions to the experimental bipolar response, and we can make a direct comparison between the two; *there are no free parameters in this prediction.* As shown in the Fig. 2, the predicted bipolar response (6) is in excellent agreement with the measured response; all deviations are well within the error bars.

4 Concluding remarks

We began by posing a theoretical question: How can we best recover the photon arrival rate from observations of the rod signals? The answer, in the form of a linear filter which we apply to the rod current, divides into two stages — a stage which is matched to the rod signal and noise characteristics, and a stage which depends on the particular characteristics of the photon source we are observing. The first-stage filter in fact is the universal pre-processor for *all* visual processing tasks at low SNR. We identified this filter with the rod-bipolar transfer function, and based on this hypothesis predicted the bipolar response to a dim, diffuse flash. Our prediction agrees extremely well with experimental bipolar responses. We emphasize once more that this is not a "model" of the bipolar cell; in fact there is nothing in our theory about the physical properties of bipolar cells. Rather our approach results in parameter-free predictions of the *computational* properties of these cells from the general theoretical principle of optimal computation. As far as we know this is the first successful quantitative prediction from a theory of neural computation.

Thus far our results are limited to the dark-adapted regime; however the theoretical analysis presented here depends only on low SNR. This observation suggests a follow-up experiment to test the role of adaptation in the rod-bipolar transfer function. If the retina is first adapted to a constant background illumination and then shown dim flashes on top of the background we can use the analysis presented here to predict the *adapted* bipolar response from the *adapted* rod impulse response and noise. Such an experiments would answer a number of interesting questions about retinal processing: (1) Does the processing remain optimal at higher light levels? (2) Does the bipolar cell still function as the universal pre-processor? (3) Do the rod and bipolar cells adapt together in such a way that the optimal first-stage filter remains unchanged, or does the rod-bipolar transfer function also adapt?

Can these ideas be extended to other systems, particularly spiking cells? A number of other signal processing systems exhibit nearly optimal performance [2]. One example we are currently studying is the extraction of movement information from the array of photoreceptor voltages in the insect compound eye [13]. In related work, Atick and Redlich [14] have argued that the receptive field characteristics of retinal ganglion cells can be quantitatively predicted from a principle of optimal encoding (see also [15]). A more general question we are currently pursuing is the efficiency of the coding of sensory information in neural spike trains. Our preliminary results indicate that the information rate in a spike train can be as high as 80% of the maximum information rate possible given the noise characteristics of spike generation [16]. From these examples we believe that "optimal performance" provides a general theoretical framework which can be used to predict the significant computational dynamics of cells in many neural systems.

Acknowledgments

We thank R. Miller and W. Hare for sharing their data and ideas, D. Warland and R. de Ruyter van Steveninck for helping develop many of the methods we have used in this analysis, and J. Atick, J. Hopfield and D. Tank for many helpful discussions. W. B. thanks the Aspen Center for Physics for the environment which catalyzed these discussions. Work at Berkeley was supported by the National Institutes of Health through Grant No. EY 03785 to WGO, and by the National Science Foundation through a Presidential Young Investigator Award to WB, supplemented by funds from Cray Research, Sun Microsystems, and the NEC Research Institute, and through a Graduate Fellowship to FR.

References

1. W. Bialek. *Ann. Rev. Biophys. Biophys. Chem.*, 16:455, 1987.
2. W. Bialek. In E. Jen, editor, *1989 Lectures in Complex Systems, SFI Studies in the Sciences of Complexity*, volume 2, pages 513–595. Addison-Wesley, Reading, Mass., 1990.
3. S. Hecht, S. Shlaer, and M. Pirenne. *J. Gen. Physiol.*, 25:819, 1942.
4. H. B. Barlow. *J. Opt. Soc. Am.*, 46:634, 1956.
5. H. B. Barlow. *Nature*, 334:296, 1988.
6. A.-C. Aho, K. Donner, C. Hydèn, L. O. Larsen, and T. Reuter. *Nature*, 324:348, 1988.
7. W. Bialek and W. Owen. *Biophys. J.*, in press.
8. W. A. Hare and W. G. Owen. *J. Physiol.*, 421:223, 1990.
9. M. Capovilla, W. A. Hare, and W. G. Owen. *J. Physiol.*, 391:125, 1987.
10. Denis Baylor, T. D. Lamb, and K.-W. Yau. *J. Physiol.*, 288:613–634, 1979.
11. D. Baylor, G. Matthews, and K. Yau. *J. Physiol.*, 309:591, 1980.
12. V. Torre and W. G. Owen. *Biophys. J.*, 41:305–324, 1983.
13. W. Bialek, F. Rieke, R. R. de Ruyter van Steveninck, and D. Warland. In D. Touretzky, editor, *Advances in Neural Information Processing Systems 2*, pages 36–43. Morgan Kaufmann, San Mateo, Ca., 1990.
14. J. J. Atick and N. Redlich. *Neural Computation*, 2:308, 1990.
15. W. Bialek, D. Ruderman, and A. Zee. In D. Touretzky, editor, *Advances in Neural Information Processing Systems 3*. Morgan Kaufmann, San Mateo, Ca., 1991.
16. F. Rieke, W. Yamada, K. Moortgat, E. R. Lewis, and W. Bialek. *Proceedings of the 9th International Symposium on Hearing*, 1991.

A four neuron circuit accounts for change sensitive inhibition in salamander retina

Jeffrey L. Teeters
Lawrence Livermore Lab
PO Box 808, L-426
Livermore CA 94550

Frank H. Eeckman
Lawrence Livermore Lab
PO Box 808, L-270
Livermore CA 94550

Frank S. Werblin
UC-Berkeley
Room 145, LSA
Berkeley CA 94720

Abstract

In salamander retina, the response of On-Off ganglion cells to a central flash is reduced by movement in the receptive field surround. Through computer simulation of a 2-D model which takes into account their anatomical and physiological properties, we show that interactions between four neuron types (two bipolar and two amacrine) may be responsible for the generation and lateral conductance of this change sensitive inhibition. The model shows that the four neuron circuit can account for previously observed movement sensitive reductions in ganglion cell sensitivity and allows visualization and prediction of the spatio-temporal pattern of activity in change sensitive retinal cells.

1 INTRODUCTION

In the salamander retina, the response of transient (On-Off) ganglion cells to a central flash is reduced by movement in the receptive field surround (Werblin, 1972; Werblin & Copenhagen, 1974) as illustrated in Fig 1. This phenomenon requires the detection of change in the surround and the lateral transmission of this change sensitive inhibition to the ganglion cell dendrites. Wunk & Werblin (1979) showed that all ganglion cells receive change-sensitive inhibition, and Barnes & Werblin (1987) implicated a change-sensitive amacrine cell with widely distributed processes. The change-sensitivity of these amacrine cells has been traced in part to a truncation of synaptic release from the bipolar terminals that presumably drive them (Maguire *et al.*, 1989). The transient response of these amacrine cells, mediated by voltage gated currents (Barnes & Werblin, 1986; Eliasof *et al.*, 1987) also contributes to this change sensitivity.

These and other experiments suggest that interactions between four neuron types underlie both the change detection and the lateral transmission of inhibition (Werblin *et al.*, 1988; Maguire *et al.*, 1989). To test this hypothesis and make predictions that could be compared with later experiments we have constructed a computational model of the four neuron circuit and incorporated it into an overall model of the retina. This model allows us to simulate the effect of inhibition generated by the four neuron circuit on ganglion cells.

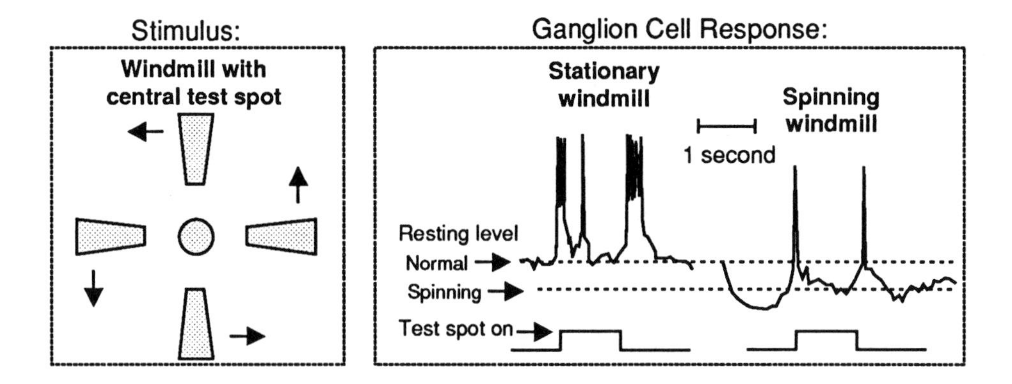

Figure 1: Change-Sensitive Inhibition. Data is from Werblin (1972).

2 IMPLEMENTING THE HYPOTHETICAL CIRCUIT

The proposed change-sensitive circuit (Werblin *et al.*, 1988; Maguire *et al.*, 1989) is reproduced in Figure 2. This is meant to describe a very local region of the retina where the receptive fields of the two bipolar cells are spatially overlapping. When a visual target enters this receptive field, the bipolar cells are both depolarized. The sustained bipolar cell activates the narrow field amacrine cell that, in turn feeds back to the synaptic terminal of the transient bipolar cell to truncate transmitter release after a brief (ca. 100 msec) delay. Because the signal reaching the wide field amacrine cell is truncated after about 100 msec, the wide field amacrine cell will receive excitation when the target enters the receptive field, but will not continue to respond in the presence of the target.

The spatial profiles of synaptic input and output for the cell types involved in the model are summarized in Figure 3. The bipolar and narrow field amacrine cell sensitivities extend over a region corresponding roughly to their dendritic spread. The wide field amacrine cell appears to receive input over a local region near the cell body, but delivers its inhibitory output over a much wider region corresponding the the full extent (ca. 500 mm) of its processes.

Figure 4 shows the electrical circuit model for each cell type, and illustrates the interactions between cells that are implemented in the model. In Figure 4, boxes contain the circuit for each cell and arrows between them represent synaptic interactions thought

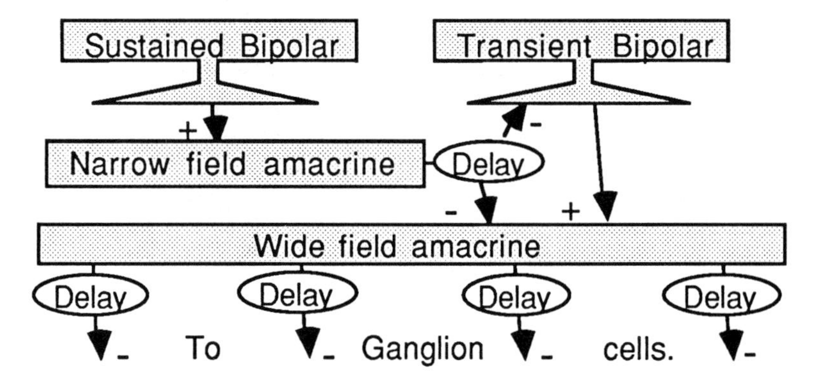

Figure 2: Circuitry to be Analyzed

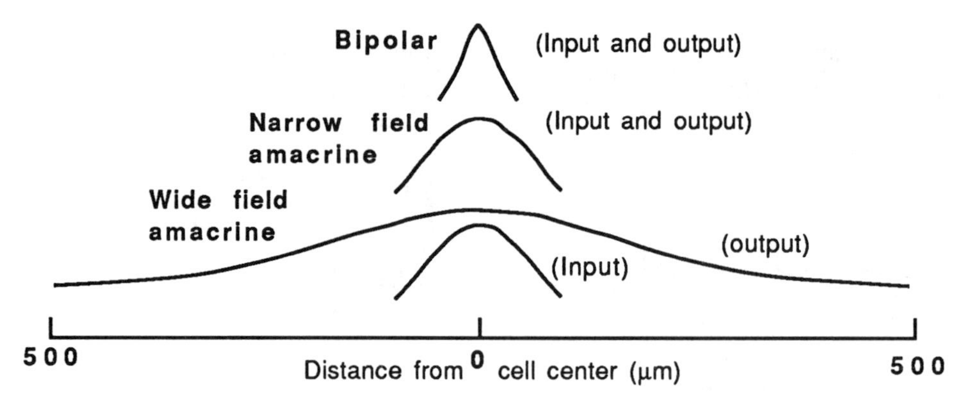

Figure 3: Spatial Profiles of Input Sensitivity and Output Transmission

to occur as determined through experiments in which a neurotransmitter is puffed onto bipolar dendrites. Bipolar cells are modeled using two compartments, corresponding to the cell body and axon terminal as suggested in Maguire *et al.* (1989). Amacrine cells are modeled using only one compartment as in Eliasof *et al.* (1987).

Each compartment has a voltage (Vbs, Vbst, Vbtt, Van, Vaw). The cell body for the sustained and transient bipolar are assumed to be the same. Batteries in the figure correspond to excitatory (E+, Ena) or inhibitory reversal potentials (E-, Ek, Ecl). Resistors represent ionic conductances. Circles and arrows through resisters indicate transmitter dependent conductances which are controlled by the voltage of a presynaptic or same cell. Functions relating voltages to conductances are mostly linear with a threshold. More details are given in Teeters *et al.* (1991).

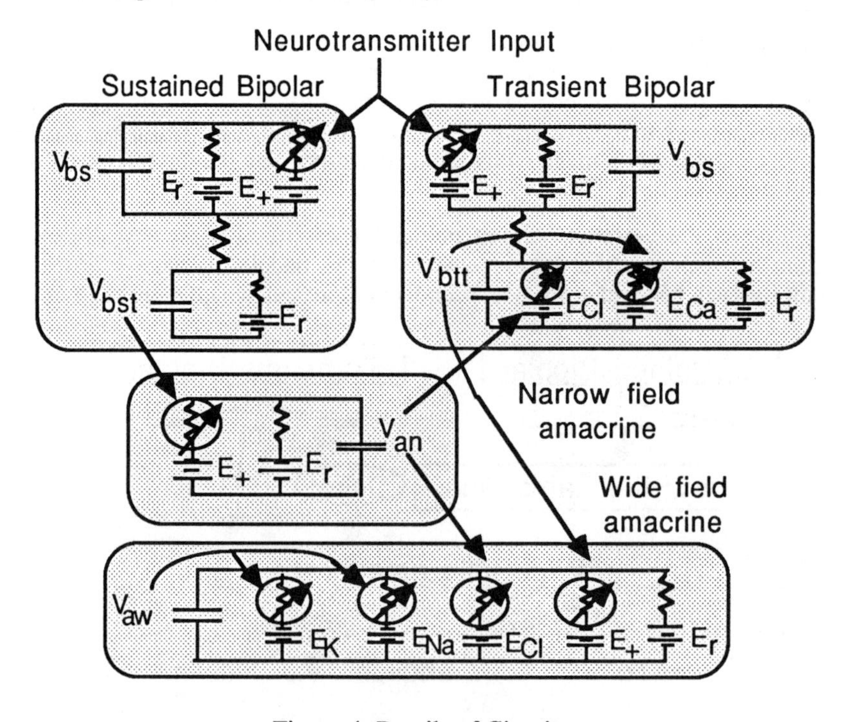

Figure 4: Details of Circuitry

3 TESTING THE COMPUTATIONAL MODEL

Computer simulation was used to tune model parameters, and test whether the single cell properties and proposed interactions between cells shown in Figure 4 are consistent with the responses recorded from the neurons during applications of a neurotransmitter puff.

Results are shown in Figure 5. Voltage clamp experiments electrically clamp the cell membrane potential to a constant voltage and determine the current required to maintain the voltage over time. Downward traces indicate that current is flowing into the cell; upward traces indicate outward current. For simplicity, scales are not shown, but in all cases the magnitude of the simulated response is close to that of the observed response.

The simulated and observed responses voltage clamps of the wide field amacrine shown in the fourth row vary because there is a sustained outward current observed experimentally that is not apparent in the simulations. This shows that the model is not perfect and is something that needs further investigation.

This difference between the model and observed response does not prevent the hypothesized function of the circuit from being simulated. This is shown on the bottom row where both the observed and simulated voltage responses from the wide field amacrine are transient.

4 SIMULATING INHIBITION TO GANGLION CELLS

Figure 5 illustrates that we have, to a large degree, succeeded in combining the characteristics of single cells into a model which can explain many of the observed properties thought to be due to the interaction between these cells in a local region.

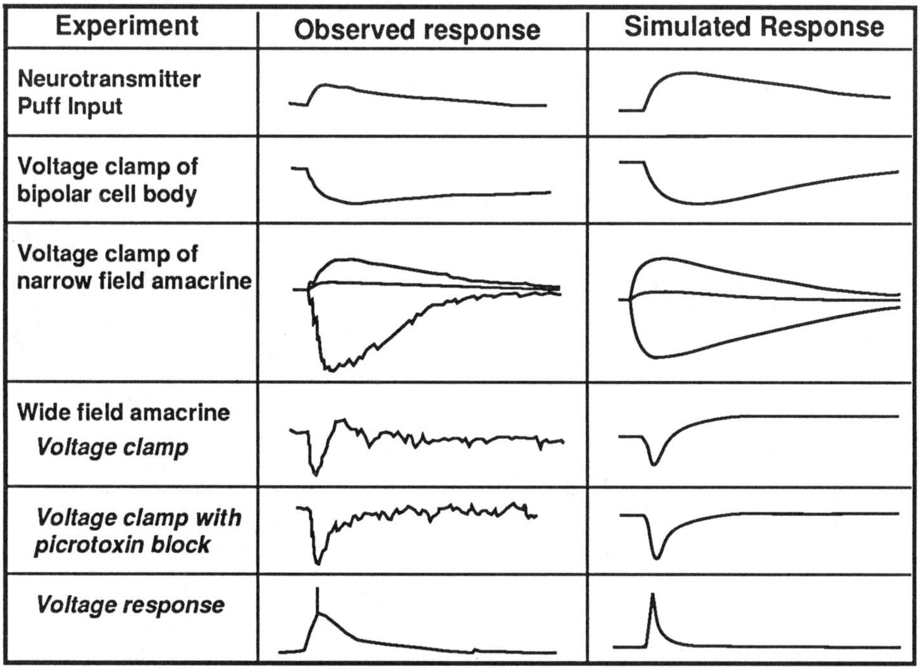

Experiment	Observed response	Simulated Response
Neurotransmitter Puff Input		
Voltage clamp of bipolar cell body		
Voltage clamp of narrow field amacrine		
Wide field amacrine *Voltage clamp*		
Voltage clamp with picrotoxin block		
Voltage response		

Figure 5: Example Puff Simulations

The next step in our analysis is to investigate how this circuit influences the response of ganglion cells. To do this requires simulating the input to the bipolar dendrites and simulating the ganglion cells which receive the transient inhibition generated by the wide field amacrine. This amounts to a integrated model of an entire patch of retina, including receptors, horizontal cells, the four neuron circuit discussed earlier, and ganglion cells. The manner in which we accomplish this is illustrated in Figure 6.

The left side of figure 6 shows the model elements. Receptors and horizontal cells are modeled as low pass filters with different time constants and different spatial inputs. The ganglion cell model receives a transient excitatory input generated phenomenologically by a thresholded high pass filter from the transient bipolar. Inhibitory input to the ganglion cell is implemented as coming from the transient wide field amacrine cells described previously. For simplicity, voltage gated currents and spiking are not implemented in the ganglion cell model, and only the off bipolar pathways are simulated.

The right hand of Figure 6 illustrates how the model is implemented spatially. The circuit for each cell type is duplicated across the retina patch in a matrix format. The known spatial properties of each cell, such as the spatial range of transmitter sensitivity and release are incorporated into the model. Details are given in Teeters *et al.* 1991.

5 SIMULATING INHIBITION TO GANGLION CELLS

To test if the model can account for the observed reduction in ganglion cell response during movement in the receptive field surround, we simulated the experiment depicted in Figure 1, mainly the flashing of a central light during the presence of a stationary and spinning windmill. The results are shown in Figure 7.

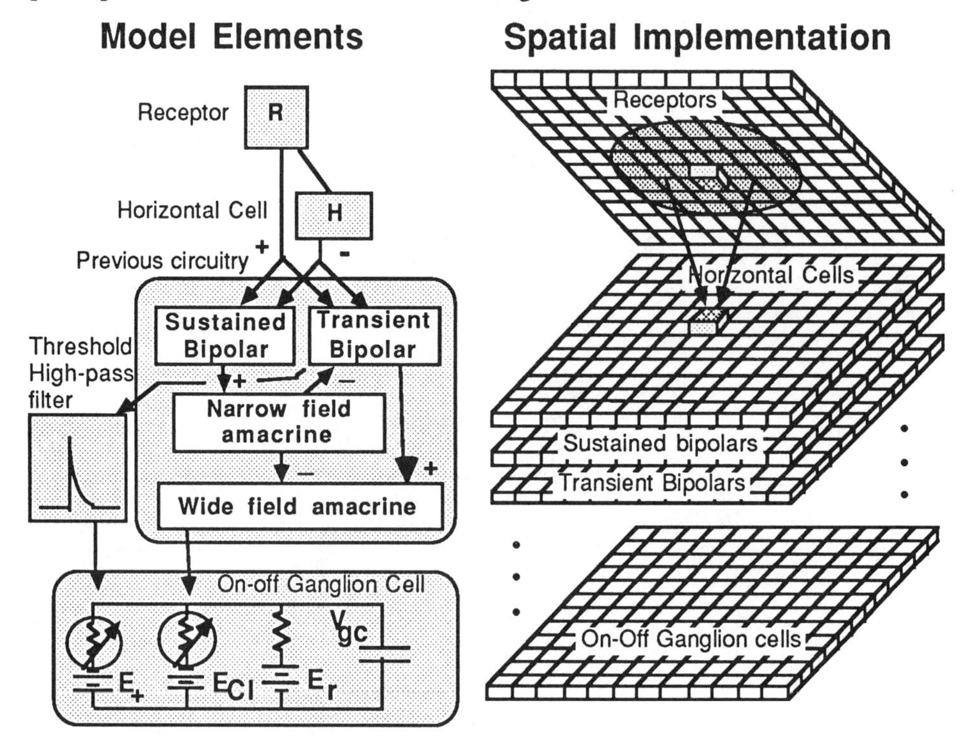

Figure 6: Integrated Retinal Model

Rather than displaying a single curve representing the response of a single unit over time, Figure 7 shows the simultaneous pattern of activity in an array of neurons spatially distributed across the retina patch at an instant in time (just after a central light spot is turned on). The neuron responses are the transient bipolar terminal, the wide field amacrine neurotransmitter release, and the ganglion cell voltage response. On the left column is shown the response to a flashing spot when the windmill is stationary. On the right is shown the response to the same flashing spot but with a spinning windmill.

When the windmill is stationary, the transient bipolar terminal responds only to the center flash. Responses to the windmill vanes are suppressed by the narrow field amacrine cell causing the appearance of four regions of hyperpolarizing responses around the center. The wide field amacrine responds to the central test flash and releases transmitter as shown in the second row. The array of ganglion cells responds to both the excitatory input generated by the spot at the bipolar terminals and the inhibitory input generated by the wide field amacrines. Because the wide field inhibition has not yet taken effect at this point in time, the ganglion cells respond well to the flashing spot.

When the windmill is spinning, as is shown on the right hand column, the transient bipolar terminals generate a response to the leading edge of the windmill vanes. The wide field amacrine cells receive excitatory input from the transient bipolar terminal responses to the vane, and consequently release inhibitory neurotransmitter over a wide area as shown in in the right column. Because inhibition is being continuously generated by the spinning windmill, the response of the ganglion cells across the retinal patch has a large

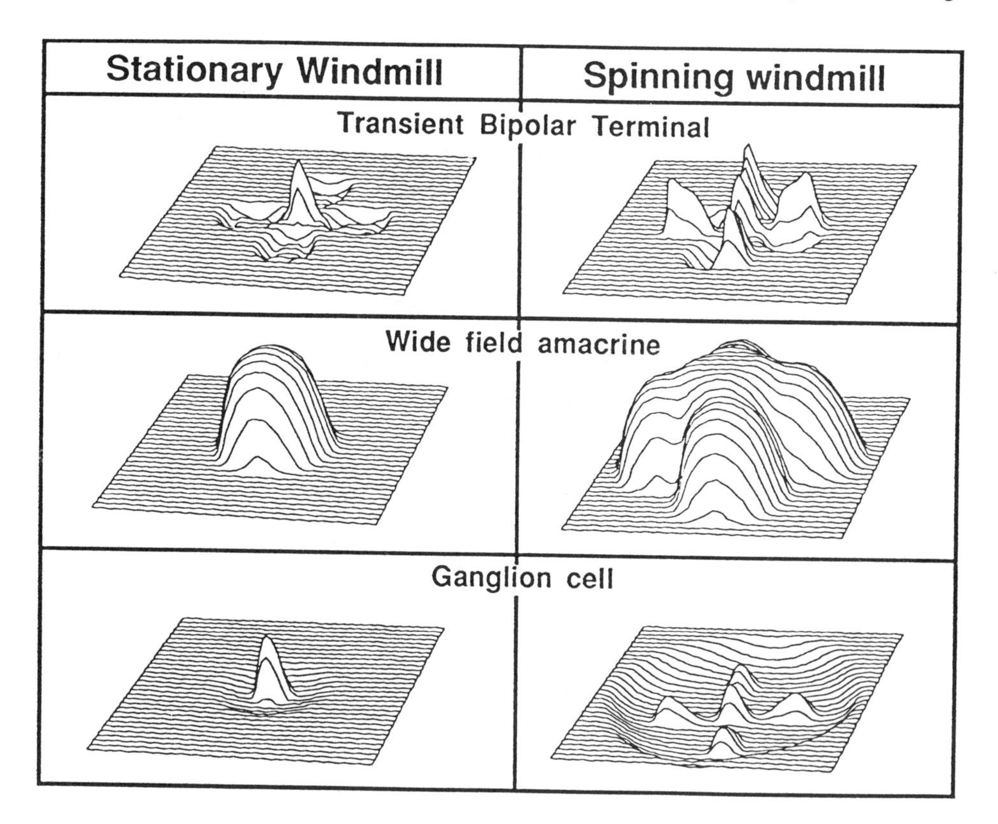

Fig. 7 - Ganglion Cell Inhibition Caused By Spinning Windmill

bowl shaped area of hyperpolarization which reduces the ganglion cell response of the cells to the central test flash. This is seen by the fact that the height of depolarization in the centrally located ganglion cells is much smaller under conditions of a spinning windmill than if the windmill is stationary. This is consistent with the results found experimentally which are illustrated in Figure 1. Experimental data not yet attained, but which are predicted by the model simulations illustrated in Figure 7, are the spatial patterns of activity generated in the bipolar, amacrine, and ganglion cells in response to the different stimuli.

6 SUMMARY

Using computer simulation of a neurophysiologically based model, we demonstrate that the experimental data describing properties of four neurons in the inner retina are compatible with the hypothesis that these neurons are involved in the detection of change and the feedforward of change-sensitive inhibition to ganglion cells. First, we build a computational model of the hypothesized four neuron circuit and determine that the proposed interactions between them are sufficient to reproduce many of the observed network properties in response to a puff of neurotransmitter. Next, we integrate this model into a full retina model to simulate their influence on ganglion cell responses.

The model verifies the consistency of presently available data, and allows formation of predictions of neural activity are subject to refutation or verification by new experiments. We are currently recording the spatio-temporal response of ganglion cells to moving stimuli so that direct comparisons to these model predictions can be made.

References

Barnes, S. and Werblin, F.S. (1986). Gated currents generate single spike activity in amacrine cells of the tiger salamander. *Proc. Natl. Acad. Sci. USA* 83: 1509 - 1512.

Barnes, S. and Werblin, F.S. (1987). Direct excitatory and lateral inhibitory synaptic inputs to amacrine cells in the tiger salamander retina. *Brain Res.* 406: 233 - 237.

Eliasof S., Barnes S. and Werblin, F.S. (1987). The interaction of ionic currents mediating single spike activity in retinal amacrine cells of the tiger salamander. *J. Neurosci.* 7: 3512 - 3524.

Maguire, G., Lukasiewicz, P. and Werblin F.S. (1989). Amacrine cell interactions underlying the response to change in the tiger salamander retina. *J. Neurosci.* 9: 726 - 735.

Teeters, J.L., Eeckman, F.H., Werblin F.S. (1991). A computer model to visualize change sensitive responses in the salamander retina. In MA. Arbib and J-P. Ewert (eds.) *Visuomotor Coordination: Amphibians, Comparisons, Models and Robots.* Plenum.

Werblin, F.S. (1972). Lateral interactions at inner plexiform layer of a vertebrate retina: antagonistic response to change. *Science.* 175: 1008 - 1010.

Werblin, F.S. and Copenhagen, D.R. (1974). Control of retinal sensitivity. III. Lateral interactions at the inner plexiform layer. *J. Gen. Physiol.* 63: 88 - 110.

Werblin, F.S., Maguire, G., Lukasiewicz, P., Eliasof, S., and Wu, S. (1988). Neural interactions mediating the detection of motion in the retina of the tiger salamander. *Visual Neurosci.* 1: 317 - 329.

Wunk, D.F. and Werblin, F.S. (1979). Synaptic inputs to ganglion cells in the tiger salamander retina. *J. Gen. Physiol.* 73: 265 - 286.

FEEDBACK SYNAPSE TO CONE AND LIGHT ADAPTATION

Josef Skrzypek
Machine Perception Laboratory
UCLA - Los Angeles, California 90024
INTERNET: SKRZYPEK@CS.UCLA.EDU

Abstract

Light adaptation (LA) allows cone vision to remain functional between twilight and the brightest time of day even though, at any one time, their intensity-response (I-R) characteristic is limited to 3 log units of the stimulating light. One mechanism underlying LA, was localized in the outer segment of an isolated cone (1,2). We found that by adding annular illumination, an I-R characteristic of a cone can be shifted along the intensity domain. Neural network involving feedback synapse from horizontal cells to cones is involved to be in register with ambient light level of the periphery. An equivalent electrical circuit with three different transmembrane channels leakage, photocurrent and feedback was used to model static behavior of a cone. SPICE simulation showed that interactions between feedback synapse and the light sensitive conductance in the outer segment can shift the I-R curves along the intensity domain, provided that phototransduction mechanism is not saturated during maximally hyperpolarized light response.

1 INTRODUCTION

1.1 Light response in cones

In the vertebrate retina, cones respond to a small spot of light with sustained hyperpolarization which is graded with the stimulus over three log units of intensity [5]. Mechanisms underlying this I-R relation was suggested to result from statistical superposition of invariant single-photon, hyperpolarizing responses involvnig sodium conductance changes that are gated by cyclic nucleotides (see 6). The shape of the response measured in cones depends on the size of the stimulating spot of light, presumably because of peripheral signals mediated by a negative feedback synapse from horizontal cells [7,8]; the hyperpolarizing response to the spot illumination in the central portion of the cone receptive field is antagonized by light in the surrounding periphery [11,12,13]. Thus the cone membrane is influenced by two antagonistic effects; 1) feedback, driven by peripheral illumination and 2) the light sensitive conductance, in the cone outer segment. Although it has been shown that key aspects of adaptation can be observed in isolated cones [1,2,3], the effects of peripheral illumination on adaptation as related to feedback input from horizontal cells have not been examined. It was reported that under appropriate stimulus conditions the resting membrane potential for a cone can be reached at two drastically different intensities for a spot/annulus combinations [8,14].

We present here experimental data and modeling results which suggests that results of feedback from horizontal cells to cones resemble the effect of the neural component of light adaptation in cones. Specifically, peripheral signals mediated via feedback synapse reset the cone sensitivity by instantaneously shifting the I-R curves to a new intensity domain. The full range of light response potentials is preserved without noticeable compression.

2 RESULTS

2.1 Identification of cones

Preparation and the general experimental procedure as well as criteria for identification of cones has been detailed in [15,8]. Several criteria were used to distinguish cones from other cells in the OPL such as: 1) the depth of recording in the retina [11, 13], 2) the sequence of penetrations concomitant with characteristic light responses, 3) spectral response curves [18], 4) receptive field diameter [8], 5) the fastest time from dark potential to the peak of the light response [8, 15], 6)domain of I-R curves and 7) staining with Lucipher Yellow [8, 11, 13]. These values represent averages derived from all intracellular recordings in 37 cones, 84 bipolar cells, more than 1000 horizontal cells, and more than 100 rods.

2.2 Experimental procedure

After identifying a cone, its I-R curve was recorded. Then, in a presence of center illumination (diameter = 100 um) which elicited maximal hyperpolarization from a cone, the periphery of the receptive field was stimulated with an annulus of inner diameter (ID) = 750 um and the outer diameter (OD) = 1500 um. The annular intensity was adjusted to elicit depolarization of the membrane back to the dark potential level. Finally, the center intensity was increased again in a stepwise manner to antagonize the effect of peripheral illumination, and this new I-R curve was recorded.

2.3 Peripheral illumination shifts the I-R curve in cones

Sustained illumination of a cone with a small spot of light, evokes a hyperpolarizing response, which after transient peak gradually repolarizes to some steady level (Fig. 1a). When the periphery of the retina is illuminated with a ring of light in the presence of center spot, the antagonistic component of response can be recorded in a form of sustained depolarization. It has been argued previously that in the tiger salamander cones, this type of response in cones is mediated via synaptic input from horizontal cells. [11, 12].

The significance of this result is that the resting membrane potential for this cone can be reached at two drastically different intensities for a spot/annulus combinations; The action of an annular illumination is a fast depolarization of the membrane; the whole process is completed in a fraction of a second unlike the previous reports where the course of light-adaptation lasted for seconds or even minutes.

Response due to spot of light measured at the peak of hyperpolarization, increased in magnitude with increasing intensity over three log units (fig. 1.a). The same data is plotted as open circles in fig. 1.b. Initially, annulus presented during the central illumination did not produce a noticeable response. Its amplitude reached maximum when the center spot intensity was increased to 3 log units. Further increase of center intensity resulted in disappearance of the annulus- elicited depolarization. Feedback action is graded with annular intensity and it depends on the balance between amount of light falling on the center and the surround of the cone receptive field. The change in cone's membrane potential, due to combined effects of central and annular illumination is plotted as filled circles in fig. 1b. This new intensity-response curve is shifted along the intensity axis by approximately two log units. Both I-R curves span approximately three log units of intensity. The I-R curve due to combined center and surround illumination can be described by the function $V/Vm = I/(I+k)$ [16] where Vm is a peak hyperpolarization and k is a constant intensity generating half-maximal response. This relationship $[x/(x+k)]$ was suggested to be an indication of the light adaptation [2]. The I-R curve plotted using peak response values (open circles), fits a continuous line drawn according to equation $(1-\exp(-kx))$. This has been argued previously to indicate absence of light adaptation [2,1]. There is little if any compression or change in gain after the shift of the cone operating point to some new domain of intensity. The results suggest that peripheral illumination can shift the center-spot elicited I-R curve of the cone thus resetting the response-generating mechanism in cones.

2.4 Simulation of a cone model

The results presented in the previous sections imply that maximal hyperpolarization for the cone membrane is not limited by the saturation in the phototransduction process alone. It seems reasonable to assume that such a limit may be in part determined by the batteries of involved ions. Furthermore, it appears that shifting I-R curves along the intensity domain is not dependent solely on the light adaptation mechanism localized to the outer segment of a cone. To test these propositions we developed a simplified compartmental model of a cone (Fig.2.) and we exercised it using SPICE (Vladimirescu et al., 1981).

All interactions can be modeled using Kirchoff's current law; membrane current is $c_{m(dV/dt)}+I_{ionic}$. The leakage current is $I_{leak} = G_{leak}(V_m-E_{leak})$, light sensitive current is $I_{light} = G_{light}*(V_m-E_{light})$ and the feedback current is $I_{fb} = G_{fb}*(V_m-E_{fb})$. The left branch represents ohmic leakage channels (G_{leak}) which are associated with a constant battery E_{leak} (-70 mV). The middle branch represents the light sensitive conductance (G_{light}) in series with +1 mV ionic battery (E_{light}) [18]. Light adaptation effects could be incorporated here by making Glight time varying and dependent on internal concentration of Calcium ions. In our preliminary studies we were only interested in examining whether the shift of I-R is possible and if it would explain the disappearance of depolarizing FB reponse with hyperpolarization by the center light. This can be done with passive measurements of membrane potential amplitude. The right-most branch represents ionic channels that are controlled by the feedback synapse. With, E_{fb} = -65 mV [11] G_{fb} is a time and voltage independent feedback conductance.

The input resistance of an isolated cone is taken to be near 500 Mohm (270 Mohm Attwell, et al., 82). Assuming specific membrane resistance of 5000 Ohm*cm*cm and that a cone is 40 microns long and has a 8 micron diameter at the base we get the leakage conductance G_{leak} = 1/(1Gohm). In our studies we assume G_{leak} to be linear altghouth there is evidence that cone membrane rectifies (Skrzypek, 79). The G_{light} and G_{fb} are assumed to be equal and add up to 1/(1Gohm). The Glight varies with light intensity in proportion of two to three log units of intensity for a tenfold change in conductance. This relation was derived empirically, by comparing intensity response data obtained from a cone {V_m=f(LogI)} to {V_m=f(LogG_{light})} generated by the model. The changes in Gfb have not been calibrated to changes in light intensity of the annulus. However, we assume that Gfb can not undergo variation larger that G_{light}.

Figure 3 shows the membrane potential changes generated by the model plotted as a function of R_{light}, at different settings of the "feedback" resistance R_{fb}. With increasing R_{fb}, there is a parallel shift along the abscissa without any changes in the shape of the curve. Increase in R_{light} corresponds to increase in light intensity and the increasing magnitude of the light response from 0mV (E_{light}) all the way down to -65 mV (E_{fb}). The increase in R_{fb} is associated with increasing intensity of the annular illumination, which causes additional hyperpolarization of the horizontal cell and consequently a decrease in "feedback" transmitter released from HC to cones. Since we assume the E_{fb} =–65mV, a more negative level than the normal resting membrane potential, a decrease in G_{fb} would cause a depolarizing response in the cone. This can be observed here as a shift of the curve along the abscissa. In our model, a hundred fold change in feedback resistance from 0.01Gohm to 1Gohm, resulted in shift of the "response-intensity" curve by approximately two log units along the abscissa. The relationship between changes in R_{fb} and the shift of the "response-intensity" curve is nonlinear and additional increases in Rfb from 1Gohm to 100Gohm results in decreasing shifts.

Membrane current undergoes similar parallel shift with changes in feedback conductance. However, the photocurrent (I_{light}) and the feedback current (I_{fb}), show only saturation with increasing G_{light} (not shown). The limits of either I_{light} or I_{fb} currents are defined by the batteries of the model. Since these currents are associated with batteries of opposite polarities, the difference between them at various settings of the feedback conductance G_{fb} determines the amount of shift for I_{leak} along the abscissa. The compression in shift of "response intensity" curves at smaller values of G_{fb} results from smaller and smaller current flowing through the feedback branch of the circuit. Consequently, a smaller G_{fb} changes are required to get response in the dark than in the light.

The shifting of the "response-intensity" curves generated by our model is not due to light adaptation as described by [1,2] although it is possible that feedback effects could be involved in modulating light-sensitive channels. Our model suggests that in order to generate additional light response after the membrane of a cone was fully hyperpolarized by light, it is insufficient to have a feedback effect alone that would depolarize the cone membrane. Light sensitive channels that were not previously closed [18] must also be available.

3 DISCUSSION

The results presented here suggest that synaptic feedback from horizontal cells to cones could contribute to the process of light adaptation at the photoreceptor level. A complete explanation of the underlying mechanism requires further studies but the results seem to suggest that depolarization of the cone membrane by a peripheral illumination, resets the response-generating process in the cone. This result can be explained withing the framework of the current hypothesis of the light adaptation, recently summarized by [6].

It is conceivable that feedback transmitter released from horizontal cells in the dark, opens channels to ions with reversal potential near -65 mV [11]. Hence, hyperpolarizing cone membrane by increasing center spot intensity would reduce the depolarizing feedback response as cone nears the battery of involved ions. Additional increase in annular illumination, further reduces the feedback transmitter and the associated feedback conductance thus pushing cone's membrane potential away from the "feedback" battery. Eventually, at some values of the center intensity, cone membrane is so close to -65 mV that no change in feedback conductance can produce a depolarizing response.

ACKNOWLEDGEMENTS

Special gratitude to Prof. Werblin for providing a superb research environment and generous support during early part of this project. We acknowledge partial support by NSF grant ECS-8307553, ARCO-UCLA Grant #1, UCLA-SEASNET Grant KF-21, MICRO-Hughes grant #541122-57442, ONR grant #N00014-86-K-0395, ARO grant DAAL03-88- K-0052

REFERENCES

1. Nakatani, K., & Yau, K.W. (1988). Calcium and light adaptation in retinal rods and cones. Nature. 334, 69-71.

2. Matthews, H.R., Murphy, R.L.W., Fain, G.L., & Lamb, T.D. (1988). Photoreceptor light adaptation is mediated by cytoplasmic calcium concentration. Nature, 334, 67-69.

3. Normann, R.A. & Werblin, F.S. (1974). Control of retinal sensitivity. I. Light and dark-adaptation of vertebrate rods and cones. J. Physiol. 63, 37-61.

4. Werblin, F.S. & Dowling, J.E. (1969). Organization of the retina of the mudpuppy, Necturus maculosus. II. Intracellular recording. J. Neurophysiol. 32, (1969),315-338.

5. Pugh, E.N. & Altman, J. Role for calcium in adaptation. Nature 334, (1988), 16-17.

6. O'Bryan P.M., Properties of the dpolarizing synaptic potential evoked by peripheral illumination in cones of the turtle retina. J.Physiol. Lond. 253, (1973), 207-223.

7. Skrzypek J., Ph.D. Thesis, University of California at Berkeley, (1979).

8. Skrzypek, J. & Werblin, F.S.,(1983). Lateral interactions in absence of feedback to cones. J. Neurophysiol. 49, (1983), 1007-1016.

9. Skrzypek, J. & Werblin, F.S., All horizontal cells have center-surround antagonistic receptive fields. ARVO Abstr., (1978).

10. Lasansky, A. Synaptic action mediating cone responses to annular illumination in the retina of the larval tiger salamander. J. Physiol. Lond. 310, (1981), 206-214.

11. Skrzypek J., Electrical coupling between horizontal vell bodies in the tiger salamander retina. Vision Res. 24, (1984), 701-711.

12. Naka, K.I. & Rushton, W.A.H. (1967). The generation and spread of S-potentials in fish (Cyprinidae) J. Physiol., 192, (1967), 437-461.

13. Attwell, D., Werblin, F.S. & Wilson, M. (1982a). The properties of single cones isolated from the tiger salamander retina. J. Physiol. 328, 259-283.

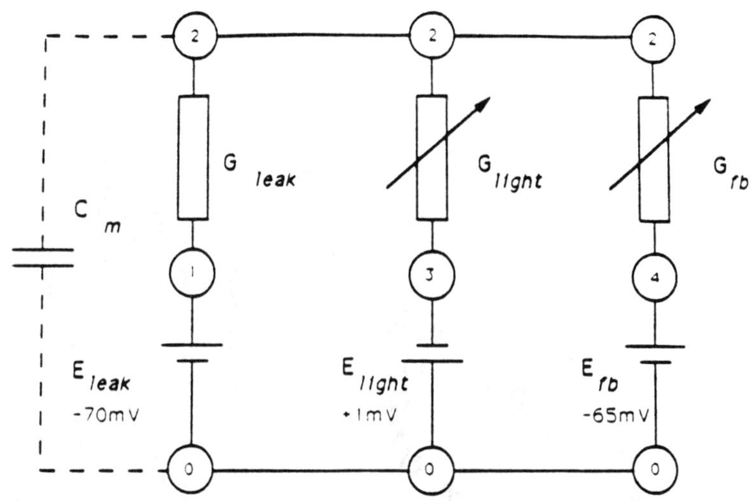

Fig. 2 Equivalent circuit model of a cone based on three different transmembrane channels. The ohmic leakage channel consists of a constant conductance G_{leak} in series with constant battery E_{leak}. Light sensitive channels are represented in the middle branch by G_{light}. Battery E_{light}, represents the reversal potential for light response at approximately OmV. Feedback synapse is shown in the right-most branch as a series combination of G_{fb} and the battery $E_{fb} = -65mV$, representing reversal potential for annulus elicited, depolarizing response measured in a cone.

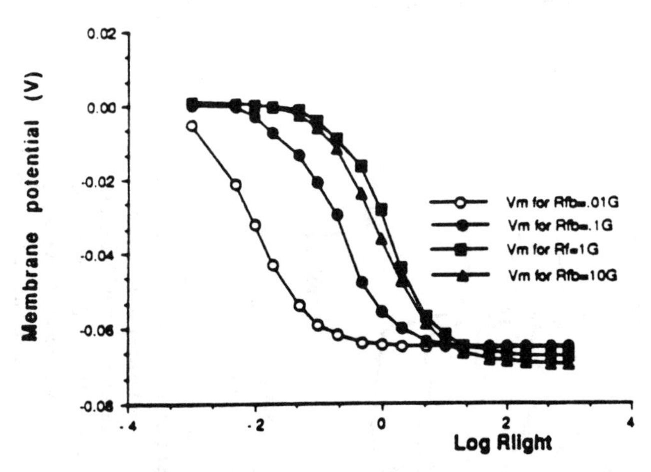

Fig. 3 Plot of the membrane potential versus the logarithm of light-sensitive resistance. The data was synthesized with the cone model simulated by SPICE. Both current and voltage curves can be fitted by x/(x+k) relation (not shown) at all different settings of Gfb (Rfb) indicated in the legend. The shift of the curves, measured at 1/2 maximal value (k=x) spans about two log units. With increasing settings of Rfb (10 Gohms), curves begin to cross (Vm at -65mV) signifying decreasing contribution of "feedback" synapse.

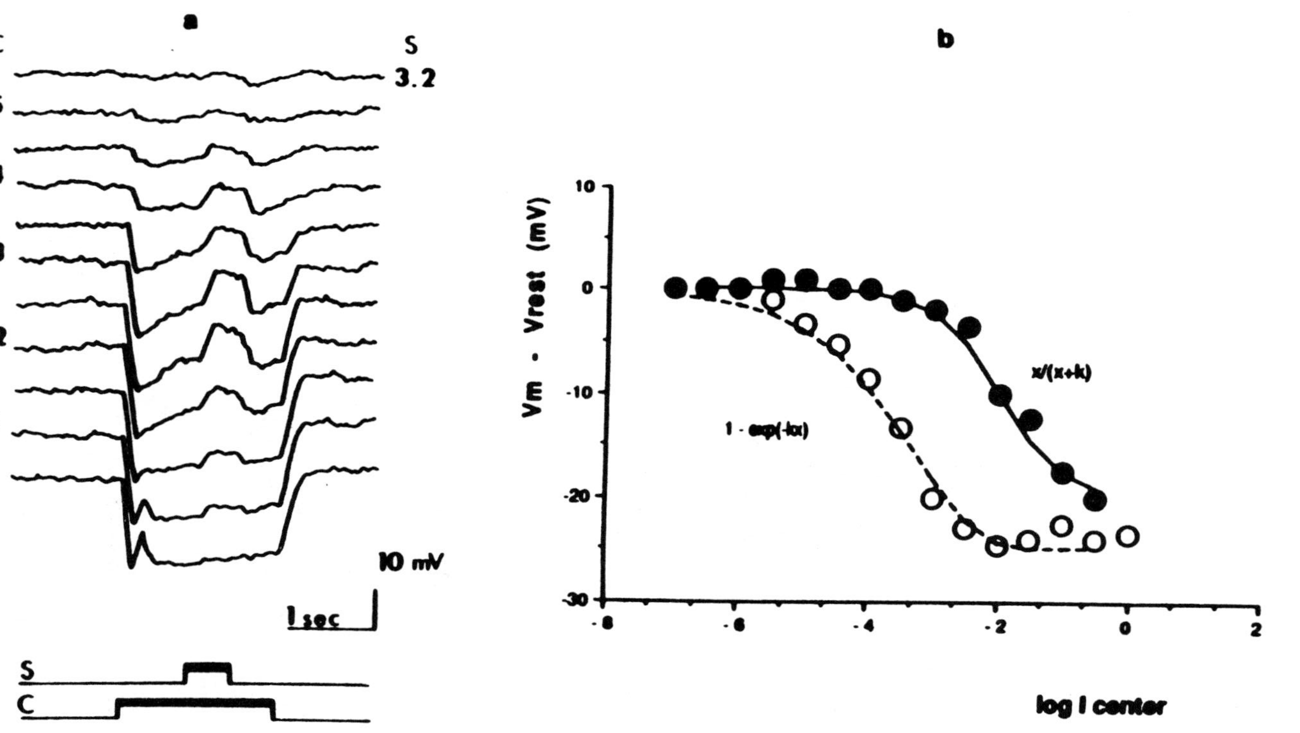

Fig. 1 (a) Series of responses to a combination of center spot and annulus. Surround illumination (S) was fixed at -3.2 l.u. throughout the experiment. Center spot intensity (C) was increased in 0.5 l.u. steps as indicated by the numbers near each trace. In the dark (upper-most trace) surround illumination had no measurable effect on the cone membrane potential. Annulus-elicited depolarizing response increased with intensity in the center up to about -3 l.u. Further increase of the spot intensity diminished the surround response. Plot of the peak hyperpolarizing response versus center spot intensity in log units in shown in (b) as open circles. It fits the dashed curve drawn according to equation 1-exp(-kx). The curve indicated by filled circles represents the membrane potential measurements taken in the middle of the depolarizing response. This data can be approximated by a continuous curve derived from x/(x+k). All membrane potential measurement are made with respect to the resting level in the dark. This result shows that in the presence of peripheral illumination, when the feedback is activated, membrane potential follows the intensity-response curve which is shifted along the Log I axis.

An Analog VLSI Chip for Finding Edges from Zero-crossings

Wyeth Bair **Christof Koch**
Computation and Neural Systems Program
Caltech 216-76
Pasadena, CA 91125

Abstract

We have designed and tested a one-dimensional 64 pixel, analog CMOS VLSI chip which localizes intensity edges in real-time. This device exploits on-chip photoreceptors and the natural filtering properties of resistive networks to implement a scheme similar to and motivated by the Difference of Gaussians (DOG) operator proposed by Marr and Hildreth (1980). Our chip computes the zero-crossings associated with the difference of two exponential weighting functions. If the derivative across this zero-crossing is above a threshold, an edge is reported. Simulations indicate that this technique will extend well to two dimensions.

1 INTRODUCTION

The zero-crossings of the Laplacian of the Gaussian, $\nabla^2 G$, are often used for detecting edges. Marr and Hildreth (1980) argued that the Mexican-hat shape of the $\nabla^2 G$ operator can be approximated by the difference of two Gaussians (DOG). In this spirit, we have built a chip that takes the difference of two resistive-network smoothings of photoreceptor input and finds the resulting zero-crossings. The Green's function of the resistive network, a symmetrical decaying exponential, differs from the Gaussian filter. Figure 1 shows the "Mexican-hat" shape of the DOG superimposed on the "witch-hat" shape of the difference of exponentials (DOE) filter implemented by our chip.

This implementation has the particular advantage of exploiting the smoothing operation performed by a linear resistive network, shown in Figure 2. In such a network, data voltages d are applied to the nodes along the network via conductances G, and the nodes are connected by resistances R. Following Kirchhoff's laws, the network node voltages v settle to values such that power dissipation is minimized. One may think of the network node voltages v as the convolution of the input with the symmetrical decaying exponential filter function. The characteristic length of this filter function is approximately $1/\sqrt{RG}$, where G is the data conductance and R the network resistance.

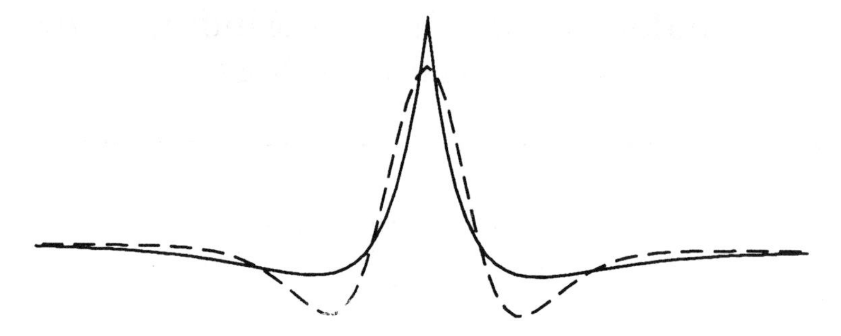

Figure 1: The Mexican-hat shape of the difference of Gaussians (dotted) and the witch-hat shape of the filter implemented by our chip.

Such a network is easily implemented in silicon and avoids the burden of additional circuitry which others have used to implement Gaussian kernels. Our simulations with digitized camera images show only minor differences between the zero-crossings from the DOE filter and those from the DOG.

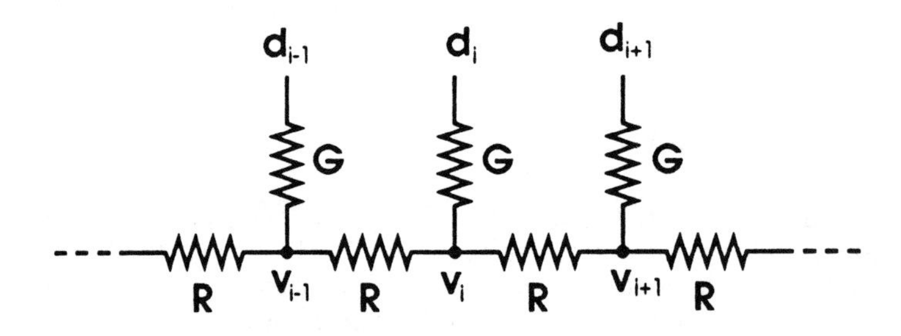

Figure 2: 1-D resistive network.

2 ANALOG VLSI IMPLEMENTATION

This chip was implemented with a 2.0μm CMOS n-well process available through the MOSIS silicon foundry. Intensity edges are detected using four stages of circuitry: photoreceptors capture incoming light, a pair of 1-D resistive networks smooth the input image, transconductance amplifiers subtract the smoothed images, and digital circuitry detects zero-crossings. Figures 3 and 4 show block diagrams for two pixels of the 64 pixel chip.

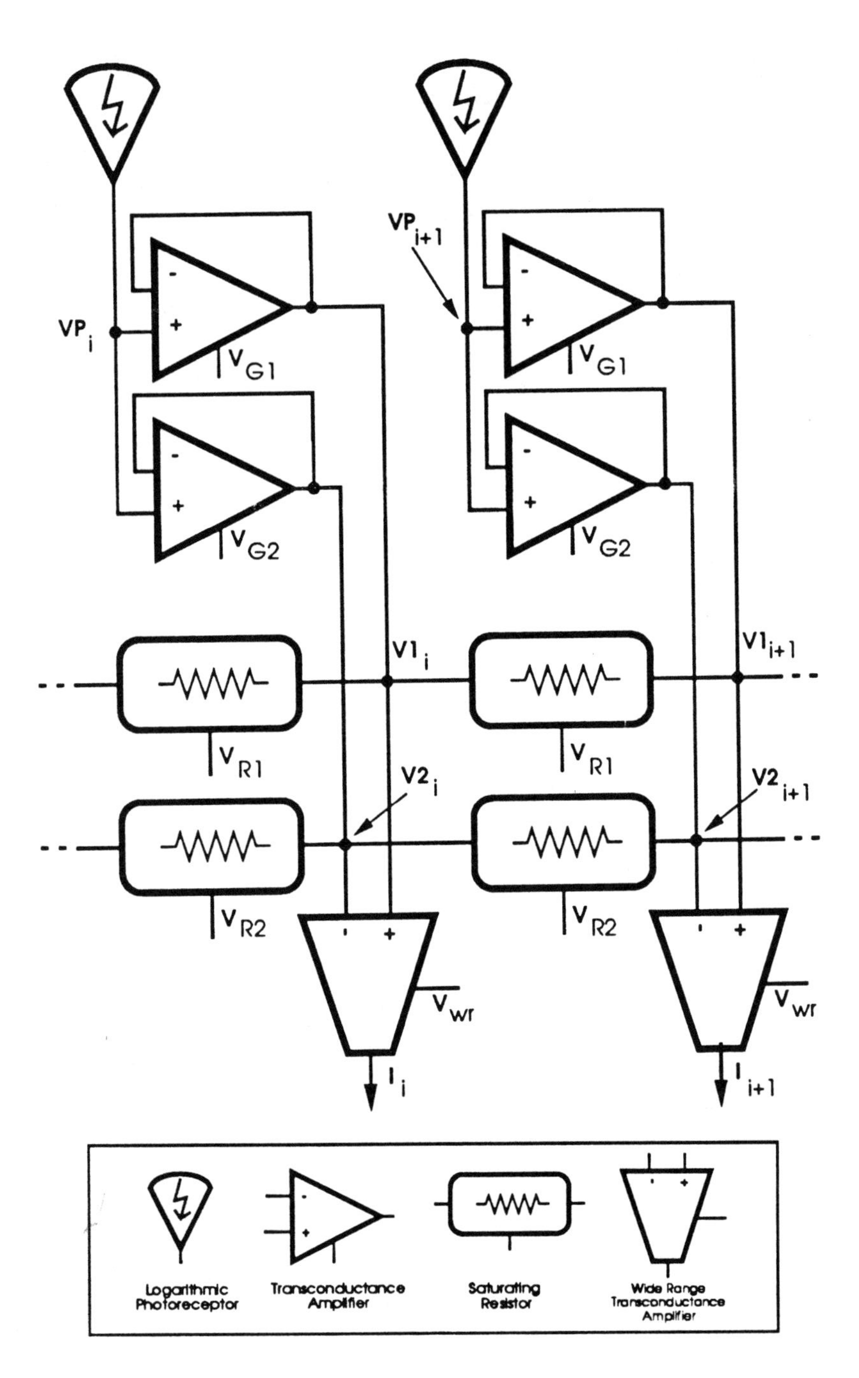

Figure 3: Block circuit diagram for two of 64 pixels as described in Section 2.

Processing begins at a line of photoreceptors spaced $100\mu m$ apart which encode the logarithm of light intensity as a voltage VP, shown in Figure 3. The set of voltages from the photoreceptors are reported to corresponding nodes of two resistive networks via transconductance amplifiers connected as followers. The followers' voltage biases, V_{G1} and V_{G2}, can be adjusted off-chip to independently set the data conductances for each resistive network. The network resistors are implemented as Mead's saturating resistors (Mead, 1989). Voltage biases V_{R1} and V_{R2} allow independent off-chip adjustment of the two network resistances. The data conductance and network resistance values determine the space constant of the smoothing filter which each network implements. The sets of voltages $V1$ and $V2$, shown in Figure 3, represent the two filtered versions of the image. Wide-range transconductance amplifiers (Mead, 1989) produce currents, I, proportional to the difference $V1 - V2$.

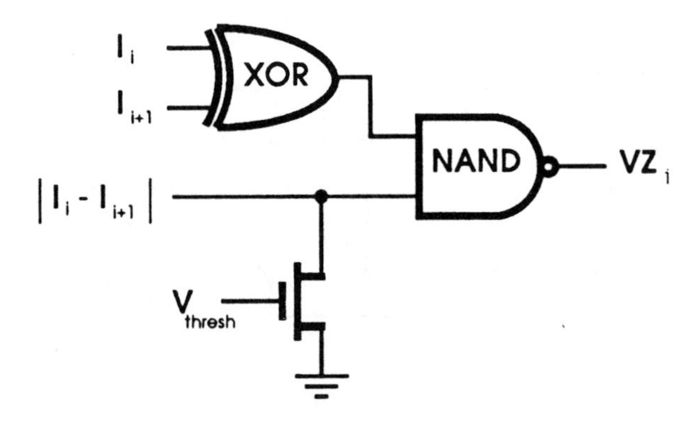

Figure 4: Zero-crossing detection and threshold circuitry.

Figure 4 shows the final stage of processing which detects zero-crossings in the sequence of currents I and implements a threshold on the slope of those zero-crossings. Currents I_i and I_{i+1} charge or discharge the inputs of an exclusive OR gate. The output of this gate is the first input to a NAND gate which is used to implement the threshold. A current proportional to the magnitude of the difference $I_i - I_{i+1}$ charges the second input of the NAND gate, while a threshold current discharges this input. If the charging current, representing the slope of the zero-crossing, is greater than the threshold current set off-chip by the bias voltage V_{thresh}, this NAND input is charged to logical 1, otherwise, this input is discharged to logical 0. The output of the NAND gate, VZ_i indicates the presence, logical 0, or the absence, logical 1, of a zero-crossing with slope greater than I_{thresh}.

A final stage of circuitry is used to multiplex the sequence of 63 bits, VZ, and corresponding currents $I_i - I_{i+1}$ indicating the slope of the zero-crossings.

3 BEHAVIOR

We tested the behavior of the chip by placing a small lens above the silicon wafer to focus an image onto the array of photoreceptors. The input light profile that we used is shown in Figure 5a. Figure 5b is an oscilloscope trace showing the smoothed voltages ($V1$ and $V2$ of Figure 3) corresponding to the filtered versions of the image. The difference of these two smoothed voltage traces is shown in Figure 5c. Arrows indicate the locations of two zero-crossings which the chip reports at the output. The reported zero-crossings accurately localize the positions of the edges in the image. The trace in Figure 5c crosses zero at other locations, but zero-crossings with slope less than the adjustable threshold are masked by the circuitry shown in Figure 4. This allows for noise and imperfections in the circuitry and can be used to filter out weaker edges which are not relevant to the application.

Figure 6 shows the response when two fingers are held one meter from the lens and swept across the field of view. The fingers appear as bright regions against a darker background. The chip accurately localizes the four edges (two per finger) as indicated by the pulses below each voltage trace. As the fingers move quickly back and forth across the field of view, the image and the zero-crossings follow the object with no perceived delay. The measured response time of the chip to the appearance of a detectable discontinuity in light intensity varies from about 100μsec in bright indoor illumination to about 10msec in a dark room. The time constant is longer for lower illumination due to the design of the logarithmic photoreceptor (Mead, 1989).

The chip has been proven to be a reliable and robust edge detector through its use in two systems. It provides data for a system designed at the Hughes Aircraft Artificial Intelligence Center which tracks edges and reports their velocities at over 300Hz. Also, we have built a hand-held battery powered device which displays the locations of edges on a bank of 63 LEDs. This device accurately detects edges in many different environments, ranging from a dimly lit room to bright outdoor sunlight.

4 SIMULATIONS OF A 2-D VERSION

We have used a computer simulation of rectangular networks of ideal linear resistors to test the extension of this technique in two dimensions. Results indicate that the zero-crossings from the difference of two symmetrical exponential filters are qualitatively similar to those from the DOG. Figure 7 compares the zero-crossing from a difference of Gaussians filter (left) to those from a difference of resistive networks filter (right). For the DOG, a Gaussian of $\sigma = 1.25$ pixels is subtracted from a Gaussian of $\sigma = 0.75$ pixels. For the resistive networks, a filter of characteristic length 1 was subtracted from one with characteristic length $1/\sqrt{2}$. Weaker zero-crossings are masked from both output images by thresholding on the slope to emphasize comparison of the stronger edges.

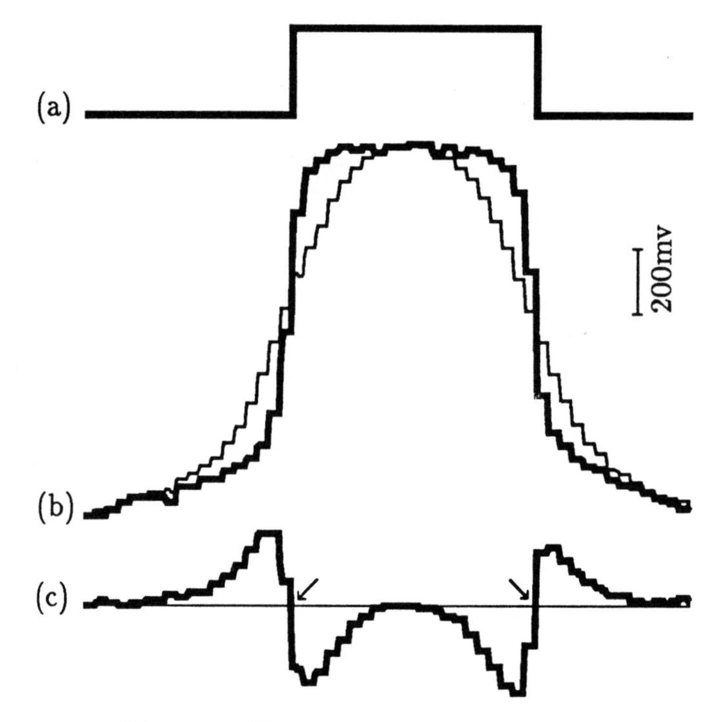

Figure 5: Chip response to a light bar stimulus.

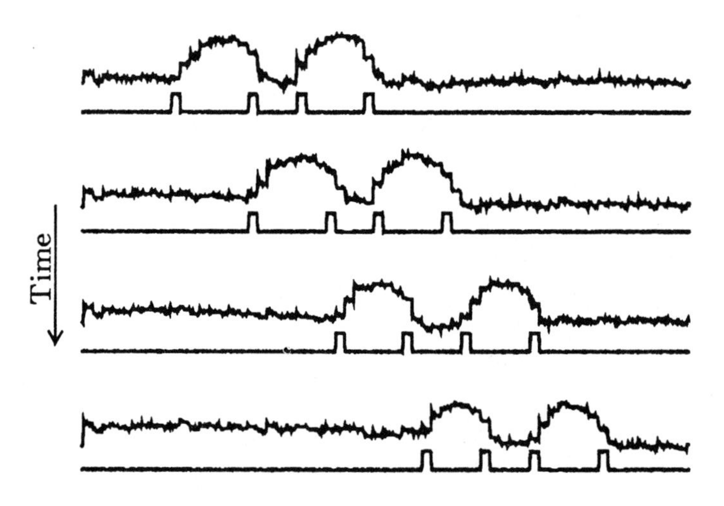

Figure 6: Chip response to two moving stimuli.

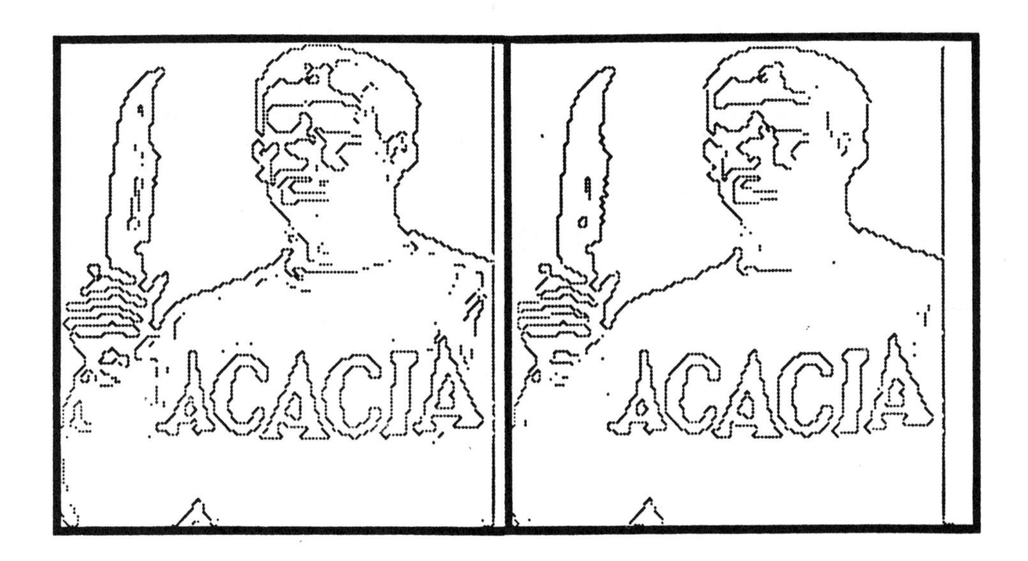

Figure 7: Zero-crossings from the difference of two Gaussians (left) and similar output from a difference of decaying exponentials (right).

5 CONCLUSION

Our analog VLSI chip shows that finding the thresholded zero-crossings of the difference of exponential filters is a robust technique for localizing intensity edges in real-time. The robust behavior of the chip in systems to track edges and determine velocity demonstrates the usefulness of implementing simple algorithms in analog VLSI and the advantages of avoiding large, more general digital systems for these purposes.

Acknowledgements

Many thanks to Carver Mead. Our laboratory is partially supported by grants from the Office of Naval Research, the Rockwell International Science Center and the Hughes Aircraft Artificial Intelligence Center. Wyeth Bair is supported by a National Science Foundation Graduate Fellowship. Thanks also to Steve DeWeerth and John Harris.

References

Marr, D. and Hildreth, E.C. (1980) Theory of edge detection. *Proc. Roy. Soc. Lond.* B 207:187-217.

Mead, C.A. (1989) *Analog VLSI and Neural Systems.* Addison-Wesley: Reading, MA.

A Delay-Line Based Motion Detection Chip

Tim Horiuchi[†] John Lazzaro[*] Andrew Moore[†] Christof Koch[†]

[†]Computation and Neural Systems Program
[*]Department of Computer Science
California Institute of Technology MS 216-76
Pasadena, CA 91125

Abstract

Inspired by a visual motion detection model for the rabbit retina and by a computational architecture used for early audition in the barn owl, we have designed a chip that employs a correlation model to report the one-dimensional field motion of a scene in real time. Using subthreshold analog VLSI techniques, we have fabricated and successfully tested a 8000 transistor chip using a standard MOSIS process.

1. INTRODUCTION

Most proposed short-range intensity-based motion detection schemes fall into two major categories: gradient models and correlation models. In gradient models, computation begins from local image qualities such as spatial gradients and temporal derivatives that can be vulnerable to noise or limited resolution. Correlation models, on the other hand, use a filtered version of the input intensity multiplied with the temporally delayed and filtered version of the intensity at a neighboring

* Present address: John Lazzaro, University of Colorado at Boulder, Campus Box 425, Boulder, Colorado, 80309–0425

receptor. Many biological motion detection systems have been shown to use a correlation model (Grzywacz and Poggio, 1990). To make use of this model, previous artificial systems, that typically look at sampled images of a scene changing in time, have had to cope with the correspondence problem, i.e. the problem of matching features between two images and measuring their shift in position. Whereas traditional digital approaches lend themselves to the measurement of image shift over a fixed time, an analog approach lends itself to the measurement of time over fixed distance. The latter is a local computation that scales to different velocity ranges gracefully without suffering from the problems of extended interconnection.

Inspired by visual motion detection models (Barlow and Levick, 1965) and by a computational architecture found in early audition (Konishi, 1986), we have designed a chip that contains a large array of velocity-tuned "cells" that correlate two events in time, using a delay-line structure. We have fabricated and successfully tested an analog integrated circuit that can can report, in real time, the field motion of a one-dimensional image projected onto the chip. The chip contains 8000 transistors and a linear photoreceptor array with 28 elements.

2. SYSTEM ARCHITECTURE

Figure 1 shows the block diagram of the chip. The input to the chip is a real-world image, focused directly onto the silicon via a lens mounted over the chip. The one-dimensional array of on-chip hysteretic photoreceptors (Delbrück and Mead, 1989) receives the light and reports rapid changes in the signal for both large and small changes. Each photoreceptor is connected to a half-wave rectifying neuron circuit (Lazzaro and Mead, 1989) that fires a single pulse of constant voltage amplitude and duration when it receives a quickly rising (but not falling) light-intensity signal.

This rising light intensity signal is interpreted to be a moving edge in the image passing over the photoreceptor. It is this signal that is the "feature" to be correlated. Note that the choice of the rising or falling intensity as a feature, from an algorithmic point of view, is arbitrary. Each neuron circuit is in turn connected to an axon circuit (Mead, 1989) that propagates the pulse down its length. By orienting the axons in alternating directions, as shown in Figure 1, any two adjacent receptors generates pulses that will "race" toward each other and meet at some point along the axon. Correlators between the axons detect when pulses pass each other, indicating the detection of a specific time difference. The width of the pulses in the axon circuits is adjustable and determines the detectable velocity range. From the summing of "votes" for different velocities by correlators across the entire chip, a winner-take-all circuit (Lazzaro et al., 1989) determines the velocity.

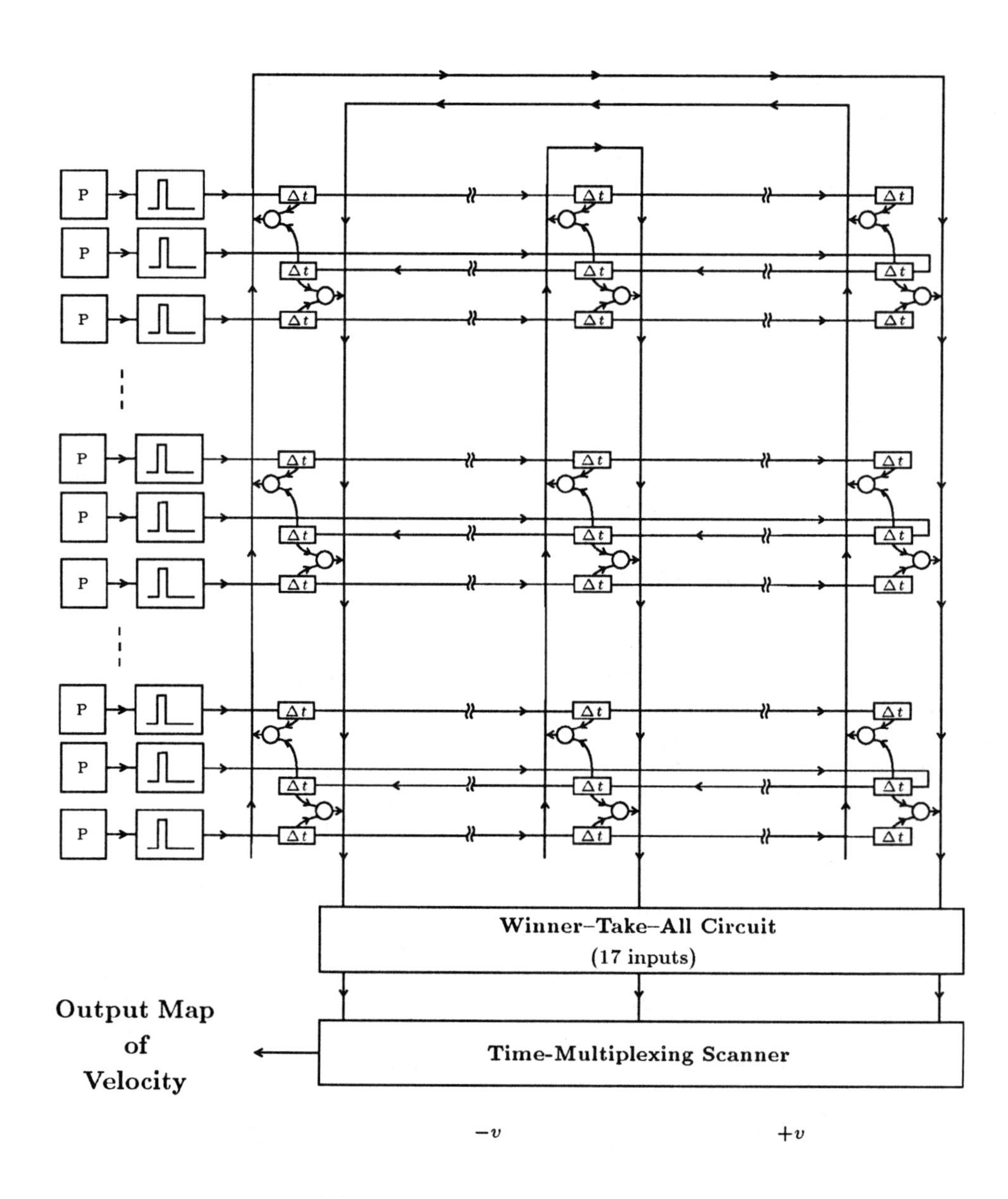

Figure 1. Block diagram of the chip, showing information flow from the photoreceptors (P), to the time-multiplexed winner-take-all output. Rising light signals are converted to pulses that propagate down the axons. Correlators are drawn as circles and axons are piecewise denoted by Δt boxes. See the text for explanation.

3. SYSTEM OPERATION AND RESULTS

3.1 READING BETWEEN THE LINES

The basic signal quantity that we are measuring is the time a "feature" takes to travel from one photoreceptor to one of its neighbors. By placing two delay lines in parallel that propagate signals in opposing directions, a temporal difference in signal start times from opposite ends will manifest itself as a difference in the location where the two signals will meet. Between the axons, correlation units perform a logical AND with the axon signals on both sides. If pulses start down adjacent axons with zero difference in start times (i.e. infinite velocity), they will meet in the center and activate a correlator in the center of the axon. If the time difference is small (i.e. the velocity is large), correlations occur near the center. As the time difference increases, correlations occur further out toward the edges. The two halves of the axon with respect to the center represent different directions of motion. When a single stimulus (e.g. a step edge) is passed over the length of the photoreceptor array with a constant velocity, a specific subset of correlators will be activated that all represent the same velocity. A current summing line is connected to each of these correlators and is passed to a winner-take-all circuit. The winner of the winner-take-all computation corresponds to the line that is receiving the largest number of correlation inputs. The output of the winner-take-all is scanned off the chip using an external input clock. Because the frequency of correlation affects the confidence of the data, scenes that are denser in edges provide more confident data as well as a quicker response.

3.2 SINGLE VS. BURSTING MODE

Until now, the circuit described uses a single pulse to indicate a passing edge. Due to the statistical nature of this system, a large number of samples are needed to make a confident statement of the detected time difference, or velocity. By externally increasing the amplitude of the signal passed to the neuron during each event, the neuron can fire multiple pulses in quick succession. With an increased number of pulses travelling down the axon, the number of correlations increase, but with a decrease in accuracy, due to the multiple incorrect correlations. The incorrect correlations are not random, however, but occur closely around the correct velocity. The end result is a net decrease in resolution in order to achieve increased confidence in the final data.

3.3 VELOCITY RANGE

The chip output is the measured time difference of two events in multiples of τ, the time-constant of a single axon section. The time difference (measured in seconds/pixel) is translated into velocity, by the equation $V = 1/\Delta t$, where V is velocity in pixels/sec and Δt can be positive or negative. Thus the linear measurement of time difference gives a non-linear velocity interpretation with the highest resolution at the slower speeds. At the slower speeds, however, we tend to have decreased confidence in the data due to the relatively smaller correlation frequency. This is expected to be less troublesome as larger photoreceptor arrays are used. The variable resolution in the computation is often an acceptable feature for control of robotic motion systems since high velocity motions are often ballistic or at least coarse, whereas fine control is needed at lower velocities.

3.4 PERFORMANCE

We have fabricated the circuit shown in Figure 1 using a double polysilicon $2\mu m$ process in the MOSIS Tiny Chip die. The chip has 17 velocity channels, and an input array of 28 photoreceptors. The voltages from the winner-take-all circuit are scanned out sequentially by on-chip scanners, the only clocked circuitry on the chip.

In testing the chip, gratings of varying spatial frequencies and natural images from newspaper photos and advertisements were mounted on a rotating drum in front of the lens. Although the most stable data was collected using the gratings, both images sources provided satisfactory data. Figure 2 shows oscilloscope traces of scanned winner-take-all channels for twelve different negative and positive velocities within a specific velocity range setting. The values to the right indicate the approximate center of the velocity range. Figure 3(a) shows the winning time interval channel vs. actual time delay. The response is linear as expected. Figure 3(b) shows the data from Figure 3(a) converted to the interpreted velocity channel vs. velocity. The horizontal bars indicate the range of velocity inside of which each channel responds. As described above, at the lower velocities, correlations occur at a lower rate, thus some of the lowest velocity channels do not respond. By increasing the number of parallel photoreceptor channels, it is expected that this situation will improve. The circuit, currently with only eight velocity channels per direction, is able to reliably measure, over different settings, velocities from 2.9 pixels/sec up to 50 pixels/sec.

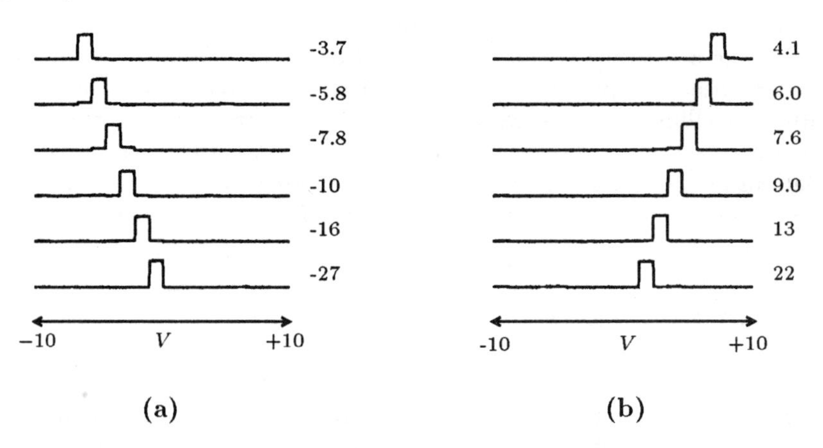

Figure 2. Winner-take-all oscilloscope traces for twelve positive (a) and negative (b) velocities. Trace labels represent the approximate center of the velocity range.

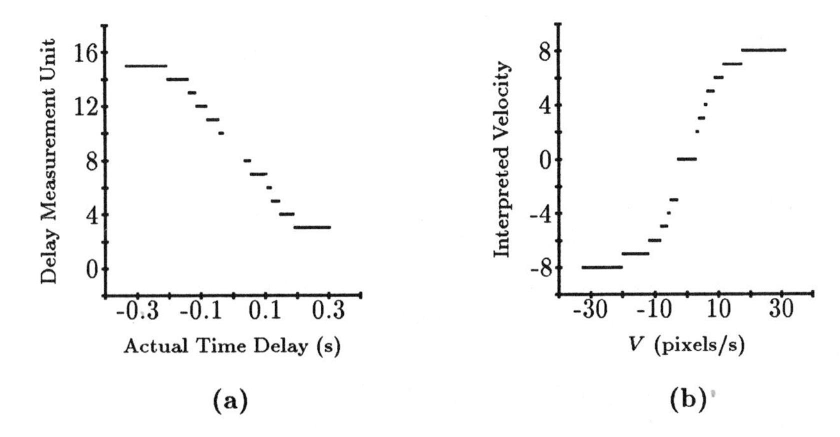

Figure 3. (a) Plot of winning time interval channel vs. actual time delay. (b) Plot of interpreted velocity channel vs. velocity (same data as in (a)).

An interesting feature of our model that also manifests itself in the visual system of the fly (Buchner 1984) is spatial aliasing, leading in the worst case to motion reversal. Spatial aliasing is due to the discrete sampling provided by photoreceptor spacing. At spatial frequencies higher than the Nyquist limit, a second stimulus can enter the neighboring axon before the first stimulus has exited, causing a sudden change in the sign of the velocity.

4 CONCLUSION

A correlation-based model for motion detection has been successfully demonstrated in subthreshold analog VLSI. The chip has shown the ability to successfully detect relatively low velocities; the slowest speed detected was 2.9 pixels/sec. and shows promise for use in different settings where other motion detection strategies have difficulty. The chip responds very well to low-light stimulus and its output is robust against changes in contrast. This is due to the high temporal derivative sensitivity of the hysteretic photoreceptor to both large and small changes. Interestingly, the statistical nature of the computation allows the system to perform successfully in noise as well as to produce a level of confidence measure. In addition, the nature of the velocity computation provides the highest resolution at the slower speeds and may be considered as an effective way to expand the detectable velocity range.

Acknowledgements

We thank Carver Mead for providing laboratory resources for the design, fabrication, and initial testing of this chip. We thank Rockwell International and the Hughes Aircraft Corporation for financial support of VLSI research in Christof Koch's laboratory, and we thank the System Development Foundation and the Office Naval Research for financial support of VLSI research in Carver Mead's laboratory. We thank Hewlett-Packard for computing support and the Defense Advanced Research

Projects Agency and the MOS Implementation Service (MOSIS) for chip fabrication.

References

Barlow, H.B. and Levick, W.R. (1965) The mechanism of directionally sensitive units in rabbit's retina. *J. Physiol.* **178:** 477-504.

Buchner, E. (1984). Behavioural Analysis of Spatial Vision in Insects. In Ali, M. A. (ed) *Photoreception and Vision in Invertebrates.* New York: Plenum Press, pp. 561-621.

Delbrück, T. and Mead, C. (1989) An Electronic Photoreceptor Sensitive to Small Changes in Intensity. In Touretzky (ed), *Neural Information Processing Systems 1.* San Mateo, CA: Morgan Kaufmann Publishers, pp. 720-727.

Grzywacz, N. and Poggio, T. (1990). Computation of Motion by Real Neurons. In Zornetzer (ed), *An Introduction to Neural and Electronic Networks.* New York: Academic Press, pp. 379-401.

Konishi, M. (1986). Centrally synthesized maps of sensory space. *Trends in Neuroscience* 4: 163-168.

Lazzaro, J. and Mead, C. (1989). Circuit models of sensory transduction in the cochlea. In Mead, C. and Ismail, M. (eds), *Analog VLSI Implementations of Neural Networks.* Norwell, MA: Kluwer Academic Publishers, pp. 85-101.

Lazzaro, J., Ryckebusch, S., Mahowald, M. A., and Mead, C. (1988). Winner-take-all networks of O(n) complexity. In Tourestzky, D. (ed), *Advances in Neural Information Processing Systems 1.* San Mateo, CA: Morgan Kaufmann Publishers, pp. 703-711.

Mead., C. (1989) *Analog VLSI and Neural Systems.* Reading, MA: Addison-Wesley, pp. 193-203.

Part VIII

Control and Navigation

Neural Networks Structured for Control Application to Aircraft Landing

Charles Schley, Yves Chauvin, Van Henkle, Richard Golden
Thomson–CSF, Inc., Palo Alto Research Operations
630 Hansen Way, Suite 250
Palo Alto, CA 94306

Abstract

We present a generic neural network architecture capable of controlling non–linear plants. The network is composed of dynamic, parallel, linear maps gated by non–linear switches. Using a recurrent form of the back–propagation algorithm, control is achieved by optimizing the control gains and task–adapted switch parameters. A mean quadratic cost function computed across a nominal plant trajectory is minimized along with performance constraint penalties. The approach is demonstrated for a control task consisting of landing a commercial aircraft in difficult wind conditions. We show that the network yields excellent performance while remaining within acceptable damping response constraints.

1 INTRODUCTION

This paper illustrates how a recurrent back–propagation neural network algorithm (Rumelhart, Hinton & Williams, 1986) may be exploited as a procedure for controlling complex systems. In particular, a simplified mathematical model of an aircraft landing in the presence of severe wind gusts was developed and simulated. A recurrent back–propagation neural network architecture was then designed to numerically estimate the parameters of an optimal non–linear control law for landing the aircraft. The performance of the network was then evaluated.

1.1 A TYPICAL CONTROL SYSTEM

A typical control system consists of a controller and a process to be controlled. The controller's function is to accept task inputs along with process outputs and to determine control signals tailored to the response characteristics of the process. The physical process to be controlled can be electro–mechanical, aerodynamic, etc. and generally has well defined behavior. It may be subjected to disturbances from its external environment.

1.2 CONTROLLER DESIGN

Many variations of both classical and modern methods to design control systems are described in the literature. Classical methods use linear approximations of the plant to be controlled and some loosely defined response specifications such as bandwidth (speed of response) and phase margin (degree of stability). Classical methods are widely used in practice, even for sophisticated control problems. Modern methods are more universal and generally assume that a performance index for the process is specified. Controllers are then designed to optimize the performance index. Our approach relates more to modern methods.

Narendra and Parthasarathy (1990) and others have noted that recurrent back–propagation networks can implement gradient descent algorithms that may be used to optimize the performance of a system. The essence of such methods is first to propagate performance errors back through the process and then back through the controller to give error signals for updating the controller parameters. Figure 1 provides an overview of the interaction of a neural control law with a complex system and possible performance indices for evaluating various control laws. The functional components needed to train the controller are shown within the shaded box of Figure 1. The objective performance measure contains factors that are written mathematically and usually represent terms such as weighted square error or other quantifiable measures. The performance constraints are often more subjective in nature and can be formulated as reward or penalty functions on categories of performance (e.g., "good" or "bad").

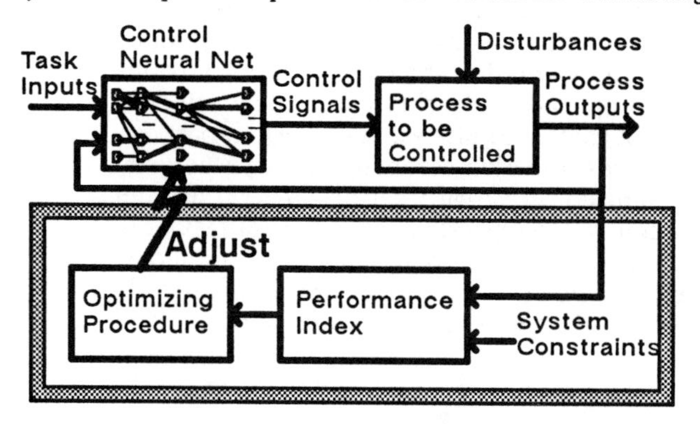

Figure 1: Neural Network Controller Design

2 A GENERIC NON–LINEAR CONTROL ARCHITECTURE

Many complex systems are in fact non–linear or "multi–modal." That is, their behavior changes in fundamental ways as a function of their position in the state space. In practice, controllers are often designed for such systems by treating them as a collection of systems linearized about a "setpoint" in state space. A linear controller can then be determined separately for each of these system "modes." These observations suggest that a reasonable approach for controlling non–linear or "multi–modal" systems would be to design a "multi–modal" control law.

2.1 THE SWITCHING PRINCIPLE

The architecture of our proposed general non–linear control law for "multi–modal" plants is shown in Figure 2. Task inputs and process outputs are entered into

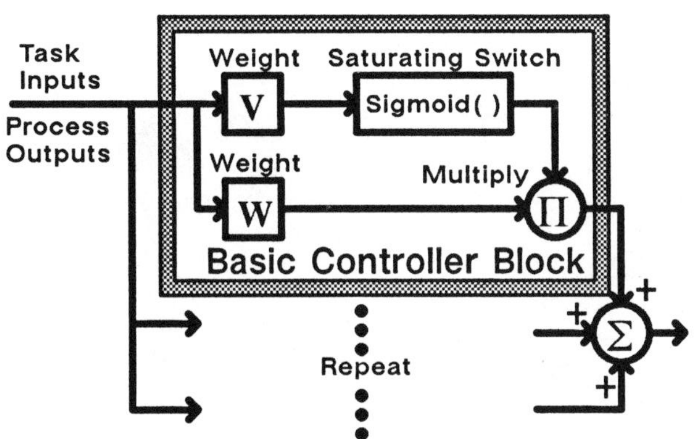

Figure 2: Neural Network Controller Architecture

multiple basic controller blocks (shown within the shaded box of Figure 2). Each basic controller block first determines a weighted sum of the task inputs and process outputs (multiplication by weights *W*). Then, the degree to which the weighted sum passes through the block is modified by means of a saturating switch and multiplier. The input to the switch is itself another weighted sum of the task inputs and process outputs (multiplication by weights *V*). If the input to the saturating switch is large, its output is unity and the weighted sum (weighted by *W*) is passed through unchanged. At the other extreme, if the saturating switch has zero output, the weighted sum of task inputs and process outputs does not appear in the output. When these basic controller blocks are replicated and their outputs are added, control signals consist of weighted sums of the controller inputs that can be selected and/or blended by the saturating switches. The overall effect is a prototypical feed–forward and feedback controller with selectable gains and multiple pathways where the overall equivalent gains are a function of the task inputs and process outputs. The resulting architecture yields a *sigma–pi* processing unit in the final controller (Rumelhart, Hinton & Williams, 1986).

2.2 MODELLING DYNAMIC MAPPINGS

Weights shown in Figure 2 may be constant and represent a static relationship between input and control. However, further controller functionality is obtained by considering the weights *V* and *W* as dynamic mappings. For example, proportional plus integral plus derivative (PID) feedback may be used to ensure that process outputs follow task inputs with adequate steady–state error and transient damping. Thus, the weights can express parameters of various generally useful control functions. These functions, when combined with the switching principle, yield rich capabilities that can be adapted to the task at hand.

3 AIRCRAFT LANDING

The generic neural network architecture of Figure 2 and the associated neural network techniques were tested with a "real–world" application: automatic landing of an aircraft. Here, we describe the aircraft and environment model during landing.

3.1 GLIDESLOPE AND FLARE

During aircraft landing, the final two phases of a landing trajectory consist of a "glideslope" phase and a "flare" phase. Figure 3 shows these two phases. Flare occurs at about 45 feet. Glideslope is characterized by a linear downward slope; flare by an exponential shaped curve. When the aircraft begins flare, its response characteristics are changed to make it more sensitive to the pilot's actions, making the process "multi–modal" or non–linear over the whole trajectory.

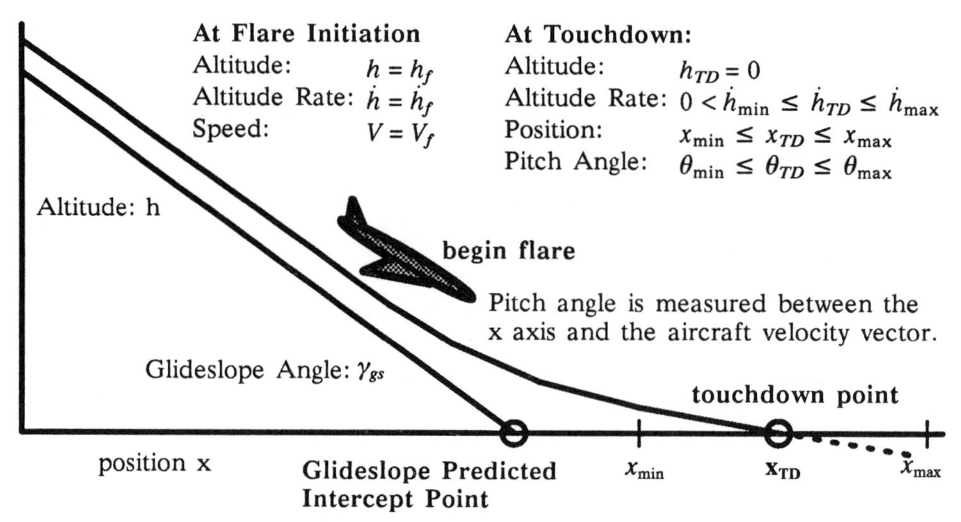

Figure 3: Glideslope and Flare Geometry

3.2 STATE EQUATIONS

Linearized equations of motion were used for the aircraft during each phase. They are adequate during the short period of time spent during glideslope and flare. A pitch stability augmentation system and an auto-throttle were added to the aircraft state equations to damp the bare airframe oscillatory behavior and provide speed control. The function of the autoland controller is to transform information about desired and actual trajectories into the aircraft pitch command. This is input to the pitch stability augmentation system to develop the aircraft elevator angle that in turn controls the aircraft's actual pitch angle. Simplifications retain the overall quality of system response (i.e., high frequency dynamics were neglected).

3.3 WIND MODEL

The environment influences the process through wind disturbances represented by constant velocity and turbulence components. The magnitude of the constant velocity component is a function of altitude (wind shear). Turbulence is a stochastic process whose mean and variance are functions of altitude. For the horizontal and vertical wind turbulence velocities, the so-called Dryden spectra for spatial turbulence distribution are assumed. These are amenable to simulation and show reasonable agreement with measured data (Neuman & Foster, 1970). The generation of turbulence is effected by applying Gaussian white noise to coloring filters.

4 NEURAL NETWORK LEARNING IMPLEMENTATION

As previously noted, modern control theory suggests that a performance index for evaluating control laws should first be constructed, and then the control law should be computed to optimize the performance index. Generally, numerical methods are used for estimating the parameters of a control law. Neural network algorithms can actually be seen as constituting such numerical methods (Narendra and Parthasarathy, 1990; Bryson and Ho, 1969; Le Cun, 1989). We present here an implementation of a neural network algorithm to address the aircraft landing problem.

4.1 DIFFERENCE EQUATIONS

The state of the aircraft (including stability augmentation and autothrottle) can be represented by a vector X, containing variables representing speed, angle of attack, pitch rate, pitch angle, altitude rate and altitude. The difference equations describing the dynamics of the controlled plant can be written as shown in equation 1.

$$X_{t+1} = A_t X_t + B_t U_t + C D_t + N_t \tag{1}$$

The matrix A represents the plant dynamics and B represents the aircraft response to the control U. D is the desired state and N is the additive noise computed from the wind model. The switching controller can be written as in equation 2 below. Referring to Figure 2, the weight matrix V in the sigmoidal switch links actual altitude to each switch unit. The weight matrix W in the linear controller links altitude error, altitude rate error and altitude integral error to each linear unit output.

$$U_t = P_t^T L_t \quad \textit{where } P_t = \textit{Sigmoidal switch and } L_t = \textit{Linear controller} \tag{2}$$

Figure 4 shows a recurrent network implementation of the entire system. Actual and desired states at time $t+1$ are fed back to the input layers. Thus, with recurrent connections between output and input, the network generates entire trajectories and is seen as a recurrent back–propagation network (Rumelhart, Hinton & Williams, 1986; Jordan & Jacobs, 1990). The network is trained using the back–propagation algorithm with given wind distributions. For the controller, we chose initially two basic PID controller blocks (see Figure 2) to represent glideslope and flare. The task of the network is then to learn the state dependent PID controller gains that optimize the cost function.

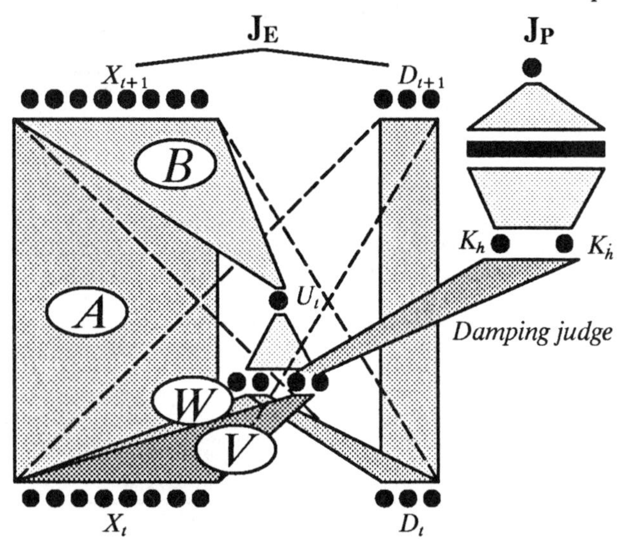

Figure 4: Recurrent Neural Network Architecture

4.2 PERFORMANCE INDEX OPTIMIZATION

The basic performance measure selected for this problem was the squared trajectory error accumulated over the duration of the landing. Trajectory error corresponds to a weighted combination of altitude and altitude rate errors.

Since minimizing only the trajectory error can lead to undesirable responses (e.g., oscillatory aircraft motions), we include relative stability constraints in the performance index. Aircraft transient responses depend on the value of a damping factor. An analysis was performed by probing the plant with a range of values for controller weight parameters. The data was used to train a "damping judge" net to categorize "good" and "bad" damping. This net was used to construct a penalty function on "bad" damping. As seen in Figure 4, additional units were added for this purpose.

The main optimization problem is now stated. Given an initial state, minimize the expected value over the environmental disturbances of performance index J.

$$J = J_E + J_P = \textit{Trajectory Error} + \textit{Performance Constraint Penalty} \tag{3}$$

$$J_E = \sum_{t=1}^{T} a_h[\, h_{cmd_t} - h_t\,]^2 + a_{\dot{h}}[\, \dot{h}_{cmd_t} - \dot{h}_t\,]^2 \quad \textit{We used } a_h = a_{\dot{h}} = 1$$

$$J_P = \sum_{t=1}^{T} Max(0, \zeta_{judge} - \zeta^*_{judge})(\zeta_{judge} - \zeta^*_{judge}) \quad \textit{Note that when } \zeta_{judge} \leq \zeta^*_{judge}, \textit{ there is no penalty. Otherwise, it is quadratic.}$$

5 SIMULATION EXPERIMENTS

We now describe our simulations. First, we introduce our training procedure. We then present statistical results of flight simulations for a variety of wind conditions.

5.1 TRAINING PROCEDURE

Networks were initialized in various ways and trained with a random wind distribution where the constant sheared speed varied from 10 ft/sec tailwind to 40 ft/sec headwind (a strong wind). Several learning strategies were used to change the way the network was exposed to various response characteristics of the plant. The exact form of the resulting *V* switch weights varied, but not the equivalent gain schedules.

5.2 STATISTICAL RESULTS

After training, the performance of the network controller was tested for different wind conditions. Table 1 shows means and standard deviations of performance variables computed over 1000 landings for five different wind conditions. Shown

Table 1: Landing Statistics (standard deviations in parenthesis).

	Overall Performance		Glide Slope Mean Squared Error		Flare Mean Squared Error		Touchdown Performance		
Wind	J/T	T	$J : h_{gs}$	$J : \dot{h}_{gs}$	$J : h_{fl}$	$J : \dot{h}_{fl}$	x_{TD}	θ_{TD}	$\dot{h}_{TD}$
H=-10	1.34 (0.56)	21.6 (0.047)	13.500 (9.8)	4.230 (2.6)	8.50 (4.4)	2.67 (1.2)	1030 (11)	0.0473 (0.0039)	-2.15 (0.052)
H=0	0.27 (0.00)	22.2 (0.000)	0.603 (0.0)	0.209 (0.0)	3.31 (0.0)	1.86 (0.0)	1080 (0)	-0.0400 (0.0000)	-1.98 (0.000)
H=10	0.96 (0.53)	23.0 (0.052)	12.500 (9.2)	4.390 (2.6)	3.17 (2.2)	2.01 (1.1)	1160 (12)	-0.1260 (0.0046)	-1.79 (0.040)
H=20	3.56 (2.10)	23.8 (0.100)	54.000 (38.0)	18.500 (11.0)	8.65 (8.2)	3.43 (2.7)	1230 (24)	-0.2170 (0.0100)	-1.64 (0.061)
H=30	8.03 (4.70)	24.6 (0.160)	130.000 (91.0)	43.200 (25.0)	19.20 (19.0)	5.73 (4.7)	1310 (39)	-0.3110 (0.0170)	-1.50 (0.076)
H=40	13.40 (7.80)	25.5 (0.220)	219.000 (150.0)	76.200 (46.0)	37.00 (36.0)	9.24 (8.0)	1400 (54)	-0.4030 (0.0230)	-1.39 (0.083)

are values for overall performance (quadratic cost J per time step, landing time T), trajectory performance (quadratic cost J on altitude and altitude rate), and landing performance (touchdown position, pitch angle, altitude rate).

5.3 CONTROL LAWS OBTAINED BY LEARNING

By examining network weights, equation 2 yields the gains of an equivalent controller over the entire trajectory (gain schedules). These gain schedules represent *optimality* with respect to a given performance index. Results show that the switch builds a *smooth* transition between glideslope and flare and provides the network controller with a *non-linear distributed* control law for the whole trajectory.

6 DISCUSSION

The architecture we propose integrates *a priori* knowledge of real plants within the structure of the neural network. The knowledge of the physics of the system and its representation in the network are part of the solution. Such *a priori* knowledge structures are not only useful for finding control solutions, but also allow interpretations of network dynamics in term of standard control theory. By observing the weights learned by the network, we can compute gain schedules and understand how the network controls the plant.

The augmented architecture also allows us to control damping. In general, integrating optimal control performance indices with constraints on plant response characteristics is not an easy task. The neural network approach and back-propagation learning represent an interesting and elegant solution to this problem. Other constraints on states or response characteristics can also be implemented with similar architectures. In the present case, the control gains are obtained to minimize the objective performance index while the plant remains within a desired stability region. The effect of this approach provides good damping and control gain schedules that make the plant robust to disturbances.

Acknowledgements

This research was supported by the Boeing High Technology Center. Particular thanks are extended to Gerald Cohen of Boeing. We would also like to thank Anil Phatak for his decisive help and Yoshiro Miyata for the use of his XNet simulator.

References

Bryson, A. & Ho, Y. C. (1969). *Applied Optimal Control.* Blaisdel Publishing Co.

Jordan, M. I. & Jacobs, R. A. (1990). Learning to control an unstable system with forward modeling. In D. S. Touretzky (Ed.), *Neural Information Processing Systems 2.* Morgan Kaufman: San Mateo, CA.

Le Cun, Y. (1989). A theoretical framework for back-propagation. In D. Touretzky, G. Hinton and T. Sejnowski (Eds.), *Proceedings of the 1988 Connectionist Models Summer School.* Morgan Kaufman: San Mateo, CA.

Narendra, K. & Parthasarathy, K. (1990). Identification and control of dynamical systems using neural networks. *IEEE Transactions on Neural Networks, 1,* 4–26.

Neuman, F. & Foster, J. D. (1970). Investigation of a digital automatic aircraft landing system in turbulence. *NASA Technical Note TN D–6066.* NASA–Ames Research Center, Moffett Field, CA.

Rumelhart, D. E., Hinton G. E., Williams R. J. (1986). Learning internal representations by error propagation. In D. E. Rumelhart & J. L. McClelland (Eds.) *Parallel Distributed Processing: Explorations in the Microstructures of Cognition (Vol. I).* Cambridge, MA: MIT Press.

Real-time autonomous robot navigation using VLSI neural networks

Lionel Tarassenko Michael Brownlow Gillian Marshall* **Jon Tombs**
Department of Engineering Science
Oxford University, Oxford, OX1 3PJ, UK

Alan Murray

Department of Electrical Engineering
Edinburgh University, Edinburgh, EH9 3JL, UK

Abstract

We describe a real time robot navigation system based on three VLSI neural network modules. These are a resistive grid for path planning, a nearest-neighbour classifier for localization using range data from a time-of-flight infra-red sensor and a sensory-motor associative network for dynamic obstacle avoidance.

1 INTRODUCTION

There have been very few demonstrations of the application of VLSI neural networks to *real world* problems. Yet there are many signal processing, pattern recognition or optimization problems where a large number of competing hypotheses need to be explored in parallel, most often in real time. The massive parallelism of VLSI neural network devices, with one multiplier circuit per synapse, is ideally suited to such problems. In this paper, we present preliminary results from our design for a real time robot navigation system based on VLSI neural network modules. This is a

*Also: RSRE, Great Malvern, Worcester, WR14 3PS

real world problem which has not been *fully* solved by traditional AI methods; even when partial solutions have been proposed and implemented, these have required vast computational resources, usually remote from the robot and linked to it via an umbilical cord.

2 OVERVIEW

The aim of our work is to develop an autonomous vehicle capable of *real-time* navigation, including obstacle avoidance, in a known indoor environment. The obstacles may be permanent (static) or unexpected and dynamic (for example, in an automated factory environment, the walls and machines are permanent but people, other moving vehicles and packages are not.) There are three neural network modules at the heart of our navigation system: a localization module (to determine, at any time, the robot's position within the environment), an obstacle detection module and a path planning module (to compute a path to the goal which avoids obstacles). These modules perform *low-level processing in real time* which can then be decoupled from higher level processing to be carried out by a simple controller. It is our view that such a hybrid system is the best way to realise the computational potential of artificial neural networks for solving a real world problem such as this without compromising overall system performance.

A short description of each module is now given. In each case, the general principles are first outlined and, where applicable, the results of our preliminary work are then reported.

3 PATH PLANNING

The use of resistive grids for parallel analog computation was first suggested by Horn in the mid-seventies (Horn, 1974) and the idea has since been exploited by Mead and co-workers, for example in a silicon retina (Mead and Mahowald, 1988). Although these resistive grids cannot be said to be neural networks in the conventional sense, they also perform parallel analog computation and they have the same advantages, in terms of speed and fault-tolerance, as any hardware realisation of neural networks.

We have taken the resistive grid concept and applied it to the path planning problem, here taken to be the computation of an obstacle-avoiding path, in a structured environment, from the robot's initial (or present) position (P) to its goal (G). In our approach, the robot's working domain is discretized and mapped onto a resistive grid of hexagonal or rectangular cells – see Figure 1 which shows the test environment for Autonomous Guided Vehicles (AGV's) in the Oxford Robotics Laboratory. Each resistor in the grid has a value of R_0, unless it is part of a region of the grid corresponding to an obstacle, in which case its resistance is infinite (R_∞).

The principle of the method is perhaps best understood by considering a continuous analog of the resistive grid (for example, a sheet of material of uniform resistivity in which holes have been cut to represent the obstacles). The current streamlines resulting from the application of an external source between P and G skirt around the obstacles; if we follow one of these streamlines from P to G, we will obtain a *guaranteed* collision-free path since current cannot flow into the obstacles (Tarassenko and

Blake, 1991). For simple cases such as circularly symmetric conductivity distributions in 2D, Laplace's equation can be solved in order to calculate the value of the potential V at every point within the workspace. Following a current streamline is then simply a matter of performing gradient descent in V.

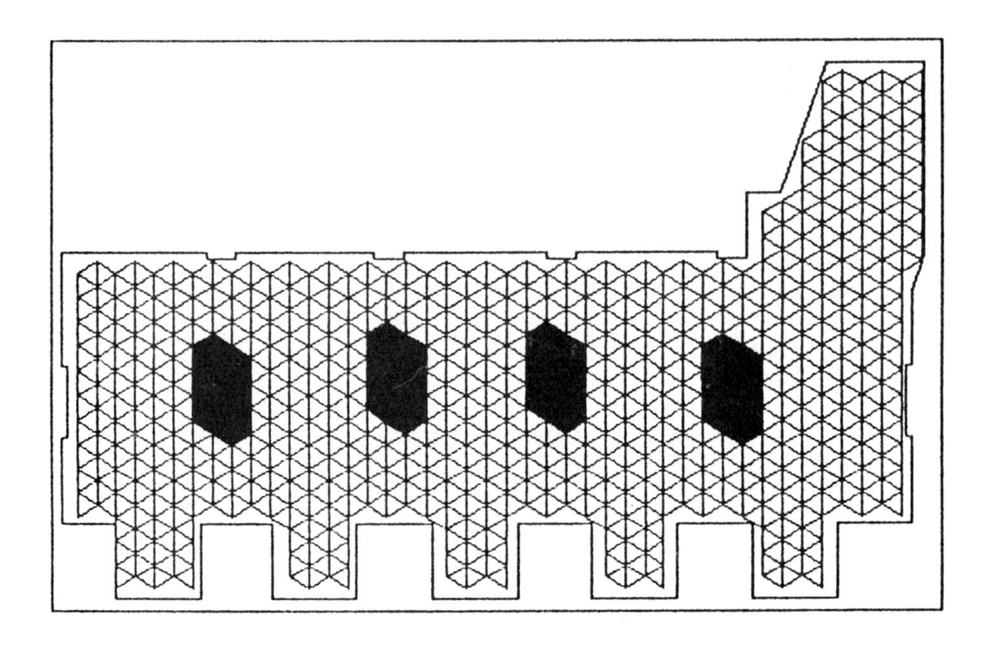

Figure 1: The Oxford test environment for AGV's mapped out as a hexagonal resistive grid. The resistors corresponding to the four pillars in the middle are open circuits. Note that the pillars are enlarged in their grid representation in order to take into account the mobile robot's finite size.

It is not possible, however, to solve Laplace's equation analytically for realistic environments. With the resistive grid, the problem is discretized and mapped onto a hardware representation which can be implemented in VLSI. As soon as an external source of power is connected between P and G, the resistive network settles into the state of least power dissipation and the node voltages can be read out (hardware computation of Kirchhoff's equations). The path from P to G is computed incrementally from *local* voltage measurements: for each node, the next move is identified by measuring the voltage drop ΔV_n between that node and each of its nearest neighbours ($n = 6$ for a hexagonal grid) and then selecting the node corresponding to $(\Delta V_n)_{max}$. This is illustrated by the example of a robot in a maze (Figure 2). As above, the resistors shown shaded are open circuits whilst all other resistors are set to be equal to R_0. The robot is initially placed at the centre of the maze (P) and a path has to be found to the goal in the top left-hand corner (G). The solid line shows the path resulting from a *single application* of the voltage between P and G. The dotted line shows the (optimal) path computed by re-applying the voltage at every node as the robot moves towards the goal. As already indicated, this is actually how we intend to use the resistive grid planner in practice, since this approach also allows us to re-compute the robot's path whenever unexpected obstacles appear in the environment (see Section 5).

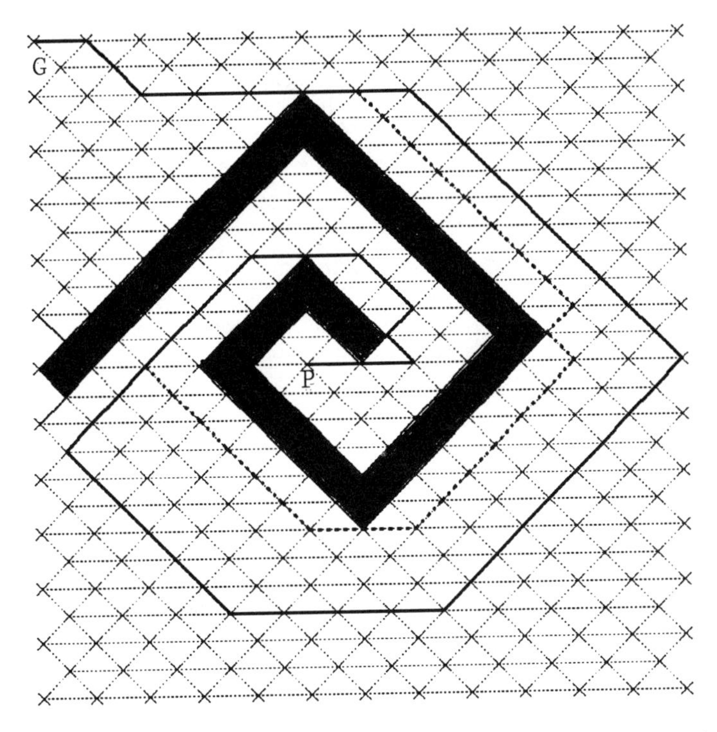

Figure 2: Path from middle of maze (P) to top left-hand corner (G)

3.1 VLSI IMPLEMENTATION

The VLSI implementation of the resistive grid method will allow us to solve the path planning for complex environments in real time. MOS switches are ideal implementations of the binary resistors in the grid. Each transistor can be programmed to be either open (R_∞) or closed (R_0) from a RAM cell connected to its gate. With the incremental computation of the path described above, the selection of the next move is a matter of identifying the largest of six voltages. Of course, the nearest neighbour voltages and that of the P node could be read out through an A/D converter and the decision made off-chip. We favour a full hardware solution instead, whereby the maximum voltage difference is directly identified on-chip.

4 LOCALIZATION

The autonomous robot should at any time be able to work out its position in the workspace so that the path to the goal can be updated if required. The grid representation of the environment used for the path planner can also be employed for localization purposes, in which case localization becomes, in the first instance, a matter of identifying the nearest node in the grid at any time during navigation.

This task can be performed by harnessing the pattern recognition capabilities of neural networks. The room environment is learnt by recording a 360° range scan at every node during a training phase prior to navigation. During navigation, the nearest node is identified using a minimum-distance classifier implemented on a single-layer neural network working on dense input data (one range value every 3°, say). In order to solve the localization problem in real-time, we have designed a time-of-flight *optical* rangefinder, which uses near infra-red light, amplitude-modulated at a frequency of just above 5 MHz, together with a heterodyne mixing technique. Our design is capable of resolving phase shifts in the received light signal of the order of 0.1° over a 50 dB dynamic range.

The rotating optical scanner gives a complete 360° scan approximately every second during navigation. The minimum-distance classifier is used to compare this scan $\mathbf{x}$ with the k patterns $\mathbf{u}_i$ recorded at each node during training. If we use a Euclidean metric for the comparison, this is equivalent to identifying the pattern $\mathbf{u}_i$ for which:

$$\| \mathbf{x} - \mathbf{u}_i \|^2 = \| \mathbf{x} \|^2 - 2\mathbf{u}_i^T \mathbf{x} + \| \mathbf{u}_i \|^2 \tag{1}$$

is a minimum. The first term in the above equation is the same for all i and can be ignored. We can therefore write:

$$g_i(\mathbf{x}) = -\frac{1}{2}(-2\mathbf{w}_i^T \mathbf{x} + \mathbf{u}_i^2) = \mathbf{w}_i^T \mathbf{x} + w_{i0} \tag{2}$$

where $g_i(\mathbf{x})$ is a linear discriminant function, $\mathbf{w}_i = \mathbf{u}_i$ and $w_{i0} = -\frac{1}{2}\mathbf{u}_i^2$. Thus each $\mathbf{w}_i$ vector is one of the learnt patterns $\mathbf{u}_i$ and the discriminant $g_i(\mathbf{x})$ matches the input $\mathbf{x}$ with $\mathbf{u}_i$, point by point. If we let $\mathbf{w}_i = \{T_{ij}\}$ and $\mathbf{x} = \{V_j\}$ and assume that there are n range values in each scan, then we can write:

$$g_i(\mathbf{x}) = \sum_{j=1}^{j=n} T_{ij} V_j + w_{i0} \tag{3}$$

Thus the synaptic weights are an exact copy of the patterns recorded at each grid point during learning and the neurons can be thought of as processors which compute distances to those patterns. During navigation, the nearest node is identified with a network of k neurons evaluating k discriminant functions in parallel, followed by a "winner-take-all" network to pick the maximum $g_i(\mathbf{x})$. This is the well-known implementation of the nearest-neighbour classifier on a neural network architecture. Since the $\mathbf{u}_i$'s are *analog* input vectors, then the synaptic weights T_{ij} will also be analog quantities and this leads to a very efficient use of the pulse-stream analog VLSI technology which we have recently developed for the implementation of neural networks (Murray *et al*, 1990).

With pulse-stream arithmetic, analog computation is performed under digital control. The neural states are represented by *pulse rates* and synaptic multiplication is achieved by pulse width modulation. This allows very compact, fully-programmable, synapse circuits to be designed (3 or 4 transistors per synapse). We have already applied one set of our working chips to the nearest-neighbour classification task described in this Section. They were evaluated on a 24-node test environment and full results have been reported elsewhere (Brownlow, Tarassenko and Murray, 1990). It was found that the $\sum T_{ij}V_j$ scalar products evaluated by our VLSI chips on this test problem were always within 1.2% of those computed on a SUN 3/80 workstation.

5 OBSTACLE DETECTION/AVOIDANCE

A more appropriate name for this module may be that of *local navigation*. The module will rely on optical flow information derived from a number of *fixed* optical sensors mounted on the robot platform. Each sensor will include a pulsed light source to illuminate the scene locally and the light reflected from nearby objects will be focussed onto a pair of gratings at right angles to each other, before being detected by a photodiode array. From the time derivatives of the received signals, it is possible to compute the relative velocities of nearby objects such as moving obstacles. We plan to use previous work on structure from motion to pre-process these velocity vectors and derive from them appropriate feature vectors to be used as inputs to a low-level neural network for motor control (see Figure 3 below).

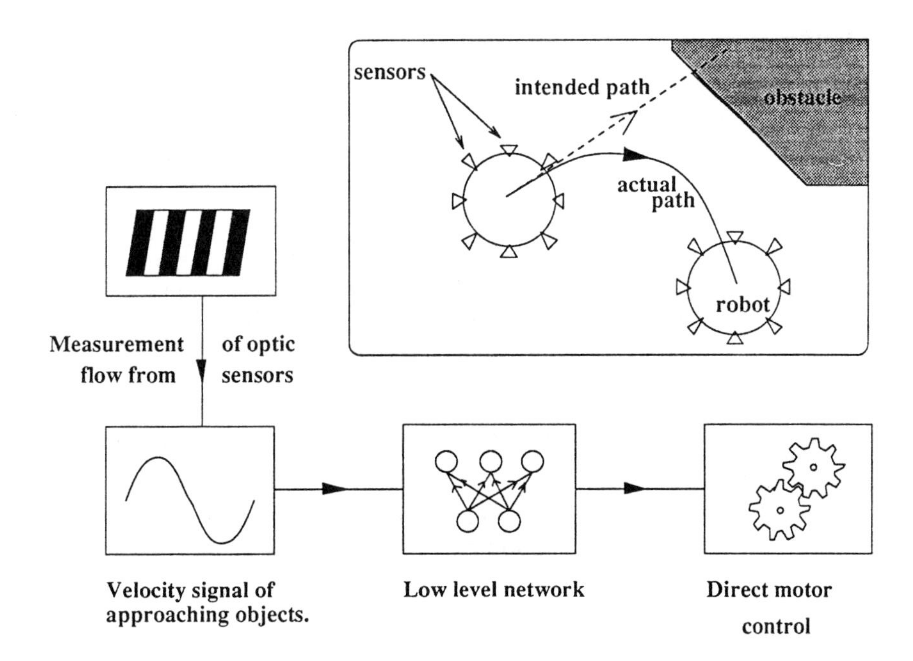

Figure 3: Sensory-motor associative network for obstacle avoidance

The obstacle avoidance network will be taught to associate appropriate motor behaviours with different types of sensory input data, for example the taking of the correct evasive action when a moving object is approaching the robot from a particular direction. This module will therefore be responsible for *path adjustment* in response to dynamic obstacles (with a bandwidth of around 100 Hz), but the path planner of Section 3 will continue to deal with *path reconfiguration* at a much lower data rate (1 Hz), once the dynamic obstacle has been avoided. Our work on this module has, so far, been mainly concerned with the design of the input sensors and associated electronics.

6 CONCLUSION

We have implemented the path planning and localization modules described in this paper on a SUN 4 workstation and used them to control a mobile robot platform via a radio link. This capability was demonstrated at the NIPS'90 Conference with a videotape recording of our mobile robot navigating around static obstacles in a laboratory environment, using real-time infra-red data for localization. It was possible to run the path planner in near real-time in simulation because no resistor value need be changed in a static environment; in order to achieve real-time path planning in a *dynamic* environment, however, the hardware solution of Section 3 will be mandatory. Our aim remains the implementation of all 3 modules in VLSI in order to demonstrate a fully autonomous real-time navigation system with all the sensors and hardware mounted on the robot platform.

Acknowledgements

We gratefully acknowledge the financial support of UK Science and Engineering Research Council and of the EEC (ESPRIT BRA). We have benefitted greatly from the help and advice of members of the Robotics Research Group, most notably Martin Adams, Gabriel Hamid and Jake Reynolds.

References

M.J. Brownlow, L. Tarassenko & A.F. Murray. (1990) Analogue computation using VLSI neural network devices. *Electronics Letters*, **26**(16):1297-1299.

B.K.P. Horn. (1974) Determining lightness from an image. *Computational Graphics & Image Processing*, **3**:277-299.

C.A. Mead & M.A. Mahowald. (1988) A silicon model of early visual processing. *Neural Networks*, **1**(1):91-97.

A.F. Murray, M.J. Brownlow, L. Tarassenko, A. Hamilton, I.S. Han & H.M. Reekie. (1990) Pulse-Firing Neural Chips for Hundreds of Neurons. In D.S. Touretzky (ed.), *Advances in Neural Information Processing Systems 2*, 785-792. San Mateo, CA: Morgan Kaufmann.

L. Tarassenko & A. Blake. (1991). Analogue computation of collision-free paths. To be published in: *Proceedings of 1991 IEEE Int. Conf. on Robotics & Automation*, Sacramento, CA:

Rapidly Adapting Artificial Neural Networks for Autonomous Navigation

Dean A. Pomerleau
School of Computer Science
Carnegie Mellon University
Pittsburgh, PA 15213

Abstract

The ALVINN (Autonomous Land Vehicle In a Neural Network) project addresses the problem of training artificial neural networks in real time to perform difficult perception tasks. ALVINN is a back-propagation network that uses inputs from a video camera and an imaging laser rangefinder to drive the CMU Navlab, a modified Chevy van. This paper describes training techniques which allow ALVINN to learn in under 5 minutes to autonomously control the Navlab by watching a human driver's response to new situations. Using these techniques, ALVINN has been trained to drive in a variety of circumstances including single-lane paved and unpaved roads, multilane lined and unlined roads, and obstacle-ridden on- and off-road environments, at speeds of up to 20 miles per hour.

1 INTRODUCTION

Previous trainable connectionist perception systems have often ignored important aspects of the form and content of available sensor data. Because of the assumed impracticality of training networks to perform realistic high level perception tasks, connectionist researchers have frequently restricted their task domains to either toy problems (e.g. the T-C identification problem [11] [6]) or fixed low level operations (e.g. edge detection [8]). While these restricted domains can provide valuable insight into connectionist architectures and implementation techniques, they frequently ignore the complexities associated with real world problems.

There are exceptions to this trend towards simplified tasks. Notable successes in high level domains such as speech recognition [12], character recognition [5] and face recognition [2] have been achieved using real sensor data. However, the results have come only in very controlled environments, after careful preprocessing of the input to segment and label the training exemplars. In addition, these successful connectionist perception systems have ignored the fact that sensor data normally becomes available gradually and not as a monolithic training set. In short, artificial neural networks previously have never been successfully trained

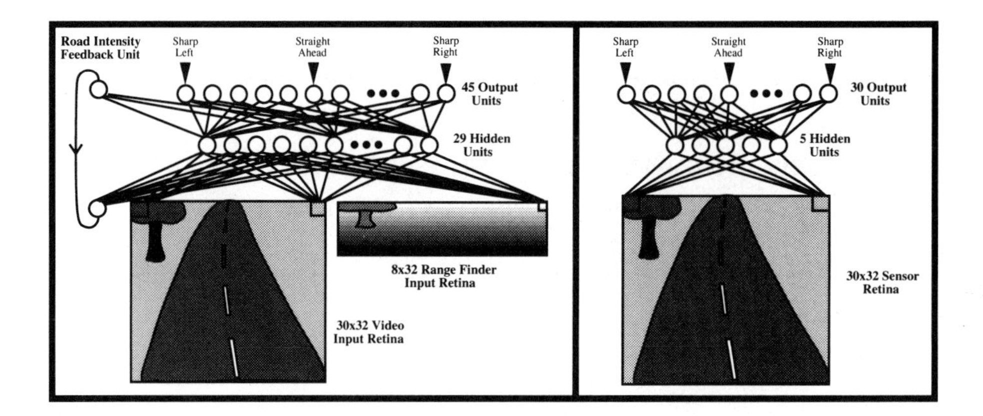

Figure 1: ALVINN's previous (left) and current (right) architectures

using sensor data in real time to perform a real world perception task.

The ALVINN (Autonomous Land Vehicle In a Neural Network) system remedies this shortcoming. ALVINN is a back-propagation network designed to drive the CMU Navlab, a modified Chevy van. Using real time training techniques, the system quickly learns to autonomously control the Navlab by watching a human driver's reactions. ALVINN has been trained to drive in a variety of circumstances including single-lane paved and unpaved roads, multilane lined and unlined roads and obstacle ridden on- and off-road environments, at speeds of up to 20 miles per hour. This paper will primarily focus on improvements and extensions made to the ALVINN system since the presentation of this work at the 1988 NIPS conference [9].

2 NETWORK ARCHITECTURE

The current architecture for an individual ALVINN driving network is significantly simpler than the previous version (See Figure 1). The input layer now consists of a single 30x32 unit "retina" onto which a sensor image from either the video camera or the laser rangefinder is projected. Each of the 960 input units is fully connected to the hidden layer of 5 units, which is in turn fully connected to the output layer. The 30 unit output layer is a linear representation of the currently appropriate steering direction which may serve to keep the vehicle on the road or to prevent it from colliding with nearby obstacles[1]. The centermost output unit represents the "travel straight ahead" condition, while units to the left and right of center represent successively sharper left and right turns.

The reductions in network complexity over previous versions have been made in response to experience with ALVINN in actual driving situations. I have found that the distributed nature of the internal representation allows a network of only 5 hidden units to accurately drive in a variety of situations. I have also learned that multiple sensor inputs to a single network are redundant and can be eliminated. For instance, when training a network on a single-lane road, there is sufficient information in the video image alone for accurate driving. Similarly, for obstacle avoidance, the laser rangefinder image is sufficient and the video image

[1]The task a particular driving network performs depends on the type of input sensor image and the driving situation it has been trained to handle.

is superfluous. The road intensity feedback unit has been eliminated on similar grounds. In the previous architecture, it provided the network with the relative intensity of the road vs. the non-road in the previous image. This information was unnecessary for accurate road following, and undefined in new ALVINN domains such as off-road driving.

To drive the Navlab, an image from the appropriate sensor is reduced to 30 x 32 pixels and projected onto the input layer. After propagating activation through the network, the output layer's activation profile is translated into a vehicle steering command. The steering direction dictated by the network is taken to be the center of mass of the "hill" of activation surrounding the output unit with the highest activation level. Using the center of mass of activation instead of the most active output unit when determining the direction to steer permits finer steering corrections, thus improving ALVINN's driving accuracy.

3 TRAINING "ON-THE-FLY"

The most interesting recent improvement to ALVINN is the training technique. Originally, ALVINN was trained with backpropagation using 1200 simulated scenes portraying roads under a wide variety of weather and lighting conditions [9]. Once trained, the network was able to drive the Navlab at up to 1.8 meters per second (3.5 mph) along a 400 meter path through a wooded area of the CMU campus in weather which included snowy, rainy, sunny and cloudy situations.

Despite its apparent success, this training paradigm had serious shortcomings. It required approximately 6 hours of Sun-4 CPU time to generate the synthetic road scenes, and then an additional 45 minutes of Warp[2] computation time to train the network. Furthermore, while effective at training the network to drive on a single-lane road, extending the synthetic training paradigm to deal with more complex driving situations like multilane and off-road driving would have required prohibitively complex artificial scene generators.

I have developed a scheme called training "on-the-fly" to deal with these problems. Using this technique, the network learns to imitate a person as he drives. The network is trained with back-propagation using the latest video camera image as input and the person's current steering direction as the desired output.

There are two potential problems associated with this simple training on-the-fly scheme. First, since the person steers the vehicle down the center of the road during training, the network will never be presented with situations where it must recover from misalignment errors. When driving for itself, the network may occasionally stray from the road center, so it must be prepared to recover by steering the vehicle back to the middle of the road. The second problem is that naively training the network with only the current video image and steering direction may cause it to overlearn recent inputs. If the person drives the Navlab down a stretch of straight road near the end of training, the network will be presented with a long sequence of similar images. This sustained lack of diversity in the training set will cause the network to "forget" what it had learned about driving on curved roads and instead learn to always steer straight ahead.

Both problems associated with training on-the-fly stem from the fact that back-propagation requires training data which is representative of the full task to be learned. To provide the necessary variety of exemplars while still training on real data, the simple training on-the-

[2]There was formerly a 100 MFLOP Warp systolic array supercomputer onboard the Navlab. It has been replaced by 3 Sun-4s, further necessitating the streamlined architecture described in the previous section.

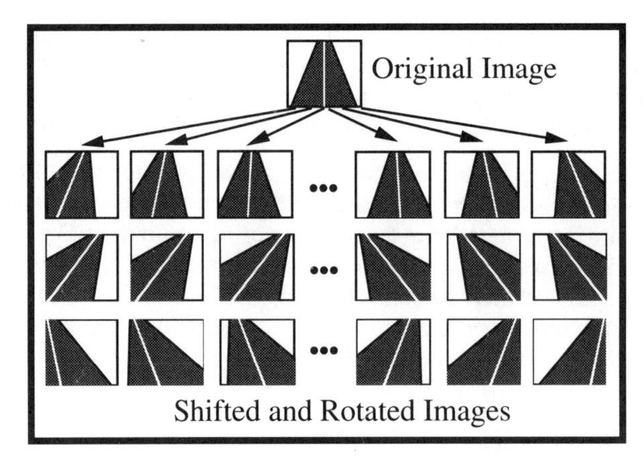

Figure 2: The single original video image is shifted and rotated to create multiple training exemplars in which the vehicle appears to be a different locations relative to the road.

fly scheme described above must be modified. Instead of presenting the network with only the current video image and steering direction, each original image is shifted and rotated in software to create 14 additional images in which the vehicle appears to be situated differently relative to the environment (See Figure 2). The sensor's position and orientation relative to the ground plane are known, so precise transformations can be achieved using perspective geometry. The correct steering direction as dictated by the driver for the original image is altered for each of the transformed images to account for the altered vehicle placement[3]. Using transformed training patterns allows the network to learn how to recover from driving errors. Also, overtraining on repetitive images is less of a problem, since the transformed training exemplars add variety to the training set. As additional insurance against the effects of repetitive exemplars, the training set diversity is further increased by maintaining a buffer of previously encountered training patterns.

In practice, training on-the-fly works as follows. A live sensor image is digitized and reduced to the low resolution image required by the network. This single original image is shifted and rotated 14 times to create 14 additional training exemplars[4]. Fifteen old exemplars from the current training set of 200 patterns are chosen and replaced by the 15 new exemplars. The 15 exemplars to be replaced in the training set are chosen on the basis of how closely they match the steering direction of one of the new tokens. Exchanging a new token for an old token with a similar steering direction helps maintain diversity in the training buffer during monotonous stretches of road by preventing novel older patterns from being replaced by recent redundant ones.

After this replacement process, one forward and one backward pass of the back-propagation algorithm is performed on the 200 exemplars to update the network's weights. The entire process is then repeated. The network requires approximately 50 iterations through this digitize-replace-train cycle to learn to drive in the domains that have been tested. Running

[3]A simple steering model is used when transforming the driver's original direction. It assumes the "correct" steering direction is the one that will eliminate the additional vehicle translation and rotation introduced by the transformation and bringing the vehicle to the point the person was originally steering towards a fixed distance ahead of the vehicle.

[4]The shifts are chosen randomly from the range -1.25 to +1.25 meters and the rotations from the range -6.0 to +6.0 degrees.

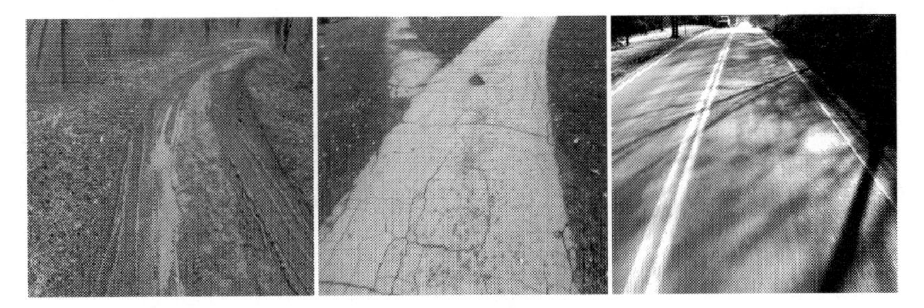

Figure 3: Video images taken on three of the test roads ALVINN has been trained to drive on. They are, from left to right, a single-lane dirt access road, a single-lane paved bicycle path, and a lined two-lane highway.

on a Sun-4, this takes about five minutes during which a person drives the Navlab at about 4 miles per hour over the training road.

4 RESULTS AND DISCUSSION

Once it has learned, the network can accurately traverse the length of road used for training and also generalize to drive along parts of the road it has never encountered under a variety of weather conditions. In addition, since determining the steering direction from the input image merely involves a forward sweep through the network, the system is able to process 25 images per second, allowing it to drive at up to the Navlab's maximum speed of 20 miles per hour[5]. This is over twice as fast as any other sensor-based autonomous system has driven the Navlab [3] [7].

The training on-the-fly scheme gives ALVINN a flexibility which is novel among autonomous navigation systems. It has allowed me to successfully train individual networks to drive in a variety of situations, including a single-lane dirt access road, a single-lane paved bicycle path, a two-lane suburban neighborhood street, and a lined two-lane highway (See Figure 3). Using other sensor modalities as input, including laser range images and laser reflectance images, individual ALVINN networks have been trained to follow roads in total darkness, to avoid collisions in obstacle rich environments, and to follow alongside railroad tracks. ALVINN networks have driven in each of these situations for up to 1/2 mile, until reaching a dead end or a difficult intersection. The development of a system for each of these domains using the "traditional approach" to autonomous navigation would require the programmer to 1) determine what features are important for the particular task, 2) program detectors (using statistical or symbolic techniques) for finding these important features and 3) develop an algorithm for determining which direction to steer from the location of the detected features.

In contrast, ALVINN is able to *learn* for each new domain what image features are important, how to detect them and how to use their position to steer the vehicle. Analysis of the hidden unit representations developed in different driving situations shows that the network forms detectors for the image features which correlate with the correct steering direction. When trained on multi-lane roads, the network develops hidden unit feature detectors for the lines painted on the road, while in single-lane driving situations, the detectors developed are

[5]The Navlab has a hydraulic drive system which allows for very precise speed control, but which prevents the vehicle from driving over 20 miles per hour.

sensitive to road edges and road-shaped regions of similar intensity in the image. For a more detailed analysis of ALVINN's internal representations see [9] [10].

This ability to utilize arbitrary image features can be problematic. This was the case when ALVINN was trained to drive on a poorly defined dirt road with a distinct ditch on its right side. The network had no problem learning and then driving autonomously in one direction, but when driving the other way, the network was erratic, swerving from one side of the road to the other. After analyzing the network's hidden representation, the reason for its difficulty became clear. Because of the poor distinction between the road and the non-road, the network had developed only weak detectors for the road itself and instead relied heavily on the position of the ditch to determine the direction to steer. When tested in the opposite direction, the network was able to keep the vehicle on the road using its weak road detectors but was unstable because the ditch it had learned to look for on the right side was now on the left. Individual ALVINN networks have a tendency to rely on *any* image feature consistently correlated with the correct steering direction. Therefore, it is important to expose them to a wide enough variety of situations during training so as to minimize the effects of transient image features.

On the other hand, experience has shown that it is more efficient to train several domain specific networks for circumstances like one-lane vs. two-lane driving, instead training a single network for all situations. To prevent this network specificity from reducing ALVINN's generality, I am currently implementing connectionist and non-connectionist techniques for combining networks trained for different driving situations. Using a simple rule-based priority system similar to the subsumption architecture [1], I have recently combined a road following network and an obstacle avoidance network. The road following network uses video camera input to follow a single-lane road. The obstacle avoidance network uses laser rangefinder images as input. It is trained to swerve appropriately to prevent a collision when confronted with obstacles and to drive straight when the terrain ahead is free of obstructions. The arbitration rule gives priority to the road following network when determining the steering direction, except when the obstacle avoidance network outputs a sharp steering command. In this case, the urgency of avoiding an imminent collision takes precedence over road following and the steering direction is determined by the obstacle avoidance network. Together, the two networks and the arbitration rule comprise a system capable of staying on the road and swerving to prevent collisions.

To facilitate other rule-based arbitration techniques, I am currently adding to ALVINN a non-connectionist module which maintains the vehicle's position on a map. Knowing its map position will allow ALVINN to use arbitration rules such as "when on a stretch of two lane highway, rely primarily on the two lane highway network". This symbolic mapping module will also allow ALVINN to make high level, goal-oriented decisions such as which way to turn at intersections and when to stop at a predetermined destination.

Finally, I am experimenting with connectionist techniques, such as the task decomposition architecture [6] and the meta-pi architecture [4], for combining networks more seamlessly than is possible with symbolic rules. These connectionist arbitration techniques will enable ALVINN to combine outputs from networks trained to perform the same task using different sensor modalities and to decide when a new expert must be trained to handle the current situation.

Acknowledgements

The principle support for the Navlab has come from DARPA, under contracts DACA76-85-C-0019, DACA76-85-C-0003 and DACA76-85-C-0002. This research was also funded in part by a grant from Fujitsu Corporation.

References

[1] Brooks, R.A. (1986) A robust layered control system for a mobile robot. *IEEE Journal of Robotics and Automation*, vol. RA-2, no. 1, pp. 14-23, April 1986.

[2] Cottrell, G.W. (1990) Extracting features from faces using compression networks: Face, identity, emotion and gender recognition using holons. In Connectionist Models: Proc. of the 1990 Summer School, David Touretzky (Ed.), Morgan Kaufmann, San Mateo, CA.

[3] Crisman, J.D. and Thorpe C.E. (1990) Color vision for road following. In *Vision and Navigation: The CMU Navlab* Charles Thorpe (Ed.), Kluwer Academic Publishers, Boston, MA.

[4] Hampshire, J.B., Waibel A.H. (1989) The meta-pi network: Building distributed knowledge representations for robust pattern recognition. Carnegie Mellon Technical Report CMU-CS-89-166-R. August, 1989.

[5] LeCun, Y., Boser, B., Denker, J.S., Henderson, D., Howard, R.E., Hubbard, W., and Jackel, L.D. (1989) Backpropagation applied to handwritten zip code recognition. *Neural Computation 1(4).*

[6] Jacobs, R.A., Jordan, M.I., Barto, A.G. (1990) Task decomposition through competition in a modular connectionist architecture: The what and where vision tasks. Univ. of Massachusetts Computer and Information Science Technical Report 90-27, March 1990.

[7] Kluge, K. and Thorpe C.E. (1990) Explicit models for robot road following. In *Vision and Navigation: The CMU Navlab* Charles Thorpe (Ed.), Kluwer Academic Publishers, Boston, MA.

[8] Koch, C., Bair, W., Harris, J.G., Horiuchi, T., Hsu, A. and Luo, J. (1990) Real-time computer vision and robotics using analog VLSI circuits. In *Advances in Neural Information Processing Systems, 2*, D.S. Touretzky (Ed.), Morgan Kaufmann, San Mateo, CA.

[9] Pomerleau, D.A. (1989) ALVINN: An Autonomous Land Vehicle In a Neural Network, *Advances in Neural Information Processing Systems, 1*, D.S. Touretzky (Ed.), Morgan Kaufmann, San Mateo, CA.

[10] Pomerleau, D.A. (1990) Neural network based autonomous navigation. In *Vision and Navigation: The CMU Navlab* Charles Thorpe (Ed.), Kluwer Academic Publishers, Boston, MA.

[11] Rumelhart, D.E., Hinton, G.E., and Williams, R.J. (1986) Learning internal representations by error propagation. In D.E. Rumelhart and J.L. McClelland (Eds.) *Parallel Distributed Processing: Explorations in the Microstructures of Cognition. Vol. 1: Foundations*. Bradford Books/MIT Press, Cambridge, MA.

[12] Waibel, A., Hanazawa, T., Hinton, G., Shikano, K., Lang, K. (1988) Phoneme recognition: Neural Networks vs. Hidden Markov Models. *Proceedings from Int. Conf. on Acoustics, Speech and Signal Processing*, New York, New York.

Learning Trajectory and Force Control of an Artificial Muscle Arm by Parallel-hierarchical Neural Network Model

Masazumi Katayama **Mitsuo Kawato**
Cognitive Processes Department
ATR Auditory and Visual Perception Research Laboratories
Seika-cho, Soraku-gun, Kyoto 619-02, JAPAN

Abstract

We propose a new *parallel-hierarchical neural network* model to enable motor learning for simultaneous control of both trajectory and force, by integrating Hogan's control method and our previous neural network control model using a *feedback-error-learning* scheme. Furthermore, two *hierarchical control laws* which apply to the model, are derived by using the Moore-Penrose pseudo-inverse matrix. One is related to the *minimum muscle-tension-change* trajectory and the other is related to the *minimum motor-command-change* trajectory. The human arm is redundant at the dynamics level since joint torque is generated by agonist and antagonist muscles. Therefore, acquisition of the inverse model is an ill-posed problem. However, the combination of these control laws and feedback-error-learning resolve the ill-posed problem. Finally, the efficiency of the parallel-hierarchical neural network model is shown by learning experiments using an artificial muscle arm and computer simulations.

1 INTRODUCTION

For humans to properly interact with the environment using their arms, both arm posture and exerted force must be skillfully controlled. The hierarchical neural network model which we previously proposed was successfully applied to trajectory control of an industrial manipulator (Kawato et al., 1987). However, this model could not directly be applied to force control, because the manipulator mechanism was essentially different from the musculo-skeletal system of a human arm. Hogan proposed a biologically motivated control method which specifies both the virtual trajectory and the mechanical impedance of a musculo-skeletal system (Hogan, 1984, 1985). One of its advantages is that both trajectory and force can be simultaneously controlled. However, this control method does not explain motor learning.

In this paper, by integrating these two previous studies, we propose a new *Parallel-Hierarchical Neural network* Model (PHNM) using a *feedback-error-learning* scheme we previously proposed (Kawato et al., 1987), as shown in Fig.1. PHNM explains the biological motor learning for simultaneous control of both trajectory and force. Arm movement depends on the static and dynamic properties of a musculo-skeletal system. From this viewpoint, its inverse model which computes a motor command from a desired trajectory and force, consists of two parallel inverse models: the Inverse Statics Model (ISM) and the Inverse Dynamics Model (ISM) (see Fig.1).

The human arm is redundant at the dynamics level since joint torque is generated by agonist and antagonist muscles. Therefore, acquisition of the inverse model is an ill-posed problem in the sense that the muscle tensions can not be uniquely determined from the prescribed trajectory and force. The central nervous system can resolve the ill-posed problem by applying suitable constraints. Based on behavioral data of human multi-joint arm movement, Uno et al. (1989) found that the trajectory was generated on the criterion that the time integral of the squared sum of the rate of change of muscle tension is minimized. From this point of view, we assume that the central nervous system controls the arm by using two hierarchical objective functions. One objective function is related to the *minimum muscle-tension-change* trajectory. The other objective function is related to the *minimum motor-command-change* trajectory. From this viewpoint, we propose two hierarchical control laws which apply to the feedback controller shown in Fig.1. These control laws are calculated with the Moore-Penrose pseudo-inverse matrix of the Jacobian matrix from muscle tensions or motor commands to joint torque. The combination of these control laws and the feedback-error-learning resolve the ill-posed problem. As a result, the inverse model related to hierarchical objective functions can be acquired by PHNM. We ascertained the efficiency of PHNM by performing experiments in learning control using an artificial-muscle arm with agonist and antagonist muscle-like rubber actuators as shown in Fig.2 (Katayama et al., 1990).

2 PARALLEL-HIERARCHICAL NEURAL NETWORK MODEL

In a simple case, the dynamics equation of a human multi-joint arm is described as follows:

$$R(\theta)\ddot{\theta} + B(\theta,\dot{\theta})\dot{\theta} = \tau + G(\theta), \tag{1a}$$

$$\tau = a_f(\theta)T_f(M_f,\theta,\dot{\theta}) - a_e(\theta)T_e(M_e,\theta,\dot{\theta}). \tag{1b}$$

Here, $R(\theta)$ is the inertia matrix, $B(\theta,\dot{\theta})$ expresses a matrix of centrifugal, coriolis and friction forces and $G(\theta)$ is the vector of joint torque due to gravity. M_f and M_e are agonist and antagonist motor commands, T_f and T_e are agonist and antagonist muscle tensions, θ is the joint-angle, τ is joint torque generated from the tensions of a pair of muscles and $a_f(\theta)$ and $a_e(\theta)$ are moment arms.

If the arm is static ($\dot{\theta} = \ddot{\theta} = 0$), (1a) and (1b) are reduced to the following:

$$0 = a_f(\theta)T_f(M_f,\theta,0) - a_e(\theta)T_e(M_e,\theta,0) + G(\theta). \tag{2}$$

Therefore, (2) is a statics equation. The problem, which calculates the motor commands from joint angles based on (2), is called the *inverse statics*. There are two difficulties: first, (2) including nonlinear functions (a_f, a_e, T_f, T_e and G), must be solved. Second, the inverse statics is an ill-posed problem as mentioned above. These difficulties are resolved by the ISM. The problem of computing dynamic torque other than (2) is called

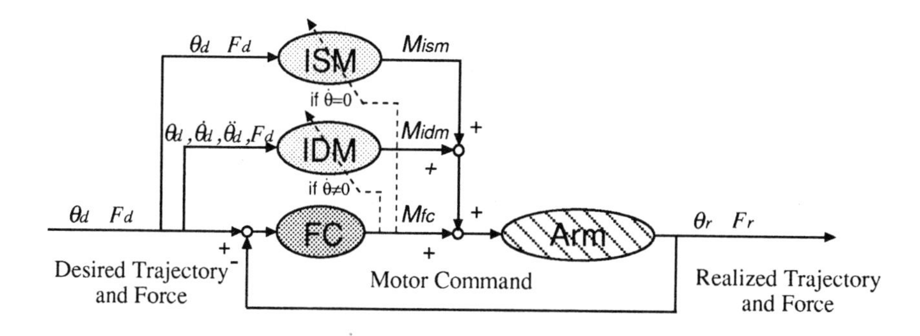

Figure 1: Parallel-Hierarchical Neural Network Model

the *inverse dynamics* and it is resolved by the IDM. The main role of the ISM is to control the equilibrium posture and mechanical stiffness (Hogan, 1984), and that of the IDM is to compensate for dynamic properties of the arm in fast movements. PHNM, in addition to a feedback controller, hierarchically arranges these parallel inverse models. The motor command is the sum of three outputs (M_{ism}, M_{idm} and M_{fc}) calculated by the ISM, the IDM and the feedback controller, respectively, as shown in Fig.1. The outputs from the ISM and IDM are calculated by feedforward neural networks with synaptic weights w from desired trajectory θ_d and desired force F_d. These neural network models can be described as the mapping from inputs θ_d and F_d to motor commands. In order to acquire the parallel inverse model, synaptic weights change according to the following *feedback-error-learning* algorithm.

$$\frac{dw}{dt} = \left(\frac{\partial \Psi}{\partial w}\right)^t M_{fc} \tag{3}$$

The ISM learns when the arm is static and the IDM learns when it is moving. The feedback motor command M_{fc} is fed only to the ISM when $\dot{\theta} = 0$ and only to the IDM when $\dot{\theta} \neq 0$ as an error signal for synaptic modification. The arm is mainly controlled by the feedback controller before learning, and the feedforward control is basically performed only by the parallel inverse model after learning because the output M_{fc} of the feedback controller is minimized after learning. Two control laws which apply to the feedback controller, are derived below.

3 HIERARCHICAL CONTROL MECHANISM

In order to acquire the parallel inverse models related to hierarchical objective functions, we propose two control laws reducing the redundancy at the dynamics level, which apply to a feedback controller in the PHNM.

3.1 MATHEMATICAL MUSCLE MODEL

Tensions (T_f, T_e) of agonist and antagonist muscles are generally modeled as follows:

$$T_f = K(M_f)\{\theta_{0,f}(M_f) - \theta\} - B(M_f)\dot{\theta}, \tag{4a}$$

$$T_e = K(M_e)\{\theta - \theta_{0,e}(M_e)\} + B(M_e)\dot{\theta}. \tag{4b}$$

Here, M consists of M_f and M_e for agonist and antagonist muscles, respectively. The mechanical impedance of a human arm can be manipulated by the stiffness $K(M)$ and viscosity $B(M)$ of the muscle itself, depending on their motor commands. $\theta_{0,f}(M_f)$ and $\theta_{0,e}(M_e)$ are joint angles at equilibrium position. $K(M)$, $B(M)$, $\theta_{0,f}(M_f)$ and $\theta_{0,e}(M_e)$ are approximately given as $K(M) \cong k_0 + kM$, $B(M) \cong b_0 + bM$, $\theta_{0,f}(M_f) \cong \theta_0 + cM_f$ and $\theta_{0,e}(M_e) \cong -\theta_0 - cM_e$, respectively. k and b are coefficients which, respectively, determine elasticity and viscosity. k_0 and b_0 are intrinsic elasticity and viscosity, respectively. θ_0 is the intrinsic equilibrium angle and c is a constant. Small changes in joint torque are expressed by using the Jacobian matrix A from small changes in motor command to small changes in joint torque. Therefore, by using the Moore-Penrose pseudo-inverse matrix $A^{\#}$, small changes in motor command are calculated as follows:

$$\begin{pmatrix} \Delta M_f \\ \Delta M_e \end{pmatrix} = A^{\#}\Delta\tau = \frac{1}{a_f(\theta)^2\left(C+g_f\right)^2 + a_e(\theta)^2\left(C-g_e\right)^2}\begin{pmatrix} a_f(\theta)\left(C+g_f\right) \\ a_e(\theta)\left(C-g_e\right)\end{pmatrix}\Delta\tau$$

$$\because C = -(k\theta + b\dot{\theta}), \qquad g_f = k_0 c + k\theta_0 + 2kcM_f$$

$$A^{\#} = A^T\left(AA^T\right)^{-1}, \qquad g_e = k_0 c + k\theta_0 + 2kcM_e \tag{5}$$

3.2 HIERARCHICAL CONTROL LAWS

Two feedback control laws are explained below, which apply to the feedback controller shown in Fig.1. Firstly, $\Delta T_f = \Delta M_f$ and $\Delta T_e = \Delta M_e$ are given from (4a) and (4b) by assuming $k=b=0$, $c \neq 0$, $a_f(\theta)=a_e(\theta)=a$ and $g_f=g_e=1$ in the simplest case. The solution $A^{\#}\Delta\tau$ in which the norm $(\Delta T_f^2+\Delta T_e^2)^{1/2}$ of vector ΔT is minimized by using the pseudo-inverse matrix $A^{\#}$, is selected. Therefore, the control law related to the minimum muscle-tension-change trajectory is derived from (5). Then the feedback control law is acquired by using $\Delta\tau = K_p\left(\theta_d - \theta_r\right) + K_d\left(\dot{\theta}_d - \dot{\theta}_r\right) + K_f\left(F_d - F_r\right)$. Here, K_p, K_d and K_f are feedback gains. Learning is performed by applying the motor commands calculated by this feedback control law to the learning algorithm of (3). As a result, the inverse model is acquired by the PHNM after learning. Only when $a_f(\theta)=a_e(\theta)=a$ does, the inverse model strictly give the optimal solution based on the minimum muscle-tension-change trajectory during the movement. a is a constant moment arm.

Next, another control law is derived from (5) by assuming $k,b \neq 0$, $c=0$, $a_f(\theta)=a_e(\theta)=a$ and $g_f=g_e=1$ by a similar way. In this case, the control law is related to the minimum motor-command-change trajectory, because the norm $(\Delta M_f^2+\Delta M_e^2)^{1/2}$ of vector ΔM is minimized by using the pseudo-inverse matrix $A^{\#}$. Then the control law explains the behavioral data of rapid arm movement, during which the mechanical impedance is increased by coactivation of agonist and antagonist muscles (Kurauchi et al., 1980). The mechanical impedance of the muscles increases when C increases. Therefore, C explains the coactivation because C increases when the arm moves rapidly. Thus, rapid arm movement can be stably executed by such coactivation. It is noted that the control law directly takes account of the variable stiffness and viscosity of the muscle itself. Learning is performed by the same algorithm above. As a result, the inverse model acquired by the PHNM gives the approximate solution related to the minimum motor-command-change trajectory, because $A^{\#}$ depends on the joint angle in this case. Furthermore, stiffness and virtual trajectory are uniquely determined from a mathematical muscle model using the outputs of the trained inverse models.

4 EFFICIENCY OF PHNM

The efficiency of the PHNM is shown by the experiment results using two hierarchical control laws.

4.1 ARTIFICIAL MUSCLE ARM

The artificial muscle arm used in our experiments is the rubber-actuator-arm (5 degrees of freedom, 16 rubber actuators, made by Bridgestone Co.), as shown in Fig.2, which is a manipulator with agonist and antagonist muscle-like actuators. The actuators are made of rubber and driven by air. In our experiment, the motor command is air-pressure.

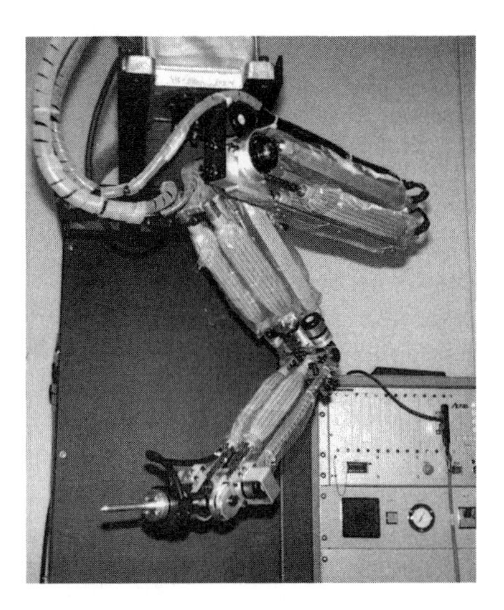

Figure 2: Artificial Muscle Arm

The mechanical structure of the artificial arm is basically the same as that of the human arm. Moreover, properties of the actuator are also similar to those of muscle. The actuator has a variable mechanical impedance which consists of stiffness and viscosity. Then, the stiffness which is mechanically realized, expresses the spring-like behavior of muscle. This property acts as a simple mechanical feedback system whose time delay is "zero". Furthermore, the ratio of the output torque and the weight of the arm is extremely high. Therefore, we hope it will be easy to control the force and trajectory at the end-effector or joint. However, it is difficult to control the trajectory of the arm because the artificial arm, like the human arm, is a very nonlinear system. We note that feedforward control using the trained ISM and IDM is necessary to control the arm.

4.2 TRAJECTORY CONTROL OF ARTIFICIAL MUSCLE ARM

Learning control experiments using an artificial muscle arm are performed with the feedback control law related to the *minimum muscle-tension-change* trajectory. The ISM and IDM use a 3-layer perceptron. The results shown in Fig.3 indicate that the conventional feedback control method can not realize accurate trajectory control, because the realized trajectory lagged behind the desired trajectory. While the results shown in Fig.4a indicate that accurate and smooth trajectory control of a slow movement can be realized only by feedforward control using the trained ISM and IDM after learning, because the realized trajectory fits the desired trajectory. Moreover, the result indicates that the PHNM can resolve the ill-posed inverse problem. The results shown in Fig.4b indicate that learning of the ISM and IDM is finished after about 2,000 iterations, because the output of

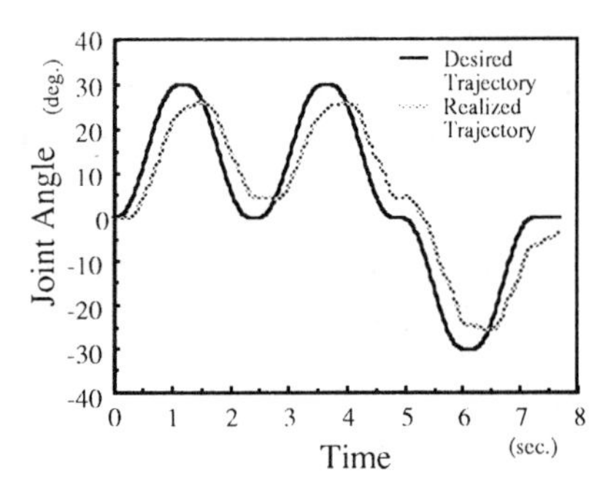

Figure 3: Feedback Control Using Conventional Feedback Controller

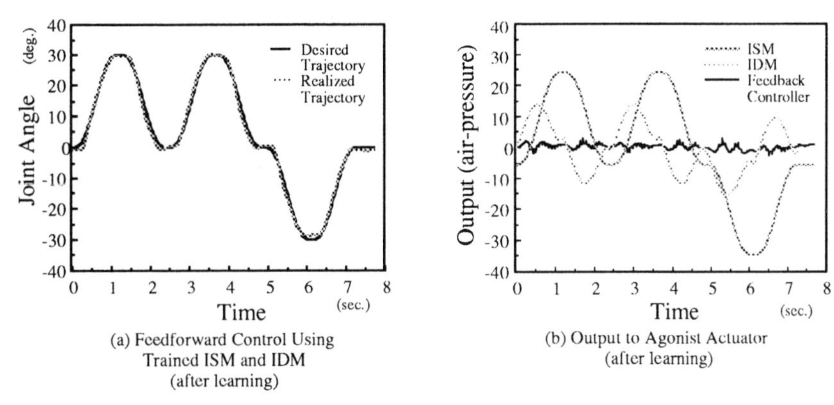

(a) Feedforward Control Using Trained ISM and IDM (after learning)

(b) Output to Agonist Actuator (after learning)

Figure 4: Trajectory Control Using Control Law Related to Minimum Muscle-Tension-Change Criterion (in slow movement using artificial muscle arm)

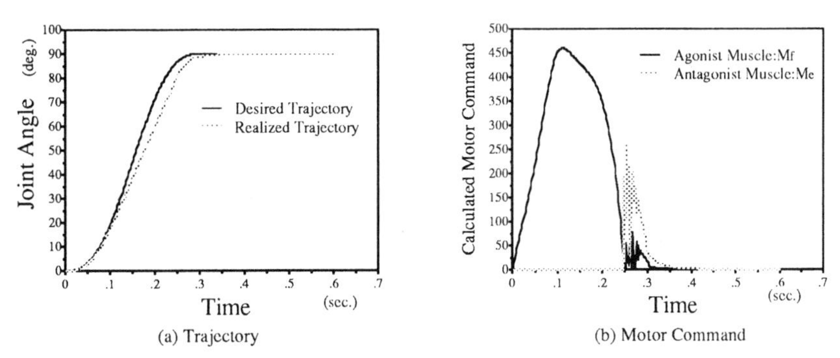

(a) Trajectory

(b) Motor Command

Figure 5: Feedback Trajectory Control Using Control Law Related to Minimum Motor-command-change Criterion (in fast movement using computer simulation)

the feedback controller is minimized. Then note that the output of the ISM is greater than the other outputs. Furthermore, we confirmed that by using an untrained trajectory, the generalization capability of the trained parallel inverse models is good.

4.3 TRAJECTORY CONTROL IN FAST MOVEMENT

One of the advantages of the control law related to the *minimum motor-command-change* criterion, is shown by a trajectory control experiment in fast movement. We confirmed that the feedback control law allowed stable trajectory control in fast movement. Control experiments were performed by computer simulation. The results shown in Fig.5a indicate that PHNM applying this feedback control law realizes stable trajectory control in rapid movement, because no oscillation characteristics can be found when the arm reaches the desired position. This is because the mechanical impedance of the joint increases when a pair of muscles are coactivated (see Fig.5b). Moreover, the results also explain behavioral data in fast arm movement (Kurauchi et al., 1980).

4.4 FORCE CONTROL

We confirmed that the feedback control law related to the *minimum motor-command-change* criterion succeeded for accurate force control. The results shown in Fig.6 indicate that accurate force control can be performed by combining the trained IDM and ISM, with PHNM using this feedback control law.

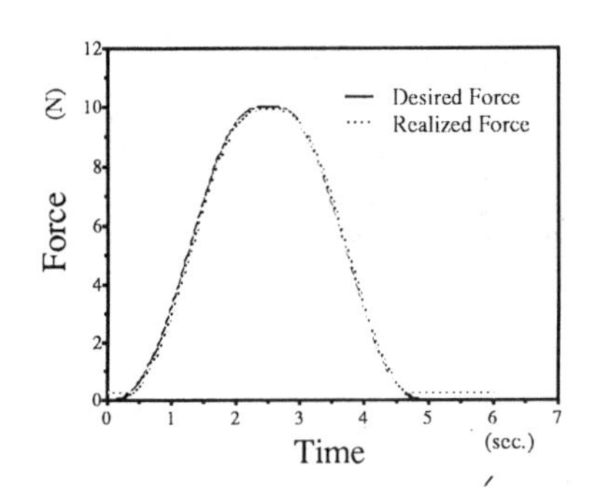

Figure 6: Force Control Using Trained ISM and IDM With Control Law Relate to Minimum Motor-command-change Criterion

5 DISCUSSION

The ISM we proposed in this paper has two advantages. The first is that it is easy to train the inverse model of the controlled object because the inverse model is separated into the ISM and IDM. The second is that control using the ISM explains Bizzi's experiment results with a deafferented rhesus monkey (Bizzi et al., 1984). Furthermore the control using the ISM relates to Hogan's control method using the virtual trajectory (Hogan, 1984, 1985).

The Parallel-Hierarchical Neural network Model proposed in this paper integrates Hogan's impedance control and our previous model, and hence can explain motor learning for simultaneous control of both trajectory and force. There is an infinite number of possible combinations of mechanical impedance and virtual trajectory that can produce the same torque and force. Thus, the problem of determining the impedance and the virtual trajectory was ill-posed in Hogan's framework. In the present paper, they were uniquely determined from (5).

References

[1] Bizzi, E., Accornero, N., Chapple, W. & Hogan, N. (1984) Posture Control and Trajectory Formation During Arm Movement. *The Journal of Neuroscience*, **4**, 11, 2738-2744.

[2] Hogan, N. (1984) An Organizing Principle for a Class of Voluntary Movements. *The Journal of Neuroscience*, **4**, 11, 2745-2754.

[3] Hogan, N. (1985) Impedance Control: An Approach to Manipulation Part I II III. *Journal of Dynamic Systems, Measurement, and Control*, **107**, 1-24.

[4] Katayama, M. & Kawato, M. (1990) Parallel-Hierarchical Neural Network Model for Motor Control of Musculo-Skeletal System. *The Transactions of The Institute of Electronics, Information and Communication Engineers*, **J73-D-II**, 8, 1328-1335. in Japanese.

[5] Kawato, M., Furukawa, K. & Suzuki, R. (1987) A Hierarchical Neural-Network Model for Control and Learning of Voluntary Movement. *Biological Cybernetics*, **57**, 169-185.

[6] Kurauchi, S., Mishima, K. & Kurokawa, T. (1980) Characteristics of Rapid Positional Movements of Forearm. *The Japanese Journal of Ergonomics*, **16**, 5, 263-270. in Japanese.

[7] Uno, Y., Suzuki, R. & Kawato, M. (1989) Minimum Muscle-Tension-Change Model which Reproduces Human Arm Movement. *Proceedings of the 4th Symposium on Biological and Physiological Engineering*, 299-302. in Japanese.

Proximity Effect Corrections in Electron Beam Lithography Using a Neural Network

Robert C. Frye
AT&T Bell Laboratories
600 Mountain Avenue
Murray Hill, NJ 08854

Kevin D. Cummings*
AT&T Bell Laboratories
600 Mountain Avenue
Murray Hill, NJ 08854

Edward A. Rietman
AT&T Bell Laboratories
600 Mountain Avenue
Murray Hill, NJ 08854

Abstract

We have used a neural network to compute corrections for images written by electron beams to eliminate the proximity effects caused by electron scattering. Iterative methods are effective, but require prohibitively computation time. We have instead trained a neural network to perform equivalent corrections, resulting in a significant speed-up. We have examined hardware implementations using both analog and digital electronic networks. Both had an acceptably small error of 0.5% compared to the iterative results. Additionally, we verified that the neural network correctly generalized the solution of the problem to include patterns not contained in its training set. We have experimentally verified this approach on a Cambridge Instruments EBMF 10.5 exposure system.

1 INTRODUCTION

Scattering imposes limitations on the minimum feature sizes that can be reliably obtained with electron beam lithography. Linewidth corrections can be used to control the dimensions of isolated features (*i.e.* intraproximity, Sewell, 1978), but meet with little success when dealing with the same features in a practical context, where they are surrounded by other features (*i.e.* interproximity). Local corrections have been proposed using a self-consistent method of computation for the desired incident dose pattern (Parikh, 1978). Such techniques require inversion of large matrices and prohibitive amounts of computation time. Lynch *et al.*, 1982, have proposed an analytical method for proximity corrections based on a solution of a set of approximate equations, resulting in a considerable improvement in speed.

The method that we present here, using a neural network, combines the computational simplicity of the method of Lynch *et al.* with the accuracy of the self-consistent methods. The first step is to determine the scattered energy profile of the electron beam which depends on the substrate structure, beam size and electron energy. This is

* Present address: Motorola Inc. Phoenix Corporate Research Laboratories, 2100 East Elliot Rd. Tempe, AZ 85284.

then used to compute spatial variations in the dosage that result when a particular image is scattered. This can be used to iteratively compute a corrected image for the input pattern. The goal of the correction is to adjust the written image so that the incident pattern of dose after scattering approximates the desired one as closely as possible. We have used this iterative method on a test image to form a training set for a neural network. The architecture of this network was chosen to incorporate the basic mathematical structure as the analytical method of Lynch *et al.*, but relies on an adaptive procedure to determine its characteristic parameters.

2 CALCULATING PROXIMITY CORRECTED PATTERNS

We determined the radial distribution of scattered dose from a single pixel by using a Monte-Carlo simulation for a variety of substrates and electron beam energies (Cummings, 1989). As an example problem, we looked at resist on a heavy metal substrate. (These are of interest in the fabrication of masks for x-ray lithography.) For a 20 KeV electron beam this distribution, or "proximity function," can be approximated by the analytical expression

$$f(r) = \frac{1}{\pi(1+\nu+\xi)}\left[\frac{e^{-(r/\alpha)^2}}{\alpha^2} + \frac{\nu e^{-(r/\gamma)}}{2\gamma^2} + \frac{\xi e^{-(r/\zeta)}}{2\zeta^2}\right]$$

where

$$\alpha = 0.038\,\mu\text{m},\quad \gamma = 0.045\,\mu\text{m},\quad \zeta = 0.36\,\mu\text{m},\quad \nu = 3.49 \text{ and } \xi = 6.42.$$

The unscattered image is assumed to be composed of an array of pixels, $I_0(x,y)$. For a beam with a proximity function f(r) like the one given above, the image after scattering will be

$$I_s(x,y) = \sum_{m=-\infty}^{\infty} \sum_{n=-\infty}^{\infty} I_0(x-m,y-n)\, f((m^2+n^2)^{1/2}),$$

which is the discrete convolution of the original image with the lineshape f(r). The approach suggested by analogy with signal processing is to deconvolve the image by an inverse filtering operation. This method cannot be used, however, because it is impossible to generate negative amounts of electron exposure. Restricting the beam to positive exposures makes the problem inherently nonlinear, and we must rely instead on an iterative, rather than analytical, solution.

Figure 1 shows the pattern that we used to generate a training set for the neural network. This pattern was chosen to include examples of the kinds of features that are difficult to resolve because of proximity effects. Minimum feature sizes in the pattern ore 0.25 μm and the overall image, using 0.125 μm pixels, is 180 pixels (22.5 μm) on a side, for a total of 32,400 pixels. The initial incident dose pattern for the iterative correction of this image started with a relative exposure value of 100% for exposed pixels and 0 for unexposed ones. The scattered intensity distribution was computed from this incident dose using the discrete two-dimensional convolution with the summation truncated to a finite range, r_0. For the example proximity function 95% of the scattered intensity is contained within a radius of 1.125 μm (9 pixels) and this value was used for r_0. The scattered intensity distribution was computed and compared with the desired pattern of 100% for exposed and 0 for unexposed pixels. The difference between the resulting scattered and desired distributions is the error. This error was subtracted from the dose pattern to be used for the next iteration. However, since negative doses are not allowed, negative regions in the correction were truncated to zero.

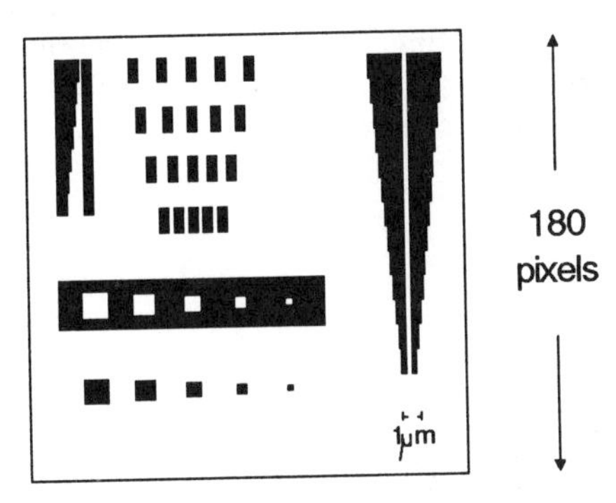

Figure 1: Training pattern

Using this algorithm, a pixel that receives a dosage that is too small will have a negative error, and on the next iteration its intensity will be increased. Unexposed pixels (*i.e.* regions where resist is to be removed) will always have some dosage scattered into them from adjacent features, and will consequently always show a positive error. Because the written dose in these regions is always zero, rather than negative, it is impossible for the iterative solution to completely eliminate the error in the final scattered distribution. However, the nonlinear exposure properties of the resist will compensate for this. Moreover, since all exposed features receive a uniform dose after correction, it is possible to choose a resist with the optimal contrast properties for the pattern.

Although this iterative method is effective, it is also time consuming. Each iteration on the test pattern required about 1 hour to run on a 386 based computer. Four iterations were required before the smallest features in the resist were properly resolved. Even the expected order of magnitude speed increase from a large mainframe computer is not sufficient to correct the image from a full sized chip consisting of several billion pixels. The purpose of the neural network is to do these same calculations, but in a much shorter time.

3 NETWORK ARCHITECTURE AND TRAINING

Figure 2 shows the relationship between the image being corrected and the neural network. The correction for one pixel takes into account the image surrounding it. Since the neighborhood must include all of the pixels that contribute appreciable scattered intensity to the central pixel being corrected, the size of the network was determined by the same maximum radius, $r_0 = 1.125\,\mu m$, that characterized the scattering proximity function. The large number of inputs would be difficult to manage in an analog network if these inputs were general analog signals, but fortunately the input data are binary, and can be loaded into an analog network using digital shift registers.

Figure 3 shows a schematic diagram of the analog network. The binary signals from the shift registers representing a portion of the image were connected to the buffer amplifiers through 10 KΩ resistors. Each was connected to only one summing node, corresponding to its radial distance from the center pixel. This stage converted the 19 x 19 binary representation of the image into 10 analog voltages that represented the radial distribution of the surrounding intensity. The summing amplifier at the output was connected to these 10 nodes by variable resistors. This resulted in an output that was a weighted sum of the radial components.

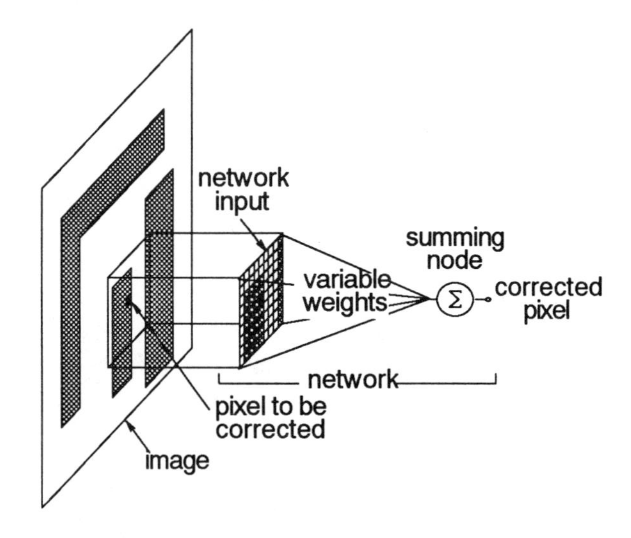

Figure 2: Network configuration

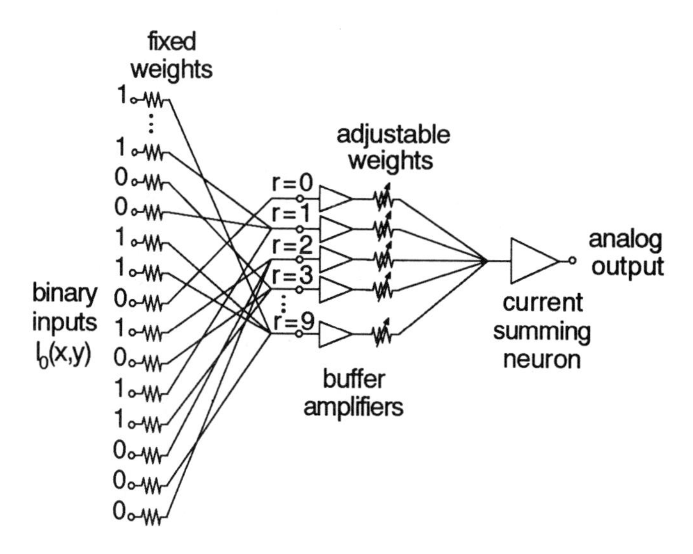

Figure 3: Schematic diagram of the analog network

Functionally, this network does the operation

$$V_{out} = \sum_{r=0}^{9} w_r \langle I_0 \rangle_r ,$$

where w_r are the weight coefficients set by the adjustable resistors and $\langle I_0 \rangle_r$ are the average values of the pixel intensity at radius r. The form of this relationship is identical to the one proposed by Lynch *et al.* but uses an adaptive method, rather than an analytical one, to determine the coefficients w_r.

The prototype analog hardware network was built on a wire wrap board using 74HC164 8 bit CMOS static shift registers and LM324 quad operational amplifiers for the active devices. The resistors in the first layer were 10 KΩ thin-film resistors in dual-in-line packages and had a tolerance of 1%. The ten adjustable resistors in the second layer of the network were 10 turn precision trimmers. Negative weights were made by inverting the sign of the voltage at the buffer amplifiers. For comparison, we also evaluated a digital hardware implementation of this network. It was implemented on a floating point array processor built by Eighteen Eight Laboratories using an AT&T DSP-32 chip operating at 8 MFLOPs peak rate. The mathematical operation performed by the network is equivalent to a two-dimensional convolution of the input image with an adaptively learned floating point kernel.

The adjustable weight values for both networks were determined using the delta rule of Widrow and Hoff (1960). For each pixel in the trial pattern of Figure 1 there was a corresponding desired output computed by the iterative method. Each pixel in the test image, its surroundings and corresponding analog corrected value (computed by the iterative method) constituted a single learning trial, and the overall image contained 32,400 of them. We found that the weight values stabilized after two passes through the test image.

4 NEURAL NETWORK PERFORMANCE

The accuracy of both the analog and digital networks, compared to the iterative solution, was comparable. Both showed an average error for the test image of 0.5%, and a maximum error of 9% on any particular pixel. The accuracy of the networks on images other than the one used to train them was comparable, averaging about 0.5% overall.

Convolution with an adaptively-learned kernel is itself a relatively efficient computational algorithm. The iterative method required 4 hours to compute the correction for the 32,400 pixel example. Equivalent results were obtained by convolution in about 6.5 minutes using the same computer. Examination of the assembled code for the software network showed that the correction for each pixel required the execution of about 30 times fewer instructions than for the iterative method.

The analog hardware generated corrections for the same example in 13.5 seconds. Almost 95% of this time was used for input/output operations between the network and the computer. It was the time required for the I/O, rather than the speed of the circuit, that limited the dynamic performance of this system. Clearly, with improved I/O hardware, the analog network could be made to compute these corrections much more quickly.

The same algorithm, running on the digital floating point array processor performed the correction for this example problem in 4.5 seconds. The factor of three improvement over the analog hardware was primarily a result of the decreased time needed for I/O in the DSP-based network. The digital network was not appreciably more accurate than the analog one, indicating that the overall accuracy of operation was determined primarily by the network architecture rather than by limitations in the implementation. These results are summarized in Table 1.

Table 1: Comparison of computational speed for various methods.

METHOD	SPEED
Iteration	6 years /mm^2
Software network	100 days /mm^2
Analog hardware network	2 days /mm^2
Digital hardware network	18 hours /mm^2

5 EXPERIMENTAL VERIFICATION

Recently, we have evaluated this method experimentally using a Cambridge Instruments EBMF 10.5 exposure system (Cummings, *et al.*, 1990). The test image was 1 mm^2 and contained 11,165 Cambridge shapes and 6.7×10^7 pixels. The substrate was silicon with 0.5 μm of SAL601-ER7 resist exposed at 20 KeV beam energy. The range of the scattered electrons is more than three times greater for these conditions than in the tests described above, requiring a network about ten times larger. The neural network computations were done using the digital floating point array processor, and required about 18 hours to correct the entire image. Input to the program was Cambridge source code, which was converted to a bit-mapped array, corrected by the neural network and then decomposed into new Cambridge source code.

Figure 4 shows SEM micrographs comparing one of the test structures written with and without the neural network correction. This test structure consists of a 10 μm square pad next to a 1 μm wide line, separated by a gap of 0.5 μm. Note in the uncorrected pattern that the line widens in the region adjacent to the large pad, and the webs of resist extending into the gap. This is caused by excess dosage scattered into these regions from the large pad. In the corrected pattern, the dosage in these regions has been adjusted, resulting in a uniform exposure after scattering and greatly improved pattern resolution.

6 CONCLUSIONS

The results of our trial experiments clearly demonstrate the computational benefits of a neural network for this particular application. The trained analog hardware network performed the corrections more than 1000 times faster than the iterative method using the same computer, and the digital processor was 3000 times faster. This technique is readily applicable to a variety of direct write exposure systems that have the capability to write with variable exposure times. Implementation of the network on more sophisticated computers with readily available coprocessors can directly lead to another order of magnitude improvement in speed, making it practical to correct full chip-sized images.

The performance of the analog network suggests that with improved speed of I/O between the computer and the network, it would be possible to obtain much faster operation. The added flexibility and generality of the digital approach, however, is a considerable advantage.

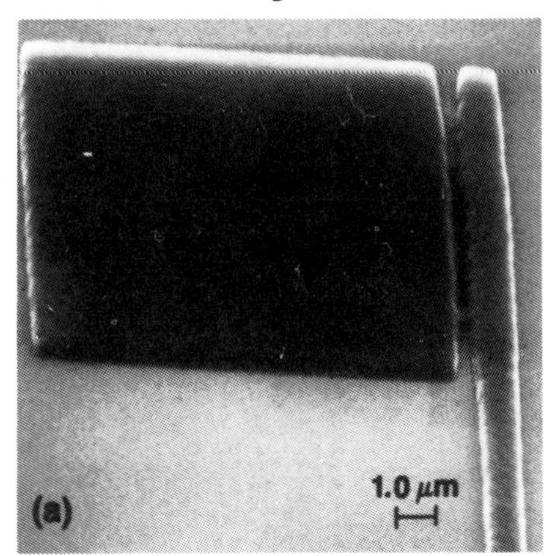

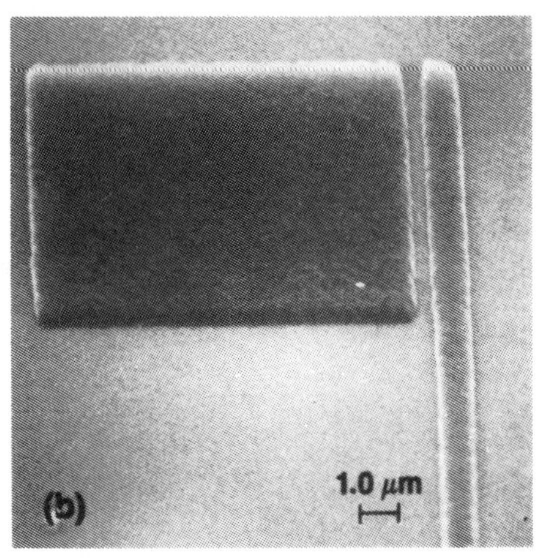

Figure 4: Comparison of a test structure written with and without correction

Acknowledgments

We thank S. Waaben and W. T. Lynch for useful discussions, suggestions and information, and J. Brereton who assisted in building the hardware and trial patterns for initial evaluation. We also thank C. Biddick, C. Lockstampfor, S. Moccio and B. Vogel for technical support in the experimental verification.

References

H. Sewell, "Control of Pattern Dimensions in Electron Lithography," J. Vac. Sci. Technol. **15**, 927 (1978).

M. Parikh, "Self-Consistent Proximity Effect Correction Technique for Resist Exposure (SPECTRE)," J. Vac. Sci. Technol. **15**, 931 (1978).

W.T. Lynch, T. E. Smith and W. Fichtner, "An Algorithm for Proximity Effect Correction with E-Beam Exposure," Int'l. Conf. on Microlithography, Microcircuit Engineering pp 309-314, Grenoble (1982).

K. D. Cummings "Determination of Proximity Parameters for Electron Beam Lithography," AT&T Bell Laboratories Internal Memorandum.

B. Widrow and M. E. Hoff, "Adaptive Switching Circuits," IRE WESCON Convention Record, Part 4, 96-104 (1960).

K. D. Cummings, R. C. Frye and E. A. Rietman, "Using a Neural Network to Proximity Correct Patterns Written with a Cambridge EBMF 10.5 Electron Beam Exposure System," Applied Phys. Lett. **57** 1431 (1990).

Planning with an Adaptive World Model

Sebastian B. Thrun
German National Research
Center for Computer
Science (GMD)
D-5205 St. Augustin, FRG

Knut Möller
University of Bonn
Department of
Computer Science
D-5300 Bonn, FRG

Alexander Linden
German National Research
Center for Computer
Science (GMD)
D-5205 St. Augustin, FRG

Abstract

We present a new connectionist planning method [TML90]. By interaction with an unknown environment, a world model is progressively constructed using gradient descent. For deriving optimal actions with respect to future reinforcement, planning is applied in two steps: an experience network proposes a plan which is subsequently optimized by gradient descent with a chain of world models, so that an optimal reinforcement may be obtained when it is actually run. The appropriateness of this method is demonstrated by a robotics application and a pole balancing task.

1 INTRODUCTION

Whenever decisions are to be made with respect to some events in the future, planning has been proved to be an important and powerful concept in problem solving. Planning is applicable if an autonomous agent interacts with a world, and if a reinforcement is available which measures only the over-all performance of the agent. Then the problem of optimizing actions yields the *temporal credit assignment problem* [Sut84], i.e. the problem of assigning particular reinforcements to particular actions in the past. The problem becomes more complicated if no knowledge about the world is available in advance.

Many connectionist approaches so far solve this problem directly, using techniques based on the interaction of an adaptive world model and an adaptive controller [Bar89, Jor89, Mun87]. Although such controllers are very fast after training, training itself is rather complex, mainly because of two reasons: a) Since future is not considered explicitly, future effects must be directly encoded into the world model. This complicates model training. b) Since the controller is trained with the world model, training of the former lags behind the latter. Moreover, if there do exist

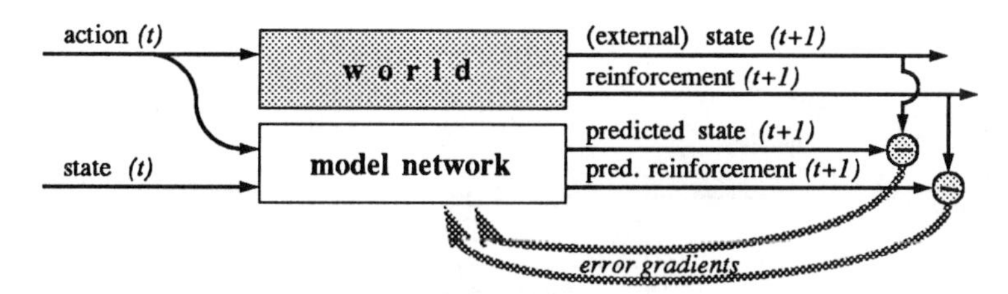

Figure 1: The training of the model network is a system identification task. Internal parameters are estimated by gradient descent, e.g. by backpropagation.

several optimal actions, such controllers will only generate at most one regardless of all others, since they represent many-to-one functions. E.g., changing the objective function implies the need of an expensive retraining.

In order to overcome these problems, we applied a planning technique to reinforcement learning problems. A model network which approximates the behavior of the world is used for looking ahead into future and optimizing actions by gradient descent with respect to future reinforcement. In addition, an experience network is trained in order to accelerate and improve planning.

2 LOOK-AHEAD PLANNING

2.1 SYSTEM IDENTIFICATION

Planning needs a world model. Training of the world model is adopted from [Bar89, Jor89, Mun87]. Formally, the world maps actions to subsequent states and reinforcements (Fig. 1). The world model used here is a standard non-recurrent or a recurrent connectionist network which is trained by backpropagation or related gradient descent algorithms [WZ88, TS90]. Each time an action is performed on the world their resulting state and reinforcement is compared with the corresponding prediction by the model network. The difference is used for adapting the internal parameters of the model in small steps, in order to improve its accuracy. The resulting model approximates the world's behavior.

Our planning technique relies mainly on two fundamental steps: Firstly, a plan is proposed either by some heuristic or by a so-called *experience network*. Secondly, this plan is optimized progressively by gradient descent in action space. First, we will consider the second step.

2.2 PLAN OPTIMIZATION

In this section we show the optimization of plans by means of gradient descent. For that purpose, let us assume an initial plan, i.e. a sequence of N actions, is given. The first action of this plan together with the current state (and, in case of a recurrent model network, its current context activations) are fed into the model network (Fig. 2). This gives us a prediction for the subsequent state and reinforcement of the world. If we assume that the state prediction is a good estimation for the next state, we can proceed by predicting the immediate next state and reinforcement from the second action of the plan correspondingly. This procedure is repeated for each of the N stages of the plan. The final output is a sequence of N reinforcement predictions, which represents the quality of the plan. In order to maximize reinforcement, we

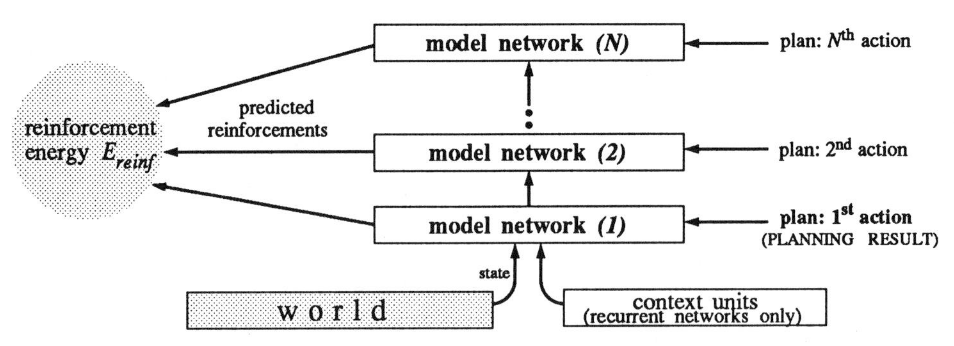

Figure 2: Looking ahead by the chain of model networks.

establish a differentiable *reinforcement energy* function E_{reinf}, which measures the deviation of predicted and desired reinforcement. The problem of optimizing plans is transformed to the problem of minimizing E_{reinf}. Since both E_{reinf} and the chain of model networks are differentiable, the gradients of the plan with respect to E_{reinf} can be computed. These gradients are used for changing the plan in small steps, which completes the gradient descent optimization.

The whole update procedure is repeated either until convergence is observed or, which makes it more convenient for real-time applications, a predefined number of iterations – note that in the latter case the computational effort is linear in N. From the planning procedure we obtain the optimized plan, the first action[1] of which is then performed on the world. Now the whole procedure is repeated.

The gradients of the plan with respect to E_{reinf} can be computed either by back-propagation through the chain of models or by a feed-forward algorithm which is related to [WZ88, TS90]:

Hand in hand with the activations we propagate also the gradients

$$\xi^j_{is}(\tau) \equiv \frac{\partial \,\text{activation}_j\,(\tau)}{\partial \,\text{action}_i\,(s)} \tag{1}$$

through the chain of models. Here i labels all action input units and j all units of the whole model network, τ $(1 \le \tau \le N)$ is the time associated with the τth model of the chain, and s $(1 \le s \le \tau)$ is the time of the sth action. Thus, for each action $(\forall i, s)$ its influence on later activations $(\forall j, \forall \tau \ge s)$ of the chain of networks, including all predictions, is measured by $\xi^j_{is}(\tau)$.

It has been shown in an earlier paper that this gradient can easily be propagated forward through the network [TML90]:

$$\xi^j_{is}(\tau) = \begin{cases} \delta_{ij}\delta_{s\tau} & \text{if } j \text{ action input unit} \\ 0 & \text{if } \tau{=}1 \wedge j \text{ state/context input unit} \\ \xi^{j'}_{is}(\tau{-}1) & \text{if } \tau{>}1 \wedge j \text{ state/context input unit} \\ & (j' \text{ corresponding output unit of preceding model}) \\ \text{logistic}'(\text{net}_j(\tau)) \cdot \sum\limits_{l \in \text{pred}(j)} \text{weight}_{jl}\, \xi^l_{is}(\tau) & \text{otherwise} \end{cases} \tag{2}$$

[1] If an unknown world is to be explored, this action might be disturbed by adding a small random variable.

The *reinforcement energy* to be minimized is defined as

$$E_{\text{reinf}} \equiv \tfrac{1}{2}\sum_{\tau=1}^{N}\sum_{k} g_k(\tau)\cdot\left(\text{reinf}'_k - \text{activation}_k(\tau)\right)^2 . \tag{3}$$

(k numbers the reinforcement output units, reinf'_k is the desired reinforcement value, usually $\forall k$: $\text{reinf}'_k \equiv 1$, and g_k weights the reinforcement with respect to τ and k, in the simplest case $g_k(\tau) \equiv 1$.) Since E_{reinf} is differentiable, we can compute the gradient of E_{reinf} with respect to each particular reinforcement prediction. From these gradients and the gradients ξ^k_{is} of the reinforcement prediction units the gradients

$$\zeta_{is} \equiv \frac{\partial\, E_{\text{reinf}}}{\partial\, \text{action}_i(s)} = -\sum_{\tau=s}^{N}\sum_{k} g_k(\tau)\cdot\left(\text{reinf}'_k - \text{activation}_k(\tau)\right)\cdot\xi^k_{is}(\tau) \tag{4}$$

are derived which indicate how to change the plan in order to minimize E_{reinf}.

Variable plan lengths: The feed-forward manner of the propagation allows it to vary the number of look-ahead steps due to the current accuracy of the model network. Intuitively, if a model network has a relatively large error, looking far into future makes little sense. A good heuristic is to avoid further look-ahead if the current linear error (due to the training patterns) of the model network is larger than the effect of the first action of the plan to the current predictions. This effect is exactly the gradients $\xi^k_{i1}(\tau)$. Using variable plan lengths might overcome the difficulties in finding an appropriate plan length N a priori.

2.3 INITIAL PLANS – THE EXPERIENCE NETWORK

It remains to show how to obtain initial plans. There are several basic strategies which are more or less problem-dependent, e.g. random, average over previous actions etc. Obviously, if some planning took place before, the problem of finding an initial plan reduces to the problem of finding a simple action, since the rest of the previous plan is a good candidate for the next initial plan.

A good way of finding this action is the *experience network*. This network is trained to predict the result of the planning procedure by observing the world's state and, in the case of recurrent networks, the temporal context information from the model network. The target values are the results of the planning procedure. Although the experience network is trained like a controller [Bar89], it is used in a different way, since outcoming actions are further optimized by the planning procedure. Thus, even if the knowledge of the experience network lags behind the model network's, the derived actions are optimized with respect to the "knowledge" of the model network rather than the experience network. On the other hand, while the optimization is gradually shifted into the experience network, planning can be progressively shortened.

3 APPROACHING A ROLLING BALL WITH A ROBOT ARM

We applied planning with an adaptive world model to a simulation of a real-time robotics task: A robot arm in 3-dimensional space was to approach a rolling ball. Both hand position (i.e. x,y,z and hand angle) and ball position (i.e. x',y') were observed by a camera system in workspace. Conversely, actions were defined as angular changes of the robot joints in configuration space. Model and experience

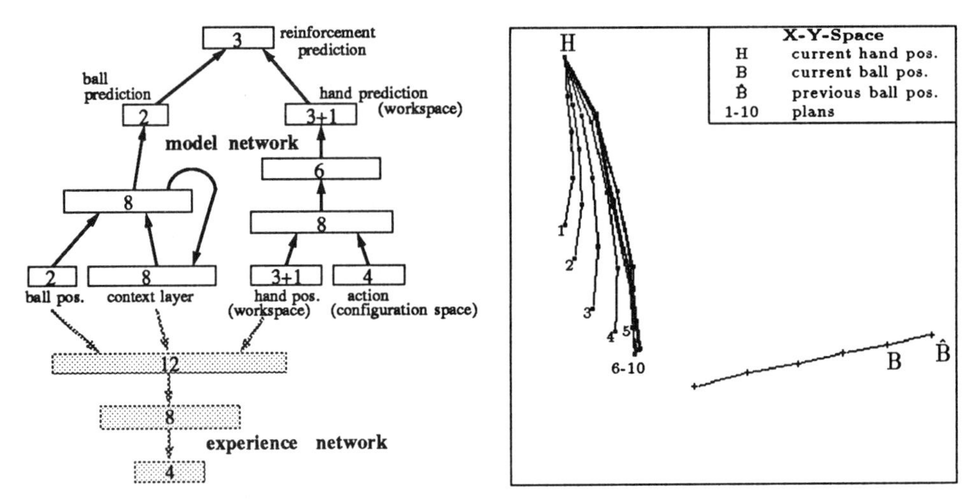

Figure 3: (a) The recurrent model network (white) and the experience network (grey) at the robotics task. (b) Planning: Starting with the initial plan 1, the approximation leads finally to plan 10. The first action of this plan is then performed on the world.

networks are shown in Fig. 3a. Note that the ball movement was predicted by a recurrent Elman-type network, since only the current ball position was visible at any time. The arm prediction is mathematically more sophisticated, because kinematics and inverse kinematics are required to solve it analytically.

The reason why planning makes sense at this task is that we did not want the robot arm to minimize the distance between hand and ball at each step – this would obviously yield trajectories in which the hand follows the ball, e.g.:

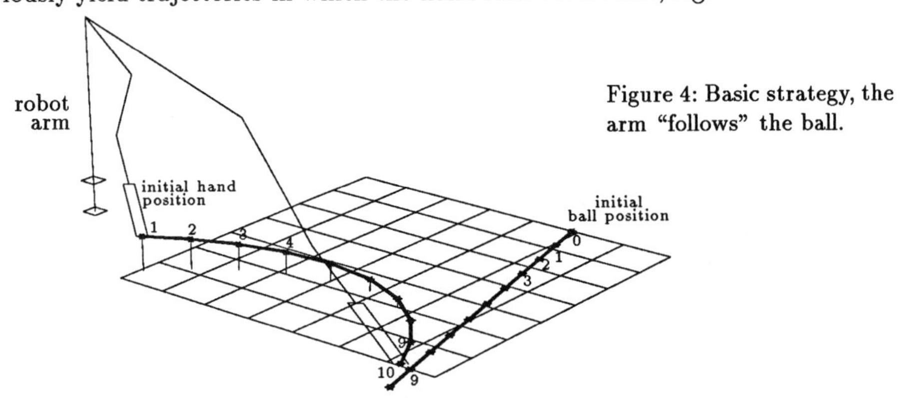

Figure 4: Basic strategy, the arm "follows" the ball.

Instead, we wanted the system to find short cuts by making predictions about the ball's next movement. Thus, the reinforcement measured the distance in workspace. Fig. 3b illustrates a "typical" planning process with look-ahead N=4, 9 iterations, $g_k(\tau) = 1.3^\tau$ (c.f. (2))[2], a weighted stepsize $\eta = 0.05 \cdot 0.9^\tau$, and well-trained model and experience networks. Starting with an initial plan 1 by the experience network

[2]This exponential function is crucial for minimizing later distances rather than the sooner.

the optimization led to plan 10. It is clear to see that the resulting action surpassed the initial plan, which demonstrates the appropriateness of the optimization.
The final trajectory was:

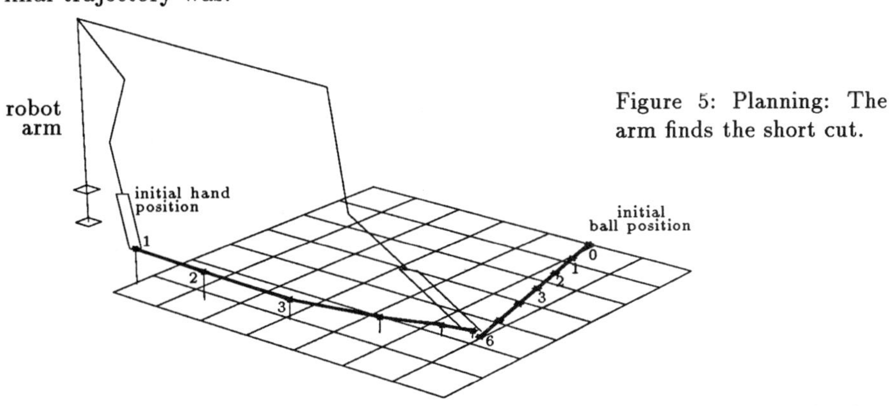

Figure 5: Planning: The arm finds the short cut.

We were now interested in modifying the behavior of the arm. Without further learning of either the model or the experience network, we wanted the arm to approach the ball from above. For this purpose we changed the energy function (7): Before the arm was to approach the ball, the energy was minimal if the arm reached a position exactly above the ball. Since the experience network was not trained for that task, we doubled the number of iteration steps. This led to:

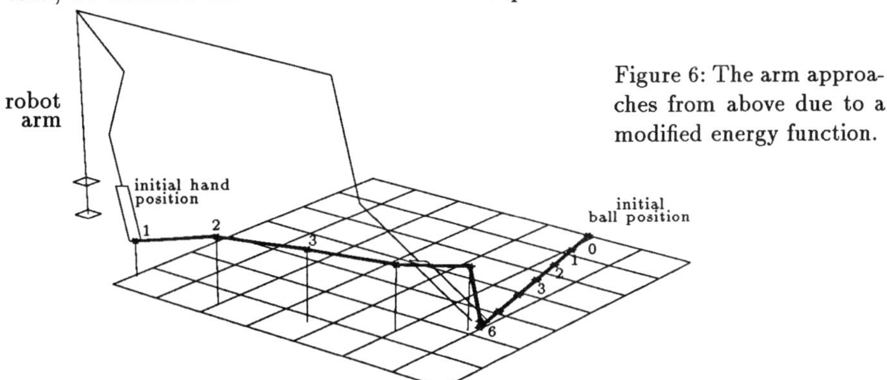

Figure 6: The arm approaches from above due to a modified energy function.

A first implementation on a real robot arm with a camera system showed similar results.

4 POLE BALANCING

Next, we applied our planning method to the pole balancing task adopted from [And89]. One main difference to the task described above is the fact that gradient descent is not applicable with binary reinforcement, since the better the approximation by the world model, the more the gradient vanishes. This effect can be prevented by using a second model network with weight decay, which is trained with the same training patterns. Weight decay smoothes the binary mapping. By using the model network for prediction only and the smoothed network for gradient propagation, the pole balancing problem became solvable. We see this as a general technique for applying gradient descent to binary reinforcement tasks.

We were especially interested in the dependency of look-ahead and the duration of balance. It turned out that in most randomly chosen initial configurations of pole and cart the look-ahead $N = 4$ was sufficient to balance the pole more than 20 000 steps. If the cart is moved randomly, after on average 10 movements the pole falls.

5 DISCUSSION

The planning procedure presented in this paper has two crucial limitations. By using a bounded look-ahead, effects of actions to reinforcement beyond this bound can not be taken into account. Even if the plan lengths are kept variable (as described above), each particular planning process must use a finite plan. Moreover, using gradient descent as search heuristic implies the danger of getting stuck in local minima. It might be interesting to investigate other search heuristics.

On the other hand this planning algorithm overcomes certain problems of adaptive controller networks, namely: a) The training is relatively fast, since the model network does not include temporal effects. b) Decisions are optimized due to the current "knowledge" in the system, and no controller lags behind the model network. c) The incorporation of additional constraints to the objective function at runtime is possible, as demonstrated. d) By using a probabilistic experience network the planning algorithm is able to act as a non-deterministic many-to-many controller. Anyway, we have not investigated the latter point yet.

Acknowledgements

The authors thank Jörg Kindermann and Frank Śmieja for many fruitful discussions and Michael Contzen and Michael Faßbender for their help with the robot arm.

References

[And89] C.W. Anderson. Learning to control an inverted pendulum using neural networks. *IEEE Control Systems Magazine*, 9(3):31–37, 1989.

[Bar89] A. G. Barto. Connectionist learning for control: An overview. Technical Report COINS TR 89-89, Dept. of Computer and Information Science, University of Massachusetts, Amherst, MA, September 1989.

[Jor89] M. I. Jordan. Generic constraints on unspecified target constraints. In *Proceedings of the First International Joint Conference on Neural Networks, Washington, DC*, San Diego, 1989. IEEE TAB NN Committee.

[Mun87] P. Munro. A dual backpropagation scheme for scalar-reward learning. In *Ninth Annual Conference of the Cognitive Science Society*, pages 165–176, Hillsdale, NJ, 1987. Cognitive Science Society, Lawrence Erlbaum.

[Sut84] R. S. Sutton. *Temporal Credit Assignment in Reinforcement Learning*. PhD thesis, University of Massachusetts, 1984.

[TML90] S. Thrun, K. Möller, and A. Linden. Adaptive look-ahead planning. In G. Dorffner, editor, *Proceedings KONNAI/OEGAI*, Springer, Sept. 1990.

[TS90] S. Thrun and F. Śmieja. A general feed-forward algorithm for gradient-descent in connectionist networks. TR 483, GMD, FRG, Nov. 1990.

[WZ88] R. J. Williams and D. Zipser. A learning algorithm for continually running fully recurrent neural networks. TR ICS Report 8805, Institute for Cognitive Science, University of California, San Diego, CA, 1988.

A Connectionist Learning Control Architecture for Navigation

Jonathan R. Bachrach
Department of Computer and Information Science
University of Massachusetts
Amherst, MA 01003

Abstract

A novel learning control architecture is used for navigation. A sophisticated test-bed is used to simulate a cylindrical robot with a sonar belt in a planar environment. The task is short-range homing in the presence of obstacles. The robot receives no global information and assumes no comprehensive world model. Instead the robot receives only sensory information which is inherently limited. A connectionist architecture is presented which incorporates a large amount of a priori knowledge in the form of hard-wired networks, architectural constraints, and initial weights. Instead of hard-wiring static potential fields from object models, my architecture learns sensor-based potential fields, automatically adjusting them to avoid local minima and to produce efficient homing trajectories. It does this without object models using only sensory information. This research demonstrates the use of a large modular architecture on a difficult task.

1 OVERVIEW

I present a connectionist learning control architecture tailored for simulated short-range homing in the presence of obstacles. The kinematics of a cylindrical robot (shown in Figure 1) moving in a planar environment is simulated. The robot has wheels that propel it independently and simultaneously in both the x and y directions with respect to a fixed orientation. It can move up to one radius per discrete time step. The robot has a 360 degree sensor belt with 16 distance sensors and 16 grey-scale sensors evenly placed around its perimeter. These 32 values form the robot's *view*.

Figure 2 is a display created by the navigation simulator. The bottom portion of

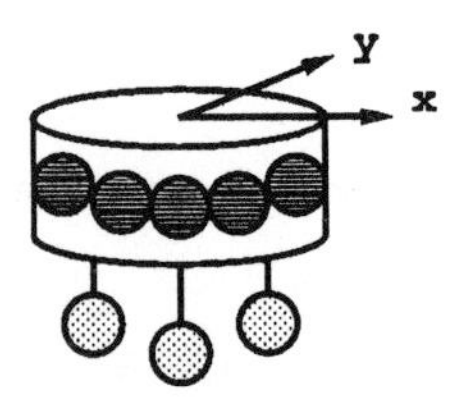

Figure 1: Simulated robot.

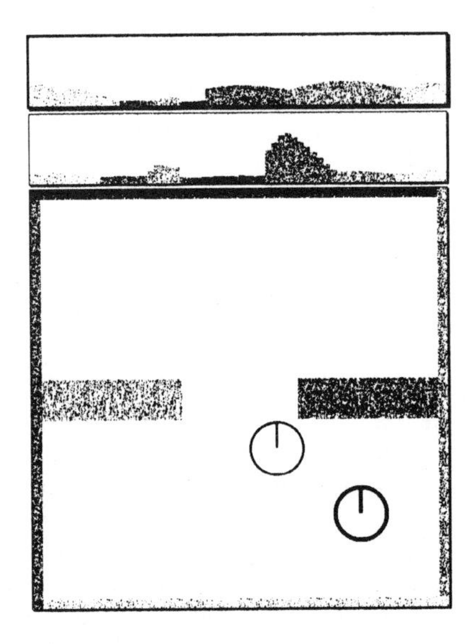

Figure 2: Navigation simulator.

the figure shows a bird's-eye view of the robot's environment. In this display, the bold circle represents the robot's "home" position, with the radius line indicating the home orientation. The other circle with radius line represents the robot's current position and orientation. The top panel shows the grey-scale view from the home position, and the next panel down shows the grey-scale view from the robot's current position. For better viewing, the distance and grey-scale sensor values are superimposed, and the height of the profile is 1/distance instead of distance. Thus as the robot gets closer to objects they get taller, and when the robot gets farther away from objects they get shorter in the display.

The robot cannot move through nor "see" through obstacles (i.e., obstacles are opaque). The task is for the robot to align itself with the home position from arbitrary starting positions in the environment while not colliding with obstacles. This task is performed using only the sensory information—the robot does not have access to the bird's-eye view.

This is a difficult control task. The sensory information forms a high-dimensional

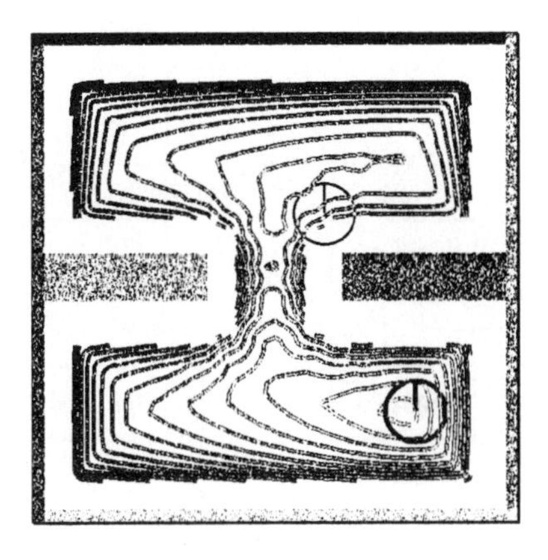

Figure 3: The potential field method. This figure shows a contour plot of a terrain created using potential fields generated from object models. The contour diagram shows level curves where the grey level of the line depicts the height of the line: the maximum height is depicted in black, and the minimum height is depicted in white.

continuous space, and successful homing generally requires a nonlinear mapping from this space to the space of real-valued actions. Further, training networks is not easily achieved on this space. The robot assumes no comprehensive world model and receives no global information, but receives only sensory information that is inherently limited. Furthermore, it is difficult to reach home using random exploration thereby making simple trial-and-error learning intractable. In order to handle this task an architecture was designed that facilitates the coding of domain knowledge in the form of hard-wired networks, architectural constraints, and initial weights.

1.1 POTENTIAL FIELDS

Before I describe the architecture, I briefly discuss a more traditional technique for navigation that uses potential fields. This technique involves building explicit object models representing the extent and position of objects in the robot's environment. Repelling potential fields are then placed around obstacles using the object models, and an attracting potential field is placed on the goal. This can be visualized as a terrain where the global minimum is located at the goal, and where there are bumps around the obstacles. The robot goes home by descending the terrain. The contour diagram in Figure 3 shows such a terrain. The task is to go from the top room to the bottom through the door. Unfortunately, there can be local minima. In this environment there are two prime examples of minima: the right-hand wall between the home location and the upper room—opposing forces exactly counteract each other to produce a local minimum in the right-hand side of the upper room, and the doorway—the repelling fields on the door frame create an insurmountable bump in the center of the door.

In contrast, my technique learns a sensor-based potential field model. Instead of hard-wiring static potential fields from the object models, the proposed architecture

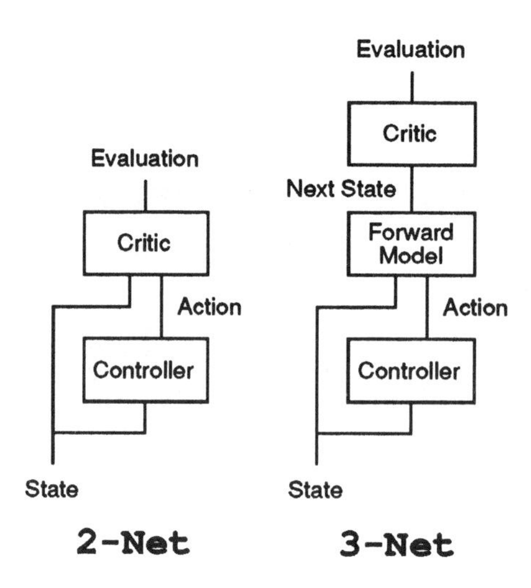

Figure 4: Control architectures.

learns potential fields, automatically adjusting them to both avoid local minima and produce efficient trajectories. Furthermore, it does this without object models, using only sensory information.

1.2 2-NET/3-NET ARCHITECTURES

I shall begin by introducing two existing architectures: the 2-net and 3-net architectures. These architectures were proposed by Werbos [9] and Jordan and Jacobs [4] and are also based on the ideas of Barto, Sutton, Watkins [2, 1, 8], and Jordan and Rumelhart [3]. The basic idea is to learn an evaluation function and then train the controller by differentiating this function with respect to the controller weights. These derivatives indicate how to change the controller's weights in order to minimize or maximize the evaluation function. The 2-net architecture consists of a controller and a critic. The controller maps states to actions, and the 2-net critic maps state/action pairs to evaluations. The 3-net architecture consists of a controller, a forward model, and a critic. The controller maps states to actions, the forward model maps state/action pairs to next states, and the 3-net critic maps states to evaluations.

It has been said that it is easier to train a 2-net architecture because there is no forward model [5]. The forward model might be very complicated and difficult to train. With a 2-net architecture, only a 2-net critic is trained based on state/action input pairs. But what if a forward model already exists or even a priori knowledge exists to aid in explicit coding of a forward model? Then it might be simpler to use the 3-net architecture because the 3-net critic would be easier to train. It is based on state-only input and not state/action pairs, and it includes more domain knowledge.

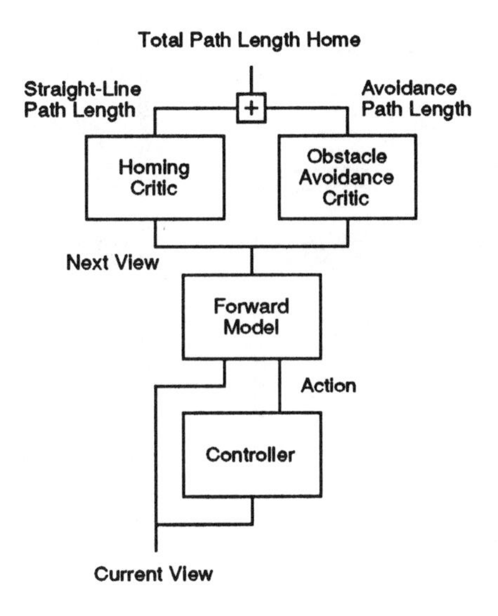

Figure 5: My architecture.

2 THE NAVIGATION ARCHITECTURE

The navigation architecture is a version of a 3-net architecture tailored for navigation, where the state is the robot's view and the evaluation is an estimate of the length of the shortest path for the robot's current location to home. It consists of a controller, a forward model, and two adaptive critics. The controller maps views to actions, the forward model maps view/action pairs to next views, the homing critic maps views to path length home using a straight line trajectory, and the obstacle avoidance critic maps views to additional path length needed to avoid obstacles. The sum of the outputs of the homing critic and the obstacle avoidance critic equals the total path length home. The forward model is a hard-wired differentiable network incorporating geometrical knowledge about the sensors and space. Both critics and the controller are radial basis networks using Gaussian hidden units.

2.1 TRAINING

Initially the controller is trained to produce straight-line trajectories home. With the forward model fixed, the homing critic and the controller are trained using dead-reckoning. Dead-reckoning is a technique for keeping track of the distance home by accumulating the incremental displacements. This distance provides a training signal for training the homing critic via supervised learning.

Next, the controller is further trained to avoid obstacles. In this phase, the obstacle avoidance critic is added while the weights of the homing critic and forward model are frozen. Using the method of temporal differences [7] the controller and obstacle avoidance critic are adjusted so that the expected path length decreases by one radius per time step. After training, the robot takes successive one-radius steps

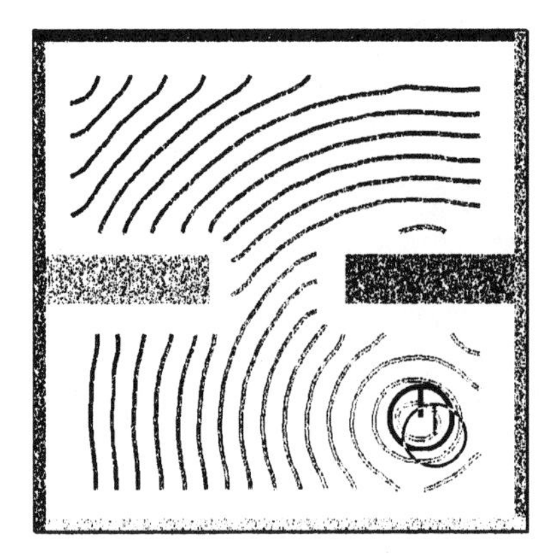
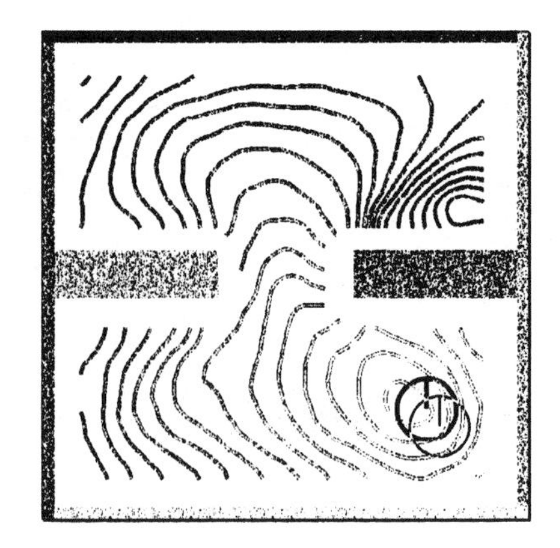

Figure 6: An example.

toward its home location.

3 AN EXAMPLE

I applied this architecture to the environment shown in Figure 2. Figure 6 shows the results of training. The left panel is a contour plot of the output of the homing critic and reflects only the straight-line distance to the home location. The right panel is a contour plot of the combined output of the homing critic and the obstacle avoidance critic and now reflects the actual path length home. After training the robot is able to form efficient homing trajectories starting from anywhere in the environment.

4 DISCUSSION

The homing task represents a difficult control task requiring the solution of a number of problems. The first problem is that there is a small chance of getting home using random exploration. The solution to this problem involves building a nominal initial controller that chooses straight-line trajectories home. Next, because the state space is high-dimensional and continuous it is impractical to evenly place Gaussian units, and it is difficult to learn continuous mappings using logistic hidden units. Instead I use Gaussian units whose initial weights are determined using expectation maximization. This is a soft form of competitive learning [6] that, in my case, creates spatially tuned units. Next, the forward model for the robot's environments is very difficult to learn. For this reason I used a hard-wired forward model whose performance is good in a wide range of environments. Here the philosophy is to learn only things that are difficult to hard-wire. Finally, the 2-net critic is difficult to train. Therefore, I split the 2-net critic into a 3-net critic and a hard-wired forward model.

There are many directions for extending this work. First, I would like to apply this architecture to real robots using realistic sensors and dynamics. Secondly, I want to to look at long range homing. Lastly, I would like to investigate navigation tasks involving multiple goals.

Acknowledgements

This material is based upon work supported by the Air Force Office of Scientific Research, Bolling AFB, under Grant AFOSR-89-0526 and by the National Science Foundation under Grant ECS-8912623. I would like to thank Richard Durbin, David Rumelhart, Andy Barto, and the UMass Adaptive Networks Group for their help on this project.

References

[1] A. G. Barto, R. S. Sutton, and C. Watkins. Sequential decision problems and neural networks. In David S. Touretzky, editor, *Advances in Neural Information Processing Systems*, P.O. Box 50490, Palo Alto, CA 94303, 1989. Morgan Kaufmann Publishers.

[2] Andrew G. Barto, Richard S. Sutton, and Charles W. Anderson. Neuronlike adaptive elements that can solve difficult learning control problems. *IEEE Transactions on Systems, Man, and Cybernetics*, SMC-13(15), September/October 1985.

[3] M. I. Jordan and D. E. Rumelhart. Supervised learning with a distal teacher. 1989. Submitted to: *Cognitive Science.*

[4] Michael I. Jordan and Robert Jacobs. Learning to control an unstable system with forward modeling. In David S. Touretzky, editor, *Advances in Neural Information Processing Systems*, P.O. Box 50490, Palo Alto, CA 94303, 1989. Morgan Kaufmann Publishers.

[5] Sridhar Mahadevan and Jonathan Connell. Automatic programming of behavior-based robots using reinforcemnt learning. Technical report, IBM Research Division, T.J. Watson Research Center, Box 704, Yorktown Heights, NY 10598, 1990.

[6] S. J. Nowlan. A generative framework for unsupervised learning. Denver, Colorado, 1989. IEEE Conference on Neural Information Processing Systems—Natural and Synthetic.

[7] Richard Sutton. Learning to predict by the methods of temporal differences. Technical report, GTE Laboratories, 1987.

[8] Richard S. Sutton. *Temporal Credit Assignment in Reinforcement Learning.* PhD thesis, Department of Computer and Information Science, University of Massachusetts at Amherst, 1984.

[9] Paul J. Werbos. Reinforcement learning over time. In T. Miller, R. S. Sutton, and P. J. Werbos, editors, *Neural Networks for Control.* The MIT Press, Cambridge, MA, In press.

Navigating through Temporal Difference

Peter Dayan
Centre for Cognitive Science & Department of Physics
University of Edinburgh
2 Buccleuch Place, Edinburgh EH8 9LW
dayan@cns.ed.ac.uk

Abstract

Barto, Sutton and Watkins [2] introduced a grid task as a didactic example of temporal difference planning and asynchronous dynamical programming. This paper considers the effects of changing the coding of the input stimulus, and demonstrates that the self-supervised learning of a particular form of hidden unit representation improves performance.

1 INTRODUCTION

Temporal difference (TD) planning [6, 7] uses prediction for control. Consider an agent moving around a finite grid such as the one in figure 1 (the agent is incapable of crossing the barrier) trying to reach a goal whose position it does not know. If it can predict how far away from the goal it is at the current step, and how far away from the goal it is at the next step, after making a move, then it can decide whether or not that move was helpful or harmful. If, in addition, it can record this fact, then it can learn how to navigate to the goal. This generation of actions from predictions is closely related to the mechanism of dynamical programming.

TD is used to learn the predictions in the first place. Consider the agent moving around randomly on the grid, receiving a negative reinforcement of -1 for every move it makes apart from moves which take it onto the goal. In this case, if it can estimate from every location it visits, how much reinforcement (discounted by how soon it arrives) it will get before it next reaches the goal, it will be predicting how far away it is, based on the random method of selecting actions. TD's mechanism of learning is to force the predictions to be consistent; the prediction from location **a** should be -1 more than the average of the predictions from the locations that can be reached in one step (hence the extra -1 reinforcement) from **a**.

If the agent initially selects each action with the same probability, then the estimate of future reinforcement from a will be monotonically related to how many steps a is away from the goal. This makes the predictions useful for criticising actions as above. In practice, the agent will modify its actions according to this criticism at the same time as learning the predictions based on those actions.

Barto, Sutton and Watkins [2] develop this example, and show how the TD mechanism coupled with a punctate representation of the stimulus (referred to as $\mathcal{R}_{BSW}$ below) finds the optimal paths to the goal. $\mathcal{R}_{BSW}$ ignores the cues shown in figure 1, and devotes one input unit to each location on the grid, which fires if and only if the agent is at that place.

TD methods can however work with more general codes. Section 2 considers alternative representations, including ones that are sensitive to the orientation of the agent as it moves through the grid, and section 3 looks at a restricted form of latent learning – what the agent can divine about its environment in the absence of reinforcement. Both techniques can improve the speed of learning.

2 ALTERNATE REPRESENTATIONS

Stimulus representations, the means by which the agent finds out from the environment where it is, can be classified along two dimensions; whether they are punctate or distributed, and whether they are directionally sensitive or in register with the world.

Over most of the grid, a 'sensible' distributed representation, such as a coarse-coded one, would be expected to make learning faster, as information about the value and action functions could be shared across adjacent grid points. There are points of discontinuity in the actions, as in the region above the right hand arm of the barrier, but they are few. In his PhD thesis [9], Watkins considers a rather similar problem to that in figure 1, and solves it using his variant of TD, Q-learning, based on a CMAC [1] coarse-coded representation of the space. Since his agent moves in a continuous bounded space, rather than being confined merely to discrete grid points, something of this sort is anyway essential. After the initial learning, Watkins arbitrarily makes the agent move ten times more slowly in a closed section of the space. This has a similar effect to the barrier in inducing a discontinuity in the action space. Despite the CMACs forcing the system to share information across such discontinuities, they were able to learn the task quickly.

The other dimension over which representations may vary involves the extent to which they are sensitive to the direction in which the agent is facing. This is of interest if the agent must construe its location from the cues around the grid. In this case, rather than moving North, South, East or West, which are actions registered with the world, the agent should only move Ahead, Left or Right (Behind is disabled as an additional constraint), whose effects are also orientation dependent. This, together with the fact that the representation will be less compact (*ie* having a larger input dimensionality) should make learning slower. Dynamical programming and its equivalents are notoriously subject to Bellman's curse of dimensionality, an engineering equivalent of exponential explosion in search.

Table 1 shows four possible representations classified along these two dimensions.

	Coarseness	
Directionally	Punctate	Distributed
Sensitive	$\mathcal{R}_{4X}$	$\mathcal{R}_{A}$
Insensitive	$\mathcal{R}_{BSW}$	$\mathcal{R}_{CMAC}$

Table 1: Representations.

$\mathcal{R}_{BSW}$ is the representation Barto, Sutton and Watkins used. $\mathcal{R}_{4X}$ is punctate and directionally sensitive - it devotes four units to every grid point, one of which fires for each possible orientation of the agent. $\mathcal{R}_{CMAC}$, the equivalent of Watkins' representation, was not simulated, because its capabilities would not differ markedly from those of the mapping-based representation developed in the next section.

$\mathcal{R}_{A}$ is rather different from the other representations; it provides a test of a representation which is more directly associated with the sensory information that might be available directly from the cues. Figure 2 shows how $\mathcal{R}_{A}$ works. Various identifiable cues, $C_1 \ldots C_c$ ($c = 7$ in the figure) are scattered around the outside of the grid, and the agent has a fictitious 'retina' which rotates with it. This retina is divided into a number of angular buckets (8 in the figure), and each bucket has c units, the ith one of which responds if the cue C_i is visible in that bucket. This representation is clearly directionally sensitive (if the agent is facing a different way, then so is its retina, and so no cue will be visible in the same bucket as it was before), and also distributed, since in general more than one cue will be visible from every location.

Note that there is no restriction on the number of units that can fire in each bucket at any time - more than one will fire if more than one cue is visible there. Also, under the present system $\mathcal{R}_{A}$ will in general not work if its coding is ambiguous – grid points must be distinguishable. Finally, it should be clear that $\mathcal{R}_{A}$ is not biologically plausible.

Figure 3 shows the learning curves for the three representations simulated. Each point is generated by switching off the learning temporarily after a certain number of iterations, starting the agent from everywhere in the grid, and averaging how many steps it takes in getting to the goal over and above the minimum necesary. It is apparent that $\mathcal{R}_{4X}$ is substantially worse, but, surprisingly, that $\mathcal{R}_{A}$ is actually better than $\mathcal{R}_{BSW}$. This implies that the added advantage of its distributed nature more than outweighs its disadvantages of having more components and being directionally sensitive.

One of the motivations behind studying alternate representations is the experimental findings on *place* cells in the hippocampi of rats (amongst other species). These are cells that fire only when the rat is at a certain location in its environment. Although their existence has led to many hypotheses about rat cognitive mapping (see [5] for a substantial discussion of place cells and mapping), it is important to note that even with a map, there remains the computationally intensive problem of navigation addressed, in this paper, by TD. $\mathcal{R}_{A}$, being closely related to the input stimuli is quite unlike a place cell code – the other representations all bear some similarities.

3 GOAL-FREE LEARNING

One of the problems with the TD system as described is that it is incapable of latent learning in the absence of reinforcement or a goal. If the goal is just taken away, but the -1 reinforcements are still applied at each step, then the values assigned to each location will tend to $-\infty$. If both are removed, then although the agent will wander about its environment with random gay abandon, it will not pick up anything that could be used to speed subsequent learning. Latent learning experiments with rats in dry mazes prove fairly conclusively that rats running mazes in the absence of rewards and punishments learn almost as much as rats that are reinforced.

One way to solve this problem is suggested by Sutton's DYNA architecture [7]. Briefly, this constructs a map of **place** $\times$ **action** $\rightarrow$ **next place**, and takes steps in the fictitious world constructed from its map in-between taking steps in the real world, as a way of ironing out the computational 'bumps' (*ie* inconsistencies) in the value and action functions.

Instead, it is possible to avoid constructing a complete map by altering the representation of the environment used for learning the prediction function and optimal actions. The section on representations concluded that coarse-coded representations are generally better than punctate ones, since information can be shared between neighbouring points. However, not all neighbouring points are amenable to this sharing, because of discontinuities in the value and action functions. If there were a way of generating a coarse coded representation (generally from a punctate one) that is sensitive to the structure of the task, rather than arbitrarily assigned by the environment, it should provide the base for faster learning still. In this case, neighbouring points should only be coded together if they are not separated by the barrier. The initial exploration would allow the agent to learn this much about the structure of the environment.

Consider a set of units whose job is to predict the future discounted sum of firings of the raw input lines. Using $\mathcal{R}_{BSW}$ during the initial stage of learning when the actions are still random, if the agent is at location (3,3) of the grid, say, then the discounted prediction of how often it will be in (3,4) (*ie* the frequency with which the single unit representing (3,4) will fire) will be high, since this location is close. However, the prediction for (7,11) will be low, because it is very unlikely to get there quickly. Consider the effect of the barrier: locations on opposite sides of it, *eg* (1,6) and (2,6), though close in the Euclidean (or Manhattan) metric on the grid, are far apart in the task. This means that the discounted prediction of how often the agent will be at (1,6) given that it starts at (2,6), will be proportionately lower.

Overall, the prediction units should act like a coarse code, sensitive to the structure of the task. As required, this information about the environment is entirely independent of whether or not the agent is reinforced during its exploration. In fact, the resulting 'map' will be more accurate if it is not, as its exploration will be more random. The output of the prediction units is taken as an additional source of information for the value and action functions.

Since their main aim is to create intelligently distributed representations from punctate ones, it is only appropriate to use these prediction units for $\mathcal{R}_{BSW}$ and $\mathcal{R}_{4X}$. Figure 4 compares average learning curves for $\mathcal{R}_{BSW}$ with and without these extra mapping units, and with and without 6000 steps of latent learning (LL) in the absence of any reinforcement. A significant improvement is apparent.

Figure 5 shows one set of predictions based on the $\mathcal{R}_{\mathrm{BSW}}$ representation[1] after a few un-reinforced iterations. The predictions are clearly fairly well developed and smooth - a predictable exponentially decaying hump. The only deviations from this are at the barrier and along the edges, where the effects of impermeability and immobility are apparent.

Figure 6 shows the same set of predictions but after 2000 reinforced iterations, by which time the agent reaches the goal almost optimally. The predictions degenerate from being roughly radially symmetric (bar the barrier) to being highly asymmetric. Once the agent has learnt how to get to the goal from some location, the path it will follow, and so the locations it will visit from there, is largely fixed. The asymptotic values of the predictions will therefore be 0 for units not on the path, and γ^r for those on the path, where r is the number of steps since the agent's start point and γ is the discounting factor weighting immediate *versus* distant reinforcement. This is a severe limitation since it implies that the topological information present in the early stages of learning disappears evaporates, and with it almost all the benefits of the prediction units.

4 DISCUSSION

Navigation comprises two problems; *where* the agent and the goals in its environment are, and *how* it can get to them. Having some form of cognitive map, as is suggested by the existence of place cells, addresses the first, but leaves open the second. For the case of one goal, the simple TD method described here is one solution.

TD planning methods are clearly robust to changes in the way the input stimulus is represented. Distributed codes, particularly ones that allow for the barrier, make learning faster. This is even true for $\mathcal{R}_{\mathrm{A}}$, which is sensitive to the orientation of the agent. All these results require each location to have a unique representation – Mozer and Bachrach [4] and Chrisley [3] and references therein look at how ambiguities can be resolved using information on the sequence of states the agent traverses.

Since these TD planning methods are totally general, just like dynamical programming, they are unlikely to scale well. Some evidence for this comes from the relatively poor performance of $\mathcal{R}_{4\mathrm{X}}$, with its quadrupled input dimension. This puts the onus back either onto dividing the task into manageable chunks, or onto more sophisticated representation.

Acknowledgements

I am very grateful to Jay Buckingham, Kate Jeffrey, Richard Morris, Toby Tyrell, David Willshaw, and the attendees of the PDP Workshop at Edinburgh, the Connectionist Group at Amherst, and a spatial learning workshop at King's College Cambridge for their helpful comments. This work was funded by SERC.

[1] Note that these are normalised to a maximum value of 10, for graphical convenience.

References

[1] Albus, JS (1975). A new approach to manipulator control: the Cerebellar Model Articulation Controller (CMAC). *Transactions of the ASME: Journal of Dynamical Systems, Measurement and Control,* **97**, pp 220-227.

[2] Barto, AG, Sutton, RS & Watkins, CJCH (1989). *Learning and Sequential Decision Making.* Technical Report 89-95, Computer and Information Science, University of Massachusetts, Amherst, MA.

[3] Chrisley, RL (1990). Cognitive map construction and use: A parallel distributed approach. In DS Touretzky, J Elman, TJ Sejnowski, & GE Hinton, editors, *Proceedings of the 1990 Connectionist Models Summer School.* San Mateo, CA: Morgan Kaufmann.

[4] Mozer, MC, & Bachrach, J (1990). Discovering the structure of a reactive environment by exploration. In D Touretzky, editor, *Advances in Neural Information Processing Systems, 2,* pp 439-446. San Mateo, CA: Morgan Kaufmann.

[5] O'Keefe, J & Nadel, L (1978). *The Hippocampus as a Cognitive Map.* Oxford, England: Oxford University Press.

[6] Sutton, RS (1988). Learning to predict by the methods of temporal difference. *Machine Learning,* **3**, pp 9-44.

[7] Sutton, RS (1990). Integrated architectures for learning, planning, and reacting based on approximating dynamic programming. In *Proceedings of the Seventh International Conference on Machine Learning.* San Mateo, CA: Morgan Kaufmann.

[8] Sutton, RS, & Barto, AG. To appear. Time-derivative models of Pavlovian conditioning. In M Gabriel & JW Moore, editors, *Learning and Computational Neuroscience.* Cambridge, MA: MIT Press.

[9] Watkins, CJCH (1989). *Learning from Delayed Rewards.* PhD Thesis. University of Cambridge, England.

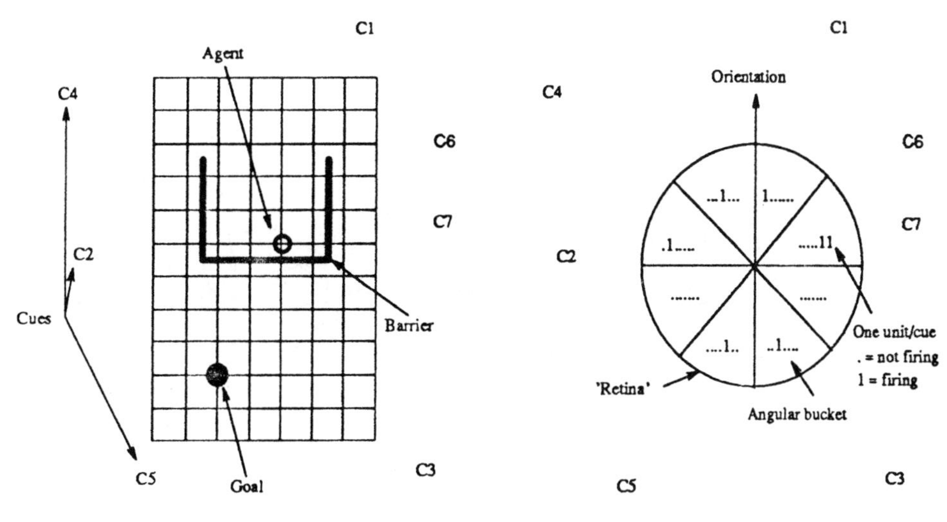

Fig 1: The grid task

Fig 2: The 'retina' for $\mathcal{R}_A$

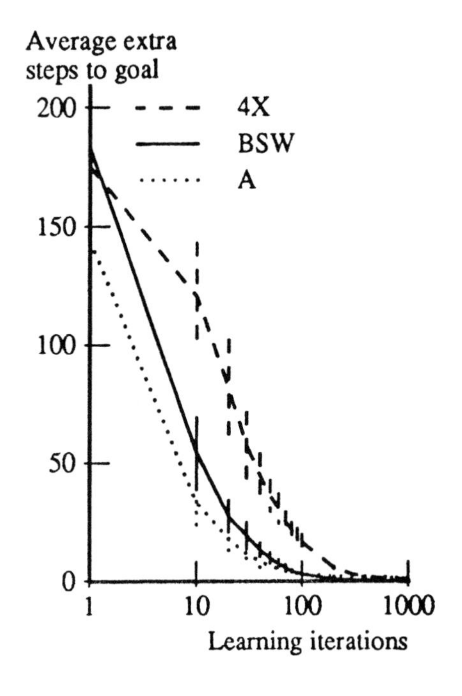

Fig 3: Different representations

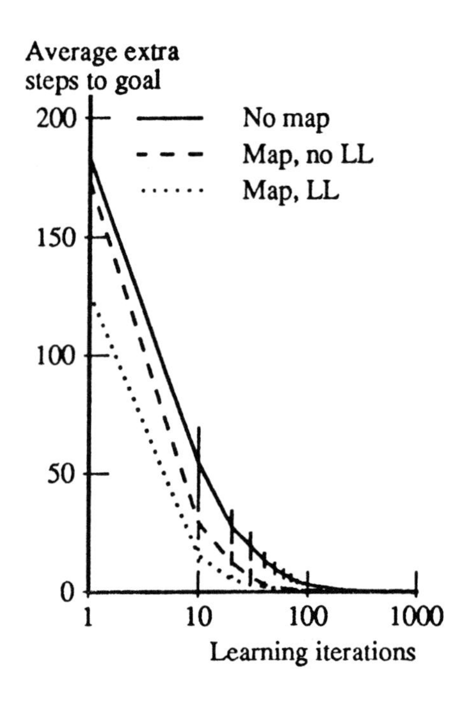

Fig 4: Mapping with $\mathcal{R}_{BSW}$

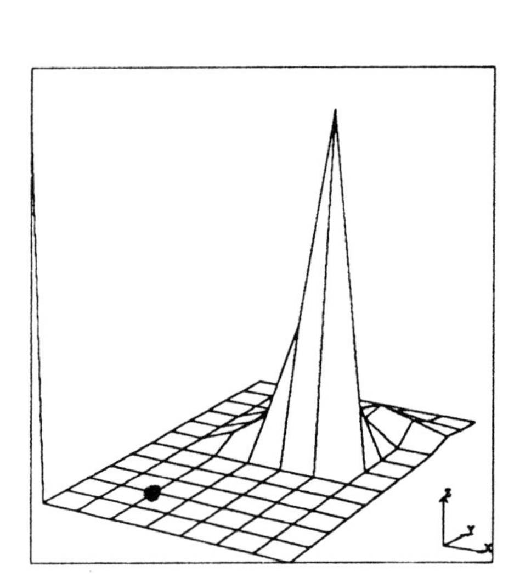

Fig 5: Initial predictions from (5,6)

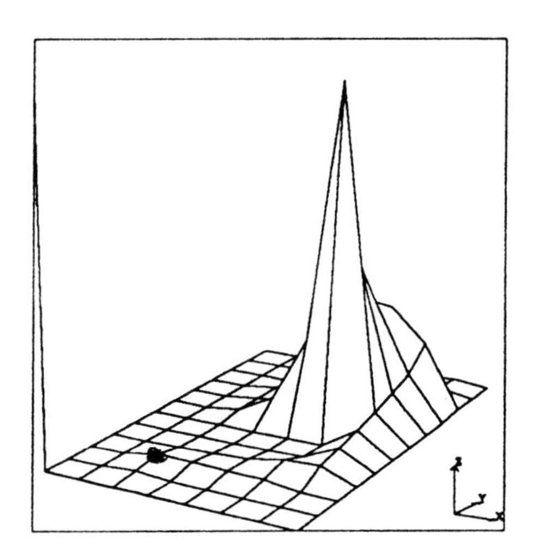

Fig 6: Predictions after 2000 iterations

Integrated Modeling and Control Based on Reinforcement Learning and Dynamic Programming

Richard S. Sutton
GTE Laboratories Incorporated
Waltham, MA 02254

Abstract

This is a summary of results with Dyna, a class of architectures for intelligent systems based on approximating dynamic programming methods. Dyna architectures integrate trial-and-error (reinforcement) learning and execution-time planning into a single process operating alternately on the world and on a learned forward model of the world. We describe and show results for two Dyna architectures, Dyna-AHC and Dyna-Q. Using a navigation task, results are shown for a simple Dyna-AHC system which simultaneously learns by trial and error, learns a world model, and plans optimal routes using the evolving world model. We show that Dyna-Q architectures (based on Watkins's Q-learning) are easy to adapt for use in changing environments.

1 Introduction to Dyna

Dyna architectures (Sutton, 1990) use learning algorithms to approximate the conventional optimal control technique known as *dynamic programming (DP)* (Bellman, 1957; Bertsekas, 1987). DP itself is not a learning method, but rather a computational method for determining optimal behavior given a complete model of the task to be solved. It is very similar to state-space search, but differs in that it is more incremental and never considers actual action *sequences* explicitly, only single actions at a time. This makes DP more amenable to incremental planning at execution time, and also makes it more suitable for stochastic or incompletely modeled environments, as it need not consider the extremely large number of sequences possible in an uncertain environment. Learned world models are likely to be stochastic and uncertain, making DP approaches particularly promising for learning systems. Dyna architectures are those that learn a world model online while using approximations to DP to learn and plan optimal behavior.

The theory of Dyna is based on the theory of DP and on DP's relationship to reinforcement learning (Watkins, 1989; Barto, Sutton & Watkins, 1989, 1990), to temporal-difference learning (Sutton, 1988), and to AI methods for planning and search (Korf, 1990). Werbos (1987) has previously argued for the general idea of building AI systems that approximate dynamic programming, and Whitehead & Ballard (1989) and others (Sutton & Barto, 1981; Sutton & Pinette, 1985; Rumelhart et al., 1986; Lin, 1991; Riolo, 1991) have presented results for the specific idea of augmenting a reinforcement learning system with a world model used for planning.

2 Dyna-AHC: Dyna by Approximating Policy Iteration

The *Dyna-AHC* architecture is based on approximating a DP method known as policy iteration (see Bertsekas, 1987). It consists of four components interacting as shown in Figure 1. The *policy* is simply the function formed by the current set of reactions; it receives as input a description of the current state of the world and produces as output an action to be sent to the world. The *world* represents the task to be solved; prototypically it is the robot's external environment. The world receives actions from the policy and produces a next state output and a reward output. The overall task is defined as maximizing the long-term average reward per time step. The architecture also includes an explicit *world model.* The world model is intended to mimic the one-step input-output behavior of the real world. Finally, the Dyna-AHC architecture includes an *evaluation function* that rapidly maps states to values, much as the policy rapidly maps states to actions. The evaluation function, the policy, and the world model are each updated by separate learning processes.

The policy is continually modified by an integrated planning/learning process. The policy is, in a sense, a *plan*, but one that is completely conditioned by current input. The planning process is incremental and can be interrupted and resumed at any time. It consists of a series of shallow seaches, each typically of one ply, and yet ultimately produces the same result as an arbitrarily deep conventional search. I call this *relaxation planning.*

Relaxation planning is based on continually adjusting the evaluation function in such a way that credit is propagated to the appropriate steps within action sequences. Generally speaking, the evaluation $e(x)$ of a state x should be equal to the best of the states y that can be reached from it in one action, taking into consideration the reward (or cost) r for that one transition:

$$e(x) \text{ ``=''} \max_{a \in Actions} E\{r + e(y) \mid x, a\}, \tag{1}$$

where $E\{\cdot \mid \cdot\}$ denotes a conditional expected value and the equal sign is quoted to indicate that this is a condition that we would like to hold, not one that necessarily does hold. If we have a complete model of the world, then the right-hand side can be computed by looking ahead one action. Thus we can generate any number of training examples for the process that learns the evaluation function: for any x,

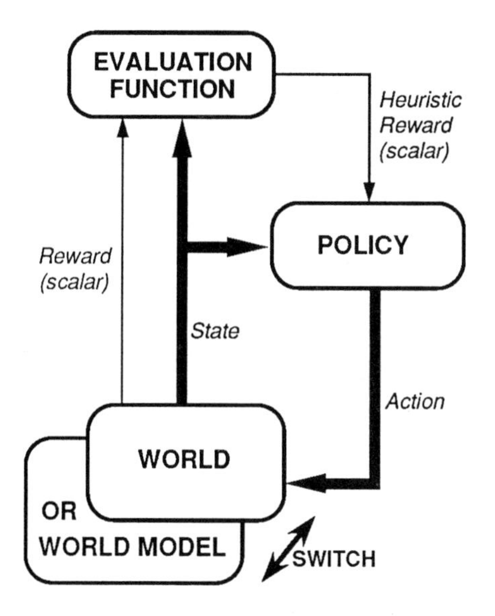

Figure 1. Overview of Dyna-AHC

1. Decide if this will be a real experience or a hypothetical one.
2. Pick a state x. If this is a real experience, use the current state.
3. Choose an action: $a \leftarrow Policy(x)$
4. Do action a; obtain next state y and reward r from world or world model.
5. If this is a real experience, update world model from x, a, y and r.
6. Update evaluation function so that $e(x)$ is more like $r + \gamma e(y)$; this is temporal-difference learning.
7. Update policy—strengthen or weaken the tendency to perform action a in state x according to the error in the evaluation function: $r+\gamma e(y)-e(x)$.
8. Go to Step 1.

Figure 2. Inner Loop of Dyna-AHC. These steps are repeatedly continually, sometimes with real experiences, sometimes with hypothetical ones.

the right-hand side of (1) is the desired output. If the learning process converges such that (1) holds in all states, then the optimal policy is given by choosing the action in each state x that achieves the maximum on the right-hand side. There is an extensive theoretical basis from dynamic programming for algorithms of this type for the special case in which the evaluation function is tabular, with enumerable states and actions. For example, this theory guarantees convergence to a unique evaluation function satisfying (1) and that the corresponding policy is optimal (Bertsekas, 1987).

The evaluation function and policy need not be tables, but can be more compact function approximators such as connectionist networks, decision trees, *k-d* trees, or symbolic rules. Although the existing theory does not apply to these machine learning algorithms directly, it does provide a theoretical foundation for exploring their use in this way.

The above discussion gives the general idea of relaxation planning, but not the exact form used in policy iteration and Dyna-AHC, in which the policy is adapted simultaneously with the evaluation function. The evaluations in this case are not supposed to reflect the value of states given optimal behavior, but rather their value given current behavior (the current policy). As the current policy gradually approaches optimality, the evaluation function also approaches the optimal evaluation function. In addition, Dyna-AHC is a *Monte Carlo* or *stochastic approximation* variant of policy iteration, in which the world model is only sampled, not examined directly. Since the real world can also be sampled, by actually taking actions and observing the result, the world can be used in place of the world model in these methods. In this case, the result is not relaxation planning, but a trial-and-error learning process much like reinforcement learning (see Barto, Sutton & Watkins,

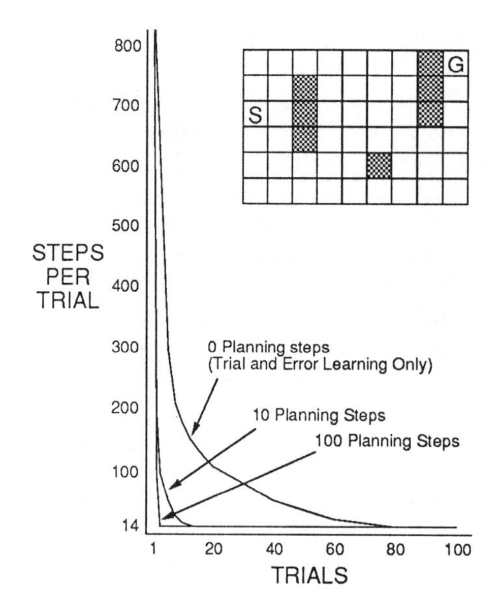

Figure 3. Learning Curves of Dyna-AHC Systems on a Navigation Task

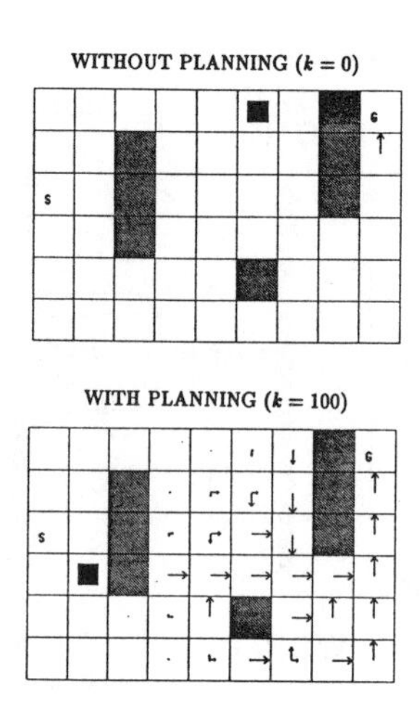

Figure 4. Policies Found by Planning and Non-Planning Dyna-AHC Systems by the Middle of the Second Trial. The black square is the current location of the system. The arrows indicate action probabilities (excess over smallest) for each direction of movement.

1989, 1990). In Dyna-AHC, both of these are done at once. The same algorithm is applied both to real experience (resulting in learning) and to hypothetical experience generated by the world model (resulting in relaxation planning). The results in both cases are accumulated in the policy and the evaluation function.

There is insufficient room here to fully justify the algorithm used in Dyna-AHC, but it is quite simple and is given in outline form in Figure 2.

3 A Navigation Task

As an illustration of the Dyna-AHC architecture, consider the task of navigating the maze shown in the upper right of Figure 3. The maze is a 6 by 9 grid of possible locations or states, one of which is marked as the starting state, "S", and one of which is marked as the goal state, "G". The shaded states act as barriers and cannot be entered. All the other states are distinct and completely distinguishable. From each there are four possible actions: UP, DOWN, RIGHT, and LEFT, which change the state accordingly, except where such a movement would take the take the system into a barrier or outside the maze, in which case the location is not changed. Reward is zero for all transitions except for those into the goal state, for which it is +1. Upon entering the goal state, the system is instantly transported back to the start state to begin the next trial. None of this structure and dynamics is known to the Dyna-AHC system a priori.

In this instance of the Dyna-AHC architecture, real and hypothetical experiences were used alternately (Step 1). For each single experience with the real world, k hypothetical experiences were generated with the model. Figure 3 shows learning curves for $k = 0$, $k = 10$, and $k = 100$, each an average over 100 runs. The $k = 0$ case involves no planning; this is a pure trial-and-error learning system entirely analogous to those used in reinforcement learning systems based on the adaptive heuristic critic (AHC) (Sutton, 1984; Barto, Sutton & Anderson, 1983). Although the length of path taken from start to goal falls dramatically for this case, it falls much *more* rapidly for the cases including hypothetical experiences, showing the benefit of relaxation planning using the learned world model. For $k = 100$, the optimal path was generally found and followed by the fourth trip from start to goal; this is very rapid learning.

Figure 4 shows why a Dyna-AHC system that includes planning solves this problem so much faster than one that does not. Shown are the policies found by the $k = 0$ and $k = 100$ Dyna-AHC systems half-way through the second trial. Without planning ($k = 0$), each trial adds only one additional step to the policy, and so only one step (the last) has been learned so far. With planning, the first trial also learned only one step, but here during the second trial an extensive policy has been developed that by the trial's end will reach almost back to the start state.

4 Dyna-Q: Dyna by Q-learning

The Dyna-AHC architecture is in essence the reinforcement learning architecture based on the adaptive heuristic critic (AHC) that my colleagues and I developed (Sutton, 1984; Barto, Sutton & Anderson, 1983) *plus* the idea of using a learned world model to generate hypothetical experience and to plan. Watkins (1989) subsequently developed the relationships between the reinforcement-learning architecture and dynamic programming (see also Barto, Sutton & Watkins, 1989, 1990) and, moreover, proposed a slightly different kind of reinforcement learning called *Q-learning*. The *Dyna-Q* architecture is the combination of this new kind of learning with the Dyna idea of using a learned world model to generate hypothetical experience and achieve planning.

Whereas the AHC reinforcement learning architecture maintains two fundamental memory structures, the evaluation function and the policy, Q-learning maintains only one. That one is a cross between an evaluation function and a policy. For each pair of state x and action a, Q-learning maintains an estimate Q_{xa} of the value of taking a in x. The value of a *state* can then be defined as the value of the state's best state-action pair: $e(x) \stackrel{\text{def}}{=} \max_a Q_{xa}$. In general, the Q-value for a state x and an action a should equal the expected value of the immediate reward r plus the discounted value of the next state y:

$$Q_{xa} \text{ “}=\text{” } E\{r + \gamma e(y) \mid x, a\}. \tag{3}$$

To achieve this goal, the updating steps (Steps 6 and 7 of Figure 2) are implemented by

$$Q_{xa} \leftarrow Q_{xa} + \beta(r + \gamma e(y) - Q_{xa}). \tag{4}$$

This is the only update rule in Q-learning. We note that it is very similar though not identical to Holland's bucket brigade and to Sutton's (1988) temporal-difference learning.

The simplest way of determining the policy on real experiences is to deterministically select the action that currently looks best—the action with the maximal Q-value. However, as we show below, this approach alone suffers from inadequate exploration. To deal with this problem, a new memory structure was added that keeps track of the degree of uncertainty about each component of the model. For each state x and action a, a record is kept of the number of time steps n_{xa} that have elapsed since a was tried in x in a real experience. An exploration bonus of $\epsilon\sqrt{n_{xa}}$ is used to make actions that have not been tried in a long time (and that therefore have uncertain consequences) appear more attractive by replacing (4) with:

$$Q_{xa} \leftarrow Q_{xa} + \beta\big(r + \epsilon\sqrt{n_{xa}} + \gamma e(y) - Q_{xa}\big). \tag{5}$$

In addition, the system is permitted to hypothetically experience actions is has never before tried, so that the exploration bonus for trying them can be propagated back by relaxation planning. This was done by starting the system with a non-empty initial model and by selecting actions randomly on hypothetical experiences. In the experiments with Dyna-Q systems reported below, actions that had never been tried were assumed to produce zero reward and leave the state unchanged.

5 Changing-World Experiments

Two experiments were performed to test the ability of Dyna systems to adapt to changes in their environments. Three Dyna systems were used: the Dyna-AHC system presented earlier in the paper, a Dyna-Q system including the exploration bonus (5), called the *Dyna-Q+* system, and a Dyna-Q system without the exploration bonus (4), called the *Dyna-Q−* system. All systems used $k = 10$.

The *blocking experiment* used the two mazes shown in the upper portion of Figure 5. Initially a short path from start to goal was available (first maze). After 1000 time steps, by which time the short path was usually well learned, that path was blocked and a longer path was opened (second maze). Performance under the new condition was measured for 2000 time steps. Average results over 50 runs are shown in Figure 5 for the three Dyna systems. The graph shows a *cumulative* record of the number of rewards received by the system up to each moment in time. In the first 1000 trials, all three Dyna systems found a short route to the goal, though the Dyna-Q+ system did so significantly faster than the other two. After the short path was blocked at 1000 steps, the graph for the Dyna-AHC system remains almost flat, indicating that it was unable to obtain further rewards. The Dyna-Q systems, on the other hand, clearly solved the blocking problem, reliably finding the alternate path after about 800 time steps.

The *shortcut experiment* began with only a long path available (first maze of Figure 6). After 3000 times steps all three Dyna systems had learned the long path, and then a shortcut was opened without interferring with the long path (second maze of Figure 6). The lower part of Figure 6 shows the results. The increase in the slope of the curve for the Dyna-Q+ system, while the others remain constant, indicates that it alone was able to find the shortcut. The Dyna-Q+ system also learned the original long route faster than the Dyna-Q− system, which in turn learned it faster than the Dyna-AHC system. However, the ability of the Dyna-Q+ system to find shortcuts does not come totally for free. Continually re-exploring the world

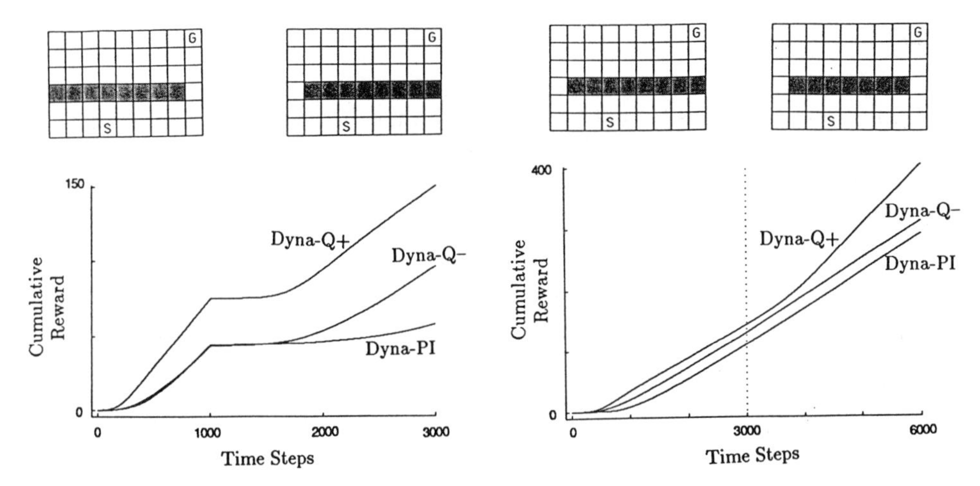

Figure 5. Performance on the Blocking Task (Slope is the *Rate* of Reward)

Figure 6. Performance on the Shortcut Task (Slope is the *Rate* of Reward)

means occasionally making suboptimal actions. If one looks closely at Figure 6, one can see that the Dyna-Q+ system actually acheives a slightly lower *rate* of reinforcement during the first 3000 steps. In a static environment, Dyna-Q+ will eventually perform worse than Dyna-Q−, whereas, in a changing environment, it will be far superior, as here. One possibility is to use a meta-level learning process to adjust the exploration parameter ϵ to match the degree of variability of the environment.

6 Limitations and Conclusions

The results presented here are clearly limited in many ways. The state and action spaces are small and denumerable, permitting tables to be used for all learning processes and making it feasible for the entire state space to be explicitly explored. In addition, these results have assumed knowledge of the world state, have used a trivial form of search control (random exploration), and have used terminal goal states. These are significant limitations of the results, but not of the Dyna architecture. There is nothing about the Dyna architecture which prevents it from being applied more generally in each of these ways (e.g., see Lin, 1991; Riolo, 1991; Whitehead & Ballard, in press).

Despite limitations, these results are significant. They show that the use of a forward model can dramatically speed trial-and-error (reinforcement) learning processes even on simple problems. Moreover, they show how planning can be done with the incomplete, changing, and oftimes incorrect world models that are contructed through learning. Finally, they show how the functionality of planning can be obtained in a completely incremental manner, and how a planning process can be freely intermixed with reaction and learning processes. Further results are needed for a thorough comparison of Dyna-AHC and Dyna-Q architectures, but the results presented here suggest that it is easier to adapt Dyna-Q architectures to changing environments.

Acknowledgements

The author gratefully acknowledges the contributions by Andrew Barto, Chris Watkins, Steve Whitehead, Paul Werbos, Luis Almeida, and Leslie Kaelbling.

References

Barto, A. G., Sutton R. S., & Anderson, C. W. (1983) *IEEE Trans. SMC-13*, 834–846.

Barto, A. G., Sutton, R. S., & Watkins, C. J. C. H. (1989) In: *Learning and Computational Neuroscience*, M. Gabriel and J.W. Moore (Eds.), MIT Press, 1991.

Barto, A. G., Sutton, R. S., & Watkins, C. J. C. H. (1990) *NIPS 2*, 686–693.

Bellman, R. E. (1957) *Dynamic Programming*, Princeton University Press.

Bertsekas, D. P. (1987) *Dynamic Programming: Deterministic and Stochastic Models*, Prentice-Hall.

Korf, R. E. (1990) *Artificial Intelligence 42*, 189–211.

Lin, Long-Ji. (1991) In: *Proceedings of the International Conference on the Simulation of Adaptive Behavior*, MIT Press.

Riolo, R. (1991) In: *Proceedings of the International Conference on the Simulation of Adaptive Behavior*, MIT Press.

Rumelhart, D. E., Smolensky, P., McClelland, J. L., & Hinton, G. E. (1986) In: *Parallel Distributed Processing: Explorations in the Microstructure of Cognition, Volume II*, by J. L. McClelland, D. E. Rumelhart, and the PDP research group, 7–57. MIT Press.

Sutton, R. S. (1984) *Temporal Credit Assignment in Reinforcement Learning.* PhD thesis, COINS Dept., Univ, of Mass.

Sutton, R.S. (1988) *Machine Learning 3*, 9–44.

Sutton, R.S. (1990) In: Proceedings of the Seventh International Conference on Machine Learning, 216–224, Morgan Kaufmann.

Sutton, R.S., Barto, A.G. (1981) *Cognition and Brain Theory 4*, 217–246.

Sutton, R.S., Pinette, B. (1985) In: *Proceedings of the Seventh Annual Conf. of the Cognitive Science Society*, 54–64, Lawrence Erlbaum.

Watkins, C. J. C. H. (1989) *Learning with Delayed Rewards.* PhD thesis, Cambridge University Psychology Department.

Werbos, P. J. (1987) *IEEE Trans. SMC-17*, 7–20.

Whitehead, S. D., Ballard, D.H. (1989) In: *Proceedings of the Sixth International Workshop on Machine Learning*, 354–357, Morgan Kaufmann.

Whitehead, S. D., Ballard, D.H. (in press) *Machine Learning.*

A Reinforcement Learning Variant for Control Scheduling

Aloke Guha
Honeywell Sensor and System Development Center
3660 Technology Drive
Minneapolis, MN 55417

Abstract

We present an algorithm based on reinforcement and state recurrence learning techniques to solve control scheduling problems. In particular, we have devised a simple learning scheme called "handicapped learning", in which the weights of the associative search element are reinforced, either positively or negatively, such that the system is forced to move towards the desired setpoint in the shortest possible trajectory. To improve the learning rate, a variable reinforcement scheme is employed: negative reinforcement values are varied depending on whether the failure occurs in handicapped or normal mode of operation. Furthermore, to realize a simulated annealing scheme for accelerated learning, if the system visits the same failed state successively, the negative reinforcement value is increased. In examples studied, these learning schemes have demonstrated high learning rates, and therefore may prove useful for in-situ learning.

1 INTRODUCTION

Reinforcement learning techniques have been applied successfully for simple control problems, such as the pole-cart problem [Barto 83, Michie 68, Rosen 88] where the goal was to maintain the pole in a quasistable region, but not at specific setpoints. However, a large class of continuous control problems require maintaining the system at a desired operating point, or setpoint, at a given time. We refer to this problem as the basic setpoint control problem [Guha 90], and have shown that reinforcement learning can be used, not surprisingly, quite well for such control tasks. A more general version of the same problem requires steering the system from some initial or starting state to a desired state or setpoint at specific times without knowledge of the dynamics of the system. We therefore wish to examine how control scheduling tasks, where the system must be steered through a sequence of setpoints at specific times, can be learned. Solving such a control problem without explicit modeling of the system or plant can prove to be beneficial in many adaptive control tasks.

To address the control scheduling problem, we have derived a learning algorithm called handicapped learning. Handicapped learning uses a nonlinear encoding of the state of the system, a new associative reinforcement learning algorithm, and a novel reinforcement scheme to explore the control space to meet the scheduling constraints. The goal of handicapped learning is to learn the control law necessary to steer the system from one setpoint to another. We provide a description of the state encoding and associative learning in Section 2, the reinforcement scheme in Section 3, the experimental results in Section 4, and the conclusions in Section 5.

2 REINFORCEMENT LEARNING STRATEGY: HANDICAPPED LEARNING

Our earlier work on regulatory control using reinforcement learning [Guha 90] used a simple linear coded state representation of the system. However, when considering multiple setpoints in a schedule, a linear coding of high-resolution results in a combinatorial explosion of states. To avoid this curse of dimensionality, we have adopted a simple nonlinear encoding of the state space. We describe this first.

2.1 STATE ENCODING

To define the states in which reinforcement must be provided to the controller, we set tolerance limits around the desired setpoint, say X_d. If the tolerance of operation defined by the level of control sophistication required in the problem is T, then the controller is defined to fail if $|X(t) - X_d| > T$ as described in our earlier work in [Guha 90].

The controller must learn to maintain the system within this tolerance window. If the range, R, of possible values of the setpoint or control variable X(t) is significantly greater than the tolerance window, then the number of states required to define the setpoint will be large. We therefore use a nonlinear coding of the control variable. Thus, if the level of discrimination within the tolerance window is 2T/n, then the number of states required to represent the control variable is (n + 2) where the two added states represent the states, $(X(t) - X_d) > T$ and $(X(t) - X_d) < -T$. With this representation scheme, any continuous range of setpoints can be represented with very high resolution but without the explosion in state space.

The above state encoding will be used in our associative reinforcement learning algorithm, handicapped learning, which we describe next.

2.2 HANDICAPPED LEARNING ALGORITHM

Our reinforcement learning strategy is derived from the Associative Search Element/Adaptive Heuristic Critic (ASE/AHC) algorithm [Barto 83, Anderson 86]. We have considered a binary control output, y(t):

$$y(t) = f(\sum_i w_i(t)x_i(t) + noise(t)) \qquad (1)$$

where f is the thresholding step function, and $x_i(t)$, $0 \le i \le N$, is the current decoded state, that is, $x_i(t) = 1$ when the system is in the ith state and 0 otherwise. As in ASE, the added term noise(t) facilitates stochastic learning. Note that the learning algorithm can be easily extended to continuous valued outputs, the nature of the continuity is determined by the thresholding function.

We incorporate two learning heuristics: state recurrence [Rosen 88] and a newly introduced heuristic called "handicapped learning". The controller is in the handicapped learning mode if a flag, H, is set high. H is defined as follows:

$$\begin{aligned} H &= 0, \text{ if } |X(t) - X_d| < T \\ &= 1, \text{ otherwise} \end{aligned} \qquad (2)$$

The handicap mode provides a mechanism to modify the reinforcement scheme. In this mode the controller is allowed to explore the search space of action sequences, to steer to a new setpoint, without "punishment" (negative reinforcement). The mode is invoked when the system is at a valid setpoint $X_1(t_1)$ at time t_1, but must be steered to the new setpoint X_2 outside the tolerance window, that is, $|X_1 - X_2| > T$, at time t_2. Since both setpoints are valid operating points, these setpoints as well as all points within the possible optimal trajectories from X_1 to X_2 cannot be deemed to be failure states. Further, by following a special reinforcement scheme during the handicapped mode, one can enable learning and facilitate the controller to find the optimal trajectory to steer the system from one setpoint to another.

The weight updating rule used during setpoint schedule learning is given by equation (3):

$$w_i(t+1) = w_i(t) + \alpha\, r_1(t)\, e_i(t) + \alpha_2\, r_2(t)\, e_{2i}(t) + \alpha_3\, r_3(t)\, e_{3i}(t) \qquad (3)$$

where the term $\alpha\, r_1(t)\, e_i(t)$ is the basic associative learning component, $r_1(t)$ the heuristic reinforcement, and $e_i(t)$ the eligibility trace of the state $x_i(t)$ [Barto 83].

The third term in equation (3) is the state recurrence component for reinforcing short cycles [Rosen 88]. Here α_2 is a constant gain, $r_2(t)$ is a positive constant reward, and e_{2i} the state recurrence eligibility is defined as follows:

$$\begin{aligned} e_{2i}(t) &= \beta_2\, x_i(t) y(t_{i,last})/(\beta_2 + t - t_{i,last}), \quad \text{if } (t - t_{i,last}) > 1 \text{ and } H = 0 \\ &= 0, \text{ otherwise} \end{aligned} \qquad (4)$$

where β_2 is a positive constant, and $t_{i,last}$ is the last time the system visited the ith state. The eligibility function in equation (4) reinforces shorter cycles more than longer cycles, and improve control when the system is within a tolerance window.

The fourth term in equation (3) is the handicapped learning component. Here α_3 is a constant gain, $r_3(t)$ is a positive constant reward and e_{3i} the handicapped learning eligibility is defined as follows:

$$e_{3i}(t) = -\beta_3 \, x_i(t) y(t_{i,last})/(\beta_3 + t - t_{i,last}), \quad \text{if } H = 1$$
$$= 0, \quad \text{otherwise} \qquad (5)$$

where β_3 is a positive constant. While state recurrence promotes short cycles around a desired operating point, handicapped learning forces the controller to move away from the current operating point $X(t)$. The system enters the handicapped mode whenever it is outside the tolerance window around the desired setpoint. If the initial operating point X_i (= $X(0)$) is outside the tolerance window of the desired setpoint X_d, $|X_i - X_d| > T$, the basic AHC network will always register a failure. This failure situation is avoided by invoking the handicapped learning described above. By setting absolute upper and lower limits to operating point values, the controller based on handicapped learning can learn the correct sequence of actions necessary to steer the system to the desired operating point X_d.

The weight update equations for the critic in the AHC are unchanged from the original AHC and we do not list them here.

3 REINFORCEMENT SCHEMES

Unlike in previous experiments by other researchers, we have constructed the reinforcement values used during learning to be multivalued, and not binary. The reinforcement to the critic is negative–both positive and negative reinforcements are used. There are two forms of failure that can occur during setpoint control. First, the controller can reach the absolute upper or lower limits. Second, there may be a timeout failure in the handicapped mode. By design, when the controller is in handicapped mode, it is allowed to remain there for only T_L, determined by the average control step A_y and the error between the current operating point and the desired setpoint:

$$T_L = k \, A_y \, (X_0 - X_d) \qquad (6)$$

where X_0 is the initial setpoint, and k some constant. The negative reinforcement provided to the controller is higher if the absolute limits of the operating point is reached.

We have implemented a more interesting reinforcement scheme that is somewhat similar to simulated annealing. If the system fails in the same state on two successive trials, the negative reinforcement is increased. The primary reinforcement function can be defined as follows:

$$r_j(k+1) = r_i(k) - r0, \quad \text{if } i = j$$
$$= r1, \quad \text{if } i \neq j \qquad (7)$$

where $r_i(k)$ is the negative reinforcement provided if the system failed in state i during trial k, and r0 and r1 are constants.

4 EXPERIMENTS AND RESULTS

Two different setpoint control experiments have been conducted. The first was the basic setpoint control of a continuous stirred tank reactor in which the temperature must be held at a desired setpoint. That experiment successfully demonstrated the use of reinforcement learning for setpoint control of a highly nonlinear and unstable process [Guha 90]. The second recent experiment has been on evaluating the handicapped learning strategy for an environmental controller where the controller must learn to control the heating system to maintain the ambient temperature specified by a time-temperature schedule. Thus, as the external temperature varies, the network must adapt the heating (ON) and (OFF) control sequence so as to maintain the environment at the desired temperature as quickly as possible. The state information describing system is composed of the time interval of the schedule, the current heating state (ON/OFF), and the error or the difference between desired and current ambient or interior temperature. The heating and cooling rates are variable: the heating rate decreases while the cooling rate increases exponentially as the exterior temperature falls below the ambient or controlled temperature.

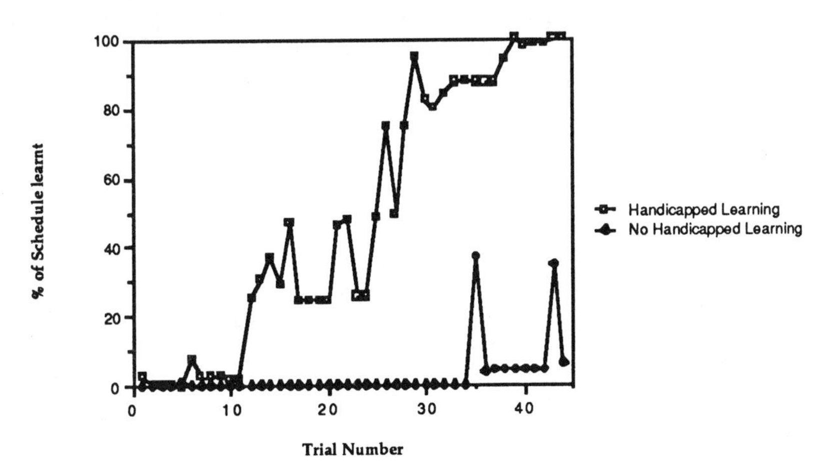

Figure 1: Rate of Learning with and without Handicapped Learning

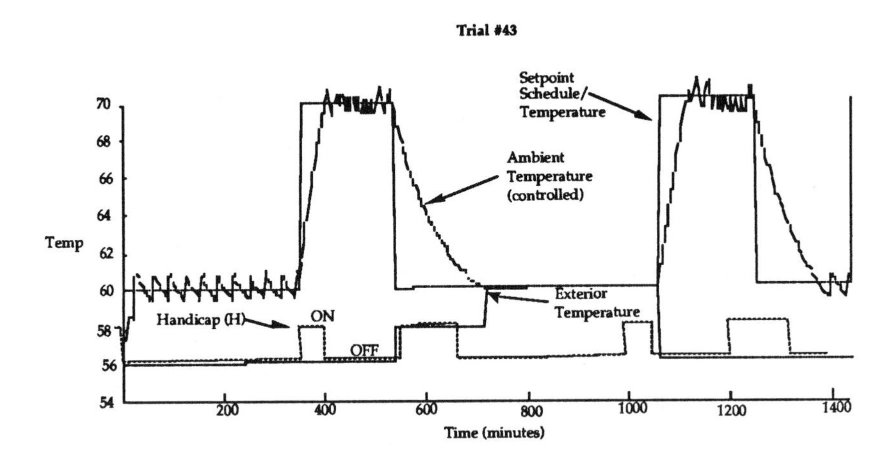

Figure 2: Time-Temperature Plot of Controlled Environment at Forty-third Trial

The experiments on the environmental controller consisted of embedding a daily setpoint schedule that contains six setpoints at six specific times. Trails were conducted to train the controller. Each trial starts at the beginning of the schedule (time = 0). The setpoints typically varied in the range of 55 to 75 degrees. The desired tolerance window was 1 degree. The upper and lower limits of the controlled temperature were set arbitrarily at 50 and 80 degrees, respectively. Control actions were taken every 5 minutes. Learning was monitored by examining how much of the schedule was learnt correctly as the number of trials increased.

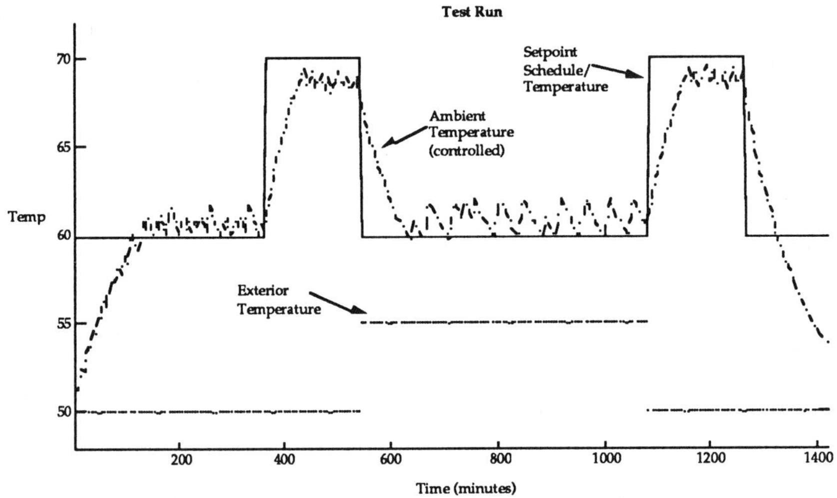

Figure 3: Time-Temperature Plot of Controlled Environment for a Test Run

Figure 1 shows how the learning progresses with the number of trials. Current results show that the learning of the complete schedule (of the six time-temperature pairs) requiring 288 control steps, can be accomplished in only 43 trials. (Given binary output, the controller could have in the worst case executed 10^{86} ($\sim 2^{288}$) trials to learn the complete schedule.)

More details on the learning ability using the reinforcement learning strategy are available from the time-temperature plots of the trial and test runs in Figures 2 and 3. As the learning progresses to the forty-third trial, the controller learns to continuously heat up or cool down to the desired temperature (Figure 2). To further test the learning generalizations on the schedule, the trained network was tested on a different environment where the exterior temperature profile (and the therefore the heating and cooling rates) was different from the one used for training. Figure 3 shows the schedule that is maintained. Because the controller encounters different cooling rates in the test run, some learning still occurs as evident form Figure 3. However, all six setpoints were reached in the proper sequence. In essence, this test shows that the controller has generalized on the heating and cooling control law, independent of the setpoints and the heating and cooling rates.

5 CONCLUSIONS

We have developed a new learning strategy based on reinforcement learning that can be used to learn setpoint schedules for continuous processes. The experimental results have demonstrated good learning performance. However, a number of interesting extensions to this work are possible. For instance, the handicapped mode exploration of control can be better controlled for faster learning, if more information on the desired or possible trajectory is known. Another area of investigation would be the area of state encoding. In our approach, the nonlinear encoding of the system state was assumed uniform at different regions of the control space. In applications where the system with high nonlinearity, different nonlinear coding could be used adaptively to improve the state representation. Finally, other formulations of reinforcement learning algorithms, besides ASE/AHC, should also be explored. One such possibility is Watkins' Q-learning [Watkins 89].

References

[Guha 90] A. Guha and A. Mathur, *Setpoint Control Based on Reinforcement Learning*, Proceedings of IJCNN 90, Washington D.C., January 1990.

[Barto 83] A.G. Barto, R.S. Sutton, and C.W. Anderson, *Neuronlike Adaptive Elements That Can Solve Difficult Learning Control Problems*, IEEE Transactions on Systems, Man, and Cybernetics, Vol. SMC-13, No. 5, September/October 1983.

[Michie 68] D. Michie and R. Chambers, *Machine Intelligence*, E. Dale and D. Michie (eds.), Oliver and Boyd, Edinburgh, 1968, p. 137.

[Rosen 88] B. E. Rosen, J. M. Goodwin, and J. J. Vidal, *Learning by State Recurrence Detection*, IEEE Conference on Neural Information Processing Systems - Natural and Synthetic, AIP Press, 1988.

[Watkins 89] C.J.C.H. Watkins, *Learning from Delayed Rewards*, Ph. D. Dissertation, King's College, May 1989.

Adaptive Range Coding

Bruce E. Rosen, James M. Goodwin, and Jacques J. Vidal
Distributed Machine Intelligence Laboratory
Computer Science Department
University of California, Los Angeles
Los Angeles, CA 90024

Abstract

This paper examines a class of neuron based learning systems for dynamic control that rely on adaptive range coding of sensor inputs. Sensors are assumed to provide binary coded range vectors that coarsely describe the system state. These vectors are input to neuron-like processing elements. Output decisions generated by these "neurons" in turn affect the system state, subsequently producing new inputs. Reinforcement signals from the environment are received at various intervals and evaluated. The neural weights as well as the *range boundaries* determining the output decisions are then altered with the goal of maximizing future reinforcement from the environment. Preliminary experiments show the promise of adapting "neural receptive fields" when learning dynamical control. The observed performance with this method exceeds that of earlier approaches.

1 INTRODUCTION

A major criticism of unsupervised learning and control techniques such as those used by Barto et al. (Barto, 1983) and by Albus (Albus, 1981) is the need for *a priori* selection of region sizes for range coding. Range coding in principle generalizes inputs and reduces computational and storage overhead, but the boundary partitioning, determined *a priori*, is often non-optimal (for example, the ranges described in (Barto, 1983) differ from those used in (Barto 1982) for the same control task differ). Determination of nearly optimal, or at least adequate, regions is left as an additional task that would require that the system dynamics be analyzed, which is not always possible.

To address this problem, we move region boundaries adaptively, progressively altering the initial partitioning to a more appropriate representation with no need for *a priori* knowledge. Unlike previous work (Michie, 1968), (Barto, 1983), (Anderson, 1982) which used fixed coders, this approach produces adaptive coders that contract and expand regions/ranges. During adaptation, frequently active regions/ranges contract, reducing the number of situations in which they will be activated, and increasing the chances that neighboring regions will receive input instead. This class of self-organization is discussed in Kohonen (Kohonen, 1984), (Ritter, 1986, 1988). The resulting self-organizing mapping will tend to track the environmental input probability density function. Adaptive range coding creates a focusing mechanism. Resources are distributed according to regional activity level. More resources can be allocated to critical areas of the state space. Concentrated activity is more finely discriminated and corresponding control decisions are more finely tuned.

Dynamic shaping of the region boundaries can be achieved without sacrificing memory or learning speed. Also, since the region boundaries are finally determined solely by the environmental dynamics, optimal *a priori* ranges and region specifications are not necessary.

As an example, consider a one dimensional state space, as shown in figures 1a and 1b. It is is partitioned into three regions by the vertical lines shown. The heavy curve indicates a theoretical optimal control surface (unknown *a priori*) of a state space which the weight in each region should approximate. The dashed horizontal lines show the best learned weight values for the respective partitionings. Weight values approximate the mean value of the true control surface weight in each of the regions.

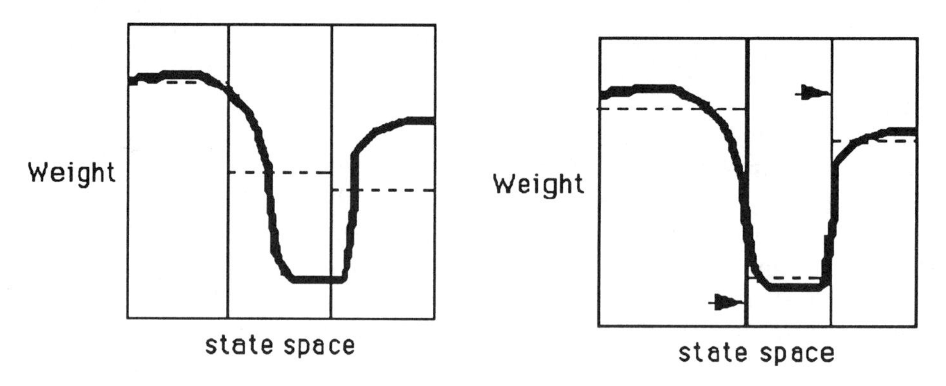

Figure 1a
Even Region Partition

Figure 1b
Adapted Region Partition

An evenly partitioned space produces the weights shown in figure 1a. Figure 1b shows the regions after the boundaries have been adjusted, and the final weight values. Although the weights in both 1a and 1b reflect the mean of the true control surface (in their respective regions), adaptive partitioning is able to represent the ideal surface with a smaller mean squared error.

2 ADAPTIVE RANGE CODING RULE

For the more general n dimensional control problem using adaptive range boundaries, the shape of each region can change from an initial n dimensional prism to an n dimensional polytope. The polytope shape is determined by the current activation state and its average activity. The heuristic for our adaptive range coding is to *move each region vertex towards or away from the current activation state according to the reinforcement.* The equation which adjusts each region boundary is adapted in part from the weight alteration formula used by Kohonen's topological mapping (Kohonen 1984). Each region (i) consists of 2^n vertices ($V_{ij}(t)$, $1 \leq j \leq 2^n$) describing that region's boundaries that move toward or away from the current state activity (A(t)) depending on the reinforcement r.

$$[1] \qquad V_{ij}(t+1) = V_{ij}(t) + K\, r\, h(V_{ij}(t) - A(t))$$

where K is the gain, r is the reinforcement (or error) used to alter the weight in the region, and h() is a Gaussian or a difference of Gaussians function.

3 SIMULATION RESULTS

In our experiments, the expected reinforcement of the ASE/ACE system $\hat{r}$ (described in (Barto 1983)) was also used as r in [1]. Simple pole balancing (see figure 2) was chosen, rather than the cart-pole balancing task in (Barto 1983). The time step τ was chosen to be large (0.05 seconds) and initial region boundaries of θ and $\dot{\theta}$ were chosen as (-12,-6,0,1,6,12) and ($-\infty$, -10,10,∞). All other parameters were identical to those described in (Barto, 1983).

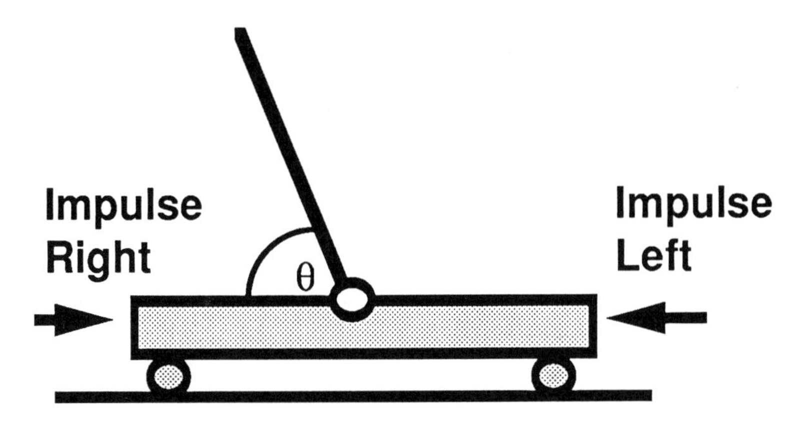

Figure 2: The Pole Balancing Task

The standard ASE, ASE/ACE, and adaptive range coding algorithms were compared on this task. One hundred runs of each algorithm were performed. Each *run* consisted of a sequence of trials and each *trial* counted the number of time steps until the pole fell. If the pole had not fallen after 20,000 time steps, the trial was considered to be *successful* and it was terminated. Each run was terminated either after 100 trials, or after the pole was successfully balanced in five successive trials. (We assumed that five successive trials indicated that the systems weights and regions had stabilized.) All region weights were initialized to zero at the start of each run.

In the adaptive range coding runs, the updated vertex state positions were determined by 3 factors: difference between the vertex and the current state, the expected reinforcement, and the gain. A Gaussian served as an appropriate decay function to modulate vertex movements. Current state to vertex differences served as function input parameters. Outputs attenuated with increasing inputs, and the standard deviation σ of the Gaussian shaped the decay function. The magnitude and position of each vertex movement were also modulated by the reinforcement $\hat{r}(t)$ which moves the vertex towards or away form the current state, and by K, a gain parameter. The user definable parameter values of K and σ were initially chosen (arbitrarily) as $K = 1$ and $\sigma = 10.0$, and were used in the following experiments. Parameters were not fine tuned or optimized.

Figure 3 shows the results of the ASE, ASE/ACE, and adaptive range coding experiments. The various runs and trials differed only in the random number generator seed. Corresponding runs and trials using the standard ASE, ASE/ACE and the adaptive range coding algorithm used the same random number seed. All other parameters were identical between the two systems. However, in adaptive range coding, region boundaries were shifted in accordance with [1] during each run.

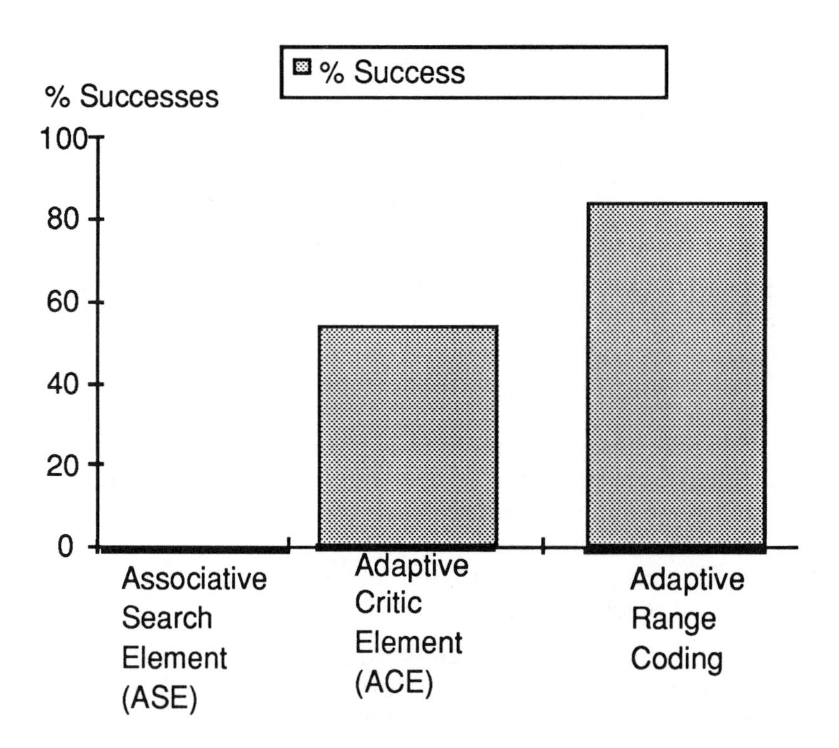

Figure 3: Comparison of the ASE, ASE/ACE, and the Adaptive Range Coding Algorithm.

We simulated 100 runs of the ASE algorithm with zero successful runs. Using the ASE/ACE algorithm, 54 runs were successful. With adaptive range coding algorithm, 84 of the 100 runs were successful. With $\sigma_{ase/ace} = 4.98$ and $\sigma_{adapt\_range\_code} = 3.66$, a χ^2 test showed the two performance sets to be statistically different ($p > 0.95$).

Figure 4 shows a comparison of the average performance values of the 100 ASE/ACE and Adaptive Range Coding (ARC) runs. Pole balancing time is shown as a function of the number of learning trials experienced.

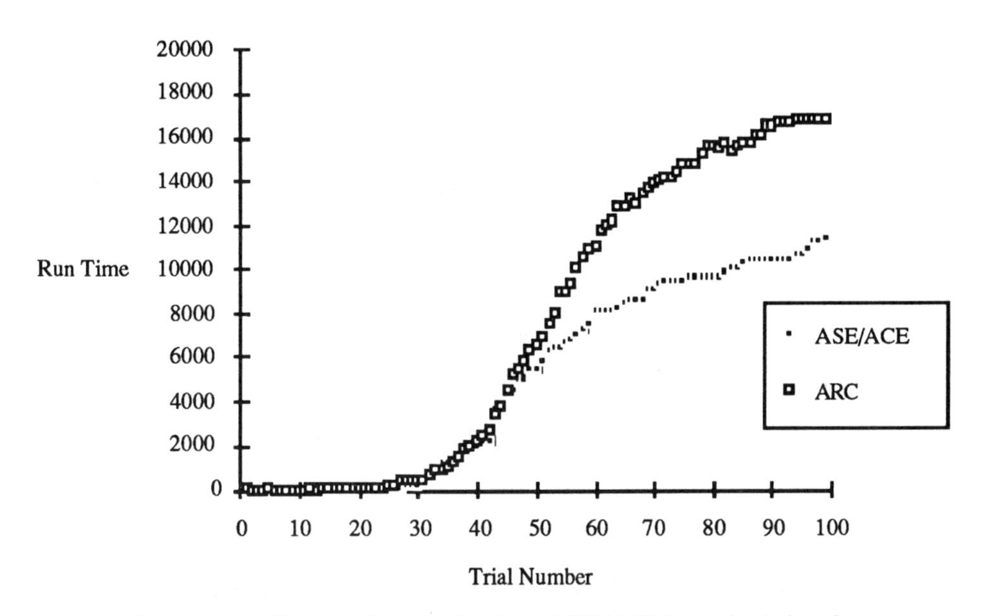

Figure 4: Comparison of the ASE/ACE and Adaptive Range Coding learning rates on the cart pole task. Pole balancing time is shown as function of learning trials. Results are averaged over 100 runs.

The disparity between the run times of the two different algorithms is due to the comparatively large number of failures of the ASE/ACE system. Statistical analysis indicates no significant difference in the learning rates or performance levels of the <u>successful</u> runs between categories, leading us to believe that adaptive range coding may lead to an "all or none" behavior, and that there is a minimum area of the state space that the system must explore to succeed.

4 CONCLUSION

The research has shown that neuron-like elements with adjustable regions can dynamically create topological cause and effect maps reflecting the control laws of dynamic systems. It is anticipated from the results of the examples presented above, that adaptive range coding will be more effective than earlier static region approaches in the control of complex systems with unknown dynamics.

References

J. S. Albus. (1981) *Brains, Behavior, and Robotics*, Peterburough, NH: McGraw-Hill Byte Books.

C. W. Anderson. (1982) Feature generation and Selection by a Layered Network of Reinforcement Learning Elements: Some Initial Experiments, *Technical Report COINS 82-12*. Amherst, MA: University of Massachusetts, Department of Computer and Information Science.

A. Barto, R. Sutton, and C. Anderson. (1982) Neuron-like elements that can solve difficult learning control problems. *Coins Tech. Rept. No. 82-20*. Amherst, MA: University of Massachusetts, Department of Computer and Information Science.

A. G. Barto, R. S. Sutton, and C. W. Anderson. (1983) Neuron-like elements that can solve difficult learning control problems, *IEEE Transactions on Systems, Man, and Cybernetics*, **13**(5): 834-846.

T. Kohonen. (1984) *Self-Organization and Associative Memory*, New York: Springer-Verlag.

D. Michie and R. Chambers. (1968) *Machine Intelligence* Edinburgh: Oliver and Boyd.

H. Ritter and K. Schulten. (1986) Topology Conserving Mappings for Learning Motor Tasks. In J. S. Denker (ed.), *Neural Networks for Computing*. Snowbird, Utah: AIP.

H. Ritter and K. Schulten. (1988) Extending Kohonen's Self-Organizing Mapping Algorithm to Learn Ballistic Movements. In R. Eckmiller (ed.), *Neural Computers*. Springer-Verlag.

Neural Network Implementation of Admission Control

Rodolfo A. Milito, Isabelle Guyon, and Sara A. Solla
AT&T Bell Laboratories, Crawfords Corner Rd., Holmdel, NJ 07733

Abstract

A feedforward layered network implements a mapping required to control an unknown stochastic nonlinear dynamical system. Training is based on a novel approach that combines stochastic approximation ideas with back-propagation. The method is applied to control admission into a queueing system operating in a time-varying environment.

1 INTRODUCTION

A controller for a discrete-time dynamical system must provide, at time t_n, a value u_n for the control variable. Information about the state of the system when such decision is made is available through the observable y_n. The value u_n is determined on the basis of the current observation y_n and the preceding control action u_{n-1}. Given the information $I_n = (y_n, u_{n-1})$, the controller implements a mapping $I_n \rightarrow u_n$.

Open-loop controllers suffice in static situations which require a single-valued control policy u^* : a constant mapping $I_n \rightarrow u^*$, regardless of I_n. Closed-loop controllers provide a dynamic control action u_n, determined by the available information I_n. This work addresses the question of training a neural network to implement a general mapping $I_n \rightarrow u_n$.

The problem that arises is the lack of training patterns: the appropriate value u_n for a given input I_n is not known. The quality of a given control policy can only be assessed by using it to control the system, and monitoring system performance. The sensitivity of the performance to variations in the control policy cannot be investigated analytically, since the system is unknown. We show that such sensitivity can be estimated within the standard framework of stochastic approximation. The usual back-propagation algorithm is used to determine the sensitivity of the output u_n to variations in the parameters $\mathbf{W}$ of the network, which can thus be adjusted so as to improve system performance.

The advantage of a neural network as a closed-loop controller resides in its ability to accept inputs $(I_n, I_{n-1}, ..., I_{n-p})$. The additional p time steps into the past provide information about the history of the controlled system. As demonstrated here, neural network controllers can capture regularities in the structure of time-varying environments, and are particularly powerful for tracking time variations driven by stationary stochastic processes.

2 CONTROL OF STOCHASTIC DYNAMICAL SYSTEMS

Consider a dynamical system for which the state x_n is updated at discrete times $t_n = n\ \delta$. The control input u_n in effect at time t_n affects the dynamical evolution, and

$$x_{n+1} = f(x_n, u_n, \xi_n). \tag{2.1}$$

Here $\{\xi_n\}$ is a stochastic process which models the intrinsic randomness of the system as well as external, unmeasurable disturbances. The variable x_n is not accessible to direct measurement, and knowledge about the state of the system is limited to the observable

$$y_n = h(x_n). \tag{2.2}$$

Our goal is to design a neural network controller which produces a specific value u_n for the control variable to be applied at time t_n, given the available information $I_n \equiv (y_n, u_{n-1})$.

In order to design a controller which implements the appropriate *control policy* $I_n \rightarrow u_n$, a specification of the purpose of controlling the dynamical system is needed. There is typically a function of the observable,

$$J_n = H(y_n), \tag{2.3}$$

which measures system performance. It follows from Eqs. (2.1)-(2.3) that the composition $G = H \circ h \circ f$ determines

$$J_n = G(x_{n-1}, u_{n-1}, \xi_{n-1}), \tag{2.4}$$

a function of the state x of the system, the control variable u, and the stochastic variable ξ. The quantity of interest is the expectation value of the system performance,

$$\langle J_n \rangle = \langle H(y_n) \rangle_\xi, \tag{2.5}$$

averaged with respect to ξ. This expectation value can be estimated by the long-run average

$$\bar{J}_N = \frac{1}{N} \sum_{n=1}^{N} H(y_n), \tag{2.6}$$

since for an ergodic system $\bar{J}_N \rightarrow \langle J_n \rangle$ as $N \rightarrow \infty$. The goal of the controller is to generate a sequence $\{u_n\}$, $1 \leq n \leq N$ of control values, such that the average performance $\langle J_n \rangle$ stabilizes to a desired value J^*.

The parameters $\mathbf{W}$ of the neural network are thus to be adapted so as to minimize a cost function

$$E(\mathbf{W}) = \frac{1}{2} (\langle J_n \rangle - J^*)^2. \tag{2.7}$$

The dependence of $E(\mathbf{W})$ on $\mathbf{W}$ is implicit: the value of $\langle J_n \rangle$ depends on the controlling sequence $\{u_n\}$, which depends on the parameters $\mathbf{W}$ of the neural network.

On-line training proceeds through a gradient descent update

$$\mathbf{W}_{n+1} = \mathbf{W}_n - \eta \nabla_{\mathbf{W}} E_n(\mathbf{W}), \tag{2.8}$$

towards the minimization of the instantaneous deviation

$$E_n(\mathbf{W}) = \frac{1}{2} (J_{n+1} - J^*)^2. \tag{2.9}$$

There is no specified target for the output u_n that the controller is expected to provide in response to the input $I_n = (y_n, u_{n-1})$. The output u_n can thus be considered as a variable u, which controls the subsequent performance: $J_{n+1} = G(x_n, u, \xi_n)$, as follows from Eq. (2.4). Then

$$\begin{aligned} \nabla_{\mathbf{W}} E_n(\mathbf{W}) &= \frac{\partial E_n(\mathbf{W})}{\partial J_{n+1}} \frac{\partial G}{\partial u} \Big|_{u=u_n} \nabla_{\mathbf{W}} u \\ &= (J_{n+1} - J^*) \frac{\partial G}{\partial u} \Big|_{u=u_n} \nabla_{\mathbf{W}} u. \end{aligned} \tag{2.10}$$

The factor $\nabla_{\mathbf{W}} u$ measures the sensitivity of the output of the neural network controller to changes in the internal parameters $\mathbf{W}$: at fixed input I_n, the output u_n is a function only of the network parameters $\mathbf{W}$. The gradient of this scalar function is easily computed using the standard back-propagation algorithm (Rumelhart et al, 1986).

The factor $\partial G / \partial u$ measures the sensitivity of the system performance J_{n+1} to changes in the control variable. The information about the system needed to evaluate this derivative is not available: unknown are the functions f which describes how x_{n+1} is affected by u_n at fixed x_n, and the function h which describes how this dependence propagates to the observable y_{n+1}. The algorithm is rendered operational through the use of stochastic approximation (Kushner, 1971): assuming that the average system performance $\langle J_n \rangle$ is a monotonically increasing function of u, the sign of the partial derivative $\partial \langle J_n \rangle / \partial u$ is positive. Stochastic approximation amounts to neglecting the unknown fluctuations of this derivative with u, and approximating it by a constant positive value, which is then absorbed in a redefinition of the step size $\eta > 0$.

The on-line update rule then becomes:

$$\mathbf{W}_{n+1} = \mathbf{W}_n - \eta (J_{n+1} - J^*) \nabla_{\mathbf{W}} u_n. \tag{2.11}$$

As with stochastic approximation, the on-line gradient update uses the instantaneous gradient based on the current measurement J_{n+1}, rather than the gradient of the expected value $<J_n>$, whose deviations with respect to the target J^* are to be minimized. The combined use of back-propagation and stochastic approximation to evaluate $\nabla_{\mathbf{W}} E_n(\mathbf{W})$, leading to the update rule of Eq. (2.11), provides a general and powerful learning rule for neural network controllers. The only requirement is that the average performance $<J_n>$ be indeed a monotonic function of the control variable u.

In the following section we illustrate the application of the algorithm to an admission controller for a traffic queueing problem. The advantage of the neural network over a standard stochastic approximation approach becomes apparent when the mapping which produces u_n is used to track a time-varying environment generated by a stationary stochastic process. A straightforward extension of the approach discussed above is used to train a network to implement a mapping $(I_n, I_{n-1}, \ldots, I_{n-p}) \rightarrow u_n$. The additional p time steps into the past provide information on the history of the controlled system, and allow the network to capture regularities in the time variations of the environment.

3 A TWO-TRAFFIC QUEUEING PROBLEM

Consider an admission controller for a queueing system. As depicted in Fig. 1, the system includes a server, a queue, a call admission mechanism, and a controller.

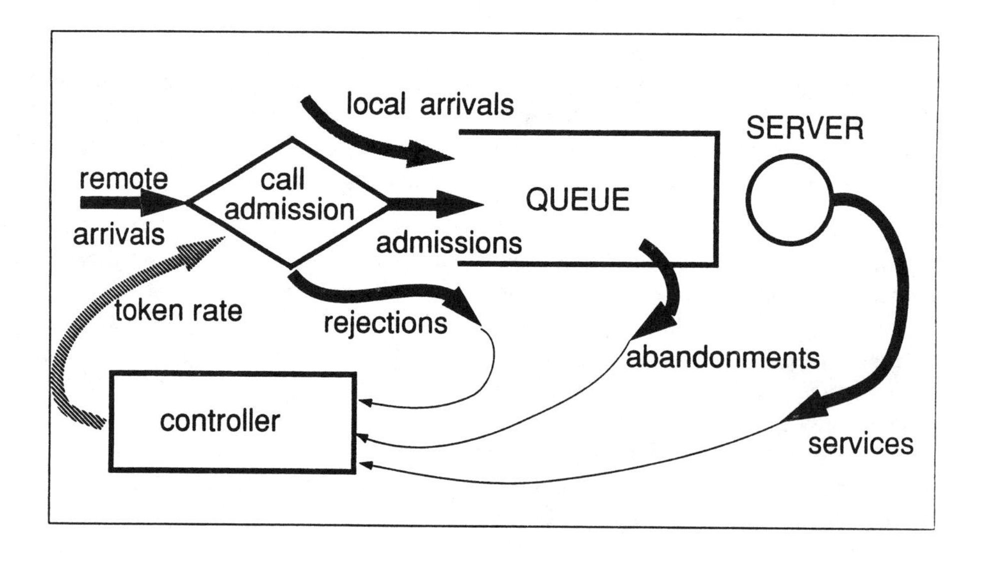

Figure 1: Admission controller for a two-traffic queuing problem.

The need to serve two independent traffic streams with a single server arises often in telecommunication networks. In a typical situation, in addition to remote arrivals which can be monitored at the control node, there are local arrivals whose admission to the queue can be neither monitored nor regulated. Within this limited information scenario, the controller must execute a policy that meets specified performance objectives. Such is the situation we now model.

Two streams are offered to the queueing system: remote traffic and local traffic. Both streams are Poisson, i.e., the interarrival times are independently and exponentially distributed, with mean $1/\lambda$. Calls originated by the remote stream can be controlled, by denying admission to the queue. Local calls are neither controlled nor monitored. While the arrival rate λ_R of remote calls is fixed, the rate $\lambda_L(t)$ of local calls is time-varying. It depends on the state of a stationary Markov chain to be described later (Kleinrock, 1975).

The service time required by a call of any type is an exponentially distributed random variable, with mean $1/\mu$.

Calls that find an empty queue on arrival get immediately into service. Otherwise, they wait in queue. The service discipline is first in first out, non-idling. Every arrival is assigned a "patience threshold" τ, independently drawn from a fixed but unknown distribution that characterizes customer behavior. If the waiting time in queue exceeds its "patience threshold", the call abandons.

Ideally, every incoming call should be admitted. The server, however, cannot process, on the average, more than μ calls per unit time. Whenever the offered load $\rho = [\lambda_R + \lambda_L(t)]/\mu$ approaches or exceeds 1, the queue starts to build up. Long queues result in long delays, which in turn induce heavy abandonments. To keep the abandonments within tolerable limits, it becomes necessary to reject some remote arrivals.

The call admission mechanism is implemented via a token-bank (not shown in the figure) rate control throttle (Berger, 1991). Tokens arrive at the token-bank at a deterministic rate λ_T. The token-bank is finite, and tokens that find a full bank are lost. A token is needed by a remote call to be admitted to the queue, and tokens are not reusable. Calls that find an empty token bank are rejected. Remote admissions are thus controlled through $u = \lambda_T/\lambda_R$.

Local calls are always admitted. The local arrival rate $\lambda_L(t)$ is controlled by an underlying q-state Markov chain, a birth-death process (Kleinrock, 1975) with transition rate γ only between neighboring states. When the Markov chain is in state i, $1 \leq i \leq q$, the local arrival rate is $\lambda_L(i)$.

Complete specification of the state x_n of the system at time t_n would require information about number of *arrivals*, *abandonments*, and *services* for both remote and local traffic during the preceding time interval of duration $\delta = 1$, as well as *rejections* for the controllable remote traffic, and *waiting time* for every queued call. But the local traffic is not monitored, and information on arrivals and waiting times is not accessible. Thus y_n only contains information about the remote traffic: the number n_r of rejected calls, the number n_a of abandonments, and the number n_s of serviced calls since t_{n-1}. The information I_n available at time t_n also includes the preceding control action u_{n-1}. The controller uses $(I_n, I_{n-1}, \ldots, I_{n-p})$ to determine u_n.

The goal of the control policy is to admit as many calls as possible, compatible with a tolerable rate of abandonment $n_a/\lambda_R \le \Delta$. The ratio n_a/λ_R thus plays the role of the performance measure J_n, and its target value is $J^* = \Delta$. Values in excess of Δ imply an excessive number of abandonments and require stricter admission control. Values smaller than Δ are penalized if obtained at the expense of avoidable rejections.

4 RESULTS

All simulations reported here correspond to a server capable of handling calls at a rate of $\mu = 200$ per unit time. The remote traffic arrival rate is $\lambda_R = 100$. The local traffic arrival rate is controlled by a $q = 10$ Markov chain with $\lambda_L(i) = 20i$ for $1 \le i \le 10$. The offered load thus spans the range $0.6 \le \rho \le 1.5$, in steps of 0.1. Transition rates $\gamma = 0.1$, 1, and 10 in the Markov chain have been used to simulate slow, moderate, and rapid variations in the offered load.

The neural network controller receives inputs $(I_n, I_{n-1}, ..., I_{n-4})$ at time t_n through 20 input units. A hidden layer with 6 units transmits information to the single output unit, which provides u_n. The bound for tolerable abandonment rate is set at $\Delta = 0.1$.

To check whether the neural network controller is capable of correct generalization, a network trained under a time-varying scenario was subject to a static one for testing. Training takes place under an offered load ρ varying at a rate of $\gamma = 1$. The network is tested at $\gamma = 0$: the underlying Markov chain is frozen and ρ is kept fixed for a long enough period to stabilize the control variable around a fixed value u^*, and obtain statistically meaningful values for n_a, n_r, and n_s. A careful numerical investigation of these quantities as a function of ρ reveals that the neural network has developed an adequate control policy: light loads $\rho \le 0.8$ spontaneously result in low values of n_a and require no control ($u = 1.25$ guarantees ample token supply, and $n_r \approx 0$), but as ρ exceeds 1, the system is controlled by decreasing the value of u below 1, thus increasing n_r to satisfy the requirement $n_a/\lambda_R \le \Delta$. Detailed results of the static performance in comparison with a standard stochastic approximation approach will be reported elsewhere.

It is in the tracking of a time-varying environment that the power of the neural network controller is revealed. A network trained under a varying offered load is tested dynamically by monitoring the distribution of abandonments and rejections as the network controls an environment varying at the same rate γ as used during training. The abandonment distribution $F_a(x) = \text{Prob}\ \{n_a/\lambda_R \le x\}$, shown in Fig. 2 (a) for $\gamma = 1$, indicates that the neural network (NN) controller outperforms both stochastic approximation[1] (SA) and the uncontrolled system (UN): the probability of keeping the abandonment rate n_r/λ_R bounded is larger for the NN controller for *all* values of the bound x. As for the goal of not exceeding $x = \Delta$, it is achieved with probability $F_a(\Delta) = 0.88$ by the NN, in comparison to only $F_a(\Delta) = 0.74$ with SA or $F_a(\Delta) = 0.51$ if UN. The rejection distribution $F_r(x) = \text{Prob}\ \{n_r/\lambda_R \le x\}$, shown in Fig. 2 (b) for $\gamma = 1$, illustrates the stricter control policy provided by NN. Results for $\gamma = 0.1$ and $\gamma = 10$, not shown here, confirm the superiority of the control policy

[1] Stochastic approximation with a fixed gain, to enable the controller to track time-varying environments. The gain was optimized numerically.

developed by the neural network.

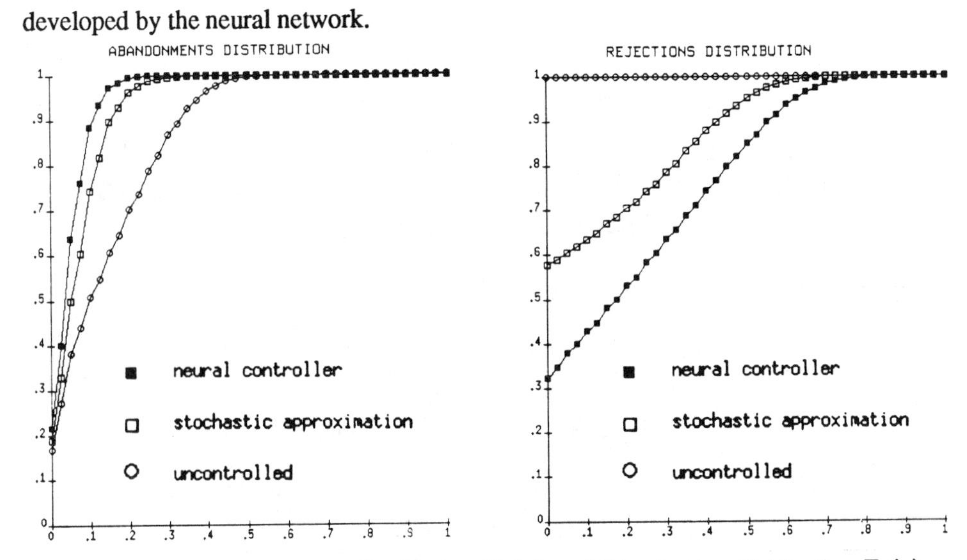

Figure 2: (a) Abandonment distribution $F_a(x)$, and (b) rejection distribution $F_r(x)$.

5 CONCLUSIONS

The control of an unknown stochastic system requires a mapping that is implemented here via a feedforward layered neural network. A novel learning rule, a blend of stochastic approximation and back-propagation, is proposed to overcome the lack of training patterns through the use of on-line performance information provided by the system under control. Satisfactorily tested for an admission control problem, the approach shows promise for a variety of applications to congestion control in telecommunication networks.

References

A.W. Berger, "Overload control using a rate control throttle: selecting token capacity for robustness to arrival rates", *IEEE Transactions on Automatic Control* **36**, 216-219 (1991).

H. Kushner, *Stochastic Approximation Methods for Constrained and Unconstrained Systems*, Springer Verlag (1971).

L. Kleinrock, *QUEUEING SYSTEMS Volume I: Theory*, John Wiley & Sons (1975).

D.E. Rumelhart, G.E. Hinton, and R.J. Williams, "Learning representations by back-propagating errors", *Nature* **323**, 533-536 (1986).

Reinforcement Learning in Markovian and Non-Markovian Environments

Jürgen Schmidhuber
Institut für Informatik
Technische Universität München
Arcistr. 21, 8000 München 2, Germany
schmidhu@tumult.informatik.tu-muenchen.de

Abstract

This work addresses three problems with reinforcement learning and adaptive neuro-control: 1. Non-Markovian interfaces between learner and environment. 2. On-line learning based on system realization. 3. Vector-valued adaptive critics. An algorithm is described which is based on system realization and on two interacting fully recurrent continually running networks which may learn in parallel. Problems with parallel learning are attacked by 'adaptive randomness'. It is also described how interacting model/controller systems can be combined with *vector-valued* 'adaptive critics' (previous critics have been *scalar*).

1 INTRODUCTION

At a given time, an agent with a *non-Markovian interface* to its environment *cannot* derive an optimal next action by considering its current input only. The algorithm described below differs from previous reinforcement algorithms in at least some of the following issues: It has a potential for on-line learning and non-Markovian environments, it is local in time and in principle it allows arbitrary time lags between actions and ulterior consequences; it does not care for something like episode-boundaries, it allows vector-valued reinforcement, it is based on two interacting fully recurrent continually running networks, and it tries to construct a full environmental model - thus providing complete 'credit assignment paths' into the past.

We dedicate one or more conventional input units (called *pain* and *pleasure units*) for the purpose of reporting the actual reinforcement to a fully recurrent control network. Pain and pleasure input units have time-invariant desired values.

We employ the IID-Algorithm (Robinson and Fallside, 1987) for training a fully recurrent model network to model the relationships between environmental inputs, output actions of an agent, and corresponding pain or pleasure. The model network (e.g. (Werbos, 1987)(Jordan, 1988)(Robinson and Fallside, 1989)) in turn allows the system to compute controller gradients for 'minimizing pain' and 'maximizing pleasure'. *Since reinforcement gradients depend on 'credit assignment paths' leading 'backwards through the environment', the model network should not only predict the pain and pleasure units but also the other input units.*

The quantity to be minimized by the model network is $\sum_{t,i}(y_i(t) - y_{ipred}(t))^2$, where $y_i(t)$ is the activation of the ith input unit at time t, and $y_{ipred}(t)$ is the model's prediction of the activation of the ith input unit at time t. The quantity to be minimized by the controller is $\sum_{t,i}(c_i - r_i(t))^2$, where $r_i(t)$ is the activation of the ith pain or pleasure input unit at time t and c_i is its desired activation for all times. t ranges over all (discrete) time steps. Weights are changed at each time step. This relieves dependence on 'episode boundaries'. Here the assumption is that the learning rates are small enough to avoid instabilities (Williams and Zipser, 1989).

There are two versions of the algorithm: the sequential version and the parallel version. With the sequential version, the model network is first trained by providing it with randomly chosen examples of sequences of interactions between controller and environment. Then the model's weights are fixed to their current values, and the controller begins to learn. With the parallel version both the controller and the model learn concurrently. One advantage of the parallel version is that the model network focusses only on those parts of the environmental dynamics with which the controller typically is confronted. Another advantage is the applicability to changing environments. Some disadvantages of the parallel version are listed next.

1. Imperfect model networks. The model which is used to compute gradient information for the controller may be wrong. However, *if we assume that the model network always finds a zero-point of its error function,* then over time we can expect the control network to perform gradient descent according to a perfect model of the visible parts of the real world. *1.A:* The assumption that the model network can always find a zero-point of its error function is not valid in the general case. One of the reasons is the old problem of local minima, for which this paper does not suggest any solutions. *1.B:* (Jordan, 1988) notes that a model network does not need to be perfect to allow increasing performance of the control network.

2. Instabilities. One source of instability could arise if the model network 'forgets' information about the environmental dynamics because the activities of the controller push it into a new sub-domain, such that the weights responsible for the old well-modeled sub-domain become over-written.

3. Deadlock. Even if the model's predictions are perfect for all actions executed by the controller, this does not imply that the algorithm will always behave as desired. Let us assume that the controller enters a local minimum relative to the current state of an imperfect model network. This relative minimum might cause the controller to execute the same action again and again (in a certain spatio-temporal context), while the model does not get a chance to learn something about the consequences of *alternative* actions (this is the *deadlock*).

The sequential version lacks the flavor of on-line learning and is bound to fail as soon as the environment changes significantly. We will introduce 'adaptive randomness' for the controller outputs to attack problems of the parallel version.

2 THE ALGORITHM

The sequential version of the algorithm can be obtained in a straight-forward manner from the description of the parallel version below. At every time step, the parallel version is performing essentially the same operations:

In step 1 of the main loop of the algorithm, actions to be performed in the external world are computed. These actions are based on both current and previous inputs and outputs. For all new activations, the corresponding derivatives with respect to all controller weights are updated. In step 2 actions are executed in the external world, and the effects of the current action and/or previous actions may become visible. In step 3 the model network sees the last input and the current output of the controller at the same time. The model network tries to predict the new input without seeing it. Again the relevant gradient information is computed. In step 4 the model network is updated in order to better predict the input (including pleasure and pain) for the controller. The weights of the control network are updated in order to minimize the cumulative differences between desired and actual activations of the pain and pleasure units. 'Teacher forcing' (Williams and Zipser, 1989) is used in the model network (although there is no teacher besides the environment). The partial derivatives of the controller's inputs with respect to the controller's weights are approximated by the partial derivatives of the corresponding predictions generated by the model network.

Notation (the reader may find it convenient to compare with (Williams and Zipser, 1989)): *C is the set of all non-input units of the control network, A is the set of its output units, I is the set of its 'normal' input units, P is the set of its pain and pleasure units, M is the set of all units of the model network, O is the set of its output units, $O_P \subset O$ is the set of all units that predict pain or pleasure, W_M is the set of variables for the weights of the model network, W_C is the set of variables for the weights of the control network, $y_{k_{new}}$ is the variable for the updated activation of the kth unit from $M \cup C \cup I \cup P$, $y_{k_{old}}$ is the variable for the last value of $y_{k_{new}}$, w_{ij} is the variable for the weight of the directed connection from unit j to unit i. δ_{ik} is the Kronecker-delta, which is 1 for $i = k$ and 0 otherwise, $p^k_{ij_{new}}$ is the variable which gives the current (approximated) value of $\frac{\partial y_{k_{new}}}{\partial w_{ij}}$, $p^k_{ij_{old}}$ is the variable which gives the last value of $p^k_{ij_{new}}$. If $k \in P$ then c_k is k's desired activation for all times, if $k \in I \cup P$, then kpred is the unit from O which predicts k. α_C is the learning rate for the control network, α_M is the learning rate for the model network.*

$\mid I \cup P \mid = \mid O \mid$, $\mid O_P \mid = \mid P \mid$. *Each unit in $I \cup P \cup A$ has one forward connection to each unit in $M \cup C$, each unit in M is connected to each other unit in M, each unit in C is connected to each other unit in C. Each weight variable of a connection leading to a unit in M is said to belong to W_M, each weight variable of a connection leading to a unit in C is said to belong to W_C. For each weight $w_{ij} \in W_M$ there are p^k_{ij}-values for all $k \in M$, for each weight $w_{ij} \in W_C$ there are p^k_{ij}-values for all $k \in M \cup C \cup I \cup P$.* The parallel version of the algorithm works as follows:

INITIALIZATION:

$\forall\ w_{ij} \in W_M \cup W_C$: $w_{ij} \leftarrow$ *random*, $\forall$ *possible* k: $p^k_{ij_{old}} \leftarrow 0, p^k_{ij_{new}} \leftarrow 0$.

$\forall\ k \in M \cup C : y_{k_{old}} \leftarrow 0, y_{k_{new}} \leftarrow 0.$

$\forall\ k \in I \cup P$: *Set* $y_{k_{old}}$ *according to the current environment,* $y_{k_{new}} \leftarrow 0.$

UNTIL TERMINATION CRITERION IS REACHED :

1. $\forall\ i \in C : y_{i_{new}} \leftarrow \frac{1}{1+e^{-\sum_j w_{ij} y_{j_{old}}}}.$

$\forall\ w_{ij} \in W_C, k \in C$: $p^k_{ij_{new}} \leftarrow y_{k_{new}}(1 - y_{k_{new}})(\sum_l w_{kl} p^l_{ij_{old}} + \delta_{ik} y_{j_{old}}).$

$\forall\ k \in C$: $y_{k_{old}} \leftarrow y_{k_{new}}$, $\forall\ w_{ij} \in W_C$: $p^k_{ij_{old}} \leftarrow p^k_{ij_{new}}$.

2. Execute all actions based on activations of units in A. Update the environment.

$\forall\ i \in I \cup P$: *Set* $y_{i_{new}}$ *according to environment.*

3. $\forall\ i \in M : y_{i_{new}} \leftarrow \frac{1}{1+e^{-\sum_j w_{ij} y_{j_{old}}}}.$

$\forall\ w_{ij} \in W_M \cup W_C, k \in M$: $p^k_{ij_{new}} \leftarrow y_{k_{new}}(1 - y_{k_{new}})(\sum_l w_{kl} p^l_{ij_{old}} + \delta_{ik} y_{j_{old}}).$

$\forall\ k \in M$: $y_{k_{old}} \leftarrow y_{k_{new}}$, $\forall\ w_{ij} \in W_C \cup W_M$: $p^k_{ij_{old}} \leftarrow p^k_{ij_{new}}$.

4. $\forall\ w_{ij} \in W_M$: $w_{ij} \leftarrow w_{ij} + \alpha_M \sum_{k \in I \cup P}(y_{k_{new}} - y_{kpred_{old}}) p^{kpred}_{ij_{old}}.$

$\forall\ w_{ij} \in W_C$: $w_{ij} \leftarrow w_{ij} + \alpha_C \sum_{k \in P}(c_k - y_{k_{new}}) p^{kpred}_{ij_{old}}.$

$\forall\ k \in I \cup P$: $y_{k_{old}} \leftarrow y_{k_{new}}$, $y_{kpred_{old}} \leftarrow y_{k_{new}}$, $\forall\ w_{ij} \in W_M$: $p^{kpred}_{ij_{old}} \leftarrow 0,$

$\forall\ w_{ij} \in W_C : p^k_{ij_{old}} \leftarrow p^{kpred}_{ij_{old}}$.

The algorithm is local in time, but not in space. The computation complexity per time step is $O(\mid W_M \cup W_C \mid\mid M \mid\mid M \cup I \cup P \cup A \mid + \mid W_C \mid\mid C \mid\mid I \cup P \cup C \mid)$. In what follows we describe some useful extensions of the scheme.

1. More network ticks than environmental ticks. For highly 'non-linear' environments the algorithm has to be modified in a trivial manner such that the involved networks perform more than one (but not more than three) iterations of step 1 and step 3 at each time step. (4-layer-operations in principle can produce an arbitrary approximation of any desired mapping.)

2. Adaptive randomness. Explicit explorative random search capabilities can be introduced by probabilistic controller outputs and 'gradient descent through random number generators' (Williams, 1988). We adjust both the mean and the variance of the controller actions. In the context of the IID algorithm, this works as follows: A probabilistic output unit k consists of a conventional unit $k\mu$ which acts as a mean generator and a conventional unit $k\sigma$ which acts as a variance generator. At a given time, the probabilistic output $y_{k_{new}}$ is computed by $y_{k_{new}} = y_{k\mu_{new}} + z y_{k\sigma_{new}}$, where z is distributed e.g. according to the normal distribution. The corresponding $p^k_{ij_{new}}$

must then be updated according to the following rule:

$$p^k_{ij_{new}} \leftarrow p^{k\mu}_{ij_{new}} + \frac{y_{k_{new}} - y_{k\mu_{new}}}{y_{k\sigma_{new}}} p^{k\sigma}_{ij_{new}}.$$

A more sophisticated strategy to improve the model network is to introduce *'adaptive curiosity and boredom'*. The priniciple of adaptive curiosity for model-building neural controllers (Schmidhuber, 1990a) says: Spend additional reinforcement whenever there is a mismatch between the expectations of the model network and reality.

3. Perfect models. Sometimes one can gain a 'perfect' model by constructing an appropriate mathematical description of the environmental dynamics. This saves the time needed to train the model. However, additional external knowledge is required. For instance, the description of the environment might be in form of differential or difference equations. In the context of the algorithm above, this means introducing new p^{η}_{ij} variables for each $w_{ij} \in W_C$ and each relevant state variable $\eta(t)$ of the dynamical environment. The new variables serve to accumulate the values of $\frac{\partial \eta(t)}{\partial w_{ij}}$. This can be done in exactly the same cumulative manner as with the activations of the model network above.

4. Augmenting the algorithm by TD-methods. The following ideas are not limited to recurrent nets, but are also relevant for feed-forward controllers in Markovian environments.

It is possible to augment model-building algorithms with an 'adaptive critic' method. To simplify the discussion, let us assume that there are no pleasure units, just pain units. The algorithm's goal is to minimize cumulative pain. We introduce the TD-principle (Sutton, 1988) by changing the error function of the units in O_P: At a given time t, the contribution of each unit $kpred \in O_P$ to the model network's error is $y_{kpred}(t) - \gamma y_{kpred}(t+1) - y_k(t+1)$, where $y_i(t)$ is the activation of unit i at time t, and $0 < \gamma < 1$ is a discount factor for avoiding predictions of infinite sums. Thus O_P is trained to predict the *sum of all* (discounted) future pain vectors and becomes a *vector-valued adaptive critic.* (This affects the first $\forall$-*loop* in step 4 .)

The controller's goal is to minimize the absolute value of M's pain predictions. Thus, the contribution of time t to the error function of the controller now becomes $\sum_{kpred \in O_P}(y_{kpred}(t))^2$. This affects the second *For-loop* in step 4 of the algorithm. Note that it is not a *state* which is evaluated by the adaptive critic component, but a *combination of a state and an action.* This makes the approach similar to (Jordan and Jacobs, 1990). (Schmidhuber, 1990a) shows how a recurrent model/controller combination can be used for look-ahead planning *without* using TD-methods.

3 EXPERIMENTS

The following experiments were conducted by the TUM-students Josef Hochreiter and Klaus Bergner. See (Schmidhuber, 1990a) and (Schmidhuber, 1990b) for the full details.

1. Evolution of a flip-flop by reinforcement learning. A controller K had to learn to behave like a flip-flop as described in (Williams and Zipser, 1989). The *main diffi-*

culty (the one which makes this different from the supervised approach as described in (Williams and Zipser, 1989)) was that there was no teacher for K's (probabilistic) output units. Instead, the system had to generate alternative outputs in a variety of spatio-temporal contexts, and to build a model of the often 'painful' consequences. K's only goal information was the activation of a pain input unit whenever it produced an incorrect output. With $\mid C \mid = 3$, $\mid M \mid = 4$, $\alpha_C = 0.1$ and $\alpha_M = 1.0$ 20 out of 30 test runs with the parallel version required less than 1000000 time steps to produce an acceptable solution.

Why does it take much more time solving the reinforcement flip-flop problem than solving the corresponding supervised flip-flop problem? One answer is: With supervised learning the controller gradient is *given* to the system, while with reinforcement learning the gradient has to be *discovered* by the system.

2. 'Non-Markovian' pole balancing. A cart pole system was modeled by the same differential equations used for a related balancing task which is described in (Anderson, 1986). In contrast to previous pole balancing tasks, however, *no information about temporal derivatives of cart position and pole angle was provided.* (Similar experiments are mentioned in (Piché, 1990).)

In our experiments the cart-pole system would not stabilize indefinitely. However, significant performance improvement was obtained. The best results were achieved by using a 'perfect model' as described above: Before learning, the average time until failure was about 25 time steps. Within a few hundred trials one could observe trials with more than 1000 time steps balancing time. 'Friendly' initial conditions could lead to balancing times of more than 3000 time steps.

3. 'Markovian' pole balancing with a vector-valued adaptive critic. The adaptive critic extension described above does not need a non-Markovian environment to demonstrate advantages over previous adaptive critics: A four-dimensional adaptive critic was tested on the pole balancing task described in (Anderson, 1986). The critic component had four output units for predicting four different kinds of 'pain', two for bumps against the two edges of the track and two for pole crashes.

None of five conducted test runs took more than 750 failures to achieve the first trial with more than 30000 time steps. (The longest run reported by (Anderson, 1986) took about 29000 time steps, more than 7000 failures had to be experienced to achieve that result.)

4 SOME LIMITATIONS OF THE APPROACHES

1. The recurrent network algorithms are not local in space.

2. As with all gradient descent algorithms there is the problem of local minima. This paper does not offer any solutions to this problem.

3. More severe limitations of the algorithm are *inherent problems* of the concepts of 'gradient descent through time' and adaptive critics. Neither gradient descent nor adaptive critics are practical when there are *long* time lags between actions and ultimate consequences. For this reason, first steps are made in (Schmidhuber, 1990c) towards *adaptive sub-goal generators* and *adaptive 'causality detectors'*.

Acknowledgements

I wish to thank Josef Hochreiter and Klaus Bergner who conducted the experiments. This work was supported by a scholarship from SIEMENS AG.

References

Anderson, C. W. (1986). *Learning and Problem Solving with Multilayer Connectionist Systems.* PhD thesis, University of Massachusetts, Dept. of Comp. and Inf. Sci.

Jordan, M. I. (1988). Supervised learning and systems with excess degrees of freedom. Technical Report COINS TR 88-27, MIT.

Jordan, M. I. and Jacobs, R. A. (1990). Learning to control an unstable system with forward modeling. In *Proc. of the 1990 Connectionist Models Summer School, in press.* San Mateo, CA: Morgan Kaufmann.

Piché, S. W. (1990). Draft: First order gradient descent training of adaptive discrete time dynamic networks. Technical report, Dept. of Electrical Engineering, Stanford University.

Robinson, A. J. and Fallside, F. (1987). The utility driven dynamic error propagation network. Technical Report CUED/F-INFENG/TR.1, Cambridge University Engineering Department.

Robinson, T. and Fallside, F. (1989). Dynamic reinforcement driven error propagation networks with application to game playing. In *Proceedings of the 11th Conference of the Cognitive Science Society, Ann Arbor*, pages 836–843.

Schmidhuber, J. H. (1990a). Making the world differentiable: On using fully recurrent self-supervised neural networks for dynamic reinforcement learning and planning in non-stationary environments. Technical Report FKI-126-90 (revised), Institut für Informatik, Technische Universität München. (Revised and extended version of an earlier report from February.).

Schmidhuber, J. H. (1990b). Networks adjusting networks. Technical Report FKI-125-90 (revised), Institut für Informatik, Technische Universität München. (Revised and extended version of an earlier report from February.).

Schmidhuber, J. H. (1990c). Towards compositional learning with dynamic neural networks. Technical Report FKI-129-90, Institut für Informatik, Technische Universität München.

Sutton, R. S. (1988). Learning to predict by the methods of temporal differences. *Machine Learning*, 3:9–44.

Werbos, P. J. (1987). Building and understanding adaptive systems: A statistical/numerical approach to factory automation and brain research. *IEEE Transactions on Systems, Man, and Cybernetics*, 17.

Williams, R. J. (1988). On the use of backpropagation in associative reinforcement learning. In *IEEE International Conference on Neural Networks, San Diego*, volume 2, pages 263–270.

Williams, R. J. and Zipser, D. (1989). Experimental analysis of the real-time recurrent learning algorithm. *Connection Science*, 1(1):87–111.

A Model of Distributed Sensorimotor Control in the Cockroach Escape Turn

R.D. Beer[1,2], G.J. Kacmarcik[1], R.E. Ritzmann[2] and H.J. Chiel[2]
Departments of [1]Computer Engineering and Science, and [2]Biology
Case Western Reserve University
Cleveland, OH 44106

Abstract

In response to a puff of wind, the American cockroach turns away and runs. The circuit underlying the initial turn of this escape response consists of three populations of individually identifiable nerve cells and appears to employ distributed representations in its operation. We have reconstructed several neuronal and behavioral properties of this system using simplified neural network models and the backpropagation learning algorithm constrained by known structural characteristics of the circuitry. In order to test and refine the model, we have also compared the model's responses to various lesions with the insect's responses to similar lesions.

1 INTRODUCTION

It is becoming generally accepted that many behavioral and cognitive capabilities of the human brain must be understood as resulting from the cooperative activity of populations of nerve cells rather than the individual activity of any particular cell. For example, distributed representation of orientation by populations of directionally-tuned neurons appears to be a common principle of many mammalian motor control systems (Georgopoulos *et al.*, 1988; Lee *et al.*, 1988). While the general principles of distributed processing are evident in these mammalian systems, however, the details of their operation are not. Without a deeper knowledge of the underlying neuronal circuitry and its inputs and outputs, it is difficult to answer such questions as how the population code is formed, how it is read out, and what precise role it plays in the operation of the nervous system as a whole. In this paper, we describe our work with an invertebrate system, the cockroach escape response, which offers the possibility of addressing these questions.

2 THE COCKROACH ESCAPE RESPONSE

Any sudden puff of wind directed toward the American cockroach (*Periplaneta americana*), such as from an attacking predator, evokes a rapid directional turn away from the wind source followed by a run (Ritzmann, 1984). The initial turn is generally completed in approximately 60 msec after the onset of the wind. During this time, the insect must integrate information from hundreds of sensors to direct a very specific set of leg movements involving dozens of muscles distributed among three distinct pairs of multisegmented legs. In addition, the response is known to exhibit various forms of plasticity, including adaptation to sensory lesions. This system has also recently been shown to be capable of multiphasic responses (e.g. an attack from the front may elicit a sequence of escape movements rather than a single turn) and context-dependent responses (e.g. if the cockroach is in antennal contact with an obstacle, it may modify its escape movements accordingly) (Ritzmann *et al.*, in preparation).

The basic architecture of the neuronal circuitry responsible for the initial turn of the escape response is known (Daley and Camhi, 1988; Ritzmann and Pollack, 1988; Ritzmann and Pollack, 1990). Characteristics of the initiating wind puff are encoded by a population of several hundred broadly-tuned wind-sensitive hairs located on the bottom of the insect's cerci (two antennae-like structures found at the rear of the animal). The sensory neurons which innervate these hairs project to a small population of four pairs of ventral giant interneurons (the vGIs). These giant interneurons excite a larger population of approximately 100 interneurons located in the thoracic ganglia associated with each pair of legs. These type A thoracic interneurons (the TI_As) integrate information from a variety of other sources as well, including leg proprioceptors. Finally, the TI_As project to local interneurons and motor neurons responsible for the control of each leg.

Perhaps what is most interesting about this system is that, despite the complexity of the response it controls, and despite the fact that its operation appears to be distributed across several populations of interneurons, the individual members of these populations are uniquely identifiable. For this reason, we believe that the cockroach escape response is an excellent model system for exploring the neuronal basis of distributed sensorimotor control at the level of identified nerve cells. As an integral part of that effort, we are constructing a computer model of the cockroach escape response.

3 NEURAL NETWORK MODEL

While a great deal is known about the overall response properties of many of the individual neurons in the escape circuit, as well as their architecture of connectivity, little detailed biophysical data is currently available. For this reason, our initial models have employed simplified neural network models and learning techniques. This approach has proven to be effective for analyzing a variety of neuronal circuits (e.g. Lockery *et al.*, 1989; Anastasio and Robinson, 1989). Specifically, using backpropagation, we train model neurons to reproduce the observed properties of identified nerve cells in the escape circuit.

In order to ensure that the resulting models are biologically relevant, we constrain

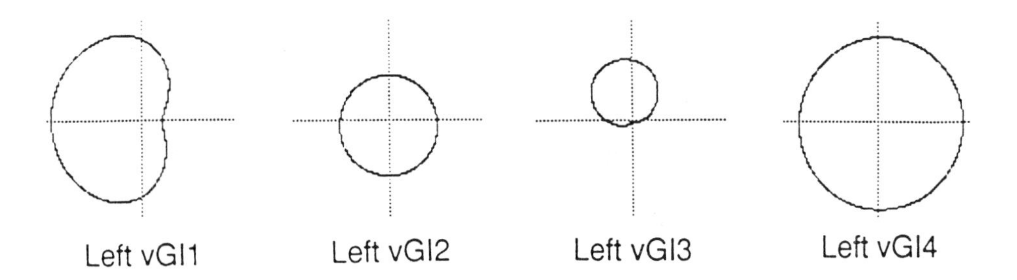

Figure 1: Windfields of Left Model Ventral Giant Interneurons

backpropagation to produce solutions which are consistent with the known structural characteristics of the circuit. The most important constraints we have utilized to date are the existence or nonexistence of specific connections between identified cells and the signs of existing connections. Other constraints that we are exploring include the firing curves and physiological operating ranges of identified neurons in the circuit. It is important to emphasize that we employed backpropagation solely as a means for finding the appropriate connection weights given the known structure of the circuit, and no claim is being made about its biological validity.

As an example of this approach, we have reconstructed the observed windfields of the eight ventral giant interneurons which serve as the first stage of interneuronal processing in the escape circuit. These windfields, which represent the intensity of a cell's response to wind puffs from different directions, have been well characterized in the insect (Westin, Langberg, and Camhi, 1977). The windfields of individual cercal sensory neurons have also been mapped (Westin, 1979; Daley and Camhi, 1988). The response of each hair is broadly tuned about a single preferred direction, which we have modeled as a cardioid. The cercal hairs are arranged in nine major columns on each cercus. All of the hairs in a single column share similar responses. Together, the responses of the hairs in all eighteen columns provide overlapping coverage of most directions around the insect's body. The connectivity between each major cercal hair column and each ventral giant interneuron is known, as are the signs of these connections (Daley and Camhi, 1988). Using these data, each model vGI was trained to reproduce the corresponding windfield by constrained backpropagation.[1] The resulting responses of the left four model vGIs are shown in Figure 1. These model windfields closely approximate those observed in the cockroach. Further details concerning vGI windfield reconstruction will be given in a forthcoming paper.

4 ESCAPE TURN RECONSTRUCTIONS

Ultimately, we are interested in simulating the entire escape response. This requires some way to connect our neural models to behavior, an approach that we have termed *computational neuroethology* (Beer, 1990). Toward that end, we have

[1]Strictly speaking, we are only using the delta rule here. The full power of backpropagation is not needed for this task since we are training only a single layer of weights.

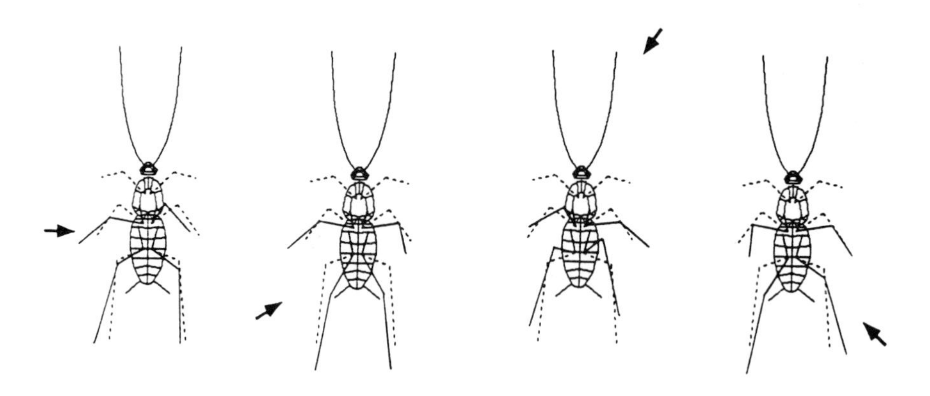

Figure 2: Model Escape Turns for Wind from Different Directions

also constructed a three dimensional kinematic model of the insect's body which accurately represents the essential degrees of freedom of the legs during escape turns. For our purposes here, the essential joints are the coxal-femur (CF) and femur-tibia (FT) joints of each leg. The leg segment lengths and orientations, as well as the joint angles and axes of rotation, were derived from actual measurements (Nye and Ritzmann, unpublished data). The active leg movements during escape turns of a tethered insect, in which the animal is suspended by a rod above a greased plate, have been shown to be identical to those of a free ranging animal (Camhi and Levy, 1988). Because an insect thus tethered is neither supporting its own weight nor generating appreciable forces with its legs, a kinematic body model can be defended as an adequate first approximation.

The leg movements of the simulated body were controlled by a neural network model of the entire escape circuit. Where sufficient data was available, the structure of this network was constrained appropriately. The first layer of this circuit was described in the previous section and is prevented from further training here. There are six groups of six representative TI_As, one group for each leg. Within a group, representative members of each identified class of TI_A are modeled. Where known, the connectivity from the vGIs to each class of TI_As was enforced and all connections from vGIs to TI_As were constrained to be excitatory (Ritzmann and Pollack, 1988). Model TI_As also receive inputs from leg proprioceptors which encode the angle of each joint (Murrain and Ritzmann, 1988). The TI_A layer for each side of the body was fully connected to 12 local interneurons, which were in turn fully connected to motor neurons which encode the change in angle of each joint in the body model.

High speed video films of the leg movements underlying actual escape turns in the tethered preparation for a variety of different wind angles and initial joint angles have been made (Nye and Ritzmann, 1990). The angles of each joint before wind onset and immediately after completion of the initial turn were used as training data for the model escape circuit. Only movements of the middle and hind legs were considered because individual joint angles of the front legs were far more variable. After training with constrained backpropagation, the model successfully reproduced the essential features of this data (Figure 2). Wind from the rear always caused

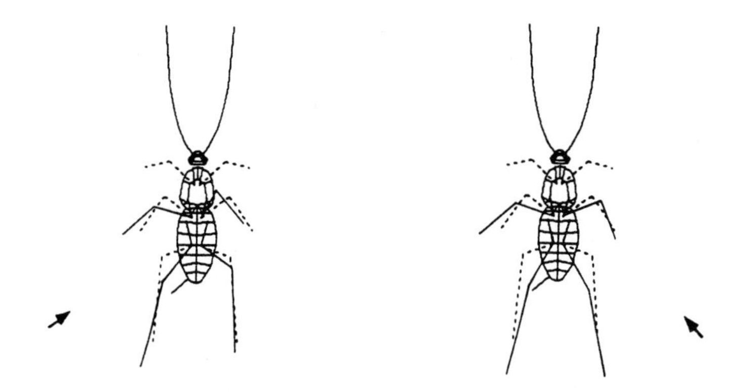

Figure 3: Model Escape Turns Following Left Cercal Ablation

the rear legs of the model to thrust back, which would propel the body forward in a freely moving insect, while wind from the front caused the rear legs to move forward, pulling the body back. The middle legs always turned the body away from the direction of the wind.

5 MODEL MANIPULATIONS

The results described above demonstrate that several neuronal and behavioral properties of this system can be reproduced using only simplified but biologically constrained neural network models. However, to serve as a useful tool for understanding the neuronal basis of the cockroach escape response, it is not enough for the model to simply reproduce what is already known about the normal operation of the system. In order to test and refine the model, we must also examine its responses to various lesions and compare them to the responses of the insect to analogous lesions. Here we report the results of two experiments of this sort.

Immediately following removal of the left cercus, cockroaches make a much higher proportion of incorrect turns (i.e. turns toward rather than away from the wind source) in response to wind from the left, while turns in response to wind from the right are largely unaffected. (Vardi and Camhi, 1982a). These results suggest that, despite the redundant representation of wind direction by each cercus, the insect integrates information from *both* cerci in order to compute the appropriate direction of movement. As shown in Figure 3, the response of the model to a left cercal ablation is consistent with these results. In response to wind from the unlesioned side, the model generates leg movements which would turn the body away from the wind. However, in response to wind from the lesioned side, the model generates leg movements which would turn the body toward the wind.

It is interesting to note that, following an approximately thirty day recovery period, the directionality of a cercally ablated cockroach's escape response is largely restored (Vardi and Camhi, 1982a). While the mechanisms underlying this adaptation are not yet fully understood, they appear to involve a reorganization of the vGI connections from the intact cercus (Vardi and Camhi, 1982b). After a cercal ablation, the windfields of the vGIs on the ablated side are significantly reduced. Following the thirty day recovery period, however, these windfields are largely restored. We have also examined these effects in the model. After cercal ablation, the model vGI windfields show some similarities to those of similarly lesioned insects. In addition, using vGI retraining to simulate the adaptation process, we have found that the model can effect a similar recovery of vGI windfields by adjusting the connections from the intact cercus. However, due to space limitations, these results will be described in detail elsewhere.

A second experimental manipulation that has been performed on this system is the selective lesion of individual ventral giant interneurons (Comer, 1985). The only result that we will describe here is the lesion of vGI1. In the animal, this results in a behavioral deficit similar to that observed with cercal ablation. Correct turns result for wind from the unlesioned side, but a much higher proportion of incorrect turns are observed in response to wind from the lesioned side. The response of the model to this lesion is also similar to its response to a cercal ablation (Figure 3) and is thus consistent with these experimental results.

6 CONCLUSIONS

With the appropriate caveats, invertebrate systems offer the possibility of addressing important neurobiological questions at a much finer level than is generally possible in mammalian systems. In particular, the cockroach escape response is a complex sensorimotor control system whose operation is distributed across several populations of interneurons, but is nevertheless amenable to a detailed cellular analysis. Due to the overall complexity of such circuits and the wealth of data which can be extracted from them, modeling must play a crucial role in this endeavor. However, in order to be useful, models must make special efforts to remain consistent with known biological data and constantly be subjected to experimental test. Experimental work in turn must be responsive to model demands and predictions. This paper has described our initial results with this cooperative approach to the cockroach escape response. Our future work will focus on extending the current model in a similar manner.

Acknowledgements

This work was supported by ONR grant N00014-90-J-1545 to RDB, a CAISR graduate fellowship from the Cleveland Advanced Manufacturing Program to GJK, NIH grant NS 17411 to RER, and NSF grant BNS-8810757 to HJC.

References

Anastasio, T.J. and Robinson, D.A. (1989). Distributed parallel processing in the vestibulo-oculomotor system. *Neural Computation* **1**:230-241.

Beer, R.D. (1990). *Intelligence as Adaptive Behavior: An Experiment in Computational Neuroethology.* Academic Press.

Camhi, J.M. and Levy, A. (1988). Organization of a complex motor act: Fixed and variable components of the cockroach escape behavior. *J. Comp. Physiology*

163:317-328.

Comer, C.M. (1985). Analyzing cockroach escape behavior with lesions of individual giant interneurons. *Brain Research* **335**:342-346.

Daley, D.L. and Camhi, J.M. (1988). Connectivity pattern of the cercal-to-giant interneuron system of the American cockroach. *J. Neurophysiology* **60**:1350-1368.

Georgopoulos, A.P., Kettner, R.E. and Schwartz, A.B. (1988). Primate motor cortex and free arm movements to visual targets in three-dimensional space. II. Coding of the direction of movement by a neuronal population. *J. Neuroscience* **8**:2928-2937.

Lee, C., Rohrer, W.H. and Sparks, D.L. (1988). Population coding of saccadic eye movements by neurons in the superior colliculus. *Nature* **332**:357-360.

Lockery, S.R., Wittenberg, G., Kristan, W.B. Jr. and Cottrell, G.W. (1989). Function of identified interneurons in the leech elucidated using neural networks trained by back-propagation. *Nature* **340**:468-471.

Murrain, M. and Ritzmann, R.E. (1988). Analysis of proprioceptive inputs to DPG interneurons in the cockroach. *J. Neurobiology* **19**:552-570.

Nye, S.W. and Ritzmann, R.E. (1990). Videotape motion analysis of leg joint angles during escape turns of the cockroach. *Society for Neurosciences Abstracts* **16**:759.

Ritzmann, R.E. (1984). The cockroach escape response. In R.C. Eaton (Ed.) *Neural Mechanisms of Startle Behavior* (pp. 93-131). New York: Plenum.

Ritzmann, R.E. and Pollack, A.J. (1988). Wind activated thoracic interneurons of the cockroach: II. Patterns of connection from ventral giant interneurons. *J. Neurobiology* **19**:589-611.

Ritzmann, R.E. and Pollack, A.J. (1990). Parallel motor pathways from thoracic interneurons of the ventral giant interneuron system of the cockroach, *Periplaneta americana*. *J. Neurobiology* **21**:1219-1235.

Ritzmann, R.E., Pollack, A.J., Hudson, S. and Hyvonen, A. (in preparation). Thoracic interneurons in the escape system of the cockroach, *Periplaneta americana*, are multi-modal interneurons.

Vardi, N. and Camhi, J.M. (1982). Functional recovery from lesions in the escape system of the cockroach. I. Behavioral recovery. *J. Comp. Physiology* **146**:291-298.

Vardi, N. and Camhi, J.M. (1982). Functional recovery from lesions in the escape system of the cockroach. II. Physiological recovery of the giant interneurons. *J. Comp. Physiology* **146**:299-309.

Westin, J. (1979). Responses to wind recorded from the cercal nerve of the cockroach *Periplaneta americana*. I. Response properties of single sensory neurons. *J. Comp. Physiology* **133**:97-102.

Westin, J., Langberg, J.J. and Camhi, J.M. (1977). Response properties of giant interneurons of the cockroach *Periplaneta americana* to wind puffs of different directions and velocities. *J. Comp. Physiology* **121**:307-324.

Flight Control in the Dragonfly: A Neurobiological Simulation

William E. Faller and Marvin W. Luttges
Aerospace Engineering Sciences,
University of Colorado, Boulder, Colorado 80309-0429.

ABSTRACT

Neural network simulations of the dragonfly flight neurocontrol system have been developed to understand how this insect uses complex, unsteady aerodynamics. The simulation networks account for the ganglionic spatial distribution of cells as well as the physiologic operating range and the stochastic cellular firing history of each neuron. In addition the motor neuron firing patterns, "flight command sequences", were utilized. Simulation training was targeted against both the cellular and flight motor neuron firing patterns. The trained networks accurately resynthesized the intraganglionic cellular firing patterns. These in turn controlled the motor neuron firing patterns that drive wing musculature during flight. Such networks provide both neurobiological analysis tools and first generation controls for the use of "unsteady" aerodynamics.

1 INTRODUCTION

Hebb (1949) proposed a theory of inter-neuronal learning, "Hebbian Learning", in which cells acting together as assemblies alter the efficacy of mutual interconnections. These neural "cell assemblies" presumably comprise the information processing "units" of the nervous system.

To provide one framework within which to perform detailed analyses of these cellular organizational "rules" a new analytical technique based on neural networks is being explored. The neurobiological data analyzed was obtained from the neural cells of the dragonfly ganglia.

The dragonfly use of unsteady separated flows to generate highly maneuverable flight is governed by the control sequences that originate in the thoracic ganglia flight motor neurons (MN). To provide this control the roughly 2200 cells of the meso- and metathoracic ganglia integrate environmental cues that include visual input, wind shear, velocity and acceleration. The cellular firing patterns coupled with proprioceptive feedback in turn drive elevator/depressor flight MNs which typically produce a 25-37 Hz wingbeat depending on the flight mode (Luttges 1989; Kliss 1989).

The neural networks utilized in the analyses incorporate the spatial distribution of cells, the physiologic operating range of each neuron and the stochastic history of the cellular spike trains (Faller and Luttges 1990). The present work describes two neural networks. The simultaneous single-unit firing patterns at time (t) were used to predict the cellular firing patterns at time ($t+\Delta$). And, the simultaneous single-unit firing patterns were used to "drive" flight-MN firing patterns at a 37 Hz wingbeat frequency.

2 METHODS

2.1 BIOLOGICAL DATA

Recordings were obtained from the mesothoracic ganglion of the dragonfly *Aeshna* in the ganglionic regions known to contain the cell bodies of flight MNs as well as small and large cell bodies (Simmons 1977; Kliss 1989). Multiple-unit recordings from many cells (~40-80) were systematically decomposed to yield simultaneously active single-unit firing patterns. The technique has been described elsewhere (Faller and Luttges in press).

During the recording of neural activity spontaneous flight episodes commonly occurred. These events were consistent with typical flight episodes (2-3 secs duration) observed in the tethered dragonfly (Somps and Luttges 1985). For analysis, a 12 second record was obtained from 58 single units, 26 rostral cells and 32 caudal cells. The continuous record was separated into 4 second behavioral epochs: pre-flight, flight and post-flight.

A simplified model of one flight mode was assumed. Each forewing is driven by 3 main elevator and 2 main depressor muscles, innervated by 11 and 14 MNs, respectively. A 37 Hz MN firing frequency, 3-5 spikes per output burst, and 180 degree phase shift between antagonistic MNs was assumed. Given the symmetrical nature of the elevator/depressor output patterns only the 11 elevator MNs were simulated.

Prior to analysis the ganglionic spatial distribution of neurons was reconstructed. The importance of this is reserved for later discussion. A method has been described (Faller and Luttges submitted:a) that resolves the spatial distribution based on two distancing criteria: the amplitude ratio across electrodes and the spike angle (width) for each cell. Cells were sorted along a rostral, cell 1, to caudal, cell 58 continuum based on this information.

The middle 2 seconds of the flight data was simulated. This was consistent with the known duration of spontaneous flight episodes. Within these 2 seconds, 44 cells remained active, 19 rostral and 25 caudal. The cell numbering (1-58) derived for the biological data was not altered. The remaining 14 inactive cells/units carry zeros in all analyses.

2.2 MIMICKING THE SINGLE CELLS

Each neuron was represented by a unique unit that mimicked both the mean firing frequency and dynamic range of the physiologic cell. The activation value ranged from zero to twice the normalized mean firing frequency for each cell. The dynamic range was calculated as a unique thermodynamic profile for each sigmoidal activation function. The technique has been described fully elsewhere (Faller and Luttges 1990).

2.3 SPIKE TRAIN REPRESENTATION

The spike trains and MN firing patterns were represented as iteratively continuous "analog" gradients (Faller and Luttges 1990 & submitted:b). Briefly, each spike train was represented in two-dimensions based on the following assumptions: (1) the mean firing frequency reflects the inherent physiology of each cell and (2) the interspike intervals encode the information transferred to other cells. Exponential functions were mapped into the intervals between consecutive spikes and these functions were then discretized to provide the spike train inputs to the neural network. These functions retain the exact spiking times and the temporal modulations (interval code) of cell firing histories.

2.4 ARCHITECTURE

The two simulation architectures were as follows:

	Simulation 1	Simulation 2
Input layer	1 cell:1 unit (44 units)	1 cell:1 unit (44 units)
Hidden layer	1 cell:2 units (88 units)	1 cell:2 unit (88 units)
Output layer	1 cell : 1 unit (44 total units)	11 main elevator MNs

The hidden units were recurrently connected and the interconnections between units were based on a 1st order exponential rise and decay. The general architecture has been described elsewhere (Faller and Luttges 1990).

For the cell-to-cell simulation no bias units were utilized. Since the MNs fire both synchronously and infrequently bias units were incorporated in the MN simulation. These units were constrained to function synchronously at the MN firing frequency. This constraining technique permitted the network to be trained despite the sparsity of the MN data set.

Training was performed using a supervised backpropagation algorithm in time. All 44 cells, 2000 points per discretized gradient (Δ=1 msec real-time) were presented synchronously to the network. The results were consistent for Δ=2-5 msec in all cases. The simulation paradigms were as follows:

	Simulation 1	Simulation 2
Input	Neural activity at time (t)	Neural activity at time (t)
Output/Target	Neural activity at time (t+Δ)	MN activity at time (t)

Initial weights were random, -0.3 and 0.3, and the learning rate was η=0.2. Training was performed until the temporal reproduction of cell spiking patterns was verified for all cells. Following training, the network was "run", η = 0.

Sum squared errors for all units were calculated and normalized to an activation value of 0 to 1. The temporal reproduction of the output patterns was verified by linear correlation against the targeted spike trains. The "effective" contribution of each unit to the flight pattern was then determined by "lesioning" individual cells from the network prior to presenting the input pattern. The effects of lesioning were judged by the change in error relative to the unlesioned network.

3 RESULTS

3.1 CELL-TO-CELL SIMULATION

Following training the complete pattern set was presented to the network. And, the sum squared error was averaged over all units, Fig. 1. Clearly the network has a different "interpretation" of the data at certain time steps. This is due both to the omission/commission of spikes as well as timing errors. However, the data needed to reproduce overall cell firing patterns is clearly available.

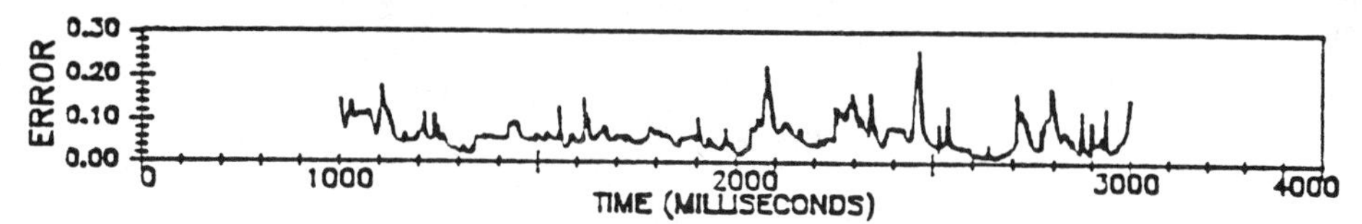

Figure 1: The network error

Unit sum squared errors were also averaged over the 2 second simulation, Fig. 2. Clearly the network predicted some unit/cell firing patterns easier than others.

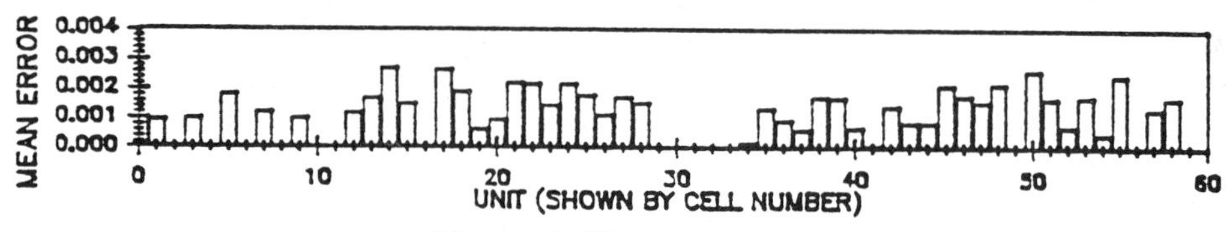

Figure 2: The unit errors

The temporal reproduction of the cell firing patterns was verified by linear correlation between the network outputs and the biological spike train representations. If the network accurately reproduces the temporal history of the spike trains these functions should be identical, r=1, Fig. 3. Clearly the network reproduces the temporal coding inherent within each spike train. The lowest correlation of roughly 0.85 is highly significant, ($p<0.01$).

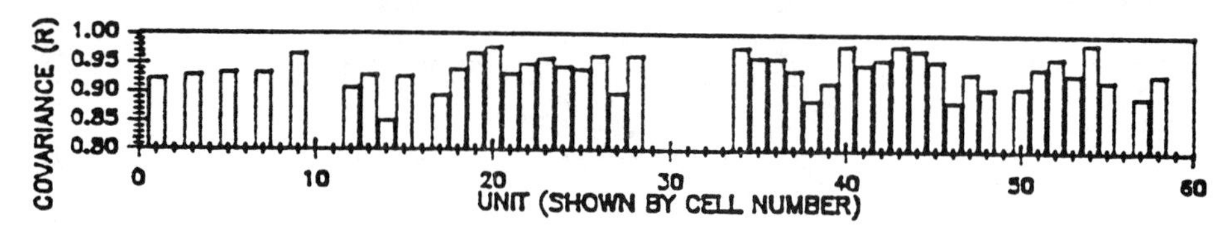

Figure 3: The unit temporal errors

One way to measure the relative importance of each unit/cell to the network is to omit/"lesion" each unit prior to presenting the cell firing patterns to the trained network. The data shown was collected by lesioning each unit individually, Fig. 4. The unlesioned network error is shown as the "0" cell. Overall the degradation of the network was minimal. Clearly some units provide more information to the network in reproducing the cell firing histories. Units that caused relatively large errors when "lesioned" were defined as primary units. The other units were defined as secondary units.

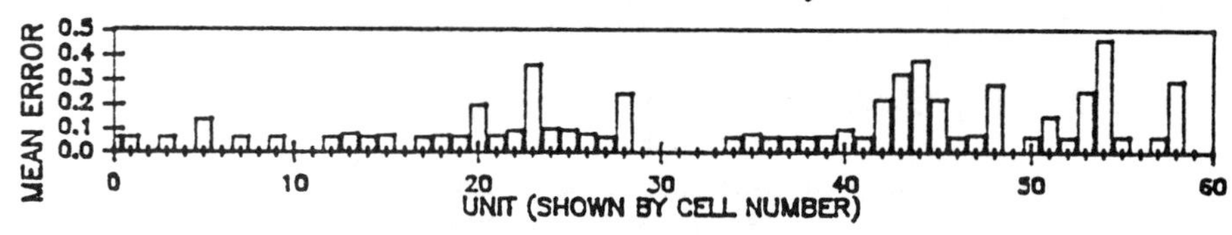

Figure 4: Lesion studies

The primary units (cells) form what might classically be termed a central pattern generator. These units can provide a relatively gross representation of both cellular and MN firing patterns. The generation of dynamic cellular and MN firing patterns, however, is apparently dependent on both primary and secondary units. It appears that the generation of functional activity patterns within the ganglia is largely controlled by the dynamic interactions between large groups of cells, ie. the "whole" network. This is consistent with other results derived from both neural network and statistical analyses of the biological data (Faller and Luttges 1990 & submitted:b).

3.2 MOTOR NEURON FIRING PATTERNS

The 44 cellular firing patterns were then used to drive the MN firing patterns. Following training, the cell firing pattern set was presented to the network and the sum squared error was averaged over the output MNs, Fig. 5. The error in this case oscillates in time at the wingbeat frequency of 37 Hz. As will be shown, however, this is an artifact and the network does accurately drive the MNs.

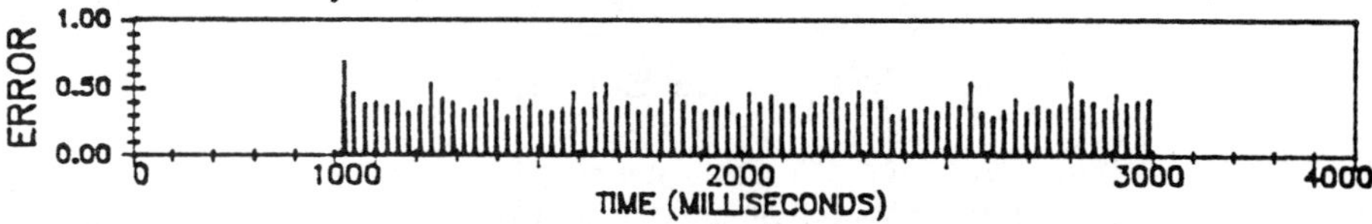

Figure 5: The network error

For each MN the sum squared error was also averaged over the 2 second simulation, Fig. 6. Clearly individual MNs contribute nearly equally to the network error.

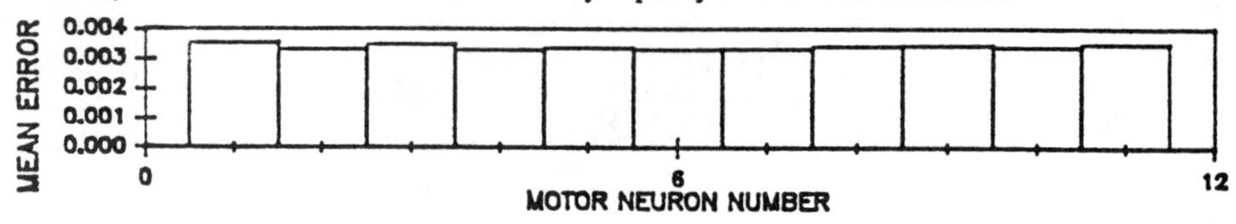

Figure 6: The unit errors

The temporal reproduction of the MN firing patterns was verified by linear correlation between the output and targeted MN firing patterns of the network. This is shown in Fig. 7. Clearly the cell inputs to the network have the spiking characteristics needed for driving the temporal firing sequences of the MNs innervating the wing musculature. All correlations are roughly 0.80, highly significant, ($p<0.01$). The output for one MN is shown relative to the targeted MN output in Fig. 8. Clearly the network does drive the MNs correctly.

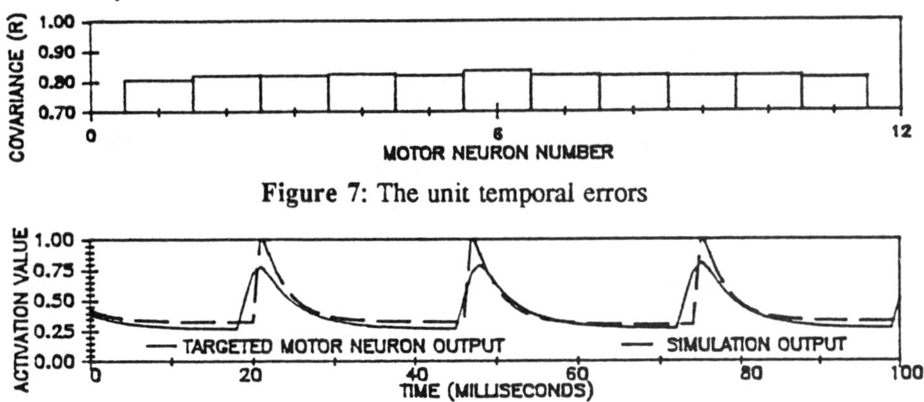

Figure 7: The unit temporal errors

Figure 8: The MN firing patterns

3.3 SUMMARY

The results indicate that synthetic networks can learn and then synthesize patterns of neural spiking activity needed for biological function. In this case, cell and MN firing patterns occurring in the dragonfly ganglia during a spontaneous flight episode.

4 DISCUSSION

Recordings from more than 50 spatially unique cells that reflect the complex network characteristics of a small, intact neural tissue were used to successfully train two neural networks. Unit sum squared errors were less than 0.003 and spike train temporal histories were accurately reproduced. There was little evidence for unexpected "cellular behavior". Functional lesioning of single units in the network caused minimal degradation of network performance, however, some lesioned cells were more important than others to overall network performance.

The capability to lesion cells permitted the contribution of individual cells to the production of the flight rhythm to be determined. The detection of primary and secondary cells underlying the dynamic generation of both cellular and MN firing patterns is one example. Such results may encourage neurobiologists to adopt neural networks as effective analytical tools with which to study and analyze spike train data.

Clearly the solution arrived at is not the biological one. However, the networks do accurately predict the future cell firing patterns based on past firing history information. It is asserted that the network must therefore contain the majority of information required to resolve biological cell interactions during flight in the dragonfly. A sample of 58 ganglionic cells was utilized, the remaining cells functional contributions are presumably statistically accounted for by this small sampling. The inherent "information" of the biological network is presumably stored in the weight matrices as a generalized statistical representation of the "rules" through which cells participate in biological assemblies.

Analyses of the weight matrices in turn may permit the operational "rules" of cell assemblies to be defined. Questions about the effects of cell size, the spatial architecture of the network and the temporal interactions between cells as they relate to cell assembly function can be addressed. For this reason the individuality of cells, the spatial architecture and the stochastic cellular firing histories of the individual cells were retained within the network architectures utilized. Crucial to these analyses will be methods that permit direct, time-incrementing evaluations of the weight matrices following training.

Biological nervous system function can now be analyzed from two points of view: direct analyses of the biological data and indirect, but potentially more approachable, analyses of the weight matrices from trained neural networks such as the ones described.

REFERENCES

Faller WE, Luttges MW (1990) A Neural Network Simulation of Simultaneous Single-Unit Activity Recorded from the Dragonfly Ganglia. ISA Paper #90-033

Faller WE, Luttges MW (in press) Recording of Simultaneous Single-Unit Activity in the Dragonfly Ganglia. J Neurosci Methods

Faller WE, Luttges MW (Submitted:a) Spatiotemporal Analysis of Simultaneous Single-Unit Activity in the Dragonfly: I. Cellular Activity Patterns. Biol Cybern

Faller WE, Luttges MW (Submitted:b) Spatiotemporal Analysis of Simultaneous Single-Unit Activity in the Dragonfly: II. Network Connectivity. Biol Cybern

Hebb DO (1949) The Organization of Behavior: A Neuropsychological Theory. Wiley, New York, Chapman and Hall, London

Kliss MH (1989) Neurocontrol Systems and Wing-Fluid Interactions Underlying Dragonfly Flight. Ph.D. Thesis, University of Colorado, Boulder, pp 70-80

Luttges MW (1989) Accomplished Insect Fliers. In: Gad-el-Hak M (ed) Frontiers in Experimental Fluid Mechanics. Springer-Verlag, Berlin Heidelberg, pp 429-456

Simmons P (1977) The Neuronal Control of Dragonfly Flight I. Anatomy. J exp Biol 71:123-140

Somps C, Luttges MW (1985) Dragonfly flight: Novel uses of unsteady separated flows. Science 228:1326-1329

Part IX

Applications

A Novel Approach to Prediction of the 3-Dimensional Structures of Protein Backbones by Neural Networks

Henrik Fredholm[1,5]
and
Henrik Bohr[2], Jakob Bohr[3], Søren Brunak[4], Rodney M.J. Cotterill[4], Benny Lautrup[5] and Steffen B. Petersen[1]

[1]MR-Senteret, SINTEF, N-7034 Trondheim, Norway.
[2]University of Illinois, Urbana, IL 61801, USA.
[3]Risø National Laboratory, DK-4000 Roskilde, Denmark.
[4]Technical Univ. of Denmark, B. 307, DK-2800 Lyngby, Denmark.
[5]Niels Bohr Institute, Blegdamsvej 17, DK-2100 Cph. Ø, Denmark.

Abstract

Three-dimensional (3D) structures of protein backbones have been predicted using neural networks. A feed forward neural network was trained on a class of functionally, but not structurally, homologous proteins, using backpropagation learning. The network generated tertiary structure information in the form of binary distance constraints for the C_α atoms in the protein backbone. The binary distance between two C_α atoms was 0 if the distance between them was less than a certain threshold distance, and 1 otherwise. The distance constraints predicted by the trained neural network were utilized to generate a folded conformation of the protein backbone, using a steepest descent minimization approach.

1 INTRODUCTION

One current aim of molecular biology is determination of the (3D) tertiary structures of proteins in their folded native state from their sequences of amino acid residues. Since Kendrew & Perutz solved the first protein structures, myoglobin and hemoglobin, and explained from the discovered structures how these proteins perform their function, it has been widely recognized that protein function is intimately linked with protein structure[1].

Within the last two decades X-ray crystallographers have solved the 3-dimensional (3D) structures of a steadily increasing number of proteins in the crystalline state, and recently 2D-NMR spectroscopy has emerged as an alternative method for small proteins in solution. Today approximately three hundred 3D structures have been solved by these methods, although only about half of them can be considered as truly different, and only around a hundred of them are solved at high resolution (that is, less than 2Å). The number of protein sequences known today is well over 20,000, and this number seems to be growing at least one order of magnitude faster than the number of known 3D protein structures.

Obviously, it is of great importance to develop tools that can predict structural aspects of proteins on the basis of knowledge acquired from known 3D structures.

1.1 THE PROTEIN FOLDING PROBLEM

It is generally accepted that most aspects of protein structure derive from the properties of the particular sequence of amino acids that make up the protein[1]. The classical experiment is that of Anfinsen *et al.* [2] who demonstrated that ribonuclease could be denatured and refolded without loss of enzymatic activity.

This has led to the formulation of the so-called protein folding problem: *given the sequence of amino acids of a protein, what will be its native folded conformation?*

1.2 SECONDARY STRUCTURE PREDICTION

Several methods have been developed for protein structure prediction. Most abundant are the methods for protein secondary structure prediction [3, 4, 5, 6]. These methods predict for each amino acid in the protein sequence what type of secondary structure the amino acid is part of. Several strategies have been suggested, most of which are based on statistical analysis of the occurrence of single amino acids or very short stretches of amino acids in secondary structural elements in known proteins. In general, these prediction schemes have a prediction accuracy of 50–60% for a three-category prediction of helix-, sheet- and coil conformations.

Recently neural networks have been applied to secondary structure prediction with encouraging results [7, 8, 9, 10]; on three-category prediction the accuracy is 65%; on two-catagory prediction of helix- and coil conformations the accuracy is 73%; and on a two-category prediction of turn- and coil conformations the accuracy is 71%. In all the three cases this is an improvement of the traditional methods.

[1]Although recent results indicate that certain proteins catalyze, but do not alter, the course of protein folding.

1.3 TERTIARY STRUCTURE PREDICTION

The methods that exist for 3D structure prediction fall in three broad categories: (1) use of sequence homology with other protein with know 3D structure; (2) prediction of secondary structure units followed by the assembly of these units into a compact structure; and (3) use of empirical energy functions *ab initio* to derive the 3D structure.

No general method for 3D structure prediction exists today, and novel methods are most often documented through case stories that illustrate best or single case performance. The most successful methods so far has been those based on sequence homology; if significant sequence and functional homology exists between a protein of interest and proteins for which the 3D structures are known, it is possible (but cumbersome) to build a reasonable 3D model of the protein structure.

2 METHOD

We here describe a new method for predicting the 3D structure of a protein backbone from its amino acid sequence [11]. The main idea behind this approach is to use a noise tolerant representation of the protein backbone that is invariant to rotation and translation of the backbone[2], and then train a neural network to map protein sequences to this representation.

2.1 REPRESENTATION OF 3D BACKBONE STRUCTURES

The folded backbone structure of a protein brings residues that are distantly positioned in sequence close to each other in space. One may identify such close contacts and use them as constraints on the backbone conformation.

We define the binary distance $D(i,j)$ between two residues i and j as 0 if the distance between the C_α atom in residue i and the C_α atom in residue j is less than a given threshold and as 1 if it is above or equal to the threshold, a typical choice of threshold being 8Å. Organizing these distances as a binary distance matrix gives rise to a two dimensional representation of the protein backbone (figure 2a depict such matrix).

Most secondary motifs can be distinguished in this representation; helices appear as thickenings of the diagonal and anti-parallel and parallel sheets appear as stripes orthogonal and parallel to the diagonal.

It is possible to reconstruct the 3D backbone from the binary distance matrix representation by minimizing the "energy function",

$$E = \sum_{i \neq j} g(d_{ij}(\mid \tilde{C}_\alpha(i) - \tilde{C}_\alpha(j) \mid - \theta))$$

where $d_{ij} = 1 - 2D(i,j)$, $g(x) = 1/(1+\exp(-x))$ and θ is the distance threshold. The initial positions of the $\tilde{C}_\alpha$ atoms are chosen at random. The motif for this

[2]The (ϕ,ψ) torsion-angle representation is also rotation- and translation invariant, but it is not noise tolerant.

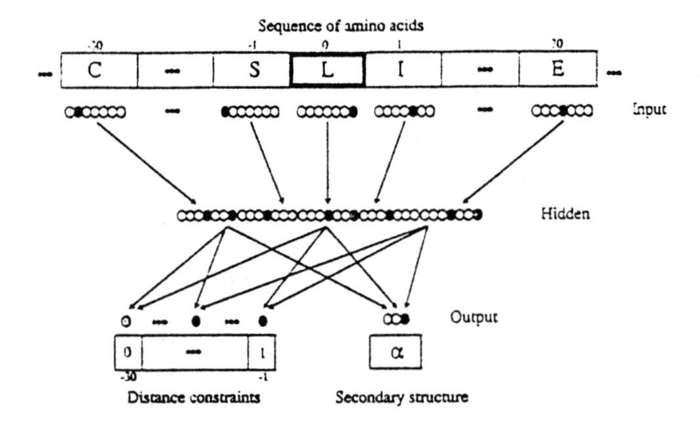

Figure 1: The input to the network consists of 61 contiguous amino acids, where each amino acid is represented by a group of 20 neurons (only seven neurons/group are illustrated). At the output layer, a set of binary distances, between the centrally positioned residue and those lying to the left of it in the input window, is produced. Secondary structure assignment for the centrally positioned residue, in the three categories of helix, sheet and coil, is also produced. Regarding the binary distance matrix, the network is trained to report which of the 30 preceding C_α atoms are positioned within a distance of 8Å to the centrally placed amino acid. The input layer had 1220 (61×20) neurons, the hidden layer had 300 neurons and the output layer had 33 neurons.

energy function is that constraints that do not hold should contribute with large values, while constraints that do hold should contribute with small values.

For small proteins of the order of 60 residues the reconstruction is very accurate. For Bovine Pancreatic Trypsin Inhibitor (6PTI), a 56 residue long protein, we were able to generate a correctly folded backbone structure. The binary distance matrix was generated from the crystallographic data of 6PTI using a distance threshold of 8Å. After convergence of the minimization procedure the errors between the reconstructed structure and the correct structure lay within 1.2Å root mean square (rms).

Preliminary results (unpublished) indicate that backbone structures for larger proteins can be reconstructed with a deviation from the correct structure down to 2Å rms, when a distance threshold of 16Å is used. When 5% random noise is added to the distance matrix the deviation from the correct structure grows to 4–5Å rms.

2.2 DISTANCE MATRIX PREDICTION

A backpropagation network [12] was used to map protein sequences to distance matrices. To simplify the task the neural network had to learn, it was not taught to predict all constraints in the distance matrix. Only a band along the diagonal was to be predicted. More specifically, the network was taught to predict for each residue in the protein sequence the binary distances to the 30 previous residues. Furthermore it had to classify the central residue in question as either helix, sheet or coil, see figure 1. Hence, the trained neural network produced, when given a protein sequence, a secondary structure prediction and a distance matrix containing

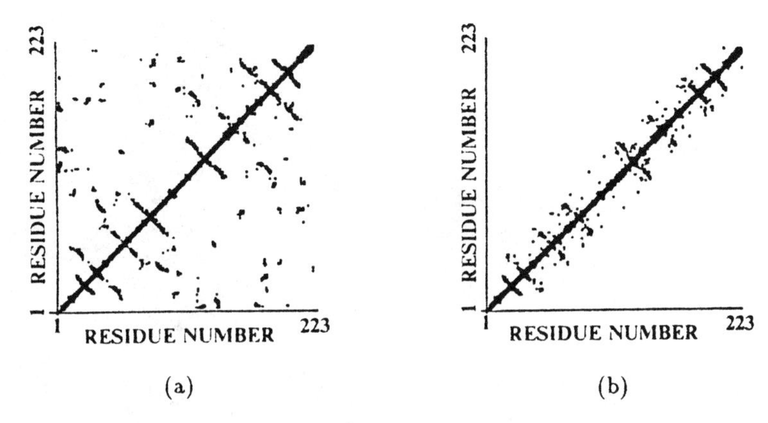

Figure 2: Binary distance matrices for 1TRM. The matrices (223 × 223) show which C_α atoms are within an 8Å distance to each other C_α atom in the folded protein. a) The matrix corresponding to the structure determined from the X-ray data. b) Neural network prediction of an 8Å distance matrix. A 61-residue band centered along the diagonal is generated. The network predicts this band with an accuracy of 96.6%.

binary distance constraints for a lower diagonal-band matrix of width 30. Due to symmetry in the distance matrix and the diagonal being always zero, the resulting binary distance matrix contained a diagonal-band of predicted distance constraints of width 61.

3 CASE STORY

A neural network with this architecture was trained on 13 different proteases [13] from the Brookhaven Protein Data Bank, all having their data collected to a nominal resolution better than 2Å. The 13 proteases were of several structural classes including trypsins and subtilisins. This training set generated 3171 different examples (input windows) which were presented to the network. After 200 presentations of each example, the network had learned the training set to perfection[3]. A 14th protease, 1TRM (Rat Trypsin), with a length of 223 residues, was used to test the network. This protease was 74% homologous to one of the 13 proteases that the network was trained on. The distance matrix derived from X-ray diffraction for this protein is shown in figure 2a. The ability of the network to correctly assign structural information is amply illustrated in figure 2b, where the network is predicting the distance constraints around the diagonal for 1TRM. Although a high degree of sequence homology exists between 1TRM and the trypsins included in the training set, not a single input window presented to the network was identical to any window in the training set. The prediction thus illustrates the ability of the network to generalize from the training set. In the prediction (figure 2b), a clear distinction can be made between helices and anti-parallel sheets as well as other tertiary motifs.

If the whole binary distances matrix had been predicted, it would have been possible

[3]The training lasted 2 weeks on an Apollo 10000 running at 10 Mflops.

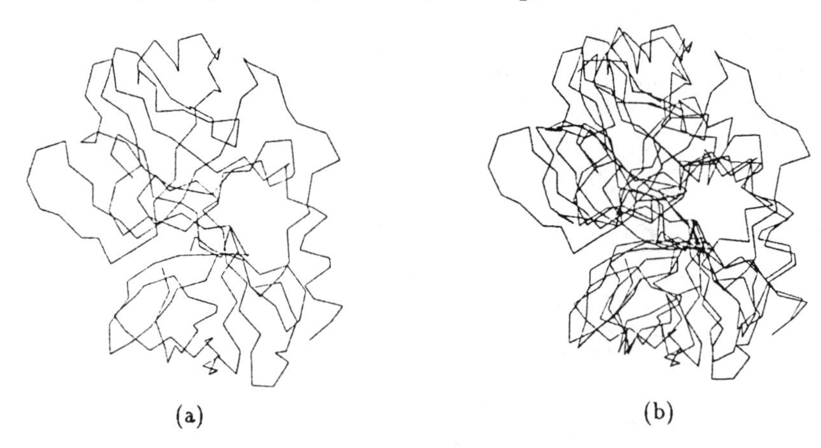

Figure 3: Backbone conformation for the 223 residue long trypsin 1TRM. a) The crystal structure for 1TRM, as determined by X-ray data. b) The predicted structure of 1TRM superimposed on the crystal structure. The rms deviation calculated over all the C_α atoms was 3Å. The largest deviations were present in surface loops, some of which are fixed by several disulphide bridges.

to construct the backbone conformation directly from the prediction. However, since only a truncated version was predicted, a good guess of the backbone conformation is needed for the minimization[4]. By using as initial guess the backbone conformation for a homologous protein, the backbone conformation of 1TRM was predicted with a 3Å rms deviation from the coordinates determined by X-ray diffraction, see figure 3. In this particular case, the length of the sequence used for the starting configuration was identical to that of the protein to be reconstructed. When the sequences are of unequal length, on the other hand, it is clear that additional considerations would have to be taken into account during the minimization process.

4 DISCUSSION

The single main achievement of this study has been the generation of a 3D structure of a protein from its amino acid sequence. The approach involved first the prediction of a distance matrix using a neural network and subsequently a minimization fitting procedure.

Binary distance matrices were introduced as a noise tolerant translation- and rotation invariant representation of 3D protein backbones, and a neural network was trained to map protein sequences to this representation.

The results reported here are predictions of folded conformations, illustrated with the trypsin 1TRM. Our neural network is clearly capable of generalizing the folding

[4]For large proteins, where the band of distance constraints does not cover all spatial contacts, local folding domains may acquire different chiralities, leading to improper packing of the domains in the protein. However, new experiments indicate that the backbone structure of proteins that are 200–300 residues long can be reconstructed with good results from a random configuration, if the width of the band in the distance matrix is 121 and the distance threshold is 16Å.

information stemming from known proteins with homologous function. Current investigations have shown that the network is robust towards mutation of amino acids in the protein sequence, whereas it is very sensitive to insertions and deletions in the sequence. Thus, new network architectures will have to be developed, if this method is to be useful for proteins with low homology; a bigger training set alone will not do it.

Distance constraints can also be derived from experimental procedures such as NMR, in which they take the form of nuclear Overhauser enhancement (nOe) factors. Structural information can be successfully derived from such data using restraint dynamics which in its essential form bears some resemblance to the approach employed here, the most salient difference being that the potential energy function in our work is much simpler.

Acknowledgements

HF thanks the Danish Research Academy, Novo-Nordisk and UNI-C for grants.

References

[1] Jaenicke, R. (1987) Prog. Biophys. Molec. Biol. **49**, 117–237.

[2] Anfinsen, C.B *et al.* (1961) Proc. Natl. Acad. Sci. USA, **47**, 1309–1314.

[3] Chou, P.Y, and Fasman, G.D. (1974) Biochemistry **13**, 211–245.

[4] Garnier, J., Osguthorpe, D.J., and Robson, B. J. (1978) Mol. Biol., **120**, 97–120.

[5] Lim, V.I. (1974) J. Mol. Biol., **88**, 857-894.

[6] Robson, D., and Suzuki, E. (1976) J. Mol. Biol., **107**, 327–356.

[7] Qian N., and Sejnowski, T.J. (1988) J. Mol. Biol., **202**, 865-884.

[8] Bohr, H., Bohr, J., Brunak, S., Cotterill, R.M.J., Lautrup, B., Nørskov, L., Olsen, O.H, and Petersen, S.B (1988) FEBS Letters, **241**, 223-228.

[9] McGregor, M.J., Flores, T.P., and Sternberg, M.J.E. (1989) Protein Engineering, **2**, 521–526.

[10] Kneller, D.G., Cohen, F.E., and Langridge, L. (1990) J. Mol. Biol., **214**, 171–182.

[11] Bohr, H., Bohr. J, Brunak, S., Cotterill, R.M.J., Fredholm, H., Lautrup, B., and Petersen, S.B. (1990) FEBS Letters, **261**, 43–46.

[12] Rummelhart, D.E., Hinton, G.E., and Williams, R.J. (1986) Parallel Distributed Processing, **1**, 318–362. Bradford Books, Cambridge, MA.

[13] Brookhaven Protein Data Bank entry codes: 1SGT (Streptomyces Trypsin), 2EST (Porcine Pancreatic Elastase), 4PTP (Bovine Pancreatic beta Trypsin), 2KAI (Porcine Pancreatic Kallikrein A), 1CHG (Bovine Chymotrypsin A), 2PRK (Fungal Proteinase K), 1SEC (Subtilisin Carlsberg), 1SGC (Streptomyces Proteinase A), 2ALP (Lysobacter Alfalytic Protease), 3APR (Rhizopus Acid Proteinase), 3RP2 (rat Mast Cell Proteinase), 2SBT (Subtilisin NOVO) and 1SAV (Subtilisin Savinase).

Training Knowledge-Based Neural Networks to Recognize Genes in DNA Sequences

Michiel O. Noordewier
Computer Science
Rutgers University
New Brunswick, NJ 08903

Geoffrey G. Towell
Computer Sciences
University of Wisconsin
Madison, WI 53706

Jude W. Shavlik
Computer Sciences
University of Wisconsin
Madison, WI 53706

Abstract

We describe the application of a hybrid symbolic/connectionist machine learning algorithm to the task of recognizing important genetic sequences. The symbolic portion of the KBANN system utilizes inference rules that provide a roughly-correct method for recognizing a class of DNA sequences known as *eukaryotic splice-junctions.* We then map this "domain theory" into a neural network and provide training examples. Using the samples, the neural network's learning algorithm adjusts the domain theory so that it properly classifies these DNA sequences. Our procedure constitutes a general method for incorporating preexisting knowledge into artificial neural networks. We present an experiment in molecular genetics that demonstrates the value of doing so.

1 Introduction

Often one has some preconceived notions about how to perform some classification task. It would be useful to incorporate this knowledge into a neural network, and then use some training examples to refine these approximately-correct rules of thumb. This paper describes the KBANN *(Knowledge-Based Artificial Neural Networks)* hybrid learning system and demonstrates its ability to learn in the complex domain of molecular genetics. Briefly, KBANN uses a knowledge base of hierarchically-structured rules (which may be both incomplete and incorrect) to form an artificial neural network (ANN). In so doing, KBANN makes it possible to apply neural learning techniques to the empirical improvement of knowledge bases.

The task to be learned is the recognition of certain DNA (deoxyribonucleic acid) subsequences important in the expression of genes. A large governmental research

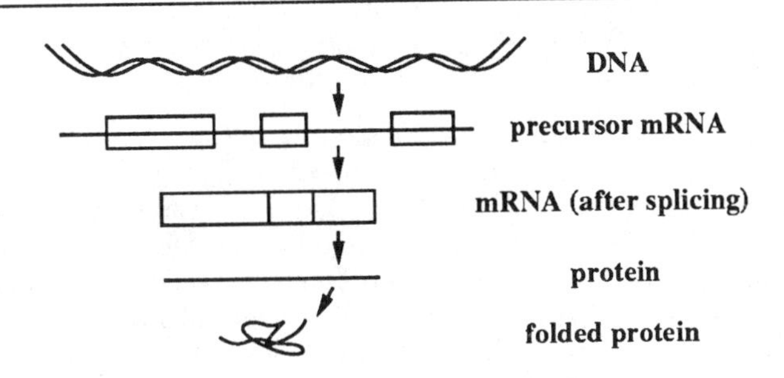

Figure 1: Steps in the Expression of Genes

program, called the Human Genome Initiative, has recently been undertaken to determine the sequence of DNA in humans, estimated to be 3×10^9 characters of information. This provides a strong impetus to develop genetic-analysis techniques based solely on the information contained in the sequence, rather than in combination with other chemical, physical, or genetic techniques. DNA contains the information by which a cell constructs protein molecules. The cellular expression of proteins proceeds by the creation of a "message" ribonucleic acid (mRNA) copy from the DNA template (Figure 1). This mRNA is then translated into a protein. One of the most unexpected findings in molecular biology is that large pieces of the mRNA are removed before it is translated further [1].

The utilized sequences (represented by boxes in Figure 1) are known as "exons", while the removed sequences are known as "introns", or intervening sequences. Since the discovery of such "split genes" over a decade ago, the nature of the splicing event has been the subject of intense research. The points at which DNA is removed (the boundaries of the boxes in Figure 1) are known as *splice-junctions.* The splice-junctions of eukaryotic[1] mRNA precursors contain patterns similar to those in Figure 2.

exon	intron	exon
... (A/C) A G	G T (A/G) A G T ... $(C/T)_6$ X (C/T) A G	G (G/T) ...

Figure 2: Canonical Splice-Junctions
DNA is represented by a string of characters from the set {A,G,C,T}. In this figure, **X** represents any character, slashes represent disjunctive options, and subscripts indicate repetitions of a pattern.

However, numerous other locations can resemble these canonical patterns. As a result, these patterns do not by themselves reliably imply the presence of a splice-junction. Evidently, if junctions are to be recognized on the basis of sequence information alone, longer-range sequence information will have to be included in

[1] Eukaryotic cells contain nuclei, unlike prokaryotic cells such as bacterial and viruses.

the decision-making criteria. A central problem is therefore to determine the extent to which sequences surrounding splice-junctions differ from sequences surrounding spurious analogues.

We have recently described a method [9, 12] that combines empirical and symbolic learning algorithms to recognize another class of genetic sequences known as *bacterial promoters.* Our hybrid KBANN system was demonstrated to be superior to other empirical learning systems including decision trees and nearest-neighbor algorithms. In addition, it was shown to more accurately classify promoters than the methods currently reported in the biological literature. In this manuscript we describe the application of KBANN to the recognition of splice-junctions, and show that it significantly increases generalization ability when compared to randomly-initialized, single-hidden-layer networks (i.e., networks configured in the "usual" way). The paper concludes with a discussion of related research and the areas which our research is currently pursuing.

2 The KBANN Algorithm

KBANN uses a knowledge base of domain-specific inference rules in the form of PROLOG-like clauses to define what is initially known about a topic. The knowledge base need be neither complete nor correct; it need only support approximately correct reasoning. KBANN translates knowledge bases into ANNs in which units and links correspond to parts of knowledge bases. A detailed explanation of the procedure used by KBANN to translate rules into an ANN can be found in [12].

As an example of the KBANN method, consider the artificial knowledge base in Figure 3a which defines membership in category A. Figure 3b represents the hierarchical structure of these rules: solid and dotted lines represent *necessary* and *prohibitory* dependencies, respectively. Figure 3c represents the ANN that results from the translation into a neural network of this knowledge base. Units X and Y in Figure 3c are introduced into the ANN to handle the disjunction in the knowledge base. Otherwise, units in the ANN correspond to consequents or antecedents in the knowledge base. The thick lines in Figure 3c represent the links in the ANN that correspond to dependencies in the explanation. The weight on thick solid lines is 3, while the weight on thick dotted lines is -3. The lighter solid lines represent the links added to the network to allow refinement of the initial rules. At present, KBANN is restricted to non-recursive, propositional (i.e., variable-free) sets of rules.

Numbers beside the unit names in Figure 3c are the biases of the units. These biases are set so that the unit is active if and only if the corresponding consequent in the knowledge base is true.

As this example illustrates, the use of KBANN to initialize ANNs has two principle benefits. First, it indicates the features believed to be important to an example's classification. Second, it specifies important derived features; through their deduction the complexity of an ANN's final decision is reduced.

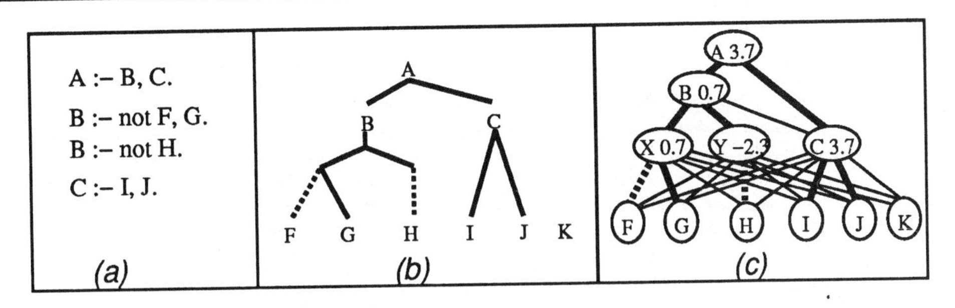

Figure 3: Translation of a Knowledge Base into an ANN

3 Problem Definition

The splice-junction problem is to determine into which of the following three categories a specified location in a DNA sequence falls: (1) exon/intron borders, referred to as *donors*, (2) intron/exon borders, referred to as *acceptors*, and (3) *neither*. To address this problem we provide KBANN with two sets of information: a set of DNA sequences 60 nucleotides long that are classified as to the category membership of their center and a domain theory that describes when the center of a sequence corresponds to one of these three categories.

Table 1 contains the initial domain theory used in the splice-junction recognition task. A special notation is used to specify locations in the DNA sequence. When a rule's antecedents refer to input features, they first state a relative location in the sequence vector, then the DNA symbol that must occur (e.g., @3=A). Positions are numbered negatively or positively depending on whether they occur before or after the possible junction location. By biological convention, position numbers of zero are not used. The set of rules was derived in a straightforward fashion from the biological literature [13]. Briefly, these rules state that a donor or acceptor sequence is present if characters from the canonical sequence (Figure 2) are present and triplets known as *stop codons* are absent in the appropriate positions.

The examples were obtained by taking the documented split genes from all primate gene entries in Genbank release 64.1 [?] that are described as complete. Each training example consists of a window that covers 30 nucleotides before and after each donor and acceptor site. This procedure resulted in 751 examples of acceptor and 745 examples of donors. Negative examples are derived from similarly-sized windows, which did not cross an intron/exon boundary, sampled at random from these sequences. Note that this differs from the usual practice of generating random sequences with base-frequency composition the same as the positive instances. However, we feel that this provides a more realistic training set, since DNA is known to be highly non-random [3]. Although many more negative examples were available, we used approximately as many negative examples are there were both donor and acceptors. Thus, the total data set we used had 3190 examples.

The network created by KBANN for the splice-junction problem has one output

Table 1: Knowledge Base for Splice-Junctions

```
donor :- @-3=M, @-2=A, @-1=G, @1=G, @2=T, @3=R,
         @4=A, @5=G, @6=T, not(don-stop).
don-stop :- @-3=T, @-2=A, @-1=A.     don-stop :- @-4=T, @-3=A, @-2=G.
don-stop :- @-3=T, @-2=A, @-1=G.     don-stop :- @-4=T, @-3=G, @-2=A.
don-stop :- @-3=T, @-2=G, @-1=A.     don-stop :- @-5=T, @-4=A, @-3=A.
don-stop :- @-4=T, @-3=A, @-2=A.     don-stop :- @-5=T, @-4=A, @-3=G.
don-stop :- @-5=T, @-4=G, @-3=A.
acceptor :- pyr-rich, @-3=Y, @-2=A, @-1=G, @1=G, @2=K, not(acc-stop).
pyr-rich :- 6 of (@-15=Y, @-14=Y, @-13=Y, @-12=Y, @-11=Y,
                  @-10=Y, @-9=Y, @-8=Y, @-7=Y, @-6=Y.)
acc-stop :- @1=T, @2=A, @3=A.        acc-stop :- @2=T, @3=A, @4=A.
acc-stop :- @1=T, @2=A, @3=G.        acc-stop :- @2=T, @3=A, @4=G.
acc-stop :- @1=T, @2=G, @3=A.        acc-stop :- @2=T, @3=G, @4=A.
acc-stop :- @3=T, @4=A, @5=A.        acc-stop :- @3=T, @4=A, @5=G.
acc-stop :- @3=T, @4=G, @5=A.
R :- A.  R :- G.  Y :- C.  Y :- T.  M :- C.  M :- A.  K :- G.  K :- T
```

units for each category to be learned; and four input units for each nucleotide in the DNA training sequences, one for each of the four values in the DNA alphabet. In addition, the rules for *acc-stop, don-stop, R, Y,* and *M* are considered definitional. Thus, the weights on the links and biases into these units were frozen. Also, the second rule only requires that six of its 11 antecedents be true. Finally, there are no rules in Table 1 for recognizing negative examples. So we added four unassigned hidden units and connected them to all of the inputs and to the output for the *neither* category. The final result is that the network created by KBANN has 286 units: 3 output units, 240 input units, 31 fixed-weight hidden units, and 12 tunable hidden units.

4 Experimental Results

Figure 4 contains a learning curve plotting the percentage of errors made on a set of "testing" examples by KBANN-initialized networks, as a function of the number of training examples. Training examples were obtained by randomly selecting examples from the population of 3190 examples described above. Testing examples consisted of all examples in the population that were not used for training. Each data point represents the average of 20 repetitions of this procedure.

For comparison, the error rate for a randomly-initialized, fully-connected, two-layer ANN with 24 hidden units is also plotted in Figure 4. (This curve is expected to have an error rate of 67% for zero training examples. Test results were slightly better due to statistical fluctuations.) Clearly, the KBANN-initialized networks learned faster than randomly-initialized ANNs, making less than half the errors of the randomly-initialized ANNs when there were 100 or fewer training examples. However, when

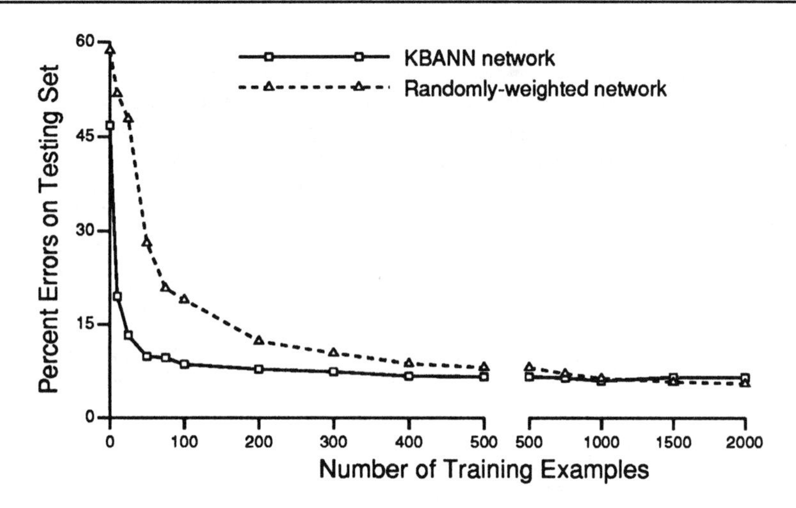

Figure 4: Learning Curve for Splice Junctions

large numbers of training examples were provided the randomly-initialized ANNs had a slightly lower error rate (5.5% vs. 6.4% for KBANN). All of the differences in the figure are statistically significant.

5 Related and Future Research

Several others have investigated predicting splice-junctions. Staden [10] has devised a weight-matrix method that uses a perceptron-like algorithm to find a weighting function that discriminates two sets (true and false) of boundary patterns in known sequences. Nakata et al. [7] employ a combination of methods to distinguish between exons and introns, including Fickett's statistical method [5]. When applied to human sequences in the Genbank database; this approach correctly identified 81% of true splice-junctions. Finally, Lapedes et al. [6] also applied neural networks and decision-tree builders to the splice-junction task. They reported neural-network accuracies of 92% and claimed their neural-network approach performed significantly better than the other approaches in the literature at that time. The accuracy we report in this paper represents an improvement over these results. However, it should be noted that these experiments were not all performed under the same conditions.

One weakness of neural networks is that it is hard to understand what they have learned. We are investigating methods for the automatic translation into symbolic rules of trained KBANN-initialized networks [11]. These techniques take advantage of the human-comprehensible starting configuration of KBANN's networks to create a small set of hierarchically-structured rules that accurately reflect what the network learned during training. We are also currently investigating the use of richer splice-junction domain theories, which we hope will improve KBANN's accuracy.

6 Conclusion

The KBANN approach allows ANNs to refine preexisting knowledge, generating ANN topologies that are well-suited to the task they are intended to learn. KBANN does this by using a knowledge base of approximately correct, domain-specific rules to determine the ANN's structure and initial weights. This provides an alternative to techniques that either shrink [2] or grow [4] networks to the "right" size. Our experiments on splice-junctions, and previously on bacterial promoters, [12] demonstrate that the KBANN approach can substantially reduce the number of training examples needed to reach a given level of accuracy on future examples.

This research was partially supported by Office of Naval Research Grant N00014-90-J-1941, National Science Foundation Grant IRI-9002413, and Department of Energy Grant DE-FG02-91ER61129.

References

[1] R. J. Breathnach, J. L. Mandel, and P. Chambon. Ovalbumin gene is split in chicken DNA. *Nature*, 270:314–319, 1977.

[2] Y. Le Cun, J. Denker, and S. Solla. Optimal brain damage. *Advances in Neural Information Processing Systems 2*, pages 598–605, 1990.

[3] G. Dykes, R. Bambara, K. Marians, and R. Wu. On the statistical significance of primary structural features found in DNA-protein interaction sites. *Nucleic Acids Research*, 2:327–345, 1975.

[4] S. Fahlman and C. Lebiere. The cascade-correlation learning architecture. *Advances in Neural Information Processing Systems 2*, pages 524–532, 1990.

[5] J. W. Fickett. Recognition of protein coding regions in DNA sequences. *Nucleic Acids Research*, 10:5303–5318, 1982.

[6] A. Lapedes, D. Barnes, C. Burks, R. Farber, and K. Sirotkin. Application of neural networks and other machine learning algorithms to DNA sequence analysis. In *Computers and DNA*, pages 157–182. Addison-Wesley, 1989.

[7] K. Nakata, M. Kanehisa, and C. DeLisi. Prediction of splice junctions in mrna sequences. *Nucleic Acids Research*, 13:5327–5340, 1985.

[8] M. C. O'Neill. Escherichia coli promoters: I. Consensus as it relates to spacing class, specificity, repeat substructure, and three dimensional orgainzation. *Journal of Biological Chemistry*, 264:5522–5530, 1989.

[9] J. W. Shavlik and G. G. Towell. An approach to combining explanation-based and neural learning algorithms. *Connection Science*, 1:233–255, 1989.

[10] R. Staden. Computer methods to locate signals in DNA sequences. *Nucleic Acids Research*, 12:505–519, 1984.

[11] G. G. Towell, M. Craven, and J. W. Shavlik. Automated interpretation of knowledge based neural networks. Technical report, University of Wisconsin, Computer Sciences Department, Madison, WI, 1991.

[12] G. G. Towell, J. W. Shavlik, and M. O. Noordewier. Refinement of approximately correct domain theories by knowledge-based neural networks. In *Proc. of the Eighth National Conf. on Artificial Intelligence*, pages 861–866, Boston, MA, 1990.

[13] J. D. Watson, N. H. Hopkins, J. W. Roberts, J. A. Steitz, and A. M. Weiner. *Molecular Biology of the Gene*, pages 634–647, 1987.

Neural Network Application to Diagnostics and Control of Vehicle Control Systems

Kenneth A. Marko
Research Staff
Ford Motor Company
Dearborn, Michigan 48121

ABSTRACT

Diagnosis of faults in complex, real–time control systems is a complicated task that has resisted solution by traditional methods. We have shown that neural networks can be successfully employed to diagnose faults in digitally controlled powertrain systems. This paper discusses the means we use to develop the appropriate databases for training and testing in order to select the optimum network architectures and to provide reasonable estimates of the classification accuracy of these networks on new samples of data. Recent work applying neural nets to adaptive control of an active suspension system is presented.

1 INTRODUCTION

This paper reports on work performed on the application of artificial neural systems (ANS) techniques to the diagnosis and control of vehicle systems. Specifically, we have examined the diagnosis of common faults in powertrain systems and investigated the problem of developing an adaptive controller for an active suspension system.

In our diagnostic investigations we utilize neural networks routinely to establish the standards for diagnostic accuracy we can expect from analysis of vehicle data. Previously we have examined the use of various ANS paradigms to diagnosis of a wide range of faults in a carefully collected data set from a vehicle operated in a narrow range of speed and load. Subsequently, we have explored the classification of a data set with a more restricted set of faults, drawn from a much broader range of operating conditions. This step was taken as concern about needs for specific, real–time continuous diagnostics superseded the need to develop well–controlled, on–demand diagnostic testing. The impetus arises from recently enacted legislation which dictates that such real-time diagnosis of powertrain systems will be required on cars sold in the U.S. by the mid-1990's. The difference between the two applications is simple: in the former studies it was presumed that an independent agent has identified that a fault is present, the root cause needs only to be identified. In the real-time problem, the diagnostic task is to detect and identify the fault as soon as it occurs. Consequently, the real-time application is more demanding. In analyzing this more difficult task, we explore some of the complications that arise in developing successful classification schemes for the virtually semi-infinite data streams that are produced in continuous operation of a vehicle fleet. The obstacles to realized applications of neural nets in this area often stem from the sophistication required of the classifier and the complexity of the problems addressed. The limited computational resources on-board vehicles will determine the scope of the diagnostic task and how implementations, such as ANS methods, will operate.

Finally, we briefly examine an extension of the ANS work to developing trainable controllers for non-linear dynamic systems such as active suspension systems. Preliminary work in this area indicates that effective controllers for non-linear plants can be developed efficiently, despite the exclusion of an accurate plant model from the training process. Although our studies were carried out in simulation, and accurate plant models were therefore available, the capability to develop controllers in the absence of such models is a significant step forward. Such controllers can be developed for existing, un-modeled hardware, and thereby reduce both the efforts required to develop control algorithms by conventional means and the time to program the real-time controllers.

2 NEURAL NET DIAGNOSTICS OF CONTROL SYSTEMS

Our interest in neural networks for diagnosis of faults in control systems stemmed from work on model-based diagnosis of faults in such systems, typically called plants. In the model-based approach, a model of the system under control is developed and used to predict the dynamic behavior of the system. With the system in operation, the plant performance is observed. The expected behavior and the observed behavior are compared, and if no differences are found, the plant is deemed to be operating normally. If deviations are found, the differences indicate that a fault of some sort is present (failure detection), and an analysis of the differences is used in an attempt to identify the cause (fault identification). Successful implementations (Min, 1987; Liubakka *et al*, 1988; Rizzoni *et al*, 1989) of fault detection and identification in complex systems linearized about selected operating points were put together utilizing mathematical constructs called failure detection filters. These filters are simply matrices which transform a set of observations (which become an input vector to the filter) of a plant into another vector space (the output vector or classification space). The form of these filters suggested to us that neural networks could be used to learn similar transforms and thereby avoid the tedious process of model development and validation and a priori identification of the detection filter matrix elements. We showed previously that complex signal patterns from operating internal combustion engines could be examined on a cycle by cycle basis (two revolutions of the common four-stroke engine cycle) and used to correctly identify faults present in the engine (Marko *et al*, 1989).

Typical data collected from an operating engine has been shown elsewhere (Marko *et al*, 1989). This demonstration was focussed on a production engine, limited to a small operating range. One might suppose that a linear model–based diagnostic system could be constructed for such a task, if one wished to expend the time and effort, and therefore this exercise was not a strenuous test of the neural network approach. Additionally, our expert diagnostician could examine the data traces and accurately identify the faults. However, we demonstrated that this problem, which had eluded automated solution by other means up to that time, could easily be handled by neural network classifiers and encouraged us to proceed to more difficult problems for which efficient, rigorous procedures did not exist. We were prepared to tolerate developing empirical solutions to our more difficult problems, since we did not expect that a thorough analytic understanding would precede a demonstrated solution. The process outlined here utilized neural network analysis almost exclusively (predominantly back–propagation) on these problems. The understanding of the relationship of neural networks, the structure of the data and the training and testing of the classifiers emerged after acceptable solutions using the neural networks methods were obtained.

Consequently, the next problem addressed was that of identifying similar faults by observing the system through the multiplex serial communication link resident on the engine control computer. The serial link provides a simple hook–up procedure to the vehicle without severing any links between plant and microcontroller. However, the chief drawback of this approach is that it greatly complicates the recognition task. The complication arises because the data from the plant is sampled too infrequently, is "contaminated" by some processing in the controller, and delivered asynchronously to the serial link with respect to events in the plant (the data output process is not permitted to interrupt the real–time control requirements). In this case, a test sample of a smaller number of faults was drawn from a vehicle operated in a similar limited range to the first example and an attempt to detect and identify the faults was made using a variety of networks. Unlike the previous case, it was impossible for any experienced technicians to identify the faults. Again, neural network classifiers were found to develop satisfactory solutions over these limited data sets, which were later verified by a number of careful statistical tests (Marko *et al*, 1990). This more complex problem also produced a wider range of performance among the various neural net paradigms studied, as shown in Figure 1, where the error rates for various classifiers on these data sets are shown in the graph. These results suggested that not only would data quality and quantity need to be controlled and improved, but that the problem itself would implicitly direct us to the choice of the classifier paradigm. These issues are more thoroughly discussed elsewhere (Marko *et al*, 1990; Weiss *et al*, 1990), but the conclusion was that a complete, acceptable solution to the real scope of this problem could not be developed with our group's resources for data collection, data verification and classifier validation.

With these two experiences in mind, we could see that the first approach was an effective means of handling the failure detection and identification (FDI) problem, while the latter, although attractive from the standpoint of easy link–up to a vehicle, was for our numerical analysis, a very difficult task. It seemed that the appropriate course was to obtain reliable data, by observing the plant directly, and to perform the classification on that data. An effective scheme to accomplish this goal is to perform the classification task in the control microprocessor which has access to the direct data. Adopting this strategy, we move the diagnostics from an off–board processor to the on–board processor, and create a new set of possibilities for diagnostics.

With diagnostics contained in the controlling processor, diagnostics can be shifted from an on-demand activity, undertaken at predetermined intervals or when the vehicle operator has detected a problem, to a continuous, real-time activity. This change implies that the diagnostic algorithms will, for the most part, be evaluating a properly operating system and only infrequently be required to detect a failure and identify the cause. Additionally, the diagnostic algorithms will have to be very compact, since the current control microprocessors have very limited time and memory for calculation compared to a off-board PC. Furthermore, the classification task will need to be learned from a sample of data which is minuscule compared to the data sets that the deployed diagnostics will have to classify. This fact imposes on the training data set the requirement that it be an accurate statistical sample of the much more voluminous real-world data. This situation must prevail because we cannot anticipate the deployment of a classifier that is undergoing continuous training. A classifier capable of continuous adaptation would require more computational capability, and quite likely a supervised learning environment. The fact is, even for relatively simple diagnostics of operating engines, assembling a large, accurate training data set off-line is a considerable task. This last issue is explored in the next paragraph, but it seems to rule out early deployment of anything other than pretrained classifiers until some experience with much larger data sets from deployed diagnostic systems is obtained.

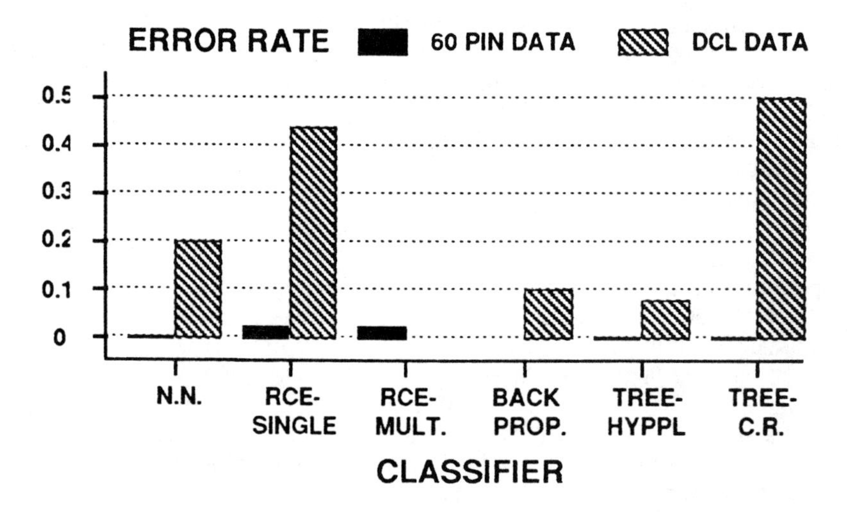

Figure 1. Comparison of the performance of various neural network paradigms on two static data sets by leave-one-out testing from measurements performed on vehicles in a service bay. The network paradigms tested are nearest neighbor, Restricted Coulomb Energy (RCE) Single Unit, RCE Multiple Units, Backpropagation, Tree Classifier using hyperplane separation, Tree Classifier using Center-Radius decision surface. The 60-Pin data is the data obtained directly from the engine, the DCL (Data Communication Link) data comes through the control microprocessor on a multiplexed two-wire link. Note that RCE-Multiple requires a priori knowledge about the problem which was unavailable for the DCL data and that the complete statistical testing of backpropagation was impractical due to the length of time required to train each network.

We have examined this issue of real–time diagnostics as it applies to engine misfire detection and identification. Data from normal and misfiring engines was required from a wide range of conditions, a task which consumes hours of test track driving. The set of measurements taken is extensive in order to be certain that the information obtained is a superset of the minimum set of information required. Additionally, great care needed to be exercised in establishing the accuracy of a training set for supervised learning. Specifically, we needed to be certain that the only samples of misfires included were those intentionally created, and not those which occurred spontaneously and were presumably mislabeled as normal because no intentional fault was being introduced at that time. In order to accomplish this purification of the training set, one must either have an independent detector of misfires (none exists for a production engine operating in a vehicle) or go through an iterative process to remove all the data vectors misclassified as misfire from the data set after the network has completed training. Since the independent assessment of misfire cannot be obtained, we must accept the latter method which is not altogether satisfactory. The problem with the iterative method is that one must initially exclude from the training set exactly the type of event that the system is being trained to classify. We have to start with the assumption that any additional misfires, beyond the number we introduce, are classification errors. We then reserve the right to amend this judgment in light of further experience as we build up confidence in the classifier. The results of our initial studies is shown in Fig. 2. Here we can see that a backpropagation neural network can classify a broad range of engine operation correctly, and that the network does quite well when we broaden the operating range almost to the performance limits of the engine. The classification errors indicated in the more exhaustive study are misfires detected when no misfire was introduced. At this stage of our investigation we cannot be certain that these are real errors, they may very well be misfires occurring spontaneously or appearing as a result of an additional, unintentional induced misfire in an engine cycle following the one in which the fault was introduced.

The results shown in Fig. 2 therefore represent a conservative estimate of the classification errors that can be expected from tests of our engine data. The backpropagation network we constructed demonstrated that misfire detection and identification is attainable if adequate computation resources are available and appropriate

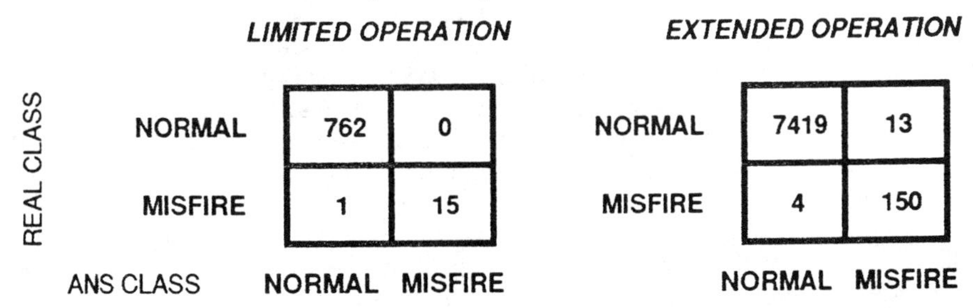

Figure 2. Classification accuracy of a backpropagation neural network trained on misfire data tabulated as confusion matrices. Data similar to that shown in Fig. 2 is collected over a modest range of dynamic conditions and then over a very wide range of conditions (potholed roads, severe accelerations and braking etc.) to estimate the performance limits of classifiers on such data. These misclassification rates are indicators of the best possible performance obtainable from such data, and therefore they are not reasonable estimates of what practical implementations of classifiers should produce.

care in obtaining a suitable training set is exercised. However. in order to make a neural net a practical means of performing this diagnosis aboard vehicles, we need to eliminate information from the input vector which has no effect on the classification accuracy; otherwise the computational task is hopelessly beyond the capability of the engine's microcontroller. This work is currently underway using a combination of a priori knowledge about the sensor information and principal component analysis of the data sets. Nonetheless, the neural network analysis has once again established that a solution exists and set standards for classification accuracy that we can hope to emulate with more compact forms of classifiers.

3 NEURAL NET CONTROL OF ACTIVE SUSPENSION

The empirical approach to developing solutions for diagnostic problems suggested that a similar tactic might be employed effectively to control problems for which developing acceptable controllers for non–linear dynamic systems by conventional means was a daunting task. We wished to explore the application of feed–forward networks to the problem of learning to control a model of a non–linear active suspension system. This problem was of interest because considerable effort had gone into designing controllers by conventional means and a performance comparison could readily be made. In addition, since active suspension systems are being investigated by a number of companies, we wished to examine the possibility of developing model–independent controllers for such systems, since effective hardware systems are usually available before thoroughly validated system models appear. The initial results of this investigation, outlined below, are quite encouraging.

A backpropagation network was trained to emulate an existing controller for an active suspension as a first exercise to establish some feel for the complexity of the network required to perform such a task. A complete description of the work can be found elsewhere (Hampo, 1990), but briefly, a network with several hidden nodes was trained to provide performance equivalent to the conventional controller. Since this exercise simply replicated an existing controller, the next step was to develop a controller in the absence of any conventional controller. Therefore, a system model with a novel non–linearity was developed and utilized to train a neural network to control such a plant. The architecture for this control system is similar to that used by Nygen and Widrow (Ngyen *et al*, 1990) and is described in detail elsewhere.(Hampo *et al*, 1991) Once again, a backpropagation network, with only 2 hidden nodes, was trained to provide an satisfactory performance in controlling the suspension system simulation running on a workstation. This small network learned the task with less than 1000 training vectors, the equivalent of less than 100 feet of bumpy road.

Finally, we examined the performance of the neural network on the same plant, but without explicit use of the plant model in the control architecture. In this scheme, the output error is derived from the difference between the observed performance and the desired performance produced by a cost function based upon conventional measures of suspension performance. In this Cost Function architecture, networks of similar size were readily trained to control non–linear plants and attain performance equivalent to conventional controllers hand–tuned for such plants. Controllers developed in this manner provide a flexible means of approaching the problem of investigating tradeoffs between the conflicting demands made on such suspension systems. These demands include ride quality, vehicle control, and energy management. This control architecture is being applied both to simulations of new systems and to actual, un-modeled hardware rigs to expedite prototype development.

4 CONCLUSIONS

This brief summary of our investigations has shown that neural networks play an important role in the development both of classification systems for diagnosis of faults in control systems and of controllers for practical non-linear plants. In these tasks, neural networks must compete with conventional methods. Conventional methods, although endowed with a more thorough analytic understanding, have usually failed to provide acceptable solutions to the problems we encountered as readily as have the neural network methods. Therefore, the ANS methods have a crucial role in developing solutions. Although neural networks provide these solutions expeditiously, we are just beginning to understand how these solutions arise. The growth of this understanding will determine the role neural networks play in the deployed implementations of these solutions.

References

1. P.S. Min, "Detection of Incipient Failures in Dynamic Systems", Ph.D. Thesis, University of Michigan, 1987.

2. M.K. Liubakka, G. Rizzoni, W.B. Ribbens and K.A. Marko, "Failure Detection Algorithms Applied to Control System Design for Improved Diagnostics and Reliability", SAE Paper #880726, Detroit, Michigan, 1988.

3. G. Rizzoni, R. Hampo, M.K. Liubakka and K.A. Marko, "Real-Time Detection Filters for On-Board Diagnosis of Incipient Failures", SAE Paper #890763, 1989.

4. K.A. Marko, J. James, J. Dosdall and J. Murphy, "Automotive Control System Diagnostics Using Neural Nets for Rapid Classification of Large Data Sets", Proceedings IJCNN, II-13, Washington, D.C., 1989.

5. K.A. Marko, L.A. Feldkamp and G.V. Puskorius, "Automotive Diagnostics Using Trainable Classifiers: Statistical Testing and Paradigm Selection", Proceedings IJCNN, I-33, San Diego, California, 1990.

6. Sholom Weiss and Casimir Kulikowski, "Computer Systems That Learn", Morgan Kaufman, San Mateo, California, 1990.

7. R.J. Hampo, "Neural Net Control of an Active Suspension System", M.S. Thesis, University of Michigan, 1990.

8. D. Ngyen and B. Widrow, "The Truck-Backer Upper: An Example of Self-Learning in Neural Networks", in Neural Networks for Control, ed. W.T. Miller, MIT Press, Cambridge, Massachusetts, 1990.

9. R.J. Hampo and K.A. Marko, "Neural Net Architectures for Active Suspension Control", paper submitted to IJCNN, Seattle, Washington, 1991.

Lg DEPTH ESTIMATION AND RIPPLE FIRE CHARACTERIZATION USING ARTIFICIAL NEURAL NETWORKS

John L. Perry and Douglas R. Baumgardt
ENSCO, Inc.
Signal Analysis and Systems Division
5400 Port Royal Road
Springfield, Virginia 22151
(703) 321-9000, perry@dewey.css.gov

Abstract

This study has demonstrated how artificial neural networks (ANNs) can be used to characterize seismic sources using high-frequency regional seismic data. We have taken the novel approach of using ANNs as a research tool for obtaining seismic source information, specifically depth of focus for earthquakes and ripple-fire characteristics for economic blasts, rather than as just a feature classifier between earthquake and explosion populations. Overall, we have found that ANNs have potential applications to seismic event characterization and identification, beyond just as a feature classifier. In future studies, these techniques should be applied to actual data of regional seismic events recorded at the new regional seismic arrays. The results of this study indicates that an ANN should be evaluated as part of an operational seismic event identification system.

1 INTRODUCTION

1.1 NEURAL NETWORKS FOR SEISMIC SOURCE ANALYSIS

In this study, we have explored the application of artificial neural networks (ANNs) for the characterization of seismic sources for the purpose of distinguishing between explosions and earthquakes. ANNs have usually been used as pattern matching algorithms, and recent studies have applied ANNs to standard classification between classes of earthquakes and explosions using waveform features (Dowla, et al, 1989), (Dysart and Pulli, 1990). However, in considering the current state-of-the-art in seismic event identification, we believe the most challenging problem is not to develop a superior classification method, but rather, to have a better understanding of the physics of seismic source and regional signal propagation.

Our approach to the problem has been to use ANN technology as a research tool for obtaining a better understanding of the phenomenology behind regional discrimination, with emphasis on high-frequency regional array data, as well as using ANNs as a pattern classifier. We have explored two applications of ANNs to seismic source characterization: (1) the use of ANNs for depth characterization and (2) the recognition of ripple-firing effects in economic explosions.

In the first study, we explored the possible use of the Lg cross-coherence matrix, measured at a regional array, as a "hidden discriminant" for event depth of focus. In the second study, we experimented with applying ANNs to the recognition of ripple-fire effects in the spectra of regional phases. Moreover, we also investigated how a small (around 5 Kt yield) possibly decoupled nuclear explosion, detonated as part of a ripple-fire sequence, would affect the spectral modulations observed at regional distances and how these effects could be identified by the ANN.

1.2 ANN DESCRIPTION

MLP Architecture: The ANN that we used was a multilayer perceptron (MLP) architecture with a backpropagation training algorithm (Rumelhart, et al, 1986). The input layer is fully connected to the hidden layer, which is fully connected to the output layer. There are no connections within an individual layer. Each node communicates with another node through a weighted connection. Associated with each connection is a weight connecting input node to hidden node, and a weight connecting hidden node to output node. The output of "activation level" of a particular node is defined as the linear weighted sum of all its inputs. For an MLP, a sigmoidal transformation is applied to this weighted sum. Two layers of our network have activation levels.

MLP Training: The MLP uses a backpropagation training algorithm which employs an iterating process where an output error signal is propagated back through the network and used to modify weight values. Training involves presenting sweeps of input patterns to the network and backpropagating the error until it is minimized. It is the weight values that represent a trained network and which can be used in the recognition/classification phase.

MLP Recognition: Recognition, on the other hand, involves presenting a pattern to a trained network and propagating node activation levels uni-directionally from the input layer, through the hidden layer(s), to the output layer, and then selecting the class corresponding to the highest output (activation) signal.

2 Lg DEPTH ESTIMATION

In theory, the Lg phase, which is often the largest regional phase on the seismogram, should provide depth information because Lg results from the superposition of numerous normal modes in the crust, whose excitation is highly depth dependent. Some studies have shown that Lg amplitudes do depend on depth (Der and Baumgardt, 1989). However, the precise dependency of Lg amplitude on depth has been hard to establish because other effects in the crustal model, such as anelastic attenuation, can also affect the Lg wave amplitude.

In this study, we have considered if the Lg coherence, measured across a regional array, might show depth dependency. This idea is based on the fact that all the normal modes which comprise Lg propagate at different phase velocities. For multilayered media, the normal modes will have frequency-dependent phase velocities because of dispersion. Our method for studying this dependency is a neural network implementation of a technique, called *matched field processing*, which has been used in underwater acoustics for source water-depth estimation (Bucker, 1976), (Baggeroer, et al, 1988). This method consists of computing the spectral matrix of an emitted signal, in our case, Lg, and comparing it against the same spectral matrix for master events at different depths. In the past, various optimal methods have been developed for the matching process. In our study, we have investigated using a neural network to accomplish the matching.

2.1 SPECTRAL MATRIX CALCULATION AND MATCHED FIELD PROCESSING

The following is a description of how the spectral matrix is computed. First, the synthetic seismograms for each of the nine elements of the hypothetical array are Fourier transformed in some time window. If $S_i(\omega)$ is the Fourier transform of a time window for the i the channel, then, the spectral matrix is written as, $H_{ij}(\omega) = S_i(\omega) S_j^*(\omega)$, where $S_i(\omega) = A_i e^{-j[\omega t + \Phi_i(\omega)]}$, the index j is the complex number, ϕ_i is the phase angle, and the * represents complex transpose. The elements, a_{ik} of the spectral matrix can be written as $a_{ik}(\omega) = A_i A_k e^{-j[\Phi_i - \Phi_k]}$ where the exponential phase shift term is $\Phi_i(\omega) - \Phi_k(\omega) = -\frac{\omega}{c_n(\omega)}(x_i - x_k) = -\omega \tau_{ik}^n(\omega)$. $c_n(\omega)$ represents the phase velocity for mode n, which is a function of frequency because of dispersion, $x_i - x_k$ is the spatial separation of the i th and k th channels of the array, and $\tau_{ik}^n(\omega)$ is the time shift of mode n at frequency ω across the two channels. The product of the synthetic eigenfunctions, A_i, and thus, the spectral matrix terms, are functions of source depth and model parameters.

The spectral matrix, $H_{ij}(\omega)$, can be computed for an entire synthetic waveform or for a window on a part of the waveform. The elements of the spectral matrix can be normalized by inter- or intra- window normalization so that its values range from 0 to 1.

2.2 ANN - MATCHED FIELD DEPTH ESTIMATION

Two different depth studies were performed during this effort. The first study evaluated using the ANN to classify deep (greater than 4 kilometers) vs. shallow (less than 4 kilometers) seismic events. The number of input nodes equaled the number of points in the spectral matrix which was 1620 (36 data points x 45 spectral elements after smoothing). The number of output nodes was dependent on the type of classification we wanted to perform. For the shallow-deep discrimination, we only required two output nodes, one for each class. Training the ANN involved compiling a training (exemplar) set of spectral matrices for various shallow and deep events and then presenting the training set to the ANN.

In the second study, we investigated if the ANN could be used to classify seismic events at different depths. Again, we used five windows on the Lg phase and implemented the interwindow and intrawindow normalization procedure. The second network was trained with a seven-element depth vector, whose elements represent the depths of 1, 3, 6, 9, 12, 16, and 20 kilometers.

3 RIPPLE-FIRE CHARACTERIZATION

In this study, we wanted to determine if spectral modulations could be recognized by the neural network and if they could be attached to concepts relating to the source parameters of ripple-fired events. Previous studies have demonstrated how such patterns could be found by looking for time-independent spectral modulations (Baumgardt and Ziegler, 1989), (Hedlin, et al, 1990). In this study, we assumed such a pattern has been found and that the input to the ANN is one of the time-independent spectra. An additional issue we considered was whether it would be possible to hide a nuclear explosion in the ripple-fire pattern, and whether or not such a pattern might be recognizable by an ANN. In this study, as in the previous depth characterization study, we relied entirely on simulated data for training and test.

3.1 ANN - RIPPLE FIRE CHARACTERIZATION

We performed two ripple-fired studies which were designed to extract different parameters from the ripple-fired events. The two studies characterized the following parameters: 1) time delay (Experiment A), and 2) normal vs. anomalous (Experiment B). The purpose of the time delay study was to estimate the time delay between explosions irrespective of the number of explosions. The goal of the second study was to determine if the ANN could extract a "normal" ripple-fired explosion from a simulated nuclear explosion buried in a ripple-fired event.

The input nodes to all three networks consisted of the elements of the seismic spectra which had 256 data points, covering the frequency range of 0 to 20 Hz. All weights were initialized to random values in the range of [-0.5, 0.5] and all networks had their momentum term set to 0.9. The number of hidden units, learning rate, and number of output nodes varied between each experiment.

In Experiment A, the number of hidden units was 24, and we used a learning rate of 0.2. We used seven output nodes to represent seven different classes with time delays of 37.5, 62.5, 87.5, 112.5, 137.5, 162.5, and 187.5 ms. These delay times are the centers of the following delay time bins: 25-50 ms, 50-75 ms, 75-100 ms, 100-125 ms, 125-150 ms, 150-175 ms, and 175-200 ms. We used five examples of each class for training derived by varying the time delay by ±5 msec. Training involved presenting the five exemplars for each class to the ANN until the squared error approached zero, as we did in the depth discrimination study. The ANN was trained to return a high activation level in the bin closest to the delay time of the ripple-fire.

In Experiment B, we wanted to determine if the ANN could discern between normal and anomalous ripple-fire patterns. The ANN was trained with 50 hidden units and a learning rate of 0.1. There were 36 exemplars of each class, which resulted from all combinations of six time delays of 5, 6, 7, 8, 9, and 10 ms between individual shots and six time delays of 5, 6, 7, 8, 9, and 10 ms between rows of shots. Each time delay was also varied ±1.0 ms to simulate the effect of errors in the blasting delays.

Two output nodes were defined which represent *anomalous* or *normal* ripple-fire. The *normal* ripple-fire class represented all the simulations done for the triangular pattern. We assumed each shot had a yield of 1000 kg. The *anomalous* class were all the simulations for when the last row of 10 shots was replaced with a single large explosion of 10,000 kg. The ANN was then trained to produce a high activation level for either of these classes depending on which kind of event it was presented. The effect of the single large explosion signal was to wash out the scalloping pattern produced by the ripple-fired explosions. We trained the ANN with normal ripple-fired patterns, with no embedded nuclear explosions, and anomalous patterns, with an embedded nuclear explosion.

4 RESULTS

4.1 RESULTS OF DEPTH STUDY

In our first study, we wanted to determine if the network could learn the simple concepts of *shallow* and *deep* from Lg synthetics when presented with only a small number of exemplar patterns. We presented the ANN with four depths, 1, 2, 12, and 20 km, and trained the network to recognize the first two as shallow and the second two as deep. We then presented the network with the rest of the synthetics, including synthetics for depths the ANN had not seen in training.

The results of the shallow-deep discrimination study are shown in Table 1. The table shows the results for both the interwindow and intrawindow normalization procedures. The test set used to generate these results were also synthetically generated events that were either less than 4 km (shallow) or greater than 4 km (deep). Our criteria for a correct match was if the correct output node had an activation level that was 0.4 or more above the other output node's activation. This is a very conservative threshold criteria, which is evident from the number of undecided values. However, the results do indicate that the percent of incorrect classifications was only 5.0% for the intrawindow case and 8.3% for the interwindow case. The percent of correct classification (PCC) for the intrawindow case was 50% and the PCC for the interwindow case was 58.3%. The network appeared to be well trained, relative to their squared error values for this study. Using a less conservative correct match criteria, where the correct output node only had to be larger than the other output node's activation, the PCC was 88.3% for the intrawindow case and 93.3% for the interwindow case.

Depth (km.)	Intra-Window / Inter-Window					
	correct		incorrect		undecided	
	0.4 criterion	greatest activation	0.4 criterion	greatest activation	0.4 criterion	greatest activation
3	2/3	5/5	0/0	0/0	3/2	0/0
4	1/2	3/3	0/2	0/2	4/1	2/0
5	2/3	4/5	0/0	0/0	3/2	1/0
6	4/3	5/5	0/1	0/0	1/1	0/0
7	2/4	4/5	1/0	1/0	2/1	0/0
8	3/2	5/5	0/0	0/0	2/3	0/0
9	3/5	4/5	1/0	0/0	1/0	1/0
10	3/3	5/5	0/0	0/0	2/2	0/0
11	1/2	4/3	1/2	1/2	3/1	0/0
13	2/2	5/5	0/0	0/0	3/3	0/0
14	4/4	5/5	0/0	0/0	1/1	0/0
15	3/2	4/5	0/0	0/0	2/3	1/0
Total	30/35	53/56	3/5	2/4	27/20	5/0

Table 1: Results of ANN for Shallow-Deep Discrimination.

4.2 RESULTS OF THE RIPPLE-FIRED STUDY

Linear Shot Patterns (Experiment A)

Table 2 summarizes all the results for the time-delay ripple-fired classification study performed during Experiment A. The table shows both two-shot training and a two- and three-shot training cases. The test set for both cases were spectra that had time delays that were in a ±5 ms range of the target time delay pattern. We set two criteria for PCC for the two-shot case. The first was that the activation level for the correct output node be larger than the activation levels of the other output nodes. This produced a PCC of 77.7%, with a 22.2% error rate and no undecided responses. All of the errors resulted from attempting to use the ANN to learn time delays from a three-shot pattern where the network was only trained on two-shot events. The second criterion was more conservative and required that the activation level of the correct output node be ≥ 0.5 than the other output nodes. This gave a PCC = 68.2%, an error percentage of 4.5%, although the number of undecided responses increased to 27.2%. Again, all the errors resulted from expecting the ANN to generalize to three-shot events from only being trained with two-shot patterns. Finally, the results for the two- and three-shot training case were much more impressive. Using both threshold criteria, the ANN achieved a PCC of 100%.

Test Set *	Threshold Criteria 0.0 / 0.5		
	correct	incorrect	undecided
Case A	7 / 6	0 / 0	0 / 1
Case B	8 / 7	0 / 0	0 / 1
3 shots	3 / 2	4 / 1	0 / 4
Total	18 / 15	4 / 1	0 / 6

* (Trained with a 2-shot pattern)

Test Set *	Threshold Criteria 0.0 / 0.5		
	correct	incorrect	undecided
Case A	7 / 7	0 / 0	0 / 0
Case B	8 / 8	0 / 0	0 / 0
3 shots	7 / 7	0 / 0	0 / 0
Total	22 / 22	0 / 0	0 / 0

* (Trained with a 2- and 3-shot pattern)

Table 2: Results of ANN for Time-Delay Ripple-Fired Discrimination

Triangular Shot Patterns - Normal Versus Anomalous (Experiment B)

Table 3 depicts the results of Experiment B for the normal vs. anomalous study. The threshold criteria for the target output node compared to the other output nodes was 0.4. Again, the test set consisted of time delays that were within ±5 ms of the target time delay pattern. The PCC was 69.4%, the error percentage was 2.7%, and the percentage of undecided responses was 27.7%. As evident from the table, the majority of undecided responses were generated from attempting to classify the anomalous event.

Test Set	Threshold Criteria 0.4		
	correct	incorrect	undecided
Normal	31	1	4
Anomalous	19	1	16
Total	50	2	20

Table 3: Results of ANN for Normal vs. Anomalous Ripple-Fired Discrimination

5 CONCLUSIONS

This study has shown that ANNs can be used to characterize seismic waveform patterns for the purpose of characterizing depth of focus, from Lg spectral matrices, and for recognizing ripple-fire patterns from spectral modulations. However, we were only able to analyze the results for simulated input data. In future studies, we intend to use real data as input.

We have demonstrated that events can be classed as shallow or deep on the basis of the Lg spectral matrix and that the ANN provided a convenient and robust methodology for matching spectral matrices. The fact that we obtained nearly the same recognition performance for interwindow and intrawindow normalizations shows that the Lg spectral matrix does in fact contain significant information about the depth of focus of a seismic event, at least for theoretically derived synthetic cases.

The results for the ripple-fire recognition study were very encouraging. We found that neural networks could easily be trained to recognize many different ripple-fire patterns. For a given blasting region, a neural network could be trained to recognize the usual, routine ripple-fire patterns generally used in the region. We have shown that it should be possible to identify unusual or anomalous ripple-fire patterns due to attempts to include a large decoupled nuclear explosion in with an ordinary ripple-fire sequence.

References

Baggeroer, A.M., W.A. Kuperman, and H. Schmidt (1988). Matched field processing: source localization in correlated noise as optimum parameter estimation, *J. Acoust. Soc. Am.*, **83**, 571-587.

Baumgardt, D.R. and K.A. Ziegler (1989). Automatic recognition of economic and underwater blasts using regional array data. *Unpublished report to Science Applications Incorporated, 11-880085-51.*

Bucker, H.P. (1976). Use of calculated sound fields and matched-field detection to locate sound sources in shallow water, *J. Acoust. Soc. Am.*, **59**, 368-373.

Der, Z.A. and D.R. Baumgardt (1989). Effect of source depth on the Lg phase, DARPA/AFTAC Research Review, November 1989.

Dowla, F.U., S.R. Taylor, and R.W. Anderson (1989). Seismic discrimination with artificial neural networks: preliminary results with regional spectral data, UCRL-102310, Lawrence Livermore National Laboratory, Livermore, CA.

Dysart, P.S. and J.J. Pulli (1990). Regional seismic event classification at the NORESS array; seismological measurements and the use of trained neural networks, abstract in *Program, Symposium on Regional Seismic Arrays and Nuclear Test Ban Verification*, Oslo, Norway, 14-17 February 1990.

Hedlin, M.A.H., J.B. Minster, J.A. Orcutt (1990). An automatic means to discriminate between earthquakes and quarry blasts, submitted to *Bull. Seism. Soc. Am.*

Rumelhart, D.E., Hinton, G.E., Williams, R.J. (1986). Learning internal representations by error propagation", in *Parallel Distributed Processing*, **1**, MIT Press, Cambridge, MA.

A B-P ANN Commodity Trader

Joseph E. Collard
Martingale Research Corporation
100 Allentown Pkwy., Suite 211
Allen, Texas 75002

Abstract

An Artificial Neural Network (ANN) is trained to recognize a buy/sell (long/short) pattern for a particular commodity future contract. The Back-Propagation of errors algorithm was used to encode the relationship between the Long/Short desired output and 18 fundamental variables plus 6 (or 18) technical variables into the ANN. Trained on one year of past data the ANN is able to predict long/short market positions for 9 months in the future that would have made $10,301 profit on an investment of less than $1000.

1 INTRODUCTION

An Artificial Neural Network (ANN) is trained to recognize a long/short pattern for a particular commodity future contract. The Back-Propagation of errors algorithm was used to encode the relationship between the Long/Short desired output and 18 fundamental variables plus 6 (or 18) technical variables into the ANN.

2 NETWORK ARCHITECTURE

The ANNs used were simple, feed forward, single hidden layer networks with no input units, N hidden units and one output unit. See Figure 1. N varied from six (6) through sixteen (16) hidden units.

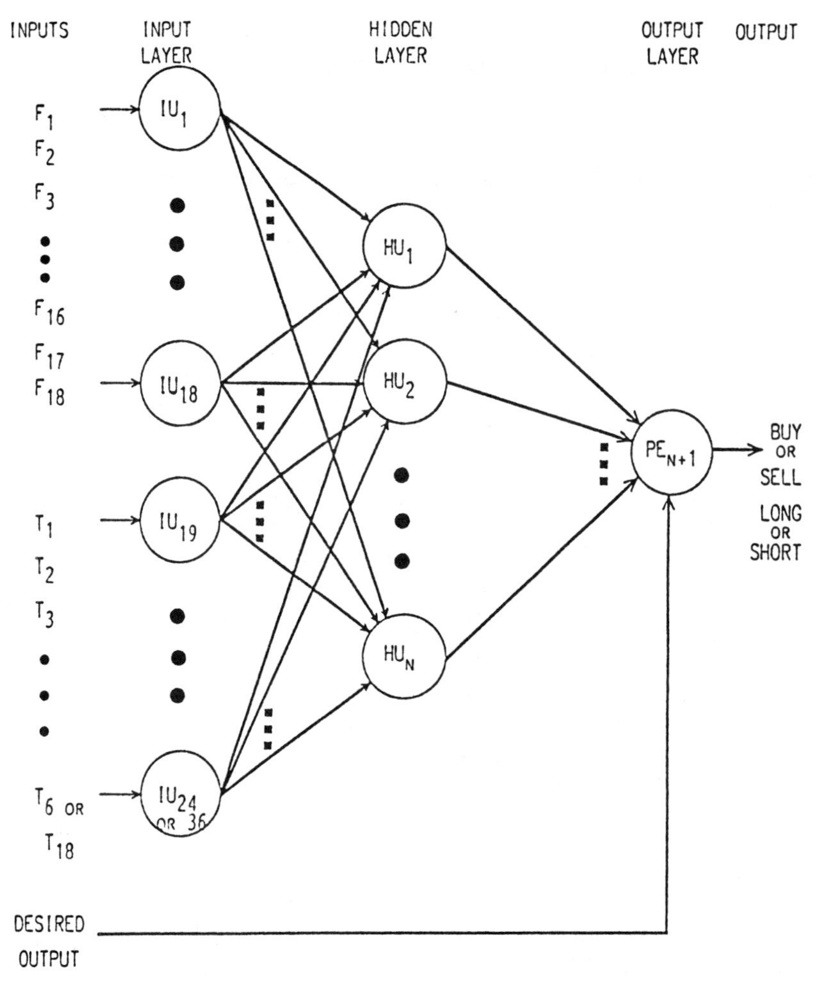

Figure 1. The Network Architecture

3 TRAINING PROCEDURE

Back Propagation of Errors Algorithm: The ANN was trained using the well known ANN training algorithm called Back Propagation of Errors which will not be elaborated on here.

A Few Mods to the Algorithm: We are using the algorithm above with three changes. The changes, when implemented and tested on the standard exclusive-or problem, resulted in a trained, one hidden unit network after 60-70 passes through the 4 pattern vectors. This compares to the 245 passes cited by Rumelhart [2]. Even with a 32 hidden unit network, Yves found the average number of passes to be 120 [2].

The modifications to standard back propagation are:

1. Minimum Slope Term in the Derivative of the Activation Function [John Denker at Bell Labs].
2. Using the Optional Momentum Term [2].
3. Weight change frequency [1].

4 DATA

In all cases, the six market technical variables (Open, High, Low, Close, Open Interest and Volume) were that trading day's data for the "front month" commodity contract (roughly speaking, the most active month's commodity contract).

The first set of training data consisted of 105 or 143 "high confidence" trading days in 1988. Each trading day had associated with it a twenty-five component pattern vector (25-vector) consisting of eighteen fundamental variables, such as weather indicators and seasonal indicators, plus the six market technical variables for the trading day, and finally, the EXPERT's hindsight long/short position. The test data for these networks was all 253 25-vectors in 1988.

The next training data set consisted of all 253 trading days in 1988. Again each trading day had associated with it a 25-vector consisting of the same eighteen fundamental variables plus the six market technical variables and finally, the EXPERT's long/short position. The test set for these networks consisted of 25-vectors from the first 205 trading days in 1989.

Finally, the last set of training data consisted of the last 251 trading days in 1988. For this set each trading day had associated with it a 37 component pattern vector (37-vector) consisting of the same eighteen fundamental variables plus six market technical variables for that trading day, six market technical variables for the previous trading day, six market technical variables for the two days previous trading day, and finally, the EXPERT's long/short position. The test set for these networks consisted of 37-vectors from the first 205 trading days in 1989.

5 RESULTS

The results for 7 trained networks are summarized in Table 1.

Table 1. Study Results

#	SIZE/IN	TRAIN.	%	@ ε-XPT	PROFIT/RTS	TEST	PROFIT/RTS
005	6-1 /24	105-'88	100	@.125		253-'88	76%
006	6-1 /24	143-'88	99	@.125-1		253-'88	82%
Targets >>>		253-'88	---------		$25,296/10	205-'89	$14,596/ 6
009	10-1/24	253-'88	98	@ .25-4	$24,173/14	205-'89	$ 7,272/ 6
010	6-1 /24	105-'88	100	@ .1	$17,534/13	253-'88	80%
Targets >>>		251-'88	---------		$24,819/10	205-'89	$14,596/ 6
011	10-1/36	251-'88	98	@ .25-4	$23,370/14	205-'89	$ 7,272/ 6
012	13-1/36	251-'88	97	@ .25-7	$22,965/12	205-'89	$ 6,554/14
013	16-1/36	251-'88	99	@ .25-3	$22,495/12	205-'89	$10,301/19

The column headings for Table 1 have the following meanings:

Heading	Meaning
#	The numerical designation of the Network.
Size/In	The hidden-output layer dimensions and the number of inputs to the network.
Train.	The number of days and year of the training set.
% @ ε-Xpt	The percent of the training data encoded in the network at less than ε error - the number of days not encoded.
Profit RTs	The profit computed for the training or test set and how many round turns (RTs) it required for that profit. Or, if the profit calculation was not yet available, then the percent the network is in agreement with the EXPERT.
Test set	The number of trading days/year of the test set.

Figure 2 shows how well the 013 network agrees with its training set's long/short positions. The NET 19 INPUT curve is the commodities price curve for 1988's 251 trading days.

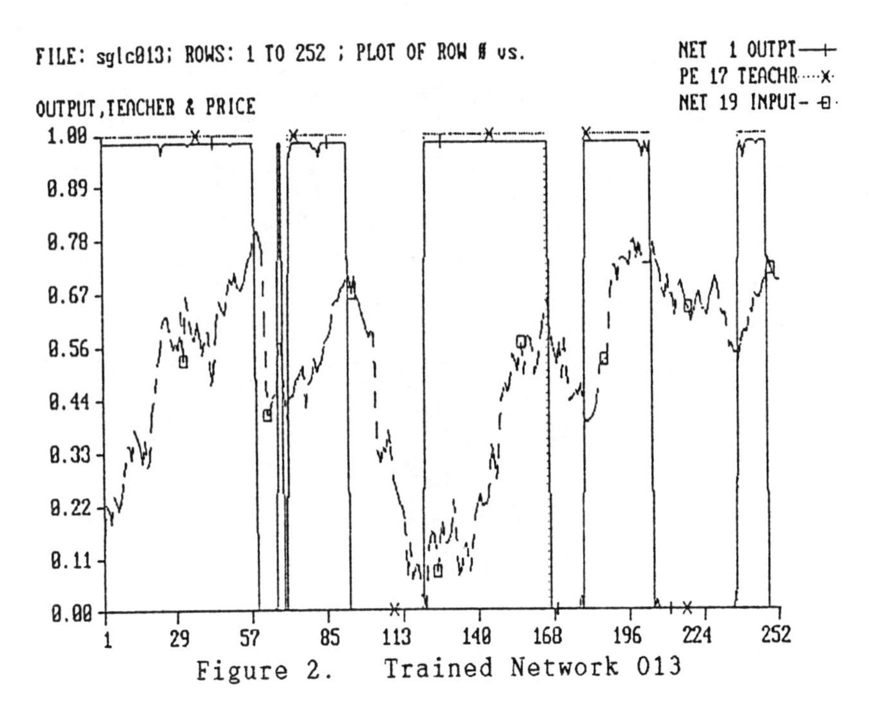

Figure 2. Trained Network 013

Figure 3 shows the corresponding profit plot on the training data for both the EXPERT and network 013.

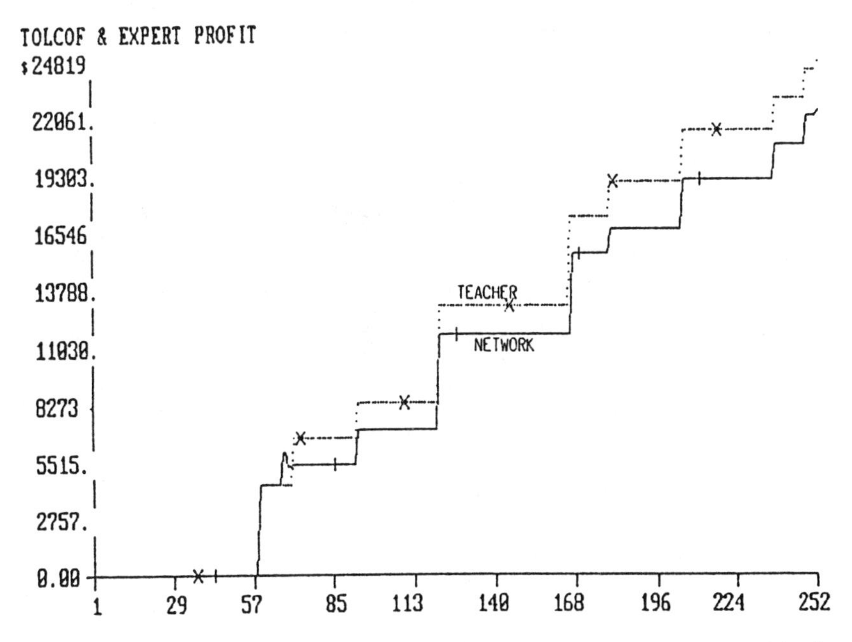

Figure 3. Network 013's and EXPERT's Profit for 1988 data

Figure 4 is the profit plot for the network when tested on the first 205 trading days in 1989. Two significant features should be noted in Figure 4. The network's profit step function is almost always increasing. The profit is never negative.

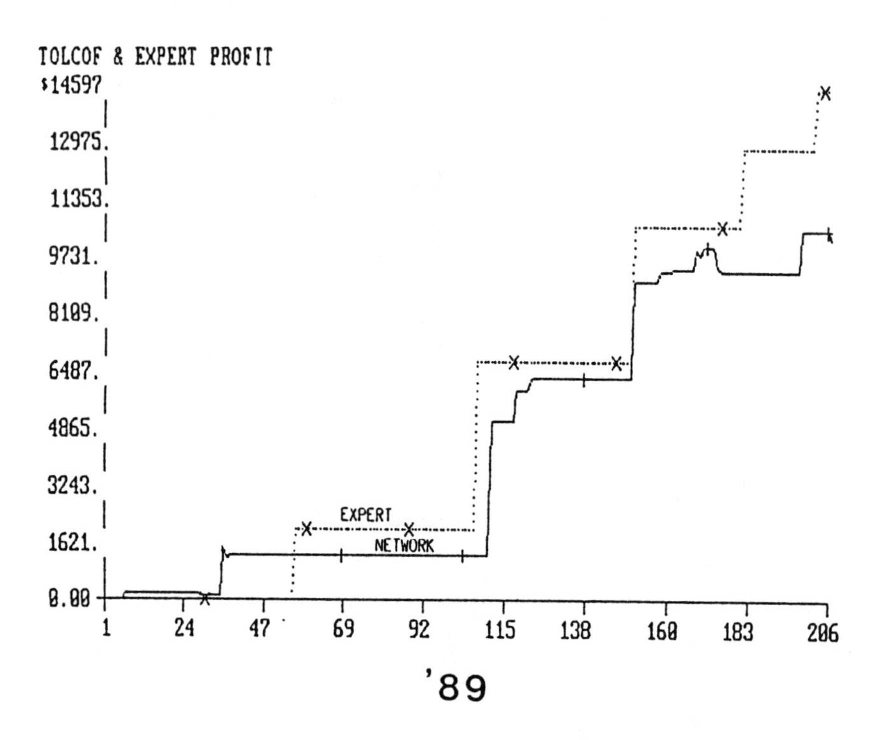

Figure 4. Network 013's and EXPERT's Profit for 1989 data

6 REFERENCES

1. Pao, Y.- H., Adaptive Pattern Recognition and Neural Networks, Addison Wesley, 1989.
2. Rumelhart, D., and McClelland, J., Parallel Distributed Processing, MIT Press, 1986.

Integrated Segmentation and Recognition of Hand-Printed Numerals

James D. Keeler*
MCC
3500 W. Balcones Ctr. Dr.
Austin, TX 78759

David E. Rumelhart
Psychology Department
Stanford University
Stanford, CA 94305

Wee-Kheng Leow
MCC and
University of Texas
Austin, TX 78759

Abstract

Neural network algorithms have proven useful for recognition of individual, segmented characters. However, their recognition accuracy has been limited by the accuracy of the underlying segmentation algorithm. Conventional, rule-based segmentation algorithms encounter difficulty if the characters are touching, broken, or noisy. The problem in these situations is that often one cannot properly segment a character until it is recognized yet one cannot properly recognize a character until it is segmented. We present here a neural network algorithm that simultaneously segments and recognizes in an integrated system. This algorithm has several novel features: it uses a supervised learning algorithm (backpropagation), but is able to take position-independent information as targets and self-organize the activities of the units in a competitive fashion to infer the positional information. We demonstrate this ability with overlapping hand-printed numerals.

1 INTRODUCTION

A major problem with standard backpropagation algorithms for pattern recognition is that they seem to require carefully segmented and localized input patterns for training. This is a problem for two reasons: first, it is often a labor intensive task to provide this information and second, the decision as to how to segment often depends on prior recognition. However, we describe below a neural network design and corresponding backpropagation learning algorithm that learns to simultane-

*Reprint requests: Jim Keeler, keeler@mcc.com or coila@mcc.com

ously segment and identify a pattern. [1]

There are two important aspects to many pattern recognition problems that we have built directly into our network and learning algorithm. The first is that the exact location of the pattern, in space or time, is irrelevant to the classification of the pattern; it should be recognized as a member of the same class wherever or whenever it occurs. This suggests that we build translation independence directly into our network. The second aspect is that feedback about *whether* or not a pattern of a particular class is present is all that should be required for training; information about the exact location and relationship to other patterns should not be required. The target information, thus, does not include information about *where* the patterns occur, only about *whether* a particular pattern occurs.

We have incorporated two design principles into our network to deal with these problems. The first is to build translation independence into the network by using linked local receptive fields. The second is to build a fixed "forward model" (c.f. Jordan and Rumelhart, 1990) which translates a location-specific recognition process into a location-independent output value. This output gives rise to a non-specific error signal which is propagated back through this fixed network to train the underlying location-specific network.

2 NETWORK ARCHITECTURE AND ALGORITHM

The basic organization of the network is illustrated in Figure 1. In the case of character recognition, the input consists of a set of pixels over which the stimulus patterns are displayed. We designate the stimulus pattern by the vector $\vec{X}$. In general, we assume that any character can be presented in any position and that characters may overlap. The input image then projects to a set of hidden units which learn to abstract features from the input field. These feature abstraction units are organized into sheets, one for each feature type. Each unit within a sheet is constrained to have the same weights as every other unit in the sheet (to enforce translational invariance). This is the same method used by Rumelhart, Hinton and Williams (1986) in solving the so-called T/C problem and the one used by LeCun et al. (1990) in their work on ZIP-code recognition.

We let the activation value of hidden unit of type i at location j be a logistic sigmoidal function of its net input and designate it h_{ij}. We interpret h_{ij} as the probability that feature f_i is present in the input at position j. The hidden units then project onto a set of sheets of position-specific character recognition units, one sheet for each character type. These units have exponential activation functions and each unit in the sheet receives inputs from a local receptive field block of feature detection units as shown in Figure 1. As with the hidden units, the weights in each exponential unit sheet are linked, enforcing translational invariance. We designate as χ_{ij} the activation of the unit for detecting character i at location j, and define

[1] The algorithm and network design presented here was first proposed by Rumelhart in a presentation entitled "Learning and Generalization in Multilayer networks" given at the NATO Advanced Research Workshop on Neuro Computing, Algorithms, Architectures and Applications held in Les Arcs, France in February, 1989. The algorithm can be viewed as a generalization and refinement of the TDNN of Lang, Hinton, & Waibel, 1990.

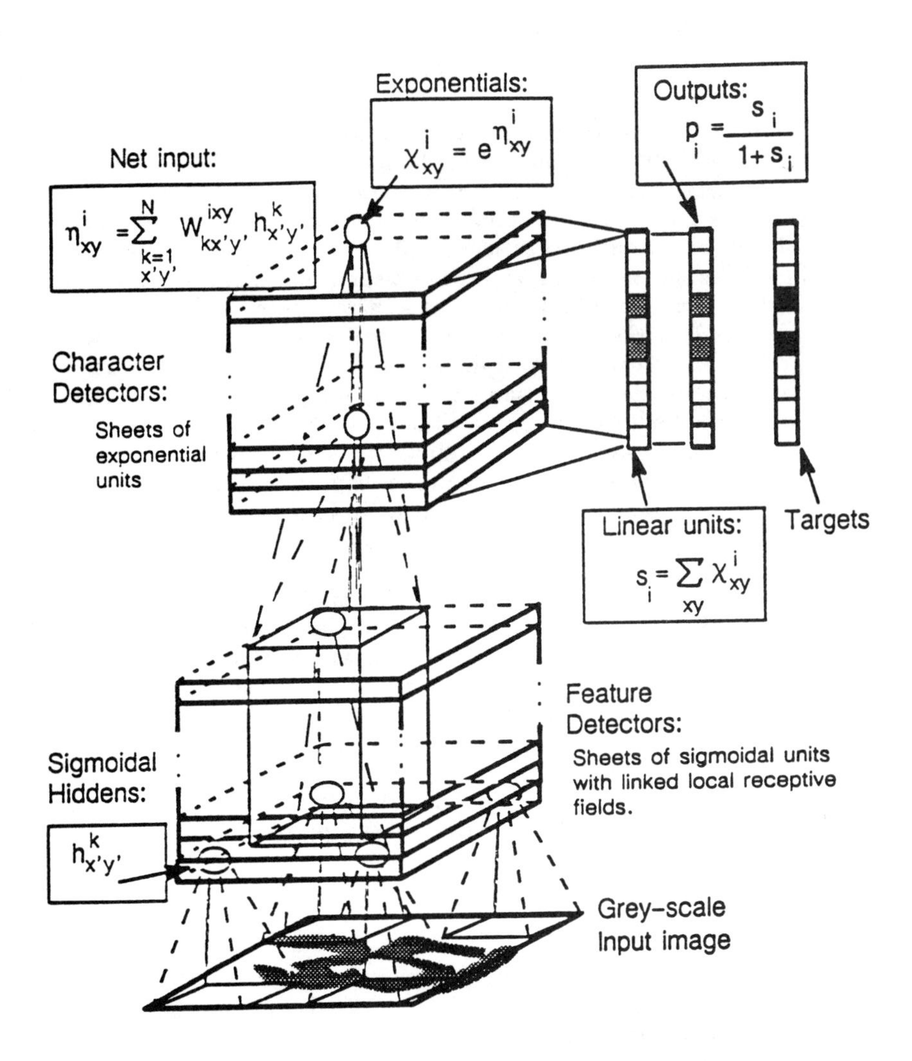

Figure 1: The Integrated Segementation and Recognition (ISR) network. The input image may contain several characters and is presented to the network in a two-dimensional array of grey-scale values. Units in the first block $h^k_{x'y'}$ have linked-local receptive fields to the input image, and detect features of type k. The exponential units in the next block receive inputs from a local receptive field of hidden sigmoidal units. The weights $W^{ixy}_{kx'y'}$ connect the hidden unit $h^k_{x'y'}$ to the exponential unit χ^i_{xy}. The architecture enforces translational invariance across the sheets of units by linking the weights and shifting the receptive fields in each dimension. Finally, the activity in each individual sheet of exponential units is summed by the linear units s_i and converted to a probability p_i. The two-dimensional input image can be thought of as a one-dimensional vector $\vec{X}$ as discussed in the text. For notational convenience we used one-dimensional indices (j) in the text rather than two-dimensional (xy) as shown in the figure. All of the mathematics goes through if one replaces $j \leftrightarrow xy$.

$\chi_{ij} = e^{\eta_{ij}}$, where the net input to the unit is

$$\eta_{ij} = \sum_k w_{ik} h_{kj} + \beta_i \tag{1}$$

and w_{ik} is the weight from hidden unit h_{kj} to the detector χ_{ij}. As we argue in Keeler Rumelhart and Leow (1991), η_{ij} can usefully be interpreted as the logarithm of the likelihood ratio favoring the hypothesis that a character of type i is at location j of the input field. Since χ_{ij} is the exponential of η_{ij}, the χ units are to be interpreted as representing the likelihood ratios themselves. Thus, we can interpret the output of the χ units directly as the *evidence* favoring the assumption that there is a character of a particular type at a particular location. If we were willing and able to carefully segment the input and tell the network the exact location of each character, we could use a standard training technique to train the network to recognize characters at any location with any degree of overlap. However, we are interested in a training algorithm in which we don't have to provide the network with such specific training information. We are interested in simply telling the network which characters are present in the input – not where each character is. This approach saves tremendous time and effort in data preparation and labeling. To implement this idea, we have built an additional network which takes the output of the χ units and computes, through a fixed output network, the probability that a given character is present anywhere in the input field. We do this by adding two additional layers of units. The first layer of units, the S units, simply sum the activity of each sheet of the χ units. The activity of unit S_i can, under certain assumptions, be interpreted as the likelihood ratio that a character of type i occurred *anywhere* in the input field. Finally in the output layer, we convert the likelihood ratio into a probability by the formula

$$p_i = \frac{S_i}{1 + S_i}. \tag{2}$$

Thus, p_i is interpreted as representing directly the probability that character i occurred in the input field.

2.1 The learning Rule

On having set up our network, it is straight-forward to compute the derivative of the error function with respect to η_{ij}. We get a particularly simple learning rule if we let the objective function be the cross-entropy function,

$$l = \sum_i t_i \ln p_i + (1 - t_i) \ln(1 - p_i) \tag{3}$$

where t_i equals 1 if character i is presented and zero otherwise. In this case, we get the following rule:

$$\frac{\partial l}{\partial \eta_{ij}} = (t_i - p_i) \frac{\chi_{ij}}{\sum_k \chi_{ik}}. \tag{4}$$

It should be noted that this is a kind of *competitive* rule in which the learning is proportional to the relative strength of the activation at the unit at a particular location in the χ layer to the strength of activation in the entire layer. This is valid if we assume that either the character appears exactly once or not at all. This ratio is the conditional probability that the target was at position j under the assumption that the target was, in fact, presented. It is also possible to derive a learning rule for the case where more than one of the same character is present[3].

3 EXPERIMENTAL RESULTS

To investigate the ability of this network to simultaneously segment and recognize characters in an integrated system, we trained the network outlined in section 2 on a database of hand-printed numerals taken from financial documents. We used a training and test set of about 9,000 and 1,800 characters respectively. We placed pairs of these grey-scaled characters on the input plane at positions determined by a distance parameter which tells how far apart to place the centers of the characters. We used a distance parameter of 1.2 which indicates that the centers were about 1.2 characters apart with an added random displacement in the x and y dimensions by $\pm.25$ and ±0.15 of the leftmost character size respectively. With these parameters, the characters touch or overlap about 15% of the time. The network had 10 output units and the target was to turn on the units of the two characters in the input window, regardless of what order or position they occurred in. Thus the pair (3,5) has the same target as (5,3): $\vec{target} = (0001010000)$.

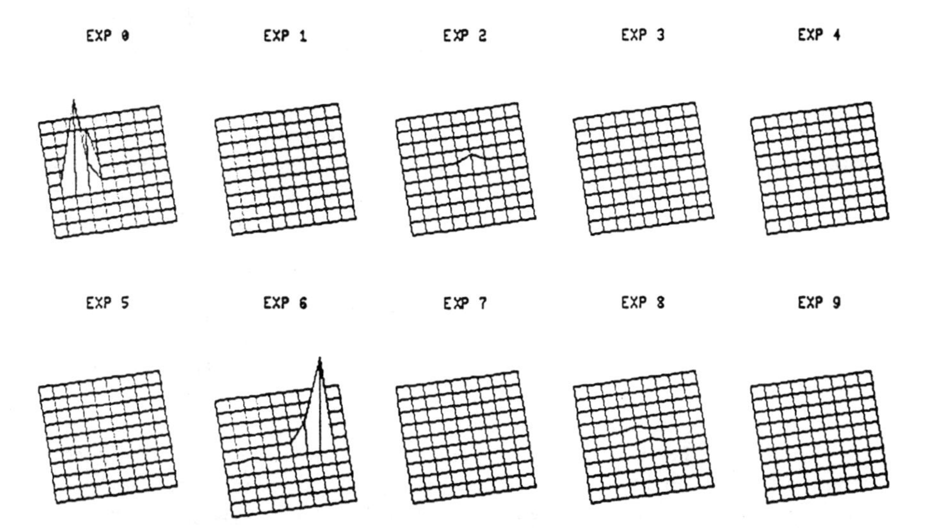

Figure 2: The ISR network's performance. This figure shows two touching characters (06, shown at left) in the input image and the corresponding activation of the sheets of exponential units. The network was never trained on these particular characters individually or as a pair, but gets the correct activation of greater than 0.9 on the 6 and 0.8 on the 0 with near 0.0 activation for all other outputs. Note the sharp peaks of activity in the 0 and 6 layers approximetely above the center of the characters, even though they are touching. In this case the maximum activity of the 6-sheet was about 14,000 and had to be scaled by a factor of about 70 to fit in the graph space. The maximum activity in the 0 sheet was approximately 196.

After training on several hundred thousand of the randomly sampled pairs of numbers from the 9,000, the network generalized correctly on about 81% of the pairs. This pair accuracy corresponds to a single-character recognition accuracy of about 90%. The network recognizes isolated single characters at an accuracy of about 95%. Note that this is an artificially generated data set, and by changing the distance parameter we can make the problem as simple or as difficult as we desire, up to the point where the characters overlap so much that a human cannot recognize them. Most conventional segmentation algorithms do not deal with touching characters, and so would presumably miss the vast majority of these characters. To see how overlap affects performance, we tested generalization in the same network on 100 pairs with the distance parameter lowered to 1.0 and 0.95. With a distance parameter of 1.0, the characters touch or overlap about 50% of the time. Of those, the network correctly identified 80%. Of the 20% that were missed, about 1/2 were unrecognizable by a human. With a distance parameter of 0.95, causing about 66% of the characters to touch, about 74% are correctly identified. As one expects, performance drops for smaller distance parameters.

The qualitative behavior of this system is quite interesting. As described in section 2, the learning rule for the exponential units contains a term that is competitive in nature. This term favors "winner-take-all" behavior for the units in that sheet in the sense that nearly equal activations are unstable under the learning rule: if one presents the same pattern again and again, the learning rule will cause one activation to grow or shrink away from the other at an exponetial rate. This causes self-organization to occur in the exponential sheets, and we would expect the exponential units to organize into highly-localized activations or "spikes" of activity on the appropriate exponential layers directly above the input characters. This is exactly the behavior that is observed in the trained network, as exemplified in Figure 2. In this figure we see two overlapping characters in the input image (06). The network generalized properly with output activity of about 0.8 for zero 0.99 for 6 and about 0.0 for everything else. Note that in the exponential layer, there are very sharp spikes of activity directly above the 0 and the 6 in the appropriate layers. Indeed, it has been our experience that even with quite noisy input images, the representation in the exponential layer is very localized, and we could presumably recover the positional information by examining the activity of the exponential units. We can thus think of these spikes in the exponential layer as "smart histograms": the exponential units in each sheet learn to look for specific combinations of features in the input layer and reject other combinations of inputs. This allows them to respond correctly even if there is a significant amount of noise in the input image, or if the characters happen to be touching or broken.

4 DISCUSSION

The system presented here demonstrates that neural networks can, in fact, be used for segmentation as well as recognition. We have by no means demonstrated that this method is better than conventional segmentation/recognition systems in overall performance. However, most conventional systems cannot deal with touching, broken, or noisy characters very well *at all*, whereas the present system handles all of these cases and recognition in a single, integrated fashion. This approach not only offers an integrated solution to the problems at hand, it also has the properties of being translation invariant, trainable with minimal information, and could be implemented in hardware for extremely fast feed-forward performance.

Note that the architecture discussed here is similar in some respects to the neocognitron model of Fukushima (1980). However, the system is different in several important aspects. First of all, the features here are learned through backpropagation rather than hand-coded as in the neocognitron. Second, the neural network self-organizes positional information via localized activation in the exponential layers. Third, the network is all feed-forward in its run-time dynamics.

Finally, it is worth pointing out that there are other aspects of the problem that we have not dealt with: Our network was trained on approximately the same size characters – to within 40% in height and no normalization in the x-dimension. We have not dealt here with the aspects of normalization, attentional focusing, or recovery of positional information, all of which would be needed in a functioning system.

Acknowledgements

We thank Peter Robinson from NCR Waterloo for providing the training data and Eric Hartman, Carsten Peterson, Richard Durbin, and Charles Rosenburg for useful discussions.

References

[1] K. Fukushima. (1980) Neocognitron: A self-organizing neural network model for a mechanism of pattern recognition unaffected by shift in position. *Biological Cybern.* **36**, 193-202.

[2] M. I. Jordan and D. E. Rumelhart (1990) Forward models: Supervised Learning with a Distal Teacher. *MIT Center for Cognitive Science, Occasional paper #* 40.

[3] J. Keeler, D. E. Rumelhart and W. K. Leow. (1991) Integrated Segmentation and Recognition of Hand-Printed Numerals. *MCC Technical Report ACT-NN-10.91*

[4] K. Lang, A. Waibel and G. Hinton. (1990) A Time Delay Neural Network Architecture for Isolated Word Recognition. *Neural Networks*, **3** 23-44.

[5] Y. Le Cun, B. Boser, J.S. Denker, S. Solla, R. Howard, and L. Jackel. (1990) Back-Propagation applied to Handwritten Zipcode Recognition. *Neural Computation* **1**(4):541-551.

[6] D.E. Rumelhart, G.E.Hinton and R.J.Williams (1986), "Learning Internal Representations by Error Propagation," in D.E.Rumelhart, J.L.McClelland and the PDP Research Group, *Parallel Distributed Processing: Explorations in the Microstructure of Cognition. Volume 1: Foundations*, Cambridge, MA: MIT Press/Bradford.

EMPATH:
Face, Emotion, and Gender Recognition Using Holons

Garrison W. Cottrell
Computer Science and Engineering Dept.
Institute for Neural Computation
University of California San Diego
La Jolla, CA 92093

Janet Metcalfe
Department of Psychology
Dartmouth College
Hanover, NH 03755

Abstract

The dimensionality of a set of 160 face images of 10 male and 10 female subjects is reduced from 4096 to 40 via an autoencoder network. The extracted features do not correspond to the features used in previous face recognition systems (Kanade, 1973), such as ratios of distances between facial elements. Rather, they are whole-face features we call *holons*. The holons are given to 1 and 2 layer back propagation networks that are trained to classify the input features for identity, feigned emotional state and gender. The automatically extracted holons provide a sufficient basis for all of the gender discriminations, 99% of the identity discriminations and several of the emotion discriminations among the training set. Network and human judgements of the emotions are compared, and it is found that the networks tend to confuse more distant emotions than humans do.

1 Introduction and motivation

We describe further research on the use of dimensionality-reduction networks for face recognition first described in (Cottrell & Fleming, 1990; Fleming & Cottrell, 1990). There, we demonstrated that an unsupervised autoencoding network was able to extract features from faces sufficient for identity discrimination. Here we extend that work to show that a network so trained can also recognize feigned emotional states.

Cottrell, Munro & Zipser (1987) showed that a back propagation network could be used for image compression. The network is trained to simply reproduce its input, and so can be seen as a non-linear version of Kohonen's (1977) auto-associator. However it must do this through a narrow channel of hidden units, so it must extract regularities from the input vectors during learning. Empirical analysis of the trained network showed that the hidden units span the principal subspace of the image vectors, with some noise on the first principal component due to network nonlinearity (Cottrell & Munro, 1988).

Although the network uses error-correction learning, no teacher other than the input is provided, so the learning can be regarded as *unsupervised*. We suggested that this network could be used for automatic feature extraction in a pattern recognition system. This is the approach taken here.

The model is shown in Figure 1. The image compression network extracts the features, and then the hidden unit representation so developed is given as input to one and two layer classification networks which yield identity, gender, and emotion as output. In previous work, we showed that the features developed by the model are holistic rather than discrete features, that they can combine to form faces that the model has never been trained on, and that they form a redintegrative memory, able to complete noisy or partial inputs (Kohonen et al., 1977). We have dubbed them *holons*.

2 Materials

The images that comprised the input to the network were selected from full face pictures taken of 10 females and 10 males. All subjects were introductory psychology students at the University of California, San Diego who received partial course credit for participating. Following the procedure outlined by Galton (1878), images were aligned along the axes of the eyes and mouth. These images were captured by a frame grabber, and reduced to 64×64 pixels by averaging. To prevent the use of first order statistics for discrimination, the images were normalized to have equal brightness and variance. The gray levels were linearly scaled to the range [0,.8]. Part of the training set and its reproduction by the autoencoder are shown in Figure 2.

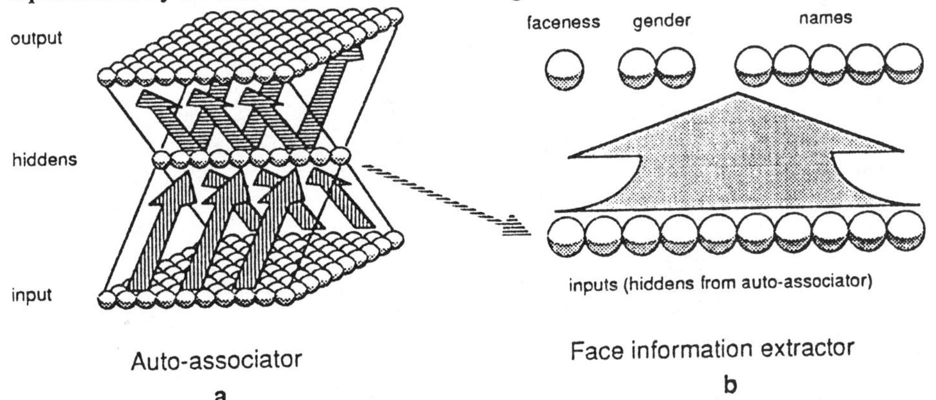

Figure 1: The face recognition model. (a) An image compression network is trained first to compress the 4096 inputs into 40 hidden units. (b) The hidden units from the first network are used as inputs to various recognition networks.

Each column corresponds to one of 8 different feigned emotional expressions. Russell (1980) has shown that subjects' judgements of adjectives describing human emotions can be represented in a two-dimensional "emotion space" (Figure 3). The horizontal dimension can be characterized as pleasure/displeasure; the vertical dimension as high arousal/low arousal. Russell and his colleagues have shown using multidimensional scaling techniques (Russell, 1980, 1983; Russell & Bullock, 1986) that most common human emotions fall on a circle within this space. We chose adjectives from this circle to be the emotions that we asked our subjects to feign. The adjectives for each class are those in the numbered circles in Figure 3. If the subject did not respond well to one of the adjectives, others from the circled region were given as encouragement to form the proper facial expression. We labeled these classes with one adjective from each region: astonished, happy, pleased, relaxed, sleepy, bored, miserable and angry. The adjectives were presented in randomized order to offset possible carry over effects.

We found that subjects were enthusiastically expressive with certain of these emotions, such as astonished and delighted. However, despite claims of negative feelings when cued with adjectives such as miserable, bored and sleepy, the subjects did not overtly express these negative emotions very clearly.

3 Procedure

The whole image is input at once to our network, so the input layer is 64×64. We used 40 hidden units, and a 64×64 output layer, with a sigmoidal activation function with range [-1,1]. Due to the extreme difference in fan-in at the hidden and output layers (4096 vs. 40), differential learning rates were used at the two layers. Use of a single learning rate led to most of the hidden units becoming pinned at full off or on regardless

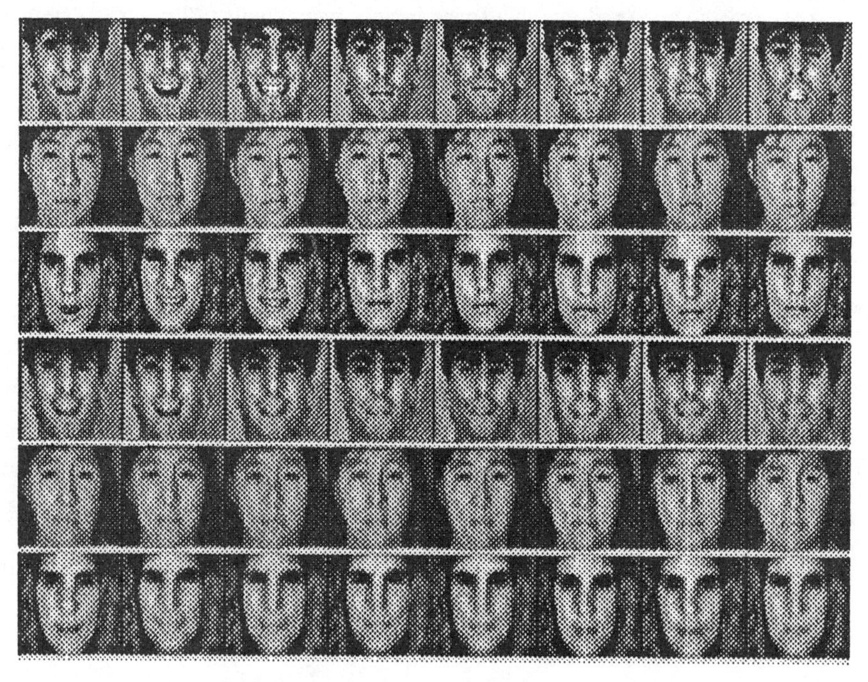

Figure 2: Three subjects and their reproductions by the compression network.

of the input. We used a learning rate of .25 at the output layer during the first epoch, in order to quickly learn the bias, or "palette", then a rate of .1 was used for the remaining 49 epochs, where an epoch corresponds to the presentation of all 160 images. The hidden layer used a constant learning rate of .0001. The initial weight span was .1 (+/- .05). We used no momentum or weight decay. The average squared error per unit at the end was .0017. This corresponds to about 12 gray levels per pixel. Sample reproductions of trained images are shown in Figure 2.

The 40-element vectors produced by the hidden units of the compression network are then given as input to a single layer network that has a localist unit for every name and a unit for gender. A two-layer network with 20 hidden units is used for identifying which of the 8 emotion adjectives that were given to the subjects pertains to each image. The network is trained to produce .5 for the wrong answer, and 1 for the correct answer. The emotion network is trained for 1000 epochs, which reduces the total sum squared error to 22. To investigate how performance changed with further training, we trained this network for 2000 more epochs. 9 other networks were trained using the features from the same compression network for 1000 epochs from different initial random weights for comparison to human subjects on the same task.

4 Results

The criteria for correctness was that the output unit with the maximum activation must correspond to the correct answer. The network learned to discriminate 99% of the training set for identity. One image of one woman was taken for another. Sex discrimination was perfect. It was found that performance was better on these tasks without a hidden layer. The emotion classification network performed better with a

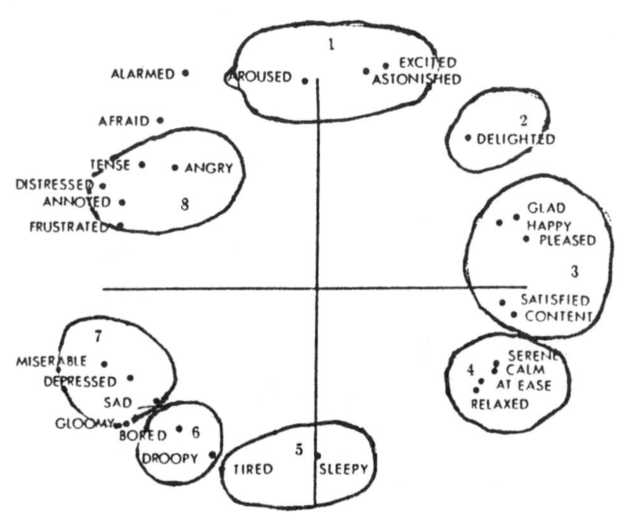

Figure 3: The two-dimensional emotion space extracted via multi-dimensional scaling from similarity ratings. Data from Russell (1980).

Table 1: Percentage hits on each emotion (Generalization in parentheses)

Emotion/Epochs	1000		2000		3000	
astonished	100	(40)	100	(60)	100	(40)
delighted	55	(20)	75	(40)	90	(40)
pleased	80	(100)	90	(40)	80	(40)
relaxed	80	(40)	35	(0)	45	(20)
sleepy	20	(0)	70	(0)	80	(0)
bored	5	(0)	85	(0)	85	(0)
miserable	65	(0)	75	(0)	80	(20)
angry	85	(40)	85	(0)	70	(0)

hidden layer. However, the observation during data acquisition that negative emotions are poorly portrayed was confirmed by the network's early performance (See Table 1).

Initially, the network was much better at detecting positive states than negative ones. Later training improved some categories at the expense of others, suggesting that the network did not have enough capacity to perform all the discriminations. Generalization tests were performed on a small set of 5 subjects (40 faces in all), with the results shown in parentheses in Table 1. Generalization gets worse with more training, suggesting the network is becoming overtrained. The network is best at generalization on the positive emotions. This also suggests that the negative emotions are not easily discriminable in our data set. The generalization results, while not spectacular, should be considered in the light of the fact that the training set only contained 20 subjects, and it should be noted that the compression network was not trained on the images in this test set.

5 Internal representation

We investigated the representation formed by the compression network. We found the receptive fields of the hidden units in this network to be white noise. In order to extract the actual features used, we recorded the hidden unit activations as the network processed all 160 images. We formed the covariance matrix of the hidden unit activations, and extracted the principal components. Note that this operation "re-localizes" the principal components from the distributed representation used. The resulting vectors may be decompressed for viewing purposes. The results are shown in Figure 4.

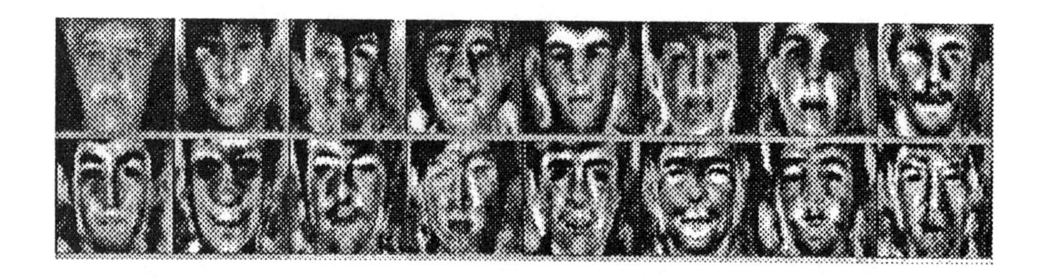

Figure 4: Sixteen holons derived by PCA from hidden unit responses.

These are similar to the "eigenfaces" found by Turk & Pentland (submitted) in their principal components analysis of faces. Such a representation, if localized by a procedure such as Sanger's (1990), or as we have found in previous work develops at higher learning rates (Cottrell & Fleming, 1990), could provide a computational basis for the kinds of single cell recordings found in the STS of monkey cortex, without resorting to the notion of localist "grandmother" cells for each face.

6 Comparison with human subjects

In order to compare our network performance to that of human subjects on the same task, we tested human subjects on the same discriminations the networks were required to perform. 10 subjects were presented with one quarter of the training set (40 images of 5 subjects) 8 times in randomized order in each block (320 presentations total). On each presentation of an image, the subject was asked to make a Yes/No discrimination as to whether the image is a good example of one of the adjective class names.

Various factors (small sample size, large heterogeneity of variance) prevented a reliable statistical test of the model vs. the subjects. However, it is informative to compare the confusion matrices for the two pools of subjects (the other 9 network simulations are included here). All "yes" responses to each kind of face with each adjective are summed across subjects for the humans and the networks. The networks' responses were converted into "yes/no" responses by thresholding the outputs of the networks for each face, producing 8 yes/no responses. The threshold was chosen to produce approximately the same overall number of "yes" responses for the 10 networks as the 10 humans. The matrices are shown in Table 2. The rows correspond to the portrayals of the emotions, the columns are the adjectives presented with them. So, for example, across 10 subjects there were 45 instances of calling a "pleased" face a good example of "delighted" (out of a possible 50).

It is clear from the tables that there is a lot of regularity in the the human subjects data that is not totally captured by the model. The first three emotions/adjectives form a cluster, as do the last four. Since these adjectives are listed in the order of a tour around the circumference of Russell's circomplex model, the confusability of nearby emotions suggests that the clustering of descriptive adjectives is matched by a perceptual clustering of the facial expressions produced by a subject in response to those adjectives. However, rather than a diagonal band of confusability, as would be predicted by the circomplex, the positive/negative dimension appears to separate into two clusters. For example, anger and astonishment are separated more than would be expected from Russell's circomplex model (there is no "wrap-around" in this matrix). In between these two clusters, the adjective "relaxed" is seen by the subjects as compatible with nearly every facial category to some degree, but the "relaxed" faces are not compatible with the first three positive emotional categories.

The networks, while displaying some of the clustering shown in the human data, have higher entries along the diagonals, due to having been trained on this data, and more unusual confusions in regions where the human subjects (upper right and lower left) have practically no entries, such as "angry" labels on "delighted" and "pleased" faces. This may be due to forcing the networks to make as many responses as the humans. We found that a minor threshold change leads to many more responses, suggesting that we are over-extracting responses from the network.

Table 2: Confusion matrices for human and network subjects

	Human								Network							
Face/Adj	ast	del	ple	rel	sle	bor	mis	ang	ast	del	ple	rel	sle	bor	mis	ang
astonished	37	24	21	9	0	1	0	0	50	8	5	14	13	9	4	9
delighted	6	29	32	24	4	6	1	0	10	44	27	7	8	6	7	20
pleased	2	45	48	18	0	0	0	0	1	29	50	1	3	2	10	23
relaxed	1	0	7	42	22	32	7	2	1	3	2	46	43	14	6	5
sleepy	0	0	0	28	31	33	19	1	13	4	2	39	49	2	10	4
bored	0	0	1	33	24	38	21	10	5	3	15	26	21	38	15	21
miserable	0	0	1	24	17	31	28	1	3	1	9	3	18	13	38	34
angry	4	0	0	16	11	12	13	3	3	4	14	3	2	11	25	49

7 Holons

This work demonstrates that, at least for our data set, dimensionality reduction is a useful preprocessing step that can maintain enough information for the recognition process. We term the representational units used by the compression network "holons". This is more than just another name for a distributed representation. By this we simply mean: Any representational element is a holon if its receptive field subtends the whole object being represented. Ideally we want to require that the information in a set of holons be maximally distributed: i.e., the average unit entropy is maximized. The latter restriction eliminates grandmother cells, insures that the representation be noise resistant, and also distributes the processing load evenly. A weak point of our definition is the difficulty of defining precisely the notion of a "whole object".

This definition applies to many distributed representational schemes, but does not apply to articulated ones such as the Wickelfeatures used by Rumelhart and McClelland (1987) in their past tense model as these only represent portions of the verb. On the other hand, we would not have holons for a "room", simply because we can not get a room to fill but not extend beyond our sensory surface at once. Given this meaning for the term, the units of area 17 are not holons, but the units in Superior Temporal Sulcus (STS) are. The main motivation for this definition is to give an alternative notion to the grandmother cell one for face cells in STS (Desimone et al., 1984).

8 Conclusions

We have shown that a network model that extracts features from its environment in an unsupervised manner can achieve near perfect recognition rates for identity discrimination and sex discrimination, even though the features were not extracted for that purpose. Where categories become "fuzzier", as in emotional states, the network's abilities are also limited. In particular, generalization to new faces is poor. In our preliminary study of human perception of these faces, we found support for the idea that when subjects are asked to produce expressions based on "near" adjectives in emotional space, they produce "near" expressions in perceptual space. These appear to fall in positive/negative clusters much more than the circomplex model would predict. However, this could be a fault of the subjects' abilities to portray the given emotions, rather than a fault of the circomplex model. Finally, we compared the networks' performance to that of humans. We found that the networks (when constrained to make as many responses as humans), while generally following the pattern of the human data, produce several category confusions that humans do not.

References

Cottrell, G. & Fleming, M. (1990). Face recognition using unsupervised feature extraction. In *Proceedings of the International Neural Network Conference*, Paris.

Cottrell, G, Munro, P. & Zipser, D. (1987). Learning internal representations of gray scale images: An example of extensional programming. In *Proc. Ninth Annual Cognitive Science Society Conference*, Seattle, Wa.

Cottrell, G.W. and Munro, P. (1988) Principal components analysis of images via back propagation. In *Proc. Soc. of Photo-Optical Instr. Eng.*, Cambridge, MA.

Desimone, R., Albright, T., Gross, C., and Bruce, C. (1984). Stimulus-selective properties of inferior temporal neurons in the Macaque. *J. Neuroscience, 4*, 2051-2062.

Fleming, M. & Cottrell, G. (1990). A neural network model of face recognition. In *Proceedings of the Int. Joint Conf. on Neural Networks*, San Diego, CA.

Galton, F. R. S. (1878). Composite Portraits. *Nature, 23*, 97-100.

Kanade, Takeo (1973). Picture processing system by computer complex and recognition of human faces. Unpublished Ph.D. Thesis, Dept. of Info. Science, Kyoto University.

Kohonen, T. Lehtio, P., Oja, E., Kortekangas, A., & Makisara, K. (1977). Demonstration of pattern processing properties of the optimal associative mappings. In *Proc Intl. Conf. on Cybernetics and Society*, Wash., D.C.

Russell, J. A. (1980). A circomplex model of affect. *Journal of Personality and Social Psychology, 39*, 1161-1178.

Russell, J. A. (1983). Pancultural aspects of the human conceptual organization of emotion. *Journal of Personality and Social Psychology, 45*, 1281-1288.

Russell, J. A. & Bullock, M. (1986). On the dimensions preschoolers use to interpret facial expressions of emotion. *Developmental Psychology, 22*, 97-102.

Rumelhart, D. E., Hinton, G. E., and Williams, R. J. (1986). Learning representations by back-propagating errors. *Nature, 323*, 533-536.

Rumelhart, D. & McClelland, J. On learning the past tenses of English verbs. In J.L. McClelland & D.E. Rumelhart (Eds.), *Parallel Distributed Processing, Vol 2.*, Cambridge, MA: MIT Press.

Sanger, T. D. (1989) Optimal unsupervised learning in a single-layer linear feedforward neural network. *Neural Networks, 2*, pp. 459-473.

Turk, M. & Pentland, A. (1990) Eigenfaces for recognition. (Submitted for publication).

SEXNET: A NEURAL NETWORK IDENTIFIES SEX FROM HUMAN FACES

B.A. Golomb, D.T. Lawrence, and T.J. Sejnowski
The Salk Institute
10010 N. Torrey Pines Rd.
La Jolla, CA 92037

Abstract

Sex identification in animals has biological importance. Humans are good at making this determination visually, but machines have not matched this ability. A neural network was trained to discriminate sex in human faces, and performed as well as humans on a set of 90 exemplars. Images sampled at 30x30 were compressed using a 900x40x900 fully-connected back-propagation network; activities of hidden units served as input to a back-propagation "SexNet" trained to produce values of 1 for male and 0 for female faces. The network's average error rate of 8.1% compared favorably to humans, who averaged 11.6%. Some SexNet errors mimicked those of humans.

1 INTRODUCTION

People can capably tell if a human face is male or female. Recognizing the sex of conspecifics is important. While some animals use pheromones to recognize sex, in humans this task is primarily visual. How is sex recognized from faces? By and large we are unable to say. Although certain features are nearly pathognomonic for one sex or the other (facial hair for men, makeup or certain hairstyles for women), even in the absence of these cues the determination is made; and even in their presence, other cues may override.

Sex-recognition in faces is thus a prototypical pattern recognition task of the sort at which humans excel, but which has vexed traditional AI. It appears to follow no simple algorithm, and indeed is modifiable according to fashion (makeup, hair etc). While ambiguous cases exist, for which we must appeal to other cues such as physical build (if visible), voice patterns (if audible), and mannerisms, humans are fairly good in most cases at discriminating sex merely from photos of faces, without resorting to such adscititious cues. Can neural networks do the same?

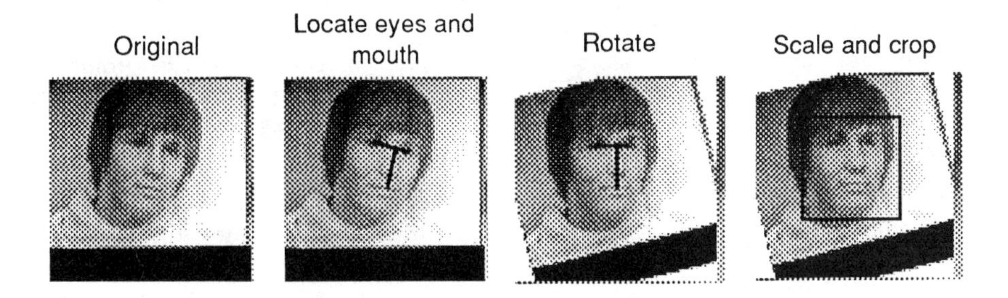

Figure 1: Preprocessing for all faces. After locating the eyes by hand, the image was rotated such that the line joining the eyes was horizontal. The distance between the eyes and the perpendicular distance to the mouth were scaled and the resulting image was cropped. Blocks of pixels were averaged to produce a final 30x30 subsampled image which served as input to the network.

2 METHOD

90 photos of young adult faces (45 male, 45 female), were used (O'Toole, Millward, & Anderson, 1988). Faces had no facial hair, no jewelry, and apparently no makeup. A white cloth was draped about each neck to eliminate possible clothing cues. Most photos were head on, but the exact angle varied.

Faces were rotated until eyes were level; scaled and translated to position eyes and mouth similarly in each image; and clipped to present a similar extent of image around eyes and mouth. Final faces were 30x30 pixels with 12 pixels between the eyes, and 8 pixels from eyes to mouth. The 256 gray-level images were adjusted to the same average brightness. (No attempt was made to equalize higher order statistics.)

Network processing entailed two stages: image compression and sex discrimination. Both networks were fully-connected three layer networks with two biases, trained with simple unadorned back-propagation (Werbos, 1974; Parker, 1986; Rumelhart, Hinton, & Williams, 1986), with a sigmoidal squashing function and a learning rate of 0.2, using Bottou and LeCun's SN2 simulator. Image compression followed the scheme of Cottrell and Fleming (1989, personal communication), who previously used compressed faces as an input to a face identity network. The compression network served to force the 30x30 images (900 inputs units) through a 40 hidden unit bottleneck, and reconstruct the image at the 900 unit output level. Thus, the input equalled the desired output. The function of this compression was twofold. First, use of compressed representations decreases the number of inputs and hence connections to the sex discrimination portion of the SexNet, allowing for faster learning and relearning of sex with different subsets of faces. Second, while simple gray-levels may adequately represent changes in face images for part of a single face in fixed lighting (Yuhas, Goldstein, Sejnowski & Jenkins, 1990), the representation of multiple faces benefits from preprocessing which extracts essential properties. In an encoder network (Cottrell, Munro & Zipser, 1987), the compression performs a principle components analysis if the hidden units are linear. The 50 leading components reproduce reasonable likenesses of faces (Kirby & Sirovich, 1990). For nonlinear hidden units, such as those used here, the compression is more efficient and fewer are needed. The compression network trained for 2000 runs on each of 90 faces, yielding output faces that were subjectively distinct and discriminable, although not identical to the inputs. This procedure served to forge a representation of each face in the activities of only 40 units, thus providing a more tractable input (40 units rather than 900) to the sex discrimination network.

The second, sex-discrimination portion, or SexNet had 40 inputs (the activities of the 40 hidden units of the compression net), 2, 5, 10, 20 and 40 hidden units, and one output unit. Training consisted of encouraging, by gradient descent (Rumelhart, et al., 1986) the network to produce a "1" for men, and a "0" for women. Values greater than 0.5 were accounted "male", and those less than 0.5 female. In a control experiment we trained a 900x40x1 backpropagation network directly on the raw images. This network performed well on the training set but was unable to generalize.

Since the proper measure of performance of the network is human performance on the same faces, a pseudorandomized face order was established, by which even vs odd sequential digits of pi coded male vs female for 45 faces, and, to equalize males and females, the order was repeated with reverse parity for the second 45 faces. No visual reference to the faces influenced the order. 5 humans were tested on these 90 faces, with two binary decisions for each face: sex and certainty (sure vs unsure). Subjects had unlimited time, and could scrutinize faces in any manner. For comparison, 8 tests of the SexNet were undertaken, each training on a different 80 faces, leaving a distinct set of 10 untrained faces for testing.

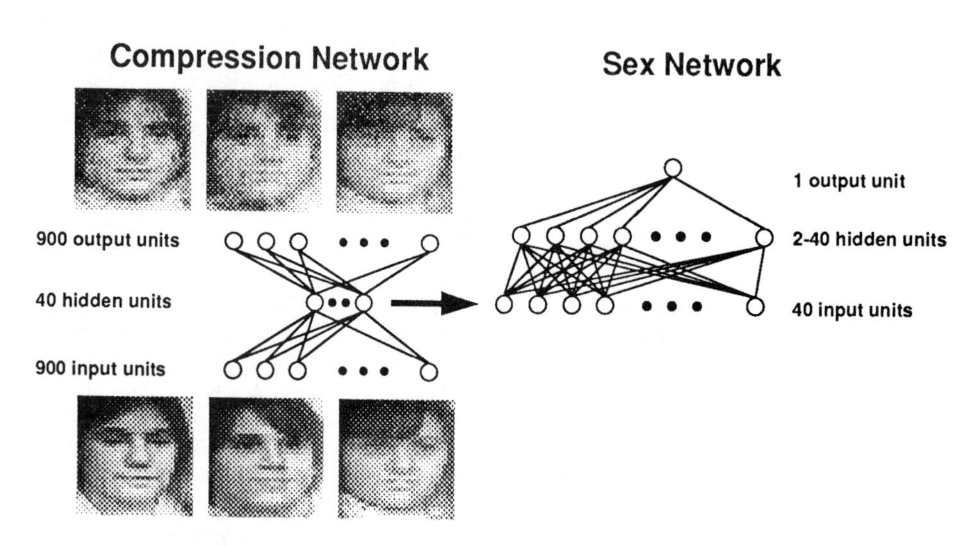

Figure 2: Two-stage network for discrimating sex from faces. The compression network encodes the normalized faces into 40 hidden units, which are then used as inputs to a sex network. The 30x30 input image has 256 gray levels per pixel. The output of the sex network is 1 for male and 0 for female.

3 RESULTS

Psychophysical studies of 5 humans on the 90 faces revealed errors of 8, 10, 12, 8 and 14, corresponding to 8.9, 11.1, 13.3, 8.9 and 15.5%, with an average error of 11.6%. The SexNet with 10 hidden units gave errors on test faces of 15, 0, 20, 0, 20, 10, 0 and 0%, for an average of 8.1%.

Similar errors seemed to affect the net and humans. One male face gave particular trouble to the SexNet, being mis-sexed when a test face, and taking long to train when a training face. This same face was (erroneously) judged "female", "sure" by all 5 human observers.

On one preliminary trial the SexNet correctly assigned all ten test faces, but misjudged two of the 80 training faces: the problematic male hitherto noted, to which it assigned the androgynous value of 0.495, and another male on which it performed wretchedly, with a value between 0.2 and 0.3, despite copious training. The SexNet proved right: The face was a clear female whose sex value had been mistranscribed.

4 DISCUSSION

Gender can be recognized by humans even when lesions of cerebral cortex in humans cause prosopagnosia, a selective impairment in the ability to recognize individual faces (Tranel, Damasio & Damasio, 1988; Damasio, Damasio & Van Hoesen, 1982). Thus, gender recognition in humans, as in our network, does not depend on the ability to identify individuals. Single neurons in the superior temporal sulcus of visual cortex, as well as the amygdala, respond selectively to faces and such neurons may participate in facial discrimination tasks similar to those of the SexNet (Rolls, 1984;Baylis, Rolls & Leonard, 1985).

We have shown that the complex visual pattern recognition task of recognizing the sex of human faces can be adequately performed by a neural network without prior feature selection and with minimal preprocessing. Human performance was matched by a using a 900x40x900 Cottrell-style back-propagation image compression network, the activities of whose hidden units served as inputs to a back-propagation SexNet; no efforts to optimize the network were needed to match human performance.

The SexNet performance was similar to humans' not just by percent errors. Not only did it correctly sex previously unseen faces as can we, but it had difficulties on faces which also posed difficulties for humans. Indeed the SexNet correctly sexed one female face despite being labeled male during training. It had evidently done a fine job of abstracting what distinguishes the sexes.

Failure of humans and the network on the same face suggests a means by which to handle the net's difficulty, in analogy with human strategies. When a face persists in being wrongly judged (say female) long after others seem stably correct, one shouldn't emend male-female categories too drastically to accommodate it; the face could be a fluke, and one may encounter another nearly identical face which is in fact female. The human strategy confronted with a "training face" (one for which sex is known by other criteria) would consist in making a special category for the individual; and having that provide input to overrule the facial information. This would permit outliers to be correctly identified without adverse consequences to generalization.

Although the SexNet task has limited utility of itself – after all, humans sex human faces fine – extensions of this work have application. For instance, it is not known whether faces differ for male and female rhesus monkeys. By training a neural network to discriminate the sex of a monkey, then comparing the network's performance on untrained faces, better than chance performance would imply that there exist facial sex differences in rhesus monkey faces – answering a question of some ethological significance.

Another important area of application is to the recognition of facial expressions. Some emotional states, such as anger, surprise, and happiness are associated with facial expressions that are stable across cultures (Ekman, 1989). Our approach to recognizing sex can also be used to recognize human emotion from facial expression. Indeed, we have devised a preliminary ExpressioNet, which capably distinguishes among (both training and test examples of) 8 different facial expressions, a precursor to network automation of Ekman and Friesen's facial action coding system (Ekman & Friesen, 1975).

A variety of congenital medical disorders (such as Down syndrome) are accompanied by craniofacial anomalies (Dyken, & Miller, 1980), resulting in distinctive "facies", or facial appearances. Some are subtle or rare, and not often recognized by physicians. It may be possible to to screen normal from affected infants or children using special purpose neural networks. We hope to extend our work to include neural nets for diagnosing William's syndrome, or infantile hypercalcemia, in which children's' faces are "elfin-like" (Bellugi, Bihrle, Trauner, Jernigan, & Doherty, 1990; Trauner, Bellugi, & Chase, 1989). Williams' faces compare to normals in a manner which recalls the male/female distinction in that no isolated well described features occur in all of one but none of the other. Early diagnosis is important because these children often have associated cardiac defects requiring surgical correction.

On a final, more frivolous note, the same strategy, using personality indices rather than sex for the second phase of the net, could, at last, scientifically test the tenets of anthroposcopy (physiognomy), according to which personality traits can be divined from features of the face and head.

Acknowledgements

We are indebted to Dr. A. O'Toole for providing the images used in this study, and to Shona Chattarji for helping with graphics. This research was supported, in part, by the Drown Foundation.

References

Baylis, G. C., Rolls, E. T., & Leonard, C. M. (1985). Selectivity between faces in the responses of as population of neurons in the cortex in the superior temporal sulcus of the monkey. Brain Research, 342, 91-102.

Bellugi, U., Bihrle, A., Trauner, D., Jernigan, T., & Doherty, S. (1990). Neuropsychological, neurological, and neuroanatomical profile of Williams syndrome children.

American Journal of Medical Genetics, In Press,

Cottrell, G. W., Munro, P., &, Zipser, D. (1987). Image compression by back propagation: An example of extensional programming. UCSD Institute for Cognitive Science Technical Report ICS-8702.

Damasio, A. R., Damasio, H., & Van Hoesen, G. W. (1982). Prosopagnosia: anatomic basis and neurobehavioral mechanisms. Neurology, 32, 331-341.

Dyken, P. R., & Miller, M. D. (1980). Facial Features of Neurologic Syndromes . St. Louis, Missouri: C.V. Mosby Company.

Ekman, P. (1989). The argument and evidence about universals in facial expressions of emotion. In H. W. a. J. Manstead (Ed.), Handbook of psychophysiology: Emotion and social behavior (pp. 143-164). London: John Wiley and Sons.

Ekman, P., & Friesen, W. V. (1975). Unmasking the face: A guide to recognizing emotions from facial clues. New Jersey: Prentice Hall.

Kirby, M., & Sirovich, L., (1990). Application of the Karhunen-Loeve procedure for the characterization of human faces. IEEE Transactions on Pattern Analysis and Machine Intelligence, 12(1), 103-108

O'Toole, A. J., Millward, R. B., & Anderson, J. A. (1988). A physical system approach to recognition memory for spatially transformed faces. Neural Networks, 1, 179-199.

Parker, D. B. (1986). A comparison of algorithms for neuron-like cells. In J. S. Denker (Ed.), Neural networks for computing New York: American Institute of Physics.

Rolls, E. T. (1984). Neurons in the cortex of the temporal lobe and in the amygdala of the monkey with responses selective for faces. Human Neurobiology, 3, 209-222.

Rumelhart, D. E., Hinton, G., & Williams, R. J. (1986). Learning internal representation by error propagation. In D. E. R. a. J. L. McClelland (Ed.), Parallel Distributed Processing, Explorations in the microstructure of cognition (pp. 318-362). Cambridge, Mass.: MIT Press.

Tranel, D., Damasio, A. R., & Damasio, H. (1988). Intact recognition of facial expression, gender, and age in patients with impaired recognition of face identity. Neurology, 38, 690-696.

Trauner, D., Bellugi, U., & Chase, C. (1989). Neurologic features of Williams and Down Syndromes. Pediatric Neurology, 5(3), 166-168.

Werbos, P. (1974). Beyond Regression: New tools for prediction and analysis in the behavioral sciences. Harvard University,

Yuhas, B. P., Goldstein, M. H. Jr., Sejnowski, T. J., & Jenkins, R. E. (1990). Neural network models of sensory integration for improved vowel recognition. Proceedings of the IEEE, 78(10), 1658-1668

A Neural Expert System with Automated Extraction of Fuzzy If-Then Rules and Its Application to Medical Diagnosis

Yoichi Hayashi*
Department of Computer and Information Sciences
Ibaraki University
Hitachi-shi, Ibaraki 316, Japan

ABSTRACT

This paper proposes a *fuzzy neural expert system* (FNES) with the following two functions: (1) Generalization of the information derived from the training data and embodiment of knowledge in the form of the fuzzy neural network; (2) Extraction of fuzzy `If-Then` rules with *linguistic relative importance* of each proposition in an antecedent (`If`-part) from a trained neural network. This paper also gives a method to extract automatically fuzzy If-Then rules from the trained neural network. To prove the effectiveness and validity of the proposed fuzzy neural expert system, a fuzzy neural expert system for medical diagnosis has been developed.

1 INTRODUCTION

Expert systems that have neural networks for their knowledge bases are sometimes called *neural expert system* (Gallant & Hayashi, 1990; Hayashi et al., 1990; Yoshida et al., 1990) or *connectionist expert system* (Gallant, 1988; Yoshida et al., 1989). This paper extends work reported in (Hayashi & Nakai, 1990; Hayashi et al., 1990) and shows a new method to give confidence measurements for all inferences and explanations to neural expert systems. In contrast with conventional expert systems, we propose a *fuzzy neural expert system* (FNES) with automated extraction of fuzzy If-Then rules. This paper also gives a method to extract automatically fuzzy If-Then rules with *linguistic relative importance* of each proposition in an antecedent (If-part) from a trained neural network. To prove the effectiveness and validity of the proposed neural expert system, a fuzzy neural expert system for diagnosing hepatobiliary disorders has been developed by using a real medical database. This paper compares the diagnostic capability provided by the neural network approach and that provided by the statistical approach. Furthermore, we evaluate the performance of extracted fuzzy If-Then rules from a neural network knowledge base.

*A part of this work was performed when the author was with the University of Alabama at Birmingham, Department of Computer and Information Sciences as a Visiting Associate Professor.

2 FUZZY NEURAL EXPERT SYSTEM WITH AUTOMATED EXTRACTION OF FUZZY IF-THEN RULES

2.1 Distributed Neural Network

Figure 1 illustrates a schematic diagram of a fuzzy neural expert system with automated extraction of fuzzy If-Then rules. For backpropagation, the configuration consisting of p input cells, q intermediate cells ("hidden units") and r output cells has been the most widely used. Connections run from every input cell to every intermediate cell, and from every intermediate cell to every output cell. In this paper, we employ a valiant of conventional perceptron network, which is called *distributed (neural) network* (Gallant, 1990). In the network, there are the same cells and connections as with the backpropagation, and in addition there are direct connections from input to output cells. See Figure 2. Each connection has an integer weight w_{ij} that roughly corresponds to the influence of cell u_j on cell u_i. Although the weights of connections from the input layer to the intermediate layer are generated by using a random number generator (in this paper, integers between -10 and +10 were used) and fixed for learning process. Cell activations are discrete, each taking on values +1, 0, or -1.

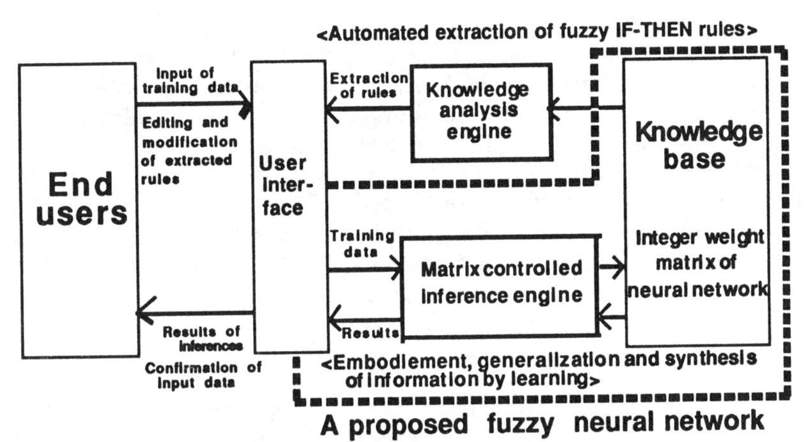

Figure 1: A Schematic Diagram of A Fuzzy Neural System with Automated Extraction of Fuzzy IF-THEN Rules

Activations of the input cells I_i $(i = 1,2,..., p)$, the intermediate cell H_j $(j = 1,2,..., q)$ and the output cell O_k $(k = 1,2,..., r)$ can be calculated using equations (1) - (4). The value of the cell I_0 is always +1, and it is connected to every other cell except for input cells.

$$SH_j = \sum_{i=0}^{p} w_{ji} I_i \qquad (1)$$

$$H_j = \begin{cases} +1 \text{ or True} & (SH_j > 0) \\ 0 \text{ or Unknown} & (SH_j = 0) \\ -1 \text{ or False} & (SH_j < 0) \end{cases} \qquad (2)$$

$$SO_k = \sum_{i=0}^{p} u_{ki} I_i + \sum_{j=1}^{q} v_{kj} H_j \qquad (3)$$

$$O_k = \begin{cases} +1 \text{ or True} & (SO_k > 0) \\ 0 \text{ or Unknown} & (SO_k = 0) \\ -1 \text{ or False} & (SO_k < 0) \end{cases} \qquad (4)$$

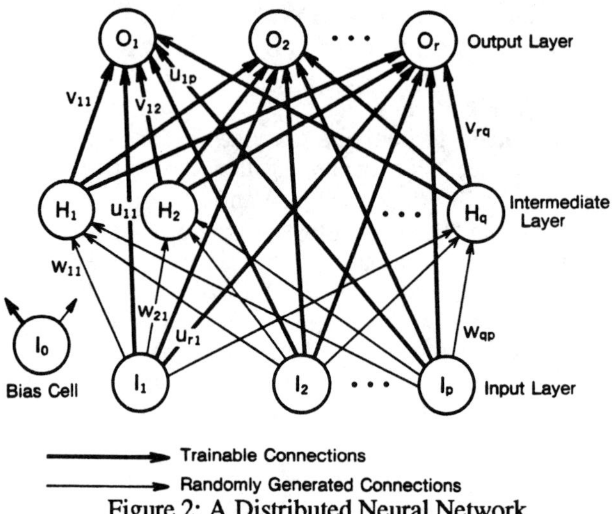

Figure 2: A Distributed Neural Network

2.2 Fuzzy Neural Network

To handle various fuzziness in the input layer of the distributed neural network, it is necessary to interpret subjective input data which has non-Boolean quantitative and/or qualitative meaning. In general, fuzzy sets defined by monotone membership functions can be "defuzzified" into a family of crisp sets by using the level set representation (Negoita, 1985) or "thermometer code" of B. Widrow. Therefore, the fuzziness can be incorporated into the training data by using only Boolean inputs. Once the training data is set up in this manner, it can be processed by the Pocket Algorithm (Gallant, 1990). In this paper, we will propose a *fuzzy neural network* to handle fuzzy data and crisp data

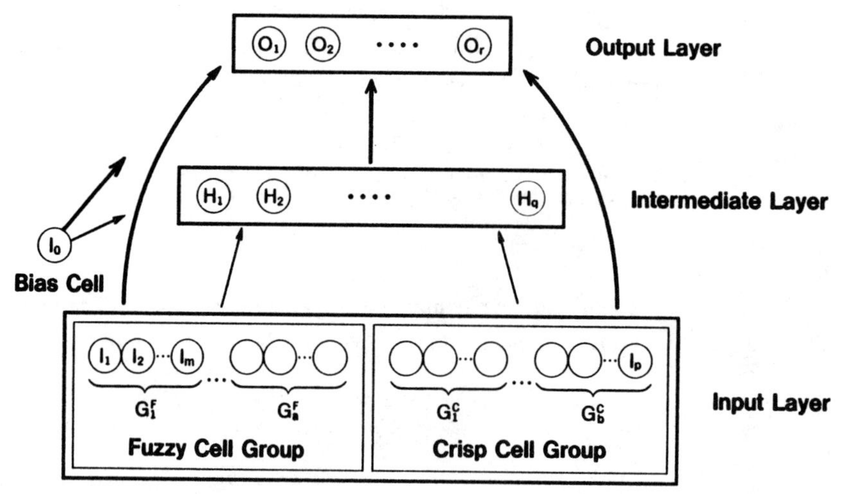

Figure 3: A Neural Network with Fuzzy Cell Groups and Crisp Cell Groups

given in the input layer. Figure 3 shows the structure of proposed fuzzy neural network whose input layer consists of fuzzy cell groups and crisp (non-fuzzy) cell groups. Here, truthfulness of fuzzy information and crisp information such as binary encoded data is represented by fuzzy cell groups and crisp cell groups, respectively. A fuzzy cell group consists of m input cells which have the level set representation using binary m-dimensional vector, each taking on values in {+1, -1}; whereas a crisp cell group also consists of m input cells which take on two values in {(+1,+1,...,+1), (-1,-1,...,-1)}.

3 AUTOMATED EXTRACTION OF FUZZY IF-THEN RULES FROM TRAINED NEURAL NETWORKS

This paper also extends previous work described in (Hayashi & Nakai, 1990) and proposes a method to extract automatically fuzzy If-Then rules with *linguistic relative importance* of each proposition in an antecedent (Hayashi & Nakai, 1989) from a trained fuzzy neural network. The method is implemented in the knowledge analysis engine in Figure 1. The linguistic relative importance such as *Very Important* and *Moderately Important*, which is defined by a fuzzy set, represents the degree of effect of each proposition on consequence. By providing linguistic relative importance for each proposition, each fuzzy If-Then rule has more flexible expression than that of ordinary If-Then rules. Furthermore, truthfulness of each fuzzy If-Then rule is given in the form of linguistic truth value such as *Very True* and *Possibly True*, which is defined by a fuzzy set. Enhancement of the presentation capability and flexibility by using fuzzy If-Then rules with linguistic relative importance facilitates the automated extraction of fuzzy If-Then rules from a trained neural network.

3.1 Automated If-Then Rule Extraction Algorithm

We have proposed some methods to extract fuzzy If-Then rules with linguistic relative importance from a trained (fuzzy) neural network. In this section, we extend work reported in (Hayashi & Nakai, 1990; Hayashi et al., 1990) and give an algorithm to extract fuzzy If-Then rules from a trained fuzzy neural network in the following. Note that an exact algorithm of Step 2 and Step 3 can be derived from algorithms shown in (Hayashi & Nakai, 1990) in the same manner. Here, we will give a brief discussion on them due to space limitation. We shall concentrate on Step1.

Step 1. Extraction of framework of fuzzy If-then rules: We select propositions in an antecedent (`If`-part) of a rule, that is, extract framework of fuzzy If-Then rules. We will give a precise algorithm for this step in section 3.2.

Step 2. Assignment of linguistic truth value to each extracted rule: A linguistic truth value such as *Very Very True* (V.V.T.) and *Possibly True* (P.T.) is given to each fuzzy If-Then rule selected in Step 1. Linguistic truth value assigned to each rule indicates the degree of certainty to draw the conclusion. The linguistic truth value is determined by the relative amount of weighted sum of output cells.

Step 3. Assignment of linguistic relative importance to each proposition: Linguistic relative importance is assigned to each proposition of antecedent in fuzzy If-Then rules. Linguistic relative importance such as *Very Important* (V.I.) and *Moderately Important* (M.I.) represents the degree of effect of each proposition on consequence.

3.2 Algorithm to extract framework of fuzzy If-Then rules

Extraction of dispensable propositions on cell groups in an antecedent (`If`-part) is required for the extraction of framework of fuzzy If-Then rules. For simplicity, it is supposed in this section that each cell consists of three input cells. Therefore, a fuzzy cell group takes on three values in {(+1,-1,-1), (+1,+1,-1), (+1,+1,+1)}; whereas a crisp cell group takes on two values in {(+1,+1,+1), (-1,-1,-1)}. In distributed neural network, we can determine activations (values) of cells using partial input information. For example, activations of intermediate cell H_j are determined as

$$H_j = \begin{cases} +1 \ \ or \ \ True & (|SH_j| > USH_j \ \ and \ \ SH_j > 0) \\ 0 \ \ or \ \ Unknown & (|SH_j| \leq USH_j) \\ -1 \ \ or \ \ False & (|SH_j| > USH_j \ \ and \ \ SH_j < 0) \end{cases} \quad (5)$$

where

$$USH_j = \sum_{j : I_i \text{ is } Unknown} |w_{ji}| \ . \quad (6)$$

In the same manner, activations of output cell O_k are determined as

$$O_k = \begin{cases} +1 \ \ or \ \ True & (|SO_k| > USO_k \ \ and \ \ SO_k > 0) \\ 0 \ \ or \ \ Unknown & (|SO_k| \leq USO_k) \\ -1 \ \ or \ \ False & (|SO_k| > USO_k \ \ and \ \ SH_k < 0) \end{cases} \quad (7)$$

where

$$USO_k = \sum_{i : I_i \text{ is } Unknown} |u_{ki}| + \sum_{j : H_j \text{ is } Unknown} |v_{kj}| \ . \quad (8)$$

Our problem is to determine the value of input cell groups so that each output cell O_k takes on values +1 or -1. Propositions (Input items) corresponding to determined input cell groups will be entrapped in an antecedent (`If`-part) of each rule. We will give an extraction algorithm for framework of fuzzy If-Then rules as follows:

Step I: Select one output cell O_k.

Step II: Select one cell group. If the selected cell group is a fuzzy cell group, set the values of the cell group in (+1,-1,-1), (+1,+1,-1) or (+1,+1,+1); whereas if the selected cell group is a crisp cell group, set the values of the cell group in (+1,+1,+1) or (-1,-1,-1). Furthermore, set the value of cell groups which were not selected to (0, 0, 0).

Step III (Forward search): Determine all the value of intermediate cells H_j by using the values of cell groups given in Step II and equation (5). Furthermore, determine the value of output cell O_k using (7). If the value of O_k is +1 or -1, go to Step V. Otherwise (the value of O_k is 0), go to Step IV. Although all the cell groups are entrapped in an antecedent (`If`-part), if the value of O_k is 0, there is no framework of fuzzy If-Then rules for the output cell O_k and go to Step VI.

Step IV (Backward search): Let v^* be the maximum value of $|v_{kj}|$ which is an absolute value of the weight of the connections between the output cell O_k and the intermediate cell H_j whose activation value is 0. Furthermore, let u^* be the maximum value of $|u_{ki}|$ which is an absolute value of the weight of the connections between the output cell O_k and the input cell I_i whose value is 0. If $u^* \geq v^*$ or values of all the intermediate cells are determined, go to Step IV-1. Otherwise, go to Step IV-2.

Step IV-1: For the input cell I_i which is incident to u_{ki} ($|u_{ki}| = u^*$), if the input cell I_i is included in the fuzzy cell group, go to Step IV-1-F; whereas in the crisp cell group, go to Step IV-1-C.

Step IV-1-F: If $SO_k \geq 0$, select one pattern of the fuzzy cell group which has the maximum value of SO_k among (+1,-1,-1), (+1,+1,-1) and (+1,+1,+1). Conversely, If $SO_k < 0$, select one pattern which has the minimum value of SO_k. Go to Step V.
Step IV-1-C: If $SO_k \geq 0$, select one pattern of the crisp cell group which has the maximum value of SO_k in (+1,+1,+1) and (-1,-1,-1). Conversely, If $SO_k < 0$, select one pattern which has the minimum value of SO_k. Go to Step V.
Step IV-2: Let w^* be he maximum value of $|w_{ji}|$ which is an absolute value of the weight of the connections between the intermediate cell H_j which is incident to v_{kj} ($|v_{kj}| = v^*$) and the input cell I_i whose activation value is 0. Select the input cell I_i which is incident to the connection w_{ji} ($|w_{ji}| = w^*$). If the input cell I_i is included in the fuzzy cell group, go to Step IV-2-F; whereas in the crisp cell group, go to Step IV-2-C.
Step IV-2-F: If $SH_j \geq 0$, select one pattern of the fuzzy cell group which has the maximum value of SH_j among (+1,-1,-1), (+1,+1,-1) and (+1,+1,+1). Conversely, If $SH_j < 0$, select one pattern which has the minimum value of SH_j. Go to Step V.
Step IV-2-C: If $SH_j \geq 0$, select one pattern of the crisp cell group which has the maximum value of SH_j in (+1,+1,+1) and (-1,-1,-1). Conversely, If $SH_j < 0$, select one pattern which has the minimum value of SH_j. Go to Step V.
Step V (Extraction of framework of If-then Rules): If the value of O_k is determined, extract input items corresponding to a determined cell group as the propositions in an antecedent (`If`-part). Here, if the value of O_k is +1, the consequence is set to "O_k is *True*"; conversely if the value of O_k is -1, the consequence is set to "O_k is *False*". If multiple frameworks of If-Then rules with same antecedent and consequence are extracted, adopt one of them.
Step VI (Termination condition of extraction algorithm for each output cell): For output cell O_k, if there are any cell groups which are not selected yet; or for selected cell groups, there are any patterns which are not selected yet, go to Step II. Otherwise, go to Step VII.
Step VII (Termination condition of whole extraction algorithm): Repeat Steps II through VI stated above until the termination condition of extraction algorithm for each output cell is satisfied. If there are any output cell O_k which are not selected yet in Step I, go to Step I. Otherwise, stop the whole extraction algorithm.

4 APPLICATION TO MEDICAL DIAGNOSIS

To prove the effectiveness and validity of the proposed neural expert system, we have developed neural expert systems for diagnosing hepatobiliary disorders (Yoshida et al., 1989 & 1990). We used a real medical database containing sex and the results of nine biochemical tests (e.g. GOT, GGT) of four hepatobiliary disorders, Alcoholic liver damage, Primary hepatoma, Liver cirrhosis and Cholelithiasis. The subjects consisted of 536 patients who were admitted to a university-affiliated hospital. The patients were clinically and pathologically diagnosed by physicians. The subjects were randomly assigned to 373 training data and 163 test (external) data. Degree of abnormality of each biochemical item is represented by a fuzzy cell group which consists of three input cells. There are four output cells. Each output cell corresponds to a hepatobiliary disorder. Fifty thousand iterations in learning process of Pocket Algorithm was performed for each output cell. The diagnosis criteria is the same as that employed in (Yoshida et al. 1989). After learning by using training data from 345 patients, the fuzzy neural network correctly diagnosed 75.5% of test (external) data from 163 previously unseen patients and correctly diagnosed 100% of the training data. Conversely, the diagnostic accuracy of the linear discriminant analysis was 65.0% of the test data and 68.4% of the training data. The proposed fuzzy neural network showed significantly higher diagnostic accuracy in training data and also had substantially higher diagnostic accuracy in test data than those of linear discriminant analysis. We extracted 48 general fuzzy If-Then rules for diagnosing hepatobiliary disorders by using the proposed algorithm given in section 3.2. The number of rules for comfirming diseases are 12 and the those for excluding diseases are 36. Hayashi and Nakai (1989) have proposed three kinds of reasoning methods using fuzzy If-Then rules with linguistic relative importance. In the present paper, we use the reasoning method-I for the evaluation of extracted fuzzy If-Then rules. Total diagnostic accuracy of the twelve extracted rules (four confirming rules and eight excluding rules) is 87.7%. We conclude that the present neural network knowledge base approach will be a promising and useful technique for generating practical knowledge bases from various databases. It should be noted that enhancement of interpretation capability of real data, and embodiment of implicit and/or subjective knowledge will lead to significant reduction of man power for knowledge acquisition in expert system development.

Acknowledgements

The author wishes to thank Dr. Stephen I. Gallant, Dr. Katsumi Yoshida and Mr. Atsushi Imura for their valuable comments and discussions.

References

Gallant, S.I. 1988 Connectionist Expert Systems, CACM, **31**(2), 152-169

Gallant, S.I. & Hayashi, Y. 1990 A Neural Network Expert System with Confidence Measurements, Proc. of the Third Int. Conf. on Infor. Proc. and Mgt. of Uncertainty in Knowledge-based Systems, pp.3-5, Paris, July 2-6; Springer Edited Volume (in press)

Gallant, S.I. 1990 Perceptron-Based Learning Algorithms, IEEE Transactions on Neural Networks, **1**(2), 179-191

Hayashi, Y. & Nakai, M. 1989 Reasoning Methods Using a Fuzzy Production Rule with Linguistic Relative Importance in an Antecedent, The Transactions of The Institute of Electrical Engineers of Japan (T. IEE Japan), **109-C**(9), 661-668

Hayashi, Y. & Nakai, M. 1990 Automated Extraction of Fuzzy IF-THEN Rules Using Neural Networks, T. IEE Japan, **110-C**(3), 198-206

Hayashi, Y., Imura, A. & Yoshida, K. 1990 A Neural Expert System under Uncertain Environments and Its Evaluation, Proc. of the 11th Knowledge and Intelligence System Symposium, pp.13-18, Tokyo

Negoita, C.V. 1985 Expert Systems and Fuzzy Systems: Benjamin Cummings Pub.

Yoshida, K., Hayashi, Y. & Imura, A. 1989 A Connectionist Expert System for Diagnosing Hepatobiliary Disorders," in MEDINFO89 (Proc. of the Sixth Conf. on Medical Informatics), B. Barber et al. eds.: North-Holland, 116-120

Yoshida, K., Hayashi, Y., Imura, A. & Shimada, N. 1990 Fuzzy Neural Expert System for Diagnosing Hepatobiliary Disorders, Proc. of the Int. Conf. on Fuzzy Logic & Neural Networks (IIZUKA '90), pp.539-543, Iizuka, Japan, July 20-24

Analog Neural Networks as Decoders

Ruth Erlanson*
Dept. of Electrical Engineering
California Institute of Technology
Pasadena, CA 91125

Yaser Abu-Mostafa
Dept. of Electrical Engineering
California Institute of Technology
Pasadena, CA 91125

Abstract

Analog neural networks with feedback can be used to implement K-Winner-Take-All (KWTA) networks. In turn, KWTA networks can be used as decoders of a class of nonlinear error-correcting codes. By interconnecting such KWTA networks, we can construct decoders capable of decoding more powerful codes. We consider several families of interconnected KWTA networks, analyze their performance in terms of coding theory metrics, and consider the feasibility of embedding such networks in VLSI technologies.

1 INTRODUCTION: THE K-WINNER-TAKE-ALL NETWORK

We have previously demonstrated the use of a continuous Hopfield neural network as a K-Winner-Take-All (KWTA) network [Majani et al., 1989, Erlanson and Abu-Mostafa, 1988]. Given an input of N real numbers, such a network will converge to a vector of K positive one components and $(N - K)$ negative one components, with the positive positions indicating the K largest input components. In addition, we have shown that the $\binom{N}{K}$ such vectors are the only stable states of the system.

One application of the KWTA network is the analog decoding of error-correcting codes [Majani et al., 1989, Platt and Hopfield, 1986]. Here, a known set of vectors (the codewords) are transmitted over a noisy channel. At the receiver's end of the channel, the initial vector must be reconstructed from the noisy vector.

*currently at: Hughes Network Systems, 10790 Roselle St., San Diego, CA 92121

If we select our codewords to be the $\binom{N}{K}$ vectors with K positive one components and $(N-K)$ negative one components, then the KWTA neural network will perform this decoding task. Furthermore, the network decodes from the noisy analog vector to a binary codeword (so no information is lost in quantization of the noisy vector). Also, we have shown [Majani et al., 1989] that the KWTA network will perform the optimal decoding, maximum likelihood decoding (MLD), if we assume noise where the probability of a large noise spike is less than the probability of a small noise spike (such as additive white Gaussian noise). For this type of noise, an MLD outputs the codeword closest to the noisy received vector. Hence, the most straightforward implementation of MLD would involve the comparison of the noisy vector to all the codewords. For large codes, this method is computationally impractical.

Two important parameters of any code are its rate and minimum distance. The rate, or amount of information transmitted per bit sent over the channel, of this code is good (asymptotically approaches 1). The minimum distance of a code is the Hamming distance between the two closest codewords in the code. The minimum distance determines the error-correcting capabilities of a code. The minimum distance of the KWTA code is 2.

In our previous work, we have found that the KWTA network performs optimal decoding of a nonlinear code. However, the small minimum distance of this code limited the system's usefulness.

2 INTERCONNECTED KWTA NETWORKS

In order to look for more useful code-decoder pairs, we have considered interconnected KWTA networks. We have found two interesting families of codes:

2.1 THE HYPERCUBE FAMILY

A decoder for this family of codes has $m = n^i$ nodes. We label the nodes $x_1, x_2, \ldots x_i$ with $x_j \in 1, 2 \ldots n$. KWTA constraints are placed on sets of n nodes which differ in only one index. For example, $\{1, 1, 1, \ldots, 1\}$, $\{2, 1, 1, \ldots, 1\}$, $\{3, 1, 1, \ldots, 1\}$, $\ldots$, $\{n, 1, 1, \ldots, 1\}$ are the nodes in one KWTA constraint.

For a two-dimensional system ($i = 2$) the nodes can be laid out in an array where the KWTA constraints will be along the rows and columns of the array. For the code associated with the two-dimensional system, we find that

$$\text{rate} \geq 1 - \frac{3 \log n}{2n}.$$

The minimum distance of this code is 4. Experimental results show that the decoder is nearly optimal.

In general, for an i-dimensional code, the minimum distance is 2^i. The rate of these codes can be bounded only very roughly.

We also consider implementing these decoders on an integrated circuit. Because of the high level of interconnectivity of these decoders and the simple processing required at each node (or neuron) we assume that the interconnections will dictate the chip's size. Using a standard model for VLSI area complexity, we determine that the circuit area scales as the square of the network size. Feature sizes of current mainstream technologies suggest that we could construct systems with $22^2 = 484$ (2-dimensional), $6^3 = 216$ (3-dimensional) and $5^4 = 625$ (4-dimensional) nodes. Thus, nontrivial systems could be constructed with current VLSI technology.

2.2 NET-GENERATED CODES

This family uses combinatorial nets to specify the nodes in the KWTA constraints. A net on n^2 points consists of parallel classes: Each class partitions the n^2 points into n disjoint lines each containing n points. Two lines from different classes intersect at exactly one point.

If we impose a KWTA constraint on the points on a line, a net can be used to generate a family of code-decoder pairs. If n is the integer power of a prime number, we can use a projective plane to generate a net with $(n + 1)$ classes. For example, in Table 1 we have the projective plane of order 2 ($n = 2$). A projective plane has $n^2 + n + 1$ points and $n^2 + n + 1$ lines where each line has $n + 1$ points and any 2 lines intersect in exactly one point.

Table 1: Projective Plane of Order 2. Points are numbered for clarity.

	points:						
	1	2	3	4	5	6	7
	1	1		1			
		1	1		1		
			1	1		1	
lines:				1	1		1
	1				1	1	
		1				1	1
	1		1				1

We can generate a net of 3 (i.e., $n+1$) classes in the following way: Pick one line of the projective plane. Without loss of generality, we select the first line. Eliminate the points in that line from all the lines in the projective plane, as shown in Table 2. Renumber the remaining $n^2 + n + 1 - (n + 1) = n^2$ points. These are the points of the net. The first class of the net is composed of the reduced lines which previously contained the first point (old label 1) of the projective plane. In our example, this class contains two lines: L_1 consists of points 2 and 3, and L_2 consists of points 1 and 4. The remaining classes of the net are formed in a corresponding manner from the other points of the first line of the projective plane.

If we use all $(n + 1)$ classes to specify KWTA constraints, the nodes are over-constrained and the network has no stable states. We can obtain n different codes by using $1, 2, \ldots,$ up to n classes to specify constraints. (The code constructed with two classes is identical to the two-dimensional code in Section 2.1!) Experimentally, we have found that these decoders perform near-optimal decoding on their corresponding code. A code constructed with i nets has a minimum distance of at least $2i$. Thus, a code of size n^2 (i.e., the codewords contain n^2 bits) can be constructed with minimum distance up to $2n$. The rate of these codes in general can be bounded only roughly.

We found that we could embed the decoder with a nets in an integrated circuit with width proportional to $\frac{1}{2}an^3$, or area proportional to the cube of the number of processors. In a typical VLSI process, one could implement systems with 484 ($a = 2$, $n = 22$), 81 ($a = 3$, $n = 9$) or 64 ($a = 4$, $n = 8$) nodes.

3 SUMMARY

We have simulated and analyzed analog neural networks which perform near-optimal decoding of certain families of nonlinear codes. Furthermore, we have shown that nontrivial implementations could be constructed. This work is discussed in more detail in [Erlanson, 1991].

References

E. Majani, R. Erlanson and Y.S. Abu-Mostafa, "On the K-Winners-Take-All Feedback Network," *Advances in Neural Information Processing Systems*, D. Touretzky (ed.), Vol. 1, pp. 634–642, 1989.

R. Erlanson and Y.S. Abu-Mostafa, "Using an Analog Neural Network for Decoding," *Proceedings of the 1988 Connectionist Models Summer School*, D. Touretzky, G. Hinton, T. Sejnowski (eds.), pp. 186–190, 1988.

J.C. Platt and J.J. Hopfield, "Analog decoding using neural networks," *AIP Conference Proceedings #151, Neural Networks for Computing*, J. Denker (ed.), pp. 364-369, 1986.

R. Erlanson, "Soft-Decision Decoding of a Family of Nonlinear Codes Using a Neural Network," PhD. Thesis, California Institute of Technology, 1991.

Table 2: Constructing a Net from a Projective Plane.

projective plane's points:	1	2	3	4	5	6	7	
	~~1~~	~~1~~		~~1~~				
		~~1~~	1		1			
			1	~~1~~		1		
lines:				~~1~~	1		1	
	~~1~~				1	1		L_1
		~~1~~				1	1	
	~~1~~		1				1	L_2
net's points:			1		2	3	4	

Part X

Language and Cognition

Distributed Recursive Structure Processing

Géraldine Legendre
Department of
Linguistics

Yoshiro Miyata
Optoelectronic
Computing Systems Center
University of Colorado
Boulder, CO 80309-0430*

Paul Smolensky
Department of
Computer Science

Abstract

Harmonic grammar (Legendre, et al., 1990) is a connectionist theory of linguistic well-formedness based on the assumption that the well-formedness of a sentence can be measured by the harmony (negative energy) of the corresponding connectionist state. Assuming a lower-level connectionist network that obeys a few general connectionist principles but is otherwise unspecified, we construct a higher-level network with an equivalent harmony function that captures the most linguistically relevant global aspects of the lower level network. In this paper, we extend the tensor product representation (Smolensky 1990) to fully recursive representations of recursively structured objects like sentences in the lower-level network. We show theoretically and with an example the power of the new technique for parallel distributed structure processing.

1 Introduction

A new technique is presented for representing recursive structures in connectionist networks. It has been developed in the context of the framework of Harmonic Grammar (Legendre et al. 1990a, 1990b), a formalism for theories of linguistic well-formedness which involves two basic levels: At the lower level, elements of the problem domain are represented as distributed patterns of activity in a network; At the higher level, the elements in the domain are represented locally and connection weights are interpreted as soft rules involving these elements. There are two aspects that are central to the framework.

*The authors are listed in alphabetical order.

First, the connectionist well-formedness measure *harmony* (or negative "energy"), which we use to model linguistic well-formedness, has the properties that it is p-reserved between the lower and the higher levels and that it is maximized in the network processing. Our previous work developed techniques for deriving harmonies at the higher level from linguistic data, which allowed us to make contact with existing higher-level analyses of a given linguistic phenomenon.

This paper concentrates on the second aspect of the framework: how particular linguistic structures such as sentences can be efficiently represented and processed at the lower level. The next section describes a new method for representing tree structures in a network which is an extension of the tensor product representation proposed in (Smolensky 1990) that allows recursive tree structures to be represented and various tree operations to be performed in parallel.

2 Recursive tensor product representations

A *tensor product representation* of a set of structures S assigns to each $s \in S$ a vector built up by superposing role-sensitive representations of its constituents. A *role decomposition* of S specifies the constituent structure of s by assigning to it an unordered set of *filler-role bindings*. For example, if S is the set of strings from the alphabet $\{\mathtt{a}, \mathtt{b}, \mathtt{c}\}$, and $s = \mathtt{cba}$, then we might choose a role decomposition in which the roles are absolute positions in the string (r_1 = first, r_2 = second, ...) and the constituents are the filler/role bindings $\{\mathtt{b}/r_2, \mathtt{a}/r_3, \mathtt{c}/r_1\}$. [1]

In a tensor product representation a constituent – i.e., a filler/role binding – is represented by the tensor (or generalized outer) product of vectors representing the filler and role in isolation: $\mathtt{f}/r$ is represented by the vector $\mathbf{v} = \mathbf{f} \otimes \mathbf{r}$, which is in fact a second-rank tensor whose elements are conveniently labelled by two subscripts and defined simply by $\mathbf{v}_{\varphi\rho} = \mathbf{f}_{\varphi}\mathbf{r}_{\rho}$.

Where do the filler and role vectors **f** and **r** come from? In the most straightforward case, each filler is a member of a simple set F (e.g. an alphabet) and each role is a member of a simple set R and the designer of the representation simply specifies vectors representing all the elements of F and R. In more complex cases, one or both of the sets F and R might be sets of structures which in turn can be viewed as having constituents, and which in turn can be represented using a tensor product representation. This recursive construction of the tensor product representations leads to tensor products of three or more vectors, creating tensors of rank three and higher, with elements conveniently labelled by three or more subscripts.

The recursive structure of trees leads naturally to such a recursive construction of a tensor product representation. (The following analysis builds on Section 3.7.2 of (Smolensky 1990.)) We consider binary trees (in which every node has at most two children) since the techniques developed below generalize immediately to trees with higher branching factor, and since the power of binary trees is well attested, e.g., by the success of Lisp, whose basic datastructure is the binary tree. Adopting the conventions and notations of Lisp, we assume for simplicity that the terminal nodes

[1] The other major kind of role decomposition considered in (Smolensky 1990) is contextual roles; under one such decomposition, one constituent of cba is "b in the role 'preceded by c and followed by a'".

of the tree (those with no children), and only the terminal nodes, are labelled by symbols or atoms. The set of structures S we want to represent is the union of a set of atoms and the set of binary trees with terminal nodes labelled by these atoms.

One way to view a binary tree, by analogy with how we viewed strings above, is as having a large number of positions with various locations relative to the root: we adopt *positional roles* r_x labelled by binary strings (or bit vectors) such as $x = 0110$ which is the position in a tree accessed by "caddar = car(cdr(cdr(car)))", that is, the left child (0; car) of the right child (1; cdr) of the right child of the left child of the root of the tree. Using this role decomposition, each constituent of a tree is an atom (the filler) bound to some role r_x specifying its location; so if a tree s has a set of atoms $\{f_i\}$ at respective locations $\{x_i\}$, then the vector representing s is $\mathbf{s} = \sum_i \mathbf{f}_i \otimes \mathbf{r}_{\mathbf{x}_i}$.

A more recursive view of a binary tree sees it as having only *two* constituents: the atoms or subtrees which are the left and right children of the root. In this *fully recursive role decomposition*, fillers may either be atoms or trees: the set of possible fillers F is the same as the original set of structures S.

The fully recursive role decomposition can be incorporated into the tensor product framework by making the vector spaces and operations a little more complex than in (Smolensky 1990). The goal is a representation obeying, $\forall \mathbf{s}, \mathbf{p}, \mathbf{q} \in S$:

$$\mathtt{s} = \mathtt{cons}(\mathtt{p}, \mathtt{q}) \Rightarrow \mathbf{s} = \mathbf{p} \otimes \mathbf{r_0} + \mathbf{q} \otimes \mathbf{r_1} \tag{1}$$

Here, $\mathtt{s} = \mathtt{cons}(\mathtt{p}, \mathtt{q})$ is the tree with left subtree $\mathtt{p}$ and right subtree $\mathtt{q}$, while $\mathbf{s}, \mathbf{p}$ and $\mathbf{q}$ are the vectors representing $\mathtt{s}, \mathtt{p}$ and $\mathtt{q}$. The only two roles in this recursive decomposition are r_0, r_1: the left and right children of root. These roles are represented by two vectors $\mathbf{r_0}$ and $\mathbf{r_1}$.

A fully recursive representation obeying Equation 1 can actually be constructed from the positional representation, by assuming that the (many) positional role vectors are constructed recursively from the (two) fully recursive role vectors according to:

$$\mathbf{r_{x0}} = \mathbf{r_x} \otimes \mathbf{r_0} \quad \mathbf{r_{x1}} = \mathbf{r_x} \otimes \mathbf{r_1}.$$

For example, $\mathbf{r_{0110}} = \mathbf{r_0} \otimes \mathbf{r_1} \otimes \mathbf{r_1} \otimes \mathbf{r_0}$. [2] Thus the vectors representing positions at depth d in the tree are tensors of rank d (taking the root to be depth 0). As an example, the tree $\mathtt{s} = \mathtt{cons}(\mathtt{A}, \mathtt{cons}(\mathtt{B}, \mathtt{C})) = \mathtt{cons}(\mathtt{p}, \mathtt{q})$, where $\mathtt{p} = \mathtt{A}$ and $\mathtt{q} = \mathtt{cons}(\mathtt{B}, \mathtt{C})$, is represented by

$$\begin{aligned} \mathbf{s} &= \mathbf{A} \otimes \mathbf{r_0} + \mathbf{B} \otimes \mathbf{r_{01}} + \mathbf{C} \otimes \mathbf{r_{11}} = \mathbf{A} \otimes \mathbf{r_0} + \mathbf{B} \otimes \mathbf{r_0} \otimes \mathbf{r_1} + \mathbf{C} \otimes \mathbf{r_1} \otimes \mathbf{r_1} \\ &= \mathbf{A} \otimes \mathbf{r_0} + (\mathbf{B} \otimes \mathbf{r_0} + \mathbf{C} \otimes \mathbf{r_1}) \otimes \mathbf{r_1} = \mathbf{p} \otimes \mathbf{r_0} + \mathbf{q} \otimes \mathbf{r_1}, \end{aligned}$$

in accordance with Equation 1.

The complication in the vector spaces needed to accomplish this recursive analysis is one that allows us to add together the tensors of different ranks representing different depths in the tree. All we need do is take the direct sum of the spaces of tensors of different rank; in effect, concatenating into a long vector all the elements

[2] By adopting this definition of $\mathbf{r_x}$, we are essentially taking the recursive structure that is implicit in the subscripts x labelling the positional role vectors, and mapping it into the structure of the vectors themselves.

of the tensors. For example, in $\mathbf{s} = \mathtt{cons}(\mathtt{A}, \mathtt{cons}(\mathtt{B}, \mathtt{C}))$, depth 0 is 0, since $\mathbf{s}$ isn't an atom; depth 1 contains A, represented by the tensor $S^{(1)}_{\varphi\rho_1} = \mathbf{A}_\varphi \mathbf{r_0}_{\rho_1}$, and depth 2 contains B and C, represented by $S^{(2)}_{\varphi\rho_1\rho_2} = \mathbf{B}_\varphi \mathbf{r_0}_{\rho_1} \mathbf{r_1}_{\rho_2} + \mathbf{C}_\varphi \mathbf{r_1}_{\rho_1} \mathbf{r_1}_{\rho_2}$. The tree as a whole is then represented by the sequence $\mathbf{s} = \{S^{(0)}_\varphi, S^{(1)}_{\varphi\rho_1}, S^{(2)}_{\varphi\rho_1\rho_2}, \ldots\}$ where the tensor for depth 0, $S^{(0)}_\varphi$, and the tensors for depths $d > 2$, $S^{(d)}_{\varphi\rho_1\cdots\rho_d}$, are all zero.

We let V denote the vector space of such sequences of tensors of rank 0, rank 1, ... , up to some maximum depth D which may be infinite. Two elements of V are added (or "superimposed") simply by adding together the tensors of corresponding rank. This is our vector space for representing trees. [3]

The vector operation **cons** for building the representation of a tree from that of its two subtrees is given by Equation 1. As an operation on V this can be written:

$$\mathbf{cons} : (\{P^{(0)}_\varphi, P^{(1)}_{\varphi\rho_1}, P^{(2)}_{\varphi\rho_1\rho_2}, \cdots\}, \{Q^{(0)}_\varphi, Q^{(1)}_{\varphi\rho_1}, Q^{(2)}_{\varphi\rho_1\rho_2}, \cdots\}) \mapsto$$
$$\{0, P^{(0)}_\varphi \mathbf{r_0}_{\rho_1}, P^{(1)}_{\varphi\rho_1} \mathbf{r_0}_{\rho_2}, \cdots\} + \{0, Q^{(0)}_\varphi \mathbf{r_1}_{\rho_1}, Q^{(1)}_{\varphi\rho_1} \mathbf{r_1}_{\rho_2}, \cdots\}$$

(Here, $\mathbf{0}$ denotes the zero vector in the space representing atoms.) In terms of matrices multiplying vectors in V, this can be written

$$\mathbf{cons}(\mathbf{p}, \mathbf{q}) = \mathbf{W_{cons0}}\ \mathbf{p} + \mathbf{W_{cons1}}\ \mathbf{q}$$

(parallel to Equation 1) where the non-zero elements of the matrix $\mathbf{W_{cons0}}$ are

$$\mathbf{W}_{\mathbf{cons0}\varphi\rho_1\rho_2\cdots\rho_d\rho_{d+1},\varphi\rho_1\rho_2\cdots\rho_d} = \mathbf{r_0}_{\rho_{d+1}}$$

and $\mathbf{W_{cons1}}$ is gotten by replacing $\mathbf{r_0}$ with $\mathbf{r_1}$.

Taking the car or cdr of a tree – extracting the left or right child – in the recursive decomposition is equivalent to *unbinding* either r_0 or r_1. As shown in (Smolensky 1990, Section 3.1), if the role vectors are linearly independent, this unbinding can be performed accurately, via a linear operation, specifically, a generalized inner product (tensor contraction) of the vector representing the tree with an unbinding vector $\mathbf{u_0}$ or $\mathbf{u_1}$. In general, the unbinding vectors are the dual basis to the role vectors; equivalently, they are the vectors comprising the inverse matrix to the matrix of all role vectors. If the role vectors are orthonormal (as in the simulation discussed below), the unbinding vectors are the same as the role vectors. The **car** operation can be written explicitly as an operation on V:

$$\mathbf{car} : \{S^{(0)}_\varphi, S^{(1)}_{\varphi\rho}, S^{(2)}_{\varphi\rho_1\rho_1}, \cdots\} \mapsto$$
$$\{\textstyle\sum_{\rho_1} S^{(1)}_{\varphi\rho_1} \mathbf{u_0}_{\rho_1}, \sum_{\rho_2} S^{(2)}_{\varphi\rho_1\rho_2} \mathbf{u_0}_{\rho 2}, \sum_{\rho_3} S^{(3)}_{\varphi\rho_1\rho_2\rho_3} \mathbf{u_0}_{\rho_3}, \cdots\}$$

---

[3] In the connectionist implementation simulated below, there is one unit for each element of each tensor in the sequence. In the simulation we report, seven atoms are represented by (binary) vectors in a three-dimensional space, so $\varphi = 0, 1, 2$; $\mathbf{r_0}$ and $\mathbf{r_1}$ are vectors in a two-dimensional space, so $\rho = 0, 1$. The number of units representing the portion of V for depth d is thus $3 \cdot 2^d$ and the total number of units representing depths up to D is $3(2^{D+1} - 1)$. In tensor product representations, exact representation of deeply embedded structure does not come cheap.

(Replacing $\mathbf{u_0}$ by $\mathbf{u_1}$ gives **cdr**.) The operation **car** can be realized as a matrix $\mathbf{W_{car}}$ mapping V to V with non-zero elements:

$$\mathbf{W_{car}}_{\varphi\rho_1\rho_2\cdots\rho_d,\varphi\rho_1\rho_2\cdots\rho_d\rho_{d+1}} = \mathbf{u_0}_{\rho_{d+1}}.$$

$\mathbf{W_{cdr}}$ is the same matrix, with $\mathbf{u_0}$ replaced by $\mathbf{u_1}$. [4]

One of the main points of developing this connectionist representation of trees is to enable massively parallel processing. Whereas in the traditional sequential implementation of Lisp, symbol processing consists of a long sequence of **car**, **cdr**, and **cons** operations, here we can compose together the corresponding sequence of $\mathbf{W_{car}}$, $\mathbf{W_{cdr}}$, $\mathbf{W_{cons0}}$ and $\mathbf{W_{cons1}}$ operations into a single matrix operation. Adding some minimal nonlinearity allows us to compose more complex operations incorporating the equivalent of conditional branching. We now illustrate this with a simple linguistically motivated example.

3 An example

The symbol manipulation problem we consider is that of transforming a tree representation of a syntactic parse of an English sentence into a tree representation of a predicate-calculus expression for the meaning of the sentence. We considered two possible syntactic structures: simple active sentences of the form A V P and passive sentences of the form P Aux V by A. Each was to be transformed into a tree representing V(A,P), namely V A P. Here, the agent A and patient P of the verb V are both arbitrarily complex noun phrase trees. (Actually, the network could handle arbitrarily complex V's as well.) Aux is a marker for passive (eg. *is* in *is feared.*)

The network was presented with an input tree of either type, represented as an activation vector using the fully recursive tensor product representation developed in the preceding section. The seven non-zero binary vectors of length three coded seven atoms; the role vectors used were technique described above. The desired output was the same tensorial representation of the tree representing V(A, B). The filler vectors for the verb and for the constituent words of the two noun phrases should be unbound from their roles in the input tree and then bound to the appropriate roles in the output tree.

Such transformation was performed, for an active sentence, by the operation cons(cadr(s), cons(car(s), cddr(s))) on the input tree s, and for a passive sentence, by cons(cdadr(s), cons(cdddr(s), car(s))). These operations were implemented in the network as two weight matrices, $\mathbf{W_a}$ and $\mathbf{W_p}$, [5] connecting the input units to the output units as shown in Figure 1. In addition, the network had a circuit for

---

[4]Note that in the case when the $\{\mathbf{r_0}, \mathbf{r_1}\}$ are orthonormal, and therefore $\mathbf{u_0} = \mathbf{r_0}$, $\mathbf{W_{car}} = \mathbf{W_{cons0}}^T$; similarly, $\mathbf{W_{cdr}} = \mathbf{W_{cons1}}^T$.

[5]The two weight matrices were constructed from the four basic matrices as $\mathbf{W_a} = \mathbf{W_{cons0}}\mathbf{W_{car}}\mathbf{W_{cdr}} + \mathbf{W_{cons1}}(\mathbf{W_{cons0}}\mathbf{W_{car}} + \mathbf{W_{cons1}}\mathbf{W_{cdr}}\mathbf{W_{cdr}})$ and $\mathbf{W_p} = \mathbf{W_{cons0}}\mathbf{W_{cdr}}\mathbf{W_{car}}\mathbf{W_{cdr}} + \mathbf{W_{cons1}}(\mathbf{W_{cons0}}\mathbf{W_{cdr}}\mathbf{W_{cdr}}\mathbf{W_{cdr}} + \mathbf{W_{cons1}}\mathbf{W_{car}})$.

Output = cons(V,cons(C,cons(A,B)))

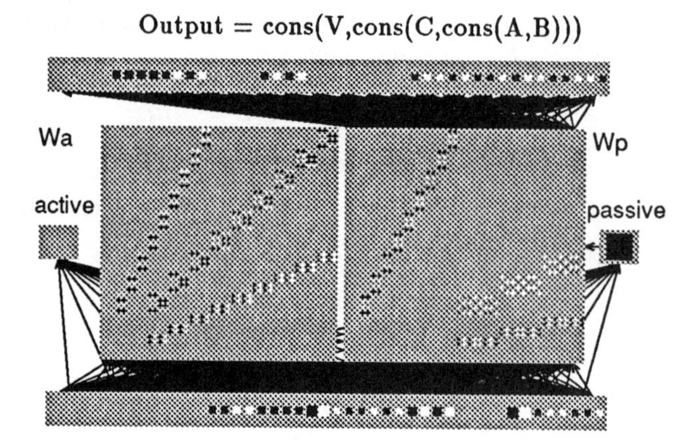

Input = cons(cons(A,B),cons(cons(Aux,V),cons(by,C)))

Figure 1: Recursive tensor product network processing a passive sentence

determining whether the input sentence was active or passive. In this example, it simply computed, by a weight matrix, the `caddr` of the input tree (where a passive sentence should have an `Aux`), and if it was the marker `Aux`, gated (with sigma-pi connections) $\mathbf{W_p}$, and otherwise gated $\mathbf{W_a}$.

Given this setting, the network was able to process arbitrary input sentences of either type, up to a certain depth (4 in this example) limited by the size of the network, properly and generated correct case role assignments. Figure 1 shows the network processing a passive sentence `((A.B).((Aux.V).(by.C)))` as in *All connectionists are feared by Minsky* and generating `(V.(C.(A.B)))` as output.

4 Discussion

The formalism developed here for the recursive representation of trees generates quite different representations depending on the choice of the two fundamental role vectors $\mathbf{r}_0$ and $\mathbf{r}_1$ and the vectors for representing the atoms. At one extreme is the trivial fully local representation in which one connectionist unit is dedicated to each possible atom in each possible position: this is the special case in which $\mathbf{r}_0$ and $\mathbf{r}_1$ are chosen to be the canonical basis vectors (1 0) and (0 1), and the vectors representing the n atoms are also chosen to be the canonical basis vectors of n-space. The example of the previous section illustrated the case of (a) linearly dependent vectors for atoms and (b) orthonormal vectors for the roles that were "distributed" in that both elements of both vectors were non-zero. Property (a) permits the representation of many more than n atoms with n-dimensional vectors, and could be used to enrich the usual notions of symbolic computation by letting "similar atoms" be represented by vectors that are closer to each other than are "dissimilar atoms." Property (b) contributes no savings in units of the purely local case, amounting to a literal rotation in role space. But it does allow us to demonstrate that fully distributed representations are as capable as fully local ones at supporting massively parallel structure processing. This point has been denied (often rather loudly) by advocates of local representations and by such critics as (Fodor & Pylyshyn 1988) and (Fodor & McLaughlin 1990) who have claimed that only connectionist implementations that preserve the concatenative structure of language-like representations of symbolic structures could be capable of true structure-sensitive processing.

The case illustrated in our example is distributed in the sense that all units corresponding to depth d in the tree are involved in the representation of all the atoms at that depth. But different depths are kept separate in the formalism and in the network. We can go further by allowing the role vectors to be linearly dependent, sacrificing full accuracy and generality in structure processing for representation of greater depth in fewer units. This case is the subject of current research, but space limitations have prevented us from describing our preliminary results here.

Returning to Harmonic Grammar, the next question is, having developed a fully recursive tensor product representation for lower-level representation of embedded structures such as those ubiquitous in syntax, what are the implications for well-formedness as measured by the harmony function? A first approximation to the natural language case is captured by context free grammars, in which the well-formedness of a subtree is independent of its level of embedding. It turns out that such depth-independent well-formedness is captured by a simple equation governing the harmony function (or weight matrix). At the higher level where grammatical "rules" of Harmonic Grammar reside, this has the consequence that the numerical constant appearing in each soft constraint that constitutes a "rule" applies at all levels of embedding. This greatly constrains the parameters in the grammar.

References

[1] J. A. Fodor and B. P. McLaughlin. Connectionism and the problem of systematicity: Why smolensky's solution doesn't work. *Cognition*, 35:183–204, 1990.

[2] J. A. Fodor and Z. W. Pylyshyn. Connectionism and cognitive architecture: A critical analysis. *Cognition*, 28:3–71, 1988.

[3] G. Legendre, Y. Miyata, and P. Smolensky. Harmonic grammar – a formal multi-level connectionist theory of linguistic well-formedness: Theoretical foundations. In *the Proceedings of the twelveth meeting of the Cognitive Science Society*, 1990a.

[4] G. Legendre, Y. Miyata, and P. Smolensky. Harmonic grammar – a formal multi-level connectionist theory of linguistic well-formedness: An application. In *the Proceedings of the twelveth meeting of the Cognitive Science Society*, 1990b.

[5] P. Smolensky. Tensor product variable binding and the representation of symbolic structures in connectionist networks. *Artificial Intelligence*, 46:159–216, 1990.

Translating Locative Prepositions

Paul W. Munro and Mary Tabasko
Department of Information Science
University of Pittsburgh
Pittsburgh, PA 15260

ABSTRACT

A network was trained by back propagation to map locative expressions of the form "noun-preposition-noun" to a semantic representation, as in Cosic and Munro (1988). The network's performance was analyzed over several simulations with training sets in both English and German. Translation of prepositions was attempted by presenting a locative expression to a network trained in one language to generate a semantic representation; the semantic representation was then presented to the network trained in the other language to generate the appropriate preposition.

1 INTRODUCTION

Connectionist approaches have enjoyed success, relative to competing frameworks, in accounting for context sensitivity and have become an attractive approach to NLP. An architecture (Figure 1) was put forward by Cosic and Munro (1988) to map locative expressions of the form "noun-preposition-noun" to a representation of the spatial relationship between the referents of the two nouns. The features used in the spatial representations were abstracted from Herskovits (1986). The network was trained using the generalized delta rule (Rumelhart, Hinton, and Williams, 1986) on a set of patterns with four components, three syntactic and one semantic. The syntactic components are a pair of nouns separated by a locative preposition [N1-LP-N2], and the semantic component is a representation of the spatial relationship [SR].

The architecture of the network includes two encoder banks, E1 and E2, inspired by Hinton (1986), to force the development of distributed representations of the nouns. This was not done to enhance the performance of the network but rather to facilitate analysis of the network's function, since an important component of Herskovits' theory is the role of nouns as modifiers of the preposition's ideal meaning.

The networks were trained to perform a pattern-completion task. That is, three components from a pattern are selected from the training set and presented to the input layer; either the LP or the SR component is missing. The task is to provide both the LP and SR components at the output. Analysis of a network after the learning phase consists of several tests, such as presenting prepositions with no accompanying nouns, in order to obtain an "ideal meaning" for each preposition, and comparing the noun representations at the encoder banks E1 and E2.

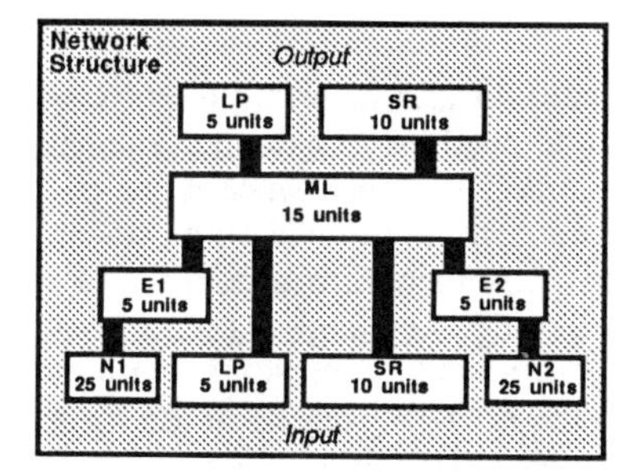

Noun Units (25)	clouds	lake	campsite	table	book
	sky	river	school	glass	flowers
	plane	road	house	bowl	grass
	boat	city	floor	crack	man
	water	island	room	chip	fish

Spatial Relation Units (10)		
	N1 over N2	N1 within border of N2
	N2 over N1	N1 touching N2
	N1 at edge of N2	N1 near N2
	N1 embedded in N2	N1 far from N2
	N2 contains N1	N2 supports N1

Preposition Units (5)	in	at	on	under	above

Figure 1: Network Architecture. Inputs are presented at the lowest layer, either across input banks N1, LP, and N2 or across input banks N1, SR, and N2. The bold lines indicate connectivity from all the units in the lower bank to all the units in the upper bank. The units used to represent the patterns are listed in the table on the right.

2 METHODOLOGY

2.1 THE TRAINING SETS

3125 (25 x 5 x 25) pattern combinations can be formed with the 25 nouns and five prepositions; of these, 137 meaningful expressions were chosen to constitute an English "training corpus". For each phrase, a set of one to three SR units was chosen to represent the position of the second noun's referent relative to the first noun's. To generate the German corpus, we picked the best German preposition to describe the spatial representation between the nouns. So, each training set consists of the same set of 137 spatial relationships between pairs of nouns. The correspondences between prepositions in the two languages across training sets is given in Table 1.

Table 1: The number of correspondences between the prepositions used in the English and German training sets.

GER \ ENG	IN	AT	ON	UNDER	ABOVE
IN	53	4	0	0	0
AN	0	9	12	0	0
AUF	0	8	20	0	0
UNTER	0	0	0	18	0
ÜBER	0	0	0	0	13

2.2 TRANSLATION OF THE PREPOSITIONS

Transforming syntactic expressions to semantic representations and inverting the process in another language is known as the interlingua approach to machine translation. The network described in this paper is particularly well-suited to this approach since it can perform this transformation in either direction (encoding or decoding). Networks trained using expressions from two languages can be attached in sequence to accomplish the translation task. A syntactic triple (N1-LP-N2) from the source language is presented to the network trained in that language. The resulting SR output is then presented with the corresponding nouns in the target language as input to the network trained in the target language, yielding the appropriate preposition in the target language as output. In this procedure, it is assumed that, relative to the prepositions, the nouns are easy to translate; that is, the translation of the nouns is assumed to be much less dependent on context. An example translation of the preposition *on* in the expression "house on lake" is illustrated in Figure 2.

3 RESULTS

Eight networks were trained using the two-stroke procedure described above; four using English language inputs and four using German, with two different learning rates in each language, and two different initializations for the random number generator in each case.

Various tests were performed on the trained network in order to determine the ideal meaning of each preposition, the network's classification of the various nouns, and the contextual interaction of the nouns with the prepositions. Also, translation of prepositions from English to German was attempted. The various test modes are described in detail below.

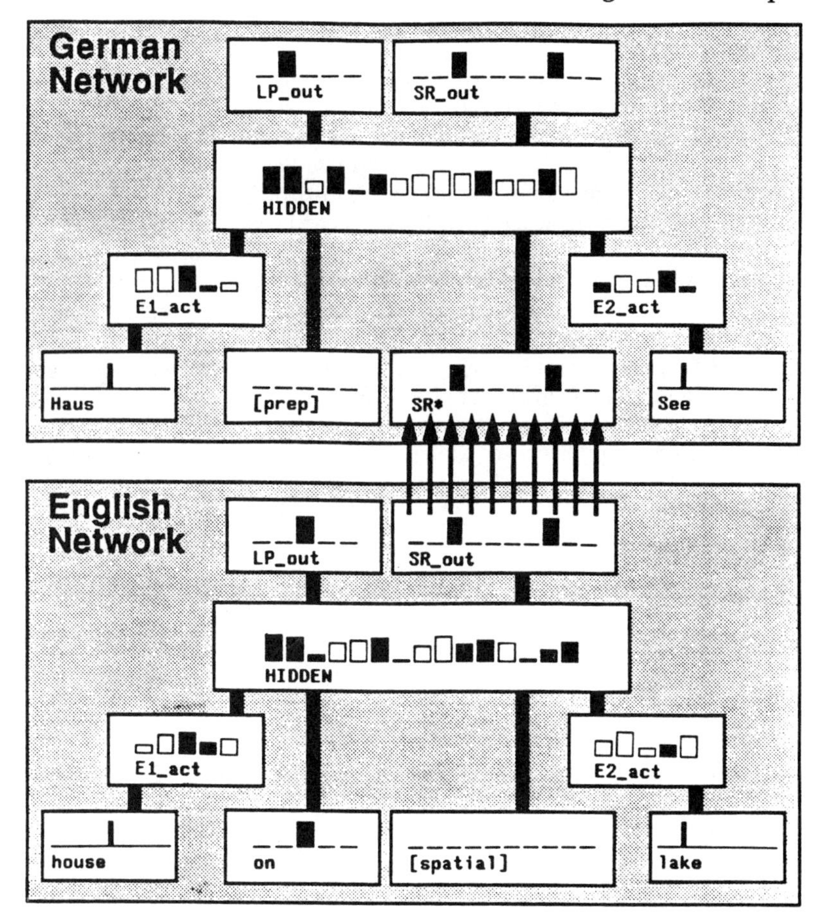

Figure 2: A Schematic View of the Translation Procedure.After training networks in two languages, a preposition can be appropriately translated from one language to the other by performing a decoding task in the source language followed by an encoding task in the target language. The figure shows the resulting activity patterns from the expression "house on lake". The system correctly translates *on* in English to *an* in German. In other contexts, *on* could correspond to the German *auf*.

3.1 CONVERGENCE

In each case, the networks converged to states of very low average error (less than 0.5%). However, in no case did a network learn to respond correctly to every phrase in the training set. The performance of each training run was measured by computing the total sum of squared error over the output units across all 137 training patterns. The errors were analyzed into four types:

LP-LP errors:	Errors in the LP output units for (N1-LP-N2) input
SR-LP errors (encoding):	Errors in the LP output units for (N1-SR-N2) input
LP-SR errors (decoding):	Errors in the SR output units for (N1-LP-N2) input
SR-SR errors:	Errors in the SR output units for (N1-SR-N2) input

In assessing the performance of the network after learning, the error measure driving the training (that is, the difference between desired and actual activity levels for every output unit) is inappropriate. In cases such as this, where the output units are being trained to binary values, it is much more informative to compare the relative activity of the output units to the desired pattern and simply count the number of inputs that are "wrong". This approach was used to determine whether each phrase had been processed correctly or incorrectly by the network. Preposition output errors were counted by identifying the most highly activated output unit and checking whether it matched the correct preposition. Since the number of active units in the SR component of each training pattern varies from one to three, a response was registered as incorrect if any of the units that should have been off were more active than any of those that should have been on. These results are reported in Table 2 as total errors out of the 137 in the training corpus.

Table 2: Number of errors for each task in each simulation (out of 137).

	LP - LP	SR-LP	LP-SR	SR - SR
ENG 1	0	0	3	0
ENG 2	0	0	2	0
ENG 3	0	0	2	0
ENG 4	0	0	2	0
ENG AVG	0.00	0.00	2.25	0.00
GER 1	0	1	2	0
GER 2	0	1	3	0
GER 3	0	0	2	0
GER 4	0	0	4	0
GER AVG	0.00	0.50	2.75	0.00

3.2 IDEAL MEANINGS OF THE PREPOSITIONS

To find the unmodified spatial representation the net associates with each preposition, the prepositions were presented individually to the net and the resulting spatial responses recorded. This gives a context-free interpretation of each preposition. Figure 3 shows the output activity on the spatial units for one simulation in each language. The results were similar for all simulations within a language, demonstrating that the network finds fairly stable representations for the prepositions. Note that the representations of German *auf*, *an*, and *in* share much of their activation with those of English *on*, *at*, and *in*, although its distribution across the prepositions varies. For example, the preposition *auf* is activated much like English *on*, but without the units indicating the first object at the edge of and near the second. These units are found weakly activated in German *an*, along with the unit indicating coincidence. The ideal meaning of *auf*, then, may be somewhere between those of *on* and *at* in English.

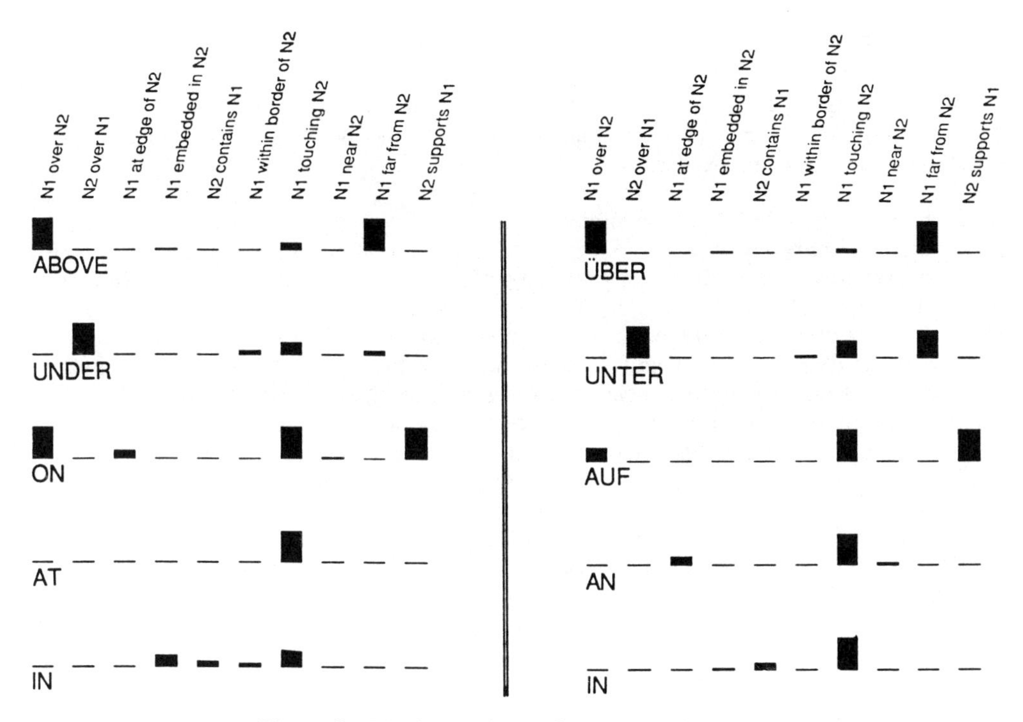

Figure 3: Ideal Meanings of the Prepositions.

3.3 TRANSLATION

We made eight translations of the 137-phrase training corpus, four from English to German and four from German to English. The performance for each network over the training corpus is shown in Table 3. The maximum number of phrases translated incorrectly was eight (94.2 percent correct), and the minimum was one wrong (99.3 percent correct). The fact that the English networks learned the training corpus better than the German networks (especially in generating a semantic description for two nouns and a preposition) shows up in the translation task. The English-to-German translations are consistently better than the German-to-English.

Table 3: Number of phrases translated incorrectly (out of 137).

SIMULATION NUMBER	ENG to GER	GER to ENG
1	1	6
2	3	7
3	2	6
4	1	8
AVG	1.75	6.75

4 DISCUSSION

Even in this highly constrained and very limited demonstration, the simulations performed using the two databases illustrate how connectionist networks can capture structures in different languages and interact.

The "interlingua" approach to machine translation has not shown promise in practical systems using frameworks based in traditional linguistic theory (Slocum, 1985). The network presented in this paper, however, supports such an approach using a connectionist framework. Of course, even if it is feasible to construct a space with which to represent semantics adequately for the limited domain of concrete uses of locative prepositions, representation of arbitrary semantics is quite another story. On the other hand, semantic representations must be components of any full-scale machine-translation system. In any event, a system that can learn bidirectional mappings between syntax and semantics from a set of examples and extend this learning to novel expressions is a candidate for machine translation (and NLP in general) that warrants further investigation.

We anticipate that any extensive application of back propagation, or any other neural network algorithm, to NLP will involve processing temporal patterns and keeping a dynamic representation of semantic hypotheses, such as the temporal scheme proposed by Elman (1988).

Acknowledgements

This research was supported in part by NSF grant IRI-8910368 to the first author and by the International Computer Science Institute, which kindly provided the first author with financial support and a stimulating research environment during the summer of 1988.

References

Cosic, C. and Munro, P. W. (1988) Learning to represent and understand locative prepositional phrases. *10th Ann. Conf. Cognitive Science Society*, 257-262.

Elman, J. L. (1988) Finding structure in time. CRL TR 8801, Center for Research in Language, University of California, San Diego.

Herskovits, Annette (1986) *Language and Spatial Cognition.* Cambridge University Press, Cambridge.

Hinton, Geoffrey (1986) Learning distributed representations of concepts. *8th Ann. Conf. Cognitive Science Society*, 1-12.

Rumelhart, D. E., Hinton, G. and Williams, R. W. (1986) Learning internal representations by error propagation. In: *Parallel Distributed Processing: Explorations in the Microstructure of Cognition.* Vol 1. D. E. Rumelhart and J. L McClelland, eds. Cambridge: MIT/Bradford.

Slocum, J. (1985) A survey of machine translation: its history, current status, and future prospects. *Computational Linguistics, 11*, 1-17.

A Short-Term Memory Architecture for the Learning of Morphophonemic Rules

Michael Gasser and Chan-Do Lee
Computer Science Department
Indiana University
Bloomington, IN 47405

Abstract

Despite its successes, Rumelhart and McClelland's (1986) well-known approach to the learning of morphophonemic rules suffers from two deficiencies: (1) It performs the artificial task of associating forms with forms rather than perception or production. (2) It is not constrained in ways that humans learners are. This paper describes a model which addresses both objections. Using a simple recurrent architecture which takes both forms and "meanings" as inputs, the model learns to generate verbs in one or another "tense", given arbitrary meanings, and to recognize the tenses of verbs. Furthermore, it fails to learn reversal processes unknown in human language.

1 BACKGROUND

In the debate over the power of connectionist models to handle linguistic phenomena, considerable attention has been focused on the learning of simple morphological rules. It is a straightforward matter in a symbolic system to specify how the meanings of a stem and a bound morpheme combine to yield the meaning of a whole word and how the form of the bound morpheme depends on the shape of the stem. In a distributed connectionist system, however, where there may be no explicit morphemes, words, or rules, things are not so simple.

The most important work in this area has been that of Rumelhart and McClelland (1986), together with later extensions by Marchman and Plunkett (1989). The networks involved were trained to associate English verb stems with the corresponding past-tense forms, successfully generating both regular and irregular forms and generalizing to novel inputs. This work established that rule-like linguistic behavior could be achieved in a system with no explicit rules. However, it did have important limitations, among them the following:

1. The representation of linguistic form was inadequate. This is clear, for example, from the fact that distinct lexical items may be associated with identical representations (Pinker & Prince, 1988).

2. The model was trained on an artificial task, quite unlike the perception and production that real hearers and speakers engage in. Of course, because it has no semantics, the model also says nothing about the issue of compositionality.

One consequence of both of these shortcomings is that there are few constraints on the kinds of processes that can be learned.

In this paper we describe a model which addresses these objections to the earlier work on morphophonemic rule acquisition. The model learns to generate forms in one or another "tense", given arbitrary patterns representing "meanings", and to yield the appropriate tense, given forms. The network sees linguistic forms one segment at a time, saving the context in a short-term memory. This style of representation, together with the more realistic tasks that the network is faced with, results in constraints on what can be learned. In particular, the system experiences difficulty learning reversal processes which do not occur in human language and which were easily accommodated by the earlier models.

2 SHORT-TERM MEMORY AND PREDICTION

Language takes place in time, and at some point, systems that learn and process language have to come to grips with this fact by accepting input in sequential form. Sequential models require some form of short-term memory (STM) because the decisions that are made depend on context. There are basically two options, window approaches, which make available stretches of input events all at once, and dynamic memory approaches (Port, 1990), which offer the possibility of a recoded version of past events. Networks with recurrent connections have the capacity for dynamic memory. We make use of a variant of a simple recurrent network (Elman, 1990), which is a pattern associator with recurrent connections on its hidden layer. Because the hidden layer receives input from itself as well as from the units representing the current event, it can function as a kind of STM for sequences of events.

Elman has shown how networks of this type can learn a great deal about the structure of the inputs when trained on the simple, unsupervised task of predicting the next input event. We are interested in what can be expected from such a network that is given a single phonological segment (hereafter referred to as a *phone*) at a time and trained to predict the next phone. If a system could learn to do this successfully, it would have a left-to-right version of what phonologists call *phonotactics*; that is, it would have knowledge of what phones tend to follow other phones in given contexts. Since word recognition and production apparently build on phonotactic knowledge of the language (Church, 1987), training on the prediction task might provide a way of integrating the two processes within a single network.

3 ARCHITECTURE

The type of network we work with is shown in Figure 1. Both its inputs and

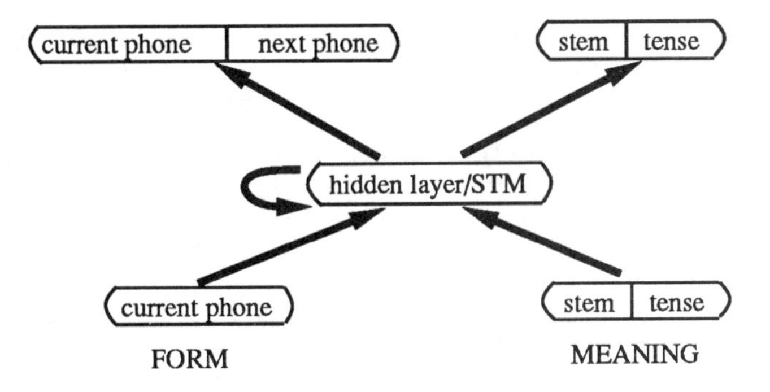

Figure 1: Network Architecture

outputs include FORM, that is, an individual phone, and what we'll call MEANING, that is, a pattern representing the stem of the word to be recognized or produced and a single unit representing a grammatical feature such as PAST or PRESENT. In fact, the meaning patterns have no real semantics, but like real meanings, they are arbitrarily assigned to the various morphemes and thus convey nothing about the phonological realization of the stem and grammatical feature. The network is trained both to auto-associate the current phone and predict the next phone.

The word recognition task corresponds to being given phone inputs (together with a default pattern on the meaning side) and generating meaning outputs. The meaning outputs are copied to the input meaning layer on each time step. While networks trained in this way can learn to recognize the words they are trained on, we have not been able to get them to generalize well. Networks which are expected only to output the grammatical feature, however, do generalize, as we shall see.

The word production task corresponds to being given a constant meaning input and generating form output. Following an initial default phone pattern, the phone input is what was predicted on the last time step. Again, however, though such a network does fine on the training set, it does not generalize well to novel inputs. We have had more success with a version using "teacher forcing". Here the correct current phone is provided on the input at each time step.

4 SIMULATIONS

4.1 STIMULI

We conducted a set of experiments to test the effectiveness of this architecture for the learning of morphophonemic rules. Input words were composed of sequences of phones in an artificial language. Each of the 15 possible phones was represented by a pattern over a set of 8 phonetic features. For each simulation, a set of 20 words was generated randomly from the set of possible words. Twelve of these were designated "training" words, 8 "test" words.

For each of these basic words, there was an associated inflected form. For each simulation, one of a set of 9 rules was used to generate the inflected form: (1) suffix (+ assimilation) (gip→gips, gib→gibz), (2) prefix (+ assimilation) (gip→zgip, kip→skip), (3) gemination (iga→igga), (4) initial deletion (gip→ip), (5) medial deletion (ipka→ipa), (6) final deletion (gip→gi), (7) tone change (gíp→gìp), (8) Pig Latin (gip→ipge), and (9) reversal (gip→pig).

In the two assimilation cases, the suffix or prefix agreed with the preceding or following phone on the voice feature. In the suffixing example, p is followed by s because it is voiceless, b by z because it is voiced. In the prefixing example, g is preceded by z because it is voiced, k by s because it is voiceless. Because the network is trained on prediction, these two rules are not symmetric. It would not be surprising if such a network could learn to generate a final phone which agrees in voicing with the phone preceding it. But in the prefixing case, the network must choose the correct prefix before it has seen the phone with which it is to agree in voicing. We thought this would still be possible, however, because the network also receives meaning input representing the stem of the word to be produced.

We hoped that the network would succeed on rule types which are common in natural languages and fail on those which are rare or non-existent. Types 1–4 are relatively common, types 5–7 infrequent or rare, type 8 apparently known only in language games, and type 9 apparently non-occurring.

For convenience, we will refer to the uninflected form of a word as the "present" and the inflected form as the "past tense" of the word in question. Each input word consisted of a present or past tense form preceded and followed by a word boundary pattern composed of zeroes. Meaning patterns consisted of an arbitrary pattern across a set of 6 "stem" units, representing the meaning of the "stem" of one of the 20 input words, plus a single bit representing the "tense" of the input word, that is, present or past.

4.2 TRAINING

During training each of the training words was presented in both present and past forms, while the test words appeared in the present form only. Each of the 32 separate words was trained in both the recognition and production directions.

For recognition training, the words were presented, one phone at a time, on the form input units. The appropriate pattern was also provided on the stem meaning units. Targets specified the current phone, next phone, and complete meaning. Thus the network was actually being trained to generate only the tense portion of the meaning for each word. The activation on the tense output unit was copied to the tense input unit following each time step.

For production training, the stem and grammatical feature were presented on the lexical input layer and held constant throughout the word. The phones making up the word were presented one at a time beginning with the initial word boundary, and the network was expected to predict the next phone in each case.

There were 10 separate simulations for each of the 9 inflectional rules. Pilot runs

Table 1: Results of Recognition and Production Tests

	RECOGNITION	PRODUCTION	
	% tenses correct	% segments correct	% affixes correct
Suffix	79	82	83
Prefix	76	62	76
Tone change	99	98	–
Gemination	90	74	42
Deletion	67	31	–
Pig Latin	61	27	–
Reversal	13	23	–

were used to find estimates of the best hidden layer size. This varied between 16 and 26. Training continued until the mean sum-of-squares error was less than 0.05. This normally required between 50 and 100 epochs. Then the connection weights were frozen, and the network was tested in both the recognition and production directions on the past tense forms of the test words.

4.3 RESULTS

In all cases, the network learned the training set quite successfully (at least 95% of the phones for production and 96% of the tenses for recognition). Results for the recognition and production of past-tense forms of test words are shown in Table 1. For recognition, chance is 37.5%. For production, the network's output on a given time step was considered to be that phone which was closest to the pattern on the phone output units.

5 DISCUSSION

5.1 AFFIXATION AND ASSIMILATION

The model shows clear evidence of having learned morphophonemic rules which it uses in both the production and perception directions. And the degree of mastery of the rules, at least for production, mirrors the extent to which the types of rules occur in natural languages. Significantly, the net is able to generate appropriate forms even in the prefix case when a "right-to-left" (anticipatory) rule is involved. That is, the fact that the network is trained only on prediction does not limit it to left-to-right (perseverative) rules because it has access to a "meaning" which permits the required "lookahead" to the relevant feature on the phone following the prefix. What makes this interesting is the fact that the meaning patterns bear no relation to the phonology of the stems. The connections between the stem meaning input units and the hidden layer are being trained to encode the voicing feature even when, in the case of the test words, this was never required during training.

In any case, it is clear that right-to-left assimilation in a network such as this is more difficult to acquire than left-to-right assimilation, all else being equal. We are unaware of any evidence that would support this, though the fact that prefixes are less common than suffixes in the world's languages (Hawkins & Cutler, 1988) means that there are at least fewer opportunities for the right-to-left process.

5.2 REVERSAL

What is it that makes the reversal rule, apparently difficult for human language learners, so difficult for the network? Consider what the network does when it is faced with the past-tense form of a verb trained only in the present. If the novel item took the form of a set rather than a sequence, it would be identical to the familiar present-tense form. What the network sees, however, is a sequence of phones, and its task is to predict the next. There is thus no sharing at all between the present and past forms and no basis for generalizing from the present to the past. Presented with the novel past form, it is more likely to base its response on similarity with a word containing a similar sequence of phones (e.g., `gip` and `gif`) than it is with the correct mirror-image sequence.

It is important to note, however, that difficulty with the reversal process does not necessarily presuppose the type of representations that result from training a simple recurrent net on prediction. Rather this depends more on the fact that the network is trained to map meaning to form and form to meaning, rather than form to form, as in the case of the Rumelhart and McClelland (1986) model. Any network of the former type which represents linguistic form in such a way that the contexts of the phones are preserved is likely to exhibit this behavior.[1]

6 LIMITATIONS AND EXTENSIONS

Despite its successes, this model is far from an adequate account of the recognition and production of words in natural language. First, although networks of the type studied here are capable of yielding complete meanings given words and complete words given meanings, they have difficulty when expected to respond to novel forms or combinations of known meanings. In the simulations, we asked the network to recognize only the grammatical morpheme in a novel word, and in production we kept it on track by giving it the correct input phone on each time step. It will be important to discover ways to make the system robust enough to respond appropriately to novel forms and combinations of meanings.

Equally important is the ability of the model to handle more complex phonological processes. Recently Lakoff (1988) and Touretzky and Wheeler (1990) have developed connectionist models to deal with complicated interacting phonological rules. While these models demonstrate that connectionism offers distinct advantages to conventional serial approaches to phonology, they do not learn phonology (at least not in a connectionist way), and they do not yet accommodate perception.

We believe that the performance of the model will be significantly improved by the capacity to make reference directly to units larger than the phone. We are currently investigating an architecture consisting of a hierarchy of networks of the type described here, each trained on the prediction task at a different time scale.

[1] We are indebted to Dave Touretzky for helping to clarify this issue.

7 CONCLUSIONS

It is by now clear that a connectionist system can be trained to exhibit rule-like behavior. What is not so clear is whether networks can discover how to map elements of form onto elements of meaning and to use this knowledge to interpret and generate novel forms. It has been argued (Fodor & Pylyshyn, 1988) that this behavior requires the kind of constituency which is not available to networks making use of distributed representations.

The present study is one attempt to demonstrate that networks are not limited in this way. We have shown that, given "meanings" and temporally distributed representations of words, a network can learn to isolate stems and the realizations of grammatical features, associate them with their meanings, and, in a somewhat limited sense, use this knowledge to produce and recognize novel forms. In addition, the nature of the training task constrains the system in such a way that rules which are rare or non-occurring in natural language are not learned.

References

Church, K. W. (1987). Phonological parsing and lexical retrieval. *Cognition, 25*, 53–69.

Elman, J. (1990). Finding structure in time. *Cognitive Science, 14*, 179–211.

Fodor, J., & Pylyshyn, Z. (1988). Connectionism and cognitive architecture: A critical analysis. *Cognition, 28*, 3–71.

Hawkins, J. A., & Cutler, A. (1988). Psychological factors in morphological asymmetry. In J. A. Hawkins (Ed.), *Explaining language universals* (pp. 280-317). Oxford: Basil Blackwell.

Lakoff, G. (1988). *Cognitive phonology.* Paper presented at the Annual Meeting of the Linguistics Society of America.

Marchman, V., & Plunkett, K. (1989). Token frequency and phonological predictability in a pattern association network: Implications for child language acquisition. *Proceedings of the Annual Conference of the Cognitive Science Society, 11*, 179–187.

Pinker, S., & Prince, A. (1988). On language and connectionism: Analysis of a parallel distributed processing model of language acquisition. *Cognition, 28*, 73–193.

Port, R. (1990). Representation and recognition of temporal patterns. *Connection Science, 2*, 151–176.

Rumelhart, D., & McClelland, J. (1986). On learning the past tense of English verbs. In J. L. McClelland & D. E. Rumelhart (Eds.), *Parallel Distributed Processing*, Vol. 2 (pp. 216–271). Cambridge, MA: MIT Press.

Touretzky, D. and Wheeler, D. (1990). A computational basis for phonology. In D. S. Touretzky (Ed.), *Advances in Neural Information Processing Systems 2*, San Mateo, CA: Morgan Kaufmann.

Exploiting Syllable Structure in a Connectionist Phonology Model

David S. Touretzky **Deirdre W. Wheeler**
School of Computer Science
Carnegie Mellon University
Pittsburgh, PA 15213-3890

Abstract

In a previous paper (Touretzky & Wheeler, 1990a) we showed how adding a clustering operation to a connectionist phonology model produced a parallel processing account of certain "iterative" phenomena. In this paper we show how the addition of a second structuring primitive, *syllabification*, greatly increases the power of the model. We present examples from a non-Indo-European language that appear to require rule ordering to at least a depth of four. By adding syllabification circuitry to structure the model's perception of the input string, we are able to handle these examples with only two derivational steps. We conclude that in phonology, derivation can be largely replaced by structuring.

1 Introduction

In linguistics a *grammar* is an abstract formal system describing a language. The term *psycho-grammar* has been suggested for systems that express the linguistic knowledge that actually exists in speakers' heads (George, 1989). Psycho-grammars may differ from grammars as a result of performance demands, limited memory capacity, or other aspects of mental representations. Psycho-grammars are still somewhat abstract, in that they are concerned with mental rather than physical phenomena. The term *physio-grammar* (George, 1989) refers to the the physical representation of grammatical knowledge in neural structures, such as (perhaps) synapse strengths. Detailed proposals for physio-grammars do not yet exist; the field of neurolinguistics is insufficiently advanced to support such proposals at present.

We are developing a theory of phonology that is compatible with gross constraints on neural processing and cognitive plausibility. Our research, then, is on the construction of psycho-grammars at the phonological level. We use a connectionist model to demonstrate

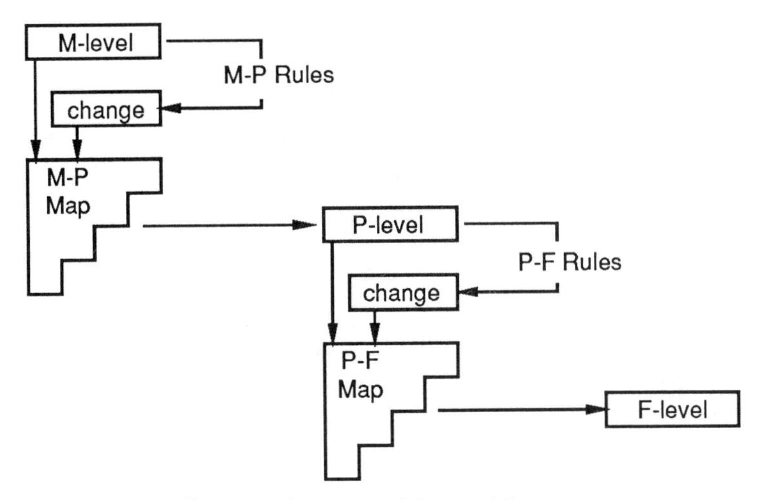

Figure 1: Structure of the model.

the computational feasibility of the psycho-grammar architecture we propose. In this paper we show how the addition of syllabification as a primitive operation greatly increases the scope and power of the model at little computational cost.

2 Structure of the Model

Our model, shown in Figure 1, has three levels of representation. Following Lakoff (1989), they are labeled M, P, and F. The M, or morpho-phonemic level, is a sequence of phonemes constructed by concatenating abstract underlying representations of morphemes. The P, or phonemic level, is an intermediate representation that is constrained to hold syllabically well-formed strings. The F, or phonetic level, is the surface level representation: a sequence of phonetic segments. Derivations are performed by mapping strings from M to P level, and then from P to F level, under the control of a set of language-specific rules. These rules alter the mapping in various ways to effect processes such as voicing assimilation and vowel harmony.

The model has a number of important constraints. Rules at a given level (M-P or P-F) apply in a single parallel step during the mapping from one level to the next. There is no iterative rule application. "Iterative" processes are instead handled by a parallel clustering mechanism described in Touretzky & Wheeler (1990a,1991). The connectionist implementation uses limited-depth, strictly feed-forward circuitry, so the model has minimal computational complexity.

Another very important constraint is that only two levels of derivation are provided, M-P and P-F, so there is no room for the long chains of ordered rules that other phonological theories permit. However, in standard analyses some languages appear to require long rule chains. The problem for those who want to eliminate such chains on grounds of cognitive implausibility[1] is to reformulate existing linguistic analyses to account for the data in some

[1]Here we are referring to Goldsmith (1990) and Lakoff (1989), as well as our own work.

/ hro+aht ũ/	"he has disappeared"
hro ht ũ	*vowel deletion*
hró ht ũ	*stress*
ró ht ũ	*initial h-deletion*
ró hdũ	*pre-son. voicing*
[ró hdũ]	

/ ʌ̃+k+hrek+?/	"I will push it"
ʌ̃́ k hrek ?	*stress*
ʌ̃́ k hreke?	*epenthesis*
ʌ̃́ k hrege?	*pre-son. voicing*
[ʌ̃́ k hrege?]	

Figure 2: Two Mohawk derivations.

other way. This is not always easy to do, especially in our model, which is more tightly constrained than either the Goldsmith or Lakoff proposals. Such reformulations help us to see how psycho-grammar diverges from grammar when computational constraints are taken into consideration.

3 A Problem From Mohawk

In Mohawk, an American Indian language, stress is placed on the penultimate syllable of a word. Since there are processes in Mohawk that add and delete vowels from words, their interaction with the stress rule is problematic. Figure 2 shows two Mohawk derivations in a standard generative account.[2] The first example shows us that vowel deletion must precede stress assignment. The penultimate vowel /a/ in the underlying form does not appear in the surface form of the word. Instead stress is assigned to the preceding vowel, /o/, which is is the penultimate vowel in the surface form. The second example shows that stress assignment must precede vowel epenthesis (insertion), because the epenthetic /e/ that appears in the surface form is not counted when determining the penultimate vowel. Since the epenthetic /e/ is also the trigger for presonorant voicing in this example, we see that voicing must be ordered after vowel epenthesis. Together these two examples indicate the following rule ordering: Vowel deletion < Stress < Epenthesis < Pre-sonorant voicing. But this is a depth of four, and our model permits only two levels of derivation. We therefore must produce an alternative account of these four processes that requires fewer derivations. To do so, we rely on three features of the model: parallel rule application, multi-level representations, and a structuring primitive: syllabification.

4 Representation of Syllable Structure

Most insertion and deletion operations are syllabically-motivated (Itô, 1989). By adding a syllabification mechanism to our model, we can replace certain derivational (string-rewriting) steps with more constrained and perhaps cognitively less taxing structuring steps. Linguists represent syllables as tree structures, as in the left portion of Figure 3. The nucleus of the syllable is normally a vowel. Any preceding consonants form the onset, and any following consonants the coda. The combined nucleus and coda make up the rime. In the middle portion of Figure 3 the syllabic structure of the English word "tokens" (phonetic transcription [tokɛnz]) is shown in this hierarchically structured form. The right portion shows how we encode the same information in our model using a set of onset, nucleus,

[2]These examples, derived from Halle & Clements (1983), are cited in Lakoff (1989). We thank Marianne Mithun (p.c.) for correcting an error in the original data.

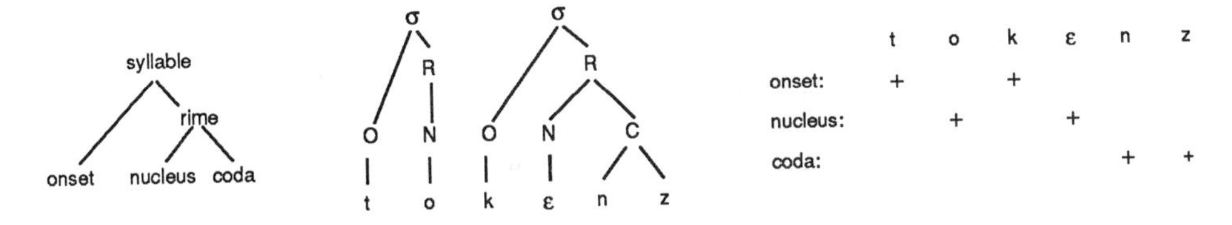

Figure 3: Representations for syllable structure.

M:	hr oaht ũ		M:	ʌ̃khr ek ʔ	
onset:	++ +		onset:	++ +	*epenthesis*
nucleus:	+ +	*vowel del.*	nucleus:	+ +	
coda:	+		coda:	+ +	
		stress (M-P)			*stress (M-P)*
P:	hr ó ht ũ		P:	ʌ̃́khr ekeʔ	
		h-del.; pre-son.			*pre-son.*
F:	r ó hdũ	*voicing (P-F)*	F:	ʌ̃́khr egeʔ	*voicing (P-F)*

Figure 4: Our solution to the Mohawk problem.

and coda bits, or ONC bits for short. We have no explicit representation for rimes, but this could be added if necessary.

In Mohawk, the vowel deletion and epenthesis processes are both syllabically motivated. Vowel deletion enforces a constraint against branching nuclei.[3] Epenthesis inserts a vowel to break up a word-final consonant cluster (/k/ followed by glottal stop /ʔ/) that would be an illegal syllable coda. Our contention is that syllabification operates on the M-level string by setting the associated ONC bits in such a way that the P-level string will be syllabically well-formed. The ONC bits share control with the M-P rules of the mapping from M to P level.

Every M-level segment must have one of its ONC bits set in order to be mapped to P-level. Thus, the syllabifier can cause a vowel to be deleted at P simply by failing to set its nucleus bit, as occurs for the /a/ in /hroahtũ/ in Figure 4. For the /ʌ̃khrekʔ/ example, note in Figure 4 that the /k/ has been marked as an onset by the syllabifier and the /ʔ/ as a coda; there is no intervening nucleus. This automatically triggers an insertion by the M-P map, so that a vowel will appear between these two segments at P-level. The vowel chosen is the default or "unmarked" vowel for that particular language; for Mohawk it is /e/. For further details of the syllabification algorithm, see Touretzky & Wheeler (1990b).

The left half of Figure 5 shows our formulation of the Mohawk stress rule, which assigns stress to the penultimate nucleus of a word. Rather than looking directly at the M-level buffer, the rule looks at the "projection" of the nucleus tier. By this we mean the M-level substring consisting of those segments whose nucleus bit is set. The # symbol indicates a word boundary. Since vowels deleted by the syllabifier have no nucleus bit set, and

[3]This constraint is not shared by all languages. Furthermore, deletion is only one possible solution; another would be to insert a consonant or glide, such as /w/, to separate the vowels into different syllables. Each language makes its own choices about how constraint violations are to be repaired.

Figure 5: Rules for Mohawk stress (M-P) and presonorant voicing (P-F).

epenthetic vowels that will be inserted by the syllabifier have no nucleus bit at M-level, insertion and deletion processes can proceed in parallel with stress assignment. At P-level, all that's left to be done in this example is pre-sonorant voicing, handled by the P-F rule shown in the right half of the figure.

5 More Complex Stress Rules

In Mohawk, stress falls on the penultimate syllable regardless of the internal structure of the syllable. This stress assignment rule is quite simple compared to some other languages. For example, "quantity sensitive" languages make distinctions among syllable types for purposes of stress assignment. A syllable consisting of an optional onset and a single, short vowel in the rime is normally said to be "light," while syllables with codas and/or long vowels (often represented as double nuclei) are designated "heavy," and typically attract stress. Thus, for example, in Aguacatec Mayan (Hayes, 1981) stress falls on the rightmost syllable with a long vowel, otherwise the final syllable.

In order to account for syllable weight distinctions we introduce an additional level of representation, as illustrated in Figure 6 using C and V to represent consonants and vowels, respectively. The "mora" bit is activated for all segments that contribute to syllable weight in the language. In this particular language only vowels are important for determining the weight of syllables, so the mora bit is activated for all and only the vocalic segments. Once moras have been identified, universal principles come into play, and bits for "syllable" and "heavy syllable" are set. The syllable bit is activated for the first of a sequence of one or more moras; the heavy syllable bit is activated for syllables containing two or more moras. With this enriched representation, the stress patterns of quantity-sensitive languages can be straightforwardly generated. To stress the last heavy syllable, we assign [+stress] to segments on the heavy syllable tier that have word boundaries to their right. (Word boundaries must be projected down to the heavy syllable tier for this purpose.)

Languages like Yana (Hayes, 1981), in which both long vowels and codas make syllables heavy, have a slightly different representation at the mora level. In these languages, coda consonants as well as vocalic segments trigger the activation of the mora bit, as illustrated in Figure 7. Here again, while specification of what counts as a mora is a language-specific parameter, once the mora bits are set the syllable and heavy syllable representations follow from universal principles. The mora bit is activated for any segment which has either the nucleus or coda bit set, essentially collapsing the nucleus and coda tiers. The Yana stress rule targets the leftmost heavy syllable in a word, no matter how far it might occur from the initial word boundary, or the first syllable if none are heavy. The latter case requires a separate rule with a slightly more complex environment; rules of this form are discussed in Wheeler & Touretzky (1991).

	#	C	V	C	V	C	V	V	C	V	C	V	V	C	#
onset		+		+		+			+		+				
nucleus			+		+		+	+		+		+	+		
coda														+	
mora			+		+		+	+		+		+	+		
syllable			+		+		+			+		+			
heavy syllable							+					+			

Figure 6: Long vowels make syllables heavy in Aguacatec Mayan.

	#	C	V	C	V	C	C	V	C	V	V	C	V	V	C	#
onset		+		+			+		+			+				
nucleus			+		+			+		+	+		+	+		
coda						+									+	
mora			+		+	+		+		+	+		+	+	+	
syllable			+		+			+		+			+			
heavy syllable					+					+			+			

Figure 7: Long vowels or codas make syllables heavy in Yana.

6 Discussion

For the linguist, it is interesting to see how structuring operations such as clustering and syllabification can take some of the pressure off derivation, thereby allowing strict limits to be maintained on derivational depth. But what is the significance of this work for connectionists? Unlike most other attempts to model phonological processes in neural networks, we demonstrate the influence computational modeling can have on the development of a linguistic theory. In designing a system for expressing linguistic processes, there must be some sort of cost metric to determine which operations are computationally feasible and which are not. A connectionist implementation provides a natural cost metric: size (depth, fanout, component count) of the required threshold logic circuity.

It is doubtful that the structure of our model corresponds to that of some cortical language area, and we reject any simplistic analogy between threshold logic units and neurons. Using circuit complexity as a cost metric can be independently justified on grounds of simplicity and theoretical elegance. If one measures cost in some more abstract way, there is a danger that computationally expensive mechanisms may lurk beneath the grammar's apparent simplicity. An example is the local rule ordering proposal of Anderson (1974), in which explicit rule ordering is eliminated by introducing a much more complex mechanism for determining, on a case-by-case basis, the order in which rules should apply.

If the mental representation of utterances is fundamentally different from the discrete symbolic form we've assumed,[4] we may be using the wrong cost metric for determining cognitive plausibility. However, we are constrained, like everyone else, to work within the computational frameworks that are presently available.

[4]For example: if phonetic strings turn out to be represented in the brain as chaotic trajectories in a high dimensional dynamical system, or something equally exotic.

There remains the question of why structuring should be preferred over derivation. First, since some mutation processes are sensitive to syllabic structure, this information would have to be computed even if insertions and deletions weren't handled by the syllabifier. Second, structuring is a highly constrained operation; it merely annotates an existing string to reflect constituency relationships, whereas derivations can make arbitrary changes to a string. We therefore assume that derivations have a higher cognitive cost, despite the fact that they can be computed fairly efficiently in our model by the mapping matrix described in Touretzky & Wheeler (1991). Finally, adding extra derivational levels increases the difficulty of phonological rule induction, a topic of current research.

Acknowledgements

This work was sponsored by a grant from the Hughes Aircraft Corporation, by National Science Foundation grant EET-8716324, and by the Office of Naval Research under contract number N00014-86-K-0678.

References

Anderson, S. R. (1974) *The Organization of Phonology.* New York: Academic Press.

George, A. (1989) How not to become confused about linguistics. In A. George (ed.), *Reflections on Chomsky*, 90-110. Oxford, UK: Basil Blackwell.

Goldsmith, J. A. (1990) *Autosegmental and Metrical Phonology.* Oxford, UK: Basil Blackwell.

Halle, M., and Clements, G. N. (1983) *Problem Book in Phonology: A Workbook for Introductory Courses in Linguistics and Modern Phonology.* Cambridge, MA: The MIT Press.

Hayes, B. (1981) *A Metrical Theory of Stress Rules.* Doctoral dissertation, MIT, Cambridge, MA.

Itô, J. (1989) A prosodic theory of epenthesis. *Natural Language and Linguistic Theory,* 7(2), 217-259.

Lakoff, G. (1989) Cognitive phonology. Draft of paper presented at the UC-Berkeley Workshop on Constraints vs. Rules, May 1989.

Touretzky, D. S., and Wheeler, D. W. (1990a) A computational basis for phonology. In D. S. Touretzky (ed.), *Advances in Neural Information Processing Systems* 2, 372-379. San Mateo, CA: Morgan Kaufmann.

Touretzky, D. S., and Wheeler, D. W. (1990b) Two derivations suffice: the role of syllabification in cognitive phonology. In C. Tenny (ed.), *The MIT Parsing Volume, 1989-1990,* 21-35. MIT Center for Cognitive Science, Parsing Project Working Papers 3.

Touretzky, D. S., and Wheeler, D. W. (1991) Sequence manipulation using parallel mapping networks. *Neural Computation* 3(1):98-109.

Wheeler, D. W., and Touretzky, D. S. (1991) From syllables to stress: a cognitively plausible model. In K. Deaton, M. Noske, and M. Ziolkowski (eds.), *CLS 26-II: Papers from the Parasession on The Syllable in Phonetics and Phonology, 1990.* Chicago Linguistic Society.

Language Induction by Phase Transition in Dynamical Recognizers

Jordan B. Pollack
Laboratory for AI Research
The Ohio State University
Columbus, OH 43210
pollack@cis.ohio-state.edu

Abstract

A higher order recurrent neural network architecture learns to recognize and generate languages after being "trained" on categorized exemplars. Studying these networks from the perspective of dynamical systems yields two interesting discoveries: First, a longitudinal examination of the learning process illustrates a new form of mechanical inference: Induction by phase transition. A small weight adjustment causes a "bifurcation" in the limit behavior of the network. This phase transition corresponds to the onset of the network's capacity for generalizing to arbitrary-length strings. Second, a study of the automata resulting from the acquisition of previously published languages indicates that while the architecture is NOT guaranteed to find a minimal finite automata consistent with the given exemplars, which is an NP-Hard problem, the architecture does appear capable of generating non-regular languages by exploiting fractal and chaotic dynamics. I end the paper with a hypothesis relating linguistic generative capacity to the behavioral regimes of non-linear dynamical systems.

1 Introduction

I expose a recurrent high-order back-propagation network to both positive and negative examples of boolean strings, and report that although the network does **not** find the minimal-description finite state automata for the languages (which is NP-Hard (Angluin, 1978)), it does induction in a novel and interesting fashion, and searches through a hypothesis space which, theoretically, is not constrained to machines of finite state. These results are of import to many related neural models currently under development, e.g. (Elman, 1990; Giles et al., 1990; Servan-Schreiber et al., 1989), and relates ultimately to the question of how linguistic capacity can arise in nature.

Although the transitions among states in a finite-state automata are usually thought of as being fully specified by a table, a transition function can also be specified as a mathematical function of the current state and the input. It is known from (McCulloch & Pitts, 1943) that even the most elementary modeling assumptions yield finite-state control, and it is worth reiterating that any network with the capacity to compute arbitrary boolean functions (say, as logical sums of products) lapedes farber how nets], white hornik .], can be used recurrently to implement arbitrary finite state machines.

From a different point of view, a recurrent network with a state evolving across k units can be considered a k-dimensional discrete-time continuous-space dynamical system, with a precise initial condition, $z_k(0)$, and a state space in Z, a subspace of R^k. The governing function, F, is parameterized by a set of weights, W, and merely computes the next state from the current state and input, $y_j(t)$, a finite sequence of patterns representing tokens from some alphabet Σ:

$$z_k(t+1) = F_W(z_k(t), y_j(t))$$

If we view one of the dimensions of this system, say z_a, as an "acceptance" dimension, we can define the language accepted by such a *Dynamical Recognizer* as all strings of input tokens evolved from the precise initial state for which the accepting dimension of the state is above a certain threshold. In network terms, one output unit would be subjected to a threshold test after processing a sequence of input patterns.

The first question to ask is how can such a dynamical system be constructed, or taught, to accept a particular language? The weights in the network, individually, do not correspond directly to graph transitions or to phrase structure rules. The second question to ask is what sort of generative power can be achieved by such systems?

2 The Model

To begin to answer the question of learning, I now present and elaborate upon my earlier work on Cascaded Networks (Pollack, 1987), which were used in a recurrent fashion to learn parity, depth-limited parenthesis balancing, and to map between word sequences and proposition representations (Pollack, 1990a). A Cascaded Network is a well-controlled higher-order connectionist architecture to which the back-propagation technique of weight adjustment (Rumelhart et al., 1986) can be applied. Basically, it consists of two subnetworks: The *function network* is a standard feed-forward network, with or without hidden layers. However, the weights are dynamically computed by the linear *context network*, whose outputs are mapped in a 1:1 fashion to the weights of the function net. Thus the input pattern to the context network is used to "multiplex" the the function computed, which can result in simpler learning tasks.

When the outputs of the function network are used as inputs to context network, a system can be built which learns to produce specific outputs for variable-length sequences of inputs. Because of the multiplicative connections, each input is, in effect, processed by a different function. Given an initial context, $z_k(0)$, and a sequence of inputs, $y_j(t)$, $t = 1...n$, the network computes a sequence of state vectors, $z_i(t)$, $t = 1...n$ by dynamically changing the set of weights, $w_{ij}(t)$. Without hidden units the forward pass computation is:

$$w_{ij}(t) = \sum_k w_{ijk} \, z_k(t-1)$$

$$z_i(t) = g(\sum_j w_{ij}(t) \, y_j(t))$$

where g is the usual sigmoid function used in back-propagation system.

In previous work, I assumed that a teacher could supply a consistent and generalizable desired-state for each member of a large set of strings, which was a significant overconstraint. In learning a two-state machine like parity, this did not matter, as the 1-bit state fully determines the output. However, for the case of a higher-dimensional system, we know what the final output of a system should be, but we *don't care* what its state should be along the way.

Jordan (1986) showed how recurrent back-propagation networks could be trained with "don't care" conditions. If there is no specific preference for the value of an output unit for a particular training example, simply consider the error term for that unit to be 0. This will work, *as long as that same unit receives feedback from other examples.* When the don't-cares line up, the weights to those units will never change. My solution to this problem involves a *backspace*, unrolling the loop only once: After propagating the errors determined on only a subset of the weights from the "acceptance" unit z_a:

$$\frac{\partial E}{\partial z_{aj}(n)} = (z_a(n) - d_a)\, z_a(n)\, (1 - z_a(n))\, y_j(n)$$

$$\frac{\partial E}{\partial w_{ajk}} = \frac{\partial E}{\partial w_{aj}(n)}\, z_k(n-1)$$

The error on the remainder of the weights ($\frac{\partial E}{\partial w_{ijk}}$, $i \neq a$) is calculated using values from the penultimate time step:

$$\frac{\partial E}{\partial z_k(n-1)} = \sum_a \sum_j \frac{\partial E}{\partial w_{ajk}} \frac{\partial E}{\partial w_{aj}(n)}$$

$$\frac{\partial E}{\partial w_{ij}(n-1)} = \frac{\partial E}{\partial z_i(n-1)}\, y_j(n-1)$$

$$\frac{\partial E}{\partial w_{ijk}} = \frac{\partial E}{\partial w_{ij}(n-1)}\, z_k(n-2)$$

This is done, in batch (epoch) style, for a set of examples of varying lengths.

3 Induction as Phase Transition

In initial studies of learning the simple regular language of odd parity, I expected the recognizer to merely implement "exclusive or" with a feedback link. It turns out that this is not quite enough. Because termination of back-propagation is usually defined as a 20% error (e.g. logical "1" is above 0.8) recurrent use of this logic tends to a limit point. In other words, mere separation of the exemplars is no guarantee that the network can recognize parity in the limit. Nevertheless, this is indeed possible as illustrated by illustrated below. In order to test the limit behavior of a recognizer, we can observe its response to a very long "characteristic string". For odd parity, the string 1* requires an alternation of responses.

A small cascaded network composed of a 1-2 function net and a 2-6 context net (requiring 18 weights) was was trained on odd parity of a small set of strings up to length 5. At each epoch, the weights in the network were saved in a file. Subsequently, each configuration was tested in its response to the first 25 characteristic strings. In figure 1, each vertical column, corresponding to an epoch, contains 25 points between 0 and 1. Initially, all strings longer than length 1 are not distinguished. From cycle 60-80, the network is improving at separating finite strings. At cycle 85, the network undergoes a "bifurcation," where the small change in weights of a single epoch leads to a phase transition from a limit point to a limit cycle.[1] This phase transition is so "adaptive" to the classification task that the network rapidly exploits it.

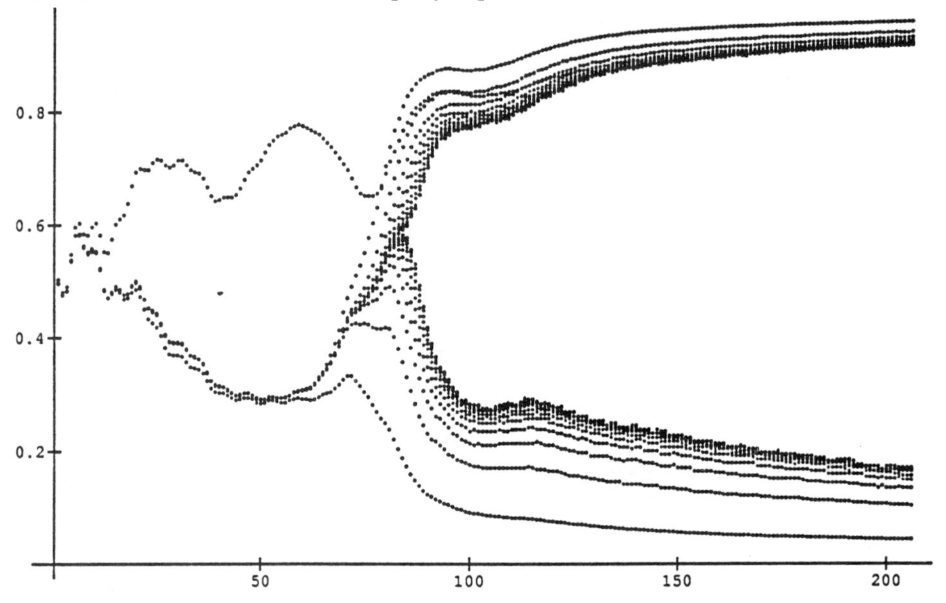

Figure 1: A bifurcation diagram showing the response of the parity-learner to the first 25 characteristic strings over 200 epochs of training.

I wish to stress that this is a new and very interesting form of mechanical induction, and reveals that with the proper perspective, non-linear connectionist networks are capable of much more complex behavior than hill-climbing. Before the phase transition, the machine is in principle **not** capable of performing the serial parity task; after the phase transition it **is**. The similarity of learning through a "flash of insight" to biological change through a "punctuated" evolution is much more than coincidence.

4 Benchmarking Results

Tomita (1982) performed elegant experiments in inducing finite automata from positive and negative evidence using hillclimbing in the space of 9-state automata. Each case was defined by two sets of boolean strings, accepted by and rejected by the regular languages

[1] For the simple low dimensional dynamical systems usually studied, the "knob" or control parameter for such a bifurcation diagram is a scalar variable; here the control parameter is the entire 32-D vector of weights in the network, and back-propagation turns the knob!

listed below.

1	1*
2	(1 0)*
3	no odd zero strings after odd 1 strings
4	no triples of zeros
5	pairwise, an even sum of 01's and 10's.
6	number of 1's - number of 0's = 3n
7	0*1*0*1*

Rather than inventing my own training data, or sampling these languages for a well-formed training set I ran all 7 Tomita training environments as given, on a sequential cascaded network of a 1-input 4-output function network (with bias, 8 weights to set) and a 3-input 8-output context network with bias, using a learning rate was of 0.3 and a momentum to 0.7. Termination was when all accepted strings returned output bits above 0.8 and rejected strings below 0.2.

Of Tomita's 7 cases, all but cases #2 and #6 converged without a problem in several hundred epochs. Case 2 would not converge, and kept treating a negative case as correct because of the difficulty for my architecture to induce a "trap" state; I had to modify the training set (by added reject strings 110 and 11010) in order to overcome this problem.[2] Case 6 took several restarts and thousands of cycles to converge, cause unknown. The complete experimental data is available in a longer report (Pollack, 1990b).

Because the states are "in a box" of low dimension,[3] we can view these machines graphically to gain some understanding of how the state space is being arranged. Based upon some intitial studies of parity, my initial hypothesis was that a set of clusters would be found, organized in some geometric fashion: i.e. an embedding of a finite state machine into a finite dimensional geometry such that each token's transitions would correspond to a simple transformation of space. Graphs of the states visited by all possible inputs up to length 10, for the 7 Tomita test cases are shown in figure 2. Each figure contains 2048 points, but often they overlap.

The images (a) and (d) are what were expected, clumps of points which closely map to states of equivalent FSA's. Images (b) and (e) have limit "ravine's" which can each be considered states as well.

5 Discussion

However, the state spaces, (c), (f), and (g) of the dynamical recognizers for Tomita cases 3, 6, and 7, are interesting, because, theoretically, they are *infinite* state machines, where the states are not arbitrary or random, requiring an infinite table of transitions, but are constrained in a powerful way by mathematical principle. In other words, the complexity is in the dynamics, not in the specifications (weights).

In thinking about such a principle, consider other systems in which extreme observed complexity emerges from algorithmic simplicity plus computational power. It is

[2] It can be argued that other FSA inducing methods get around this problem by presupposing rather than learning trap states.

[3] One reason I have succeeded in such low dimensional induction is because my architecture is a Mealy, rather than Moore Machine (Lee Giles, Personal Communication)

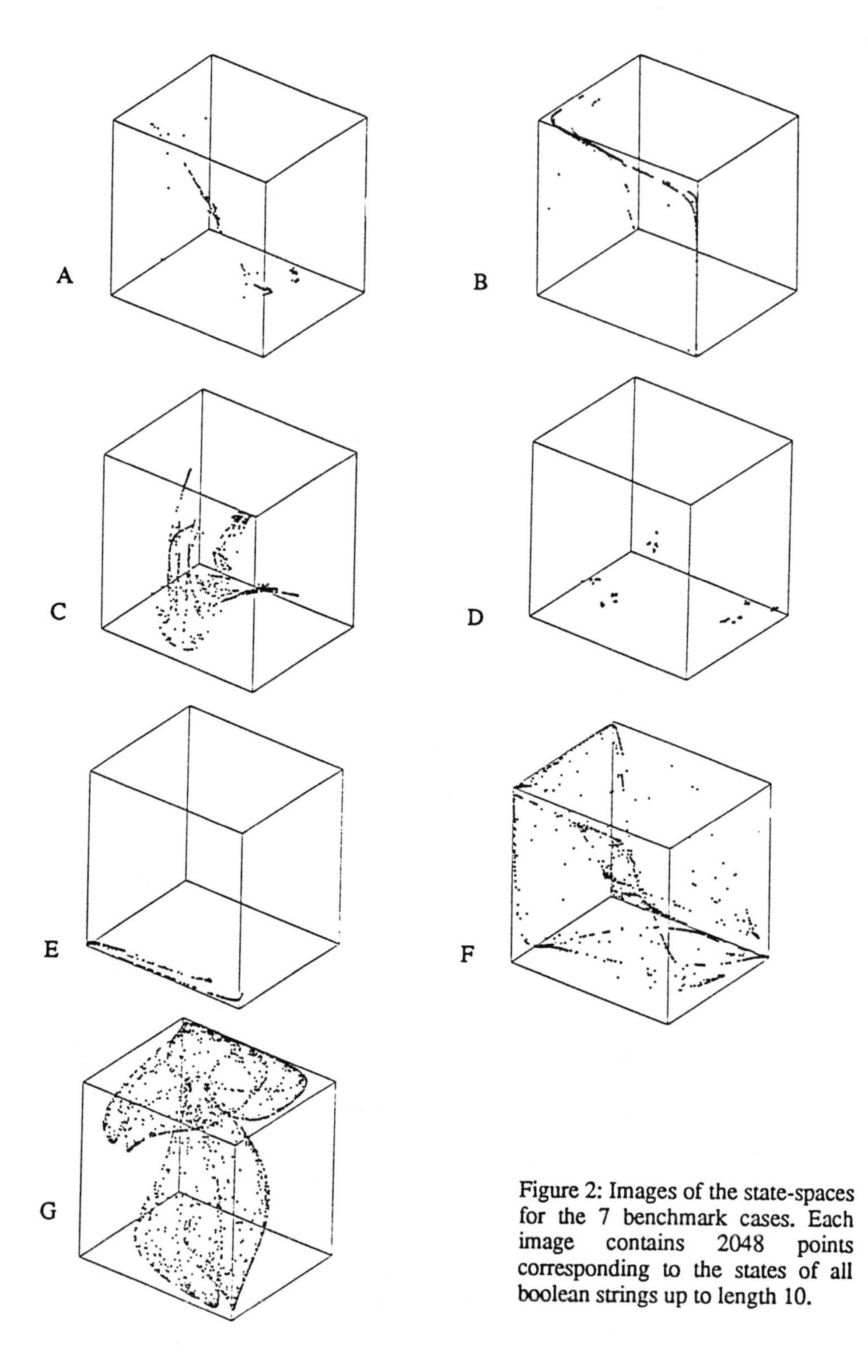

Figure 2: Images of the state-spaces for the 7 benchmark cases. Each image contains 2048 points corresponding to the states of all boolean strings up to length 10.

interesting to note that by eliminating the sigmoid and commuting the y_j and z_k terms, the forward equation for higher order recurrent networks with is identical to the generator of an Iterated Function System (IFS) (Barnsley et al., 1985). Thus, my figures of state-spaces, which emerge from the projection of Σ^* into Z, are of the same class of mathematical object as Barnsley's fractal attractors (e.g. the widely reproduced fern). Using the method of (Grassberger & Procaccia, 1983), the correlation dimension of the attractor in Figure 2(g) was found to be about 1.4.

The link between work in complex dynamical systems and neural networks is well-established both on the neurobiological level (Skarda & Freeman, 1987) and on the mathematical level (Derrida & Meir, 1988; Huberman & Hogg, 1987; Kurten, 1987; Smolensky, 1986). This paper expands a theme from an earlier proposal to link them at the "cognitive" level (Pollack, 1989).

There is an interesting formal question, which has been brought out in the work of (Wolfram, 1984) and others on the universality of cellular automata, and more recently in the work of (Crutchfield & Young, 1989) on the descriptive complexity of bifurcating systems: What is the relationship between complex dynamics (of neural systems) and traditional measures of computational complexity? From this work and other supporting evidence, I venture the following hypothesis:

> The state-space limit of a dynamical recognizer, as $\Sigma^* \rightarrow \Sigma^\infty$, is an Attractor, which is cut by a threshold (or similar decision) function. The complexity of the language recognized is regular if the cut falls between disjoint limit points or cycles, context-free if it cuts a "self-similar" (recursive) region, and context-sensitive if it cuts a "chaotic" (pseudo-random) region.

Acknowledgements

This research has been partially supported by the Office of Naval Research under grant N00014-89-J-1200.

References

Angluin, D. (1978). On the complexity of minimum inference of regular sets. *Information and Control, 39*, 337-350.

Barnsley, M. F., Ervin, V., Hardin, D. & Lancaster, J. (1985). Solution of an inverse problem for fractals and other sets. *Proceedings of the National Academy of Science, 83*.

Crutchfield, J. P & Young, K. (1989). Computation at the Onset of Chaos. In W. Zurek, (Ed.), *Complexity, Entropy and the Physics of INformation*. Reading, MA: Addison-Wesley.

Derrida, B. & Meir, R. (1988). Chaotic behavior of a layered neural network. *Phys. Rev. A, 38*.

Elman, J. L. (1990). Finding Structure in Time. *Cognitive Science, 14*, 179-212.

Giles, C. L., Sun, G. Z., Chen, H. H., Lee, Y. C. & Chen, D. (1990). Higher Order Recurrent Networks and Grammatical Inference. In D. Touretzky, (Ed.), *Advances in Neural Information Processing Systems*. Los Gatos, CA: Morgan Kaufman.

Grassberger, P. & Procaccia, I. (1983). Measuring the Strangeness of Strange Attractors. *Physica, 9D*, 189-208.

Huberman, B. A. & Hogg, T. (1987). Phase Transitions in Artificial Intelligence Systems. *Artificial Intelligence, 33*, 155-172.

Jordan, M. I. (1986). Serial Order: A Parallel Distributed Processing Approach. ICS report 8608, La Jolla: Institute for Cognitive Science, UCSD.

Kurten, K. E. (1987). Phase transitions in quasirandom neural networks. In *Institute of Electrical and Electronics Engineers First International Conference on Neural Networks.* San Diego, II-197-20.

McCulloch, W. S. & Pitts, W. (1943). A logical calculus of the ideas immanent in nervous activity. *Bulletin of Mathematical Biophysics, 5*, 115-133.

Pollack, J. B. (1987). Cascaded Back Propagation on Dynamic Connectionist Networks. In *Proceedings of the Ninth Conference of the Cognitive Science Society.* Seattle, 391-404.

Pollack, J. B. (1989). Implications of Recursive Distributed Representations. In D. Touretzky, (Ed.), *Advances in Neural Information Processing Systems.* Los Gatos, CA: Morgan Kaufman.

Pollack, J. B. (1990). Recursive Distributed Representation. *Artificial Intelligence, 46*, 77-105.

Pollack, J. B. (1990). The Induction of Dynamical Recognizers. Tech Report 90-JP-Automata, Columbus, OH 43210: LAIR, Ohio State University.

Rumelhart, D. E., Hinton, G. & Williams, R. (1986). Learning Internal Representations through Error Propagation. In D. E. Rumelhart, J. L. McClelland & the PDP research Group, (Eds.), *Parallel Distributed Processing: Experiments in the Microstructure of Cognition*, Vol. 1. Cambridge: MIT Press.

Servan-Schreiber, D., Cleeremans, A. & McClelland, J. L (1989). Encoding Sequential Structure in Simple Recurrent Networks. In D. Touretzky, (Ed.), *Advances in Neural Information Processing Systems.* Los Gatos, CA: Morgan Kaufman.

Skarda, C. A. & Freeman, W. J. (1987). How brains make chaos. *Brain & Behavioral Science, 10.*

Smolensky, P. (1986). Information Processing in Dynamical Systems: Foundations of Harmony Theory. In D. E. Rumelhart, J. L. McClelland & the PDP research Group, (Eds.), *Parallel Distributed Processing: Experiments in the Microstructure of Cognition*, Vol. 1. Cambridge: MIT Press.

Tomita, M. (1982). Dynamic construction of finite-state automata from examples using hill-climbing. In *Proceedings of the Fourth Annual Cognitive Science Conference.* Ann Arbor, MI, 105-108.

Wolfram, S. (1984). Universality and Complexity in Cellular Automata. *Physica, 10D*, 1-35.

Discovering Discrete Distributed Representations with Iterative Competitive Learning

Michael C. Mozer
Department of Computer Science
and Institute of Cognitive Science
University of Colorado
Boulder, CO 80309-0430

Abstract

Competitive learning is an unsupervised algorithm that classifies input patterns into mutually exclusive clusters. In a neural net framework, each cluster is represented by a processing unit that competes with others in a winner-take-all pool for an input pattern. I present a simple extension to the algorithm that allows it to construct discrete, *distributed* representations. Discrete representations are useful because they are relatively easy to analyze and their information content can readily be measured. Distributed representations are useful because they explicitly encode similarity. The basic idea is to apply competitive learning iteratively to an input pattern, and after each stage to subtract from the input pattern the component that was captured in the representation at that stage. This component is simply the weight vector of the winning unit of the competitive pool. The subtraction procedure forces competitive pools at different stages to encode different aspects of the input. The algorithm is essentially the same as a traditional data compression technique known as multistep vector quantization, although the neural net perspective suggests potentially powerful extensions to that approach.

1 INTRODUCTION

Competitive learning (Grossberg, 1976; Kohonen, 1982; Rumelhart & Zipser, 1985; von der Malsburg, 1973) is an unsupervised algorithm that classifies input patterns into mutually exclusive clusters. In a neural net framework, each cluster is represented by a processing unit that competes with others in a winner-take-all pool for each input pattern. Competitive learning thus constructs a local representation in which a single unit is activated in response to an input. I present a simple extension to the algorithm that allows it to construct discrete, *distributed* representations. Discrete representations are useful because they are relatively easy to analyze and their information content can readily be measured. Distributed representations are useful because they explicitly encode similarity. I begin by describing the standard competitive learning algorithm.

2 COMPETITIVE LEARNING

Consider a two layer network with α input units and β competitive units. Each competitive unit represents a different classification of the input. The competitive units are activated by the input units and are connected in a winner-take-all pool such that a single competitive unit becomes active. Formally,

$$y_i = \begin{cases} 1 & \text{if } |\mathbf{w}_i - \mathbf{x}| \le |\mathbf{w}_j - \mathbf{x}| \text{ for all } j \\ 0 & \text{otherwise,} \end{cases}$$

where y_i is the activity of competitive unit i, $\mathbf{x}$ is the input activity vector, $\mathbf{w}_i$ is the vector of connection strengths from the input units to competitive unit i, and $|\cdot|$ denotes the L2 vector norm. The conventional weight update rule is:

$$\Delta \mathbf{w}_i = \varepsilon y_i (\mathbf{x} - \mathbf{w}_i),$$

where ε is the step size. This algorithm moves each weight vector toward the center of a cluster of input patterns.

The algorithm attempts to develop the best possible representation of the input with only β discrete alternatives. This representation is simply the weight vector of the winning competitive unit, $\mathbf{w}_{winner}$. What does it mean to develop the *best* representation? Following Durbin (1990), competitive learning can be viewed as performing gradient descent in the error measure

$$E = - \sum_{p=1}^{\#patterns} \ln \sum_{i=1}^{\beta} e^{-|\mathbf{w}_i - \mathbf{x}(p)|^2/T} \qquad (1)$$

as $T \rightarrow 0$, where p is an index over patterns. T is a parameter in a soft competitive learning model (Bridle, 1989; Rumelhart, in press) which specifies the degree of competition; the winner-take-all version of competitive learning is obtained at the limit of $T = 0$.

3 EXTENDING COMPETITIVE LEARNING

Competitive learning constructs a *local* representation of the input. How might competitive learning be extended to construct *distributed* representations? One idea is to have several independent competitive pools, each of which may form its own partition of the input space. This often fails because all pools will discover the *same* partitioning if this partitioning is unequivocally better than others. Thus, we must force different pools to encode different components of the input.

In the one-pool competitive learning network, the component of the input not encoded is simply

$$\mathbf{x}' = \mathbf{x} - \mathbf{w}_{winner}.$$

If competitive learning is reapplied with $\mathbf{x}'$ instead of $\mathbf{x}$, the algorithm is guaranteed to extract information not captured by the first pool of competitive units because this information has been subtracted out. This procedure can be invoked iteratively to capture different aspects of the input in an arbitrary number of competitive pools, hence the name *iterative competitive learning* or *ICL*. The same idea is at the heart of Sanger's (1989) and Hrycej's (1989) algorithms for performing principal components analysis. Whereas these algorithms discover continuous-valued feature dimensions, ICL is concerned with the discovery of discrete-valued features. Of course, the continuous features can be quantized to form discrete features, an idea that both Sanger and Hrycej explore, but there is a cost to this, as I elaborate later.

To formalize the ICL model, consider a network composed of an arbitrary number of *stages* (Figure 1). Each stage, s, consists of α input units and $\beta^{(s)}$ competitive units. Both the input and competitive units at a given stage feed activity to the input units at the next higher stage. The activity of the input units at stage 1, $\mathbf{x}^{(1)}$, is given by the external input. At subsequent stages, s,

$$\mathbf{x}^{(s)} = \mathbf{x}^{(s-1)} - \left[\mathbf{W}^{(s-1)}\right]^{\mathrm{T}} \mathbf{y}^{(s-1)}$$

where $\mathbf{W}$ and $\mathbf{y}$ are as before with an additional index for the stage number.

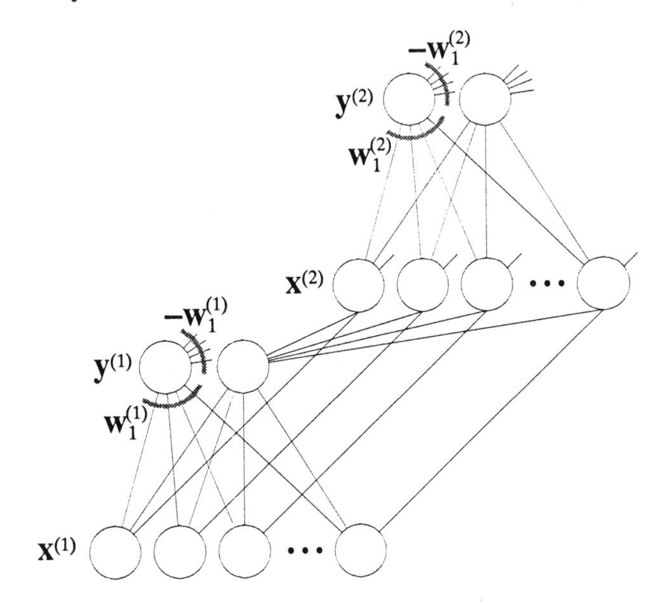

Figure 1: The Iterative Competitive Learning Model

To reconstruct the original input pattern from the activities of the competitive units, the components captured by the winning unit at each stage are simply summed together:

$$\hat{\mathbf{x}} = \sum_{s} \left[\mathbf{W}^{(s)}\right]^{\mathrm{T}} \mathbf{y}^{(s)}. \tag{2}$$

A variant of ICL has been independently proposed by Ambros-Ingerson, Granger, and Lynch (1990).[1] Their algorithm, inspired by a neurobiological model, is the same as ICL except for the competitive unit activation rule which uses an inner product instead of distance measure:

---

[1] I thank Todd Leen and Steve Rehfuss for bringing this work to my attention.

$$y_i = \begin{cases} 1 & \text{if } \mathbf{x}^T\mathbf{w}_i \geq 0 \text{ and } \mathbf{x}^T\mathbf{w}_i \geq \mathbf{x}^T\mathbf{w}_j \text{ for all } j \\ 0 & \text{otherwise.} \end{cases}$$

The problem with this rule is that it is difficult to interpret what exactly the network is computing, e.g., what aspect of the input is captured by the winning unit, whether the input can be reconstructed from the resulting activity pattern, and what information is discarded. The ICL activation rule, in combination with the learning rule, has a clear computational justification by virtue of the underlying objective measure (Equation 1) that is being optimized.

It also turns out, much to my dismay, that ICL is virtually identical to a conventional technique in data compression known as multistep vector quantization (Gray, 1984). More on this later.

4 A SIMPLE EXAMPLE

Consider a set of four input patterns forming a rectangle in 2D space, located at (−1,−.5), (−1,.5), (1,−.5), and (1,.5), and an ICL network with two stages each containing two competitive units. The first stage discovers the primary dimension of variation — along the x-axis. That is, the units develop weight vectors (−1,0) and (1,0). Removing this component from the input, the four points become (0,−.5), (0,.5), (0,−.5), (0,.5). Thus, the two points on the left side of the rectangle are collapsed together with the two points on the right side. The second stage of the network then discovers the secondary dimension of variation — along the y-axis.

The response of the ICL network to each input pattern can be summarized by the set of competitive units, one per stage, that are activated. If the two units at each stage are numbered 0 and 1, four response patterns will be generated: {0,0}, {0,1}, {1,0}, {1,1}. Thus, ICL has discovered a two-bit code to represent the four inputs. The result will be the same if instead of just four inputs, the input environment consists of four *clusters* of points centered on the corners of the rectangle. In this case, the two-bit code will not describe each input uniquely, but it will distinguish the clusters.

5 IMAGE COMPRESSION

Because ICL discovers compact and discrete codes, the algorithm should be useful for data and image compression. In such problems, a set of raw data must be transformed into a compact representation which can then be used to reconstruct the original data. ICL performs such a transformation, with the resulting code consisting of the competitive unit response pattern. The reconstruction is achieved by Equation 2.

I experimented with a 600×460 pixel image having 8 bits of gray level information per pixel. ICL was trained on random 8×8 patches of the image for a total of 125,000 training trials. The network had 64 input units and 80 stages, each with two competitive units. The initial weights were random, selected from a Normal distribution with mean zero and standard deviation .0001. A fixed ε of .01 was used. Figure 2 shows incoming connection strengths to the competitive units in the first nine stages. The connection strengths are depicted as an 8×8 grid of cells whose shading indicates the weight from the corresponding position in the image patch to the competitive unit.

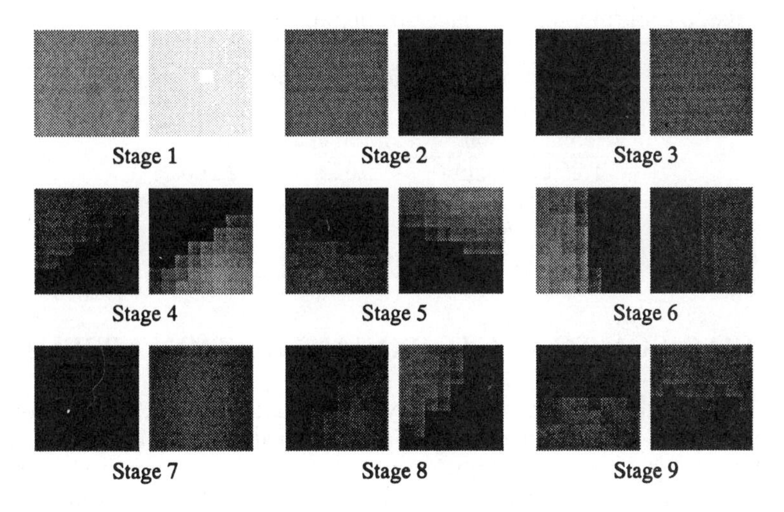

Figure 2: Input-to-Competitive Unit Connection Strengths at Stages 1-9

Following training, the image is compressed by dividing the image into nonoverlapping 8×8 patches, presenting each in turn to ICL, obtaining the compressed code, and then reconstructing the patch from the code. With an s stage network and two units per stage, the compressed code contains s bits. Thus, the number of bits per pixel in the compressed code is $s/(8\times8)$. To obtain different levels of compression, the number of stages in ICL can be varied. Fortunately, this does not require retraining ICL because the features detected at each stage do not depend on the number of stages; the earlier stages capture the most significant variation in the input. Thus, if the network is trained with 80 stages, one can use just the first 32 to compress the image, achieving a .5 bit per pixel encoding.

The image used to train ICL was originally used in a neural net image compression study by Cottrell, Munro, and Zipser (1989). Their compression scheme used a three-layer back propagation autoencoder to map an image patch back to itself through a hidden layer. The hidden layer, with fewer units than the input layer, served as the encoding. Because hidden unit activities are continuous valued, it was necessary to quantize the activities. Using a standard measure of performance, the signal-to-noise ratio (the logarithm of the average energy relative to the average reconstruction error), ICL outperforms Cottrell et al.'s network (Table 1).

This result is not surprising. In the data compression literature, vector quantization approaches — similar to ICL — usually work better than transformation-based approaches — e.g., Cottrell et al. (1989), Sanger (1989). The reason is that transformation-based approaches do not take quantization into account in the development of the code. That is, in transformation-based approaches, the training procedure, which discovers the code, and the quantization step, which turns this code into a form that can be used for digital data transmission or storage, are two distinct processes. In Cottrell et al.'s network, a hidden unit encoding is learned without considering the demands of quantization. There is no assurance that the quantized code will retain the information in the signal. In contrast, ICL takes quantization into account *during* training.

Table 1: Signal-to-Noise Ratio for Different Compression Levels

compression	Cottrell et al.	ICL
1.25 bits/pixel	2.324	2.366
1 bit/pixel	2.170	2.270
.75 bits/pixel	1.746	2.146
.5 bits/pixel	not available	1.975

6 COMPARISON TO VECTOR QUANTIZATION APPROACHES

As I mentioned previously, ICL is essentially a neural net reformulation of a conventional data compression scheme called multistep vector quantization. However, adopting a neural net perspective suggests several promising variants of the approach. These variants result from viewing the encoding task as an optimization problem (i.e., finding weights that minimize Equation 1). I mention three variants, the first two of which are methods for finding the solution more efficiently and consistently, the final one is a powerful extension to algorithm that I believe has not yet been studied in the vector quantization literature.

6.1 AVOIDING LOCAL OPTIMA

As Rumelhart and Zipser (1985) and others have noted, competitive learning experiences a serious problem from locally optimal solutions in which one competitive unit captures most or all of the input patterns while others capture none. To eliminate such situations, I have introduced a secondary error term whose purpose is to force the competitive units to win equally often:

$$E_{sec} = \sum_{i=1}^{\beta} \left(\frac{1}{\beta} - \bar{y}_i\right)^2 ,$$

where $\bar{y}_i$ is the mean activity of competitive unit i over trials. Based on the soft competitive learning model with $T>0$, this yields the weight update rule

$$\Delta \mathbf{w}_i = \gamma\,(\mathbf{x}-\mathbf{w}_i)(1-\beta\bar{y}_i) ,$$

where γ is the step size. Because this constraint should not be part of the ultimate solution, γ must gradually be reduced to zero. In the image compression simulation, γ was set to .005 initially and was decreased by .0001 every 100 training trials. This is a more principled solution to the local optimum problem than the "leaky learning" idea suggested by Rumelhart and Zipser. It can also be seen as an alternative or supplement to the schemes proposed for selecting the initial code (weights) in the vector quantization literature.

6.2 CONSTRAINTS ON THE WEIGHTS

I have explored a further idea to increase the likelihood of converging on a good solution and to achieve more rapid convergence. The idea is based on two facts. First, in an optimal solution, the weight vector of a competitive unit should be the mean of the inputs captured by that unit. This gives rise to the second observation: beyond stage 1, the mean input, $\bar{\mathbf{x}}^{(s)}$, should be zero.

If the competitive pools contain two units, these facts lead to a strong constraint on the weights:

$$0 = \bar{\mathbf{x}}^{(s)}$$

$$= \frac{\sum_{p \in PART_1} \mathbf{x}^{(s)}(p) + \sum_{p \in PART_2} \mathbf{x}^{(s)}(p)}{n_1 + n_2}$$

$$= \frac{n_1 \mathbf{w}_1^{(s)} + n_2 \mathbf{w}_2^{(s)}}{n_1 + n_2},$$

where $\mathbf{x}^{(s)}(p)$ is the input vector in stage s for pattern p, $PART_1$ and $PART_2$ are the two clusters of input patterns partitioned by the competitive units at stage $s-1$, and n_1 and n_2 are the number of elements in each cluster.

The consequence is that, in an optimal solution,

$$\mathbf{w}_1 = -\frac{n_2}{n_1}\mathbf{w}_2 .$$

(This property is observed in Figure 2.) Constraining the weights in this manner, and performing gradient descent in the ratio n_2/n_1, as well as in the weight parameters themselves, the quality of the solution and the convergence rate are dramatically improved.

6.3 GENERALIZING THE TRANSFORMATION BETWEEN STAGES

At each stage s, the winning competitive unit specifies a transformation of $\mathbf{x}^{(s)}$ to obtain $\mathbf{x}^{(s+1)}$. In ICL, this transformation is simply a translation. There is no reason why this could not be generalized to include rotation and dilation as well, i.e.,

$$\mathbf{x}^{(s+1)} = \mathbf{T}_{winner}^{(s)} \mathbf{x}^{(s)},$$

where $\mathbf{T}_{winner}$ is a transformation matrix that includes the translation specified by $\mathbf{w}_{winner}$. (For this notation to be formally correct, $\mathbf{x}$ must be augmented by an element having constant value 1 to allow for translations.) The rotation and dilation parameters can be learned via gradient descent search in the error measure given in Equation 1. Reconstruction involves inverting the sequence of transformations:

$$\hat{\mathbf{x}} = \left[\mathbf{T}_{winner}^{(1)}\right]^{-1} \cdots \left[\mathbf{T}_{winner}^{(s)}\right]^{-1} (0\,0\,0 \cdots 1)^{\mathrm{T}} .$$

A simple example of a situation in which this generalized transformation can be useful is depicted in Figure 3. After subtracting out the component detected at stage 1, the two clusters may be rotated into alignment, allowing the second stage to capture the remaining variation in the input. Whether or not this extension proves useful has yet to be tested. However, the connectivity patterns in Figure 2 certainly suggest that factoring out variations in orientation might permit an even more compact representation of the input data.

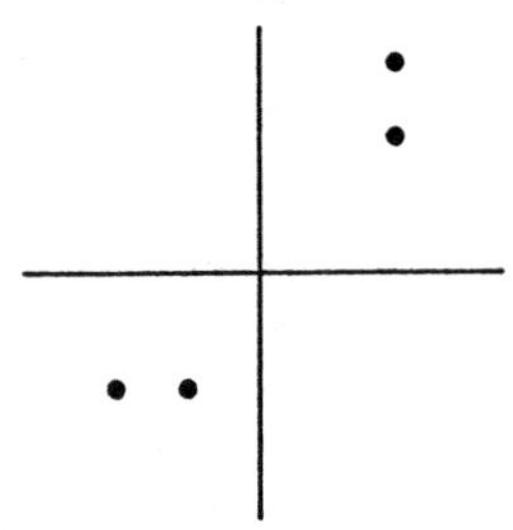

Figure 3: A Sample Input Space With Four Data Points

Acknowledgements

This research was supported by NSF grant IRI-9058450 and grant 90-21 from the James S. McDonnell Foundation. My thanks to Paul Smolensky for helpful comments on this work and to Gary Cottrell for providing the image data and associated software.

References

Ambros-Ingerson, J., Granger, G., & Lynch, G. (1990). Simulation of paleocortex performs hierarchical clustering. *Science, 247*, 1344-1348.

Bridle, J. (1990). Training stochastic model recognition algorithms as networks can lead to maximum mutual information estimation of parameters. In D. S. Touretzky (Ed.), *Advances in neural information processing systems 2* (pp. 211–217). San Mateo, CA: Morgan Kaufmann.

Cottrell, G. W., Munro, P., & Zipser, D. (1989). Image compression by back propagation: An example of extensional programming. In N. Sharkey (Ed.), *Models of cognition: A review of cognitive science* (pp. 208–240). Norwood, NJ: Ablex.

Durbin, R. (April, 1990). Principled competitive learning in both unsupervised and supervised networks. Poster presented at the conference on Neural Networks for Computing, Snowbird, Utah.

Gray, R. M. (1984). Vector quantization. *IEEE ASSP Magazine*, 4–29.

Grossberg, S. (1976). Adaptive pattern classification and universal recoding. I: Parallel development and coding of neural feature detectors. *Biological Cybernetics, 23*, 121–134.

Hrycej, T. (1989). Unsupervised learning by backward inhibition. *Proceedings of the Eleventh International Joint Conference on Artificial Intelligence* (pp. 170-175). Los Altos, CA: Morgan Kaufmann.

Kohonen, T. (1982). Clustering, taxonomy, and topological maps of patterns. In M. Lang (Ed.), *Proceedings of the Sixth International Conference on Pattern Recognition* (pp. 114–125). Silver Spring, MD: IEEE Computer Society Press.

Rumelhart, D. E. (in press). Connectionist processing and learning as statistical inference. In Y. Chauvin & D. E. Rumelhart (Eds.), *Backpropagation: Theory, architectures, and applications*. Hillsdale, NJ: Erlbaum.

Rumelhart, D. E., & Zipser, D. (1985). Feature discovery by competitive learning. *Cognitive Science, 9*, 75–112.

Sanger, T. D. (1989). Optimal unsupervised learning in a single-layer linear feedforward neural network. *Neural Networks, 2*, 459–473.

von der Malsburg, C. (1973). Self-organization of orientation sensitive cells in the striate cortex. *Kybernetik, 14*, 85–100.

Direct memory access using two cues: Finding the intersection of sets in a connectionist model

Janet Wiles, Michael S. Humphreys, John D. Bain and Simon Dennis
Departments of Psychology and Computer Science
University of Queensland QLD 4072 Australia
email: janet@psych.psy.uq.oz.au

Abstract

For lack of alternative models, search and decision processes have provided the dominant paradigm for human memory access using two or more cues, despite evidence against search as an access process (Humphreys, Wiles & Bain, 1990). We present an alternative process to search, based on calculating the intersection of sets of targets activated by two or more cues. Two methods of computing the intersection are presented, one using information about the possible targets, the other constraining the cue-target strengths in the memory matrix. Analysis using orthogonal vectors to represent the cues and targets demonstrates the competence of both processes, and simulations using sparse distributed representations demonstrate the performance of the latter process for tasks involving 2 and 3 cues.

1 INTRODUCTION

Consider a task in which a subject is asked to name a word that rhymes with *oast.* The subject answers "most", (or post, host, toast, boast, ...). Now the subject is asked to find a word that means *a mythical being that rhymes with oast.* She or he pauses slightly and replies "ghost".

The difference between the first and second questions is that the first requires the use of one cue to access memory. The second question requires the use of two cues – either combining them before the access process, or combining the targets they access. There are many experimental paradigms in psychology in which a subject uses two or more cues to perform a task (Rubin & Wallace, 1989). One default assumption underlying many explanations for the effective use of two cues relies on a search process through memory.

Models of human memory based on associative access (using connectionist models) have provided an alternative paradigm to search processes for memory access using a single cue (Anderson, Silverstein, Ritz & Jones, 1977; McClelland & Rumelhart, 1986), and for two cues which have been studied together (Humphreys, Bain & Pike 1989). In some respects, properties of these models correspond very closely to the characteristics of human memory (Rumelhart, 1989). In addition to the evidence against search processes for memory access using a single cue, there is also experimental evidence against sequential search in some tasks requiring the combination of two cues, such as cued recall with an extra-list cue, cued recall with a part-word cue, lexical access and semantic access (Humphreys, Wiles & Bain, 1990). Furthermore, in some of these tasks it appears that the two cues have never jointly occurred with the target. In such a situation, the tensor product employed by Humphreys et. al. to bind the two cues to the target cannot be employed, nor can the co-occurrences of the two cues be encoded into the hidden layer of a three-layer network. In this paper we present the computational foundation for an alternative process to search and decision, based on parallel (or direct) access for the intersection of sets of targets that are retrieved in response to cues that have not been studied together.

Definition of an intersection in the cue-target paradigm: Given a set of cue-target pairs, and two (or more) access cues, then the intersection specified by the access cues is defined to be the set of targets which are associated with both cues. If the cue-target strengths are not binary, then they are constrained to lie between 0 and 1, and targets in the intersection are weighted by the product of the cue-target strengths. A complementary definition for a union process could be the set of targets associated with any one or more of the access cues, weighted by the sum of the target strengths.

In the models that are described below, we assume that the access cues and targets are represented as vectors, the cue-target associations are represented in a memory matrix and the set of targets retrieved in response to one or more cues is represented as a linear combination, or *blend*, of target vectors associated with that cue or cues. Note that under this definition, if there is more than one target in the intersection, then a second stage is required to select a unique target to output from the retrieved linear combination. We do not address this second stage in this paper.

A task requiring intersection: In the rhyming task described above, the rhyme and semantic cues have extremely low separate probabilities of accessing the target, *ghost*, but a very high joint probability. In this study we do not distinguish between the representation of the semantic and part-word cues, although it would be required for a more detailed model. Instead, we focus on the task of retrieving a target weakly associated with two cues. We simulate this condition in a simple task using two cues, C_1 and C_2, and three targets, T_1, T_2 and T_3. Each cue is strongly associated with one target, and weakly associated with a second target, as follows (strengths of association are shown above the arrows):

$$C_1 \xrightarrow{.9} T_1,\ C_1 \xrightarrow{.1} T_2,\ C_2 \xrightarrow{.1} T_2, \text{ and } C_2 \xrightarrow{.9} T_3.$$

The intersection of the targets retrieved to the two cues, C_1 and C_2, is the target, T_2, with a strength of 0.01. Note that in this example, a model based on vector addition would be insufficient to select target, T_2, which is weakly associated with both cues, in preference to either target, T_1 or T_3, which are strongly associated with one cue each.

2 IMPLEMENTATIONS OF INTERSECTION PROCESSES

2.1 LOCAL REPRESENTATIONS

Given a local representation for two sets of targets, their intersection can be computed by multiplying the activations elicited by each cue. This method extends to sparse representations with some noise from cross product terms, and has been used by Dolan and Dyer (1989) in their tensor model, and Touretzky and Hinton (1989) in the Distributed Connectionist Production System (for further discussion see Wiles, Humphreys, Bain & Dennis, 1990). However, multiplying activation strengths does not extend to fully distributed representations, since multiplication depends on the basis representation (i.e., the target patterns themselves) and the cross-product terms do not necessarily cancel. One strong implication of this for implementing an intersection process, is that the choice of patterns is not critical in a linear process (such as vector addition) but can be critical in a non-linear process (which is necessary for computing intersections). An intersection process requires more information about the target patterns themselves.

It is interesting to note that the inner product of the target sets (equivalent to the match process in Humphreys et. al.'s (1989) Matrix model) can be used to determine whether or not the intersection of targets is empty, if the target vectors are orthogonal, although it cannot be used to find the particular vectors which are in the intersection.

2.2 USING INFORMATION ABOUT TARGET VECTORS

A local representation enables multiplication of activation strengths because there is implicit knowledge about the allowable target vectors in the local representation itself. The first method we describe for computing the intersection of fully distributed vectors uses information about the targets, explicitly represented in an auto-associative memory, to filter out cross-product terms: In separate operations, each cue is used to access the memory matrix and retrieve a composite target vector (the linear combination of associated targets). A temporary matrix is formed from the outer product of these two composite vectors. This matrix will contain product terms between all the targets in the intersection set as well as noise in the form of cross-product terms. The cross-product terms can be filtered from the temporary matrix by using it as a retrieval cue for accessing a three-dimensional auto-associator (a tensor of rank 3) over all the targets in the original memory. If the target vectors are orthonormal, then this process will produce a vector which contains no noise from cross-product terms, and is the linear combination of all targets associated with both cues (see Box 1).

Box 1. Creating a temporary matrix from the product of the target vectors, then filtering out the noise terms: Let the cues and targets be represented by vectors which are mutually orthonormal (i.e., $C_i.C_i = T_i.T_i = 1$, $C_i.C_j = T_i.T_j = 0$, $i, j = 1,2,3$). The memory matrix, **M**, is formed from cue-target pairs, weighted by their respective strengths, as follows:

$$\mathbf{M} = 0.9C_1 T_1' + 0.1C_1 T_2' + 0.1C_2 T_2' + 0.9C_2 T_3'$$

where T' represents the transpose of T, and $C_i T_i'$ is the outer product of C_i and T_i.
In addition, let **Z** be a three-dimensional auto-associative memory (or tensor of rank 3) created over three orthogonal representations of each target (i.e., T_i is a column vector, T_i' is a row vector which is the transpose of T_i, and T_i'' is the vector in a third direction orthogonal to both, where i=1,2,3), as follows:

$$\mathbf{Z} = \Sigma_i T_i T_i' T_i''$$

Let a two-dimensional temporary matrix, **X**, be formed by taking the outer product of target vectors retrieved to the access cues, as follows:

$$\mathbf{X} = (C_1 \mathbf{M})(C_2 \mathbf{M})'$$

$$= (0.9T_1 + 0.1T_2)(0.1T_2 + 0.9T_3)'$$

$$= 0.09T_1T_2' + 0.81T_1T_3' + 0.01T_2T_2' + 0.09T_2T_3'$$

Using the matrix **X** to access the auto-associator **Z**, will produce a vector from which all the cross-product terms have been filtered, as follows:

$$\mathbf{X\,Z} = (0.09T_1T_2' + 0.81T_1T_3' + 0.01T_2T_2' + 0.09T_2T_3')\,(\Sigma_i T_i T_i' T_i'')$$

$$= (0.09T_1T_2')(\Sigma_i T_i T_i' T_i'') + (0.81T_1T_3')(\Sigma_i T_i T_i' T_i'')$$

$$+ (0.01T_2T_2')(\Sigma_i T_i T_i' T_i'') + (0.09T_2T_3')(\Sigma_i T_i T_i' T_i'')$$

$$= (0.01T_2T_2')(T_2 T_2' T_2'') \quad \text{since all other terms cancel.}$$

$$= 0.01T_2''$$

This vector is the required intersection of the linear combination of target vectors associated with both the input cues, C_1 and C_2 weighted by the product of the strengths of associations from the cues to the targets.

A major advantage of the above process is that only matrix (or tensor) operations are used, which simplifies both the implementation and the analysis. The behaviour of the system can be analysed either at the level of behaviours of patterns, or using a coordinate system based on individual units, since in a linear system these two levels of description are isomorphic. In addition, the auto-associative target matrix could be created incrementally when the target vectors are first learnt by the system using the matrix memory. The disadvantages include the requirement for dynamic creation and short term storage of the two dimensional product-of-targets matrix, and the formation and much longer term storage of the three dimensional auto-associative matrix. It is possible, however, that an auto-associator may be part of the output process.

2.3 ADDITIVE APPROXIMATIONS TO MULTIPLICATIVE PROCESSES

An alternative approach to using the target auto-associator for computing the intersection, is to incorporate a non-linearity at the time of memory storage, rather than memory access. The aim of this transform would be to change the cue-target strengths so that linear addition of vectors could be used for computing the intersection. An operation that is equivalent to multiplication is the addition of logarithms. If the logarithm of each cue-target strength was calculated and stored at the time of association, then an additive access process would retrieve the intersection of the inputs. More generally, it may be possible to use an operation that preserves the same order relations (in terms of strengths) as multiplication. It is always possible to find a restricted range of association strengths such that the sum of a number of weak cue-target associations will produce a stronger target activation than the sum of a smaller number of strong cue-target associations. For example, by scaling the target strengths to the range $[(n-1)/n, 1]$ where n is the number of simultaneously available cues, vector addition can be made to approximate multiplication of target strengths.

This method has the advantage of extending naturally to non-orthogonal vectors, and to the combination of three or more cues, with performance limits determined solely by cross-talk between the vectors. Time taken is proportional to the number of cues, and noise is proportional to the product of the set sizes and cross-correlation between the vectors.

3 SIMULATIONS OF THE ADDITIVE PROCESS

Two simulations of the additive process using scaled target strengths were performed to demonstrate the feasibility of the method producing a target weakly associated with two cues, in preference to targets with much higher probabilities of being produced in response to a single cue. As a work-around for the problem of how (and when) to decompose the composite output vector, the target with the strongest correlation with the composite output was selected as the winner. To simulate the addition of some noise, non-orthogonal vectors were used.

The first simulation involved two cues, C_1 and C_2, and three targets, T_1, T_2 and T_3, represented as randomly generated 100 dimensional vectors, 20% 1s, the remainder 0s. Cue C_1 was strongly associated with target T_1 and weakly associated with target T_2, cue C_2 was strongly associated with target T_3 and weakly associated with target T_2. A trial consisted of generating random cue and target vectors, forming a memory matrix from their outer products (multiplied by 0.9 for strong associates and 0.6 for weak associates; note that these strengths have been scaled to the range, [0,1]), and then pre-multiplying the memory matrix by the appropriate cue (i.e., either C_1 or C_2 or $C_1 + C_2$).

The memory matrix, **M**, was formed as shown in Box 1. Retrieval to a cue, C_1 , was as follows: C_1 $\mathbf{M} = 0.9\, C_1 .C_1 T_1' + 0.6\, C_1 .C_1 T_2' + 0.6\, C_1 .C_2 T_2' + 0.9\, C_1.C_2 T_3'$. In this case, the cross product terms, $C_1.C_2$, do not cancel since the vectors are not orthogonal, although their expected contribution to the output is small (expected correlation 0.04). The winning target vector was the one that had the strongest correlation (smallest normalized dot product) with the resulting output vector. The results are shown in Table 1.

Table 1: Number of times each target was retrieved in 100 trials.

	t1	*t2*	*t3*
c1	92	8	0
c2	0	9	91
c1+c2	11	80	9

Over 100 trials, the results show that when either cue C_1 or C_2 was presented alone, the target with which it was most strongly paired was retrieved in over 90% of cases. Target T_2 had very low probabilities of recall given either C_1 or C_2 (8% and 9% respectively), however, it was very likely to be recalled if both cues were presented (80%).

The first simulation demonstrated the multi-cue paradigm with the simple two-cue and three-target case. In a second simulation, the system was tested for robustness in a similar case involving three cues, C_1 to C_3, and four targets, T_1 to T_4. The results show that T_4 had low probabilities of recall given either C_1 , C_2 or C_3 (13%, 22% and 18% respectively), medium probabilities of recall given a combination of two cues (36%, 31% and 28%), and was most likely to be recalled if all three cues were presented (44%). For this task, when three cues are presented concurrently, in the ideal intersection only T_4 should be produced. The results show that it is produced more often than the other targets (44% compared with 22%, 18% and 16%), each of which is strongly associated with two out of the three cues, but there is considerably more noise than in the two-cue case. (See Wiles, Humphreys, Bain & Dennis, 1990, for further details.)

4 DISCUSSION

The simulation results demonstrated the effect of the initial scaling of the cue-target strengths, and non-linear competition between the target outputs. It is important to note the difference between the *association strengths* from cues to targets and the *cued recall probability* of each target. In memory research, the association strengths have been traditionally identified with the probability of recall. However, in a connectionist model the association strengths are related to the weights in the network and the cued recall probability is the probability of recall of a given target to a given cue.

This paper builds on the idea that direct access is the default access method for human memory, and that all access processes are cue based. The immediate response from memory is a blend of patterns, which provide a useful intermediate stage. Other processes may act on the blend of patterns before a single target is selected for output in a successive stage. One such process that may act on the intermediate representation is an intersection process that operates over blends of targets. Such a process would provide an alternative to search as a computational technique in psychological paradigms that use two or more cues. We don't claim that we have described the way to implement such a process – much more is required to investigate these issues. The two methods presented here have served to demonstrate that direct access intersection is a viable neural network technique. This demonstration means that more processing can be performed in the network dynamics, rather than by the control structures that surround memory.

Acknowledgements

Our thanks to Anthony Bloesch, Michael Jordan, Julie Stewart, Michael Strasser and Roland Sussex for discussions and comments. This work was supported by grants from the Australian Research Council, a National Research Fellowship to J. Wiles and an Australian Postgraduate Research Award to S. Dennis.

References

Anderson, J.A., Silverstein, J.W., Ritz, S.A. and Jones, R.S. Distinctive features, categorical perception, and probability learning: Some applications of a neural model. *Psychological Review, 84*, 413-451, 1977.

Dolan, C. and Dyer, M.G. Parallel retrieval and application of conceptual knowledge. *Proceedings of the 1988 Connectionist Models Summer School, San Mateo, Ca: Morgan Kaufmann*, 273-280, 1989.

Humphreys, M.S., Bain, J.D. and Pike, R. Different ways to cue a coherent memory system: A theory for episodic, semantic and procedural tasks. *Psychological Review, 96:2*, 208-233, 1989.

Humphreys, M.S., Wiles, J. and Bain, J.D. Direct Access: Cues with separate histories. Paper presented at Attention and Performance 14, Ann Arbor, Michigan, July, 1990.

McClelland, J.L. and Rumelhart, D.E. A distributed model of memory. In McClelland, J.L. and Rumelhart, D.E. (eds.) *Parallel Distributed Processing: Explorations in the microstructure of cognition*, 170-215, MIT Press, Cambridge, MA, 1986.

Rubin, D.C. and Wallace, W.T. Rhyme and reason: Analysis of dual retrieval cues. *Journal of Experimental Psychology: Learning, Memory and Cognition, 15:4*, 698-709, 1989.

Rumelhart, D.S. The architecture of mind: A connectionist approach. In Posner, M.I. (ed.) *Foundations of Cognitive Science*, 133-159, MIT Press, Cambridge, MA, 1989.

Touretzky, D.S. and Hinton, G.E. A distributed connectionist production system. *Cognitive Science, 12*, 423-466, 1988.

Wiles, J., Humphreys, M.S., Bain, J.D. and Dennis, S. Control processes and cue combinations in a connectionist model of human memory. Department of Computer Science Technical Report, #186, University of Queensland, October 1990, 40pp.

An Attractor Neural Network Model of Recall and Recognition

Eytan Ruppin
Department of Computer Science
School of Mathematical Sciences
Sackler Faculty of Exact Sciences
Tel Aviv University
69978, Tel Aviv, Israel

Yechezkel Yeshurun
Department of Computer Science
School of Mathematical Sciences
Sackler Faculty of Exact Sciences
Tel Aviv University
69978, Tel Aviv, Israel

Abstract

This work presents an Attractor Neural Network (ANN) model of Recall and Recognition. It is shown that an ANN model can qualitatively account for a wide range of experimental psychological data pertaining to the these two main aspects of memory access. Certain psychological phenomena are accounted for, including the effects of list-length, word-frequency, presentation time, context shift, and aging. Thereafter, the probabilities of successful Recall and Recognition are estimated, in order to possibly enable further quantitative examination of the model.

1 Motivation

The goal of this paper is to demonstrate that a Hopfield-based [Hop82] ANN model can qualitatively account for a wide range of experimental psychological data pertaining to the two main aspects of memory access, Recall and Recognition. *Recall* is defined as the ability to retrieve an item from a list of items (words) originally presented during a previous learning phase, given an appropriate cue (*cued Recall*), or spontaneously (*free Recall*). *Recognition* is defined as the ability to successfully acknowledge that a certain item has or has not appeared in the tutorial list learned before.

The main prospects of ANN modeling is that some parameter values, that in former, 'classical' models of memory retrieval (see e.g. [GS84]) had to be explicitly assigned, can now be shown to be emergent properties of the model.

2 The Model

The model consists of a Hopfield ANN, in which distributed patterns representing the learned items are stored during the learning phase, and are later presented as inputs during the test phase. In this framework, successful Recall and Recognition is defined. Some additional components are added to the basic Hopfield model to enable the modeling of the relevant psychological phenomena.

2.1 The Hopfield Model

The Hopfield model's dynamics are composed of a non-linear, iterative, asynchronous transformation of the network state [Hop82]. The process may include a stochastic noise which is analogous to the 'temperature' T in statistical mechanics. Formally, the Hopfield model is described as follows: Let neuron's i state be a binary variable S_i, taking the values ± 1 denoting a firing or a resting state, correspondingly. Let the network's state be a vector S specifying the binary values of all its neurons. Let J_{ij} be the synaptic strength between neurons i and j. Then, h_i, the input 'field' of neuron i is given by $h_i = \sum_{j \neq i}^{N} J_{ij} S_j$. The neuron's dynamic behavior is described by

$$S_i(t+1) = \begin{cases} 1, & \text{with probability } \frac{1}{2}(1 + tgh(\frac{h_i}{T})) \\ -1, & \text{with probability } \frac{1}{2}(1 - tgh(\frac{h_i}{T})) \end{cases}$$

Storing a new memory pattern ξ^μ in the network is performed by modifying every ij element of the synaptic connection matrix according to $J_{ij}^{new} = J_{ij}^{old} + \frac{1}{N}\xi^{\mu}{}_i \xi^{\mu}{}_j$.

A Hopfield network will always converge to a stable state, and every stored memory is an *attractor* having an area surrounding it termed its *basin of attraction* [Hop82]. In addition to the stored memories, also other, non-memory states exist as stable states (local minima) of the network [AGS85]. The maximal number m of (randomly generated) memory patterns which can be stored in the basic Hopfield network of n neurons is $m = \alpha_c \cdot n$, $\alpha_c \approx 0.14$ [AGS85].

2.2 Recall and Recognition in the model's framework

2.2.1 Recall

Recall is considered successful when upon starting from an initial cue the network converges to a stable state which corresponds to the learned memory nearest to the input pattern. Inter-pattern distance is measured by the Hamming distance between the input and the learned item encodings. If the network converges to a non-memory stable state, its output will stand for a 'failure of recall' response. [1].

[1]The question of "How do such non-memory states bear the meaning of 'recall failure'?" is out of the scope of this work. However, a possible explanation is that during the learning phase 'meaning' is assigned to the stored patterns via connections formed with external patterns, and since non-memory states lack such associations with external patterns, they are 'meaningless', yielding the 'recall failure' response. Another possible mechanism is that every output pattern generated in the recall process passes also a recognition phase so that non-memory states are rejected, (see the following paragraph describing recognition in our model).

2.2.2 Recognition

Recognition is considered successful when the network arrives at a stable state during a time interval Δ, beginning from input presentation. In general, the shorter the distance between an input and its nearest memory, the faster is its convergence [AM88, KP88, RY90]. Since non-memory (non-learned) stable states have higher energy levels and much shallower basins of attraction than memorized stable states [AGS85, LN89], convergence to such states takes significantly longer timer. Therefore, there exists a range of possible values of Δ that enable successful recognition only of inputs similar to one of the stored memories.

2.3 Other features of the model

- The context of the psychological experiments is represented as a substring of the input's encoding. In order to minimize inter-pattern correlation, the size of the context encoding relative to the total size of the memory encoding is kept small.
- The total associational linkage of a learned item, is modeled as an external field vector E. When a learned memory pattern ξ^{μ} is presented to the network, the value of the external field vector generated is $E_i = h \cdot \xi^{\mu}$, where h is an 'orientation' coefficient, expressing the association strength.

Additional features, including a modified storage equation accounting for learning taking place at the test phase, and a storage decay parameter, are described in [RY90].

3 The Modeling of experimental data.

Regarding every phenomenon discussed, a brief description of the psychological findings is followed by an account of its modeling. We rely on the known results pertaining to Hopfield models to show that qualitatively, the psychological phenomena reviewed are emergent properties of the model. When such analytical evidence is lacking, simulations were performed in order to account for the experimental data. For a review of the psychological literature supporting the findings modeled see [GS84].

The List-Length Effect: It is known that the probability of successful Recall or Recognition of a particular item decreases as the length of list of learned items increases.

List length is expressed in memory load. Since It has been shown that the width of the memories basins of attraction monotonically decreases following an approximately inverse parabolic curve [Wei85], Recall performance should decrease as memory load is increased. We have examined the convergence time of the same set of input patterns at different values of memory load. As demonstrated in Fig. 1, it was found that, as the memory load is increased, successful convergence has occurred (on the average) only after an increasingly growing number of asynchronous iterations. Hence, convergence takes more time and can result in Recognition failure, although memories' stability is maintained till the critical capacity α_c is reached.

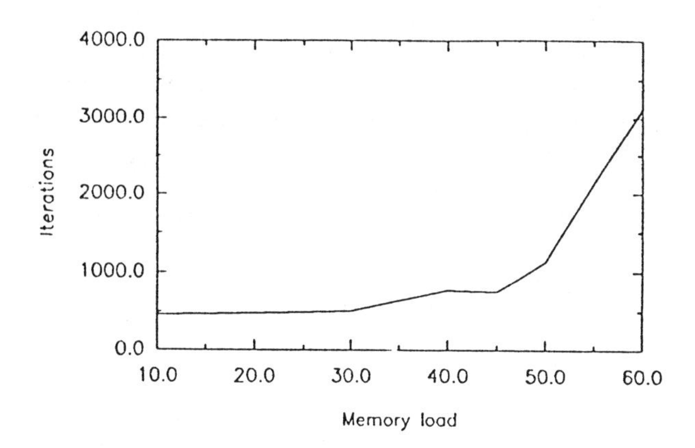

Figure 1: Recognition speed (No. of asynchronous iterations) as a function of memory load (No. of stored memories). The network's parameters are $n = 500$, $T = 0.28$

The word-frequency effect: The more frequent a word is in language, the probability of recalling it increases, while the probability of recognizing it decreases.

A word's frequency in the language is assumed to effect its retrieval through the stored word's semantic relations and associations [Kat85, NCBK87]. It is assumed, that relative to low frequency words, high frequency words have more semantic relations and therefore more connections between the patterns representing them and other patterns stored in the memory (i.e., in other networks). This one-to-many relationship is assumed to be reciprocal, i.e., each of the externally stored patterns has also connections projected to several of the stored patterns in the allocated network.

The process leading to the formation of the external field E (acting upon the allocated network), generated by an input pattern nearest to some stored memory pattern ξ^μ is assumed to be characterized as follows:

1. There is a threshold degree of overlap θ_{min}, such that $E > 0$ only when the allocated network's state overlap H^μ is higher than θ_{min}.
2. At overlap values H^μ which are only moderately larger than θ_{min}, h^μ is monotonically increasing, but as H^μ continues to rise, a certain 'optimal' point is reached, beyond which h^μ is monotonically decreasing.
3. High-frequency words have lower θ_{min} values than low-frequency words.

Recognition tests are characterized by a high initial value of overlap H^μ, to some memory ξ^μ. The value of h^μ and E^μ generated is post-optimal and therefore smaller than in the case of low-frequency words which have higher θ_{min} values.

In Recall tests the initial situation is characterized by low values of overlap H^μ to some nearest memory ξ^μ. only the overlap value of high-frequency words is sufficient for activating associated items, i.e. $H^\mu > \theta_{min}$.

Presentation Time: Increasing the presentation time of learned words is known to improve both their Recall and Recognition.

This is explained by the phenomenon of maintenance rehearsal; The memories' basins of attraction get deeper, since the 'energy' E of a given state equals to $\sum_{\mu=1}^{m} H^{\mu 2}$. Deeper basins of attraction are also wider [HFP83, KPKP90]. Therefore, the probability of successful Recall and Recognition of rehearsed items is increased. The effect of a uniform rehearsal is equivalent to a temperature decrease. Hence, increasing presentation time will attenuate and delay the List length phenomenon, till a certain limit. In a similar way, the Test Delay phenomenon is accounted for [RY90].

Context Shift: The term Context Shift refers to the change in context from the tutorial period to the test period. Studies examining the effect of context shift have shown a decrement in Recall performance with context shift, but little change in Recognition performance.

As demonstrated in [RY90], when a context shift is simulated by flipping some of the context string's bits, Recall performance severely deteriorates while memories stability remains intact. No significant increase in the time (i.e. number of asynchronous iterations) required for convergence was found, thus maintaining the pre-shift probability of successful Recognition.

Age differences in Recall and Recognition: It was found that older people perform more poorly on Recall tasks than they do on Recognition tasks [CM87]. These findings can be accounted for by the assumption that synapses are being weakened and deleted with aging, which although being controversial has gained some experimental support (see [RY90]). We have investigated the retrieval performance as a function of the input's initial overlap, various levels of synaptic dilution, and memory load: As demonstrated in Fig. 2, when the synaptic dilution is increased, a 'critical' phase is reached where memory retrieval of far-away input patterns is decreased but the retrieval of input patterns with a high level of initial overlap remains intact. As the memory load is increased, this 'critical' phase begins at lower levels of synaptic dilution. On the other hand, only a mild increase (of 15%) in recognition speed was found.

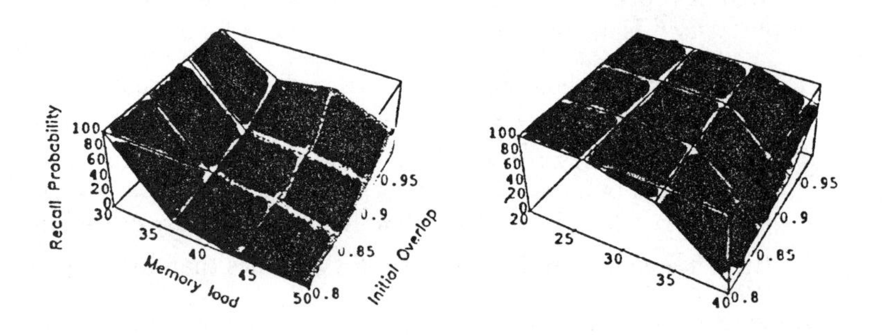

Figure 2: The probability of successful retrieval performance as a function of memory load and the input pattern's initial overlap, at two different degrees of synaptic dilution; 50% in the right-sided figure, and 55% in the left-sided figure. The network's parameters are $n = 500$, $T = 0.05$.

The interested reader can find a description of the modeling of additional phenomena, including test position, word fragment completion, and distractor similarity, in [RY90].

4 On a quantitative test of the model.

4.1 Estimating Recall performance

In a given network, with n neurons and m memories, the radius r of the basins of attraction of the memories decreases as the memory load parameter ($\alpha = m/n$) is increased. According to [MPRV87], n, m, and r are related according to the expression $m = \frac{(1-2\cdot r)^2}{4} \cdot \frac{n}{\log n}$.

The concept of the basins of attraction implies a non-linear probability function with low probability when input vectors are further than the radius of attraction and high probability otherwise. The slope of this non-linearity increases as the noise level T is decreased.

The probability P_c that a *random* input vector will converge to one of the stored memories can be estimated by $P_c \approx \frac{\sum_{d=1}^{rn} \binom{n}{d}}{2^n} \cdot m$. It is interesting to note that the rates of change of r and of P_c have distinct forms; Recall tests beginning from randomly generated cues would yield a very low rate of successful Recall (P_c). Yet, if one examines Recall by picking a stored memory, flipping some of its encoding bits, and presenting it as an input to the network (determining r), 'reasonable' levels of successful Recall can still be obtained even when a 'considerable' number of encoding bits are flipped. P_c can be also estimated by considering the context representation [RY90].

4.2 Estimating Recognition performance

The probability of correct Recognition depends mainly on the the length of the interval Δ; assume that after an input pattern is presented to a network of n neurons, during the time interval Δ, k iterations steps of a Monte Carlo simulation are performed: In each such step, a neuron is randomly selected, and then it examines whether or not it should flip its state, according to its input.

We show that the probability $P_g\{d\}$ that an input pattern will be successfully recognized is is bounded by $P_g\{d\} \geq 1 - d \cdot e^{\frac{-k}{n}}$. It can be seen that Recognition's success depends strongly on the initial input proximity to a stored memory, and even more strongly dependent on the number of allowed asynchronous iteration k, determined by the length of Δ. For a selection of $k = n(ln(d) + c)$, one obtains $P_g \geq 1 - e^{-c}$. The expected number of iterations, (denoted as $Exp(X)$) till successful convergence is achieved is $E(X) = \sum_{i=1}^{d} E(X_i) = n \cdot \sum_{i=1}^{d} \frac{1}{i} \approx n \cdot ln(d)$.

In the more general case, Let o denote the Hamming distance (between the network's state S and a stored memory) below which retrieval is considered successful. Then, the corrected estimations of retrieval performance are $P_g \geq 1 - \binom{d}{o} \cdot e^{\frac{-k \cdot o}{n}}$, and $E(X) \approx n \cdot ln(\frac{d}{o})$. In simulations we have performed, ($n = 500$, $d = 20$, $o = 10$), the average number of iterations until successful convergence was in the range of 300 - 400, in excellent correspondence with the predicted expectation, $E(X) = 500 \cdot ln(2)$.

References

[AGS85] D. J. Amit, H. Gutfreund, and H. Sompolinsky. Storing infinite numbers of patterns in a spin-glass model of neural networks. *Phys. Rev. Lett.*, 55:1530, 1985.

[AM88] S. I. Amari and K. Maginu. Statistical neurodynamics of associative memory. *Neural Networks*, 1:63, 1988.

[CM87] F.I.M. Craik and J.M. McDowd. Age differences in recall and recognition. *Journal of Experimental Psychology; Learning, Memory, and Cognition*, 13(3):474, 1987.

[GS84] G. Gillund and M. Shiffrin. A retrieval model for both recognition and recall. *Psychological Review*, 91:1, 1984.

[HFP83] J.J. Hopfield, D. I. Fienstien, and R. G. Palmer. Unlearning' has a stabilizing effect in collective memories. *Nature*, 304:158, 1983.

[Hop82] J.J. Hopfield. Neural networks and physical systems with emergent collective abilities. *Proc. Nat. Acad. Sci. USA*, 79:2554, 1982.

[Kat85] T. Kato. Semantic-memory sources of episodic retrieval failure. *Memory & Cognition*, 13(5):442, 1985.

[KP88] J. Komĺos and R. Paturi. Convergence results in an associative memory model. *Neural Networks*, 1:239, 1988.

[KPKP90] B. Kagmar-Parsi and B. Kagmar-Parsi. On problem solving with hopfield neural networks. *Biol. Cybern.*, 62:415, 1990.

[LN89] M. Lewenstein and A. Nowak. Fully connected neural networks with self-control of noise levels. *Phys. Rev. Lett.*, 62(2):225, 1989.

[MPRV87] R.J. McEliece, E.C. Posner, E.R. Rodemich, and S.S. Venkatesh. The capacity of the hopfield associative memory. *IEEE Transactions on Information theory*, IT-33(4):461, 1987.

[NCBK87] D.L Nelson, J.J. Canas, M.T. Bajo, and P.D. Keelan. Comparing word fragment completion and cued recall with letter cues. *Journal of Experimental Psychology: Learning, Memory and Cognition*, 13(4):542, 1987.

[RY90] E. Ruppin and Y. Yeshurun. Recall and recognition in an attractor neural network model of memory retrieval. Technical report, Dept. of Computer Science, Tel-Aviv University, 1990.

[Wei85] G. Weisbuch. Scaling laws for the attractors of hopfield networks. *J. Physique Lett.*, 46:L–623, 1985.

ALCOVE: A Connectionist Model of Human Category Learning

John K. Kruschke
Department of Psychology and Cognitive Science Program
Indiana University, Bloomington IN 47405-4201 USA
e-mail: kruschke@ucs.indiana.edu

Abstract

ALCOVE is a connectionist model of human category learning that fits a broad spectrum of human learning data. Its architecture is based on well-established psychological theory, and is related to networks using radial basis functions. From the perspective of cognitive psychology, ALCOVE can be construed as a combination of exemplar-based representation and error-driven learning. From the perspective of connectionism, it can be seen as incorporating constraints into back-propagation networks appropriate for modelling human learning.

1 INTRODUCTION

ALCOVE is intended to accurately model human, perhaps non-optimal, performance in category learning. While it is a feed-forward network that learns by gradient descent on error, it is unlike standard back propagation (Rumelhart, Hinton & Williams, 1986) in its architecture, its behavior, and its goals. Unlike the standard back-propagation network, which was motivated by generalizing neuron-like perceptrons, the architecture of ALCOVE was motivated by a molar-level psychological theory, Nosofsky's (1986) generalized context model (GCM). The psychologically constrained architecture results in behavior that captures the detailed course of human category learning in many situations where standard back propagation fares less well. And, unlike most applications of standard back propagation, the goal of ALCOVE is not to discover new (hidden-layer) representations after lengthy training, but rather to model the course of learning itself (Kruschke, 1990c), by determining which dimensions of the given representation are most relevant to the task, and how strongly to associate exemplars with categories.

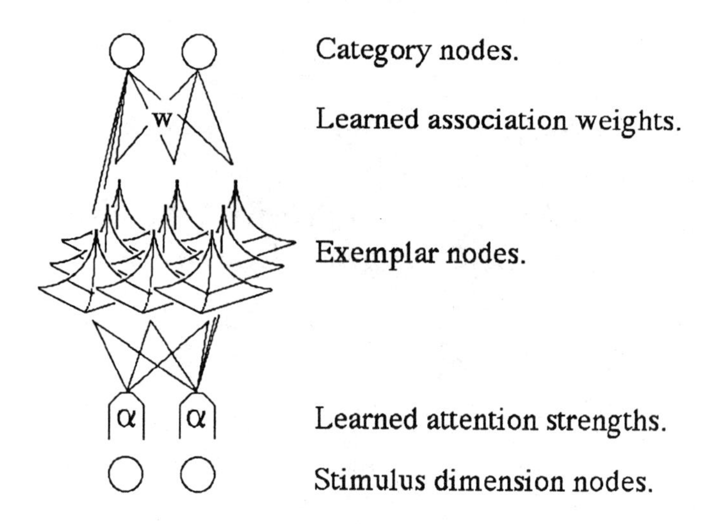

Figure 1: The architecture of ALCOVE (Attention Learning COVEring map). Exemplar nodes show their activation profile when $r = q = 1$ in Eqn. 1.

2 THE MODEL

Like the GCM, ALCOVE assumes that input patterns can be represented as points in a multi-dimensional psychological space, as determined by multi-dimensional scaling algorithms (e.g., Shepard, 1962). Each input node encodes a single psychological dimension, with the activation of the node indicating the value of the stimulus on that dimension. Figure 1 shows the architecture of ALCOVE, illustrating the case of just two input dimensions.

Each input node is gated by a dimensional *attention strength* α_i. The attention strength on a dimension reflects the relevance of that dimension for the particular categorization task at hand, and the model learns to allocate more attention to relevant dimensions and less to irrelevant dimensions.

Each hidden node corresponds to a position in the multi-dimensional stimulus space, with one hidden node placed at the position of every training exemplar. Each hidden node is activated according to the psychological similarity of the stimulus to the exemplar represented by the hidden node. The similarity function comes from the GCM and the work of Shepard (1962; 1987): Let the position of the jth hidden node be denoted as $(h_{j1}, h_{j2}, \ldots)$, and let the activation of the jth hidden node be denoted as a_j^{hid}. Then

$$a_j^{hid} = \exp\left(-c \left(\sum_i \alpha_i \left| h_{ji} - a_i^{in} \right|^r \right)^{q/r} \right) \tag{1}$$

where c is a positive constant called the *specificity* of the node, where the sum is taken over all input dimensions, and where r and q are constants determining the similarity metric and similarity gradient, respectively. For separable psychological

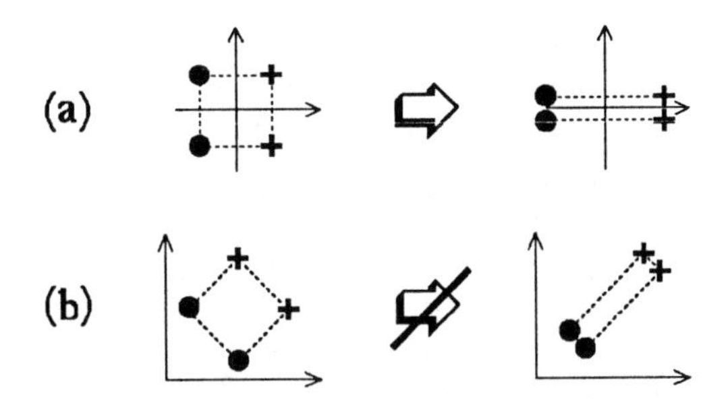

Figure 2: (a) Increasing attention on the horizontal axis and decreasing attention on the vertical axis causes exemplars of the two categories (denoted by dots and +'s) to have greater between-category dissimilarity and greater within-category similarity. (After Nosofsky, 1986, Fig. 2.) (b) ALCOVE cannot differentially attend to diagonal axes.

dimensions, the city-block metric ($r = 1$) is used, while integral dimensions might call for a Euclidean metric ($r = 2$). An exponential similarity gradient ($q = 1$) is used here (Shepard, 1987; this volume), but a Gaussian similarity gradient ($q = 2$) can sometimes be appropriate.

The dimensional attention strengths adjust themselves so that exemplars from different categories become less similar, and exemplars within categories become more similar. Consider a simple case of four stimuli that form the corners of a square in input space, as in Figure 2(a). The two left stimuli are mapped to one category (indicated by dots) and the two right stimuli are mapped to another category (indicated by +'s). ALCOVE learns to increase the attention strength on the horizontal axis, and to decrease the attention strength on the vertical axis. On the other hand, ALCOVE cannot stretch or shrink diagonally, as suggested in Figure 2(b). This constraint is an accurate reflection of human performance, in that categories separated by a diagonal boundary tend to take longer to learn than categories separated by a boundary orthogonal to one dimension.

Each hidden node is connected to output nodes that correspond to response categories. The connection from the jth hidden node to the kth category node has a connection weight denoted w_{kj}, called the *association weight* between the exemplar and the category. The output (category) nodes are activated by the linear rule used in the GCM and the network models of Gluck and Bower (1988a,b):

$$a_k^{out} = \sum_{j}^{hid} w_{kj} a_j^{hid} . \tag{2}$$

In ALCOVE, unlike the GCM, the association weights are learned and can take on any real value, including negative values. Category activations are mapped to response probabilities using the same choice rule as was used in the GCM and network models. Thus,

$$\Pr(K) = \exp(\phi\, a_K^{out}) \Big/ \sum_{k}^{out} \exp(\phi\, a_k^{out}) \tag{3}$$

where ϕ is a real-valued scaling constant. In other words, the probability of classifying the given stimulus into category K is determined by the magnitude of category K's activation relative to the sum of all category activations.

The dimensional attention strengths, α_i, and the association weights, w_{kj}, are learned by gradient descent on sum-squared error, as used in standard back propagation (Rumelhart *et al.*, 1986) and in the network models of Gluck and Bower (1988a,b). Details can be found in Kruschke (1990a,b). In fitting ALCOVE to human learning data, there are four free parameters: the fixed specificity c in Equation 1; the probability mapping constant ϕ in Equation 3; the association weight learning rate; and, the attention strength learning rate.

In summary, ALCOVE extends Nosofsky's (1986) GCM by having a learning mechanism and by allowing any positive or negative values for association weights, and it extends Gluck and Bower's (1988a,b) network models by including explict attention strengths and by using continuous input dimensions. It is a combination of exemplar-based category representations with error-driven learning, as alluded to by Estes *et al.* (1989; see also Hurwitz, 1990). ALCOVE can also be construed as a form of (non-)radial basis function network, if $r = q = 2$ in Equation 1. In the form described here, the hidden nodes are placed at positions where training exemplars occur, but another option, described by Kruschke (1990a,b), is to scatter hidden nodes over the input space to form a covering map. Both these methods work well in fitting human data in some situations, but the exemplar-based approach has advantages (Kruschke, 1990a,b). ALCOVE can also be compared to a standard back-propagation network that has adaptive attentional multipliers on its input nodes (*cf.* Mozer and Smolensky, 1989), but with fixed input-to-hidden weights (Kruschke 1990b, p.33). Such a network behaves similarly to a covering-map version of ALCOVE. Moreover, such back-prop networks are susceptible to catastrophic retroactive interference (Ratcliff, 1990; McCloskey & Cohen, 1989), unlike ALCOVE.

3 APPLICATIONS

Several applications of ALCOVE to modelling human performance are detailed elsewhere (Kruschke, 1990a,b); a few will be summarized here.

3.1 RELATIVE DIFFICULTY OF CATEGORY STRUCTURES

The classic work of Shepard, Hovland and Jenkins (1961) explored the relative difficulty of learning different category structures. As a simplified example, the linearly separable categories in Figure 2(a) are easier to learn than the exclusive-or problem (which would have the top-left and bottom-right exemplars mapped to one category, and the top-right and bottom-left mapped to the other). Shepard *et al.* carefully considered several candidate explanations for the varying difficulties, and concluded that some form of attentional learning was necessary to account for their results. That is, people seemed to be able to determine which dimensions were relevant or irrelevant, and they allocated attention to dimensions accordingly. Category structures with fewer relevant dimensions were easier to learn. ALCOVE has just the sort of attentional learning mechanism called for, and can match the relative difficulties observed by Shepard *et al.*

3.2 BASE-RATE NEGLECT

A recent series of experiments (Gluck & Bower, 1988b; Estes *et al.*, 1989; Shanks, 1990; Nosofsky *et al.*, 1991) investigated category learning when the assignment of exemplars to categories was probabilistic and the base rates of the categories were unequal. In these experiments, there were two categories (one "rare" and the other "common") and four binary-valued stimulus dimensions. The stimulus values were denoted s1 and s1* for the first dimension, s2 and s2* for the second dimension, and so on. The probalities were arranged such that over the course of training, the normative probability of each category, given s1 alone, was 50%. However, when presented with feature s1 alone, human subjects classified it as the rare category significantly more than 50% of the time. It was as if people were neglecting the base rates of the categories.

Gluck and Bower (1988b) and Estes *et al.* (1989) compared two candidate models to account for the apparent base-rate neglect. One was a simple exemplar-based model that kept track of each training exemplar, and made predictions of categorizations by summing up frequencies of occurence of each stimulus value for each category. The exemplar-based model was unable to predict base-rate neglect. The second model they considered, the "double-node network," was a one-layer error-driven network that encoded each binary-valued dimension with a pair of input nodes. The double-node model was able show base-rate neglect.

ALCOVE is an exemplar-based model, and so it is challenged by those results. In fact, Kruschke (1990a,b) and Nosofsky *et al.* (1991) show that ALCOVE fits the trail-by-trial learning and base-rate neglect data as well as or better than the double-node model.

3.3 THREE-STAGE LEARNING OF RULES AND EXCEPTIONS

One of the best-known connectionist models of human learning is Rumelhart and McClelland's (1986) model of verb past tense acquistion. One of the main phenomena they wished to model was three-stage learning of irregular verbs: First a few high-frequency irregulars are learned; second, many regular verbs are learned with some interference to the previously learned irregulars; and third, the high-frequency irregulars are re-learned.[1] In order to reproduce three-stage learning in their model, Rumelhart and McClelland had to change the training corpus during learning, so that early on the network was trained with ten verbs, 80% of which were irregular, and later the network was trained with 420 verbs, only 20% of which were irregular. It remains a challenge to connectionist models to show three-stage learning of rules and exceptions while keeping the training set constant.

While ALCOVE has not been applied to the verb-learning situation (and perhaps should not be, as a multi-dimensional similarity-space might not be a tractable representation for verbs), it can show three-stage learning of rules and exceptions in simpler but analogous situations. Figure 3 shows an arrangement of training exemplars, most of which can be classified by the simple rule, "if it's to the right

[1] There is evidence that three-stage learning is only very subtle in verb past tense acquisition (*e.g.*, Marcus, 1990), but whether it exists more robustly in the simpler category learning domains addressed by ALCOVE is still an open question.

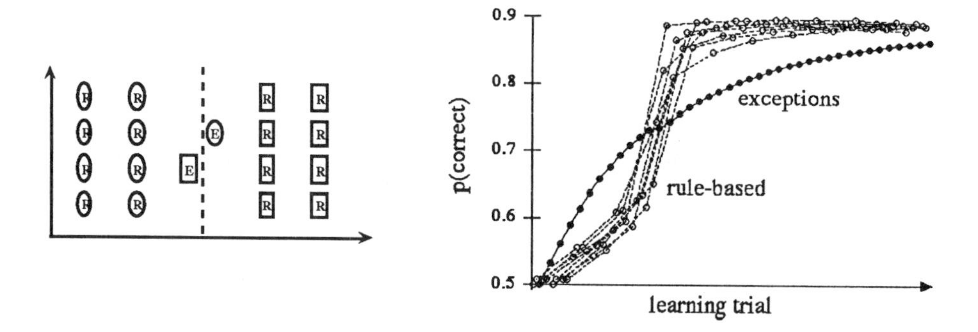

Figure 3: Left panel shows arrangement of rule-following (R) and exceptional (E) cases. Right panel shows the performance of ALCOVE. The ratio of E to R cases and all parameters of the model were fixed throughout training.

of the dashed line, then it's in the 'rectangle' category, otherwise it's in the 'oval' category." The rule-following cases are marked with an "R." There are two exceptional cases near the dashed line, marked with an "E." Exceptional exemplars occurred 4 times as often as rule-following exemplars. The right panel of Figure 3 shows that ALCOVE initially learns the E cases better than the R cases, but that later in learning the R cases surpass the E's. The reason is that early in learning, ALCOVE is primarily building up association weights and has not yet shifted much attention away from the irrelevant dimension. Associations from the E cases grow more quickly because they are more frequent. Once the associations are established, then there is a basis for attention to be shifted away from the irrelevant dimension, rapidly improving performance on the R cases. At the time of this writing, these results have the status of a provocative demonstration, but experiments with human subjects in similar learning situations are presently being undertaken.

Acknowledgment

This research was supported in part by Biomedical Research Support Grant RR 7031-25 from the National Institutes of Health.

References

Estes, W. K., Campbell, J. A., Hatsopoulos, N., & Hurwitz, J. B. (1989). Base-rate effects in category learning: A comparison of parallel network and memory storage-retrieval models. *J. Exp. Psych. Learning, Memory and Cognition*, **15**, 556-576.

Gluck, M. A. & Bower, G. H. (1988a). Evaluating an adaptive network model of human learning. *J. of Memory and Language*, **27**, 166-195.

Gluck, M. A. & Bower, G. H. (1988b). From conditioning to category learning: An adaptive network model. *J. Exp. Psych. General*, **117**, 227-247.

Hurwitz, J. B. (1990). A hidden-pattern unit network model of category learning. Doctoral dissertation, Harvard University.

Kruschke, J. K. (1990a). A connectionist model of category learning. Doctoral dissertation, University of California at Berkeley. Available from University Microfilms International.

Kruschke, J. K. (1990b). ALCOVE: A connectionist model of category learning. Research Report 19, Cognitive Science Program, Indiana University.

Kruschke, J. K. (1990c). How connectionist models learn: The course of learning in connectionist networks. *Behavioral and Brain Sciences*, **13**, 498-499.

Marcus, G. F., Ullman, M., Pinker, S., Hollander, M., Rosen, T. J., & Xu, F. (1990). Overregularization. Occasional Paper #41, MIT Center for Cognitive Science.

McCloskey, M. & Cohen, N. J. (1989). Catastrophic interference in connectionist networks: the sequential learning problem. In: G. Bower (ed.), *The Psychology of Learning and Motivation, Vol. 24.* New York: Academic Press.

Mozer, M. C., & Smolensky, P. (1989). Skeletonization: A technique for trimming the fat from a network via relevance assessment. In: D. S. Touretzky (ed.), *Advances in Neural Information Processing Systems, I*, pp. 107-115. San Mateo, CA: Morgan Kaufmann.

Nosofsky, R. M. (1986). Attention, similarity and the identification-categorization relationship. *J. Exp. Psych. General*, **115**, 39-57.

Nosofsky, R. M., Kruschke, J. K., & McKinley, S. (1991). Comparisons between adaptive network and exemplar models of classification learning. Research Report 35, Cognitive Science Program, Indiana University.

Ratcliff, R. (1990). Connectionist models of recognition memory: Constraints imposed by learning and forgetting functions. *Psychological Review*, **97**, 285-308.

Rumelhart, D. E., Hinton, G. E., & Williams, R. J. (1986). Learning internal representations by back-propagating errors. In: D. E. Rumelhart & J. L. McClelland (eds.), *Parallel Distributed Processing, Vol. 1*, pp. 318-362. Cambridge, MA: MIT Press.

Rumelhart, D. E., & McClelland, J. L. (1986). On learning the past tenses of english verbs. In: J. L. McClelland & D. E. Rumelhart (eds.), *Parallel Distributed Processing, Vol. 2*, pp. 216-271. Cambridge, MA: MIT Press.

Shanks, D. R. (1990). Connectionism and the learning of probabilistic concepts. *Quarterly J. Exp. Psych.*, **42A**, 209-237.

Shepard, R. N. (1962). The analysis of proximities: Multidimensional scaling with an unknown distance function, I & II. *Psychometrika*, **27**, 125-140, 219-246.

Shepard, R. N. (1987). Toward a universal law of generalization for psychological science. *Science*, **237**, 1317-1323.

Shepard, R. N., Hovland, C. L., & Jenkins, H. M. (1961). Learning and memorization of classifications. *Psychological Monographs*, **75**(13), Whole No. 517.

Spherical Units as Dynamic Consequential Regions: Implications for Attention, Competition and Categorization

Stephen José Hanson*
Learning and Knowledge
Acquisition Group
Siemens Corporate Research
Princeton, NJ 08540

Mark A. Gluck
Center for Molecular &
Behavioral Neuroscience
Rutgers University
Newark, NJ 07102

Abstract

Spherical Units can be used to construct dynamic reconfigurable consequential regions, the geometric bases for Shepard's (1987) theory of stimulus generalization in animals and humans. We derive from Shepard's (1987) generalization theory a particular multi-layer network with dynamic (centers and radii) spherical regions which possesses a specific mass function (Cauchy). This learning model generalizes the configural-cue network model (Gluck & Bower 1988): (1) configural cues can be learned and do not require pre-wiring the power-set of cues, (2) Consequential regions are continuous rather than discrete and (3) Competition amoungst receptive fields is shown to be increased by the global extent of a particular mass function (Cauchy). We compare other common mass functions (Gaussian; used in models of Moody & Darken; 1989, Krushke, 1990) or just standard backpropogation networks with hyperplane/logistic hidden units showing that neither fare as well as models of human generalization and learning.

1 The Generalization Problem

Given a favorable or unfavorable consequence, what should an organism assume about the contingent stimuli? If a moving shadow overhead appears prior to a hawk attack what should an organism assume about other moving shadows, their shapes and positions? If a dense food patch is occasioned by a particular density of certain kinds of shrubbery what should the organism assume about other shurbbery, vegetation or its spatial density? In an pattern recognition context, given a character of a certain shape, orientation, noise level etc.. has been recognized correctly what should the system assume about other shapes, orientations, noise levels it has yet to encounter?

* Also a member of Cognitive Science Laboratory, Princeton University, Princeton, NJ 08544

Many "generalization" theories assume stimulus similarity represents a "failure to discriminate", rather than a cognitive decision about what to assume is consequential about the stimulus event. In this paper we implement a generalization theory with multilayer architecture and localized kernel functions (cf. Cooper, 1962; Albus 1975; Kanerva, 1984; Hanson & Burr, 1987,1990; Niranjan & Fallside, 1988; Moody & Darken, 1989; Nowlan, 1990; Krushke, 1990) in which the learning system constructs hypotheses about novel stimulus events.

2 Shepard's (1987) Generalization Theory

Considerable empirical evidence indicates that when stimuli are represented within an multi-dimensional psychological space, similarity, as measured by stimulus generalization, drops off in an approximate exponential decay fashion with psychological distance (Shepard, 1957, 1987). In comparison to a linear function, a similarity-distance relationship with upwards concave curvature, such as an exponential-decay curve, exaggerates the similarity of items which are nearby in psychological space and minimizes the impact of items which are further away.

Recently, Roger Shepard (1987) has proposed a "Universal Law of Generalization" for stimulus generalization which derives this exponential decay similarity-distance function as a "rational" strategy given minimal information about the stimulus domain (see also Shepard & Kannappan, this volume). To derive the exponential-decay similarity-distance rule, Shepard (1987) begins by assuming that stimuli can be placed within a psychological space such that the response learned to any one stimulus will generalize to another according to an invariant monotonic function of the distance between them. If a stimulus, **O**, is known to have an important consequence, what is the probability that a novel test stimulus, **X**, will lead to the same consequence? Shepard shows, through arguments based on probabilistic reasoning that regardless of the *a priori* expectations for regions of different sizes, this expectation will almost always yield an approximate exponentially decaying gradient away from a central memory point. In particular, very simple geometric constraints can lead to the exponential generalization gradient. Shepard (1987) assumes (1) that the consequential region overlaps the consequential stimulus event. and (2) bounded center symmetric consequential regions of unknown shape and size In the 1-dimensional case it can be shown that g(x) is robust over a wide variety of assumptions for the distribution of p(s); although for p(s) exactly the Erlangian or discrete Gamma, g(x) is exactly Exponential.

We now investigate possible ways to implement a model which can learn consequential regions and appropriate generalization behavior (cf. Shepard, 1990).

3 Gluck & Bower's Configural-cue Network Model

The first point of contact is to discrete model due to Gluck and Bower: The configural-cue network model (Gluck & Bower, 1988) The network model adapts its weights (associations) according to Rescorla and Wagner's (1972) model of classical conditioning which is a special case of Widrow & Hoff's (1961) Least-Mean-Squares (LMS) algorithm for training one-layer networks. Presentation of a stimulus pattern is represented by activating nodes on the input layer which correspond to the pattern's elementary features and pair-wise conjunctions of features.

The configural-cue network model implicitly embodies an exponential generalization (similarity) gradient (Gluck, 1991) as an emergent property of it's stimulus representation scheme. This equivalence can be seen by computing how the number of overlapping active input nodes (similarity) changes as a function of the number of overlapping component cues (distance). If a stimulus pattern is associated with some outcome, the configural-cue model will generalize this association to other stimulus patterns in proportion to the number of common input nodes they both activate.

Although the configural cue model has been successful with various categorization data, there are several limitations of the configural cue model: (1) it is discrete and can not deal adequately with continuous stimuli (2) it possesses a non-adaptable internal representation (3) it can involve the pre-wiring the power set of possible cues Nonetheless, there are several properties that make the Configural Cue model successful that are important to retain for generalizations of this model: (a) the competitive stimulus properties deriving from the delta rule (b) the exponential stimulus generalization property deriving from the successive combinations of higher-order features encoded by hidden units.

4 A Continuous Version of Shepard's Theory

We derive in this section a new model which generalizes the configural cue model and derives directly from Shepard's generalization theory. In Figure 1, is shown a one dimensional depiction of the present theory. Similar to Shepard we assume there is a consequential

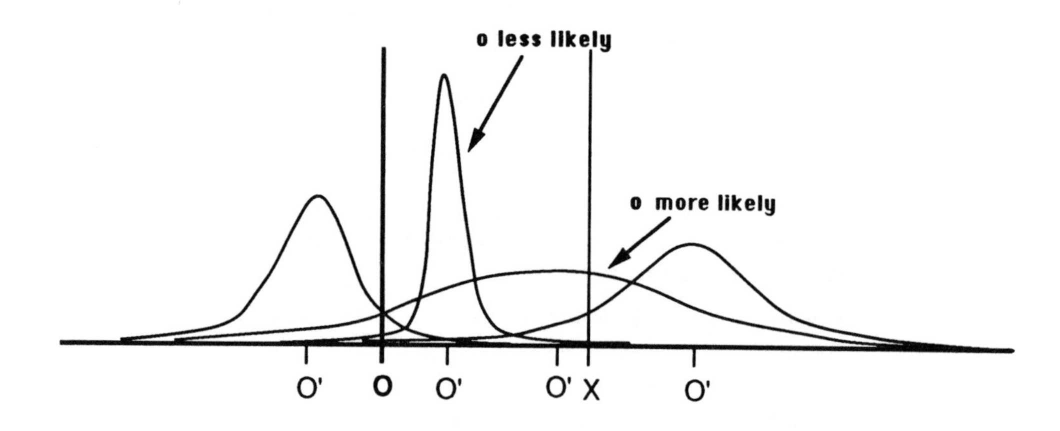

Figure 1: Hypothesis Distributions based on Consequential Region

region associated with a significant stimulus event, **O**. Also similar to Shepard we assume the learning system knows that the significant stimulus event is contained in the consequential region, but does not know the size or location of the consquential region. In absence of this information the learning system constructs hypothesis distributions

(**O'**) which may or maynot be contained in the consequential region but at least overlap the significant stimulus event with some finite probablity measure. In some hypothesis distributions the significant stimulus event is "typical" in the consequential region, in other hypothesis distributions the significant stimulus event is "rare". Consequently, the present model differs from Shepard's approach in that the learning system uses the consequential region to project into a continuous hypothesis space in order to construct the conditional probability of the novel stimulus, X, given the significant stimulus event **O**.

Given no further information on the location and size of the consequential region the learning system averages over all possible locations (equally weighted) and all possible (equally weighted) variances over the known stimulus dimension:

$$g(x) = \int_{s1}^{s2} p(s) \int_{c1}^{c2} p(c) H(x,s,c)\, dc\, ds \qquad (1)$$

In order to derive particular gradients we must assume particular forms for the hypothesis distribution, H(x,s,c). Although we have investigated many different hypothesis distributions and wieghting functions (p(c), p(s)), we only have space here to report on two bounding cases, one with very "light tails", the Gaussian, and one with very "heavy tails", the Cauchy (see Figure 2). These two distributions are extremes and provide a test of the robustness of the generalization gradient. At the same time they represent different commitments to the amount of overlap of hidden unit receptive fields and the consequent amount of stimulus competition during learning.

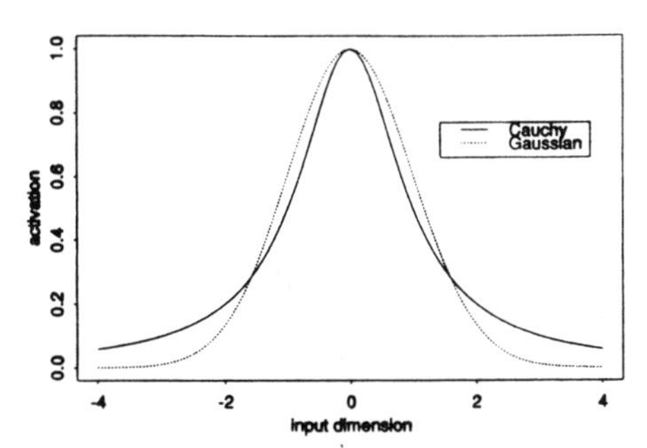

Figure 2: Gaussian compared to the Cauchy: Note heavier Cauchy tail

Equation 2 was numerically integrated (using mathematica), over a large range of variances and a large range of locations using uniform densities representing the weighting functions and both Gaussian and Cauchy distributions representing the hypothesis distributions. Shown in Figure 3 are the results of the integrations for both the Cauchy and Gaussian distributions. The resultant gradients are shown by open circles (Cauchy) or stars (Gaussian) while the solid lines show the best fitting exponential gradient. We note that they approximate the derived gradients rather closely in spite of the fact the underlying forms are quite complex, for example the curve shown for the Cauchy integration is actually:

$$-5Arctan\left(\frac{x-c2}{5}\right)+0.01\left[Arctan(100(x-c1))\right]+5Arctan\left(\frac{x+c1}{5}\right)- \quad (2)$$

$$0.01\left[Arctan(100(x+c2))\right]-\tfrac{1}{2}((c2+x)\log(1-s1x+x2)+(c1-x)\log(s2-s1x+x2))-$$

$$\tfrac{1}{2}(c1-x)\log(1+s1x+x2)+(c2+x)\log(s2+s1x+x2))$$

Consequently we confirm Shepard's original observation for a continuous version[1] of his theory that the exponential gradient is a robust consequence of minimum information set of assumptions about generalization to novel stimuli.

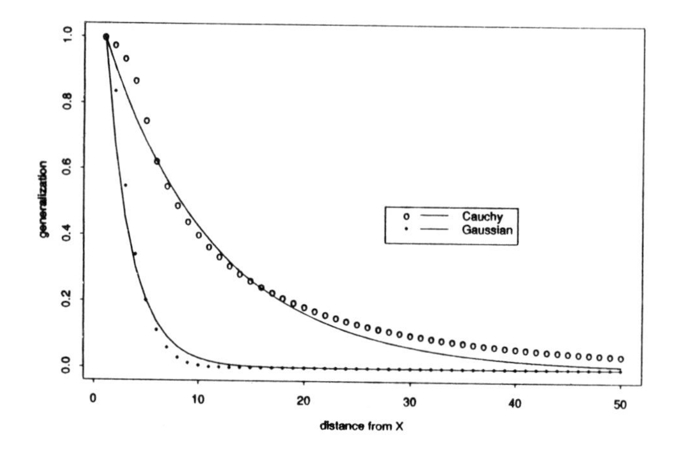

Figure 3: Generalization Gradients Compared to Exponential (Solid Lines)

4.1 Cauchy vs Gaussian

As pointed out before the Cauchy has heavier tails than the Gaussian and thus provides more global support in the feature space. This leads to two main differences in the hypothesis distributions:

(1) Global vs Local support: Unlike back-propagation with hyperplanes, Cauchy can be local in the feature space and unlike the Gaussian can have more global effect.

(2) Competition not Dimensional scaling: Dimensional "Attention" in CC and Cauchy multilayer network model is based on competition and effective allocation of resources during learning rather than dimensional contraction or expansion.

---

[1] N-Dimensional Versions: we generalize the above continuous 1-d model to an N-dimensional model by assuming that a network of Cauchy units can be used to construct a set of consequential regions each possibly composed of several Cauchy receptive fields. Consequently, dimensions can be differentially weighted by subsets of cauchy units acting in concert could produce metrics like L-1 norms in separable (e.g., shape, size of arbitrary forms) dimension cases while equally weighting dimensions similar to metrics like L-2 norms in integral (e.g., lightness, hue in color) dimension cases.

Since the stimulus generalization properites of both hypothesis distributions are indistinguishable (both close to exponential) it is important to compare categorization results based on a multilayer gradient descent model using both the Cauchy and Gaussian as hidden node functions.

5 Comparisons with Human Categorization Performance

We consider in the final section two experiments from human learning literature which constrain categorization results. The model was a multilayer network using standard gradient descent in the radius, location and second layer weights of either Cauchy or Gaussian functions in hidden units.

5.1 Shepard, Hovland and Jenkins (1961)

In order to investigate adults ability to learn simple classification SH&J used eight 3-dimensional stimuli (corners of the cube) representing seperable stimuli like shape, color or size. Of the 70 possible 4-exempler dichotomies there are only six unique 4 exemplar dichotomies which ignor the specific stimulus dimension.

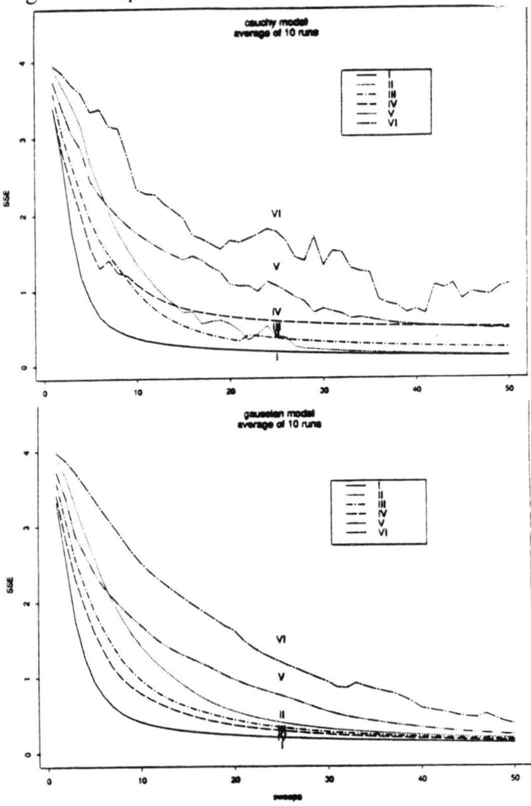

Figure 4: Classification Learning Rate for Gaussian and Cauchy on SHJ stimuli

These dichotomies involve both linearly separable and nonlinearly separable classifications as well as selective dependence on a specific dimension or dimensions.

For both measures of trials to learn and the number of errors made during learning the order of difficulty was (easiest) I<II<III<IV<V<VI (hardest).

In Figure 4, both the Cauchy model and the Gaussian model was compared using the SHJ stimuli. Note that the Gaussian model misorders the 6 classification tasks: I<IV<III<II<V<VI while the Cauchy model conforms with the human performance.

5.2 Medin and Schwanenflugel (1981)

Data suitable to illustrate the implications of this non-linear stimulus generalization gradient for classification learning, are provided by Medin and Schwanenflugel (1981). They contrasted performance of groups of subjects learning pairs of classification tasks, one of which was *linearly separable* and one of which was not. One of the classifications is linearly separable (LS) and the other is not (NLS).

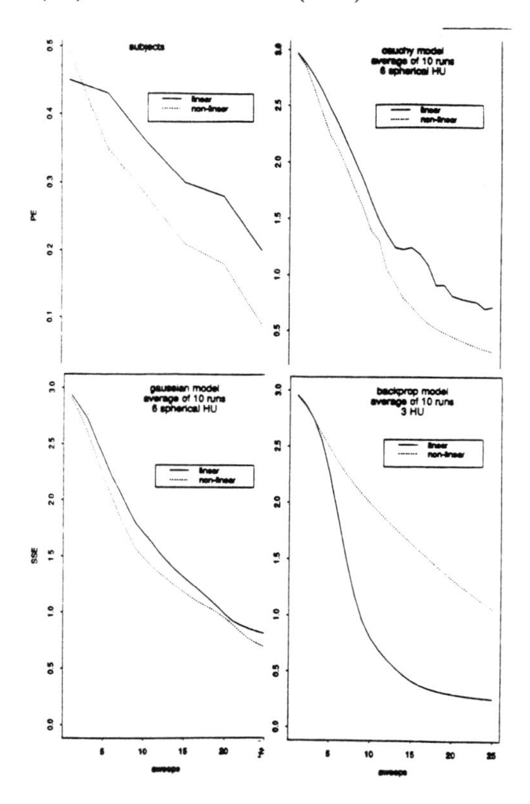

Figure 5: Subjects (a) Cauchy (b) Gaussian (c) and Backprop (d) Learning performance on the M&S stimuli.

An important difference between the tasks lies in how the between-category and within-category distances are distributed. The linearly separable task is composed of many "close" (Hamming distance=1) and some "far" (Hamming distance=3) relations, while the non-separable task has a broader distribution of "close", "medium", and "far" between-category distances. These unequal distributions have important implications for models which use a non-linear mapping from distance to similarity. Medin and Schwanenflugel reported reliable and complete results with a four-dimensional task that embodied the same controls for linear separability and inter-exemplar similarities. To evaluate the relative difficulty of the two tasks, Medin & Schwanenflugel compared the average learning curves of subjects trained on these stimuli. Subjects found the linearly separable task (LS) more difficult than the non-linearly separable task (NLS), as indicated by the reduced percentage of errors for the NLS task at all points during training (see next Figure 5--Subjects, top left) In Figure 5 is shown 10 runs of the Cauchy model (top right) note that it, similar to the human performance, had more difficulty with the LS than the NLS separable task. Below this frame is the results for the Gaussian model (bottom left) which does show a slight advantage of learning the NLS task over the LS task. While in the final frame (bottom right) of this series standard backprop actually reverses the speed of learning of each task relative to human performance.

6 Conclusions

A continuous version of Shepard's (1987) generalization theory was derived providing for a specific Mass/Activation function (Cauchy) and receptive field distribution. The Cauchy activation function is shown to account for a range of human learning performance while another Mass/Activation function (Gaussian) does not. The present model also generalizes the Configural Cue model to continuous, dynamic, internal representation.

Attention like effects are obtained through competition of Cauchy units as a fixed resource rather than dimensional "shrinking" or "expansion" as in an explicit rescaling of each axes.

Cauchy units are a compromise; providing more global support in approximation than gaussian units and more local support than the hyperplane/logistic units in backpropagation models.

References

Albus, J. S. (1975) A new approach to manipulator control: The cerebellar model articulation controller (CMAC), American Society of Engineers, Transactions G (Journal of Dynamic Systems, Measurement and Control) 97(3):220-27.

Cooper, P. (1962) The hypersphere in pattern recognition. Information and Control, 5, 324-346.

M. A. Gluck (1991) Stimulus generalization and representation in adaptive network models of category learning. Psychological Science, 2, 1, 1-6.

M. A. Gluck & G. H. Bower, (1988), Evaluating an adaptive network model of human learning. Journal of Memory and Language, 27, 166-195.

Hanson, S. J. and Burr, D. J. (1987) Knowledge Representation in Connectionist Networks, Bellcore Technical Report.

Hanson, S. J. and Burr, D. J. (1990) What Connectionist models learn: Learning and Representation in Neural Networks. Behavioral and Brain Sciences.

Kanerva, P. (1984) Self propagating search : A unified theory of memory; Ph.D. Thesis, Stanford University.

Kruschke, J. (1990) A connectionist model of category learning, Ph.D. Thesis, UC Berkeley.

Medin D. L., & Schanwenflugel, P. J. (1981) Linear seperability in classification learning. Journal of Experimental Psychology: Human Learning and Memory, 7, 355-368.

Moody .J. and Darken, C (1989) Fast learning in networks of locally-tuned processing units, Neural Computation, 1, 2, 281-294.

Niranjan M. & Fallside, F. (1988) Neural networks and radial basis functions in classifying static speech patterns, Technical Report, CUED/FINFENG TR22, Cambridge University.

Nowlan, S. (1990) Max Likelihood Competition in RBF Networks. Technical Report CRG-TR-90-2, University of Toronto.

R. A. Rescorla A. R. Wagner (1972) A theory of Pavlovian conditioning: Variations in the effectiveness of reinforcement and non-reinforcement. A. H. Black W. F. Prokasy (Eds.) Classical conditioning II: Current research and theory, 64-99 Appleton-Century-Crofts: New York.

R. N. Shepard (1958), Stimulus and response generalization: Deduction of the generalization gradient from a trace model, Psychological Review 65, 242-256

Shepard, R. N. (1987) Toward a Universal Law of Generalization for Psychological Science. Science, 237.

R. N. Shepard, C. I. Hovland & H. M. Jenkins (1961), Learning and memorization of classifications, Psychological Monographs, 75, 1-42

A B. Widrow & M. E. Hoff (1960) Adaptive switching circuits, Institute of Radio Engineers, Western Electronic Show and Convention, Convention Record, 4, 96-194

Connectionist Implementation of a Theory of Generalization

Roger N. Shepard
Department of Psychology
Stanford University
Stanford, CA 94305-2130

Sheila Kannappan
Department of Physics
Harvard University
Cambridge, MA 02138

Abstract

Empirically, generalization between a training and a test stimulus falls off in close approximation to an exponential decay function of distance between the two stimuli in the "stimulus space" obtained by multidimensional scaling. Mathematically, this result is derivable from the assumption that an individual takes the training stimulus to belong to a "consequential" region that includes that stimulus but is otherwise of unknown location, size, and shape in the stimulus space (Shepard, 1987). As the individual gains additional information about the consequential region—by finding other stimuli to be consequential or not—the theory predicts the shape of the generalization function to change toward the function relating actual probability of the consequence to location in the stimulus space. This paper describes a natural connectionist implementation of the theory, and illustrates how implications of the theory for generalization, discrimination, and classification learning can be explored by connectionist simulation.

1 THE THEORY OF GENERALIZATION

Because we never confront exactly the same situation twice, anything we have learned in any previous situation can guide us in deciding which action to take in the present situation only to the extent that the similarity between the two situations is sufficient to justify generalization of our previous learning to the present situation. Accordingly, principles of generalization must be foundational for any theory of behavior.

In Shepard (1987) nonarbitrary principles of generalization were sought that would be optimum in any world in which an object, however distinct from other objects, is generally a member of some class or *natural kind* sharing some dispositional property of potential consequence for the individual. A newly encountered plant or animal might be edible or poisonous, for example, depending on the hidden genetic makeup of its natural kind.

This simple idea was shown to yield a quantitative explanation of two very general empirical regularities that emerge when generalization date are submitted to methods of *multidimensional scaling*. The first concerns the shape of the *generalization gradient*, which describes how response probability falls off with distance of a test stimulus from the training stimulus in the obtained representational space. The second, which is not treated in the present (unidimensional) connectionist implementation, concerns the metric of multidimensional representational spaces. (See Shepard, 1987.)

These results were mathematically derived for the simplest case of an individual who, in the absence of any advance knowledge about particular objects, now encounters one such object and discovers it to have an important consequence. From such a learning event, the individual can conclude that all objects are consequential that are of the same kind as that object and that therefore fall in some *consequential region* that overlaps the point corresponding to that object in representational space. The individual can only estimate the probability that a given new object is consequential as the conditional probability, given that a region of unknown size and shape overlaps that point, that it also overlaps the point corresponding to the new object. The gradient of generalization then arises because a new object that is closer to the old object in the representational space is more likely to fall within a random region that overlaps the old object.

In order to obtain a quantitative estimate of the probability that the new stimulus is consequential, the individual must integrate over all candidate regions in representational space—with, perhaps, different probabilities assigned, a priori, to different sizes and shapes of region. The results turn out to depend remarkably little on the prior probabilities assigned (Shepard, 1987). For any reasonable choice of these probabilities, integration yields an approximately exponential gradient. And, for the single most reasonable choice in the absence of any advance information about size or shape, namely, the choice of maximum entropy prior probabilities, integration yields exactly the exponential decay function.

These results were obtained by separating the *psychological* problem of the form of generalization in a psychological space from the *psychophysical* problem of the mapping from any physical parameter space to that psychological space. The psychophysical mapping, having been shaped by natural selection, would favor a representational space in which regions that correspond to natural kinds, though variously sized and shaped, are not on average systematically elogated or compressed in any particular direction or location of the space. Such a regularized space would provide the best basis for generalization from objects of newly encountered kinds.

The psychophysical mapping thus corresponds to an optimum mapping from input to hidden units in a connectionist system. Indeed, Rumelhart (1990) has recently suggested that the power of the connectionist approach comes from the ability of a set of hidden units to represent the relations among possible inputs according to their significances for the system as a whole rather than according to their superficial relations at the input level. Although in biologically evolved individuals the psychophysical mapping is likely to have been shaped more through evolution than through learning (Shepard, 1989; see also Miller & Todd, 1990) the connectionist implementation to be described here does provide for some fine tuning of this mapping through learning.

Beyond the exponential form of the gradient of generalization following training on a single stimulus, three basic phenomena of discrimination and classification learning that the theory of generalization should be able to explain are the following: First, when all and only the stimuli within a compact subset are followed by an important consequence (reinforcement), an individual should eventually learn to respond to all and only the stimuli in that subset (Shepard, 1990)—at least to the degree possible, given any noise-induced uncertainty about locations in the representational space (Shepard, 1986, 1990). Second, when the positive stimuli do not form a compact subset but are interspersed among negative (nonreinforced) stimuli, generalization should entail a slowing of classification learning (Nosofsky, 1986; Shepard & Chang, 1963). Third, repeated discrimination or classification learning, in which a boundary between positive and negative stimuli remains fixed, should induce a "fine tuning" stretching of the representational space at that boundary such that any subsequent learning will generalize less fully across that boundary.

Our initial connectionist explorations have been for relatively simple cases using a unidemensional stimulus set and a linear learning rule. These simulations serve to illustrate how information about the probable disposition of a consequential region accrues, in a Bayesian manner, from successive encounters with different stimuli, each of which is or is not followed by the consequence. In complex cases, the cumulative effects on probability of generalized response, on latency of discriminative response, and on fine tuning of the psychophysical mapping may sometimes be easier to establish by simulation than by mathematical derivation. Fortunately for this purpose, the theory of generalization has a connectionist embodiment that is quite direct and neurophysiologically plausible.

2 A CONNECTIONIST IMPLEMENTATION

In the implementation reported here, a linear array of 20 input units represents a set of 20 stimuli differing along a unidimensional continnuum, such as the continuum of pitches of tones. The activation level of a given input unit is 1 when its corresponding stimulus is presented and 0 when it is not. (This localist representation of the "input" may be considered the output of a lower-level, massively parallel network for perpetual analysis.)

When such an "input unit" is activated, its activation propagates upward and outward through successively higher layers of hidden units, giving rise to a *cone of activation* of that input unit (Figure 1a). Higher units are activated by wider ranges of input units (i.e., have larger "receptive fields"). The hidden units thus represent potential consequential regions, with higher units corresponding to regions of greater sizes in representational space.

The activation from any input unit is also subject to progressive attenuation as it propagates to succesively higher layers of hidden units. In the present form of the model, this attenuation comes about because the weights of the connections from input to hidden units fall off exponentially with the heights of the hidden units. (Connection weights are pictorially indicated in Figure 1 by the heavinesses of the connecting lines.) An exponential fall off of connection weight with height is natural, in that it corresponds to a decrement of fixed proportion as the activation propagates through each layer to the next. According to the generalizaton theory (Shepard, 1987), an exponential fall off is also optimum for the case of minimum prior knowledge, because it corresponds to the maximum entropy probability density distribution of possible sizes of a consequential region.

When a response, R_k, is followed by a positive consequence in the presence of a stimulus, S_1, a simple linear rule (either a Hebbian or a delta rule) will increase the weight of the connection from each representational unit, j, (whether input or hidden unit) to that response

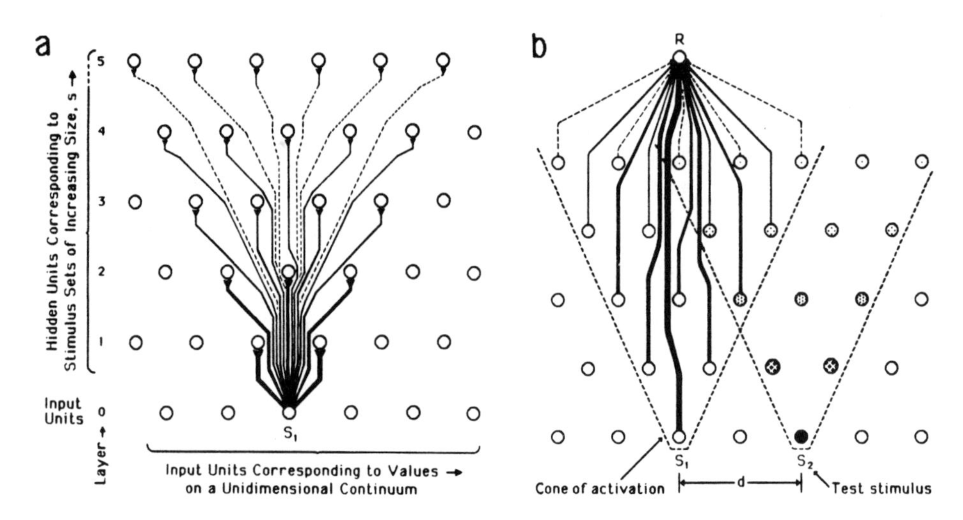

Figure 1: Schematic portrayal of the connectionist embodiment. (a) Initial connections from an input unit to hidden units in its "cone of activation." (b) Connections from these hidden units to a response unit following reinforcement of the response.

unit, R_k, in proportion to the current level of activation, a_j, of that representational unit. In the initial implementation considered here, the change in weight from representational unit j to the response unit R_k is simply

$$\Delta w_{jk} = \begin{cases} \lambda a_j(1 - a_k) & \text{upon a positive outcome (reinforcement)} \\ -\lambda a_j a_k & \text{upon a negative outcome (nonreinforcement)} \end{cases}$$

where λ is a learning rate parameter and a_k is the current activation level of the response unit R_k (which, tending to be confined between 0 and 1, represents an estimate of the probability of the positive consequence). Following a positive outcome, then, positive weights will connect all the units in the cone of activation for S_1 to R_k, but with values that decay exponentially with the height of a unit in that cone (Figure 1b).

If, now, a different stimulus, S_2, is encountered, some but not all of the representational units that are in the cone of activation of S_1 and, hence, that are already connected to R_k will also fall in the cone of activation of S_2 (Figure 1b). It is these units in the overlap of the two cones that mediate generalization of the response from S_1 to S_2. Not only is this simple connectionist scheme neurophysiologically plausible, it is also isomorphic to the theory of generalization (Shepard, 1987) based solely on considerations of optimal behavior in a world consisting of natural kinds.

3 PRELIMINARY CONNECTIONIST EXPLORATIONS

The simulation results for generalization and discrimination learning are summarized in Figure 2. Panel a shows, for different stages of training on stimulus S_{10}, the level of response activation produced by activation of each of the 20 input units. In accordance with theory, this activation decayed exponentially with distance from the training stimulus. The obtained functions differ only by a multiplicative scale factor that increased (toward asymptote) with the amount of training. Following this training, the response connection weights decreased exponentially with the heights of the hidden units (Panel b). Later training on a second positive stimulus, S_{12}, created a secondary peak in the activation function (Panel c), and still later nonreinforced presentation of a third stimulus, S_9, produced a sharp drop in the activation function at the discrimination boundary (Panel d).

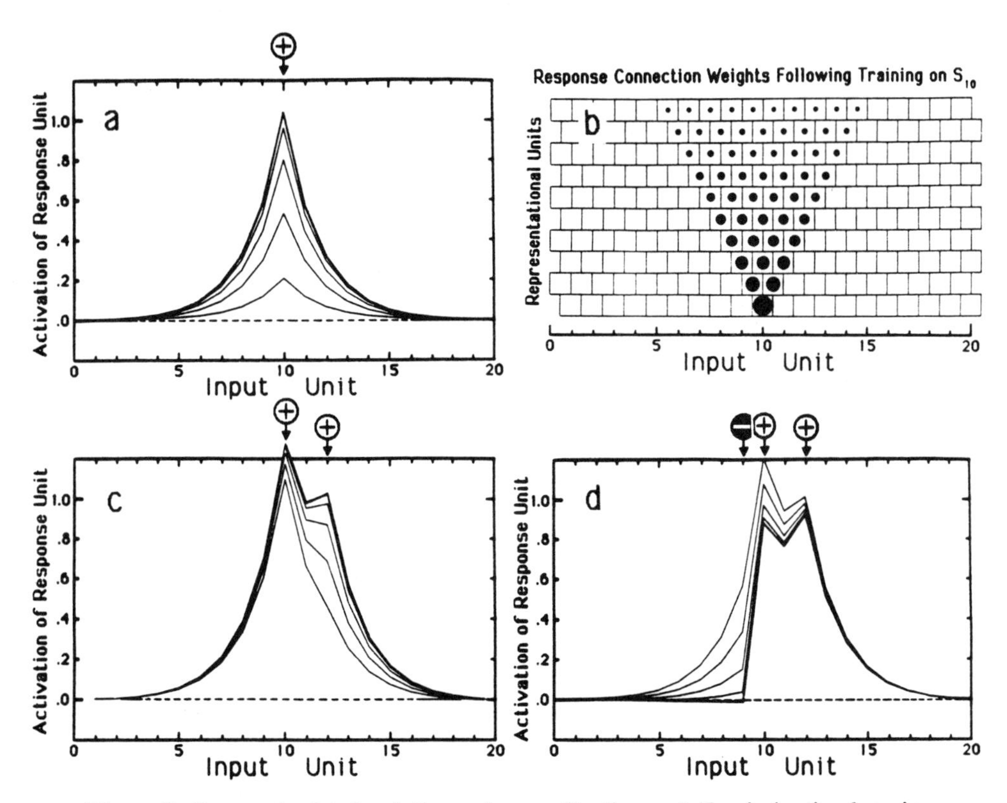

Figure 2: Connectionist simulations of generalization and discrimination learning.

Figure 3 presents the results for classification learning in which all stimuli were presented but with response reinforcement for stimuli in the positive set only. When the positive set was compact (Panel a) sharp discrimination boundaries formed and response activation approached 1 for all positive stimuli and 0 for all negative stimuli. In accordance with theory and empirical data, generalization entailed slower classification learning when the positive stimuli were dispersed among negative stimuli (Panel b)—as shown by a (mean square) error measure (Panel c).

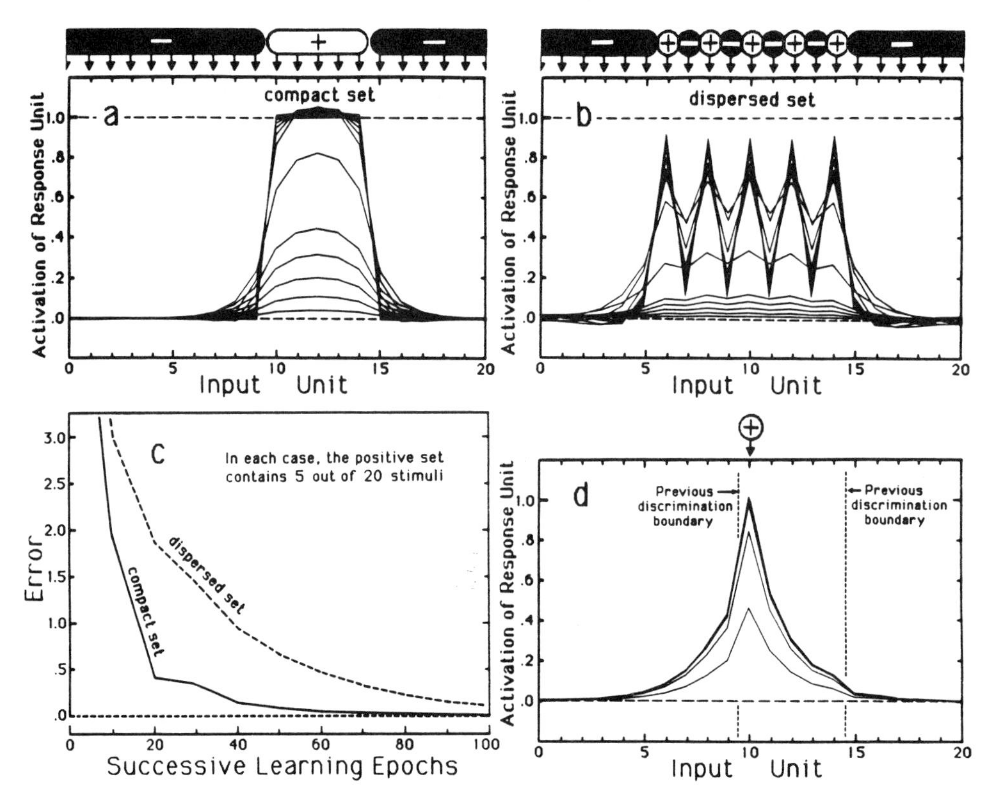

Figure 3: Connectionist simulations of classification learning.

Finally, Panel d illustrates fine tuning of the psychophysical mapping when discrimination boundaries have the same locations for many successively learned classifications. In contrast to the preceding simulations, in which only the response connection weights were allowed to change, here the connection weights from the input units to the hidden units were also allowed to change through "back propagation" (Rumelhart, Hinton, & Williams, 1986). For 400 learning epochs each, each of ten different responses was successively associated with the same five positive stimuli, S_{10} through S_{14}, while reinforcement was withheld for all the remaining stimuli. Then, yet another response was associated with the single stimulus S_{10}. Although the resulting activation curves for this new response (Panel d) are similar to the original generalization curves (Figure 2a), they drop more sharply where classification boundaries were previously located. This fine tuning of the psychophysical mapping proceeded, however, much more slowly than the learning of the classificatory responses themselves.

4 CONCLUDING REMARKS

This is just the beginning of the connectionist exploration of the implications of the generalization theory in more complex cases. In addition to accounting for generalization and classification along a unidimensional continuum, the approach can account for generalization and classification of stimuli differing with respect to multidimensional continua (Shepard, 1987) and also with respect to discrete features (Gluck, 1991; Russell, 1986). Finally, the connectionist implementation should facilitate a proposed extension to the treatment of response latencies as well as probabilities (Shepard, 1987).

Connectionists have sometimes assumed an exponential decay generalization function, and their notion of radial basis functions is not unlike the present concept of consequential regions (see Hanson & Gluck, this volume). What has been advocated here (and in Shepard, 1987) is the derivation of such functions and concepts from first principles.

Acknowledgements

This work was supported by National Science Foundation grant BNS85-11685 to the first author. For help and guidance, we thank Jonathan Bachrach, Geoffrey Miller, Mark Monheit, David Rumelhart, and Steven Sloman.

References

Gluck, M. A. (1991). Stimulus generalization and representation in adaptive network models of category learning. *Psychological Science, 2*. (in press).

Hanson, S. J. & Gluck, M. A. (1991). Spherical units as dynamic consequential regions: Implications for attention, competition, and categorization. (This volume).

Miller, G. F. & Todd, P. M. (1990). Exploring adaptive agency I: Theory and methods for simulating the evolution of learning. In D. S. Touretzky, J. L. Elman, T. J. Sejnowski, & G. E. Hinton (Eds.), *Proceedings of the 1990 Connectionist Models Summer School*. San Mateo, CA: Morgan Kaufmann.

Nosofsky, R. M. (1986). Attention, similarity, and the identification-categorization relationship. *Journal of Experimental Psychology: General, 114*, 39–57.

Rumelhart, D. E. (1990). Representation in connectionist models (The Association Lecture). *Attention & Performance Meeting*. Ann Arbor, Michigan, July 9.

Rumelhart, D. E., Hinton, G. E., & Williams, R. J. (1986). Learning representations by back-propagating errors. *Nature, 323*, 533–536.

Russell, S. J. (1986). A quantitative analysis of analogy by similarity. In *Proceedings of the National Conference on Artificial Intelligence*. Philadelphia, PA: American Association for Artificial Intelligence.

Shepard, R. N. (1986). Discrimination and generalization in identification and classification: Comment on Nosofsky. *Journal of Experimental Psychology: General, 115*, 50–61.

Shepard, R. N. (1987). Toward a universal law of generalization for psychological science. *Science, 237*, 1317–1323.

Shepard, R. N. (1989). Internal representation of universal regularities: A challenge for connectionism. In L. Nadel, L. A. Cooper, P. Culicover, & R. M. Harnish (Eds.), *Neural Connections, Mental Computation* (pp. 103–104). Cambridge, MA: MIT Press.

Shepard, R. N. (1990). Neural nets for generalization and classification: Comment on Staddon and Reid. *Psychological Review, 97*, 579–580.

Shepard, R. N. & Chang, J. J. (1963). Stimulus generalization in the learning of classifications. *Journal of Experimental Psychology, 65*, 94–102.

Part XI

Local Basis Functions

ADAPTIVE SPLINE NETWORKS

Jerome H. Friedman
Department of Statistics and
Stanford Linear Accelerator Center
Stanford University
Stanford, CA 94305

Abstract

A network based on splines is described. It automatically adapts the number of units, unit parameters, and the architecture of the network for each application.

1 INTRODUCTION

In supervised learning one has a system under study that responds to a set of simultaneous input signals $\{x_1 \cdots x_n\}$. The response is characterized by a set of output signals $\{y_1, y_2, \cdots, y_m\}$. The goal is to learn the relationship between the inputs and the outputs. This exercise generally has two purposes: prediction and understanding. With prediction one is given a set of input values and wishes to predict or forecast likely values of the corresponding outputs without having to actually run the system. Sometimes prediction is the only purpose. Often, however, one wishes to use the derived relationship to gain understanding of how the system works. Such knowledge is often useful in its own right, for example in science, or it may be used to help improve the characteristics of the system, as in industrial or engineering applications.

The learning is accomplished by taking training data. One observes the outputs produced by the system in response to varying sets of input values

$$\{y_{1i} \cdots y_{mi} \mid x_{1i} \cdots x_{ni}\}_1^N. \tag{1}$$

These data (1) are then used to train an "artificial" system (usually a computer program) to learn the input/output relationship. The underlying framework or model is usually taken to be

$$y_k = f_k(x_1 \cdots x_n) + \epsilon_k, \quad k = 1, m \tag{2}$$

with $\text{ave}(\epsilon_k \mid x_1 \cdots x_n) = 0$. Here (2) y_k is the kth responding output signal, f_k is a single valued deterministic function of an n-dimensional argument (inputs) and ϵ_k is a random (stochastic) component that reflects the fact that (if nonzero) y_k is not completely specified by the observed inputs, but is also responding to other quantities that are neither controlled nor observed. In this framework the learning goal is to use the training data to derive a function $\hat{f}(x_1 \cdots x_n)$ that can serve as a reasonable approximation (estimate) of the true underlying ("target") function f_k (2). The supervised learning problem can in this way be viewed as one of function or surface approximation, usually in high dimensions ($n >> 2$).

2 SPLINES

There is an extensive literature on the theory of function approximation (see Cheney [1986] and Chui [1988], and references therein). From this literature spline methods have emerged as being among the most successful (see deBoor [1978] for a nice introduction to spline methods). Loosely speaking, spline functions have the property that they are the smoothest for a given flexibility and vice versa. This is important if one wishes to operate under the least restrictive assumptions concerning $f_k(x_1 \cdots x_n)$ (2), namely, that it is relatively smooth compared to the noise ϵ_k but is otherwise arbitrary. A spline approximation is characterized by its order q [$q = 1$ (linear), $q = 2$ (quadratic), and $q = 3$ (cubic) are the most popular orders]. The procedure is to first partition the input variable space into a set of disjoint regions. The approximation $\hat{f}(x_1 \cdots x_n)$ is taken to be a separate n-dimensional polynomial in each region with maximum degree q in any one variable, constrained so that $\hat{f}$ and all of its derivatives to order $q - 1$ are continuous across all region boundaries. Thus, a particular spline approximation is determined by a choice for q, which tends not to be very important, and the particular set of chosen regions, which tends to be crucial. The central problem associated with spline approximations is how to choose a good set of associated regions for the problem at hand.

2.1 TENSOR-PRODUCT SPLINES

The most popular method for partitioning the input variable space is by the tensor or outer product of interval sets on each of the n axes. Each input axis is partitioned into $K + 1$ intervals delineated by K points ("knots"). The regions in the n-dimensional space are taken to be the $(K + 1)^n$ intersections of all such intervals. Figure 1 illustrates this procedure for $K = 4$ knots on each of two axes producing 25 regions in the corresponding two-dimensional space.

Owing to the regularity of tensor-product representations, the corresponding spline approximation can be represented in a simple form as a basis function expansion. Let $\mathbf{x} = (x_1 \cdots x_n)$. Then

$$\hat{f}(\mathbf{x}) = \sum_{\ell} w_\ell B_\ell(\mathbf{x}) \tag{3}$$

where $\{w_\ell\}$ are the coefficients (weights) for each respective basis function $B_\ell(\mathbf{x})$, and the basis function set $\{B_\ell(\mathbf{x})\}$ is obtained by taking the tensor product of the set of functions

$$\{x_j^i\}_{i=0}^{q}, \ \{(x_j - t_{kj})_+^q\}_{k=1}^{K} \tag{4}$$

over all of the axes, $j = 1, n$. That is, each of the $K + q + 1$ functions on each axis j ($j = 1, n$) is multiplied by all of the functions (4) corresponding to all of the other axes k ($k = 1, n$; $k \neq j$). As a result the total number of basis functions (3) defining the tensor-product spline approximation is

$$(K + q + 1)^n. \tag{5}$$

The functions comprising the second set in (4) are known as the truncated power functions:

$$(x_j - t_{kj})_+^q = \begin{cases} 0 & x_j \leq t_{kj} \\ (x_j - t_{kj})^q & x_j > t_{kj} \end{cases} \tag{6}$$

and there is one for each knot location t_{kj} ($k = 1, K$) on each input axis j ($j = 1, n$).

Although conceptually quite simple, tensor-product splines have severe limitations that preclude their use in high dimensional settings ($n >> 2$). These limitations stem from the exponentially large number of basis functions that are required (5). For cubic splines ($q = 3$) with five inputs ($n = 5$) and only five knots per axis ($K = 5$) 59049 basis functions are required. For $n = 6$ that number is 531441, and for $n = 10$ it is approximately 3.5×10^9. This poses severe statistical problems in fitting the corresponding number of weights unless the training sample is large compared to these numbers, and computational problems in any case since the computation grows as the number of weights (basis functions) cubed. These are typical manifestations of the so-called "curse-of-dimensionality" (Bellman [1961]) that afflicts nearly all high-dimensional problems.

3 ADAPTIVE SPLINES

This section gives a very brief overview of an adaptive strategy that attempts to overcome the limitations of the straightforward application of tensor-product splines, making practical their use in high-dimensional settings. This method, called MARS (multivariate adaptive regression splines), is described in detail in Friedman [1991] along with many examples of its use involving both real and artificially generated data. (A FORTRAN program implementing the method is available from the author.)

The method (conceptually) begins by generating a tensor-product partition of the input variable space using a large number of knots, $K \lesssim N$, on each axis. Here N (1) is the training sample size. This induces a very large $(K + 1)^n$ number of regions. The procedure then uses the training data to select particular unions of these (initially large number of) regions to define a relatively small number of (larger) regions most suitable for the problem at hand.

This strategy is implemented through the basis function representation of spline approximations (3). The idea is to select a relatively small subset of basis functions

$$\{B_m^*(\mathbf{x})\}_0^M \underset{\text{small}}{\subset} \{B_\ell(\mathbf{x})\}_0^{\text{huge}} \tag{7}$$

from the very large set (3) (4) (5) induced by the initial tensor-product partition. The particular subset for a problem at hand is obtained through standard statistical variable subset selection, treating the basis functions as the "variables". At the first step the best single basis function is chosen. The second step chooses the basis function that works best in conjunction with the first. At the mth step, the one that works best with the $m-1$ already selected, is chosen, and so on. The process stops when including additional basis functions fails to improve the approximation.

3.1 ADAPTIVE SPLINE NETWORKS

This section describes a network implementation that approximates the adaptive spline strategy described in the previous section. The goal is to synthesize a good set of spline basis functions (7) to approximate a particular system's input/output relationship, using the training data. For the moment, consider only one output y; this is generalized later. The basic observation leading to this implementation is that the approximation takes the form of sums of products of very simple functions, namely the truncated power functions (6), each involving a single input variable,

$$B_m^*(\mathbf{x}) = \prod_{k=1}^{K_m} (x_{j(k)} - t_{kj})_+^q, \tag{8}$$

and

$$\hat{f}(\mathbf{x}) = \sum_{m=0}^{M} w_m B_m^*(\mathbf{x}). \tag{9}$$

Here $1 \leq j(k) \leq n$ is an input variable and $1 \leq K_m \leq n$ is the number of factors in the product (interaction level).

The network is comprised of an ordered set of interconnected units. Figure 2 shows a diagram of the interconnections for a (small) network. Figure 3 shows a schematic diagram of each individual unit. Each unit has as its inputs all of the system inputs $x_1 \cdots x_n$ and all of the outputs from the previous units in the network $B_0 \cdots B_M$. It is also characterized by three parameters: j, ℓ, t. The triangles in Figure 3 represent selectors. The upper triangle selects one of the system inputs, x_j; the left triangle selects one of the previous unit outputs, B_ℓ. These serve as inputs, along with the parameter t, to two internal units that each produce an output. The first output is $B_\ell \cdot (x_j - t)_+^q$ and the second is $B_\ell \cdot (t - x_j)_+^q$. The whole unit thereby produces two outputs B_{M+1} and B_{M+2}, that are available to serve as inputs to future units. In addition to units of this nature, there is an initial unit (B_0) that produces the constant output $B_0 = 1$, that is also available to be selected as an input to all units. The output of the entire network, $\hat{f}$, is a weighted sum (9) of all of the unit outputs (including $B_0 = 1$). This is represented by the bottom trapezoid in Figure 2.

The parameters associated with the network are the number of units Nu, the parameters associated with each one

$$\{\ell_i, j_i, t_i\}_1^{Nu}, \tag{10}$$

and the weights in the final adder

$$\{w_k\}_0^{M=2\cdot Nu}. \tag{11}$$

The goal of training the network is to choose values for these parameters (10) (11) that minimize average future prediction error (squared), that is the squared error on (test) data not used as part of the training sample. An estimate of this quantity is provided by the generalized cross-validation model selection criterion (Craven and Wahba [1979])

$$GCV = \frac{1}{N}\sum_{i=1}^{N}(y_i - \hat{f}_i)^2 / \left[1 - \frac{5 \cdot Nu + 1}{N}\right]^2. \quad (12)$$

The numerator in (12) is the average squared-error over the training data. The denominator is an (inverse) penalty for adding units. The quantity $(5 \cdot Nu+1)$ is just the number of adjustable parameters in the network. This GCV criterion (12) has its roots in ordinary (leave-one-out) cross-validation and serves as an approximation to it (see Craven and Wahba [1979]).

The training strategy used is a semi-greedy one. The units are considered in order. For the mth unit the weights of all later units are set to zero, that is

$$w_{2m+1} = \cdots = w_{2M_{\max}} = 0$$

where $M_{\max}$ is the maximum number of units in the network. The GCV criterion (12) is then minimized with respect to the parameters of the mth unit (ℓ_m, j_m, t_m), and the weights associated with all previous units as well as the unit under consideration $\{w_k\}_0^{2m}$, given the parameter values associated with the previous units $\{\ell_i, j_i, t_i\}_1^{m-1}$. This optimization can be done very rapidly, $O(nm^2N)$, using least squares updating formulae (see Friedman [1991]). This process is repeated until $M_{\max}$ units have been added to the network. A post optimization procedure (weight elimination) is then applied to select an optimal subset of weights to be set to zero, so as to minimize the GCV criterion (12). This will (usually) decrease the GCV value since it includes a penalty for increasing the number of nonzero weights

The semi-greedy training strategy has the advantage of being quite fast. The total computation is $O(nNM_{\max}^3)$ where n is the number of system inputs, N is the training sample size, and $M_{\max}$ is the maximum number of units to be included in the network (before weight elimination). On a SUN SPARCstation, small to moderate sized problems train in seconds to minutes, and very large ones in a few hours. A potential disadvantage of this strategy is possible loss of prediction accuracy compared to a more thorough optimization strategy. This tends not to be the case. Experiments with more complete optimization seldom resulted in even moderate improvement. This is because units added later to the network can compensate for the suboptimal settings of parameters introduced earlier.

Figure 4 illustrates a (very small) network that might be realized with the MARS procedure. The number above each unit is the system input that it selected. The letter within each unit represents its knot parameter. The first unit necessarily has as its input the constant $B_0 = 1$. Its first output goes to the final adder but was not selected as an input to any future units. Its second output serves as the selected input to the next two units, but was eliminated from the adder by the final weight elimination, and so on. The final approximation for this network is

$$\hat{f}(\mathbf{x}) = w_0 + w_1(x_3 - s)_+^q + w_2(s - x_3)_+^q(x_7 - t)_+^q$$
$$+ w_3(s - x_3)_+^q(x_2 - u)_+^q + w_4(s - x_3)_+^q(u - x_2)_+^q(x_8 - v)_+^q$$
$$+ w_5(s - x_3)_+^q(u - x_2)_+^q(v - x_8)_+^q.$$

Two possible network topologies that might be realized are of special interest. One is where all units happen to select the constant line $B_0 = 1$ as their unit input. In this case the resulting approximation will be a sum of spline functions each involving only one input variable. This is known as an additive function (no interactions)

$$\hat{f}(\mathbf{x}) = \sum_{j=1}^{J} f_j(x_j). \tag{13}$$

An additive function has the property that the functional dependence on any variable is independent of the values of all other input variables up to an overall additive constant. Additive function approximations are important because many true underlying functions $f(\mathbf{x})$ (2) are close to additive and thus well approximated by additive functions. MARS can realize additive functions as a subclass of its potential models.

Another potential network topology that can be realized by MARS is one in which every unit output serves either as an input to one (and only one) other unit or goes to the final weighted adder (but not both). This is a binary tree topology similar to those generated by recursive partitioning strategies like CART (Breiman, Friedman, Olshen and Stone [1984]). In fact, if one were to impose this restriction and employ $q = 0$ splines, the MARS strategy reduces to that of CART (see Friedman [1991]). Thus, MARS can also realize CART approximations as a subclass of its potential models.

MARS can be viewed as a generalization of CART. First by allowing $q > 0$ splines continuous approximations are produced. This generally results in a dramatic increase in accuracy. In addition, all unit outputs are eligible to contribute to the final adder, not just the terminal ones; and finally, all previous unit outputs are eligible to be selected as inputs for new units, not just the currently terminal ones.

Both additive and CART approximations have been highly successful in largely complementary situations: additive modeling when the true underlying function is close to additive, and CART when it dominately involves high order interactions between the input variables. MARS unifies both into a single framework. This lends hope that MARS will be successful at both these extremes as well as the broad spectrum of situations in between where neither works well.

Multiple response outputs $y_1 \cdots y_m$ (1) (2) are incorporated in a straightforward manner. The internal units and their interconnections are the same as described above and shown in Figures 2 and 3. Only the final weighted adder unit (Figure 2) is modified to incorporate a set of weights

$$\{w_{mk}\}_{0\ 1}^{M\ m} \tag{14}$$

for each response output ($k = 1, m$). The approximation for each output is

$$\hat{f}_k(\mathbf{x}) = \sum_{m=0}^{M} w_{mk} B_m, \quad k = 1, m.$$

The numerator in the GCV criterion (12) is replaced by

$$\frac{1}{mN} \sum_{k=1}^{m} \sum_{i=1}^{N} (y_{ik} - \hat{f}_{ik})^2$$

and it is minimized with respect to the internal network parameters (10) and all of the weights (14).

4 DISCUSSION

This section (briefly) compares and contrasts the MARS approach with radial basis functions and sigmoid "back-probagation" networks. An important consequence of the MARS strategy is input variable subset selection. Each unit individually selects the best system input so that it can best contribute to the approximation. It is often the case that some or many of the inputs are never selected. These will be inputs that tend to have little or no effect on the output(s). In this case excluding them from the approximation will greatly increase statistical accuracy. It also aids in the interpretation of the produced model. In addition to global variable subset selection, MARS is able to do input variable subset selection locally in different regions of the input variable space. This is a consequence of the restricted support (nonzero value) of the basis functions produced. Thus, if in any local region, the target function (2) depends on only a few of the inputs, MARS is able to use this to advantage even if the relevant inputs are different in different local regions. Also, MARS is able to produce approximations of low interaction order even if the number of selected inputs is large.

Radial basis functions are not able to do local (or usually even global) input variable subset selection as a part of the procedure. All basis functions involve all of the inputs at the same relative strength everywhere in the input variable space. If the target function (2) is of this nature they will perform well in that no competing procedure will do better, or likely even as well. If this is not the case, radial basis functions are not able to take advantage of the situation to improve accuracy. Also, radially symmetric basis functions produce approximations of the highest possible interaction order (everywhere in the input space). This results in a marked disadvantage if the target function tends to dominately involve interactions in at most a few of the inputs (such as additive functions (13)).

Standard networks based on sigmoidal units of linear combinations of inputs share the properties described above for radial basis functions. Including "weight elimination" (Rumelhart [1988]) provides an (important) ability to do global (but not local) input variable subset selection. The principal differences between MARS and this approach center on the use of splines rather than sigmoids, and products rather than linear combinations of the input variables. Splines tend to be more flexible in that two spline functions can closely approximate any sigmoid whereas it can take many sigmoids to approximate some splines. MARS' use of product expansions enables it to produce approximations that are local in nature. Local approximations have the property that if the target function is badly behaved in any local region of the input space, the quality of the approximation is not affected in the other regions. Also, as noted above, MARS can produce approximations of low interaction order. This is difficult for approximations based on linear combinations.

Both radial basis functions and sigmoidal networks produce approximations that are difficult to interpret. Even in situations where they produce high accuracy, they provide little information concerning the nature of the target function. MARS approximations on the other hand can often provide considerable interpretable information. Interpreting MARS models is discussed in detail in Friedman [1991]. Finally, training MARS networks tends to be computationally much faster than other types of learning procedures.

References

Bellman, R. E. (1961). *Adaptive Control Processes.* Princeton University Press, Princeton, NJ.

Breiman, L., Friedman, J. H., Olshen, R. A. and Stone, C. J. (1984). *Classification and Regression Trees.* Wadsworth, Belmont, CA.

Cheney, E. W. (1986). *Multivariate Approximation Theory: Selected Topics.* Monograph: SIAM CBMS-NSF Regional Conference Series in Applied Mathematics, Vol. 51.

Chui, C. K. (1988). *Multivariate Splines.* Monograph: SIAM CBMS-NSF Regional Conference Series in Applied Mathematics, Vol. 54.

Craven, P. and Wahba, G. (1979). Smoothing noisy data with spline functions. Estimating the correct degree of smoothing by the method of generalized cross-validation. *Numerische Mathematik* **31** 317–403.

deBoor, C. (1978). *A Practical Guide to Splines.* Springer-Verlag, New York, NY.

Friedman, J. H. (1991). Multivariate adaptive regression splines (with discussion). *Annals of Statistics*, March.

Rumelhart, D. E. (1988). Learning and generalization. IEEE International Conference on Neural Networks, San Diego, plenary address.

FIGURE 1

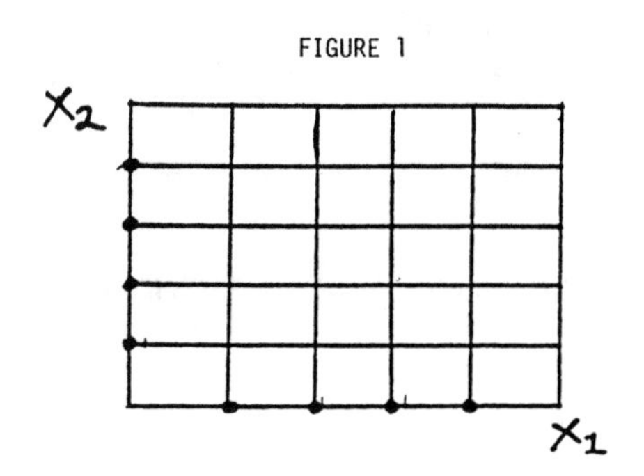

FIGURE 2

General Adaptive Spline Network

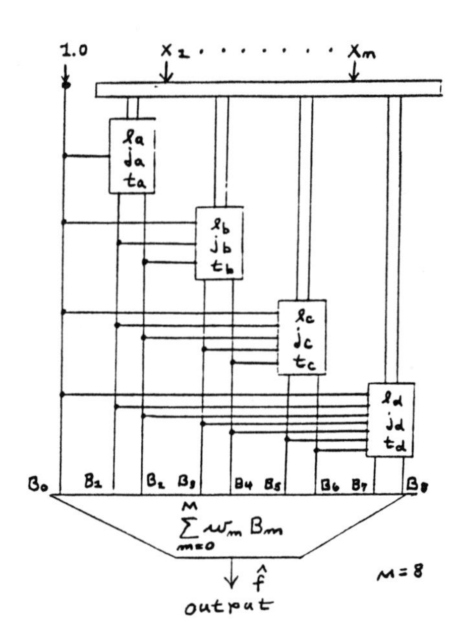

FIGURE 3

Adaptive Spline Unit

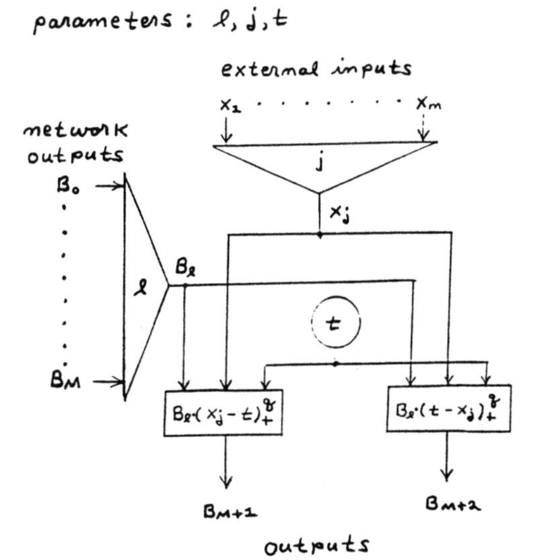

FIGURE 4

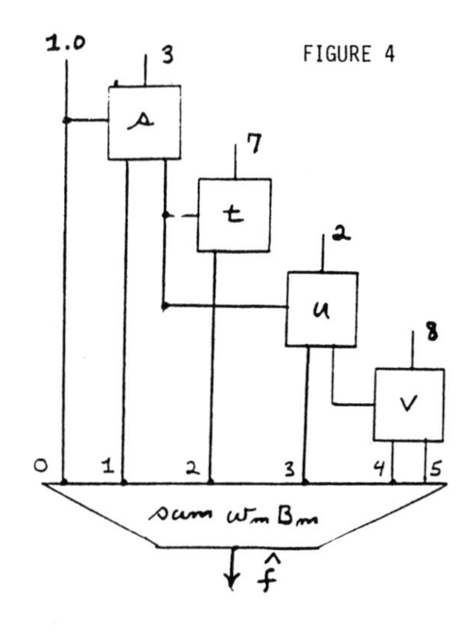

Multi-Layer Perceptrons with B-Spline Receptive Field Functions

Stephen H. Lane, Marshall G. Flax, David A. Handelman and Jack J. Gelfand

Human Information Processing Group
Department of Psychology
Princeton University
Princeton, New Jersey 08544

ABSTRACT

Multi-layer perceptrons are often slow to learn nonlinear functions with complex local structure due to the global nature of their function approximations. It is shown that standard multi-layer perceptrons are actually a special case of a more general network formulation that incorporates B-splines into the node computations. This allows novel spline network architectures to be developed that can combine the generalization capabilities and scaling properties of ***global*** multi-layer feedforward networks with the computational efficiency and learning speed of ***local*** computational paradigms. Simulation results are presented for the well known spiral problem of Weiland and of Lang and Witbrock to show the effectiveness of the Spline Net approach.

1. INTRODUCTION

Recently, it has been shown that multi-layer feedforward neural networks, such as Multi-Layer Perceptrons (MLPs), are theoretically capable of representing arbitrary mappings, provided that a sufficient number of units are included in the hidden layers (Hornik et al., 1989). Since all network weights are updated with each training exemplar, these networks construct ***global*** approximations to multi-input/multi-output function data in a manner analogous to fitting a low-order polynomial through a set of data points. This is illustrated by the cubic polynomial "Global Fit" of the data points in Fig. 1.

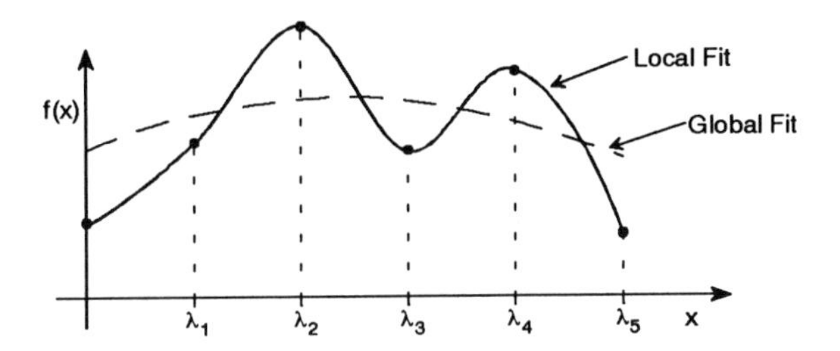

Figure 1. Global vs. Local Function Approximation

Consequently, multi-layer perceptrons are capable of generalizing (extrapolating/ interpolating) their response to regions of the input space where little or no training data is present, using a quantity of connection weights that typically scales quadratically with the number of hidden nodes. The global nature of the weight updating, however, tends to blur the details of local structures, slows the rate of learning, and makes the accuracy of the resulting function approximation sensitive to the order of presentation of the training data.

It is well known that many sensorimotor structures in the brain are organized using neurons that possess locally-tuned overlapping receptive fields (Hubel and Wiesel, 1962). Several neural network computational paradigms such as CMACs (Cerebellar Model Articulation Controllers) (Albus, 1973) and Radial Basis Functions (RBFs) (Moody and Darken, 1988) have been quite successful representing complex nonlinear functions using this same organizing principle. These networks construct ***local*** approximations to multi-input/multi-output function data that are analogous to fitting a least-squares spline through a set of data points using piecewise polynomials or other basis functions. This is illustrated as the cubic spline "Local Fit" in Fig. 1. The main benefits of using local approximation techniques to represent complex nonlinear functions include fast learning and reduced sensitivity to the order of presentation of training data. In many cases, however, in order to represent the function to the desired degree of smoothness, the number of basis functions required to adequately span the input space can scale exponentially with the number of inputs (Lane et al., 1991a,b).

The work presented in this paper is part of a larger effort (Lane et al, 1991a) to develop a general neural network formulation that can combine the generalization capabilities and scaling properties of ***global*** multi-layer feedforward networks with the computational efficiency and learning speed of ***local*** network paradigms. It is shown in the sequel that this can be accomplished by incorporating B-Spline receptive fields into the node connection functions of Multi-Layer Perceptrons.

2. MULTI-LAYER PERCEPTRONS WITH B-SPLINE RECEPTIVE FIELD FUNCTIONS

Standard Multi-Layer Perceptrons (MLPs) can be represented using node equations of the form,

$$y_i^L = \sigma\left(\sum_{j=0}^{\eta_{L-1}} c_{ij}^L\right) = \frac{1}{1+\exp\left(-\sum_{j=0}^{\eta_{L-1}} c_{ij}^L\right)} \quad (1)$$

where η_L is the number of nodes in layer L and the c_{ij}^L are linear connection functions between nodes in layers L and (L-1) such that,

$$c_{ij}^L = w_{ij}^L y_j^{L-1} \quad (2)$$

$\sigma(\bullet)$ is the standard sigmoidal nonlinearity, y_i^{L-1} is the output of a node in layer L-1, $y_0^{L-1} = 1$, and the w_{ij}^L are adjustable network weights. Some typical linear connection functions are shown in Fig. 2. c_{10}^L corresponds to a threshold input.

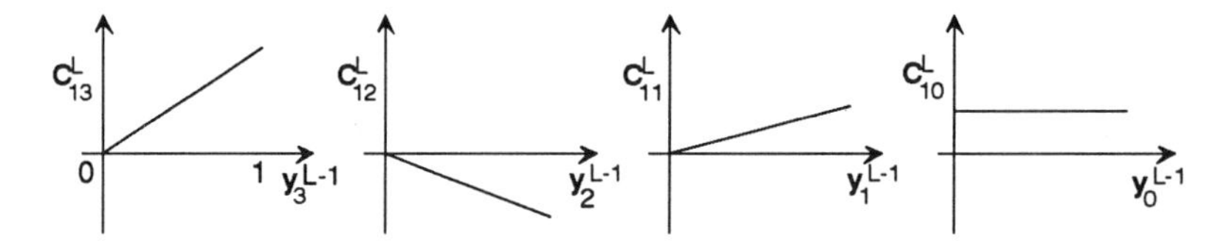

Figure 2. Typical MLP Node Connection Functions

Incorporating B-Spline receptive field functions (Lane et al., 1991a) into the node computations of eq. (1) allows more general connection functions (e.g. piecewise linear, quadratic, cubic, etc.) to be formulated. The corresponding B-Spline MLP (Spline Net) is derived by redefining the connection functions of eq. (2) such that,

$$c_{ij}^L(y_j^{L-1}) = \sum_k w_{ijk}^L B_{nk}^G(y_j^{L-1}) \quad (3)$$

This enables the construction of a more general neural network architecture that has node equations of the form,

$$y_i^L = \sigma\left[\sum_{j=1}^{\eta_{L-1}} c_{ij}^L(y_j^{L-1})\right] = \frac{1}{1+\exp\left[-\sum_{j=1}^{\eta_{L-1}} c_{ij}^L(y_j^{L-1})\right]} \quad (4)$$

The $B_{nk}^{G}(y_j^{L-1})$ are B-spline receptive field functions (Lane et al, 1989,1991a) of order n and support G, while the w_{ijk}^{L} are the spline network weights. The order, n, corresponds to the number of coefficients in the polynomial pieces. For example, linear splines are of order n=2, whereas cubic splines are of order n=4. The advantage of the more general B-Spline connection functions of eq. (3) is that it allows varying degrees of "locality" to be added to the network computations since network weights are now activated based on the value of y_j^{L-1}. The w_{ijk}^{L} are modified by backpropagating the output error only to the G weights in each connection function associated with active (i.e. nonzero) receptive field functions. The Lth-layer weights are updated using the method of steepest descent learning such that,

$$w_{ijk}^{L} \leftarrow w_{ijk}^{L} + \beta e_i^L y_i^L (1 - y_i^L) B_{nk}^{G}(y_j^{L-1}) \tag{5}$$

where e_i^L is the output error back-propagated to the ith node in layer L and β is the learning rate (Lane et al., 1991a). In the more general Spline Net formulation of eqs. (3-5), each node input has $P+G$-1 receptive fields and $P+G$-1 weights associated with it, but only G are active at any one time. P determines the number of partitions in the input space of the connection functions. Standard MLP networks are a degenerate case of the Spline Net architecture, as they can be realized with B-Spline receptive field functions of order n=2, with P=1 and G=2. Due to the connectivity of the B-Spline receptive field functions, for the case when P>1, the resulting network architecture corresponds to multiply-connected MLPs, where any given MLP is active within only one hypercube in the input space, but has weights that are shared with MLPs on the neighboring hypercubes. The amount of computation required in each layer of a Spline Net during both learning and function approximation is proportional to G, and independent of P.

Formulating the connection functions of eq. (3) with linear (n=2) B-Splines allows connection functions such as those shown in Fig. 3 to be learned.

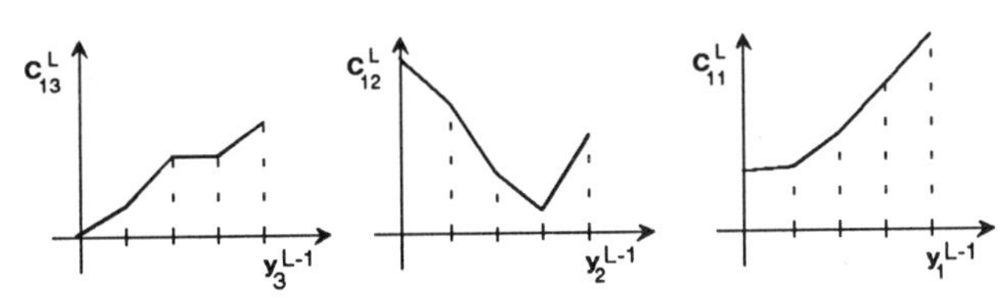

Figure 3. Spline Net Connection Functions Using Linear B-Splines (n=2)

The connection functions shown in Fig. 3 have P=4 partitions (5 knots) on the interval $y_j^{L-1} \in [0,1]$. The number of input partitions, P, determines the degree of locality of the resulting function approximation since the local shape of the connection function is determined from the current node input activation interval.

Networks constructed using the Spline Net formulation are reminiscent of the form and function of Kolmogorov-Lorenz networks (Baron and Baron, 1988). A neurobiological interpretation of a Spline Net is that it is composed of neurons that have dendritic branches with synapses that operate as a function of the level of activation at a given node or network input. This is shown in the network architecture of Fig. 4b where the standard three-layer MLP network of Fig. 4a has been redrawn using B-Spline receptive field functions with n=2, P=4 and G=2.

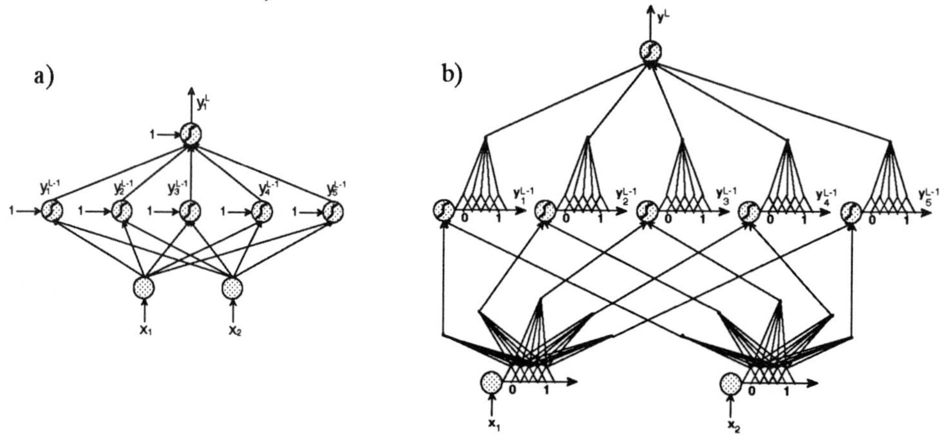

Figure 4. Three-Layer Spline Net Architecture, n=2,P=4,G=2

The horizontal arrows projecting from the right of each network node in Fig. 4b represent the node outputs. The overlapping triangles on the node output represent the receptive field functions of neurons in the next layer. These receptive field functions are summed with weighted connections in the dendritic branches to form the inputs to the next network layer. In the architecture shown in Fig. 4b, only two receptive fields are active for any given value of a node output. Therefore for this single hidden-layer network architecture, given any value for the inputs (x_1,x_2), at most N_w = 30 weights will be active where,

$$N_w = (s+1)\eta G \tag{6}$$

s is the number of network inputs and η is the number of nodes in the hidden layer, which for this case is $2s$+1 = 5.

3. SIMULATION RESULTS

In order to evaluate the impact of local computation on MLP performance, the well known spiral problem of Weiland and of Lang and Witbrock (1988) was chosen as a benchmark. Simulations were conducted using a Spline Net architecture having one hidden layer with 5 hidden nodes and linear B-Splines with support, G=2 (Fig. 4). All trials used the "vanilla" back-prop learning rule of eq. (5) with $\beta = 1/(2P)$. The connection function weights were initialized in each node such that the resulting connection functions were continuous linear functions with arbitrary slope. From previous experience (Lane et al., 1989), it was known that the number of receptive field partitions can drastically affect network learning and performance. Therefore, the connection function partitions were bifurcated during training to see the effect on network generalization capability and learning speed. The bifurcation consisted of splitting every receptive field in half after increments of 100K (100,000) training points, each time doubling the number of connection function partitions and weights in the network nodes. A more adaptive approach would monitor the slope of the learning curve to determine when to split the partitions. New weights were initializing such that the connection functions before and after the bifurcation retained the same shape. All simulation results presented in Figs. 5-12 were generated using 800K training points.

The left-most column of Fig. 5 represents the two learned connection functions that lead to each hidden node depicted in Fig. 4. The elements in the second column are the hidden node response to excitation over the unit square, while the plots in the third column are the connection functions from the hidden layer to the output node. The fourth column shows the hidden node outputs after being passed through their respective connection functions. The network output shown in the fifth column is the algebraic sum of the hidden node responses shown in the fourth column. The Spline Net was initialized as a standard MLP with P=1. Figure 6 shows the evolution of the two connection functions to the third hidden node in Fig. 4 after every 100K training points. Around 400K (P=8) the connection functions start to take on a characteristic shape. For P>8, the creation of additional partitions has little effect on the shape of the connection functions. Figure 7 shows the associated learning curve, while Fig. 8 is an enlarged version of the network output. These results indicate that the bifurcation schedule introduces additional degrees of freedom (weights) to the network in such a way as to carve out coarse global features first, then incrementally capture finer and finer localized details later. This is in contrast to the results shown in Figs. 9 and 10 where the training (using the same 800K points as in Figs. 7 and 8) was begun on a network having P=128 initial partitions. Figure 11 shows the Spline Net output after 800K training iterations using 112 discrete points located on the two spirals. Lang and Witbrock (1988) state that similar spiral results could only be obtained using a MLP network with 3 hidden layers (including jump connections) and 50,000,000 training iterations. The use of a Spline Net with a bifurcation schedule enabled the learning to be sped up by almost two orders of magnitude, indicating there is a significant performance advantage in trading-off number of hidden layers for node complexity.

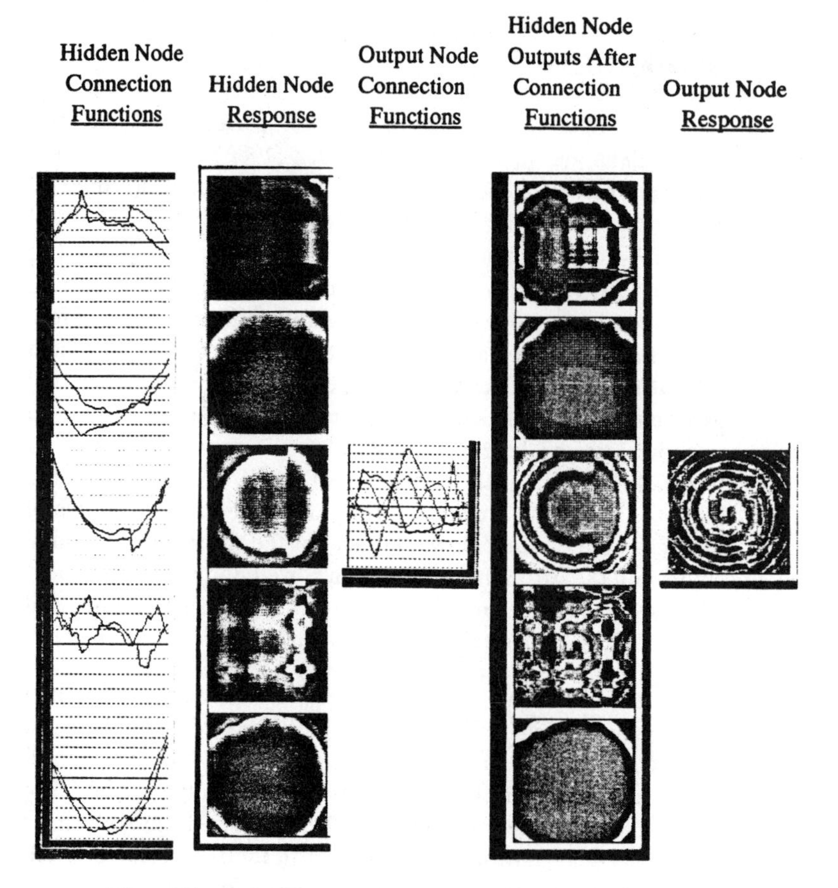

Figure 5. Spiral Learning with Bifurcation Schedule

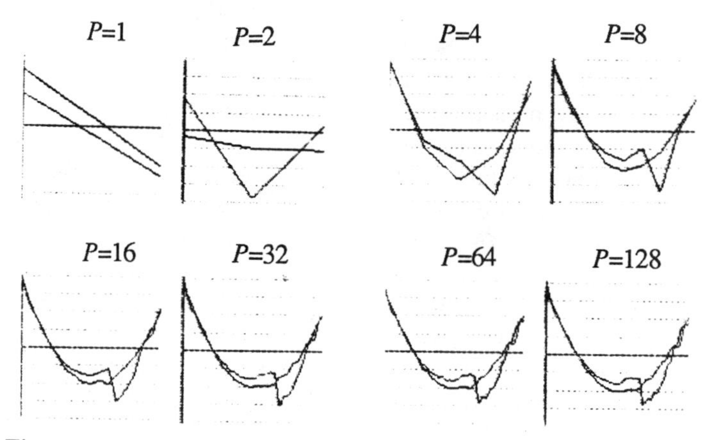

Figure 6. Evolution of Connection Functions to Third Hidden Node

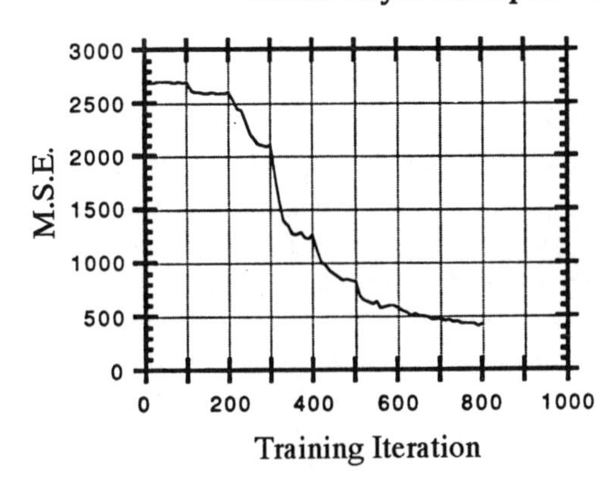

Figure 7. Learning Curve with Bifurcation Schedule
Mean Square Error vs. Training Iteration

Figure 8. Output Node Response with Bifurcation

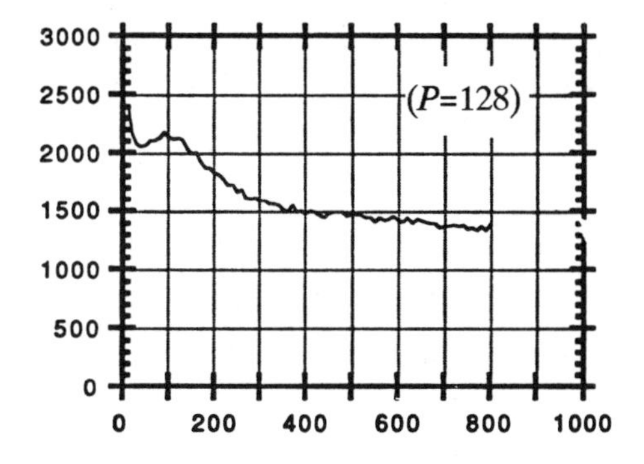

Figure 9. Learning Curve without Bifurcation Schedule
Mean Square Error vs. Training Iteration

Figure 10. Output Node Response without Bifurcation

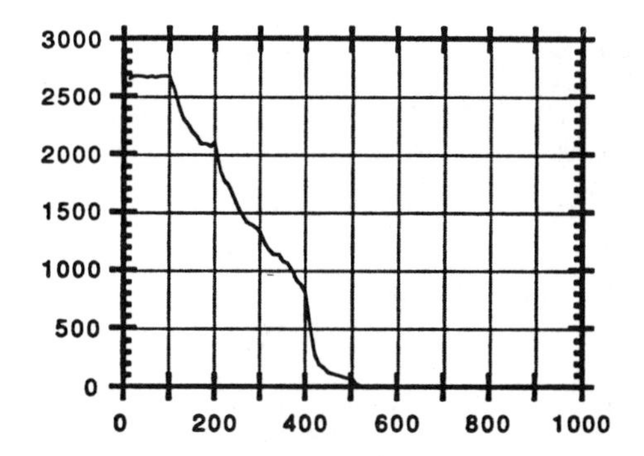

Figure 11. Learning Curve with Bifurcation Schedule
Mean Square Error vs. Training Iteration
(112 Discrete Points)

Figure 12. Output Node Response with Bifurcation
(112 Discrete Points)

4. CONCLUSIONS

It was shown that the introduction of B-Splines into the node connection functions of Multi-Layer Perceptrons allows more general neural network architectures to be developed. The resulting Spline Net architecture combines the fast learning and computational efficiency of strictly local neural network approaches with the scaling and generalization properties of the more established global MLP approach. Similarity to Kolmogorov-Lorenz networks can be used to suggest an initial number of hidden layer nodes. The number of node connection function partitions chosen affects both network generalization capability and learning performance. It was shown that use of a bifurcation schedule to determine the number of node input partitions speeds learning and improves network generalization. Results indicate that Spline Nets solve difficult learning problems by trading-off number of hidden layers for node complexity.

Acknowledgements

Stephen H. Lane and David A. Handelman are also employed by Robicon Systems Inc., Princeton, NJ. This research has been supported through a grant from the James S. McDonnell Foundation and a contract from the DARPA Neural Network Program.

References

Albus, J. (1975) "A New Approach to Manipulator Control: The Cerebellar Model Articulation Controller (CMAC)," *J. Dyn. Sys. Meas. Control*, vol. 97, pp. 270-277.

Barron, A.R. and Barron, R.L. (1988) "Statistical Learning Networks: A Unifying View," *Proc. 20th Symp. on the Interface - Computing and Statistics*, pp. 192-203.

Hornik, K. Stinchcombe, M. and White, H. (1989) "Multi-layer Feedforward Networks are Universal Approximators," *Neural Networks*, vol. 2, pp. 359-366.

Hubel, D. and Wiesel, T.N. (1962) "Receptive Fields, Binocular Interaction and Functional Architecture in Cat's Visual Cortex," *J. Physiology*, vol. 160, no. 106.

Lane, S.H., Handelman, D.A. and Gelfand, J.J. (1989) "Development of Adaptive B-Splines Using CMAC Neural Networks", *1989 IJCNN*, Wash. DC., June 1989.

Lane, S.H., Flax, M.B., Handelman, D.A. and Gelfand, J.J. (1991a) "Function Approximation in Multi-Layer Neural Networks with B-Spline Receptive Field Functions," Princeton University Cognitive Science Lab Report No. 42, in prep for *J. of Int'l Neural Network Society.*

Lane, S.H., Handelman, D.A. and Gelfand, J.J. (1991b) "Higher-Order CMAC Neural Networks-Theory and Practice," to appear Amer. Contr. Conf., Boston, MA, June,1991.

Lang, K.J. and Witbrock, M.J. (1988) "Learning to Tell Two Spirals Apart," *Proc. 1988 Connectionist Model Summer School*, D. Touretzky, G. Hinton, and T. Sejnowski, Eds.

Moody, J. and Darken, C. (1988) "Learning with Localized Receptive Fields," *Proc. 1988 Connectionist Model Summer School*, D. Touretzky, G. Hinton, T.Sejnowski, Eds.

Bumptrees for Efficient Function, Constraint, and Classification Learning

Stephen M. Omohundro
International Computer Science Institute
1947 Center Street, Suite 600
Berkeley, California 94704

Abstract

A new class of data structures called "bumptrees" is described. These structures are useful for efficiently implementing a number of neural network related operations. An empirical comparison with radial basis functions is presented on a robot arm mapping learning task. Applications to density estimation, classification, and constraint representation and learning are also outlined.

1 WHAT IS A BUMPTREE?

A bumptree is a new geometric data structure which is useful for efficiently learning, representing, and evaluating geometric relationships in a variety of contexts. They are a natural generalization of several hierarchical geometric data structures including oct-trees, k-d trees, balltrees and boxtrees. They are useful for many geometric learning tasks including approximating functions, constraint surfaces, classification regions, and probability densities from samples. In the function approximation case, the approach is related to radial basis function neural networks, but supports faster construction, faster access, and more flexible modification. We provide empirical data comparing bumptrees with radial basis functions in section 2.

A bumptree is used to provide efficient access to a collection of functions on a Euclidean space of interest. It is a complete binary tree in which a leaf corresponds to each function of interest. There are also functions associated with each internal node and the defining constraint is that each interior node's function must be everwhere larger than each of the functions associated with the leaves beneath it. In many cases the leaf functions will be peaked in localized regions, which is the origin of the name. A simple kind of bump function is spherically symmetric about a center and vanishes outside of a specified ball. Figure 1 shows the structure of a two-dimensional bumptree in this setting.

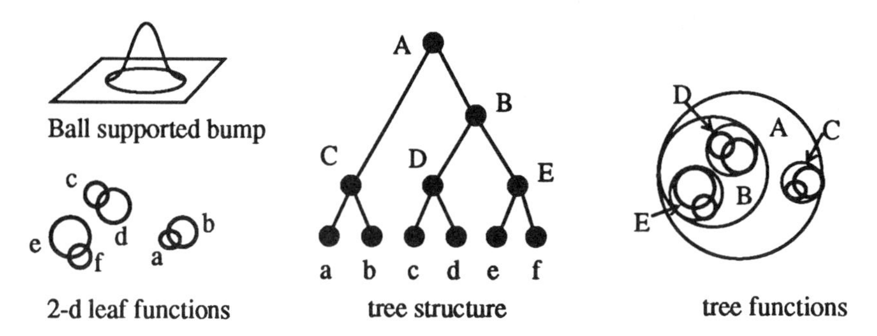

Figure 1: A two-dimensional bumptree.

A particularly important special case of bumptrees is used to access collections of Gaussian functions on multi-dimensional spaces. Such collections are used, for example, in representing smooth probability distribution functions as a Gaussian mixture and arises in many adaptive kernel estimation schemes. It is convenient to represent the quadratic exponents of the Gaussians in the tree rather than the Gaussians themselves. The simplest approach is to use quadratic functions for the internal nodes as well as the leaves as shown in Figure 2, though other classes of internal node functions can sometimes provide faster access.

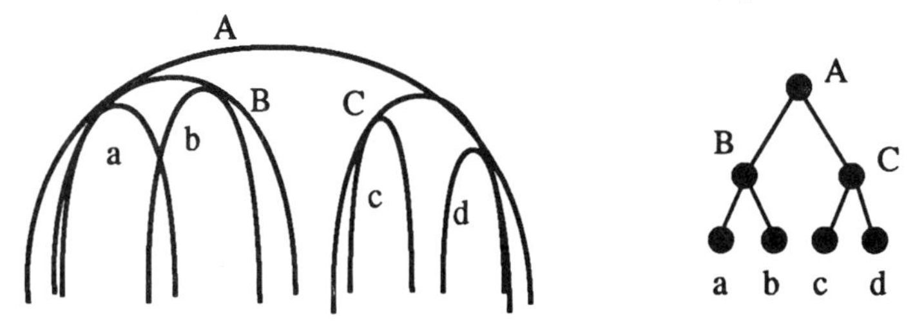

Figure 2: A bumptree for holding Gaussians.

Many of the other hierarchical geometric data structures may be seen as special cases of bumptrees by choosing appropriate internal node functions as shown in Figure 3. Regions may be represented by functions which take the value 1 inside the region and which vanish outside of it. The function shown in Figure 3D is aligned along a coordinate axis and is constant on one side of a specified value and decreases quadratically on the other side. It is represented by specifying the coordinate which is cut, the cut location, the constant value (0 in some situations), and the coefficient of quadratic decrease. Such a function may be evaluated extremely efficiently on a data point and so is useful for fast pruning operations. Such evaluations are effectively what is used in (Sproull, 1990) to implement fast nearest neighbor computation. The bumptree structure generalizes this kind of query to allow for different scales for different points and directions. The empirical results presented in the next section are based on bumptrees with this kind of internal node function.

Figure 3: Internal bump functions for A) oct-trees, kd-trees, boxtrees (Omohundro, 1987), B) and C) for balltrees (Omohundro, 1989), and D) for Sproull's higher performance kd-tree (Sproull, 1990).

There are several approaches to choosing a tree structure to build over given leaf data. Each of the algorithms studied for balltree construction in (Omohundro, 1989) may be applied to the more general task of bumptree construction. The fastest approach is analogous to the basic k-d tree construction technique (Friedman, *et. al*, 1977) and is top down and recursively splits the functions into two sets of almost the same size. This is what is used in the simulations described in the next section. The slowest but most effective approach builds the tree bottom up, greedily deciding on the best pair of functions to join under a single parent node. Intermediate in speed and quality are incremental approaches which allow one to dynamically insert and delete leaf functions.

Bumptrees may be used to efficiently support many important queries. The simplest kind of query presents a point in the space and asks for all leaf functions which have a value at that point which is larger than a specified value. The bumptree allows a search from the root to prune any subtrees whose root function is smaller than the specified value at the point. More interesting queries are based on branch and bound and generalize the nearest neighbor queries that k-d trees support. A typical example in the case of a collection of Gaussians is to request all Gaussians in the set whose value at a specified point is within a specified factor (say .001) of the Gaussian whose value is largest at that point. The search proceeds down the most promising branches first, continually maintains the largest value found at any point, and prunes away subtrees which are not within the given factor of the current largest function value.

2 THE ROBOT MAPPING LEARNING TASK

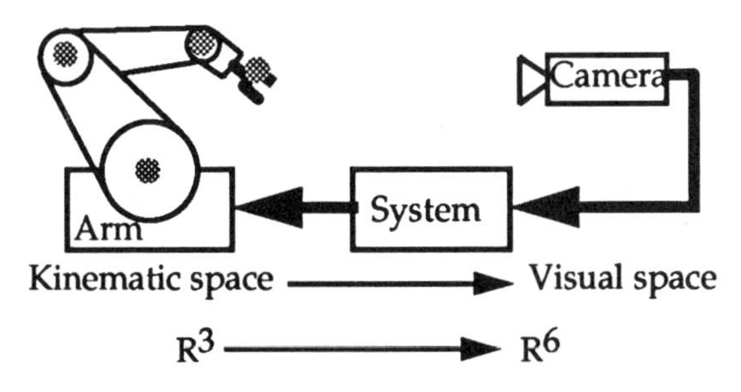

Figure 4: Robot arm mapping task.

Figure 4 shows the setup which defines the mapping learning task we used to study the effectiveness of the balltree data structure. This setup was investigated extensively by (Mel, 1990) and involves a camera looking at a robot arm. The kinematic state of the arm is defined by three angle control coordinates and the visual state by six visual coordinates of highlighted spots on the arm. The mapping from kinematic to visual space is a nonlinear map from three dimensions to six. The system attempts to learn this mapping by flailing the arm around and observing the visual state for a variety of randomly chosen kinematic states. From such a set of random input/output pairs, the system must generalize the mapping to inputs it has not seen before. This mapping task was chosen as fairly representative of typical problems arising in vision and robotics.

The radial basis function approach to mapping learning is to represent a function as a linear combination of functions which are spherically symmetric around chosen centers $f(x) = \sum_i w_i g_i (x - x_i)$. In the simplest form, which we use here, the basis functions are centered on the input points. More recent variations have fewer basis functions than sample points and choose centers by clustering. The timing results given here would be in terms of the number of basis functions rather than the number of sample points for a variation of this type. Many forms for the basis functions themselves have been suggested. In our study both Gaussian and linearly increasing functions gave similar results. The coefficients of the radial basis functions are chosen so that the sum forms a least squares best fit to the data. Such fits require a time proportional to the cube of the number of parameters in general. The experiments reported here were done using the singular value decomposition to compute the best fit coefficients.

The approach to mapping learning based on bumptrees builds local models of the mapping in each region of the space using data associated with only the training samples which are nearest that region. These local models are combined in a convex way according to "influence" functions which are associated with each model. Each influence function is peaked in the region for which it is most salient. The bumptree structure organizes the local models so that only the few models which have a great influence on a query sample need to be evaluated. If the influence functions vanish outside of a compact region, then the tree is used to prune the branches which have no influence. If a model's influence merely dies off with distance, then the branch and bound technique is used to determine contributions that are greater than a specified error bound.

If a set of bump functions sum to one at each point in a region of interest, they are called a "partition of unity". We form influence bumps by dividing a set of smooth bumps (either Gaussians or smooth bumps that vanish outside a sphere) by their sum to form an easily computed partiton of unity. Our local models are affine functions determined by a least squares fit to local samples. When these are combined according to the partition of unity, the value at each point is a convex combination of the local model values. The error of the full model is therefore bounded by the errors of the local models and yet the full approximation is as smooth as the local bump functions. These results may be used to give precise bounds on the average number of samples needed to achieve a given approximation error for functions with a bounded second derivative. In this approach, linear fits are only done on a small set of local samples, avoiding the computationally expensive fits over the whole data set required by radial basis functions. This locality also allows us to easily update the model online as new data arrives.

If $b_i(x)$ are bump functions such as Gaussians, then $n_i(x) = \frac{b_i(x)}{\sum_j b_j(x)}$ forms a partition of unity. If $m_i(x)$ are the local affine models, then the final smoothly interpolated approximating function is $f(x) = \sum_i n_i(x) m_i(x)$. The influence bumps are centered on the sample points with a width determined by the sample density. The affine model associated with each influence bump is determined by a weighted least squares fit of the sample points nearest the bump center in which the weight decreases with distance.

Because it performs a global fit, for a given number of samples points, the radial basis function approach achieves a smaller error than the approach based on bumptrees. In terms of construction time to achieve a given error, however, bumptrees are the clear winner.Figure 5 shows how the mean square error for the robot arm mapping task decreases as a function of the time to construct the mapping.

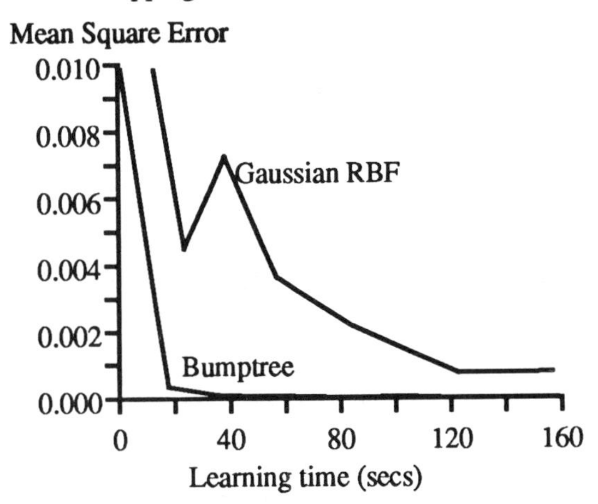

Figure 5: Mean square error as a function of learning time.

Perhaps even more important for applications than learning time is retrieval time. Retrieval using radial basis functions requires that the value of each basis function be computed on each query input and that these results be combined according to the best fit weight matrix. This time increases linearly as a function of the number of basis functions in the representation. In the bumptree approach, only those influence bumps and affine models which are not pruned away by the bumptree retrieval need perform any computation on an input. Figure 6 shows the retrieval time as a function of number of training samples for the robot mapping task. The retrieval time for radial basis functions crosses that for balltrees at about 100 samples and increases linearly off the graph. The balltree algorithm has a retrieval time which empirically grows very slowly and doesn't require much more time even when 10,000 samples are represented.

While not shown here, the representation may be improved in both size and generalization capacity by a best first merging technique. The idea is to consider merging two local models and their influence bumps into a single model. The pair which increases the error the least is merged first and the process is repeated until no pair is left whose meger wouldn't exceed an error criterion. This algorithm does a good job of discovering and representing linear parts of a map with a single model and putting many higher resolution models in areas with strong nonlinearities.

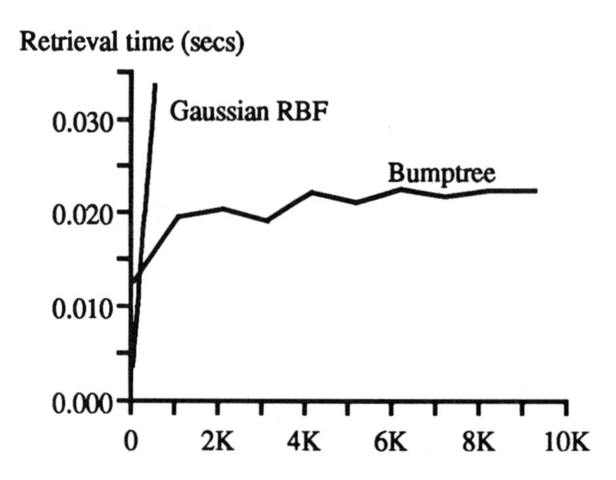

Figure 6: Retrieval time as a function of number of training samples.

3 EXTENSIONS TO OTHER TASKS

The bumptree structure is useful for implementing efficient versions of a variety of other geometric learning tasks (Omohundro, 1990). Perhaps the most fundamental such task is density estimation which attempts to model a probability distribution on a space on the basis of samples drawn from that distribution. One powerful technique is adaptive kernel estimation (Devroye and Gyorfi, 1985). The estimated distribution is represented as a Gaussian mixture in which a spherically symmetric Gaussian is centered on each data point and the widths are chosen according to the local density of samples. A best-first merging technique may often be used to produce mixtures consisting of many fewer non-symmetric Gaussians. A bumptree may be used to find and organize such Gaussians. Possible internal node functions include both quadratics and the faster to evaluate functions shown in Figure 3D.

It is possible to efficiently perform many operations on probability densities represented in this way. The most basic query is to return the density at a given location. The bumptree may be used with branch and bound to achieve retrieval in logarithmic expected time. It is also possible to quickly find marginal probabilities by integrating along certain dimensions. The tree is used to quickly identify the Gaussian which contribute. Conditional distributions may also be represented in this form and bumptrees may be used to compose two such distributions.

Above we discussed mapping learning and evaluation. In many situations there are not the natural input and output variables required for a mapping. If a probability distribution is peaked on a lower dimensional surface, it may be thought of as a constraint. Networks of constraints which may be imposed in any order among variables are natural for describing many problems. Bumptrees open up several possibilities for efficiently representing and propagating smooth constraints on continuous variables. The most basic query is to specify known external constraints on certain variables and allow the network to further impose whatever constraints it can. Multi-dimensional product Gaussians can be used to represent joint ranges in a set of variables. The operation of imposing a constraint surface may be thought of as multiplying an external constraint Gaussian by the function representing the constraint distribution. Because the product of two Gaussians is a Gaussian, this operation always produces Gaussian mixtures and bumptrees may be used to facilitate the operation.

A representation of constraints which is more like that used above for mappings constructs surfaces from local affine patches weighted by influence functions. We have developed a local analog of principle components analysis which builds up surfaces from random samples drawn from them. As with the mapping structures, a best-first merging operation may be used to discover affine structure in a constraint surface.

Finally, bumptrees may be used to enhance the performance of classifiers. One approach is to directly implement Bayes classifiers using the adaptive kernel density estimator described above for each class's distribution function. A separate bumptree may be used for each class or with a more sophisticated branch and bound, a single tree may be used for the whole set of classes.

In summary, bumptrees are a natural generalization of several hierarchical geometric access structures and may be used to enhance the performance of many neural network like algorithms. While we compared radial basis functions against a different mapping learning technique, bumptrees may be used to boost the retrieval performance of radial basis functions directly when the basis functions decay away from their centers. Many other neural network approaches in which much of the network does not perform useful work for every query are also susceptible to sometimes dramatic speedups through the use of this kind of access structure.

References

L. Devroye and L. Gyorfi. (1985) *Nonparametric Density Estimation: The L1 View*, New York: Wiley.

J. H. Friedman, J. L. Bentley and R. A. Finkel. (1977) An algorithm for finding best matches in logarithmic expected time. *ACM Trans. Math. Software* **3**:209-226.

B. Mel. (1990) *Connectionist Robot Motion Planning, A Neurally-Inspired Approach to Visually-Guided Reaching*, San Diego, CA: Academic Press.

S. M. Omohundro. (1987) Efficient algorithms with neural network behavior. *Complex Systems* **1**:273-347.

S. M. Omohundro. (1989) Five balltree construction algorithms. *International Computer Science Institute Technical Report* TR-89-063.

S. M. Omohundro. (1990) Geometric learning algorithms. *Physica D* **42**:307-321.

R. F. Sproull. (1990) Refinements to Nearest-Neighbor Searching in k-d Trees. *Sutherland, Sproull and Associates Technical Report* SSAPP #184c, *to appear in Algorithmica.*

Basis-Function Trees as a Generalization of Local Variable Selection Methods for Function Approximation

Terence D. Sanger
Dept. Electrical Engineering and Computer Science
Massachusetts Institute of Technology, E25-534
Cambridge, MA 02139

Abstract

Local variable selection has proven to be a powerful technique for approximating functions in high-dimensional spaces. It is used in several statistical methods, including CART, ID3, C4, MARS, and others (see the bibliography for references to these algorithms). In this paper I present a tree-structured network which is a generalization of these techniques. The network provides a framework for understanding the behavior of such algorithms and for modifying them to suit particular applications.

1 INTRODUCTION

Function approximation on high-dimensional spaces is often thwarted by a lack of sufficient data to adequately "fill" the space, or lack of sufficient computational resources. The technique of local variable selection provides a partial solution to these problems by attempting to approximate functions locally using fewer than the complete set of input dimensions.

Several algorithms currently exist which take advantage of local variable selection, including AID (Morgan and Sonquist, 1963, Sonquist *et al.*, 1971), k-d Trees (Bentley, 1975), ID3 (Quinlan, 1983, Schlimmer and Fisher, 1986, Sun *et al.*, 1988), CART (Breiman *et al.*, 1984), C4 (Quinlan, 1987), and MARS (Friedman, 1988), as well as closely related algorithms such as GMDH (Ivakhnenko, 1971, Ikeda *et al.*, 1976, Barron *et al.*, 1984) and SONN (Tenorio and Lee, 1989). Most of these algorithms use tree structures to represent the sequential incorporation of increasing numbers of input variables. The differences between these techniques lie in the representation ability of the networks they generate, and the methods used to grow and prune the trees. In the following I will show why trees are a natural structure for these techniques, and how all these algorithms can be seen as special cases of a general method I call "Basis Function Trees". I will also propose a new algorithm called an "LMS tree" which has a simple and fast network implementation.

2 SEPARABLE BASIS FUNCTIONS

Consider approximating a scalar function $f(x)$ of d-dimensional input x by

$$f(x_1, \ldots, x_d) \approx \sum_{i=1}^{L} c_i \sigma_i(x_1, \ldots, x_d) \tag{1}$$

where the σ_i's are a finite set of nonlinear basis functions, and the c_i's are constant coefficients. If the σ_i's are separable functions we can assume without loss of generality that there exists a finite set of scalar-input functions $\{\phi_n\}_{n=1}^{N}$ (which includes the constant function), such that we can write

$$\sigma_i(x_1, \ldots, x_d) = \phi_{r_1^i}(x_1) \cdots \phi_{r_d^i}(x_d) \tag{2}$$

where x_p is the p'th component of x, $\phi_{r_p^i}(x_p)$ is a scalar function of scalar input x_p, and r_p^i is an integer from 1 to N specifying which function ϕ is chosen for the p'th dimension of the i'th basis function σ_i.

If there are d input dimensions and N possible scalar functions ϕ_n, then there are N^d possible basis functions σ_i. If d is large, then there will be a prohibitively large number of basis functions and coefficients to compute. This is one form of Bellman's "curse of dimensionality" (Bellman, 1961). The purpose of local variable selection methods is to find a small basis which uses products of fewer than d of the ϕ_n's. If the ϕ_n's are local functions, then this will select different subsets of the input variables for different ranges of their values. Most of these methods work by incrementally increasing both the number and order of the separable basis functions until the approximation error is below some threshold.

3 TREE STRUCTURES

Polynomials have a natural representation as a tree structure. In this representation, the output of a subtree of a node determines the weight from that node to its parent. For example, in figure 1, the subtree computes its output by summing the weights a and b multiplied by the inputs x and y, and the result $ax + by$ becomes the weight from the input x at the first layer. The depth of the tree gives the order of the polynomial, and a leaf at a particular depth p represents a monomial of order p which can be found by taking products of all inputs on the path back to the root.

Now, if we expand equation 1 to get

$$f(x_1, \ldots, x_d) \approx \sum_{i=1}^{L} c_i \phi_{r_1^i}(x_1) \cdots \phi_{r_d^i}(x_d) \tag{3}$$

we see that the approximation is a polynomial in the terms $\phi_{r_p^i}(x_p)$. So the approx-

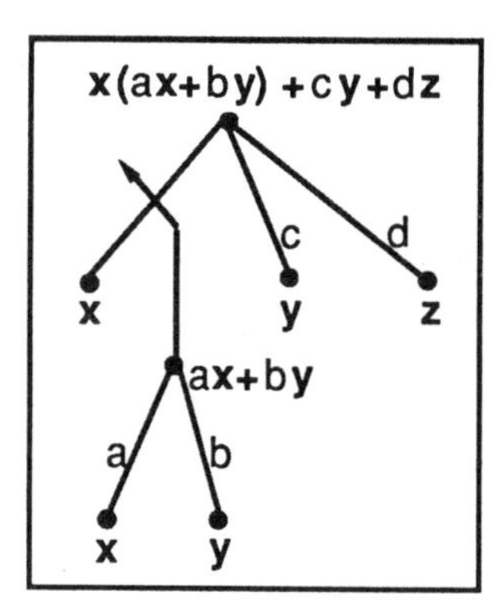

Figure 1: Tree representation of the polynomial $ax^2 + bxy + cy + dz$.

imation on separable basis functions can be described as a tree where the "inputs" are the one-dimensional functions $\phi_n(x_p)$, as in figure 2.

Most local variable selection techniques can be described in this manner. The differences in representation abilities of the different networks are determined by the choice of the one-dimensional basis functions ϕ_n. Classification algorithms such as CART, AID, C4, or ID3 use step-functions so that the resulting approximation is piecewise constant. MARS uses a cubic spline basis so that the result is piecewise cubic.

I propose that these algorithms can be extended by considering many alternate bases. For example, for bandlimited functions the Fourier basis may be useful, for which $\phi_n(x_p) = \sin(nx_p)$ for n odd, and $\cos(nx_p)$ for n even. Alternatively, local Gaussians may be used to approximate a radial basis function representation. Or the bits of a binary input could be used to perform Boolean operations. I call the class of all such algorithms "Basis Function Trees" to emphasize the idea that the basis functions are arbitrary.

It is important to realize that Basis Function Trees are fundamentally different from the usual structure of multi-layer neural networks, in which the result of a computation at one layer provides the data input to the next layer. In these tree algorithms, the result of a computation at one layer determines the *weights* at the next layer. Lower levels control the behavior of the processing at higher levels, but the input data never traverses more than a single level.

4 WEIGHT LEARNING AND TREE GROWING

In addition to the choice of basis functions, one also has a choice of learning algorithm. Learning determines both the tree structure and the weights.

There are many ways to adjust the weights. Since the entire network is equivalent to a single-layer network described by (1), The mean-squared output error can be minimized either directly using pseudo-inverse techniques, or iteratively using

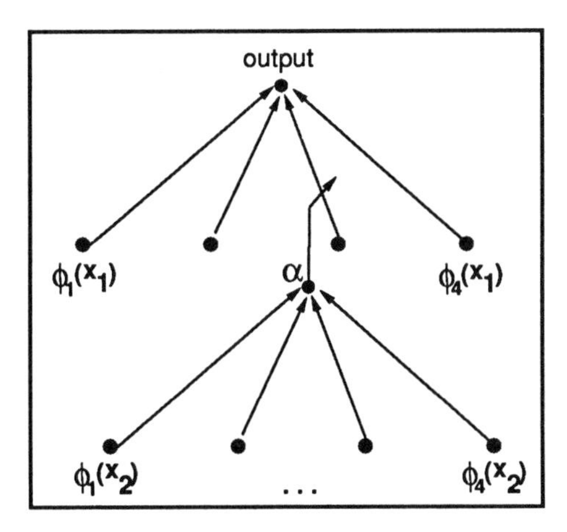

Figure 2: Tree representation of an approximation over separable basis functions.

recursive least squares (Ljung and Soderstrom, 1983) or the Widrow-Hoff LMS algorithm (Widrow and Hoff, 1960). Iterative techniques are often less robust and can take longer to converge than direct techniques, but they do not require storage of the entire data set and can adapt to nonstationary input distributions.

Since the efficiency of local variable selection methods will depend on the size of the tree, good tree growing and pruning algorithms are essential for performance. Tree-growing algorithms are often called "splitting rules", and the choice of rule should depend on the data set as well as the type of basis functions. AID and the "Regression Tree" method in CART split below the leaf with maximum mean-squared prediction error. MARS tests all possible splits by forming the new trees and estimating a "generalized cross-validation" criterion which penalizes both for output error and for increasing tree size. This method is likely to be more noise-tolerant, but it may also be significantly slower since the weights must be re-trained for every subtree which is tested. Most methods include a tree-pruning stage which attempts to reduce the size of the final tree.

5 LMS TREES

I now propose a new member of the class of local variable selection algorithms which I call an "LMS Tree" (Sanger, 1991, Sanger, 1990a, Sanger, 1990b). LMS Trees can use arbitrary basis functions, but they are characterized by the use of a recursive algorithm to learn the weights as well as to grow new subtrees.

The LMS tree will be built using one dimension of the input at a time. The approximation to $f(x_1, \ldots, x_d)$ using only the first dimension of the input is given by

$$f(x_1, \ldots, x_d) \approx \hat{f}(x_1) = \sum_{n=1}^{N} \alpha_n \phi_n(x_1). \tag{4}$$

I use the Widrow-Hoff LMS learning rule (Widrow and Hoff, 1960) to minimize the mean-squared approximation error based on only the first dimension:

$$\Delta\alpha_n = \eta(f(x_1,\ldots,x_d) - \hat{f}(x_1))\phi_n(x_1) \quad (5)$$

where η is a rate term, and $\Delta\alpha_n$ is the change in the weight α_n made in response to the current value of x_1. After convergence, $\hat{f}(x_1)$ is the best approximation to f based on linear combinations of $\phi_1(x_1),\ldots,\phi_N(x_1)$, and the expected value of the weight change $E[\Delta\alpha_n]$ will be zero. However, there may still be considerable variance of the weight changes, so that $E[(\Delta\alpha_n)^2] \neq 0$. The weight change variance indicates that there is "pressure" to increase or decrease the weights for certain input values, and it is related to the output error by

$$\frac{\sum_{n=1}^{N} E[(\Delta\alpha_n)^2]}{\min_{x_1} \sum_{n=1}^{N} \phi_n^2(x_1)} \geq E[(f-\hat{f})^2] \geq \max_n \frac{E[(\Delta\alpha_n)^2]}{E[(\phi_n(x_1))^2]} \quad (6)$$

(Sanger, 1990b). So the output error will be zero if and only if $E[(\Delta\alpha_n)^2] = 0$ for all n.

We can decrease the weight change variance by using another network based on x_2 to add a variable term to the weight α_{r_1} with largest variance, so that the new network is given by

$$\hat{f}(x_1,x_2) = \sum_{n\neq r_1} \alpha_n\phi_n(x_1) + \left(\alpha_{r_1} + \sum_{m=1}^{N} \alpha_{r_1,m}\phi_m(x_2)\right)\phi_{r_1}(x_1). \quad (7)$$

$\Delta\alpha_{r_1}$ becomes the error term used to train the second-level weights $\alpha_{r_1,m}$, so that $\Delta\alpha_{r_1,m} = \Delta\alpha_{r_1}\phi_m(x_2)$. In general, the weight change at any layer in the tree is the error term for the layer below, so that

$$\Delta\alpha_{r_1,\ldots,r_{p+1}} = \Delta\alpha_{r_1,\ldots,r_p}\phi_{r_{p+1}}(x_{p+1}) \quad (8)$$

where the root of the recursion is $\Delta\alpha_\emptyset = \eta(f(x_1,\ldots,x_d) - \hat{f})$, and $\alpha_\emptyset$ is a constant term associated with the root of the tree.

As described so far, the algorithm imposes an arbitrary ordering on the dimensions $x_1,\ldots,x_d$. This can be avoided by using all dimensions at once. The first layer tree would be formed by the additive approximation

$$f(x_1,\ldots,x_d) \approx \sum_{p=1}^{d}\sum_{n=1}^{N} \alpha_{(n,p)}\phi_n(x_p). \quad (9)$$

New subtrees would include all dimensions and could be grown below any $\phi_n(x_p)$. Since this technique generates larger trees, tree pruning becomes very important. In practice, most of the weights in large trees are often close to zero, so after a network has been trained, weights below a threshold level can be set to zero and any leaf with a zero weight can be removed.

LMS trees have the advantage of being extremely fast and easy to program. (For example, a 49-input network was trained to a size of 20 subtrees on 40,000 data

Method	Basis Functions	Tree Growing
MARS	Truncated Cubic Polynomials	Exhaustive search for split which minimizes a cross-validation criterion
CART (Regression), **AID**	Step functions	Split leaf with largest mean-squared prediction error (= weight variance)
CART (Classification), **ID3, C4**	Step functions	Choose split which maximizes an information criterion
k-d Trees	Step functions	Split leaf with the most data points
GMDH, SONN	Data Dimensions	Find product of existing terms which maximizes correlation to desired function
LMS Trees	Any. All dimensions present at each level.	Split leaf with largest weight change variance

Figure 3: Existing tree algorithms.

samples in approximately 30 minutes of elapsed time on a sun-4 computer. The LMS tree algorithm required 22 lines of C code (Sanger, 1990b).) The LMS rule trains the weights and automatically provides the weight change variance which is used to grow new subtrees. The data set does not have to be stored, so no memory is required at nodes. Because the weight learning and tree growing both use the recursive LMS rule, trees can adapt to slowly-varying nonstationary environments.

6 CONCLUSION

Figure 3 shows how several of the existing tree algorithms fit into the framework presented here. Some aspects of these algorithms are not well described by this framework. For instance, in MARS the location of the spline functions can depend on the data, so the ϕ_n's do not form a fixed finite basis set. GMDH is not well described by a tree structure, since new leaves can be formed by taking products of existing leaves, and thus the approximation order can increase by more than 1 as each layer is added. However, it seems that the essential features of these algorithms and the way in which they can help avoid the "curse of dimensionality" are well explained by this formulation.

Acknowledgements

Thanks are due to John Moody for introducing me to MARS, to Chris Atkeson for introducing me to the other statistical methods, and to the many people at NIPS who gave useful comments and suggestions. The LMS Tree technique was inspired by a course at MIT taught by Chris Atkeson, Michael Jordan, and Marc Raibert. This report describes research done within the laboratory of Dr. Emilio Bizzi in the department of Brain and Cognitive Sciences at MIT. The author was supported by an NDSEG fellowship from the U.S. Air Force.

References

Barron R. L., Mucciardi A. N., Cook F. J., Craig J. N., Barron A. R., 1984, Adaptive learning networks: Development and application in the United States of algorithms related to GMDH, In Farlow S. J., ed., *Self-Organizing Methods in Modeling*, Marcel Dekker, New York.

Bellman R. E., 1961, *Adaptive Control Processes*, Princeton Univ. Press, Princeton, NJ.

Bentley J. H., 1975, Multidimensional binary search trees used for associated searching, *Communications ACM*, 18(9):509–517.

Breiman L., Friedman J., Olshen R., Stone C. J., 1984, *Classification and Regression Trees*, Wadsworth Belmont, California.

Friedman J. H., 1988, Multivariate adaptive regression splines, Technical Report 102, Stanford Univ. Lab for Computational Statistics.

Ikeda S., Ochiai M., Sawaragi Y., 1976, Sequential GMDH algorithm and its application to river flow prediction, *IEEE Trans. Systems, Man, and Cybernetics*, SMC-6(7):473–479.

Ivakhnenko A. G., 1971, Polynomial theory of complex systems, *IEEE Trans. Systems, Man, and Cybernetics*, SMC-1(4):364–378.

Ljung L., Soderstrom T., 1983, *Theory and Practice of Recursive Identification*, MIT Press, Cambridge, MA.

Morgan J. N., Sonquist J. A., 1963, Problems in the analysis of survey data, and a proposal, *J. Am. Statistical Assoc.*, 58:415–434.

Quinlan J. R., 1983, Learning efficient classification procedures and their application to chess end games, In Michalski R. S., Carbonell J. G., Mitchell T. M., ed.s, *Machine Learning: An Artificial Intelligence Approach*, chapter 15, pages 463–482, Tioga P., Palo Alto.

Quinlan J. R., 1987, Simplifying decision trees, *Int. J. Man-Machine Studies*, 27:221–234.

Sanger T. D., 1990a, Basis-function trees for approximation in high-dimensional spaces, In Touretzky D., Elman J., Sejnowski T., Hinton G., ed.s, *Proceedings of the 1990 Connectionist Models Summer School*, pages 145–151, Morgan Kaufmann, San Mateo, CA.

Sanger T. D., 1990b, A tree-structured algorithm for function approximation in high dimensional spaces, *IEEE Trans. Neural Networks*, in press.

Sanger T. D., 1991, A tree-structured algorithm for reducing computation in networks with separable basis functions, *Neural Computation*, 3(1), in press.

Schlimmer J. C., Fisher D., 1986, A case study of incremental concept induction, In *Proc. AAAI-86, Fifth National Conference on AI*, pages 496–501, Los Altos, Morgan Kaufmann.

Sonquist J. A., Baker E. L., Morgan J. N., 1971, Searching for structure, Institute for Social Research, Univ. Michigan, Ann Arbor.

Sun G. Z., Lee Y. C., Chen H. H., 1988, A novel net that learns sequential decision process, In Anderson D. Z., ed., *Neural Information Processing Systems*, pages 760–766, American Institute of Physics, New York.

Tenorio M. F., Lee W.-T., 1989, Self organizing neural network for optimum supervised learning, Technical Report TR-EE 89-30, Purdue Univ. School of Elec. Eng.

Widrow B., Hoff M. E., 1960, Adaptive switching circuits, In *IRE WESCON Conv. Record, Part 4*, pages 96–104.

Generalization Properties of Radial Basis Functions

Sherif M. Botros **Christopher G. Atkeson**

Brain and Cognitive Sciences Department
and the Artificial Intelligence Laboratory
Massachusetts Institute of Technology
Cambridge, MA 02139

Abstract

We examine the ability of radial basis functions (RBFs) to generalize. We compare the performance of several types of RBFs. We use the inverse dynamics of an idealized two-joint arm as a test case. We find that without a proper choice of a norm for the inputs, RBFs have poor generalization properties. A simple global scaling of the input variables greatly improves performance. We suggest some efficient methods to approximate this distance metric.

1 INTRODUCTION

The Radial Basis Functions (RBF) approach to approximating functions consists of modeling an input-output mapping as a linear combination of radially symmetric functions (Powell, 1987; Poggio and Girosi, 1990; Broomhead and Lowe, 1988; Moody and Darken, 1989). The RBF approach has some properties which make it attractive as a function interpolation and approximation tool. The coefficients that multiply the different basis functions can be found with a linear regression. Many RBFs are derived from regularization principles which optimize a criterion combining fitting error and the smoothness of the approximated function. However, the optimality criteria may not always be appropriate, especially when the input variables have different measurement units and affect the output differently. A natural extension to RBFs is to vary the distance metric (equivalent to performing a linear transformation on the input variables). This can be viewed as changing the cost function to be optimized (Poggio and Girosi, 1990). We first use an exact interpolation approach with RBFs centered at the data in the training set. We then explore the effect of optimizing the distance metric for Gaussian RBFs using a smaller number of functions than data in the training set. We also suggest and test different methods to approximate this metric for the case of Gaussian RBFs that work well for the two joint arm example that we examined. We refer the reader to several other studies addressing the generalization performance of RBFs (Franke, 1982; Casdagli, 1989; Renals and Rohwer, 1989).

2 EXACT INTERPOLATION APPROACH

In the exact interpolation model the number of RBFs is equal to the number of experiences. The centers of the RBFs are chosen to be at the location of the experiences. We used an idealized horizontal planar two joint arm model with no friction and no noise (perfect measurements) to test the performance of RBFs:

$$\begin{aligned}
T_1 &= \ddot{\theta}_1(I_1 + I_2 + 2m_2c_{x_2}l_1\cos\theta_2 - 2m_2c_{y_2}l_1\sin\theta_2) \\
&\quad +\ddot{\theta}_2(I_2 + m_2c_{x_2}l_1\cos\theta_2 - m_2c_{y_2}l_1\sin\theta_2) \\
&\quad -2l_1\dot{\theta}_1\dot{\theta}_2(m_2c_{x_2}\sin\theta_2 + m_2c_{y_2}\cos\theta_2) \\
&\quad -l_1\dot{\theta}_2^{\,2}(m_2c_{x_2}\sin\theta_2 + m_2c_{y_2}\cos\theta_2) \\
T_2 &= \ddot{\theta}_1(m_2c_{x_2}l_1\cos\theta_2 - m_2c_{y_2}l_1\sin\theta_2 + I_2) + \ddot{\theta}_2 I_2 \\
&\quad +l_1\dot{\theta}_1^{\,2}(m_2c_{x_2}\sin\theta_2 + m_2c_{y_2}\cos\theta_2) \qquad (1)
\end{aligned}$$

where θ_i, $\dot{\theta}_i$, $\ddot{\theta}_i$ are the angular position, velocity and acceleration of joint i. T_i is the torque at joint i. I_i, m_i, l_i, c_{xi} and c_{y_i} are respectively the moment of inertia, mass, length and the x and y components of the center of mass location of link i. The input vector is $(\theta_1, \theta_2, \dot{\theta}_1, \dot{\theta}_2, \ddot{\theta}_1, \ddot{\theta}_2)$. The training and test sets are formed of one thousand random experiences each; uniformly distributed across the space of the inputs. The different inputs were selected from the following ranges: [-4, 4] for the joint angles, [-20, 20] for the joint angular velocities and [-100, 100] for the joint angular accelerations. For the exact interpolation case, we scaled the input variables such that the input space is limited to the six dimensional hypercube $[-1, 1]^6$. This improved the results we obtained. The torque to be estimated at each joint is modeled by the following equation:

$$T_k(\mathbf{x}_i) = \sum_{j=1}^{n} C_{kj}\phi(||\mathbf{x}_i - \mathbf{x}_j||) + \sum_{j=1}^{p} \mu_{kj}P_j^m(\mathbf{x}_i) \qquad (2)$$

where $T_k, k = 1, 2$, is the estimated torque at the kth joint, n is the number of experiences/RBFs, $\mathbf{x}_i$ is the ith input vector, $||\cdot||$ is the Euclidean norm and $P_j^m(\cdot), j = 1, \ldots, p$, is the space of polynomials of order m. The polynomial terms are not always added and it was found that adding the polynomial terms by themselves does not improve the performance significantly, which is in agreement with the conclusion made by Franke (Franke, 1982). When a polynomial is present in the equation, we add the following extra constraints (Powell, 1987):

$$\sum_{j=1}^{n} C_{kj}P_i^m(\mathbf{x}_j) = 0 \qquad i = 1, \ldots, p \qquad (3)$$

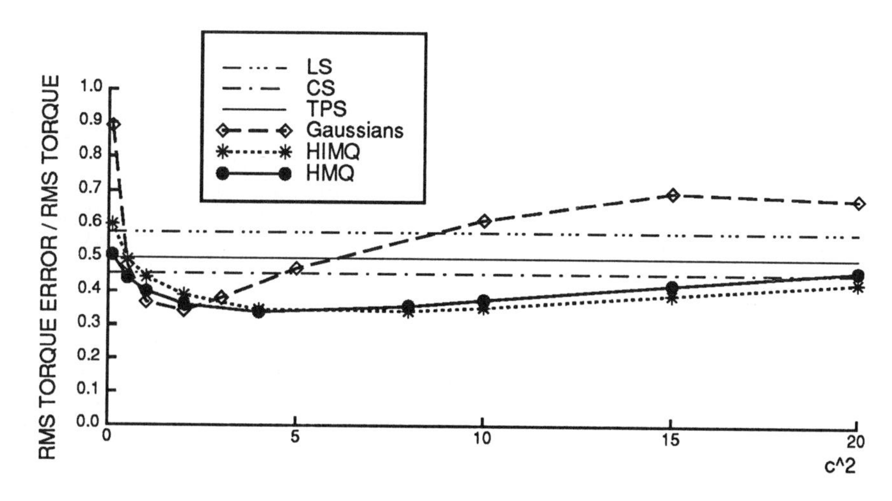

Figure 1: Normalized errors for the different RBFs using exact interpolation. c^2 is the width parameter when relevant.

To find the coefficients C_{kj} and μ_{kj} , we have to invert a square matrix which is nonsingular for distinct inputs for the basis functions we considered (Micchelli, 1986). We used the training set to find the parameters $C_{kj},\ j = 1, n,$ and when relevant $\mu_{kj},\ j = 1, p,$ for the following RBFs:

- Gaussians $\phi(r) = \exp(\frac{-r^2}{c^2})$
- Hardy Multiquadrics [HMQ] $\phi(r) = \sqrt{r^2 + c^2}$
- Hardy Inverse Multiquadrics [HIMQ] $\phi(r) = \frac{1}{\sqrt{r^2+c^2}}$
- Thin Plate Splines [TPS] $\phi(r) = r^2 \log r$
- Cubic Splines [CS] $\phi(r) = r^3$
- Linear Splines [LS] $\phi(r) = r$

where $r = \|\mathbf{x}_i - \mathbf{x}_j\|$. For the last three RBFs, we added polynomials of different orders, subject to the constraints in equation 3 above. Since the number of independent parameters is equal to the number of points in the training set, we can train the system so that it exactly reproduces the training set. We then tested its performance on the test set. The error was measured by equation 4 below:

$$E = \sqrt{\frac{\sum_{k=1}^{2}\sum_{i=1}^{n}(T_{ki} - \hat{T}_{ki})^2}{\sum_{k=1}^{2}\sum_{i=1}^{n} T_{ki}^2}} \tag{4}$$

The normalized error obtained on the test set for the different RBFs are shown in figure 1. The results for LS and CS shown in this figure are obtained after the addition of a first order polynomial to the RBFs. We also tried adding a third order polynomial for TPS. As shown in this figure, the normalized error was more sensitive to the width parameter (i.e. c^2) for the Gaussian RBFs than for

Hardy multiquadrics and inverse multiquadrics. This is in agreement with Franke's observation (Franke, 1982). The best normalized error for any RBF that we tested was 0.338 for HMQ with a value of $c^2 = 4$. Also, contrary to our expectations and to results reported by others (Franke, 1982), the TPS with a third order polynomial had a normalized error of 0.5003. This error value did not change significantly when only lower order polynomials are added to the $(r^2 \log r)$ RBFs. Using Generalized Cross Validation (Bates *et al.*, 1987) to optimize the tradeoff between smoothness and fitting the data, we got similar normalized error for TPS.

3 GENERALIZED RBF

The RBF approach has been generalized (Poggio and Girosi, 1990) to have adjustable center locations, fewer centers than data, and to use a different distance metric. Instead of using a Euclidean norm, we can use a general weighted norm:

$$||\mathbf{x}_i - \mathbf{x}_j||_W^2 = (\mathbf{x}_i - \mathbf{x}_j)^T \mathbf{W}^T \mathbf{W} (\mathbf{x}_i - \mathbf{x}_j) \tag{5}$$

where $\mathbf{W}$ is a square matrix. This approach is also referred to as Hyper Basis Functions (Poggio and Girosi, 1990). The problem of finding the weight matrix and the location of the centers is nonlinear. We simplified the problem by only considering a diagonal matrix $\mathbf{W}$ and fixing the locations of the centers of the RBFs. The center locations were chosen randomly and were uniformly distributed over the input space. We tested three different methods to find the different parameters for Gaussian RBFs that we will describe in the next three subsections.

3.1 NONLINEAR OPTIMIZATION

We used a Levenberg-Marquardt nonlinear optimization routine to find the coefficients of the RBFs $\{C_i\}$ and the diagonal scaling matrix $\mathbf{W}$ that minimized the sum of the squares of the errors in estimating the training set. We were able to find a set of parameters that reduced the normalized error to less than 0.01 in both the training and the test sets using 500 Gaussian RBFs randomly and uniformly spaced over the input space. One disadvantage we found with this method is the possible convergence to local minima and the long time it takes to converge using general purpose optimization programs. The diagonal elements of the matrix $\mathbf{W}$ are shown in the L-M columns of table 1. As expected, θ_1 has a very small scale for both joints compared to θ_2, since θ_1 does not affect the output of either joint in the horizontal model described by equation 1. Also the scaling of θ_2 is much larger than the scaling of the other variables. This suggests that the scaling could be dependent on both the range of the input variables as well as the sensitivity of the output to the different input variables. We found empirically that a formula of the form of equation 6 approximates reasonably well the scaling weights found using nonlinear optimization.

$$w_{ii} = \frac{\overline{|\nabla f_i|}}{||\nabla f||} \frac{k}{\sqrt{E\{(x_i - t_i)^2\}}} \tag{6}$$

where $\frac{\overline{|\nabla f_i|}}{||\nabla f||}$ is the normalized average absolute value of the gradient of the correct model of the function to be approximated. The term $\frac{k}{\sqrt{E\{(x_i - t_i)^2\}}}$ normalizes the

Table 1: Scaling Weights Obtained Using Different Methods.

W	L-M ALG.		TRUE FUNC.		GRAD. APPROX.	
	Joint 1	Joint 2	Joint 1	Joint 2	Joint 1	Joint 2
$W_{11}(\theta_1)$	0.000021	5.48237e-06	0.000000	0.000000	0.047010	0.005450
$W_{22}(\theta_2)$	0.382014	0.443273	0.456861	0.456449	0.400615	0.409277
$W_{33}(\dot{\theta}_1)$	0.004177	0.0871921	0.005531	0.010150	0.009898	0.038288
$W_{44}(\dot{\theta}_2)$	0.004611	0.000120948	0.007490	0.000000	0.028477	0.008948
$W_{55}(\ddot{\theta}_1)$	0.000433	0.00134168	0.000271	0.000110	0.006365	0.002166
$W_{66}(\ddot{\theta}_2)$	0.000284	0.000955884	0.000059	0.000116	0.000556	0.001705

density of the input variables in each direction by taking into account the expected distances from the RBF centers to the data. The constant k in this equation is inversely proportional to the width of the Gaussian used in the RBF. For the inverse dynamics problem we tested, and using 500 Gaussian functions randomly and uniformly distributed over the entire input space, a k between 1 and 2 was found to be good and results in scaling parameters which approximate those obtained by optimization. The scaling weights obtained using equation 6 and based on the knowledge of the functions to be approximated are shown in the TRUE FUNC. columns of table 1. Using these weight values the error in the test set was about 0.0001

3.2 AVERAGE GRADIENT APPROXIMATION

In the previous section we showed that the scaling weights could be approximated using the derivatives of the function to be approximated in the different directions. If we can approximate these derivatives, we can then approximate the scaling weights using equation 6. A change in the output Δy could be approximated by a first order Taylor series expansion as shown in equation 7 below:

$$\Delta y = \sum_{i=1}^{d} \frac{\partial y}{\partial x_i} \Delta x_i \tag{7}$$

We first scaled the input variables so that they have the same range, then selected all pairs of points from the training set that are below a prespecified distance (since equation 7 is only valid for nearby points), and then computed Δx_i and Δy for each pair. We used least squares regression to estimate the values of $\frac{\partial y}{\partial x_i}$. Using the estimated derivatives and equation 6, we got the scaling weights shown in the last two columns of table 1. Note the similarity between these weights and the ones obtained using the nonlinear optimization or the derivatives of the true function. The normalized error in this case was found to be 0.012 for the training set and 0.033 for the test set. One advantage of this method is that it is much faster than the nonlinear optimization method. However, it is less accurate.

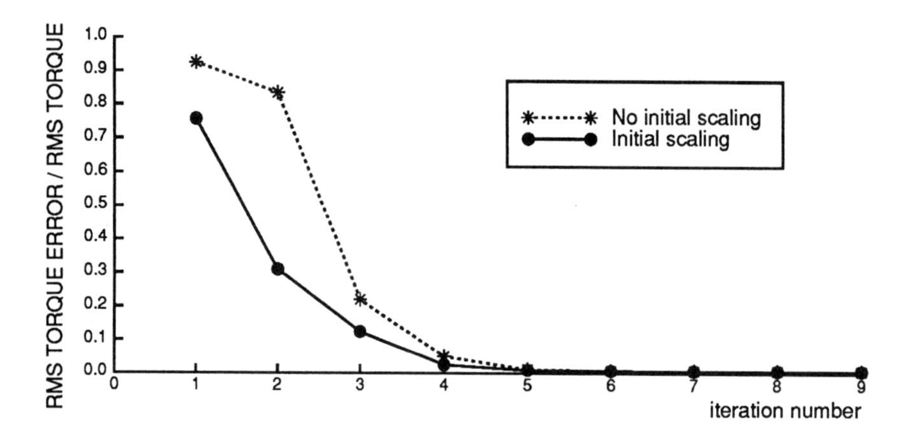

Figure 2: Normalized error vs. the number of iterations using the recursive method with and without initial scaling.

3.3 RECURSIVE METHOD

Another possible method to approximate the RMS values of the derivatives is to first approximate the function using RBFs of "reasonable" widths and then use this first approximation to compute the derivatives which are then used to modify the Gaussian widths in the different directions. The procedure is then repeated. We used 100 RBFs with Gaussian units randomly and uniformly distributed to find the coefficients of the RBFs. We explored two different scalings of the input data. In the first case we used the raw data without scaling, and in the second case the different input variables were scaled so that they have the same range from [-1, 1]. The width of the Gaussians used as specified by the variance c^2 was equal to 200 in the first case, and 2 in the second case. We then used the estimated values of the derivatives to change the width of the Gaussians in the different directions and iterated the procedure. The normalized error is plotted versus the number of iterations for both cases in figure 2. As shown in this figure, the test set error dropped to around 0.001 in about only 4 iterations. This technique is also much faster than the nonlinear optimization approach. Also it can be easily made local, which is desirable if the dependence of the function to be approximated on the input variables changes from one region of the input space to the other. One disadvantage of this approach is that it is not guaranteed to converge especially if the initial approximation of the function is very bad.

4 CONCLUSION

In this paper we tested the ability of RBFs to generalize from the training set. We found that the choice of the distance metric used may be crucial for good generalization. For the problem we tested, a bad choice of a distance metric resulted in very poor generalization. However, the performance of Gaussian RBFs improved significantly if we optimized the distance metric. We also tested some empirical methods for efficiently estimating this metric that worked well in our test problem. Additional work has to be done to identify the conditions under which the techniques we presented here may or may not work. Although a simple global scaling of the input variables worked well in our test example, it may not work in general. One problem that we found when we optimized the distance metric is that the values of the coefficients C_i become very large, even if we imposed a penalty on their values. The reason for this, we think, is that the estimation problem was close to singular. Choice of the training set and optimizing the centers of the RBFs may solve this problem. The recursive method we described could probably be modified to approximate a complete linear coordinate transformation and local scaling.

Acknowledgments

Support was provided under Office of Naval Research contract N00014-88-K-0321 and under Air Force Office of Scientific Research grant AFOSR-89-0500. Support for CGA was provided by a National Science Foundation Engineering Initiation Award and Presidential Young Investigator Award, an Alfred P. Sloan Research Fellowship, the W. M. Keck Foundation Assistant Professorship in Biomedical Engineering, and a Whitaker Health Sciences Fund MIT Faculty Research Grant.

References

D. M. Bates, M. J. Lindstorm, G. Wahba and B. S. Yandel (1987) "GCVPACK - Routines for generalized cross validation". *Commun. Statist.-Simulat.* **16** (1): 263-297.

D. S. Broomhead and D. Lowe (1988) "Multivariable functional interpolation and adaptive networks". *Complex Systems* **2**:321-323.

M. Casdagli (1989) "Nonlinear prediction of chaotic time series". *Physica D* **35**: 335-356.

R. Franke (1982) "Scattered data interpolation: Tests of some methods". *Math. Comp.* **38**(5):181-200.

C. A. Micchelli (1986) "Interpolation of scattered data: distance matrices and conditionally positive definite functions". *Constr. Approx.* **2**:11-22.

J. Moody and C. Darken (1989) "Fast learning in networks of locally tuned processing units". *Neural Computation* **1**(2):281-294.

T. Poggio and F. Girosi (1990) "Networks for approximation and learning". *Proceedings of the IEEE* **78**(9):1481-1497.

M. J. D. Powell (1987) "Radial basis functions for multivariable interpolation: A review". In J. C. Mason and M. G. Cox (ed.), *Algorithms for Approximation*, 143-167. Clarendon Press, Oxford.

S. Renals and R. Rohwer (1989) "Phoneme classification experiments using radial basis functions". In *Proceedings of the International Joint Conference on Neural Networks*, I-462 - I-467, Washington, D.C., IEEE TAB Neural Network Committee.

Learning by Combining Memorization and Gradient Descent

John C. Platt
Synaptics, Inc.
2860 Zanker Road, Suite 206
San Jose, CA 95134

ABSTRACT

We have created a radial basis function network that allocates a new computational unit whenever an unusual pattern is presented to the network. The network learns by allocating new units and adjusting the parameters of existing units. If the network performs poorly on a presented pattern, then a new unit is allocated which memorizes the response to the presented pattern. If the network performs well on a presented pattern, then the network parameters are updated using standard LMS gradient descent. For predicting the Mackey Glass chaotic time series, our network learns much faster than do those using back-propagation and uses a comparable number of synapses.

1 INTRODUCTION

Currently, networks that perform function interpolation tend to fall into one of two categories: networks that use gradient descent for learning (e.g., back-propagation), and constructive networks that use memorization for learning (e.g., k-nearest neighbors).

Networks that use gradient descent for learning tend to form very compact representations, but use many learning cycles to find that representation. Networks that memorize their inputs need to only be exposed to examples once, but grow linearly in the training set size.

The network presented here strikes a compromise between memorization and gradient descent. It uses gradient descent for the "easy" input vectors and memorization for the "hard" input vectors. If the network performs well on a particular input vector, or the particular input vector is already close to a stored vector, then the network adjusts its parameters using gradient descent. Otherwise, it memorizes the input vector and the corresponding output vector by allocating a new unit. The explicit storage of an input-output pair means that this pair can be used immediately to improve the performance of the system, instead of merely using that information for gradient descent.

The network, called the resource-allocation network (RAN), uses units whose response is localized in input space. A unit with a non-local response needs to undergo gradient descent, because it has a non-zero output for a large fraction of the training data.

Because RAN is a constructive network, it automatically adjusts the number of units to reflect the complexity of the function that is being interpolated. Fixed-size networks either use too few units, in which case the network memorizes poorly, or too many, in which case the network generalizes poorly. Parzen windows and K-nearest neighbors both require a number of stored patterns that grow linearly with the number of presented patterns. With RAN, the number of stored patterns grows sublinearly, and eventually reaches a maximum.

1.1 PREVIOUS WORK

Previous workers have used networks with localized basis functions (Broomhead & Lowe, 1988) (Moody & Darken, 1988 & 89) (Poggio & Girosi, 1990). Moody has further extended his work by incorporating a hash table lookup (Moody, 1989). The hash table is a resource-allocating network where the values in the hash table only become non-zero if the entry in the hash table is activated by the corresponding presence of non-zero input probability.

The RAN adjusts the centers of the Gaussian units based on the error at the output, like (Poggio & Girosi, 1990). Networks with centers placed on a high-dimensional grid, such as (Broomhead & Lowe, 1988) and (Moody, 1989), or networks that use unsupervised clustering for center placement, such as (Moody & Darken, 1988 & 89) generate larger networks than RAN, because they cannot move the centers to increase the accuracy.

Previous workers have created function interpolation networks that allocate fewer units than the size of training set. Cascade-correlation (Fahlman & Lebiere, 1990), SONN (Tenorio & Lee, 1989), and MARS (Friedman, 1988) all construct networks by adding additional units. These algorithms work well. The RAN algorithm improves on these algorithms by making the addition of a unit as simple as possible. RAN uses simple algebra to find the parameters of a new unit, while cascade-correlation and MARS use gradient descent and SONN uses simulated annealing.

2 THE ALGORITHM

This section describes a resource-allocating network (RAN), which consists of a network, a strategy for allocating new units, and a learning rule for refining the network.

2.1 THE NETWORK

The RAN is a two-layer radial-basis-function network. The first layer consists of units that respond to only a local region of the space of input values. The second layer linearly aggregates outputs from these units and creates the function that approximates the input-output mapping over the entire space.

A simple function that implements a locally tuned unit is a Gaussian:

$$\begin{aligned} z_j &= \sum_k (c_{jk} - I_k)^2, \\ x_j &= \exp(-z_j/w_j^2). \end{aligned} \tag{1}$$

We use a C^1 continuous polynomial approximation to speed up the algorithm, without loss of network accuracy:

$$x_j = \begin{cases} \left(1 - (z_j/qw_j^2)\right)^2, & \text{if } z_j < qw_j^2; \\ 0, & \text{otherwise;} \end{cases} \tag{2}$$

where $q = 2.67$ is chosen empirically to make the best fit to a Gaussian.

Each output of the network y_i is a sum of the outputs x_j, each weighted by the synaptic strength h_{ij} plus a global polynomial. The x_j represent information about local parts of the space, while the polynomial represents global information:

$$y_i = \sum_j h_{ij} x_j + \sum_k L_{ik} I_k + \gamma_i. \tag{3}$$

The $h_{ij} x_j$ term can be thought of as a bump that is added or subtracted to the polynomial term $\sum_k L_{ik} I_k + \gamma_i$ to yield the desired function.

The linear term is useful when the function has a strong linear component. In the results section, the Mackey-Glass equation was predicted with only a constant term.

2.2 THE LEARNING ALGORITHM

The network starts with a blank slate: no patterns are yet stored. As patterns are presented to it, the network chooses to store some of them. At any given point the network has a current state, which reflects the patterns that have been stored previously.

The allocator may allocate a new unit to memorize a pattern. After the new unit is allocated, the network output is equal to the desired output $\vec{T}$. Let the index of this new unit be n.

The peak of the response of the newly allocated unit is set to the memorized input vector,

$$\vec{c}_n = \vec{I}. \tag{4}$$

The linear synapses on the second layer are set to the difference between the output of the network and the novel output,

$$\vec{h}_n = \vec{T} - \vec{y}. \tag{5}$$

The width of the response of the new unit is proportional to the distance from the nearest stored vector to the novel input vector,

$$w_n = \kappa||\vec{I} - \vec{c}_{\text{nearest}}||, \tag{6}$$

where κ is an overlap factor. As κ grows larger, the responses of the units overlap more and more.

The RAN uses a two-part memorization condition. An input-output pair $(\vec{I}, \vec{T})$ should be memorized if the input is far away from existing centers,

$$||\vec{I} - \vec{c}_{\text{nearest}}|| > \delta(t), \tag{7}$$

and if the difference between the desired output and the output of the network is large

$$||\vec{T} - \vec{y}(\vec{I})|| > \epsilon. \tag{8}$$

Typically, ϵ is a desired accuracy of output of the network. Errors larger than ϵ are immediately corrected by the allocation of a new unit, while errors smaller than ϵ are gradually repaired using gradient descent. The distance $\delta(t)$ is the scale of resolution that the network is fitting at the tth input presentation. The learning starts with $\delta(t) = \delta_{\text{max}}$, which is the largest length scale of interest, typically the size of the entire input space of non-zero probability density. The distance $\delta(t)$ shrinks until the it reaches δ_{min}, which is the smallest length scale of interest. The network will average over features that are smaller than δ_{min}. We used a function:

$$\delta(t) = \max(\delta_{\text{max}} \exp(-t/\tau), \delta_{\text{min}}), \tag{9}$$

where τ is a decay constant.

At first, the system creates a coarse representation of the function, then refines the representation by allocating units with smaller and smaller widths. Finally, when the system has learned the entire function to the desired accuracy and length scale, it stops allocating new units altogether.

The two-part memorization condition is necessary for creating a compact network. If only condition (7) is used, then the network will allocate units instead of using gradient descent to correct small errors. If only condition (8) is used, then fine-scale units may be allocated in order to represent coarse-scale features, which is wasteful.

By allocating new units the RAN eventually represents the desired function ever more closely as the network is trained. Fewer units are needed for a given accuracy if the first-layer synapses c_{jk}, the second-level synapses h_{ij}, and the parameters for the global polynomial γ_i and L_{ik} are adjusted to decrease the error: $\mathcal{E} = ||\vec{y} - \vec{T}||^2$ (Widrow & Hoff, 1960). We use gradient descent on the second-layer synapses to decrease the error whenever a new unit is not allocated:

$$\begin{aligned} \Delta h_{ij} &= \alpha(T_i - y_i)x_j, \\ \Delta \gamma_i &= \alpha(T_i - y_i), \\ \Delta L_{ik} &= \alpha(T_i - y_i)I_k. \end{aligned} \tag{10}$$

In addition, we adjust the centers of the responses of units to decrease the error:

$$\Delta c_{jk} = 2\frac{\alpha}{w_j}(I_k - c_{jk})x_j \left[\sum_i (T_i - y_i)h_{ij}\right]. \tag{11}$$

Equation (11) is derived from gradient descent and equation (1). Empirically, equation (11) also works for the polynomial approximation (2).

3 RESULTS

One application of an interpolating RAN is to predict complex time series. As a test case, a chaotic time series can be generated with a nonlinear algebraic or differential equation. Such a series has some short-range time coherence, but long-term prediction is very difficult.

The RAN was tested on a particular chaotic time series created by the Mackey-Glass delay-difference equation:

$$x(t+1) = (1-b)x(t) + a\frac{x(t-\tau)}{1+x(t-\tau)^{10}}, \tag{12}$$

for $a = 0.2$, $b = 0.1$, and $\tau = 17$. We trained the network to predict the value $x(T + \Delta T)$, given the values $x(T), x(T-6), x(T-12)$, and $x(T-18)$ as inputs.

The network was tested using two different learning modes: off-line learning with a limited amount of data, and on-line learning with a large amount of data. The Mackey-Glass equation has been learned off-line, by other workers, using the back-propagation algorithm (Lapedes & Farber, 1987), and radial basis functions (Moody & Darken, 1989). We used RAN to predict the Mackey-Glass equations with the following parameters: $\alpha = 0.02$, 400 learning epochs, $\delta_{\text{max}} = 0.7$, $\kappa = 0.87$ and $\delta_{\text{min}} = 0.07$ reached after 100 epochs. RAN was simulated using $\epsilon = 0.02$ and $\epsilon = 0.05$. In all cases, $\Delta T = 85$.

Figure 1 shows the efficiency of the various learning algorithms: the smallest, most accurate algorithms are towards the lower left. When optimized for size of network ($\epsilon = 0.05$), the RAN has about as many weights as back-propagation and is just as accurate. The efficiency of RAN is roughly the same as back-propagation, but requires much less computation: RAN takes approximately 8 minutes of SUN-4 CPU time to reach the accuracy listed in figure 4, while back-propagation took approximately 30–60 minutes of Cray X-MP time.

The Mackey-Glass equation has been learned using on-line techniques by hashing B-splines (Moody, 1989). We used on-line RAN using the following parameters: $\alpha = 0.05$, $\delta_{\text{max}} = 0.7$, $\delta_{\text{min}} = 0.07$, $\kappa = 0.87$, and δ_{min} reached after 5000 input presentations. Table 1 compares the on-line error versus the size of network for both RAN and the hashing B-spline (Moody, personal communication). In both cases, $\Delta T = 50$. The RAN algorithm has similar accuracy to the hashing B-splines, but the number of units allocated is between a factor of 2 and 8 smaller.

For more detailed results on the Mackey-Glass equation, see (Platt, 1991).

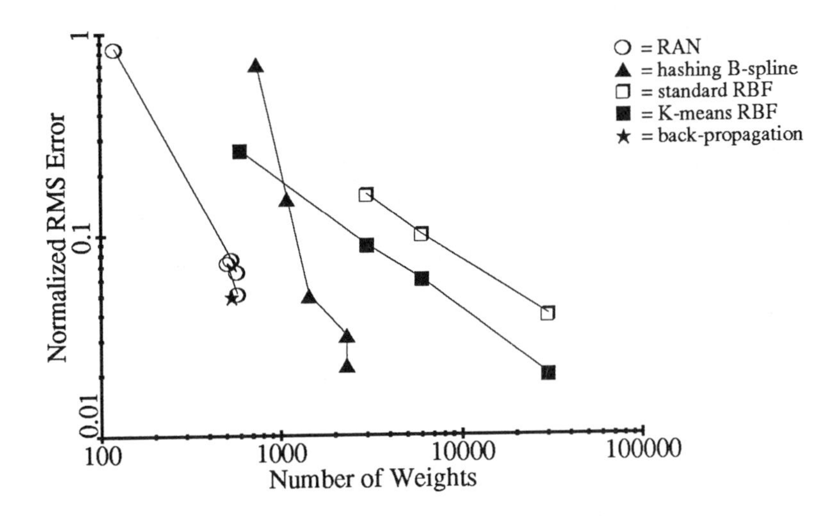

Figure 1: The error on a test set versus the size of the network. Back-propagation stores the prediction function very compactly and accurately, but takes a large amount of computation to form the compact representation. RAN is as compact and accurate as back-propagation, but uses much less computation to form its representation.

Table 1: Comparison between RAN and hashing B-splines

Method	Number of Units	Normalized RMS Error
RAN, $\epsilon = 0.05$	50	0.071
RAN, $\epsilon = 0.02$	143	0.054
Hashing B-spline 1 level of hierarchy	284	0.074
Hashing B-spline 2 levels of hierarchy	1166	0.044

4 CONCLUSIONS

There are various desirable attributes for a network that learns: it should learn quickly, it should learn accurately, and it should form a compact representation. Formation of a compact representation is particularly important for networks that are implemented in hardware, because silicon area is at a premium. A compact representation is also important for statistical reasons: a network that has too many parameters can overfit data and generalize poorly.

Many previous network algorithms either learned quickly at the expense of a compact representation, or formed a compact representation only after laborious computation. The RAN is a network that can find a compact representation with a reasonable amount of computation.

Acknowledgements

Thanks to Carver Mead, Carl Ruoff, and Fernando Pineda for useful comments on the paper. Special thanks to John Moody who not only provided useful comments on the paper, but also provided data on the hashing B-splines.

References

Broomhead, D., Lowe, D., 1988, Multivariable function interpolation and adaptive networks, *Complex Systems,* **2,** 321–355.

Fahlman, S. E., Lebiere, C., 1990, The Cascade-Correlation Learning Architecture, *In:* Advances in Neural Information Processing Systems 2, D. Touretzky, ed., 524–532, Morgan-Kaufmann, San Mateo.

Friedman, J. H., 1988, Multivariate Adaptive Regression Splines, Department of Statistics, Stanford University, Tech. Report LCS102.

Lapedes, A., Farber, R., 1987, *Nonlinear Signal Processing Using Neural Networks: Prediction and System Modeling,* Technical Report LA-UR-87-2662, Los Alamos National Laboratory, Los Alamos, NM.

Moody, J, Darken, C., 1988, Learning with Localized Receptive Fields, *In:* Proceedings of the 1988 Connectionist Models Summer School, D. Touretzky, G. Hinton, T. Sejnowski, eds., 133–143, Morgan-Kaufmann, San Mateo.

Moody, J, Darken, C., 1989, Fast Learning in Networks of Locally-Tuned Processing Units, *Neural Computation,* **1(2),** 281–294.

Moody, J., 1989, Fast Learning in Multi-Resolution Hierarchies, *In:* Advances in Neural Information Processing Systems 1, D. Touretzky, ed., 29–39, Morgan-Kaufmann, San Mateo.

Platt., J., 1991, A Resource-Allocating Network for Function Interpolation, *Neural Computation,* **3(2),** to appear.

Poggio, T., Girosi, F., 1990, Regularization Algorithms for Learning that are Equivalent to Multilayer Networks, *Science,* **247,** 978–982.

Powell, M. J. D., 1987, Radial Basis Functions for Multivariable Interpolation: A Review, *In:* Algorithms for Approximation, J. C. Mason, M. G. Cox, eds., Clarendon Press, Oxford.

Tenorio, M. F., Lee, W., 1989, Self-Organizing Neural Networks for the Identification Problem, *In:* Advances in Neural Information Processing Systems 1, D. Touretzky, ed., 57–64, Morgan-Kaufmann, San Mateo.

Widrow, B., Hoff, M., 1960, Adaptive Switching Circuits, *In:* 1960 IRE WESCON Convention Record, 96–104, IRE, New York.

Sequential Adaptation of Radial Basis Function Neural Networks and its Application to Time-series Prediction

V. Kadirkamanathan
Engineering Department
Cambridge University
Cambridge CB2 1PZ, UK

M. Niranjan

F. Fallside

Abstract

We develop a sequential adaptation algorithm for radial basis function (RBF) neural networks of Gaussian nodes, based on the method of successive $\mathcal{F}$-Projections. This method makes use of each observation efficiently in that the network mapping function so obtained is consistent with that information and is also optimal in the least L_2-norm sense. The RBF network with the $\mathcal{F}$-Projections adaptation algorithm was used for predicting a chaotic time-series. We compare its performance to an adaptation scheme based on the method of stochastic approximation, and show that the $\mathcal{F}$-Projections algorithm converges to the underlying model much faster.

1 INTRODUCTION

Sequential adaptation is important for signal processing applications such as time-series prediction and adaptive control in nonstationary environments. With increasing computational power, complex algorithms that can offer better performance can be used for these tasks. A sequential adaptation scheme, called the method of successive $\mathcal{F}$-Projections [Kadirkamanathan & Fallside, 1990], makes use of each observation efficiently in that, the function so obtained is consistent with that observation and is the optimal posterior in the least L_2-norm sense.

In this paper we present an adaptation algorithm based on this method for the radial basis function (RBF) network of Gaussian nodes [Broomhead & Lowe, 1988]. It is a memoryless adaptation scheme since neither the information about the past samples nor the previous adaptation directions are retained. Also, the observations are presented only once. The RBF network employing this adaptation scheme was used for predicting a chaotic time-series. The performance of the algorithm is compared to a memoryless sequential adaptation scheme based on the method of stochastic approximation.

2 METHOD OF SUCCESSIVE $\mathcal{F}$-PROJECTIONS

The *principle of $\mathcal{F}$-Projection* [Kadirkamanathan *et al.*, 1990] is a general method of choosing a posterior function estimate of an unknown function f^*, when there exists a prior estimate and new information about f^* in the form of constraints. The principle states that, of all the functions that satisfy the constraints, one should choose the posterior f_n that has the least L_2-norm, $||f_n - f_{n-1}||$, where f_{n-1} is the prior estimate of f^*. *viz.*,

$$f_n = \arg\min_f ||f - f_{n-1}|| \qquad \text{such that} \qquad f_n \in H_I \tag{1}$$

where H_I is the set of functions that satisfy the new constraints, and

$$||f - f_{n-1}||^2 = \int_{\underline{x} \in C} ||f(\underline{x}) - f_{n-1}(\underline{x})||^2 |d\underline{x}| = D(f, f_{n-1}) \tag{2}$$

where $\underline{x}$ is the input vector, $|d\underline{x}|$ is the infinitesimal volume in the input space domain C.

In functional analysis theory, the metric $D(.,.)$ describes the L_2-normed linear space of square integrable functions. Since an inner product can be defined in this space, it is also the Hilbert space of square integrable functions [Linz, 1984]. Constraints of the form $y_n = f(\underline{x}_n)$ are linear in this space, and the functions that satisfy the constraint lie in a hyperplane subspace H_I. The posterior f_n, obtained from the principle can be seen to be a projection of f_{n-1} onto the subspace H_I containing f^*, the underlying function that generates the observation set, and hence is optimal (i.e., best possible choice), see Figure 1.

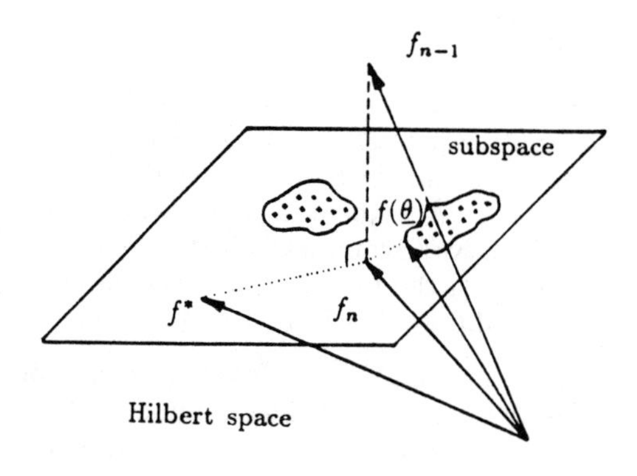

Figure 1: Principle of $\mathcal{F}$-Projection

Neural networks can be viewed as constructing a function in its input space. The structure of the neural network and the finite number of parameters restrict the class of functions that can be constructed to a subset of functions in the Hilbert space. Neural networks, therefore approximate the underlying function that describes the set of observations. Hence, the principle of $\mathcal{F}$-Projection now yields a posterior $f(\underline{\theta}_n) \in H_I$ that is an approximation of f_n (see Figure 1).

The *method of successive $\mathcal{F}$-Projections* is the application of the principle of $\mathcal{F}$-Projection on a sequence of observations or information [Kadirkamanathan *et al.*, 1990]. For neural networks, the method gives an algorithm that has the following two steps.

- Initialise parameters with random values or values based on a priori knowledge.
- For each pattern $(\underline{x}_i, y_i)$ $i = 1 \ldots n$, determine the posterior parameter estimate

$$\underline{\theta}_i = \arg\min_{\underline{\theta}} \int_{\underline{x} \in C} \|f(\underline{x}, \underline{\theta}) - f(\underline{x}, \underline{\theta}_{i-1})\|^2 |d\underline{x}|$$

  such that $f(\underline{x}_i, \underline{\theta}_i) = y_i$.

where $(\underline{x}_i, y_i)$, for $i = 1 \ldots n$ constitutes the observation set, $\underline{\theta}$ is the neural network parameter set and $f(\underline{x}, \underline{\theta})$ is the function constructed by the neural network.

3 $\mathcal{F}$-PROJECTIONS FOR AN RBF NETWORK

The class of radial basis function (RBF) neural networks were first introduced by Broomhead & Lowe [1988]. One such network is the RBF network of Gaussian nodes. The function constructed at the output node of the RBF network of Gaussian nodes, $f(\underline{x})$, is derived from a set of basis functions of the form,

$$\phi_i(\underline{x}) = \exp\{-(\underline{x} - \underline{\mu}_i)^T C_i^{-1} (\underline{x} - \underline{\mu}_i)\} \qquad i = 1 \ldots m \tag{3}$$

Each basis function $\phi_i(\underline{x})$ is described at the output of each hidden node and is centered on $\underline{\mu}_i$ in the input space. $\phi_i(\underline{x})$ is a function of the radial weighted distance between the input vector $\underline{x}$ and the node centre $\underline{\mu}_i$. In general, C_i is diagonal with elements $[\sigma_{i1}, \sigma I2, \ldots, \sigma_{iN}]$. $f(\underline{x})$ is a linear combination of the m basis functions.

$$f(\underline{x}) = \sum_{i=1}^{m} \alpha_i \phi_i(\underline{x}) \tag{4}$$

and $\underline{\theta} = [\cdots, \alpha_i, \underline{\mu}_i, \underline{\sigma}_i, \cdots]$ is then the parameter vector for the RBF network.

There are two reasons for developing the sequential adaptation algorithm for the RBF network of Gaussian nodes. Firstly, the method of successive $\mathcal{F}$-Projections is based on minimizing the hypervolume change in the hypersurface when learning new patterns. The RBF network of Gaussian nodes construct a localized hypersurface and therefore the changes will also be local. This results in the adaptation of a few nodes and therefore the algorithm is quite stable. Secondly, the L_2-norm measure of the hypervolume change can be solved analytically for the RBF network of Gaussian nodes.

The method of successive $\mathcal{F}$-Projections is developed under deterministic noise-free conditions. When the observations are noisy, the constraint that $f(\underline{\theta}_i, \underline{x}_i) = y_i$ must be relaxed to,

$$\|f(\underline{\theta}_i, \underline{x}) - y_i\|^2 \leq \epsilon \tag{5}$$

Hence, the sequential adaptation scheme is modified to,

$$\underline{\theta}_n = \arg\min_{\underline{\theta}} J(\underline{\theta}) \tag{6}$$

$$J(\underline{\theta}) = \int \|f(\underline{\theta}, \underline{x}) - f(\underline{\theta}_{i-1}, \underline{x})\|^2 |d\underline{x}| \quad + \quad c_i \|f(\underline{\theta}, \underline{x}_i) - y_i\|^2 \tag{7}$$

c_i is the penalty parameter that trades off between the importance of learning the new pattern and losing the information of the past patterns. This minimization can be performed by the gradient descent procedure. The minimization procedure is halted when the change ΔJ falls below a threshold. The complete adaptation algorithm is as follows:

- Choose $\underline{\theta}_0$ randomly
- For each pattern $(i = 1 \dots P)$
  - $\underline{\theta}_i^{(0)} = \underline{\theta}_{i-1}$
  - Repeat (k^{th} iteration)

$$\underline{\theta}_i^{(k)} = \underline{\theta}_i^{(k-1)} - \eta \nabla J \Big|_{\underline{\theta} = \underline{\theta}_i^{(k-1)}}$$

Until $\Delta J^{(k)} < \varepsilon_{th}$

where ∇J is the gradient vector of $J(\underline{\theta})$ with respect to $\underline{\theta}$, $\Delta J^{(k)} = J(\underline{\theta}_i^{(k)}) - J(\underline{\theta}_i^{(k-1)})$ is the change in the cost function and ε_{th} is a threshold. Note that $\alpha_i, \underline{\mu}_i, \underline{\sigma}_i$ for $i = 1 \dots m$ are all adapted. The details of the algorithm can be found in the report by Kadirkamanathan *et al.*, [Kadirkamanathan, Niranjan & Fallside, 1991].

4 TIME SERIES PREDICTION

An area of application for sequential adaptation of neural networks is the prediction of time-series in nonstationary environments, where the underlying model generating the time-series is time-varying. The adaptation algorithm must also result in the convergence of the neural network to the underlying model under stationary conditions. The usual approach to predicting time-series is to train the neural network on a set of training data obtained from the series [Lapedes & Farber, 1987; Farmer & Sidorowich, 1988; Niranjan, 1991]. Our sequential adaptation approach differs from this in that the adaptation takes place for each sample.

In this work, we examine the performance of the $\mathcal{F}$-Projections adaptation algorithm for the RBF network of Gaussian nodes in predicting a deterministic chaotic series. The chaotic series under investigation is the *logistic map* [Lapedes & Farber, 1987], whose dynamics is governed by the equation,

$$x_n = 4x_{n-1}(1 - x_{n-1}) \tag{8}$$

This is a first order nonlinear process where only the previous sample determines the value of the present sample. Since neural networks offer the capability of constructing any arbitrary mapping to a sufficient accuracy, a network with input nodes equal to the process order will find the underlying model. Hence, we use the RBF network of Gaussian nodes with a single input node. We are thus able to compare the map the RBF network constructed with that of the actual map given by eqn (8).

First, RBF network with 2 input nodes and 8 Gaussian nodes was used to predict the logistic map chaotic series of 100 samples. Each sample was presented only once for training. The training was temporarily halted after 0, 20, 40, 60, 80 and 100 samples, and in each case the prediction error residual was found. This is given in Figure 2 where the increasing darkness of the curves stand for the increasing number of patterns used for training. It is evident from this figure that the prediction model improves very quickly from the initial state and then slowly keeps on improving as the number of training patterns used is increased.

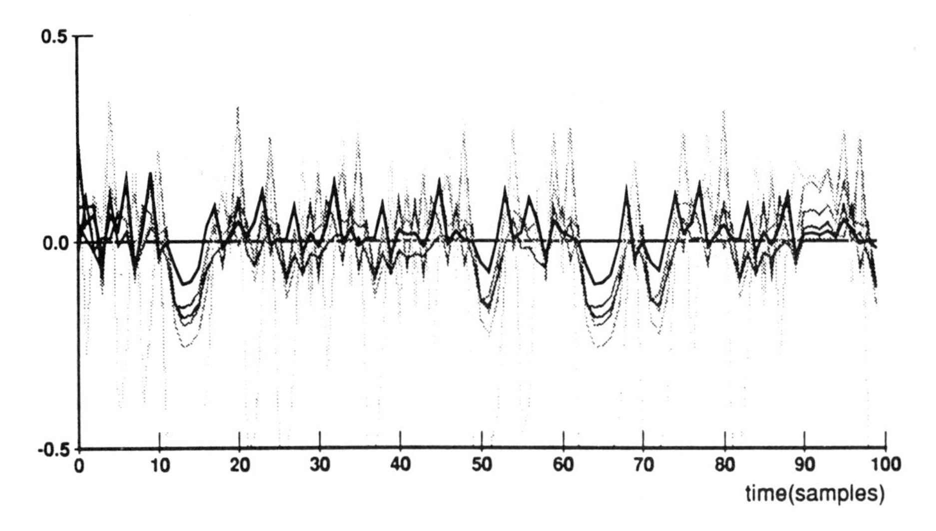

Figure 2: Evolution of prediction error residuals

In order to compare the performance of the sequential adaptation algorithm, a memoryless adaptation scheme was also used to predict the chaotic series. The scheme is the LMS or stochastic approximation (sequential back propagation [White, 1987]), where for each sample, one iteration takes place. The iteration is given by,

$$\underline{\theta}_i = \underline{\theta}_{i-1} - \eta \nabla J \Big|_{\underline{\theta}=\underline{\theta}_i} \tag{9}$$

where,

$$J(\underline{\theta}) = ||f(\underline{\theta}, \underline{x}_i) - y_i||^2 \tag{10}$$

and $J(\underline{\theta})$ is the squared prediction error for the present sample.

Next, the RBF network with a single input node and 8 Gaussian units was used to predict the chaotic series. The $\mathcal{F}$-Projections and the stochastic approximation adaptation algorithms were used for training this network on 60 samples. Results on the map constructed by a network trained by each of these schemes for 0, 20 and 60 samples and the samples used for training are shown in Figure 3. Again, each sample was presented only once for training.

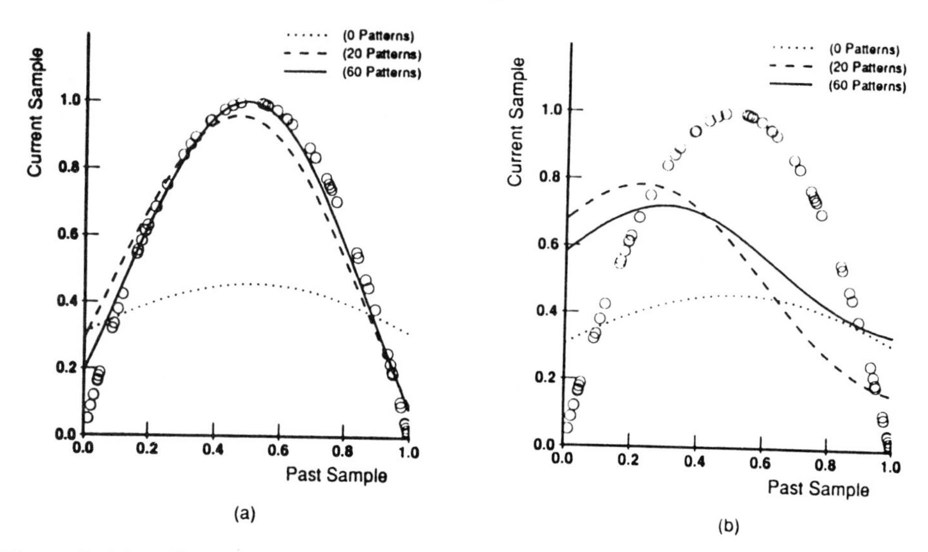

Figure 3: Map f(x) constructed by the RBF network. (a) f-projections (b) stochastic approximation.

The stochastic approximation algorithm fails to construct a close-fit mapping of the underlying function after training on 60 samples. The $\mathcal{F}$-Projections algorithm however, provides a close-fit map after training on 20 samples. It also shows stability by maintaining the map up to training on 60 samples. The speed of convergence achieved, in terms of the number of samples used for training, is much higher for the $\mathcal{F}$-Projections.

Comparing the cost functions being minimized for the $\mathcal{F}$-Projections and the stochastic approximation algorithms, given by eqns (7) and (10), it is clear that the difference is only an additional integral term in eqn (7). This term is not a function of the present observation, but is a function of the *a priori* parameter values. The addition of such a term is to incorporate a priori knowledge of the network to that of the present observation in determining the posterior parameter values. The faster convergence result for the $\mathcal{F}$-Projections indicate the importance of the extended cost function. Even though the cost term for the $\mathcal{F}$-Projections was developed for a recursive estimation algorithm, it can be applied to a block estimation method as well. The cost function given by eqn (7) can be seen to be an extension of the nonlinear least squared error to incorporate *a priori* knowledge.

5 CONCLUSIONS

The *principle of $\mathcal{F}$-Projection* proposed by Kadirkamanathan *et al.*, [1990], provides an optimal posterior estimate of a function, from the prior estimate and new information. Based on it, they propose a sequential adaptation scheme called, the *method of successive f-projections.* We have developed a sequential adaptation algorithm for the RBF network of Gaussian nodes based on this method.

Applying the RBF network with the $\mathcal{F}$-Projections algorithm to the prediction of a chaotic series, we have found that the RBF network was able to map the underlying function. The prediction error residuals at the end of training with different number of samples, indicate that, after a substantial reduction in the error in the initial stages, with increasing number of samples presented for training the error was steadily decreasing. By comparing with the performance of the stochastic approximation algorithm, we show the superior convergence achieved by the $\mathcal{F}$-Projections.

Comparing the cost functions being minimized for the $\mathcal{F}$-Projections and the stochastic approximation algorithms reveal that the $\mathcal{F}$-Projections uses both the prediction error for the current sample and the *a priori* values of the parameters, whereas the stochastic approximation algorithms use only the prediction error. We also point out that such a cost term that includes a priori knowledge of the network can be used for training a trained network upon receipt of further information.

References

[1] Broomhead.D.S & Lowe.D, (1988), *"Multi-variable Interpolation and Adaptive Networks"*, RSRE memo No.4148, Royal Signals and Radar Establishment, Malvern.

[2] Farmer.J.D & Sidorowich.J.J, (1988), *"Exploiting chaos to predict the future and reduce noise"*, Technical Report, Los Alamos National Laboratory.

[3] Kadirkamanathan.V & Fallside.F (1990), *"$\mathcal{F}$-Projections: A nonlinear recursive estimation algorithm for neural networks"*, Technical Report CUED/F-INFENG/TR.53, Cambridge University Engineering Department.

[4] Kadirkamanathan.V, Niranjan.M & Fallside.F (1991), *"Adaptive RBF network for time-series prediction"*, Technical Report CUED/F-INFENG/TR.56, Cambridge University Engineering Department.

[5] Lapedes.A.S & Farber.R, (1987), *"Non-linear signal processing using neural networks: Prediction and system modelling"*, Technical report, Los Alamos National Laboratory, Los Alamos, New Mexico 87545.

[6] Linz.P, (1984), *"Theoretical Numerical Analysis"*, John Wiley, New York.

[7] Niranjan.M, (1991), *"Implementing threshold autoregressive models for time series prediction on a multilayer perceptron"*, Technical Report CUED/F-INFENG/TR.50, Cambridge University Engineering Department.

[8] White.H, 1987, *"Some asymptotic results for learning in single hidden layer feedforward network models"*, Technical Report, Department of Economics, Univeristy of California, San Diego.

Oriented Non-Radial Basis Functions for Image Coding and Analysis

Avijit Saha[1] **Jim Christian** **D. S. Tang**

Microelectronics and Computer Technology Corporation
3500 West Balcones Center Drive
Austin, TX 78759

Chuan-Lin Wu

Department of Electrical and Computer Engineering
University of Texas at Austin,
Austin, TX 78712

ABSTRACT

We introduce oriented non-radial basis function networks (ONRBF) as a generalization of Radial Basis Function networks (RBF)- wherein the Euclidean distance metric in the exponent of the Gaussian is replaced by a more general polynomial. This permits the definition of more general regions and in particular- hyper-ellipses with orientations. In the case of hyper-surface estimation this scheme requires a smaller number of hidden units and alleviates the "curse of dimensionality" associated kernel type approximators.In the case of an image, the hidden units correspond to features in the image and the parameters associated with each unit correspond to the rotation, scaling and translation properties of that particular "feature". In the context of the ONBF scheme, this means that an image can be represented by a small number of features. Since, transformation of an image by rotation, scaling and translation correspond to identical transformations of the individual features, the ONBF scheme can be used to considerable advantage for the purposes of image recognition and analysis.

1 INTRODUCTION

Most, "neural network" or "connectionist" models have evolved primarily as adaptive function approximators. Given a set of input-output pairs <x,y> (x from an underlying function f (i.e. y = f(x)), a feed forward, time-independent neural network estimates a

---

1. Alternate address: Dept. of ECE, Univ. of Texas at Austin, Austin, TX 78712

function y' = g(**p**,**x**) such that E= ρ(y - y') is arbitrarily small over all <**x**,y> pairs. Here, **p** is the set of parameters associated with the network model and ρ is a metric that measures the quality of approximation, usually the Euclidean norm. In this paper, we shall restrict our discussion to approximation of real valued functions of the form $f{:}R^n \rightarrow R$. For a network of fixed structure (determined by g), all or part of the constituent parameter set **p**, that minimize E are determined adaptively by modifying the set of parameters. The problem of approximation or hypersurface reconstruction is then one of determining what class of g to use, and then the choice of a suitable algorithm for determining the parameters **p**- given a set of samples {<**x**,y>}.By far the most popular method for determining network parameters has been the gradient descent method. If the error surface is quadratic or convex, gradient descent methods will yield an optimal value for the network parameters.However, the burning problem in still remains the determination of network parameters when the error function is infested with local minimas. One way of obviating the problem of local minimas is to match a network architecture with an objective function such that the error surface is free of local minimas. However, this might limit the power of the network architecture such as in the case of linear perceptrons[1]. Another approach is to obtain algebraic transformations of the objective functions such that algorithms can be readily designed around the transformed functions to avoid local minimas. Random optimization method of Matyas and its variations have been studied recently [2], as alternate avenues for determining the parameter set **p**. Perhaps the most probable reason for the BP algorithms popularity is that the error surface is relatively smooth [1],[3]

The problem of local minimas is circumvented somewhat differently in local or kernel type estimators. The input space in such a method is partitioned into a number of local regions and if the number of regions defined is sufficiently large, then the output response in each local region is sufficiently uniform or smooth and the error will remain bounded i.e. a local minima will be close to the global minima. The problem with kernel type of estimators is that the number of “bins”, ”kernels” or “regions” that need to be defined increases exponentially with the dimension of the input space. An improvement such as the one considered by [4] is to define the kernels only in regions of the input space where there is data. However, our experiments indicate that even this may not be sufficient to lift the curse of dimensionality. If instead of limiting the shape of the kernels to be boxes or even hyperspheres we select the kernels to be shapes defined by a second order polynomials then a larger class of shapes or regions can be defined resulting in significant reductions in the number of kernels required. This was the principal motivation behind our generalization of ordinary RBF networks. Also, we have determined that radial basis function networks will, given sufficiently large widths, linearize the output response between two hidden units. This gives rise to hyperacuity or coarse coding, whereby a high resolution of stimuli can be observed at the signal level despite poor resolution in the sensor array. In the context of function approximation this means that if the hyper-surface being approximated varies linearly in a certain region, the output behavior can be captured by suitably placing a single widely tuned receptive field in that region. Therefore, it is advantageous to choose the regions with proper knowledge of the output response in that region as opposed to choosing the bins based on the inputs alone. These were some of the principal motivations for our generalization.

In addition to the architectural and learning issues, we have been concerned with approximation schemes in which the optimal parameter values have readily interpretable forms that may allow other useful processing elsewhere. In the following section we present ONBF as a generalization to RBF [4] and GRBF [5]. We show how rotation, scaling and translation (center) information of these regions can be readily extracted from the parameter values associated with each hidden unit. In subsequent sections we present experimental results illustrating the performance of ONRBF as a function approximator and feasibility of ONRBF for the purposes of image coding and analysis.

2 ORIENTED NON-RADIAL BASIS FUNCTION NETWORKS

Radial Basis Function networks can be described by the formula:

$$f(x) = \sum_{\alpha=0}^{k} w_\alpha R_\alpha(x)$$

where f(x) is the output of the network, k is the number of hidden units, w_α is the weight associated with hidden unit α, and $R_\alpha(x)$ is the response of unit α, The response $R_\alpha(x)$ of unit α is given by

$$R_\alpha = e^{-\left(\frac{\| c_\alpha - x \|}{\sigma_\alpha}\right)^2}$$

Poggio and Girosi [5] have considered the generalization where a different width parameter σ_{α_i} is associated with each input dimension i. The response function R_α is then defined as

$$R_\alpha(x) = e^{-\sum_{i=1}^{d} \left(\frac{c_{\alpha_i} - x_i}{\sigma_{\alpha_i}}\right)^2}$$

Now each σ_{α_i} can influence the response of the αth unit and the effect is that widths associated with irrelevant or correlated inputs will tend to be increased. It has been shown that if one of the input components has a random input and a constant width (constant for that particular dimension) is used for each receptive field, then the width for that particular receptive field is maximum [6].

The generalization we consider in this paper is a further shaping of the response R_α by composing it with a rotation function S_α designed to rotate the unit about its center in d-space, where d is the input dimension. This composition can be represented compactly by a response function of the form:

$$R_\alpha = e^{-\| M_\alpha [x_1, \ldots, x_d, 1] \|^2}$$

where M_α is a d by d+1 matrix. The matrix transforms the input vectors and these transformations correspond to translation (center information), scaling and rotation of the input vectors. The response function presented above is the restricted form of a more general response function of the form:

$$R_\alpha = e^{-[P(x)]}$$

where the exponent is a general polynomial in the input variables. In the following sections we present the learning rules and we show how center, rotation and scaling information can be extracted from the matrix elements. We do this for the case when the input dimension is 2 (as is the case for 2-dimensional images) but the results are generalized easily.

2.1 LEARNING RULES

Consider the n-dimensional case where $<x_1,...x_n>$ represents the input vector and $m_{\alpha jk}$ represents the matrix element of the jth row and k^{th} column of the matrix M_α associated with the αth unit. Then the response of the αth unit is given by:

$$R_\alpha(x,y) = e^{-\left(\sum_{j=1}^{n}\left(\sum_{i=1}^{n+1} m_{\alpha ji} x_i\right)\right)}$$

The total sum square error over b patterns is given by:

$$TE = \sum_\beta \left[f(\mathbf{x}_\beta) - F(\mathbf{x}_\beta)\right]^2 = \sum_\beta E_\beta = \sum_\beta L_\beta^2$$

Then the derivative of the error due to the βth pattern with respect to the matrix element $m_{\alpha ij}$ of the αth unit is given by:

$$\therefore \frac{\partial}{\partial m_{\alpha_{ij}}}(E_\beta) = 2\,[f(\mathbf{x}_\beta) - F(\mathbf{x}_\beta)\,]\frac{\partial}{\partial m_{\alpha_{ij}}} f = 2\,[L_\beta]\frac{\partial}{\partial m_{\alpha_{ij}}} f$$

and:

$$\frac{\partial}{\partial m_{\alpha_{ij}}} f = -2 m_{\alpha_i} \langle x_\beta, 1\rangle^T x_j R_\alpha(x_\beta)$$

where,

$m_{\alpha i}$: is the ith row of the matrix corresponding to the αth unit
x_β : is the input vector
x_j : is the jth variable in the input space.

Then the update rule for the matrix elements with learning rate η is given by:

$$m_{\alpha_{ij}}^{t+1} = m_{\alpha_{ij}}^{t} - \eta \frac{\partial}{\partial m_{\kappa_{ij}}}(E_\beta)$$

and the learning rule for the weights w_α is given by:

$$w_\alpha^{t+1} = w_\alpha^{t} - \eta L_\beta R_\alpha(x_\beta)$$

2.2 EXTRACTING ROTATION, SCALE AND CENTER VALUES

In this section we present the equations for extracting the rotation, translation and scaling values (widths) of the αth receptive field from its associated matrix elements. We present these for the special case when n the input dimension is equal to 2, since that is the case for images. The input vector **x** is represented by $<x,y>$ and the rules for converting the matrix elements into center, scaling and rotation information is as follows:

- center (x_0, y_0)

$$x_0 = \frac{(m_{12}m_{11} + m_{21}m_{22})(m_{11}m_{13} + m_{23}m_{21}) - (m_{11}^2 + m_{21}^2)(m_{13}m_{12} + m_{23}m_{22})}{\Delta}$$

$$y_0 = \frac{(m_{12}m_{11}+m_{21}m_{22})(m_{12}m_{13}+m_{23}m_{22}) - (m_{12}^2+m_{22}^2)(m_{13}m_{11}+m_{23}m_{21})}{\Delta}$$

where,

$$\Delta = (m_{11}^2+m_{21}^2)(m_{12}^2+m_{22}^2) - (m_{11}m_{12}+m_{22}m_{21})$$

- rotation (θ)

$$\theta = \frac{1}{2}\tan^{-1}\left(\frac{m_{21}m_{22}+m_{12}m_{11}}{m_{11}^2+(m_{21}^2-m_{12}^2-m_{22}^2)}\right)$$

- scaling or receptive field widths or sigmas

$$d_1 = \frac{1}{2}(m_{11}^2+m_{21}^2+m_{12}^2+m_{22}^2)+\frac{m_{12}m_{11}+m_{22}m_{21}}{\sin 2\theta} \equiv \frac{1}{\sqrt{2}\sigma_1}$$

$$d_2 = \frac{1}{2}(m_{11}^2+m_{21}^2+m_{12}^2+m_{22}^2)-\frac{m_{12}m_{11}+m_{22}m_{21}}{\sin 2\theta} \equiv \frac{1}{\sqrt{2}\sigma_2}$$

2.3 HIERARCHICAL CLUSTERING

We use a multi-resolution, hierarchical approach to determine where to place hidden units to maximize the accuracy of approximation and to locate image features. For illustration, we consider our method in the context of image processing, though the idea will work for any type of function approximation problem. The process begins with a small number of widely tuned receptive field units. The widths are made high my multiplying the value obtained from the nearest neighbor-heuristic by a large overlap parameter. The large widths force the units to excessively smooth the image being approximated. Then, errors will be observed in regions where detailed features occur. Those pixels for which high error (say, greater than one standard deviation from the mean) occurred are collected and new units are added in locations chosen randomly from this set. The entire process can be repeated until a desired level of accuracy is reached. Notice that, when the network is finally trained, the top levels in the hierarchy provide global information about the image under consideration. This scheme is slightly different than the one presented in [7], where units in each resolution learn the error observed in the previous resolution-- in our method, after the addition of the new units all the units learn the original function as opposed to the some error function.

3 RESULTS

3.1 ONRBF AS AN APPROXIMATOR

Oriented non-radial basis function networks allow the definition of larger regions or receptive fields- this is due to the fact that rotation, along with the elliptical hyper-spheres as opposed to mere spheres, permits the grouping of more nearby points into a single region.

Therefore, the approximation accuracy of such a network can be quite good with even a small number of units. For instance, Table 1 compares ordinary radial basis function networks with oriented non-radial basis function networks in terms of the number of units required to achieve various levels of accuracy. The function approximated is the Mackey-Glass differential delay equation:

$$\frac{dx_t}{dt} = -bx_t + a\frac{x_{t-T}}{1+x_{t-T}}$$

TABLE 1. Normalized approximation error for radial and non-radial basis functions

	RBF Train	ONBF Train	RBF Test 1	ONBF Test 1	RBF Test 2	ONBF Test 2
10 units	.426	.229	.267	.161	.522	.298
20 units	.377	.119	.167	.071	.497	.166
40 units	.236	.057	.134	.065	.310	.105
80 units	.197		.123		.271	
160 units	.159		.126		.228	
320 units	.107		.131		.207	
500 units	.061		.121		.208	

The series used was generated with t = 17, a = 0.1 and b = 0.2. A series of 500 consecutive points was used for training, and the next two sets of 500 points were used for cross-validation. The training vector at time t is the tuple $(x_t, x_{t-6}, x_{t-12}, x_{t-18}, x_{t+85})$, where the first four components form the input vector and the last forms the target, and x_t is the value of the series at time t. Table 1 lists the normalized error for each experiment- that is, the root mean square prediction error divided by the standard deviation of the data series. Oriented non-radial basis function networks yield higher accuracy than do radial basis function networks with the same number of units. In addition, ONRBF nets were found to generalize better.

3.2 IMAGE CODING AND ANALYSIS

For images each hidden unit corresponds some feature in the input space. This implies that there is some invariant property associated with the region spanned by the receptive field. For bitmaps this property could be the probability density function (ignoring higher order statistics) and a feature is a region over which the probability density function remains the same. For grey level images, instead of the linear weight this property could be described by a low order polynomial. We have found that when the parameters of an image function are determined adaptively using the learning rules in section 2.1-- the receptive fields organize themselves so as to capture features in the input space. This is illustrated in Figure 1, where the input image is a bitmap for a set of Chinese characters. The property of a feature in this case is the value of the pixel (0 or 1) in the coordinate location specified by the input- and therefore a linear term (for the weight) as used in section 2.1 is sufficient. Figure 1.a is the input bitmap image and figure 1.b shows the plot of the regions of influence of the individual receptive fields. Notice that the individual receptive fields tend to become "responsible" for entire strokes of the character.

We would like to point out that if the initial positions of the hidden units are chosen randomly, then with each new start of the approximation process a single feature may be represented by a collection of hidden units in many different manners- and the task of

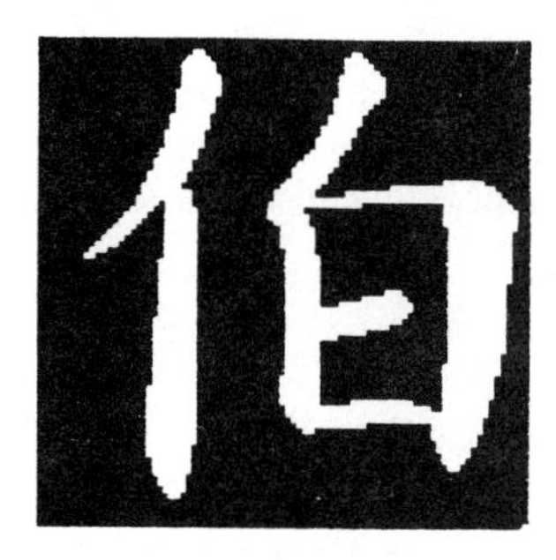

Figure1.a: Bitmap Of Chinese Character Which Is The Input Image

Figure 1.b: Plot Of Regions Of Influence Of Receptive Fields After Training

recognition becomes difficult. Therefore, for consistent approximation, a node deletion or region growing algorithm is needed. Such an algorithm has been developed and will be presented elsewhere. If with every approximation of the same image, we get the same features (parameters for the hidden units), then images under rotation and scaling can also be recognized easily-- since there will be a constant scaling and rotational change in all the hidden units.

4 CONCLUSIONS

We have presented a generalization of RBF networks that allows interpretation of the parameter values associated with the hidden units and performs better as a function approximator. The number of parameters associated with each hidden units grow quickly with the input dimension ($O(d^2)$). However, the number of hidden units required is significantly lower if the function is relatively smooth. Alternatively, one can compose the Gaussian response of the original RBF by using a suitable clipping function in which the number of associated parameters grow linearly with the input dimension d. For images, the input dimension is 2 and the number of parameters associated with each hidden unit is 6 as opposed to 5- when the multidimensional Gaussian is represented by the superposition of 1-dimensional Gaussians, and 4 with RBF networks.

References

[1] Widrow, Bernard and Michael A. Lehr,"30 Years of Adaptive Neural Networks: Perceptron, Madaline, and Backpropagation", Proc. of the IEEE, vol.78, No. 9, Sept 1990, pp 1415-1442.

[2] Baba, Norio,"A New Approach for Finding the Global Minimum of Error Function of Neural Networks", Neural Networks, Vol. 2, pp 367-373, 1989.

[3] Baldi, Pierre and Kurt Hornik,"Neural Networks and Principal Component Analysis: Learning from Examples Without Local Minima", Neural Networks, Vol. 2,pp 53-58, 1989.

[4] Moody, John and Darken, Christen, " Learning with Localized Receptive Fields", Proc. of the 1988 Connectionist Models Summer School,CMU.

[5] Poggio Tomaso and Fedrico Giorsi,"Networks for Approximation and Learning", Proc. of IEEE, vol. 78, no. 9, September 1990, pp 1481- 1496.

[6] Saha, Avijit , D. S. Tang and Chuan-Lin Wu,."Dimension Reduction Using Networks of Linear Superposition of Gaussian Units",MCC Technical Report,, Sept. 1990.

[7] Moody, John and Darken, Christen, " Learning with Localized Receptive Fields", Proc. of the 1988 Connectionist Models Summer School, CMU.

Computing with Arrays of Bell-Shaped and Sigmoid Functions

Pierre Baldi*
Jet Propulsion Laboratory
California Institute of Technology
Pasadena, CA 91109

Abstract

We consider feed-forward neural networks with one non-linear hidden layer and linear output units. The transfer function in the hidden layer are either bell-shaped or sigmoid. In the bell-shaped case, we show how Bernstein polynomials on one hand and the theory of the heat equation on the other are relevant for understanding the properties of the corresponding networks. In particular, these techniques yield simple proofs of universal approximation properties, i.e. of the fact that any reasonable function can be approximated to any degree of precision by a linear combination of bell-shaped functions. In addition, in this framework the problem of learning is equivalent to the problem of reversing the time course of a diffusion process. The results obtained in the bell-shaped case can then be applied to the case of sigmoid transfer functions in the hidden layer, yielding similar universality results. A conjecture related to the problem of generalization is briefly examined.

1 INTRODUCTION

Bell-shaped response curves are commonly found in biological neurons whenever a natural metric exist on the corresponding relevant stimulus variable (orientation, position in space, frequency, time delay, ...). As a result, they are often used in neural models in different context ranging from resolution enhancement and interpolation to learning (see, for instance, Baldi et al. (1988), Moody et al. (1989)

*and Division of Biology, California Institute of Technology. The complete title of this paper should read: "Computing with arrays of bell-shaped and sigmoid functions. Bernstein polynomials, the heat equation and universal approximation properties".

and Poggio et al. (1990)). Consider then the problem of approximating a function $y = f(x)$ by a weighted sum of bell-shaped functions $B(k, x)$, i. e. of finding a suitably good set of weights $H(k)$ satisfying

$$f(x) \approx \sum_k H(k)B(k, x). \tag{1}$$

In neural network terminology, this corresponds to using a feed-forward network with a unique hidden layer of bell-shaped units and a linear ouput layer. In this note, we first briefly point out how this question is related to two different mathematical concepts: Bernstein Polynomials on one hand and the Heat Equation on the other. The former shows how such an approximation is always possible for any reasonable function whereas through the latter the problem of learning, that is of finding $H(k)$, is equivalent to reversing the time course of a diffusion process. For simplicity, the relevant ideas are presented in one dimension. However, the extension to the general setting is straightforward and will be sketched in each case. We then indicate how these ideas can be applied to similar neural networks with sigmoid transfer functions in the hidden layer. A conjecture related to the problem of generalization is briefly examined.

2 BERNSTEIN POLYNOMIALS

In this section, without any loss of generality, we assume that all the functions to be considered are defined over the interval [0,1]. For a fixed integer n, there are n Bernstein polynomials of degree n (see, for instance, Feller (1971)) given by

$$B_n(k, x) = \binom{n}{k} x^k (1-x)^{n-k}. \tag{2}$$

$B_n(k, x)$ can be interpreted as being the probability of having k successes in a coin flipping experiment of duration n, where x represents the probability of a single success. It is easy to see that $B_n(k, x)$ is bell-shaped and reaches its maximum for $x = k/n$. Can we then approximate a function f using linear combinations of Bernstein polynomials of degree n? Let us first consider, as an example, the simple case of the identity function $f(x) = x$ ($x \in [0, 1]$). If we interpret x as the probability of success on a single coin toss, then the expected number of successes in n trials is given by

$$nx = \sum_{k=0}^{n} k \binom{n}{k} x^k (1-x)^{n-k} \tag{3}$$

or equivalently

$$f(x) = \sum_{k=0}^{n} f(\frac{k}{n}) \binom{n}{k} x^k (1-x)^{n-k}. \tag{4}$$

The remarkable theorem of Bernstein is that (4) remains approximately true for a general function f. More precisely:

Theorem: *Assume f is a bounded function defined over the interval* $[0, 1]$. *Then*

$$\lim_{n \to \infty} \sum_{k=0}^{n} f(\frac{k}{n}) \binom{n}{k} x^k (1-x)^{n-k} = f(x) \tag{5}$$

at any point x where f is continuous. Moreover, if f is continuous everywhere, the sequence in (5) approaches f uniformly.

Proof: The proof is beautiful and elementary. It is easy to see that

$$|f(x) - \sum_{k=0}^{n} f(\frac{k}{n})\binom{n}{k} x^k(1-x)^{n-k}| \leq \sum_{|x-\frac{k}{n}|<\delta} |f(x) - f(\frac{k}{n})|\binom{n}{k} x^k(1-x)^{n-k}$$

$$+ \sum_{|x-\frac{k}{n}|\geq\delta} |f(x) - f(\frac{k}{n})|\binom{n}{k} x^k(1-x)^{n-k}$$

for any $0 \leq \delta \leq 1$. To bound the first term in the right hand side of this inequality, we use the fact that for fixed ϵ and for n large enough, at a point of continuity x, we can find a δ such that $|f(x) - f(\frac{k}{n})| < \epsilon$ as soon as $|x - \frac{k}{n}| < \delta$. Thus the first term is bounded by ϵ. If f is continuous everywhere, then it is uniformly continuous and δ can be found independently of x. For the second term, since f is bounded ($|f(x)| \leq M$), we have $|f(x) - f(\frac{k}{n})| \leq 2M$. Now we use Tchebycheff inequality ($P(|X - E(X)| \geq a) \leq (\text{Var}X)/a^2$) to bound the tail of the binomial series

$$|\sum_{|x-\frac{k}{n}|\geq\delta} \binom{n}{k} x^k(1-x)^{n-k}| \leq \frac{nx(1-x)}{\delta^2 n^2} \leq \frac{1}{4n\delta^2}.$$

Collecting terms, we finally get

$$|f(x) - \sum_{k=0}^{n} f(\frac{k}{n})\binom{n}{k} x^k(1-x)^{n-k}| \leq \epsilon + \frac{M}{2n\delta^2}.$$

which completes the proof.

Bernsteins's theorem provides a probabilistic constructive proof of Weierstrass theorem which asserts that every continuous function over a compact set can be uniformly approximated by a sequence of polynomials. Its "connectionist" interpretation is that every reasonable function can be computed by a two layer network consisting of one array of equally spaced bell-shaped detectors feeding into one linear output unit. In addition, the weighting function $H(k)$ is the function f itself (see also Baldi et al. (1988)). Notice that the shape of the functions $B_n(k, x)$ in the array depends on k: in the center ($k \approx n/2$) they are very symmetric and similar to gaussians, as one moves towards the periphery the shape becomes less symmetric. Two additional significant properties of Bernstein polynomials are that, for fixed n, they form a partition of unity: $\sum_k B_n(k, x) = (x + (1-x))^n = 1$ and that they have constant energy $\int_0^1 B_n(k, x) = 1/(n+1)$. One important advantage of the approximation defined by (5) is its great smoothness. If f is differentiable, then not only (5) holds but also

$$\lim_{n\to\infty} \frac{d}{dx}(\sum_{k=0}^{n} f(\frac{k}{n})\binom{n}{k} x^k(1-x)^{n-k}) \to \frac{df}{dx} \tag{6}$$

uniformly on [0, 1] and the same is true for higher order derivatives (see, for instance, Davis (1963)). Thus the Bernstein polynomials provide simultaneous approximation of a function and of its derivatives. In particular, they preserve the convexity properties of the function f being approximated and mimic extremely well its qualitative behavior. The price to be paid is in precision, for the convergence in (5) can sometimes be slow. Good qualitative properties of the approximation may be relevant for biological systems, whereas precision there may not be a problem, especially in light of the fact that n is often large.

Finally, this approach can be extended to the general case of an input space with d dimensions by defining the generalized Bernstein polynomials

$$B_{n_1,\dots,n_d}(k_1,\dots,k_d,x_1,\dots,x_d) = \binom{n_1}{k_1}\dots\binom{n_d}{k_d} x_1^{k_1}(1-x_1)^{n_1-k_1}\dots x_d^{k_d}(1-x_d)^{n_d-k_d}. \tag{7}$$

If $f(x_1,\dots,x_d)$ is a continuous function over the hypercube $[0,1]^d$, then

$$\sum_{k_1=0}^{n_1}\dots\sum_{k_d=0}^{n_d} f(\frac{k_1}{n_1},\dots,\frac{k_d}{n_d})B_{n_1,\dots,n_d}(k_1,\dots,k_d,x_1,\dots,x_d) \tag{8}$$

approaches uniformly f on $[0,1]^d$ as $\min n_i \rightarrow \infty$.

3 LEARNING AND THE HEAT EQUATION

Consider again the general problem of approximating a function f by a linear combination of bell-shaped functions, but where now the bell-shaped functions are gaussians $B(w,x)$, of the form

$$B(w,x) = \frac{1}{\sqrt{2\pi}\sigma}e^{-(x-w)^2/2\sigma^2}. \tag{9}$$

The fixed centers w of the gaussians are distributed in space according to a density $\mu(w)$ (this enables one to treat the continuous and discrete case together and also to include the case where the centers are not evenly distributed). This idea was directly suggested by a presentation of R. Durbin (1990), where the limiting case of an infinite number of logistic hidden units in a connectionist network was considered. In this setting, we are trying to express f as

$$f(x) \approx \int_{-\infty}^{+\infty} h(w)\frac{1}{\sqrt{2\pi}\sigma}e^{-(x-w)^2/2\sigma^2}\mu(w)dw \tag{10}$$

or

$$f(x) \approx \int_{-\infty}^{+\infty} \frac{1}{\sqrt{2\pi}\sigma}H(w)e^{-(x-w)^2/2\sigma^2}dw \tag{11}$$

where $H = h\mu$. Now, diffusion processes or propagation of heat are usually modeled by a partial differential equation of the type

$$\frac{\partial u}{\partial t} = \frac{\partial^2 u}{\partial x^2} \tag{12}$$

(the heat equation) where $u(x,t)$ represents the temperature (or the concentration) at position x at time t. Given a set of initial conditions of the form $u(x,0) = g(x)$, then the distribution of temperatures at time t is given by

$$u(x,t) = \int_{-\infty}^{+\infty} g(w) \frac{1}{\sqrt{4\pi t}} e^{-(x-w)^2/4t} dw. \tag{13}$$

Technically, (13) can be shown to give the correct distribution of temperatures at time t provided g is continuous, $|g(x)| = O(\exp(hx^2))$ and $0 \leq t < 1/4h$. Under these conditions, it can be seen that $u(x,t) = O(\exp(kx^2))$ for some constant $k > 0$ (depending on h) and is the unique solution satisfying this property (see Friedman (1964) and John (1975) for more details).

The connection to our problem now becomes obvious. If the initial set of temperatures is equal to the weights in the network ($H(w) = g(w)$), then the function computed by the network is equal to the temperature at x at time $t = \sigma^2/2$. Given a function $f(x)$ we can view it as a description of temperature values at time $\sigma^2/2$; *the problem of learning, i. e. of determining the optimal $h(w)$ (or $H(w)$) consists in finding a distribution of initial temperatures at time $t = 0$ from which f could have evolved.* In this sense, learning is equivalent to reversing time in a diffusion process. If the continuous case is viewed as a limiting case where units with bell-shaped tuning curves are very densely packed, then it is reasonable to consider that, as the density is increased, the width σ of the curves tends to 0. As $\sigma \to 0$, the final distribution of temperatures approaches the initial one and this is another heuristic way of seeing why the weighting function $H(w)$ is identical to the function being learnt.

In the course of a diffusion or heat propagation process, the integral of the concentration (or of the temperature) remains constant in time. Thus the temperature distribution is similar to a probability distribution and we can define its entropy

$$E(u(x,t)) = -\int_{-\infty}^{+\infty} u(x,t) \ln u(x,t) dx. \tag{14}$$

It is easy to see that the heat equation tends to increase E. Therefore learning can also be viewed as a process by which E is minimized (within certain time boundaries constraints). This is intuitively clear if we think of learning as an attempt to evolve an initially random distribution of connection weights and concentrate it in one or a few restricted regions of space.

In general, the problem of solving the heat equation backwards in time is difficult: physically it is an irreversible process and mathematically the problem is ill-posed in the sense of Hadamard. The solution does not always exist (for instance, the final set of temperatures must be an analytic function), or exists only over a limited period of time and, most of all, small changes in the final set of temperatures can lead to large changes in the initial set of temperatures) (see, for instance, John (1955)). However, the problem becomes well-posed if the final set of temperatures has a compact Fourier spectrum (see Miranker (1961); alternatively, one could use a regularization approach as in Franklin (1974)). In a connectionist framework, one usually seeks a least square approximation to a given function. The corresponding error functional is convex (the heat equation is linear) and therefore a solution always exists. In addition, the problem is usually not ill-posed because the functions to be learnt have a bounded spectrum and are often known only through a finite sample. Thus learning from examples in networks consisting of one hidden layer of gaussians units and a linear output unit is relatively straightforward, for the landscape of the usual error function has no local minima and the optimal set of weights can be found by gradient descent or directly, essentially by linear regression. To be more precise, we can write the error function in the most general case in the form:

$$E(h(w)) = \int [f(x) - \int h(u) e^{-(x-u)^2/2\sigma^2} \mu(u) du]^2 \nu(x) dx \tag{15}$$

where μ and ν are the measures defined on the weights and the examples respectively. The gradient, as in the usual back-propagation of errors, is given by:

$$\frac{\partial E}{\partial h(w)} = -2 \int [f(x) - \int H(u) e^{-(x-u)^2/2\sigma^2} du] e^{-(x-w)^2/2\sigma^2} \mu(w) \nu(x) dx. \tag{16}$$

Thus the critical weights of (15) where $\mu(w) \neq 0$ are characterized by the relation

$$\int f(x) e^{-(x-w)^2/2\sigma^2} \nu(x) dx = \int \int H(u) e^{-(x-w)^2/2\sigma^2} e^{-(x-u)^2/2\sigma^2} \nu(x) du dx. \tag{17}$$

If now we assume that the centers of the gaussians in the hidden layer occupy a (finite or infinite) set of isolated points w_i, (17) can be rewritten in matrix form as

$$B = AH(u) \tag{18}$$

where $B_i = \int f(x) \exp(-(x - w_i)^2/2\sigma^2) \nu(x) dx$, $H(u)_i = h(u_i)\mu(u_i)$ and A is the real symmetric matrix with entries

$$A_{ij} = \int e^{-(x-w_i)^2/2\sigma^2} e^{-(x-u_j)^2/2\sigma^2} \nu(x) dx. \tag{19}$$

Usually A is invertible, so that $H(u) = A^{-1}B$ which, in turn, yields $h(u_i) = H(u_i)/\mu(u_i)$.

Finally, everything can be extended without any difficulty to d dimensions, where the typical solution of $\nabla^2 u = \partial u / \partial t$ is given by

$$u(x_1, ..., x_d, t) = \int_{-\infty}^{+\infty} ... \int_{-\infty}^{+\infty} g(w) \frac{1}{(4\pi t)^{d/2}} e^{-\sum_i (x_i - w_i)^2/4t} dw_1 ... dw_d \tag{20}$$

with, under some smoothness assumptions, $u(x,t) \to g(x)$ as $t \to 0$.

Remark

For an application to a discrete setting consider, as in Baldi et al. (1988), the sum

$$l(x) = \sum_{k=-\infty}^{+\infty} \frac{k}{\sqrt{2\pi}\sigma} e^{-(x-k)^2/2\sigma^2}.$$

For an initial gaussian distribution of temperatures $u(x,0)$ of the form $(1/\sqrt{2\pi}) \exp(-x^2/2\eta^2)$, the distribution $u(x,t)$ of temperatures at time t is also gaussian, centered at the origin, but with a larger standard deviation which, using (13), is given by $(\eta^2 + 2t)^{1/2}$. Thus, if we imagine that at time 0 a temperature equal to k has been injected (with a very small η) at each integer location along the real axis, then $l(x)$ represents the distribution of temperatures at time $t = (\sigma^2 - \eta^2)/2$. Intuitively, it is clear that as σ is increased (i.e. as we wait longer) the distribution of temperatures becomes more and more linear.

(2) It is aesthetically pleasing that the theory of the heat equation can also be used to give a proof of Weierstrass theorem. For this purpose, it is sufficient to observe that, for a given continuous function g defined over a closed interval $[a, b]$, the function $u(x,t)$ given by (13) is an analytic function in x at a fixed time t. By letting $t \rightarrow 0$ and truncating the corresponding series, one can get polynomial approximations converging uniformly to g.

4 THE SIGMOID CASE

We now consider the case of a neural network with one hidden layer of sigmoids and one linear output unit. The output of the network can be written as a transform

$$out(x) = \int \sigma(w.x)h(w)\mu(w)dw \tag{21}$$

where x is the input vector and w is a weight vector which is characteristic of each hidden unit (i. e. each hidden units is characterized by the vector of weights on its incoming input lines rather than, for instance, its spatial location). Assume that the inputs and the weights are normalized, i.e. $||x|| = ||w|| = 1$ and that the weight vectors cover the n-dimensional sphere uniformly (or, in the limit, that there is a vector for each point on the sphere). Then for a given input x, the scalar products $w.x$ are maximal and close to 1 in the region of the sphere corresponding to hidden units where w and x are colinear and decay as we move away till they reach negative values close to -1 in the antipodal region. When these scalar products are passed through an appropriate sigmoid, a bell-shaped pattern of activity is created on the surface of the sphere and from then on we are reduced to the previous case. Thus the previous results can be extended and in particular we have a heuristic simple proof that the corresponding networks have universal approximation properties (see, for instance, Hornik et al. (1989)). Notice that intuitively the reason is simple for we end up we something like a grand-mother cell per pattern or cluster of patterns.

If we assume that initially $\mu(w) \neq 0$ everywhere, then it is clear that for learning via LMS optimization we can take μ to be fixed and adjust only the output weights h. But the problem then is convex and without local minima. This suggests that in the limit of an extremely large number of hidden units, the landscape of the error function is devoid of local minima and learning becomes very smooth. This result is consistent with the conjecture that under reasonable assumptions, as we progressively increase the number of hidden units, learning goes from being impossible, to being possible but difficult and lengthy, to being relatively easy and quick to trivial. And if so what is the nature of these transitions? This picture is also consistent with certain simulation results reported by several authors, whereby optimal performance and generalization is not best obtained by training for a very long time a minimal size highly constrained network, but rather by training for a shorter time (until the validation error begins to go up (see Baldi and Chauvin (1991))) a larger network with extra hidden units.

Acknowledgements

This work is supported by NSF grant DMS-8914302 and ONR contract NAS7-100/918. We would like to thank Y. Rinott for useful discussions.

References

Baldi, P. and Heiligenberg, W. (1988) How sensory maps could enhance resolution through ordered arrangements of broadly tuned receivers. Biological Cybernetics, **59**, 313-318.

Baldi, P. and Chauvin, Y. (1991) A study of generalization in simple networks. Submitted for publication.

Davis, P. J. (1963) Interpolation and approximation. Blaisdell.

Durbin, R. (1990) Presented at the Neural Networks for Computing Conference, Snowbird, Utah.

Feller, W. (1971) An introduction to probability theory and its applications. John Wiley & Sons

Franklin, J. N. (1974) On Tikhonov's method for ill-posed problems. Mathematics of Computation, 28, 128, 889-907.

Friedman, A. (1964) Partial differential equations of parabolic type. Prentice-Hall.

Hornik, K., Stinchcombe, M. and White, H. (1989) Multilayer feedforward networks are universal approximators. Neural Networks, **2**, 5, 359-366.

John, F. (1955) Numerical solutions of the equation of heat conduction for preceding times. Ann. Mat. Pura Appl., ser. IV, vol. 40, 129-142.

John, F. (1975) Partial differential equations. Springer Verlag.

Miranker, W. L. (1961) A well posed problem for the backward heat equation. Proceedings American Mathematical Society, **12**, 243-247.

Moody, J. and Darken, C. J. (1989) Fast learning in networks of locally-tuned processing units. Neural Computation, **1**, 2, 281-294.

Poggio, T. and Girosi, F. (1990) Regularization algorithms for learning that are equivalent to multilayer networks. Science, **247**, 978-982.

Discrete Affine Wavelet Transforms For Analysis And Synthesis Of Feedforward Neural Networks

Y. C. Pati and **P. S. Krishnaprasad**
Systems Research Center and Department of Electrical Engineering
University of Maryland, College Park, MD 20742

Abstract

In this paper we show that discrete affine wavelet transforms can provide a tool for the analysis and synthesis of standard feedforward neural networks. It is shown that wavelet frames for $L^2(\mathbb{R})$ can be constructed based upon sigmoids. The spatio-spectral localization property of wavelets can be exploited in defining the topology and determining the weights of a feedforward network. Training a network constructed using the synthesis procedure described here involves minimization of a convex cost functional and therefore avoids pitfalls inherent in standard backpropagation algorithms. Extension of these methods to $L^2(\mathbb{R}^N)$ is also discussed.

1 INTRODUCTION

Feedforward type neural network models constructed from empirical data have been found to display significant predictive power [6]. Mathematical justification in support of such predictive power may be drawn from various density and approximation theorems [1, 2, 5]. Typically this latter work doesn't take into account the spectral features apparent in the data. In the present paper, we note that the discrete affine wavelet transform provides a natural framework for the analysis and synthesis of feedforward networks. This new tool takes account of spatial and spectral localization properties present in the data.

Throughout most of this paper we restrict discussion to networks designed to approximate mappings in $L^2(\mathbb{R})$. Extensions to $L^2(\mathbb{R}^N)$ are briefly discussed in Section 4 and will be further developed in [10].

2 WAVELETS AND FRAMES

Consider a function f of one real variable as a static feedforward input-output map

$$y = f(x)$$

For simplicity assume $f \in \mathrm{L}^2(\mathbb{R})$ the space of square integrable functions on the real line. Suppose a sequence $\{f_n\} \subset \mathrm{L}^2(\mathbb{R})$ is given such that, for suitable constants $A > 0,\ B < \infty$,

$$A\|f\|^2 \leq \sum_n |< f, f_n >|^2 \leq B\|f\|^2 \tag{1}$$

for *all* $f \in \mathrm{L}^2(\mathbb{R})$. Such a sequence is said to be a *frame*. In particular orthonormal bases are frames. The above definition (1) also applies in the general Hilbert space setting with the appropriate inner product. Let T denote the bounded operator from $\mathrm{L}^2(\mathbb{R})$ to $l^2(\mathbb{Z})$, the space of square summable sequences, defined by

$$(Tf) = \{< f, f_n >\}_{n \in \mathbb{Z}}.$$

In terms of the *frame operator* T, it is possible to give series expansions,

$$\begin{aligned} f &= \sum_n \widetilde{f_n} < f, f_n > \\ &= \sum_n f_n < f, \widetilde{f_n} >, \end{aligned} \tag{2}$$

where $\{\widetilde{f_n} = (T^*T)^{-1} f_n\}$ is the *dual frame*.

A particular class of frames leads to affine wavelet expansions. Consider a family of functions $\{\psi_{mn}\}$ of the form,

$$\psi_{mn}(x) = a^{-m/2}\psi(a^{-m}x - nb) \tag{3}$$

where, the function ψ satisfies appropriate admissibility conditions [3, 4] (e.g. $\int \psi = 0$). Then for suitable choices of $a > 1,\ b > 0$, the family $\{\psi_{mn}\}$ is a frame for $\mathrm{L}^2(\mathbb{R})$. Hence there exists a convergent series representation,

$$\begin{aligned} f(x) &= \sum_m \sum_n c_{mn} \psi_{mn}(x) \\ &= \sum_m \sum_n c_{mn} a^{-m/2} \psi(a^{-m}x - nb) \end{aligned} \tag{4}$$

The frame condition (1) guarantees that the operator (T^*T) is boundedly invertible. Also since $\|I - (2(A+B)^{-1}T^*T)\| < 1,\ (T^*T)^{-1}$ is given by a Neumann series [3]. Hence, given f, the expansion coefficients c_{mn} can be computed.

The representation (4) of f above as a series in *dilations* and *translations* of a single function ψ is called a wavelet expansion and the function ψ is known as the *analyzing* or *mother wavelet* for the expansion.

3 FEEDFORWARD NETWORKS AND WAVELET EXPANSIONS

Consider the input-output relationship of a feedforward network with one input, one output, and a single hidden layer,

$$\tilde{f}(x) = \sum_n c_n g(a_n x - b_n) \tag{5}$$

where a_n are the weights from the the input node to the hidden layer, b_n are the biases on the hidden layer nodes, c_n are the weights from the hidden layer to the output layer and g defines the activation function of the hidden layer nodes. It is clear from (5) that the output of such a network is given in terms of dilations and translations of a single function g.

3.1 WAVELET ANALYSIS OF FEEDFORWARD NETWORKS

Let g be a 'sigmoidal' function e.g. $g(x) = \frac{1}{1+e^{-x}}$ and let ψ be defined as

$$\psi(x) = g(x+2) + g(x-2) - 2g(x). \tag{6}$$

Then it is possible (see [9] for details) to determine a translation stepsize b and

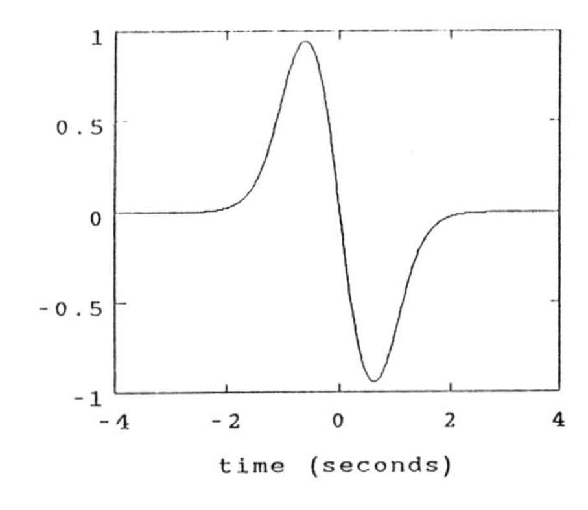

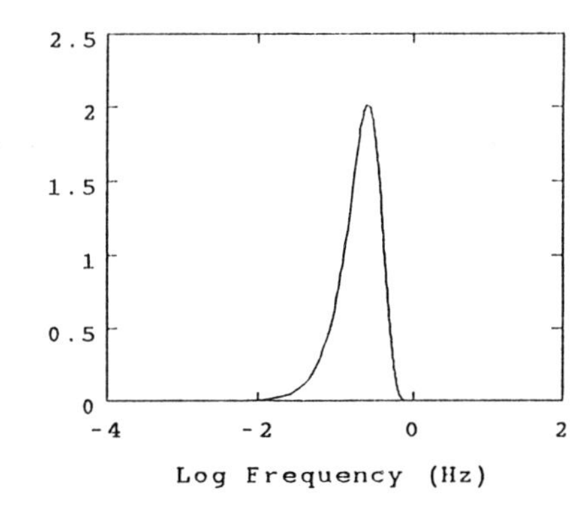

Figure 1: Mother Wavelet ψ (Left) And Magnitude Of Fourier Transform $|\hat{\psi}|^2$

a dilation stepsize a for which the family of functions ψ_{mn} as defined by (3) is a frame for $L^2(\mathbb{R})$. Note that wavelet frames for $L^2(\mathbb{R})$ can be constructed based upon other combinations of sigmoids (e.g $\psi(x) = g(x+p)+g(x-p)-2g(x),\ \ p > 0$) and that we use the mother wavelet of (6) only to illustrate some properties which are common to many such combinations.

It follows from the above discussion that a feedforward network having one hidden layer with sigmoidal activation functions can represent any function in $L^2(\mathbb{R})$. In such a network (6) says that the sigmoidal nodes should be grouped together in sets of three so as to form the mother wavelet ψ.

3.2 WAVELETS AND SYNTHESIS OF FEEDFORWARD NETWORKS

In defining the topology of a feedforward network we make use of the fact that the function ψ is well concentrated in both spatial and spectral domains (see Figure 1). Dilating ψ corresponds to shifting the spectral concentration and translating ψ corresponds to shifting the spatial concentration.

The synthesis procedure we describe here is based upon estimates of the spatial and spectral localization of the unknown mapping as determined from samples provided by the training data. Spatial locality of interest can easily be determined by examination of the training data or by introducing *a priori* assumptions as to the region over which it is desired to approximate the unknown mapping. Estimates of the appropriate spectral locality are also possible via preprocessing of the training data.

Let $\mathcal{Q}_{mn}$ and $\mathcal{Q}_f$ respectively denote the spatio-spectral concentrations of the wavelet ψ_{mn} and of f. Thus $\mathcal{Q}_{mn}$ and $\mathcal{Q}_f$ are rectangular regions in the spatio-spectral plane (see Figure 2) which contain 'most' of the energy in the functions ψ_{mn} and f. More precise definitions of these concentrations can be found in [9]. Assuming that $\mathcal{Q}_f$ has been estimated from the training data. We choose only those

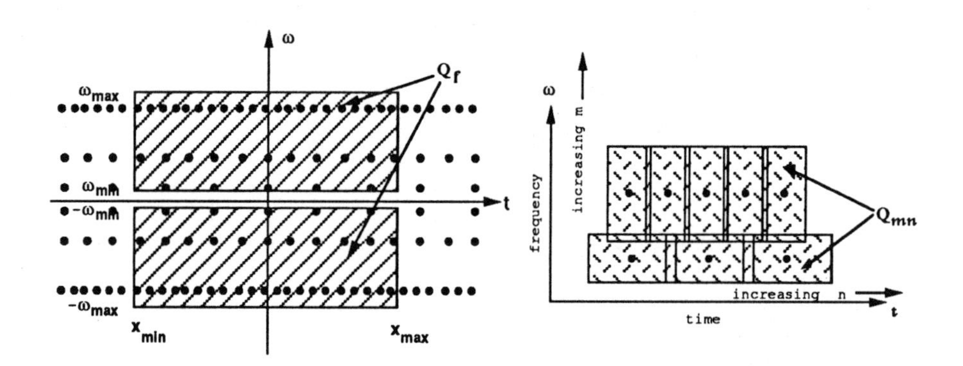

Figure 2: Spatio-Spectral Concentrations $\mathcal{Q}_{mn}$ And $\mathcal{Q}_f$ Of Wavelets ψ_{mn} And Unknown Map f.

elements of the frame $\{\psi_{mn}\}$ which contribute 'significantly' to the region $\mathcal{Q}_f$ by defining an index set $\mathcal{I}_f \subseteq \mathbb{Z}^2$ in the following manner,

$$\mathcal{I}_f = \{(m,n) \in \mathbb{Z} : \ \mu(\mathcal{Q}_f \bigcap \mathcal{Q}_{mn}) > 0\}$$

where, μ is the Lesbegue measure on $\mathbb{R}^2$. Since f is concentrated in $\mathcal{Q}_f$, by choosing $\mathcal{I}_f$ as above, a 'good' approximation of f can be obtained in terms of the *finite* set of frame elements with indices in $\mathcal{I}_f$. That is f can be approximated by $\tilde{f}$ where,

$$\tilde{f} = \sum_{(m,n)\in\mathcal{I}_f} c_{mn}\psi_{mn} \tag{7}$$

for some coefficients $\{c_{mn}\}_{(m,n)\in\mathcal{I}_f}$.

Having determined $\mathcal{I}_f$, a network is constructed to implement the appropriate wavelets ψ_{mn}. This is easily accomplished by choosing the number of sigmoidal hidden layer nodes to be $M = 3 \times \sharp\mathcal{I}_f$ and then grouping them together in sets of three to implement ψ as in (6). Weights from the input to the hidden layer are set to provide the required dilations of ψ and biases on the hidden layer nodes are set to provide the required translations.

3.2.1 Computation of Coefficients

By the above construction, all weights in the network have been fixed except for the weights from the hidden layer to the output which specify the coefficients c_{mn} in (7). These coefficients can be computed using a simple gradient descent algorithm on the standard cost function of backpropagation. Since the cost function is convex in the remaining weights, only globally minimizing solutions exist.

3.2.2 Simulations

Figure 3 shows the results of a simple simulation example. The solid line in Figure 3 indicates the original mapping f which was defined via the inverse Fourier transform of a randomly generated approximately bandlimited spectrum. Using a single dilation of ψ which covered the frequency band sufficiently well and the required translations, the dashed curve shows the learned network approximation.

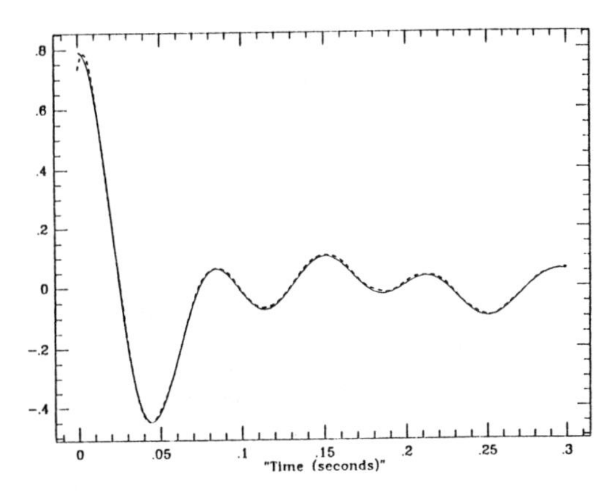

Figure 3: Simulation Using Network Synthesis Procedure. Solid Curve: Original Function, Dashed Curve: Network Reconstruction.

4 DISCUSSION AND CONCLUSIONS

It has been demonstrated here that affine wavelet expansions provide a framework within which feedforward networks designed to approximate mappings in $L^2(\mathbb{R})$ can be understood. In the case when the mapping is known, the expansion coefficients, and therefore *all* weights in the network can be computed. Hence the wavelet transform method (and in general any transform method) not only gives us representability of certain classes of mappings by feedforward networks, but also tells us what the representation should be. Herein lies an essential difference between the wavelet methods discussed here and arguments based upon density in function spaces.

In addition to providing arguments in support of the approximating power of feedforward networks, the wavelet framework also suggests one method of choosing network topology (in this case the number of hidden layer nodes) and reducing the training problem to a convex optimization problem. The synthesis technique suggested is based upon spatial and spectral localization which is provided by the wavelet transform.

Most useful applications of feedforward networks involve the approximation of mappings with higher dimensional domains e.g. mappings in $L^2(\mathbb{R}^N)$. Discrete affine wavelet transforms can be applied in higher dimensions as well (see e.g. [7] and [8]). Wavelet transforms in $L^2(\mathbb{R}^N)$ can also be defined with respect to mother wavelets constructed from sigmoids combined in a manner which doesn't deviate from standard feedforward network architectures [10]. Figure 4 shows a mother wavelet for $L^2(\mathbb{R}^2)$ constructed from sigmoids. In higher dimensions it is possible to use more than one analyzing wavelet [7], each having certain orientation selectivity in addition to spatial and spectral localization. If orientation selectivity is not essential, an isotropic wavelet such as that in Figure 4 can be used.

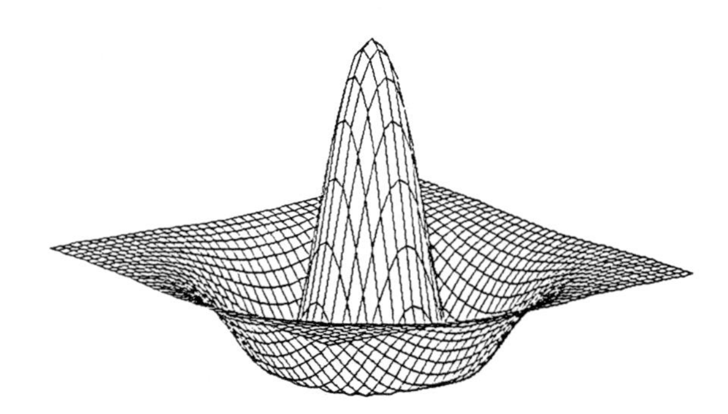

Figure 4: Two-Dimensional Isotropic Wavelet From Sigmoids

The wavelet formulation of this paper can also be used to generate an orthonormal basis of compactly supported wavelets within a standard feedforward network architecture. If the sigmoidal function g in Equation (6) is chosen as a discontinuous threshold function, the resulting wavelet ψ is the Haar function which thereby results in the Haar transform. Dilations of the Haar function in powers of 2 ($a = 2$) together with integer translations ($b = 1$), generate an orthonormal basis for $L^2(\mathbb{R})$. Multidimensional Haar functions are defined similarly. The Haar transform is the earliest known example of a wavelet transform which however suffers due to the discontinuous nature of the mother wavelet.

Acknowledgements

The authors wish to thank Professor Hans Feichtinger of the University of Vienna, and Professor John Benedetto of the University of Maryland for many valuable discussions. This research was supported in part by the National Science Foundation's Engineering Research Centers Program: NSFD CDR 8803012, the Air Force Office of Scientific Research under contract AFOSR-88-0204 and by the Naval Research Laboratory.

References

[1] G. Cybenko. *Approximations by Superpositions of a Sigmoidal Function.* Technical Report CSRD 856, Center for Supercomputing Research and Development, University of Illinois, Urbana, February 1989.

[2] G. Cybenko. *Continuous Valued Neural Networks with Two Hidden Layers are Sufficient.* Technical Report, Department of Computer Science, Tufts University, Medford, MA, March 1988.

[3] I. Daubechies. The Wavelet Transform, Time-Frequency Localization and Signal Analysis. *IEEE Transactions on Information Theory*, 36(5):961–1005,September 1990.

[4] C. E. Heil and D. F. Walnut. Continuous and Discrete Wavelet Transforms. *SIAM Review*, 31(4):628–666, December 1989.

[5] K. Hornik, M. Stinchcombe, and H. White. Multilayer Feedforward Networks are Universal Approximators. *Neural Networks*, 2:359–366, 1989.

[6] A. Lapedes, and R. Farber. *Nonlinear Signal Processing Using Neural Networks: Prediction and System Modeling.* Technical Report LA-UR-87-2662, Los Alamos National Laboratory, 1987.

[7] S. G. Mallat. Multifrequency Channel Decompositions of Images and Wavelet Models. *IEEE Transactions On Acoustics Speech and Signal Processing*, 37(12):2091–2110, December 1989.

[8] R. Murenzi, "Wavelet Transforms Associated To The n-Dimensional Euclidean Group With Dilations: Signals In More Than One Dimension," in *Wavelets Time-Frequency Methods And Phase Space* (J. M. Combes, A. Grossman and Ph. Tchamitchian, eds.), pp. 239–246, Springer-Verlag, 1989.

[9] Y. C. Pati and P. S. Krishnaprasad, "Analysis and Synthesis of Feedforward Neural Networks Using Discrete Affine Wavelet Transforms," Technical Report SRC TR 90-44, University of Maryland, Systems Research Center, 1990.

[10] Y. C. Pati and P. S. Krishnaprasad, In preparation.

Extensions of a Theory of Networks for Approximation and Learning: Outliers and Negative Examples

Federico Girosi
AI Lab. M.I.T.
Cambridge, MA 02139

Tomaso Poggio
AI Lab. M.I.T.
Cambridge, MA 02139

Bruno Caprile
I.R.S.T.
Povo, Italy, 38050

Abstract

Learning an input-output mapping from a set of examples can be regarded as synthesizing an approximation of a multi-dimensional function. From this point of view, this form of learning is closely related to regularization theory, and we have previously shown (Poggio and Girosi, 1990a, 1990b) the equivalence between regularization and a class of three-layer networks that we call regularization networks. In this note, we extend the theory by introducing ways of dealing with two aspects of learning: learning in presence of unreliable examples or outliers, and learning from positive *and* negative examples.

1 Introduction

In previous papers (Poggio and Girosi, 1990a, 1990b) we have shown the equivalence between certain regularization techniques and a class of three-layer networks – that we call regularization networks – which are related to the Radial Basis Functions interpolation method (Powell, 1987). In this note we indicate how it is possible to extend our theory of learning in order to deal with 1) occurence of unreliable examples, 2) negative examples. Both problems are also interesting from the point of view of classical approximation theory:

1. discounting "bad" examples corresponds to discarding, in the approximation of a function, data points that are outliers.
2. learning by using negative examples – in addition to positive ones – corresponds to approximating a function considering not only points which the function

ought to be close to, but also points – or regions – that the function must avoid.

2 Unreliable data

Suppose that a set $g = \{(\mathbf{x}_i, y_i) \in R^n \times R\}_{i=1}^N$ of data has been obtained by randomly sampling a function f, defined in R^n, in presence of noise, in a way that we can write

$$y_i = f(\mathbf{x}_i) + \epsilon_i, \quad i = 1, \ldots, N$$

where ϵ_i are independent random variables. We are interested in recovering an estimate of the function f from the set of data g. Taking a probabilistic approach, we can regard the function f as the realization of a random field with specified prior probability distribution. Consequently, the data g and the function f are non independent random variables, and, by using Bayes rule, it is possible to express the conditional probability $\mathcal{P}[f|g]$ of the function f, given the examples g, in terms of the prior probability of f, $\mathcal{P}[f]$, and the conditional probability of g given f, $\mathcal{P}[g|f]$:

$$\mathcal{P}[f|g] \propto \mathcal{P}[g|f]\ \mathcal{P}[f]. \tag{1}$$

A common choice (Marroquin et al., 1987) for the prior probability distribution $\mathcal{P}[f]$ is

$$\mathcal{P}[f] \propto e^{-\lambda \|Pf\|^2} \tag{2}$$

where P is a differential operator (the so called *stabilizer*), $\|\cdot\|$ is the L^2 norm, and λ is a positive real number. This form of probability distribution assignes significant probability only to those functions for which the term $\|Pf\|^2$ is "small", that is to functions that do not vary too "quickly" in their domain.

If the noise is Gaussian, the probability $\mathcal{P}[g|f]$ can be written as:

$$\mathcal{P}[g|f] = \frac{2^N}{\pi^{\frac{N}{2}}} \prod_{i=1}^{N} \sqrt{\beta_i} e^{-\beta_i \epsilon_i^2} \tag{3}$$

where $\beta_i = \frac{1}{2\sigma_i^2}$, and σ_i is the variance of the noise related to the i-th data point. The values of the variances are usually assumed to be equal to some known value σ, that reflects the accuracy of the measurement apparatus. However, in many cases we do not have access to such an information, and weaker assumptions have to be made. A fairly natural and general one consists in regarding the variances of the noise, as well as the function f, as random variables. Of course, some a priori knowledge about these variables, represented by an appropriate prior probability distribution, is needed. Let us denote by β the set of random variables $\{\beta_i\}_{i=1}^N$. By means of Bayes rule we can compute the joint probability of the variables f and β. Assuming that the field f and the set β are conditionally independent we obtain:

$$\mathcal{P}[f,\beta|g] \propto \mathcal{P}[g|f,\beta]\ \mathcal{P}[f]\ \mathcal{P}[\beta] \tag{4}$$

where $\mathcal{P}[\beta]$ is the prior probability of the set of variances β and $\mathcal{P}[g|f,\beta]$ is the same as in eq. (3). Given the posterior probability (4) we are mainly interested in computing an estimate of f. Thus what we really need to compute is the marginal posterior probability of f, $P_m[f]$, that is obtained integrating equation (4) over the variables β_i:

$$P_m[f] \propto \int_0^\infty \mathcal{P}[f,\beta|g] \prod_{i=1}^N d\beta_i \tag{5}$$

A simple way to obtain an estimate of the function f from the probability distribution (5) consists in computing the so called MAP (Maximum A Posteriori) estimate, that is the function that maximizes the posterior probability $P_m[f]$. The problem of recovering the function f from the set of data g, with partial information about the amount of Gaussian noise affecting the data, is therefore equivalent to solving an appropriate variational problem. The specific form of the functional that has to be maximized – or minimized – depends on the probability distributions $\mathcal{P}[f]$ and $\mathcal{P}[\beta]$.

Here we consider the following situation: we have knowledge that a given percentage, $(1-\epsilon)$ of the data is characterized by a Gaussian noise distribution of variance $\sigma_1 = (2\beta_1)^{-\frac{1}{2}}$, whereas for the rest of the data the variance of the noise is a very large number $\sigma_2 = (2\beta_2)^{-\frac{1}{2}}$ (we will call these data "outliers"). This situation yields the following probability distribution:

$$\mathcal{P}[\beta] = \prod_{i=1}^N [(1-\epsilon)\delta(\beta_i - \beta_1) + \epsilon\ \delta(\beta_i - \beta_2)]\ . \tag{6}$$

In this case, choosing $\mathcal{P}[f]$ as in eq. (2), we can show that $P_m[f] \propto e^{-H[f]}$, where

$$H[f] = \sum_{i=1}^N V(\epsilon_i) + \lambda \|Pf\|^2\ . \tag{7}$$

Here V represents the *effective potential*

$$V(x) = \beta_1 x^2 - \ln\left(1 + \frac{\epsilon}{1-\epsilon}\sqrt{\frac{\beta_2}{\beta_1}} e^{x^2(\beta_1-\beta_2)}\right)\ . \tag{8}$$

depicted in fig. (1) for different values of β_2.

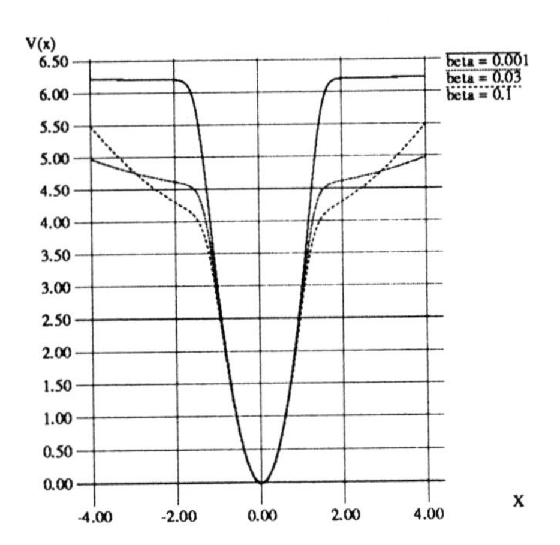

Figure 1: The effective potential $V(x)$ for $\epsilon = 0.1$, $\beta_1 = 3.0$ and three different values of β_2: 0.1, 0.03, 0.001

The MAP estimate is therefore obtained minimizing the functional (7). The first term enforces closeness to the data, while the second term enforces smoothness of the solution, the trade off between these two opposite tendencies being controlled by the parameter λ. Looking at fig. (1) we notice that, in the limit of $\beta_2 \rightarrow 0$, the effective potential V is quadratic if the absolute value of its argument is smaller than a threshold, and constant otherwise (fig. 1). Therefore, data points are taken in account when the interpolation error is smaller than a threshold, and their contribution neglected otherwise.

If $\beta_1 = \beta_2 = \bar{\beta}$, that is if the distribution of the variables β_i is a delta function centered on some value $\bar{\beta}$, the effective potential $V(x) = \bar{\beta}x^2$ is obtained. Therefore, this method becomes equivalent to the so called "regularization technique" (Tikhonov and Arsenin, 1977) that has been extensively used to solve *ill-posed problems*, of which the one we have just outlined is a particular example (Poggio and Girosi, 1990a, 1990b). Suitable choices of distribution $\mathcal{P}[\beta]$ result in other effective potentials (for example the potential $V(x) = \sqrt{\alpha^2 + x^2}$ can be obtained), and the corresponding estimators turn out to be similar to the well known *robust smoothing splines* (Eubank, 1988).

The functional (7), with the choice expressed by eq. (2), admits a simple physical interpretation. Let us consider for simplicity a function defined on a one-dimensional lattice. The value of the function $f(\mathbf{x}_i)$ at site i is regarded as the position of a particle that can move only in the vertical direction. The particle is attracted – according to a spring-like potential V – towards the data point and the neighboring particles as well. The natural trend of the system will be to minimize its total energy which, in this scheme, is expressed by the functional (7): the first term is associated to the springs connecting the particle to the data point, and the second one, being associated to the the springs connecting neighboring particles, enforces the smoothness of the final configuration. Notice that the potential energy of the springs connecting the particle to the data point is not quadratic, as for the "standard" springs, resulting this in a non-linear relationship between the force and the elongation. The potential energy becomes constant when the elongation is larger than a fixed threshold, and the force (which is proportional to the first derivative of the potential energy) goes to zero. In this sense we can say that the springs "break" when we try to stretch them too much (Geiger and Girosi, 1990).

3 Negative examples

In many situations, further information about a function may consist in knowing that its value at some given point has to be far from a given value (which, in this context, can be considered as a "negative example"). We shall account for the presence of negative examples by adding to the functional (7) a quadratic repulsive term for each negative example (for a related trick, see Kass et al., 1987). However, the introduction of such a "repulsive spring" may make the functional (7) unbounded from below, because the repulsive terms tend to push the value of the function up to infinity. The simplest way to prevent this occurency is either to allow the spring constant to decrease with the increasing elongation, or, in the extreme case, to break at some point. Hence, we can use the same model of nonlinear spring of the previous section, and just reverse the sign of the associated potential. If $\{(\mathbf{t}_\alpha, y_\alpha) \in R^n \times R\}_{i=1}^K$ is the set of negative examples, and if we define $\Delta_\alpha = y_\alpha - f(\mathbf{t}_\alpha)$ the functional (7) becomes:

$$H[f] = \sum_{i=1}^{N} V(\Delta_i) - \sum_{\alpha=1}^{K} V(\Delta_\alpha) + \lambda \|Pf\|^2 \ .$$

4 Solution of the variational problem

An exhaustive discussion of the solution of the variational problem associated to the functional (7) cannot be given here. We refer the reader to the papers of Poggio and Girosi (1990a, 1990b) and Girosi, Poggio and Caprile (1990), and just sketch the form of the solution. In both cases of unreliable and negative data, it can be shown that the solution of the variational problem always has the form

$$f^*(\mathbf{x}) = \sum_{i=1}^{N} c_i G(\mathbf{x}; \mathbf{x}_i) + \sum_{i=1}^{k} \alpha_i \phi_i(\mathbf{x}) \tag{9}$$

where G is the Green's function of the operator $\hat{P}P$ ($\hat{P}$ denoting the adjoint operator of P), and $\{\phi_i(\mathbf{x})\}_{i=1}^k$ is a basis of functions for the null space of P (usually polynomials of low degree) and $\{c_i\}_{i=1}^N$ and $\{\alpha_i\}_{i=1}^k$ are coefficients to be computed.

Substituting the expansion (9) in the functional (7), the function $H^*(\mathbf{c}, \boldsymbol{\alpha}) = H[f^*]$ is defined. The vectors $\mathbf{c}$ and $\boldsymbol{\alpha}$ can then be found by minimizing the function $H^*(\mathbf{c}, \boldsymbol{\alpha})$.

We shall finally notice that the solution (9) has a simple interpretation in terms of feedforward networks with one layer of hidden units, of the same class of the regularization networks introduced in previous papers (Poggio and Girosi, 1990a, 1990b). The only difference between these networks and the regularization networks previously introduced consists in the function that has to be minimized in order to find the weights of the network.

5 Experimental Results

In this section we report two examples of the application of these techniques to very simple one-dimensional problems.

5.1 Unreliable data

The data set consisted of seven examples, randomly taken, within the interval $[-1, 1]$, from the graph of $f(x) = \cos(x)$. In order to create an outlier in the data set, the value of the fourth point has been substituted with the value 1.5. The Green's function of the problem was a Gaussian of variance $\sigma = 0.3$, the parameter ϵ was set to 0.1, the value of the regularization parameter λ was 10^{-2}, and the parameters β_1 and β_2 were set respectively to 10.0 and 0.003. With this choice of the parameters the effective potential was approximately constant for values of its argument larger than 1. In figure (2a) we show the result that is obtained after only 10 iterations of gradient descent: the spring of the outlier breaks, and it does not influence the solution any more. The "hole" that the solution shows nearby the outlier is a combined effect of the fact that the variance of the Gaussian Green's function is small ($\sigma = 0.3$), and of the lack of data next to the outlier itself.

5.2 Negative examples

Again data to be approximated came from a random sampling of the function $f(x) = \cos(x)$, in the interval $[-1, 1]$. The fourth data point was selected as the negative example, and the parameters were set in a way that its spring would break when the elongation exceeded the value 1. In figure (2b) we show a result obtained with 500 iterations of a stochastic gradient descent algorithm, with a Gaussian Green's function of variance $\sigma = 0.4$.

Acknowledgements We thank Cesare Furlanello for useful discussions and for a critical reading of the manuscript.

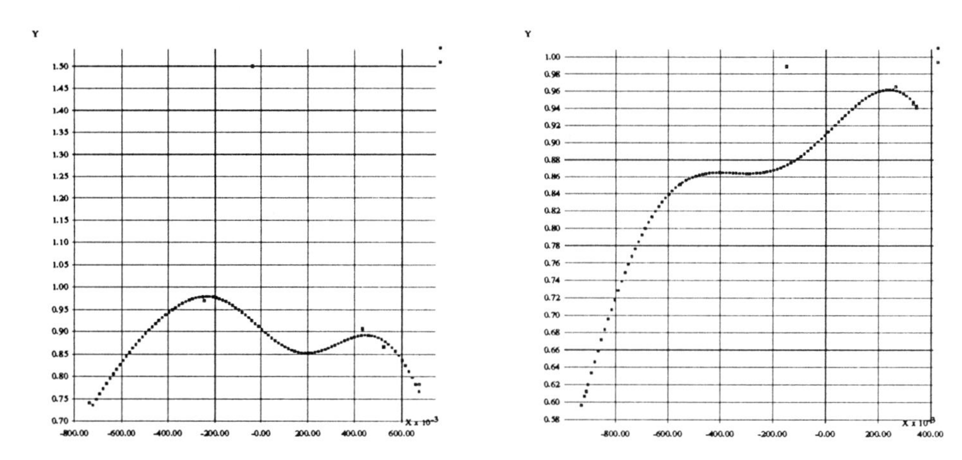

Figure 2: (a) Approximation in presence of an outlier (the data point whose value is 1.5). (b) Approximation in presence of a negative example.

References

[1] R.L. Eubank. *Spline Smoothing and Nonparametric Regression*, volume 90 of *Statistics: Textbooks and Monographs*. Marcel Dekker, Inc., New York, 1988.

[2] D. Geiger and F. Girosi. Parallel and deterministic algorithms for MRFs: surface reconstruction and integration. In O. Faugeras, editor, *Lecture Notes in Computer Science, Vol. 427: Computer Vision – ECCV 90*. Springer-Verlag, Berlin, 1990.

[3] F. Girosi, T. Poggio, and B. Caprile. Extensions of a theory of networks for approximation and learning: outliers and negative examples. A.I. Memo 1220, Artificial Intelligence Laboratory, Massachusetts Institute of Technology, 1990.

[4] M. Kass, A. Witkin, and D. Terzopoulos. Snakes: Active contour models. In *Proceedings of the First International Conference on Computer Vision*, London, 1987. IEEE Computer Society Press, Washington, D.C.

[5] J. L. Marroquin, S. Mitter, and T. Poggio. Probabilistic solution of ill-posed problems in computational vision. *J. Amer. Stat. Assoc.*, 82:76–89, 1987.

[6] T. Poggio and F. Girosi. A theory of networks for learning. *Science*, 247:978–982, 1990a.

[7] T. Poggio and F. Girosi. Networks for approximation and learning. *Proceedings of the IEEE*, 78(9), September 1990b.

[8] M. J. D. Powell. Radial basis functions for multivariable interpolation: a review. In J. C. Mason and M. G. Cox, editors, *Algorithms for Approximation*. Clarendon Press, Oxford, 1987.

[9] A. N. Tikhonov and V. Y. Arsenin. *Solutions of Ill-posed Problems*. W. H. Winston, Washington, D.C., 1977.

How Receptive Field Parameters Affect Neural Learning

Bartlett W. Mel
CNS Program
Caltech, 216-76
Pasadena, CA 91125

Stephen M. Omohundro
ICSI
1947 Center St., Suite 600
Berkeley, CA 94704

Abstract

We identify the three principle factors affecting the performance of learning by networks with localized units: unit noise, sample density, and the structure of the target function. We then analyze the effect of unit receptive field parameters on these factors and use this analysis to propose a new learning algorithm which dynamically alters receptive field properties during learning.

1 LEARNING WITH LOCALIZED RECEPTIVE FIELDS

Locally-tuned representations are common in both biological and artificial neural networks. Several workers have analyzed the effect of receptive field size, shape, and overlap on representation accuracy: (Baldi, 1988), (Ballard, 1987), and (Hinton, 1986). This paper investigates the additional interactions introduced by the task of function learning. Previous studies which have considered learning have for the most part restricted attention to the use of the input probability distribution to determine receptive field layout (Kohonen, 1984) and (Moody and Darken, 1989). We will see that the structure of the function being learned may also be advantageously taken into account.

Function learning using radial basis functions (RBF's) is currently a popular technique (Broomhead and Lowe, 1988) and serves as an adequate framework for our discussion. Because we are interested in constraints on biological systems, we must explictly consider the effects of unit noise. The goal is to choose the layout of receptive fields so as to minimize average performance error.

Let $y = f(\mathbf{x})$ be the function the network is attempting to learn from example

$(\mathbf{x}, y)$ pairs. The network consists of N units whose locally-tuned receptive fields are distributed across the input space. The activity of the ith unit is the sum of a radial basis function $\phi_i(\mathbf{x})$ and a mean-zero noise process $\eta_i(\mathbf{x})$. A typical form for ϕ_i is an n-dimensional Gaussian parametrized by its center $\mathbf{x}_i$ and width σ_i,

$$\phi_i(\mathbf{x}) = e^{\frac{-\|\mathbf{x}_i - \mathbf{x}\|^2}{2\sigma_i^2}}. \tag{1}$$

The function $f(\mathbf{x})$ is approximated as a weighted sum of the output of N of these units:

$$F(\mathbf{x}) = \sum_{i=1}^{N} w_i[\phi_i(\mathbf{x}) + \eta_i(\mathbf{x})]. \tag{2}$$

The weights w_i are trained using the LMS (least mean square) rule, which attempts to minimize the mean squared distance between f and F over the set of training patterns p for the current layout of receptive fields. In the next section we address the additional considerations that arise when the receptive field centers and sizes are allowed to vary in addition to the weights.

2 TWO KINDS OF ERROR

To understand the effect of receptive field properties on performance we must distinguish two basic sources of error. The first we call *estimation error* and is due to the intrinsic unit noise. The other we call *approximation error* and arises from the inability of the unit activity functions to represent the target function.

2.1 ESTIMATION ERROR

The *estimation error* can be characterized by the variance in $F(\mathbf{x}) \mid \mathbf{x}$. Because of the intrinsic unit noise, repeated stimulation of a network with the same input vector $\mathbf{x}_0$ will generate a distribution of outputs $F(\mathbf{x}_0)$. If this variance is large, it can be a significant contribution to the MSE (fig. 1). Consideration of noisy units is most relevant to biological networks and analog hardware implementations of artificial units. Averaging is a powerful statistical technique for reducing the variance of a distribution. In the current context, averaging corresponds to receptive field overlap. In general, the more overlap the better the noise reduction in $F(\mathbf{x})$ (though see section 2.2). The overlap of units at $\mathbf{x}_0$ can be increased by either increasing the density of receptive field centers there, or broadening the receptive fields of units in the neighborhood.

From equation 2, $F(\mathbf{x})$ may be rewritten

$$F(\mathbf{x}) = \sum_{i=1}^{N} \phi_i(\mathbf{x}) w_i + \xi(\mathbf{x}), \tag{3}$$

where the summation term is the noise-free LMS approximation to $f(\mathbf{x})$, and the second term

$$\xi(\mathbf{x}) = \sum_{i=1}^{N} \eta_i(\mathbf{x}) w_i, \tag{4}$$

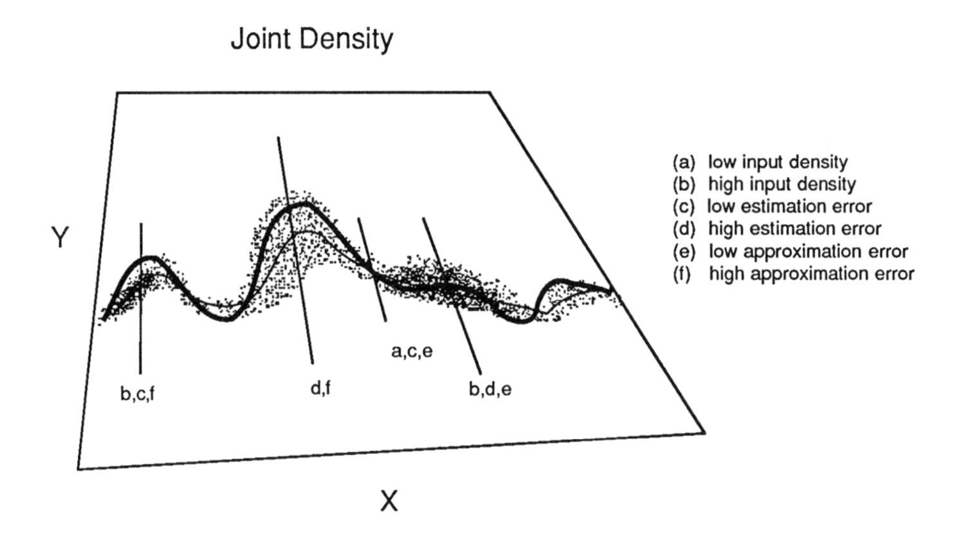

Figure 1: A. Estimation error arises from the variance of $F(\mathbf{x}) \mid \mathbf{x}$. B. Approximation error is the deviation of the mean from the desired response $(f(\mathbf{x}) - \langle F(\mathbf{x}) \rangle)^2$.

is the estimation error. Since $\xi(\mathbf{x})$ has mean zero for all $\mathbf{x}$, its variance is

$$\mathrm{Var}[\xi(\mathbf{x})] = \mathrm{E}[\xi^2(\mathbf{x})] = \mathrm{E}[\sum_{i=1}^{N} \eta_i^2(\mathbf{x}) w_i^2]. \tag{5}$$

If each unit has the same noise profile, this reduces to

$$\mathrm{Var}[\xi] = \mathrm{Var}[\eta] \sum_{i=1}^{N} w_i^2. \tag{6}$$

The dependence of estimation error ξ on the size of weights explains why increasing the density of receptive fields in the input space reduces noise in the output of the learning network. Though the *number* of units, and hence weights, that contribute to the output is increased in this manipulation, the estimation error is proportional to the sum of *squared* weights (6). The benefit achieved by making weights smaller outruns the cost of increasing their number. For example, each receptive field with weight w_i may be replaced by two copies of itself with weight $w_i/2$ and leave $F(\mathbf{x})$ unchanged. The new sum of squared weights, $\sum_{i=1}^{N} 2(\frac{w_i}{2})^2$, and hence the estimation error, is reduced by a factor of two, however.

A second strategy that may lead to a reduction in the size of weights involves *broadening* receptive fields (see section 2.2 for conditions). In general, broadening receptive fields increases the unweighted output of the network $\sum_{i=1}^{N} \phi_i(\mathbf{x})$, implying that the weights w_i must be correspondingly reduced in order that $\| F(\mathbf{x}) \|$ remain approximately constant.

These observations suggest that the effects of noise are best mitigated by allocating receptive field resources in regions of the input space where units are heavily weighted. It is interesting to note that under the assumption of additive noise, the functional form ϕ of the receptive fields themselves has no direct effect on the estimation error in $F(\mathbf{x})$. The response profiles may, however, *indirectly* affect estimation error via the weight vector, since LMS weights on receptive fields of different functional forms will generally be different.

2.2 APPROXIMATION ERROR

The second fundamental type of error, which we call *approximation error*, persists even for noise-free input units, and is due to error in the "fit" of the approximating function F to the target function f (fig. 1). Two aspects of approximation error are distinguished in the following sections.

2.2.1 MISMATCH OF FUNCTIONAL FORM

First, there may be mismatch between the specific functional form of the basis functions and that of the target function. For example, errors naturally arise when linear RBF's are used to approximate nonlinear target functions, since curves cannot be perfectly fit with straight lines. However, these errors may be made vanishingly small by increasing the density of receptive fields. For example, if linear receptive fields are trained to best fit a curved region of $f(\mathbf{x})$ with second derivative c, then the mean squared error, $\int_{-d/2}^{d/2}(\frac{c}{2}x^2 - a)^2$ has a value $O(c^2d^5)$. This type of error falls off as the 5th power of d, where d is the spacing of the receptive fields. In a similar result, (Baldi and Heilegenberg, 1988) show that approximations to both linear and quadratic functions improve exponentially fast with increasing density of Gaussian receptive fields.

2.2.2 MISMATCH OF SPATIAL SCALE

A more general source of error in fitting target functions occurs when receptive fields are either too broad or too widely spaced relative to the fine spatial structure of f. Both of these factors can act to locally limit the high frequency content of the approximation F, which may give rise to severe approximation errors.

The Nyquist (and Shannon) result on signal sampling says that the highest frequency which may be recovered from a sampled signal is half the sampling frequency. If the receptive field density is not high enough then this kind of result shows that high frequency fine structure in the function being approximated will be lost.

When the unit receptive fields are excessively wide, they can also wash out the high frequency fine structure of the function. One can think of F as a "blurred" version of the the weight vector which in turn is a sampled version of f. The blurring is greater for wide receptive fields. The density and width should be chosen to match their frequency transfer characteristics and best approximate the function. For one-dimensional Gaussian receptive fields of width σ, we choose the receptive field spacing d to be

$$d = \frac{\pi}{2}\sigma. \qquad (7)$$

A density that satisfies this type of condition will be referred to in the next section as a "frequency-matched" density.

3 A RECEPTIVE FIELD DESIGN STRATEGY

In this section we describe an adaptive learning strategy based on the results above. Figure 2 shows the results of an experimental implementation of this procedure.

It is possible to empirically measure the magnitude of the two sources of error analyzed above. Since we wish to minimize the expected performance error for the network as a whole, we weight our measurements of each type of error at each $\mathbf{x}$ by the input probability $\rho(\mathbf{x})$. Errors in high density regions count more. Small magnitude errors may be important in high probability regions while even large errors may be neglected in low probability regions. The learning algorithm adjusts the layout of receptive fields to adjust to each form of error in turn. The steps involved follow.

1. Uniformly distribute broad receptive fields at frequency-matched density throughout regions of the input space that contain data. (In our 1-d example, data, and hence receptive fields, are present across the entire domain.)
2. Train the network weights to an LMS solution with fixed receptive fields. Using the trained network, accrue approximation errors across the input space.
3. Where the approximation error exceeds a threshold τ anywhere within a unit's receptive field, split the receptive field into two subfields that are as small as possible while still locally maintaining frequency-matched density. (This depends on receptive field profile). Repeat steps 2 and 3 until the approximation error is under threshold across entire input space. We now have a layout where receptive field width and density are locally matched to the spatial frequency content of the target function, and approximation error is small and uniform across the input space. Note that since errors accrue according to $\rho(\mathbf{x})$, we have preferentially allocated resources (through splitting) in regions with both high error and high input probability.
4. Using the current network, measure and accrue estimation errors across the input space.
5. Where the estimation error exceeds τ anywhere within a unit's receptive field, replace the receptive field by two of the same size, adding a small random pertubation to each center. Repeat from 4 until estimation error is below threshold across entire input space. We now have a layout where receptive field *density* is highest where the effects of noise were most severe, such that estimation error is now small and uniform across the input space. Once again, we have preferentially allocated resources in regions with both high error and high input probability.

Figure 2 illustrates this process for a noisy, one-dimensionsal learning problem. Each frame shows the estimation error, the approximation error, the target func-

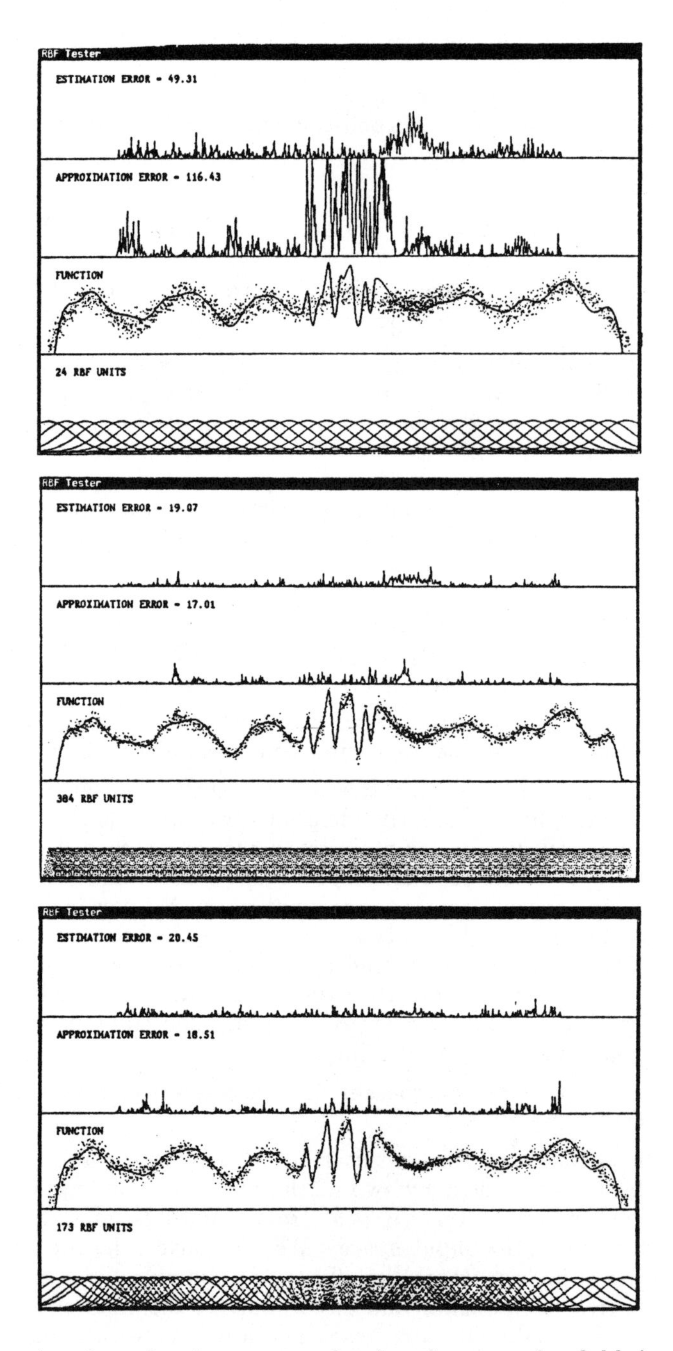

Figure 2: Results of an adaptive strategy for choosing receptive field size and density. See text for details.

tion and network output, and the unit response functions. In the top frame 24 units with broad, noisy receptive fields have been LMS-trained to fit the target function. Estimation error is visible across the entire domain, though it is concentrated in the small region just to the right of center where the input probability is peaked. Approximation error is concentrated in the central region which contains high spatial frequencies, with minor secondary peaks in other regions, including the region of high input probability.

In the second frame, the receptive field width was uniformly decreased and density was uniformly increased to the point where MSE fell below τ; 384 units were required. In the third frame, the adaptive strategy presented above was used to allocate units and choose widths. Fewer than half as many units (173) were needed in this example to achieve the same MSE as in the second frame. In higher dimensions, and with sparser data, this kind of recursive splitting and doubling strategy should be even more important.

4 CONCLUSIONS

In this paper we have shown how receptive field size, shape, density, and noise characteristics interact with the frequency content of target functions and input probability density to contribute to both estimation and approximation errors during supervised function learning. Based on these interrelationships, a simple, adaptive, error-driven strategy for laying out receptive fields was demonstrated that makes efficient use of unit resources in the attempt to minimize mean squared performance error.

An improved understanding of the role of receptive field structure in learning may in the future help in the interpretation of patterns of coarse-coding seen in many biological sensory and motor systems.

References

Baldi, P. & Heiligengerg, W. How sensory maps could enhance resolution through ordered arrangements of broadly tuned receptors. *Biol. Cybern.*, 1988, *59*, 313-318.

Ballard, D.H. Interpolation coding: a representation for numbers in neural models. *Biol. Cybern.*, 1987, *57*, 389-402.

Broomhead, D.S. & Lowe, D. Multivariable functional interpolation and adaptive networks. *Complex Systems*, 1988, *2*, 321-355.

Hinton, G.E. (1986) Distributed representations. In *Parallel distributed processing: explorations in the microstructure of cognition, vol. 1*, D.E. Rumelhart, J.L. McClelland, (Eds.), Bradford, Cambridge.

Kohonen, T. *Self organization and associative memory.* Springer-Verlag: Berlin, 1984.

MacKay, D. Hyperacuity and coarse-coding. In preparation.

Moody, J. & Darken, C. Fast learning in networks of locally-tuned processing units. *Neural Computation*, 1989, *1*, 281-294.

Part XII

Learning Systems

A competitive modular connectionist architecture

Robert A. Jacobs and **Michael I. Jordan**
Department of Brain & Cognitive Sciences
Massachusetts Institute of Technology
Cambridge, MA 02139

Abstract

We describe a multi–network, or modular, connectionist architecture that captures that fact that many tasks have structure at a level of granularity intermediate to that assumed by local and global function approximation schemes. The main innovation of the architecture is that it combines associative and competitive learning in order to learn task decompositions. A task decomposition is discovered by forcing the networks comprising the architecture to compete to learn the training patterns. As a result of the competition, different networks learn different training patterns and, thus, learn to partition the input space. The performance of the architecture on a "what" and "where" vision task and on a multi–payload robotics task are presented.

1 INTRODUCTION

A dichotomy has arisen in recent years in the literature on nonlinear network learning rules between *local* approximation of functions and *global* approximation of functions. Local approximation, as exemplified by lookup tables, nearest–neighbor algorithms, and networks with units having local receptive fields, has the advantage of requiring relatively few learning trials and tends to yield interpretable representations. Global approximation, as exemplified by polynomial regression and fully–connected networks with sigmoidal units, has the advantage of requiring less storage capacity than local approximators and may yield superior generalization.

In this paper, we report a multi–network, or modular, connectionist architecture that captures the fact that many tasks have structure at a level of granularity intermediate to that assumed by local and global approximation schemes. It does so

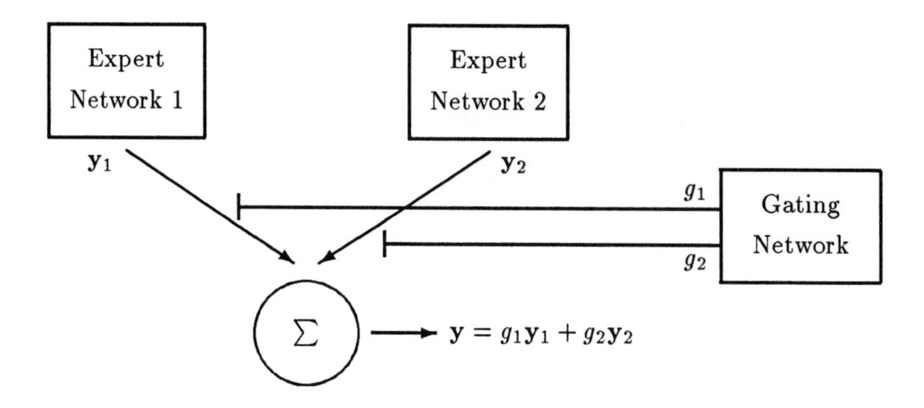

Figure 1: A Modular Connectionist Architecture

by combining the desirable features of the approaches embodied by these disparate approximation schemes. In particular, it uses different networks to learn training patterns from different regions of the input space. Each network can itself be a local or global approximator for a particular region of the space.

2 A MODULAR CONNECTIONIST ARCHITECTURE

The technical issues addressed by the modular architecture are twofold: (a) detecting that different training patterns belong to different tasks and (b) allocating different networks to learn the different tasks. These issues are addressed in the architecture by combining aspects of competitive learning and associative learning. Specifically, task decompositions are encouraged by enforcing a competition among the networks comprising the architecture. As a result of the competition, different networks learn different training patterns and, thus, learn to compute different functions. The architecture was first presented in Jacobs, Jordan, Nowlan, and Hinton (1991), and combines earlier work on learning task decompositions in a modular architecture by Jacobs, Jordan, and Barto (1991) with the mixture models view of competitive learning advocated by Nowlan (1990) and Hinton and Nowlan (1990). The architecture is also presented elsewhere in this volume by Nowlan and Hinton (1991).

The architecture, which is illustrated in Figure 1, consists of two types of networks: *expert networks* and a *gating network*. The expert networks compete to learn the training patterns and the gating network mediates this competition. Whereas the expert networks have an arbitrary connectivity, the gating network is restricted to have as many output units as there are expert networks, and the activations of these output units must be nonnegative and sum to one. To meet these constraints, we use the "softmax" activation function (Bridle, 1989); specifically, the activation of the ith output unit of the gating network, denoted g_i, is

$$g_i = \frac{e^{s_i}}{\sum_{j=1}^{n} e^{s_j}} \tag{1}$$

where s_i denotes the weighted sum of unit i's inputs and n denotes the number of expert networks. The output of the entire architecture, denoted $\mathbf{y}$, is

$$\mathbf{y} = \sum_{i=1}^{n} g_i \mathbf{y}_i \tag{2}$$

where $\mathbf{y}_i$ denotes the output of the ith expert network. During training, the weights of the expert and gating networks are adjusted simultaneously using the backpropagation algorithm (le Cun, 1985; Parker, 1985; Rumelhart, Hinton, and Williams, 1986; Werbos, 1974) so as to maximize the function

$$\ln L = \ln \sum_{i=1}^{n} g_i e^{-\frac{1}{2\sigma_i^2}\|\mathbf{y}^* - \mathbf{y}_i\|^2} \tag{3}$$

where $\mathbf{y}^*$ denotes the target vector and σ_i^2 denotes a scaling parameter associated with the ith expert network.

This architecture is best understood if it is given a probabilistic interpretation as an "associative gaussian mixture model" (see Duda and Hart (1973) and McLachlan and Basford (1988) for a discussion of non–associative gaussian mixture models). Under this interpretation, the training patterns are assumed to be generated by a number of different probabilistic rules. At each time step, a rule is selected with probability g_i and a training pattern is generated by the rule. Each rule is characterized by a statistical model of the form $\mathbf{y}^* = f_i(\mathbf{x}) + \epsilon_i$, where $f_i(\mathbf{x})$ is a fixed nonlinear function of the input vector, denoted $\mathbf{x}$, and ϵ_i is a random variable. If it is assumed that ϵ_i is gaussian with covariance matrix $\sigma_i^2 \mathbf{I}$, then the residual vector $\mathbf{y}^* - \mathbf{y}_i$ is also gaussian and the cost function in Equation 3 is the log likelihood of generating a particular target vector $\mathbf{y}^*$.

The goal of the architecture is to model the distribution of training patterns. This is achieved by gradient ascent in the log likelihood function. To compute the gradient consider first the partial derivative of the log likelihood with respect to the weighted sum s_i at the ith output unit of the gating network. Using the chain rule and Equation 1 we find that this derivative is given by:

$$\frac{\partial \ln L}{\partial s_i} = g(i \mid \mathbf{x}, \mathbf{y}^*) - g_i \tag{4}$$

where $g(i \mid \mathbf{x}, \mathbf{y}^*)$ is the a posteriori probability that the ith expert network generates the target vector:

$$g(i \mid \mathbf{x}, \mathbf{y}^*) = \frac{g_i e^{-\frac{1}{2\sigma_i^2}\|\mathbf{y}^* - \mathbf{y}_i\|^2}}{\sum_{j=1}^{n} g_j e^{-\frac{1}{2\sigma_j^2}\|\mathbf{y}^* - \mathbf{y}_j\|^2}}. \tag{5}$$

Thus the weights of the gating network are adjusted so that the network's outputs—the a priori probabilities g_i—move toward the a posteriori probabilities.

Consider now the gradient of the log likelihood with respect to the output of the ith expert network. Differentiation of $\ln L$ with respect to $\mathbf{y}_i$ yields:

$$\frac{\partial \ln L}{\partial \mathbf{y}_i} = g(i \mid \mathbf{x}, \mathbf{y}^*) \frac{(\mathbf{y}^* - \mathbf{y}_i)}{\sigma_i^2}. \tag{6}$$

These derivatives involve the error term $\mathbf{y}^* - \mathbf{y}_i$ weighted by the a posteriori probability associated with the ith expert network. Thus the weights of the network are adjusted to correct the error between the output of the ith network and the global target vector, but only in proportion to the a posteriori probability. For each input vector, typically only one expert network has a large a posteriori probability. Consequently, only one expert network tends to learn each training pattern. In general, different expert networks learn different training patterns and, thus, learn to compute different functions.

3 THE WHAT AND WHERE VISION TASKS

We applied the modular connectionist architecture to the object recognition task ("what" task) and spatial localization task ("where" task) studied by Rueckl, Cave, and Kosslyn (1989).[1] At each time step of the simulation, one of nine objects is placed at one of nine locations on a simulated retina. The "what" task is to identify the object; the "where" task is to identify its location.

The modular architecture is shown in Figure 2. It consists of three expert networks and a gating network. The expert networks receive the retinal image and a task specifier indicating whether the architecture should perform the "what" task or the "where" task at the current time step. The gating network receives the task specifier. The first expert network contains 36 hidden units, the second expert network contains 18 hidden units, and the third expert network doesn't contain any hidden units (i.e., it is a single-layer network).

There are at least three ways that this modular architecture might successfully learn the "what" and "where" tasks. One of the multi-layer expert networks could learn to perform both tasks. Because this solution doesn't show any task decomposition, we consider it to be unsatisfactory. A second possibility is that one of the multi-layer expert networks could learn the "what" task, and the other multi-layer expert network could learn the "where" task. Although this solution exhibits task decomposition, a shortcoming of this solution is apparent when it is noted that, using the retinal images designed by Rueckl et al. (1989), the "where" task is linearly separable. This means that the structure of the single-layer expert network most closely matches the "where" task. Consequently, a third and possibly best solution would be one in which one of the multi-layer expert networks learns the "what" task and the single-layer expert network learns the "where" task. This solution would not only show task decomposition but also the appropriate allocation of tasks to expert networks. Simulation results show that the third possible solution is the one that

[1]For a detailed presentation of the application of an earlier modular architecture to the "what" and "where" tasks see Jacobs, Jordan, and Barto (1991).

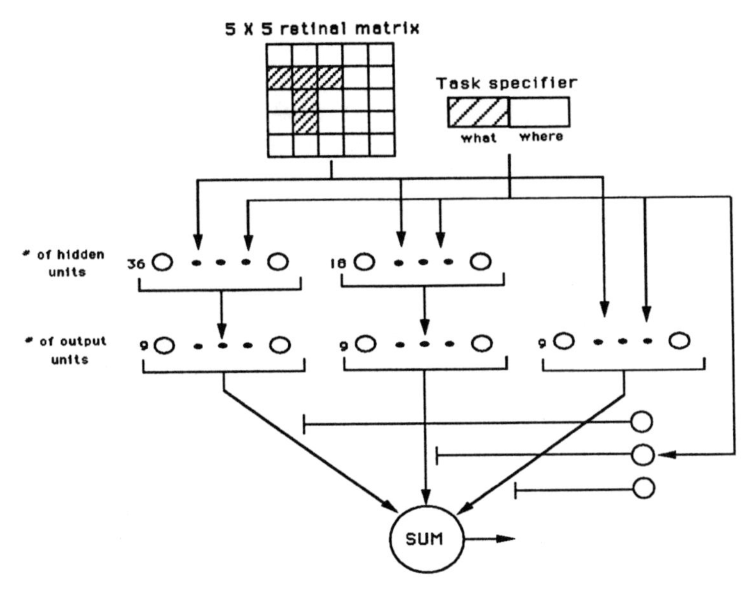

Figure 2: The Modular Architecture Applied to the What and Where Tasks

is always achieved. These results provide evidence that the modular architecture is capable of allocating a different network to different tasks and of allocating a network with an appropriate structure to each task.

4 THE MULTI–PAYLOAD ROBOTICS TASK

When designing a compensator for a nonlinear plant, control engineers frequently find it impossible or impractical to design a continuous control law that is useful in all the relevant regions of a plant's parameter space. Typically, the solution to this problem is to use *gain scheduling*; if it is known how the dynamics of a plant change with its operating conditions, then it may be possible to design a piecewise controller that employs different control laws when the plant is operating under different conditions. From our viewpoint, gain scheduling is an attractive solution because it involves task decomposition. It circumvents the problem of determining a fixed global model of the plant dynamics. Instead, the dynamics are approximated using local models that vary with the plant's operating conditions.

Task decomposition is a useful strategy not only when the control law is designed, but also when it is learned. We suggest that an ideal controller is one that, like gain scheduled controllers, uses local models of the plant dynamics, and like learning controllers, learns useful control laws despite uncertainties about the plant or environment. Because the modular connectionist architecture is capable of both task decomposition and learning, it may be useful in achieving both of these desiderata.

We applied the modular architecture to the problem of learning a feedforward con-

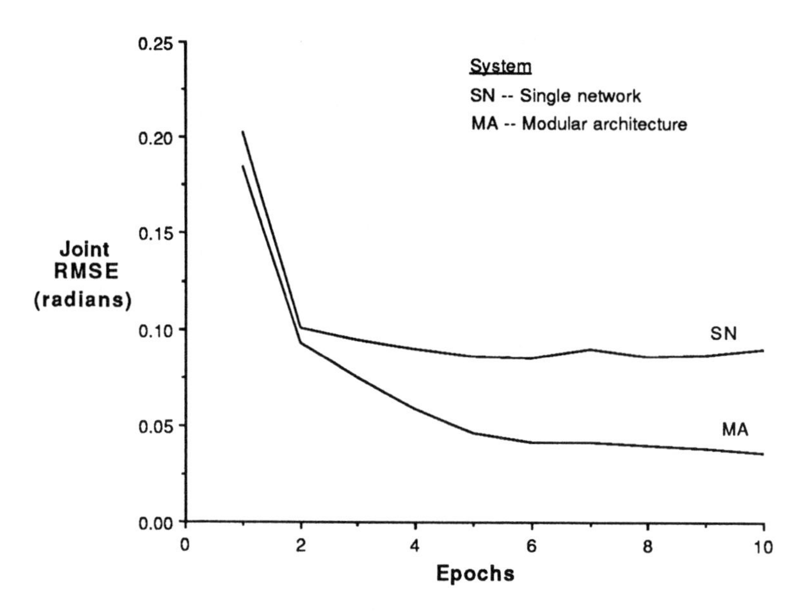

Figure 3: Learning Curves for the Multi–Payload Robotics Task

troller for a robotic arm in a multiple payload task.[2] The task is to drive a simulated two–joint robot arm with a variety of payloads, each of a different mass, along a desired trajectory. The architecture is given the payload's identity (e.g., payload *A* or payload *B*) but not its mass.

The modular architecture consisted of six expert networks and a gating network. The expert networks received as input the state of the robot arm and the desired acceleration. The gating network received the payload identity. We also trained a single multi–layer network to perform this task. The learning curves for the two systems are shown in Figure 3. The horizontal axis gives the training time in epochs. The vertical axis gives the joint root mean square error in radians. Clearly, the modular architecture learned significantly faster than the single network. Furthermore, the modular architecture learned to perform the task by allocating different expert networks to control the arm with payloads from different mass categories (e.g., light, medium, or heavy payloads).

Acknowledgements

This research was supported by a postdoctoral fellowship provided to the first author from the McDonnell–Pew Program in Cognitive Neuroscience, by funding provided to the second author from the Siemens Corporation, and by NSF grant IRI-9013991 awarded to both authors.

[2]For a detailed presentation of the application of the modular architecture to the multiple payload robotics task see Jacobs and Jordan (1991).

References

Bridle, J. (1989) Probabilistic interpretation of feedforward classification network outputs, with relationships to statistical pattern recognition. In F. Fogelman-Soulie & J. Hérault (Eds.), *Neuro-computing: Algorithms, Architectures, and Applications.* New York: Springer-Verlag.

Duda, R.O. & Hart, P.E. (1973) *Pattern Classification and Scene Analysis.* New York: John Wiley & Sons.

Hinton, G.E. & Nowlan, S.J. (1990) The bootstrap Widrow-Hoff rule as a cluster-formation algorithm. *Neural Computation*, 2, 355-362.

Jacobs, R.A. & Jordan, M.I. (1991) Learning piecewise control strategies in a modular connectionist architecture. Submitted to *IEEE Transactions on Neural Networks.*

Jacobs, R.A., Jordan, M.I., & Barto, A.G. (1991) Task decomposition through competition in a modular connectionist architecture: The what and where vision tasks. *Cognitive Science*, in press.

Jacobs, R.A., Jordan, M.I., Nowlan, S.J., & Hinton, G.E. (1991) Adaptive mixtures of local experts. *Neural Computation*, in press.

le Cun, Y. (1985) Une procédure d'apprentissage pour réseau a seuil asymétrique [A learning procedure for asymmetric threshold network]. *Proceedings of Cognitiva*, 85, 599-604.

McLachlan, G.J. & Basford, K.E. (1988) *Mixture Models: Inference and Applications to Clustering.* New York: Marcel Dekker.

Nowlan, S.J. (1990) Maximum likelihood competitive learning. In D.S. Touretzky (Ed.), *Advances in Neural Information Processing Systems 2.* San Mateo, CA: Morgan Kaufmann Publishers.

Nowlan, S.J. & Hinton, G.E. (1991) Evaluation of an associative mixture architecture on a vowel recognition task. In R.P. Lippmann, J. Moody, & D.S. Touretzky (Eds.), *Advances in Neural Information Processing Systems 3.* San Mateo, CA: Morgan Kaufmann Publishers.

Parker, D.B. (1985) Learning logic. Technical Report TR-47, Massachusetts Institute of Technology, Cambridge, MA.

Rueckl, J.G., Cave, K.R., & Kosslyn, S.M. (1989) Why are "what" and "where" processed by separate cortical visual systems? A computational investigation. *Journal of Cognitive Neuroscience*, 1, 171-186.

Rumelhart, D.E., Hinton, G.E., & Williams, R.J. (1986) Learning internal representations by error propagation. In D.E. Rumelhart, J.L. McClelland, & the PDP Research Group, *Parallel Distributed Processing: Explorations in the Microstructure of Cognition. Volume 1: Foundations.* Cambridge, MA: The MIT Press.

Werbos, P.J. (1974) *Beyond Regression: New Tools for Prediction and Analysis in the Behavioral Sciences.* Ph.D. thesis, Harvard University, Cambridge, MA.

Evaluation of Adaptive Mixtures of Competing Experts

Steven J. Nowlan and **Geoffrey E. Hinton**
Computer Science Dept.
University of Toronto
Toronto, ONT M5S 1A4

Abstract

We compare the performance of the modular architecture, composed of competing expert networks, suggested by Jacobs, Jordan, Nowlan and Hinton (1991) to the performance of a single back-propagation network on a complex, but low-dimensional, vowel recognition task. Simulations reveal that this system is capable of uncovering interesting decompositions in a complex task. The type of decomposition is strongly influenced by the nature of the input to the gating network that decides which expert to use for each case. The modular architecture also exhibits consistently better generalization on many variations of the task.

1 Introduction

If back-propagation is used to train a single, multilayer network to perform different subtasks on different occasions, there will generally be strong interference effects which lead to slow learning and poor generalization. If we know in advance that a set of training cases may be naturally divided into subsets that correspond to distinct subtasks, interference can be reduced by using a system (see Fig. 1) composed of several different "expert" networks plus a gating network that decides which of the experts should be used for each training case.

Systems of this type have been suggested by a number of authors (Hampshire and Waibel, 1989; Jacobs, Jordan and Barto, 1990; Jacobs et al., 1991) (see also the paper by Jacobs and Jordan in this volume (1991)). Jacobs, Jordan, Nowlan and Hinton (1991) show that this system can be trained by performing gradient descent

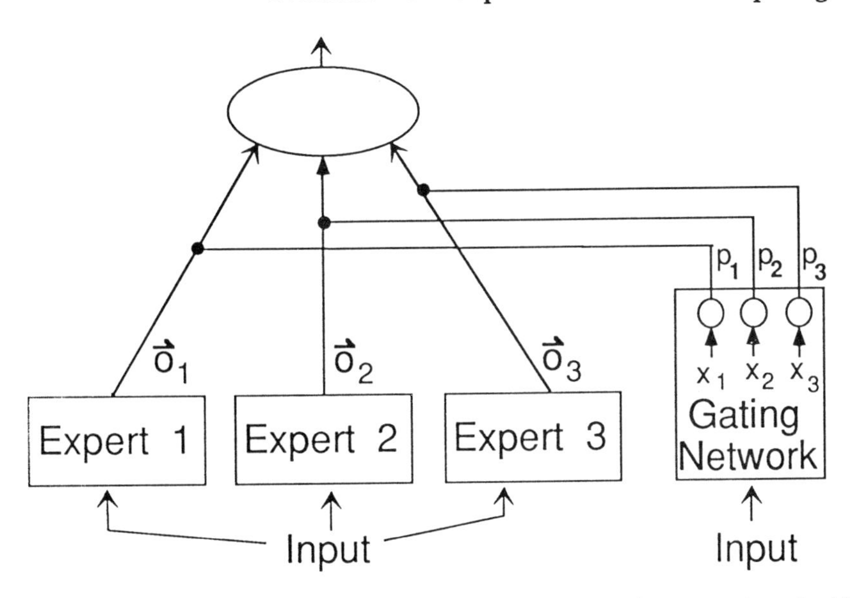

Figure 1: A system of expert and gating networks. Each expert is a feedforward network and all experts receive the same input and have the same number of outputs. The gating network is also feedforward and may receive a different input than the expert networks. It has normalized outputs $p_j = \exp(x_j)/\sum_i \exp(x_i)$, where x_j is the total weighted input received by output unit j of the gating network. p_j can be viewed as the probability of selecting expert j for a particular case.

in the following error function:

$$E^c = -\log \sum_i p_i^c e^{-\|\vec{d}^c - \vec{o}_i^c\|^2 / 2\sigma^2} \quad (1)$$

where E^c is the error on training case c, p_i^c is the output of the gating network for expert i, $\vec{d}^c$ is the desired output vector and $\vec{o}_i^c$ is the output vector of expert i, and σ is constant.

The error defined by Equation 1 is simply the negative log probability of generating the desired output vector under a mixture of gaussians model of the probability distribution of possible output vectors given the current input. The output vector of each expert specifies the mean of a multidimensional gaussian distribution. These means are a function of the inputs to the experts. The outputs of the gating network specify the mixing proportions of the experts, so these too are determined by the current input.

During learning, the gradient descent in E has two effects. It raises the mixing proportion of experts that do better than average in predicting the desired output vector for a particular case, and it also makes each expert better at predicting the desired output for those cases for which it has a high mixing proportion. The result of these two effects is that, after learning, the gating network nearly always assigns a mixing proportion near 1 to one expert on each case. So towards the end of the learning, each expert can focus on modelling the cases it is good at without interference from the cases for which it has a negligible mixing proportion.

In this paper, we compare mixtures of experts to single back-propagation networks on a vowel recognition task. We demonstrate that the mixtures are better at fitting the training data and better at generalizing than comparable single back-propagation networks.

2 Data and Experimental Procedures

The data used in these experiments consisted of the frequencies of the first and second formants for 10 vowels from 75 speakers (32 Males, 28 Females, and 15 Children) (Peterson and Barney, 1952).[1] The vowels, which were uttered in an **hVd** context, were {*heed, hid, head, had, hud, hod, hawed, hood, who'd, heard*}. The word list was repeated twice by each speaker, with the words in a different random order for each presentation. The resulting spectrograms were hand segmented and the frequencies of the formants extracted from the middle portion of the vowel.

The simulations were performed using a conjugate gradient technique, with one weight change after each pass through the training set. For the back-propagation experiments, each simulation was initialised randomly with weight values in the range $[-0.5, 0.5]$. For the mixture systems, the last layer of weights in the gating network was always initialised to 0 so that all experts initially had equal *a priori* selection probabilities, $p_{i,k}$, while all other weights in the gating and expert networks were initialized randomly with values in the range $[-0.5, 0.5]$ to break symmetry. The value of σ used was 0.25 for all of the mixture simulations. In all cases, the input formant values were linearly scaled by dividing them by 1000, so the first formant was in the range $(0, 1.5)$ and the second was in the range $(0, 4)$.

Two sets of experiments were performed: one in which the performance of different systems on the training data was compared and a second in which the ability of different systems to generalize was compared.

Five different types of input were used in each set of experiments:

1. Frequencies of first and second formants only (Form.).
2. Form. plus a localist encoding of the speaker identity (Form. + Speaker ID).
3. Form. plus a localist encoding of whether the speaker was a male, female, or child (Form. + MFC).
4. Form. plus the minimum and maximum frequency for the first and second formant (as real values) over all samples from the speaker (Form. + Range).
5. Form. + MFC + Range.

For the simulations in which a single back-propagation network was used the network received the entire set of input values. However, for the mixture systems the expert networks saw *only* the formant frequencies, while the gating network saw everything *but* the formant frequencies (except of course when the input consisted only of the formant frequencies).

[1]Obtained, with thanks, from Ray Watrous, who originally obtained the data from Ann Syrdal at AT&T Bell Labs.

Type of Input	# Experts	# Hid per Expert	# Hid Gating
Form.	20	3 – 5	10
Form. + Speaker ID	10	25	0
Form. + MFC	10	25	0
Form. + MFC + Range	10	25	5
Form. + Range	10	25	5

Table 1: Summary of mixture architecture used with each type of input.

Type of Input	Mixture Error %	BP Error %	Sig.(p)
Formants only	13.9 ± 0.9	21.8 ± 0.6	$\gg 0.9999$
Form. + Speaker ID	4.6 ± 0.7	6.2 ± 0.6	> 0.97
Form. + MFC	13.0 ± 0.4	15.4 ± 0.3	$\gg 0.9999$
Form. + MFC + Range	5.6 ± 0.6	13.1 ± 1.0	$\gg 0.9999$
Form. + Range	11.6 ± 0.9	13.5 ± 0.4	> 0.998

Table 2: Performance comparison of associative mixture systems and single back-propagation networks on vowel classification task. Results reported are based on an average over 25 simulations for each back-propagation network or mixture system.

The BP networks used in the single network simulations contained one layer of hidden units.[2] In the mixture systems, the expert networks also contained one layer of hidden units although the number of hidden units in each expert varied. The gating network in some cases contained hidden units, while in other cases it did not (see Table 1). Further details of the simulations may be found in (Nowlan, 1991).

3 Results of Performance Studies

In the set of *performance* experiments, each system was trained with the entire set of 1494 tokens until the magnitude of the gradient vector was $< 10^{-8}$. The error rate (as percent of total cases) was evaluated on the *training* data (generalization studies are described in the next section). The very high degree of class overlap in this task makes it extremely difficult to find good solutions with a gradient descent procedure and this is reflected by the far from optimal average performance of all systems on the training data (see Table 2). For purposes of comparison, the best performance ever obtained on this vowel data using *speaker dependant* classification methods is about 2.5% (Gerstman, 1968; Watrous, 1990).

Table 2 reveals that in every case the mixture system performs significantly better[3] than a single network given the same input. The most striking, and interesting,

[2]The number of hidden units was selected by performing a number of initial simulations with different numbers of hidden units for each network and choosing the smallest number which gave near optimal performance. These numbers were 50, 150, 60, 150, and 80 respectively for the five types of input listed above.

[3]Based on a t-test with 48 degrees of freedom.

Spec. #	% Male	% Female	% Child	% Total
0	0.0	0.0	6.7	1.3
4	3.1	3.6	0.0	2.7
5	84.4	17.8	0.0	42.7
7	9.4	7.1	6.7	8.0
8	3.1	42.9	0.0	17.3
9	0.0	28.6	86.7	28.0

Table 3: Speaker decomposition in terms of Male, Female and Child categories for a mixture with speaker identity as input to the gating network.

result in Table 2 is contained in the fourth row of the table. While the associative mixture architecture is able to combine the two separate cues of MFC categories and speaker formant range quite effectively, the single back-propagation network fails to do so. The combination of these two different cues in the associative mixture system was obtained by a hierarchical training procedure in which three different experts were first created using the MFC cue alone, and copies of these networks were further specialized when the formant range cue was added to the input received by the gating network (see (Nowlan, 1990; Nowlan, 1991) for details). Since the single back-propagation network is much less modular than the associative mixture system, it is difficult to implement such a hierarchical training procedure in the single network case. (A variety of techniques were explored and details may again be found in (Nowlan, 1991).)

Another interesting aspect of the mixture systems, not revealed in Table 2, is the manner in which the training cases were divided among the different expert networks. Once the network was trained, the training cases were clustered by assigning each case to the expert that was selected most strongly by the gating network.

The mixture which used only the formant frequencies as input to both the gating and expert networks tended to cluster training cases according to the position of the tongue hump when the vowel is uttered. In all simulations, the four *front* vowels were always clustered together and handled by a single expert. The *low back* and *high back* vowels also tended to be grouped together, but each of these groups was divided among several experts and not always in exactly the same way.

The mixture which received speaker identity as well as formant frequencies as input tended to group speakers roughly according to the categories male, female, and child. A typical grouping of speakers by the mixture is shown in Table 3.

4 Results of Generalization Studies

In the set of *generalization* experiments, for all but the input which contained the speaker identity, each system was trained on data from 65 speakers until the magnitude of the gradient vector was $< 10^{-4}$. The performance was then tested on the data from the 10 speakers not in the training set. Twenty different test sets were created by leaving out different speakers for each, and results are an average over one simulation with each of the test sets. Each test set consisted of 4 male, 3

Type of Input	Mixture Error %	BP Error %	Sig.(p)
Formants only	15.1 ± 0.9	23.3 ± 1.2	$\gg 0.9999$
Form. + Speaker ID	6.4 ± 1.3	–	$\gg 0.9999$
Form. + MFC	13.5 ± 0.6	18.4 ± 1.1	$\gg 0.9999$
Form. + MFC + Range	6.2 ± 0.9	16.1 ± 1.0	$\gg 0.9999$
Form. + Range	12.8 ± 0.9	16.2 ± 0.8	> 0.9999

Table 4: Generalization comparison of associative mixture systems and single back-propagation networks on vowel classification task. Results reported are based on an average over 20 simulations for each back-propagation network or mixture system.

female and 3 child speakers.

The generalization tests for the mixture in which speaker identity was part of the input used a different testing strategy. In this case, the training set consisted of 70 speakers and the testing set contained the remaining 5 speakers (2 male, 2 female, 1 child). Again, results are averaged over 20 different testing sets. After the mixture was trained, an expert was selected for each test speaker using one utterance of each of the first 3 vowels, and the performance of the selected expert was tested on the remaining 17 utterances of that speaker. No generalization results are reported for the single back-propagation network which received the speaker identity as well as the first and second formant values, since there is no straightforward way to perform rapid speaker adaptation with this architecture. (See Watrous (Watrous, 1990) for some approaches to speaker adaptation in single networks.) The percentage of misclassifications on the *test* set for the mixture systems and corresponding single back-propagation networks are summarized in Table 4, and in all cases the mixture system generalizes significantly better[4] than a single network.

The relatively poor generalization performance of the single back-propagation networks is not due to overfitting on the training data because the single back-propagation networks perform worse on the *training* data than the mixture systems on the *test* data. Also, the associative mixture systems initially contained even more parameters than the corresponding back-propagation networks. (The associative mixture which received formant range data for gating input initially contained almost 3600 parameters, while the corresponding single back-propagation network contained only slightly more than 1200 parameters.) Part of the explanation for the good generalization performance of the mixtures is the pruning of excess parameters as the system is trained. The number of effective parameters in the final mixture is very often less than half the number in the original system, because a large number of experts have negligible mixing proportions in the final mixture.

5 Discussion

The mixture systems outperform single back-propagation networks which receive the same input, and show much better generalization properties when forced to deal with relatively small training sets. In addition, the mixtures can easily be

[4]Based on a t-test with 38 degrees of freedom.

refined hierarchically by learning a few experts and then making several copies of each and adding additional contextual input to the gating network.

The best performance for either single networks or mixture systems is obtained by including the speaker identity as part of the input. When given such input, the mixture systems are capable of discovering speaker categories which give levels of classification performance close to those obtained by speaker dependent classification schemes. Good performance can also be obtained on novel speakers by determining which existing speaker category the new speaker is most similar to (using a small number of labelled utterances). If, instead, the speaker is represented in terms of features such as male, female, child, and formant range, the mixtures also exhibit good generalization to novel speakers described in terms of these features.

Acknowledgements

This research was supported by grants from the Natural Sciences and Engineering Research Council, the Ontario Information Technology Research Center, and Apple Computer Inc. Hinton is the Noranda fellow of the Canadian Institute for Advanced Research.

References

Gerstman, L. J. (1968). Classification of self-normalized vowels. *IEEE Trans. on Audio and Electroacoustics*, AU-16(1):78–80.

Hampshire, J. and Waibel, A. (1989). The Meta-Pi network: Building distributed knowledge representations for robust pattern recognition. Technical Report CMU-CS-89-166, Carnegie-Mellon, Pittsburgh, PA.

Jacobs, R. A. and Jordan, M. I. (1991). A competitive modular connectionist architecture. In Touretzky, D. S., editor, *Neural Information Processing Systems 3*. Morgan Kauffman, San Mateo, CA.

Jacobs, R. A., Jordan, M. I., and Barto, A. G. (1990). Task decomposition through competition in a modular connectionist architecture: The what and where vision tasks. *Cognitive Science*. In Press.

Jacobs, R. A., Jordan, M. I., Nowlan, S. J., and Hinton, G. E. (1991). Adaptive mixtures of local experts. *Neural Computation*, 3(1).

Nowlan, S. J. (1990). Competing experts: An experimental investigation of associative mixture models. Technical Report CRG-TR-90-5, Department of Computer Science, University of Toronto.

Nowlan, S. J. (1991). *Soft Competitive Adaptation: Neural Network Learning Algorithms based on Fitting Statistical Mixtures.* PhD thesis, School of Computer Science, Carnegie Mellon University, Pittsburgh, PA.

Peterson, G. E. and Barney, H. L. (1952). Control methods used in a study of vowels. *The Journal of the Acoustical Society of America*, 24:175–184.

Watrous, R. L. (1990). Speaker normalization and adaptation using second order connectionist networks. Technical Report CRG-TR-90-6, University of Toronto.

A Framework for the Cooperation of Learning Algorithms

Léon Bottou **Patrick Gallinari**

Laboratoire de Recherche en Informatique
Université de Paris XI
91405 Orsay Cedex
France

Abstract

We introduce a framework for training architectures composed of several modules. This framework, which uses a statistical formulation of learning systems, provides a unique formalism for describing many classical connectionist algorithms as well as complex systems where several algorithms interact. It allows to design hybrid systems which combine the advantages of connectionist algorithms as well as other learning algorithms.

1 INTRODUCTION

Many recent achievements in the connectionist area have been carried out by designing systems where different algorithms interact. For example (Bourlard & Morgan, 1991) have mixed a Multi-Layer Perceptron (MLP) with a Dynamic Programming algorithm. Another impressive application (Le Cun, Boser & al., 1990) uses a very complex multi-layer architecture, followed by some statistical decision process. Also, in speech or image recognition systems, input signals are sequentially processed through different modules. Modular systems are the most promising way to achieve such complex tasks. They can be built using simple components and therefore can be easily modified or extended, also they allow to incorporate into their architecture some *structural a priori knowledge* about the task decomposition. Of course, this is also true for connectionism, and important progresses in this field could be achieved if we were able to train multi-modules architectures.

In this paper, we introduce a formal framework for designing and training such cooperative systems. It provides a unique formalism for describing both the different modules and the global system. We show that it is suitable for many connectionist algorithms, which allows to make them cooperate in an optimal way according to the goal of learning. It also allows to train hybrid systems where connectionist and classical algorithms interact. Our formulation is based on a probabilistic approach to the problem of learning which is described in section 2. One of the advantages of this approach is to provide a formal definition of the *goal of learning*. In section 3, we introduce modular architectures where each module can be described using this framework, and we derive explicit formulas for training the global system through a stochastic gradient descent algorithm. Section 4 is devoted to examples, including the case of hybrid algorithms combining MLP and Learning Vector Quantization (Bollivier, Gallinari & Thiria, 1990).

2 LEARNING SYSTEMS

The probabilistic formulation of the problem of learning has been extensively studied for three decades (Tsypkin 1971), and applied to control, pattern recognition and adaptive signal processing. We recall here the main ideas and refer to (Tsypkin 1971) for a detailed presentation.

2.1 EXPECTED COST

Let $\mathbf{x}$ be an instance of the concept to learn. In the case of a pattern recognition problem for example, $\mathbf{x}$ would be a pair (pattern, class). The concept is mathematically defined by an unknown probability density function $p(\mathbf{x})$ which measures the likelihood of instance $\mathbf{x}$.

We shall use a system parameterized by $\mathbf{w}$ to perform some task that depends on $p(\mathbf{x})$. Given an example $\mathbf{x}$, we can define a *local cost*, $J(\mathbf{x},\mathbf{w})$, that measures how well our system behaves on that example. For instance, for classification J would be zero if the system puts a pattern in the correct class, or positive in case of misclassification.

Learning consists in finding a parameter $\mathbf{w}^*$ that optimises some functional of the model parameters. For instance, one would like to minimize the *expected cost* (1).

$$C(\mathbf{w}) = \int J(\mathbf{x},\mathbf{w})\, p(\mathbf{x})d\mathbf{x} \tag{1}$$

The expected cost cannot be explicitely computed, because the density $p(\mathbf{x})$ is unknown. Our only knowledge of the process comes from a series of observations $\{\mathbf{x}_1 \ldots \mathbf{x}_n\}$ drawn from the unknown density $p(\mathbf{x})$. Therefore, the quality of our system can only be measured through the realisations $J(\mathbf{x},\mathbf{w})$ of the local cost function for the different observations.

2.2 STOCHASTIC GRADIENT DESCENT

Gradient descent algorithms are the simplest minimization algorithms. We cannot, however, compute the gradient of the expected cost (1), because $p(\mathbf{x})$ is unknown. Estimating these derivatives on a training set $\{\mathbf{x}_1 \ldots \mathbf{x}_n\}$, gives the gradient algorithm (2), where ∇J denotes the gradient of $J(\mathbf{x},\mathbf{w})$ with respect to $\mathbf{w}$, and ε_t, a small positive constant, the "learning rate".

$$\mathbf{w}_{t+1} = \mathbf{w}_t - \varepsilon_t \frac{1}{n} \sum_{i=1}^{n} \nabla J(\mathbf{x}_i,\mathbf{w}_t) \tag{2}$$

The *stochastic gradient descent* algorithm (3) is an alternative to algorithm (2). At each iteration, an example $\mathbf{x}_t$ is drawn at random, and a new value of $\mathbf{w}$ is computed.

$$\mathbf{w}_{t+1} = \mathbf{w}_t - \varepsilon_t \nabla J(\mathbf{x}_t,\mathbf{w}_t) \tag{3}$$

Algorithm (3) is faster and more reliable than (2), it is the only solution for training adaptive systems like Neural networks (NN). Such stochastic approximations have been extensively studied in adpative signal processing (Benveniste, Metiver & Priouret, 1987), (Ljung & Soderström, 1983). Under certain conditions, algorithm (3) converges almost surely (Bottou, 1991), (White, 1991) and allows to reach an optimal state of the system.

3 MODULAR LEARNING SYSTEMS

Most often, when the goal of learning is complex, it can be achieved more easily by using a decomposition of the global task into several simpler subtasks which for instance reflect some a priori knowledge about the structure of the problem. One can use this decomposition to build modular architectures where each module will correspond to one of the subtasks.

Within this framework, we will use the expected risk (1) as the goal of learning. The problem now is to change the analytical formulation of the functional (1) so as to introduce the modular decomposition of the global task. In (1), the analytic expression of the local cost $J(\mathbf{x},\mathbf{w})$ has two meanings: it describes a parametric relationship between the inputs and the outputs of the system, and measures the quality of the system. To introduce the decomposition, one may write this local cost $J(\mathbf{x},\mathbf{w})$ as the composition of several functions. One of them will take into account the local error and therefore measure the quality of the system; the others will correspond to the decomposition of the parametric relationship between the inputs and the outputs of the system (Figure 1). Each of the modules will therefore receive some inputs from other modules or the external world and produce some outputs which will be sent to other modules.

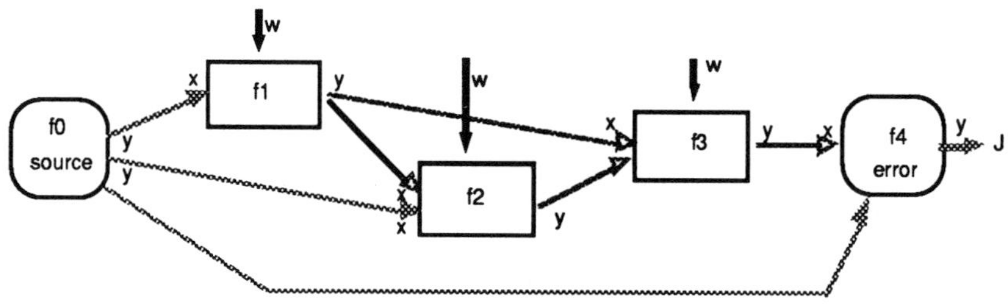

Figure 1: A modular system

In classical systems, these modules correspond to well defined processing stages like e.g. signal processing, filtering, feature extraction, classification. They are trained sequentially and then linked together to build a complete processing system which takes some inputs (e.g. raw signals) and produces some outputs (e.g. classes). Neither the assumed decomposition, nor the behavior of the different modules is guaranteed to optimally contribute to the global goal of learning. We will show in the following that it is possible to optimally train such systems.

3.1 TRAINING MODULAR SYSTEMS

Each function in the above composition defines a local processing stage or module whose outputs are defined by a parametric function of its inputs (4).

$$\forall j \in Y^{-1}(n),\ y_j = f_j\Big((x_k)_{k \in X^{-1}(n)},\ (w_i)_{i \in W^{-1}(n)} \Big) \tag{4}$$

$Y^{-1}(n)$ (resp. $X^{-1}(n)$, and $W^{-1}(n)$) denotes the set of subscripts associated to the outputs y (resp. inputs x and parameters w) of module n. Conversely, output y_j (resp. input x_k and parameter w_i) belongs to module $Y(j)$ (resp. $X(k)$ and $W(i)$).

Modules are linked so as to build a feed-forward topology which is expressed by a function ϕ.

$$\forall k,\ x_k = y_{\phi(k)} \tag{5}$$

We shall consider that the first module only feeds the system with examples and that the last module only computes $y_{last} = J(\mathbf{x},\mathbf{w})$.

Following (Le Cun, 1988), we can compute the derivatives of J with a Lagrangian method. Let α and β be the Lagrange coefficients for constraints (4) and (5).

$$L = J - \sum_k \beta_k (x_k - y_{\phi(k)}) - \sum_j \alpha_j \Big(y_j - f_j\big((x_k)_{k \in X^{-1}Y(j)},\ (w_i)_{i \in W^{-1}Y(j)} \big)\Big) \tag{6}$$

By equating the derivatives of L with respect to x and y to zero, we get recursive formulas for computing α and β in a single backward pass along the acyclic graph ϕ.

$$\alpha_{last} = 1, \quad \beta_k = \sum_{j \in Y^{-1}X(k)} \alpha_j \frac{\partial f_j}{\partial x_k}, \quad \alpha_j = \sum_{k \in \phi^{-1}(j)} \beta_k \text{ (if } j \neq \text{last)} \tag{7}$$

Then, the derivatives of J with respect to the weights are:

$$\frac{\partial J}{\partial w_i}(w) = \frac{\partial L}{\partial w_i}(\alpha,\beta,w) = \sum_{j \in Y^{-1}W(i)} \alpha_j \frac{\partial f_j}{\partial w_i} \tag{8}$$

Once we have computed the derivatives of the local cost $J(\mathbf{x},\mathbf{w})$, we can apply the stochastic gradient descent algorithm (3) for minimizing of the expected cost $C(\mathbf{w})$.

We shall say that each module is defined by the equations in (7) and (8) that characterize its behavior. These equations are:

- a forward equation (F) $\quad y_j = f_j((x_k)_{k \in X^{-1}(n)}, (w_i)_{i \in W^{-1}(n)})$
- a backward equation (B) $\quad \beta_k = \sum_{j \in Y^{-1}X(k)} \alpha_j \frac{\partial f_j}{\partial x_k}$
- a gradient equation (G) $\quad \Delta_i = \frac{\partial J}{\partial w_i} = \sum_{j \in Y^{-1}W(i)} \alpha_j \frac{\partial f_j}{\partial w_i}$

The remaining equations do not depend on the nature of the modules. They describe how modules interact during training. Like back-propagation, they address the credit assignment problem between modules by globally minimizing a single cost function. Training such a complex system actually consists in *cooperatively training* its components.

4 EXAMPLES

Most learning algorithms, as well as new algorithms may be expressed as modular learning systems. Here are some simple examples of modules and systems.

4.1 LINEAR AND QUASI-LINEAR SYSTEMS

MODULE	SYMBOL	FORWARD	BACKWARD	GRADIENT
Matrix product	Wx	$y_i=\sum_k w_{ik}x_k$	$\beta_k=\sum_i \alpha_i w_{ik}$	$\Delta_{ik}=\alpha_i x_k$
Mean square error	MSE	$J=\sum_k (d_k-x_k)^2$	$\beta_k=-2\ (d_k-x_k)$	---
Perceptron error	Perceptron	$J=-\sum_k (d_k-1_{\Re+}(x_k))x_k$	$\beta_k=-\ (d_k-1_{\Re+}(x_k))$	---
Sigmoid	sigmoïd	$y_k=f(x_k)$	$\beta_k=f'(x_k)\alpha_k$	---

A few basic modules are defined in the above table. Figure 2 gives examples of linear and quasi linear algorithms derived by combining these modules.

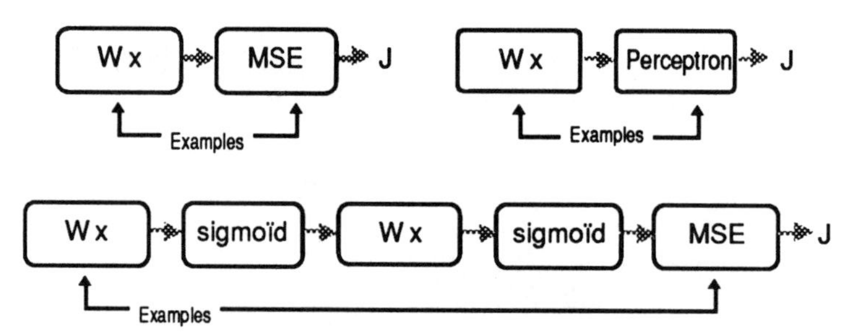

Figure 2: An Adaline, a Perceptron, and a 2-Layer Perceptron.

Some MLP architectures, Time Delay Networks for instance, use local connections and shared weights. Such complex architectures may be constructed by defining either quasi-linear unit modules or complex matrix operations modules like convolutions. The latter solution leads to more efficient implementations. Figure 3 gives an example of convolution module, composed of several matrix products modules.

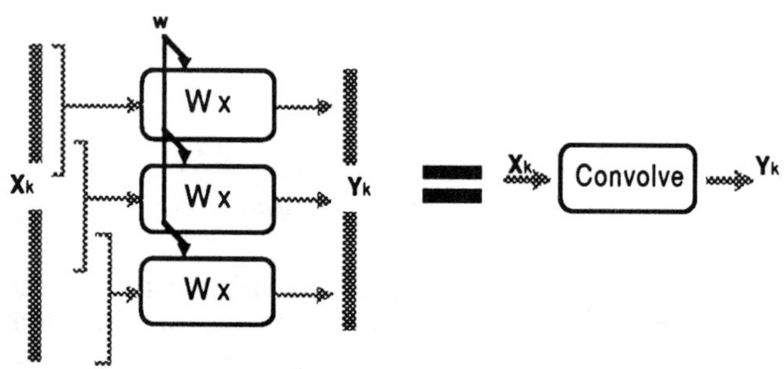

Figure 3: A convolution module, composed of several matrix product modules.

4.2 EUCLIDIAN DISTANCE BASED ALGORITHMS

A wide class of learning systems are based on the measure of euclidian distances. Again, defining an euclidian distance module and some adequate cost functions allows for handling most euclidian distance based algorithms. Here are some examples:

MODULE	SYMBOL	FORWARD	BACKWARD	GRADIENT
Euclidian distance	$(x\text{-}w)^2$	$y_j=\sum_k (w_{jk}x_k)^2$	$\beta_k=-2\sum_k \alpha_j(w_{jk}-x_k)$	$\Delta_{jk}=2\alpha_j(w_{jk}-x_k)$
Minimum	Min	$J=x_{k^*}=\mathrm{Min}\{x_k\}$	$\beta_{k^*}=1,\ \beta_{k\neq k^*}=0$	---
LVQ 1 error	LVQ1	If the nearest reference x_{k^*} is associated to the correct class		
		$J = x_{k^*}=\mathrm{Min}\{x_k\}$	$\beta_{k^*}=1,\ \beta_{k\neq k^*}=0$	---
		else		
		$J = -x_{k^*}=-\mathrm{Min}\{x_k\}$	$\beta_{k^*}=-1,\ \beta_{k\neq k^*}=0$	---

Combining an euclidian distance module with a "minimum" error module gives a K-means algorithm; combining it with a LVQ1 error module gives the LVQ1 algorithm (Figure 4).

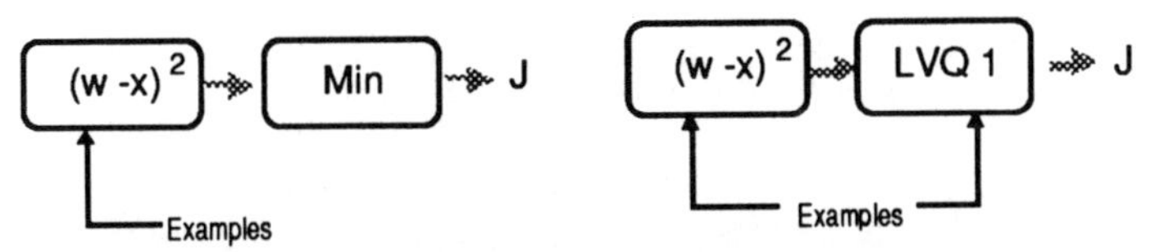

Figure 4: K-Means and Learning Vector Quantization.

4.3 HYBRID ALGORITHMS

Hybrid algorithms which may combine classical and connectionist learning algorithms are easily defined by chaining appropriate modules. Figure 5, for instance, depicts an algorithm combining a MLP layer and LVQ1. This algorithm has been described and empirically compared to other pattern recognition algorithms in (Bollivier, Gallinari & Thiria, 1990).

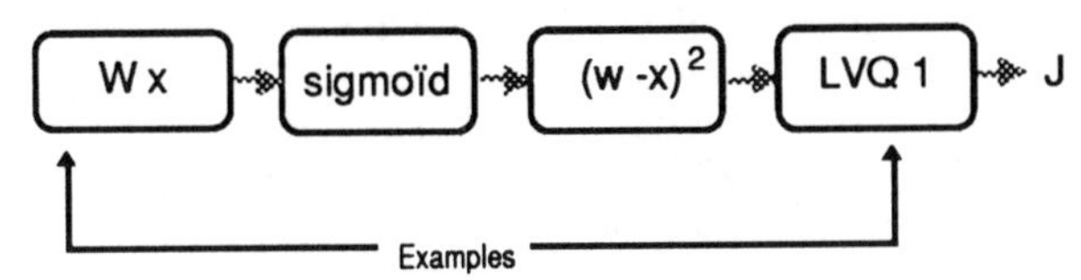

Figure 5: An hybrid algorithm combining a MLP and LVQ.

Cooperative training gives a framework and a possible implementation for such algorithms. Nevertheless, there are still specific problems (e.g. convergence, initialization) which require a careful study. More complex hybrid systems, including combinations of Markov Models and Time Delay Networks, have been described within this framework in (Bottou,1991).

5 CONCLUSION

Cooperative training of modular systems provides a unified view of many learning algorithms, as well as hybrid systems which combine classical or connectionist algorithms. Our formalism provides a way to define specific modules and to combine them into a cooperative system. This allows to design and implement complex learning systems which eventually incorporate structural a priori knowledge about the task.

Acknowledgements

During this work, L.B. was supported by DRET grant n° 87/808/19.

References

Benveniste A., Metivier M., Priouret P. (1987) *Algorithmes adaptatifs et approximations stochastiques*, Masson

Bollivier M. de, Gallinari P. & Thiria S. (1990) Cooperation of neural nets for robust classification, *Procedings of IJCNN 90*, San Diego, vol1, 113-120.

Bottou L. (1991) *Une approche théorique de l'apprentissage connexionniste; applications à la reconnaissance de la parole*. PhD Thesis, Université de Paris XI

Bourlard H., Morgan N. (1991) A Continuous Speech Recognition System Embedding MLP into HMM - In Touretzky D.S., Lipmann R. (eds.) *Advances in Neural Information Processing Systems 3* (this volume), Morgan-Kaufman

Le Cun Y.: A theoretical framework for back-propagation (1988) in Touretzky D., Hinton G. & Sejnowsky T. (eds.) *Proceedings of the 1988 Connectionist Models Summer School*, 21-28, Morgan Kaufmann (1988)

Le Cun Y., Boser B., & al., (1990): Handwritten Digit Recognition with a Back-Propagation Network- in D.Touretzky (ed.) *Advances in Neural Information Processing Systems 2* , 396-404, Morgan Kaufmann

Ljung L. & Söderström T. (1983) *Theory and Practice of Recursive Identification*, MIT Press

Tsypkin Ya. (1971) *Adaptation and Learning in Automatic systems*, Mathematics in science and engineering, vol 73, Academic Press

White H. (1991) An Overview of Representation and Convergence results for Multilayer feed-forward Networks, Touretzky D.S., Lipmann R. (eds.) *Advances in Neural Information Processing Systems 3* (this volume), Morgan-Kaufman

Connectionist Music Composition Based on Melodic and Stylistic Constraints

Michael C. Mozer
Department of Computer Science
and Institute of Cognitive Science
University of Colorado
Boulder, CO 80309-0430

Todd Soukup
Department of Electrical
and Computer Engineering
University of Colorado
Boulder, CO 80309-0425

Abstract

We describe a recurrent connectionist network, called CONCERT, that uses a set of melodies written in a given style to compose new melodies in that style. CONCERT is an extension of a traditional algorithmic composition technique in which transition tables specify the probability of the next note as a function of previous context. A central ingredient of CONCERT is the use of a psychologically-grounded representation of pitch.

1 INTRODUCTION

In creating music, composers bring to bear a wealth of knowledge about musical conventions. If we hope to build automatic music composition systems that can mimic the abilities of human composers, it will be necessary to incorporate knowledge about musical conventions into the systems. However, this knowledge is difficult to express: even human composers are unaware of many of the constraints under which they operate.

In this paper, we describe a connectionist network that composes melodies. The network is called CONCERT, an acronym for connectionist composer of erudite tunes. Musical knowledge is incorporated into CONCERT via two routes. First, CONCERT is trained on a set of sample melodies from which it extracts rules of note and phrase progressions. Second, we have built a representation of pitch into CONCERT that is based on psychological studies of human perception. This representation, and an associated theory of generalization proposed by Shepard (1987), provides CONCERT with a basis for judging the similarity among notes, for selecting a response, and for restricting the set of alternatives that can be considered at any time.

2 TRANSITION TABLE APPROACHES TO COMPOSITION

We begin by describing a traditional approach to algorithmic music composition using Markov *transition tables*. This simple but interesting technique involves selecting notes sequentially according to a table that specifies the probability of the next note as a function of the current note (Dodge & Jerse, 1985). The tables may be hand-constructed according to certain criteria or they may be set up to embody a particular musical style. In the latter case, statistics are collected over a set of examples (hereafter, the *training set*) and the table entries are defined to be the transition probabilities in these examples.

In melodies of any complexity, musical structure cannot be fully described by pairwise statistics. To capture additional structure, the transition table can be generalized from a two-dimensional array to n dimensions. In the n-dimensional table, often referred to as a table of order $n-1$, the probability of the next note is indicated as a function of the previous $n-1$ notes. Unfortunately, extending the transition table in this manner gives rise to two problems. First, the size of the table explodes exponentially with the amount of context and rapidly becomes unmanageable. Second, a table representing the high-order structure masks whatever low-order structure is present.

Kohonen (1989) has proposed a scheme by which only the *relevant* high-order structure is represented. The scheme is symbolic algorithm that, given a training set of examples, produces a collection of rules — a context-sensitive grammar — sufficient for reproducing most or all of the structure inherent in the set. However, because the algorithm attempts to produce deterministic rules — rules that always apply in a given context — the algorithm will not discover regularities unless they are absolute; it is not equipped to deal with statistical properties of the data. Both Kohonen's musical grammar and the transition table approach suffer from the further drawback that a symbolic representation of notes does not facilitate generalization. For instance, invariance under transposition is not directly representable. In addition, other similarities are not encoded, for example, the congruity of octaves.

Connectionist learning algorithms offer the potential of overcoming the various limitations of transition table approaches and Kohonen musical grammars. Connectionist algorithms are able to discover relevant structure and statistical regularities in sequences (e.g., Elman, 1990; Mozer, 1989), and to consider varying amounts of context, noncontiguous context, and combinations of low-order and high-order regularities. Connectionist approaches also promise better generalization through the use of distributed representations. In a local representation, where each note is represented by a discrete symbol, the sort of statistical contingencies that can be discovered are among notes. However, in a distributed representation, where each note is represented by a set of continuous feature values, the sort of contingencies that can be discovered are among *features*. To the extent that two notes share features, featural regularities discovered for one note may transfer to the other note.

3 THE CONCERT ARCHITECTURE

CONCERT is a recurrent network architecture of the sort studied by Elman (1990). A melody is presented to it, one note at a time, and its task at each point in time is to predict the next note in the melody. Using a training procedure described below, CONCERT's connection strengths are adjusted so that it can perform this task correctly for a set of training examples. Each example consists of a sequence of notes, each note being characterized by a pitch and a duration. The current note in the sequence is represented in the input layer of CONCERT, and the prediction of the next note is represented in the output layer. As Figure 1 indicates, the next note is encoded in two different ways: The next-note-distributed (or *NND*) layer contains CONCERT's internal representation of the note, while the next-note-local (or *NNL*) layer contains one unit for each alternative. For now, it should suffice to say that the representation of a note in the NND layer, as well as in the input layer, is distributed, i.e., a note is indicated by a *pattern* of activity across the units. Because such patterns of activity can be quite difficult to interpret, the NNL layer provides an alternative, explicit representation of the possibilities.

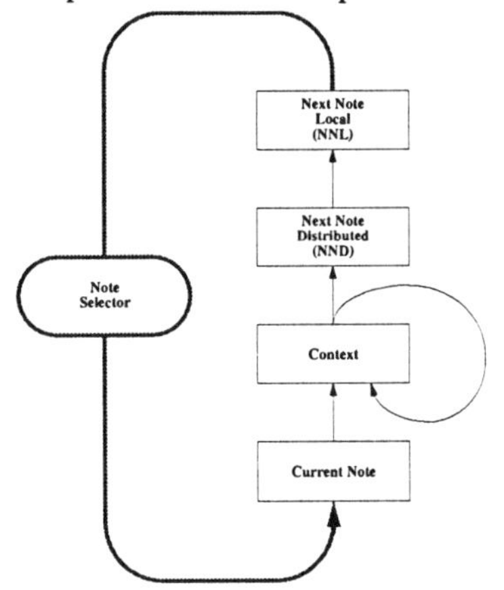

Figure 1: The CONCERT Architecture

The context layer represents the the temporal context in which a prediction is made. When a new note is presented in the input layer, the current context activity pattern is integrated with the new note to form a new context representation. Although CONCERT could readily be wired up to behave as a k-th order transition table, the architecture is far more general. The training procedure attempts to determine which aspects of the input sequence are relevant for making future predictions and retain only this task-relevant information in the context layer. This contrasts with Todd's (1989) seminal work on connectionist composition in which the recurrent context connections are prewired and fixed, which makes the nature of the information Todd's model retains independent of the examples on which it is trained.

Once CONCERT has been trained, it can be run in *composition mode* to create new pieces. This involves first seeding CONCERT with a short sequence of notes, perhaps the initial notes of one of the training examples. From this point on, the output of CONCERT can be fed back to the input, allowing CONCERT to continue generating notes without further external input. Generally, the output of CONCERT does not specify a single note with absolute certainty; instead, the output is a probability distribution over the set of candidates. It is thus necessary to select a particular note in accordance with this distribution. This is the role of the selection process depicted in Figure 1.

3.1 ACTIVATION RULES AND TRAINING PROCEDURE

The activation rule for the context units is

$$c_i(n) = s\,[\sum_j w_{ij} x_j(n) + \sum_j v_{ij} c_j(n-1)]\,, \tag{1}$$

where $c_i(n)$ is the activity of context unit i following processing of input note n (which we refer to as *step* n), $x_j(n)$ is the activity of input unit j at step n, w_{ij} is the connection strength from unit j of the input to unit i of the context layer, and v_{ij} is the connection strength from unit j to unit i within the context layer, and s is a sigmoid activation function rescaled to the range (-1,1). Units in the NND layer follow a similar rule:

$$nnd_i(n) = s\left[\sum_j u_{ij} c_j(n)\right],$$

where $nnd_i(n)$ is the activity of NND unit i at step n and u_{ij} is the strength of connection from context unit j to NND unit i.

The transformation from the NND layer to the NNL layer is achieved by first computing the distance between the NND representation, $\mathbf{nnd}(n)$, and the target (distributed) representation of each pitch i, $\boldsymbol{\rho}_i$:

$$d_i = \left| \mathbf{nnd}(n) - \boldsymbol{\rho}_i \right|,$$

where $|\cdot|$ denotes the L2 vector norm. This distance is an indication of how well the NND representation matches a particular pitch. The activation of the NNL unit corresponding to pitch i, nnl_i, increases inversely with the distance:

$$nnl_i(n) = e^{-d_i} / \sum_j e^{-d_j} .$$

This normalized exponential transform (proposed by Bridle, 1990, and Rumelhart, in press) produces an activity pattern over the NNL units in which each unit has activity in the range (0,1) and the activity of all units sums to 1. Consequently, the NNL activity pattern can be interpreted as a probability distribution — in this case, the probability that the next note has a particular pitch.

CONCERT is trained using the back propagation unfolding-in-time procedure (Rumelhart, Hinton, & Williams, 1986) using the log likelihood error measure

$$E = -\sum_{p,n} \log nnl_{tgt}(n,p),$$

where p is an index over pieces in the training set and n an index over notes within a piece; tgt is the target pitch for note n of piece p.

3.2 PITCH REPRESENTATION

Having described CONCERT's architecture and training procedure, we turn to the representation of pitch. To accommodate a variety of music, CONCERT needs the ability to represent a range of about four octaves. Using standard musical notation, these pitches are labeled as follows: `C1`, `D1`, ..., `B1`, `C2`, `D2`, ... `B2`, `C3`, ... `C5`, where `C1` is the lowest pitch and `C5` the highest. Sharps are denoted by a #, e.g., `F#3`. The range `C1-C5` spans 49 pitches.

One might argue that the choice of a pitch representation is not critical because back propagation can, in principle, discover an alternative representation well suited to the task. In practice, however, researchers have found that the choice of external representation is a critical determinant of the network's ultimate performance (e.g., Denker et al., 1987; Mozer, 1987). Quite simply, the more task-appropriate information that is built into the network, the easier the job the learning algorithm has. Because we are asking the network to make predictions about melodies that *people* have composed or to generate melodies that *people* perceive as pleasant, we have furnished CONCERT with a psychologically-motivated representation of pitch. By this, we mean that notes that people judge to be similar have similar representations in the network, indicating that the representation in the head matches the representation in the network.

Shepard (1982) has studied the similarity of pitches by asking people to judge the perceived similarity of pairs of pitches. He has proposed a theory of generalization (Shepard, 1987) in which the similarity of two items is exponentially related to their distance in an internal or "psychological" representational space. (This is one justification for the NNL layer computing an exponential function of distance.) Based on psychophysical experiments, he has proposed a five-dimensional space for the representation of pitch, depicted in Figure 2.

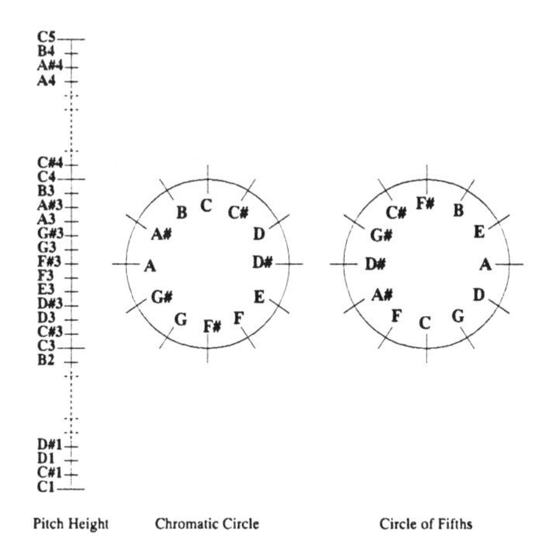

Figure 2: Pitch Representation Proposed by Shepard (1982)

In this space, each pitch specifies a point along the *pitch height* (or *PH*) dimension, an (x,y) coordinate on the *chromatic circle* (or *CC*), and an (x,y) coordinate on the *circle of fifths* (or *CF*). we will refer to this representation as PHCCCF, after its three components. The pitch height component specifies the logarithm of the frequency of a pitch; this logarithmic transform places tonal half-steps at equal spacing from one another along the pitch height axis. In the chromatic circle, neighboring pitches are a tonal half-step apart. In the circle of fifths, the perfect fifth of a pitch is the next pitch immediately counterclockwise. Figure 2 shows the relative magnitude of the various components to scale. The proximity of two pitches in the five-dimensional PHCCCF space can be determined simply by computing the Euclidean distance between their representations.

A straightforward scheme for translating the PHCCCF representation into an activity pattern over a set of connectionist units is to use five units, one for pitch height and two pairs to encode the (x,y) coordinates of the pitch on the two circles. Due to several problems, we have represented each circle over a set of 6 binary-valued units that preserves the essential distance relationships among tones on the circles (Mozer, 1990). The PHCCCF representation thus consists of 13 units altogether. Rests (silence) are assigned a code that distinguish them from all pitches. The end of a piece is coded by several rests.

4 SIMULATION EXPERIMENTS

4.1 LEARNING THE STRUCTURE OF DIATONIC SCALES

In this simulation, we trained CONCERT on a set of diatonic scales in various keys over a one octave range, e.g., `D1 E1 F#1 G1 A1 B1 C#2 D2`. Thirty-seven such scales can be made using pitches in the `C1-C5` range. The training set consisted of 28 scales — roughly 75% of the corpus — selected at random, and the test set consisted of the remaining 9. In 10 replications of the simulation using 20 context units, CONCERT mastered the training set in approximately 55 passes. Generalization performance was tested by presenting the scales in the test set one note at a time and examining CONCERT's prediction. Of the 63 notes to be predicted in the test set, CONCERT achieved remarkable performance: 98.4% correct. The few errors were caused by transposing notes one full octave or one tonal half step.

To compare CONCERT with a transition table approach, we built a second-order transition table from the training set data and measured its performance on the test set. The transition table prediction (i.e., the note with highest probability) was correct only 26.6% of the time. The transition table is somewhat of a straw man in this environment: A transition table that is based on absolute pitches is simply unable to generalize correctly. Even if the transition table encoded relative pitches, a third-order table would be required to master the environment. Kohonen's musical grammar faces the same difficulties as a transition table.

4.2 LEARNING INTERSPERSED RANDOM WALK SEQUENCES

The sequences in this simulation were generated by interspersing the elements of two simple random walk sequences. Each interspersed sequence had the following form: a_1, b_1, a_2, b_2, $\cdots$, a_5, b_5, where a_1 and b_1 are randomly selected pitches, a_{i+1} is one step up or down from a_i on the C major scale, and likewise for b_{i+1} and b_i. Each sequence consisted of ten notes. CONCERT, with 25 context units, was trained on 50 passes through a set of 200 examples and was then tested on an additional 100. Because it is impossible to predict the second note in the interspersed sequences (b_1) from the first (a_1), this prediction was ignored for the purpose of evaluating CONCERT's performance. CONCERT achieved a performance of 91.7% correct. About half the errors were ones in which CONCERT transposed a correct prediction by an octave. Excluding these errors, performance improved to 95.8% correct.

To capture the structure in this environment, a transition table approach would need to consider at least the previous two notes. However, such a transition table is not likely to generalize well because, if it is to be assured of predicting a note at step n correctly, it must observe the note at step $n-2$ in the context of *every possible* note at step $n-1$. We constructed a second-order transition table from CONCERT's training set. Using a testing criterion analogous to that used to evaluate CONCERT, the transition table achieved a performance level on the test set of only 67.1% correct. Kohonen's musical grammar would face the same difficulty as the transition table in this environment.

4.3 GENERATING NEW MELODIES IN THE STYLE OF BACH

In a final experiment, we trained CONCERT on the melody line of a set of ten simple minuets and marches by J. S. Bach. The pieces had several voices, but the melody generally appeared in the treble voice. Importantly, to naive listeners the extracted melodies sounded pleasant and coherent without the accompaniment.

In the training data, each piece was terminated with a rest marker (the only rests in the pieces). This allowed CONCERT to learn not only the notes within a piece but also when the end of the piece was reached. Further, each major piece was transposed to the key of C major and each minor piece to the key of A minor. This was done to facilitate learning because the pitch representation does not take into account the notion of musical key; a more sophisticated pitch representation might avoid the necessity of this step.

In this simulation, each note was represented by a duration as well as a pitch. The duration representation consisted of five units and was somewhat analogous the PHCCCF representation for pitch. It allowed for the representation of sixteenth, eighth, quarter, and half notes, as well as triplets. Also included in this simulation were two additional input ones. One indicated whether the piece was in a major versus minor key, the other indicated whether the piece was in 3/4 meter versus 2/4 or 4/4. These inputs were fixed for a given piece.

Learning the examples involves predicting a total of 1,260 notes altogether, no small feat. CONCERT was trained with 40 hidden units for 3000 passes through the training set. The learning rate was gradually lowered from .0004 to .0002. By the completion of training, CONCERT could correctly predict about 95% of the pitches and 95% of the durations correctly. New pieces can be created by presenting a few notes to start and then running CONCERT in composition mode. One example of a composition produced by CONCERT is shown in Figure 3. The primary deficiency of CONCERT's compositions is that they are lacking in global coherence.

Figure 3: A Sample Composition Produced by CONCERT

5 DISCUSSION

Initial results from CONCERT are encouraging. CONCERT is able to learn musical structure of varying complexity, from random walk sequences to Bach pieces containing nearly 200 notes. We presented two examples of structure that CONCERT can learn but that cannot be captured by a simple transition table or by Kohonen's musical grammar.

Beyond a more systematic examination of alternative architectures, work on CONCERT is heading in two directions. First, the pitch representation is being expanded to account for the perceptual effects of musical context and musical key. Second, CONCERT is being extended to better handle the processing of global structure in music. It is unrealistic to expect that CONCERT, presented with a linear string of notes, could induce not only local relationships among the notes, but also more global phrase structure, e.g., an AABA phrase pattern. To address the issue of global structure, we have designed a network that operates at several different temporal resolutions simultaneously (Mozer, 1990).

Acknowledgements

This research was supported by NSF grant IRI-9058450, grant 90-21 from the James S. McDonnell Foundation. Our thanks to Paul Smolensky, Yoshiro Miyata, Debbie Breen, and Geoffrey Hinton for helpful comments regarding this work, and to Hal Eden and Darren Hardy for technical assistance.

References

Bridle, J. (1990). Training stochastic model recognition algorithms as networks can lead to maximum mutual information estimation of parameters. In D. S. Touretzky (Ed.), *Advances in neural information processing systems 2* (pp. 211–217). San Mateo, CA: Morgan Kaufmann.

Dodge, C., & Jerse, T. A. (1985). *Computer music: Synthesis, composition, and performance.* New York: Shirmer Books.

Elman, J. L. (1990). Finding structure in time. *Cognitive Science, 14*, 179–212.

Kohonen, T. (1989). A self-learning musical grammar, or "Associative memory of the second kind". *Proceedings of the 1989 International Joint Conference on Neural Networks*, 1–5.

Mozer, M. C. (1987). RAMBOT: A connectionist expert system that learns by example. In M. Caudill & C. Butler (Eds.), *Proceedings fo the IEEE First Annual International Conference on Neural Networks* (pp. 693–700). San Diego, CA: IEEE Publishing Services.

Mozer, M. C. (1989). A focused back-propagation algorithm for temporal pattern recognition. *Complex Systems, 3*, 349–381.

Mozer, M. C. (1990). *Connectionist music composition based on melodic, stylistic, and psychophysical constraints* (Tech Report CU–CS–495–90). Boulder, CO: University of Colorado, Department of Computer Science.

Rumelhart, D. E., Hinton, G. E., & Williams, R. J. (1986). Learning internal representations by error propagation. In D. E. Rumelhart & J. L. McClelland (Eds.), *Parallel distributed processing: Explorations in the microstructure of cognition. Volume I: Foundations* (pp. 318–362). Cambridge, MA: MIT Press/Bradford Books.

Rumelhart, D. E. (in press). Connectionist processing and learning as statistical inference. In Y. Chauvin & D. E. Rumelhart (Eds.), *Backpropagation: Theory, architectures, and applications.* Hillsdale, NJ: Erlbaum.

Shepard, R. N. (1982). Geometrical approximations to the structure of musical pitch. *Psychological Review, 89*, 305–333.

Shepard, R. N. (1987). Toward a universal law of generalization for psychological science. *Science, 237*, 1317–1323. Shepard (1987)

Todd, P. M. (1989). A connectionist approach to algorithmic composition. *Computer Music Journal, 13*, 27–43.

Using Genetic Algorithms to Improve Pattern Classification Performance

Eric I. Chang and **Richard P. Lippmann**
Lincoln Laboratory, MIT
Lexington, MA 02173-9108

Abstract

Genetic algorithms were used to select and create features and to select reference exemplar patterns for machine vision and speech pattern classification tasks. For a complex speech recognition task, genetic algorithms required no more computation time than traditional approaches to feature selection but reduced the number of input features required by a factor of five (from 153 to 33 features). On a difficult artificial machine-vision task, genetic algorithms were able to create new features (polynomial functions of the original features) which reduced classification error rates from 19% to almost 0%. Neural net and k nearest neighbor (KNN) classifiers were unable to provide such low error rates using only the original features. Genetic algorithms were also used to reduce the number of reference exemplar patterns for a KNN classifier. On a 338 training pattern vowel-recognition problem with 10 classes, genetic algorithms reduced the number of stored exemplars from 338 to 43 without significantly increasing classification error rate. In all applications, genetic algorithms were easy to apply and found good solutions in many fewer trials than would be required by exhaustive search. Run times were long, but not unreasonable. These results suggest that genetic algorithms are becoming practical for pattern classification problems as faster serial and parallel computers are developed.

1 INTRODUCTION

Feature selection and creation are two of the most important and difficult tasks in the field of pattern classification. Good features improve the performance of both conventional and neural network pattern classifiers. Exemplar selection is another task that can reduce the memory and computation requirements of a KNN classifier. These three tasks require a search through a space which is typically so large that exhaustive search is impractical. The purpose of this research was to explore the usefulness of Genetic search algorithms for these tasks. Details concerning this research are available in (Chang, 1990).

Genetic algorithms depend on the generation-by-generation development of possible solutions, with selection eliminating bad solutions and allowing good solutions to replicate and be modified. There are four stages in the genetic search process: creation, selection, crossover, and mutation. In the creation stage, a group of possible solutions to a search problem is randomly generated. In most genetic algorithm applications, each solution is a bit string with each bit initially randomly set to 1 or 0.

After the creation stage, each solution is evaluated using a fitness function and assigned a fitness value. The fitness function must be tightly linked to the eventual goal. The usual criterion for success in pattern classification tasks is the percentage of patterns classified correctly on test data. This was approximated in all experiments by using a leave-one-out cross-validation measure of classification accuracy obtained using training data and a KNN classifier. After solutions are assigned fitness values, a selection stage occurs, where the fitter solutions are given more chance to reproduce. This gives the fitter solutions more and more influence over the changes in the population so that eventually fitter solutions dominate.

A crossover operation occurs after two fitter solutions (called parent solutions) have been selected. During crossover, portions of the parent solutions are exchanged. This operation is performed in the hope of generating new solutions which will contain the useful parts of both parent solutions and be even better solutions. Crossover is responsible for generating most of the new solutions in genetic search. When all solutions are similar, the crossover operation loses its ability to generate new solutions since exchanging portions of identical solutions generates the same solutions. Mutation (randomly altering bits) is performed on each new solution to prevent the whole population from becoming similar. However, mutation does not generally improve solutions by itself. The combination of both crossover and mutation is required for good performance.

There are many varieties of genetic algorithms. A relatively new incremental static population model proposed by (Whitley, 1989) was used in all experiments. In the regular genetic algorithm model, the whole population undergoes selection and reproduction, with a large portion of the strings replaced by new strings. It is thus possible for good strings to be deleted from the population. In the static population model, the population is ranked according to fitness. At each recombination cycle, two strings are picked as parents according to their fitness values, and two new strings are produced. These two new strings replace the lowest ranked strings in the original population. This model automatically protects the better strings in the population.

2 FEATURE SELECTION

Adding more input features or input dimensions to a pattern classifier often degrades rather than improves performance. This is because as the number of input features increases, the number of training patterns required to maintain good generalization and adequately describe class distributions also often increases rapidly. Performance with limited training data may thus degrade. Feature selection (dimensionality

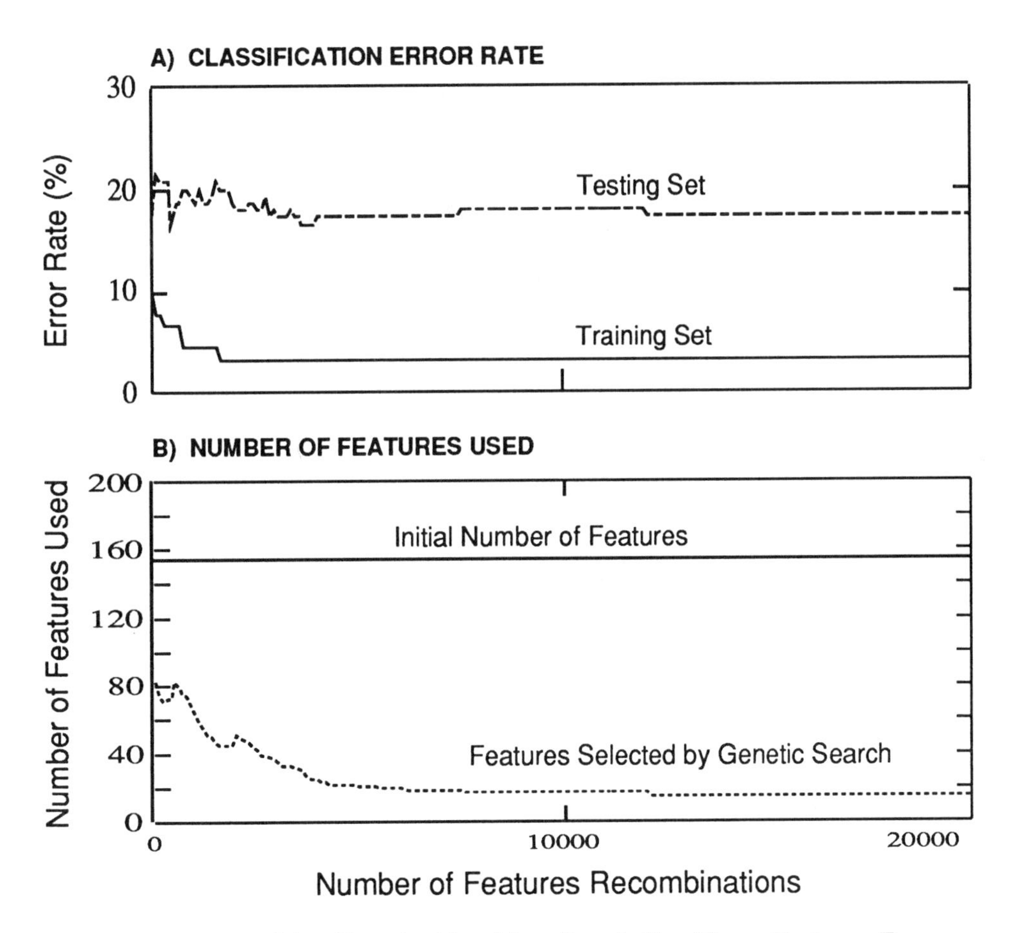

Figure 1: Progress Of a Genetic Algorithm Search For Those Features From an Original 153 Features That Provide High Accuracy in "E" Set Classification For One Female Talker: (A) Classification Error Rate and (B) Number Of Features Used.

reduction) is often required when training data is limited to select the subset of features that best separates classes. It can improve performance and/or reduce computation requirements.

Feature selection is difficult because the number of possible combinations of features grows exponentially with the number of original features. For a moderate size problem with 64 features, there are 2^{64} possible subsets of features. Clearly an exhaustive evaluation of each possible combination is impossible. Frequently, finding a near optimal feature subset is adequate. An overview of many different approaches to feature selection is available in (Siedlecki and Sklansky, 1988).

This work applies genetic search techniques to the problem of feature selection. Every feature set is represented by a bit string with d bits, where d is the maximum input dimension. Each bit determines whether a feature is used. The accuracy of a KNN classifier with the leave-one-out approach to error rate estimation was used as an evaluation function as described above. A KNN classifier has the advantage of requiring no training time and providing results directly related to performance.

"E-set" words (9 letters from the English alphabet that rhyme with the letter "E") taken from a Texas Instruments 46-word speech database were used for experiments. Waveforms were spectrally analyzed and encoded with a hidden Markov Model speech recognizer as described in (Huang and Lippmann, 1990). Features were the average log likelihood distance and duration from all the hidden Markov nodes determined using Viterbi decoding. The final output of the hidden Markov model was also included in the feature set. This resulted in 17 features per word class. The 9 different word classes result in a total of 153 features. For each talker there were 10 patterns in the training set and 16 patterns in the testing set per word class. All experiments were talker dependent.

An experiment was performed using the data from one female talker. More conventional sequential forward and backward searches for the best feature subset were first performed. The total number of KNN evaluations for each sequential search was 11,781. The best feature subset found with sequential searches contained 33 features and the classification error rates were 2.2% and 18.5% on training and testing sets respectively. Genetic algorithms provided a lower error rate on the testing set with fewer than half as many features. Fig. 1 shows the progress of the genetic search. The bottom plot shows that near recombination 12,100, the number of features used was reduced to 15. The top plot shows that classification error rates were 3.3% and 17.5% for the training and testing sets respectively.

3 FEATURE CREATION

One of the most successful techniques for improving pattern classification performance with limited training data is to find more effective input features. An approach to creating more effective input features is to search through new features that are polynomial functions of the original features. This difficult search problem was explored using genetic algorithms. The fitness function was again determined using the performance of a KNN classifier with leave-one-out testing.

Polynomial functions of the original features taken two at a time were created as new features. New features were represented by a bit string consisting of substrings identifying the original features used, their exponents, and the operation to be applied between the original features. A gradual buildup of feature complexity over multiple stages was enforced by limiting the complexity of the created features. Once the accuracy of a KNN classifier had converged at one stage, another stage was begun where more complex high order features were allowed. This improves generalization by creating simple features first and by creating more complicated features only when simpler features are not satisfactory.

A parallel vector problem, where the input data consists of $\Delta x, \Delta y$ of two vectors, was used. Parallel vectors are identified as one class while nonparallel vectors are identified as another. There were 300 training patterns and 100 testing patterns. During an experiment, the ratio features $\Delta x2/\Delta x1$ and $\Delta y2/\Delta y1$ were first found near recombination 700. After the error rate had not changed for 2,000 recombinations, the complexity of the created features was allowed to increase at recombination 2,700. At this point the two ratio features and the four original features were treated as if they were six original features. The final feature found after this point was $(\Delta x_2 * \Delta y_2)/(\Delta x_1 * \Delta y_1)$. Classification error rates for the training set and the testing set decreased to 0% with this feature. The classification error rate on the testing set using the original four features was 19% using a KNN classifier. Tests using the original features with two more complex classifiers also used in (Ng and Lippmann, 1991) resulted in error rates of 13.3% for a GMDH classifier and 8.3% for a radial basis function classifier. Feature creation with a simple KNN classifier was thus more effective than the use of more complex classifiers with the original features.

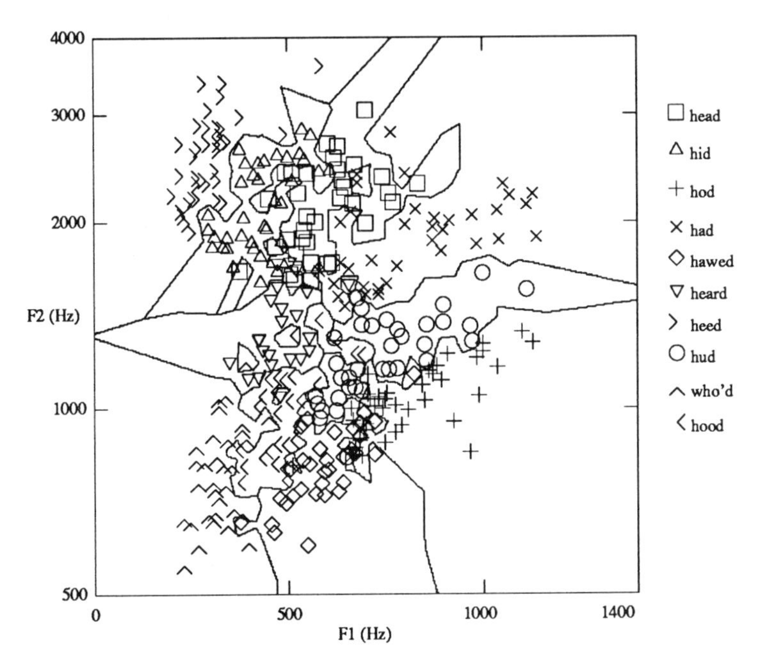

Figure 2: Decision Boundaries Of a Nearest Neighbor Classifier For The Vowel Problem Using All 338 Original Exemplars.

4 EXEMPLAR SELECTION

The performance of a KNN classifier typically improves as more training patterns are stored. This often makes KNN classifiers impractical because both classification time and memory requirements increase linearly with the number of training patterns. Previous approaches to reducing the classification time and memory requirements of KNN classifiers include using KD trees and condensed k nearest neighbor (CKNN) classifiers as described in (Ng and Lippmann, 1991). KD trees, however, are effective only if the input dimensionality is low, and CKNN classifiers use a heuristic that may not result in minimal memory requirements. An alternate

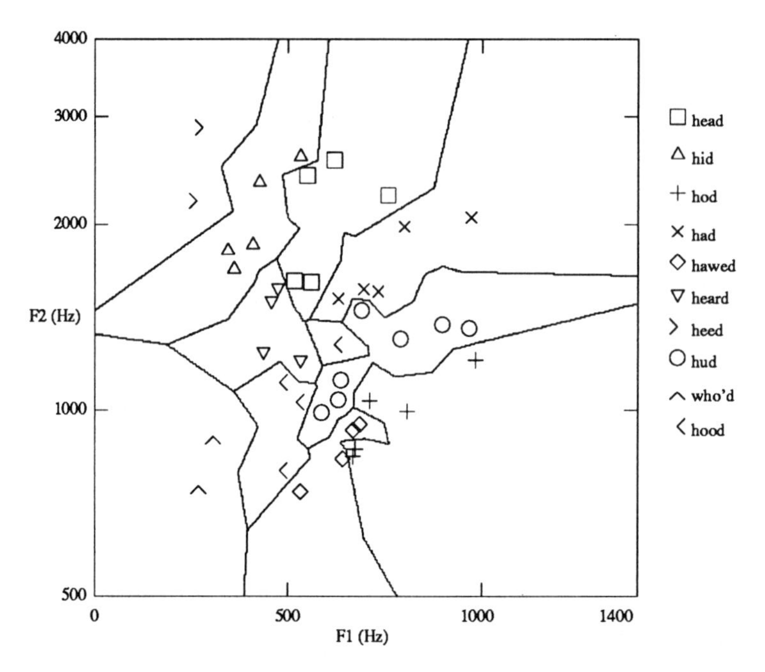

Figure 3: Decision Boundaries Of a Nearest Neighbor Classifier For The Vowel Problem Using 43 Exemplars selected Using Genetic Search.

approach is to use genetic algorithms.

Genetic algorithms were used to manipulate bit strings identifying useful exemplar patterns. A bonus proportional to the number of unused exemplars was given to strings with classifier accuracy above a user-preset threshold. The value k was also selected by genetic algorithms in some experiments. The k value was encoded with three bits which were attached to the end of each string. Exemplar selection was tested with the vowel database used by (Ng and Lippmann, 1991). There were ten classes, each class being a word starting with "h" and ending with "d", with a vowel in between ("head", "hid", "hod", "had", "hawed", "heard", "heed", "hud", "who'd", and "hood"). A total of 338 patterns was used as the training set and 333 patterns were used as the testing set. Each pattern consisted of two features which were the two formant frequencies of the vowel determined by spectrographic analysis.

Genetic algorithms were effective in both reducing the number of exemplars and selecting k. Classification error rates with selected exemplars were roughly 20% on both training and test data. Selecting k typically resulted in fewer exemplars and the number of exemplars required was reduced by a factor of roughly 8 (from 338 to 43). Genetic search was thus much more effective than the CKNN classifier described in (Ng and Lippmann, 1991) which reduced the number of exemplars by a factor of roughly 2 (from 338 to 152). Decision boundaries with all 338 original exemplars are shown in Fig. 2. Boundaries are excessively complex and provide perfect performance on the training patterns but perform poorly on the testing patterns (25% error rate). Decision boundaries with the 43 exemplars selected using genetic algorithms are shown in Fig. 3. Boundaries with the smaller number of exemplars are smoother and provide an error rate of 20.1% on test data.

5 CONCLUSIONS

Genetic algorithms proved to be a good search technique which is widely applicable in pattern classification. Genetic algorithms were relatively easy to apply to feature selection, feature creation, and exemplar selection problems. Solutions were found that were better than those provided by heuristic approaches including forward and backward feature selection and condensed k nearest neighbor algorithms. Genetic algorithms also required far fewer evaluations than required by exhaustive search and sometimes required only little more computation than heuristic approaches. Run times on a Sun-3 workstation were long (hours and sometimes one or two days) but not impractical. Run times are becoming become less of an issue as single-processor workstations become more powerful and as parallel computers become more available. Compared to developing a heuristic search technique for each type of search problem, genetic algorithms offer the benefit of simplicity and good performance on all problems. Further experiments should explore the use of genetic algorithms in other application areas and also compare alternative search techniques including simulated annealing.

Acknowledgements

This work was sponsored by the Air Force Office of Scientific Research and the Department of the Air Force.

References

Eric I. Chang. Using Genetic Algorithms to Select and Create Features for Pattern Classification. Master's Thesis, Massachusetts Institute of Technology, Department of Electrical Engineering and Computer Science, Cambridge, MA, May 1990.

William Y. Huang and Richard P. Lippmann. HMM Speech Recognition Systems with Neural Net Discrimination. In D. Touretzky (Ed.) *Advances in Neural Information Processing Systems 2*, 194–202, 1990.

Kenney Ng and Richard P. Lippmann. A Comparative Study of the Practical Characteristics of Neural Network and Conventional Pattern Classifiers. In Lippmann, R., Moody, J., Touretzky, D., (Eds.) *Advances in Neural Information Processing Systems 3*, 1991.

W. Siedlecki and J. Sklansky. On Automatic Feature Selection. *International Journal of Pattern Recognition and Artificial Intelligence*, 2:197–220, 1988.

Darrel Whitley. The GENITOR Algorithm and Selection Pressure: Why Rank-Based Allocation of Reproductive Trials is Best. In *Proceedings Third International Conference on Genetic Algorithms*, Washington, DC, June 1989.

EVOLUTION AND LEARNING IN NEURAL NETWORKS: THE NUMBER AND DISTRIBUTION OF LEARNING TRIALS AFFECT THE RATE OF EVOLUTION

Ron Keesing and **David G. Stork***

Ricoh California Research Center
2882 Sand Hill Road Suite 115
Menlo Park, CA 94025
stork@crc.ricoh.com

and

*Dept. of Electrical Engineering
Stanford University
Stanford, CA 94305
stork@psych.stanford.edu

Abstract

Learning can increase the rate of evolution of a population of biological organisms (the Baldwin effect). Our simulations show that in a population of artificial neural networks solving a pattern recognition problem, no learning or too much learning leads to slow evolution of the genes whereas an intermediate amount is optimal. Moreover, for a given total number of training presentations, fastest evoution occurs if different individuals within each generation receive *different* numbers of presentations, rather than *equal* numbers. Because genetic algorithms (GAs) help avoid local minima in energy functions, our hybrid learning-GA systems can be applied successfully to complex, high-dimensional pattern recognition problems.

INTRODUCTION

The structure and function of a biological network derives from both its evolutionary precursors and real-time learning. Genes specify (through development) coarse attributes of a neural system, which are then refined based on experience in an environment containing more information — and more *unexpected* information — than the genes alone can represent. Innate neural structure is essential for many high level problems such as scene analysis and language [Chomsky, 1957].

Although the Central Dogma of molecular genetics [Crick, 1970] implies that information *learned* cannot be *directly* transcribed to the genes, such information *can* appear in the genes through an indirect Darwinian process (see below). As such, learning can change the rate of evolution — the Baldwin effect [Baldwin, 1896]. Hinton and Nowlan [1987] considered a closely related process in artificial neural networks, though they used stochastic search and not learning *per se*. We present here analyses and simulations of a hybrid evolutionary-learning system which uses gradient-descent learning as well as a genetic algorithm, to determine network connections.

Consider a population of networks for pattern recognition, where initial synaptic weights (weights "at birth") are determined by genes. Figure 1 shows the Darwinian fitness of networks (i.e., how many patterns each can correctly classify) as a function the weights. Iso-fitness contours are *not* concentric, in general. The tails of the arrows represent the synaptic weights of networks at birth. In the case of evolution *without* learning, network **B** has a higher fitness than does **A**, and thus would be preferentially selected. In the case of gradient-descent learning before selection, however, network **A** has a higher after-learning fitness, and would be preferentially selected (tips of arrows). Thus learning can change which individuals will be selected and reproduce, in particular favoring a network (here, **A**) whose genome is "good" (i.e., initial weights "close" to the optimal), despite its poor performance at birth. Over many generations, the choice of "better" genes for reproduction leads to new networks which require less learning to solve the problem — they are closer to the optimal. The rate of gene evolution is increased by learning (the Baldwin effect).

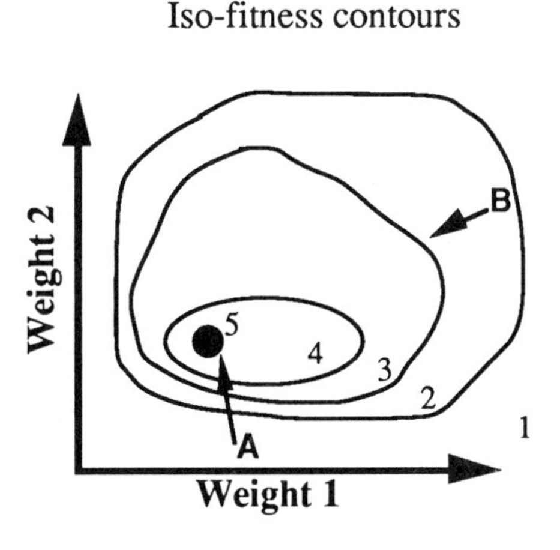

Figure 1: Iso-fitness contours in synaptic weight space. The black region corresponds to perfect classifications (fitness = 5). The weights of two networks are shown *at birth* (tails of arrows), and *after learning* (tips of arrows). At birth, **B** has a higher fitness score (2) than does **A** (1); a pure genetic algorithm (without learning) would preferentially reproduce **B**. *With* learning, though, **A** has a higher fitness score (4) than **B** (2), and would thus be preferentially reproduced. Since **A**'s genes are "better" than **B**'s, learning can lead to selection of better genes.

Surprisingly, *too much* learning leads to *slow* evolution of the genome, since after sufficient training in each generation, *all* networks can perform perfectly on the pattern recognition task, and thus are equally likely to pass on their genes, regardless of whether they are "good" or "bad." In Figure 1, if both **A** and **B** continue learning, eventually both will identify all five patterns correctly. **B** will be just as likely to reproduce as **A**, even though **A**'s genes are "better." Thus the rate of evolution will be decreased — too much learning is worse than an intermediate amount — or even no — learning.

SIMULATION APPROACH

Our system consists of a population of 200 networks, each for classifying pixel images of the first five letters of the alphabet. The 9 x 9 input grid is connected to four 7 x 7 sets of overlapping 3 x 3 orientation detectors; each detector is fully connected by modifiable weights to an output layer containing five category units (Fig. 2).

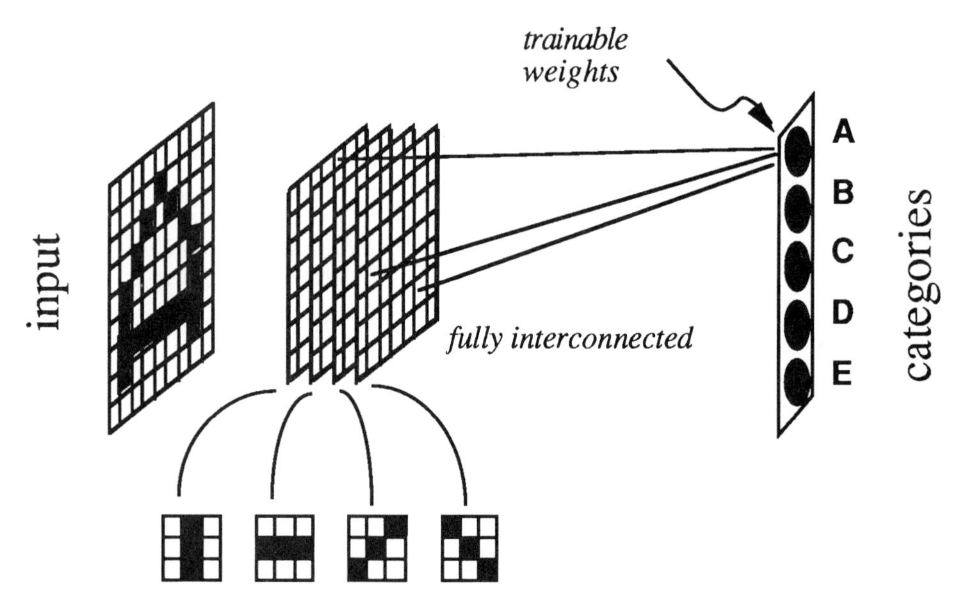

Figure 2: Individual network architecture. The 9x9 pixel input is detected by each of four orientation selective input layers (7x7 unit arrays), which are fully connected by trainable weights to the five category units. The network is thus a simple perceptron with 196 (=4x7x7) inputs and 5 outputs. Genes specify the initial connection strengths.

Each network has a 490-bit gene specifying the initial weights (Figure 3). For each of the 49 filter positions and 5 categories, the gene has two bits which specify *which* orientation is initially most strongly connected to the category unit (by an arbitrarily chosen factor of 3:1). During training, the weights from the filters to the output layer are changed by (supervised) perceptron learning. Darwinian fitness is given by the number of patterns correctly classified *after* training. We use fitness-proportional reproduction and the standard genetic algorithm processes of replication, mutation, and cross-over [Holland, 1975]. Note that while fitness may be measured after training, reproduction is of the genes present at birth, in accord with the Central Dogma. This is not a Lamarkian process.

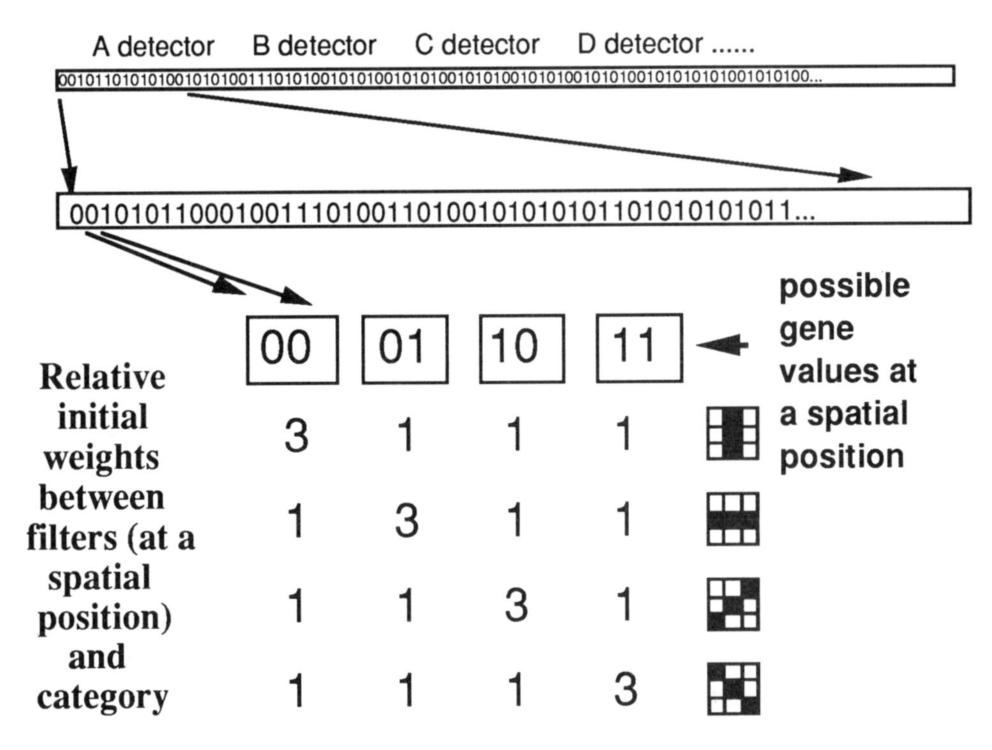

Figure 3: The genetic representation of a network. For each of the five category units, 49 two-bit numbers describe which of the four orientation units is most strongly connected at each position within the 7x7 grid. This unit is given a relative connection strength of 3, while the other three orientation units at that position are given a relative strength of 1.

For a given total number of teaching presentations, reproductive fitness might be defined in many ways, including categorization score at the end of learning or during learning; such functions will lead to different rates of evolution. We show simulations for two schemes: in *uniform learning* each network received the same number (e.g., 20) of training presentations; in *distributed learning* networks received a randomly chosen number (10, 34, 36, 16, etc.) of presentations.

RESULTS AND DISCUSSION

Figure 4 shows the population average fitness *at birth*. The lower curve shows the performance of the genetic algorithm alone; the two upper curves represent genetypic evolution — the amount of information within the genes — when the genetic algorithm is combined with gradient-descent learning. Learning increases the rate of evolution — both uniform and distributed learning are significantly better than no learning. The fitness *after* learning in a generation (not shown) is typically only 5% higher than the fitness at birth. Such a small improvement at a *single* generation cannot account for the overall high performance at later generations. A network's performance — even after learning — is more dependent upon its *ancestors* having learned than upon *its* having learned the task.

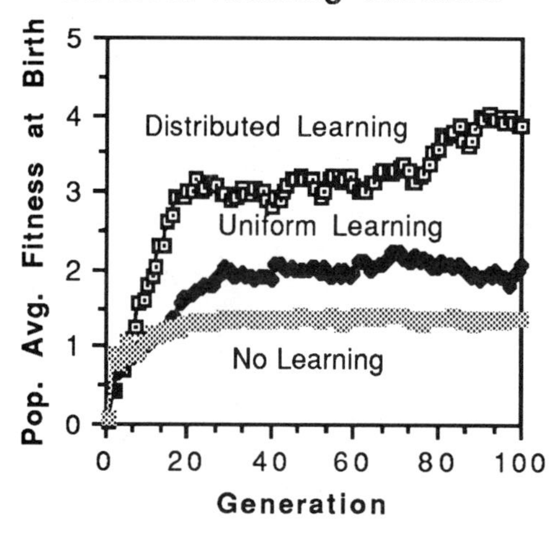

Figure 4: Learning guides the rate of evolution. In uniform learning, every network in every generation receives 20 learning presentations; in the distributed learning scheme, any network receives a number of patterns randomly chosen between 0 and 40 presentations (mean = 20). Clearly, evolution with learning leads to superior genes (fitness *at birth*) than evolution without learning.

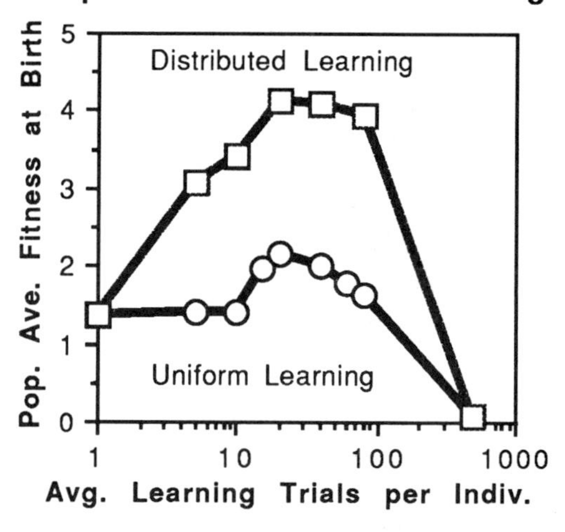

Figure 5: Selectivity of learning-evolution interactions. Too little or too much learning leads to slow evolution (population fitness at birth at generation 100) while an intermediate amount of learning leads to significantly higher such fitness. This effect is significant in both learning schemes. (Each point represents the mean of five simulation runs.)

Figure 5 illustrates the tuning of these learning-evolution interactions, as discussed above: too little or too much learning leads to poorer evolution than does an intermediate amount of learning. Given excessive learning (e.g., 500 presentations) *all* networks perform perfectly. This leads to the *slowest* evolution, since selection is independent of the quality of the genes.

Note too in Fig. 4 that distributed learning leads to significantly faster evolution (higher fitness at any particular generation) than uniform learning. In the uniform learning scheme, once networks have evolved to a point in weight space where they (and their offspring) can identify a pattern after learning, there is no more "pressure" on the genes to evolve. In Figure 6, both **A** and **B** are able to identify three patterns correctly after uniform learning, and hence both will reproduce equally. However, in the distributed learning scheme, one of the networks may (randomly) receive a small amount of learning. In such cases, **A**'s reproductive fitness will be unaffected, because it is able to solve the patterns without learning, while **B**'s fitness will decrease significantly. Thus in the distributed learning scheme (and in schemes in which fitness is determined in part *during* learning), there is "pressure" on the genes to improve at every generation. Diversity is, a driving force for evolution. Our distributed learning scheme leads to a greater diversity of fitness throughout a population.

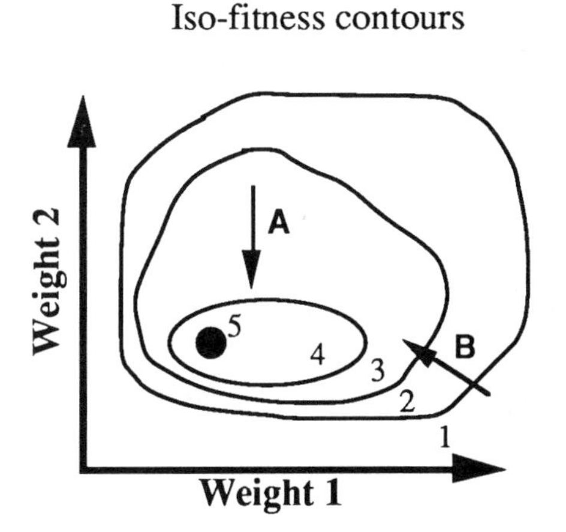

Figure 6: Distributed learning leads to faster evolution than uniform learning. In uniform learning, (shown above) **A** and **B** have equal reproductive fitness, even though **A** has "better" genes. In distributed learning, **A** will be more likely to reproduce when it (randomly) receives a small amount of learning (shorter arrow) than **B** will under similar circumstances. Thus "better" genes will be more likely to reproduce, leading to faster evolution.

CONCLUSIONS

Evolutionary search via genetic algorithms is a powerful technique for avoiding local minima in complicated energy landscapes [Goldberg, 1989; Peterson, 1990], but is often slow to converge in large problems. Conventional genetic approaches consider only the reproductive fitness of the genes; the slope of the fitness landscape in the immediate vicinity of the genes is ignored. Our hybrid evolutionary-learning approach utilizes the gradient of the local fitness landscape, along with the fitness of the genes, in determining survival and reproduction.

We have shown that this technique offers advantages over evolutionary search alone in the single-minimum landscape given by perceptron learning. In a simple pattern recognition problem, the hybrid system performs twice as well as a genetic algorithm alone. A hybrid system with distributed learning, which increases the "pressure" on the genes to evolve at every generation, performs four times as well as a genetic algorithm. In addition, we have demonstrated that there exists an optimal average amount of learning in order to increase the rate of evolution — too little or too much learning leads to slower evolution. In the extreme case of too much learning, where all networks are trained to perfect performance, there is no improvement of the genes. The advantages of the hybrid approach in landscapes with *multiple* minima can be even more pronounced [Stork and Keesing, 1991].

Acknowledgments

Thanks to David Rumelhart, Marcus Feldman, and Aviv Bergman for useful discussions.

References

Baldwin, J. M. "A new factor in evolution," *American Naturalist* **30**, 441-451 (1896)

Chomsky, N. ***Syntactic Structures*** The Hague: Mouton (1957)

Crick, F. W. "Central Dogma of Molecular Biology," *Nature* **227**, 561-563 (1970)

Goldberg, D. E. ***Genetic Algorithms in Search, Optimization & Machine Learning*** Reading, MA: Addison-Wesley (1989).

Hinton, G. E. and Nowlan, S. J. "How learning can guide evolution," *Complex Systems* **1**, 495-502 (1987)

Holland, J. H. ***Adaptation in Natural and Artificial Systems*** University of Michigan Press (1975)

Peterson, C. "Parallel Distributed Approaches to Combinatorial Optimization: Benchmanrk Studies on Traveling Salesman Problem," *Neural Computation* **2**, 261-269 (1990).

Stork, D. G. and Keesing, R. "The distribution of learning trials affects evolution in neural networks" (1991, submitted).

Designing Linear Threshold Based Neural Network Pattern Classifiers

Terrence L. Fine
School of Electrical Engineering
Cornell University
Ithaca, NY 14853

Abstract

The three problems that concern us are identifying a natural domain of pattern classification applications of feedforward neural networks, selecting an appropriate feedforward network architecture, and assessing the tradeoff between network complexity, training set size, and statistical reliability as measured by the probability of incorrect classification. We close with some suggestions, for improving the bounds that come from Vapnik-Chervonenkis theory, that can narrow, but not close, the chasm between theory and practice.

1 Speculations on Neural Network Pattern Classifiers

(1) The goal is to provide rapid, reliable classification of new inputs from a pattern source. Neural networks are appropriate as pattern classifiers when the pattern sources are ones of which we have little understanding, beyond perhaps a nonparametric statistical model, but we have been provided with classified samples of features drawn from each of the pattern categories. Neural networks should be able to provide rapid and reliable computation of complex decision functions. The issue in doubt is their statistical response to new inputs.

(2) The pursuit of optimality is misguided in the context of Point (1). Indeed, it is unclear what might be meant by 'optimality' in the absence of a more detailed mathematical framework for the pattern source.

(3) The well-known, oft-cited 'curse of dimensionality' exposed by Richard Bellman may be a 'blessing' to neural networks. Individual network processing nodes (e.g., linear threshold units) become more powerful as the number of their inputs increases. For a large enough number n of points in an input space of d dimensions, the number of dichotomies that can be generated by such a node grows exponentially in d. This suggests that, unlike all previous efforts at pattern classification that required substantial effort directed at the selection of low-dimensional feature vectors so as to make the decision rule calculable, we may now be approaching a

position from which we can exploit raw data (e.g., the actual samples in a time series or pixel values in an image). Even if we are as yet unable to achieve this, it is clear from the reports on actual pattern classifiers that have been presented at NIPS90 and the accompanying Keystone Workshop that successful neural network pattern classifiers have been constructed that accept as inputs feature vectors having hundreds of components (e.g., Guyon, et al. [1990]).

(4) The blessing of dimensionality is not granted if there is either a large subset of critically important components that will force the network to be too complex or a small subset that contains almost all of the information needed for accurate discrimination. The network is liable to be successful in those cases where the input or feature vector $\underline{x}$ has components that are individually nearly irrelevant, although collectively they enable us to discriminate well. Examples of such feature vectors might be the responses of individual fibers in the optic nerve, a pixel array for an image of an alphanumeric character, or the set of time samples of an acoustic transient. No one fiber, pixel value, or time sample provides significant information as to the true pattern category, although all of them taken together may enable us to do nearly error-free classification. An example in which all components are critically important is the calculation of parity. On our account, this is the sort of problem for which neural networks are inappropriate, albeit it has been repeatedly established that they can calculate parity.

We interpret 'critically important' very weakly as meaning that the subspace spanned by the subset of critically important features/inputs needs to be partitioned by the classifier so that there is at least one bounded region. If the nodes are linear threshold units then to carve out a bounded region, minimally a simplex, in a subspace of dimension c, where c is the size of the subset of critically important inputs, will require a network having at least $c + 1$ nodes in the first layer.

(5) Neural networks have opened up a new application domain wherein in practice we can intelligently construct nonlinear pattern classifiers characterized by thousands of parameters. In practice, nonlinear statistical models, ones not defined in terms of a covariance matrix, seem to be restricted to a few parameters.

(6) Nonetheless, Occam's Razor advises us to be sparing of parameters. We should be particularly cautious about the problem of overfitting when the number of parameters in the network is not much less than the number of training samples. Theory needs to provide practice with better insight and guidelines for avoiding overfitting and for the use of restrictions on training time as a guard against overfitting a system with almost as many adjustable parameters as there are data points.

(7) Points (1) and (5) combine to suggest that analytical approaches to network performance evaluation based upon typical statistical ideas may either be difficult to carry out or yield conclusions of little value to practice. There is no mismatch between statistical theory and neural networks in principle, but there does seem to be a significant mismatch in practice. While we are usually dealing with thousands of training samples, the complexity of the network means that we are not in a regime where asymptotic analyses (large sample behavior) will prove informative. On the other hand, the problem is far to complex to be resolved by 'exact' small sample analyses. These considerations serve to validate the widespread use of simulation studies to assess network design and performance.

2 The QED Architecture

2.1 QED Overview

One may view a classifier as either making the decision as to the correct class or as providing 'posterior' probabilities for the various classes. If we adopt the latter approach, then the use of sigmoidal units having a continuum of responses is appropriate. If, however, we adopt the first approach, then we require hard-limiting devices to select one of only finitely many (in our case only two) pattern classes. This is the approach that we adopt and it leads us to reliance upon linear threshold units (LTUs).

We have focused our attention upon a flexible architecture consisting of a first hidden layer that is viewed as a *quantizer* of the input feature vector $\underline{x}$ and is therefore referred to as the Q-layer. The binary outputs from the Q-layer are then input to a second hidden layer whose function is to *expand* the dimension of the set of Q-layer outputs. The E-layer enables us to exploit the blessing of dimensionality in that by choosing it wide enough we can ensure that all Boolean functions of the binary outputs of the Q-layer are now implementable as linearly separable functions of the E-layer outputs. Hence, to implement a binary classifier we need a third layer consisting of only a single node to effect the desired *decision*, and this output layer is referred to as the D-layer. The layers taken together are called a QED architecture.

2.2 Constructing the Q-Layer

The first layer in a feedforward neural network having LTUs can always be viewed as a quantizer. Subsequent layers in the network only see the input $\underline{x}$ through the window provided by the first layer quantization. We do not expect to be able to quantize/partition the input space, say $\mathbf{R}^{\mathbf{d}}$ for large d, into many small compact regions; to do so would require that $m >> d$, as noted in Point (4) of the preceding section. Hence, asymptotic results drawn from deterministic approximation theory are unlikely to be helpful here. One might have recourse to the large literature on vector quantization (e.g., the special issue on quantization of the *IEEE Transactions on Information Theory*, March 1982), but we expect to quantize vectors of high dimension into a relatively small number of regions. Most of the information-theoretic literature on vector quantization does not address this domain of very low information rate (bits/coordinate). A more promising direction is that of clustering algorithms (e.g., k-means as in Pollard [1982], Darken and Moody [1990]) to guide the choice of Q-layer.

2.3 Constructing the E,D-Layers

Space limitations prevent us from detailed discussion of the formation of the E,D layers. In brief, the E-layer can be composed of 2^m, often fewer, nodes where the weights to the ith node from the m Q-layer nodes are a binary representation of the index i with '0' replaced by '-1'. No training is required for the E-layer. The desired D-layer responses of 0 or 1 are formed simply by assigning weight t to connections from E-layer nodes corresponding to input patterns from class t, and summing and thresholding at 1/2. The training set $\mathcal{T}$ must be consulted to determine, say, on the basis of majority rule, the category $t \in \{0, 1\}$ to assign to a given E-layer node.

2.4 The Width of the Q-Layer

The overall complexity of the QED net depends upon the number m of nodes in the Q-layer. Hence, our proposal will only be of practical interest if m need not be large. As a first argument concerning the size of this parameter, if $m \leq d$ then m hyperplanes in general position partition $\mathbf{R}^{\mathbf{d}}$ into 2^m regions/cells. These cells are only of interest to us if we know how to assign them to pattern classes. From the perspective of Point (1) in the preceding section, we can only determine a classification of a cell if we have classified data points lying in the cell. Thus, if we wish to make rational use of m nodes in the Q-layer, then we should have in excess of 2^m data points in our training set. If we have fewer data points in $\mathcal{T}$ then we will be generating a multitude of cells about whose categorization we know no more than that provided by possibly known prior class probabilities. Another estimate of the required sample size is obtained by assuming that data points are placed at random in the cells. In this case results summarized and improved on in Flatto [1982] suggest that we will need in excess of $m2^m$ points to have a reasonable probability of having all cells occupied by data points. Many of the experimental studies reported at the meeting and workshops of NIPS90 assumed training set sizes no larger than about 10,000, implying that we need not consider m in excess of about 10. This number of nodes still yields a tractable QED architecture.

A second argument on which to base an *a priori* determination of m can be made by considering the problem-average performance analyses carried out by Hughes [1968]. He found that the probability of correct classification for a randomly selected classification problem, with equal prior probabilities for selecting a class, varied with the number M of possible feature values as $\frac{3M-2}{4M-2}$. This conclusion would suggest that a Q-layer containing as few as five properly selected nodes would suffice (Point (2)) for the design of a good pattern classifier.

In any event, both of our arguments suggest that a QED net having no more than about 10 Q-layer nodes might be adequate for many applications. At worst we would have to contemplate about 1,000 nodes in the E-layer, and this is not a prohibitively large number given current directions in hardware development. Nonetheless, the contradiction between our suggestions and current practice suggests that our conclusions are only tentative, and they need to be explored through applications, simulations, and studies of statistical generalization ability.

3 Sketch of Vapnik-Chervonenkis Theory of Statistical Generalization

We assume that there are two pattern classes labelled by $t \in \{0, 1\}$. A pattern sample is reduced by a preprocessor to a feature vector $\underline{x} \in \mathbf{R}^{\mathbf{d}}$. Point (3) expresses the goal of having this reduction be significantly less than would be required by an approach that does not use neural networks. Neural networks are generically labelled by $\eta : \mathbf{R}^{\mathbf{d}} \to \{0, 1\}$, $\eta(\underline{x}) = t$. $\mathcal{N} = \{\eta\}$ denotes the family of networks described by an architecture. As above, m denotes the width of the first hidden layer, and M denotes the number of cells/regions into which a net in $\mathcal{N}$ can partition $\mathbf{R}^d$. Typically, $M = 2^m$. The training set $\mathcal{T} = \{(\underline{x}_i, t_i), i = 1, n\}$. We hypothesize that the elements of $\mathcal{T}$ are *i.i.d.* as $\mathcal{P}(\underline{x}, t)$, which is unknown.

Performance is measured by error probabilities,

$$\mathcal{E}(\eta) = \mathcal{P}(\eta(\underline{x}) \neq t).$$

A good (it need not be unique) net in the family $\mathcal{N}$ is

$$\eta^0 = \text{argmin}_{\eta \in \mathcal{N}} \mathcal{E}(\eta), \qquad \mathcal{E}(\eta^0) = \min_{\eta \in \mathcal{N}} \mathcal{E}(\eta).$$

$\mathcal{E}_B$ denotes the Bayes error probability calculated on the basis of $\mathcal{P}(\underline{x}, t)$.

The empirical error frequency $\nu_{\mathcal{T}}(\eta)$ sustained by net η applied to $\mathcal{T}$ is

$$\nu_{\mathcal{T}}(\eta) = \frac{1}{n} \sum_{i=1}^{n} |\eta(\underline{x}_i) - t_i|.$$

A net in $\mathcal{N}$ having good classification performance on the training set $\mathcal{T}$ is

$$\eta^* = \text{argmin}_{\eta \in \mathcal{N}} \nu_{\mathcal{T}}(\eta).$$

By definition,

$$\mathcal{E}(\eta^*) \geq \mathcal{E}(\eta^0) \geq \mathcal{E}_B.$$

Let $m_{\mathcal{N}}(n)$ denote the VC growth function– the maximum, taken over all sets of n points in the input space, of the number of subsets that can be generated by the classification functions in $\mathcal{N}$. Let $V_{\mathcal{N}}$ denote the VC capacity, the largest n for which $\mathcal{N}$ can generate all 2^n of the subsets of some such set of n points.

For $n > V_{\mathcal{N}}$, Vapnik-Chervonenkis theory (Vapnik [1982], Pollard [1984], Baum and Haussler [1989]) can be adapted to yield the VC upper bound

$$\mathcal{P}(\mathcal{E}(\eta^*) - \mathcal{E}(\eta^0) \geq \epsilon) \leq 6 \frac{(2n)^{V_{\mathcal{N}}}}{V_{\mathcal{N}}\,!} e^{-n\epsilon^2/16} = 6 e^{V_{\mathcal{N}} \log 2n - \log V_{\mathcal{N}}\,! - n\epsilon^2/16}.$$

Let n_c denote the critical value of sample size n for which the exponent first becomes negative. If $n < n_c$ then the upper bound will exceed unity and be uninformative. However, if $n > n_c$ then the upper bound will converge to zero exponentially fast in sample size. An approximate solution for n_c from the VC upper bound yields

$$n_c \approx \frac{16}{\epsilon^2} V_{\mathcal{N}} \left(\log \frac{32e}{\epsilon^2} + \log\log \frac{32e}{\epsilon^2}\right).$$

If for purposes of illustration we take $\epsilon = .1, V_{\mathcal{N}} = 50$, then we find that $n_c \approx 902,000$. This conclusion, obtained by a direct application of Vapnik-Chervonenkis theory, disagrees by orders of magnitude with the experience of practitioners gained in training such low-complexity networks (about 50 connections).

4 Tightening the VC Argument

There are several components of the derivation of VC bounds that involve approximations and these, therefore, can be sources for improving these bounds. These approximations include recourses to Chernoff/Hoeffding bounds, union bounds, estimates of $m_{\mathcal{N}}(n)$, and the relation between $\mathcal{E}(\eta^*)-\mathcal{E}(\eta^0)$ and $2\sup_\eta |\nu_{\mathcal{T}}(\eta)-\mathcal{E}(\eta)|$. There is a belief among members of the neural network community that the weakness of the VC argument lies in the fact that by dealing with all possible underlying distributions $\mathcal{P}$ it is dealing with the worst case, and this worst case forces the large sample sizes. We agree with all but the last part of this belief. VC arguments being independent of the choice of $\mathcal{P}$ do indeed have to deal with worst cases. However, the worst case is dealt with through recourse to Chernoff/Hoeffding inequalities, and it is easily shown that these inequalities are not the source of our difficulties. A more promising direction in which to seek realistic estimates of training set size is through reductions in $m_{\mathcal{N}}(n)$ achieved through constraints on the architecture $\mathcal{N}$. One such restriction is through training time bounds that in effect restrict the portion of $\mathcal{N}$ that can be explored. Two other restrictions are discussed below.

5 Restricting the Architecture

5.1 Parameter Quantization

We can control the growth function contribution by quantizing all network parameters to k bits and thereby restricting $\mathcal{N}$. The VC dimension of a LTU with parameters quantized to $k \geq 1$ bits equals the VC dimension of the LTU with real-valued parameters. Hence, VC arguments show no improvement. However, there are now only $2^{km(d+1)}$ distinct first layers of m nodes accepting vectors from $\mathbf{R}^{\mathbf{d}}$. Hence, there are no more than $2^{2^m+km(d+1)}$ QED nets, and the restricted $\mathcal{N}$ has only finitely many members.

Direct application of the union bound and Chernoff inequality yield

$$\mathcal{P}(\mathcal{E}(\eta^*) - \mathcal{E}(\eta^0) \geq \epsilon) \leq 2^{2+2^m+km(d+1)}e^{-n\epsilon^2/2}.$$

When $\epsilon = .1, m = 5, d = 10$ this bound becomes less than unity for $n > n_c = 4710 + 7625k$. Thus, even 1-bit quantization suggests a training sample size in excess of 4700 for reliable generalization of even this simple network.

5.2 Clustering

The growth function $m_{\mathcal{N}}(n)$ 'overestimates' the number of cases we need to be concerned with in dealing with the random variable $Z(\eta) = |\nu_{\mathcal{T}}(\eta) - \nu_{\mathcal{T}'}(\eta)|$ encountered in VC theory derivations. We are only interested in whether Z exceeds a prescribed precision level ϵ, and not whether, say, $Z(\eta_1)$ differs from $Z(\eta_2)$ by as little as $\frac{1}{n}$ due to η_2 disagreeing with η_1 at only a single sample point.

To enforce consideration of networks as being different only if they yield classifications of $\mathcal{T}$ disagreeing substantially with each other we might proceed by clustering the points in $\mathcal{T}$ into κ clusters for each of the two classes. We then train the network so that decision boundaries do not subdivide individual clusters (see also Devroye and Wagner [1979]). The union bound and Chernoff inequality yield

$$\mathcal{P}(\mathcal{E}(\eta^*) - \mathcal{E}(\eta^0) \geq \epsilon) \leq 2^{2+4\kappa}e^{-n\epsilon^2/2},$$

a result that is independent of the input dimension d.

If we again choose $\epsilon = .1$ then the sample size n required to make this upper bound less than unity is about $280 + 560\kappa$. For accuracy at the precision level ϵ we should expect to have $\kappa \geq 1/\epsilon$. Hence, the least acceptable sample size should exceed 5,880. If we hope to make full use of the capabilities of the net, then we should expect to have clusters in almost all of the 2^m cells. If we take this to mean that $2\kappa = 2^m$, then $n > 9,240$ for $m = 5$. If clusters were equally likely to fall into each of the M cells then we would require $M(\log M + \alpha)$ clusters for a probability of no empty cell being approximately $e^{-e^{-\alpha}}$ (e.g., Flatto [1982]). Roughly, for $m = 5$ we should then aim for $2\kappa = 110$ and a sample size exceeding 31,000. Large as this estimate is, it is still a factor of 30 below what a direct application of VC theory yields.

Acknowledgements

I wish to thank Thomas W. Parks for insightful remarks on several of the topics discussed above.

This paper was prepared with partial support from DARPA through AFOSR-90-0016A.

References

Baum, E., D. Haussler [1989], What size net gives valid generalization?, in D. Touretzky, ed., *Advances in Neural Information Processing Systems 1*, Morgan Kaufman Pub., 81-90.

Darken, C., J. Moody [1990], Fast adaptive k-means clustering, NIPS90.

Devroye, L., T. Wagner [1979], Distribution-free bounds with the resubstitution error estimate, *IEEE Trans. on Information Theory*, **IT-25**, 208-210.

Flatto, L. [1982], Limit theorems for some random variables associated with urn models, *Annals of Probability*, **10**, 927-934.

Guyon, I., P. Albrecht, Y. Le Cun, J. Denker, W. Hubbard [1990], Design of a neural network character recognizer for a touch terminal, listed as to appear in *Pattern Recognition*, presented orally by Le Cun at the 1990 Keystone Workshop.

Hughes, G. [1968], On the mean accuracy of statistical pattern recognizers, *IEEE Trans. on Information Theory*, **14**, 55-63.

Pollard, D. [1982], A central limit theorem for k-means clustering, *Annals of Probability*, **10**, 919-926.

Pollard, D. [1984], *Convergence of Stochastic Processes*, Springer Verlag.

Vapnik, V. [1982], *Estimation of Dependences Based on Empirical Data*, Springer Verlag.

On Stochastic Complexity and Admissible Models for Neural Network Classifiers

Padhraic Smyth
Communications Systems Research
Jet Propulsion Laboratory
California Institute of Technology
Pasadena, CA 91109

Abstract

Given some training data how should we choose a particular network classifier from a family of networks of different complexities? In this paper we discuss how the application of stochastic complexity theory to classifier design problems can provide some insights into this problem. In particular we introduce the notion of *admissible* models whereby the complexity of models under consideration is affected by (among other factors) the class entropy, the amount of training data, and our prior belief. In particular we discuss the implications of these results with respect to neural architectures and demonstrate the approach on real data from a medical diagnosis task.

1 Introduction and Motivation

In this paper we examine in a general sense the application of Minimum Description Length (MDL) techniques to the problem of selecting a good classifier from a large set of candidate models or hypotheses. Pattern recognition algorithms differ from more conventional statistical modeling techniques in the sense that they typically choose from a very large number of candidate models to describe the available data. Hence, the problem of searching through this set of candidate models is frequently a formidable one, often approached in practice by the use of greedy algorithms. In this context, techniques which allow us to eliminate portions of the hypothesis space are of considerable interest. We will show in this paper that it is possible to use the intrinsic structure of the MDL formalism to eliminate large numbers of candidate models given only minimal information about the data. Our results depend on the very simple notion that models which are obviously too complex for the problem (e.g., models whose complexity exceeds that of the data itself) can be discarded from further consideration in the search for the most parsimonious model.

2 Background on Stochastic Complexity Theory

2.1 General Principles

Stochastic complexity prescribes a general theory of inductive inference from data, which, unlike more traditional inference techniques, takes into account the *complexity* of the proposed model in addition to the standard goodness-of-fit of the model to the data. For a detailed rationale the reader is referred to the work of Rissanen (1984) or Wallace and Freeman (1987) and the references therein. Note that the Minimum Description Length (MDL) technique (as Rissanen's approach has become known) is implicitly related to Maximum A Posteriori (MAP) Bayesian estimation techniques if cast in the appropriate framework.

2.2 Minimum Description Length and Stochastic Complexity

Following the notation of Barron and Cover (1991), we have N data-points, described as a sequence of tuples of observations $\{x_i^1, \ldots, x_i^K, y_i\}, 1 \leq i \leq N$, to be referred to as $\{\underline{x_i}, y_i\}$ for short. The x_i^k correspond to values taken on by the K random variables X^k (which may be continuous or discrete), while, for the purposes of this paper, the y_i are elements of the finite alphabet of the discrete m-ary class variable Y. Let $\Gamma_N = \{M_1, \ldots, M_{|\Gamma_N|}\}$ be the family of candidate models under consideration. Note that by defining Γ_N as a function of N, the number of data points, we allow the possibility of considering more complicated models as more data arrives. For each $M_j \in \Gamma_N$ let $C(M_j)$ be non-negative numbers such that

$$\sum_j 2^{-C(M_j)} \leq 1.$$

The $C(M_j)$ can be interpreted as the cost in bits of specifying model M_j — in turn, $2^{-C(M_j)}$ is the prior probability assigned to model M_j (suitably normalized). Let us use $\mathcal{C} = \{C(M_1), \ldots, C(M_{|\Gamma_N|})\}$ to refer to a particular coding scheme for Γ_N. Hence the total *description length* of the data plus a model M_j is defined as

$$L(M_j, \{\underline{x_i}, y_i\}) = C(M_j) + \log\left(\frac{1}{p(\{y_i\}|M_j(\{\underline{x_i}\}))}\right)$$

i.e., we first describe the model and then the class data relative to the given model (as a function of $\{\underline{x_i}\}$, the feature data). The *stochastic complexity* of the data $\{\underline{x_i}, y_i\}$ relative to $\mathcal{C}$ and Γ_N is the minimum description length

$$I(\{\underline{x_i}, y_i\}) = \min_{M_j \in \Gamma_N} \{L(M_j, \{\underline{x_i}, y_i\})\}.$$

The problem of finding the model of *shortest* description length is intractable in the general case — nonetheless the idea of finding the best model we can is well motivated, works well in practice and is far preferable to the alternative approach of ignoring the complexity issue entirely.

3 Admissible Stochastic Complexity Models

3.1 Definition of Admissibility

We will find it useful to define the notion of an *admissible* model for the classification problem: the set of admissible models Ω_N ($\subseteq \Gamma_N$) is defined as all models whose complexity is such that there exists no other model whose description length is known to be smaller. In other words we are saying that inadmissible models are those which have complexity in bits greater than any *known* description length — clearly they cannot be better than the best known model in terms of description length and can be eliminated from consideration. Hence, Ω_N is defined dynamically and is a function of how many description lengths we have already calculated in our search. Typically Γ_N may be pre-defined, such as the class of all 3-layer feed-forward neural networks with particular activation functions. We would like to restrict our search for a good model to the set $\Omega_N \subseteq \Gamma_N$ as far as possible (since non-admissible models are of no practical use). In practice it may be difficult to determine the exact boundaries of Ω_N, particularly when $|\Gamma_N|$ is large (with decision trees or neural networks for example). Note that the notion of admissibility described here is particularly useful when we seek a *minimal* description length, or equivalently a model of *maximal a posteriori* probability — in situations where one's goal is to average over a number of possible models (in a Bayesian manner) a modification of the admissibility criterion would be necessary.

3.2 Results for Admissible Models

Simple techniques for eliminating obvious non-admissible models are of interest: for the classification problem a necessary condition that a model M_j be admissible is that

$$C(M_j) \leq N \cdot H(X) \leq N \log(m)$$

where $H(X)$ is the entropy of the m-ary class variable X. The obvious interpretation in words is that any admissible model must have complexity less than that of the data itself. It is easy to show in addition that the complexity of any admissible model is upper bounded by the parameters of the classification problem:

$$p(M_j) \geq 2^{-N.H(X)} \geq 2^{-N \log(m)}, \qquad \forall M_j \in \Omega_N.$$

Hence, the size of the space of admissible models can also be bounded:

$$|\Omega_N| \leq 2^{N \cdot H(X)} \leq 2^{N.\log(m)}.$$

Our approach suggests that for classification at least, once we know N and the number of classes m, there are strict limitations on how many *admissible* models we can consider. Of course the theory does not state that considering a larger subset will necessarily result in a less optimal model being found, however, it is difficult to argue the case for including large numbers of models which are clearly too complex for the problem. At best, such an approach will lead to an inefficient search, whereas at worst a very poor model will be chosen perhaps as a result of the use of a poor coding scheme for the unnecessarily large hypothesis space.

3.3 Admissible Models and Bayes Risk

The notion of *minimal* compression (the minimum achievable goodness-of-fit) is intimately related in the classification problem to the minimal Bayes risk for the problem (Kovalevsky, 1980). Let M_B be any model (not necessarily unique) which achieves the optimal Bayes risk (i.e., minimizes the classifier error) for the classification problem. In particular, $C(\{x_i\}|M_B(\{y_i\}))$ is not necessarily zero, indeed in most practical problems of interest it is non-zero, due to the ambiguity in the mapping from the feature space to the class variable. In addition, M_B may not be defined in the set Γ_N, and hence, M_B need not even be admissible. If, in the limit as $N \rightarrow \infty$, $M_B \notin \Gamma_\infty$ then there is a fundamental *approximation* error in the representation being used, i.e., the family of models under consideration is not flexible enough to optimally represent the mapping from $\{x_i\}$ to $\{y_i\}$. Smyth (1991) has shown how information about the Bayes error rate for the problem (if available) can be used to further tighten the bounds on admissibility.

4 Applying Minimum Description Length Principles to Neural Network Design

In principle the admissibility results can be applied to a variety of classifier design problems — applications to Markov model selection and decision tree design are described elsewhere (Smyth, 1991). In this paper we limit our attention to the problem of automatically selecting a feedforward multi-layer network architecture.

4.1 Calculation of the Goodness-of-Fit

As is clear from the preceding discussion, application of the MDL principle to classifier selection requires that the classifier produce a posterior probability estimate of the class labels. In the context of a network model this is not a problem provided the network is trained to provide such estimates. This requires a simple modification of the objective function to a log-likelihood function $-\sum_{i=1}^{N} \log(\hat{p}(y_i|x_i))$, where y_i is the class label of the ith training datum and $\hat{p}()$ is the network's estimate of $p()$. This function has been proposed in the literature in the past under the guise of a cross-entropy measure (for the special case of binary classes) and more recently it has been derived from the more basic arguments of Minimum Mutual Information (MMI) (Bridle, 1990) and Maximum Likelihood (ML) Estimation (Gish, 1990). The cross-entropy function for network training is nothing more that the goodness-of-fit component of the description length criterion. Hence, both MMI and ML (since they are equivalent in this case) are special cases of the MDL procedure wherein the complexity term is a constant and is left out of the optimization (all models are assumed to be equally likely and likelihood alone is used as the decision criterion).

4.2 Complexity Penalization for Multi-layer Perceptron Models

It has been proposed in the past (Barron, 1989) to use a penalty term of $(k/2)\log N$, where k is the number of parameters (weights and biases) in the network. The origins of this complexity measure lie in general arguments originally proposed by Rissanen (1984). However this penalty term is too large. Cybenko (1990) has pointed out that existing successful applications of networks have far more parameters than could possibly be justified by a statistical analysis, given the amount of training data used to construct the network. The critical factor lies in the *precision* to which these parameters are stated in the final model. In essence the principle of MDL (and Bayesian techniques) dictates that the data only justifies the stating of any parameter in the model to some finite precision, inversely proportional to the inherent variance of the estimate. Approximate techniques for the calculation of the complexity terms in this manner have been proposed (Weigend, Huberman and Rumelhart, this volume) but a complete description length analysis has not yet appeared in the literature.

4.3 Complexity Penalization for a Discrete Network Model

It turns out that there are alternatives to multi-layer perceptrons whose complexity is much easier to calculate. We will look in particular at the rule-based network of Goodman et al. (1990). In this model the hidden units correspond to Boolean combinations of discrete input variables. The link weights from hidden to output (class) nodes are proportional to log conditional probabilities of the class given the activation of a hidden node. The output nodes form estimates of the posterior class probabilities by a simple summation followed by a normalization. The implicit assumption of conditional independence is ameliorated in practice by the fact that the hidden units are chosen in a manner to ensure that the assumption is violated as little as possible.

The complexity penalty for the network is calculated as being $(1/2)\log N$ per link from the hidden to output layers, plus an appropriate coding term for the specification of the hidden units. Hence, the description length of a network with k hidden units would be

$$L = -\sum_{i=1}^{N} \log(\hat{p}(y_i|\underline{x_i})) + k/2 \log N - \sum_{i=1}^{k} \log \pi(o_i)$$

where o_i is the order of the ith hidden node and $\pi(o_i)$ is a prior probability on the orders. Using this definition of description length we get from our earlier results on admissible models that the number of hidden units in the architecture is upper bounded by

$$k \leq \frac{NH(C)}{0.5\log N + \log K + 1}$$

where K is the number of binary input attributes.

4.4 Application to a Medical Diagnosis Problem

We consider the application of our techniques to the discovery of a parsimonious network for breast cancer diagnosis, using the discrete network model. A common technique in breast cancer diagnosis is to obtain a fine needle aspirate (FNA) from the patient. The FNA sample is then evaluated under a microscope by a physician who makes a diagnosis. Ground truth in the form of binary class labels ("benign" or "malignant") is obtained by re-examination or biopsy at a later stage. Wolberg and Mangasarian (1991) described the collection of a database of such information.

The feature information consisted of subjective evaluations of nine FNA sample characteristics such as uniformity of cell size, marginal adhesion and mitoses. The training data consists of 439 such FNA samples obtained from real patients which were later assigned class labels. Given that the prior class entropy is almost 1 bit, one can immediately state from our bounds that networks with more than 51 hidden units are inadmissible. Furthermore, as we evaluate different models we can narrow the region of admissibility using the results stated earlier. Figure 1 gives a graphical interpretation of this procedure.

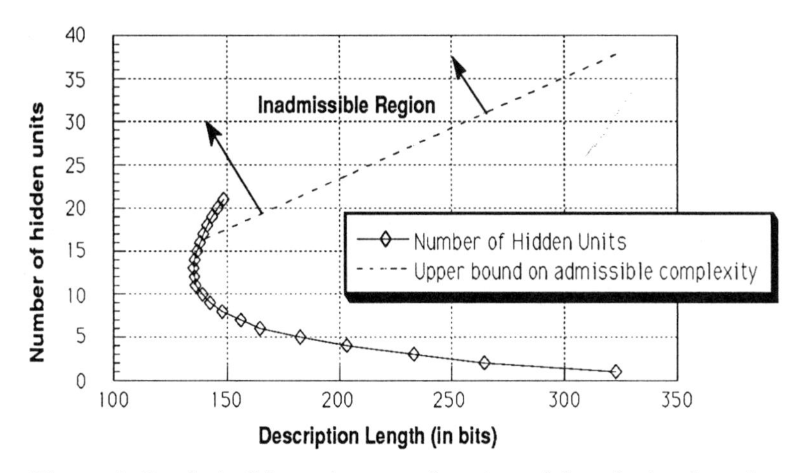

Figure 1. Inadmissible region as a function of description length

The algorithm effectively moves up the left-hand axis, adding hidden units in a greedy manner. Initially the description length (the lower curve) decreases rapidly as we capture the gross structure in the data. For each model that we calculate a description length, we can in turn calculate an upper bound on admissibility (the upper curve) — this bound is linear in description length. Hence, for example by the time we have 5 hidden units we know that any models with more than 21 hidden units are inadmissible. Finally a local minimum of the description length function is reached at 12 units, at which point we know that the optimal solution can have at most 16 hidden units. As matter of interest, the resulting network with 12 hidden units correctly classified 94 of 96 independent test cases.

5 Conclusion

There are a variety of related issues which arise in this context which we can only briefly mention due to space constraints. For example, how does the prior "model entropy", $H(\Omega_N) = -\sum_i p(M_i)\log(p(M_i))$, affect the complexity of the search problem? Questions also naturally arise as to how Ω_N should grow as a function of N in an *incremental* learning scenario.

In conclusion, it should not be construed from this paper that consideration of admissible models is the major factor in inductive inference — certainly the choice of description lengths for the various models and the use of efficient optimization techniques for seeking the parameters of each model remain the cornerstones of success. Nonetheless, our results provide useful theoretical insight and are practical to the extent that they provide a "sanity check" for model selection in MDL.

Acknowledgments

The research described in this paper was performed at the Jet Propulsion Laboratories, California Institute of Technology, under a contract with the National Aeronautics and Space Administration. In addition this work was supported in part by the Air Force Office of Scientific Research under grant number AFOSR–90–0199.

References

A. R. Barron (1989), 'Statistical properties of artificial neural networks,' in *Proceedings of 1989 IEEE Conference on Decision and Control.*

A. R. Barron and T. M. Cover (1991), 'Minimum complexity density estimation,' to appear in *IEEE Trans. Inform. Theory.*

J. Bridle (1990), 'Training stochastic model recognition algorithms as networks can lead to maximum mutual information estimation of parameters,' in D. S. Touretzky (ed.), *Advances in Neural Information Processing Systems 1*, pp.211–217, San Mateo, CA: Morgan Kaufmann.

G. Cybenko (1990), 'Complexity theory of neural networks and classification problems,' preprint.

H. Gish (1991), 'Maximum likelihood training of neural networks,' to appear in *Proceedings of the Third International Workshop on AI and Statistics*, (D. Hand, ed.), Chapman and Hall: London.

R. M. Goodman, C. Higgins, J. W. Miller, and P. Smyth (1990), 'A rule-based approach to neural network classifiers,' in *Proceedings of the 1990 International Neural Network Conference*, Paris, France.

V. A. Kovalevsky (1980), *Image Pattern Recognition*, translated from Russian by A. Brown, New York: Springer Verlag, p.79.

J. Rissanen (1984), 'Universal coding, information, prediction, and estimation,' *IEEE Trans. Inform. Theory*, vol.30, pp.629–636.

P. Smyth (1991), 'Admissible stochastic complexity models for classification problems,' to appear in *Proceedings of the Third International Workshop on AI and Statistics*, (D. Hand, ed.), Chapman and Hall: London.

C. S. Wallace and P. R. Freeman (1987), 'Estimation and inference by compact coding,' *J. Royal Stat. Soc. B*, vol.49, no.3, pp.240–251.

W. H. Wolberg and O. L. Mangasarian (1991), Multi-surface method of pattern separation applied to breast cytology diagnosis, *Proceedings of the National Academy of Sciences*, in press.

A Method for the Efficient Design of Boltzmann Machines for Classification Problems

Ajay Gupta and Wolfgang Maass*
Department of Mathematics, Statistics, and Computer Science
University of Illinois at Chicago
Chicago IL, 60680

Abstract

We introduce a method for the efficient design of a Boltzmann machine (or a Hopfield net) that computes an arbitrary given Boolean function f. This method is based on an efficient simulation of acyclic circuits with threshold gates by Boltzmann machines. As a consequence we can show that various concrete Boolean functions f that are relevant for classification problems can be computed by scalable Boltzmann machines that are guaranteed to converge to their global maximum configuration with high probability after constantly many steps.

1 INTRODUCTION

A Boltzmann machine ([AHS], [HS], [AK]) is a neural network model in which the units update their states according to a stochastic decision rule. It consists of a set $\mathcal{U}$ of units, a set $\mathcal{C}$ of *unordered* pairs of elements of $\mathcal{U}$, and an assignment of connection strengths $S : \mathcal{C} \rightarrow \mathbf{R}$. A configuration of a Boltzmann machine is a map $k : \mathcal{U} \rightarrow \{0,1\}$. The consensus $C(k)$ of a configuration k is given by $C(k) = \sum_{\{u,v\} \in \mathcal{C}} S(\{u,v\}) \cdot k(u) \cdot k(v)$. If the Boltzmann machine is currently in configuration k and unit u is considered for a state change, then the acceptance

*This paper was written during a visit of the second author at the Department of Computer Science of the University of Chicago.

probability for this state change is given by $\frac{1}{1+e^{-\Delta C/c}}$. Here ΔC is the change in the value of the consensus function C that would result from this state change of u, and $c > 0$ is a fixed parameter (the "temperature").

Assume that n units of a Boltzmann machine B have been declared as input units and m other units as output units. One says that B computes a function $f : \{0,1\}^n \to \{0,1\}^m$ if for any clamping of the input units of B according to some $\underline{a} \in \{0,1\}^n$ the only global maxima of the consensus function of the clamped Boltzmann machine are those configurations where the output units are in the states given by $f(\underline{a})$.

Note that even if one leaves the determination of the connection strengths for a Boltzmann machine up to a learning procedure ([AHS], [HS], [AK]), one has to know in advance the required number of hidden units, and how they should be connected (see section 10.4.3 of [AK] for a discussion of this open problem).

Ad hoc constructions of efficient Boltzmann machines tend to be rather difficult (and hard to verify) because of the cyclic nature of their "computations".

We introduce in this paper a new method for the construction of efficient Boltzmann machines for the computation of a given Boolean function f (the same method can also be used for the construction of Hopfield nets). We propose to construct first an acyclic Boolean circuit T with threshold gates that computes f (this turns out to be substantially easier). We show in section 2 that any Boolean threshold circuit T can be simulated by a Boltzmann machine $B(T)$ of the same size as T. Furthermore we show in section 3 that a minor variation of $B(T)$ is likely to converge very fast. In Section 4 we discuss applications of our method for various concrete Boolean functions.

2 SIMULATION OF THRESHOLD CIRCUITS BY BOLTZMANN MACHINES

A threshold circuit T (see [M], [PS], [R], [HMPST]) is a labeled *acyclic directed* graph. We refer to the number of edges that are directed into (out of) a node of T as the indegree (outdegree) of that node. Its nodes of indegree 0 are labeled by input variables $x_i (i \in \{1, \ldots, n\})$. Each node g of indegree $l > 0$ in T is labeled by some arbitrary Boolean threshold function $F_g : \{0,1\}^l \to \{0,1\}$, where $F_g(y_1, \ldots, y_l) = 1$ if and only if $\sum_{i=1}^{l} \alpha_i y_i \geq t$ (for some arbitrary parameters $\alpha_1, \ldots, \alpha_l, t \in \mathbf{R}$; w.l.o.g. $\alpha_1, \ldots, \alpha_l, t \in \mathbf{Z}$ [M]). One views such node g as a threshold gate that computes F_g. If m nodes of a threshold circuit T are in addition labeled as output nodes, one defines in the usual manner the Boolean function $f : \{0,1\}^n \to \{0,1\}^m$ that is computed by T.

We simulate T by the following Boltzmann machine $B(T) = \langle \mathcal{U}, \mathcal{C}, S \rangle$ (note that T has *directed* edges, while $B(T)$ has *undirected* edges). We reserve for each node g of T a separate unit $b(g)$ of $B(T)$. We set

$$\begin{aligned} \mathcal{U} &:= \{b(g) | g \text{ is a node of } T\} \text{ and} \\ \mathcal{C} &:= \{\{b(g'), b(g)\} | g', g \text{ are nodes of } T \text{ so that either } g' = g \text{ or} \\ &\qquad g', g \text{ are connected by an edge in } T\}. \end{aligned}$$

Consider an arbitrary unit $b(g)$ of $B(T)$. We define the connection strengths $S(\{b(g)\})$ and $S(\{b(g'), b(g)\})$ (for edges $< g', g >$ of T) by induction on the length of the longest path in T from g to a node of T with outdegree 0.

If g is a gate of T with outdegree 0 then we define $S(\{b(g)\}) := -2t + 1$, where t is the threshold of g, and we set $S(\{b(g'), b(g)\}) := 2\alpha(< g', g >)$ (where $\alpha(< g', g >)$ is the weight of the directed edge $< g', g >$ in T).

Assume that g is a threshold gate of T with outdegree > 0. Let $g_1, \ldots, g_k$ be the immediate successors of g in T. Set $w := \sum_{i=1}^{k} |S(\{b(g), b(g_i)\})|$ (we assume that the connection strengths $S(\{b(g), b(g_i)\})$ have already been defined). We define $S(\{b(g)\}) := -(2w + 2) \cdot t + w + 1$, where t is the threshold of gate g. Furthermore for every edge $< g', g >$ in T we set $S(\{b(g'), b(g)\}) := (2w + 2) \cdot \alpha (< g', g >)$.

Remark: It is obvious that for problems in TC^0 (see section 4) the size of connection strengths in $B(T)$ can be bounded by a polynomial in n.

Theorem 2.1 *For any threshold circuit T the Boltzmann machine $B(T)$ computes the same Boolean function as T.*

Proof of Theorem 2.1:

Let $\underline{a} \in \{0, 1\}^n$ be an arbitrary input for circuit T. We write $g(\underline{a}) \in \{0, 1\}$ for the output of gate g of T for circuit input $\underline{a}$.

Consider the Boltzmann machine $B(T)_{\underline{a}}$ with the n units $b(g)$ for input nodes g of T clamped according to $\underline{a}$. We show that the configuration $K_{\underline{a}}$ of $B(T)_{\underline{a}}$ where $b(g)$ is on if and only if $g(\underline{a}) = 1$ is the only global maximum (in fact: the only *local* maximum) of the consensus function C for $B(T)_{\underline{a}}$.

Assume for a contradiction that configuration K of $B(T)_{\underline{a}}$ is a global maximum of the consensus function C and $K \neq K_{\underline{a}}$. Fix a node g of T of minimal depth in T so that $K(b(g)) \neq K_{\underline{a}}(b(g)) = g(\underline{a})$. By definition of $B(T)_{\underline{a}}$ this node g is not an input node of T. Let K' result form K by changing the state of $b(g)$. We will show that $C(K') > C(K)$, which is a contradiction to the choice of K.

We have (by the definition of C)

$$C(K') - C(K) = (1 - 2K(b(g))) \cdot (S_1 + S_2 + S(\{b(g)\})), \text{ where}$$
$$S_1 := \sum\{K(b(g')) \cdot S(\{b(g'), b(g)\}) | < g', g > \text{ is an edge in } T\}$$
$$S_2 := \sum\{K(b(g')) \cdot S(\{b(g), b(g')\}) | < g, g' > \text{ is an edge in } T\}.$$

Let w be the parameter that occurs in the definition of $S(\{b(g)\})$ (set $w := 0$ if g has outdegree 0). Then $|S_2| \leq w$. Let $p_1, \ldots, p_m$ be the immediate predecessors of g in T, and let t be the threshold of gate g. Assume first that $g(\underline{a}) = 1$. Then $S_1 = (2w+2) \cdot \sum_{i=1}^{m} \alpha(< p_i, g >) \cdot p_i(\underline{a}) \geq (2w+2) \cdot t$. This implies that $S_1 + S_2 > (2w+2) \cdot t - w - 1$, and therefore $S_1 + S_2 + S(\{b(g)\}) > 0$, hence $C(K') - C(K) > 0$.

If $g(\underline{a}) = 0$ then we have $\sum_{i=1}^{m} \alpha(< p_i, g >) \cdot p_i(\underline{a}) \leq t - 1$, thus $S_1 = (2w + 2) \cdot \sum_{i=1}^{m} \alpha(< p_i, g >) \cdot p_i(\underline{a}) \leq (2w + 2) \cdot t - 2w - 2$. This implies that $S_1 + S_2 < (2w + 2) \cdot t - w - 1$, and therefore $S_1 + S_2 + S(\{b(g)\}) < 0$. We have in this case $K(b(g)) = 1$, hence $C(K') - C(K) = (-1) \cdot (S_1 + S_2 + S(\{b(g)\})) > 0$. □

3 THE CONVERGENCE SPEED OF THE CONSTRUCTED BOLTZMANN MACHINES

We show that the constructed Boltzmann machines will converge relatively fast to a global maximum configuration. This positive result holds both if we view $B(T)$ as a sequential Boltzmann machine (in which units are considered for a state change one at a time), and if we view $B(T)$ as a parallel Boltzmann machine (where several units are simultaneously considered for a state change). In fact, it even holds for unlimited parallelism, where *every* unit is considered for a state change at every step. Although unlimited parallelism appears to be of particular interest in the context of brain models and for the design of massively parallel machines, there are hardly any positive results known for this case (see section 8.3 in [AK]).

If g is a gate in T with outdegree > 1 then the current state of unit $b(g)$ of $B(T)$ becomes relevant at several different time points (whenever one of the immediate successors of g is considered for a state change). This effect increases the probability that unit $b(g)$ may cause an "error." Therefore the error probability of an output unit of $B(T)$ does not just depend on the number of nodes in T, but on the number $N(T)$ of nodes in a tree T' that results if we replace in the usual fashion the directed graph of T by a tree T' of the same depth (one calls a directed graph a *tree* if all of its nodes have outdegree ≤ 1).

To be precise, we define by induction on the depth of g for each gate g of T a tree Tree(g) that replaces the subcircuit of T below g. If $g_1, \ldots, g_k$ are the immediate predecessors of g in T then Tree(g) is the tree which has g as root and Tree(g^1), ..., Tree(g_k) as immediate subtrees (it is understood that if some g_i has another immediate successor $g' \neq g$ then different copies of Tree(g_i) are employed in the definition of Tree(g) and Tree(g')).

We write $|\text{Tree}(g)|$ for the number of nodes in Tree(g) , and $N(T)$ for $\sum\{|\text{Tree}(g)|\ |g$ is an output node of $T\}$. It is easy to see that if T is synchronous (i.e. depth $(g'') = \text{depth}(g') + 1$ for all edges $< g', g'' >$ in T) then $|\text{Tree}(g)| \leq s^{d-1}$ for any node g in T of depth d which has s nodes in the subcircuit of T below g. Therefore $N(T)$ is polynomial in n if T is of constant depth and polynomial size (this can be achieved for all problems in TC^0, see Section 4).

We write $B^\delta(T)$ for the variation of the Boltzmann machine $B(T)$ of section 2 where each connection strength in $B(T)$ is multiplied by δ ($\delta > 0$). Equivalently one could view $B^\delta(T)$ as a machine with the *same* connection strengths as $B(T)$ but a lower "temperature" (replace c by c/δ).

Theorem 3.1 *Assume that T is a threshold circuit of depth d that computes a Boolean function $f : \{0,1\}^n \to \{0,1\}^m$. Let $B^\delta(T)_{\underline{a}}$ be the Boltzmann machine that results from clamping the input units of $B^\delta(T)$ according to $\underline{a}$ ($\underline{a} \in \{0,1\}^n$).*

Assume that $0 = q_0 < q_1 < \ldots < q_d$ are arbitrary numbers such that for every $i \in \{1, \ldots, d\}$ and every gate g of depth i in T the corresponding unit $b(g)$ is considered for a state change at some step during interval $(q_{i-1}, q_i]$. There is no restriction on how many other *units are considered for a state change at any step.*

Let t be an arbitrary time step with $t \geq q_d$. Then the output units of $B(T)$ are at *the end of step t with probability* $\geq 1 - N(T) \cdot \frac{1}{1+e^{\delta/c}}$ *in the states given by* $f(\underline{a})$.

Remarks:

1. For $\delta := n$ this probability converges to 1 for $n \to \infty$ if T is of constant depth and polynomial size.
2. The condition on the timing of state changes in Theorem 3.1 has been formulated in a very general fashion in order to make it applicable to all of the common types of Boltzmann machines.For a sequential Boltzmann machine (see [AK], section 8.2) one can choose $q_i - q_{i-1}$ sufficiently large (for example polynomially in the size of T) so that with high probability every unit of $B(T)$ is considered for a state change during the interval $(q_{i-1}, q_i]$. On the other hand, for a synchronous Boltzmann machine with limited parallelism ([AK], section 8.3) one may apply the result to the case where every unit $b(g)$ with g of depth i in T is considered for a state change at step i (set $q_i := i$). Theorem 3.1 also remains valid for unlimited parallelism ([AK], section 8.3), where every unit is considered for a state change at every step (set $q_i := i$). In fact, not even synchronicity is required for Theorem 3.1, and it also applies to asynchronous parallel Boltzmann machines ([AK], section 8.3.2).
3. For sequential Boltzmann machines in general the available upper bounds for their convergence speed are very unsatisfactory. In particular no upper bounds are known which are polynomial in the number of units (see section 3.5 of [AK]). For Boltzmann machines with unlimited parallelism one can in general not even prove that they converge to a global maximum of their consensus function (section 8.3 of [AK]).

Proof of Theorem 3.1: We prove by induction on i that for every gate g of depth i in T and every step $t \geq q_i$ the unit $b(g)$ is at the end of step t with probability $\geq 1 - |\text{Tree}(g)| \cdot \frac{1}{1+e^{\delta/c}}$ in state $g(\underline{a})$.

Assume that $g_1, \ldots, g_k$ are the immediate predecessors of gate g in T. By definition we have $|\text{Tree}(g)| = 1 + \sum_{j=1}^{k} |\text{Tree}(g_j)|$. Let $t' \leq t$ be the last step before t at which $b(g)$ has been considered for a state change. Since $T \geq q_i$ we have $t' > q_{i-1}$. Thus for each $j = 1, \ldots, k$ we can apply the induction hypothesis to unit $b(g_j)$ and step $t' - 1 \geq q_{\text{depth}(g_j)}$. Hence with probability $\geq 1 - (|\text{Tree}(g)| - 1) \cdot \frac{1}{1+e^{\delta/c}}$ the state of the units $b(g_1), \ldots, b(g_k)$ at the end of step $t' - 1$ are $g_1(\underline{a}), \ldots, g_k(\underline{a})$. Assume now that the unit $b(g_j)$ is at the end of step $t' - 1$ in state $g_j(\underline{a})$, for $j = 1, \ldots, k$. If g is at the beginning of step t' not in state $g(\underline{a})$, then a state change of unit $b(g)$ would increase the consensus function by $\Delta C \geq \delta$ (independently of the current status of units $b(\tilde{g})$ for immediate successors $\tilde{g}$ of g in T). Thus $b(g)$ accepts in this case the change to state $g(\underline{a})$ with probability $\frac{1}{1+e^{-\Delta C/c}} \geq \frac{1}{1+e^{-\delta/c}} = 1 - \frac{1}{1+e^{\delta/c}}$. On the other hand, if $b(g)$ is already at the beginning of step t' in state $g(\underline{a})$, then a change of its state would decrease the consensus by at least δ. Thus $b(g)$ remains with probability $\geq 1 - \frac{1}{1+e^{\delta/c}}$ in state $g(\underline{a})$. The preceding considerations imply that unit $b(g)$ is at the end of step t' (and hence at the end of step t) with probability $\geq 1 - |\text{Tree}(g)| \cdot \frac{1}{1+e^{\delta/c}}$ in state $g(\underline{a})$. □

4 APPLICATIONS

The complexity class TC^0 is defined as the class of all Boolean functions $f : \{0,1\}^* \to \{0,1\}^*$ for which there exists a family $(T_n)_{n \in N}$ of threshold circuits of some constant depth so that for each n the circuit T_n computes f for inputs of length n, and so that the number of gates in T_n and the absolute value of he weights of threshold gates in T_n (all weights are assumed to be integers) are bounded by a polynomial in n ([HMPST], [PS]).

Corollary 4.1 (to Theorems 2.1, 3.1): *Every Boolean function f that belongs to the complexity class TC^0 can be computed by scalable (i.e. polynomial size) Boltzmann machines whose connection strengths are integers of polynomial size and which converge for state changes with unlimited parallelism with high probability in constantly many steps to a global maximum of their consensus function.*

The following Boolean functions are known to belong to the complexity class TC^0: AND, OR, PARITY; SORTING, ADDITION, SUBTRACTION, MULTIPLICATION and DIVISION of binary numbers; DISCRETE FOURIER TRANSFORM, and approximations to arbitrary analytic functions with a convergent rational power series ([CVS], [R], [HMPST]).

Remarks:

1. One can also use the method from this paper for the efficient construction of a Boltzmann machine $B_{\mathbf{p_1},\ldots,\mathbf{p_k}}$ that can decide very fast to which of k stored "patterns" $\mathbf{p_1},\ldots,\mathbf{p_k} \in \{0,1\}^n$ the current input $\underline{x} \in \{0,1\}^n$ to the Boltzmann machine has the closest "similarity."
   For arbitrary fixed "patterns" $\mathbf{p}_1,\cdots,\mathbf{p}_k \in \{0,1\}^n$ let $f_{\mathbf{p}_1,\ldots,\mathbf{p}_k} : \{0,1\}^n \to \{0,1\}^k$ be the *pattern classification function* whose ith output bit is 1 if and only if the Hamming distance between the input $\underline{x} \in \{0,1\}^n$ and $\mathbf{p}_i$ is less or equal to the Hamming distance between $\underline{x}$ and $\mathbf{p}_j$, for all $j \neq i$.
   We write $HD(\underline{x},\underline{y})$ for the Hamming distance $\sum_{i=1}^n |x_i - y_i|$ of strings $\underline{x},\underline{y}, \in \{0,1\}^n$. One has $HD(\underline{x},\underline{y}) = \sum_{y_i=0} x_i + \sum_{y_i=1}(1-x_i)$, and therefore $HD(\underline{x},\mathbf{p}_j) - HD(\underline{x},\mathbf{p}_l) = \sum_{i=1}^n \alpha_i x_i + c$ for suitable coefficients $\alpha_i \in \{-2,-1,0,1,2\}$ and $c \in \mathbf{Z}$ (that depend on the fixed patterns $\mathbf{p}_j, \mathbf{p}_l \in \{0,1\}^n$). Thus there is a threshold circuit that consists of a single threshold gate which outputs 1 if $HD(\underline{x},\mathbf{p}_j) \leq HD(\underline{x},\mathbf{p}_l)$, and 0 otherwise.
   The function $f_{\mathbf{p}_1,\ldots,\mathbf{p}_k}$ can be computed by a threshold circuit T of depth 2 whose jth output gate is the AND of $k-1$ gates as above which check for $l \in \{1,\ldots,k\} - \{j\}$ whether $HD(\underline{x},\mathbf{p}_j) \leq HD(\underline{x},\mathbf{p}_l)$ (note that the underlying graph of T is the same for any choice of the patterns $\mathbf{p}_1,\ldots,\mathbf{p}_k$). The desired Boltzmann machine $B_{\mathbf{p}_1,\ldots,\mathbf{p}_k}$ is the Boltzmann machine $B(T)$ for this threshold circuit T.
2. Our results are also of interest in the context of *learning algorithms* for Boltzmann machines. For example, the previous remark provides a *single* graph $< \mathcal{U},\mathcal{C} >$ of a Boltzmann machine with n input units, k output units, and $k^2 - k$ hidden units, that is able to compute with a suitable assignment of

connection strengths (that may arise from a learning algorithm for Boltzmann machines) *any* function $f_{\mathbf{p}_1,\ldots,\mathbf{p}_k}$ (for any choice of $\mathbf{p}_1,\ldots,\mathbf{p}_k \in \{0,1\}^n$).

Similarly we get from Theorem 2.1 together with a result from [M] the graph $< \mathcal{U}, \mathcal{C} >$ of a Boltzmann machine with n input units, n hidden units, and one output unit, that can compute with a suitable assignment of connection strengths *any* symmetric function $f : \{0,1\}^n \rightarrow \{0,1\}$ (f is called symmetric if $f(x_i,\cdots,x_n)$ depends only on $\sum_{i=1}^{n} x_i$; examples of symmetric functions are AND, OR, PARITY).

Acknowledgment: We would like to thank Georg Schnitger for his suggestion to investigate the convergence speed of the constructed Boltzmann machines.

References

[AK] E. Aarts, J. Korst, Simulated Annealing and Boltzmann Machines, John Wiley & Sons (New York, 1989).

[AHS] D.H. Ackley, G.E. Hinton, T.J. Sejnowski, A learning algorithm for Boltzmann machines, Cognitive Science, 9, 1985, pp. 147-169.

[HS] G.E. Hinton, T.J. Sejinowski, Learning and relearning in Boltzmann machines, in: D.E. Rumelhart, J.L McCelland, & the PDP Research Group (Eds.), Parallel Distributed Processing: Explorations in the Microstructure of Cognition, MIT Press (Cambridge, 1986), pp. 282-317.

[CVS] A.K. Chandra, L.J. Stockmeyer, U. Vishkin, Constant depth reducibility, SIAM, J. Comp., 13, 1984, pp. 423-439.

[HMPST] A. Hajnal, W. Maass, P. Pudlak, M. Szegedy, G. Turan, Threshold circuits of bounded depth, to appear in J. of Comp. and Syst. Sci. (for an extended abstract see Proc. of the 28th IEEE Conf. on Foundations of Computer Science, 1987, pp.99-110).

[M] S. Muroga, Threshold Logic and its Applications, John Wiley & Sons (New York, 1971).

[PS] I. Parberry, G. Schnitger, Relating Boltzmann machines to conventional models of computation, Neural Networks, 2, 1989, pp. 59-67.

[R] J. Reif, On threshold circuits and polynomial computation, Proc. of the 2nd Annual Conference on Structure in Complexity Theory, IEEE Computer Society Press, Washington, 1987, pp. 118-123.

Note on Learning Rate Schedules for Stochastic Optimization

Christian Darken and John Moody
Yale University
P.O. Box 2158 Yale Station
New Haven, CT 06520
Email: moody@cs.yale.edu

Abstract

We present and compare learning rate schedules for stochastic gradient descent, a general algorithm which includes LMS, on-line backpropagation and k-means clustering as special cases. We introduce "search-then-converge" type schedules which outperform the classical constant and "running average" ($1/t$) schedules both in speed of convergence and quality of solution.

1 Introduction: Stochastic Gradient Descent

The optimization task is to find a parameter vector W which minimizes a function $G(W)$. In the context of learning systems typically $G(W) \equiv \mathcal{E}_X E(W, X)$, i.e. G is the average of an objective function over the exemplars, labeled E and X respectively. The stochastic gradient descent algorithm is

$$\Delta W(t) = -\eta(t) \nabla_W E(W(t), X(t)).$$

where t is the "time", and $X(t)$ is the most recent independently-chosen random exemplar. For comparison, the deterministic gradient descent algorithm is

$$\Delta W(t) = -\eta(t) \nabla_W \mathcal{E}_X E(W(t), X).$$

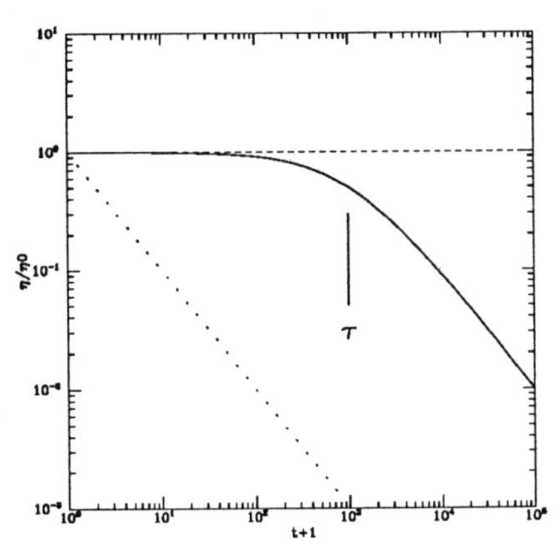

Figure 1: Comparison of the shapes of the schedules. Dashed line = constant, Solid line = search-then-converge, Dotted line = "running-average"

While on average the stochastic step is equal to the deterministic step, for any particular exemplar $X(t)$ the stochastic step may be in any direction, even uphill in $\mathcal{E}_X E(W(t), X)$. Despite its noisiness, the stochastic algorithm may be preferable when the exemplar set is large, making the average over exemplars expensive to compute.

The issue addressed by this paper is: which function should one choose for $\eta(t)$ (the learning rate schedule) in order to obtain fast convergence to a good local minimum? The schedules compared in this paper are the following (Fig. 1):

- **Constant:** $\eta(t) = \eta_0$
- **"Running Average":** $\eta(t) = \eta_0/(1+t)$
- **Search-Then-Converge:** $\eta(t) = \eta_0/(1+t/\tau)$

"Search-then-converge" is the name of a novel class of schedules which we introducein this paper. The specific equation above is merely one member of this class and was chosen for comparison because it is the simplest member of that class. We find that the new schedules typically outperform the classical constant and running average schedules. Furthermore the new schedules are capable of attaining the optimal asymptotic convergence rate for any objective function and exemplar distribution. The classical schedules cannot.

Adaptive schedules are beyond the scope of this short paper (see however Darken and Moody, 1991). Nonetheless, all of the adaptive schedules in the literature of which we are aware are either second order, and thus too expensive to compute for large numbers of parameters, or make no claim to asymptotic optimality.

2 Example Task: K-Means Clustering

As our sample gradient-descent task we choose a k-means clustering problem. Clustering is a good sample problem to study, both for its inherent usefulness and its illustrative qualities. Under the name of vector-quantization, clustering is an important technique for signal compression in communications engineering. In the machine learning field, clustering has been used as a front-end for function learning and speech recognition systems. Clustering also has many features to recommend it as an illustrative stochastic optimization problem. The adaptive law is very simple, and there are often many local minima even for small problems. Most significantly however, if the means live in a low dimensional space, visualization of the parameter vector is simple: it has the interpretation of being a set of low-dimensional points which can be easily plotted and understood.

The k-means task is to locate k points (called "means") to minimize the expected distance between a new random exemplar and the nearest mean to that exemplar. Thus, the function being minimized in k-means is $\mathcal{E}_X||X - M_{nrst}||^2$, where M_{nrst} is the nearest mean to exemplar X. An equivalent form is $\int dXP(X)\sum_{\alpha=1}^{k} I_\alpha(X)||X - M_\alpha||^2$, where $P(X)$ is the density of the exemplar distribution and $I_\alpha(X)$ is the indicator function of the Veronois region corresponding to the αth mean. The stochastic gradient descent algorithm for this function is

$$\Delta M_{nrst}(t) = -\eta(t_{nrst})[M_{nrst}(t) - X(t)],$$

i.e. the nearest mean to the latest exemplar moves directly towards the exemplar a fractional distance $\eta(t_{nrst})$. In a slight generalization from the stochastic gradient descent algorithm above, t_{nrst} is the total number of exemplars (including the current one) which have been assigned to mean M_{nrst}.

As a specific example problem to compare various schedules across, we take $k = 9$ (9 means) and X uniformly distributed over the unit square. Although this would appear to be a simple problem, it has several observed local minima. The global minimum is where the means are located at the centers of a uniform 3x3 grid over the square. Simulation results are presented in figures 2 and 3.

3 Constant Schedule

A constant learning rate has been the traditional choice for LMS and backpropagation. However, a constant rate generally does not allow the parameter vector (the "means" in the case of clustering) to converge. Instead, the parameters hover around a minimum at an average distance proportional to η and to a variance which depends on the objective function and the exemplar set. Since the statistics of the exemplars are generally assumed to be unknown, this residual misadjustment cannot be predicted. The resulting degradation of other measures of system performance, mean squared classification error for instance, is still more difficult to predict. Thus the study of how to make the parameters converge is of significant practical interest.

Current practice for backpropagation, when large misadjustment is suspected, is to restart learning with a smaller η. Shrinking η does result in less residual misadjustment, but at the same time the speed of convergence drops. In our example clustering problem, a new phenomenon appears as η drops—metastable local minima. Here the parameter vector hovers around a relatively poor solution for a very long time before slowly transiting to a better one.

4 Running Average Schedule

The running average schedule ($\eta(t) = \eta_0/(1+t)$) is the staple of the stochastic approximation literature (Robbins and Monro, 1951) and of k-means clustering (with $\eta_0 = 1$) (MacQueen, 1967). This schedule is optimal for $k = 1$ (1 mean), but performs very poorly for moderate to large k (like our example problem with 9 means). From the example run (Fig. 2A), it is clear that η must decrease more slowly in order for a good solution to be reached. Still, an advantage of this schedule is that the parameter vector has been proven to converge to a local minimum (MacQueen, 1967). We would like a class of schedules which is guaranteed to converge, and yet converges as quickly as possible.

5 Stochastic Approximation Theory

In the stochastic approximation literature, which has grown steadily since it began in 1951 with the Robbins and Monro paper, we find conditions on the learning rate to ensure convergence with optimal speed [1].

From (Ljung, 1977), we find that $\eta(t) \to At^{-p}$ asymptotically for any $1 \geq p > 0$, is sufficient to guarantee convergence. Power law schedules may work quite well in practice (Darken and Moody, 1990), however from (Goldstein, 1987) we find that in order to converge at an optimal rate, we must have $\eta(t) \to c/t$ asymptotically, for c greater than some threshold which depends on the objective function and exemplars [2]. When the optimal convergence rate is achieved, $||W - W^*||^2$ goes like $1/t$.

The running average schedule goes as η_0/t asymptotically. Unfortunately, the convergence rate of the running average schedule often cannot be improved by enlarging η_0, because the resulting instability for small t can outweigh the improvements in asymptotic convergence rate.

6 Search-Then-Converge Schedules

We now introduce a new class of schedules which are guaranteed to converge and furthermore, can achieve the optimal $1/t$ convergence rate without stability problems. These schedules are characterized by the following features. The learning rate stays high for a "search time" τ in which it is hoped that the parameters will find and hover about a good minimum. Then, for times greater than τ, the learning rate decreases as c/t, and the parameters converge.

[1] The cited theory generally does not directly apply to the full nonlinear setting of interest in much practical work. For more details on the relation of the theory to practical applications and a complete quantitative theory of asymptotic misadjustment, see (Darken and Moody, 1991).

[2] This choice of asymptotic η satisfies the necessary conditions given in (White, 1989).

We choose the simplest of this class of schedules for study, the "short-term linear" schedule ($\eta(t) = \eta_0/(1+t/\tau)$), so called because the learning rate decreases linearly during the search phase. This schedule has $c \equiv \tau\eta_0$ and reduces to the running average schedule for $\tau = 1$.

7 Conclusions

We have introduced the new class of "search-then-converge" learning rate schedules. Stochastic approximation theory indicates that for large enough τ, these schedules can achieve optimally fast asymptotic convergence for any exemplar distribution and objective function. Neither constant nor "running average" (1/t) schedules can achieve this. Empirical measurements on k-means clustering tasks are consistent with this expectation. Furthermore asymptotic conditions obtain surprisingly quickly. Additionally, the search-then-converge schedule improves the observed likelihood of escaping bad local minima.

As implied above, k-means clustering is merely one example of a stochastic gradient descent algorithm. LMS and on-line backpropagation are others of great interest to the learning systems community. Due to space limitations, experiments in these settings will be published elsewhere (Darken and Moody, 1991). Preliminary experiments seem to confirm the generality of the above conclusions.

Extensions to this work in progress includes application to algorithms more sophisticated than simple gradient descent, and adaptive search-then-converge algorithms which automatically determine the search time.

Acknowledgements

The authors wish to thank Hal White for useful conversations and Jon Kauffman for developing the animator which was used to produce figure 2. This work was supported by ONR Grant N00014-89-J-1228 and AFOSR Grant 89-0478.

References

C. Darken and J. Moody. (1990) Fast Adaptive K-Means Clustering: Some Empirical Results. In *International Joint Conference on Neural Networks 1990*, **2**:233-238. IEEE Neural Networks Council.

C. Darken and J. Moody. (1991) Learning Rate Schedules for Stochastic Optimization. In preparation.

L. Goldstein. (1987) Mean square optimality in the continuous time Robbins Monro procedure. Technical Report DRB-306. Department of Mathematics, University of Southern California.

L. Ljung. (1977) Analysis of Recursive Stochastic Algorithms. *IEEE Trans. on Automatic Control.* **AC-22**(4):551-575.

J. MacQueen. (1967) Some methods for classification and analysis of multivariate observations. In *Proc. 5th Berkeley Symp. Math. Stat. Prob.* **3**:281.

H. Robbins and S. Monro. (1951) A Stochastic Approximation Method. *Ann. Math. Stat.* **22**:400-407.

H. White. (1989) Learning in Artificial Neural Networks: A Statistical Perspective. *Neural Computation.* **1**:425-464.

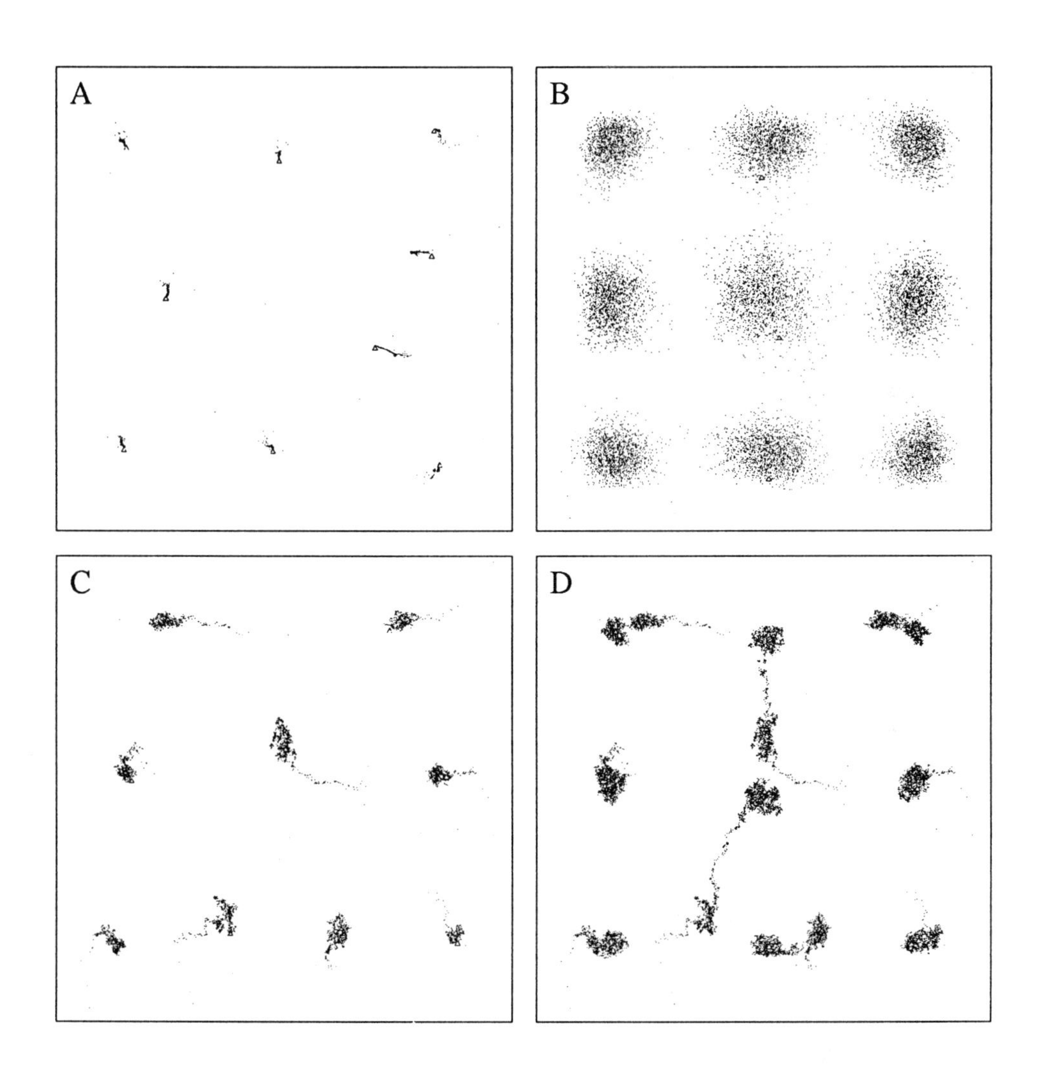

Figure 2: Example runs with classical schedules on 9-means clustering task. Exemplars are uniformly distributed over the square. Dots indicate previous locations of the means. The triangles (barely visible) are the final locations of the means. (A) "Running average" schedule ($\eta = 1/(1+t)$), 100k exemplars. Means are far from any minimum and progressing very slowly. (B) Large constant schedule (η=0.1), 100k exemplars. Means hover around global minimum at large average distance. (C) Small constant schedule (η=0.01), 50k exemplars. Means stuck in metastable local minimum. (D) Small constant schedule (η=0.01), 100k exemplars (later in the run pictured in C). Means tunnel out of local minimum and hover around global minimum.

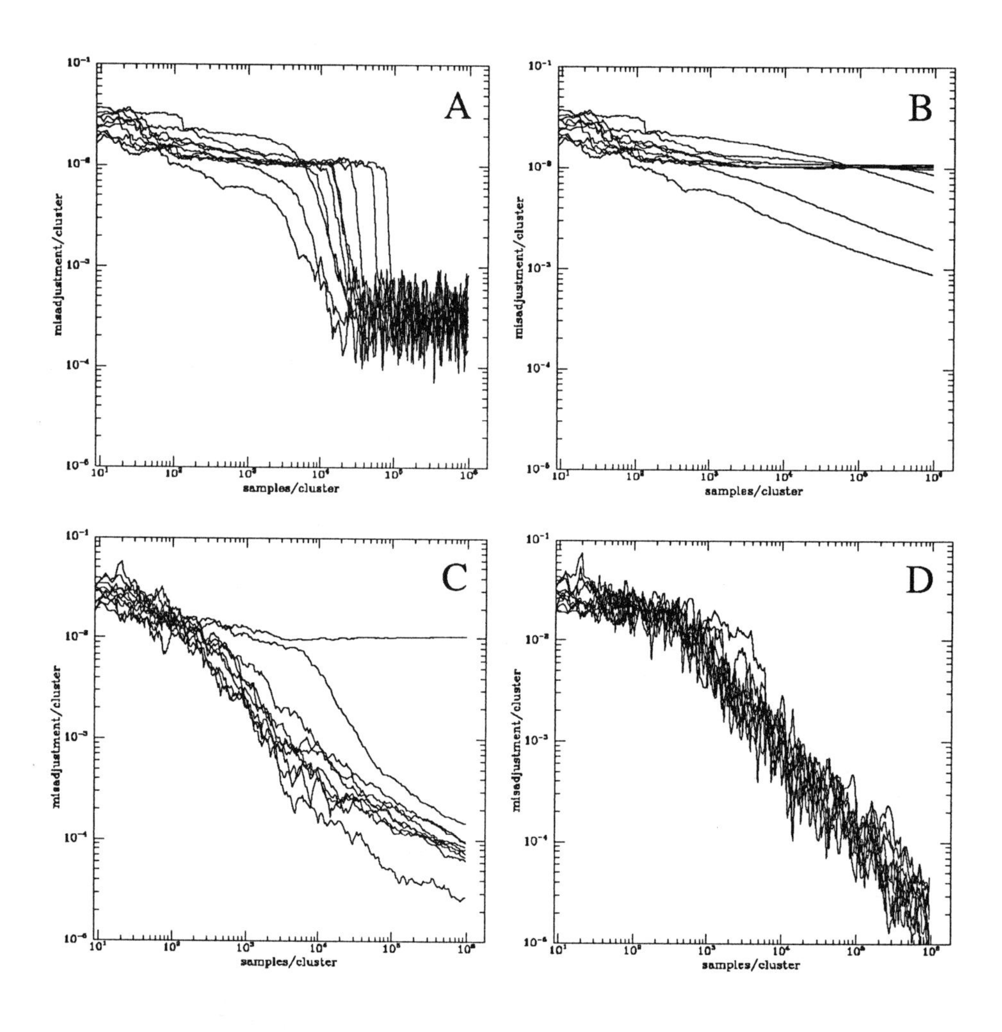

Figure 3: Comparison of 10 runs over the various schedules on the 9-means clustering task (as described under Fig. 1). The exemplars are the same for each schedule. Misadjustment is defined as $||W - W^{best}||^2$. (A) Small constant schedule (η=0.01). Note the well-defined transitions out of metastable local minima and large misadjustment late in the runs. (B) "Running average" schedule ($\eta = 1/(1+t)$). 6 out of 10 runs stick in a local minimum. The others slowly head for the global minimum. (C) Search-then-converge schedule ($\eta = 1/(1+t/4)$). All but one run head for global minimum, but at a suboptimal rate (asymptotic slope less than -1). (D) Search-then-converge schedule ($\eta = 1/(1+t/32)$). All runs head for global minimum at optimally quick rate (asymptotic slope of -1).

Convergence of a Neural Network Classifier

John S. Baras
Systems Research Center
University of Maryland
College Park, Maryland 20705

Anthony LaVigna
Systems Research Center
University of Maryland
College Park, Maryland 20705

Abstract

In this paper, we prove that the vectors in the LVQ learning algorithm converge. We do this by showing that the learning algorithm performs stochastic approximation. Convergence is then obtained by identifying the appropriate conditions on the learning rate and on the underlying statistics of the classification problem. We also present a modification to the learning algorithm which we argue results in convergence of the LVQ error to the Bayesian optimal error as the appropriate parameters become large.

1 Introduction

Learning Vector Quantization (LVQ) originated in the neural network community and was introduced by Kohonen (Kohonen [1986]). There have been extensive simulation studies reported in the literature demonstrating the effectiveness of LVQ as a classifier and it has generated considerable interest as the training times associated with LVQ are significantly less than those associated with backpropagation networks.

In this paper we analyse the convergence properties of LVQ. Using a theorem from the stochastic approximation literature, we prove that the update algorithm converges under the suitable conditions. We also present a modification to the algorithm which provides for more stable learning. Finally, we discuss the decision error associated with this "modified" LVQ algorithm.

2 A Review of Learning Vector Quantization

Let $\{(x_i, d_{x_i})\}_{i=1}^N$ be the training data or past observation set. This means that x_i is observed when pattern d_{x_i} is in effect. We assume that the x_i's are statistically independent (this assumption can be relaxed). Let θ_j be a Voronoi vector and let $\Theta = \{\theta_1, \ldots, \theta_k\}$ be the set of Voronoi vectors. We assume that there are many more observations than Voronoi vectors (Duda & Hart [1973]). Once the Voronoi vectors are initialized, training proceeds by taking a sample (x_j, d_{x_j}) from the training set, finding the closest Voronoi vector and adjusting its value according to equations (1) and (2). After several passes through the data, the Voronoi vectors converge and training is complete.

Suppose θ_c is the closest vector. Adjust θ_c as follows:

$$\theta_c(n+1) = \theta_c(n) + \alpha_n \; (x_j - \theta_c(n)) \tag{1}$$

if $d_{\theta_c} = d_{x_j}$ and

$$\theta_c(n+1) = \theta_c(n) - \alpha_n \; (x_j - \theta_c(n)) \tag{2}$$

if $d_{\theta_c} \neq d_{x_j}$. The other Voronoi vectors are not modified.

This update has the effect that if x_j and θ_c have the same decision then θ_c is moved closer to x_j, however if they have different decisions then θ_c is moved away from x_j. The constants $\{\alpha_n\}$ are positive and decreasing, e.g., $\alpha_n = 1/n$. We are concerned with the convergence properties of $\Theta(n)$ and with the resulting detection error.

For ease of notation, we assume that there are only two pattern classes. The equations for the case of more than two pattern classes are given in (LaVigna [1989]).

3 Convergence of the Learning Algorithm

The LVQ algorithm has the general form

$$\theta_i(n+1) = \theta_i(n) + \alpha_n \, \gamma(d_{x_n}, d_{\theta_i(n)}, x_n, \Theta_n) \; (x_n - \theta_i(n)) \tag{3}$$

where x_n is the currently chosen past observation. The function γ determines whether there is an update and what its sign should be and is given by

$$\gamma(d_{x_n}, d_{\theta_i}, x_n, \Theta_n) = \begin{cases} -1 & \text{if } d_{x_n} = d_{\theta_i} \text{ and } x_n \in V_{\theta_i} \\ 1 & \text{if } d_{x_n} \neq d_{\theta_i} \text{ and } x_n \in V_{\theta_i} \\ 0 & \text{otherwise} \end{cases} \tag{4}$$

Here V_{θ_i} represents the set of points closest to θ_i and is given by

$$V_{\theta_i} = \{\, x \in \Re^d \; : \; ||\theta_i - x|| < ||\theta_j - x||, \; j \neq i\} \qquad i = 1, \ldots, k. \tag{5}$$

The update in (3) is a stochastic approximation algorithm (Benveniste, Metivier & Priouret [1987]). It has the form

$$\Theta_{n+1} = \Theta_n + \alpha_n \; H(\Theta_n, z_n) \tag{6}$$

where Θ is the vector with components θ_i; $H(\Theta, z)$ is the vector with components defined in the obvious manner from (3) and $z_n = (x_n, d_{x_n})$ is the random pair consisting of the observation and the associated *true* pattern number. If the appropriate conditions are satisfied by α_n, H, and z_n, then Θ_n approaches the solution of

$$\frac{d}{dt}\bar{\Theta}(t) = h(\bar{\Theta}(t)) \tag{7}$$

for the appropriate choice of $h(\Theta)$.

For the two pattern case, we let $p_1(x)$ represent the density for pattern 1 and π_1 represent its prior. Likewise for $p_0(x)$ and π_0. It can be shown (Kohonen [1986]) that

$$h_i(\Theta) = \int_{V_{\theta_i}} (x - \Theta_i)\, q_i(x)\, dx \tag{8}$$

where

$$q_i(\Theta) = \begin{cases} p_1(x)\pi_1 - p_0(x)\pi_0 & \text{if } d_{\theta_i} = 1 \\ p_0(x)\pi_0 - p_1(x)\pi_1 & \text{if } d_{\theta_i} = 1 \end{cases} \tag{9}$$

If the following hypotheses hold then using techniques from (Benveniste, Metivier & Priouret [1987]) or (Kushner & Clark [1978]) we can prove the convergence theorem below:

[H.1] $\{\alpha_n\}$ is a nonincreasing sequence of positive reals such that $\sum_n \alpha_n = \infty$, $\sum_n \alpha_n^\lambda < \infty$.

[H.2] Given d_{x_n}, x_n are independent and distributed according to $p_{d_{x_n}}(x)$.

[H.3] The pattern densities, $p_i(x)$, are continuous.

Theorem 1 *Assume that [H.1]-[H.3] hold. Let $\bar{\Theta}^*$ be a locally asymptotic stable equilibrium point of (7) with domain of attraction D^*. Let Q be a compact subset of D^*. If $\Theta_n \in Q$ for infinitely many n then*

$$\lim_{n\to\infty} \Theta_n = \bar{\Theta}^* \quad a.s. \tag{10}$$

Proof: (see (LaVigna [1989]))

Hence if the initial locations and decisions of the Voronoi vectors are close to a locally asymptotic stable equilibrium of (7) and if they do not move too much then the vectors converge.

Given the form of (8) one might try to use Lyapunov theory to prove convergence with

$$L(\Theta) = \sum_{i=1}^{K} \int_{V_{\theta_i}} \|x - \Theta_i\|^2\, q_i(x), dx \tag{11}$$

as a candidate Lyapunov function. This function will not work as is demonstrated by the following calculation in the one dimensional case. Suppose that $K = 2$ and $\theta_1 < \theta_2$ then

$$\frac{\partial}{\partial \theta_1} L(\Theta) \quad = \quad \frac{\partial}{\partial \theta_1} \sum_{i=1}^{2} \int_{V_{\theta_i}} \|x - \Theta_i\|^2\, q_i(x), dx \tag{12}$$

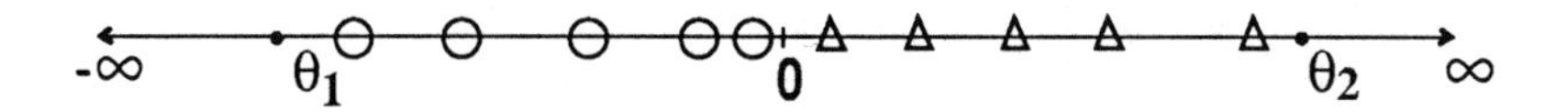

Figure 1: *A possible distribution of observations and two Voronoi vectors.*

$$= \frac{\partial}{\partial\theta_1}(\int_{V_{\theta_1}} ||x-\Theta_1||^2\, q_1(x), dx + \int_{V_{\theta_2}} ||x-\Theta_2||^2\, q_2(x), dx \quad (13)$$

$$= \frac{\partial}{\partial\theta_1}(\int_{-\infty}^{(\theta_1+\theta_2)/2} ||x-\Theta_1||^2\, q_1(x), dx + \int_{(\theta_1+\theta_2)/2}^{\infty} ||x-\Theta_2||^2\, q_2(x), dx \quad (14)$$

$$= -2\int_{-\infty}^{(\theta_1+\theta_2)/2} (x-\Theta_1)\, q_1(x), dx + ||(\theta_1-\theta_2)/2||^2\, q_1((\theta_1+\theta_2)/2) \quad (15)$$

$$= -h_1(\Theta) + ||(\theta_1-\theta_2)/2||^2\, q_1((\theta_1+\theta_2)/2) \quad (16)$$

$$(17)$$

Likewise

$$\frac{\partial}{\partial\theta_2} L(\Theta) = -h_2(\Theta) + ||(\theta_2-\theta_1)/2||^2\, q_2((\theta_1+\theta_2)/2) \quad (18)$$

Therefore

$$\nabla L(\Theta)\dot{\Theta} = -h_1(\Theta)^2 - h_2(\Theta)^2 + ||(\theta_1-\theta_2)/2||^2\, q_1((\theta_1+\theta_2)/2)(h_1(\Theta)-h_2(\Theta)) \quad (19)$$

In order for this to be a Lyapunov function (19) would have to be strictly nonpositive which is not the case. The problem with this candidate occurs because the integrand $q_i(x)$ is not strictly positive as is the case for ordinary vector quantization and adaptive K-means.

4 Modified LVQ Algorithm

The convergence results above require that the initial conditions are close to the stable points of (7) in order for the algorithm to converge. In this section we present a modification to the LVQ algorithm which increases the number of stable equilibrium for equation (7) and hence increases the chances of convergence. First we present a simple example which emphasizes a defect of LVQ and suggests an appropriate modification to the algorithm.

Let ◯ represent an observation from pattern 2 and let △ represent an observation from pattern 1. We assume that the observations are scalar. Figure 1 shows a possible distribution of observations. Suppose there are two Voronoi vectors θ_1 and θ_2 with decisions 1 and 2, respectively, initialized as shown in Figure 1. At each update of the LVQ algorithm, a point is picked at random from the observation set and the closest Voronoi vector is modified. We see that during this update, it is possible for $\theta_2(n)$ to be pushed towards ∞ and $\theta_1(n)$ to be pushed towards $-\infty$, hence the Voronoi vectors may not converge.

Recall that during the update procedure in (3), the Voronoi cells are changed by changing the location of one Voronoi vector. After an update, the majority vote of the observations in each new Voronoi cell may not agree with the decision previously assigned to that cell. This discrepency can cause the divergence of the algorithm. In order to prevent this from occuring the decisions associated with the Voronoi vectors should be updated to agree with the majority vote of the observations that fall within their Voronoi cells. Let

$$g_i(\Theta; N) = \begin{cases} 1 & \text{if } \frac{1}{N}\sum_{j=1}^{N} 1_{\{y_j \in V_{\theta_i}\}} 1_{\{d_{y_j}=1\}} > \frac{1}{N}\sum_{j=1}^{N} 1_{\{y_j \in V_{\theta_i}\}} 1_{\{d_{y_j}=2\}} \\ 2 & \text{otherwise.} \end{cases} \quad (20)$$

Then g_i represents the decision of the majority vote of the observations falling in V_{θ_i}. With this modification, the learning for θ_i becomes

$$\theta_i(n+1) = \theta_i(n) + \alpha_n \, \gamma(d_{x_n}, g_i(\Theta_n; N), x_n, \Theta_n) \, \nabla_{\theta_i(n)}(\theta_i(n) - x_n). \quad (21)$$

This equation has the same form as (3) with the function $\overline{H}(\Theta, z)$ defined from (21) replacing $H(\Theta, z)$.

This divergence happens because the decisions of the Voronoi vectors do not agree with the majority vote of the observations closest to each vector. As a result, the Voronoi vectors are pushed away from the origin. This phenomena occurs even though the observation data is bounded. The point here is that, if the decision associated with a Voronoi vector does not agree with the majority vote of the observations closest to that vector then it is possible for the vector to diverge. A simple solution to this problem is to correct the decisions of all the Voronoi vectors after every adjustment so that their decisions correspond to the majority vote. In practice this correction would only be done during the beginning iterations of the learning algorithm since that is when α_n is large and the Voronoi vectors are moving around significantly. With this modification it is possible to show convergence to the Bayes optimal classifier (LaVigna [1989]) as the number of Voronoi vectors become large.

5 Decision Error

In this section we discuss the error associated with the modified LVQ algorithm. Here two results are discussed. The first is the simple comparison between LVQ and the nearest neighbor algorithm. The second result is if the number of Voronoi vectors is allowed to go to infinity at an appropriate rate as the number of observations goes to infinity, then it is possible to construct a convergent estimator of the Bayes risk. That is, the error associated with LVQ can be made to approach the optimal error. As before, we concentrate on the binary pattern case for ease of notation.

5.1 Nearest Neighbor

If a Voronoi vector is assigned to each observation then the LVQ algorithm reduces to the nearest neighbor algorithm. For that algorithm, it was shown (Cover & Hart [1967]) that its Bayes minimum probability of error is less than twice that of the optimal classifier. More specifically, let r^* be the Bayes optimal risk and let r be the nearest neighbor risk. It was shown that

$$r^* \leq r \leq 2r^*(1 - r^*) \leq 2r^*. \tag{22}$$

Hence in the case of no iteration, the Bayes' risk associated with LVQ is given from the nearest neighbor algorithm.

5.2 Other Choices for Number of Voronoi Vectors

We saw above that if the number of Voronoi vectors equals the number of observations then LVQ coincides with the nearest neighbor algorithm. Let k_N represent the number of Voronoi vectors for an observation sample size of N. We are interested in determining the probability of error for LVQ when k_N satisfies (1) $\lim k_N = \infty$ and (2) $\lim(k_N/N) = 0$. In this case, there are more observations than vectors and hence the Voronoi vectors represent averages of the observations. It is possible to show that with k_N satisfying (1)-(2) the decision error associated with modified LVQ can be made to approach the Bayesian optimal decision error as N becomes large (LaVigna [1989]).

6 Conclusions

We have shown convergence of the Voronoi vectors in the LVQ algorithm. We have also presented the majority vote modification of the LVQ algorithm. This modification prevents divergence of the Voronoi vectors and results in convergence for a larger set of initial conditions. In addition, with this modification it is possible to show that as the appropriate parameters go to infinity the decision regions associated with the modified LVQ algorithm approach the Bayesian optimal (LaVigna [1989]).

7 Acknowledgements

This work was supported by the National Science Foundation through grant CDR-8803012, Texas Instruments through a TI/SRC Fellowship and the Office of Naval Research through an ONR Fellowship.

8 References

A. Benveniste, M. Metivier & P. Priouret [1987], *Algorithmes Adaptatifs et Approximations Stochastiques*, Mason, Paris.

T. M. Cover & P. E. Hart [1967], "Nearest Neighbor Pattern Classification," *IEEE Transactions on Information Theory* IT-13, 21–27.

R. O. Duda & P. E. Hart [1973], *Pattern Classification and Scene Analysis*, John Wiley & Sons, New York, NY.

T. Kohonen [1986], "Learning Vector Quantization for Pattern Recognition," Technical Report TKK-F-A601, Helsinki University of Technology.

H. J. Kushner & D. S. Clark [1978], *Stochastic Approximation Methods for Constrained and Unconstrained Systems* , Springer-Verlag, New York–Heidelberg–Berlin.

A. LaVigna [1989], "Nonparametric Classification using Learning Vector Quantization," Ph.D. Dissertation, Department of Electrical Engineering, University of Maryland.

Learning Theory and Experiments with Competitive Networks

Griff L. Bilbro
North Carolina State University
Box 7914
Raleigh, NC 27695-7914

David E. Van den Bout
North Carolina State University
Box 7914
Raleigh, NC 27695-7914

Abstract

We apply the theory of Tishby, Levin, and Solla (TLS) to two problems. First we analyze an elementary problem for which we find the predictions consistent with conventional statistical results. Second we numerically examine the more realistic problem of training a competitive net to learn a probability density from samples. We find TLS useful for predicting average training behavior.

1 TLS APPLIED TO LEARNING DENSITIES

Recently a theory of learning has been constructed which describes the learning of a relation from examples (Tishby, Levin, and Solla, 1989), (Schwartz, Samalan, Solla, and Denker, 1990). The original derivation relies on a statistical mechanics treatment of the probability of independent events in a system with a specified average value of an additive error function.

The resulting theory is not restricted to learning relations and it is not essentially statistical mechanical. The TLS theory can be derived from the ***principle of maximum entropy***, a general inference tool which produces probabilities characterized by certain values of the averages of specified functions(Jaynes, 1979). A TLS theory can be constructed whenever the specified function is additive and associated with independent examples. In this paper we treat the problem of learning a probability density from samples.

Consider the model as some function $p(x|\omega)$ of fixed form and adjustable parameters ω which are to be chosen to approximate $\overline{p}(x)$ where the overline denotes the true density. All we know about $\overline{p}$ are the elements of a training set $\mathcal{T}$ which are drawn from it. Define an error $\epsilon(x|\omega)$. By the principal of maximum entropy

$$p(x|\omega) = \frac{1}{z(\beta)} e^{-\beta\epsilon(x|\omega)}, \tag{1}$$

can be interpreted as the unique density which contains no other information except a specified value of the average error

$$\langle\epsilon\rangle = \int dx\ p(x|\omega)\epsilon(x|\omega). \tag{2}$$

In Equation 1 z is a normalization that is assumed to be independent of the value of ω; the parameter β is called the ***sensitivity*** and is adjusted so that the average error is equal to some ϵ_T, the specified target error on the training set. We will use the convention that an integral operates on the entire expression that follows it.

The usual Bayes rule produces a density in ω from $p(x|\omega)$ and from a prior density $\rho^{(0)}(\omega)$ which reflects at best a genuine prior probability or at least a restriction to the acceptable portion of the search space. Posterior to training on m certain examples,

$$\rho^{(m)}(\omega) = \frac{\rho^{(0)}(\omega)}{Z_m} \exp(-\beta \sum_{i=1}^{m} \epsilon(x_i|\omega)) \tag{3}$$

where Z_m is a normalization that depends on the particular set of examples as well as their number. In order to remove the effect of any particular set of examples, we can average this posterior density over all possible m examples

$$\langle\rho^{(m)}(\omega)\rangle_x = \int dx^{(m)}\overline{p}(x_1)\overline{p}(x_2)...\overline{p}(x_m)\rho^{(m)}(\omega). \tag{4}$$

This average posterior density models the expected density of nets or ω after training. This distribtution in ω implies the following expected posterior density for a new example x_{m+1}

$$\int d\omega p(x_{m+1}|\omega)\langle\rho^{(m)}(\omega)\rangle_x. \tag{5}$$

TLS compare this probability in x_{m+1} with the true target probability to obtain the *Average Prediction Probability* or APP after training

$$p^{(m)} = \int dx_{m+1}\overline{p}(x_{m+1}) \int d\omega p(x_{m+1}|\omega)\langle\rho^{(m)}(\omega)\rangle_x, \tag{6}$$

the average over both the training set $x^{(m)}$ and an independent test example x_{m+1}.

In the averages of Equations 4 and 6 are inconvenient to evaluate exactly because of the Z_m term in Equation 3. TLS propose an "annealed approximation" to APP in which the average of the ratio of Equation 4 is replaced by the ratio of the averages. Equation 6 becomes

$$p^{(m)} = \frac{\int d\omega \rho^{(0)}(\omega) g^{m+1}(\omega)}{\int d\omega \rho^{(0)}(\omega) g^{m}(\omega)} \tag{7}$$

where

$$g(\omega) = \int dx \overline{p}(x) p(x|\omega). \tag{8}$$

Equation 7 is well suited for theoretical analysis and is also convenient for numerical predictions. To apply Equation 7 numerically, we will produce Monte Carlo estimates for the moments of g that involve sampling $\rho^{(0)}(\omega)$. If the dimension of ω is larger than 50, it is preferable to histogram g rather than evaluate the moments directly.

1.1 ANALYSIS OF AN ELEMENTARY EXAMPLE

In this section we theoretically analyze a learning problem with the TLS theory. We will study the adjustment of the mean of a Gaussian density to represent a finite number of samples. The utility of this elementary example is that it admits an analytic solution for the APP of the previous section. All the relevant integrals can be computed with the identity

$$\int_{-\infty}^{\infty} dx \, \exp\left(-a_1(x-b_1)^2 - a_2(x-b_2)^2\right) = \sqrt{\frac{\pi}{a_1+a_2}} \, \exp\left(-\frac{a_1 a_2}{a_1+a_2}(b_1-b_2)^2\right). \tag{9}$$

We take the true density to be a Gaussian of mean $\overline{\omega}$ and variance $1/2\alpha$

$$\overline{p}(x) = \sqrt{\frac{\alpha}{\pi}} e^{-\alpha(x-\overline{\omega})^2}. \tag{10}$$

We model the prior density as a Gaussian with mean ω_0 and variance $1/2r$

$$\rho^{(0)}(\omega) = \sqrt{\frac{r}{\pi}} e^{-r(\omega-\omega_0)^2}. \tag{11}$$

We choose the simplest error function

$$\epsilon(x|\omega) = (x-\omega)^2, \tag{12}$$

the squared error between a sample x and the Gaussian "model" defined by its mean ω, which is to become our estimate of $\overline{\omega}$. In Equation 1, this error function leads to

$$p(x|\omega) = \frac{1}{z(\beta)} e^{-\beta(x-\omega)^2} \tag{13}$$

with $z(\beta) = \sqrt{\frac{\pi}{\beta}}$ which is independent of ω as assumed. We determine β by solving for the error on the training set to get $\beta = \frac{1}{2\epsilon_T}$.

The generalization, Equation 8, can now be evaluated with Equation 9

$$g(\omega) = \sqrt{\frac{\kappa}{\pi}} e^{-\kappa(\omega-\overline{\omega})^2}, \tag{14}$$

where

$$\kappa = \frac{\alpha\beta}{\alpha+\beta}, \tag{15}$$

is less than either α or β. The denominator of Equation 7 becomes

$$\left(\frac{\kappa}{\pi}\right)^{m/2} \sqrt{\frac{r}{r+m\kappa}} \, \exp\left(-\frac{m\kappa r}{m\kappa+r}(\overline{\omega}-\omega_0)^2\right) \tag{16}$$

with a similar expression for the numerator.

The case of many examples or little prior knowledge is interesting. Consider Equations 7 and 16 in the limit $m\kappa >> r$

$$p^{(m)} = \sqrt{\frac{\kappa}{\pi}}\sqrt{\frac{m}{m+1}}, \tag{17}$$

which climbs to an asymptotic value of $\sqrt{\frac{\kappa}{\pi}}$ for $m \longrightarrow \infty$. In order to compare this with intuition, consider that the sample mean of $\{x_1, x_2, ..., x_m\}$ approaches $\overline{\omega}$ to within a variance of $1/2m\alpha$, so that

$$\langle \rho^{(m)}(\omega) \rangle_x \approx \sqrt{\frac{m\alpha}{\pi}} e^{-m\alpha(x-\overline{\omega})^2} \tag{18}$$

which makes Equation 6 agree with Equation 17 for large enough β. In this sense, the statistical mechanical theory of learning differs from conventional Bayesian estimation only in its choice of an unconventional performance criterion APP.

2 GENERAL NUMERICAL PROCEDURE

In this section we apply the theory to the more realistic problem of learning a continuous probability density from a finite sample set. We can estimate the moments of Equation 7 by the following Monte Carlo procedure. Given a training set $\mathcal{T} = \{x_t\}_{t=1}^{t=T}$ drawn from the unknown density $\overline{p}$ on domain X with finite volume V, an error function $\epsilon(x|\omega)$, a training error $\epsilon_{\mathcal{T}}$, and a prior density $\rho^{(0)}(\omega)$ of vectors such that each ω specifies a candidate function,

1. Construct two sample sets: a prior set of P functions $\mathcal{P} = \{\omega_p\}$ drawn from $\rho^{(0)}(\omega)$ and a set of U input vectors $\mathcal{U} = \{x_u\}$ drawn uniformly from X. For each p in the prior set, tabulate the error $\epsilon_{up} = \epsilon(x_u|\omega_p)$ for every point in $\mathcal{U}$ and the error $\epsilon_{tp} = \epsilon(x_t|\omega_p)$ for every point in $\mathcal{T}$.
2. Determine the sensitivity β by solving the equation $\langle \epsilon \rangle = \epsilon_{\mathcal{T}}$ where
$$\langle \epsilon \rangle = \frac{\sum_u e^{-\beta\epsilon_{up}}\epsilon_{up}}{\sum_u e^{-\beta\epsilon_{up}}}. \tag{19}$$
3. Estimate the average generalization of a given ω_p from Equation 8
$$g(\omega_p) = \frac{1}{V}\frac{1/T\sum_t e^{-\beta\epsilon_{tp}}}{1/U\sum_u e^{-\beta\epsilon_{up}}}. \tag{20}$$
4. The performance after m examples is the ratio of Equation 7. By construction $\mathcal{P}$ is drawn from $\rho^{(0)}$ so that
$$p^{(m)} = \frac{\sum_p g^{m+1}(\omega_p)}{\sum_p g^m(\omega_p)}. \tag{21}$$

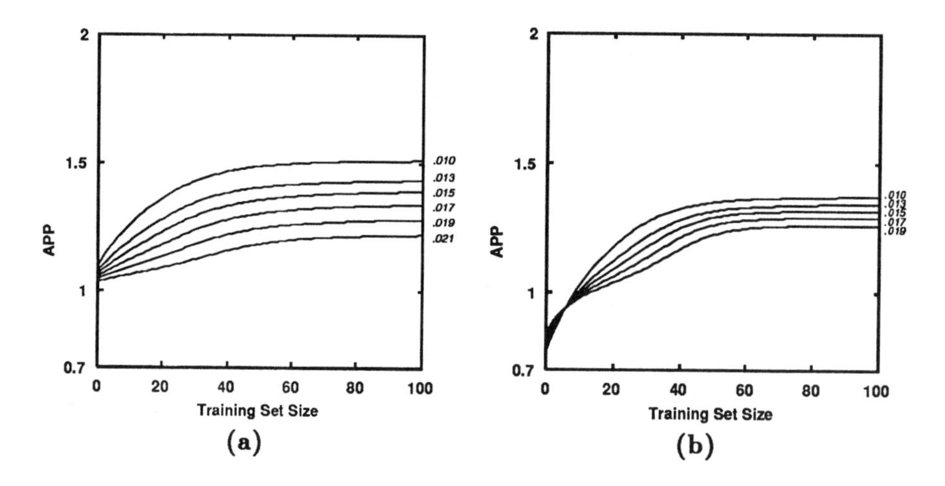

Figure 1: Predicted APP versus number of training samples for a 20-neuron competitive network trained to various target errors where the neuron weights were initialized from **(a)** a uniform density, **(b)** an antisymmetrically skewed density.

3 COMPETITIVE LEARNING NETS

We consider competitive learning nets (CLNs) because they are familiar and useful to us (Van den Bout and Miller, 1990), because there exist two widely known training strategies for CLNs (the neurons can learn either independently or under a global interaction called conscience (DeSieno, 1988), and because CLNs can be applied to one-dimensional problems without being too trivial. Competitive learning nets with conscience qualitatively change their behavior when they are trained on finite sample sets containing fewer examples than neurons; except for that regime we found the theory satisfactory. All experiments in this section were conducted upon the following one-dimensional training density

$$\overline{p}(x) = \begin{cases} \frac{1}{2\sqrt{x}} & 0 \le x \le 1, \\ 0 & \text{otherwise.} \end{cases}$$

In Figure 1 is the Average Prediction Probability (APP) for $k = 20$ versus m, for several values of target error ϵ_T and for two prior densitsities; first consider predictions from the uniform prior. For $\epsilon_T = 0.01$, APP practically attains its asymptote of 1.5 by $m = 40$ examples. Assuming the APP to be dominated in the limit by the largest g, we expect a CLN trained to an error of 0.01 on a set of 40 examples to perform 1.5 times better than an untrained net on unseen samples drawn from the same probability density. This leads to a predicted probable error of about

$$\epsilon_{prob} = \frac{1}{2\ k\ p^{(m)}}. \tag{22}$$

For $k = 20$, $\epsilon_{prob} = 0.017$ for $\epsilon_T = .01$ and $\epsilon_{prob} = 0.021$ for $\epsilon_T = 0.02$.

We performed 5,000 training trials of a 20-neuron CLN on randomly selected sets of

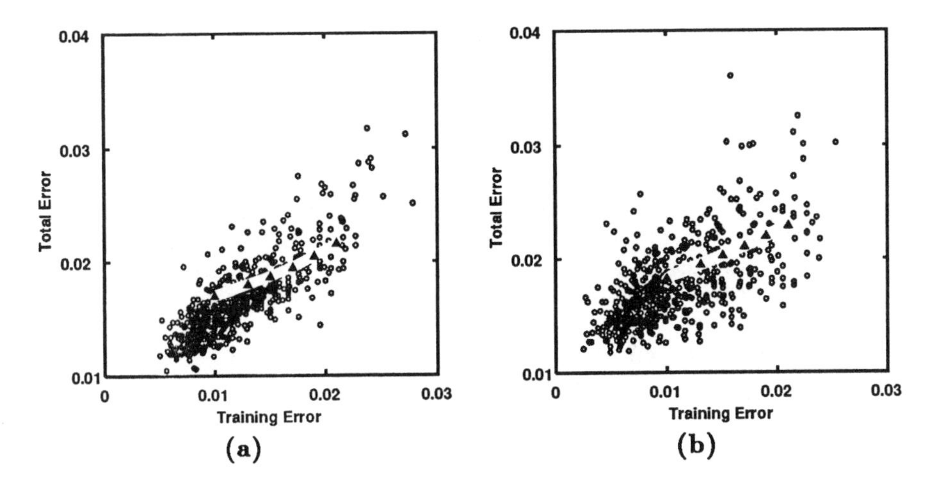

Figure 2: Experimentally determined and predicted values of total error across the training density after competitive learning was performed using a 20-neuron network trained to various target errors **(a)** with 40 samples, **(b)** with 20 samples.

40 samples from the training density. Each network was trained to a target error in the range $[0.005, 0.03]$ on its 40 samples, and the average error on the total density was then calculated for the trained network. Figure 2 is a plot of 500 of these trials along with the predicted errors for various target errors. The probable error is qualitatively correct and the scatter of actual experiments increases in width by about the ratio of APPs for $m = 20$ and $m = 40$. For the case of $m = 20$ examples, the same net can only be expected to exhibit probable errors of .019 and .023 for corresponding training target errors, which is compared graphically in Figure 2 with the experimentally determined errors for $m = 20$.

The APP curves saturate at a value of m that is insensitive to the prior density from which the nets are drawn. The vertical scale does depend somewhat on the prior however. Consider Figure 1, which also shows the APP curves for the same $k = 20$ net with the prior density antisymmetrically skewed *away* from the true density by the following function:

$$\rho^{(0)}(\omega) = \begin{cases} \frac{1}{2\sqrt{1-\omega}} & 0 \leq \omega \leq 1, \\ 0 & \text{otherwise.} \end{cases}$$

For $m > 20$ the *shapes* of the curves are almost unchanged, even though the vertical scale is different: saturation occurs at about the same value of m. Even when the prior greatly overrepresents poor nets, their effect on the prediction rapidly diminishes with training set size. This is important because in actual training, the effect of the initial configuration is also quickly lost. For $m < 20$ the predictions are not valid in any case, since our simple error function does not reflect the actual probability even approximately for $m < k$ in these nets. It is for $m < 20$ where the only significant differences between the two families of curves occur. We have also been able to draw the same conclusions from less structured prior densities generated by assigning positive normalized random numbers to intervals of the domain. Moreover, we generally find that TLS predicts that about twice as many samples as neurons are needed to train competitive nets of other sizes.

4 CONCLUSION

TLS can be applied to learning densities as well as relations. We considered the effects of varying the number of examples, the target training error, and the choice of prior density. In these experiments on learning a density as well as others dealing with learning a binary output (Bilbro and Snyder, 1990), a ternary output (Chow, Bilbro, and Yee, 1990), and a continuous output (Bilbro and Klenin, 1990) we find if saturation occurs for m substantially less than the total number of available samples, say $m < |T|/2$, that m is a good predictor of sufficient training set size. Moreover there is evidence from a reformulation of the learning theory based on the grand canonical ensemble that supports this statistical approach (Klenin,1990).

References

G. L. Bilbro and M. Klenin. (1990) Thermodynamic Models of Learning: Applications. Unpublished.

G. L. Bilbro and W. E. Snyder. (1990) Learning theory, linear separability, and noisy data. CCSP-TR-90/7, Center for Communications and Signal Processing, Box 7914, Raleigh, NC 27695-7914.

M. Y. Chow, G. L. Bilbro and S. O. Yee. (1990) Application of Learning Theory to Single-Phase Induction Motor Incipient Fault Detection Artificial Neural Networks. Submitted to *International Journal of Neural Systems.*

D. DeSieno. (1988) Adding a conscience to competitive learning. In *IEEE International Conference on Neural Networks*, pages I:117–I:124.

E. T. Jaynes. (1979) Where Do We Stand on Maximum Entropy?. In R. D. Leven and M. Tribus (Eds.), *Maximum Entropy Formalism*, M. I. T. Press, Cambridge, pages 17-118.

M. Klenin. (1990) Learning Models and Thermostatistics: A Description of Overtraining and Generalization Capacities. NETR-90/3, Center for Communications and Signal Processing, Neural Engineering Group, Box 7914, Raleigh, NC 27695-7914.

D. B. Schwartz, V. K. Samalan, S. A. Solla & J. S. Denker. (1990) Exhaustive Learning. *Neural Computation.*

N. Tishby, E. Levin, and S. A. Solla. (1989) Consistent inference of probabilities in layered networks: Predictions and generalization. *IJCNN*, IEEE, New York, pages II:403-410.

D. E. Van den Bout and T. K. Miller III. (1990) TInMANN: The integer markovian artificial neural network. Accepted for publication in the *Journal of Parallel and Distributed Computing.*

Transforming Neural-Net Output Levels to Probability Distributions

John S. Denker and Yann leCun
AT&T Bell Laboratories
Holmdel, NJ 07733

Abstract

(1) The outputs of a typical multi-output classification network do not satisfy the axioms of probability; probabilities should be positive and sum to one. This problem can be solved by treating the trained network as a *preprocessor* that produces a *feature vector* that can be further processed, for instance by classical statistical estimation techniques. (2) We present a method for computing the first two moments of the probability distribution indicating the range of outputs that are consistent with the input and the training data. It is particularly useful to combine these two ideas: we implement the ideas of section 1 using Parzen windows, where the shape and relative size of each window is computed using the ideas of section 2. This allows us to make contact between important theoretical ideas (e.g. the ensemble formalism) and practical techniques (e.g. back-prop). Our results also shed new light on and generalize the well-known "softmax" scheme.

1 Distribution of Categories in Output Space

In many neural-net applications, it is crucial to produce a set of C numbers that serve as estimates of the probability of C mutually exclusive outcomes. For example, in speech recognition, these numbers represent the probability of C different phonemes; the probabilities of successive segments can be combined using a Hidden Markov Model. Similarly, in an Optical Character Recognition ("OCR") application, the numbers represent C possible characters. Probability information for the "best guess" category (and probable runner-up categories) is combined with context, cost information, etcetera, to produce recognition of multi-character strings.

According to the axioms of probability, these C numbers should be constrained to be positive and sum to one. We find that rather than modifying the network architecture and/or training algorithm to satisfy this constraint directly, it is advantageous to use a network without the probabilistic constraint, followed by a statistical post-processor. Similar strategies have been discussed before, e.g. (Fogelman, 1990).

The obvious starting point is a network with C output units. We can train the network with targets that obey the probabilistic constraint, e.g. the target for category "0" is $[1, 0, 0, \cdots]$, the target for category "1" is $[0, 1, 0, \cdots]$, etcetera. This would not, alas, guarantee that the *actual* outputs would obey the constraint. Of course, the actual outputs can always be shifted and normalized to meet the requirement; one of the goals of this paper is to understand the best way to perform such a transformation. A more sophisticated idea would be to construct a network that had such a transformation (e.g. softmax (Bridle, 1990; Rumelhart, 1989)) "built in" even during training. We tried this idea and discovered numerous difficulties, as discussed in (Denker and leCun, 1990).

The most principled solution is simply to collect statistics on the trained network. Figures 1 and 2 are scatter plots of output from our OCR network (Le Cun et al., 1990) that was trained to recognize the digits "0" through "9." In the first figure, the outputs tend to cluster around the target vectors [the points (T^-, T^+) and (T^+, T^-)], and even though there are a few stragglers, decision regions can be found that divide the space into a high-confidence "0" region, a high-confidence "1" region, and a quite small "rejection" region. In the other figure, it can be seen that the "3 versus 5" separation is very challenging.

In all cases, the plotted points indicate the output of the network when the input image is taken from a special "calibration" dataset $\mathcal{L}$ that is distinct both from the training set $\mathcal{M}$ (used to train the network) and from the testing set $\mathcal{G}$ (used to evaluate the generalization performance of the final, overall system).

This sort of analysis is applicable to a wide range of problems. The architecture of the neural network (or other adaptive system) should be chosen to suit the problem in each case. The network should then be trained using standard techniques. The hope is that the output will constitute a *sufficent statistic.*

Given enough training data, we could use a standard statistical technique such as Parzen windows (Duda and Hart, 1973) to estimate the probability density in output space. It is then straightforward to take an unknown input, calculate the corresponding output vector O, and then estimate the probability that it belongs to each class, according to the density of points of category c "at" location O in the scatter plot.

We note that methods such as Parzen windows tend to fail when the number of dimensions becomes too large, because it is exponentially harder to estimate probability densities in high-dimensional spaces; this is often referred to as "the curse of dimensionality" (Duda and Hart, 1973). Since the number of output units (typically 10 in our OCR network) is much smaller than the number of input units (typically 400) the method proposed here has a tremendous advantage compared to classical statistical methods applied directly to the input vectors. This advantage is increased by the fact that the distribution of points in network-output space is much more regular than the distribution in the original space.

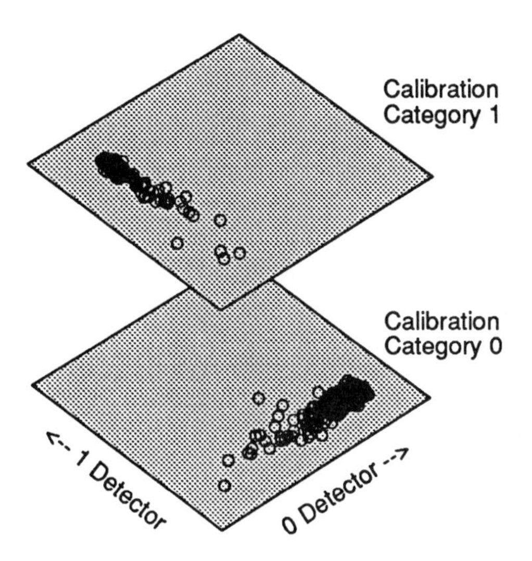

Figure 1: Scatter Plot: Category 1 versus 0

One axis in each plane represents the activation level of output unit j=0, while the other axis represents activation level of output unit j=1; the other 8 dimensions of output space are suppressed in this projection. Points in the upper and lower plane are, respectively, assigned category "1" and "0" by the calibration set. The clusters appear elongated because there are so many ways that an item can be neither a "1" nor a "0." This figure contains over 500 points; the cluster centers are heavily overexposed.

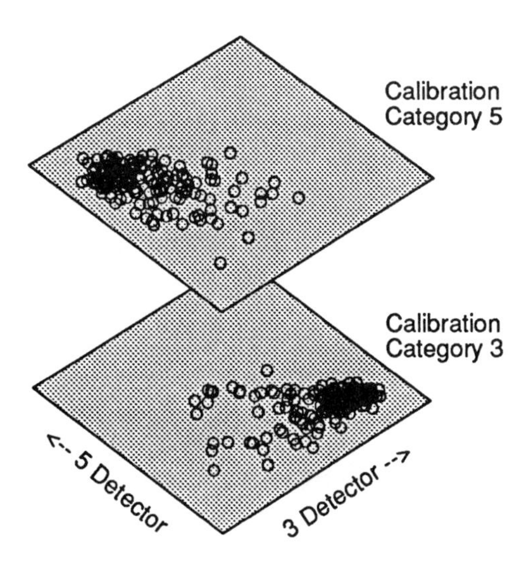

Figure 2: Scatter Plot: Category 5 versus 3

This is the same as the previous figure except for the choice of data points and projection axes.

2 Output Distribution for a Particular Input

The purpose of this section is to discuss the effect that limitations in the quantity and/or quality of training data have on the reliability of neural-net outputs. Only an outline of the argument can be presented here; details of the calculation can be found in (Denker and leCun, 1990). This section does not use the ideas developed in the previous section; the two lines of thought will converge in section 3. The calculation proceeds in two steps: (1) to calculate the range of weight values consistent with the training data, and then (2) to calculate the sensitivity of the output to uncertainty in weight space. The result is a network that not only produces a "best guess" output, but also an "error bar" indicating the confidence interval around that output.

The best formulation of the problem is to imagine that the input-output relation of the network is given by a probability distribution $P(O, I)$ [rather than the usual function $O = f(I)$] where I and O represent the input vector and output vector respectively. For any specific input pattern, we get a probability distribution $P_{OI}(O|I)$, which can be thought of as a histogram describing the probability of various output values.

Even for a definite input I, the output will be probabilistic, because there is never enough information in the training set to determine the precise value of the weight vector W. Typically there are non-trivial error bars on the training data. Even when the training data is absolutely noise-free (e.g. when it is generated by a mathematical function on a discrete input space (Denker et al., 1987)) the output can still be uncertain if the network is underdetermined; the uncertainty arises from lack of data quantity, not quality. In the real world one is faced with *both* problems: less than enough data to (over)determine the network, and less than complete confidence in the data that does exist.

We assume we have a handy method (e.g. back-prop) for finding a (local) minimum $\bar{W}$ of the loss function $E(W)$. A second-order Taylor expansion should be valid in the vicinity of $\bar{W}$. Since the loss function E is an additive function of training data, and since probabilities are multiplicative, it is not surprising that the likelihood of a weight configuration is an exponential function of the loss (Tishby, Levin and Solla, 1989). Therefore the probability can be modelled locally as a multidimensional gaussian centered at $\bar{W}$; to a reasonable (Denker and leCun, 1990) approximation the probability is proportional to:

$$\rho_m(W) = \rho_0(W) \exp[-\beta \sum_i h_{ii}(W_i - \bar{W}_i)^2/2] \tag{1}$$

where h is the second derivative of the loss (the Hessian), β is a scale factor that determines our overall confidence in the training data, and ρ_0 expresses any information we have about prior probabilities. The sums run over the dimensions of parameter space. The width of this gaussian describes the range of networks in the ensemble that are reasonably consistent with the training data.

Because we have a probability distribution on W, the expression $O = f_W(I)$ gives a probability distribution on outputs O, even for fixed inputs I. We find that the most probable output $\bar{O}$ corresponds to the most probable parameters $\bar{W}$. This unsurprising result indicates that we are on the right track.

We next would like to know what *range* of output values correspond to the allowed range of parameter values. We start by calculating the sensitivity of the output $O = f_W(I)$ to changes in W (holding the input I fixed). For each output unit j, the derivative of O_j with respect to W can be evaluated by a straightforward modification of the usual back-prop algorithm.

Our distribution of output values also has a second moment, which is given by a surprisingly simple expression:

$$\sigma_j^2 = \langle (O_j - \bar{O}_j)^2 \rangle_{\rho_m} = \sum_i \frac{\gamma_{j,i}^2}{\beta h_{ii}} \tag{2}$$

where $\gamma_{j,i}$ denotes the gradient of O_j with respect to W_i. We now have the first two moments of the output probability distribution ($\bar{O}$ and σ); we could calculate more if we wished.

It is reasonable to expect that the weighted sums (*before* the squashing function) at the last layer of our network are approximately normally distributed, since they are sums of random variables. If the output units are arranged to be reasonably linear, the output distribution is then given by

$$P_{jI}(O_j|I) = \mathcal{N}[\bar{O}_j, \sigma_j](O_j) \tag{3}$$

where $\mathcal{N}$ is the conventional Normal (Gaussian) distribution with given mean and variance, and where $\bar{O}$ and σ depend on I. For multiple output units, we must consider the joint probability distribution $P_{OI}(O|I)$. If the different output units' distributions are independent, P_{OI} can be factored:

$$P_{OI}(O|I) = \prod_j P_{jI}(O_j|I) \tag{4}$$

We have achieved the goal of this section: a formula describing a distribution of outputs consistent with a given input. This is a much fancier statement than the vanilla network's statement that $\bar{O}$ is "the" output. For a network that is not underdetermined, in the limit $\beta \to \infty$, P_{OI} becomes a δ function located at $\bar{O}$, so our formalism contains the vanilla network as a special case. For general β, the region where P_{OI} is large constitutes a "confidence region" of size proportional to the fuzziness $1/\beta$ of the data and to the degree to which the network is underdetermined.

Note that algorithms exist (Becker and Le Cun, 1989), (Le Cun, Denker and Solla, 1990) for calculating γ and h very efficiently — the time scales linearly with the time of calculation of $\bar{O}$. Equation 4 is remarkable in that it makes contact between important theoretical ideas (e.g. the ensemble formalism) and practical techniques (e.g. back-prop).

3 Combining the Distributions

Our main objective is an expression for $P(c|I)$, the probability that input I should be assigned category c. We get it by combining the idea that elements of the calibration set $\mathcal{L}$ are scattered in output space (section 1) with the idea that the network output for each such element is uncertain because the network is underdetermined (section 2). We can then draw a scatter plot in which the calibration data is represented not by zero-size *points* but by *distributions* in output space. One can imagine each element of $\mathcal{L}$ as covering the area spanned by its "error bars" of size σ as given by equation 2. We can then calculate $P(c|I)$ using ideas analogous to Parzen windows, with the advantage that the shape and relative size of each window is calculated, not assumed. The answer comes out to be:

$$P(c|I) = \int \frac{\sum_{l \in \mathcal{L}^c} P_{OI}(O|I^l)}{\sum_{l \in \mathcal{L}} P_{OI}(O|I^l)} P_{OI}(O|I) \, dO \tag{5}$$

where we have introduced $\mathcal{L}^c$ to denote the subset of $\mathcal{L}$ for which the assigned category is c. Note that P_{OI} (given by equation 4) is being used in two ways in this formula: to calibrate the statistical postprocessor by summing over the elements of $\mathcal{L}$, and also to calculate the fate of the input I (an element of the testing set).

Our result can be understood by analogy to Parzen windows, although it differs from the standard Parzen windows scheme in two ways. First, it is pleasing that we have a way of calculating the shape and relative size of the windows, namely P_{OI}. Secondly, after we have summed the windows over the calibration set $\mathcal{L}$, the standard scheme would probe each window at the single point $\bar{O}$; our expression (equation 5) accounts for the fact that the network's response to the testing input I is blurred over a region given by $P_{OI}(O|I)$ and calls for a convolution.

Correspondence with Softmax

We were not surprised that, in suitable limits, our formalism leads to a generalization of the highly useful "softmax" scheme (Bridle, 1990; Rumelhart, 1989). This provides a deeper understanding of softmax and helps put our work in context.

The first factor in equation 5 is a perfectly well-defined function of O, but it could be impractical to evaluate it from its definition (summing over the calibration set) whenever it is needed. Therefore we sought a closed-form approximation for it. After making some ruthless approximations and carrying out the integration in equation 5, it reduces to

$$P(c|I) = \frac{\exp[T^\Delta (O_c - T^0)/\sigma_{cc}^2]}{\sum_{c'} \exp[T^\Delta (O_{c'} - T^0)/\sigma_{c'c'}^2]} \tag{6}$$

where T^Δ is the difference between the target values $(T^+ - T^-)$, T^0 is the average of the target values, and σ_{cj} is the second moment of output unit j for data in category c. This can be compared to the standard softmax expression

$$P(c|I) = \frac{\exp[\Gamma O_c]}{\sum_{c'} \exp[\Gamma O_{c'}]} \tag{7}$$

We see that our formula has three advantages: (1) it is clear how to handle the case where the targets are not symmetric about zero (non-vanishing T^0); (2) the "gain" of the exponentials depends on the category c; and (3) the gains can be calculated from measurable[1] properties of the data. Having the gain depend on the category makes a lot of sense; one can see in the figures that some categories

[1]Our formulas contain the overall confidence factor β, which is not as easily measurable as we would like.

are more tightly clustered than others. One weakness that our equation 6 shares with softmax is the assumption that the output distribution of each output j is circular (i.e. independent of c). This can be remedied by retracting some of the approximations leading to equation 6.

Summary: In a wide range of applications, it is extremely important to have good estimates of the probability of correct classification (as well as runner-up probabilities). We have shown how to create a network that computes the parameters of a probability distribution (or confidence interval) describing the set of outputs that are consistent with a given input and with the training data. The method has been described in terms of neural nets, but applies equally well to any parametric estimation technique that allows calculation of second derivatives. The analysis outlined here makes clear the assumptions inherent in previous schemes and offers a well-founded way of calculating the required probabilities.

References

Becker, S. and Le Cun, Y. (1989). Improving the Convergence of Back-Propagation Learning with Second-Order Methods. In Touretzky, D., Hinton, G., and Sejnowski, T., editors, *Proc. of the 1988 Connectionist Models Summer School*, pages 29–37, San Mateo. Morgan Kaufman.

Bridle, J. S. (1990). Training Stochastic Model Recognition Algorithms as Networks can lead to Maximum Mutual Information Estimation of Parameters. In Touretzky, D., editor, *Advances in Neural Information Processing Systems*, volume 2, (Denver, 1989). Morgan Kaufman.

Denker, J. and leCun, Y. (1990). Transforming Neural-Net Output Levels to Probability Distributions. Technical Memorandum TM11359-901120-05, AT&T Bell Laboratories, Holmdel NJ 07733.

Denker, J., Schwartz, D., Wittner, B., Solla, S. A., Howard, R., Jackel, L., and Hopfield, J. (1987). Automatic Learning, Rule Extraction and Generalization. *Complex Systems*, 1:877–922.

Duda, R. and Hart, P. (1973). *Pattern Classification And Scene Analysis*. Wiley and Son.

Fogelman, F. (1990). personal communication.

Le Cun, Y., Boser, B., Denker, J. S., Henderson, D., Howard, R. E., Hubbard, W., and Jackel, L. D. (1990). Handwritten Digit Recognition with a Back-Propagation Network. In Touretzky, D., editor, *Advances in Neural Information Processing Systems*, volume 2, (Denver, 1989). Morgan Kaufman.

Le Cun, Y., Denker, J. S., and Solla, S. (1990). Optimal Brain Damage. In Touretzky, D., editor, *Advances in Neural Information Processing Systems*, volume 2, (Denver, 1989). Morgan Kaufman.

Rumelhart, D. E. (1989). personal communication.

Tishby, N., Levin, E., and Solla, S. A. (1989). Consistent Inference of Probabilities in Layered Networks: Predictions and Generalization. In *Proceedings of the International Joint Conference on Neural Networks*, Washington DC.

It is a pleasure to acknowledge useful conversations with John Bridle.

Back Propagation is Sensitive to Initial Conditions

John F. Kolen **Jordan B. Pollack**
Laboratory for Artificial Intelligence Research
The Ohio State University
Columbus, OH 43210, USA
kolen-j@cis.ohio-state.edu
pollack@cis.ohio-state.edu

Abstract

This paper explores the effect of initial weight selection on feed-forward networks learning simple functions with the back-propagation technique. We first demonstrate, through the use of Monte Carlo techniques, that the magnitude of the initial condition vector (in weight space) is a very significant parameter in convergence time variability. In order to further understand this result, additional deterministic experiments were performed. The results of these experiments demonstrate the extreme sensitivity of back propagation to initial weight configuration.

1 INTRODUCTION

Back Propagation (Rumelhart *et al.*, 1986) is the network training method of choice for many neural network projects, and for good reason. Like other weak methods, it is simple to implement, faster than many other "general" approaches, well-tested by the field, and easy to mold (with domain knowledge encoded in the learning environment) into very specific and efficient algorithms.

Rumelhart *et al.* made a confident statement: for many tasks, "the network rarely gets stuck in poor local minima that are significantly worse than the global minima."(p. 536) According to them, initial weights of exactly 0 cannot be used, since symmetries in the environment are not sufficient to break symmetries in initial weights. Since their paper was published, the convention in the field has been to choose initial weights with a uniform distribution between plus and minus ρ, usually set to 0.5 or less.

The convergence claim was based solely upon their empirical experience with the back propagation technique. Since then, Minsky & Papert (1988) have argued that there exists no proof of convergence for the technique, and several researchers (*e.g.* Judd 1988) have found that the convergence time must be related to the difficulty of the problem, otherwise an unsolved computer science question ($P \stackrel{?}{=} NP$) would finally be answered. We do not wish to make claims about convergence of the technique in the limit (with vanishing stepsize), or the relationship between task and performance, but wish to talk about a pervasive behavior of the technique which has gone unnoticed for several years: the sensitivity of back propagation to initial conditions.

2 THE MONTE-CARLO EXPERIMENT

Initially, we performed empirical studies to determine the effect of learning rate, momentum rate, and the range of initial weights on t-convergence (Kolen and Goel, to appear). We use the term *t-convergence* to refer to whether or not a network, starting at a precise initial configuration, could learn to separate the input patterns according to a boolean function (correct outputs above or below 0.5) within t epochs. The experiment consisted of training a 2-2-1 network on exclusive-or while varying three independent variables in 114 combinations: learning rate, η, equal to 1.0 or 2.0; momentum rate, α, equal to 0.0, 0.5, or 0.9; and initial weight range, ρ, equal to 0.1 to 0.9 in 0.1 increments, and 1.0 to 10.0 in 1.0 increments. Each combination of parameters was used to initialize and train a number of networks.[1] Figure 1 plots the percentage of t-convergent (where $t \cong 50,000$ epochs of 4 presentations) initial conditions for the 2-2-1 network trained on the exclusive-or problem. From the figure we thus conclude the choice of $\rho \leq 0.5$ is more than a convenient symmetry-breaking default, but is quite necessary to obtain low levels of nonconvergent behavior.

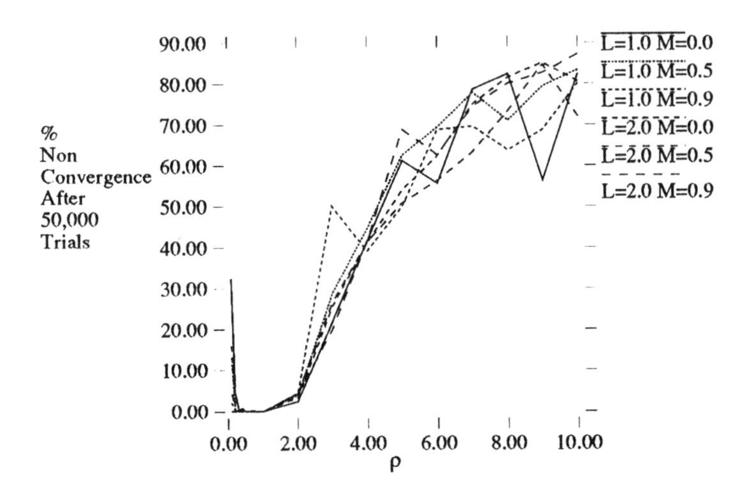

Figure 1: Percentage T-Convergence vs. Initial Weight Range

3 SCENES FROM EXCLUSIVE-OR

Why do networks exhibit the behavior illustrated in Figure 1? While some might argue that very high initial weights (i.e. $\rho > 10.0$) lead to very long convergence times since the derivative of the semi-linear sigmoid function is effectively zero for large weights, this

1. Numbers ranged from 8 to 8355, depending on availability of computational resources. Those data points calculated with small samples were usually surrounded by data points with larger samples.

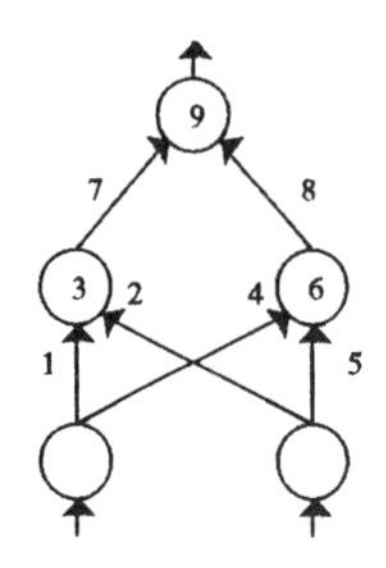

Figure 2:
(Schematic Network)

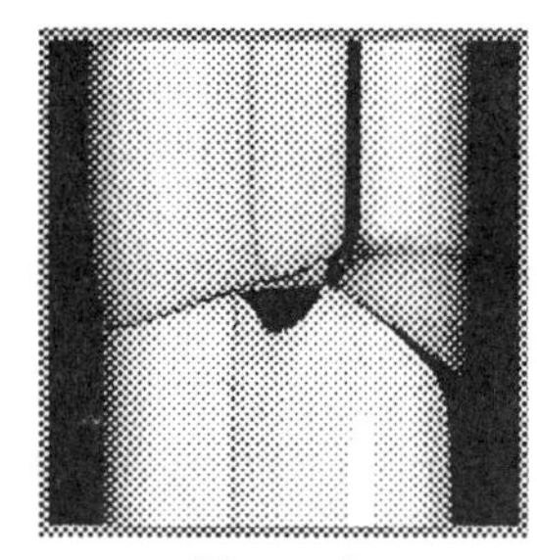

Figure 3:
(-5-3+3+6Y-1-6+7X)
η=3.25 α=0.40

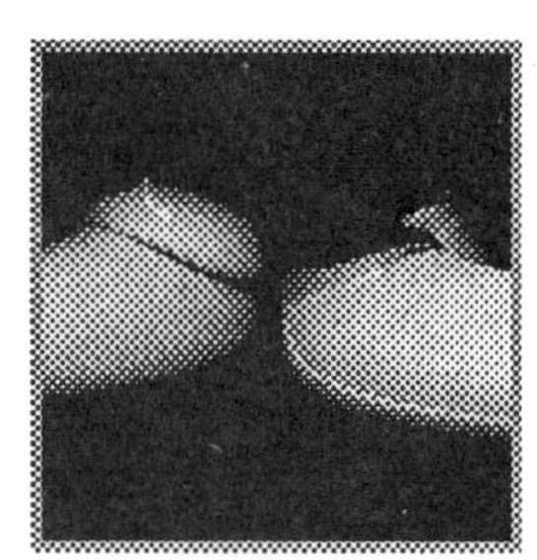

Figure 4:
(+4-7+6+0-3Y+1X+1)
η=2.75 α=0.00

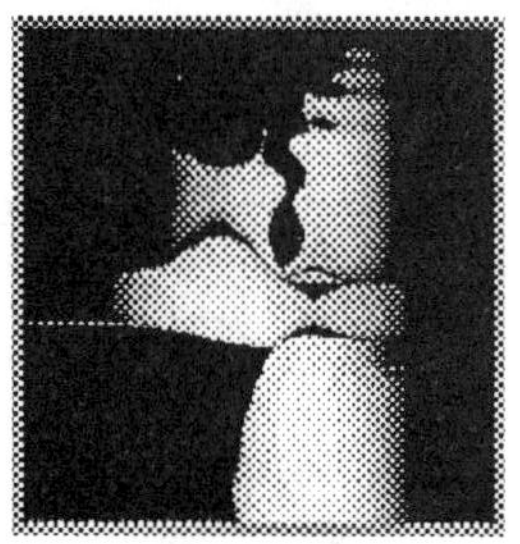

Figure 5:
(-5+5+1-6+3XY+8+3)
η=2.75 α=0.80

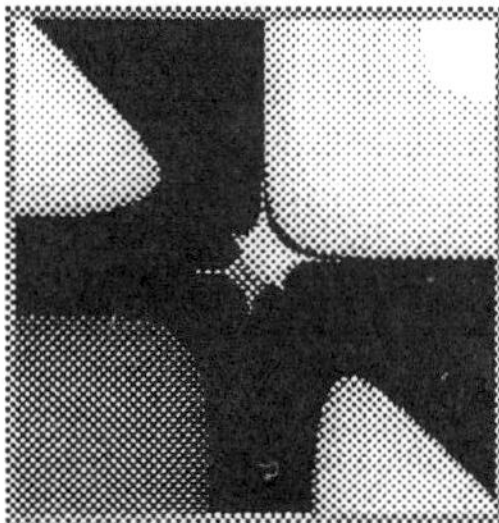

Figure 6:
(YX-3+6+8+3+1+7-3)
η=3.25 α=0.00

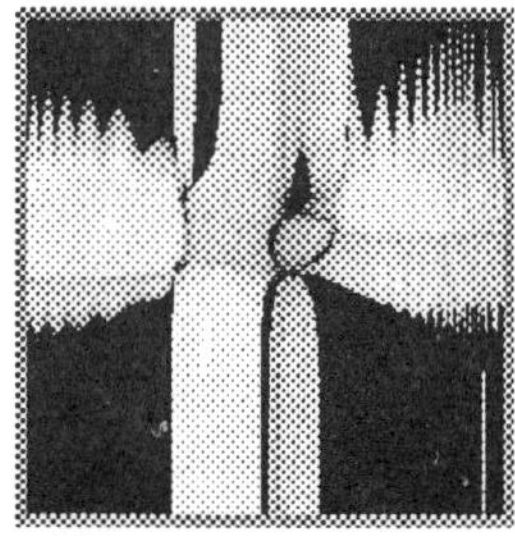

Figure 7:
(Y+3-9-2+6+7-3X+7)
η=3.25 α=0.60

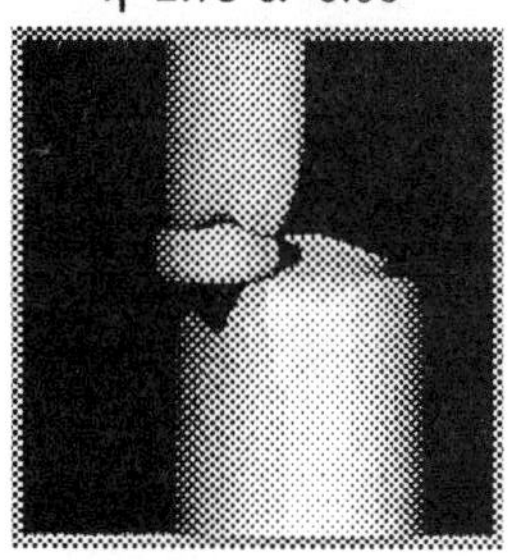

Figure 8:
(-6-4XY-6-6+9-4-9)
η=3.00 α=0.50

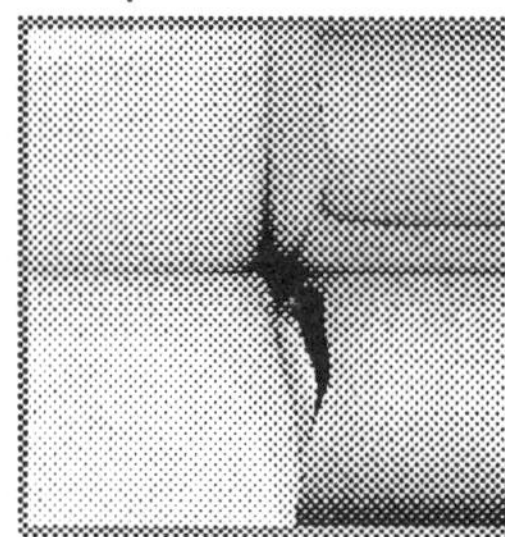

Figure 9:
(-2+1+9-1X-3+8Y-4)
η=2.75 α=0.20

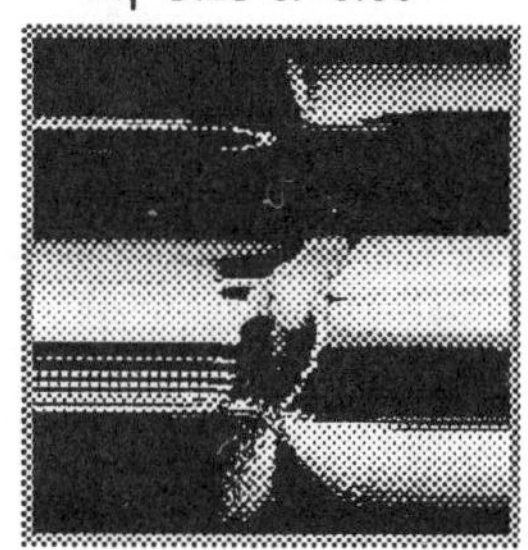

Figure 10:
(+1+8-3-6X-1+1+8Y)
η=3.50 α=0.90

Figure 11:
(+7+4-9-9-5Y-3+9X)
η=3.00 α=0.70

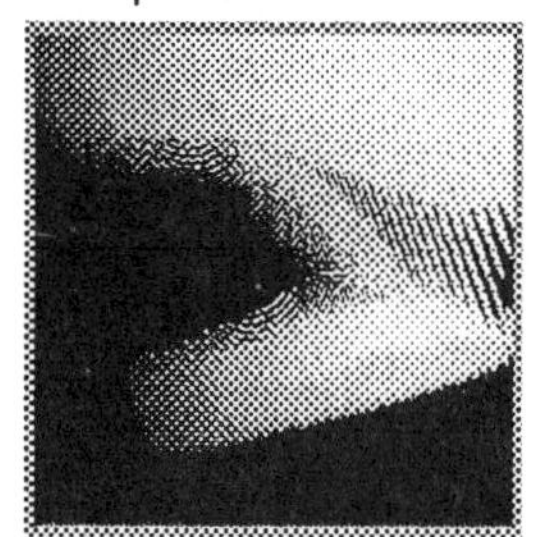

Figure 12:
(-9.0,-1.8)
step 0.018

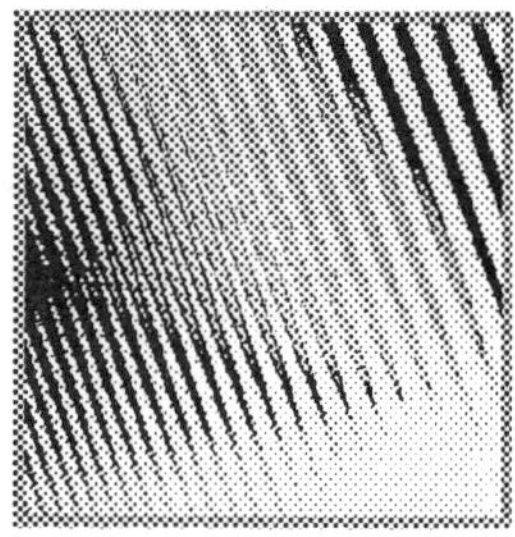

Figure 13:
(-6.966,-0.500)
step 0.004

does not explain the fact that when ρ is between 2.0 and 4.0, the non-t-convergence rate varies from 5 to 50 percent.

Thus, we decided to utilize a more deterministic approach for eliciting the structure of initial conditions giving rise to t-convergence. Unfortunately, most networks have many weights, and thus many dimensions in initial-condition space. We can, however, examine 2-dimensional slices through the space in great detail. A slice is specified by an origin and two orthogonal directions (the X and Y axes). In the figures below, we vary the initial weights regularly throughout the plane formed by the axes (with the origin in the lower left-hand corner) and collect the results of running back-propagation to a particular time limit for each initial condition. The map is displayed with grey-level linearly related to time of convergence: black meaning not t-convergent and white representing the fastest convergence time in the picture. Figure 2 is a schematic representation of the networks used in this and the following experiment. The numbers on the links and in the nodes will be used for identification purposes. Figures 3 through 11 show several interesting "slices" of the the initial condition space for 2-2-1 networks trained on **exclusive-or**. Each slice is compactly identified by its 9-dimensional weight vector and associated learning/ momentum rates. For instance, the vector (-3+2+7-4X+5-2-6Y) describes a network with an initial weight of -0.3 between the left hidden unit and the left input unit. Likewise, "+5" in the sixth position represents an initial bias of 0.5 to the right hidden unit. The letters "X" and "Y" indicate that the corresponding weight is varied along the X- or Y-axis from -10.0 to +10.0 in steps of 0.1. All the figures in this paper contain the results of 40,000 runs of back-propagation (*i.e.*200 pixels by 200 pixels) for up to 200 epochs (where an epoch consists of 4 training examples).

Figures 12 and 13 present a closer look at the sensitivity of back-propagation to initial conditions. These figures zoom into a complex region of Figure 11; the captions list the location of the origin and step size used to generate each picture.

Sensitivity behavior can also be demonstrated with even simpler functions. Take the case of a 2-2-1 network learning the **or** function. Figure 14 shows the effect of learning "or" on networks (+5+5-1X+5-1Y+3-1) and varying weights 4 (X-axis) and 7 (Y-axis) from -20.0 to 20.0 in steps of 0.2. Figure 15 shows the same region, except that it partitions the display according to equivalent solution networks after t-convergence (200 epoch limit), rather than the time to convergence. Two networks are considered equivalent[2] if their weights have the same sign. Since there are 9 weights, there are 512 ($2 sup 9$) possible network equivalence classes. Figures 16 through 25 show successive zooms into the central swirl identified by the XY coordinate of the lower-left corner and pixel step size. After 200 iterations, the resulting networks could be partitioned into 37 (both convergent and nonconvergent) classes. Obviously, the smooth behavior of the t-convergence plots can be deceiving, since two initial conditions, arbitrarily alike, can obtain quite different final network configuration.

Note the triangles appearing in Figures 19, 21, 23 and the mosaic in Figure 25 corresponding to the area which did not converge in 200 iterations in Figure 24. The triangular boundaries are similar to fractal structures generated under iterated function systems (Barnsley 1988): in this case, the iterated function is the back propagation

2. For rendering purposes only. It is extremely difficult to know precisely the equivalence classes of solutions, so we approximated.

Figure 14 :
(-20.00000, -20.00000)
Step 0.200000

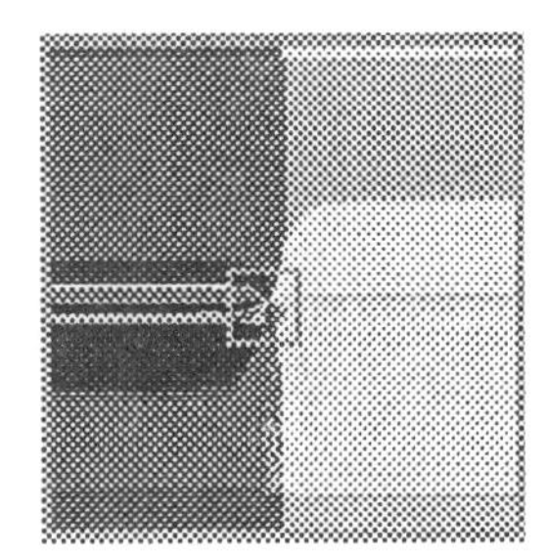

Figure 15 :
Solution Networks

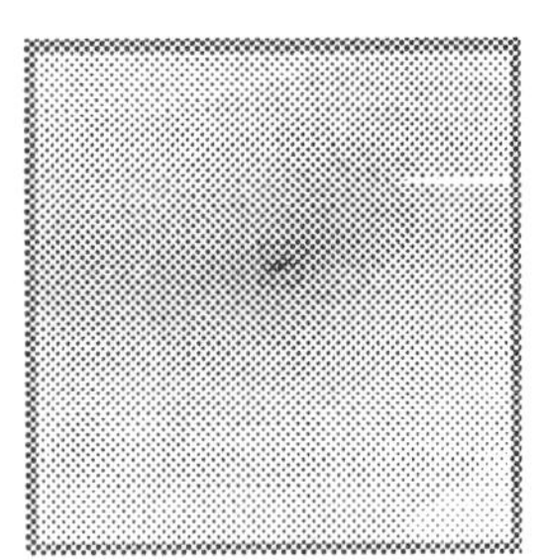

Figure 16 :
(-4.500000, -4.500000)
Step 0.030000

Figure 17 :
Solution Networks

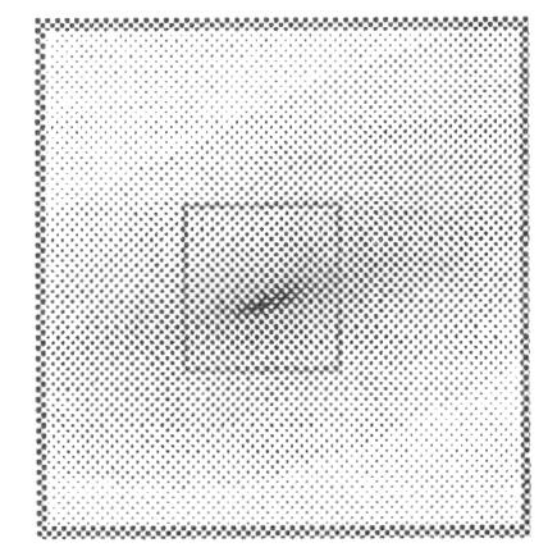

Figure 18 :
(-1.680000, -1.350000)
Step 0.002400

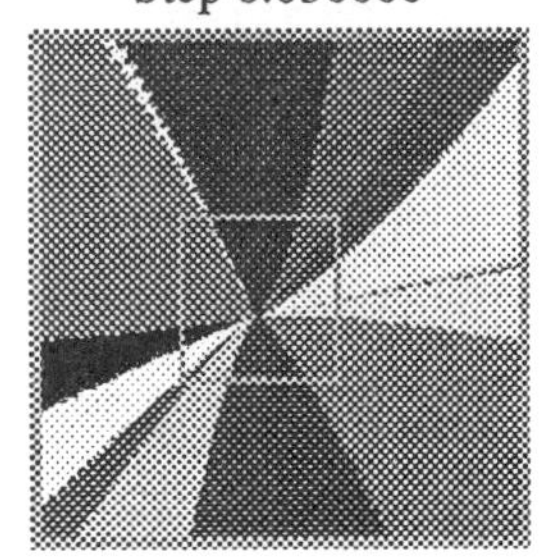

Figure 19 :
Solution Networks

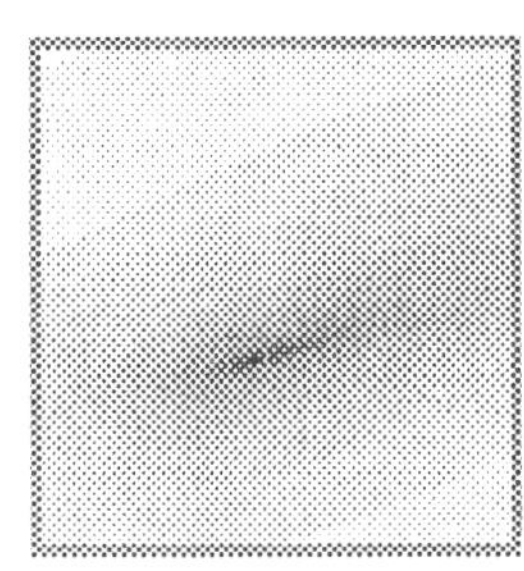

Figure 20 :
(-1.536000, -1.197000)
Step 0.000780

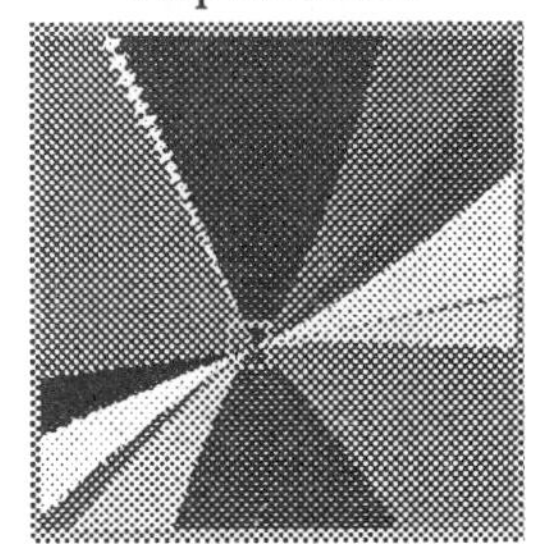

Figure 21 :
Solution Networks

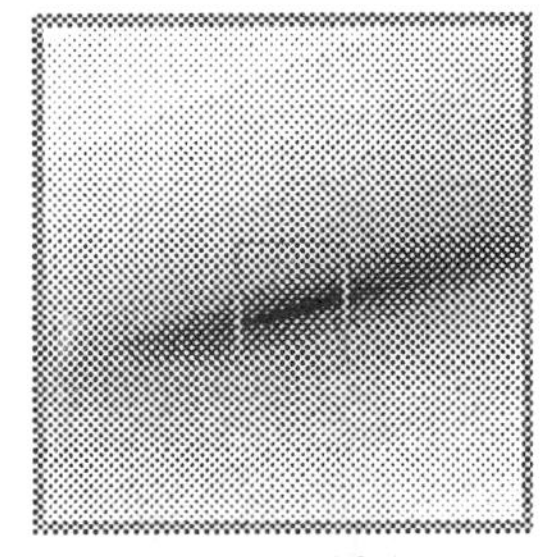

Figure 22 :
(-1.472820, -1.145520)
Step 0.000070

Figure 23 :
Solution Networks

Figure 24 :
(-1.467150, -1.140760)
Step 0.000016

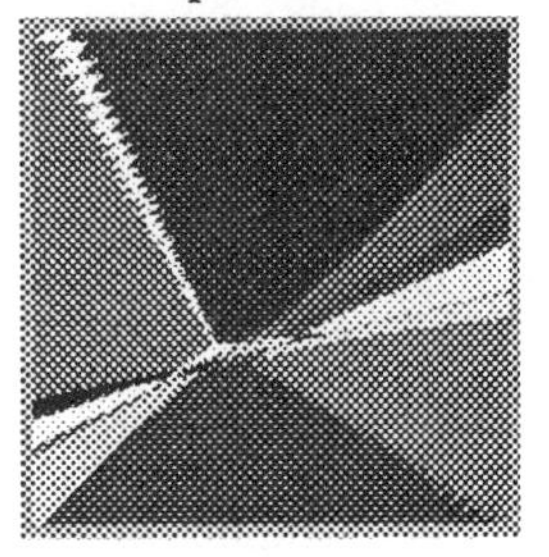

Figure 25 :
Solution Networks

	Figure 26	Figure 28	Figure 27 Figure 29 Figure 30
Weight 1	-0.34959000	-0.34959000	-0.34959000
Weight 2	0.00560000	0.00560000	0.00560000
Weight 3	-0.26338813	0.39881098	0.65060705
Weight 4	0.75501968	-0.16718577	0.75501968
Weight 5	0.47040862	-0.28598450	0.91281711
Weight 6	-0.18438011	-0.18438011	-0.19279729
Weight 7	0.46700363	-0.06778983	0.56181073
Weight 8	-0.48619500	0.66061292	0.20220653
Weight 9	0.62821201	-0.39539510	0.11201949
Weight 10	-0.90039973	0.55021922	0.67401200
Weight 11	0.48940201	0.35141364	-0.54978875
Weight 12	-0.70239312	-0.17438740	-0.69839197
Weight 13	-0.95838741	-0.07619988	-0.19659844
Weight 14	0.46940394	0.88460041	0.89221204
Weight 15	-0.73719884	0.67141031	-0.56879740
Weight 16	0.96140103	-0.10578894	0.20201484

Table 1: Network Weights for Figures 26 through 30

learning method. We propose that these fractal-like boundaries arise in back-propagation due to the existence of multiple solutions (attractors), the non-zero learning parameters, and the non-linear deterministic nature of the gradient descent approach. When more than one hidden unit is utilized, or when an environment has internal symmetry or is very underconstrained, then there will be multiple attractors corresponding to the large number of hidden-unit permutations which form equivalence classes of functionality. As the number of solutions available to the gradient descent method increases, the more complicated the non-local interactions between them. This explains the puzzling result that several researchers have noted, that as more hidden units are added, instead of speeding up, back-propagation slows down (*e.g.* Lippman and Gold, 1987). Rather than a hill-climbing metaphor with local peaks to get stuck on, we should instead think of a many-body metaphor: The existence of many bodies does not imply that a particle will take a simple path to land on one. From this view, we see that Rumelhart *et al.*'s claim of back-propagation usually converging is due to a very tight focus inside the "eye of the storm".

Could learning and momentum rates also be involved in the storm? Such a question prompted another study, this time focused on the interaction of learning and momentum rates. Rather than alter the initial weights of a set of networks, we varied the learning rate along the X axis and momentum rate along the Y axis. Figures 26, 27, and 28 were produced by training a 3-3-1 network on 3-bit parity until t-convergence (250 epoch limit). Table 1 lists the initial weights of the networks trained in Figures 26 through 31. Examination of the fuzzy area in Figure 26 shows how small changes in learning and/or momentum rate can drasticly affect t-convergence (Figures 30 and 31).

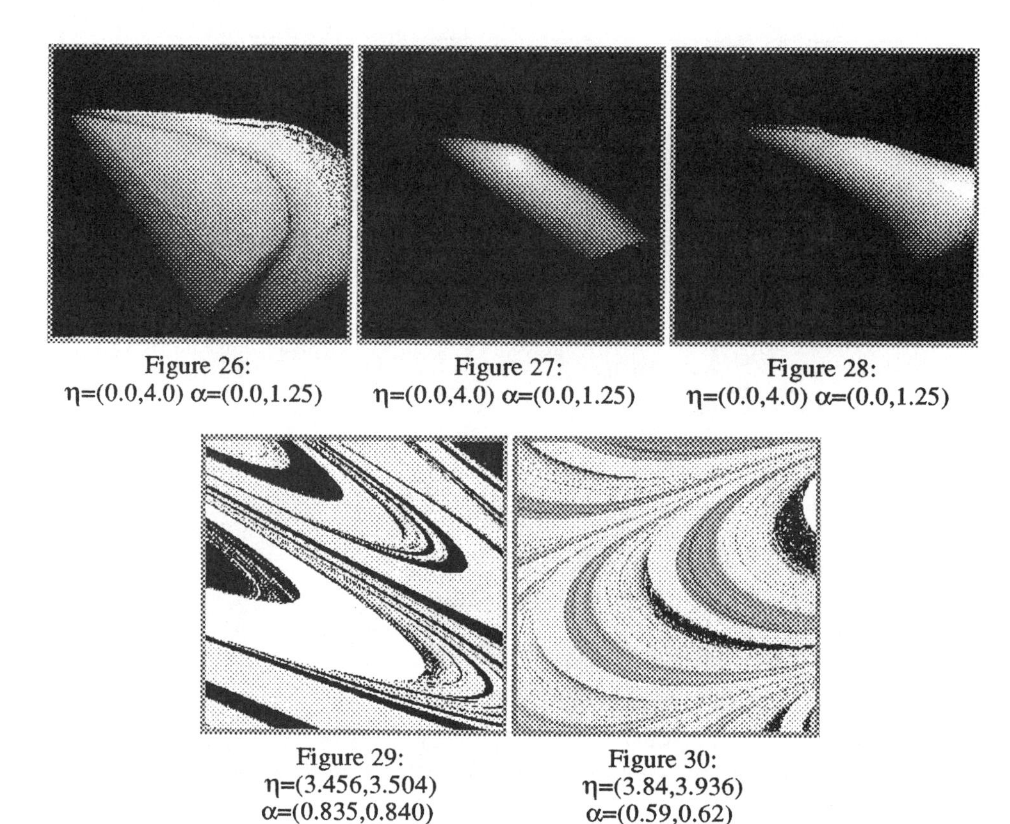

Figure 26: $\eta=(0.0,4.0)$ $\alpha=(0.0,1.25)$

Figure 27: $\eta=(0.0,4.0)$ $\alpha=(0.0,1.25)$

Figure 28: $\eta=(0.0,4.0)$ $\alpha=(0.0,1.25)$

Figure 29: $\eta=(3.456,3.504)$ $\alpha=(0.835,0.840)$

Figure 30: $\eta=(3.84,3.936)$ $\alpha=(0.59,0.62)$

4 DISCUSSION

Chaotic behavior has been carefully circumvented by many neural network researchers (through the choice of symmetric weights by Hopfield (1982), for example), but has been reported in increasing frequency over the past few years (*e.g.* Kurten and Clark, 1986). Connectionists, who use neural models for cognitive modeling, disregard these reports of extreme non-linear behavior in spite of common knowledge that non-linearity is what enables network models to perform non-trivial computations in the first place, All work to date has noticed various forms of chaos in network dynamics, but not in learning dynamics. Even if back-propagation is shown to be non-chaotic in the limit, this still does not preclude the existance of fractal boundaries between attractor basins since other non-chaotic non-linear systems produce such boundaries (i.e. forced pendulums with two attractors (D'Humieres *et al.*, 1982))

What does this mean to the back-propagation community? From an engineering applications standpoint, where only the solution matters, nothing at all. When an optimal set of weights for a particular problem is discovered, it can be reproduced through digital means. From a scientific standpoint, however, this sensitivity to initial conditions demands that neural network *learning* results must be specially treated to guarantee replicability. When theoretical claims are made (from experience) regarding the power of an adaptive network to model some phenomena, or when claims are made regarding the similarity between psychological data and network performance, **the initial conditions for the network need to be precisely specified or filed in a public scientific database.**

What about the future of back-propagation? We remain neutral on the issue of its ultimate convergence, but our result points to a few directions for improved methods. Since the slowdown occurs as a result of global influences of multiple solutions, an algorithm for first factoring the symmetry out of both network and training environment (*e.g.* domain knowledge) may be helpful. Furthermore, it may also turn out that search methods which harness "strange attractors" ergodically guaranteed to come arbitrarily close to somesubset of solutions might work better than methods based on strict gradient descent. Finally, we view this result as strong impetus to discover how to exploit the information-creative aspects of non-linear dynamical systems for future models of cognition (Pollack 1989).

Acknowledgements

This work was supported by Office of Naval Research grant number N00014-89-J1200. Substantial free use of over 200 Sun workstations was generously provided by our department.

References

M. Barnsley,*Fractals Everywhere*, Academic Press, San Diego, CA, (1988).

J. J. Hopfield, "Neural Networks and Physical Systems with Emergent Collective Computational Abilities", *Proceedings US National Academy of Science*, **79**:2554-2558, (1982).

D. D'Humieres, M. R. Beasley, B. A. Huberman, and A. Libchaber, "Chaotic States and Routes to Chaos in the Forced Pendulum", *Physical Review A*, **26**:3483-96, (1982).

S. Judd, "Learning in Networks is Hard", *Journal of Complexity*, **4**:177-192, (1988).

J. Kolen and A. Goel, "Learning in Parallel Distributed Processing Networks: Computational Complexity and Information Content", *IEEE Transactions on Systems, Man, and Cybernetics*, in press.

K. E. Kürten and J. W. Clark, "Chaos in Neural Networks", *Physics Letters*, **114**A, 413-418, (1986).

R. P. Lippman and B. Gold, "Neural Classifiers Useful for Speech Recognition", In *1st International Conference on Neural Networks* ,IEEE, IV:417-426, (1987).

M. L. Minsky and S. A. Papert, *Perceptrons*. MIT Press, (1988).

J. B. Pollack, "Implications of Recursive Auto Associative Memories", In *Advances in Neural Information Processing Systems*. (ed. D. Touretzky) pp 527-536, Morgan Kaufman, San Mateo, (1989) .

D. E. Rumelhart, G. E. Hinton, and R. J. Williams, "Learning Representation by Back-Propagating Errors", *Nature*, **323**:533-536, (1986).

Closed-Form Inversion of Backpropagation Networks: Theory and Optimization Issues

Michael L. Rossen
HNC, Inc.
5501 Oberlin Drive
San Diego, CA 92121
rossen@amos.ucsd.edu

Abstract

We describe a closed-form technique for mapping the output of a trained backpropagation network into input activity space. The mapping is an *inverse mapping* in the sense that, when the image of the mapping in input activity space is propagated forward through the normal network dynamics, it reproduces the output used to generate that image. When more than one such inverse mappings exist, our inverse mapping is special in that it has no projection onto the nullspace of the activation flow operator for the entire network. An important by-product of our calculation, when more than one inverse mappings exist, is an orthogonal basis set of a significant portion of the activation flow operator nullspace. This basis set can be used to obtain an alternate inverse mapping that is optimized for a particular real-world application.

1 Overview

This paper describes a closed-form technique for mapping a particular output of a trained backpropagation network into input activity space. The mapping produced by our technique is an *inverse mapping* in the sense that, when the image in input space of the mapping of an output activity is propagated forward through the normal network dynamics, it reproduces the output used to generate it.[1] When multiple inverse mappings exist, our inverse mapping is unique in that it has no

[1] It is possible that no such inverse mappings exist. This point is addressed in section 4.

projection onto the nullspace of the activation flow operator for the entire network. An important by-product of our calculation is an orthogonal basis set of a significant portion of this nullspace. Any vector within this nullspace can be added to the image from the inverse mapping, producing a new point in input space that is still an inverse mapping image in the above sense. Using this nullspace, the inverse mapping can be optimized for a particular application by minimizing a cost function over the input elements, relevant to that application, to obtain the vector from the nullspace to add to the original inverse mapping image. For this reason and because of the closed-form we obtain for calculation of the network inverse mapping, our method compares favorably to previously proposed iterative methods of network inversion [Widrow & Stearns, 1985, Linden & Kinderman, 1989]. We now briefly summarize our method of closed-form inversion of a backpropagation network.

2 The Inverse Mapping Operator

To outline the calculation of our inverse mapping operator, we start by considering a trained feed-forward backpropagation network with one hidden layer and bipolar sigmoidal activation functions. We calculate this inverse as a sequence of the inverses of the sub-operations constituting the dynamics of activation flow. If we use the 'I, H, O' as subscripts indicating input, hidden and output modules of model neurons, respectively, the activation flow from input through hidden module to output module is:

$$\begin{aligned} \underline{\mathbf{f}}_{(O)} &= \sigma \odot \mathcal{W}_{(O,H)} \odot \underline{\mathbf{f}}_{(H)} \\ &= \sigma \odot \mathcal{W}_{(O,H)} \odot \sigma \odot \mathcal{W}_{(H,I)} \odot \underline{\mathbf{f}}_{(I)} \\ &\doteq \mathcal{A} \odot \underline{\mathbf{f}}_{(I)}, \end{aligned} \tag{1}$$

where

σ : bipolar sigmoid function;

$\mathcal{W}_{(dest,source)}$: Matrix operator of connection weights, indexed by 'source' and 'dest'(destination) modules;

$\underline{\mathbf{f}}_{(k)}$: Vector of activities for module 'k'.

$\mathcal{A}$ is defined here as the activation flow operator for the entire network. The symbol $\odot$ separates operators sequentially applied to the argument.

Since the sub-operators constituting $\mathcal{A}$ are applied sequentially, the inverse that we calculate, $\mathcal{A}^+$, is equal to a composition of inverses of the individual sub-operators, with the order of the composition reversed from the order in activation flow. The closed-form mapping of a specified output $\underline{\mathbf{f}}_{(O)}$ to input space is then:

$$\begin{aligned} \underline{\mathbf{f}}_{(I)} &= \mathcal{A}^+ \odot \underline{\mathbf{f}}_{(O)} \\ &= \mathcal{W}^+_{(O,H)} \odot \sigma^{-1} \odot \mathcal{W}^+_{(H,I)} \odot \sigma^{-1} \odot \underline{\mathbf{f}}_{(O)}, \end{aligned} \tag{2}$$

where

σ^{-1} : Inverse of the bipolar logistic sigmoid;

$\mathcal{W}^+_{(dest,source)}$: Pseudo-inverse of $\mathcal{W}_{(dest,source)}$.

Subject to the existence conditions discussed in section 4, $\hat{\underline{\mathbf{f}}}_{(I)}$ is an inverse mapping of $\underline{\mathbf{f}}_{(O)}$ in that it reproduces $\underline{\mathbf{f}}_{(O)}$ when it is propagated forward through the network:

$$\underline{\mathbf{f}}_{(O)} = \mathcal{A} \odot \hat{\underline{\mathbf{f}}}_{(I)}. \tag{3}$$

We use singular value decomposition (SVD), a well-known matrix analysis method (e.g., [Lancaster, 1985]), to calculate a particular matrix inverse, the pseudo-inverse $\mathcal{W}^{+}_{(j,i)}$ (also known as the Moore-Penrose inverse) of each connection weight matrix block. In the case of $\mathcal{W}_{(H,I)}$, for example, SVD yields the two unitary matrices, $\mathcal{S}_{(H,I)}$ and $\mathcal{V}_{(H,I)}$, and a rectangular matrix $\mathcal{D}_{(H,I)}$, all zero except for the singular values on its diagonal, such that

$$\mathcal{W}_{(H,I)} = \mathcal{S}_{(H,I)}\mathcal{D}_{(H,I)}\mathcal{V}^{*}_{(H,I)} \tag{4}$$

$$\mathcal{W}^{+}_{(H,I)} = \mathcal{V}_{(H,I)}\mathcal{D}^{+}_{(H,I)}\mathcal{S}^{*}_{(H,I)}, \tag{5}$$

where

$\mathcal{V}^{*}_{(H,I)}, \mathcal{V}^{*}_{(H,I)}$: Transposes of $\mathcal{S}_{(H,I)}$, $\mathcal{V}_{(H,I)}$, respectively;

$\mathcal{D}^{+}_{(H,I)}$: Pseudo-inverse of $\mathcal{D}_{(H,I)}$, which is simply its transpose with each non-zero singular value replaced by its inverse.

3 Uniqueness and Optimization Considerations

The pseudo-inverse (calculated by SVD or other methods) is one of a class of solutions to the inverse of a matrix operator that may exist, called generalized inverses. For our purposes, each of these generalized inverses, if they exist, are inverses in the useful sense that when substitued for $\mathcal{W}^{+}_{(j,i)}$ in eq. (2), the resultant $\hat{\underline{\mathbf{f}}}_{(I)}$ will be and inverse mapping image as defined by eq. (3).

When a matrix operator $\mathcal{W}$ does not have a nullspace, the pseudo-inverse is the only generalized inverse that exists. If $\mathcal{W}$ does have a nullspace, the pseudo-inverse is special in that its range contains no projection onto the nullspace of $\mathcal{W}$. It follows that if either of the matrix operators $\mathcal{W}_{(H,I)}$ or $\mathcal{W}_{(O,H)}$ in eq. (1) have a nullspace, then multiple inverse mapping operators will exist. However, the inverse mapping operator $\mathcal{A}^{+}$ calculated using pseudo-inverses will be the only inverse mapping operator that has no projection in the nullspace of $\mathcal{A}$. The derivation of these properties follow in a straightforward manner from the discussion of generalized inverses in [Lancaster, 1985]. An interesting result of using SVD to obtain the pseudo-inverse is that:

SVD provides a direct method for varying $\hat{\underline{\mathbf{f}}}_{(I)}$ within the space of inverse mapping images in input space of $\underline{\mathbf{f}}_{(O)}$.

This becomes clear when we note that if $r = \rho(\mathcal{W}_{(H,I)})$ is the rank of $\mathcal{W}_{(H,I)}$, only the first r singular values in $\mathcal{D}_{(H,I)}$ are non-zero. Thus, only the first r columns of $\mathcal{S}_{(H,I)}$ and $\mathcal{V}_{(H,I)}$ participate in the activity flow of the network from input module to hidden module.

The columns $\{\underline{\mathbf{v}}_{(H,I)(i)}\}_{i>r}$ of $\mathcal{V}_{(H,I)}$ span the nullspace of $\mathcal{W}_{(H,I)}$. This nullspace is also the nullspace of $\mathcal{A}$, or at least a significant portion thereof.[2] If $\hat{\underline{\mathbf{f}}}_{(I)}$ is an inverse mapping image of $\underline{\mathbf{f}}_{(O)}$, then the addition of any vector from the nullspace to $\hat{\underline{\mathbf{f}}}_{(I)}$ would still be an inverse mapping image of $\underline{\mathbf{f}}_{(O)}$, satisfying eq. (3). If an inverse mapping image $\hat{\underline{\mathbf{f}}}_{(I)}$ obtained from eq. (2) is unphysical, or somehow inappropriate for a particular application, it could possibly be optimized by combining it with a vector from the nullspace of $\mathcal{A}$.

4 Existence and Stability Considerations

There are still implementational issues of importance to address:

1. For a given $\underline{\mathbf{f}}_{(O)}$, can eq. (2) produce some mapping image $\hat{\underline{\mathbf{f}}}_{(I)}$?
2. For a given $\underline{\mathbf{f}}_{(O)}$, will the image $\hat{\underline{\mathbf{f}}}_{(I)}$ produced by eq. (2) be a true inverse mapping image; i.e., will it satisfy eq. (3)? If not, is it a best approximation in some sense?
3. How stable is an inverse mapping from $\underline{\mathbf{f}}_{(O)}$ that produces the answer 'yes' to questions 1 and 2; i.e., if $\underline{\mathbf{f}}_{(O)}$ is perturbed to produce a new output point, will this new output point satisfy questions 1 and 2?

In general, eq. (2) will produce an image for any output point generated by the forward dynamics of the network, eq. (1). If $\underline{\mathbf{f}}_{(O)}$ is chosen arbitrarily, however, then whether it is in the domain of $\mathcal{A}^+$ is purely a function of the network weights. The domain is restricted because the domain of the inverse sigmoid sub-operator is restricted to (-1,+1).

Whether an image produced by eq. (2) will be an *inverse* mapping image, i.e., satisfying eq. (3), is dependent on both the network weights and the network architecture. A strong sufficient condition for guaranteeing this condition is that the network have a *convergent* architecture; that is:

- The dimension of input space is greater than or equal to the dimension of output space.
- The rank of $\mathcal{D}_{(H,I)}$ is greater than or equal to the rank of $\mathcal{D}_{(O,H)}$.

The stability of inverse mappings of a desired output away from such an actual output depends wholly on the weights of the network. The range of singular values of weight matrix block $\mathcal{W}_{(O,H)}$ can be used to address this issue. If the range is much more than one order of magnitude, then random perturbations about a given point in output space will often be outside the domain of $\mathcal{A}^+$. This is because the columns of $\mathcal{S}_{(O,H)}$ and $\mathcal{V}_{(O,H)}$ associated with small singular values during forward

[2]Since its first sub-operation is linear, and the sigmoid non-linearity we employ maps zero to zero, the non-linear operator $\mathcal{A}$ can still have a nullspace. Subsequent layers of the network might add to this nullspace, however, and the added region may not be a linear subspace.

activity flow are associated with proportionately large inverse singular values in the inverse mapping. Thus, if singular value $d_{O,Hi}$ is small, a random perturbation with a projection on column $\underline{s}_{(O,H)(i)}$ of $\mathcal{S}_{(O,H)}$ will cause a large magnitude swing in the inverse sub-operator $\mathcal{W}^{+}_{(O,H)}$, with the result possibly outside the domain of σ^{-1}.

5 Summary

- We have shown that a closed-form inverse mapping operator of a backpropagation network can be obtained using a composition of pseudo-inverses and inverse sigmoid operators.
- This inverse mapping operator, specified in eq. (2), operating on any point in the network's output space, will obtain an inverse image of that point that satisfies eq. (3), if such an inverse image exists.
- When many inverse images of an output point exist, an extension of the SVD analyses used to obtain the original inverse image can be used to obtain an alternate inverse image optimized to satisfy the problem constraints of a particular application.
- The existence of an inverse image of a particular output point depends on that output point and the network weights. The dependence on the network can be expressed conveniently in terms of the singular values and the singular value vectors of the network weight matrices.
- Application for these techniques include explanation of network operation and process control.

References

[Lancaster, 1985] Lancaster, P., & Tismenetsky, M. (1985). *The Theory of Matrices.* Orlando: Academic.

[Linden & Kinderman, 1989] Linden, A., & Kinderman, J. (1989). Inversion of multilayer nets. *Proceedings of the Third Annual International Joint Conference on Neural Networks, Vol II*, 425-430.

[Widrow & Stearns, 1985] Widrow, B., & Stearns, S.D. (1985). *Adpative Signal Processing.* Englewood Cliffs: Prentice-Hall.

Part XIII

Learning and Generalization

Generalization by Weight-Elimination with Application to Forecasting

Andreas S. Weigend
Physics Department
Stanford University
Stanford, CA 94305

David E. Rumelhart
Psychology Department
Stanford University
Stanford, CA 94305

Bernardo A. Huberman
Dynamics of Computation
Xerox PARC
Palo Alto, CA 94304

Abstract

Inspired by the information theoretic idea of minimum description length, we add a term to the back propagation cost function that penalizes network complexity. We give the details of the procedure, called weight-elimination, describe its dynamics, and clarify the meaning of the parameters involved. From a Bayesian perspective, the complexity term can be usefully interpreted as an assumption about prior distribution of the weights. We use this procedure to predict the sunspot time series and the notoriously noisy series of currency exchange rates.

1 INTRODUCTION

Learning procedures for connectionist networks are essentially statistical devices for performing inductive inference. There is a trade-off between two goals: on the one hand, we want such devices to be as general as possible so that they are able to learn a broad range of problems. This recommends large and flexible networks. On the other hand, the true measure of an inductive device is not how well it performs on the examples it has been shown, but how it performs on cases it has not yet seen, *i.e.*, its out-of-sample performance.

Too many weights of high precision make it easy for a net to fit the idiosyncrasies or "noise" of the training data and thus fail to generalize well to new cases. This *overfitting problem* is familiar in inductive inference, such as polynomial curve fitting. There are a number of potential solutions to this problem. We focus here on the so-called minimal network strategy. The underlying hypothesis is: if several nets fit the data equally well, the simplest one will on average provide the best generalization. Evaluating this hypothesis requires *(i)* some way of measuring simplicity and *(ii)* a search procedure for finding the desired net.

The complexity of an algorithm can be measured by the length of its minimal description in some language. Rissanen [Ris89] and Cheeseman [Che90] formalized the old but vague intuition of Occam's razor as the information theoretic *minimum description length (MDL) criterion:* Given some data, the most probable model is the model that minimizes

$$\underbrace{\text{description length}}_{\text{cost}} = \underbrace{\text{description length(data|model)}}_{\text{error}} + \underbrace{\text{description length(model)}}_{\text{complexity}} .$$

This sum represents the trade-off between residual error and model complexity. The goal is to find a net that has the lowest complexity while fitting the data adequately. The complexity is dominated by the number of bits needed to encode the weights. It is roughly proportional to the number of weights times the number of bits per weight. We focus here on the procedure of weight-elimination that tries to find a net with the smallest *number of weights.* We compare it with a second approach that tries to minimize the *number of bits per weight*, thereby creating a net that is not too dependent on the precise values of its weights.

2 WEIGHT-ELIMINATION

In 1987, Rumelhart proposed a method for finding minimal nets within the framework of back propagation learning. In this section we explain and interpret the procedure and, for the first time, give the details of its implementation. [1]

2.1 METHOD

The idea is indeed simple in conception: add to the usual cost function a term which counts the number of parameters, and *minimize the sum* of performance error and the number of weights by back propagation,

$$\sum_{k \in \mathcal{T}} (\text{target}_k - \text{output}_k)^2 + \lambda \sum_{i \in \mathcal{C}} \frac{w_i^2/w_0^2}{1 + w_i^2/w_0^2} \quad . \tag{1}$$

The first term measures the performance of the net. In the simplest case, it is the sum squared error over the set of training examples $\mathcal{T}$. The second term measures the size of the net. Its sum extends over all connections $\mathcal{C}$. λ represents the relative importance of the complexity term with respect to the performance term.

The learning rule is then to change the weights according to the gradient of the *entire* cost function, continuously doing justice to the trade-off between error and complexity. This differs from methods that consider a set of fixed models, estimate the parameters for each of them, and then compare between the models by considering the number of parameters.

The complexity cost as function of w_i/w_0 is shown in Figure 1(b). The extreme regions of very large and very small weights are easily interpreted. For $|w_i| \gg w_0$, the cost of a weight approaches unity (times λ). This justifies the interpretation of the complexity term as a counter of significantly sized weights. For $|w_i| \ll w_0$, the cost is close to zero. "Large" and "small" are defined with respect to the scale w_0, a free parameter of the weight-elimination procedure that has to be chosen.

[1] The original formulation benefited from conversations with Paul Smolensky. Variations, and alternatives have been developed by Hinton, Hanson and Pratt, Mozer and Smolensky, le Cun, Denker and Solla, Ji, Snapp and Psaltis and others. They are discussed in Weigend [Wei91].

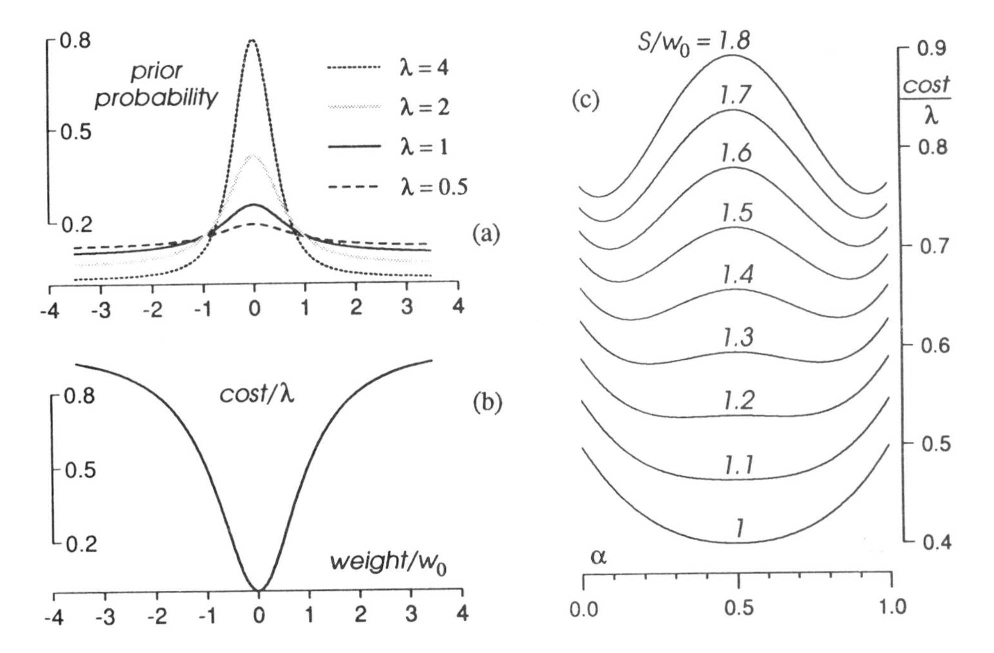

Figure 1: (a) Prior probability distribution for a weight. (b) Corresponding cost. (c) Cost for different values of S/w_0 as function of $\alpha = w_1/S$, where $S = w_1 + w_2$.

To clarify the meaning of w_0, let us consider a unit which is connected—redundantly—by two weights (w_1 and w_2) to the same signal source. Is it cheaper to have two smaller weights or just one large weight? Interestingly, as shown in Figure 1(c), the answer depends on the ratio S/w_0, where $S = w_1 + w_2$ is the relevant sum for the receiving unit. For values of S/w_0 up to about 1.1, there is only one minimum at $\alpha := w_1/S = 0.5$, *i.e.*, both weights are present and equal. When S/w_0 increases, this symmetry gets broken; it is cheaper to set one weight $\approx S$ and eliminate the other one.

Weight-*decay*, proposed by Hinton and by le Cun in 1987, is contained in our method of weight-*elimination* as the special case of large w_0. In the statistics community, this limit (cost $\propto w_i^2$) is known as *ridge regression*. The scale parameter w_0 thus allows us to express a preference for fewer large weights (w_0 small) or many small weights (w_0 large). In our experience, choosing w_0 of order unity is good for activations of order unity.

2.2 INTERPRETATION AS PRIOR PROBABILITY

Further insight can be gained by viewing the *cost as the negative log likelihood of the network, given the data.* In this framework[2], the error term is the negative logarithm of the probability of the data given the net, and the complexity term is the negative logarithm of the prior probability of the weights.

The cost function corresponds approximately to the assumption that the weights come from a mixture of two distributions. Relevant weights are drawn from a uniform distribution (to

[2]This perspective is expanded in a forthcoming paper by Rumelhart *et al.* [RDGC92].

allow for normalization of the probability, up to a certain maximum size). Weights that are merely the result of "noise" are drawn from a Gaussian-like distribution centered on zero; they are expected to be small. We show the prior probability for our complexity term for several values of λ in Figure 1(a). If we wish to approximate the bump around zero by a Gaussian, its variance is given by $\sigma^2 = w_0^2/\lambda$. Its width scales with w_0.

Perhaps surprisingly the innocent weighting factor λ now influences the width: the variance of the "noise" is inversely proportional to λ. The larger λ is, the closer to zero a weight must be to have a reasonable probability of being a member of the "noise" distribution. Also, the larger λ is, the more "pressure" small weights feel to become even smaller.

The following technical section describes how λ is dynamically adjusted in training. From the perspective taken in Section 2.1, the usual increase of λ during training corresponds to attaching more importance to the complexity term. From the perspective developed in this section, it corresponds to sharpening the peak of the weight distribution around zero.

2.3 DETAILS

Although the basic form of the weight-elimination procedure is simple, it is sensitive to the choice of λ.[3] If λ is too small, it will have no effect. If λ is too large, all of the weights will be driven to zero. Worse, a value of λ which is useful for a problem that is easily learned may be too large for a hard problem, and a problem which is difficult in one region (at the start, for example) may require a larger value of λ later on. We have developed some rules that make the performance relatively insensitive to the exact values of the parameters.

We start with $\lambda = 0$ so that the network can initially use all of its resources. λ is changed after each epoch. It is usually gently incremented, sometimes decremented, and, in emergencies, cut down. The choice among these three actions depends on the value of the error on the training set $\mathcal{E}_n$.
The subscript n denotes the number of the epoch that has just finished. (Note that $\mathcal{E}_n$ is only the first term of the cost function (Equation 1). Since gradient descent minimizes the sum of both terms, $\mathcal{E}_n$ by itself can decrease or increase.) $\mathcal{E}_n$ is compared to three quantities, the first two derived from previous values of that error itself, the last one given externally:

- $\mathcal{E}_{n-1}$ Previous error.
- $\mathcal{A}_n$ Average error (exponentially weighted over the past).
  It is defined as $\mathcal{A}_n = \gamma\mathcal{A}_{n-1} + (1-\gamma)\mathcal{E}_n$ (with γ relatively close to 1).
- $\mathcal{D}$ Desired error, the externally provided performance criterion.
  The strategy for choosing $\mathcal{D}$ depends on the specific problem. For example, "solutions" with an error larger than $\mathcal{D}$ might not be acceptable. Or, we may have observed (by monitoring the out-of-sample performance during training) that overfitting starts when a certain in-sample error is reached. Or, we may have some other estimate of the amount of noise in the training data. For toy problems, derived from approximating analytically defined functions (where perfect performance on the training data can be expected), a good choice is $\mathcal{D} = 0$. For hard problems, such as the prediction of currency exchange rates, $\mathcal{D}$ is set just below the error that corresponds to chance performance, since overfitting would occur if the error was reduced further.

After each epoch in training, we evaluate whether $\mathcal{E}_n$ is above or below each of these quantities. This gives eight possibilities. Three actions are possible:

- $\lambda \leftarrow \lambda + \Delta\lambda$
  In six cases, we increment λ slightly. These are the situations in which things are going well: the error is already below than the criterion ($\mathcal{E}_n < \mathcal{D}$) and/or is still falling ($\mathcal{E}_n < \mathcal{E}_{n-1}$).

[3]The reason that λ appears at all is because weight-elimination only deals with a part of the complete network complexity, and this only approximately. In a theory rigidly derived from the minimum description length principle, no such parameter would appear.

Incrementing λ means attaching more importance to the complexity term and making the Gaussian a little sharper. Note that the primary parameter is actually $\Delta\lambda$. Its size is fairly small, of order 10^{-6}.

In the remaining two cases, the error is worse than the criterion and it has grown compared to just before ($\mathcal{E}_n \geq \mathcal{E}_{n-1}$). The action depends on its relation to its long term average $\mathcal{A}_n$.

- $\underline{\lambda \leftarrow \lambda - \Delta\lambda}$ $\quad$ $\left[\text{if } \mathcal{E}_n \geq \mathcal{E}_{n-1} \wedge \mathcal{E}_n < \mathcal{A}_n \wedge \mathcal{E}_n \geq \mathcal{D}\right]$
  In the less severe of those two cases, the performance is still improving with respect to the long term average ($\mathcal{E}_n < \mathcal{A}$). Since the error can have grown only slightly, we reduce λ slightly.
- $\underline{\lambda \leftarrow 0.9\,\lambda}$ $\quad$ $\left[\text{if } \mathcal{E}_n \geq \mathcal{E}_{n-1} \wedge \mathcal{E}_n \geq \mathcal{A}_n \wedge \mathcal{E}_n \geq \mathcal{D}\right]$
  In this last case, the error has increased and exceeds its long term average. This can happen for two reasons. The error might have grown a lot in the last iteration. Or, it might not have improved by much in the whole period covered by the long term average, *i.e.*, the network might be trapped somewhere before reaching the performance criterion. The value of λ is cut, hopefully prevent weight-elimination from devouring the whole net.

We have found that this set of heuristics for finding a minimal network while achieving a desired level of performance on the training data works rather well on a wide range of tasks. We give two examples of applications of weight-elimination. In the second example we show how λ changes during training.

3 APPLICATION TO TIME SERIES PREDICTION

A central problem in science is predicting the future of temporal sequences; examples range from forecasting the weather to anticipating currency exchange rates. The desire to know the future is often the driving force behind the search for laws in science. The ability to forecast the behavior of a system hinges on two types of knowledge. The first and most powerful one is the knowledge of the laws underlying a given phenomenon. When expressed in the form of equations, the future outcome of an experiment can be predicted. The second, albeit less powerful, type of knowledge relies on the discovery of empirical regularities without resorting to knowledge of the underlying mechanism. In this case, the key problem is to determine which aspects of the data are merely idiosyncrasies and which aspects are truly indicators of the intrinsic behavior. This issue is particularly serious for real world data, which are limited in precision and sample size. We have applied nets with weight-elimination to time series of sunspots and currency exchange rates.

3.1 SUNSPOT SERIES [4]

When applied to predict the famous yearly sunspot averages, weight-elimination reduces the number of hidden units to three. Just having a small net, however, is not the ultimate goal: predictive power is what counts. The net has one half the out-of-sample error (on iterated single step predictions) of the benchmark model by Tong [Ton90].

What happens when we enlarge the input size from twelve, the optimal size for the benchmark model, to four times that size? As shown in [WRH90], the performance does not deteriorate (as might have been expected from a less dense distribution of data points in higher dimensional spaces). Instead, the net manages to ignore irrelevant information.

[4] We here only briefly summarize our results on sunspots. Details have been published in [WHR90] and [WRH90].

3.2 CURRENCY EXCHANGE RATES [5]

We use daily exchange rates (or *prices* with respect to the US Dollar) for five currencies (German Mark (DM), Japanese Yen, Swiss Franc, Pound Sterling and Canadian Dollar) to predict the *returns* at day t, defined as

$$r_t := \ln \frac{p_t}{p_{t-1}} = \ln \left(1 + \frac{p_t - p_{t-1}}{p_{t-1}}\right) \approx \frac{p_t - p_{t-1}}{p_{t-1}} \quad . \tag{2}$$

For small changes, the return is the difference to the previous day normalized by the price p_{t-1}. Since different currencies and different days of the week may have different dynamics, we pick for one day (Monday) and one currency (DM). We define the task to be to learn *Monday DM dynamics:* given exchange rate information through a Monday, predict the DM - US$ rate for the following day.

The net has 45 inputs for past daily DM returns, 5 inputs for the present Monday's returns of all available currencies, and 11 inputs for additional information (trends and volatilities), solely derived from the original exchange rates. The *k day trend* at day t is the mean of the returns of the k last days, $\frac{1}{k}\sum_{t-k+1}^{t} r_t$. Similarly, the *k day volatility* is defined to be the standard deviation of the returns of the k last days.

The inputs are fully connected to the *5 sigmoidal hidden units* with range $(-1, 1)$. The hidden units are fully connected to *two output units.* The first one is to predict the next day return, r_{t+1}. This is a linear unit, trained with quadratic error. The second output unit focuses on the *sign* of the change. Its target value is one when the price goes up and zero otherwise. Since we want the unit to predict the probability that the return is positive, we choose a sigmoidal unit with range $(0, 1)$ and minimize cross entropy error.

The central question is whether the net is able to extract any signal from the training set that generalizes to the test sets. The performance is given as function of training time in epochs in Figure 2. [6]

The result is that the out-of-sample prediction is *significantly better than chance.* Weight-elimination reliably extracts a signal that accounts for between 2.5 and 4.0 per cent of the variance, corresponding to a correlation coefficient of 0.21 ± 0.03 for both test sets. In contrast, nets without precautions against overfitting show hopeless out-of-sample performance almost before the training has started. Also, none of the control experiments (randomized series and time-reversed series) reaches any significant predictability.

The dynamics of weight-elimination, discussed in Section 2.3, is also shown in Figure 2. λ first grows very slowly. Then, around epoch 230, the error reaches the performance

[5] We thank Blake LeBaron for sending us the data.

[6] The error of the unit predicting the return is expressed as the *average relative variance*

$$\mathtt{arv}_S = \frac{\sum_{k\in S}\left(\text{target}_k - \text{prediction}_k\right)^2}{\sum_{k\in S}\left(\text{target}_k - \text{mean}_S\right)^2} = \frac{1}{\sigma_S^2}\,\frac{1}{N_S}\sum_{k\in S}\left(r_k - \hat{r}_k\right)^2 \quad . \tag{3}$$

The averaging (division by N_S, the number of observations in set S) makes the measure independent of the size of the set. The normalization (division by σ_S^2, the estimated variance of the data in S), removes the dependence on the dynamic range of the data. Since the mean of the returns is close to zero, the random walk hypothesis corresponds to $\mathtt{arv} = 1.0$.

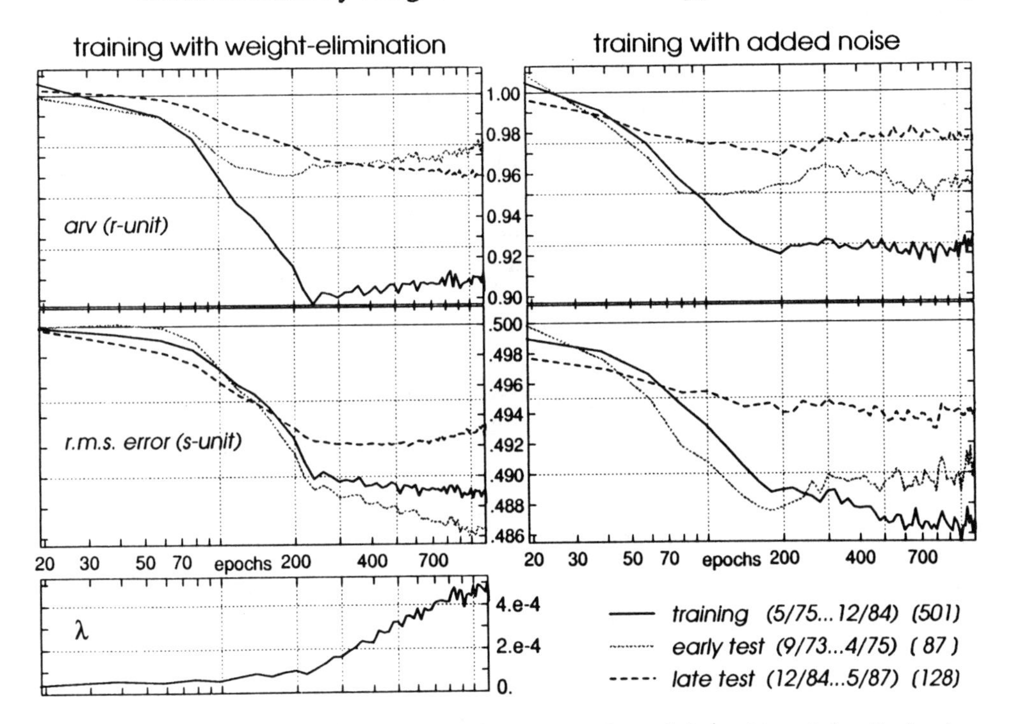

Figure 2: Learning curves of currency exchange rates for training with weight-elimination (left) and training with added noise (right). In-sample predictions are shown as solid lines, out-of sample predictions in grey and dashed. Top: average relative variance of the unit predicting the return (r-unit). Center: root-mean-square error of the unit predicting the sign (s-unit). Bottom: Weighting of the complexity term.

criterion. [7] The network starts to focus on the elimination of weights (indicated by growing λ) without further reducing its in-sample errors (solid lines), since that would probably correspond to overfitting.

We also compare training with weight-elimination with a method intended to make the parameters more robust. We add noise to the inputs, independently to each input unit, different at each presentation of each pattern.[8] This can be viewed as artificially enlarging the training set by smearing the data points around their centers. Smoother boundaries of the "basins of attraction" are the result. Viewed from the description length angle, it means saving bits by specifying the (input) weights with less precision, as opposed to eliminating some of them. The corresponding learning curves are shown on the right hand side of Figure 2. This simple method also successfully avoids overfitting.

[7] Guided by cross-validation, we set the criterion (for the sum of the squared errors from both outputs) to 650. With this value, the choice of the other parameters is not critical, as long as they are fairly small. We used a learning rate of 2.5×10^{-4}, no momentum, and an increment $\Delta\lambda$ of 2.5×10^{-6}. If the criterion was set to zero, the balance between error and complexity would be fragile in such a hard problem.

[8] We add Gaussian noise with a rather large standard deviation of 1.5 times the signal. The exact value is not crucial: similar performance is obtained for noise levels between 0.7 and 2.0 .

Finally, we analyze the weight-eliminated network solution. The weights from the hidden units to the outputs are in a region where the complexity term acts as a counter. In fact only one or two hidden units remain. The weights from the inputs to the dead hidden units are also eliminated. For time series prediction, weight-elimination acts as hidden-unit elimination.

The weights between inputs and remaining hidden units are fairly small. Weight-elimination is in its quadratic region and prevents them from growing too large. Consequently, the activation of the hidden units lies in $(-0.4, 0.4)$. This prompted us to try a linear net where our procedure also works surprisingly well, yielding comparable performance to sigmoids.

Since all inputs are scaled to zero mean and unit standard deviation, we can gauge the importance of different inputs directly by the size of the weights. With weight-elimination, it becomes fairly clear which quantities are important, since connections that do not manage to reduce the error are not worth their price. A detailed description will be published in [WHR91]. Weight-elimination enhances the interpretability of the solution.

To summarize, we have a working procedure that finds small nets and can help prevent overfitting. With our rules for the dynamics of λ, weight-elimination is fairly stable. values of most parameters. In the examples we analyzed, the network manages to pick out some significant part of the dynamics underlying the time series.

References

[Che90] Peter C. Cheeseman. **On finding the most probable model.** In J. Shrager and P. Langley (eds.) *Computational Models of Scientific Discovery and Theory Formation*, p. 73. Morgan Kaufmann, 1990.

[RDGC92] David E. Rumelhart, Richard Durbin, Richard Golden, and Yves Chauvin. **Backpropagation: theoretical foundations.** In Y. Chauvin and D. E. Rumelhart (eds.) *Backpropagation and Connectionist Theory.* Lawrence Erlbaum, 1992.

[Ris89] Jorma Rissanen. **Stochastic Complexity in Statistical Inquiry**. World Scientific, 1989.

[Ton90] Howell Tong. **Non-linear Time Series: a Dynamical System Approach.** Oxford University Press, 1990.

[Wei91] Andreas S. Weigend. **Connectionist Architectures for Time Series Prediction.** PhD thesis, Stanford University, 1991. (in preparation)

[WHR90] Andreas S. Weigend, Bernardo A. Huberman, and David E. Rumelhart. **Predicting the future: a connectionist approach.** *International Journal of Neural Systems*, 1:193, 1990.

[WHR91] Andreas S. Weigend, Bernardo A. Huberman, and David E. Rumelhart. **Predicting sunspots and currency rates with connectionist networks.** In M. Casdagli and S. Eubank (eds.) *Proceedings of the 1990 NATO Workshop on Nonlinear Modeling and Forecasting (Santa Fe).* Addison-Wesley, 1991.

[WRH90] Andreas S. Weigend, David E. Rumelhart, and Bernardo A. Huberman. **Back-propagation, weight-elimination and time series prediction.** In D. S. Touretzky, J. L. Elman, T. J. Sejnowski, and G. E. Hinton (eds.) *Proceedings of the 1990 Connectionist Models Summer School*, p 105. Morgan Kaufmann, 1990.

The Devil and the Network: What Sparsity Implies to Robustness and Memory

Sanjay Biswas and **Santosh S. Venkatesh**
Department of Electrical Engineering
University of Pennsylvania
Philadelphia, PA 19104

Abstract

Robustness is a commonly bruited property of neural networks; in particular, a folk theorem in neural computation asserts that neural networks—in contexts with large interconnectivity—continue to function efficiently, albeit with some degradation, in the presence of component damage or loss. A second folk theorem in such contexts asserts that dense interconnectivity between neural elements is a *sine qua non* for the efficient usage of resources. These premises are formally examined in this communication in a setting that invokes the notion of the "devil"[1] in the network as an agent that produces sparsity by snipping connections.

1 ON REMOVING THE FOLK FROM THE THEOREM

Robustness in the presence of component damage is a property that is commonly attributed to neural networks. The content of the following statement embodies this sentiment.

> *Folk Theorem 1: Computation in neural networks is not substantially affected by damage to network components.*

While such a statement is manifestly not true in general—witness networks with "grandmother cells" where damage to the critical cells fatally impairs the computational ability of the network—there is anecdotal evidence in support of it in

[1] Well, maybe an imp.

situations where the network has a more "distributed" flavour with relatively dense interconnectivity of elements and a distributed format for the storage of information. Qualitatively, the phenomenon is akin to holographic modes of storing information where the distributed, non-localised format of information storage carries with it a measure of security against component damage.

The flip side to the robust folk theorem is the following observation, robustness notwithstanding:

> *Folk Theorem 2: Dense interconnectivity is a sine qua non for efficient usage of resources; in particular, sparser structures exhibit a degradation in computational capability.*

Again, disclaimers have to be thrown in on the applicability of such a statement. In recurrent network architectures, however, this might seem to have some merit. In particular, in associative memory applications, while structural robustness might guarantee that the loss in memory storage capacity with increased interconnection sparsity may not be catastrophic, nonetheless intuitively a drop in capacity with increased sparsity may be expected.

This communication represents an effort to mathematically codify these tenets. In the setting we examine we formally introduce sparse network interconnectivity by invoking the notion of a (puckish) devil in the network which severs interconnection links between neurons. Our results here involve some surprising consequences—viewed in the light of the two folk theorems—of sparse interconnectivity to robustness and to memory storage capability. Only the main results are stated here; for extensions and details of proofs we refer the interested reader to Venkatesh (1990) and Biswas and Venkatesh (1990).

Notation We denote by $\mathbb{B}$ the set $\{-1, 1\}$. For every integer k we denote the set of integers $\{1, 2, \ldots, k\}$ by $[k]$. By ordered multiset we mean an ordered collection of elements with repetition of elements allowed, and by k-set we mean an ordered multiset of k elements. All logarithms in the exposition are to base e.

2 RECURRENT NETWORKS

2.1 INTERCONNECTION GRAPHS

We consider a recurrent network of n formal neurons. The allowed pattern of neural interconnectivity is specified by the edges of a *(bipartite) interconnectivity graph*, G_n, on vertices, $[n] \times [n]$. In particular, the existence of an edge $\{i, j\}$ in G_n is indicative that the state of neuron j is input to neuron i.[2] The network is characterised by an $n \times n$ matrix of weights, $\mathbf{W} = [w_{ij}]$, where w_{ij} denotes the (real) weight modulating the state of neuron j at the input of neuron i. If $\mathbf{u} \in \mathbb{B}^n$ is the current state of the system, an update, $u_i \mapsto u_i'$ of the state of neuron i is

[2]Equivalently, imagine a devil loose with a pair of scissors snipping those interconnections for which $\{i, j\} \notin G_n$. For a complementary discussion of sparse interconnectivity see Komlós and Paturi (1988).

specified by the linear threshold rule

$$u_i' = \operatorname{sgn}\left(\sum_{j:\{i,j\}\in G} w_{ij}u_j\right).$$

The network dynamics describe trajectories in a state space comprised of the vertices of the n-cube.[3] We are interested in an associative memory application where we wish to store a desired set of states—the *memories*—as fixed points of the network, and with the property that errors in an input representation of a memory are corrected and the memory retrieved.

2.2 DOMINATORS

Let $\mathbf{u} \in \mathbb{B}^n$ be a memory and $0 \leq \rho < 1$ a parameter. Corresponding to the memory $\mathbf{u}$ we generate a probe $\hat{\mathbf{u}} \in \mathbb{B}^n$ by independently specifying the components, $\hat{u}_j$, of the probe as follows:

$$\hat{u}_j = \begin{cases} u_j & \text{with probability } 1-\rho \\ -u_j & \text{with probability } \rho. \end{cases} \tag{1}$$

We call $\hat{\mathbf{u}}$ a *random probe with parameter* ρ.

Definition 2.1 We say that a memory, $\mathbf{u}$, *dominates over a radius* ρn if, with probability approaching one as $n \to \infty$, the network corrects all errors in a random probe with parameter ρ in one synchronous step. We call ρ the *(fractional) dominance radius*. We also say that $\mathbf{u}$ is *stable* if it is a 0-dominator.

REMARKS: Note that stable memories are just fixed points of the network. Also, the expected number of errors in a probe is ρn.

2.3 CODES

For given integers $m \geq 1$, $n \geq 1$, a *code*, $\mathcal{K}_n^m$, is a collection of ordered multisets of size m from $\mathbb{B}^n$. We say that an m-set of memories is *admissible* iff it is in $\mathcal{K}_n^m$.[4] Thus, a code just specifies which m-sets are allowable as memories. Examples of codes include: the set of all multisets of size m from $\mathbb{B}^n$; a single multiset of size m from $\mathbb{B}^n$; all collections of m mutually orthogonal vectors in $\mathbb{B}^n$; all m-sets of vectors in $\mathbb{B}^n$ in general position.

Define two ordered multisets of memories to be *equivalent* if they are permutations of one another. We define the *size* of a code, $\mathcal{K}_n^m$, to be the number of distinct equivalence classes of m-sets of memories. We will be interested in codes of relatively large size: $\log |\mathcal{K}_n^m|/n \to \infty$ as $n \to \infty$. In particular, we require at least an exponential number of choices of (equivalence classes of) admissible m-sets of memories.

[3] As usual, there are Liapunov functions for the system under suitable conditions on the interconnectivity graph and the corresponding weights.

[4] We define admissible m-sets of memories in terms of ordered multisets rather than sets so as to obviate certain technical nuisances.

2.4 CAPACITY

For each fixed n and interconnectivity graph, G_n, an *algorithm*, $\mathcal{X}$, is a prescription which, given an m-set of memories, produces a corresponding set of interconnection weights, w_{ij}, $i \in [n]$, $\{i,j\} \in G_n$. For $m \geq 1$ let $\mathcal{A}(\mathbf{u}^1, \ldots, \mathbf{u}^m)$ be some attribute of m-sets of memories. (The following, for instance, are examples of attributes of admissible sets of memories: all the memories are stable in the network generated by $\mathcal{X}$; almost all the memories dominate over a radius ρn.) *For given n and m, we choose a random m-set of memories, $\mathbf{u}^1, \ldots, \mathbf{u}^m$, from the uniform distribution on $\mathcal{K}_n^m$.*

Definition 2.2 Given interconnectivity graphs G_n, codes $\mathcal{K}_n^m$, and algorithm $\mathcal{X}$, a sequence, $\{C_n\}_{n=1}^{\infty}$, is a *capacity function for the attribute $\mathcal{A}$* (or *$\mathcal{A}$-capacity* for short) if for $\lambda > 0$ arbitrarily small:

a) $\mathbf{P}\{\mathcal{A}(\mathbf{u}^1, \ldots, \mathbf{u}^m)\} \to 1$ as $n \to \infty$ whenever $m \leq (1-\lambda)C_n$;

b) $\mathbf{P}\{\mathcal{A}(\mathbf{u}^1, \ldots, \mathbf{u}^m)\} \to 0$ as $n \to \infty$ whenever $m \geq (1+\lambda)C_n$.

We also say that C_n is a *lower $\mathcal{A}$-capacity* if property (a) holds, and that C_n is an *upper $\mathcal{A}$-capacity* if property (b) holds.

For $m \geq 1$ let $\mathbf{u}^1, \ldots, \mathbf{u}^m \in \mathbb{B}^n$ be an m-set of memories chosen from a code $\mathcal{K}_n^m$. The *outer-product algorithm* specifies the interconnection weights, w_{ij}, according to the following rule: for $i \in [n]$, $\{i,j\} \in G_n$,

$$w_{ij} = \sum_{\beta=1}^{m} u_i^\beta u_j^\beta. \tag{2}$$

In general, if the interconnectivity graph, G_n, is symmetric then, under a suitable mode of operation, there is a Liapunov function for the network specified by the outer-product algorithm. *Given graphs G_n, codes $\mathcal{K}_n^m$, and the outer-product algorithm, for fixed $0 \leq \rho < 1/2$ we are interested in the attribute $\mathcal{D}_\rho$ that each of the m memories dominates over a radius ρn.*

3 RANDOM GRAPHS

We investigate the effect of a random loss of neural interconnections in a recurrent network of n neurons by considering a random bipartite interconnectivity graph RG_n on vertices $[n] \times [n]$ with

$$\mathbf{P}\ \{\{i,j\} \in RG_n\} = p$$

for all $i \in [n]$, $j \in [n]$, and with these probabilities being mutually independent. The interconnection probability p is called the *sparsity parameter* and may depend on n. The system described above is formally equivalent to beginning with a fully-interconnected network of neurons with specified interconnection weights w_{ij}, and then invoking a devil which randomly severs interconnection links, independently retaining each interconnection weight w_{ij} with probability p, and severing it (replacing it with a zero weight) with probability $q = 1 - p$.

Let $\mathcal{CK}_n^m$ denote the *complete code* of all choices of ordered multisets of size m from $\mathbb{B}^n$.

Theorem 3.1 *Let $0 \le \rho < 1/2$ be a fixed dominance radius, and let the sparsity parameter p satisfy $pn^2 \to \infty$ as $n \to \infty$. Then $(1-2\rho)^2 pn/2 \log pn^2$ is a $\mathcal{D}_\rho$-capacity for random interconnectivity graphs RG_n, complete codes $\mathcal{CK}_n^m$, and the outer-product algorithm.*

REMARKS: The above result graphically validates Folk Theorem 1 on the fault-tolerant nature of the network; specifically, the network exhibits a *graceful degradation* in storage capacity as the loss in interconnections increases. Catastrophic failure occurs only when p is smaller than $\log n/n$: *each neuron need retain only of the order of $\Omega(\log n)$ links of a total of n possible links with other neurons for useful associative properties to emerge.*

4 BLOCK GRAPHS

One of the simplest (and most regular) forms of sparsity that a favourably disposed devil might enjoin is block sparsity where the neurons are partitioned into disjoint subsets of neurons with full-interconnectivity within each subset and no neural interconnections between subsets. The weight matrix in this case takes on a block diagonal form, and the interconnectivity graph is composed of a set of disjoint, complete bipartite sub-graphs.

More formally, let $1 \le b \le n$ be a positive integer, and let $\{I_1, \ldots, I_{n/b}\}$ partition $[n]$ such that each subset of indices, I_k, $k = 1, \ldots, n/b$, has size $|I_k| = b$.[5] We call each I_k a *block* and b the *block size*. We specify the edges of the *(bipartite) block interconnectivity graph* BG_n by $\{i, j\} \in BG_n$ iff i and j lie in a common block.

Theorem 4.1 *Let the block size b be such that $b = \Omega(n)$ as $n \to \infty$, and let $0 \le \rho < 1/2$ be a fixed dominance radius. Then $(1-2\rho)^2 b/2 \log bn$ is a $\mathcal{D}_\rho$-capacity for block interconnectivity graphs BG_n, complete codes $\mathcal{CK}_n^m$, and the outer-product algorithm.*

Corollary 4.2 *Under the conditions of theorem 4.1 the fixed point memory capacity is $b/2 \log bn$.*

Corollary 4.3 *For a fully-interconnected graph, complete codes $\mathcal{CK}_n^m$, and the outer-product algorithm, the fixed point memory capacity is $n/4 \log n$.*

Corollary 4.3 is the main result shown by McEliece, Posner, Rodemich, and Venkatesh (1987). Theorem 4.1 extends the result and shows (formally validating the intuition espoused in Folk Theorem 2) that increased sparsity causes a loss in capacity if the code is complete, i.e., all choices of memories are considered admissible. It is possible, however, to design codes to take advantage of the sparse interconnectivity structure, rather at odds with the Folk Theorem.

[5] Here, as in the rest of the paper, we ignore details with regard to integer rounding.

Without loss of generality let us assume that block I_1 consists of the first b indices, $[b]$, block I_2 the next b indices, $[2b]-[b]$, and so on, with the last block $I_{n/b}$ consisting of the last b indices, $[n]-[n-b]$. We can then partition any vector $\mathbf{u} \in \mathbb{B}^n$ as

$$\mathbf{u} = \begin{pmatrix} \mathbf{u}_1 \\ \mathbf{u}_2 \\ \vdots \\ \mathbf{u}_{n/b} \end{pmatrix}, \tag{3}$$

where for $k = 1, \ldots, n/b$, $\mathbf{u}_k$ is the vector of components corresponding to block I_k. For $M \geq 1$ we form the *block code* $\mathcal{BK}_n^{M^{n/b}}$ as follows: to each ordered multiset of M vectors, $\mathbf{u}^1, \ldots, \mathbf{u}^M$ from $\mathbb{B}^n$, we associate a unique ordered multiset in $\mathcal{BK}_n^{M^{n/b}}$ by lexicographically ordering all $M^{n/b}$ vectors of the form

$$\begin{pmatrix} \mathbf{u}_1^{\alpha_1} \\ \mathbf{u}_2^{\alpha_2} \\ \vdots \\ \mathbf{u}_{n/b}^{\alpha_{n/b}} \end{pmatrix}, \qquad \alpha_1, \alpha_2, \ldots, \alpha_{n/b} \in [M].$$

Thus, we obtain an admissible set of $M^{n/b}$ memories from any ordered multiset of M vectors in $\mathbb{B}^n$ by "mixing" the blocks of the vectors. We call each M-set of vectors, $\mathbf{u}^1, \ldots, \mathbf{u}^M \in \mathbb{B}^n$, the *generating vectors* for the corresponding admissible set of memories in $\mathcal{BK}_n^{M^{n/b}}$.

EXAMPLE: Consider a case with $n = 4$, block size $b = 2$, and $M = 2$ generating vectors. To any 2-set of generating vectors there corresponds a unique $4(=M^{n/b})$-set in the block code as follows:

$$\left(\begin{array}{c} u_1^1 \\ u_2^1 \\ \hline u_3^1 \\ u_4^1 \end{array}\right), \left(\begin{array}{c} u_1^2 \\ u_2^2 \\ \hline u_3^2 \\ u_4^2 \end{array}\right) \longmapsto \left(\begin{array}{c} u_1^1 \\ u_2^1 \\ \hline u_3^1 \\ u_4^1 \end{array}\right), \left(\begin{array}{c} u_1^1 \\ u_2^1 \\ \hline u_3^2 \\ u_4^2 \end{array}\right), \left(\begin{array}{c} u_1^2 \\ u_2^2 \\ \hline u_3^1 \\ u_4^1 \end{array}\right), \left(\begin{array}{c} u_1^2 \\ u_2^2 \\ \hline u_3^2 \\ u_4^2 \end{array}\right).$$

Theorem 4.4 *Let $0 \leq \rho < 1/2$ be a fixed dominance radius. Then we have the following capacity estimates for block interconnectivity graphs BG_n, block codes $\mathcal{BK}_n^m$, and the outer-product algorithm:*

a) If the block size b satisfies $n \log\log bn / b \log bn \to 0$ as $n \to \infty$ then the $\mathcal{D}_\rho$-capacity is

$$\left[\frac{(1-2\rho)^2 b}{2 \log bn}\right]^{n/b}.$$

b) Define for any ν

$$C_n(\nu) = 2^{\frac{n \log b}{b \log 2}\left[1 - \frac{\log\log bn + \log\left(2(1-2\rho)^{-2}\right)}{\log b} + \frac{\nu \log\log bn}{(\log b)(\log bn)}\right]}.$$

If the block size b satisfies $b/\log n \to \infty$ and $b \log bn / \log\log bn = O(n)$ as $n \to \infty$, then $C_n(\nu)$ is a lower $\mathcal{D}_\rho$-capacity for any choice of $\nu < 3/2$ and $C_n(\nu)$ is an upper $\mathcal{D}_\rho$-capacity for any $\nu > 3/2$.

Corollary 4.5 *If, for fixed $t \geq 1$, we have $b = n/t$, then, under the conditions of theorem 4.4, the $\mathcal{D}_\rho$-capacity is*

$$(1 - 2\rho)^{2t} t^{-t} 4^{-t} \left(\frac{n}{\log n} \right)^t .$$

Corollary 4.6 *For any fixed dominance radius $0 \leq \rho < 1/2$, and for any $\tau < 1$, a constant $c > 0$ and a code of size $\Omega\left(2^{cn^{2-\tau}}\right)$ can be found such that it is possible to achieve lower $\mathcal{D}_\rho$-capacities which are $\Omega\left(2^{n^\tau}\right)$ in recurrent neural networks with interconnectivity graphs of degree $\Theta\left(n^{1-\tau}\right)$.*

REMARKS: If the number of blocks is kept fixed as n grows (i.e., the block size grows linearly with n) then capacities polynomial in n are attained. If the number of blocks increases with n (i.e., the block size grows sub-linearly with n) then super-polynomial capacities are attained. Furthermore, we have the surprising result rather at odds with Folk Theorem 2 that very large storage capacities can be obtained at the expense of code size (while still retaining large code sizes) in *increasingly sparse networks.*

Acknowledgements

The support of research grants from E. I. Dupont de Nemours, Inc. and the Air Force Office of Scientific Research (grant number AFOSR 89–0523) is gratefully acknowledged.

References

Biswas, S. and S. S. Venkatesh (1990), "Codes, sparsity, and capacity in neural associative memory," submitted for publication.

Komlós, J. and R. Paturi (1988), "Effects of connectivity in associative memory models," Technical Report CS88–131, University of California, San Diego, 1988.

McEliece, R. J., E. C. Posner, E. R. Rodemich, and S. S. Venkatesh (1987), "The capacity of the Hopfield associative memory," *IEEE Trans. Inform. Theory*, vol. IT–33, pp. 461–482.

Venkatesh, S. S. (1990), "Robustness in neural computation: random graphs and sparsity," to appear *IEEE Trans. Inform. Theory.*

Generalization Dynamics in LMS Trained Linear Networks

Yves Chauvin*
Psychology Department
Stanford University
Stanford, CA 94305

Abstract

For a simple linear case, a mathematical analysis of the training and generalization (validation) performance of networks trained by gradient descent on a Least Mean Square cost function is provided as a function of the learning parameters and of the statistics of the training data base. The analysis predicts that generalization error dynamics are very dependent on *a priori* initial weights. In particular, the generalization error might sometimes weave within a computable range during extended training. In some cases, the analysis provides bounds on the optimal number of training cycles for minimal validation error. For a speech labeling task, predicted weaving effects were qualitatively tested and observed by computer simulations in networks trained by the linear *and* non-linear back-propagation algorithm.

1 INTRODUCTION

Recent progress in network design demonstrates that non-linear feedforward neural networks can perform impressive pattern classification for a variety of real-world applications (e.g., Le Cun et al., 1990; Waibel et al., 1989). Various simulations and relationships between the neural network and machine learning theoretical literatures also suggest that too large a number of free parameters ("weight overfitting") could substantially reduce generalization performance. (e.g., Baum, 1989 1989).

A number of solutions have recently been proposed to decrease or eliminate the overfitting problem in specific situations. They range from *ad hoc* heuristics to theoretical considerations (e.g., Le Cun et al., 1990; Chauvin, 1990a; Weigend et al.,

*Also with Thomson-CSF, Inc., 630 Hansen Way, Suite 250, Palo Alto, CA 94304.

In Press). For a phoneme labeling application, Chauvin showed that the overfitting phenomenon was actually observed only when networks were overtrained far beyond their "optimal" performance point (Chauvin, 1990b). Furthermore, generalization performance of networks seemed to be independent of the size of the network during early training but the rate of decrease in performance with overtraining was indeed related the number of weights.

The goal of this paper is to better understand training and generalization error dynamics in Least-Mean-Square trained *linear* networks. As we will see, gradient descent training on linear networks can actually generate surprisingly rich and insightful validation dynamics. Furthermore, in numerous applications, even non-linear networks tend to function in their linear range, as if the networks were making use of non-linearities only when necessary (Weigend et al., In Press; Chauvin, 1990a). In Section 2, I present a theoretical illustration yielding a better understanding of training and validation error dynamics. In Section 3, numerical solutions to obtained analytical results make interesting predictions for validation dynamics under overtraining. These predictions are tested for a phonemic labeling task. The obtained simulations suggest that the results of the analysis obtained with the simple theoretical framework of Section 2 might remain qualitatively valid for non-linear complex architectures.

2 THEORETICAL ILLUSTRATION

2.1 ASSUMPTIONS

Let us consider a linear network composed of n input units and n output units fully connected by a $n.n$ weight matrix W. Let us suppose the network is trained to reproduce a noiseless output "signal" from a noisy input "signal" (the network can be seen as a linear filter). We write F as the "signal", N the noise, X the input, Y the output, and D the desired output. For the considered case, we have $X = F + N$, $Y = WX$ and $D = F$.

The statistical properties of the data base are the following. The signal is zero-mean with covariance matrix C_F. We write λ_i and e_i as the eigenvalues and eigenvectors of C_F (e_i are the so-called *principal components*; we will call λ_i the "signal power spectrum"). The noise is assumed to be zero-mean, with covariance matrix $\bar{C}_N = \bar{\nu}.I$ where I is the identity matrix. We assume the noise is uncorrelated with the signal: $\bar{C}_{FN} = 0$. We suppose two sets of patterns have been sampled for training and for validation. We write C_F, C_N and C_{FN} the resulting covariance matrices for the training set and C'_F, C'_N and C'_{FN} the corresponding matrices for the validation set. We assume $C_F \simeq C'_F \simeq \bar{C}_F$, $C_{FN} \simeq C'_{FN} \simeq \bar{C}_{FN} = 0$, $C_N = \nu.I$ and $C'_N = \nu'.I$ with $\nu' > \nu$. (Numerous of these assumptions are made for the sake of clarity of explanation: they can be relaxed without changing the resulting implications.)

The problem considered is much simpler than typical realistic applications. However, we will see below that (i) a formal analysis becomes complex very quickly (ii) the validation dynamics are rich, insightful and can be mapped to a number of results observed in simulations of realistic applications and (iii) an interesting number of predictions can be obtained.

2.2 LEARNING

The network is trained by gradient descent on the Least Mean Square (LMS) error: $\Delta W = -\eta \nabla_W E$ where η is the usual learning rate and, in the case considered, $E = \sum_p^P (F_p - Y_p)^T (F_p - Y_p)$. We can write the gradient as a function of the various covariance matrices: $\nabla_W E = (I - W)C_F + (I - 2W)C_{FN} - WC_N$. From the general assumptions, we get:

$$\nabla_W E \simeq C_F - WC_F - WC_N \tag{1}$$

We assume now that the principal components e_i are also eigenvectors of the weight matrix W at iteration k with corresponding eigenvalue α_{ik}: $W_k.e_i = \alpha_{ik} e_i$. We can then compute the image of each eigenvector e_i at iteration $k+1$:

$$W_{k+1}.e_i = \eta \lambda_i.e_i + \alpha_{ik}[1 - \eta(\lambda_i + \nu)].e_i \tag{2}$$

Therefore, e_i is also an eigenvector of W_{k+1} and $\alpha_{i,k+1}$ satisfies the induction:

$$\alpha_{i,k+1} = \eta \lambda_i + \alpha_{ik}[1 - \eta(\lambda_i + \nu)] \tag{3}$$

Assuming $W_0 = 0$, we can compute the *alpha-dynamics* of the weight matrix W:

$$\alpha_{ik} = \frac{\lambda_i}{\lambda_i + \nu}[1 - (1 - \eta(\lambda_i + \nu))^k] \tag{4}$$

As k goes to infinity, provided $\eta < 1/\lambda_M + \nu$, α_i approaches $\lambda_i/(\lambda_i + \nu_i)$, which corresponds to the optimal (Wiener) value of the linear filter implemented by the network. We will write the convergence rates $a_i = 1 - \eta\lambda_i - \eta\nu$. These rates depend on the signal "power spectrum", on the noise power and on the learning rate η.

If we now assume $W_0.e_i = \alpha_{i0}.e_i$ with $\alpha_{i0} \neq 0$ (this assumption can be made more general), we get:

$$\alpha_{ik} = \frac{\lambda_i}{\lambda_i + \nu}[1 - b_i a_i^k] \tag{5}$$

where $b_i = 1 - \alpha_{i0} - \alpha_{i0}\nu/\lambda_i$. Figure 1 represents possible alpha dynamics for arbitrary values of λ_i with $\alpha_{i0} = \alpha_0 \neq 0$.

We can now compute the learning error dynamics by expanding the LMS error term E at time k. Using the general assumptions on the covariance matrices, we find:

$$E_k = \sum_i^n E_{ik} = \sum_i^n \lambda_i (1 - \alpha_{ik})^2 + \nu \alpha_{ik}^2 \tag{6}$$

Therefore, training error is a sum of *error components*, each of them being a quadratic function of α_i. Figure 2 represents a training error component E_i as a function of α. Knowing the *alpha-dynamics*, we can write these error components as a function of k:

$$E_{ik} = \frac{\lambda_i}{\lambda_i + \nu}(\nu + \lambda_i b^2 a^{2k}) \tag{7}$$

It is easy to see that E is a monotonic decreasing function (generated by gradient descent) which converges to the bottom of the quadratic error surface, yielding the residual asymptotic error:

$$E_\infty = \sum_i^n \frac{\lambda_i \nu_i}{\lambda_i + \nu_i} \tag{8}$$

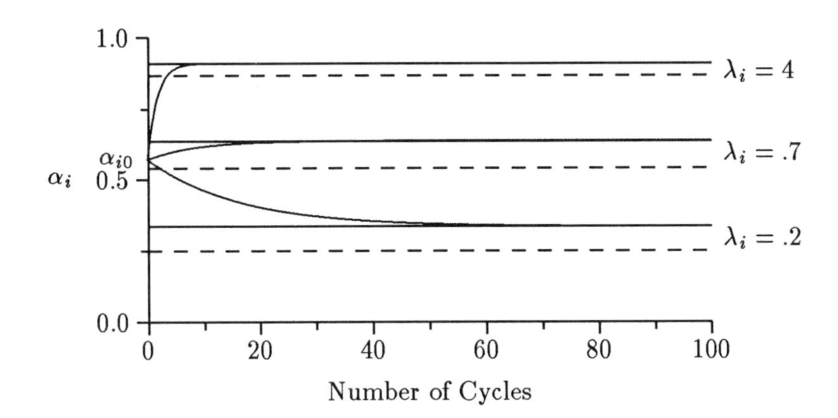

Figure 1: Alpha dynamics for different values of λ_i with $\eta = .01$ and $\alpha_{i0} = \alpha_0 \neq 0$. The solid lines represent the optimal values of α_i for the training data set. The dashed lines represent corresponding optimal values for the validation data set.

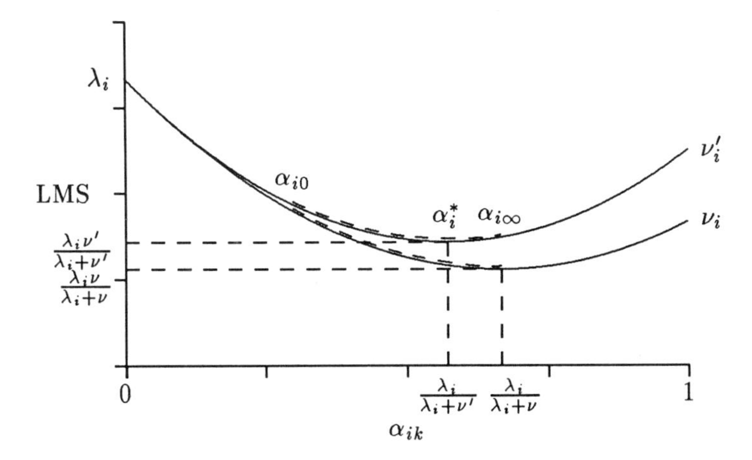

Figure 2: Training and validation error dynamics as a function of α_i. The dashed curved lines represent the error dynamics for the initial conditions α_{i0}. Each training error component follows the gradient of a quadratic learning curve (bottom). Note the overtraining phenomenon (top curve) between α_i^* (optimal for validation) and $\alpha_{i\infty}$ (optimal for training).

2.3 GENERALIZATION

Considering the general assumptions on the statistics of the data base, we can compute the validation error E' (Note that "validation error" strictly applies to the validation data set. "Generalization error" can qualify the validation data set or the whole population, depending on context.):

$$E'_k = \sum_i^n E'_{ik} = \sum_i^n \lambda_i(1-\alpha_{ik})^2 + \nu'\alpha_{ik}^2 \tag{9}$$

where the alpha-dynamics are imposed by gradient descent learning on the training data set. Again, the validation error is a sum of error components E'_i, quadratic functions of α_i. However, because the alpha-dynamics are adapted to the training sample, they might generate complex dynamics which will strongly depend on the inital values α_{i0} (Figure 1). Consequently, the resulting error components E'_i are not monotonic decreasing functions anymore. As seen in Figure 2, each of the validation error components might (i) decrease (ii) decrease then increase (overtraining) or (iii) increase as a function of α_{i0}. For each of these components, in the case of overtraining, it is possible to compute the value of α_{ik} at which training should be stopped to get minimal validation error:

$$k_i^* = \frac{Log\frac{\lambda_i}{\lambda_i+\nu'} + Log\frac{\nu'-\nu}{\lambda_i - \alpha_{i0}(\lambda_i+\nu')}}{Log(1-\eta\lambda_i - \eta\nu)} \tag{10}$$

However, the validation error dynamics become much more complex when we consider sums of these components. If we assume $\alpha_{i0} = 0$, the minimum (or minima) of E' can be found to correspond to possible intersections of hyper-ellipsoids and power curves. In general, it is possible to show that there exists at least one such minimum. It is also possible to find simple bounds on the optimal training time for minimal validation error:

$$\frac{Log\frac{\nu'-\nu}{\lambda_m+\nu'}}{Log(1-\eta\lambda_m-\eta\nu)} \le k^* \le \frac{Log\frac{\nu'-\nu}{\lambda_M+\nu'}}{Log(1-\eta\lambda_M-\eta\nu)} \tag{11}$$

These bounds are tight when the noise power is small compared to the signal "power spectrum". For $\alpha_{i0} \neq 0$, a formal analysis of the validation error dynamics becomes intractable. Because some error components might increase while others decrease, it is possible to imagine multiple minima and maxima for the total validation error (see simulations below). Considering each component's dynamics, it is nonetheless possible to compute bounds within which E' might vary during training:

$$\sum_i^n \frac{\lambda_i\nu'}{\lambda_i+\nu'} \le E'_k \le \sum_i^n \frac{\lambda_i(\nu^2+\nu'\lambda_i)}{(\lambda_i+\nu)^2} \tag{12}$$

Because of the "exponential" nature of training (Figure 1), it is possible to imagine that this "weaving" effect might still be observed after a long training period, when the training error itself has become stable. Furthermore, whereas the training error will qualitatively show the same dynamics, validation error will very much depend on α_{i0}: for sufficiently large initial weights, validation dynamics might be very dependent on particular simulation "runs".

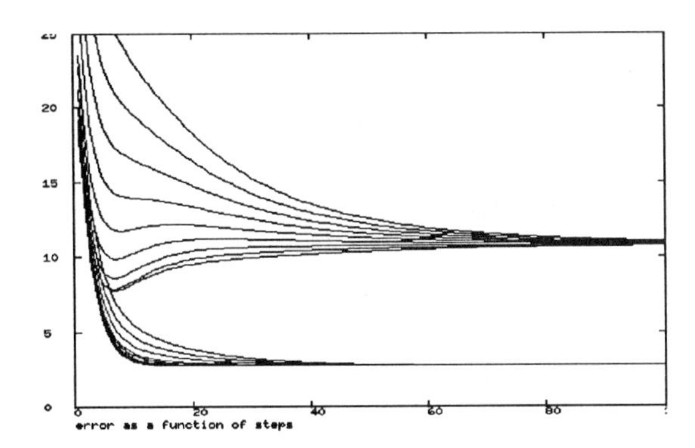

Figure 3: Training (bottom curves) and validation (top curves) error dynamics in a two-dimensional case for $\lambda_1 = 17, \lambda_2 = 1.7, \nu = 2, \nu' = 10, \alpha_{10} = 0$ as α_{20} varies from 0 to 1.6 (bottom-up) in .2 increments.

3 SIMULATIONS

3.1 CASE STUDY

Equations 7 and 9 were simulated for a two-dimensional case ($n = 2$) with $\lambda_1 = 17, \lambda_2 = 1.7, \nu = 2, \nu' = 10$ and $\alpha_{10} = 0$. The values of α_{20} determined the relative dominance of the two error components during training. Figure 3 represents training and validation dynamics as a function of k for a range of values of α_{20}. As shown analytically, training dynamics are basically unaffected by the initial conditions of the weight matrix W_0. However, a variety of validation dynamics can be observed as α_{20} varies from 0 to 1.6. For $1.6 \geq \alpha_{20} \geq 1.4$, the validation error is monotically decreasing and looks like a typical "gradient descent" training error. For $1.2 \geq \alpha_{20} \geq 1.0$, each error component in turn imposes a descent rate: the validation error looks like two "connected descents". For $.8 \geq \alpha_{20} \geq .6$, E'_2 is monotically decreasing with a slow convergence rate, forcing the validation error to decrease long after E'_1 has become stable. This creates a minimum, followed by a maximum, followed by a minimum for E'. Finally, for $.4 \geq \alpha_{20} \geq 0$, both error components have a single minimum during training and generate a single minimum for the total validation error E'.

3.2 PHONEMIC LABELING

One of the main predictions obtained from the analytical results and from the previous case study is that validation dynamics can demonstrate multiple local minima and maxima. To my knowledge, this phenomenon has not been described in the literature. However, the theory also predicts that the phenomenon will probably appear very late in training, well after the training error has become stable, which might explain the absence of such observations. The predictions were tested for a phonemic labeling task with spectrograms as input patterns and phonemes as output patterns. Various architectures were tested (direct connections or back-propagation networks with linear or non-linear hidden layers). Due to the limited length of this article, the complete simulations will be reported elsewhere. In all cases, as predicted, multiple mimina/maxima were observed for the validation dynamics, provided the networks were trained way beyond usual training times. Furthermore, these generalization dynamics were very dependent on the initial weights (provided sufficient variance on the initial weight distribution).

4 DISCUSSION

It is sometimes assumed that optimal learning is obtained when validation error starts to increase during the course of training. Although for the theoretical study presented, the first minimum of E' is probably always a global minimum, independently of α_{i0}, simulations of the speech labeling task show it is not always the case with more complex architectures: late validation minima can sometimes (albeit rarely) be deeper than the first "local" minimum. These observations and a lack of theoretical understanding of statistical inference under limited data set raise the question of the significance of a validation data set. As a final comment, we are not really interested in minimal validation error (E') but in minimal *generalization* error ($\bar{E}'$). Understanding the dynamics of the "population" error as a function of training and validation errors necessitates, at least, an evaluation of the sample statistics as a function of the number of training and validation patterns. This is beyond the scope of this paper.

Acknowledgements

Thanks to Pierre Baldi and Julie Holmes for their helpful comments.

References

Baum, E. B. & Haussler, D. (1989). What size net gives valid generalization? *Neural Computation, 1*, 151–160.

Chauvin, Y. (1990a). Dynamic behavior of constrained back-propagation networks. In D. S. Touretzky (Ed.), *Neural Information Processing Systems (Vol. 2)* (pp. 642–649). San Mateo, CA: Morgan Kaufman.

Chauvin, Y. (1990b). Generalization performance of overtrained back-propagation networks. In L. B. Almeida & C. J. Wellekens (Eds.), *Lecture Notes in Computer Science (Vol. 412)* (pp. 46–55). Berlin: Germany: Springer-Verlag.

Cun, Y. L., Boser, B., Denker, J. S., Henderson, D., Howard, R. E., Hubbard, W., & Jackel, L. D. (1990). Handwritten digit recognition with a back-propagation network. In D. S. Touretzky (Ed.), *Neural Information Processing Systems (Vol. 2)* (pp. 396–404). San Mateo, CA: Morgan Kaufman.

Waibel, A., Sawai, H., & Shikano, K. (1989). Modularity and scaling in large phonemic neural networks. *IEEE Transactions on Acoustics, Speech and Signal Processing, ASSP-37*, 1888–1898.

Weigend, A. S., Huberman, B. A., & Rumelhart, D. E. (In Press). Predicting the future: a connectionist approach. *International Journal of Neural Systems.*

Dynamics of Generalization in Linear Perceptrons

Anders Krogh
Niels Bohr Institute
Blegdamsvej 17
DK-2100 Copenhagen, Denmark

John A. Hertz
NORDITA
Blegdamsvej 17
DK-2100 Copenhagen, Denmark

Abstract

We study the evolution of the generalization ability of a simple linear perceptron with N inputs which learns to imitate a "teacher perceptron". The system is trained on $p = \alpha N$ binary example inputs and the generalization ability measured by testing for agreement with the teacher on all 2^N possible binary input patterns. The dynamics may be solved analytically and exhibits a phase transition from imperfect to perfect generalization at $\alpha = 1$. Except at this point the generalization ability approaches its asymptotic value exponentially, with critical slowing down near the transition; the relaxation time is $\propto (1 - \sqrt{\alpha})^{-2}$. Right at the critical point, the approach to perfect generalization follows a power law $\propto t^{-\frac{1}{2}}$. In the presence of noise, the generalization ability is degraded by an amount $\propto (\sqrt{\alpha} - 1)^{-1}$ just above $\alpha = 1$.

1 INTRODUCTION

It is very important in practical situations to know how well a neural network will generalize from the examples it is trained on to the entire set of possible inputs. This problem is the focus of a lot of recent and current work [1-11]. All this work, however, deals with the asymptotic state of the network after training. Here we study a very simple model which allows us to follow the evolution of the generalization ability in time under training. It has a single linear output unit, and the weights obey adaline learning. Despite its simplicity, it exhibits nontrivial behaviour: a dynamical phase transition at a critical number of training examples, with power-law decay right at the transition point and critical slowing down as one approaches it from either side.

2 THE MODEL

Our simple linear neuron has an output $V = N^{-\frac{1}{2}} \sum_i w_i \xi_i$, where ξ_i is the ith input. It learns to imitate a teacher [1] whose weights are u_i by training on p examples of input-output pairs (ξ_i^μ, ζ^μ) with

$$\zeta^\mu = N^{-\frac{1}{2}} \sum_i u_i \xi_i^\mu \tag{1}$$

generated by the teacher. The adaline learning equation [11] is then

$$\dot{w}_i = \frac{1}{\sqrt{N}} \sum_{\mu=1}^{p} (\zeta^\mu - \frac{1}{\sqrt{N}} \sum_j w_j \xi_j^\mu) \xi_i^\mu = \frac{1}{N} \sum_{\mu j} (u_j - w_j) \xi_j^\mu \xi_i^\mu . \tag{2}$$

By introducing the difference between the teacher and the pupil,

$$v_i \equiv u_i - w_i , \tag{3}$$

and the training input correlation matrix

$$A_{ij} = \frac{1}{N} \sum_{\mu=1}^{p} \xi_j^\mu \xi_i^\mu , \tag{4}$$

the learning equation becomes

$$\dot{v}_i = - \sum_j A_{ij} v_j . \tag{5}$$

We let the example inputs ξ_i^μ take the values ± 1, randomly and independently, but it is straightforward to generalize it to any distribution of inputs with $\langle \xi_i^\mu \xi_j^\nu \rangle_\xi \propto \delta_{ij} \delta_{\mu\nu}$. For a large number of examples ($p = O(N) \gg 1$), the resulting generalization ability will be independent of just which p of the 2^N possible binary input patterns we choose. All our results will then depend only on the fact that we can calculate the spectrum of the matrix A.

3 GENERALIZATION ABILITY

To measure the generalization ability, we test whether the output of our perceptron with weights w_i agrees with that of the teacher with weights u_i on all possible binary inputs. Our objective function, which we call the generalization error, is just the square of the error, averaged over all these inputs:

$$\begin{aligned} F &= \frac{1}{N 2^N} \sum_{\{\sigma\}} \left(\sum_i (u_i - w_i) \sigma_i \right)^2 = \frac{1}{N} \sum_{ij} v_i v_j \frac{1}{2^N} \sum_{\{\sigma\}} \sigma_i \sigma_j \\ &= \frac{1}{N} \sum_i v_i^2 \end{aligned} \tag{6}$$

(We used that $\frac{1}{2^N} \sum_{\{\sigma\}} \sigma_i \sigma_j$ is zero unless $i = j$.) That is, F is just proportional to the square of the difference between the teacher and pupil weight vectors. With the

N^{-1} normalization factor F will then vary between 1 (*tabula rasa*) and 0 (perfect generalization) if we normalize $\vec{u}$ to length $\sqrt{N}$. During learning, w_i and thus v_i depends on time, so F is a function of t. The complementary quantity $1 - F(t)$ could be called the generalization ability.

In the basis where A is diagonal, the learning equation (5) is simply

$$\dot{v}_r = -A_r v_r \tag{7}$$

where A_r are the eigenvalues of A. This has the solution

$$v_r(t) = v_r(0)e^{-A_r t} = u_r(0)e^{-A_r t}, \tag{8}$$

where it is assumed that the weights are zero at time $t = 0$ (we will come back to the more general case later). Thus we find

$$F(t) = \frac{1}{N}\sum_r v_r^2(t) = \frac{1}{N}\sum_r u_r^2 e^{-2A_r t} \tag{9}$$

Averaging over all possible training sets of size p this can be expressed in terms of the density of eigenvalues of A, $\rho(\epsilon)$:

$$F(t) = \frac{|\vec{u}\,|^2}{N}\int d\epsilon \rho(\epsilon) e^{-2\epsilon t}. \tag{10}$$

In the following it will be assumed that the length of $\vec{u}$ is normalized to $\sqrt{N}$, so the prefactor disappears.

For large N, the eigenvalue density is (see, e.g. [11], where it can be obtained simply from the imaginary part of the Green's function in eq.(57))

$$\rho(\epsilon) = \frac{1}{2\pi\epsilon}\sqrt{(\epsilon_+ - \epsilon)(\epsilon - \epsilon_-)} + (1-\alpha)\theta(1-\alpha)\delta(\epsilon), \tag{11}$$

where

$$\epsilon_\pm = (1 \pm \sqrt{\alpha})^2 \tag{12}$$

and $\theta(\,)$ is the unit step function. The density has two terms: a 'deformed semicircle' between the roots ϵ_- and ϵ_+, and for $\alpha < 1$ a delta function at $\epsilon = 0$ with weight $1 - \alpha$. The delta-function term appears because no learning takes place in the subspace orthogonal to that spanned by the training patterns. For $\alpha > 1$ the patterns span the whole space, and therefore the delta-function is absent.

The results at infinite time are immediately evident. For $\alpha < 1$ there is a nonzero limit, $F(\infty) = 1 - \alpha$, while $F(\infty)$ vanishes for $\alpha \geq 1$, indicating perfect generalization (the solid line in Figure 1). While on the one hand it may seem remarkable that perfect generalization can be obtained from a training set which forms an infinitesimal fraction of the entire set of possible examples, the meaning of the result is just that N points are sufficient to determine an $N-1$-dimensional hyperplane in N dimensions.

Figure 2 shows $F(t)$ as obtained numerically from (10) and (11). The qualitative form of the approach to $F(\infty)$ can be obtained analytically by inspection. For $\alpha \neq 1$, the asymptotic approach is governed by the smallest nonzero eigenvalue ϵ_-. Thus we have critical slowing down, with a divergent relaxation time

$$\tau = \frac{1}{\epsilon_-} = \frac{1}{|\sqrt{\alpha} - 1|^2} \tag{13}$$

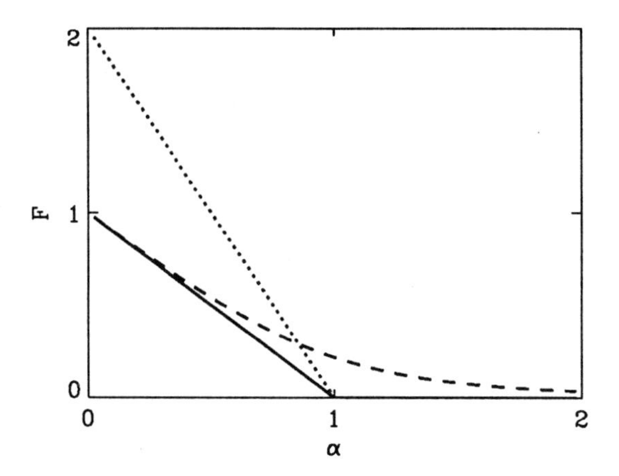

Figure 1: The asymptotic generalization error as a function of α. The full line corresponds to $\lambda = 0$, the dashed line to $\lambda = 0.2$, and the dotted line to $w_0 = 1$ and $\lambda = 0$.

as the transition at $\alpha = 1$ is approached. Right at the critical point, the eigenvalue density diverges for small ϵ like $\epsilon^{-\frac{1}{2}}$, which leads to the power law

$$F(t) \propto \frac{1}{\sqrt{t}} \tag{14}$$

at long times. Thus, while exactly N examples are sufficient to produce perfect generalization, the approach to this desirable state is rather slow. A little bit above $\alpha = 1$, $F(t)$ will also follow this power law for times $t \ll \tau$, going over to (slow) exponential decay at very long times ($t \gg \tau$). By increasing the training set size well above N (say, to $\frac{3}{2}N$), one can achieve exponentially fast generalization. Below $\alpha = 1$, where perfect generalization is never achieved, there is at least the consolation that the approach to the generalization level the network does reach is exponential (though with the same problem of a long relaxation time just below the transition as just above it).

4 EXTENSIONS

In this section we briefly discuss some extensions of the foregoing calculation. We will see what happens if the weights are non-zero at $t = 0$, discuss weight decay, and finally consider noise in the learning process.

Weight decay is a simple and frequently-used way to limit the growth of the weights, which might be desirable for several reasons. It is also possible to approximate the problem with binary weights using a weight decay term (the so-called spherical model, see [11]). We consider the simplest kind of weight decay, which comes in as an additive term, $-\lambda w_i = -\lambda(u_i - v_i)$, in the learning equation (2), so the equation

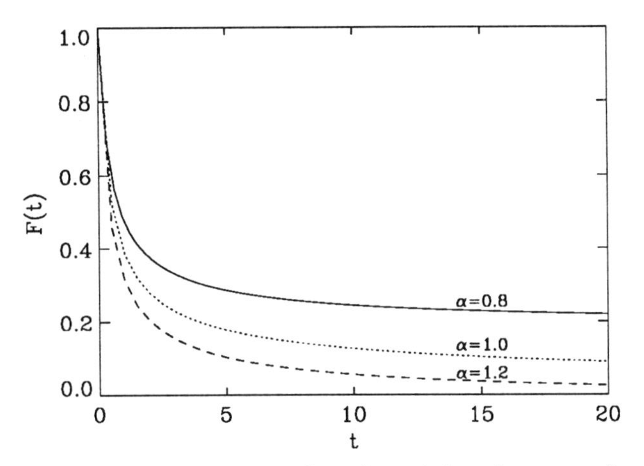

Figure 2: The generalization error as a function of time for a couple of different α.

(5) for the difference between teacher and pupil is now

$$\dot{v}_i = -\sum_j A_{ij} v_j + \lambda(u_i - v_i) = -\sum_j (A_{ij} + \lambda\delta_{ij})v_j + \lambda u_i. \tag{15}$$

Apart from the last term this just shifts the eigenvalue spectrum by λ.

In the basis where A is diagonal we can again write down the general solution to this equation:

$$v_r = \frac{(1 - e^{-(A_r+\lambda)t})\lambda u_r}{A_r + \lambda} + v_r(0)e^{-(A_r+\lambda)t}. \tag{16}$$

The square of this is

$$v_r^2 = u_r^2 \left[\frac{\lambda(1 - e^{-(A_r+\lambda)t})}{A_r + \lambda} + e^{-(A_r+\lambda)t} + \frac{w_r(0)}{u_r} e^{-(A_r+\lambda)t}\right]^2. \tag{17}$$

As in (10) this has to be integrated over the eigenvalue spectrum to find the averaged generalization error. Assuming that the initial weights are random, so that $\overline{w_r(0)} = 0$, and that they have a relative variance given by

$$\overline{\left(\frac{w_r(0)}{u_r}\right)^2} = w_0^2, \tag{18}$$

the average of $F(t)$ over the distibution of initial conditions now becomes

$$F(t) = \int d\epsilon \rho(\epsilon) \left[\left(\frac{\lambda(1 - e^{-(\epsilon+\lambda)t})}{\epsilon + \lambda} + e^{-(\epsilon+\lambda)t}\right)^2 + w_0^2 e^{-2(\epsilon+\lambda)t}\right]. \tag{19}$$

(Again it is assumed the length of $\vec{u}$ is $\sqrt{N}$.)

For $\lambda = 0$ we see the result is the same as before except for a factor $1 + w_0^2$ in front of the integral. This means that the asymptotic generalization error is now

$$F(\infty) = \begin{cases} (1 + w_0^2)(1 - \alpha) & \text{for } \alpha \le 1 \\ 0 \quad \text{for } \alpha > 1, \end{cases} \tag{20}$$

which is shown as a dotted line in Figure 1 for $w_0 = 1$. The excess error can easily be understood as a contribution to the error from the non-relaxing part of the initial weight vector in the subspace orthogonal to the space spanned by the patterns. The relaxation times are unchanged for $\lambda = 0$.

For $\lambda > 0$ the relaxation times become finite even at $\alpha = 0$, because the smallest eigenvalue is shifted by λ, so (13) is now

$$\tau = \frac{1}{\epsilon_- + \lambda} = \frac{1}{|\sqrt{\alpha} - 1|^2 + \lambda}. \tag{21}$$

In this case the asymptotic error can easily be obtained numerically from (19), and is shown by the dashed line in Figure 1. It is *smaller* than for $\lambda = 0$ for $w_0^2 > 1$ at sufficiently small α. This is simply because the weight decay makes the part of $\vec{w}(0)$ orthogonal to the pattern space decay away exponentially, thereby eliminating the excess error due to large initial weight components in this subspace.

This phase transition is very sensitive to noise. Consider adding a noise term $\eta_i(t)$ to the right-hand side of (2), with

$$\langle \eta_i(t) \eta_j(t') \rangle = 2T\delta(t - t'). \tag{22}$$

Here we restrict our attention to the case $\lambda = 0$. Carrying the extra term through the succeeding manipulations leads, in place of (7), to

$$\dot{v}_r = -A_r v_r + \eta_r(t). \tag{23}$$

The additional term leads to a correction (after Fourier transforming)

$$\delta v_r(\omega) = \frac{\eta_r(\omega)}{-i\omega + A_r} \tag{24}$$

and thus to an extra (time-independent) piece of the generalization error $F(t)$:

$$\delta F = \frac{1}{N} \sum_r \int \frac{d\omega}{2\pi} \frac{\langle |\eta_r(\omega)|^2 \rangle}{| -i\omega + A_r|^2} = \frac{1}{N} \sum_r \frac{T}{A_r}. \tag{25}$$

For $\alpha > 1$, where there are no zero eigenvalues, we have

$$\delta F = T \int_{\epsilon_-}^{\epsilon_+} d\epsilon \frac{\rho(\epsilon)}{\epsilon} \tag{26}$$

which has the large α-limit T/α, as found in equilibrium analyses (also for threshold perceptrons [2,3,5,6,7,8,9]). Equation (26) gives a generalization error which diverges as one approaches the transition at $\alpha = 1$:

$$\delta F \propto T \epsilon_-^{-1/2} = \frac{T}{\sqrt{\alpha} - 1}. \tag{27}$$

Equation (25) blows up for $\alpha < 1$, where some of the A_r are zero. This divergence just reflects the fact that in the subspace orthogonal to the training patterns, $\vec{v}$ feels only the noise and so exhibits a random walk whose variance diverges as $t \to \infty$. Keeping more careful track of the dynamics in this subspace leads to

$$\begin{aligned} \delta F &= 2T(1 - \alpha)t + T \int_{\epsilon_-}^{\epsilon_+} d\epsilon \frac{\rho(\epsilon)}{\epsilon} \\ &\underset{\alpha \to 1^-}{\longrightarrow} 2T \left[(1 - \alpha)t + O\left(\tfrac{1}{1 - \sqrt{\alpha}}\right) \right] \end{aligned} \tag{28}$$

5 CONCLUSION

Generalization in the linear perceptron can be understood in the following picture. To get perfect generalization the training pattern vectors have to span the whole input space — N points (in general position) are enough to specify any hyperplane. This means that perfect generalization appears only for $\alpha \geq 1$. As α approaches 1 the relaxation time – i.e. learning time – diverges, signaling a phase transition, as is common in physical systems. Noise has a severe effect on this transition. It leads to a degradation of the generalization ability which diverges as one reduces the number of training examples toward the critical number.

This model is of course much simpler than most real-life training problems. However, it does allow us to examine in detail the dynamical phase transition separating perfect from imperfect generalization. Further extensions of the model can also be solved and will be reported elsewhere.

References

[1] Gardner, E. and B. Derrida: Three Unfinished Works on the Optimal Storage Capacity of Networks. *Journal of Physics A* **22**, 1983–1994 (1989).

[2] Schwartz, D.B., V.K. Samalam, S.A. Solla, and J.S. Denker: Exhaustive Learning. *Neural Computation* **2**, 371–382 (1990).

[3] Tishby, N., E. Levin, and S.A. Solla: Consistent Inference of Probabilities in Layered Networks: Predictions and Generalization. Proc. IJCNN Washington 1989, vol. 2 403–410, Hillsdale: Erlbaum (1989).

[4] Baum, E.B. and D. Haussler: What Size Net Gives Valid Generalization. *Neural Computation* **1**, 151–160 (1989).

[5] Györgyi, G. and N. Tishby: Statistical Theory of Learning a Rule. In *Neural Networks and Spin Glasses*, eds W.K. Theumann and R. Koeberle. Singapore: World Scientific (1990).

[6] Hansel, D. and H. Sompolinsky: Learning from Examples in a Single-Layer Neural Network. *Europhysics Letters* **11**, 687–692 (1990).

[7] Vallet, F., J. Cailton and P. Refregier: Linear and Nonlinear Extension of the Pseudo-Inverse Solution for Learning Boolean Functions. *Europhysics Letters* **9**, 315-320 (1989).

[8] Opper, M., W. Kinzel, J. Kleinz, and R. Nehl: On the Ability of the Optimal Perceptron to Generalize. *Journal of Physics A* **23**, L581–L586 (1990).

[9] Levin, E., N. Tishby, and S. A. Solla: A Statistical Approach to Learning and Generalization in Layered Neural Networks. AT&T Bell Labs, preprint (1990).

[10] Györgyi, G.: Inference of a Rule by a Neural Network with Thermal Noise. *Physical Review Letters* **64**, 2957–2960 (1990).

[11] Hertz, J.A., A. Krogh, and G.I. Thorbergsson: Phase Transitions in Simple Learning. *Journal of Physics A* **22**, 2133–2150 (1989).

Constructing Hidden Units using Examples and Queries

Eric B. Baum   Kevin J. Lang
NEC Research Institute
4 Independence Way
Princeton, NJ 08540

ABSTRACT

While the network loading problem for 2-layer threshold nets is NP-hard when learning from examples alone (as with backpropagation), (Baum, 91) has now proved that a learner can employ queries to evade the hidden unit credit assignment problem and PAC-load nets with up to four hidden units in polynomial time. Empirical tests show that the method can also learn far more complicated functions such as randomly generated networks with 200 hidden units. The algorithm easily approximates Wieland's 2-spirals function using a single layer of 50 hidden units, and requires only 30 minutes of CPU time to learn 200-bit parity to 99.7% accuracy.

1 Introduction

Recent theoretical results (Baum & Haussler, 89) promise good generalization from multi-layer feedforward nets that are consistent with sufficiently large training sets. Unfortunately, the problem of finding such a net has been proved intractable due to the hidden unit credit assignment problem — even for nets containing only 2 hidden units (Blum & Rivest, 88). While back-propagation works well enough on simple problems, its luck runs out on tasks requiring more than a handful of hidden units. Consider, for example, Alexis Wielands "2-spirals" mapping from $\Re^2$ to $\{0, 1\}$. There are many sets of weights that would cause a 2-50-1 network to be consistent with the training set of figure 3a, but backpropagation seems unable to find any of them starting from random initial weights. Instead, the procedure drives the net into a suboptimal configuration like the one pictured in figure 2b.

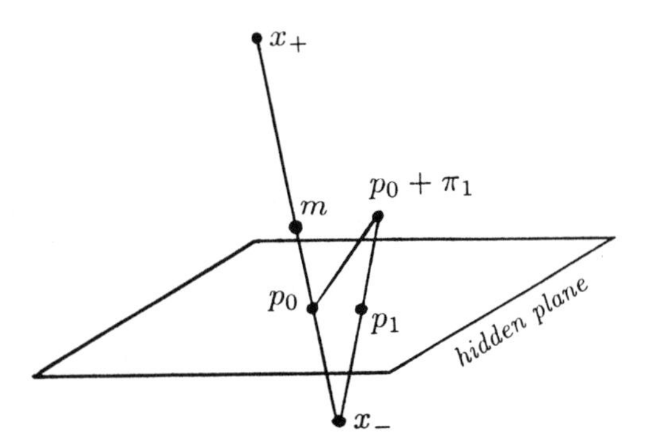

Figure 1: The geometry of query learning.

In 1984, Valiant proposed a *query learning* model in which the learner can ask an oracle for the output values associated with arbitrary points in the input space. In the next section we shall see how this additional source of information can be exploited to locate and pin down a network's hidden units one at a time, thus avoiding the combinatorial explosion of possible hidden unit configurations which can arise when one attempts to learn from examples alone.

2 How to find a hidden unit using queries

For now, assume that our task is to build a 2-layer network of binary threshold units which computes the same function as an existing "target" network. Our first step will be to draw a positive example x_+ and a negative example x_- from our training set. Because the target net maps these points to different output values, its hidden layer representations for the points must also be different, so the hyperplane through input space corresponding to one of the net's hidden units must intersect the line segment bounded by the two points (see figure 1). We can reduce our uncertainty about the location of this intersection point by a factor of 2 by asking the oracle for the target net's output at m, the line segment's midpoint. If, for example, m is mapped to the same output as x_+, then we know that the hidden plane must intersect the line segment between x_- and m, and we can then further reduce our uncertainty by querying the midpoint of *this* segment. By performing b of queries of this sort, we can determine to within b bits of accuracy the location of a point p_0 that lies on the hidden plane. Assuming that our input space has n dimensions, after finding $n-1$ more points on this hyperplane we can solve n equations in n unknowns to find the weights of the corresponding hidden unit.[1]

[1] The additional points p_i are obtained by perturbing p_0 with various small vectors π_i and then diving back to the plane via a search that is slightly more complicated than the bisection method by which we found p_0. (Baum, 91) describes this search procedure in detail, as well as a technique for verifying that all the points p_i lie on the *same* hidden plane.

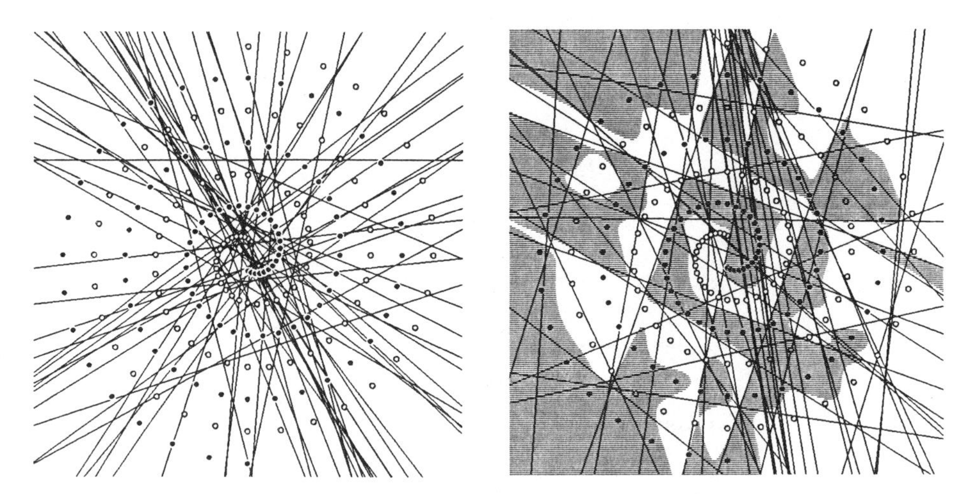

Figure 2: A backprop net before and after being trained on the 2-spirals task. In these plots over input space, the net's hidden units are shown by lines while its output is indicated by grey-level shading.

3 Can we find all of a network's hidden units?

Here is the crucial question: now that we have a procedure for finding *one* hidden unit whose hyperplane passes between a given pair of positive and negative examples,[2] can we discover *all* of the net's hidden units by invoking this procedure on a sequence of such example pairs? If the answer is yes, then we have got a viable learning method because the net's output weights can be efficiently computed via the linear programming problem that arises from forward-propagating the training set through the net's first layer of weights. (Baum, 91) proves that for target nets with four or fewer hidden units we can always find enough of them to compute the required function. This result is a direct counterpoint to the theorem of (Blum & Rivest, 88): by using queries, we can PAC learn in polynomial time small threshold nets that would be NP-hard to learn from examples alone.

However, it is possible for an adversary to construct a larger target net and an input distribution such that we may not find enough hidden units to compute the target function even by searching between every pair of examples in our training set. The problem is that more than one hidden plane can pass between a given pair of points, so we could repeatedly encounter some of the hidden units while never seeing others.

[2]This "positive" and "negative" terminology suggests that the target net possesses a single output unit, but the method is not actually restricted to this case.

Figure 3: 2-spirals oracle, and net built by query learning.

Fortunately, the experiments described in the next section suggest that one can find most of a net's hidden units in the average case. In fact, we may not even need to find all of a network's hidden units in order to achieve good generalization. Suppose that one of a network's hidden units is hard to find due to the rarity of nearby training points. As long as our test set is drawn from the same distribution as the training set, examples that would be misclassified due to the absence of this plane will also be rare. Our experiment on learning 200-bit parity illustrates this point: only 1/4 of the possible hidden units were needed to achieve 99.7% generalization.

4 Learning random target nets

Although query learning might fail to discover hidden units in the worse case, the following empirical study suggests that the method has good behavior in the average case. In each of these learning experiments the target function was computed by a 2-layer threshold net whose k hidden units were each chosen by passing a hyperplane through a set of n points selected from the uniform distribution on the unit n-sphere. The output weights of each target net corresponded to a random hyperplane through the origin of the unit k-sphere. Our training examples were drawn from the uniform distribution on the corners of the unit n-cube and then classified according to the target net.

To establish a performance baseline, we attempted to learn several of these functions using backpropagation. For ($n = 20$, $k = 20$) we succeeded in training a net to 97% accuracy in less than a day, but when we increased the size of the problem to ($n = 100$, $k = 50$) or ($n = 200$, $k = 30$), 150 hours of CPU time dumped our backprop nets into local minima that accounted for only 90% of the training data.

In contrast, query learning required only 1.5 hours to learn either of the latter two functions to 99% accuracy. The method continued to function well when we increased the problem size to ($n = 200$, $k = 200$). In each of five trials at this scale, a check of 10^4 training pairs revealed 197 or more hidden planes. Because the networks were missing a couple of hidden units, their hidden-to-output mappings were not quite linearly separable. Nevertheless, by running the perceptron algorithm on $100 \times k$ random examples, in each trial we obtained approximate output weights whose generalization was 98% or better.

5 Learning 200-bit parity

Because the learning method described above needs to make real-valued queries in order to localize a hidden plane, it cannot be used to learn a function that is only defined on boolean inputs. Thus, we defined the parity of a real-valued vector to be the function computed by the 2-layer parity net of (Rumelhart, Hinton & Williams, 1986), which has input weights of 1, hidden unit thresholds of $\frac{1}{2}, \frac{3}{2}, \ldots, n - \frac{1}{2}$, and output weights alternating between 1 and -1. The n parallel hidden planes of this net carve the input space into $n+1$ diagonal slabs, each of which contains all of the binary patterns with a particular number of 1's.

After adopting this definition of parity (which agrees with the standard definition on boolean inputs), we applied the query learning algorithm to 200-dimensional input patterns. A search of 30,000 pairs of examples drawn randomly and uniformly from the corners of the unit cube revealed 46 of the 200 decision planes of the target function. Using approximate output weights computed by the perceptron algorithm, we found the nets generalization rate to be 99.7%. If it seems surprising that the net could perform so well while lacking so many hidden planes, consider the following. The target planes that we did find were the middle ones with thresholds near 100, and these are the relevant ones for classifying inputs that contain about the same number of 1's and 0's. Because vectors of uniform random bits are unlikely to contain many more 1's than 0's or *vice versa*, we had little chance of stumbling across hidden planes with high or low thresholds while learning, but we were also unlikely to need them for classifying any given test case.

6 Function approximation using queries

Suppose now that our goal in building a threshold net is to approximate an arbitrary function rather than to duplicate an existing threshold net. Earlier, we were worried about whether we could locate all of a target net's hidden units, but at least we knew how many of them there were, and we knew that we had made real progress when we found one of them. Now, the hidden units constructed by our algorithm are merely tangents to the true decision boundaries of the target fuction, and we do not know ahead of time how many such units will be required to construct a decent approximation to the function.

While one could keep adding hidden units to a net until the hidden layer representation of the training set becomes linearly separable, the fact that there are

learning algorithm	additional heuristics	hidden units min	hidden units max	train errors	test errors min	test errors max
queries	none	90	160	0	70	136
	reject redundant units	65	80	0	47	72
	two-stage construction	49	59	0	15	45
conjugate gradient backprop		60		avg=9	80	125

Table 1: 2-spirals performance summary.

infinitely many of tangents to a given curve can result in the creation of an over-sized net which generalizes poorly. This problem can be addressed heuristically by rejecting new hidden units that are too similar to existing ones. For example, the top two rows of the above table summarize the results of 10 learning trials on the two-spirals problem with and without such a heuristic.[3] By imposing a floor on the difference between two hidden units,[4] we reduced the size of our nets and the rate of generalization errors by 40%.

The following two-stage heuristic training method resulted in even better networks. During the first stage of learning we attempted to create a minimally necessary set of hidden units by searching only between training examples that were not yet divided by an existing hidden unit. During the second stage of learning we tried to increase the separability of our hidden codes by repeatedly computing an approximate set of output weights and then searching for hidden units between misclassified examples and nearby counterexamples. This heuristic was motivated by the observation that examples tend to be misclassified when a nearby piece of the target function's decision boundary has not been discovered. Ten trials of this method resulted in networks containing an average of just 54 hidden units, and the nets committed an average of only 29 mistakes on the test set. An example of a network generated by this method is shown in figure 3b.

For comparison, we made 10 attempts to train a 60-hidden-unit backprop net on the 2-spirals problem starting from uniform random weights and using conjugate gradient code provided by Steve Nowlan. While these nets had more than enough hidden units to compute the required function, not one of them succeeded in learning the complete training set.[5]

[3] To employ query learning, we defined the oracle function indicated by shading in figure 3a. The 194 training points are shown by dots in the figure. Our 576-element test set consisted of 3 points between each pair of adjacent same-class training points.

[4] Specifically, we required a minimum euclidean distance of 0.3 between the weights of two hidden units (after first normalizing the weight vectors so that the length of the non-threshold part of each vector was 1.

[5] Interestingly, a 2-50-1 backprop net whose initial weights were drawn from a handcrafted distribution (hidden units with uniform random positions together with the appropriate output weights) came much closer to success than 2-50-1 nets with uniform random initial weights (compare figures 4 and 2). We can sometimes address tough problems with backprop when our prior knowledge gives us a head start.

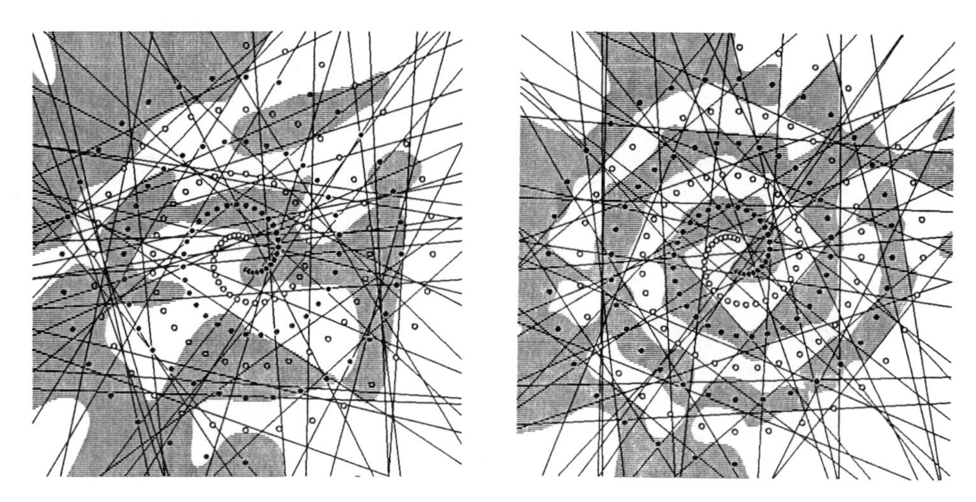

Figure 4: Backprop works better when started near a solution.

These results illustrate the main point of this paper: the currently prevalent training methodology (local optimization of random initial weights) is too weak to solve the NP-hard problem of hidden unit deployment. We believe that methods such as query learning which avoid the credit assignment problem are essential to the future of connectionism.

References

E. Baum & D. Haussler. (1989) What size net gives valid generalization? *Neural Computation* **1**(1): 151-160.

E. Baum. (1991) *Neural Net Algorithms that Learn in Polynomial Time from Examples and Queries.* IEEE Transactions on Neural Networks **2**(1), January, 1991.

A. Blum & R. L. Rivest. (1988) Training a 3-node neural network is NP-complete. In D. S. Touretzky (ed.), *Advances in Neural Information Processing Systems 1*, 494-501. San Mateo, CA: Morgan Kaufmann.

K. Lang & M. Witbrock. (1988) *Learning to Tell Two Spirals Apart.* Proceedings of the 1988 Connectionist Models Summer School, Morgan Kaufmann.

D. Rumelhart, G. Hinton, & R. Williams. (1986) Learning internal representations by error propagation. In D. Rumelhart & J. McClelland (eds.) *Parallel Distributed Processing*, MIT Press.

L. G. Valiant. (1984) A theory of the learnable. *Comm. ACM* **27**(11): 1134-1142.

Can neural networks do better than the Vapnik-Chervonenkis bounds?

David Cohn
Dept. of Comp. Sci. & Eng.
University of Washington
Seattle, WA 98195

Gerald Tesauro
IBM Watson Research Center
P.O. Box 704
Yorktown Heights, NY 10598

Abstract

We describe a series of careful numerical experiments which measure the average generalization capability of neural networks trained on a variety of simple functions. These experiments are designed to test whether average generalization performance can surpass the worst-case bounds obtained from formal learning theory using the Vapnik-Chervonenkis dimension (Blumer et al., 1989). We indeed find that, in some cases, the average generalization is significantly better than the VC bound: the approach to perfect performance is exponential in the number of examples m, rather than the $1/m$ result of the bound. In other cases, we do find the $1/m$ behavior of the VC bound, and in these cases, the numerical prefactor is closely related to prefactor contained in the bound.

1 INTRODUCTION

Probably the most important issue in the study of supervised learning procedures is the issue of generalization, i.e., how well the learning system can perform on inputs not seen during training. Significant progress in the understanding of generalization was made in the last few years using a concept known as the Vapnik-Chervonenkis dimension, or VC-dimension. The VC-dimension provides a basis for a number of powerful theorems which establish worst-case bounds on the ability of arbitrary learning systems to generalize (Blumer et al., 1989; Haussler et al., 1988). These theorems state that under certain broad conditions, the generalization error ϵ of a learning system with VC-dimension D trained on m random examples of an arbitrary function will with high confidence be no worse than a bound roughly of order D/m. The basic requirements for the theorems to hold are that the training and testing examples are generated from the same probability distribution, and that the learning system is able to correctly classify the training examples.

Unfortunately, since these theorems do not calculate the expected generalization error but instead only bound it, the question is left open whether expected error might lie significantly below the bound. Empirical results of (Ahmad and Tesauro, 1988) indicate that in at least one case, average error was in fact significantly below the VC bound: the error decreased exponentially with the number of examples, $\epsilon \sim \exp(-m/m_0)$, rather than the $1/m$ result of the bound. Also, recent statistical learning theories (Tishby et al., 1989; Schwartz et al., 1990), which provide an analytic means of calculating expected performance, indicate that an exponential approach to perfect performance could be obtained if the spectrum of possible network generalizations has a "gap" near perfect performance.

We have addressed the issue of whether average performance can surpass worst-case performance through numerical experiments which measure the average generalization of simple neural networks trained on a variety of simple functions. Our experiments extend the work of (Ahmad and Tesauro, 1988). They test both the relevance of the worst-case VC bounds to average generalization performance, and the predictions of exponential behavior due to a gap in the generalization spectrum.

2 EXPERIMENTAL METHODOLOGY

Two pairs of N-dimensional classification tasks were examined in our experiments: two linearly separable functions ("majority" and "real-valued threshold"), and two higher-order functions ("majority-XOR" and "threshold-XOR"). Majority is a Boolean predicate in which the output is 1 if and only if more than half of the inputs are 1. The real-valued threshold function is a natural extension of majority to the continuous space $[0,1]^N$: the output is 1 if and only if the sum of the N real-valued inputs is greater than $N/2$. The majority-XOR function is a Boolean function where the output is 1 if and only if the N'th input disagrees with the majority computed by the first $N-1$ inputs. This is a natural extension of majority which retains many of its symmetry properties, e.g., the positive and negative examples are equally numerous and somewhat uniformly distributed. Similarly, threshold-XOR is natural extension of the real-valued threshold function which maps $[0,1]^{N-1} \times \{0,1\} \mapsto \{0,1\}$. Here, the output is 1 if and only if the N'th input, which is binary, disagrees with the threshold function computed by the first $N-1$ real-valued inputs. Networks trained on these tasks used sigmoidal units and had standard feed-forward fully-connected structures with at most a single hidden layer. The training algorithm was standard back-propagation with momentum (Rumelhart et al., 1986).

A simulator run consisted of training a randomly initialized network on a training set of m examples of the target function, chosen uniformly from the input space. Networks were trained until all examples were classified within a specified margin of the correct classification. Runs that failed to converge within a cutoff time of 50,000 epochs were discarded. The generalization error of the resulting network was then estimated by testing on a set of 2048 novel examples independently drawn from the same distribution. The average generalization error for a given value of m was typically computed by averaging the results of 10-40 simulator runs, each with a different set of training patterns, test patterns, and random initial weights. A wide range of values of m was examined in this way in each experiment.

2.1 SOURCES OF ERROR

Our experiments were carefully controlled for a number of potential sources of error. Random errors due to the particular choice of random training patterns, test patterns, and initial weights were reduced to low levels by performing a large number of runs and varying each of these in each run.

We have also looked for systematic errors due to the particular values of learning rate and momentum constants, initial random weight scale, frequency of weight changes, training threshold, and training cutoff time. Within wide ranges of parameter values, we find no significant dependence of the generalization performance on the particular choice of any of these parameters except k, the frequency of weight changes. (However, the parameter values can affect the rate of convergence or probability of convergence on the training set.) Variations in k appear to alter the numerical coefficients of the learning curve, but not the overall functional form.

Another potential concern is the possibility of overtraining: even though the training set error should decrease monotonically with training time, the test set error might reach a minimum and then increase with further training. We have monitored hundreds of simulations of both the linearly separable and higher-order tasks, and find no significant overtraining in either case.

Other aspects of the experimental protocol which could affect measured results include order of pattern presentation, size of test set, testing threshold, and choice of input representation. We find that presenting the patterns in a random order as opposed to a fixed order improves the probability of convergence, but does not alter the average generalization of runs that do converge. Changing the criterion by which a test pattern is judged correct alters the numerical prefactor of the learning curve but the functional form. Using test sets of 4096 patterns instead of 2048 patterns has no significant effect on measured generalization values. Finally, convergence is faster with a $[-1, 1]$ coding scheme than with a $[0, 1]$ scheme, and generalization is improved, but only by numerical constants.

2.2 ANALYSIS OF DATA

To determine the functional dependence of measured generalization error ϵ on the number of examples m, we apply the standard curve-fitting technique of performing linear regression on the appropriately transformed data. Thus we can look for an exponential law $\epsilon = Ae^{-m/m_0}$ by plotting $\log(\epsilon)$ vs. m and observing whether the transformed data lies on a straight line. We also look for a polynomial law of the form $\epsilon = B/(m + a)$ by plotting $1/\epsilon$ vs. m. We have not attempted to fit to a more general polynomial law because this is less reliable, and because theory predicts a $1/m$ law.

By plotting each experimental curve in both forms, $\log(\epsilon)$ vs. m and $1/\epsilon$ vs. m, we can determine which model provides a better fit to the data. This can be done both visually and more quantitatively by computing the linear correlation coefficient r^2 in a linear least-squares fit. To the extent that one of the curves has a higher value of r^2 than the other one, we can say that it provides a better model of the data than the other functional form.

We have also developed the following technique to assess absolute goodness-of-fit. We generate a set of artificial data points by adding noise equivalent to the error bars on the original data points to the best-fit curve obtained from the linear regression. Regression on the artificial data set yields a value of r^2, and repeating this process many times gives a distribution of r^2 values which should approximate the distribution expected with the amount of noise in our data. By comparing the value r^2 from our original data to this generated distribution, we can estimate the probability that our functional model would produce data like that we observed.

3 EXPERIMENTS ON LINEARLY-SEPARABLE FUNCTIONS

Networks with 50 inputs and no hidden units were trained on majority and real-valued threshold functions, with training set sizes ranging from $m = 40$ to $m = 500$ in increments of 20 patterns. Twenty networks were trained for each value of m. A total of 3.8% of the binary majority and 7.7% of the real-valued threshold simulation runs failed to converge and were discarded.

The data obtained from the binary majority and real-valued threshold problems was tested for fit to the exponential and polynomial functional models, as shown in Figure 1. The binary majority data had a correlation coefficient of $r^2 = 0.982$ in the exponential fit; this was better than 40% of the "artificial" data sets described previously. However, the polynomial fit only gave a value of $r^2 = 0.966$, which was better than only 6% of the artificial data sets. We conclude that the binary majority data is consistent with an exponential law and not with a $1/m$ law.

The real-valued threshold data, however, behaved in the opposite manner. The exponential fit gave a value of $r^2 = 0.943$, which was better than only 14% of the artificial data sets. However, the polynomial fit gave a value of $r^2 = 0.996$, which was better than 40% of the artificial data sets. We conclude that the real-valued threshold data closely approximates a $1/m$ law and was not likely to have been generated by an exponential law.

4 EXPERIMENTS ON HIGHER-ORDER FUNCTIONS

For the majority-XOR and threshold-XOR problems, we used $N = 26$ input units: 25 for the "majority" (or threshold) and a single "XOR" unit. In theory, these problems can be solved with only two hidden units, but in practice, at least three hidden units were needed for reliable convergence. Training set sizes ranging from $m = 40$ to $m = 1000$ in increments of 20 were studied for both tasks. At each value of m, 40 simulations were performed. Of the 1960 simulations, 1702 of the binary and 1840 of the real-valued runs converged. No runs in either case achieved a perfect score on the test data.

With both sets of runs, there was a visible change in the shape of the generalization curve when the training set size reached 200 samples. We are interested primarily

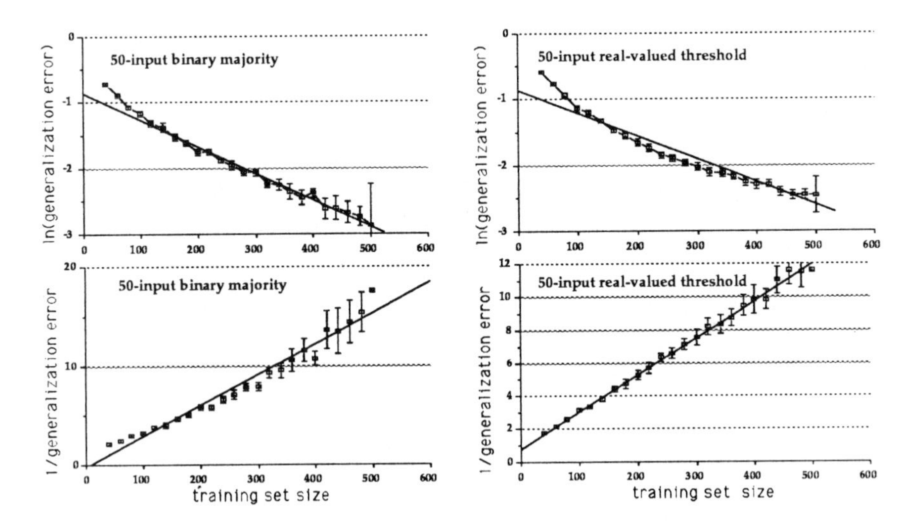

Figure 1: Observed generalization curves for binary majority and real-valued threshold, and their fit to the exponential and polynomial models. Error bars denote 95% confidence intervals for the mean.

in the asymptotic behavior of these curves, so we restricted our analysis to sample sizes 200 and above. As with the single-layer problems, we measured goodness of fit to appropriately linearized forms of the exponential and polynomial curves in question. Results are plotted in Figure 2.

It appears that the generalization curve of the threshold-XOR problem is not likely to have been generated by an exponential, but is a plausible $1/m$ polynomial. The correlation coefficient in the exponential fit is only $r^2 = 0.959$ (better than only 10% of the artificial data sets), but in the polynomial fit is $r^2 = 0.997$ (better than 62% of the artificial data sets).

The binary majority-XOR data, however, appears both visually and from the relative r^2 values to fit the exponential model better than the polynomial model. In the exponential fit, $r^2 = 0.994$, while in the polynomial fit, $r^2 = 0.940$. However, we are somewhat cautious because the artificial data test is inconclusive. The exponential fit is better than 40% of artificial data sets, but the polynomial fit is better than 60% of artificial data sets. Also, there appears to be a small component of the curve that is slower than a pure exponential.

5 COMPARISON TO THEORY

Figure 3 plots our data for both the first-order and higher-order tasks compared to the thoretical error bounds of (Blumer et al., 1989) and (Haussler et al., 1988). In the higher-order case we have used the total number of weights as an estimate of the VC-dimension, following (Baum and Haussler, 1989). (Even with this low estimate, the bound of (Blumer et al., 1989) lies off the scale.) All of our experimental curves fall below both bounds, and in each case the binary task does asymptotically better than the corresponding real-valued task. One should note that the bound in

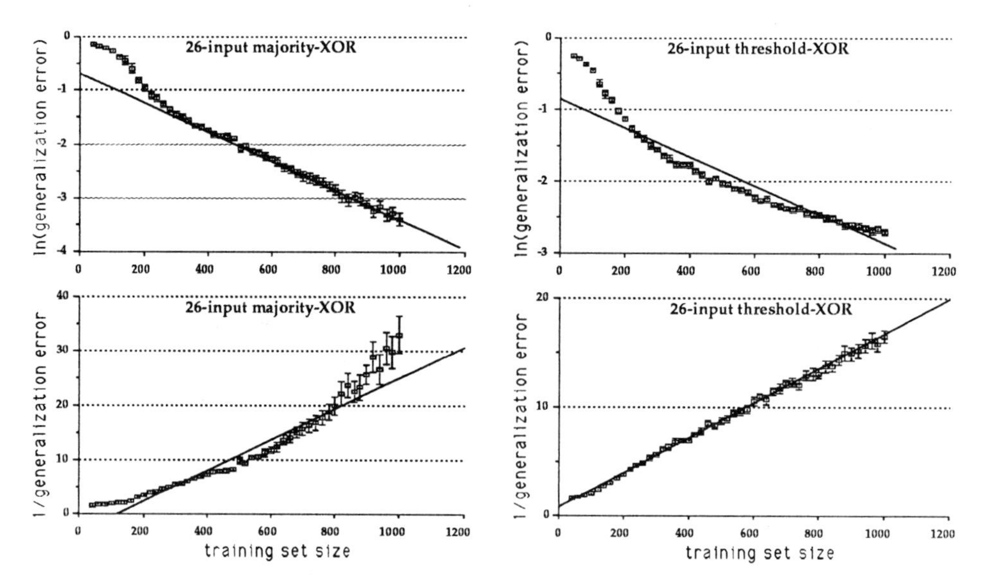

Figure 2: Generalization curves for 26-3-1 nets trained on majority-XOR and threshold-XOR, and their fit to the exponential and polynomial models.

(Haussler et al., 1988) fits the real-valued data to within a small numerical constant. However, strictly speaking it may not apply to our experiments because it is for Bayes-optimal learning algorithms, and we do not know whether back-propagation is Bayes-optimal.

6 CONCLUSIONS

We have seen that two problems using strict binary inputs (majority and majority-XOR) exhibited distinctly exponential generalization with increasing training set size. This indicates that there exists a class of problems that is asymptotically much easier to learn than others of the same VC-dimension. This is not only of theoretical interest, but it also has potential bearing on what kinds of large-scale applications might be tractable with network learning methods. On the other hand, merely by making the inputs real instead of binary, we found average error curves lying close to the theoretical bounds. This indicates that the worst-case bounds may be more relevant to expected performance than has been previously realized.

It is interesting that the statistical theories of (Tishby et al., 1989; Schwartz et al., 1990) predict the two classes of behavior seen in our experiments. Our future research will focus on whether or not there is a "gap" as suggested by these theories. Our preliminary findings for majority suggest that there is in fact no gap, except possibly an "inductive gap" in which the learning process for some reason tends to avoid the near-perfect solutions. If such an inductive gap does not exist, then either the theory does not apply to back-propagation, or it must have some other mechanism to generate the exponential behavior.

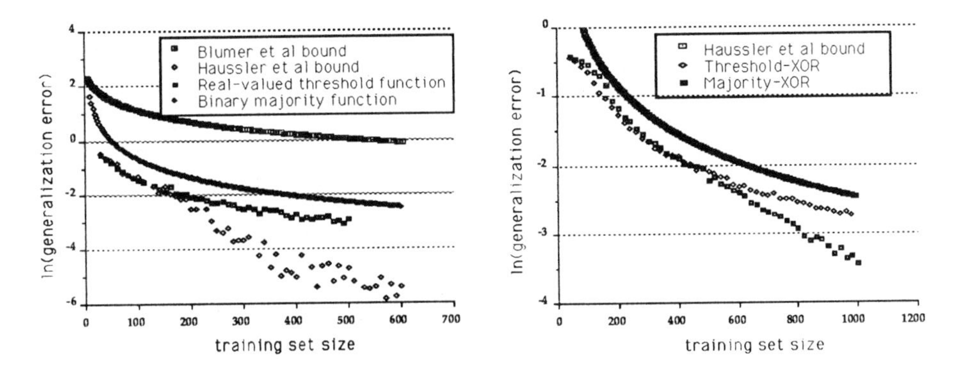

Figure 3: (a) The real-valued threshold problem performs roughly within a constant factor of the upper bounds predicted in (Blumer et al., 1989) and (Haussler et al., 1988), while the binary majority problem performs asymptotically better. (b) The threshold-XOR performs roughly within a constant factor of the predicted bound, while majority-XOR performs asymptotically better.

References

S. Ahmad and G. Tesauro. (1988) Scaling and generalization in neural networks: a case study. In D. S. Touretzky et al., eds., *Proceedings of the 1988 Connectionist Models Summer School*, 3-10, Morgan Kaufmann.

E. B. Baum and D. Haussler. (1989) What size net gives valid generalization? *Neural Computation* **1**(1):151-160.

A. Blumer, A. Ehrenfeucht, D. Haussler, and M. Warmuth. (1989) Learnability and the Vapnik-Chervonenkis dimension. *JACM* **36**(4):929-965.

D. Haussler, N. Littlestone, and M. Warmuth. (1990) Predicting {0, 1}-Functions on Randomly Drawn Points. *Tech Report UCSC-CRL-90-54*, Univ. of California at Santa Cruz, CA.

D. E. Rumelhart, G. E. Hinton and R. J. Williams. (1986) Learning internal representations by error propagation. In *Parallel Distributed Processing*, **1**:381-362 MIT Press.

D. B. Schwartz, V. K. Samalam, S. A. Solla and J. S. Denker. (1990) Exhaustive learning. *Neural Computation* **2**:374-385.

N. Tishby, E. Levin and S. A. Solla. (1989) Consistent inference of probabilities in layered networks: Predictions and generalizations. In *IJCNN Proceedings*, **2**:403-409, IEEE.

Second Order Properties of Error Surfaces : Learning Time and Generalization

Yann Le Cun
AT&T Bell Laboratories
Crawfords Corner Rd.
Holmdel, NJ 07733, USA

Ido Kanter
Department of Physics
Bar Ilan University
Ramat Gan, 52100 Israel

Sara A. Solla
AT&T Bell Laboratories
Crawfords Corner Rd.
Holmdel, NJ 07733, USA

Abstract

The learning time of a simple neural network model is obtained through an analytic computation of the eigenvalue spectrum for the Hessian matrix, which describes the second order properties of the cost function in the space of coupling coefficients. The form of the eigenvalue distribution suggests new techniques for accelerating the learning process, and provides a theoretical justification for the choice of centered versus biased state variables.

1 INTRODUCTION

Consider the class of learning algorithms which explore a space $\{W\}$ of possible couplings looking for optimal values W^* for which a cost function $E(W)$ is minimal. The dynamical properties of searches based on gradient descent are controlled by the second order properties of the E(W) surface. An analytic investigation of such properties provides a characterization of the time scales involved in the relaxation to the solution W^*.

The discussion focuses on layered networks with no feedback, a class of architectures remarkably successful at perceptual tasks such as speech and image recognition. We derive rigorous results for the learning time of a single linear unit, and discuss their generalization to multi-layer nonlinear networks. Causes for the slowest time constants are identified, and specific prescriptions to eliminate their effect result in practical methods to accelerate convergence.

2 LEARNING BY GRADIENT DESCENT

Multi-layer networks are composed of model neurons interconnected through a feed-forward graph. The state x_i of the i-th neuron is computed from the states $\{x_j\}$ of the set S_i of neurons that feed into it through the total input (or *induced local field*) $a_i = \sum_{j \in S_i} w_{ij} x_j$. The coefficient w_{ij} of the linear combination is the coupling from neuron j to neuron i. The local field a_i determines the state x_i through a nonlinear differentiable function f called the *activation function* : $x_i = f(a_i)$. The activation function is often chosen to be the hyperbolic tangent or a similar sigmoid function.

The connection graph of multi-layer networks has no feedback loops, and the stable state is computed by propagating state information from the input units (which receive no input from other units) to the output units (which propagate no information to other units). The initialization of the state of the input units through an input vector X results in an output vector $\mathcal{O}$ describing the state of the output units. The network thus implements an input-output map, $\mathcal{O} = \mathcal{O}(X, W)$, which depends on the values assigned to the vector W of synaptic couplings.

The learning process is formulated as a search in the space W, so as to find an optimal configuration W^* which minimizes a function $E(W)$. Given a training set of p input vectors X^μ and their desired outputs D^μ, $1 \leq \mu \leq p$, the cost function

$$E(W) = \frac{1}{2p} \sum_{\mu=1}^{p} ||D^\mu - \mathcal{O}(X^\mu, W)||^2 \tag{2.1}$$

measures the discrepancy between the actual behavior of the system and the desired behavior. The minimization of E with respect to W is usually performed through iterative updates using some form of gradient descent:

$$W(k+1) = W(k) - \eta \nabla E, \tag{2.2}$$

where η is used to adjust the size of the updating step, and ∇E is an estimate of the gradient of E with respect to W. The commonly used Back-Propagation algorithm popularized by (Rumelhart, Hinton, and Williams, 1986), provides an efficient way of estimating ∇E for multi-layer networks.

The dynamical behavior of learning algorithms based on the minimization of $E(W)$ through gradient descent is controlled by the properties of the $E(W)$ surface. The goal of this work is to gain better understanding of the structure of this surface through an investigation of its second derivatives, as contained in the Hessian matrix $\mathbf{H}$.

3 SECOND ORDER PROPERTIES

We now consider a simple model which can be investigated analytically: an N-dimensional input vector feeding onto a single output unit with a linear activation function $f(a) = a$. The output corresponding to input X^μ is given by

$$\mathcal{O}^\mu = \sum_{i=1}^{N} w_i x_i^\mu = W^T X^\mu, \tag{3.1}$$

where x_i^μ is the i-th component of the μ-th input vector, and w_i is the coupling from the i-th input unit to the output.

The rule for weight updates

$$W(k+1) = W(k) - \frac{\eta}{p}\sum_{\mu=1}^{p}(\mathcal{O}^\mu - d^\mu)X^\mu \tag{3.2}$$

follows from the gradient of the cost function

$$E(W) = \frac{1}{2p}\sum_{\mu=1}^{p}(d^\mu - \mathcal{O}^\mu)^2 = \frac{1}{2p}\sum_{\mu=1}^{p}(d^\mu - W^T X^\mu)^2. \tag{3.3}$$

Note that the cost function of Eq. (3.3) is quadratic in W, and can be rewritten as

$$E(W) = \frac{1}{2}(W^T\mathbf{R}W - 2Q^T W + c), \tag{3.4}$$

where $\mathbf{R}$ is the covariance matrix of the input, $R_{ij} = 1/p\sum_{\mu=1}^{p} x_i^\mu x_j^\mu$, a symmetric and nonnegative $N \times N$ matrix; the N-dimensional vector Q has components $q_i = 1/p\sum_{\mu=1}^{p} d^\mu x_i^\mu$, and the constant $c = 1/p\sum_{\mu=1}^{p}(d^\mu)^2$. The gradient is given by $\nabla E = \mathbf{R}W - Q$, while the Hessian matrix of second derivatives is $\mathbf{H} = \mathbf{R}$.

The solution space of vectors W^* which minimize $E(W)$ is the subspace of solutions of the linear equation $\mathbf{R}W = Q$, resulting from $\nabla E = 0$. This subspace reduces to a point if $\mathbf{R}$ is full rank. The diagonalization of $\mathbf{R}$ provides a diagonal matrix $\mathbf{\Lambda}$ formed by its eigenvalues, and a matrix $\mathbf{U}$ formed by its eigenvectors. Since $\mathbf{R}$ is nonnegative, all eigenvalues satisfy $\lambda \geq 0$.

Consider now a two-step coordinate transformation: a translation $V' = W - W^*$ provides new coordinates centered at the solution point; it is followed by a rotation $V = \mathbf{U}V' = \mathbf{U}(W - W^*)$ onto the principal axes of the error surface. In the new coordinate system

$$E(V) = \frac{1}{2}V^T\mathbf{\Lambda}V + E_0, \tag{3.5}$$

with $\mathbf{\Lambda} = \mathbf{U}^T\mathbf{R}\mathbf{U}$ and $E_0 = E(W^*)$. Then $\partial E/\partial v_j = \lambda_j v_j$, and $\partial^2 E/\partial v_j \partial v_k = \lambda_j \delta_{jk}$. The eigenvalues of the input covariance matrix give the second derivatives of the error surface with respect to its principal axes.

In the new coordinate system the Hessian matrix is the diagonal matrix $\mathbf{\Lambda}$, and the rule for weight updates becomes a set of N decoupled equations:

$$V(k+1) = V(k) - \eta\mathbf{\Lambda}V(k), \tag{3.6}$$

The evolution of each component along a principal direction is given by

$$v_j(k) = (1 - \eta\lambda_j)^k v_j(0), \tag{3.7}$$

so that v_j will converge to zero (and thus w_j to the solution w_j^*) provided that $0 < \eta < 2/\lambda_j$. In this regime v_j decays to zero exponentially, with characteristic time $\tau_j = (\eta\lambda_j)^{-1}$. The range $1/\lambda_j < \eta < 2/\lambda_j$ corresponds to underdamped dynamics: the step size is large and convergence to the solution occurs through oscillatory behavior. The range $0 < \eta < 1/\lambda_j$ corresponds to overdamped dynamics: the step size is small and convergence requires many iterations. Critical damping occurs for $\eta = 1/\lambda_j$; if such choice is possible, the solution is reached in one iteration (Newton's method).

If all eigenvalues are equal, $\lambda_j = \lambda$ for all $1 \leq j \leq N$, the Hessian matrix is diagonal: $\mathbf{H} = \mathbf{\Lambda}$. Convergence can be obtained in one iteration, with optimal step size $\eta = 1/\lambda$, and learning time $\tau = 1$. This highly symmetric case occurs when cross-sections of $E(W)$ are hyperspheres in the N-dimensional space $\{W\}$. Such high degree of symmetry is rarely encountered: correlated inputs result in nondiagonal elements for $\mathbf{H}$, and the principal directions are rotated with respect to the original coordinates. The cross-sections of $E(W)$ are elliptical, with different eigenvalues along different principal directions. Convergence requires $0 < \eta < 2/\lambda_j$ for all $1 \leq j \leq N$, thus η must be chosen in the range $0 < \eta < 1/\lambda_{max}$, where λ_{max} is the largest eigenvalue. The slowest time constant in the system is $\tau_{max} = (\eta\lambda_{min})^{-1}$, where λ_{min} is the lowest nonzero eigenvalue. The optimal step size $\eta = 1/\lambda_{max}$ thus leads to $\tau_{max} = \lambda_{max}/\lambda_{min}$ for the decay along the principal direction of smallest nonzero curvature. A distribution of eigenvalues in the range $\lambda_{min} \leq \lambda \leq \lambda_{max}$ results in a distribution of learning times, with average $< \tau >= \lambda_{max} < 1/\lambda >$.

This analysis demonstrates that learning dynamics in quadratic surfaces are fully controlled by the eigenvalue distribution of the Hessian matrix. It is thus of interest to investigate such eigenvalue distribution.

4 EIGENVALUE SPECTRUM

The simple linear unit of Eq. (3.1) leads to the error function (3.4), for which the Hessian is given by the covariance matrix

$$R_{ij} = 1/p \sum_{\mu=1}^{p} x_i^\mu x_j^\mu . \tag{4.1}$$

It is assumed that the input components $\{x_i^\mu\}$ are independent, and drawn from a distribution with mean m and variance v. The size of the training set is quantified by the ratio $\alpha = p/N$ between the number of training examples and the dimensionality of the input vector . The eigenvalue spectrum has been computed (Le Cun, Kanter, and Solla, 1990), and it exhibits three dominant features:

(a) If $p < N$, the rank of the matrix $\mathbf{R}$ is p. The existence of $(N-p)$ zero eigenvalues out of N results in a delta function contribution of weight $(1-\alpha)$ at $\lambda = 0$ for $\alpha < 1$.

(b) A continuous part of the spectrum,

$$\rho(\lambda) = \frac{[4\alpha v^2 - (\lambda\alpha - v(1+\alpha))^2]^{1/2}}{2\pi\lambda v} \tag{4.2}$$

within the bounded interval $\lambda_- < \lambda < \lambda_+$, with $\lambda\pm = (1 \pm \sqrt{\alpha})^2 v/\alpha$ (Krogh and Hertz, 1991). Note that $\rho(\lambda)$ is controlled only by the variance v of the distribution from which the inputs are drawn. The bounds $\lambda_\pm$ are well defined, and of order one. For all $\alpha < 1$, $\lambda_- > 0$, indicating a gap at the lower end of the spectrum.

(c) An isolated eigenvalue of order N, λ_N, present in the case of biased inputs ($m \neq 0$).

True correlations between pairs (x_j, x_k) of input components might lead to a quite different spectrum from the one described above.

The continuous part (4.2) of the eigenvalue spectrum has been computed in the $N \to \infty$ limit, while keeping α constant and finite. The magnitude of finite size effects has been investigated numerically for $N \leq 200$ and various values of α. Results for $N = 200$, shown in Fig. 1, indicate that finite size effects are negligible: the distribution $\rho(\lambda)$ is bounded within the interval $[\lambda_-, \lambda_+]$, in good agreement with the theoretical prediction, even for such small systems. The result (4.2) is thus applicable in the finite $p = \alpha N$ case, an important regime given the limited availability of training data in most learning problems.

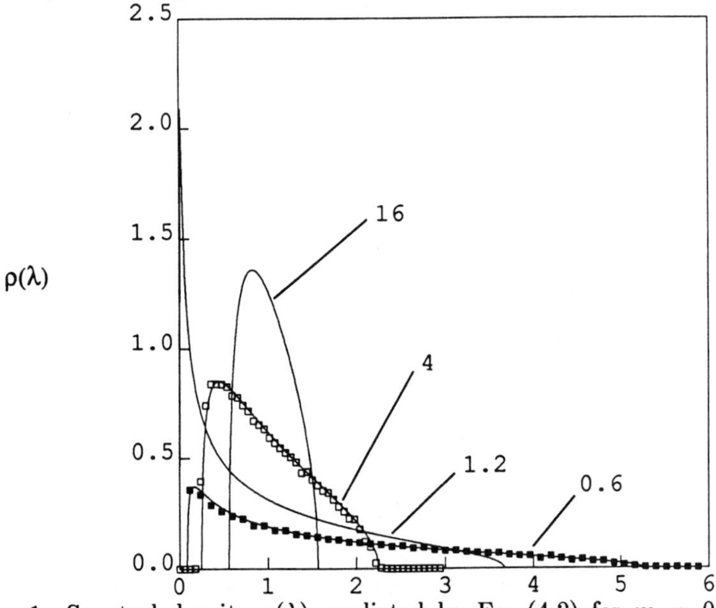

Figure 1: Spectral density $\rho(\lambda)$ predicted by Eq. (4.2) for $m = 0$, $v = 1$, and $\alpha = 0.6, 1.2, 4$, and 16. Experimental histograms for $\alpha = 0.6$ (full squares) and $\alpha = 4$ (open squares) are averages over 100 trials with $N = 200$ and $x_i^\mu = \pm 1$ with probability 1/2 each.

The existence of a large eigenvalue λ_N is easily understood by considering the structure of the covariance matrix $\mathbf{R}$ in the $p \to \infty$ limit, a regime for which a detailed analysis is available in the adaptive filters literature (Widrow and Stearns, 1985). In this limit, all off-diagonal elements of $\mathbf{R}$ are equal to m^2, and all diagonal elements are equal to $v + m^2$. The eigenvector $U_N = (1...1)$ thus corresponds to the eigenvalue $\lambda_N = Nm^2 + v$. The remaining $(N-1)$ eigenvalues are all equal to v (note that the continuous part of the spectrum collapses onto a delta function at $\lambda_- = \lambda_+ = v$ as $p \to \infty$), thus satisfying $\text{tr}\mathbf{R} = N(m^2 + v)$. The large part of λ_N is eliminated for centered distributions with $m = 0$, such as $x_i^\mu = \pm 1$ with probability 1/2, or $x_i^\mu = 3, -1, -2$ with probability 1/3. Note that although m is crucial in controlling the existence of an isolated eigenvalue of order N, it plays no role in the spectral density of Eq. (4.2).

5 LEARNING TIME

Consider the learning time $\tau = \alpha(\lambda_{max}/\lambda_{min})$. The eigenvalue ratio $(\lambda_{max}/\lambda_{min})$ measures the maximum number of iterations, and the factor of α accounts for the time needed for each presentation of the full training set.

For $m = 0$, $\lambda_{max} = \lambda_+$, and $\lambda_{min} = \lambda_-$. The learning time $\tau = \alpha(\lambda_+/\lambda_-)$ can be easily computed using Eq. (4.2): $\tau = \alpha(1+\sqrt{\alpha})^2/(1-\sqrt{\alpha})^2$. As a function of α, τ diverges at $\alpha = 1$, and, surprisingly, goes through a minimum at $\alpha = (1+\sqrt{2})^2 = 5.83$ before diverging linearly for $\alpha \to \infty$. Numerical simulations were performed to estimate τ by counting the number T of presentations of training examples needed to reach an allowed error level $\tilde{E}$ through gradient descent. If the prescribed error $\tilde{E}$ is sufficiently close to the minimum error E_0, T is controlled by the slowest mode, and it provides a good estimate for τ. Numerical results for T as a function of α, shown in Fig. 2, were obtained by training a single linear neuron on randomly generated vectors. As predicted, the curve exhibits a clear maximum at $\alpha = 1$, as well as a minimum between $\alpha = 4$ and $\alpha = 5$. The existence of such optimal training set size for fast learning is a surprising result.

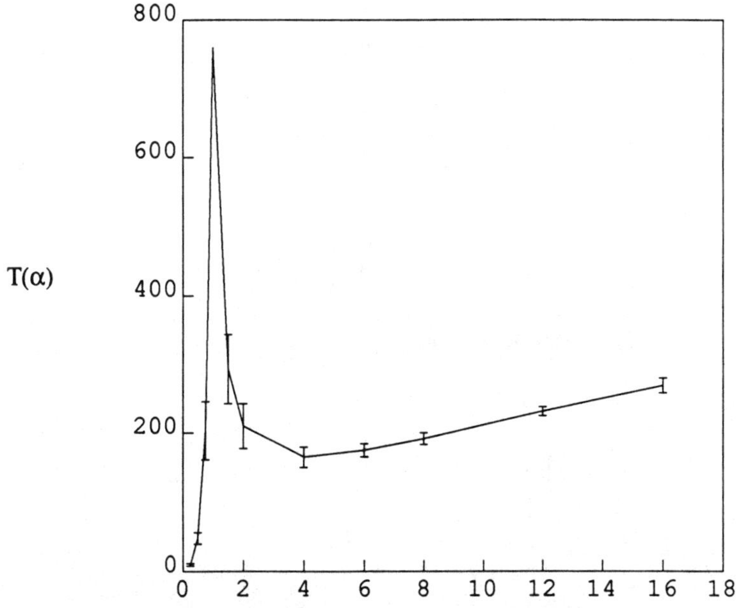

Figure 2: Number of iterations T (averaged over 20 trials) needed to train a linear neuron with $N = 100$ inputs. The x_j^μ are uniformly distributed between -1 and +1. Initial and target couplings W are chosen randomly from a uniform distribution within the $[-1,+1]^N$ hypercube. Gradient descent is considered complete when the error reaches the prescribed value $\tilde{E} = 0.001$ above the $E_0 = 0$ minimum value.

Biased inputs $m \neq 0$ produce a large eigenvalue $\lambda_{\max} = \lambda_N$, proportional to N and responsible for slow convergence. A simple approach to reducing the learning time is to center each input variable x_j by subtracting its mean. An obvious source of systematic bias m is the use of activation functions which restrict the state variables to the [0,1] interval. Symmetric activation functions such as the hyperbolic tangent are empirically known to yield faster convergence than their nonsymmetric counterparts such as the logistic function. Our results provide an explanation to this observation.

The extension of these results to multi-layer networks rests on the observation that each neuron i receives state information $\{x_j\}$ from the $j \in S_i$ neurons that feed into it, and can be viewed as minimizing a local objective function E_i whose Hessian involves the the covariance matrix of such inputs. If all input variables are uncorrelated and have zero mean, no large eigenvalues will appear. But states with $\overline{x_j} = m \neq 0$ produce eigenvalues proportional to the number of input neurons N_i in the set S_i, resulting in slow convergence if the connectivity is large. An empirically known solution to this problem, justified by our theoretical analysis, is to use individual learning rates η_i inversely proportional to the number of inputs N_i to the i-th neuron. Yet another approach is to keep a running estimate of the average $\overline{x_j}$ and use centered state variables $\widetilde{x_j} = x_j - \overline{x_j}$. Such algorithm results in considerable reductions in learning time.

6 CONCLUSIONS

Our results are based on a rigorous calculation of the eigenvalue spectrum for a symmetric matrix constructed from the outer product of random vectors. The spectral density provides a full description of the relaxation of a single adaptive linear unit, and yields a surprising result for the optimal size of the training set in batch learning. Various aspects of the dynamics of learning in multi-layer networks composed of nonlinear units are clarified: the theory justifies known empirical methods and suggests novel approaches to reduce learning times.

References

A. Krogh and J. A. Hertz (1991), 'Dynamics of generalization in linear perceptrons', in *Advances in Neural Information Processing Systems 3*, ed. by D. S. Touretzky and R. Lippman, Morgan Kaufmann (California).

Y. Le Cun, I. Kanter, and S. A. Solla (1990), 'Eigenvalues of covariance matrices: application to neural-network learning', *Phys. Rev.*, to be published.

D. E. Rumelhart, G. E. Hinton, and R. J. Williams (1986), 'Learning representations by back-propagating errors', *Nature* **323**, 533-536.

B. Widrow and S. D. Stearns (1985), *Adaptive Signal Processing*, Prentice-Hall (New Jersey).

Chaitin-Kolmogorov Complexity and Generalization in Neural Networks

Barak A. Pearlmutter
School of Computer Science
Carnegie Mellon University
Pittsburgh, PA 15213

Ronald Rosenfeld
School of Computer Science
Carnegie Mellon University
Pittsburgh, PA 15213

Abstract

We present a unified framework for a number of different ways of failing to generalize properly. During learning, sources of random information contaminate the network, effectively augmenting the training data with random information. The complexity of the function computed is therefore increased, and generalization is degraded. We analyze replicated networks, in which a number of identical networks are independently trained on the same data and their results averaged. We conclude that replication almost always results in a decrease in the expected complexity of the network, and that replication therefore increases expected generalization. Simulations confirming the effect are also presented.

1 BROKEN SYMMETRY CONSIDERED HARMFUL

Consider a one-unit backpropagation network trained on exclusive or. Without hidden units, the problem is insoluble. One point where learning would stop is when all weights are zero and the output is always $\frac{1}{2}$, resulting in an mean squared error of $\frac{1}{4}$. But this is a saddle point; by placing the discrimination boundary properly, one point can be gotten correctly, two with errors of $\frac{1}{3}$, and one with error of $\frac{2}{3}$, giving an MSE of $\frac{1}{6}$, as shown in figure 1.

Networks are initialized with small random weights, or noise is injected during training to break symmetries of this sort. But in breaking this symmetry, something has been lost. Consider a kNN classifier, constructed from a kNN program and the training data. Anyone who has a copy of the kNN program can construct an *identical* classifier if they receive the training data. Thus, considering the classification as an abstract entity, we know its complexity cannot exceed that of the training data plus the overhead of the complexity of the program, which is fixed.

But this is not necessarily the case for the backpropagation network we saw! Because of the introduction of randomly broken symmetries, the complexity of the classification itself can exceed that of the training data plus the learning procedure. Thus an identical classifier can no longer be constructed just from the program and the training data, because random factors have been introduced. For a striking example, consider presenting a "32 bit parity with 10,000 exceptions" stochastic learner with one million exemplars. The complexity of the resulting function will be high, since in order to specify it we must specify not only the regularities of training set, which we just did in a couple words, but also which of the 4 billion possibilities are among the 10,000 exceptions.

Applying this idea to undertraining and overtraining, we see that there are two kinds of symmetries that can be broken. First, if not all the exemplars can be loaded, which of the outliers are not loaded can be arbitrary. Second, underconstrained networks that behave the same on the training set may behave differently on other inputs. Both phenomena can be present simultaneously.

2 A COMPLEXITY BOUND

The expected value of the complexity of the function implemented by a network b trained on data d, where b is a potentially stochastic mapping, satisfies

$$E(\mathcal{C}(b(d))) \leq \mathcal{C}(d) + \mathcal{C}(b) + I(b(d)|d)$$

where $I(b(d)|d)$ is the negative of the entropy of the bias distribution of b trained on d,

$$I(b(d)|d) = -H(b(d)) = -\sum_{f} \log P(b(d) = f)$$

where f ranges over *functions* that the network could end up performing, with the network regarded as a black box. This in turn is bounded by the information contained in the random internal parameters, or by the entropy of the watershed structure; but these are both potentially unbounded.

A number of techniques for improving generalization, when viewed in this light, work because they tighten this bound.

- Weight decay [2] and the statistical technique of ridge regression impose an extra constraint on the parameters, reducing their freedom to arbitrarily break symmetry when underconstrained.
- Cross validation attempts to stop training before too many symmetries have been broken.
- Efforts to find the perfect number of hidden units attempt to minimize the number of symmetries that must be broken.

These techniques strike a balance between undertraining and overtraining. Since in any realistic domain both of these effects will be simultaneously present, it would seem advantageous to attack the problem at the root. One approach that has been

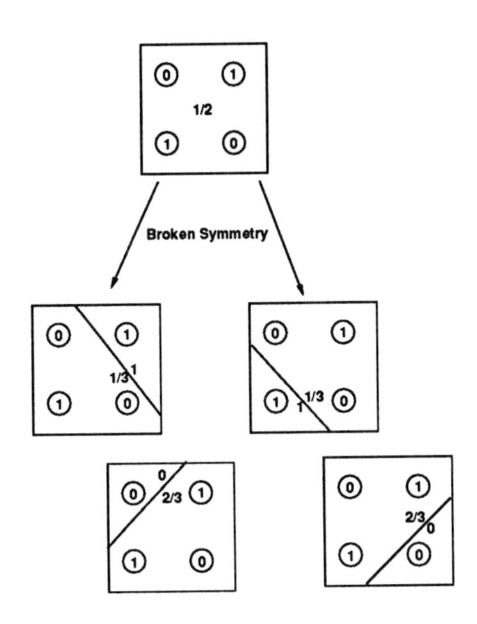

Figure 1: The bifurcation of a perceptron trained on xor.

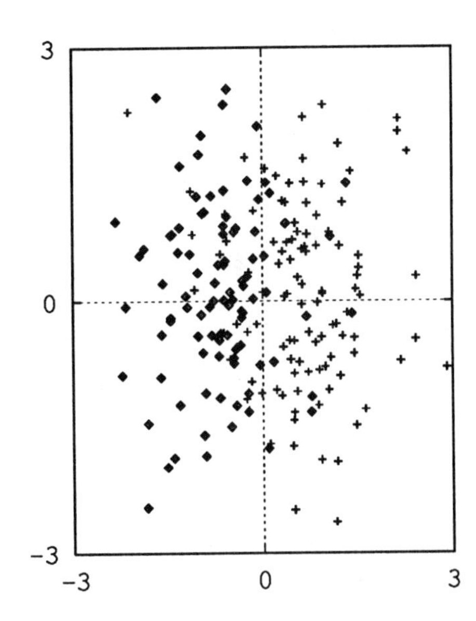

Figure 2: The training set. Crosses are negative examples and diamonds are positive examples.

rediscovered a number of times [1, 3], and systematically explored in its pure form by Lincoln and Skrzypek [4], is that of replicated networks.

3 REPLICATED NETWORKS

One might think that the complexity of the average of a collection of networks would be the sum of the complexities of the components; but this need not be the case. Consider an ensemble network, in which an infinite number of networks are taught the training data simultaneously, each making its random decisions according to whatever distributions the training procedure calls for, and their output averaged.

We have seen that the complexity of a single network can exceed that of its training data plus the training program. But this is not the case with ensemble networks, since the ensemble network output can be determined solely from the program and the training data, i.e. $\mathcal{C}(E(b(d))) \leq \mathcal{C}(b)+\mathcal{C}(d)+\mathcal{C}(\text{"replicate"})$ where $\mathcal{C}(\text{"replicate"})$ is the complexity of the instruction to replicate and average (a small constant).

A simple way to approximate the ensemble machine is to train a number of networks simultaneously and average the results. As the number of networks is increased, the composite model approaches the ensemble network, which cannot have higher complexity than the training data plus the program plus the instruction to replicate.

Note that even if one accidentally stumbles across the perfect architecture and training regime, resulting in a net that always learns the training set perfectly but with no leftover capacity, and which generalizes as well as anything could, then making a replicated network can't hurt, since all the component networks would do exactly the same thing anyway.

A number of researchers seem to have inadvertently exploited this fact. For instance, Hampshire et al. [1] train a number of networks on a speech task, where the networks differed in choice of objective function. The networks' outputs were averaged to form the answer used in the recognition phase, and the generalization performance of the composite network was significantly higher than that of any of its component networks. Replicated implementations programmed from identical specifications is a common technique in software engineering of highly reliable systems.

4 THE ISSUE OF INDUCTIVE BIAS

The representational power of an ensemble is greater that that of a single network. By the usual logic, one would expect the ensemble to have worse generalization, since its inductive bias is weaker. Counterintuitively, this is not the case. For instance, the VC dimension of an ensemble of perceptrons is infinite, because it can implement an arbitrary three layer network, using replication to implement weights. This is much greater than the finite VC dimension of a single perceptron within the ensemble, but our analysis predicts better generalization for the ensemble than for a single stochastic perceptron when the bounds are tight, that is, when

$$H(b(d)) \geq \mathcal{C}(\text{“replicate”}). \tag{1}$$

This leads to the conclusion that just knowing the inductive bias of a learner is not enough information to make strong conclusions about its expected generalization. Thus, distribution free results based purely on the inductive bias, such as VC dimension based PAC learning theory [5], may sometimes be unduly pessimistic.

As to replicated networks, we have seen that they can not help but improve generalization when (1) holds. Thus, if one is training the same network over and over, perhaps with slightly different training regimes, and getting worse generalization than was hoped for, but on different cases each time, then one can improve generalization in a seemingly principled manner by putting all the trained networks in a box and calling it a finite sample of the ensemble network (and perhaps buying a bigger computer to run it on).

5 EMPIRICAL SUPPORT

We conducted the following experiment: 17 standard backpropagation networks (Actually 20, but 3 were lost to a disk failure) were trained on a binary classification task. The nets all had identical architectures (2–20–1) but different initial weights, chosen uniformly from the interval $[-1, 1]$. The same training set was used to train all the networks. The functions implemented by each of the networks were then calculated in detail, and the performance of individual networks compared to that of their ensemble.

The classification task was a stochastic 2D linear discriminator. Each point was obtained from a Gaussian centered at (0.0) with stdev 1. A classification of 1 was

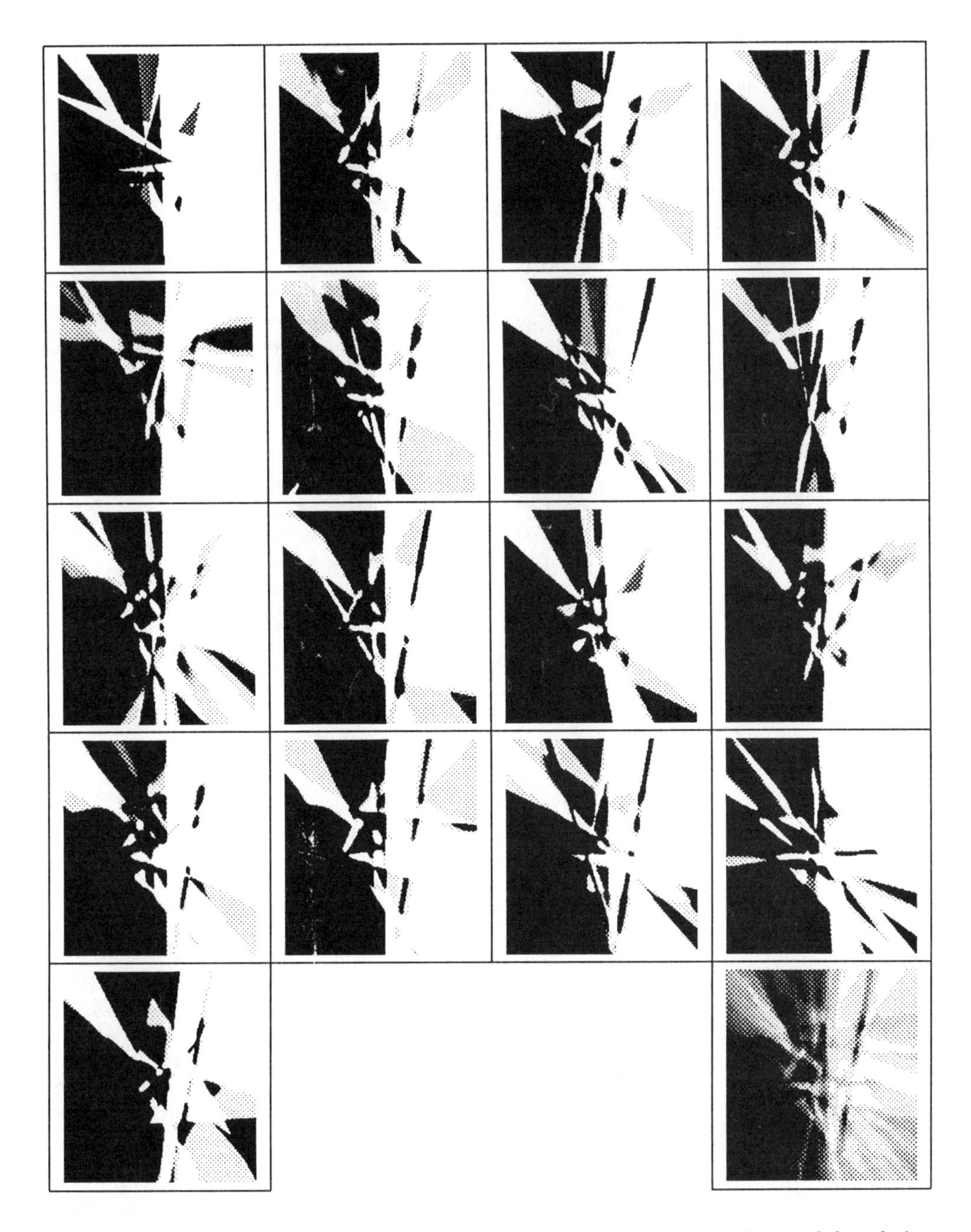

Figure 3: The functions implemented by the 17 trained networks, and by their average (bottom right). Both the x and y axes run from -3 to 3, and grey levels are used to represent intermediate values in the interval $[0, 1]$.

Table 1: Mean squared error and number of mislabeled exemplars for each network on the training set of 200.

net	MSE	errors	
12	0.0150837	3	***
9	0.0200039	4	****
16	0.0200026	4	****
5	0.0250207	5	*****
7	0.0250213	5	*****
10	0.0228319	5	*****
13	0.0250156	5	*****
17	0.0250018	5	*****
19	0.0175466	5	*****
6	0.0300099	6	******
15	0.0300075	6	******
18	0.0300060	6	******
8	0.0350609	7	*******
11	0.0350006	7	*******
20	0.0400013	8	********
14	0.0305254	9	*********
4	0.0408391	13	*************
mean	0.027469 ± 0.007226	6.058824	$\pm$ 2.261457
ensemble	0.016286	4	****
nohidden	0.060314	31	

assigned to points with $x \geq 0$, and 0 to points with $x < 0$, but reversed with an independent probability of 0.1. The final position of each point was then determined by adding a zero mean Gaussian with stdev .25. 200 points were so generated for the training set (shown in figure 2) and another 1000 points for the test set.

Looking at figure 3, each net appears to correctly classify as many of the inputs as possible, within the bounds imposed on it by its inductive bias. Each function implemented by such a net is roughly equivalent to a linear combination of 20 independent linear discriminators. It is therefore clear why each map consists of regions delineated by up to 20 straight lines. Since the initial conditions were different for each net, so were the resultant regions. All networks misclassified some of the exemplars (see table 1), but the missclassifications were different for each network, illustrating symmetry breaking due to an overconstraining data set.

Note that the ensemble's performance on the training set is comparable to that of the best of the trained networks, while its performance on the test set is far superior. The MSE error of the ensemble is much much better than the bound obtained from Jensen's inequality, the average MSE. In fact, the ensemble network gets a lower MSE than all but one individual network on the training sets, and a much lower MSE than any individual network on the test set; and it generalizes much better than any of the individual networks by a misclassification count metric.

Table 2: Mean squared error and number of mislabeled samples for each network on the test set of 1000. The performance of a theoretically perfect classifier (sign x) on the test set is 170 misclassifications, which is about what the network without hidden units gets.

net	MSE	errors
16	0.201	205
9	0.207	213
4	0.206	215
5	0.209	216
11	0.208	216
15	0.207	216
6	0.212	219
19	0.213	220
7	0.214	222
8	0.214	224
12	0.212	225
17	0.219	225
18	0.220	227
20	0.223	229
13	0.223	231
14	0.227	237
10	0.226	254
mean	0.214 ± 0.007	223 ± 10.7
ensemble	0.160	200
nohidden	0.0715	169

Table 3: Histogram of the networks' performance by number of misclassified training exemplars.

error count	networks
0	
1	
2	
3	*
4	**
5	******
6	***
7	**
8	*
9	*
10	
11	
12	
13	*
14	
15	
16	

References

[1] J. Hampshire and A. Waibel. A novel objective function for improved phoneme recognition using time delay neural networks. Technical Report CMU-CS-89-118, Carnegie Mellon University School of Computer Science, March 1989.

[2] Geoffrey E. Hinton, Terrence J. Sejnowski, and David H. Ackley. Boltzmann Machines: Constraint satisfaction networks that learn. Technical Report CMU-CS-84-119, Carnegie-Mellon University, May 1984.

[3] Nathan Intrator. A neural network for feature extraction. In D. S. Touretzky, editor, *Advances in Neural Information Processing Systems 2*, pages 719–726, San Mateo, CA, 1990. Morgan Kaufmann.

[4] Willian P. Lincoln and Josef Skrzypek. Synergy of clustering multiple back propagation networks. In D. S. Touretzky, editor, *Advances in Neural Information Processing Systems 2*, pages 650–657, San Mateo, CA, 1990. Morgan Kaufmann.

[5] L. G. Valiant. A theory of the learnable. *Communications of the ACM*, 27(11):1134–1142, 1984.

Asymptotic slowing down of the nearest-neighbor classifier

Robert R. Snapp
CS/EE Department
University of Vermont
Burlington, VT 05405

Demetri Psaltis
Electrical Engineering
Caltech 116–81
Pasadena, CA 91125

Santosh S. Venkatesh
Electrical Engineering
University of Pennsylvania
Philadelphia, PA 19104

Abstract

If patterns are drawn from an n-dimensional feature space according to a probability distribution that obeys a weak smoothness criterion, we show that the probability that a random input pattern is misclassified by a nearest-neighbor classifier using M random reference patterns asymptotically satisfies

$$P_M(\text{error}) \sim P_\infty(\text{error}) + \frac{a}{M^{2/n}},$$

for sufficiently large values of M. Here, $P_\infty(\text{error})$ denotes the probability of error in the infinite sample limit, and is at most twice the error of a Bayes classifier. Although the value of the coefficient a depends upon the underlying probability distributions, the exponent of M is largely distribution free. We thus obtain a concise relation between a classifier's ability to generalize from a finite reference sample and the dimensionality of the feature space, as well as an analytic validation of Bellman's well known "curse of dimensionality."

1 INTRODUCTION

One of the primary tasks assigned to neural networks is pattern classification. Common applications include recognition problems dealing with speech, handwritten characters, DNA sequences, military targets, and (in this conference) sexual identity. Two fundamental concepts associated with pattern classification are *generalization* (how well does a classifier respond to input data it has never encountered before?) and *scalability* (how are a classifier's processing and training requirements affected by increasing the number of features that describe the input patterns?).

Despite recent progress, our present understanding of these concepts in the context of neural networks is obstructed by complexities in the functional form of the network and in the classification problems themselves.

In this correspondence we will present analytic results on these issues for the nearest-neighbor classifier. Noted for its algorithmic simplicity and nearly optimal performance in the infinite sample limit, this pattern classifier plays a central role in the field of pattern recognition. Furthermore, because it uses proximity in feature space as a measure of class similarity, its performance on a given classification problem should yield qualitative cues to the performance of a neural network. Indeed, a nearest-neighbor classifier can be readily implemented as a "winner-take-all" neural network.

2 THE TASK OF PATTERN CLASSIFICATION

We begin with a formulation of the two-class problem (Duda and Hart, 1973):

> Let the labels ω_1 and ω_2 denote two states of nature, or pattern classes. A pattern belonging to one of these two classes is selected, and a vector of n features, $\mathbf{x}$, that describe the selected pattern is presented to a pattern classifier. The classifier then attempts to guess the selected pattern's class by assigning $\mathbf{x}$ to either ω_1 or ω_2.

As an example, the two class labels might represent the states *benign* and *malignant* as they pertain to the diagnosis of cancer tumors; the feature vector could then be a 1024×1024 pixel, real-valued representation of an electron-microscope image. A pattern classifier can thus be viewed as a mapping from an n-dimensional feature space to the discrete set $\{\omega_1, \omega_2\}$, and can be specified by demarcating the regions in the n-dimensional feature space that correspond to ω_1 and ω_2. We define the decision region $\mathcal{R}_1$ as the set of feature vectors that the pattern classifier assigns to ω_1, with an analogous definition for $\mathcal{R}_2$. A useful figure of merit is the probability that the feature vector of a randomly selected pattern is assigned to the correct class.

2.1 THE BAYES CLASSIFIER

If sufficient information is available, it is possible to construct an optimal pattern classifier. Let $P(\omega_1)$ and $P(\omega_2)$ denote the *prior probabilities* of the two states of nature. (For our cancer diagnosis problem, the prior probabilities can be estimated by the relative frequency of each type of tumor in a large statistical sample.) Further, let $p(\mathbf{x} \mid \omega_1)$ and $p(\mathbf{x} \mid \omega_2)$ denote the *class-conditional probability densities* of the feature vector for the two class problem. The total probability density is now defined by $p(\mathbf{x}) = p(\mathbf{x} \mid \omega_1)P(\omega_1) + p(\mathbf{x} \mid \omega_2)P(\omega_2)$, and gives the unconditional distribution of the feature vector. Where $p(\mathbf{x}) \neq 0$ we can now use Bayes' rule to compute the *posterior probabilities*:

$$P(\omega_1 \mid \mathbf{x}) = \frac{p(\mathbf{x} \mid \omega_1)P(\omega_1)}{p(\mathbf{x})} \qquad \text{and} \qquad P(\omega_2 \mid \mathbf{x}) = \frac{p(\mathbf{x} \mid \omega_2)P(\omega_2)}{p(\mathbf{x})}.$$

The Bayes classifier assigns an unclassified feature vector $\mathbf{x}$ to the class label having the greatest posterior probability. (If the posterior probabilities happen to be equal, then the class assignment is arbitrary.) With $\mathcal{R}_1$ and $\mathcal{R}_2$ denoting the two decision regions induced by this strategy, the probability of error of the Bayes classifier, P_B, is just the probability that $\mathbf{x}$ is drawn from class ω_1 but lies in the Bayes decision region $\mathcal{R}_2$, or conversely, that $\mathbf{x}$ is drawn from class ω_2 but lies in the Bayes decision region $\mathcal{R}_1$:

$$P_B = \int_{\mathcal{R}_2} P(\omega_1 \mid \mathbf{x})\, p(\mathbf{x})\, d^n x + \int_{\mathcal{R}_1} P(\omega_2 \mid \mathbf{x})\, p(\mathbf{x})\, d^n x.$$

The reader may verify that the Bayes classifier minimizes the probability of error.

Unfortunately, it is usually impossible to obtain expressions for the class-conditional densities and prior probabilities in practice. Typically, the available information resides in a set of correctly labeled patterns, which we collectively term a *training* or *reference sample*. Over the last few decades, numerous pattern classification strategies have been developed that attempt to learn the structure of a classification problem from a finite training sample. (The backpropagation algorithm is a recent example.) The underlying hope is that the classifier's performance can be made acceptable with a sufficiently large reference sample. In order to understand how large a sample may be needed, we turn to what is perhaps the simplest learning algorithm of this class.

3 THE NEAREST-NEIGHBOR CLASSIFIER

Let $\mathcal{X}_M = \{(\mathbf{x}^{(1)}, \theta^{(1)}), (\mathbf{x}^{(2)}, \theta^{(2)}), \ldots, (\mathbf{x}^{(M)}, \theta^{(M)})\}$ denote a finite reference sample of M feature vectors, $\mathbf{x}^{(i)} \in \mathbf{R}^n$, with corresponding known class assignments, $\theta^{(i)} \in \{\omega_1, \omega_2\}$. The *nearest-neighbor rule* assigns each feature vector $\mathbf{x}$ to class ω_1 or ω_2 as a function of the reference M-sample as follows:

- *Identify* $(\mathbf{x}', \theta') \in \mathcal{X}_M$ such that $\|\mathbf{x} - \mathbf{x}'\| \leq \|\mathbf{x} - \mathbf{x}^{(i)}\|$ for i ranging from 1 through M;
- *Assign* $\mathbf{x}$ to class θ'.

Here, $\|\mathbf{x} - \mathbf{y}\| = \sqrt{\sum_{j=1}^{n} (x_j - y_j)^2}$ denotes the Euclidean metric in $\mathbf{R}^n$.[1] The nearest-neighbor rule hence classifies each feature vector $\mathbf{x}$ according to the label, θ', of the closest point, $\mathbf{x}'$, in the reference sample. As an example, we sketch the nearest-neighbor decision regions for a two-dimensional classification problem in Fig. 1.

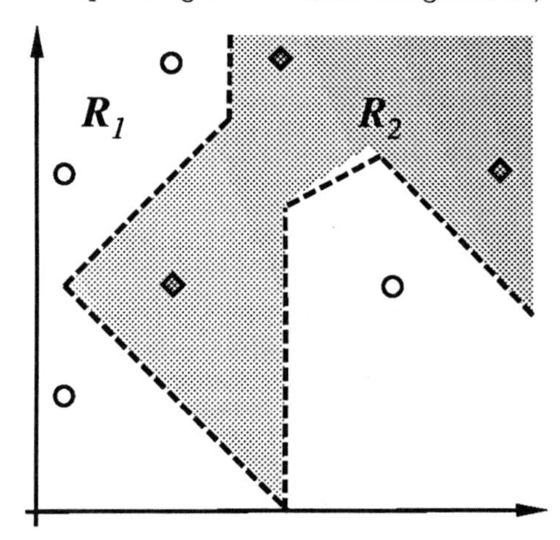

Figure 1: The decision regions induced by a nearest-neighbor classifier with a seven-element reference set in the plane.

[1] Other metrics, such as the more general Minkowski-r metric, are also possible.

It is interesting to consider how the performance of this classifier compares with that of a Bayes classifier. To facilitate this analysis, we assume that the reference patterns are selected from the total probability density $p(\mathbf{x})$ in a statistically independent manner (i.e., the choice of $\mathcal{X}_j$ does not in any way bias the selection of $\mathbf{x}^{(j+1)}$ and $\theta^{(j+1)}$). Furthermore, let $P_M(\text{error})$ denote the probability of error of a nearest-neighbor classifier working with the reference sample $\mathcal{X}_M$, and let $P_\infty(\text{error})$ denote this probability in the infinite sample limit ($M \to \infty$). We will also let $\mathcal{S}$ denote the volume in feature space over which $p(\mathbf{x})$ is nonzero. The following well known theorem shows that the nearest-neighbor classifier, with an infinite reference sample, is nearly optimal (Cover and Hart, 1967).[2]

Theorem 1 *For the two-class problem in the infinite sample limit, the probability of error of a nearest-neighbor classifier tends toward the value,*

$$P_\infty(\text{error}) = 2\int_{\mathcal{S}} P(\omega_1 \mid \mathbf{x})P(\omega_2 \mid \mathbf{x})p(\mathbf{x})\, d^n x,$$

which is furthermore bounded by the two inequalities,

$$P_B \le P_\infty(\text{error}) \le 2P_B(1 - P_B),$$

where P_B is the probability of error of a Bayes classifier.

This encouraging result is not so surprising if one considers that, with probability one, about every feature vector $\mathbf{x}$ is centered a ball of radius ϵ that contains an *infinite* number of reference feature vectors for every $\epsilon > 0$. The annoying factor of two accounts for the event that the nearest neighbor to $\mathbf{x}$ belongs to the class with smaller posterior probability.

3.1 THE ASYMPTOTIC CONVERGENCE RATE

In order to satisfactorily address the issues of generalization and scalability for the nearest-neighbor classifier, we need to consider the rate at which the performance of the classifier approaches its infinite sample limit. The following theorem applicable to nearest-neighbor classification in *one-dimensional* feature spaces was shown by Cover (1968).

Theorem 2 *Let $p(x \mid \omega_1)$ and $p(x \mid \omega_2)$ have uniformly bounded third derivatives and let $p(\mathbf{x})$ be bounded away from zero on $\mathcal{S}$. Then for sufficiently large M,*

$$P_M(\text{error}) = P_\infty(\text{error}) + O\left(\frac{1}{M^2}\right).$$

Note that this result is also very encouraging in that an order of magnitude increase in the sample size, decreases the error rate by *two* orders of magnitude.

The following theorem is our main result which extends Cover's theorem to n-dimensional feature spaces:

[2] Originally, this theorem was stated for multiclass decision problems; it is here presented for the two class problem only for simplicity.

Theorem 3 *Let $p(\mathbf{x} \mid \omega_1)$, $p(\mathbf{x} \mid \omega_2)$, and $p(\mathbf{x})$ satisfy the same conditions as in Theorem 2. Then, there exists a scalar a (depending on n) such that*

$$P_M(\text{error}) \sim P_\infty(\text{error}) + \frac{a}{M^{2/n}},$$

where the right-hand side describes the first two terms of an asymptotic expansion in reciprocal powers of $M^{2/n}$. Explicitly,

$$a = \frac{\Gamma\left(1+\frac{2}{n}\right)\left(\Gamma\left(\frac{n}{2}+1\right)\right)^{2/n}}{n\pi} \sum_{i=1}^{n} \int_{\mathcal{S}} \left(\frac{\beta_i(\mathbf{x}) p_i(\mathbf{x})}{p(\mathbf{x})} + \frac{1}{2}\gamma_{ii}(\mathbf{x}) \right) (p(\mathbf{x}))^{1-2/n} \, d^n x.$$

where,

$$\begin{aligned} p_i(\mathbf{x}) &= \frac{\partial p(\mathbf{x})}{\partial x_i} \\ \beta_i(\mathbf{x}) &= P(\omega_1 \mid \mathbf{x}) \frac{\partial P(\omega_2 \mid \mathbf{x})}{\partial x_i} + \frac{\partial P(\omega_1 \mid \mathbf{x})}{\partial x_i} P(\omega_2 \mid \mathbf{x}) \\ \gamma_{ii}(\mathbf{x}) &= P(\omega_1 \mid \mathbf{x}) \frac{\partial^2 P(\omega_2 \mid \mathbf{x})}{\partial x_i^2} + \frac{\partial^2 P(\omega_1 \mid \mathbf{x})}{\partial x_i^2} P(\omega_2 \mid \mathbf{x}). \end{aligned}$$

For $n = 1$ this result agrees with Cover's theorem. With increasing n, however, the convergence rate significantly slows down. Note that the constant a depends on the way in which the class-conditional densities overlap. If a is bounded away from zero, then for sufficiently small $\delta > 0$, $P_M(\text{error}) - P_\infty(\text{error}) < \delta$ is satisfied only if $M > (a/\delta)^{n/2}$ so that the sample size required to achieve a given performance criterion is exponential in the dimensionality of the feature space. The above provides a sufficient condition for Bellman's well known "curse of dimensionality" in this context.

It is also interesting to note that one can easily construct classification problems for which a vanishes. (Consider, for example, $p(\mathbf{x} \mid \omega_1) = p(\mathbf{x} \mid \omega_2)$ for all $\mathbf{x}$.) In these cases the higher-order terms in the asymptotic expansion are important.

4 A NUMERICAL EXPERIMENT

A conspicuous weakness in the above theorem is the requirement that $p(\mathbf{x})$ be bounded away from zero over $\mathcal{S}$. In exchange for a uniformly convergent asymptotic expansion, we have omitted many important probability distributions, including normal distributions. Therefore we numerically estimate the asymptotic behavior of $P_M(\text{error})$ for a problem consisting of two normally distributed classes in $\mathbf{R}^n$:

$$\begin{aligned} p(\mathbf{x} \mid \omega_1) &= \frac{1}{(2\pi\sigma^2)^{n/2}} \exp\left[-\frac{1}{2\sigma^2}\left((x_1-\mu)^2 + \sum_{j=2}^{n} x_j^2\right)\right], \\ p(\mathbf{x} \mid \omega_2) &= \frac{1}{(2\pi\sigma^2)^{n/2}} \exp\left[-\frac{1}{2\sigma^2}\left((x_1+\mu)^2 + \sum_{j=2}^{n} x_j^2\right)\right]. \end{aligned}$$

Assuming that $P(\omega_1) = P(\omega_2) = 1/2$, we find

$$P_\infty(\text{error}) = \frac{1}{\sigma\sqrt{2\pi}} e^{-\mu^2/2\sigma^2} \int_0^\infty e^{-x^2/2\sigma^2} \operatorname{sech}\left(\frac{\mu x}{\sigma^2}\right) dx.$$

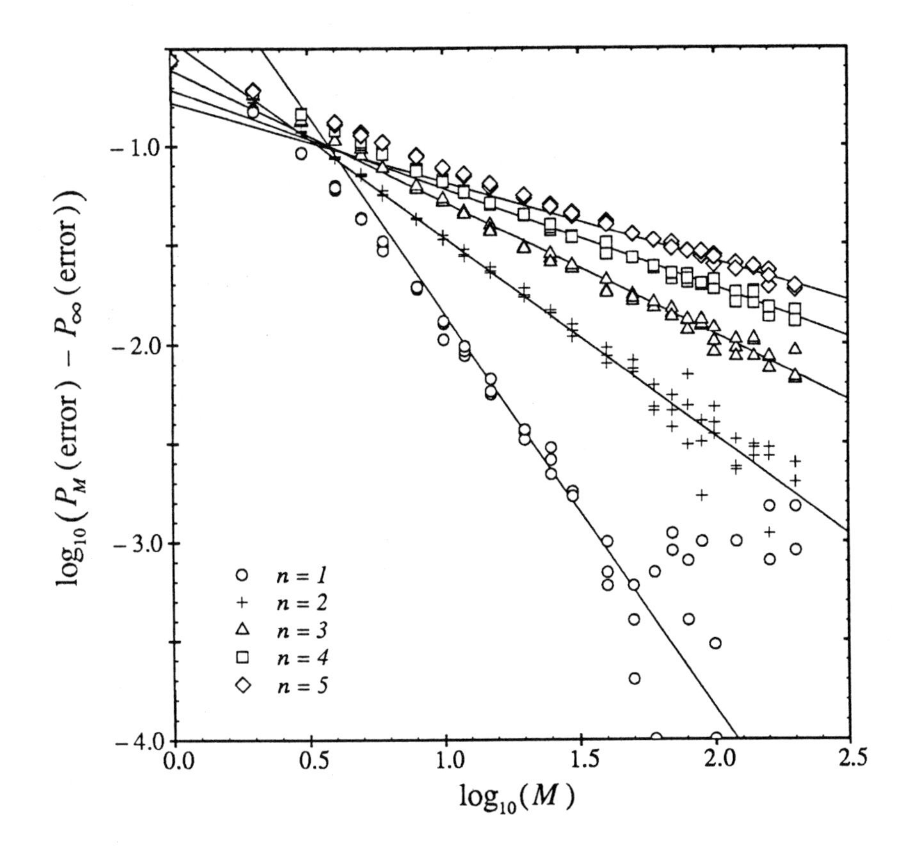

Figure 2: Numerical validation of the nearest-neighbor scaling hypothesis for two normally distributed classes in $\mathbf{R}^n$.

For $\mu = \sigma = 1$, $P_\infty(\text{error})$ is numerically found to be 0.22480, which is consistent with the Bayes probability of error, $P_B = (1/2)\text{erfc}(1/\sqrt{2}) = 0.15865$. (Note that the expression for a given in Theorem 3 is undefined for these distributions.) For n ranging from 1 to 5, and M ranging from 1 to 200, three estimates of $P_M(\text{error})$ were obtained, each as the fraction of "failures" in 160,000 or more Bernoulli trials. Each trial consists of constructing a pseudo-random sample of M reference patterns, followed by a single attempt to correctly classify a random input pattern. These estimates of P_M are represented in Figure 2 by circular markers for $n = 1$, crosses for $n = 2$, etc. The lines in Figure 2 depict the power law

$$P_M(\text{error}) = P_\infty(\text{error}) + bM^{-2/n},$$

where, for each n, b is chosen to obtain an appealing fit. The agreement between these lines and data points suggests that the asymptotic scaling hypothesis of Theorem 3 can be extended to a wider class of distributions.

5 DISCUSSION

The preceding analysis indicates that the convergence rate of the nearest-neighbor classifier slows down dramatically as the dimensionality of the feature space increases. This rate reduction suggests that proximity in feature space is a less effective measure of class identity in higher dimensional feature spaces. It is also clear that some degree of smoothness in the class-conditional densities is necessary, as well as sufficient, for the asymptotic behavior described by our analysis to occur: in the absence of smoothness conditions, one can construct classification problems for which the nearest-neighbor convergence rate is arbitrarily slow, even in one dimension (Cover, 1968). Fortunately, the most pressing classification problems are typically smooth in that they are constrained by regularities implicit in the laws of nature (Marr, 1982). With additional prior information, the convergence rate may be enhanced by selecting a fewer number of descriptive features.

Because of their smooth input-output response, neural networks appear to use proximity in feature space as a basis for classification. One might, therefore, expect the required sample size to scale exponentially with the dimensionality of the feature space. Recent results from computational learning theory, however, imply that with a sample size proportional to the *capacity*—a combinatorial quantity which is characteristic of the network architecture and which typically grows polynomially in the dimensionality of the feature space—one can in principle identify network parameters (weights) which give (close to) the smallest classification error for the given architecture (Baum and Haussler, 1989). There are two caveats, however. First, the information-theoretic sample complexities predicted by learning theory give no clue as to whether, given a sample of the requisite size, there exist any *algorithms* that can specify the appropriate parameters in a reasonable time frame. Second, and more fundamental, one cannot in general determine whether a particular architecture is intrinsically well suited to a given classification problem. The best performance achievable may be substantially poorer than that of a Bayes classifier. Thus, without sufficient prior information, one must search through the space of all possible network architectures for one that does fit the problem well. This situation now effectively resembles a non-parametric classifier and the analytic results for the sample complexities of the nearest-neighbor classifier should provide at least qualitative indications of the corresponding case for neural networks.

References

Baum, E. B. and Haussler, D. (1989), "What size net gives valid generalization," *Neural Computation*, **1**, pp. 151–160.

Cover, T. M. (1968), "Rates of convergence of nearest neighbor decision procedures," *Proc. First Annual Hawaii Conference on Systems Theory*, pp. 413–415.

Cover, T. M. and P. E. Hart (1967), "Nearest neighbor pattern classification," *IEEE Trans. Info. Theory*, vol. IT–13, pp. 21–27.

Duda, R. O. and P. E. Hart (1973), *Pattern Classification and Scene Analysis.* New York: John Wiley & Sons.

Marr, D. (1982), *Vision*, San Francisco: W. H. Freeman.

REMARKS ON INTERPOLATION AND RECOGNITION USING NEURAL NETS

Eduardo D. Sontag*
SYCON - Center for Systems and Control
Rutgers University
New Brunswick, NJ 08903

Abstract

We consider different types of single-hidden-layer feedforward nets: with or without direct input to output connections, and using either threshold or sigmoidal activation functions. The main results show that direct connections in threshold nets double the recognition but not the interpolation power, while using sigmoids rather than thresholds allows (at least) doubling both. Various results are also given on VC dimension and other measures of recognition capabilities.

1 INTRODUCTION

In this work we continue to develop the theme of comparing threshold and sigmoidal feedforward nets. In (Sontag and Sussmann, 1989) we showed that the "generalized delta rule" (backpropagation) can give rise to pathological behavior –namely, the existence of spurious local minima even when no hidden neurons are used,– in contrast to the situation that holds for threshold nets. On the other hand, in (Sontag and Sussmann, 1989) we remarked that *provided that the right variant be used*, separable sets do give rise to globally convergent backpropagation, in complete analogy to the classical perceptron learning theorem. These results and those obtained by other authors probably settle most general questions about the case of no hidden units, so the next step is to look at the case of single hidden layers. In (Sontag, 1989) we announced the fact that sigmoidal activations (at least) double recognition power. Here we provide details, and we make several further remarks on this as well as on the topic of interpolation.

Nets with one hidden layer are known to be in principle sufficient for arbitrary recognition tasks. This follows from the approximation theorems proved by various

*E-mail: sontag@hilbert.rutgers.edu

authors: (Funahashi,1988), (Cybenko,1989), and (Hornik et. al., 1989). However, what is far less clear is *how many* neurons are needed for achieving a given recognition, interpolation, or approximation objective. This is of importance both in its practical aspects (having rough estimates of how many neurons will be needed is essential when applying backpropagation) and in evaluating generalization properties (larger nets tend to lead to poorer generalization). It is known and easy to prove (see for instance (Arai, 1989), (Chester, 1990)) that one can basically interpolate values at any $n+1$ points using an n-neuron net, and in particular that any $n+1$-point set can be dichotomized by such nets. Among other facts, we point out here that allowing direct input to output connections permits doubling the recognition power to $2n$, and the same result is achieved if sigmoidal neurons are used but such direct connections are not allowed. Further, we remark that approximate interpolation of $2n-1$ points is also possible, provided that sigmoidal units be employed (but direct connections in threshold nets do not suffice).

The dimension of the input space (that is, the number of "input units") can influence the number of neurons needed, are least for dichotomy problems for suitably chosen sets. In particular, Baum had shown some time back (Baum, 1988) that the VC dimension of threshold nets with a fixed number of hidden units is at least proportional to this dimension. We give lower bounds, in dimension two, at least doubling the VC dimension if sigmoids or direct connections are allowed.

Lack of space precludes the inclusion of proofs; references to technical reports are given as appropriate. A full-length version of this paper is also available from the author.

2 DICHOTOMIES

The first few definitions are standard. Let N be a positive integer. A *dichotomy* or *two-coloring* (S_-, S_+) on a set $S \subseteq \mathbb{R}^N$ is a partition $S = S_- \bigcup S_+$ of S into two disjoint subsets. A function $f : \mathbb{R}^N \to \mathbb{R}$ will be said to *implement* this dichotomy if it holds that

$$f(u) > 0 \text{ for } u \in S_+ \text{ and } f(u) < 0 \text{ for } u \in S_- \ .$$

Let $\mathcal{F}$ be a class of functions from $\mathbb{R}^N$ to $\mathbb{R}$, assumed to be nontrivial, in the sense that for each point $u \in \mathbb{R}^N$ there is some $f_1 \in \mathcal{F}$ so that $f_1(u) > 0$ and some $f_2 \in \mathcal{F}$ so that $f_2(u) < 0$. This class *shatters* the set $S \subseteq R^N$ if each dichotomy on S can be implemented by some $f \in \mathcal{F}$.

Here we consider, for any class of functions $\mathcal{F}$ as above, the following measures of classification power. First we introduce $\overline{\mu}$ and $\underline{\mu}$, dealing with "best" and "worst" cases respectively: $\overline{\mu}(\mathcal{F})$ denotes the largest integer $l \geq 1$ (possibly ∞) so that there is at least *some* set S of cardinality l in $\mathbb{R}^N$ which can be shattered by $\mathcal{F}$, while $\underline{\mu}(\mathcal{F})$ is the largest integer $l \geq 1$ (possibly ∞) so that *every* set of cardinality l can be shattered by $\mathcal{F}$. Note that by definition, $\underline{\mu}(\mathcal{F}) \leq \overline{\mu}(\mathcal{F})$ for every class $\mathcal{F}$.

In particular, the definitions imply that no set of cardinality $\overline{\mu}(\mathcal{F}) + 1$ can be shattered, and that there is at least some set of cardinality $\underline{\mu}(\mathcal{F})+1$ which cannot be shattered. The integer $\overline{\mu}$ is usually called the *Vapnik-Chervonenkis (VC) dimension* of the class $\mathcal{F}$ (see for instance (Baum,1988)), and appears in formalizations of learning in the distribution-free sense.

A set may fail to be shattered by $\mathcal{F}$ because it is very special (see the example below with colinear points). In that sense, a more robust measure is useful: $\mu(\mathcal{F})$ is the largest integer $l \geq 1$ (possibly ∞) for which the class of sets S that can be shattered by $\mathcal{F}$ is dense, in the sense that given every l-element set $S = \{s_1, \ldots, s_l\}$ there are points $\widetilde{s}_i$ arbitrarily close to the respective s_i's such that $\widetilde{S} = \{\widetilde{s}_1, \ldots, \widetilde{s}_l\}$ can be shattered by $\mathcal{F}$. Note that

$$\underline{\mu}(\mathcal{F}) \leq \mu(\mathcal{F}) \leq \overline{\mu}(\mathcal{F}) \tag{1}$$

for all $\mathcal{F}$.

To obtain an upper bound m for $\mu(\mathcal{F})$ one needs to exhibit an open class of sets of cardinality $m+1$ none of which can be shattered.

Take as an example the class $\mathcal{F}$ consisting of all affine functions $f(x) = ax + by + c$ on $\mathbb{R}^2$. Since any three points can be shattered by an affine map provided that they are not colinear (just choose a line $ax + by + c = 0$ that separates any point which is colored different from the rest), it follows that $3 \leq \mu$. On the other hand, no set of four points can ever be dichotomized, which implies that $\overline{\mu} \leq 3$ and therefore the conclusion $\mu = \overline{\mu} = 3$ for this class. (The negative statement can be verified by a case by case analysis: if the four points form the vertices of a 4-gon color them in "XOR" fashion, alternate vertices of the same color; if 3 form a triangle and the remaining one is inside, color the extreme points differently from the remaining one; if all colinear then use an alternating coloring). Finally, since there is some set of 3 points which cannot be dichotomized (any set of three colinear points is like this), but every set of two can, $\underline{\mu} = 2$.

We shall say that $\mathcal{F}$ is *robust* if whenever S can be shattered by $\mathcal{F}$ also every small enough perturbation of S can be shattered. For a robust class and $l = \mu(\mathcal{F})$, every set in an open dense subset in the above topology, i.e. *almost every* set of l elements, can be shattered.

3 NETS

We define a "neural net" as a function of a certain type, corresponding to the idea of feedforward interconnections, via additive links, of neurons each of which has a scalar response or *activation function* θ.

Definition 3.1 Let $\theta : \mathbb{R} \to \mathbb{R}$ be any function. A function $f : \mathbb{R}^N \to \mathbb{R}$ is a *single-hidden-layer neural net with k hidden neurons of type θ and N inputs*, or just a *(k,θ)-net*, if there are real numbers $w_0, w_1, \ldots, w_k, \tau_1, \ldots, \tau_k$ and vectors $v_0, v_1, \ldots, v_k \in \mathbb{R}^N$ such that, for all $u \in \mathbb{R}^N$,

$$f(u) \;=\; w_0 \;+\; v_0.u \;+\; \sum_{i=1}^{k} w_i\, \theta(v_i.u - \tau_i) \tag{2}$$

where the dot indicates inner product. *A net with no direct i/o connections* is one for which $v_0 = 0$.

For fixed θ, and under mild assumptions on θ, such neural nets can be used to approximate uniformly arbitrary continuous functions on compacts. In particular, they can be used to implement arbitrary dichotomies.

In neural net practice, one often takes θ to be the *standard sigmoid* $\sigma(x) = \frac{1}{1+e^{-x}}$ or equivalently, up to translations and change of coordinates, the hyperbolic tangent $\tanh(x)$. Another usual choice is the hardlimiter, threshold, or *Heaviside* function

$$\mathcal{H}(x) = \begin{cases} 0 & \text{if } x \leq 0 \\ 1 & \text{if } x > 0 \end{cases}$$

which can be approximated well by $\sigma(\gamma x)$ when the "gain" γ is large. Yet another possibility is the use of the piecewise linear function

$$\pi(x) = \begin{cases} -1 & \text{if } x \leq -1 \\ 1 & \text{if } x \geq 1 \\ x & \text{otherwise.} \end{cases}$$

Most analysis has been done for $\mathcal{H}$ and no direct connections, but numerical techniques typically use the standard sigmoid (or equivalently tanh). The activation π will be useful as an example for which sharper bounds can be obtained. The examples σ and π, but not $\mathcal{H}$, are particular cases of the following more general type of activation function:

Definition 3.2 A function $\theta : \mathbb{R} \to \mathbb{R}$ will be called a *sigmoid* if these two properties hold:

(S1) $t_+ := \lim_{x\to+\infty} \theta(x)$ and $t_- := \lim_{x\to-\infty} \theta(x)$ exist, and $t_+ \neq t_-$.

(S2) There is some point c such that θ is differentiable at c and $\theta'(c) = \mu \neq 0$. □

All the examples above lead to robust classes, in the sense defined earlier. More precisely, assume that θ is continuous except for at most finitely many points x, and it is left continuous at such x, and let $\mathcal{F}$ be the class of (k, θ)-nets, for any fixed k. Then $\mathcal{F}$ is robust, and the same statement holds for nets with no direct connections.

4 CLASSIFICATION RESULTS

We let $\mu(k, \theta, N)$ denote $\mu(\mathcal{F})$, where $\mathcal{F}$ is the class of (k, θ)-nets in $\mathbb{R}^N$ with *no direct connections*, and similarly for $\underline{\mu}$ and $\overline{\mu}$, and a superscript d is used for the class of arbitrary such nets (with possible direct connections from input to output). The lower measure $\underline{\mu}$ is independent of dimension:

Lemma 4.1 For each k, θ, N, $\underline{\mu}(k, \theta, N) = \underline{\mu}(k, \theta, 1)$ and $\underline{\mu}^d(k, \theta, N) = \underline{\mu}^d(k, \theta, 1)$.

This justifies denoting these quantities just as $\underline{\mu}(k, \theta)$ and $\underline{\mu}^d(k, \theta)$ respectively, as we do from now on, and giving proofs only for $N = 1$.

Lemma 4.2 For any sigmoid θ, and for each k, N,

$$\mu(k+1, \theta, N) \geq \mu^d(k, \mathcal{H}, N)$$

and similarly for $\underline{\mu}$ and $\overline{\mu}$.

The main results on classification will be as follows.

Theorem 1 *For any sigmoid θ, and for each k,*

$$\begin{aligned}\underline{\mu}(k,\mathcal{H}) &= k+1\\ \underline{\mu}^d(k,\mathcal{H}) &= 2k+2\\ \underline{\mu}(k,\theta) &\geq 2k\,.\end{aligned}$$

Theorem 2 *For each k,*

$$\begin{aligned}4\left\lfloor\frac{k}{2}\right\rfloor \leq \mu(k,\mathcal{H},2) &\leq 2k+1\\ \mu^d(k,\mathcal{H},2) &\leq 4k+3\,.\end{aligned}$$

Theorem 3 *For any sigmoid θ, and for each k,*

$$\begin{aligned}2k+1 &\leq \overline{\mu}(k,\mathcal{H},2)\\ 4k+3 &\leq \overline{\mu}^d(k,\mathcal{H},2)\\ 4k-1 &\leq \overline{\mu}(k,\theta,2)\,.\end{aligned}$$

These results are proved in (Sontag, 1990a). The first inequality in Theorem 2 follows from the results in (Baum, 1988), who in fact established a lower bound of $2N\lfloor\frac{k}{2}\rfloor$ for $\mu(k,\mathcal{H},N)$ (and hence for $\overline{\mu}$ too), for every N, not just $N=2$ as in the Theorem above. We conjecture, but have as yet been unable to prove, that direct connections or sigmoids should also improve these bounds by at least a factor of 2, just as in the two-dimensional case and in the worst-case analysis. Because of Lemma 4.2, the last statements in Theorems 1 and 3 are consequences of the previous two.

5 SOME PARTICULAR ACTIVATION FUNCTIONS

Consider the last inequality in Theorem 1. For arbitrary sigmoids, this is far too conservative, as the number $\underline{\mu}$ can be improved considerably from $2k$, even made infinite (see below). We conjecture that for the important practical case $\theta(x)=\sigma(x)$ it is close to optimal, but the only upper bounds that we have are still too high. For the piecewise linear function π, at least, one has equality:

Lemma 5.1 $\underline{\mu}(k,\pi)=2k$.

It is worth remarking that there are sigmoids θ, as differentiable as wanted, even real-analytic, where all classification measures are infinite. Of course, the function θ is so complicated that there is no reasonably "finite" implementation for it. This remark is only of theoretical interest, to indicate that, unless further restrictions are made on (S1)-(S2), much better bounds can be obtained. (If only μ and $\overline{\mu}$ are desired to be infinite, one may also take the simpler example $\theta(x)=\sin(x)$. Note that for any l rationally independent real numbers x_i, the vectors of the form $(\sin(\gamma_1 x_1),\ldots,\sin(\gamma_l x_l))$, with the γ_i's real, form a dense subset of $[-1,1]^l$, so all dichotomies on $\{x_1,\ldots,x_l\}$ can be implemented with $(1,\sin)$-nets.)

Lemma 5.2 There is some sigmoid θ, which can be taken to be an analytic function, so that $\underline{\mu}(1,\theta)=\infty$.

6 INTERPOLATION

We now consider the following approximate interpolation problem. Assume given a sequence of k (distinct) points $x_1, \ldots, x_k$ in R^N, any $\varepsilon > 0$, and any sequence of real numbers $y_1, \ldots, y_k$, as well as some class $\mathcal{F}$ of functions from $\mathbb{R}^N$ to $\mathbb{R}$. We ask if there exists some

$$f \in \mathcal{F} \text{ so that } |f(x_i) - y_i| < \varepsilon \text{ for each } i\,. \tag{3}$$

Let $\underline{\lambda}(\mathcal{F})$ be the largest integer $k \geq 1$, possibly infinite, so that for every set of data as above (3) can be solved. Note that, obviously, $\underline{\lambda}(\mathcal{F}) \leq \underline{\mu}(\mathcal{F})$. Just as in Lemma 4.1, $\underline{\lambda}$ is independent of the dimension N when applied to nets. Thus we let $\underline{\lambda}^d(k, \theta)$ and $\underline{\lambda}(k, \theta)$ be respectively the values of $\underline{\lambda}(\mathcal{F})$ when applied to (k, θ)-nets with or without direct connections.

We now summarize properties of $\underline{\lambda}$. The next result —see (Sontag,1991), as well as the full version of this paper, for a proof— should be compared with Theorem 1. The main difference is in the second equality. Note that one can prove $\underline{\lambda}(k, \theta) \geq \underline{\lambda}^d(k-1, \mathcal{H})$, in complete analogy with the case of $\underline{\mu}$, but this is not sufficient anymore to be able to derive the last inequality in the Theorem from the second equality.

Theorem 4 *For any continuous sigmoid θ, and for each k,*

$$\begin{aligned} \underline{\lambda}(k, \mathcal{H}) &= k+1 \\ \underline{\lambda}^d(k, \mathcal{H}) &= k+2 \\ \underline{\lambda}(k, \theta) &\geq 2k-1\,. \end{aligned}$$

Remark 6.1 Thus we can approximately interpolate any $2k-1$ points using k sigmoidal neurons. It is not hard to prove as a corollary that, for the standard sigmoid, this approximate interpolation property holds in the following stronger sense: for an open dense set of $2k-1$ points, one can achieve an open dense set of values; the proof involves looking first at points with rational coordinates, and using that on such points one is dealing basically with rational functions (after a diffeomorphism), plus some theory of semialgebraic sets. We conjecture that one should be able to interpolate at $2k$ points. Note that for $k = 2$ this is easy to achieve: just choose the slope d so that some $z_i - z_{i+1}$ becomes zero and the z_i are allowed to be nonincreasing or nondecreasing. The same proof, changing the signs if necessary, gives the wanted net. For some examples, it is quite easy to get $2k$ points. For instance, $\underline{\lambda}(k, \pi) = 2k$ for the piecewise linear sigmoid π. □

7 FURTHER REMARKS

The main conclusion from Theorem 1 is that sigmoids at least double recognition power for arbitrary sets. It may be the case that $\overline{\mu}(k, \sigma, N)/\overline{\mu}(k, \mathcal{H}, N) \approx 2$ for all N; this is true for $N = 1$ and is strongly suggested by Theorem 3 (the first bound appears to be quite tight). Unfortunately the proof of this theorem is based on a result from (Asano et. al., 1990) regarding arrangements of points in the plane, a fact which does not generalize to dimension three or higher.

One may also compare the power of nets with and without connections, or threshold vs sigmoidal processors, on Boolean problems. For instance, it is a trivial consequence from the given results that parity on n bits can be computed with $\lceil \frac{n+1}{2} \rceil$

hidden sigmoidal units and no direct connections, though requiring (apparently, though this is an open problem) n thresholds. In addition, for some families of Boolean functions, the gap between sigmoidal nets and threshols nets may be infinitely large (Sontag, 1990a). See (Sontag, 1990b) for representation properties of *two*-hidden-layer nets

Acknowledgements

This work was supported in part by Siemens Corporate Research, and in part by the CAIP Center, Rutgers University.

References

Arai, M., "Mapping abilities of three-layer neural networks," *Proc. IJCNN Int.Joint Conf.on Neural Networks, Washington, June 18-22, 1989*, IEEE Publications, 1989, pp. I-419/424.

Asano,T., J. Hershberger, J. Pach, E.D. Sontag, D. Souivaine, and S. Suri, "Separating Bi-Chromatic Points by Parallel Lines," *Proceedings of the Second Canadian Conference on Computational Geometry*, Ottawa, Canada, 1990, p. 46-49.

Baum, E.B., "On the capabilities of multilayer perceptrons," *J.Complexity* **4**(1988): 193-215.

Chester, D., "Why two hidden layers and better than one," *Proc. Int. Joint Conf. on Neural Networks*, Washington, DC, Jan. 1990, IEEE Publications, 1990, p. I.265-268.

Cybenko, G., "Approximation by superpositions of a sigmoidal function," *Math. Control, Signals, and Systems* **2**(1989): 303-314.

Funahashi, K., "On the approximate realization of continuous mappings by neural networks," *Proc. Int. Joint Conf. on Neural Networks*, IEEE Publications, 1988, p. I.641-648.

Hornik, K.M., M. Stinchcombe, and H. White, "Multilayer feedforward networks are universal approximators," *Neural Networks* **2**(1989): 359-366.

Sontag, E.D., "Sigmoids distinguish better than Heavisides," *Neural Computation* **1**(1989): 470-472.

Sontag, E.D., "On the recognition capabilities of feedforward nets," Report SYCON-90-03, *Rutgers Center for Systems and Control*, April 1990.

Sontag, E.D., "Feedback Stabilization Using Two-Hidden-Layer Nets," Report SYCON-90-11, *Rutgers Center for Systems and Control*, October 1990.

Sontag, E.D., "Capabilities and training of feedforward nets," in *Theory and Applications of Neural Networks* (R. Mammone and J. Zeevi, eds.), Academic Press, NY, 1991, to appear.

Sontag, E.D., and H.J. Sussmann, "Backpropagation can give rise to spurious local minima even for networks without hidden layers," *Complex Systems* **3**(1989): 91-106.

Sontag, E.D., and H.J. Sussmann, "Backpropagation separates where perceptrons do," *Neural Networks*(1991), to appear.

ε-Entropy and the Complexity of Feedforward Neural Networks

Robert C. Williamson
Department of Systems Engineering
Research School of Physical Sciences and Engineering
Australian National University
GPO Box 4, Canberra, 2601, Australia

Abstract

We develop a new feedforward neural network representation of Lipschitz functions from $[0,\rho]^n$ into $[0,1]$ based on the level sets of the function. We show that

$$\frac{n\rho L}{2\varepsilon_r} + \frac{1}{\sqrt{2}\varepsilon_r} + \left(1 + \frac{n}{\sqrt{2}}\right)\left(\frac{\rho L}{4\varepsilon_r}\right)^n$$

is an upper bound on the number of nodes needed to represent f to within uniform error ε_r, where L is the Lipschitz constant. We also show that the number of bits needed to represent the weights in the network in order to achieve this approximation is given by

$$O\left(\frac{n^2\rho L}{\sqrt{2}\,4^n\varepsilon_r}\left(\frac{\rho L}{\varepsilon_r}\right)^n\right).$$

We compare this bound with the ε-entropy of the functional class under consideration.

1 INTRODUCTION

We are concerned with the problem of the number of nodes needed in a feedforward neural network in order to represent a function to within a specified accuracy. All results to date (e.g. [7, 10, 15]) have been in the form of existence theorems, stating that there does exist a neural network which achieves a certain accuracy of representation, but no indication is given of the number of nodes necessary in order to achieve this. The two techniques we use are the notion of ε-entropy (also known

Table 1: Hierarchy of theoretical problems to be solved.

ABSTRACT

1. Determination of the general approximation properties of feedforward neural networks. (Non-constructive results of the form mentioned above [15].)
2. Explicit constructive approximation theorems for feedforward neural networks, indicating the number (or bounds on the number) of nodes needed to approximate a function from a given class to within a given accuracy. (This is the subject of the present paper. We are unaware of any other work along these lines apart from [6].)
3. Learning in general. That is, results on learning that are not dependent on the particular representation chosen. The exciting new results using the Vapnik-Chervonenkis dimension [4, 9] fit into this category, as do studies on the use of Shortest Description Length principles [2].
4. Specific results on capabilities of learning in a given architecture [11].
5. Specific algorithms for learning in a specific architecture [14].

CONCRETE

as metric entropy) originally introduced by Kolmogorov [16] and a representation of a function in terms of its level sets, which was used by Arnold [1]. The place of the current paper with respect to other works in the literature can be judged from table 1.

We study the question of representing a function f in the class $F_{L,C}^{(\rho_1,\ldots,\rho_n),n}$, which is the space of real valued functions defined on the n-dimensional closed interval $\times_{i=1}^{n}[0,\rho_i]$ with a Lipschitz constant L and bounded in absolute value by C. If $\rho_i = \rho$ for $i = 1,\ldots,n$, we denote the space $F_{L,C}^{\rho,n}$. The error measure we use is the uniform or sup metric:

$$\varepsilon = \sup_{x\in[0,\rho]^n} |\tilde{f}(x) - f(x)|, \tag{1}$$

where $\tilde{f}$ is the approximation of f.

2 ε-ENTROPY OF FUNCTIONAL CLASSES

The ε-entropy $\mathcal{H}_\varepsilon$ gives an indication of the number of bits required to represent with accuracy ε an *arbitrary* function f in some functional class. It is defined as the logarithm to base 2 of the number of elements in the smallest ε-cover of the functional class. Kolmogorov [16] has proved that

$$\mathcal{H}_\varepsilon\left(F_{L,C}^{\rho,n}\right) = B(n)\left(\frac{\rho L}{\varepsilon}\right)^n \tag{2}$$

where $B(n)$ is a constant which depends only on n. We use this result as a yardstick for our neural network representation. A more powerful result is [18, p.86]:

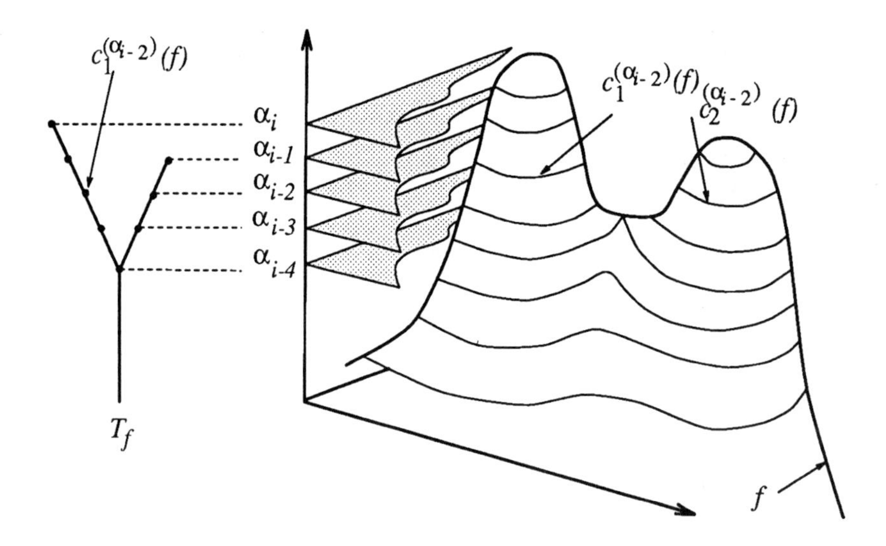

Figure 1: Illustration of some level sets of a function on $\mathbb{R}^2$.

Theorem 1 *Let p be a non-negative integer and let $\alpha \in (0,1]$. Set $s = p + \alpha$. Let $F^{\rho,n}_{s,L,C(0)}$ denote the space of real functions f defined on $[0,\rho]^n$ all of whose partial derivatives of order p satisfy a Lipschitz condition with constant L and index α, and are such that*

$$\left|\frac{\partial^{k_1+k_2+\cdots+k_n} f(0)}{\partial x_1^{k_1} \partial x_2^{k_2} \cdots \partial x_n^{k_n}}\right| \leq C \qquad for \quad \sum_{i=1}^{n} k_i \leq p. \tag{3}$$

Then for sufficiently small ε,

$$A(s,n)\rho^n \left(\frac{L}{\varepsilon}\right)^{\frac{n}{s}} \leq \mathcal{H}_\varepsilon\left(F^{\rho,n}_{s,L,C(0)}\right) \leq B(s,n)\rho^n \left(\frac{L}{\varepsilon}\right)^{\frac{n}{s}}, \tag{4}$$

where $A(s,n)$ and $B(s,n)$ are positive constants depending only on s and n.

We discuss the implication of this below.

3 A NEURAL NETWORK REPRESENTATION BASED ON LEVEL SETS

We develop a new neural network architecture for representing functions from $[0,\rho]^n$ onto $[0,1]$ (the restriction of the range to $[0,1]$ is just a convenience and can be easily dropped). The basic idea is to represent approximations $\tilde{f}$ of the function f in terms of the level sets of f (see figure 1). Then neural networks are used to approximate the *above sets* $\bar{l}_\alpha(f)$ of f, where $\bar{l}_\alpha(f) \triangleq \{x\colon f(x) \geq \alpha\} = \bigcup_{\beta \geq \alpha} l_\beta(f)$ and $l_\alpha(f)$ is the αth level set: $l_\alpha(f) \triangleq \{x\colon f(x) = \alpha\}$. The approximations $\tilde{l}_\alpha(f)$ can be implemented using three layer neural nets with threshold logic neurons. These approximations are of the form

$$\tilde{l}_{\alpha_i}(f) = \overbrace{\bigcup_{m=1}^{C_{\alpha_i}} \bigcup_{\lambda_m=1}^{\Lambda_m} \underbrace{\bigcap_{j=1}^{n} \left[S(h_{U_j,\theta_j^{\lambda_m}}) \cap S(h_{-U_j,-(\theta_j^{\lambda_m}+\psi_j^{\lambda_m})}) \right]}_{n\text{-rectangle of dimensions } \psi_1^{\lambda_m} \times \cdots \times \psi_n^{\lambda_m}}}^{\text{Isothetic approximation to the } m\text{th component of } \tilde{l}_{\alpha_i}(f).}, \qquad (5)$$

where $\psi_j^{\lambda_m}$ is the "width" in the jth dimension of the λ_mth rectangular *part* of the mth *component* (disjoint connected subset) $\tilde{c}_m^{(\alpha_i)}$ of the ith approximate above-set $\tilde{l}_{\alpha_i}$, C_{α_i} is the number of components of the above-set $\tilde{l}_{\alpha_i}(f)$, Λ_m is the number of *convex* n-rectangles (*parts*) that are required to form an ε_l-cover for $c_m^{(\alpha_i)}(f)$, $U_j \triangleq (u_j^{(1)}, \ldots, u_j^{(n)})$, $u_j^{(m)} = \delta_{jm}$, $S(h_{w,\theta})$ is the n-half-space defined by the hyperplane $h_{w,\theta}$:

$$S(h_{w,\theta}) = \{x: h_{w,\theta(x)} \geq 0\}, \qquad (6)$$

where $h_{w,\theta}(x) = wx - \theta$ and $w = (w_1, \ldots, w_n)$.

The function f is then approximated by

$$\tilde{f}^{N\text{-uas}}(x) \triangleq \frac{1}{2N} + \frac{1}{N} \sum_{i=1}^{N} \mathbf{1}_{\tilde{l}_{\alpha_i}(f)}(x), \qquad (7)$$

where $\alpha_i = \frac{i-1}{N}$, $i = 1, \ldots, N$ and $\mathbf{1}_S$ is the indicator function of a set S. The approximation $\tilde{f}^{N\text{-uas}}(x)$ is then further approximated by implementing (5) using N 3-layer neural nets in parallel:

$$\tilde{f}^{\text{NN}}(x) = \frac{1}{2N} + \underbrace{\sum_{i=1}^{N} s_\alpha}_{\text{last}} \underbrace{\bigvee_{m=1}^{\nu_2^{(i)}}}_{\text{third}} \underbrace{\bigwedge_{k_m=1}^{K_m^{(i)}}}_{\text{second}} \underbrace{\text{sgn}\left(\sum_{q=1}^{n} w_{k_m,q}^{(i)} x_q - \theta_{k_m}^{(i)} \right)}_{\text{first}} \qquad x \in \times_{i=1}^{n} [0, \rho_i], \quad (8)$$

where $x = (x_1, \ldots, x_n)^T$, $s_\alpha = \frac{1}{N}$ and $\nu_2^{(i)}$ is the number of nodes in the second layer. The last layer combines the above-sets in the manner of (7). The general architecture of the network is shown in figure 2.

4 NUMBER OF BITS NEEDED TO REPRESENT THE WEIGHTS OF THE NETWORK

The two main results of this paper are bounds on the number of nodes needed in such a neural network in order to represent $f \in F_{L,C}^{\rho,n}$ with uniform error ε_r, and bounds on the number of bits needed to represent the weights in such an approximation.

Theorem 2 *The number of nodes needed in a neural network of the above architecture in order to represent any $f \in F_{L,C}^{\rho,n}$ to within ε_r in the sup-metric is given by*

$$\frac{n\rho L}{2\varepsilon_r} + \frac{1}{\sqrt{2}\varepsilon_r} + \left(1 + \frac{n}{\sqrt{2}}\right) \left(\frac{\rho L}{4\varepsilon_r}\right)^n. \qquad (9)$$

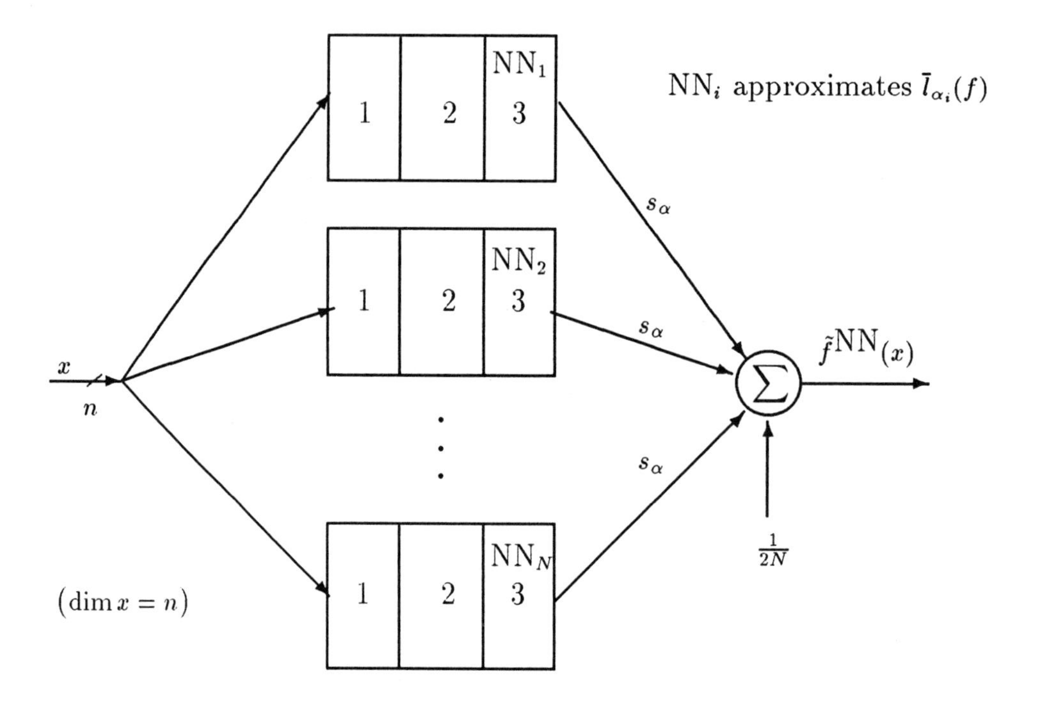

Figure 2: The Neural Network architecture we adopt.

This theorem is proved in a straight-forward manner by taking account of all the errors incurred in the approximation of a worst-case function in $F^{\rho,n}_{L,C}$.

Since comparing the number of nodes alone is inadequate for comparing the complexity of neural nets (because the nodes themselves could implement quite complex functions) we have also calculated the number of bits needed to represent all of the weights (including zero weights which denote no connection) in order to achieve an ε_r-approximation:[1]

Theorem 3 *The number of bits needed to specify the weights in a neural network with the above architecture in order to represent an arbitrary function $f \in F^{\rho,n}_{L,C}$ with accuracy ε_r in the sup-metric is bounded above by*

$$O\left(\frac{n^2 \rho L}{\sqrt{2}\, 4^n \varepsilon_r}\left(\frac{\rho L}{\varepsilon_r}\right)^n\right). \tag{10}$$

Equation 10 can be compared with (2) to see that the neural net representation is close to optimal. It is suboptimal by a factor of $O(\frac{\rho L}{\varepsilon})$. The $\frac{n^2}{\sqrt{2}\,4^n}$ term is considered subsumed into the $B(n)$ term in (2).

[1]The idea of using the number of bits as a measure of network complexity has also recently been adopted in [5].

5 FURTHER WORK

Theorem 3 shows that the complexity of representing an arbitrary $f \in F_{L,C}^{\rho,n}$ is exponential in n. This is not so much a limitation of the neural network as an indication that our problem is too hard. Theorem 1 shows that if smoothness constraints are imposed, then the complexity can be considerably reduced. It is an open problem to determine whether the construction of the network presented in this paper can be extended to make good use of smoothness constraints.

Of course the most important question is whether functions can be *learned* using neural networks. Apropos of this is Stone's result on rates of convergence in non-parametric regression [17]. Although we do not have space to give details here, suffice it say that he shows that the gains suggested by theorem 1 by imposing smoothness constraints in the representation problem, are also achievable in the learning problem. A more general statement of this type of result, making explicit the connexion with ε-entropy is given by Yatracos [19]:

Theorem 4 *Let M be a L_1-totally bounded set of measures on a probability space. Let the metric defined on the space be the L_1-distance between measures. Then there exists a uniformly consistent estimator $\hat{\theta}_i$ for some parameter θ from a possibly infinite dimensional family of measures $\Theta \subset M$ whose rate of convergence in i asymptotically satisfies the equation*

$$a_i = \left[\frac{\mathcal{H}_{a_i}(\Theta)}{i}\right]^{1/2} \tag{11}$$

where $\mathcal{H}_\varepsilon(\Theta)$ is the ε-entropy of Θ.

Similar results have been discussed by Ben-David *et al.* [3] (who have made use of Dudley's (loose) relationships between ε-entropy and Vapnik-Chervonenkis dimension [8]) and others [12, 13]. There remain many open problems in this field. One of the main difficulties however is the calculation of $\mathcal{H}_\varepsilon$ for non-trivial function classes. One of the most significant results would be a complete and tight determination of the ε-entropy for a feedforward neural network.

Acknowledgements

This work was supported in part by a grant from ATERB. I thank Andrew Paice for many useful discussions.

References

[1] V. I. Arnold, Representation of Continuous Functions of Three Variables by the Superposition of Continuous Functions of Two Variables, *Matematicheshii Sbornik (N.S.)*, **48** (1959), pp. 3–74, Translation in *American Mathematical Society Translations Series 2*, **28** (1959) pp. 61–147.

[2] A. R. Barron, Statistical Properties of Artificial Neural Networks, in *Proceedings of the 28th Conference on Decision and Control*, 1989, pp. 280–285.

[3] S. Ben-David, A. Itai and E. Kushilevitz, Learning by Distances, in *Proceedings of the Third Annual Workshop on Computational Learning Theory*, M. Fulk and J. Case, eds., Morgan Kaufmann, San Mateo, 1990, pp. 232–245.

[4] A. Blumer, A. Ehrenfeucht, D. Haussler and M. K. Warmuth, Learnability and the Vapnik-Chervonenkis Dimension, *Journal of the Association for Computing Machinery*, **36** (1989), pp. 929–965.

[5] J. Bruck and J. W. Goodman, On the Power of Neural Networks for Solving Hard Problems, *Journal of Complexity*, **6** (1990), pp. 129–135.

[6] S. M. Carroll and B. W. Dickinson, Construction of Neural Nets using the Radon Transform, in *Proceedings of the International Joint Conference on Neural Networks*, 1989, pp. 607–611, (Volume I).

[7] G. Cybenko, Approximation by Superpositions of a Sigmoidal Function, *Mathematics of Control, Signals, and Systems*, **2** (1989), pp. 303–314.

[8] R. M. Dudley, A Course on Empirical Processes, in *École d'Été de Probabilités de Saint-Flour XII–1982*, R. M. Dudley, H. Kunitay and F. Ledrappier, eds., Springer-Verlag, Berlin, 1984, pp. 1–142, Lecture Notes in Mathematics **1097**.

[9] A. Ehrenfeucht, D. Haussler, M. Kearns and L. Valiant, A General Lower Bound on the Number of Examples Needed for Learning, *Information and Computation*, **82** (1989), pp. 247–261.

[10] K. -I. Funahashi, On the Approximate Realization of Continuous Mappings by Neural Networks, *Neural Networks*, **2** (1989), pp. 183–192.

[11] S. I. Gallant, A Connectionist Learning Algorithm with Provable Generalization and Scaling Bounds, *Neural Networks*, **3** (1990), pp. 191–201.

[12] S. van de Geer, A New Approach to Least-Squares Estimation with Applications, *The Annals of Statistics*, **15** (1987), pp. 587–602.

[13] R. Hasminskii and I. Ibragimov, On Density Estimation in the View of Kolmogorov's Ideas in Approximation Theory, *The Annals of Statistics*, **18** (1990), pp. 999–1010.

[14] R. Hecht-Nielsen, Theory of the Backpropagation Neural Network, in *Proceedings of the International Joint Conference on Neural Networks*, 1989, pp. 593–605, Volume 1.

[15] K. Hornik, M. Stinchcombe and H. White, Multilayer Feedforward Networks are Universal Approximators, *Neural Networks*, **2** (1989), pp. 359–366.

[16] A. N. Kolmogorov and V. M. Tihomirov, ε-Entropy and ε-Capacity of Sets in Functional Spaces, *Uspehi Mat. (N.S.)*, **14** (1959), pp. 3–86, Translation in *American Mathematical Society Translations, Series 2*, **17** (1961) pp. 277–364.

[17] C. J. Stone, Optimal Global Rates of Convergence for Nonparametric Regression, *The Annals of Statistics*, **10** (1982), pp. 1040–1053.

[18] A. G. Vitushkin, *Theory of the Transmission and Processing of Information*, Pergamon Press, Oxford, 1961, Originally published as *Otsenka slozhnosti zadachi tabulirovaniya* (Estimation of the Complexity of the Tabulation Problem), Fizmatgiz, Moscow, 1959.

[19] Y. G. Yatracos, Rates of Convergence of Minimum Distance Estimators and Kolmogorov's Entropy, *The Annals of Statistics*, **13** (1985), pp. 768–774.

On The Circuit Complexity of Neural Networks

V. P. Roychowdhury
Information Systems Laboratory
Stanford University
Stanford, CA, 94305

K. Y. Siu
Information Systems Laboratory
Stanford University
Stanford, CA, 94305

A. Orlitsky
AT&T Bell Laboratories
600 Mountain Avenue
Murray Hill, NJ, 07974

T. Kailath
Information Systems Laboratory
Stanford University
Stanford, CA, 94305

Abstract

We introduce a geometric approach for investigating the power of threshold circuits. Viewing n-variable boolean functions as vectors in $\mathcal{R}^{2^n}$, we invoke tools from linear algebra and linear programming to derive new results on the realizability of boolean functions using threshold gates.

Using this approach, one can obtain: (1) upper-bounds on the number of spurious memories in Hopfield networks, and on the number of functions implementable by a depth-d threshold circuit; (2) a lower bound on the number of orthogonal input functions required to implement a threshold function; (3) a necessary condition for an arbitrary set of input functions to implement a threshold function; (4) a lower bound on the error introduced in approximating boolean functions using sparse polynomials; (5) a limit on the effectiveness of the only known lower-bound technique (based on computing correlations among boolean functions) for the depth of threshold circuits implementing boolean functions, and (6) a constructive proof that every boolean function f of n input variables is a threshold function of polynomially many input functions, none of which is significantly correlated with f. Some of these results lead to generalizations of key results concerning threshold circuit complexity, particularly those that are based on the so-called spectral or Harmonic analysis approach. Moreover, our geometric approach yields simple proofs, based on elementary results from linear algebra, for many of these earlier results.

1 Introduction

An S-input threshold gate is characterized by S real weights $w_1, \ldots, w_S$. It takes S inputs: $x_1, \ldots, x_S$, each either $+1$ or -1, and outputs $+1$ if the linear combination $\sum_{i=1}^{S} w_i x_i$ is positive and -1 if the linear combination is negative. Threshold gates were recently used to implement several functions of practical interest (including: Parity, Addition, Multiplication, Division, and Comparison) with fewer gates and reduced depth than conventional circuits using AND, OR, and NOT gates [12, 4, 11].

This success has led to a considerable amount of research on the power of threshold circuits [1, 10, 9, 11, 3, 13]. However, even simple questions remain unanswered. It is not known, for example, whether there is a function that can be computed by a depth-3 threshold circuit with polynomially many gates but cannot be computed by any depth-2 circuit with polynomially many threshold gates.

Geometric approaches have proven useful for analyzing threshold gates. An S-input threshold gate corresponds to a hyperplane in $\mathcal{R}^S$. This has been used for example to count the number of boolean functions computable by a single threshold gate [6], and also to determine functions that cannot be implemented by a single threshold gate. However, threshold circuits of depth two or more do not carry a simple geometric interpretation in $\mathcal{R}^S$. The inputs to gates in the second level are themselves threshold functions, hence the linear combination computed at the second level is a non-linear function of the inputs. Lacking a geometric view, researchers [5, 3] have used indirect approaches, applying harmonic-analysis techniques to analyze threshold gates. These techniques, apart from their complexity, restricted the input functions of the gates to be of very special types: input variables or parities of the input variables, thus not applying even to depth-two circuits.

In this paper, we describe a simple geometric relation between the output function of a threshold gate and its set of input functions. This applies to arbitrary sets of input functions. Using this relation, we can prove the following results: (1) upper bounds on (a) the number of threshold functions of any set of input functions, (b) the number of spurious memories in a Hopfield network, and (c) the number of functions implementable by threshold circuits of depth d; (2) a lower bound on the number of orthogonal input functions required to implement a threshold function; (3) a quantifiable necessary condition for a set of functions to implement a threshold function; (4) a lower bound on the error in approximating boolean functions using sparse polynomials; (5) a limit on the effectiveness of the correlation method used in [7] to prove that a certain function cannot be implemented by depth two circuits with polynomially many gates and polynomially bounded weights; (6) a proof that every function f is a threshold function of polynomially many input functions, none of which is significantly correlated with f.

Special cases of some of these results, where the input functions to a threshold gate are restricted to the input variables, or parities of the input variables, were proven in [5, 3] using harmonic-analysis tools. Our technique shows that these tools are not needed, providing simpler proofs for more general results.

Due to space limitations, we cannot present the full details of our results. Instead, we shall introduce the basic definitions followed by a technical summary of the results; the emphasis will be on pointing out the motivation and relating our results with those in the literature. The proofs and other technical details will appear in a complete journal paper.

2 Definitions and Background

An *n-variable boolean function* is a mapping $f : \{-1,1\}^n \rightarrow \{-1,1\}$. We view f as a (column) vector in $\mathcal{R}^{2^n}$. Each of f's 2^n components is either -1 or $+1$ and represents $f(x)$ for a distinct value assignment x of the n boolean variables. We view the S weights of an S-input threshold gate as a *weight vector* $\mathbf{w} = (w_1, \cdots, w_S)^T$ in $\mathcal{R}^S$.

Let the functions $f_1, \ldots, f_S$ be the inputs of a threshold gate $\mathbf{w}$. The gate *computes* a function f (or f is the *output* of the gate) if the following vector equation holds:

$$f = sgn\left(\sum_{i=1}^{S} f_i w_i\right) \tag{1}$$

where

$$sgn(x) = \begin{cases} +1 & \text{if } x > 0, \\ -1 & \text{if } x < 0, \\ \text{undefined} & \text{if } x = 0. \end{cases}$$

Note that this definition requires that *all components of* $\sum_{i=1}^{S} f_i w_i$ *be nonzero*. It is convenient to write Equation (1) in a matrix form:

$$f = sgn(Y\mathbf{w})$$

where the *input matrix*

$$Y = [f_1 \cdots f_S]$$

is a 2^n by S matrix whose columns are the input functions. The function f, is a *threshold function* of $f_1, \ldots, f_S$ if there exists a threshold gate (i.e., $\mathbf{w}$) with inputs $f_1, \ldots, f_S$ that computes f.

These definitions form the basis of our approach. Each function, being a ± 1 vector in $\mathcal{R}^{2^n}$, determines an *orthant* in $\mathcal{R}^{2^n}$. A function f is the output of a threshold gate whose input functions are $f_1, \ldots, f_S$ if and only if the linear combination $\sum_{i=1}^{S} f_i w_i$ defined by the gate lies inside the orthant determined by f.

Definition 1 *The correlation of two n-variable boolean functions f_1 and f_2 is:*

$$C_{f_1 f_2} = (f_1^T f_2)/2^n;$$

the two functions are uncorrelated or orthogonal *if* $C_{f_1 f_2} = 0$.

Note that $C_{f_1 f_2} = 1 - 2d_H(f_1, f_2)/2^n$, where $d_H(f_1, f_2)$ is the Hamming distance between f_1 and f_2; thus, the correlation can be interpreted as a measure of how 'close' the two functions are.

Fix the input functions $f_1, \ldots f_S$ to a threshold gate. The *correlation vector* of a function f, with the input functions is

$$C_{fY} = (Y^T f)/2^n = (C_{ff_1}\ C_{ff_2} \cdots C_{ff_S})^T.$$

Next, we define $\hat{C}$ as the maximum in magnitude among the correlation coefficients, *i.e.* , $\hat{C} = \{|C_{ff_i}| \,:\, 1 \leq i \leq S\}$.

3 Summary of Results

The correlation between two n-variable functions is a multiple of $2^{-(n-1)}$, bounded between -1 and 1, hence can assume $2^n + 1$ values. The correlation vector $C_{fY} = (C_{ff_1}, \ldots, C_{ff_1})^T$ can therefore assume at most $(2^n+1)^S$ different values. There are 2^{2^n} Boolean functions of n Boolean variables, hence many share the same correlation vector. However, the next theorem says that a threshold function of $f_1, \ldots, f_S$ does not share its correlation vector with any other function.

Uniqueness Theorem *Let f be a threshold function of $f_1, \ldots, f_S$. Then, for all $g \neq f$,*

$$C_{gY} \neq C_{fY}$$

Corollary 1 *There are at most $(2^n + 1)^S$ threshold functions of any set of S input functions.*

The special case of the Uniqueness Theorem where the functions $f_1, \ldots, f_S$ are the input variables had been proven in [5, 9]. The proof used harmonic-analysis tools such as Parseval's theorem. It relied on the mutual orthogonality of the input functions (namely, $C_{x_i,x_j} = 0$ for all $i \neq j$). Another special case where the input functions are parities of the input variables was proven in [3]. The same proof was used; see *e.g.* , pages 419-422 of [9]. Our proof shows that the harmonic-analysis tools and assumptions are not needed thereby (1) significantly simplifying the proof, and (2) showing that the functions $f_1, \ldots, f_S$ need not be orthogonal: the Uniqueness Theorem holds for all collections of functions. The more general result of the Uniqueness Theorem can be applied to obtain the following two new counting results.

Corollary 2 *The number of stable states in a Hopfield network with n elements which is programmed by the outer product rule to store s given vectors is $\leq 2^{s\log(n+1)}$.*

Corollary 3 *Let $F_n(S(n), d)$ be the number of n-variable boolean functions computed by depth-d threshold circuits with fan-in bounded by $S(n)$ (we assume $S(n) \geq n$). Then, for all $d, n \geq 1$,*

$$F_n(S(n), d) \leq 2^{O(n^2 S(n)^{d-1})} .$$

It follows easily from our geometric framework that if $C_{fY} = 0$ then f is not a threshold function of $f_1, \ldots, f_S$: every linear combination of $f_1, \ldots, f_S$ is orthogonal to f, hence cannot intersect the orthant determined by f.

Next, we consider the case where $C_{fY} \neq 0$. Define the *generalized spectrum* to be the S-dimensional vector:

$$\beta = (\beta_1, \ldots, \beta_S)^T = (Y^TY)^{-1}Y^Tf$$

(the reason for the definition and the name will be clarified soon).

Spectral-bound Theorem *If f is a linear threshold function of $f_1, \ldots, f_S$, then*

$$\sum_{i=1}^{S} |\beta_i| \geq 1, \quad \textit{hence,}$$

$$S \geq 1/\hat{\beta}, \quad \textit{where } \hat{\beta} = \max\{|\beta_i| : 1 \leq i \leq S\}$$

The Spectral-Bound theorem provides a way of *lower bounding* the number S of input functions. Specifically, if β_i is exponentially small (in n) for all $i \in \{1, \ldots, S\}$, then S must be exponentially large.

In the special case where the input functions are parities of the input variables, all input functions are orthogonal; hence $Y^T Y = 2^n I_S$ and

$$\beta = \frac{1}{2^n} Y^T f = C_{fY} \ .$$

Note that every parity function p is a basis function of the Hadamard transform, hence C_{fp} is the *spectral coefficient* corresponding to p in the transform (see [8, 2] for more details on spectral representation of boolean functions). Therefore, the generalized spectrum in this case is the real spectrum of f. In that case, the Spectral-Bound Theorem implies that $S \geq \frac{1}{\max\{|C_{ff_i}|:1\leq i\leq S\}}$. Therefore, the number of input functions needed is at least the reciprocal of the maximum magnitude among the spectral coefficients (*i.e.* , $\hat{C}$). This special case was proved in [3]. Again, their proofs used harmonic-analysis tools and assumptions that we prove are unnecessary, thereby generalizing them to arbitrary input functions. Moreover, our geometric approach considerably simplifies the exposition by presenting simple proofs based on elementary results from linear algebra.

In general, we can show that if the input functions f_i are orthogonal (*i.e.* , $C_{f_i f_j} = 0$ for $i \neq j$) or asymptotically orthogonal (*i.e.* , $\lim_{n\to\infty} C_{f_i f_j} = 0$) then the number of input functions $S \geq 1/\hat{C}$, where $\hat{C}$ is the largest (in magnitude) correlation of the output function with any of its input function.

We can also use the generalized spectrum to derive a lower bound on the *error* incurred in approximating a boolean function, f, using a set of basis functions. The lower bound can then be applied to show that the Majority function cannot be *closely approximated* by a sparse polynomial. In particular, it can be shown that if a polynomial of the input variables with only polynomially many (in n) monomials is used to approximate an n variable Majority function then the approximation error is $\Omega(1/(\log\log n)^{3/2})$. This provides a direct spectral approach for proving lower bounds on the approximation error.

The method of proving lower bounds on S in terms of the correlation coefficients C_{ff_i} of f with the possible input functions, can be termed the *method of correlations*. Hajnal et. al. [7] used a different aspect of this method[1] to prove a lower bound on the depth of a threshold circuit that computes the Inner-product-mod-2 function.

[1]They did not exactly use the correlation approach introduced in this paper, rather an equivalent framework.

Our techniques can be applied to investigate the method of correlations in more detail and prove some limits to its effectiveness. We can show that the number, S, of input functions need not be inversely proportional to the largest correlation coefficient $\hat{C}$. In particular, we give two *constructive procedures* showing that any function f is a threshold function of $O(n)$ input functions each having an exponentially small correlation with f: $|C_{ff_i}| \leq 2^{-(n-1)}$.

Construction 1 *Every boolean function f of n variables (for n even) can be expressed as a threshold function of $3n$ boolean functions: $f_1, f_2, \cdots, f_{3n}$ such that (1) $C_{ff_i} = 0$, $\forall\ 1 \leq i \leq 3n-1$, and (2) $C_{ff_{3n}} = 2^{-(n-1)}$.*

Construction 2 *Every boolean function f of n variables can be expressed as a threshold function of $2n$ boolean functions: $f_1, f_2, \cdots, f_{2n}$ such that (1) $C_{ff_i} = 0$, $\forall\ 1 \leq i \leq 2n-2$, and (2) $C_{ff_{2n-1}} = C_{ff_{2n}} = 2^{-(n-1)}$.*

The results of the above constructions are surprising. For example, in Construction 1, the output function of the threshold gate is uncorrelated with all but one of the input functions, and the only non-zero correlation is the smallest possible ($= 2^{-(n-1)}$). Note that f is not a threshold function of a set of input functions, each of which is orthogonal to f.

The above results thus provide a comprehensive understanding of the so-called method of correlations. In particular: (1) If the input functions are mutually orthogonal (or asymptotically orthogonal), then the method of correlations is effective even if exponential weights are allowed, *i.e.* , if a function is exponentially small correlated with every function from a pool of possible input functions, then one would require exponentially many inputs to implement the given function using a threshold gate; (2) If the input functions are not mutually orthogonal, then the method of correlations need not be effective, *i.e.* , one can construct examples, where the output function is correlated exponentially small with every input function, and yet it can be implemented as a threshold function of polynomially many input functions.

Furthermore, the constructive procedures can also be considered as constituting a *preliminary* answer to the following question: Given an n-variable boolean function f, are there efficient procedures for expressing it as threshold functions of polynomially many (in n) input functions? A procedure for so decomposing a given function f will be referred to as a *threshold-decomposition* procedure; moreover, a decomposition procedure can be considered as efficient if the input functions have simpler threshold implementations than f (i.e., easier to implement or require less depth/size). Constructions 1 and 2 present two such threshold-decomposition procedures. At present, the efficiency of these constructions is not clear and further work is necessary. We hope, however, that the general methodology introduced here may lead to subsequent work resulting in more efficient threshold-decomposition procedures.

4 Concluding Remarks

We have outlined a new geometric approach for investigating the properties of threshold circuits. In the process, we have developed a unified framework where many of the previous results can be derived simply as special cases, and without introducing too many seemingly difficult concepts. Moreover, we have derived several new results that quantify the input/output relationships of threshold gates, derive lower bounds on the number of input functions required to implement a given function using a threshold gate, and also analyze the limitations of a well-known lower bound technique for threshold circuit.

Acknowledgements

This work was supported in part by the Joint Services Program at Stanford University (US Army, US Navy, US Air Force) under Contract DAAL03-88-C-0011, the SDIO/IST, managed by the Army Research Office under Contract DAAL03-90-G-0108, and the Department of the Navy, NASA Headquarters, Center for Aeronautics and Space Information Sciences under Grant NAGW-419-S6.

References

[1] E. Allender. A note on the power of threshold circuits. *IEEE Symp. Found. Comp. Sci.*, 30, 1989.

[2] Y. Bradman, A. Orlitsky, and J. Hennessy. A Spectral Lower Bound Technique for the size of Decision Trees and Two level AND/OR Circuits. *IEEE Trans. on Computers*, 39, No. 2:282–287, February 1990.

[3] J. Bruck. Harmonic Analysis of Polynomial Threshold Functions. *SIAM Journal on Discrete Mathematics*, May 1990.

[4] A. K. Chandra, L. Stockmeyer, and U. Vishkin. Constant depth reducibility. *Siam J. Comput.*, 13:423–439, 1984.

[5] C. K. Chow. On The Characterization of Threshold Functions. *Proc. Symp. on Switching Circuit Theory and Logical Design*, pages 34–38, 1961.

[6] T. M. Cover. Geometrical and Statistical Properties of Systems of Linear Inequalities with Applications in Pattern Recognition. *IEEE Trans. on Electronic Computers*, EC-14:326–34, 1965.

[7] A. Hajnal, W. Maass, P. Pudlak, M. Szegedy, and G. Turan. Threshold circuits of bounded depth. *IEEE Symp. Found. Comp. Sci.*, 28:99–110, 1987.

[8] R. J. Lechner. *Harmonic analysis of switching functions.* In A. Mukhopadhyay, editor, Recent Development in Switching Theory. Academic Press, 1971.

[9] P. M. Lewis and C. L. Coates. *Threshold Logic.* John Wiley & Sons, Inc., 1967.

[10] I. Parberry and G. Schnitger. Parallel Computation with Threshold Functions. *Journal of Computer and System Sciences*, 36(3):278–302, 1988.

[11] J. Reif. On Threshold Circuits and Polynomial Computation. In *Structure in Complexity Theory Symp.*, pages 118–123, 1987.

[12] K. Y. Siu and J. Bruck. On the Power of Threshold Circuits with Small Weights. to appear in SIAM J. Discrete Math.

[13] K. Y. Siu, V. P. Roychowdhury, and T. Kailath. Computing with Almost Optimal Size Threshold Circuits. submitted to JCSS, 1990.

Part XIV

Performance Comparisons

Comparison of three classification techniques, CART, C4.5 and Multi-Layer Perceptrons

A C Tsoi
Department of Electrical Engineering
University of Queensland
St Lucia, Queensland 4072
Australia

R A Pearson
Department of Computer Science
Aust Defence Force Academy
Campbell, ACT 2600
Australia

Abstract

In this paper, after some introductory remarks into the classification problem as considered in various research communities, and some discussions concerning some of the reasons for ascertaining the performances of the three chosen algorithms, viz., CART (Classification and Regression Tree), C4.5 (one of the more recent versions of a popular induction tree technique known as ID3), and a multi-layer perceptron (MLP), it is proposed to compare the performances of these algorithms under two criteria: classification and generalisation. It is found that, in general, the MLP has better classification and generalisation accuracies compared with the other two algorithms.

1 Introduction

Classification of data into categories has been pursued by a number of research communities, viz., applied statistics, knowledge acquisition, neural networks.

In applied statistics, there are a number of techniques, e.g., clustering algorithms (see e.g., Hartigan), CART (Classification and Regression Trees, see e.g., Breiman et al). Clustering algorithms are used when the underlying data naturally fall into a number of groups, the distance among groups are measured by various metrics [Hartigan]. CART [Breiman, et al] has been very popular among applied statisticians. It assumes that the underlying data can be separated into categories, the decision boundaries can either be parallel to the axis or they can be a linear combination of these axes[1]. Under certain assumptions on the input data and their associated

[1] In CART, and C4.5, the axes are the same as the input features

output categories, its properties can be proved rigorously [Breiman et al]. The way in which CART organises its data set is quite sophisticated. For example, it grows a number of decision trees by a cross validation method.

Knowledge acquisition is an important topic in expert systems studies, see e.g., Charniak, McDermott. In this case, one is presented with a subset of input output examples drawn from the set of all possible input output examples exhibited by the underlying system. The problem is how to "distill" a set of rules describing the set of input output examples. The rules are often expressed in the form of "if statement 1, then statement 2, else statement 3". Once this set of rules is obtained, it can be used in a knowledge base for inference or for consulting purposes. It is trivial to observe that the rules can be represented in the form of a binary tree structure. In the process of building this binary tree, the knowledge acquisition system must learn about the set of input output examples. Often this problem is pursued in the machine learning community, see e.g., Michalski et al.

One of the most popular induction tree algorithms is known as ID3, or its later variants, known as C4 (see e.g., Quinlan, Utgoff). There has not been any explicit mention of the underlying assumptions on the data. However, it can be postulated that for an induction tree technqiue to work efficiently, there must be some underlying assumptions on the data set considered. By analogy with CART, it can be observed that an important underlying assumption must be that the data can be divided into categories, the decision boundaries must be parallel to the axes (i.e., it does not find a linear combination of the underlying axes to form a possible decision boundary). In contrast to CART, and similar technqiues, it does not yet have a rigorous theoretical basis. Its learning algorithm, and the way in which it organises the data set are somewhat different from CART.

Recently, there is considerable activities in the study of yet another classification method, known generally as an artificial neural network (ANN) approach (see e.g., Hecht-Nielson). In this approach, the idea is to use a system consisting of artificial neurons with very simple internal dynamics, interconnected to each other for modelling a given set of input output examples. In this approach, one selects an architecture of interconnection of artificial neurons, and a learning algorithm for finding the unknown parameters in the architecture. A particular popular ANN architecture is known as a multi-layer perceptron (MLP). In this architecture, signal travels in only one direction, i.e., there is no feedback from the output to the input. A simple version of this architecture, consisting of only input and output layers of neurons was popularised by Rosenblatt in the 1950's and 1960's. An improved version incorporating possibly more than one layer of hidden layer neurons has been used in the more recent past. A learning algorithm for finding the set of unknown parameters in this architecture while minimising a least square criterion is known as a back propagation algorithm. (see e.g., Rumelhart, McClelland).

There have been much analysis recently in understanding why a MLP can be used in classifying given input output examples, and what underlying assumptions are required (see e.g., Cybenko, Hornik et al). It can be proved that the MLP can be used to approximate any given nonlinear input output mapping given certain not too restrictive assumptions on the mapping, and the underlying input output variables.

Given that the three methods mentioned above, viz., CART, C4.5 (the latest version of the C4 Induction Tree methodology), and MLP, all enjoy popularity in their respective research communities, and that they all perform classification based on a given set of input output examples, a natural question to ask is: how do they perform as compared with one another.

There might be some objections to why a comparison among these algorithms is necessary, since each is designed to operate under some predetermined conditions. Secondly, even if it is shown that a particular algorithm performs better for a set of particular examples, there is no guarantee that the algorithm will perform better under a different set of circumstances. Thus, this may throw some doubt on the desirability of making a comparison among these algorithms.

As indicated above, each algorithm has some underlying assumptions on the construction of a data model, whether these assumptions are made explicit or not. In a practical problem, e.g., power system forecasting [Atlas et al] it is not possible to determine the underlying assumptions in the data. But on an artificially generated example, it is possible to constrain the data so that they would have the desirable characteristics. From this, it is possible to at least make some qualitative statements concerning the algorithms. These qualitative statements may guide a practitioner to watch out for possible pitfalls in applying a particular algorithm to practical problems. Hence, it is worthwhile to carry out comparison studies.

The comparison question is not new. In fact there are already a number of studies carried out to compare the performances of some of or all three algorithms mentioned[2]. For example, Atlas et al compared the performances of CART and MLP. In addition they have considered the performances of these two algorithms to a practical problem, viz., the power system forecasting. Dietterich et al compared the performances of ID3 and MLP, and have applied them to the Text to Speech mapping problem. In general, their conclusions are that the MLP is more accurate in performing generalisation on unseen examples, while the ID3 or CART is much faster in performing the classficiation task.

In this paper, we will consider the performances of all three algorithms, viz., CART, C4.5 and MLP on two criteria:

- Classification capabilities
- Generalisation capabilities

In order to ascertain how these algorithms will perform, we have chosen to study their performances using a closed set of input output examples. In this aspect, we have chosen a version of the Penzias example, first considered by Denker et al. This class of problems has been shown to require at least one hidden layer in a MLP architecture, indicating that the relationship between the input and output is non-linear. Secondly, the problem complexity depends on the number of input neurons (in Cart and C4.5, input features). Hence it is possible to test the algorithms using a progressively complex set of examples.

We have chosen to compare the algorithms under the two critieria because of the

[2]Both Atlas et al, and Diettrich et al were brought to our attention during the conference. Hence some of their conclusions were only communicated to us at that time

fact that some of them, at least, in the case of CART, were designed for classification purposes. It was not originally intended for generalisation purposes. By generalisation, we mean that the trained system is used to predict the categories of unseen examples when only the input variables are given. The predicted categories are then compared with the true categories to ascertain how well the trained system has performed.

The separate comparison is necessary because of the fact that classification and generalisation are rather different. In classification studies, the main purpose is to train a system to classify the given set of input output examples. The characteristics are: good model of the data; good accuracy in classifying the given set of examples. In generalisation, the main goal is to provide a good accuracy of prediction of output categories on the set of unseen examples. It does not matter much if the results of applying the trained data model to the training data set are less accurate.

An important point to note is that all the algorithms have a number of parameters or procedures which allow them to perform better. For example, it is possible to vary the a priori assumption on the occurrence of different output categories in CART, while to perform a similar task in C4.5 or MLP is rather more difficult. It is possible to train the MLP by ever increasing iterations until the error is small, given sufficient number of hidden layer neurons. On the other hand, in C4.5, or CART, the number of iterations is not an externally adjustable parameter.

In order to avoid pitfalls like these, as well as to avoid the criticism of favoring one algorithm over against another, the results presented here have not consciously tuned to give the best performance. For example, even though from observations, we know that the distribution of different output categories is uneven, we have not made any adjustments to the a priori probabilities in running CART. We will assume that the output categories occur with equal prior probabilities. We have not tuned the number of hidden layer neurons in the MLP, except we have taken a particular number which has been used by others. We have not tuned the learning rate, nor the momentum rate in the MLP except just a nominal default value which appears to work for other examples. We have not tuned the C4.5 nor CART apart from using the default values. Hopefully by doing this, the comparison will appear fairer.

The structure of the paper is as follows: in section 2, we will describe the classification results, while in section 3 we will present generalisation results.

2 Comparison of classification performances

Before we present the results of comparing the performances of the algorithms, we will give a brief description of the testing example used. This example is known as a clump example in Denker et al, while in Maxwell et al it is refered as the contiguity example (see [Webb, Lowe]).

There are N input features, each feature can take only the values of 0 or 1. Thus there are altogether 2^N examples. The output class of a particular input feature vector is the number of clumps involving 1's in the input feature vector. Thus, for example, if the input feature vector is 00110100, then this is in class 2 as there are two distinct clumps of 1's in the input features. Hence it is possible to generate the closed set of all input output examples given a particular value of N. For convenience, we will call this an Nth order Penzias example. In our case considered here, we have used $N = 8$, i.e., there are 256 examples in the entire set. The input features are binary equivalent of their ordinal numbers. For example, example 10 is 00001010. This allows us to denote any sample within the set more conveniently. The distribution of the output classes are as follows:

class	total number
1	37
2	126
3	84
4	9

For classification purposes, we use all 256 examples as both the training and testing data sets. The following table summarises the classificiation results.

name	# of errors	accur %
cart	96	0.625
c4.5	105	0.59
mlp1	117	0.54
mlp2	47	0.82

where mlp1 and mlp2 are the values related to the MLP when it has run for 10000 iterations and 100000 iterations respectively. We have run the MLP in the following fashion: we run it 10000 times and then in steps of 10000 iterations but at the beginning of each 10000 iterations it is run with a different initial parameter estimate. In this way, we can ensure that the MLP will not fall into a local minimum. Secondly, we can observe how the MLP accuracies will improve with increasing number of iterations. We found that in general, the MLP converges in about 20000 iterations. After that the number of iterations the results do not improve by a significant amount. In addition, becasue of the way in which we run the experiemnt the convergence would be closer to the average convergence rather than the convergence for a particular initial condition.

The parameter values used in running the experiments are as follows: In the MLP, both the learning rate and the momentum are set at 0.1. The architeture used is: 8 input neurons, 5 hidden layer neurons, and 4 output neurons. In CART, the prior probability is set to be equi-probable. The pruning is performed when the probability of the leaf node is equal 0.5. In C4.5, all the default values are used.

We have also examined the ways in which each algorithm predicts the output categories. We found that none of the algorithms ever predict an output category of 4. This is interesting in that the output category 4 occurs only 9 times out of a total possible of 256. Thus each algorithm, even though it may or may not be able to adjust the prior probability of the output categories, has made an implicit assumption of equal prior probability. This leads to the non occurrence of prediction of category 4 as it is the least frequent occurred one.

Secondly, all algorithms have a default prediction. For example, in CART, the default is class 2, being the most frequently occurred output category in the training examples, while in the case of C4.5, the default is determined by the algorithm. On the other hand, in the cases of CART, or MLP, it is not clear how the default cases are determined.

Thirdly, the algorithms make mistaken predictions at different places. For example, for sample 1, C4.5 makes the wrong prediction of category 3 while MLP makes the wrong prediction of 2, and CART makes the correct prediction. For sample 9, both CART and C4.5 make a wrong prediction, while MLP makes the correct prediction.

3 Comparison of generalisation performances

We have used the same set of input output examples generated by an 8th order Penzias example. For testing the generalisation capabilties, We have used the first 200 examples as the training vector set, and the rest of the vectors in the testing data set.

The results are summarised in the following table:

	training		testing	
name	# of errors	accur %	# of errors	accur %
cart	84	0.58	34	39.3
c4.5	97	51.5	25	55.4
mlp1	100	50	28	50
mlp2	50	75	25	55.4

It is noted that the generalisation accuracy of the MLP is better than CART, and is comparable to C4.5.

We have also examined closely the mistakes made by the algorithms as well as the default predictions. In this case, the comments made in section 2 also appear to be true.

4 Conclusions

In this paper, we considered three classification algorithms, viz., CART, C4.5, and MLP. We compared their performance both in terms of classification, and generalisation on one example, an 8th order generalised Penzias example. It is found that the MLP once it is converged, in general, has a better classification and generalisation accuracies compared with CART, or C4.5. On the other hand it is also noted that the prediction errors made by each algorithm are different. This indicates that there may be a possibility of combining these algorithms in such a way that their prediction accuracies could be improved. This is presented as a challenge for future research.

References

J. Hartigan. (1974) *Clustering Algorithms.* J. Wiley, New York.

L. Breiman, J.H. Friedman, R.A. Olshen, J. Stone. (1984) *Classification and Regression Trees.* Wadsworth and Brooks, Monterey, Calif.

E. Charniak, D. McDermott. (1985) *Introduction to Artificial Intelligence.* Addision Wesley, Reading, Mass.

R. Michalski, J.G. Carbonell, T. Mitchell. (1983) *Machine Learning: An Artificial Intelligence Approach.* Tioga, Palo Alto, Calif.

J.R. Quinlan. (1983) Learning efficient classification procedures and their application to Chess End Games. In R. Michalski et al (ed.), *Machine Learning: An Artificial Intelligence Approach.* Tioga, Palo Alto, Calif.

J. R. Quinlan. (1986) Induction of Decision Trees. *Machine Learning*, **1**, 81-106.

P. Utgoff. Incremental Induction of Decision Trees. *Machine Learning*, **4**, 161-186.

R. Hecht-Nielson. (1990) *Neurocomputing* Addison Wesley, New York.

F. Rosenblatt. (1962) *Principles of Neurodynamics.* Spartan Books, Washington, DC.

D. Rumelhart, J. McClelland. (1987) *Parallel Distributed Processing: Exploration in the Microstructure of Cognition* Volume 1. MIT Press: Bradford Books.

G. Cybenko. (1989) Approximation by superpositions of sigmoidal function. *Mathematics of Control, Signal, and Systems*, **2**:4.

K. Hornik, M. Stinchcombe, H. White. (1989) Multi-layer feedforward networks are universal approximators. *Neural Networks*, **2**:5, 359-366.

L. Atlas, R. Cole, Y. Muthusamy, A. Lippman, J. Connor, D. Park, M. El-Sharkawi, R. Marks II. (1990). A Performance Comparison of Trained Multilayer Perceptrons and Trained Classification Trees. *Proc IEEE*, **78**:10, 1614-1619.

T. Dietterich, H. Hild, G. Bakiri, (1990), "A Comparison of ID3 and Backpropagation for English Text-to-Speech Mapping", Preprint.

J. Denker, et al. (1987) Large automatic learning, rule extraction, and generalisation. *Complex Systems*, **3** 877-922.

T. Maxwell, L. Giles, Y.C. Lee. (1987) Generalisation in neural networks, the contiguity problem. *Proc IEEE 1st Int Conf on Neural Networks*, San Diego, Calif.

A.R. Webb, D. Lowe. (1990) The Optimised internal representation of multilayered classifier networks performs nonlinear discriminant analysis. *Neural Networks* **3**:4, 367-376.

A Comparative Study of the Practical Characteristics of Neural Network and Conventional Pattern Classifiers

Kenney Ng
BBN Systems and Technologies
Cambridge, MA 02138

Richard P. Lippmann
Lincoln Laboratory, MIT
Lexington, MA 02173-9108

Abstract

Seven different pattern classifiers were implemented on a serial computer and compared using artificial and speech recognition tasks. Two neural network (radial basis function and high order polynomial GMDH network) and five conventional classifiers (Gaussian mixture, linear tree, K nearest neighbor, KD-tree, and condensed K nearest neighbor) were evaluated. Classifiers were chosen to be representative of different approaches to pattern classification and to complement and extend those evaluated in a previous study (Lee and Lippmann, 1989). This and the previous study both demonstrate that classification error rates can be equivalent across different classifiers when they are powerful enough to form minimum error decision regions, when they are properly tuned, and when sufficient training data is available. Practical characteristics such as training time, classification time, and memory requirements, however, can differ by orders of magnitude. These results suggest that the selection of a classifier for a particular task should be guided not so much by small differences in error rate, but by practical considerations concerning memory usage, computational resources, ease of implementation, and restrictions on training and classification times.

1 INTRODUCTION

Few studies have compared practical characteristics of adaptive pattern classifiers using real data. There has frequently been an over-emphasis on back-propagation classifiers and artificial problems and a focus on classification error rate as the main performance measure. No study has compared the practical trade-offs in training time, classification time, memory requirements, and complexity provided by the many alternative classifiers that have been developed (e.g. see Lippmann 1989).

The purpose of this study was to better understand and explore practical characteristics of classifiers not included in a previous study (Lee and Lippmann, 1989; Lee 1989). Seven different neural network and conventional pattern classifiers were evaluated. These included radial basis function (RBF), high order polynomial GMDH network, Gaussian mixture, linear decision tree, K nearest neighbor (KNN), KD tree, and condensed K nearest neighbor (CKNN) classifiers. All classifiers were implemented on a serial computer (Sun 3-110 Workstation with FPA) and tested using a digit recognition task (7 digits, 22 cepstral inputs, 16 talkers, 70 training and 112 testing patterns per talker), a vowel recognition task (10 vowels, 2 formant frequency inputs, 67 talkers, 338 training and 333 testing patterns), and two artificial tasks with two input dimensions that require either a single convex or two disjoint decision regions. Tasks are as in (Lee and Lippmann, 1989) and details of experiments are described in (Ng, 1990).

2 TUNING EXPERIMENTS

Internal parameters or weights of classifiers were determined using training data. Global free parameters that provided low error rates were found experimentally using cross-validation and the training data or by using test data. Global parameters included an overall basis function width scale factor for the RBF classifier, order of nodal polynomials for the GMDH network, and number of nearest neighbors for the KNN, KD tree, and CKNN classifiers.

Experiments were also performed to match the complexity of each classifier to that of the training data. Many classifiers exhibit a characteristic divergence between training and testing error rates as a function of their complexity. Poor performance results when a classifier is too simple to model the complexity of training data and also when it is too complex and "over-fits" the training data. Cross-validation and statistical techniques were used to determine the correct size of the linear tree and GMDH classifiers where training and test set error rates diverged substantially. An information theoretic measure (Predicted Square Error) was used to limit the complexity of the GMDH classifier. This classifier was allowed to grow by adding layers and widening layers to find the number of layers and the layer width which minimized predicted square error. Nodes in the linear tree were pruned using 10-fold cross-validation and a simple statistical test to determine the minimum size tree that provides good performance. Training and test set error rates did not diverge for the RBF and Gaussian mixture classifiers. Test set performance was thus used to determine the number of Gaussian centers for these classifiers.

A new multi-scale radial basis function classifier was developed. It has multiple radial basis functions centered on each basis function center with widths that vary over 1 1/2 orders of magnitude. Multi-scale RBF classifiers provided error rates that were similar to those of more conventional RBF classifiers but eliminated the need to search for a good value of the global basis function width scale factor.

The CKNN classifier used in this study was also new. It was developed to reduce memory requirements and dependency on training data order. In the more conventional CKNN classifier, training patterns are presented sequentially and classified using a KNN rule. Patterns are stored as exemplars only if they are classified incorrectly. In the new CKNN classifier, this conventional CKNN training procedure is repeated N times with different orderings of the training patterns. All exemplar patterns stored using any ordering are combined into a new reduced set of training patterns which is further pruned by using it as training data for a final pass of conventional CKNN training. This approach typically required less memory than a KNN or a conventional CKNN classifier. Other experiments described in (Chang and Lippmann, 1990) demonstrate how genetic search algorithms can further reduce KNN classifier memory requirements.

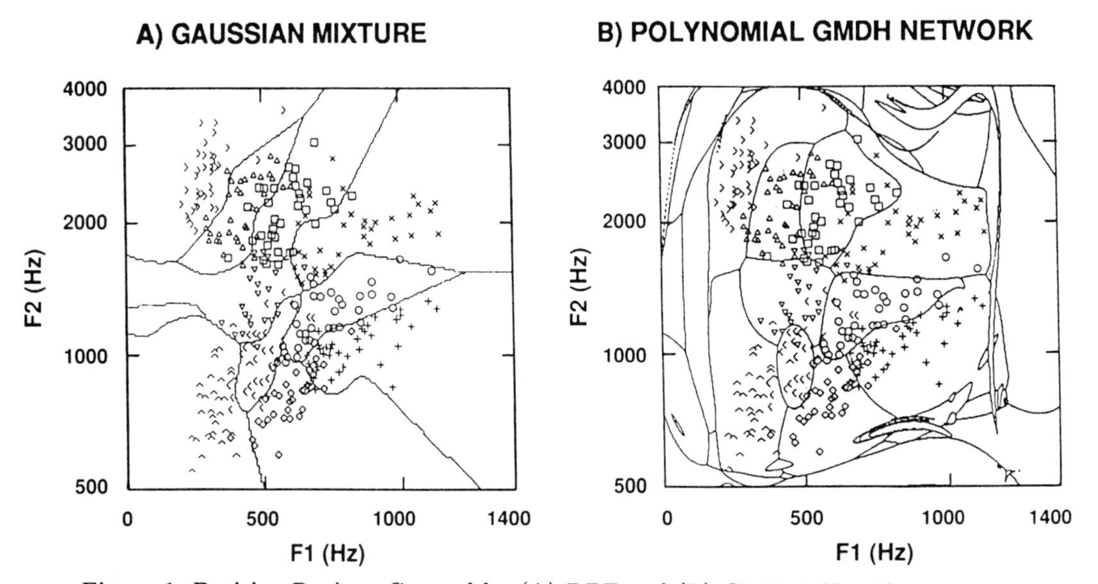

Figure 1: Decision Regions Created by (A) RBF and (B) GMDH Classifiers for the Vowel Problem.

3 DECISION REGIONS

Classifiers differ not only in their structure and training but also in how decision regions are formed. Decision regions formed by the RBF classifier for the vowel problem are shown in Figure 1A. Boundaries are smooth spline-like curves that can form arbitrarily complex regions. This improves generalization for many real problems where data for different classes form one or more roughly ellipsoidal clusters. Decision regions for the high-order polynomial (GMDH) network classifier are shown in Figure 1B. Decision region boundaries are smooth and well behaved only in regions of the input space that are densely sampled by the training data. Decision boundaries are erratic in regions where there is little training data due to the high polynomial order of the discriminant functions formed by the GMDH classifier. As a result, the GMDH classifier generalizes poorly in regions with little training data. Decision boundaries for the linear tree classifier are hyperplanes. This classifier may also generalize poorly if data is in ellipsoidal clusters.

4 ERROR RATES

Figure 2 shows the classification (test set) error rates for all classifiers on the bullseye, disjoint, vowel, and digit problems. The solid line in each plot represents the

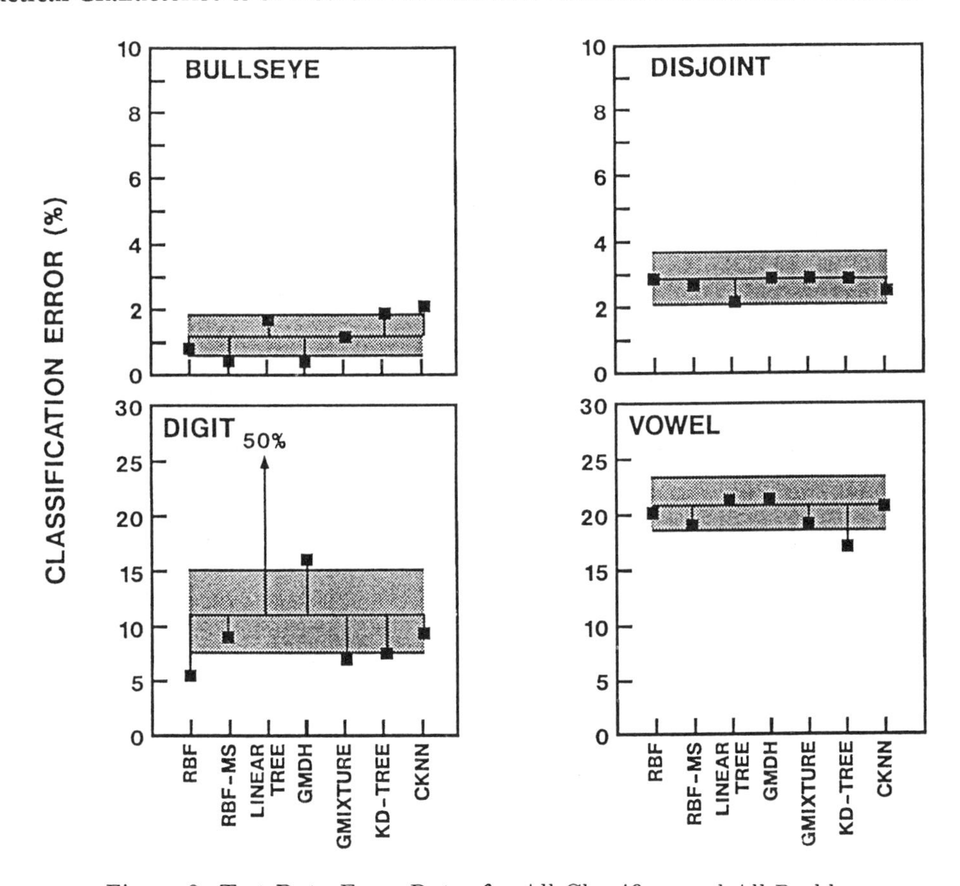

Figure 2: Test Data Error Rates for All Classifiers and All Problems.

mean test set error rate across all the classifiers for that problem. The shaded regions represent one binomial standard deviation, σ, above and below. The binomial standard deviation was calculated as $\sigma = \sqrt{\mathcal{E}(1-\mathcal{E})/N}$, where $\mathcal{E}$ is the estimated average problem test set error rate and N is the number of test patterns for each problem. The shaded region gives a rough measure of the range of expected statistical fluctuation if the error rates for different classifiers are identical. A more detailed statistical analysis of the test set error rates for classifiers was performed using McNemar's significance test. At a significance level of $\alpha = 0.01$, the error rates of the different classifiers on the bullseye, disjoint, and vowel problems do *not* differ significantly from each other.

Performance on the more difficult digit problem, however, did differ significantly across classifiers. This problem has very little training data (10 training patterns per class) and high dimensional inputs (an input dimension of 22). Some classifiers, including the RBF and Gaussian mixture classifiers, were able to achieve very low error rates on this problem and generalize well even in this high dimensional space with little training data. Other classifiers, including the multi-scale RBF, KD-tree, and CKNN classifiers, provided intermediate error rates. The GMDH network classifier and the linear tree classifier provided high error rates.

The linear tree classifier performed poorly on the digit problem because there is not enough training data to sample the input space densely enough for the training algorithm to form decision boundaries that can generalize well. The poor performance of the GMDH network classifier is due, in part, to the inability of the GMDH network classifier to extrapolate well to regions with little training data.

5 PERFORMANCE TRADE-OFFS

Although differences in the error rates of most classifiers are small, differences in practical performance characteristics are often large. For example, on the vowel problem, although both the Gaussian mixture and KD tree classifiers perform well, the Gaussian mixture classifier requires 20 times *less* classification memory than the KD tree classifier, but takes 10 times *longer* to train.

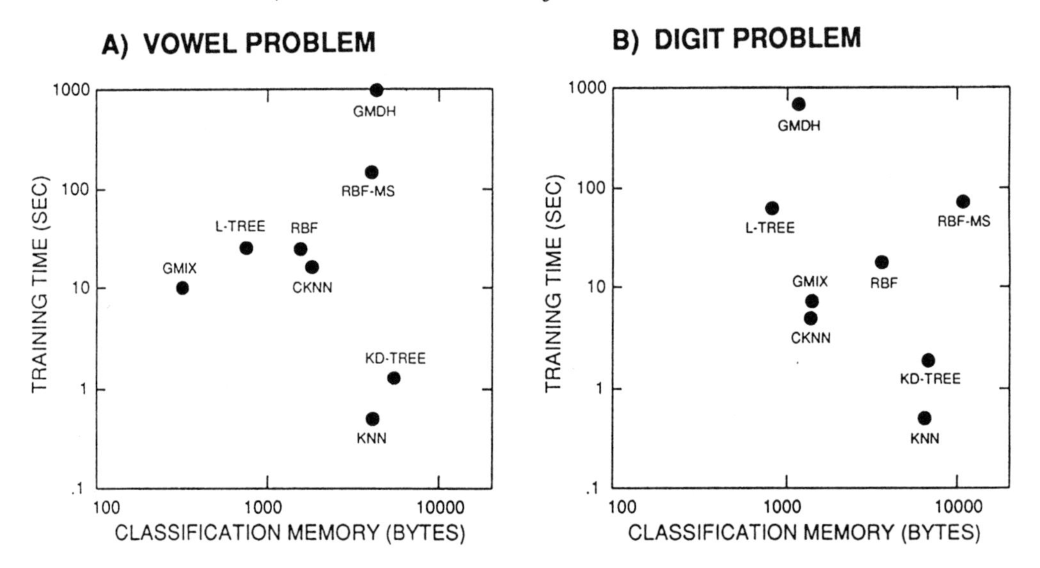

Figure 3: Training Time Versus Classification Memory Usage For All Classifiers On The (A) Vowel And (B) Digit Problems.

Figure 3 shows the relationship between training time (in CPU seconds measured on a Sun 3/110 with FPA) and classification memory usage (in bytes) for the different classifiers on the vowel and digit problems. On these problems, the KNN and KD-tree classifiers train quickly, but require large amounts of memory. The Gaussian mixture (GMIX) and linear tree (L-TREE) classifiers use little memory, but require more training time. The RBF and CKNN classifiers have intermediate memory and training time requirements. Due to the extra basis functions, the multiscale RBF (RBF-MS) classifier requires more training time and memory than the conventional RBF classifier. The GMDH classifier has intermediate memory requirements, but takes the longest to train. On average, the GMDH classifier takes 10 times longer to train than the RBF classifier, and 100 times longer than the KD tree classifier. In general, classifiers that use little memory require long training times, while those that train rapidly are not memory efficient.

Figure 4 shows the relationship between classification time (in CPU milliseconds

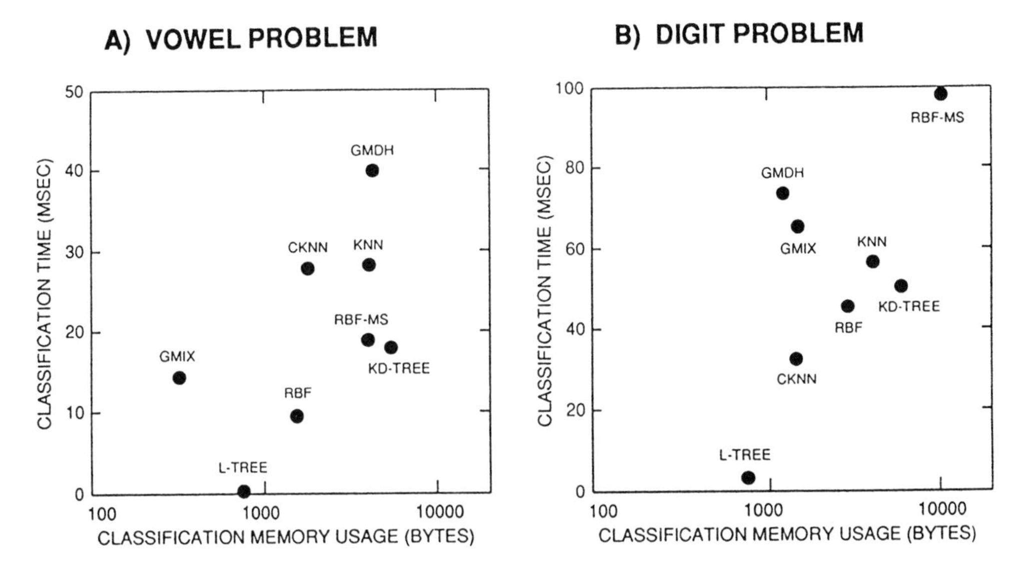

Figure 4: Classification Time Versus Classification Memory Usage For All Classifiers On The (A) Vowel And (B) Digit Problems.

for one pattern) and classification memory usage (in bytes) for the different classifiers on the vowel and digit problems. At one extreme, the linear tree classifier requires very little memory and classifies almost instantaneously. At the other, the GMDH classifier takes the longest to classify and requires a large amount of memory. Gaussian mixture and RBF classifiers are intermediate. On the vowel problem, the CKNN and the KD tree classifiers are faster than the conventional KNN classifier. On the digit problem, the CKNN classifier is faster than both the KD tree and KNN classifiers because of the greatly reduced number of stored patterns (15 out of 70). The speed up in search provided by the KD tree is greatly reduced for the digit problem due to the increase in input dimensionality. In general, the trend is for classification time to be proportional to the amount of classification memory. It is important to note, however, that trade-offs in performance characteristics depend on the particular problem and can vary for different implementations of the classifiers.

6 SUMMARY

Seven different neural network and conventional pattern classifiers were compared using artificial and speech recognition tasks. High order polynomial GMDH classifiers typically provided intermediate error rates and often required long training times and large amounts of memory. In addition, the decision regions formed did not generalize well to regions of the input space with little training data. Radial basis function classifiers generalized well in high dimensional spaces, and provided low error rates with training times that were much less than those of back-propagation classifiers (Lee and Lippmann, 1989). Gaussian mixture classifiers provided good performance when the numbers and types of mixtures were selected carefully to model class densities well. Linear tree classifiers were the most computationally efficient but performed poorly with high dimensionality inputs and when the number of training patterns was small. KD-tree classifiers reduced classification time by a factor of four over conventional KNN classifiers for low 2-input dimension problems. They provided little or no reduction in classification time for high 22-input dimension problems. Improved condensed KNN classifiers reduced memory requirements over conventional KNN classifiers by a factor of two to fifteen for all problems, without increasing the error rate significantly.

7 CONCLUSION

This and a previous study (Lee and Lippmann, 1989) explored the performance of 18 neural network, AI, and statistical pattern classifiers. Both studies demonstrated the need to carefully select and tune global parameters and the need to match classifier complexity to that of the training data using cross-validation and/or information theoretic approaches. Two new variants of existing classifiers (multi-scale RBF and improved versions of the CKNN classifier) were developed as part of this study. Classification error rates on speech problems in both studies were equivalent with most classifiers when classifiers were powerful enough to form minimum error decision regions, when sufficient training data was available, and when classifiers were carefully tuned. Practical classifier characteristics including training time, classification time, and memory usage, however, differed by orders of magnitude. These results suggest that the selection of a classifier for a particular task should be guided not so much by small differences in error rate, but by practical considerations concerning memory usage, ease of implementation, computational resources, and restrictions on training and classification times. Researchers should take time to understand the wide range of classifiers that are available and the practical tradeoffs that these classifiers provide.

Acknowledgements

This work was sponsored by the Air Force Office of Scientific Research and the Department of the Air Force.

References

Eric I. Chang and Richard P. Lippmann. Using Genetic Algorithms to Improve Pattern Classification Performance. In Lippmann, R. Moody, J., Touretzky, D., (Eds.) *Advances in Neural Information Processing Systems 3*, 1990.

Yuchun Lee. Classifiers: Adaptive modules in pattern recognition systems. Master's Thesis, Massachusetts Institute of Technology, Department of Electrical Engineering and Computer Science, Cambridge, MA, May 1989.

Yuchun Lee and R. P. Lippmann. Practical Characteristics of Neural Network and Conventional Pattern Classifiers on Artificial and Speech Problems. In D. Touretzky (Ed.) *Advances in Neural Information Processing Systems 2*, 168-177, 1989.

R. P. Lippmann. Pattern Classification Using Neural Networks. *IEEE Communications Magazine*, 27(27):47-54, 1989.

Kenney Ng. A Comparative Study of the Practical Characteristics of Neural Network and Conventional Pattern Classifiers. Master's Thesis, Massachusetts Institute of Technology, Department of Electrical Engineering and Computer Science, Cambridge, MA, May 1990.

Time Trials on Second-Order and Variable-Learning-Rate Algorithms

Richard Rohwer
Centre for Speech Technology Research
Edinburgh University
80, South Bridge
Edinburgh EH1 1HN, SCOTLAND

Abstract

The performance of seven minimization algorithms are compared on five neural network problems. These include a variable-step-size algorithm, conjugate gradient, and several methods with explicit analytic or numerical approximations to the Hessian.

1 Introduction

There are several minimization algorithms in use which in the nth iteration vary the ith coordinate x_i in the direction

$$s_i^{n+1} = r_i^n s_i^n + h_i^n \nabla_i^n \tag{1}$$

where $\nabla_i^n = \left.\frac{dE}{dx_i}\right|_{\boldsymbol{x}^n}$ is the ith component of the gradient of the error measure E at $\boldsymbol{x}^n$, $\boldsymbol{s}^0 = \boldsymbol{\nabla}^0$, and $\boldsymbol{r}^n$ and $\boldsymbol{h}^n$ are chosen differently in different algorithms. Algorithms also use various methods for choosing the step size η^n to be taken along direction $\boldsymbol{s}^n$. In this study, 7 algorithms were compared on a suite of 5 neural network problems. These algorithms are defined in table 1.

1.1 The algorithms

The algorithms investigated are Silva and Almeida's variable-step-size algorithm (Silva, 1990) which closely resembles Toolenaere's "SuperSAB" algorithm (Toole-

Table 1: The minimization methods studied.

Iteration rule:	$x_i^{n+1} = \eta_i^{n+1} s_i^{n+1}$		$s_i^{n+1} = r_i^n s_i^n + h_i^n \nabla_i^n$		
Method	r_i^n	h_i^n	η^{n+1}	other	Parameter settings
Silva/ Toolenaere	$\alpha\gamma_i^n$	$\gamma_i^n h_i^{n-1}$	$\begin{matrix} 1, & E^{n+1} < E^n \\ 0, & E^{n+1} \geq E^n \end{matrix}$	$\gamma_i^n = \begin{cases} u, & \nabla_i^n \cdot \nabla_i^{n-1} > 0 \\ 1, & \nabla_i^n \cdot \nabla_i^{n-1} = 0 \\ d, & \nabla_i^n \cdot \nabla_i^{n-1} < 0 \end{cases}$	$u = 1.2$, $d = 0.7$, $\alpha = 0.9$, $h_i^0 = 0.5$, $\beta_i^0 = 0$
Conjugate Gradient	$\frac{(\nabla^n - \nabla^{n-1}) \cdot \nabla^n}{\nabla^{n-1} \cdot \nabla^{n-1}}$	1	linesearch		
Analytic (signed)	0	$\frac{1}{B(\beta_i^n;\epsilon)}$	linesearch	$\beta_i^n = cD_i^n + (1-c)\beta_i^{n-1}$	$c = 0.2$, $\beta_i^0 = 1.0$, $\epsilon = 10^{-14}$
Analytic (abs)	0	$\frac{1}{B(\beta_i^n;\epsilon)}$	linesearch	$\beta_i^n = c\lvert D_i^n\rvert + (1-c)\beta_i^{n-1}$	$c = 0.2$, $\beta_i^0 = 1.0$, $\epsilon = 10^{-14}$
Analytic (signed, 1-step)	0	$\frac{1}{B(\beta_i^n;\epsilon)}$	$\frac{2a\lvert\nabla^n\rvert / \lvert s^{n+1}\rvert}{\sum_j \hat{D}_j^n D_j^n \hat{D}_j^n}$	$\beta_i^n = cD_i^n + (1-c)\beta_i^{n-1}$	$c = 0.2$, $\beta_i^0 = 1.0$, $a = 0.1$, $\epsilon = 10^{-14}$
Analytic (abs, 1-step)	0	$\frac{1}{B(\beta_i^n;\epsilon)}$	$\frac{2a\lvert\nabla^n\rvert / \lvert s^{n+1}\rvert}{\sum_j \hat{D}_j^n D_j^n \hat{D}_j^n}$	$\beta_i^n = c\lvert D_i^n\rvert + (1-c)\beta_i^{n-1}$	$c = 0.2$, $\beta_i^0 = 1.0$, $a = 0.1$, $\epsilon = 10^{-14}$
Max (abs) of analytic & numerical	0	$\frac{1}{B(\beta_i^n;\epsilon)}$	linesearch	$\beta_i^n = c\max\left(\lvert D_i^n\rvert, \left\lvert\frac{\nabla_i^n - \nabla_i^{n-1}}{B(s_i^n - s_i^{n-1};\epsilon)}\right\rvert\right) + (1-c)\beta_i^{n-1}$	$c = 0.2$, $\beta_i^0 = 1.0$, $a = 0.1$, $\epsilon = 10^{-14}$
Definitions:	$\nabla_i = \frac{dE}{dx_i}$	$D_i = \frac{d^2E}{dx_i^2}$	$\hat{D} = \frac{D}{\lvert D\rvert}$	$B(x,\epsilon) = \begin{cases} x & \lvert x\rvert > \epsilon \\ \epsilon & \lvert x\rvert \leq \epsilon \end{cases}$	$E^n = E(x^n)$

naere, 1990), conjugate gradient (Press, 1988), and 5 variants of an algorithm advocated by LeCun (LeCun, 1989), which employs an analytic calculation of the diagonal terms of the matrix of second derivatives. (Algorithms involving an approximation of the full Hessian, the inverse of the matrix of second derivatives, were studied by Watrous (Watrous, 1987).) In 4 of these methods the gradient is divided component-wise by a decaying average of either the second derivatives or their absolute values. Dividing by the absolute values assures that $\boldsymbol{s} \cdot \boldsymbol{\nabla} < 0$, and reflects the philosophy that directions with high curvature, be it positive or negative, are not good ones to follow because the quadratic approximation is likely to break down at short distances. In the remaining method, sketched in (Rohwer, 1990a,b), the gradient is divided componentwise by the maximum of the absolute values of an analytic and numerical calculation of the second derivitives. Again the philosopy is that curvature is to be avoided. The numerical calculation may detect evidence of nearby high curvature at a point where the analytic calculation finds low curvature.

Some algorithms conventionally use a multi-step 1-dimensional "linesearch" to determine how far to proceed in direction $\boldsymbol{s}$, whereas others take a single step according to some formula. A linesearch guarantees descent (more precisely, non-ascent), which is beneficial if local minima pose no threat. Table ?? shows the step-size methods used in this study; the decisions are rather arbitrary. The theoretical basis of the conjugate gradient method is lost if exact linesearches are not used, but it is lost anyway on any non-quadratic function. Silva and Toolenaere's use a single-step method which guarantees descent by retracting any step which does not produce ascent. The method is not a linesearch however, because the step following a retracted step will be in a different direction. Space limitations prohibit a detailed specification of the of the linesearch algorithm and the convergence criteria used. These details may be very important. A longer paper is planned in which they are to be specified, and their influence on performance studied.

1.2 The test problems

Two types of problems are used in these tests. One is a strictly-layered 3-layer back propagation network in which the minimization variables are the weights. The test problems are 4-bit parity using 4 hidden nodes, auto-association of 10-bit random patterns using 7 hidden nodes, and the Peterson and Barney vowel classification problem (Peterson, 1952), which uses 2 inputs, 10 hidden nodes, and 10 target nodes. The other type is a fully connected recurrent network trained by the Moving Targets method (Rohwer, 1990a,b). In this case the minimization variables are the weights and the moving targets, which can be regarded as variable training data for the hidden nodes. The limit cycle switching problem and the 100-step context sensitivity problem from these references are the test problems used. In the limit-cycle switching problem, a single target node is required to regularly generate pulses of width proportional to a 2-bit binary number indicated by 2 input nodes. In the 100-step context problem, the training data always has an input pulse at time step 100, and sometimes has an input pulse at time 0. The target node is required to turn on at time 100 if and only if there was an input pulse at time 0.

Each method is tested on each problem with 10 different random initial conditions, except for the parity problem which was done with 100 different initial conditions.

1.3 Unconventional nonlinearity

An unconventional form of nonlinearity was used in these tests. The usual $f(x) = 1/(1+e^{-x})$ presents difficulties when $x \rightarrow \pm\infty$ because its derivative becomes very small. This makes the system learn slowly if activations become large. Also, numerical noise becomes serious if expressions such as $f(x)(1-f(x))$ are used in the derivative calculations. Various cutoff schemes are sometimes used to prevent these problems, but these introduce discontinuities and/or incorrect derivative

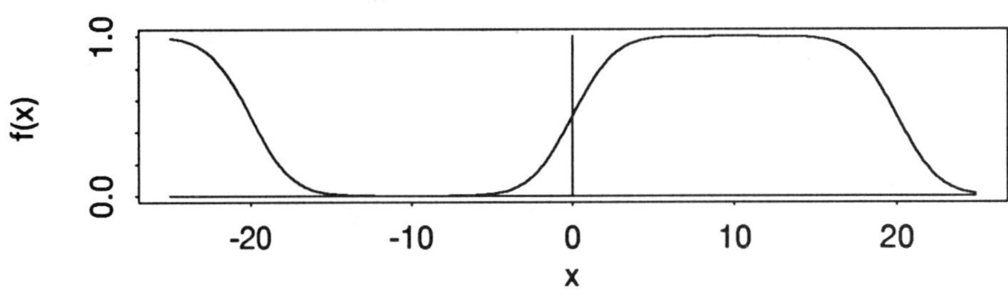

Figure 1: The nonlinearity used.

calculations which present further problems for second-derivative methods. In early work it was found that algorithm performance was highly sensitive to cutoff value (More systematic work on this subject is wanting.), so an entirely different nonlinearity was introduced which is bounded but has reasonably large derivatives for most arguments. This combination of properties can only be had with an oscillatory function. It was also desired to retain the property of $1/(1+e^{-x})$ that it has large "saturated regions" in which it is approximately constant. The function used is

$$f(x) = \frac{1}{2} + \frac{1}{2(1+\beta)}(1+\beta \sin(\frac{\pi x}{2\alpha})^2) \sin(\frac{\pi}{2} \sin(\frac{\pi}{2} \sin(\frac{\pi x}{2\alpha}))) \tag{2}$$

with $\alpha = 10$ and $\beta = 0.02$. This function is graphed in figure 1.

2 Results

An algorithm is useful if it produces good solutions quickly. The data for each algorithm-problem pair is divided into separate sets for successful and unsuccessful runs. Success is defined rather arbitrarily as less than 1% error on any target node for all training data in the backpropagation problems. In the Moving Target problems, it is defined in terms of the maximum error on any target node in the freely-running network, the threshold being 5% for the 4-limit-cycle problem and 10% for the 100-step-context problem.

The speed data, measured in number of gradient evaluations, is presented in figure 2, which contains 4 tables, one for each problem except random autoassociation. A maximum of 10000 evaluations was allowed. Each table is divided into 7 columns, one for each algorithm. From left to right, the algorithms are Rohwer's algorithm (max_abs), conjugate gradient (cg), division by unsigned (an_abs) or signed (an_sgn) analytically computed second derivatives and using a linesearch, these two with the linesearch replaced by a single variably-sized step (an_abs_ss and an_sgn_ss) and Silva's algorithm (silva_ss). The data in each of these 7 columns is divided into 3 subcolumns, the first (a) shows all data points, the second (s) shows data for successful runs only, and the third (f) shows data for the failures. Each error bar shows the mean and standard deviation of the data in its column. The all-important little boxes at the base of each column show the proportions of runs in that column's category.

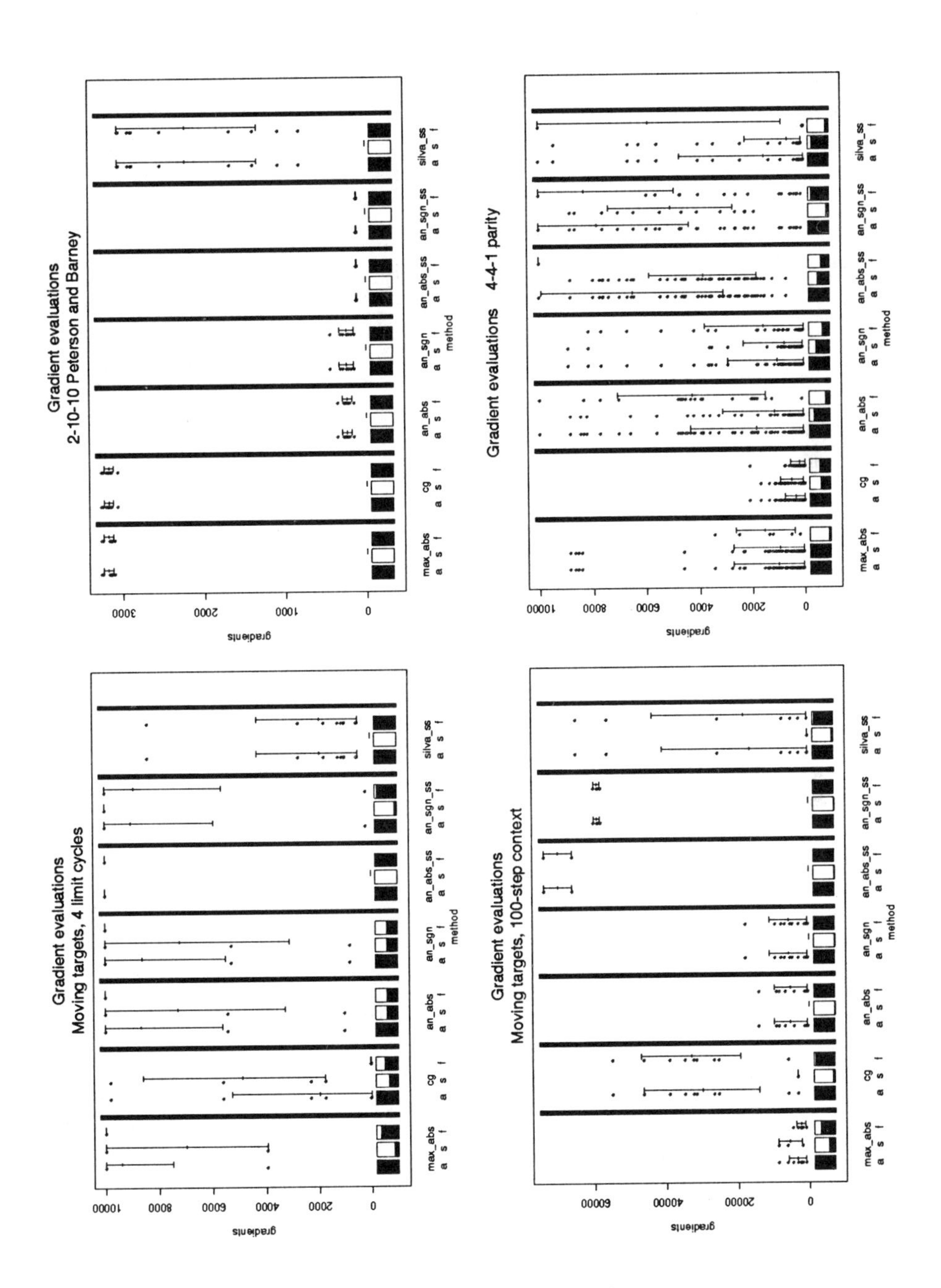

Figure 2: Gradient computations.

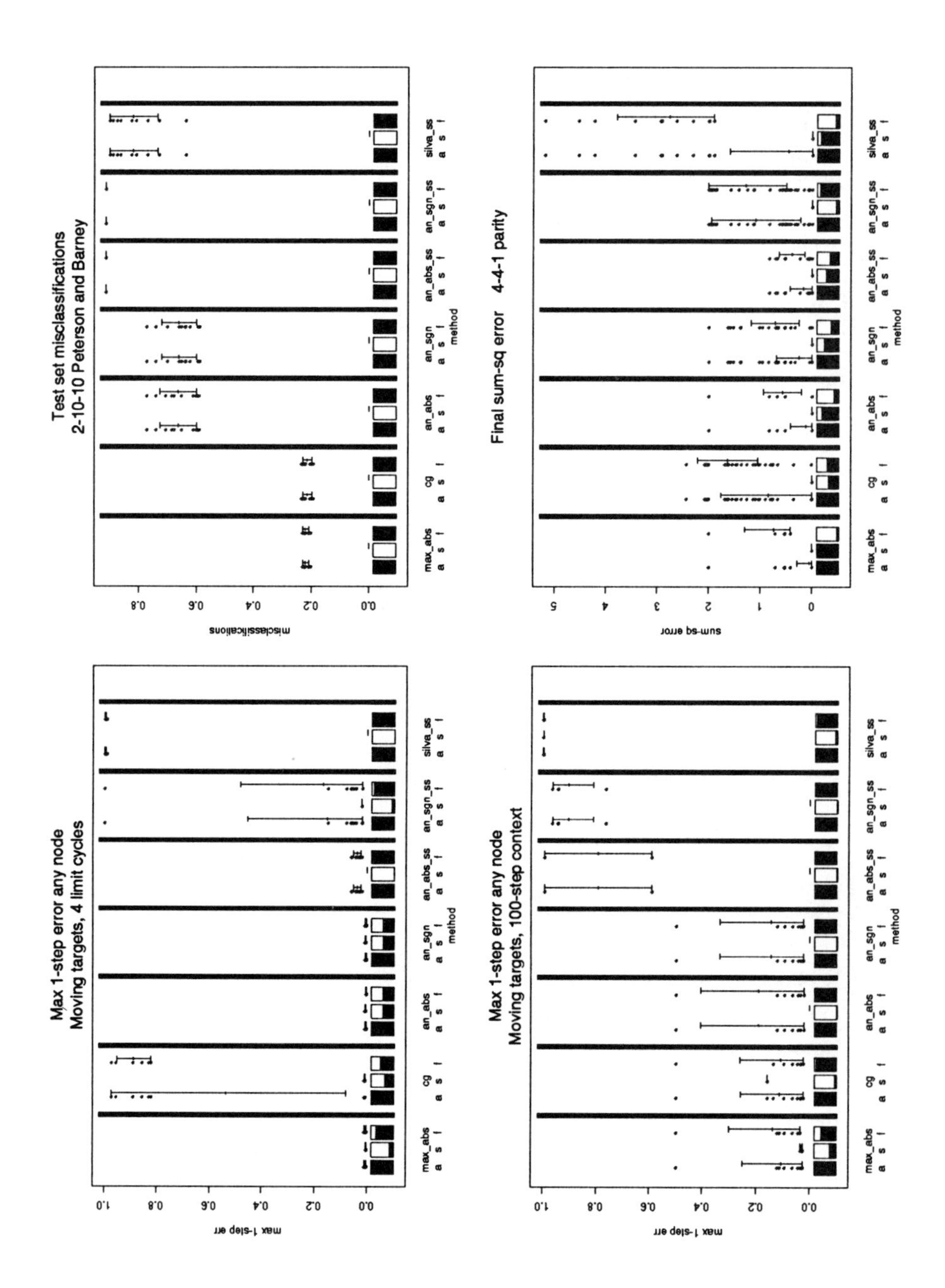

Figure 3: Network performance at error minimum.

The success criteria are quite arbitrary and innapropriate in many cases, so more detailed information on the quality of the solutions is given in Table 3. The maximum error on any target node after one time step, given the moving target values on the previous time step is shown for the Moving Target problems. Test set misclassifications are shown for the Peterson and Barney data, and final sum-squared error is shown for the parity problem.

The random autoassociation results are omitted here to save space. They qualitatively resemble the Peterson and Barney results.

Firm conclusions cannot be drawn, but the linesearch-based algorithms tend to outperform the others. Of these, the conjugate gradient algorithm and Rohwer's algorithm (Rohwer 1990a,b) are usually best.

In recent correspondence with the author, Silva has suggested small changes in his algorithm. In particular, when the algorithm fails to find descent for 5 consecutive iterations, all the learning-rate parameters are halved. Preliminary tests suggest that this change may bring enormous improvements.

Acknowledgements

This work was supported in part by ESPRIT Basic Research Action 3207 ACTS.

References

Y. LeCun, et. al. (1989) Generalization and network design strategies. In R. Pfeifer, (ed.), *Connectionism in Perspective*, 143–155. Amsterdam: North Holland.

G. E. Peterson & H. L. Barney. (1952) Control methods used in a study of vowels. *J. Acoustical Soc. of America* **24**:175–184.

W. H. Press, et. al. (1988) *Numerical Recipes in C: The Art of Scientific Computing.* Cambridge: Cambridge U. Press

R. Rohwer. (1990a) The 'moving targets' training algorithm. In L. B. Almeida & C. J. Wellekens (eds), *Neural Networks*, Lecture Notes in Computer Science **412**:100–109. Berlin: Springer-Verlag.

R. Rohwer. (1990b) The 'moving targets' training algorithm. In D. S. Touretzky (ed.), *Advances in Neural Information Processing Systems* **2**:558–565. San Mateo CA: Morgan Kaufmann.

F. M. Silva & L. B. Almeida. (1990). Acceleration techniques for the backpropagation algorithm. In L. B. Almeida & C. J. Wellekens (eds), *Neural Networks*, Lecture Notes in Computer Science **412**:110-119. Berlin: Springer-Verlag.

T. Toolenaere. (1990) SuperSAB: Fast Adaptive Back Propagation with Good Scaling Properties. *Neural Networks* **3**(5):561–574.

R. Watrous. (1987) Learning algorithms for connectionist networks: Applied gradient methods of nonlinear optimization. In Caudill & Butler (eds.), *IEEE Intl. Conf. on Neural Networks*, **II**:619–627. San Diego: IEEE.

Kohonen Networks and Clustering: Comparative Performance in Color Clustering

Wesley Snyder
Department of Radiology
Bowman Gray School of Medicine
Wake Forest University
Winston-Salem, NC 27103

Daniel Nissman, David Van den Bout, and Griff Bilbro
Center for Communications and Signal Processing
North Carolina State University
Raleigh, NC 27695

Abstract

The problem of color clustering is defined and shown to be a problem of assigning a large number (hundreds of thousands) of 3-vectors to a small number (256) of clusters. Finding those clusters in such a way that they best represent a full color image using only 256 distinct colors is a burdensome computational problem. In this paper, the problem is solved using "classical" techniques -- *k*-means clustering, vector quantization (which turns out to be the same thing in this application), competitive learning, and Kohonen self-organizing feature maps. Quality of the result is judged subjectively by how much the pseudo-color result resembles the true color image, by RMS quantization error, and by run time. The Kohonen map provides the best solution.

1 INTRODUCTION

"Clustering", "vector quantization", and "unsupervised learning" are all words which describe the same process: assigning a few exemplars to represent a large set of samples. Performing that process is the subject of a substantial body of literature. In this paper, we are concerned with the comparison of various clustering techniques to a particular, practical application: color clustering.

The color clustering problem is as follows: an image is recorded in full color -- that is, three components, RED, GREEN, and BLUE, each of which has been measured to 8 bits of precision. Thus, each pixel is a 24 bit quantity. We must find a representation in which 2563 possible colors are represented by only 8 bits per pixel. That is, for a problem with 256000 variables (512 x 512) variables, assign each variable to one of only 256 classes.

The color clustering problem is currently of major economic interest since millions of display systems are sold each year which can only store 8 bits per pixel, but on which users would like to be able to display "true" color (or at least as near true color as possible).

In this study, we have approached the problem using the standard techniques from the literature (including *k*-means -- ISODATA clustering[1,3,6], LBG[4]), competitive learning (referred to as CL herein)[2], and Kohonen feature maps[5,7,9]. The Kohonen feature map (referred to as KFM herein) was found to win "hands down", providing both the best quality image (subjectively) and objectively (based on quantization error), as well as the fastest run times.

2 BACKGROUND - METHODS TESTED

In almost all clustering algorithms, we begin with some (usually ad-hoc) determination of initial cluster centers. The number of such centers generally remains the same, although some algorithms (e.g. ISODATA[10]) allow the number to evolve through the running of the algorithm. In this work, we know that we want to find 256 distinct clusters. The basic idea behind most of these methods is to update the cluster closest to the current data point by moving it some small increment towards that data point. After the data has been presented to the algorithm sufficiently often, the clusters should converge to the real cluster means. Typically, one has to cycle through the training set several times (sometimes a large number of times) to get an acceptable solution. Each run though the training set is termed an *epoch*.

2.1 *K*-MEANS

The well-known [6] *k*-means algorithm for clustering is as follows (see [10] for a tutorial explanation).

1. Begin with an arbitrary assignment of samples to clusters or begin with an arbitrary set of cluster centers and assign samples to nearest centers.
2. Compute the sample mean of each cluster.
3. Reassign each sample to the cluster with the nearest mean.
4. If the classification of all samples has not changed, stop; else go to step 2.

2.2 LBG VECTOR QUANTIZATION

In this method, 256 colors are picked randomly from the scene. These are referred to as the "codebook". Each pixel in the image is then assigned to the "nearest" entry in the codebook. After assignment of all pixels, the mean of each bin[1] is calculated. If the difference between the codebook entry and the mean of the corresponding bin is below threshold for all entries, the "optimal" codebook has been located. In [4], the algorithm is shown to work for a large variety of distance functions; however, for applications (such as this one) where the Euclidean metric is most appropriate, the algorithm becomes identical to *k*-means. In [8], results similar to those we found are reported in the color clustering problem.

2.3 KOHONEN MAPS AND COMPETITIVE LEARNING

In competitive learning algorithms, data examples are presented sequentially to the system. The cluster center most similar to the data example is determined, and that center is moved slightly toward the example.

[1] That is, all the pixels assigned to that entry in the codebook.

The update rule for competitive learning can be described as follows:

$$\omega_i^{new} = \omega_i^{old} + n\,(data - \omega_i^{old}) \qquad \text{(EQ 1)}$$

where w_i is the weight vector (or mean) corresponding to cluster i and h is the learning parameter (typically on the order of 0.01).

In the case of Kohonen maps, however, the algorithm is slightly more complicated. All clusters are connected to each other according to a *topological* map. When the closest cluster to a data point (the primary cluster) is updated, so are its immediate neighbors (the proximity clusters) in terms of the topological map. In feature space, it is possible, initially, for the neighbors of the primary cluster to not be its topological neighbors. By the nature of the update rule, the neighbors of the primary cluster in topological space will become its neighbors in feature space after some period of time. This is very desirable for applications in which a minimum distance between related clusters is desired (the Traveling Salesman Problem, for example).

Often, it is the case that a single cluster is chosen much of the time, if not all of the time, because of the order in which data is presented and the manner in which the clusters are initialized. In order to make clustering work in a practical context, one needs to include a term in the distance calculation which reduces the probability of updating an often-used cluster. Such a term is called the *conscience*[2]. Its effect is to increase the effective distance of a cluster from a data point. An alternative approach to the use of a conscience is to increment a counter for each cluster which has been passed over for updating and then subtract some multiple of this counter from the calculated distance. We call this the *loneliness* term, and used it because the implementation turned out to be more convenient, and the performance similar to that of conscience.

For KFM, the primary cluster is updated as indicated in Eqn. 1. The proximity clusters are updated in a similar fashion

$$\omega_j^{new} = \omega_j^{old} + F(\eta, d_{ij})\,(data - \omega_j^{old}) \qquad \text{(EQ 2)}$$

where w_j is the weight vector corresponding to the proximity cluster j, d_{ij} is the topological distance between clusters i and j, and $F(\eta, d_{ij})$ is some decreasing function of the distance between i and j with a maximum at η.

3 Application to Color Clustering

Making no assumptions concerning the input image, we chose an appropriate topology for the KFM algorithm which would easily lend itself to describing a uniform distribution of colors in RGB space. Such a distribution is a rectangular solid in the 3-D color space. We chose the dimensions of this block to be 6x7x6 -- corresponding to 252 clusters rather than the 256 allowable -- under the assumption that the omission of those four clusters would not make a perceptible difference. The clusters were initialized as a small block positioned at the center of RGB space with the long axis in the green direction. This orientation was chosen because human eyes are most sensitive to green wavelengths and, hence, more resolution may be required along this axis. The exact initial orientation does not matter in the final solution, but was chosen to aid in speed of convergence.

In an attempt to significantly speed up training, each data point was assigned to one of the eight subcubes of RGB space, and then only a specified subset of clusters was searched for an appropriate candidate for updating. The clusters were subdivided, roughly, into eight subcubes as well. The effect of this is to decrease training time by approximately a factor of eight. Also, in the interest of processing time, only the six most immediate topological neighbors (those with a topological distance of one from the primary cluster) were updated. This same heuristic was applied for both CL and KFM experiments.

4 RESULTS

We applied all the techniques discussed, in various implementations, to actual color images, including in particular, pictures of faces. Although also tested on larger images, all times given in this report are against a baseline case of a 128x128 image: three bands of input (red, green, blue -- 8 bits each), and one band (8 bits) of output, plus a lookup table output indicating what 24 bit color each of the 8 bit pattern represented. Given sufficient training, all the techniques produced pseudo-color images which were extremely lifelike. Comparing the images closely on a CRT, a trained observer will note variations in the color rendering, particularly in sparse colors (e.g. blue eyes in a facial scene), and will also observe color contouring. However, these details are subtle, and are not easily reproducible in a conference proceedings. Map files and corresponding images were generated for 5, 10, and 15 epochs using $h = 0.05$ and proximity $h = 0.00625$. Direct comparisons were made between Kohonen feature maps, competitive learning, and the results from k-means (and the LBG formulation of k-means). For the training runs using competitive learning, all clusters were initialized to random values within the unit sphere located in the center of RGB space. The conscience concept was used here.

In this section all timing comparisons are done on a Microvax 2000, although we have also run many of the same programs on a Decstation. The Decstation typically runs 10-15 times as fast as the Microvax. In order to compare techniques fairly, all timing is reported for the same image.

4.1 *K*-MEANS AND LBG EXPERIMENTS

The performance of k-means and LBG algorithms were strongly dependent on how long they were allowed to run. After approximately 90 minutes of execution of k-means, the results were as good (subjectively) as from Kohonen maps. In different experiments, k-means was started from the following initial configurations:

1. 256 points randomly (uniformly) distributed over RGB space

2. The 256 points on the main diagonal of color space (red=green=blue)

3. A uniform (3D) grid spread over RGB

4. Uniformly distributed over the surface of the color cube

5. Randomly distributed near the origin

Choice 2 gave the best overall performance, where "best" is determined by the time required to converge to a point where the resulting image looked "equally good" subjectively. K-means required 87 minutes to reach this *standard* quality, although it took 9 hours to completely converge (until no cluster center moved more than .5 units in one iteration).

4.2 EXPERIMENTS ON KOHONEN AND COMPETITIVE LEARNING

KFM gave an excellent rendering of color images. In particular, blue eyes were rendered extremely well in images of faces. Depending on the value of the conscience parameter, the competitive learning algorithm tended to rendered blue eyes as brown, since the dominant skin tones in facial images are shades of brown.

Speed comparisons. All of these runs were done on Microvaxen.

Algorithm	**Total time**	**Time/epoch**
Kohonen	15:42	1:34
Comp Learn	8:38	:52

Converting the image:
1:34 for Kohonen
4:16 for Competitve Learning

The subjective judgments of picture quality were made using the 10 epoch case of Kohonen maps as a reference. To quantitatively compare the performance of Kohonen maps and competitive learning, we computed the RMS color error:

$$E = \sum_i (v_i - c_i)^2 \qquad \text{(EQ 3)}$$

where v_i is the actual color 3-vector at pixel i, and c_i is the color represented by the mean of the cluster to which pixel i is currently assigned. Plotting E vs. epoch number for both Kohonen and competitive learning, we find the results in the figure below.

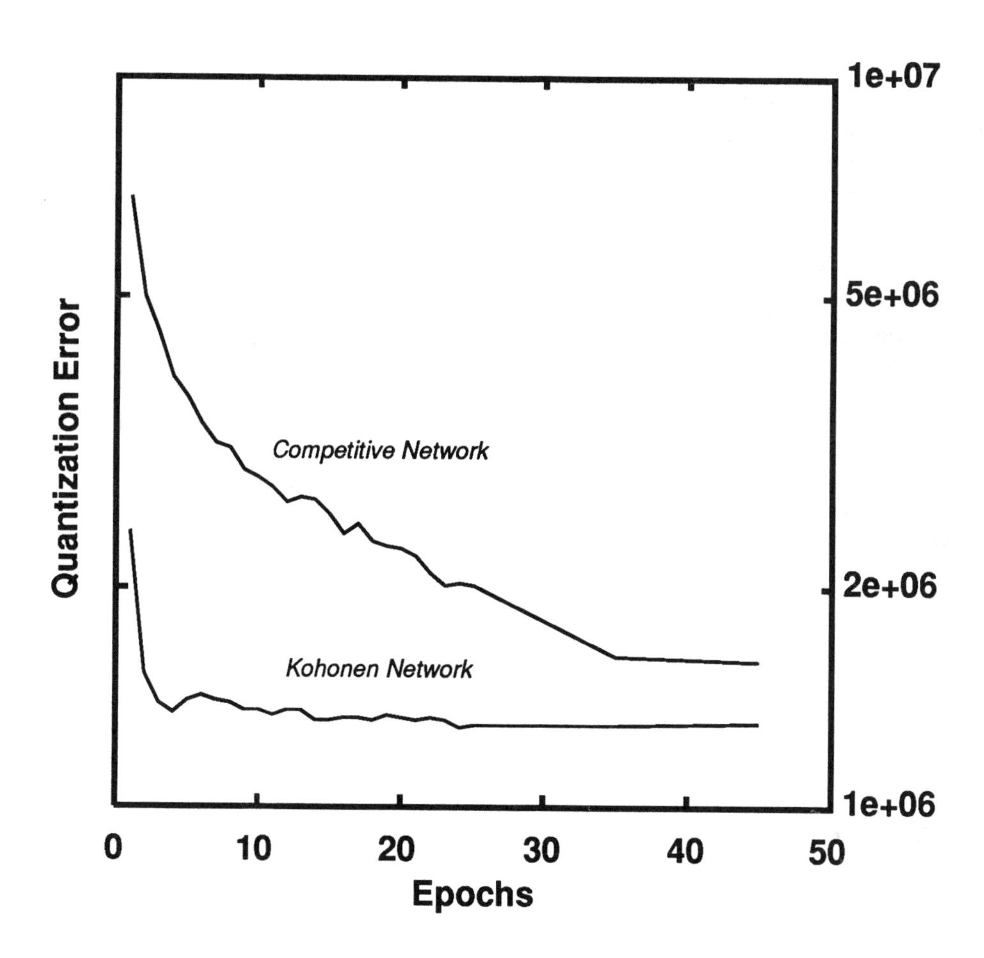

It is clear from this figure that the KFM network converges more rapidly to a stable solution with much lower error than does the competitive network. Such figures can be deceiving in image processing, however, since RMS error is a notoriously bad quality measure (small regions may have very large errors in order to make the overall average error low). In this case, however, the Kohonen map preserves the accuracy of color rendering in small regions quite well.

To evaluate the sensitivity to initial cluster center choices, both competitive learning and KFM were applied with different choices of centers. We found that competitive learning often converged to undesirable renderings, whereas KFM always yielded a good solution, even when the initial centers were all at 0,0,0.

5 DISCUSSION

The quality of rendering attained by these algorithms is due to the nature of facial images. There is a great deal of density in the flesh colored region and a comparatively smaller, but nonetheless sizable, amount in the background colors. The competitive learning algorithm found these high density regions with no problem. Greater difficulty was had with the blue eyes, since there are few examples of blue to be trained on and hence the algorithm was swamped by the high density regions. If one let the competitive learning algorithm run for a large number of epochs, it eventually found the blue cluster. The assignment of clusters to subdivisions of feature space guarantees that no region of the image was particularly emphasized, therefore allowing clusters that were solely influenced by less represented colors. However, this can also "waste" clusters in regions where there are few examples.

Furthermore, the topological structure of the Kohonen map allows one to make certain assumptions to speed up the algorithm.

Despite a minor penalty in computational speed per epoch, the Kohonen algorithm produces the image with the least error in the least amount of time. With appropriate choice of parameters, the clustered image becomes indistinguishable from the original in less than ten epochs, for essentially arbitrary initial conditions (as opposed to competitive learning). The other clustering techniques require significantly longer times.

6 REFERENCES

1. G. H. Ball and D. J. Hall, "ISODATA, A Novel Method of Data Analysis and Pattern Classification" SRI Technical Report (NTIS AD699616), Stanford, CA, 1965
2. D. DeSieno, "Adding a Conscience to Competitive Learning", International Conference On Neural Networks, Vol. 1, pp. 117-124, 1988
3. K. Fukunaga, *Introduction to Pattern Recognition*, Academic Press, Orlando FL, 1972
4. Y. Linde, A. Buzo, and R. Gray, "An Algorithm for Vector Quantizer Design", *IEEE Trans. Com.* Vol. COM-28, No. 1, pp. 84-95, Jan. 1980
5. T. Kohonen, "Self-Organized Formation of Topologically Correct Feature Maps", *Biological Cybernetics*, 43:56-69, 1982
6. J. Mac Queen "Some Methods for Classification and Analysis of Multivariate Observations", Proc. 5th Berkeley Symposium, 1, pp. 281-297, 1967
7. N. Nasrabadi and Y. Feng, "Vector Quantization of Images Based upon Kohonen Self-organizing Feature Maps", IEEE International Conference on Neural Networks, Vol. 1, pp. 101-108, 1986
8. H. Potlapalli, M. Jaisimha, H. Barad, A. Martinez, M. Lohrenz, J. Ryan, and J. Pollard. "Classification Techniques for Digital Map Compression" 21st Southeastern Symposium on System Theory, pp. 268-272. 1989. Tallahasee, Fl, March, 1989
9. H. Ritter and K. Schulten, "Kohonen Self-organizing Maps: Exploring their Computational Capabilities" IEEE International Conference on Neural Networks, Vol. 1, pp. 109-116, 1988
10. C. W. Therrien, *Design, Estimation, and Classification*, Wiley, NY, 1989

Part XV

VLSI

VLSI Implementations of Learning and Memory Systems: A Review

Mark A. Holler
Intel Corporation
2250 Mission College Blvd.
Santa Clara, Ca. 95052-8125

ABSTRACT

A large number of VLSI implementations of neural network models have been reported. The diversity of these implementations is noteworthy. This paper attempts to put a group of representative VLSI implementations in perspective by comparing and contrasting them. Design trade-offs are discussed and some suggestions for the direction of future implementation efforts are made.

IMPLEMENTATION

Changing the way information is represented can be beneficial. For example a change of representation can make information more compact for storage and transmission. Implementation of neural computational models is just the process of changing the representation of a neural model from mathmatical symbolism to a physical embodiement for the purpose of shortening the time it takes to process information according to the neural model.

FLEXIBILITY VS. PERFORMANCE

Today most neural models are already implemented in silicon VLSI, in the form of programs running on general purpose digital von Neumann computers. These machines are available at low cost and are highly flexible. Their flexibility results from the ease with which their programs can be changed. Maximizing flexibility, however, usually results in reduced performance. A program will often have to specify several simple operations to carry out one higher level operation. An example is performing a sequence of shifts and adds to accomplish a multiplication. Higher level functions can be directly implemented but more hardware is required and that hardware can't be used to execute other high level functions. Flexibility is lost. This trade-off between flexibility and performance is a fundamental issue in computational device design and will be observed in the devices reviewed here.

GROUND RULES

The neural network devices which will be discussed each consist of a set of what could loosely be called "artificial neurons". The artificial neurons typically calculate the inner product of an input vector and a stored weight vector, a sum of products of inputs times weights. An artificial synapse stores one weight and calculates one product or connection each time a new input is provided. The basic unit of computation is a "connection" and the basic measure of performance is the number of connections the neural network can perform per second, (CPS). The CPS number is directly related to how fast the chip will be able to perform mappings from input to output or recognize input patterns. The artificial neurons also include a non-linear thresholding function.

The comparison done here is restricted to devices which fit within this definition and as a result a number of important neural devices such as those which perform early vision processing or dynamical processing for optimization are not considered. In the interest of brevity only representative state of the art devices are presented.

COMPARISON CRITERIA

The criteria for comparison are based on what would be important to a user: *Performance, Capability, Cost, Flexibility/ Ease of Application.*

In addition to the CPS measure of performance there is also a measure of how fast a chip can learn. How many connection or weight updates the chip can calculate and store per second, (CUPS) is an important performance measure for the chips which have learning capability. Three of the nine chips examined have learning on chip.

Important capabilities to consider are how big a network the chip can simulate, what precision of calculation the chip provides and how independent the chip is during learning. Table 1 provides neuron and synapse counts which indicate the maximum size network each chip can implement. The synaptic function and precision are noted in another column and comments about learning capability are also provided.

An interesting figure of merit is the ratio of CPS to the number of weights. This CPS per weight ratio will be referred to as the CPSPW. This figure of merit varies by over a factor of 1000 for the 9 chips considered and all have ratios much higher than typical von Neumann machines or the human brain. See the last column of Table 1. The significance of this disparity will be discussed later.

TABLE 1. VLSI Neural Network Implementations

	CPS	Connect Type	CUPS	Learning Algorithm	Neurons	Synapses	Technology	Weights	Config.	Avail.	Price	Synapse Area u^2	CPSPW
Micro Devices [1] MD1220 Neural Bit Slice	0.01B	1b x 16b Product	NA	Off chip	8	2048	?	Ext.	Board Level	Avail.	$45	5100	4883
H.Graf, D.Henderson, [2] AT&T Bell Labs	80B	1b x 1-4b Product	NA	Off chip	256	8K-32K	.9u CMOS	No	Chip Level	Board in 92	?	1760	2.5-10M
Alspector, J., Allen, R. [3] Jayakumar, A., Bellcore	0.1B	5b x 5b Product	.1B	Boltzmann	32	992	1.2u CMOS	No	Board Level	No	Reseach	58344	100806
Arima, Y., et al [4] Mitsubishi Electric	5.6B	1b x 6b product	1.4B	Boltzmann	336	28000	1u CMOS	No	Chip Level	No	Research	4900	200000
Hammerstrom, D., et al, [5] Adaptive Solutions	1.6B	1-16b x 1-16b multiple	.24B	Many; Back-Prop etc.	64	128K-2M	.8u CMOS Multi-Field die	No	Chip Level	No	NA	1400	800-3.1K
Agranat, R., et al [6] Ca. Inst. Tech.	0.5B	5b x 5b product	NA	Off chip	256	65536	2u CMOS CCD	No	Board Level	No	Research	560	7629
Yasunaga, M., et al [7] Hitach; Wafer Scale	2.3B	6b x 6b product	NA	Off wafer	1152	73700	.8u CMOS Gate Array 8- 5" wafers	No	Wafer Level	No	>$10K	410000	31208
Tomlinson, M., et al [8] Neural Semiconductor	0.1B	4b x 4b product	NA	Off chip	32	1024	1.2u CMOS	No	Board Level	4/91	$900	23000	97656
Holler, M., et al [9] Intel Corp. 80170, ETANN	2B	6b x 6b product	NA	Off chip	64	10240	1u CMOS EEPROM	Non-Vol.	Chip Level	Avail. w/Tools	$940	2009	195313
												Brain	100
												PC	1

In addition to pricing information, what little exists, Table 1 includes the effective synapse area and process technology to give some indication of the relative cost of the various designs.

Finally to include something which suggests how flexible the chips are, comments are included in Table 1 to indicate whether or not the synaptic function, the learning algorithm and the network architecture, of each chip can be changed. Also to be considered is how hard it is to set or continuously refresh weights whether analog or digital. Analog vs. Digital I/O is a consideration as is availability and development tools. Demonstration in real applications would be another indicator of success but, none of these chips has yet reached this milestone.

COMPARISON

The first device[1], from Micro Devices, is a digital neural network which leaves the weight memory off chip. Its eight 16 bit by one bit serial synapse multipliers are multiplexed which keeps the effective synapse cell size down. Using a single synaptic multiplier per neuron makes the total compute time for a neuron's sum of products dependent on how many inputs are supplied to a neuron. One positive aspect of this architecture is that any arbitrary number of inputs per neuron can be processed as long as the neuron accumulator is wide enough not to overflow when a worst case large sum of products is accumulated.

The Micro Devices chip shares this multiplexed synapse approach with the Adaptive Solutions X1 [5]and the CCD based design [6] by Agranat et al at Cal-Tech although these two chips include weight memory on chip to attain much better data transfer performance from the weight store to the synaptic processors. The multiplexed synapse approach is a good one for reducing the effective synapse size as can be seen by comparing the synapse area for these three chips[1,5,6] to those of the other chips. [5,6] have the two smallest cell sizes.

Micro Devices was first to introduce a commercial neural network chip and developent tools. They also have the lowest cost chip available. Its all digital interface makes it easy to design in. It's only significant limitations are its low neuron count and the fact that it can only accept binary inputs and output binary activations.

Hitachi's wafer scale neural network[7] designed with gate array technology uses pulse stream data representations as does the Neural Semiconductor implementation[8]. Pulse stream representations make the implementation of a digital multiplier trivial. It becomes just an AND gate. One drawback of this approach is that the user must convert his input data to uncorrelated pulse streams. The Hitachi design is also interesting because it is clearly designed to take advantage of the fault tolerant aspect of neural networks. The system they have built consists of eight wafers which are very likely to have at least several bad die. The automated gate array design used in the Hitachi resulted in the largest synapse area at 410,000 u^2.

Neural Semiconductor's design puts the neuron units on a separate chip from its synaptic units. This allows variable width input vectors with a large upper bound.

The CCD based design from Cal-Tech[6] is most noteworthy for its small cell size, 560 u^2, and high synapse count which results from the use of multiplexed synaptic processors and analog storage in a CCD. The drawback of this type of weight storage is that it must be refreshed every few milliseconds at higher temperatures.

Intel's 80170 [9] uses analog non-volatile weight storage and uses a basic characteristic of neural networks to advantage. It uses the adaptation that is going on during learning to adapt to variations in the analog circuit computing elements on the chip. This is noteworthy because it is another example of putting one of the properties of neural networks to use to enable a design approach different from conventional digital VLSI design.

The AT&T chip reported by Graf &Henderson [2] has achieved the highest CPS rate, 80B, of any of the chips. It was designed with handprinted character recognition in mind and as a result accepts only binary inputs (black and white). It uses a hybrid circuit design approach, digital for inputs and weight storage but analog summation in the form of currents. This chip is flexible in that its weight precision can be traded off for higher synapse count.

The last three chips[3,4,5] all have learning on chip. Two of them use Boltzmann learning which has been shown by Hinton [11] to be a form of gradient decent learning like Back-Propagation. These are the Bellcore chip[3] reported by J. Alspector, R. Allen and A. Jayakumar and the chip reported by Y. Arima et al at Mitsubishi[4]. The Misubishi chip has the most impressive number for learning performance and the second best mapping performance at 5.6B CPS. Its one drawback is that the analog weights it learns are volatile and must be refreshed. Bellcore's Boltzmann machine uses digital weight storage which does not require refresh. However, as you will notice the Bellcore synapse cell size is 10X larger due to the use of digital storage and a slightly lower density 1.2u technology.

The Adaptive Solutions chip with programmable learning and programmable synaptic function represents the flexibility end of the performance/flexibility trade-off. It is a single instruction multiple data path (SIMD) von Neumann machine. Its 64 synaptic processors are multiplexed up to 4096 times for eight bit weights making the effective synapse cell size very small, 1400 u^2 in spite of using digital SRAM for weight storage and fully digital synapse processors. This chip has the second smallest cell size primarily due to its multiplexing of the synaptic processing elements and because it multiplexes them more times than any of the other designs.

CONNECTIONS PER SECOND PER WEIGHT (CPSPW)

The ratio of connections/second per weight can be estimated for biological systems to be on the order of 100 assuming one weight is stored in each synapse. If neurons are firing 100 times per second then each of the synapses must be processing pulses about 100 times per second hence the CPSPW of 100. This number is clearly related to neuron firing rate. Less obvious is how CPSPW might be connected with the precison of the biological computing elements and the time frame in which the whole network seeks to produce final results.

Following von Neumann's arguments[12] arithmetical error grows in proportion to the number of steps of processing. This is partly due to round off errors and partly due to amplification of errors that occur early in the calculations. Biological neurons have limited precision due to their analog nature. If their calculations are accurate to within 1% and they are involved in a calculation that involves propagation of results through 100 neurons in sequence then the accumulated error could be as high as 100% meaning that the answer could be competely wrong. Any further calculations using this result would be useless. In other words, a 100 step calculation is the longest calculation you might expect a biological system to attempt to do because of its limited precision. Since the time frame that biological systems are typically concerned with is around 1 second one might expect to see these biological systems executing about 100 operations for each processing element in this interval. This appears to be the case. Executing any more operations than this would produce meaningless results due to the accumulation of numerical error.

A rule of thumb which summarizes the suggested relationship between CPSPW, precision and the time frame of interest would be: ***The number of connections executed per weight in the interval of interest should be equal to the dynamic range of the weights.*** The dynamic range of a weight is just the inverse of its precision or the maximum possible weight value minus the minimum weight value divided by the smallest increment in a weight which has significance.

Motor control, vision, handwriting and speech recognition tasks all fall within the "human time frame". The rule of thumb suggests that if neural network implementations with limited precision weights are used to solve these problems then these systems are likely to work best with the same CPSPW as biological neural systems, around 100. Since all of the neural network implementations reviewed here have CPSPW's well above 100 we might conclude that they are not optimal for these human time frame tasks. They don't have enough weights relative to their processing power. Standard von Neumann computers have CPSPW's which are much lower than those of biological systems. The number of operations per second per word of memory in a typical von Neumann machine is around 1. Von Neumann machines today don't have enough processing power relative to their memory size to be optimal for executing neural network solutions to problems in the human time frame.

For systems where results are sought in a time frame shorter than the human time frame a higher CPSPW should be used according to the rule of thumb. All of the designs reviewed here have a CPSPW much higher than 100. See the right most column of

Table-1. The AT&T chip [2] has a CPSPW ratio in the millions and many of the chips[3,4,7,8,9] have a ratio around 100,000. Chips with low CPSPW's are the same chips that multiplex the synaptic processors [1,5,6]. They can store more weights because they don't replicate the synaptic processor for every weight. Their processing rates are lowered which also lowers their CPSPW because they have fewer synaptic processors working simultaneously. This is not particularly desirable but results in a better balance between processing power and memory for tasks which don't need to be done any faster than in the human time frame.

FUTURE DIRECTION

Von Neumann machines with their high degree of flexibility will continue to be critical in the near term as neural models continue their rapid evolution. Multiprocessor (>10) von Neumann machines optimized for neural type calculations are sorely needed. One such device [5] is already on the horizon. Hennessy and Patterson's quantitative approach [10] to computer design would be appropriate.

Neural network implementations with more weights are needed for making further progress in solving the difficult "human time domain" problems of speech and vision. A 1B CPS machine with 10M weights is needed. . Devices which multiplex the synaptic processing elements appear to be the best candidates for accomplishing this goal. The challenge here is to keep the bandwidth high even after the weight cache is moved off chip.

Using DRAM or "floating gate" memory cells which normally store digital information to store analog information instead in the same space is an approach which can be used in conjunction with multiplexed analog synapse processors to achieve a 6-8X improvement in the number of weights per synaptic processor with little penalty in die area. This general direction is largely unexplored except for the CCD implementation done by Agranat et al. [6].

VLSI implementations with fully parallel processing synaptic arrays represent a new computational capability; higher performance than can be achieved by any other means with given power and space. The availability of this new computing capability will open up new applications but, will likely take time. The majority of chips reviewed in this paper fall into this category [2,3,4,7,8,9].

SUMMARY

The VLSI implementations to date are mostly high performance devices with limited memory. An image of slugs crawling at the speed of sound comes to mind. There will be applications for these "supersonic slugs", but, they are unlikely to make VLSI neural networks a big business any time soon. Implementations with more flexibility or more storage relative to processing power seem to be needed.

References

[1] Yestrebsky, J., Basehore, P. , Reed, J., "Neural Bit SliceComputing Element", Product Ap. Note TP102600, Micro Devices, Orlando, Fla.

[2] Graf, H., Henderson, D., "A Reconfigurable CMOS Neural Network", *1990 Int'l Solid State Circuits Conference*, San Francisco, Ca.

[3] Alspector, J., Allen, R., Jayakumar, A., "Relaxation Networks for Large Supervised Learning Problems", *Advances in Neural Information Processing Systems 3,* 1991 San Mateo, Ca.: Morgan Kaufmann

[4] Arima, Y., et al, "336 Neuron 28K Synapse Self-Learning Neural Network Chip with Branch Neuron-Unit Architecture", *1991 IEEE Int'l Solid State Circuits Conference*

[5]Griffin, M., Hammerstrom, D., et al, "An 11 Million Transistor Digital Neural Network Execution Engine", *1991 IEEE Int'l Solid State Circuits Conference*

[6] Agranat, R., Neugebauer, C., Yariv, A., "A CCD Based Neural Network Integrated Circuit with 64K Analog Programmable Synapses", *Int'l Joint Conference on Neural Networks,* June 1990.

[7] Gold, M., "Hitachi Unveils Prototype Neural Computer", *EE-Times,* Dec. 3, 1990.

[8] SU3232, NU32 Data Sheet, Neural Semiconductor Inc. , Carlsbad, Ca.

[9] 80170NW Electrically Trainable Analog Neural Network, Data Sheet, Intel Corp. Santa Clara, Ca. May 1990.

[10] Hennessy, J.L., Patterson, D. A. , *Computer Architecture, A Quantitative Approach*", p17, Morgan Kaufmann, San Mateo, Ca., 1990

[11] Hinton, G., "Deterministic Boltzmann Learning performs Steepest Decent in Weight-Space".

[12] Von Neumann, John, *The Computer and the Brain*, p26, 78 Yale University Press, New Haven, 1958

[13] Tam, S. et al, "Learning on an Analog VLSI Neural Network Chip", *1990 IEEE Int'l Conf. on Systems, Man and Cybernetics.*

Compact EEPROM-based Weight Functions

A. Kramer, C. K. Sin, R. Chu, and P. K. Ko
Department of Electrical Engineering and Computer Science
University of California at Berkeley
Berkeley, CA 94720

Abstract

We are focusing on the development of a highly compact neural net weight function based on the use of EEPROM devices. These devices have already proven useful for analog weight storage, but existing designs rely on the use of conventional voltage multiplication as the weight function, requiring additional transistors per synapse. A parasitic capacitance between the floating gate and the drain of the EEPROM structure leads to an unusual I-V characteristic which can be used to advantage in designing a compact synapse. This novel behavior is well characterized by a model we have developed. A single-device circuit results in a 1-quadrant synapse function which is nonlinear, though monotonic. A simple extension employing 2 EEPROMs results in a 2 quadrant function which is much more linear. This approach offers the potential for more than a ten-fold increase in the density of neural net implementations.

1 INTRODUCTION - ANALOG WEIGHTING

The recent surge of interest in neural networks and parallel analog computation has motivated the need for compact analog computing blocks. Analog weighting is an important computational function of this class. Analog weighting is the combining of two analog values, one of which is typically varying (the input) and one of which is typically fixed (the weight) or at least varying more slowly. The varying value is "weighted" by the fixed value through the "weighting function", typically multiplication. Analog weighting is most interesting when the overall computational task involves computing the "weighted sum of the inputs." That is, to compute $\sum_{i=1}^{n} f(w_i, v_i)$ where $f()$ is the weighting function and $W = \{w_1, w_2, ..., w_n\}$ and

$V = \{v_1, v_2, ..., v_n\}$ are the n-dimensional analog-valued weight and input vectors. This weighted sum is simply the dot product in the case where the weighting function is multiplication.

For large n, the only way to perform this computation efficiently is to use compact weighting functions and to take advantage of current summing. Using "conductive multiplication" as the weighting function (weights stored as conductances of single devices) results in an efficient implementation such as that shown in figure 1a. This implementation is probably optimal, but in practice it is not possible to implement small single-device programmable conductances which are linear.

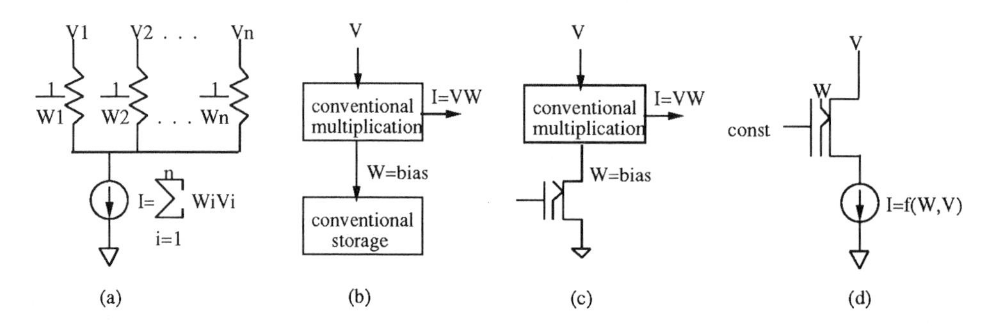

Figure 1: Weighting function implementations: (a) ideal, (b) conventional, (c) EEPROM-based storage, (d) compact EEPROM-based nonlinear weight function

1.1 CONVENTIONAL APPROACHES

The problem of implementing analog weighting is often divided into the separate tasks of storing the fixed value (the weight) and combining the two analog values through the weighting function (figure 1b). Conventional approaches to storing a fixed analog weight value are to use either digital storage with some form of D/A conversion or to use volatile analog storage, which requires a large capacitor. Both of these storage technologies require a large area.

The simplest and most widespread weighting function is multiplication $[f(w,i) = wi]$. Multiplication is attractive because of its mathematical and computational simplicity. Multiplication is also a fairly straightforward operation to implement in analog circuitry. When conventional technologies are used for weight storage, the additional area required to provide a multiplication function is not significant. Of course, the problem with this approach is that since a large area is required for weight storage, the result is not sufficiently compact.

2 EEPROMS

EEPROMs are "electrically erasable, programmable, read-only memories". They are essentially a JFET with a floating gate and a thin-oxide tunneling region between the floating gate and the drain (figure 2). A sufficiently high field across the tunneling oxide will cause electrons to tunnel into or out of the floating gate, effectively altering the threshold voltage of the device as seen from the top gate. Normal operating (reading) voltages are sufficiently small to cause only insignificant "disturbance programming" of the charge on the floating gate, so an EEPROM can be viewed as a compact storage capacitor with a very long storage lifetime.

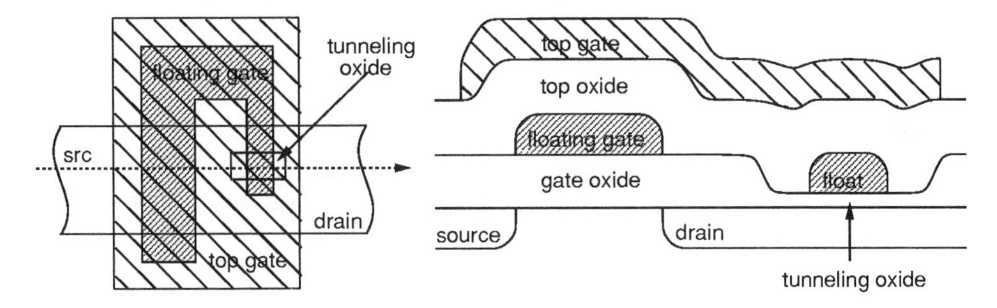

Figure 2: EEPROM layout and cross section

Several groups have found that charge leakage on EEPROMs is sufficiently small to guarantee that the threshold of a device can be retained with 4-8 bits of precision for a period of years [Kramer, 1989][Holler, 1989]. There are several drawbacks to the use of EEPROMs. Correct programming of these devices to the desired value is hard to control and requires feedback. While the programming time for a single device is less than a millisecond, because devices must be programmed one-at-a-time, the time to program all the devices on a chip can be prohibitive. In addition, fabrication of EEPROMs is a non-standard process requiring several additional masks and the ability to make a thin tunneling oxide.

2.1 EEPROM-BASED WEIGHT STORAGE

The most straightforward manner to use an EEPROM in a weighting function is to store the weight with the device. For example, the threshold of an EEPROM device could be programmed to produce the desired bias current for an analog amplifier (figure 1c). There are two advantages to this approach. Firstly, the weight storage mechanism is divorced from the actual weight function computation and hence places few constraints on it, and secondly, if the EEPROM is used in a static mode (all applied voltages are constant), the exact I-V characteristics of the EEPROM device are inconsequential.

The major disadvantage of this approach is that of inefficiency, as additional circuitry is needed to perform the weight function computation. An example of this can be seen in a recent EEPROM-based neural net implementation developed by the Intel corporation [Holler, 1989]. Though the weight value in this implementation is stored on only two EEPROMs, an additional 4 transistors are needed for the multiplication function. In addition, though the circuit was designed to perform multiplication the output is not quite linear under the best of conditions and, under certain conditions, exhibits severe nonlinearity. Despite these limitations, this design demonstrates the advantage of EEPROM storage technology over conventional approaches, as it is the most dense neural network implementation to date.

3 EEPROM I-V CHARACTERISTICS

Since linearity is difficult to implement and not a strict requirement of the weighting function, we have investigated the possibility of using the I-V characteristics of an EEPROM as the weight function. This approach has the advantage that a single device could be used for both weight storage and weight function computation, providing a very compact implementation. It is our hope that this approach will lead to useful synapses of less than $200um^2$ in area, less than a tenth the area used by the Intel synapse.

Though an EEPROM is a JFET device, a parasitic capacitance of the structure results in an I-V characteristic which is unique. Conventional use of EEPROM devices in digital circuitry does not make use of this fact, so that this effect has not before been characterized or modeled. The floating gate of an EEPROM is controlled via capacitive coupling by the top gate. In addition, the thin-ox tunneling region between the floating gate and the drain creates a parasitic capacitor between these two nodes. Though the area of this drain capacitor is small relative to that of the top-gate floating-gate overlap area, the tunneling oxide is much thinner than the insulating oxide between the two gates, resulting in a significant drain capacitance (figure 3).

We have developed a model for an EEPROM which includes this parasitic drain capacitance (figure 3). The basic contribution of this capacitance is to couple the floating-gate voltage to the drain voltage. This is most obvious when the device is saturated; while the current through a standard JFET is to first order independent of drain voltage in this region, in the case of an EEPROM, the current has a square law dependence on the drain voltage (equation 3). While this artifact of EEPROMs makes them behave poorly as current sources, it may make them more useful as single-device weighting functions.

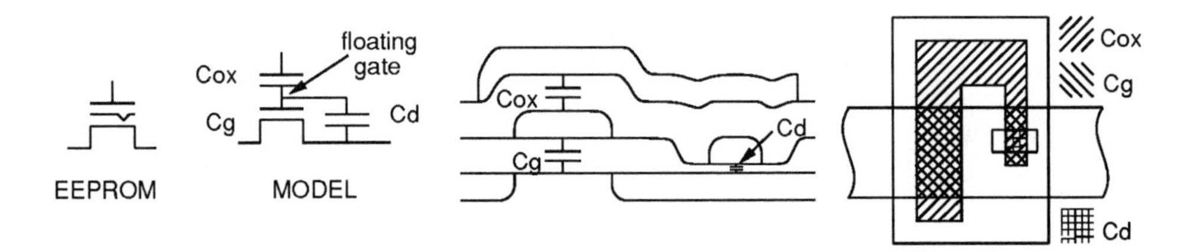

Figure 3: EEPROM model and capacitor areas

There are several ways to analyze our model depending on the level of accuracy desired [Sin, 1991]. We present here the results of simplest of these which captures the essential behavior of an EEPROM. This analysis is based on a linear channel approximation and the equations which result are similar in form to those for a normal JFET, with the addition of the dependence between the floating gate voltage and the drain voltage and all capacitive coupling factors. The equations for drain saturation voltage ($V_{ds_{sat}}$), nonsaturated drain current ($I_{ds_{lin}}$) and saturated drain current ($I_{ds_{sat}}$) are:

$$V_{ds_{sat}} = \frac{C_g V_g - V_t(C_{ox} + C_g + C_d)}{0.5C_{ox} + C_g} \quad (1)$$

$$I_{ds_{lin}} = K_p \left[\left(\frac{C_g V_g}{C_{ox} + C_g + C_d} - V_t \right) - \frac{V_{ds}^2}{2} \left(\frac{C_g - C_d}{C_{ox} + C_g + C_d} \right) \right] \quad (2)$$

$$I_{ds_{sat}} = K_p \left[\frac{C_g V_g + C_d V_{ds} - V_t(C_{ox} + C_g + C_d)}{0.5C_{ox} + C_g + C_d} \right]^2 \quad (3)$$

On EEPROM devices we have fabricated in house, our model matches measured I-V data well, especially in capturing the dependence of saturated drain current on drain voltage (figure 4).

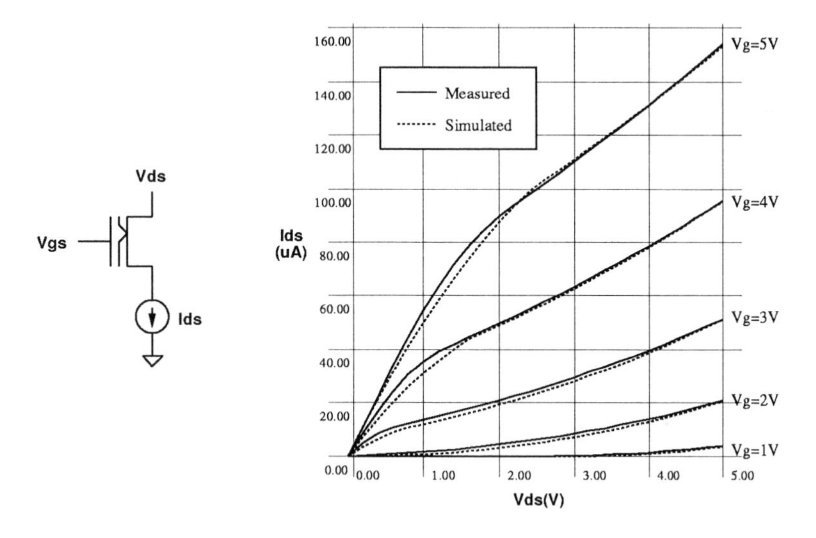

Figure 4: EEPROM I-V, measured and simulated.

4 EEPROM-BASED WEIGHTING FUNCTIONS

One way to make a compact weight function using an EEPROM is to use the device I-V characteristics directly. This could be accomplished by storing the weight as the device threshold voltage (V_t), applying the input value as the drain-source voltage (Vds) and setting the top gate voltage to a constant reference value (figure 1d). In this case the synapse would look exactly like the I-V measuring circuit and the weighting function would be exactly the EEPROM I-V shown in figure 4, except that rather than leaving the threshold voltage fixed and varying the gate voltage, as was done to generate the curves shown, the gate voltage would be fixed to a constant value and different curves would be generated by programming the device threshold to different values.

While extremely compact (a single device), this function is only a one quadrant function (both weight and input values must be positive or output is zero) and for many applications this is not sufficient. An easy way to provide a two-quadrant function based on a similar approach is to use two EEPROMs configured in a common-input, differential-output ($I_{out} = I_{ds+} - I_{ds-}$) scheme, as in the circuit depicted in figure 5. By programming the EEPROMs so that one is always active and one is always inactive, the output of the weight function can now be a "positive" or a "negative" current, depending on which device is chosen. Again, the weighting function is exactly the EEPROM I-V in this case.

In addition to providing a two-quadrant function, this two-device circuit offers another interesting possibility. The same differential output scheme can be made to provide a much more linear two quadrant function if both "positive" and "negative devices are programmed to be active (negative thresholds). The "weight" in this case is the difference in threshold values between the two devices ($W = V_{t-} - V_{t+}$). This scheme "subtracts" one device curve from the other. The model we have developed indicates that this has the effect of canceling out much of the nonlinearity and results in a function which has three distinct regions, two of which are linear in the input voltage and the weight value.

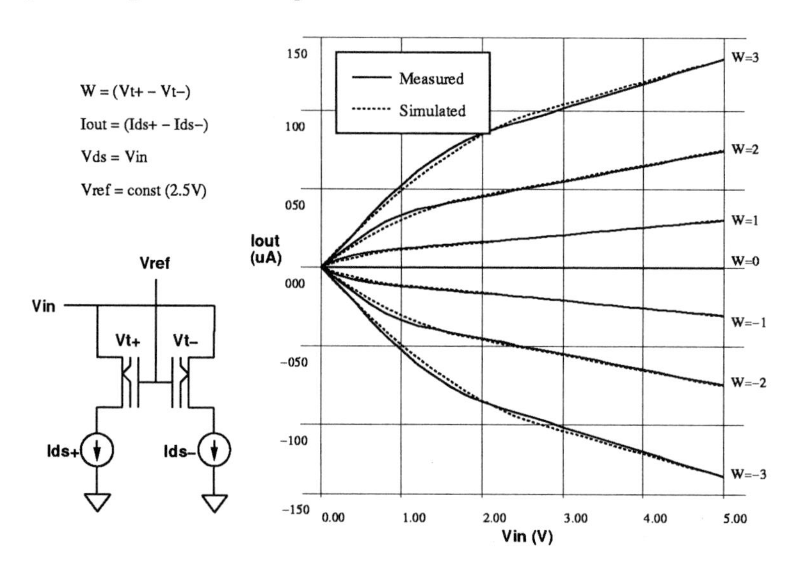

Figure 5: 2-quadrant, 2-EEPROM weighting function.

The first of these linear regions occurs when both devices are active and neither is saturated (both devices modeled by equation 2). In this case, subtracting I_{ds-} from I_{ds+} cancels all nonlinearities and the differential is exactly the product of the input value (V_{ds}) and the weight ($V_{t-} - V_{t+}$), with a scaling factor of Kp:

$$I_{ds_+} - I_{ds_-} \quad = \quad K_p V_{ds} \left(V_{t_-} - V_{t_+} \right) \tag{4}$$

The other linear region occurs when both devices are saturated (both modeled by equation 3). All nonlinearities also cancel in this case, but there is an offset remaining and the scaling factor is modified:

$$I_{ds+} - I_{ds-} = K_p \left(\frac{C_d}{0.5C_{ox} + C_g + C_d} \right) V_{ds} \left(V_{t-} - V_{t+} \right) + K_p \left(V_{t-} - V_{t+} \right) \left(\frac{C_g V_g}{0.5C_{ox} + C_g + C_d} - \left(V_{t+} + V_{t-} \right) \right) \quad (5)$$

We have fabricated structures of this type and measured, as well as simulated their function characteristics. Measured data again agreed with our model (figure 5). Note that the slope in this last region [scaling factor of $K_p C_g/(0.5C_{ox} + C_g + C_d)$] will be strictly less that in the first region [scaling factor K_p]. The model indicates that one way to minimize this difference in slopes is to increase the size of the parasitic drain capacitance (C_d) relative to the gate capacitance (C_g).

5 CONCLUSIONS

While EEPROM devices have already proven useful for nonvolatile analog storage, we have discovered and characterized novel functional characteristics of the EEPROM device which should make them useful as analog weighting functions. A parasitic drain-floating gate capacitance has been included in a model which accurately captures this behavior. Several compact nonlinear EEPROM-based weight functions have been proposed, including a single-device one-quadrant function and a more linear two-device two-quadrant function. Problems such as the usability of nonlinear weighting functions, selection of optimal EEPROM device parameters and potential fanout limitations of feeding the input into a low impedance node (drain) must all be resolved before this technology can be used for a full blown implementation. Our model will be helpful in this work. The approach of using inherent device characteristics to build highly compact weighting functions promises to greatly improve the density and efficiency of massively parallel analog computation such as that performed by neural networks.

Acknowledgements

Research sponsored by the Air Force Office of Scientific Research (AFSOR/JSEP) under Contract Number F49620-90-C-0029.

References

M. Holler, et. al., (1989) "An Electrically Trainable Artificial Neural Network (ETANN) with 10240 'Floating Gate' Synapses," *Proceedings of the ICJNN-89,* Washington D. C., 1989.

A. Kramer, et. al, (1989) "EEPROM Device as a Reconfigurable Analog Element for Neural Networks," *1989 IEDM Technical Digest,* Beaver Press, Alexandria, VA, Dec. 1989.

C. K. Sin, (1990) *EEPROM as an Analog Storage Element,* Master's Thesis, Dept. of EECS, University of California at Berkeley, Berkeley, CA, Sept. 1990.

An Analog VLSI Splining Network

Daniel B. Schwartz and Vijay K. Samalam
GTE Laboratories, Inc.
40 Sylvan Rd.
Waltham, MA 02254

Abstract

We have produced a VLSI circuit capable of learning to approximate arbitrary smooth of a single variable using a technique closely related to splines. The circuit effectively has 512 knots space on a uniform grid and has full support for learning. The circuit also can be used to approximate multi-variable functions as sum of splines.

An interesting, and as of yet, nearly untapped set of applications for VLSI implementation of neural network learning systems can be found in adaptive control and non-linear signal processing. In most such applications, the learning task consists of approximating a real function of a small number of continuous variables from discrete data points. Special purpose hardware is especially interesting for applications of this type since they generally require real time on-line learning and there can be stiff constraints on the power budget and size of the hardware. Frequently, the already difficult learning problem is made more complex by the non-stationary nature of the underlying process.

Conventional feed-forward networks with sigmoidal units are clearly inappropriate for applications of this type. Although they have exhibited remarkable performance in some types of time series prediction problems (for example, Wiegend, 1990 and Atlas, 1990), their learning rates in general are too slow for on-line learning. On-line performance can be improved most easily by using networks with more constrained architecture, effectively making the learning problem easier by giving the network a hint about the learning task. Networks that build local representations of the data, such as radial basis functions, are excellent candidates for these type of problems. One great advantage of such networks is that they require only a single layer of units. If the position and width of the units are fixed, the learning problem is linear in the coefficients and local. By local we mean the computation of a weight change requires only information that is locally available to each weight, a highly desirable property for VLSI implementation. If the learning algorithm is allowed to adjust both the position and width of the units then many of the advantages of locally tuned units are lost.

A number of techniques have been proposed for the determination of the width and placement of the units. One of the most direct is to center a unit at every data point and to adjust the widths of the units so the receptive fields overlap with those of neighboring data points (Broomhead, 1989). The proliferation of units can be limited by using unsupervised clustering techniques to clump the data followed by the allocation of units to fit the clumps (Moody, 1989). Others have advocated assigning new units only when the error on a new data point is larger than a threshold and otherwise making small adjustments in the weights and parameters of the existing units (Platt, 1990). All of these methods suffer from the common problem of requiring an indeterminate quantity of resources in contrast with the fixed resources available from most VLSI circuits. Even worse, when used with non-stationary processes a mechanism is needed to deallocate units as well as to allocate them. The resource allocation/deallocation problem is a serious barrier to implementing these algorithms as autonomous VLSI microsystems.

A Splining Network

To avoid the resource allocation problem we propose a network that uses all of its weights and units regardless of the problem. We avoid over parameterization of the training data by building constraints on smoothness into the network, thus reducing the number of degrees of freedom available to the training process. In its simplest guise, the network approximates arbitrary 1-d smooth functions with a linear superposition of locally tuned units spaced on a uniform grid,

$$g(x) = \sum_i \omega_i f_\sigma(x - i\Delta x) \tag{1}$$

where σ is the radius of the unit's receptive field and the ω_i are the weights. f_σ is a bump of width σ such as a gaussian or a cubic spline basis function. Mathematically the network is closely related to function approximation using B-splines (Lancaster, 1986) with uniformly spaced knots. However, in B-spline interpolation the overlap of the basis functions is normally determined by the degree of the spline whereas we use the degree of overlap as a free parameter to constrain the smoothness of the network's output. As mentioned earlier, the network is linear in its weights so gradient descent with a quadratic cost function (LMS) is an effective training procedure.

The weights needed for this network can easily be implemented in CMOS with an array of transconductance amplifiers. The amplifiers are wired as voltage followers with their outputs tied together and the weights are represented by voltages V_i at the non-inverting inputs of the amplifiers. If the outputs of the locally tuned units are represented by unipolar currents I_i these currents can be used to bias the transconductance amplifiers and the result is (Mead,1989)

$$V_{out} = \frac{\sum_i I_i V_i}{\sum_i I_i}$$

provided that care is taken to control the non-linearities of the amplifiers. However, while the weights have a simple implementation in analog VLSI circuitry, the input units do not. A number of circuits exist whose transfer characteristics can be shaped to be a suitable bump but none of those known to the authors allow the width of the bump to be adjusted over a wide range without the use of resistors.

Generating the Receptive Fields

Input units with tunable receptive fields can be generated quite efficiently by breaking them up into two layers of circuitry as shown in figure 1. The input layer place encodes the input signal – i.e. only one or perhaps a small cluster of units is active at a time. The output of the place encoding units either injects or controls the

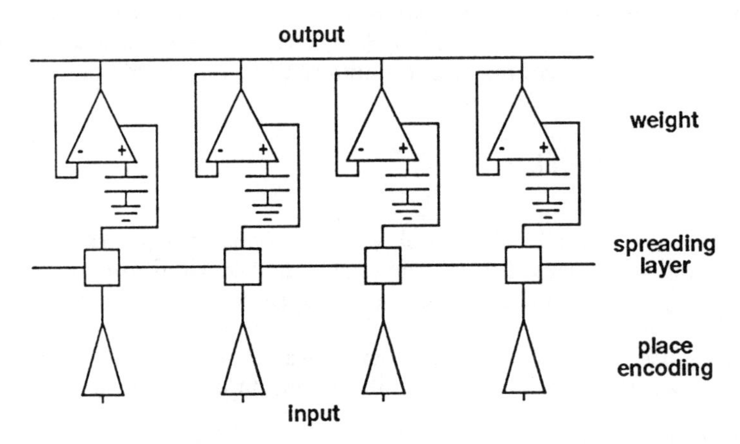

Figure 1: An architecture that allows the width and shape of the receptive fields to be varied over a wide range. The elements of the 'spreading layer' are passive and can sink current to ground.

injection of current into the laterally connected spreading layer. The elements in the spreading layer all contain ground terminals and the current sunk by each one determines the bias current applied to the associated weight. Clearly, the distribution of currents flowing to ground through the spreading layer form a smooth bump such that when excitation is applied to tap j of the spreading layer,

$$I_i = I_o f_\sigma(i - j)$$

where $f_\sigma(i)$ is the bump called for by equation 1. In our earliest realizations of this network the input layer was a crude flash A-to-D converter and the input to the circuit was analog. In the current generation the input is digital with the place encoding performed by a conventional address decoder. If desired, input quantization can be avoided by using a layer of amplifiers that generate smooth bumps of fixed width to generate the input place encoding.

The simplest candidate to implement the spreading layer in conventional CMOS is a set of diode connected n-channel transistors laterally connected by n-channel pass transistors. The gate voltages of the diode connected transistors determine the bias currents I_i of the weights. Ignoring the body effect and assuming weak inversion in the current sink, this type of networks tends to gives bumps with rather sharp peaks, $I_i \approx \sum_j I_o e^{-\alpha|j|}$, where $|j|$ is the distance from the point where the excitation is applied. Figure 2 shows a more sophisticated version of this circuit in which the output of the place encoding units applies excitation to the spreading network through a p-channel transistor. The shape of the bumps can be softened by

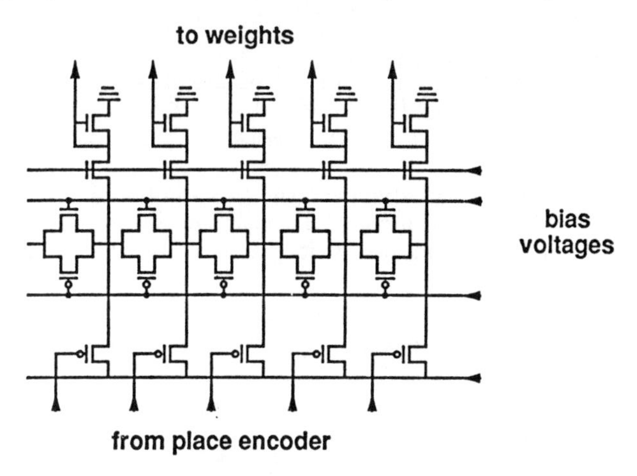

Figure 2: A schematic of a section of the spreading layer. Roughly speaking, the n-channel pass transistor controls the extent of the tails of the bumps and the p-channel pass transistor and the cascode transistor control its width.

limiting the amount of current drawn by the current sinks with an n-channel cascode transistor in series with the current sink. Some experimental results for this type of circuit are shown in figure 3a. More control can be obtained by using complementary pass transistors. The use of p-channel pass transistors alone unexpectedly results in bumps that are nearly square (figure 3b). These can be smoothed by using a using both flavors of pass transistor simultaneously (figure 3c).

The Weights

As described earlier, the implementation of the output weights is based on the computation of means by the well known follower-aggregation circuit. With typical transconductance amplifiers, this averaging is linear only when the voltages being averaged are distributed over a voltage range of no more than a few time $U_Q = kT/e$ in weak inversion. In the circuits described here the linear range has been widened to nearly a volt by reducing the transconductance of the readout amplifiers through the combination of low width to length ratio input transistors and relatively large tail currents.

The weights V_i are stored on MOS capacitors and are programmed by the gated transconductance amplifier shown in figure 4. Since this amplifier computes the

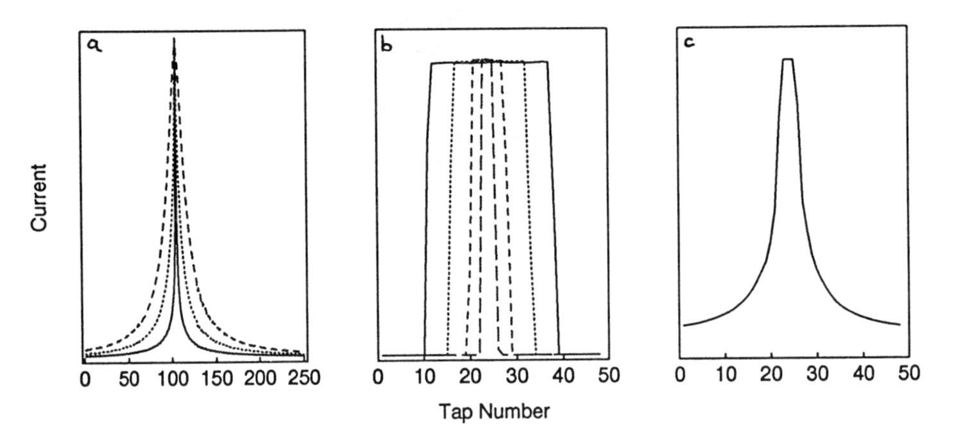

Figure 3: Experimental measurements of the receptive field shapes obtained from different types of networks. (a) n-channel transistors for several gate voltages. (b) p-channel transistors for several gate voltages. (c) Both n-channel and p-channel pass transistors.

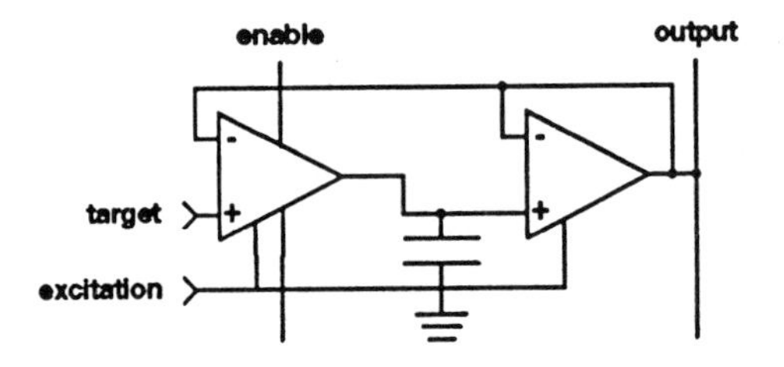

Figure 4: Schematic of an output weight including the circuitry to generate weight updates. To minimize leakage and charge injection simultaneously, the pass transistors used to gate the weight change amplifier are of minimum size and a separate transistor turns off the output transistors of the amplifier.

difference between the target voltage and the actual output of the network, the learning rule is just LMS,

$$\Delta V_i = \frac{g_i \tau}{C}(V_{target} - V_{out}),\ \Delta V_i << V_{target} - V_{out}$$

where C is the capacitance of the storage capacitor and τ is the duration of weight changes. The transconductance g_i of the weight change amplifier is determined by the strength of excitation current from the spreading layer, $g_i \propto I_i$ in weak inversion. Since the weight changes are governed by strengths of the excitation currents from the spreading layer, clusters of weights are changed at a time. This enhances the fault tolerance of the circuit since the group of weights surrounding a bad one can compensate for it.

Experimental Evaluation

Several different chips have been fabricated in 2μ p-well CMOS and tested to evaluate the principles described here. The most recent of these has 512 weights arranged in a 64×8 matrix connected to form a one dimensional array. The active area of this chip is $4.1mm \times 3.7mm$. The input signal is digital with the place encoding performed by a conventional address decoder. To maximize the flexibility of the chip, the excitation is applied to the spreading layer by a register located in each cell. By writing to multiple registers between resets, the spreading layer can be excited at multiple points simultaneously. This feature allows the chip to be treated as a single 1-dimensional spline with 512 weights or, for example, as the sum of four distinct 1-dimensional splines each made up of 128 weights. One of the most noticeable virtues of this design is the simplicity of the layout due to the absence of any clear distinction between 'weights' and 'units'. The primitive cell consists of a register, a piece of the spreading network, a weight change amplifier, a storage capacitor and output amplifier. All but a tiny fraction of the chip is a tiling of this primitive cell. The excess circuitry consists of the address decoders, a timing circuit to control the duration of weight changes and some biasing circuitry for the spreading layer.

To execute LMS learning, the user need only provide a sequence of target voltages and a current proportional to the duration of weight changes. Under reasonable operating conditions a weight updates cycle takes less than $1\mu s$ implying a weight change rate of 5×10^8 connections/second. The response of the chip to a single weight change after initialization is shown in in figure 5a. One feature of this plot is striking – even though the distribution of offsets in the individual amplifiers has a variance of $13mV$, the ripple in the output of the chip is about a 1mV. For some computations, it appears the limiting factor on the accuracy of the chip is the rate of weight decay, about $10mV/s$.

As a more strenuous test of the functionality of the chip we trained it to predict chaotic time series generated by the well know logistic equation,

$$x_{t+1} = 4\alpha x_t(1 - x_t), \ \alpha < 1.$$

Some experimental results for the mean prediction error are shown in figure 5b. In these experiments, a mean prediction error of 3% is achieved, which is well above the intrinsic accuracy of the circuit. A detailed examination of the error rate as a function of the size and shape of the bumps indicates that the problem lies in the long tails exhibited by the spreading layer when the n-channel pass transistors are turned on. This tail falls off very slowly due to the body effect. One remedy to this problem is to actively bias the gates of the n-channel pass transistors to be a programmed offset above their source voltages (Mead, 1989). A simpler solution is to subtract a fixed current from each of the bias current defined by the spreading layer. This solution costs a mere 4 transistors and has the added benefit of guaranteeing that the bumps will always have a finite support.

Conclusion

We have demonstrated that neural network learning can be efficiently mapped onto analog VLSI provided that the network architecture and training procedure are

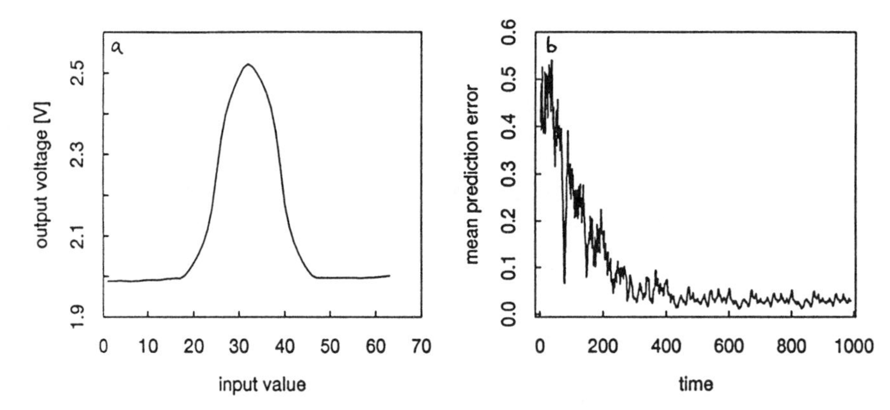

Figure 5: Some experimental results from a splining circuit. (a) The response of the circuit to learning one data point after initialization of the weights to a constant value. (b) Experimental mean prediction while learning a chaotic time series.

tailored to match the constraints imposed by VLSI. Besides the computational speed and low power consumption ($300\mu A$) that follow directly from this mapping onto VLSI, the circuit also demonstrates intrinsic fault tolerance to defects in the weights.

Acknowledgements

This work was initially inspired by a discussion with A. G. Barto and R. S. Sutton. A discussion with J. Moody was also helpful.

References

[1] L. Atlas, R. Cole, Y. Muthusamy, A. Lippman, J. Connor, D. Park, M. El-Sharkawi, and R. J. Marks II. A performance comparison of trained multi-layer perceptrons and trained classification trees. *IEEE Proceedings*, 1990.

[2] D. S. Broomhead and D. Lowe. Multivariable function interpolation and adaptive networks. *Complex Systems*, 2:321-355, 1988.

[3] P. Lancaster and K. Šalkauskas. *Curve and Surface Fitting.* Academic Press, 1986.

[4] C. Mead. *Analog VLSI and Neural Systems.* Addison-Wesley, 1989.

[5] J. Moody and C.J. Darken. Fast learning in networks of locally-tuned processing units. *Neural Computation*, 1(2), 1989.

[6] J. Platt. A resource-allocating neural network for function interpolation. In Richard P. Lippman, John Moody, and David S. Touretzky, editors, *Advances in Neural Information Processing Systems 3*, 1991.

[7] A. S. Weigend, , B. A. Huberman, and D. E. Rummlehart. Predicting the future : A connectionist approach. *International Journal of Neural Systems*, 3, 1990.

Relaxation Networks for Large Supervised Learning Problems

Joshua Alspector Robert B. Allen Anthony Jayakumar
Torsten Zeppenfeld and Ronny Meir
Bellcore
Morristown, NJ 07962-1910

Abstract

Feedback connections are required so that the teacher signal on the output neurons can modify weights during supervised learning. Relaxation methods are needed for learning static patterns with full-time feedback connections. Feedback network learning techniques have not achieved wide popularity because of the still greater computational efficiency of back-propagation. We show by simulation that relaxation networks of the kind we are implementing in VLSI are capable of learning large problems just like back-propagation networks. A microchip incorporates deterministic mean-field theory learning as well as stochastic Boltzmann learning. A multiple-chip electronic system implementing these networks will make high-speed parallel learning in them feasible in the future.

1. INTRODUCTION

For supervised learning in neural networks, feedback connections are required so that the teacher signal on the output neurons can affect the learning in the network interior. Even though back-propagation[1] networks are feedforward in processing, they have implicit feedback paths during learning for error propagation. Networks with explicit, full-time feedback paths can perform pattern completion[2] and can have interesting temporal and dynamical properties in contrast to the single forward pass processing of multilayer perceptrons trained with back-propagation or other means. Because of the potential for complex dynamics, feedback networks require a reliable method of relaxation for learning and retrieval of static patterns. The Boltzmann machine[3] uses stochastic settling while the mean-field theory (MFT) version[4] [5] uses a more computationally efficient deterministic technique.

Neither of these feedback network learning techniques has achieved wide popularity because of the greater computational efficiency of back-propagation. However, this is likely to change in the near future because the feedback networks will be implemented in VLSI[6] making them available for learning experiments on high-speed parallel hardware.

In this paper, we therefore raise the following questions: whether these types of learning networks have the same representational and learning power as the more thoroughly studied back-propagation methods, how learning in such networks scales with problem size, and whether they can solve usefully large problems. Such questions are difficult to answer with computer simulations because of the large amount of computer time required compared to back-propagation, but, as we show, the indications are promising.

2. SIMULATIONS

2.1 Procedure

In this section, we compare back-propagation, Boltzmann machine, and MFT networks on a variety of test problems. The back-propagation technique performs gradient descent in weight space by differentiation of an objective function, usually the error,

$$\varepsilon = \sum_{outputs\ k} (s_k^+ - s_k^-)^2$$

where s_k^+ is the target output and s_k^- is the actual output. We choose to use the function

$$G = \sum_{outputs\ k} [s_k^+ \log(s_k^+/s_k^-) + (1-s_k^+)\log[(1-s_k^+)/(1-s_k^-)]] \tag{1}$$

for a more direct comparison to the Boltzmann machine[7] which has

$$G = \sum_{global\ states\ g} p_g^+ \log(p_g^+/p_g^-) \tag{2}$$

where p_g is the probability of a global state.

Individual neurons in the Boltzmann machine have a probabilistic decision rule such that neuron k is in state $s_k = 1$ with probability

$$p_i = \frac{1}{1+e^{-net_i/T}} \tag{3}$$

where $net_i = \sum_j w_{ij} s_j$ is the net input to each neuron and T is a parameter that acts like temperature in a physical system and is represented by the noise term in Eq. (4), which follows. In the relaxation models, each neuron performs the activation computation

$$s_i = f\,(gain^* (net_i + noise_i)) \tag{4}$$

where f is a monotonic non-linear function such as *tanh*. In simulations of the Boltzmann machine, this is a step function corresponding to a high value of *gain*. The noise is chosen from a zero mean gaussian distribution whose width is proportional to the temperature. This closely approximates the distribution in Eq. (3) and matches our hardware implementation, which supplies uncorrelated noise to each neuron. The noise is slowly reduced as annealing proceeds. For MFT learning, the noise is zero but the gain term has a finite value proportional to $1/T$ taken from the annealing schedule. Thus the non-linearity sharpens as 'annealing' proceeds.

The network is annealed in two phases, + and –, corresponding to clamping the outputs in the desired state and allowing them to run free at each pattern presentation. The learning rule which adjusts the weights w_{ij} from neuron j to neuron i is

$$\Delta w_{ij} = sgn\,[\,(s_i s_j)^+ - (s_i s_j)^-\,]. \tag{5}$$

Note that this measures the instantaneous correlations after annealing. For both phases each synapse memorizes the correlations measured at the end of the annealing cycle and weight adjustment is then made, (i.e., online). The *sgn* matches our hardware implementation which changes weights by one each time.

2.2 Scaling

To study learning time as a function of problem size, we chose as benchmarks the parity and replication (identity) problems. The parity problem is the generalization of exclusive-OR for arbitrary input size, n. It is difficult because the classification regions are disjoint with every change of input bit, but it has only one output. The goal of the replication problem is for the output to duplicate the bit pattern found on the input after being transformed by the hidden layer. There are as many output neurons as input. For the replication problem, we chose the hidden layer to have the same number of neurons as the input layer, while for parity we chose the hidden layer to have twice the number as the input layer.

For back-propagation simulations, we used a learning rate of 0.3 and zero momentum. For MFT simulations, we started at a high temperature of $T_{hi} = K\ (1.4)^{10} \sqrt{(fanin)}$ where $K = 1{-}10$. We annealed in 20 steps dividing the temperature by 1.4 each time. The *fanin* parameter is the number of inputs from other neurons to a neuron in the hidden layer. We did 3 neuron update cycles at each temperature. For Boltzmann, we increased this to 11 updates because of the longer equilibration time. We used high gain rather than strictly binary units because of the possibility that the binary Boltzmann units would have exactly zero net input making annealing fruitless.

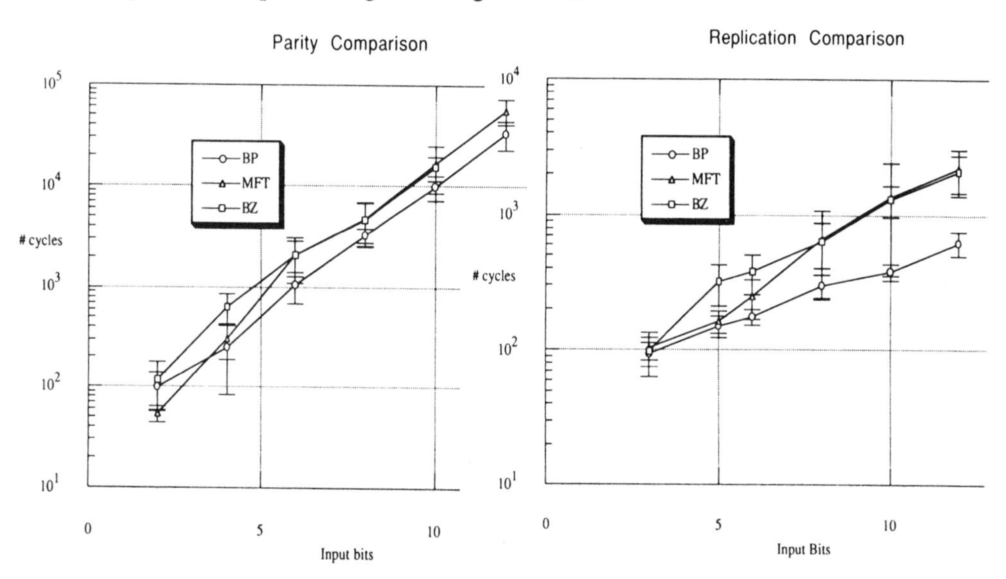

Figure 1. Scaling of Parity (1a) and Replication (1b) Problem with Input Size

Fig. 1a plots the results of an average of 10 runs and shows that the number of patterns required to learn to 90% correct for parity scales as an exponential in n for all three networks. This is not surprising since the training set size is exponential and no constraints were imposed to help the network generalize from a small amount of data. An activation range of -1 to 1 was used on both this problem and the replication problem. There is no appreciable difference in learning as a function of patterns presented. Actual computer time is larger by an additional factor of n^2 to account for the increase in the number of connections. Direct parallel implementation will reduce this additional factor to less than n. Computer time for MFT learning was an additional factor of 10 slower than back-propagation and stochastic Boltzmann learning was yet another factor of 10 slower. The hardware implementation will make these techniques roughly equal in speed and far faster than any simulation of back-propagation. Fig. 1b shows analogous results for the replication problem.

2.3 NETtalk

As an example of a large problem, we chose the NETtalk[8] corpus with 20,000 words. Fig. 2 shows the learning curves for back-propagation, Boltzmann, and MFT learning. An activation range of 0 to 1 gave the best results on this problem, possibly due to the sparse coding of text and phonemes. We can see that back-propagation does better on this problem which we believe may be due to the ambiguity in mapping letters to multiple phonemic outputs.

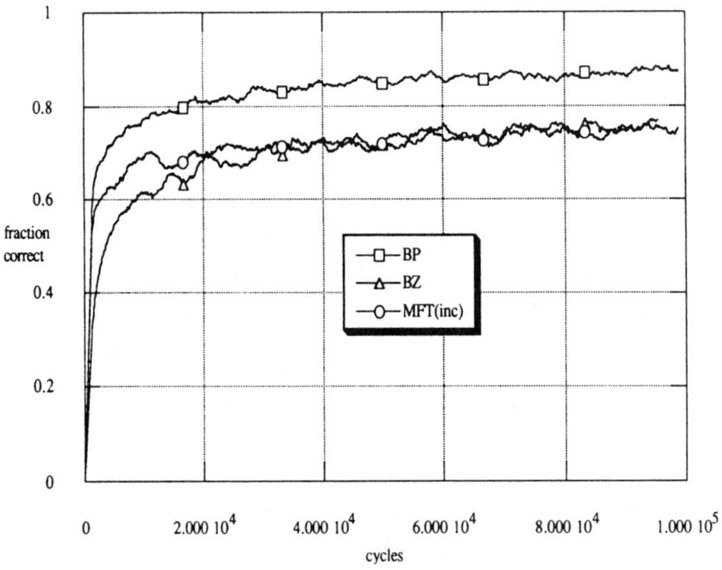

Figure 2. Learning Curves for NETtalk

2.4 Dynamic Range Manipulation

For all problems, we checked to see if reducing the dynamic range of the weights to 5 bits, equivalent to our VLSI implementation, would hinder learning. In most cases, there was no effect. Dynamic range was a limitation for the two largest replication problems with MFT. By adding an occasional global decay which decremented the absolute value of the weights, we were able to achieve good learning. Our implementation is capable of doing this. There was also a degradation of performance on the back-propagation version of the parity problem which took about a factor of three longer to learn with a 5 bit weight range.

3. VLSI IMPLEMENTATION

The previous section shows that relaxation networks are as capable as back-propagation networks of learning large problems even though they are slower in computer simulations. We are, however, implementing these feedback networks in VLSI which will speed up learning by many orders of magnitude. Our choice of learning technique for implementation is due mainly to the local learning rule which makes it much easier to cast these networks into electronics than back-propagation.

Figure 3. Photo of 32-Neuron Bellcore Learning Chip

Fig. 3 shows a microchip which has been fabricated. It contains 32 neurons and 992 connections (496 bidirectional synapses). On the extreme right is a noise generator which supplies 32 uncorrelated pseudo-random noise sources[9] to the neurons to their left. These noise sources are summed along with the weighted post-synaptic signals from other neurons at the input to each neuron in order to implement the simulated annealing process of the stochastic Boltzmann machine. The neuron amplifiers implement a non-linear activation function which has variable gain to provide for the gain sharpening function of the MFT technique. The range of neuron gain can also be adjusted to allow for scaling in summing currents due to adjustable network size.

Most of the area is occupied by the synapse array. Each synapse digitally stores a weight ranging from -15 to +15 as 4 bits plus a sign. It multiples the voltage input from the presynaptic neuron by this weight to output a current. One conductance direction can be disconnected so that we can experiment with asymmetric networks in accordance with our recent findings[10]. Although the synapses can have their weights set externally, they are designed to be adaptive. They store correlations using the local learning rule of Eq.

(5) and adjust their weights accordingly.

Although the chip is still being tested, some measurements can be reported. Fig. 4a shows a family of transfer functions of a neuron, showing how the gain is continually adjustable by varying a control voltage. Fig. 4b shows the transfer function of a synapse as different weights are loaded. The input linear range is about 2 volts.

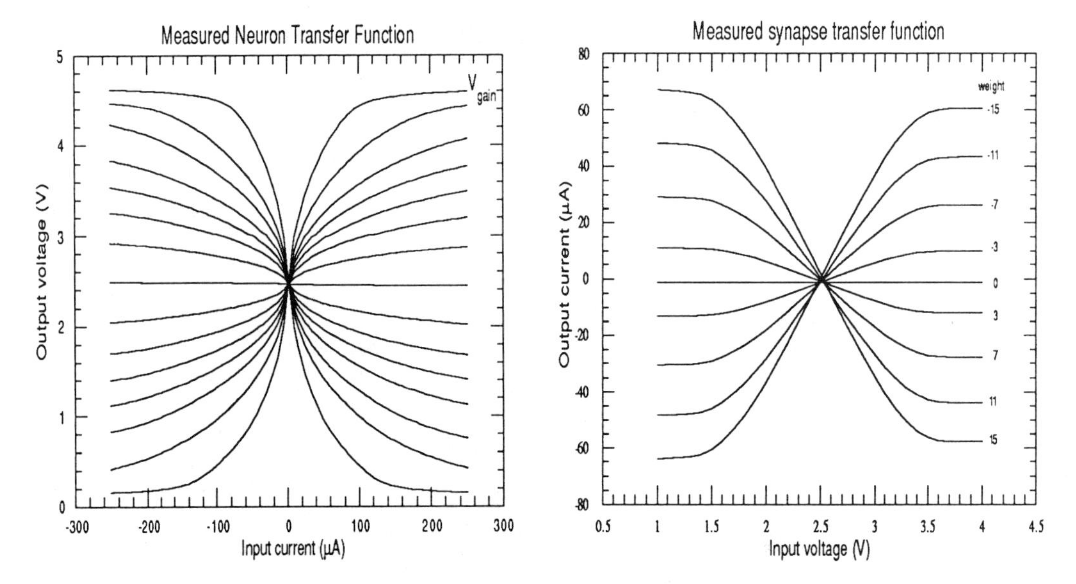

Figure 4. Transfer Functions of Electronic Neuron and Synapse

Fig. 5 shows two different neuron outputs with a decreasing noise signal added in. The upper trace shows a neuron driven by a function generator while the center trace shows an undriven neuron. The lower trace is the noise control voltage common to all neurons.

The chip is designed to be cascaded with other similar chips in a board-level system which can be accessed by a computer. The nodes which sum current from synapses for net input into a neuron are available externally for connection to other chips and for external clamping of neurons or other external input. We expect to be able to present roughly 100,000 patterns per second to the chip for learning as was determined from a previous prototype system[6] that was not cascadable. This speed will not be strongly affected by the increased network size of a multiple-chip system because of the inherent parallelism whereby each neuron and synapse updates its own state.

4. CONCLUSION

We have shown by simulation that relaxation networks of the kind we are implementing are as capable of learning large problems as back-propagation networks. A multiple-chip electronic system implementing these networks will make high-speed parallel learning in them feasible in the future.

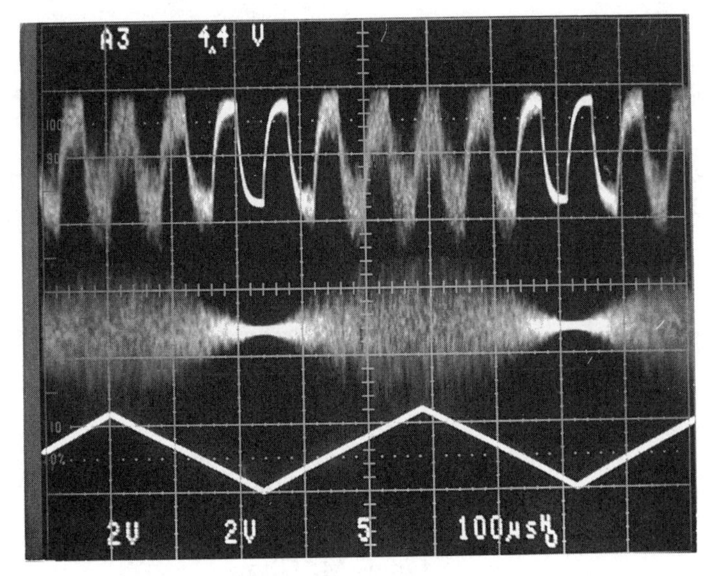

Figure 5. Neuron Signals in the Presence of Noise Generator Input

REFERENCES

1. D.E. Rumelhart, G.E. Hinton, & R.J. Williams, "Learning Internal Representations by Error Propagation", in *Parallel Distributed Processing: Explorations in the Microstructure of Cognition. Vol. 1: Foundations*, D.E. Rumelhart & J.L. McClelland (eds.), MIT Press, Cambridge, MA (1986), p. 318.

2. J.J. Hopfield, "Neural Networks and Physical Systems with Emergent Collective Computational Abilities", *Proc. Natl. Acad. Sci. USA*, **79** , 2554-2558 (1982).

3. D.H. Ackley, G.E. Hinton, & T.J. Sejnowski, "A Learning Algorithm for Boltzmann Machines", *Cognitive Science* **9** (1985) pp. 147-169.

4. C. Peterson & J.R. Anderson, "A Mean Field Learning Algorithm for Neural Networks", *Complex Systems*, **1:5**, 995-1019, (1987).

5. G. Hinton, "Deterministic Boltzmann Learning Performs Steepest Descent in Weight-Space", Neural Computation, **1,** 143-150 (1989).

6. J. Alspector, B. Gupta, & R.B. Allen, "Performance of a Stochastic Learning Microchip" in *Advances in Neural Information Processing Systems* edited by D. Touretzky (Morgan-Kaufmann, Palo Alto), pp. 748-760. (1989).

7. J.J. Hopfield, "Learning Algorithms and Probability Distributions in Feed-Forward and Feed-Back networks", *Proc. Natl. Acad. Sci. USA*, **84**, 8429-8433 (1987).

8. T.J. Sejnowski & C.R. Rosenberg, "Parallel Networks that Learn to Pronounce English Text", *Complex Systems*, **1**, 145-168 (1987).

9. J. Alspector, J.W. Gannett, S. Haber, M.B. Parker, & R. Chu, "A VLSI-Efficient Technique for Generating Multiple Uncorrelated Noise Sources and Its Application to Stochastic Neural Networks", *IEEE Trans. Circuits & Systems*, **38**, 109, (Jan., 1991).

10. R.B. Allen & J. Alspector, "Learning of Stable States in Stochastic Asymmetric Networks", *IEEE Trans. Neural Networks*, **1**, 233-238, (1990).

Design and Implementation of a High Speed CMAC Neural Network Using Programmable CMOS Logic Cell Arrays

W. Thomas Miller, III, Brian A. Box, and Erich C. Whitney
Department of Electrical and Computer Engineering
Kingsbury Hall
University of New Hampshire
Durham, New Hampshire 03824

James M. Glynn
Shenandoah Systems Company
1A Newington Park
West Park Drive
Newington, New Hampshire 03801

Abstract

A high speed implementation of the CMAC neural network was designed using dedicated CMOS logic. This technology was then used to implement two general purpose CMAC associative memory boards for the VME bus. Each board implements up to 8 independent CMAC networks with a total of one million adjustable weights. Each CMAC network can be configured to have from 1 to 512 integer inputs and from 1 to 8 integer outputs. Response times for typical CMAC networks are well below 1 millisecond, making the networks sufficiently fast for most robot control problems, and many pattern recognition and signal processing problems.

1 INTRODUCTION

We have been investigating learning techniques for the control of robotic manipulators which utilize extensions of the CMAC neural network as developed by Albus

(1972; 1975; 1979). The learning control techniques proposed have been studied in our laboratory in a series of real time experimental studies (Miller, 1986; 1987; 1989; Miller et al., 1987; 1988; 1990). These studies successfully demonstrated the ability to learn the kinematics of a robot/video camera system interacting with randomly oriented objects on a moving conveyor, and to learn the dynamics of a multi-axis industrial robot during high speed motions. We have also investigated the use of CMAC networks for pattern recognition (Glanz and Miller, 1987; Herold et al., 1988) and signal processing (Glanz and Miller, 1989) applications, with encouraging results. The primary goal of this project was to implement a compact, high speed version of the CMAC neural network using CMOS logic cell arrays. Two prototype CMAC associative memory systems for the industry standard VME bus were then constructed.

2 THE CMAC NEURAL NETWORK

Figure 1 shows a simple example of a CMAC network with two inputs and one output. Each variable in the input state vector is fed to a series of input sensors with overlapping receptive fields. The width of the receptive field of each sensor produces input generalization, while the offset of the adjacent fields produces input quantization. The binary outputs of the input sensors are combined in a series of threshold logic units (called state space detectors) with thresholds adjusted to produce logical AND functions. Each of these units receives one input from the group of sensors for each input variable, and thus its input receptive field is the interior of a hypercube in the input hyperspace. The input sensors are interconnected in a sparse and regular fashion, so that each input vector excites a fixed number of state space detectors. The outputs of the state space detectors are connected randomly to a smaller set of threshold logic units (called multiple field detectors) with thresholds adjusted such that the output will be on if any input is on. The receptive field of each of these units is thus the union of the fields of many of the state space detectors. Finally, the output of each multiple field detector is connected, through an adjustable weight, to an output summing unit. The output for a given input is thus the sum of the weights selected by the excited multiple field detectors.

The nonlinear nature of the CMAC network is embodied in the interconnections of the input sensors, state space detectors, and multiple field detectors, which perform a fixed nonlinear associative mapping of the continuous valued input vector to a many dimensional binary valued vector (which has tens or hundreds of thousands of dimensions in typical implementations). The adaptation problem is linear in this many dimensional space, and all of the convergence theorems for linear adaptive elements apply.

3 THE CMAC HARDWARE DESIGN

The custom implementation of the CMAC associative memory required the development of two devices. The first device performs the input associative mapping, converting application relevant input vectors into traditional RAM addresses. The second device performs CMAC response accumulation, summing the weights from all excited receptive fields. Both devices were implemented using 70 MHz XILINX

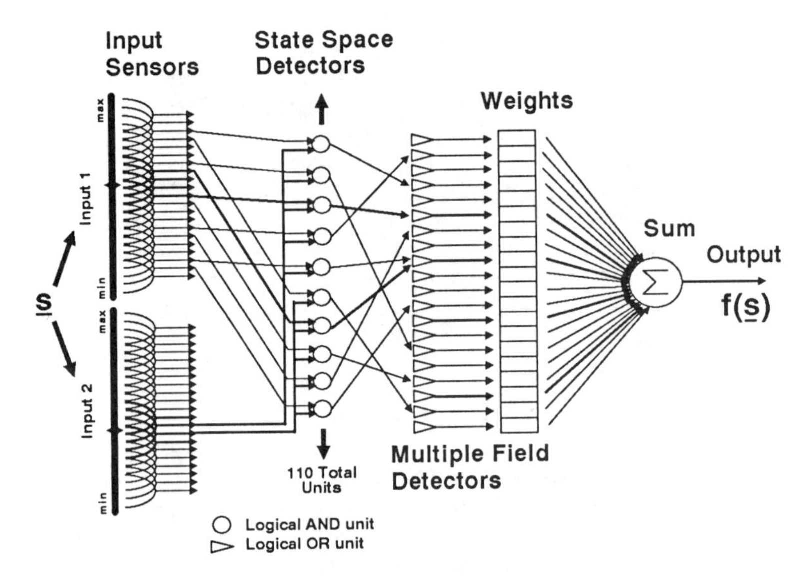

Figure 1: A Simple Example of a CMAC Neural Network

3090 programmable logic cell arrays.

The associative mapping device uses a bit recursive mapping scheme developed at UNH, which is similar in philosophy to the CMAC mapping proposed by Albus, but is structured for efficient implementation using discrete logic. The "address" of each excited virtual receptive field is formed recursively by clocking the input vector components sequentially from a buffer FIFO. The hashing of the virtual receptive field address to a physical RAM address is performed simultaneously, using pipelined logic. The resulting associative mapping generates one 18 bit RAM address for a given input vector. The multiple addresses, corresponding to the multiple receptive fields excited by a single input vector could be generated simultaneously using parallel addressing circuits, or sequentially using a single circuit.

The second CMAC device serves basically as an accumulator during CMAC response generation. As successive addresses are produced by the associative mapping circuit, the accumulator sums the corresponding values from the data RAM. During memory training, the response accumulation circuit adds the training adjustment to each of the addressed memory locations, placing the result back in the RAM. Eight independent CMAC output channels were placed on a single device.

In the final VME system design (Figure 2), a single CMAC associative mapping device was used. Overlapping receptive fields were implemented sequentially using the same device. A single CMAC response accumulation device was used, providing eight parallel output channels. A weight vector memory containing 1 million 8 bit weights was provided using 85 nanosecond 512 KByte static RAM SIMMs. A TMS320E15 microcontroller was utilized to supervise communications with the VME bus. The operational firmware for the microcontroller chip was designed to

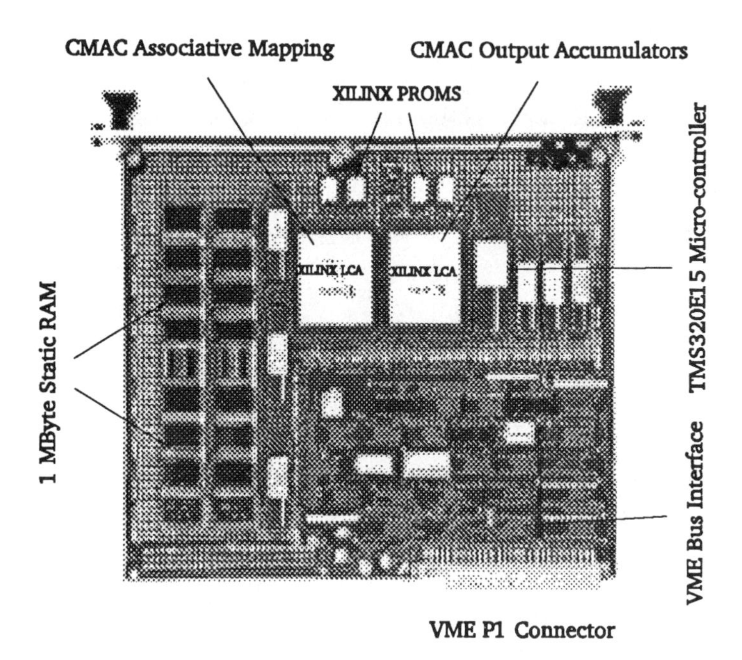

Figure 2: The Component Side of the VME Based CMAC Associative Memory Card. The two large XILINX 3090 logic cell arrays implement the CMAC associative mapping and the response accumulation/weight adjustment circuitry. The weights are stored in the 1 Mbyte static RAM. The TMS320E15 microcontroller supervises communications between the CMAC hardware and the VME host.

provide maximum flexibility in the logical organization of the CMAC associative memory, as viewed by the VME host system. The board can be initialized to act as from 1 to 8 independent virtual CMAC networks. For each network, the number of 16 bit inputs is selectable from 1 to 512, the number of 16 bit outputs is selectable from 1 to 8, and the number of overlapping receptive fields is selectable from 2 to 256.

Figure 3 shows typical response times during training and response generation operations for a CMAC network with 1 million adjustable weights. The data shown represent networks with 32 integer inputs and 8 integer outputs, with the number of overlapping receptive fields varied between 8 and 256. Throughout most of this range CMAC training and response times are well below 1 millisecond. These performance specifications should accommodate typical real time control problems (allowing 1000 cycle per second control rates), as well as many problems in pattern recognition.

A similar CMAC system for the 16 bit PC-AT bus has been developed by the Shenandoah Systems Company for commercial applications. This CMAC system supports both 8 and 16 bit adjustable weights (1 Mbyte total storage), and 8 independent virtual CMAC networks on a single card. Response times for the commercial CMAC-AT card are similar to those shown in Figure 3. A commercial version

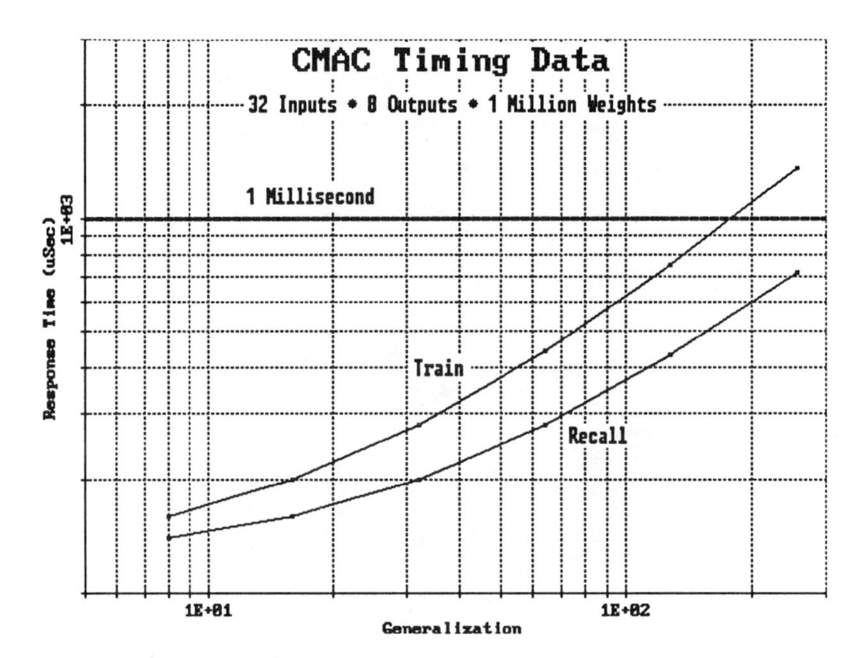

Figure 3: CMAC Associative Memory Response and Training Times. Response times are shown for values of the generalization parameter (the number of overlapping receptive fields) between 8 and 256. In each case the CMAC had 32 integer inputs, 8 integer outputs, and one million adjustable weights.

of the VME bus design is currently under development.

Acknowledgements

This work was sponsored in part by the Office of Naval Research (ONR Grant Number N00014-89-J-1686) and the National Institute of Standards and Technology.

References

Albus, J. S., *Theoretical and Experimental Aspects of a Cerebellar Model.* PhD Thesis, University of Maryland, Dec. 1972.

Albus, J. S., A New Approach to Manipulator Control: The Cerebellar Model Articulation Controller (CMAC). *Trans. of the ASME, Journal of Dynamic Systems, Measurement and Control,* vol. 97, pp. 220-227, September, 1975.

Albus, J. S., Mechanisms of Planning and Problem Solving in the Brain. *Mathematical Biosciences,* vol. 45, pp. 247-293, August, 1979.

Miller, W. T., A Nonlinear Learning Controller for Robotic Manipulators. *Proc. of the SPIE: Intelligent Robots and Computer Vision,* vol 726, pp. 416-423, October, 1986.

Miller, W. T., Sensor Based Control of Robotic Manipulators Using A General Learning Algorithm. *IEEE J. of Robotics and Automation,* vol. RA-3, pp. 157-165, April, 1987.

Miller, W. T., Glanz, F. H., and Kraft, L. G., Application of a General Learning Algorithm to the Control of Robotic Manipulators. *The International Journal of Robotics Research,* vol. 6.2, pp. 84-98, Summer, 1987.

Miller, W.T., and Hewes, R.P., Real Time Experiments in Neural Network Based Learning Control During High Speed, Nonrepetitive Robot Operations. *Proceedings of the Third IEEE International Symposium on Intelligent Control,* Washington, D.C., August 24-26, 1988.

Miller, W, T., Real Time Application of Neural Networks for Sensor-Based Control of Robots with Vision. *IEEE Transactions on Systems, Man, and Cybernetics.* Special issue on Information Technology for Sensory-Based Robot Manipulators, vol. 19, pp. 825-831, 1989.

Miller, W. T., Hewes, R. P., Glanz, F. H., and Kraft, L. G., Real Time Dynamic Control of an Industrial Manipulator Using a Neural Network Based Learning Controller. *IEEE J. of Robotics and Automation* vol. 6, pp. 1-9, 1990.

Glanz, F. H., Miller, W. T., Shape Recognition Using a CMAC Based Learning System. *Proceedings SPIE: Intelligent Robots and Computer Vision,* Cambridge, Mass., Nov., 1987.

Herold, D. J., Miller, W. T., Kraft, L. G., and Glanz, F. H., Pattern Recognition Using a CMAC Based Learning System. *Proceedings SPIE: Automated Inspection and High Speed Vision Architectures II,* vol. 1004, pp. 84-90, 1988.

Glanz, F. H., and Miller, W. T., Deconvolution and Nonlinear Inverse Filtering Using a Neural Network. *Proc. ICASSP 89,* Glasgow, Scotland, May 23-26, 1989, vol. 4, pp. 2349-2352.

Back Propagation Implementation on the Adaptive Solutions CNAPS Neurocomputer Chip

Hal McCartor
Adaptive Solutions Inc.
1400 N.W. Compton Drive
Suite 340
Beaverton, OR 97006

Abstract

The Adaptive Solutions CNAPS architecture chip is a general purpose neurocomputer chip. It has 64 processors, each with 4 K bytes of local memory, running at 25 megahertz. It is capable of implementing most current neural network algorithms with on chip learning. This paper discusses the implementation of the Back Propagation algorithm on an array of these chips and shows performance figures from a clock accurate hardware simulator. An eight chip configuration on one board can update 2.3 billion connections per second in learning mode and process 9.6 billion connections per second in feed forward mode.

1 Introduction

The huge computational requirements of neural networks and their natural parallelism have led to a number of interesting hardware innovations for executing such networks. Most investigators have created large parallel computers or special purpose chips limited to a small subset of algorithms. The Adaptive Solutions CNAPS architecture describes a general-purpose 64-processor chip which supports on chip learning and is capable of implementing most current algorithms. Implementation of the popular Back Propagation (BP) algorithm will demonstrate the speed and versatility of this new chip.

2 The Hardware Resources

The Adaptive Solutions CNAPS architecture is embodied in a single chip digital neurocomputer with 64 processors running at 25 megahertz. All processors receive the same instruction which they conditionally execute. Multiplication and addition are performed in parallel allowing 1.6 billion inner product steps per second per chip. Each processor has a 32-bit adder, 9-bit by 16-bit multiplier (16 by 16 in two clock cycles), shifter, logic unit, 32 16-bit registers, and 4096 bytes of local memory. Input and output are accomplished over 8-bit input and output buses common to all processors. The output bus is tied to the input bus so that output of one processor can be broadcast to all others. When multiple chips are used, they appear to the user as one chip with more processors. Special circuits support finding the maximum of values held in each processor and conserving weight space for sparsely connected networks. An accompanying sequencer chip controls instruction flow, input and output.

3 The Back Propagation Algorithm Implementation

Three critical issues must be addressed in the parallel implementation of BP on efficient hardware. These are the availability of weight values for back propagating the error, the scaling and precision of computations, and the efficient implementation of the output transfer function.

BP requires weight values at different nodes during the feed forward and back propagation phases of computation. This problem is solved by having a second set of weights which is the transpose of the output layer weights. These are located on hidden node processors. The two matrices are updated identically. The input to the hidden layer weight matrix is not used for error propagation and is not duplicated.

BP implementations typically use 32-bit floating point math. This largely eliminates scaling, precision and dynamic range issues. Efficient hardware implementation dictates integer arithmetic units with precision no greater than required. Baker [Bak90] has shown 16-bit integer weights are sufficient for BP training and much lower values adequate for use after training.

With fixed point integer math, the position of the binary point must be chosen. In this implementation weights are 16 bits and use 12 bits to the right of the binary point and four to the left including a sign bit. They range from -8 to +8. Input and output are represented as 8-bit unsigned integers with binary point at the left. The leaning rate is represented as an 8-bits integer with two bits to the left of the binary point and values ranging from .016 to 3.98. Error is represented as 8 bit signed integers at the output layer and with the same representation as the weights at the hidden layer.

This data representation has been used to train benchmark BP applications with results comparable to the floating point versions [HB91].

The BP sigmoid output function is implemented as an 8-bit by 256 lookup table.

During the forward pass input values are broadcast to all processors from off chip via the input bus or from hidden nodes via the output bus to the input bus. During the backward error propagation, error values are broadcast from the output nodes to hidden nodes.

The typical BP network has two computational layers, the hidden and output layers. They can be assigned to the same or different processor nodes (PNs) depending on available memory for weights. PNs used for the hidden layer contain the transpose weights of the output layer for back propagating error. If momentum or periodic weight update are used, additional storage space is allocated with each weight.

In this implementation BP can be mapped to any set of contiguous processors allowing multiple networks in CNAPS memory simultaneously. Thus, the output of one algorithm can be directly used as input to another. For instance, in speech recognition, a Fourier transform performed on the PN array could be input to a series of matched BP networks whose hidden layers run concurrently. Their output could be directed to an LVQ2 network for final classification. This can all be accomplished without any intermediate results leaving the chip array.

4 Results

BP networks have been successfully run on a hardware clock accurate simulator which gives the following timing results. In this example an eight-chip implementation (512 processors) was used. The network had 1900 inputs, 500 hidden nodes and 12 outputs. Weights were updated after each input and no momentum was used. The following calculations show BP performance:

TRAINING PHASE

Overhead clock cycles per input vector = 360
Cycles per input vector element = 4
Cycles per hidden node = 4
Cycles per output node = 7
Cycles per vector = 360+(1900*4)+(500*4)+(12*7) = 10,044
Vectors per second = 25,000,000 / 10,044 = 2,489
Total forward weights = (1900*500)+(500*12) = 956,000

Weight updates per second = 956,000*2,489 = 2,379,484,000

FEED FORWARD ONLY

Overhead cycles per input vector = 59
Cycles per input vector element = 1
Cycles per hidden node = 1
Cycles per output node = 1 (for output of data)
Cycles per vector = 59+1900+500+12 = 2,471
Vectors per second = 25,000,000/2,471 = 10,117

Connections per second = 956,000*10,117 = 9,671,852,000

5 Comparative Performance

An array of eight Adaptive Solutions CNAPS chips would execute the preceding BP network at 2.3 billion training weight updates per second or 9.6 billion feed forward connections per second. These results can be compared with the results on other computers shown in table 1.

MACHINE	MCUPS	MCPS	WTS
SUN 3 [D88]	.034	0.25	fp
SAIC SIGMA-1 [D88]		8	fp
WARP [PGTK88]	17		fp
CRAY 2 [PGTK88]	7		fp
CRAY X-MP [D88]		50	fp
CM-2 (65,536) [ZMMW90]	40	182	fp
GF-11 (566) [WZ89]	901		fp
8 ADAPTIVE CNAPS chips	2,379	9,671	16 bit int

Table 1. Comparison of BP performance for various computers and 8 Adaptive Solutions CNAPS chips on one board. MCUPS is Millions of BP connection updates per second in training mode. MCPS is millions of connections processed per second in feed forward mode. WTS is representation used for weights.

6 Summary

The Adaptive Solutions CNAPS chip is a very fast general purpose digital neurocomputer chip. It is capable of executing the Back Propagation algorithm quite efficiently. An 8 chip configuration can train 2.3 billion connections per second and evaluate 9.6 billion BP feed forward connections per second.

References

[Bak90] T Baker. Implementation limits for artificial neural networks. Master's thesis, Oregon Graduate Institute, 1990.

[D88] DARPA Neural Network Study. pp309-310 AFCEA International Press, Fairfax Virginia. 1988

[HB91] J. Holt and T. Baker. Back Propagation Simulations using Limited Precision Calculations. Submitted to IJCNN, Seattle WA 1991.

[RM86] D. Rummelhart, J. McClelland. Parallel Distributed Processing. (1986) MIT Press, Cambridge, MA.

[WZ89] M. Witbrock and M Zagha. An Implementation of Back-Propagation Learning on GF11, a Large SIMD Parallel Computer. 1989. Tech report CMU-CS-89-208 Carnegie Mellon University.

[ZMMW90] X. Zhang, M. Mckenna, J Misirov, D Waltz. An Efficient Implementation of the Back-propagation Algorithm on the Connection Machine CM-2 (1990) in Adv. in Neural Information Processing Systems 2. Ed. D. Touretzky. Morgan Kaufmann, San Mateo, CA.

Reconfigurable Neural Net Chip with 32K Connections

H.P. Graf, R. Janow, D. Henderson, and R. Lee
AT&T Bell Laboratories, Room 4G320, Holmdel, NJ 07733

Abstract

We describe a CMOS neural net chip with a reconfigurable network architecture. It contains 32,768 binary, programmable connections arranged in 256 'building block' neurons. Several 'building blocks' can be connected to form long neurons with up to 1024 binary connections or to form neurons with analog connections. Single- or multi-layer networks can be implemented with this chip. We have integrated this chip into a board system together with a digital signal processor and fast memory. This system is currently in use for image processing applications in which the chip extracts features such as edges and corners from binary and gray-level images.

1 INTRODUCTION

A key problem for a hardware implementation of neural nets is to find the proper network architecture. With a fixed network structure only few problems can be solved efficiently. Therefore, we opted for a programmable architecture that can be changed under software control. A large, fully interconnected network can, in principle, implement any architecture, but this usually wastes a lot of the connections since many have to be set to zero. To make better use of the silicon, other designs implemented a programmable architecture - either by connecting several chips with switching blocks (Mueller89), or by placing switches between blocks of synapses on one chip (Satyanarayana90). The present design (Graf90) consists of building blocks that can be connected to form many different network configurations. Single-layer nets or multi-layer nets can be implemented. The connections can be binary or can have an analog depth of up to four bits.

We designed this neural net chip mainly for pattern recognition applications, which typically require nets far too large for a single chip. However, the nets can often be structured so that the neurons have local receptive fields, and many neurons share the same receptive field. Such nets can be split into smaller parts that fit onto a chip, and the small nets are then scanned sequentially over an image. The circuit has been optimized for this type of network by adding shift registers for the data transport.

The neural net chip implementation uses a mixture of analog and digital electronics. The weights, the neuron states and all the control signals are digital, while summing the contributions of all the weights is performed in analog form. All the data going on and off the chip are digital, which makes the integration of the network into a digital system straight-forward.

2 THE CIRCUIT ARCHITECTURE

2.1 The Building Block

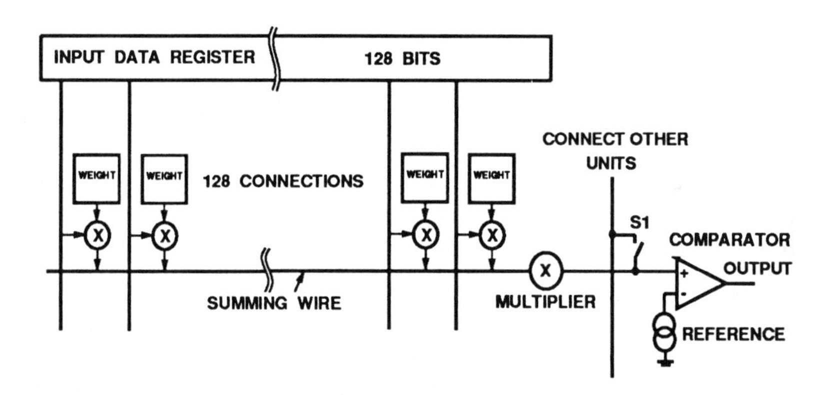

Figure 1: One of the building blocks, a "neuron"

Figure 1 shows schematically one of the building blocks. It consists of an array of 128 connections which receive input signals from other neurons or from external sources. The weights as well as the inputs have binary values, +1 or -1. The output of a connection is a current representing the result of the multiplication of a weight with a state, and on a wire the currents from all the connections are summed. This sum is multiplied with a programmable factor and can be added to the currents of other neurons. The result is compared with a reference and is thresholded in a comparator. A total of 256 such building blocks are contained on the chip.

Up to 8 of the building blocks can be connected to form a single neuron with up to 1024 connections. The network is not restricted to binary connections. Connections with four bits of analog depth are obtained by joining four building blocks and by setting each of the multipliers to a different value: 1, 1/2, 1/4, 1/8 (see Figure

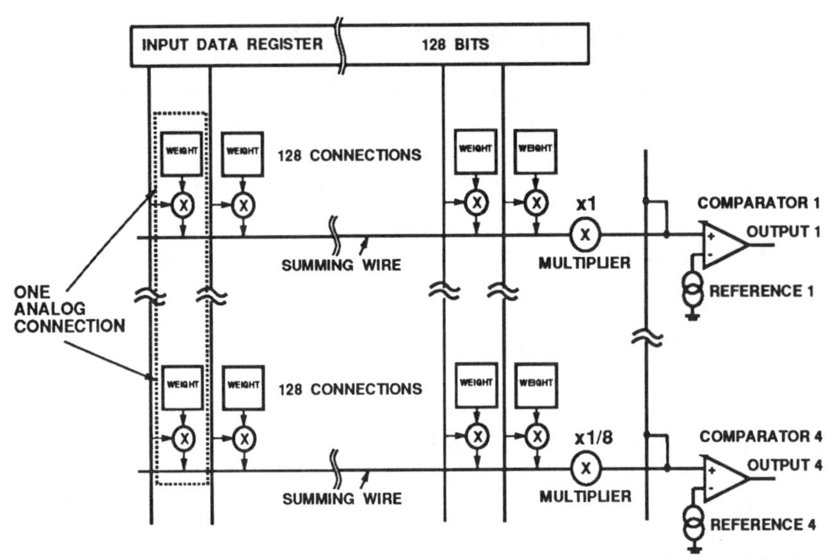

Figure 2: Connecting four building blocks to form connections with four bits of resolution

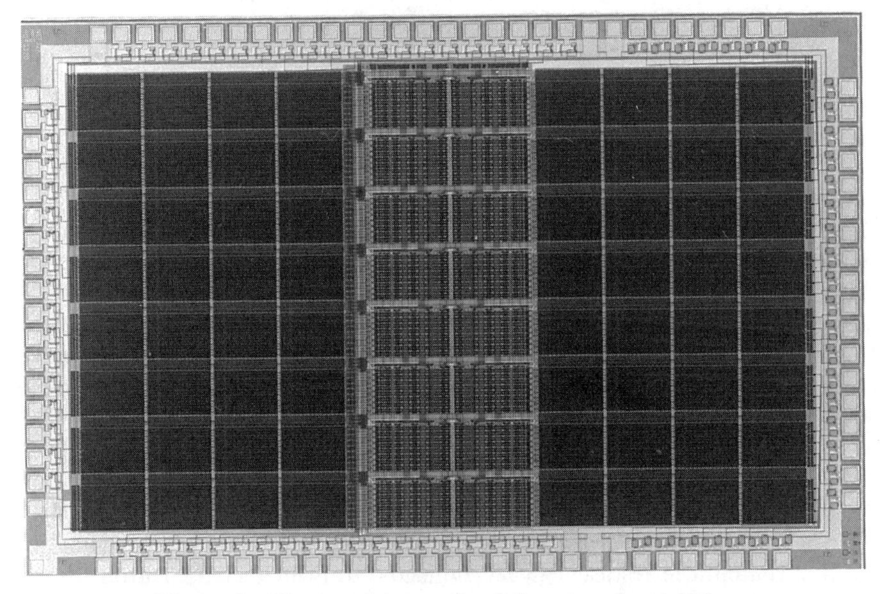

Figure 3: Photo micrograph of the neural net chip

2). In this case four binary connections, one in each building block, form one connection with an analog depth of four bits. Alternatively, the network can be configured for two-bit input signals and two-bit weights or four-bit inputs and one-bit weights. The multiplications of the input signals with the weights are four-quadrant multiplications, whether binary signals are used or multi-bit signals. With this approach only one scaling multiplier is needed per neuron, instead of one per connection as would be the case if connections were implemented with multiplying D/A converters.

The transfer function of a neuron is provided by the comparator. With a single comparator the transfer function has a hard threshold. Other types of transfer functions can be obtained when several building blocks are connected. Then, several comparators receive the same analog input and for each comparator a different reference can be selected (compare figure 2). In this way, for example, eight comparators may work as a three-bit A/D converter. Other transfer functions, such as sigmoids, can be approximated by selecting appropriate thresholds for the comparators.

The neurons are arranged in groups of 16. For each group there is one register of 128 bits providing the input data. The whole network contains 16 such groups, split in two halfs, each with eight groups. These groups of neurons can be recognized in Figure 3 that shows a photomicrograph of the circuit. The chip contains 412,000 transistors and measures 4.5mm x 7mm. It is fabricated in 0.9μm CMOS technology with one level of poly and two levels of metal.

2.2 Moving Data Through The Circuit

From a user's point of view the chip consists of the four different types of registers listed in table 1. Programming of the chip consists in moving the data over a high-speed bus of 128 bits width between these registers. Results produced by the network can be loaded directly into data-input registers and can be used for a next computation. In this way some multi-layer networks can be implemented without loading data off chip between layers.

Table 1: Registers in the neural net chip

REGISTER	FUNCTION
Shift register	Input and output of the data
Data-input registers	Provide input to the connections
Configuration registers	Determine the connectivity of the network
Result registers	Contain the output of the network

In a typical operation 16 bits are loaded from the outside into a shift register. From that register the main bus distributes the data through the whole circuit. They are loaded into one or several of the data-input registers. The analog computation is then started and the results are latched into the result registers. These results are loaded either into data-input registers if a network with feedback or a multi-layer network is implemented, or they are loaded into the output shift register and off chip.

In addition to the main bus, the chip contains two 128 bit wide shift registers, one through each half of the connection matrix. All the shift registers were added to speed up the operation when networks with local fields of view are scanned over a signal. In such an application shift registers drastically reduce the amount of new data that have to be loaded into the chip from one run to the next. For example, when an input field of 16 x 16 pixels is scanned over an image, only 16 new data values have to be loaded for each run instead of 256. Loading the data on and off the chip is often the speed-limiting operation. Therefore, it is important to provide some support in hardware.

3 TEST RESULTS

The speed of the circuit is limited by the time it takes the analog computation to settle to its final value. This operation requires less than 50 ns. The chip can be operated with instruction cycles of 100ns, where in the first 50 ns the analog computation settles down and during the following 50 ns the results are read out. Simultaneously with reading out the results, new data are loaded into the data-input registers. In this way 32k one-bit multiply-accumulates are executed every 100ns, which amounts to 320 billion connections/second.

The accuracy of the analog computation is about ±5%. This means, for example, that a comparator whose threshold is set to a value of 100 connections may already turn on when it receives the current from 95 connections. This limited accuracy is due to mismatches of the devices used for the analog computation. However, the threshold for each comparator may be individually adjusted at the cost of dedicating neurons to the task. Then a threshold can be adjusted to ±1%. The operation of the digital part of the network and the analog part has been synchronized in such a way that the noise generated by the digital part has a minimal effect on the analog computation.

4 THE BOARD SYSTEM

A system was developed to use the neural net chip as a coprocessor of a workstation with a VME bus. A schematic of this system is shown in figure 4. Beside the neural net chip, the board contains a digital signal processor to control the whole system and 256k of fast memory. Pictures are loaded from the host into the board's memory and are then scanned with the neural net chip. The results are loaded back into the board memory and from there to the host.

Loading pictures over the VME bus limits the overall speed of this system to about one frame of 512 x 512 pixels per second. Although this corresponds to less than 10% of the chips maximum data throughput, operations such as scanning an image with 32 16 x 16 kernels can be done in one second. The same operation would take around 30 minutes on the workstation alone. Therefore, this system represents a very useful tool for image processing, in particular for developing algorithms. Its architecture makes it very flexible since part of a problem can be solved by the digital signal processor and the computationally intensive parts on the neural net chip. An extra data path for the signals will be added later to take full advantage of the neural net's speed.

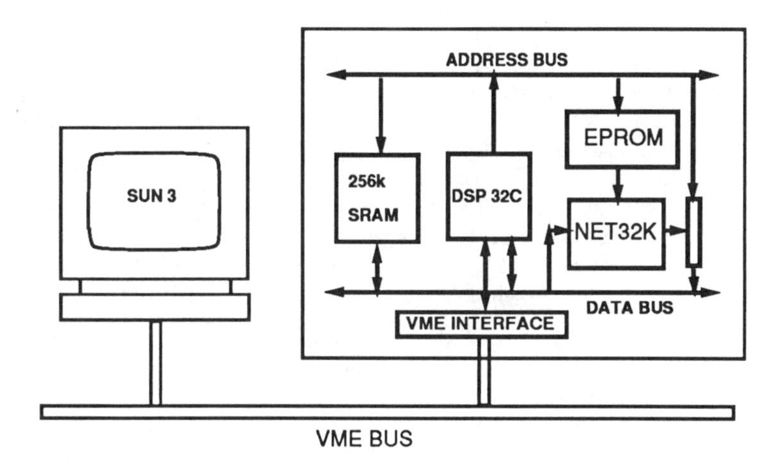

Figure 4: Schematic of the board system for the neural net chip

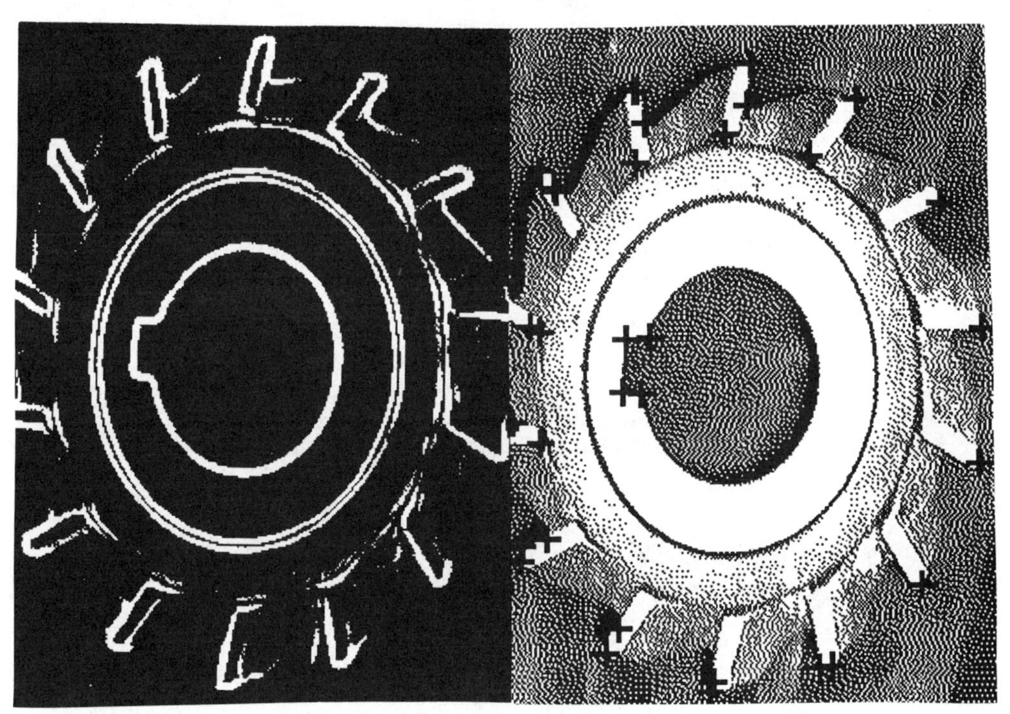

Figure 5: Result of a feature extraction application. Left image: Edges extracted from the milling cutter. Right image: The crosses mark where corners were detected. A total of 16 features were extracted simultaneously with detectors of 16 x 16 pixels in size.

5 APPLICATIONS

Figure 5 shows the result of an application, where the net is used for extracting simultaneously edges and corners from a gray-level image. The network actually handles only a small resolution in the pixel values. Therefore, the picture is first half-toned with a standard error-diffusion algorithm and then, the halftoned image is scanned with the network. To extract these features, kernels with three levels in the weights are loaded into the network. One neuron with 256 two-bit connections represents one kernel. There are a total of 16 such kernels in the network, each one tuned to a corner or an edge of a different orientation. For each comparator an extra neuron is used to set the threshold. This whole task fills 50% of the chip.

Edges and corners are important features that are often used to identify objects or to determine their positions and orientations. We are applying them now to segment complex images. Convolutional algorithms have long been recognized as reliable methods for extracting features. However, they are computationally very expensive so that often special-purpose hardware is required. To our knowledge, no other circuit can extract such a large number of features at a comparable rate.

This application demonstrates, how a large number of connections can compensate for a limited resolution in the weights and the states. We took a gray level image and clipped its pixels to binary values. Despite this coarse quantization of the signal the relevant information can be extracted reliably. Since many connections are contributing to each result, uncorrelated errors due to quantization are averaged out. The key to a good result is to make sure that the quantization errors are indeed uncorrelated, at least approximately.

This circuit has been designed with pattern matching applications in mind. However, its flexibility makes it suitable for a much wider range of applications. In particular, since its connections as well as its architecture can be changed fast, in the order of 100ns, it can be integrated in an adaptive or a learning system.

Acknowledgements

We acknowledge many stimulating discussions with the other members of the neural network group at AT&T in Holmdel. Part of this work was supported by the USASDC under contract #DASG60-88-0044.

References

H. P. Graf & D. Henderson. (1990) A Reconfigurable CMOS Neural Network. in *Digest IEEE Int. Solid State Circuits Conf.* , 144-145.

P. Mueller, J. van der Spiegel, D. Blackman, T. Chiu, T. Clare, J. Dao, Ch. Donham, T.P. Hsieh & M. Loinaz. (1989) A Programmable Analog Neural Computer and Simulator. In D.S. Touretzky (ed.), *Advances in Neural Information Processing Systems 1*, 712 - 719. San Mateo, CA: Morgan Kaufmann.

S. Satyanarayana, Y. Tsividis & H. P. Graf. (1990) A Reconfigurable Analog VLSI Neural Network Chip. In D.S. Touretzky (ed.), *Advances in Neural Information Processing Systems 2*, 758 - 768. San Mateo, CA: Morgan Kaufmann.

Simulation of the Neocognitron on a CCD Parallel Processing Architecture

Michael L. Chuang and Alice M. Chiang
M.I.T Lincoln Laboratory
Lexington, MA 02173
e-mail: *chuang@micro.ll.mit.edu*

Abstract

The neocognitron is a neural network for pattern recognition and feature extraction. An analog CCD parallel processing architecture developed at Lincoln Laboratory is particularly well suited to the computational requirements of shared-weight networks such as the neocognitron, and implementation of the neocognitron using the CCD architecture was simulated. A modification to the neocognitron training procedure, which improves network performance under the limited arithmetic precision that would be imposed by the CCD architecture, is presented.

1 INTRODUCTION

Multilayer neural networks characterized by local interlayer connectivity and groups of nodes that are constrained to have the same weights on their input lines are often refered to as shared-weight networks. A group of nodes with identical weights where each node is connected to a different portion of the layer immediately beneath can be thought of as a collection of spatially replicated receptive fields. Among the desirable attributes of shared-weight networks is the fact that substantially less storage is required for weights than would be required by a more conventional network with a comparable number of nodes. Furthermore, reducing the number of free parameters through use of shared weights and local receptive fields, as opposed to simply reducing the number of hidden nodes, may be an effective way of obtaining good generalization when only a small training set is available (Martin and Pittman, 1989). However, the most immediately obvious attribute of a shared-weight architecture is that the replicated receptive fields allow a learned feature to be detected anywhere within the input. This feature is particularly useful in tasks where position invariance is required (Le Cun, 1989). Neural networks using shared weights have been applied successfully to areas ranging from handwritten digit recognition (Le Cun, Boser, et. al., 1989) to phoneme extraction in speech preprocessing (Waibel, et. al., 1989).

A CCD architecture that is well suited to implementing shared-weight networks has been developed at Lincoln Laboratory (Chiang and LaFranchise, 1991). This architecture performs high-speed inner product computations and is able to accommodate the often complicated data access patterns of a shared-weight network without imposing the burden of this complexity on the host computer; input and output to devices built using this architecture are simple. The neocognitron (Fukushima, 1988) was selected as a candidate for implementation by the CCD architecture. In particular, we were interested the effect that limited precision arithmetic might have on network performance.

2 THE NEOCOGNITRON

The neocognitron is a multilayer feed-forward neural network for pattern recognition. The nodes or cells in each layer or level of the neocognitron are further subdivided into cell planes, where all the nodes in a given cell plane are feature detectors tuned to the same feature but connected to a different portion of the level immediately beneath (the first level has cell planes connected directly to the input). Each cell plane can be viewed as an array of identical, overlapping receptive fields.

Three types of processing elements or nodes are used in the neocognitron. S-cells perform feature extraction, c-cells compensate for local shifts of features, and v-cells are intended to prevent random excitation of s-cells. A given cell plane contains only one type of node. A cell plane containing only s-cells, for example, is thus called an s-plane. Each level of the network contains several s-planes, an identical number of c-planes, and exactly one v-plane. The function of an s-cell is to generate a nonlinear function of the inner product of a stored weight template $a_\lambda(k, \kappa, i, j)$ and the contents of its receptive field. (In this notation λ denotes the level of the s-plane with which the template is associated, and the k and κ indicate the particular s- and c-planes between which the template serves as a connection. The i, j are spatial coordinates within the template.) An s-plane is therefore a feature map of its input. Each c-plane is paired with a single s-plane of the same level. A c-cell has a small receptive field on its correpsonding s-plane and performs a weighted average of the values of the s-cells to which it is connected. This implements a form of local feature-shift invariance, and a c-plane is a feature map of its input which is unchanged by small translations of features in the input. A schematic of a three-level neocognitron is shown in Figure 1.

The cell planes in the first level of the network typically correspond to maps of simple features such as oriented line segments. The second level of the neocognitron is given the output of the first-level c-planes as input, and tends to form more complicated features from the first-level cell planes. Successively higher levels correspond to even more complex features; at the top level, each c-cell (of which there is exactly one in each top-level c-plane) corresponds to one input pattern in a trained neocognitron. The basic idea is to break up each input pattern into simple components such as line segments and corners, then to put the pieces back together, allowing a certain

An image feature extractor (IFE) device suitable for performing the inner products required by a neural network with local receptive fields and shared weights has been fabricated (Chiang and LaFranchise, 1991). The IFE consists of a 775-stage CCD tapped delay line for holding and shifting input pixels or node values, 49 eight-bit, four-quadrant multiplying digital-to-analog converters (MDACs), and on-chip storage for 980 eight-bit digital weights. Figure 2 is a photomicrograph of the chip, which has an area of 29 mm^2 and performs over one billion arithmetic operations/second when clocked at 10 MHz. The device dissipates less than 1 W.

The 49 MDACs of the IFE are arranged in a 7×7 array; each MDAC nondestructively senses the value held in an appropriate point along the 775-stage tapped delay line, which holds six 128-pixel lines, plus seven pixels of the following line, of the input image. Image pixels are continuously loaded into the device in row-by-row fashion. Each MDAC has a local memory of twenty eight-bit digital weights for holding inner product kernel or template values. Conceptually, the device scans a 7×7 "window" over an input array, shifting one position at each step, and computes the inner product of each of the twenty templates with the portion of the image beneath the window. The multiplications of each inner product are performed in parallel and the partial sums are connected to a common output line, allowing the complete inner product to be computed in one clock. In actuality, the device passes the input image under the 7×7 window, performing twenty inner products with each shift of the image. A schematic of data flow through the IFE device is shown in Figure 3.

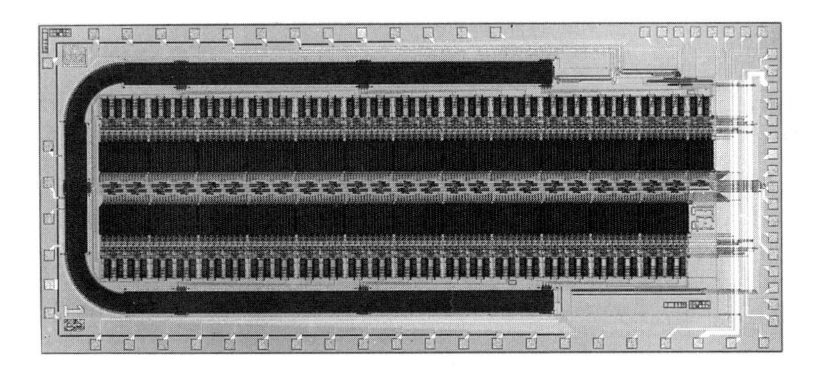

Figure 2: Photomicrograph of the CCD Image Feature Extractor

4 A MODIFIED TRAINING ALGORITHM

Most computer simulations of the neocognitron have used floating point arithmetic as well as weights which are, for all practical purposes, real numbers. However, a neocognitron implemented using an IFE device would use fairly low precision

amount of relative position shift between the pieces at each stage of reassembly. This allows the network to identify deformed or shifted inputs. The extent to which a particular network is able to tolerate deformation of input patterns depends on the amount of overlap between adjacent receptive fields as well as the size and weighting of c-cell receptive fields.

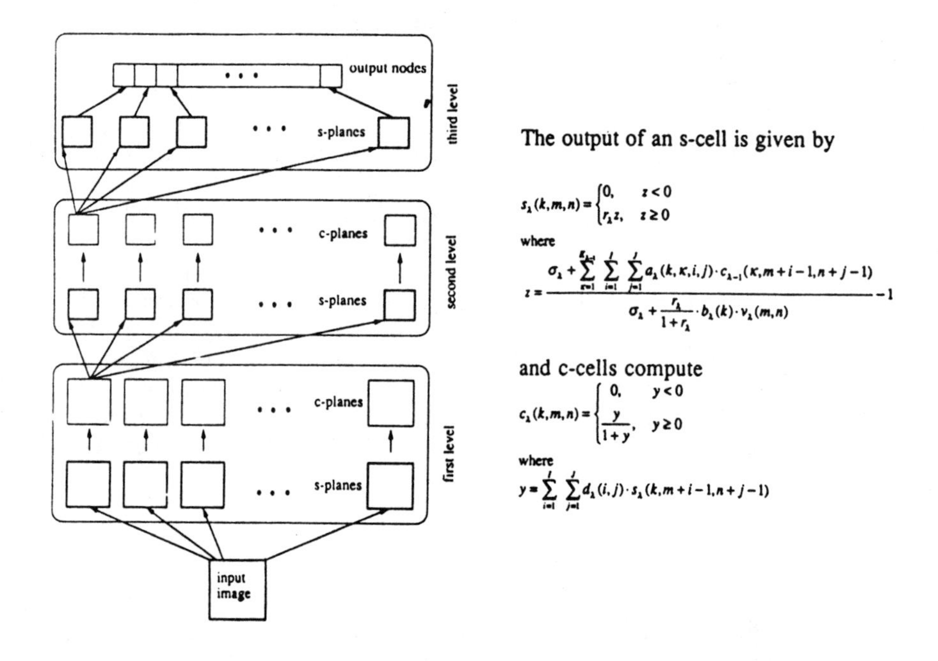

Figure 1: Schematic of a Three-Level Neocognitron

The majority of the computation in the neocognitron consists of the inner products. A good implementation of shared-weight networks such as the neocognitron must be capable of performing high speed inner product computations as well as supporting the data access patterns of the algorithm efficiently. A device which meets both these requirements is described in the following section.

3 THE IMAGE FEATURE EXTRACTOR

The neocognitron is most easily visualized as a three-dimensional structure built of the s-, c- and v-cells, but the s- and c-planes can be generated by raster scanning weight templates whose values are the $a_\lambda(k, \kappa, i, j)$ or the $d_\lambda(i, j)$, respectively, over the appropriate input. This operation can be performed efficiently by the CCD architecture alluded to in the Introduction. In this architecture, analog node values are represented using charge packets while fully programmable weight values are stored digitally on-chip. The multiplications of the generic weighted sum computation are performed in parallel, with the summation performed in the charge domain, yielding a complete inner product sum on each clock.

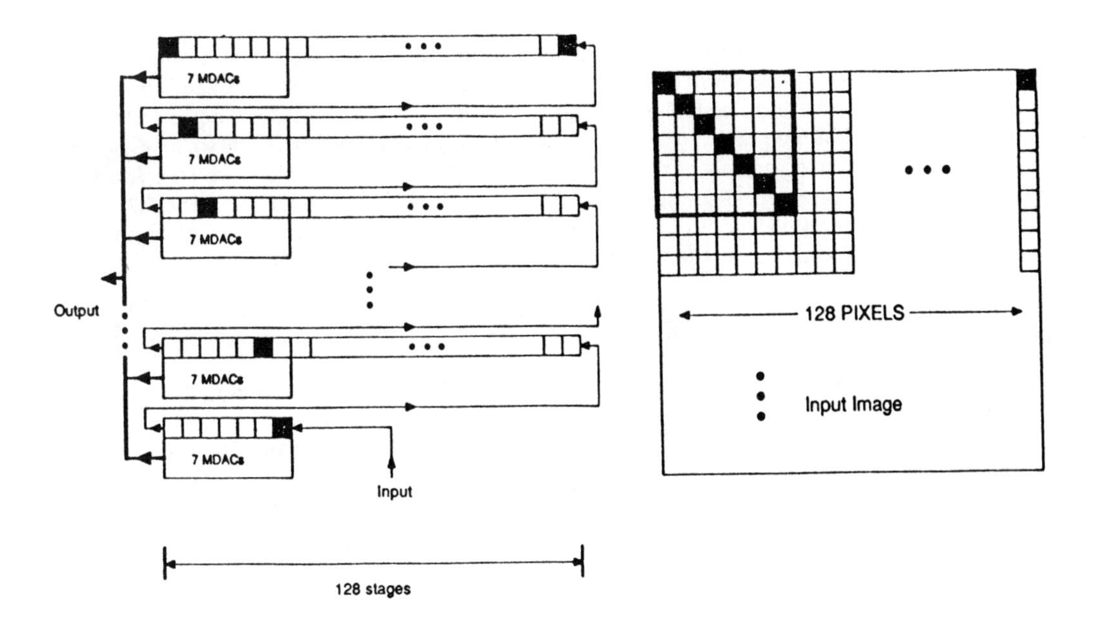

Figure 3: Dataflow in the Image Feature Extractor

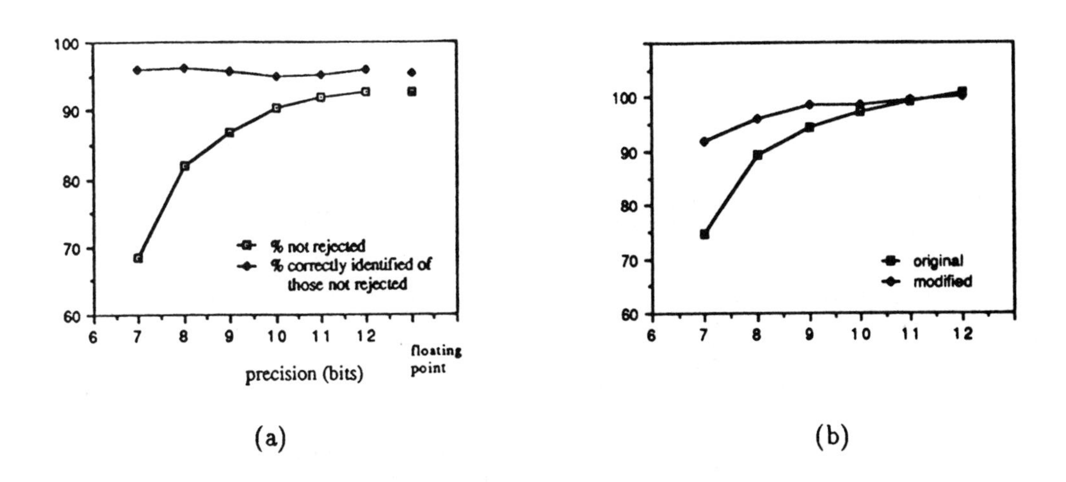

Figure 4: (a) Effect of Arithmetic Precision on Classification (b) Comparision of Original and Modified Training Procedures

arithmetic and quantized weights. In order to determine whether the neocognitron would continue to perform under such restrictions, a software simulation of neocognitrons using low precision arithmetic was implemented. Weights were taken from a network that was previously trained using floating point arithmetic and quantized to a number of bits equal to the arithmetic precision. As can be seen from Figure 4(a), the fraction of inputs correctly identified (bottom curve) from a test set of handwritten letters decreases substantially as arithmetic precision is reduced. Although the error rate (top curve) remains approximately constant, lower arithmetic precision tends to increase the number of rejections.

4.1 EFFECT OF LIMITED PRECISION

Inspection of the weights revealed that the range of weights from previously trained nets was too large to be represented using the number of bits available. Either small weights were set to zero, large weights were clipped, or both. Networks trained using low precision arithmetic tended to group all input patterns into a single category. This can again be attributed to the restricted range of possible weight values. The neocognitron training algorithm consists of assigning small random initial values to weights and presenting training inputs. The connection weights that produce strong responses are increased according to

$$a_\lambda^\gamma(k,\kappa,i,j) = a_\lambda^{\gamma-1}(k,\kappa,i,j) + \Delta a_\lambda^\gamma(k,\kappa,i,j)$$
$$\Delta a_\lambda^\gamma(k,\kappa,i,j) = q_\lambda \cdot f_{\lambda-1}(i,j) \cdot c_{\lambda-1}^\gamma(\kappa, m_\gamma + i - 1, n_\gamma + j - 1) \geq 0$$

$$b_\lambda^\gamma(k) = b_\lambda^{\gamma-1}(k) + \Delta b_\lambda^\gamma(k)$$
$$\Delta b_\lambda^\gamma(k) = q_\lambda \cdot v_\lambda^\gamma(m_\gamma, n_\gamma) \geq 0$$

where γ is an update index. Restricted to a fairly small range of numbers, weights could not be increased to the point where the contribution of the cell planes whose initial random weights were unchanged became negligible. Those initial weights that were not updated contribute random features to the recognition process; the effect is that of adding noise.

4.2 WEIGHT NORMALIZATION

In order to reduce the effects of clipping on the quantized weights, the weight update algorithm was modified. As can be seen from the weight update equations, the standard training procedure allows the $a_\lambda(k,\kappa,i,j)$ values to grow without bound. The inner product of the weights and the input is normalized implicitly when computing the s-cell output. Rather than using the available numerical range so lavishly, the algorithm was modified to normalize the $a_\lambda(k,\kappa,i,j)$ templates explicitly during training after they reached a prespecified bound. The reduction in classification performance as computational precision decreases is compared between neocognitrons trained using the modified algorithm and networks trained using the original algorithm in Figure 4(b). Networks trained using the modified algorithm have somewhat higher (less than 5 percent) rejection and error rates compared to original networks when using floating point arithmetic, but demonstrate significantly better performance when computational precision is limited to eight bits or less.

5 SUMMARY

We have presented a CCD architecture that is well matched to the computational requirements of shared-weight neural networks with local connectivity. The implementation of the neocognitron, a shared-weight network for pattern recognition and feature extraction, was simulated and a new training procedure that significantly improves classification when limited precision arithmetic is used, is presented.

Acknowledgements

This work was supported by the Office of Naval Resarch, DARPA, and the Department of the Air Force.

References

A. M. Chiang and J. R. LaFranchise, "A Programmable Image Processor," to appear in the *ISSCC Digest of Technical Papers 1991.*

M. L. Chuang, *A Study of the Neocognitron Pattern Recognition Algorithm.* Master's Thesis, Massachusetts Institute of Technology, Dept. of Electrical Engineering and Computer Science, Cambridge, MA, June 1990.

K. Fukushima, "A Neural Network for Visual Pattern Recogniton," *IEEE Computer*, vol. 21, no. 3. pp. 65-75, March, 1988.

Y. Le Cun, "Generalization and Network Design Strategies," *Technical Report CRG-TR-89-4*, Department of Computer Science, University of Toronto, 1989.

Y. Le Cun, B. Boser, J. Denker, J. Henderson, D. Howard, R. Hubbard, and L. Jackel, "Handwritten Digit Recognition with a Back-Propagation Network," in D. S. Touretzky (ed.), *Advances in Neural Information Processing Systems 2*, pp. 396-404, San Mateo, CA: Morgan Kaufmann, 1989.

G. L. Martin and J. A. Pittman, "Recognizing Hand-Printed Letters and Digits," in D. S. Touretzky (ed.), *Advances in Neural Information Processing Systems 2*, pp. 405-414, San Mateo, CA: Morgan Kaufmann, 1989.

A. Waibel, T. Hanazawa, G. Hinton, K. Shikano, and K. J. Lang, "Phoneme Recognition Using Time-Delay Neural Networks," *IEEE Trans. on Acoustics, Speech and Signal Processing*, vol. 37, no. 3, pp. 329-339, March 1989.

VLSI Implementation of TInMANN

Matt Melton Tan Phan Doug Reeves Dave Van den Bout
Electrical and Computer Engineering Dept.
North Carolina State University
Raleigh, NC 27695-7911

Abstract

A massively parallel, all-digital, stochastic architecture — TInMANN — is described which performs competitive and Kohonen types of learning. A VLSI design is shown for a TInMANN neuron which fits within a small, inexpensive MOSIS TinyChip frame, yet which can be used to build larger networks of several hundred neurons. The neuron operates at a speed of 15 MHz which allows the network to process 290,000 training examples per second. Use of level sensitive scan logic provides the chip with 100% fault coverage, permitting very reliable neural systems to be built.

1 INTRODUCTION

Uniprocessor simulation of neural networks has been the norm, but benefiting from the parallelism in neural networks is impossible without specialized hardware. Most hardware-based neural network simulators use a single high-speed ALU or multiple DSP chips connected through communication buses. The first approach does not allow exploration of the effects of parallelism, while the complex processors used in the second approach hinder investigations into the minimal hardware needs of an implementation. Such knowledge can be gained only if an implementation possess the same characteristics as a neural network — i.e. that it be built from many simple, cooperating processing elements. However, constructing and connecting large numbers of processing elements (or *neurons*) is difficult. Highly-connected, densely-packed analog neurons can be practically realized on a single VLSI chip, but interconnecting several such chips into a larger system would require many I/O pins. In addition, external parasitic capacitances and noise can affect the reliable transfer of data between the chips. These problems are avoided in neural systems based on noise-resistant digital signals that can be multiplexed over a small number of wires.

The next section of this paper describes the basic theory, algorithm, and architecture of the TInMANN digital neural network. The third section illustrates the VLSI design of a TInMANN neuron that operates at 15 MHz, is completely testable, and can be cascaded to form large Kohonen or competitive networks.

2 TInMANN ALGORITHM AND ARCHITECTURE

In the competitive learning algorithm (Rumelhart, 1986), training vectors of length W, $\mathbf{v}=(v_1, v_2, \ldots, v_W)$, are presented to a winner-take-all network of N neurons. Each neuron i possesses a weight vector of length W, $\mathbf{w}_i = (w_{i1}, w_{i2}, \ldots, w_{iW})$, and a winning neuron k is selected as the one whose weight vector is closest to the current training vector. Neuron k is then moved closer to the training vector by modifying its weights as follows

$$w_{kj} \Leftarrow w_{kj} + \epsilon \cdot (v_j - w_{kj}) \quad 0 < \epsilon < 1, \ 1 \leq j \leq W .$$

If the network is trained with a set of vectors that are naturally clustered into N groups, then each neural weight vector will eventually reside in the center of a different group. Thereafter, an input vector applied to the network is encoded by the neuron that has been sensitized to the cluster containing the input.

Kohonen's self-organizing feature maps (Kohonen, 1982) are trained using a generalization of competitive learning where each neuron i is provided with an additional X-element vector, $\mathbf{x}_i = (x_{i1}, x_{i2}, \ldots, x_{iX})$, that defines its topological position with relation to the other neurons in the network. As before, neuron k of the N neurons wins if it is the closest to the current training vector, but the weight adjustment now affects *all* neurons as determined by a decreasing function f of their topological distance from neuron k and a threshold distance d_T:

$$w_{ij} \Leftarrow w_{ij} + \epsilon \cdot f(||\mathbf{x}_k - \mathbf{x}_i||, d_T) \cdot (v_j - w_{ij}) \quad 0 < \epsilon < 1, \ 1 \leq j \leq W, \ 1 \leq i \leq N .$$

This function allows the winning neuron to *drag* its neighbors toward a given section of the input space so that topologically close neurons will eventually react similarly to closely spaced input vectors.

The integer Markovian learning algorithm of Figure 1 simplifies the Kohonen learning procedure by noting that the neuron weights slowly *integrate* the effects of stimuli. This integration can be done by stochastically updating the weights with a probability proportional to the neural input. The stochastic update of the neural weights is done by generating two uncorrelated random numbers, R_1 and R_2, on the interval $[0, d_T]$ that each neuron compares to its distance from the current training vector and its topological distance from the winning neuron, respectively. A neuron will try to increment or decrement the elements of its weight vector closer to the training vector if the absolute value of the intervening distance is greater than R_1, thus creating a total movement proportional to the distance when averaged over many cycles. This movement is inversely modulated by the topological distance to the winning neuron k via a comparison with R_2. The total effect produced by these two stochastic processes is equivalent to that produced in Kohonen's original algorithm, but only simple additive operations are now needed. Figure 2 shows

```
for( i ⇐ 1; i ≤ N; i ⇐ i + 1 )
        for( j ⇐ 1; j ≤ W; j ⇐ j + 1 )
                w_ij ⇐ random()
for( v∈ {training set} )
        parallelfor( all neurons i )
                d_i ⇐ c_i
                for( j ⇐ 1; j ≤ W; j ⇐ j + 1 )
                        d_i ⇐ d_i + |v_j − w_ij|
        k ⇐ 1
        for( i ⇐ 1; i ≤ N; i ⇐ i + 1 )
                if( d_i < d_k )
                        k ⇐ i
        parallelfor( all neurons i )
                d_i ⇐ 0
                for( j ⇐ 1; j ≤ X; j ⇐ j + 1 )
                        d_i ⇐ d_i + |x_ij − x_kj|
        for( j ⇐ 1; j ≤ W; j ⇐ j + 1 )
                R_1 ⇐ random(d_T)
                R_2 ⇐ random(d_T)
                parallelfor( all neurons i )
                        /* stochastic weight update */
                        if( |v_j − w_ij| > R_1 and d_i ≤ R_2 )
                                w_ij ⇐ w_ij + sign(v_j − w_ij)
        d_T ⇐ α_d · d_T
```

Figure 1: The integer Markovian learning algorithm.

our simplified algorithm operates correctly on a problem that has often been solved using Kohonen networks.

The integer Markovian learning algorithm is practical to implement since only simple neurons are needed to do the additive operations and a single global bus can handle all the broadcast transmissions. The high-level architecture for such an implementation is shown in Figure 3. TInMANN consists of a global controller that coordinates the actions of a linear array of neurons. The neurons contain circuitry for comparing and updating their weights, and for enabling and disabling themselves during the conditional portions of the algorithm. The network topology is configured by arranging the neurons in an X-dimensional space rather than by storing a graph structure in the hardware. This allows the calculation of the topological distance between neurons using the same circuitry as is used in the weight calculations. TInMANN performs the following operations for each training vector:

1. The global controller broadcasts the W elements of $\mathbf{v}$ while each neuron accumulates in A the absolute value of the difference between the elements of its weight vector (stored in the small, local RAM) and those of the training vector.
2. The global controller does a binary search for the neuron closest to the training

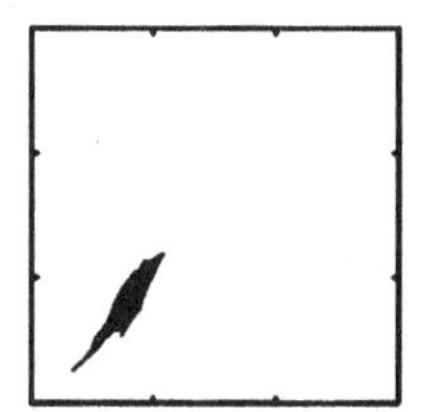 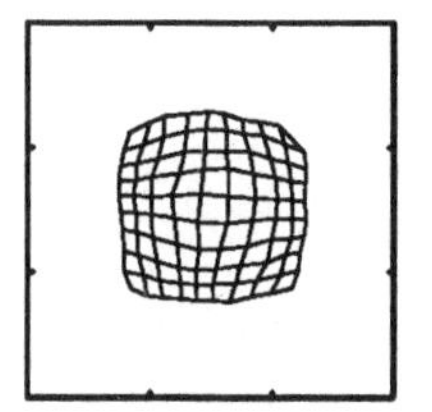 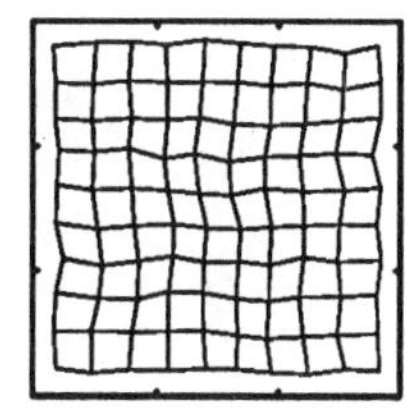

Figure 2: The evolution of 100 TInMANN neurons when learning a two-dimensional vector quantization.

vector by broadcasting distance values bisecting the range containing the winning neuron. The neurons do a comparison and signal on the wired-OR status line if their distance is less than the broadcast value (i.e. the carry bit c is set). Neurons with distances greater than the broadcast value are disabled by resetting their e flags. However, if no neuron is left enabled, the controller restores the enable bits and adjusts its search region (this action is needed on $\approx M/2$ of the search steps, where M is the machine word length used by TInMANN). The last neuron left enabled is the winner of the competition (ties are resolved by the conditional logic in each neuron).

3. The topological vector of the winning neuron is broadcast to the other neurons through gate G. The other neurons accumulate into A and store into T_1 the absolute value of the difference between their topological vectors and that of the winning neuron.
4. Random number R_2 is broadcast by the global controller and those neurons having topological distances in T_1 greater than R_2 are disabled. The remaining neurons each compute the distance between a component of their weight vector and that of the training vector broadcast by the global controller. All neurons whose calculated distances are greater than random number R_1 broadcast by the controller will increment or decrement their weight elements depending on the carry bits left in the c flags during the distance calculations. Then all neurons are re-enabled and this step is repeated for the remaining $W-1$ elements of the training vector.

A single training vector can be processed in $11W + X + 2.5M + 15$ clock cycles (Van den Bout, 1989). A word-width of 10 bits and a clock cycle of 15 MHz would allow TInMANN to learn at a rate of 200,000 three-dimensional vectors per second or 290,000 one-dimensional vectors per second.

3 THE VLSI IMPLEMENTATION OF TInMANN

Figure 4 is a block diagram for the VLSI TInMANN neuron built from the components listed in Table 1. The design was driven by the following requirements:

Size: The TInMANN neuron had to fit within a MOSIS TinyChip frame, so we used small, dense, ripple-carry adders. A 10-bit word size was selected as a

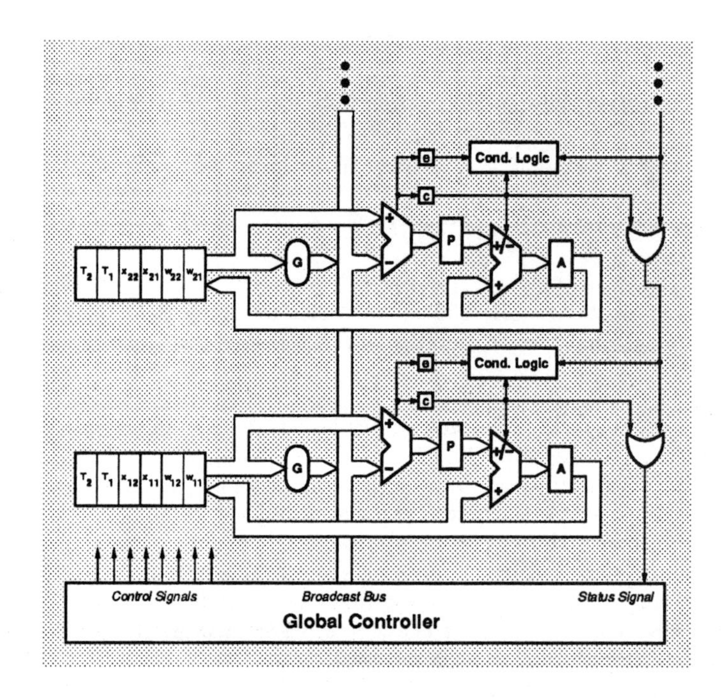

Figure 3: The TInMANN architecture.

Table 1: Components of the VLSI TInMANN neuron.

Component	Function
ABDiff	10-bit, two's-complement, ripple-borrow subtractor that calculates differences between data in the neuron and data broadcast on the global bus (B_Bus).
P	10-bit pipeline register that temporarily stores the difference output by ABDiff.
CFLAG	Records the sign bit of the difference stored in P.
PASum	10-bit, two's-complement, ripple-carry adder/subtractor that adds or subtracts P from the accumulator depending on the sign bit in CFLAG. This implements the absolute value function.
A	Accumulates the absolute values from PASum to form the Manhattan distance between a neuron and a training vector.
8-word memory	Stores the weight and topology vectors, the *conscience* register (DeSieno, 1988), and one working register.
MUX	Steers the output of A or the memory to the input of ABDiff.
EFLAG	Stores the enable bit used for conditionally controlling the neuron function during the binary search and weight update phases.

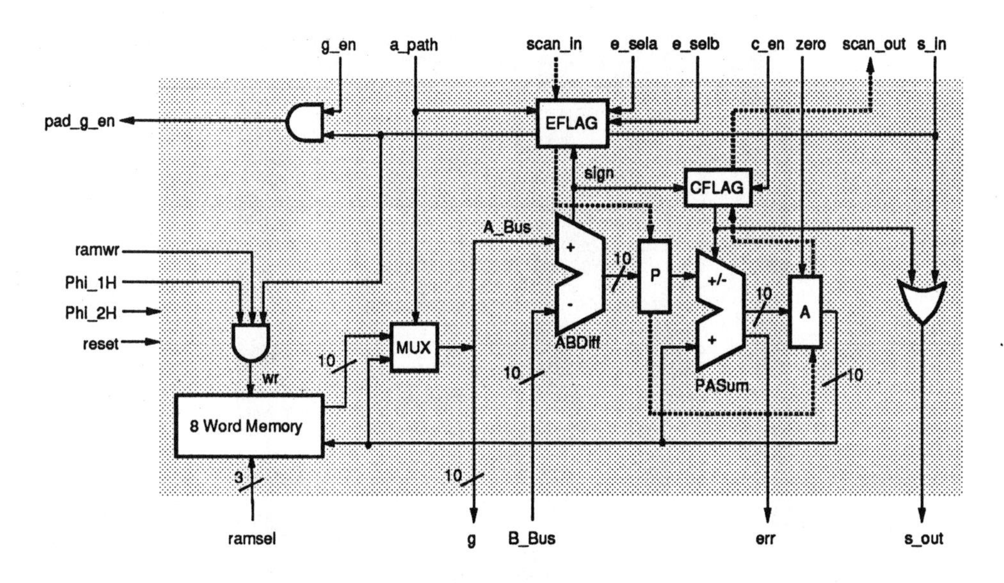

Figure 4: Block Diagram of the VLSI TInMANN neuron.

compromise between saving area and retaining numeric precision. The multiplexer was added so that A could be used as another temporary register. The neuron logic was built with the OASIS silicon compiler (Kedem, 1990), but the memory was hand-crafted to reduce its area. In the final TInMANN neuron, 4000 transistors are divided between the arithmetic logic ($770\mu \times 1300\mu$) and the memory ($710\mu \times 1160\mu$).

Expandability: The use of broadcast communications reduces the total TInMANN chip I/O to only 35 pins. This low connectivity makes it practical to build large Kohonen networks. At the chip level, the use of a silicon compiler lets us expand the design if more silicon area becomes available. For example, the word-size could be readily expanded and the layout automatically regenerated by changing a single-statement in the hardware description. Also, higher-dimensional vector spaces could be supported by adding more memory.

Speed: In the worst case, the memory access time is 12 ns, each adder delay is 45 ns, and the write time for A is 10 ns. This would have limited TInMANN to a top speed of 9 MHz. P was added to break the critical path through the adders and bring the clock frequency to 15 MHz. At the board level, the ripple of status information through the OR gates is sped up by connecting the status lines through an OR-tree.

Testability: To speed the diagnosis of system failures caused by defective chips, the TInMANN neuron was made 100% testable by building EFLAG, CFLAG, P, and A from level-sensitive scannable latches. Test patterns are shifted into the chip through the scan_in pin and the results are shifted out through scan_out. All faults are covered by only 27 test patterns. A 100% testable neural system is built by concatenating the scan_in and scan_out pins of all the chips.

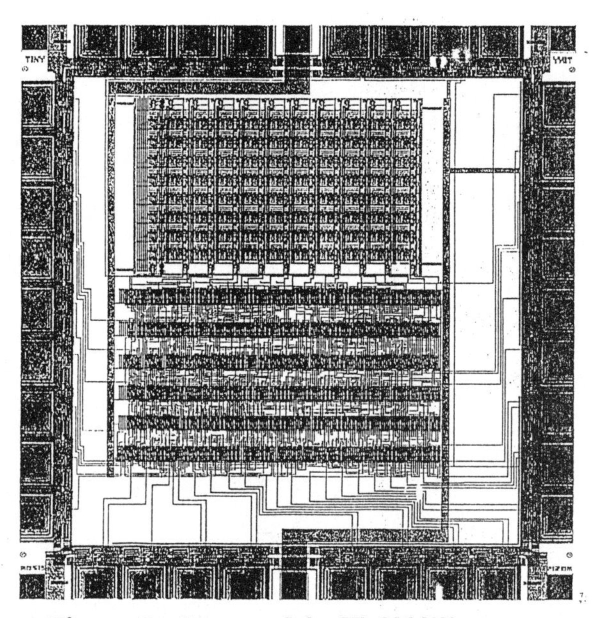

Figure 5: Layout of the TInMANN neuron.

Each component of the TInMANN neuron was extensively simulated to check for correct operation. To test the chip I/O, we performed a detailed circuit simulation of two TInMANN neurons organized as a competitive network. The simulation demonstrated the movement of the two neurons towards the centroids of two data clusters used to provide training vectors.

Four of the TInMANN neurons in Figure 5 were fabricated by MOSIS. Using the built-in scan path, each was found to function at 20 MHz (the maximum speed of our tester). These chips are now being connected into a linear neural array and attached to a global controller.

References

D. E. Van den Bout and **T. K. Miller III**. "TInMANN: The Integer Markovian Artificial Neural Network". In *IJCNN*, pages II:205–II:211, 1989.

D. DeSieno. "Adding a Conscience to Competitive Learning". In *IEEE International Conference on Neural Networks*, pages I:117–I:124, 1988.

G. Kedem, F. Brglez, and **K. Kozminski**. "OASIS: A Silicon Compiler for Rapid Implementation of Semi-custom Designs". In *International Workshop on Rapid Systems Prototyping*, June 1990.

T. Kohonen. "Self-Organized Formation of Topologically Correct Feature Maps". *Biological Cybernetics*, 43:56–69, 1982.

D. Rumelhart and **J. McClelland**. *Parallel Distributed Processing: Explorations in the Microstructure of Cognition*, chapter 5. MIT Press, 1986.

A

B

C

Page numbers refer to the first page of the paper.

D

E

F

G

H

Page numbers refer to the first page of the paper.

M

N

O

P

Q

R

S

T

U

V

W

X

Z

Author Index